Germany from Napoleon to Bismarck
1800–1866

Thomas Nipperdey

Germany from Napoleon to Bismarck

1800–1866

Translated by Daniel Nolan

Princeton University Press
Princeton, New Jersey

Published by Princeton University Press
41 William Street, Princeton, New Jersey 08540

All Rights Reserved

ISBN 0-691-02636-X

Library of Congress Cataloging-in-Publication Data
A CIP catalog record for this book is available from the Library of Congress

First published in Germany in 1983
by Verlag C. H. Beck, Munich as
Deutsche Geschichte
1800–1866
Bürgerwelt und starker Staat
© C. H. Beck'sche Verlagsbuchhandlung (Oscar Beck), München 1983
© English translation Gill & Macmillan 1996
Translated by Daniel Nolan
Index compiled by Helen Litton

This book has been composed in New Caledonia

Princeton University Press books are printed on acid-free paper and meet the guidelines for permanence and durability of the Committee on Production Guidelines for Book Longevity of the Council on Library Resources

Printed in Great Britain

1   3   5   7   9   10   8   6   4   2

Contents

List of Tables   vii

I *The Great Upheaval*   1

1. The End of Empire: Germany under Napoleon   1
2. The Great Reforms   19
3. The Great War and a Difficult Peace   67

II *Life, Work, Business*   85

1. Population   85
2. Family, Gender, Generations   97
3. Everyday Life   111
4. Agriculture and Rural Society   125
5. Industrialisation   155
6. Crafts   182
7. The Lower Classes, Factories, Industrial Workers, Social Problems   191
8. The Problem of Minorities: the Jews   217
9. Bourgeois Society   223

III *Restoration and Vormärz, 1815–48*   237

1. The End of the Reforms: Constitutions and Restoration   237
2. The Great Movements   250
3. The State and the States   280
4. German and European Politics   313
5. The Effects of the July Revolution   323
6. The Formation and Restructuring of the German Political Parties   333
7. Vormärz   350

IV *Faith and Knowledge; Education and Art*   356

1. Religion, Church, De-Christianisation   356
2. Education: School and University   398
3. The Sciences   428
4. Aesthetic Culture: Music, Art and Literature   472
5. The Reading Revolution and the Rise of the Press   520

V *The Revolution of 1848–49* 527

    1. The March Revolution 527
    2. The Road to the Paulskirche 537
    3. Extraparliamentary Movements: Denominational and Social Problems 547
    4. Germany and Europe 553
    5. Between Radicalisation and Counter-Revolution 560
    6. The Imperial Constitution and the Empire 579
    7. The End 588
    8. The Failed Revolution 590
    9. Epilogue: Germany as a Union of the States? 595

VI *Between Reaction and Liberalism: Bismarck and the Problem of
German Unity, 1849–66* 599

    1. Reaction in Germany, 1849–59 599
    2. German Policy in the 1850s 608
    3. Germany in Europe: From the Crimean War to the Italian War 612
    4. The New Era 620
    5. The German Question, 1859–63 627
    6. Politics and Society: Changes in the Parties 636
    7. The Constitutional Conflict in Prussia and Bismarck's
       Minister-Presidency 667
    8. The Decision concerning Germany: German and European
       Politics, 1863–66 684
    9. Consequences 704

Epilogue 716
Index 717

List of Tables

Table 1:   Population of the states of the German Confederation   86
Table 2:   Selected population densities   88
Table 3:   Live births, deaths, excess of births over deaths per year
             in 25-year averages   89
Table 4:   Birth rate, mortality rate, excess births over deaths in
             selected 5-year averages   91
Table 5:   Average proportion of illegitimate births out of the total
             number of births, 1830–69   93
Table 6a: Proportion of the total population aged under 14   94
Table 6b: Proportion of population aged over 60   94
Table 7:   Proportion of inhabitants in communities of over 5,000 inhabitants   95
Table 8:   Population of German cities   96
Table 9:   Emigration   97
Table 10:   Illegitimate births   109
Table 11a: Estimated yields   132
Table 11b: Total yields   133
Table 12a: Increase in livestock numbers   133
Table 12b: Output   133
Table 12c: Index figures for livestock production   134
Table 13a: Land lost and gained by the peasants in Prussia   136
Table 13b: Land gained by the large landowners in Prussia   137
Table 14:   Relative proportions of the various sizes of property (from large
             landed estates to the smallest smallholdings) in Prussia in 1855   138
Table 15:   Payment in kind/payment in currency   143
Table 16:   Average yearly population growth by social class in rural
             East Prussia 1805–67   143
Table 17:   Losses in feudal revenues   147
Table 18:   The cotton industry   160
Table 19:   Workers employed in crafts and industry in the later Reich,
             c.1800 and 1846–48   170
Table 20:   Coal-mining in the Ruhr   170
Table 21:   Iron production in Prussia   171
Table 22:   Economic comparison between Austria and the German
             Reich of 1871   177

Table 23: Craft workers within the borders of the later German Reich 183

Table 24: Development of crafts in Prussia 184

Table 25: Index figures for the development of crafts in Prussia, 1816–46 185

Table 26: Shift in the distribution of persons employed in individual crafts sectors in Prussia, 1816–46 185

Table 27: Numbers of masters and assistants within the populations of individual states, 1846–49 185

Table 28: Numbers of craftsmen by region 186

Table 29: Weekly wages in various trade sectors for the period 1840–49 196

Table 30: Incomes of selected groups of employees in the territory of the later German Reich for 1810–49 197

Table 31: Income of workers in industry and crafts in the territory of the later German Reich for 1850–70 207

Table 32: Wages in mining, 1850–70 208

Table 33: Average wages of workers in the engineering works in Esslingen, 1848–70 209

Table 34: Jewish social structure within the borders of the later Reich 220

Table 35a: Number of Germans and those of other nations involved in vital discoveries in the field of physiology 437

Table 35b: Number of Germans, as compared with French and English, involved in discoveries in the study of heat, electricity, magnetism and optics 437

Table 35c: Number of Germans, as compared with French and English, involved in medical discoveries 438

Table 36: Electoral turnout in Prussia 644

I

The Great Upheaval

1. The End of Empire:
Germany under Napoleon

In the beginning was Napoleon. His influence upon the history of the German people, their lives and experiences was overwhelming at a time when the initial foundations of a modern German state were being laid. The destiny of a nation is its politics, and those politics were Napoleon's — the politics of war and conquest, of exploitation and repression, of imperialism and reform. The nations and the other states were left with no option but to acquiesce or to resist. Rarely have power politics and pressure from without so dominated every sphere of life. The great reforms which so altered the state and society were themselves shaped by these forces. True, it was with the French Revolution that the ideas on which the modern world is based, and which went on to become an integral part of modern consciousness, first came into being. The French Revolution marked a new era in world history. For the Germans, however, the collapse of the old order became a reality only under Napoleon, and in the form of a military imperium. Only those blinded by ideology to the phenomenon of power, those who concentrate all their attention on the movements within society, on 'internal' politics, and on structures, could ignore this basic fact.

The German nation's fate was shaped by the larger political events taking place around it. The revolutionary wars — from 1792 onwards — had ended with the defeat of the German and other European powers. Napoleon, the revolution's general, was also its tamer. His victory was absolutely without precedent. In 1801, the territories on the left bank of the Rhine finally fell under French rule. In 1803, the map of Germany was redrawn; the princeling rulers were to be 'compensated' for their territorial losses. This triggered a revolution from above by the 'old' Germany. The ecclesiastical states were 'secularised'; most of the imperial cities, hitherto 'imperial sovereignties', and a whole series of smaller secular states (including what remained of the Electorate of the Palatinate) were 'mediatised', i.e. dissolved as political unities and absorbed into the large and medium-sized states. The German map was effectively simplified in a settlement agreed to by the Deputation of the Imperial Diet. In general, the new acquisitions heavily outnumbered the losses.

This geographical reform took place under the auspices of the two major continental powers, France and Russia, and in accordance with the plan and model laid down by them. Many personal alliances and a good deal of corruption played a significant role. France's dominant position and her interests were politically decisive for this revolution from above. France was now the puppet-master of German affairs, a fact which had two direct consequences. First, it caused the dissolution of the old Empire, which had relied on the imperial church and the aristocracy outside the larger territories for its power and legal system. Secondly, unified medium-sized states (*Mittelstaaten*) capable of supporting themselves were created or consolidated in the south and south-west by the enormous territorial expansion. Baden, Württemberg, Bavaria, Hesse–Darmstadt and the Nassau principalities were the big winners in this reorganisation. Both the princes and the chief ministers of these states seized the opportunity for expansion with both hands, guided by an almost undiluted pragmatism, and allowing no legitimistic, patriotic or nationalist scruples to deter them.

The medium-sized states now found themselves squeezed between the major German powers of Prussia and Austria, and they became fierce opponents of the old imperial structure. This was their first taste of genuine sovereignty, and no Kaiser or Empire was going to get in their way. Individual states which had aspired to full sovereignty during the early modern era in the development of the German state now attained their goal. This new sovereignty, however, was not viable in itself. It relied on France for its political legitimacy and power, and it was in the interests of Napoleonic France to uphold them, thereby making impossible any other form of national organisation of Germany, whether of the older or the newer variety. In this respect, the medium-sized states were not simply a result of German history, but, first and foremost, the product of the policies through which Napoleon had sought to establish his hegemony. Thus, the pragmatism of the princes and ministers was inevitably linked to a need to fall into line with French policies.

Last-ditch attempts to reform the Reich either remained futile or came to grief — like that of the Imperial Chancellor and sole remaining ecclesiastical Elector, Dalberg. It was he who tried to consolidate the imperial church and the Empire by means of a Reich Concordat — with the Kaiser, the new sovereigns or the Pope. The Reich was on the brink of bankruptcy, with only a shadow existence. When Napoleon crowned himself Emperor of the French in 1804, the German Kaiser Franz II renounced his imperial title and became Emperor of Austria, seeing this as the only office which would grant him a semblance of parity.

Yet the issue of France's supremacy in Europe remained unresolved. Austria and Prussia appeared powerless, but by 1803 England was again at war with Napoleon. He wasted no time in taking possession of Hanover, which was bound by personal union to England. This signalled the end of north German neutrality, which had been maintained under Prussia's protection. A new alliance was formed between the Netherlands, Switzerland and Italy, the powers on the flanks of England and Russia. This 'Third Coalition' aimed at resisting Napoleon's galloping expansionism, ending the economic war and putting a stop to his despotism (exemplified in the kidnapping and subsequent shooting of Duc d'Enghien in Baden in 1804). The objectives of the Third Coalition were to contain France, reverse her military conquest and to re-establish the balance of power in Europe. Austria, though still seriously weakened after its earlier revolutionary wars, and less decisive and astute in its political decisions, joined this alliance in 1805. An excuse for hostilities was provided by ever-increasing French expansionism in Italy, which went so far as to establish a Napoleonic kingdom of Italy. Napoleon had assembled his troops near Boulogne, either to prepare for an invasion of England or a continental war against the Eastern powers. In September 1805, he surprised the Austrians by sending his troops, not to Italy, but to southern Germany with breathtaking speed. Once there, he forged alliances with the south German states, and on 17 October 1805 forced an Austrian army under the incompetent Supreme Commander Mack to capitulate at Ulm. His request to Austria on 21 October to stop fighting England's war — in defence of its monopoly of the seas, colonies and trade — fell on deaf ears, and Nelson's rout of the French fleet at Trafalgar left Napoleon no other option but to fight a continental war. The Austrians were ill-prepared. The coalition was uncoordinated and they lost the initiative right from the start. Before the Russian troops were ready, Napoleon had marched into Vienna on 13 November. He won a brilliant victory at Austerlitz on 2 December (the Battle of the Three Emperors), partly because the ambitious Tsar had launched his attack too early, before all the troops of the coalition could be assembled. The Russians beat a hasty retreat. Austria had to make peace at Pressburg. She lost the Habsburg dependencies of the Upper Rhine and Upper Swabia to Baden and Württemberg. Tyrol, Lindau and Vorarlberg went to Bavaria, while Venice, Istria and Dalmatia were lost to Napoleonic Italy. Austria was reduced to owning only the territories along the Danube and was, furthermore, left with an enormous reparations bill of forty million francs.

The war had finally cleared the way for Napoleon to extend his hegemony over central Europe. France, no longer satisfied with her so-called natural boundaries and her satellite states (the Netherlands, Switzerland and Italy), began to construct a 'Great Empire' which would dominate the continent of Europe. Bavaria and Württemberg became kingdoms, Baden and Hesse–Darmstadt grand duchies. Napoleon wanted the Holy Roman Empire, now only a shadow, erased once and for all; strictly speaking, no one had any genuine or effective interest in preserving that antiquated order, not even imperial Austria. Dalberg's plan to combine the old Roman Empire with that of Napoleon in order to keep it independent from Austria and Prussia (he even appointed Napoleon's uncle as his co-regent and successor) was a lost cause. On 16 July 1806, Napoleon amalgamated the south German states in a defensive and offensive alliance called the Confederation of the Rhine. Napoleon himself was the supreme 'Protector' of this confederation, and the affiliated states were forced to provide him with troops. Once again, a whole range of smaller imperial sovereignties, including those of the Imperial Knights, were demoted and absorbed by the medium-sized states. The larger states of south Germany would have preferred to forge only military alliances with France, but Napoleon forced them to organise into a confederacy. For these states themselves, membership meant on the one hand self-preservation in the face of the strongest power on the continent, especially as Prussia was holding on to its neutrality and Austria remained a threat to at least Bavaria's continued existence as a state. On the other hand, their assertion of sovereignty over the small feudal estates was vital. This required them to renounce finally their old imperial allegiance, which could only be achieved at the price of dependence on the new hegemonial power. It was Napoleon's threat to run these territories along French lines which proved the most effective means of overcoming their objections. Amalgamation into the Confederation of the Rhine met with the approval of all influential as well as popular forces. Only then did south Germany really take shape in the political sense.

French hegemony, the sovereignty of the *Mittelstaaten* and the dissolution of the old Roman Empire are inextricably linked. The states of the Confederation of the Rhine declared that in their eyes the Empire no longer existed and made a formal withdrawal. The Kaiser eventually relinquished his imperial crown on 6 August 1806, following Napoleon's ultimatum, and, in a rather wooden proclamation, declared the Empire to have ended. It was quietly buried without ceremony and the death certificate issued. Goethe wrote that at the time a quarrel between his coachman and a servant had interested him more than this news.

The Holy Roman Empire, which had lasted for nearly a thousand years, was at an end. Out of date, cumbersome, devoid of any real power, it had not kept pace with the revolutionary changes in European relations. Many things had finally killed it off: the tremendous pressure exerted by the French revolutionary armies; the explosive force of its internal conflicts; the Austro–Prussian dualism and the territorial princes' struggle for sovereignty; the outmoded and fragmented ruling imperial orders of church, aristocracy and cities. The Empire had long maintained the balance of power in Europe and the coexistence of the individual sovereign powers in Germany, whose conflicts it regulated or checked. A bastion of the status quo, it had retained the feudal system and social hierarchy. All of this now disappeared. The new agenda was for sweeping changes, reorganisation, the end of the existing order. 'Germany' was relegated for the time being to a mere geographical concept.

The political demise of this old Empire had a very odd long-term effect. The concept of the Empire was exported from the real world to a world of dreams and symbols. The dream of the 'Reich' has since developed a dynamic all of its own in the history of the German people. A phantom, an unreality, had the power to change reality.

Prussia had made territorial gains during its ten years of neutrality between 1795 and 1805, but it had suffered a decisive loss of power and the capacity to act. In 1805 Prussia's politics, tied to the illusion of neutrality, were hesitant. Napoleon's march through Ansbach brought it closer to a coalition, but Napoleon stalled Prussia's initial attempt at mediation until after the battle of Austerlitz. Then, submitting to the dictates of Napoleon, Prussia took control of Hanover from the English as compensation for Kleve and Ansbach. A potential enemy had been turned into a rather weak-kneed ally, an accomplice of the Emperor. Prussia was forced to align itself with the anti-English front, against its best political and economic interests. England declared war on Prussia and started a blockade. At the same time, Prussia was almost helplessly at the mercy of every threat and exhortation from Napoleon, having lost practically all freedom of action. In 1806, Prussia was negotiating both with Napoleon's last continental opponent, Russia, as well as with Napoleon, on matters such as a Prussian-led north German empire. In August 1806, the news broke that Napoleon had offered Hanover back to the English, jeopardising Prussia's reward for submission to French continental policy. While the king and his foreign minister were reeling from the pressure of an anti-French 'patriotic' opposition movement among the people and the ruling classes, Prussia mobilised its armies. When Napoleon demanded they be sent back to the barracks, Prussia issued an ultimatum at the end of September for the withdrawal of

French troops from south Germany and the formation of a north German confederation. Prussia was taking the offensive out of desperation, although it was by no means determined to enter into a war in which there was little prospect of victory.

However irresolute and foolish Prussia's politics were — it had not even waited for concrete coalition agreements with Russia — war was inevitable, especially since Napoleon's claims to hegemony and Prussia's demands for some semblance of an independent role as partner in an alliance were irreconcilable. Napoleon gave the order to march; Prussia declared war on 9 October. The Prussian army was badly equipped, ill-prepared, devoid of fighting spirit, and above all lacking in mobility. Led by ageing and incompetent generals lacking in initiative, it was smashed without trace by Napoleon at Jena and Auerstedt on 14 October. Most of the remaining forces and fortresses also capitulated quietly and most of the civilian authorities surrendered. Some fled, some abandoned their positions, while others co-operated with the occupying forces. The old Prussian state collapsed. The public notice pinned up by the Berlin Chief of Police captures the mood perfectly: 'The king has lost a battle. The citizen's first duty now is to remain calm.' Even on its knees, the regime stubbornly persisted in the strict separation of dynastic and military politics from that governing the fate of its subjects. There were a few exceptions, however. For example, Blücher and Scharnhorst made it to Lübeck; Gneisenau, together with Major Schill and the burgher Joachim Nettelbeck, masterminded the successful defence of Kolberg. Nevertheless, the king, under pressure from opponents of his previous course of action, came down against the armistice which had already been initialled, and decided to continue the war in alliance with Russia. It was astonishing, after such a collapse, to hear the first rumblings of a decisive policy of resistance. Hardenburg became chief minister, but Stein was dismissed because of his obstinate disagreement with the rest of the royal cabinet.

Napoleon's attempt to soften up the Russians for a peace settlement through military victory was initially unsuccessful; the battle of Eylau on 8 February 1807 was indecisive. Even his political attempts to persuade Austria or even Prussia to enter into an alliance came to nought. Nevertheless, Napoleon mobilised a Polish uprising against Prussia and a Turkish revolt against the Tsar. This left one section of the Russian army committed. His victory at Friedland on 14 June 1807 brought the Russians to the negotiating table, and thus the two emperors met on a raft on the River Niemen. Napoleon made a profound impression on the Tsar. The Peace of Tilsit ended the war and Prussia retained its statehood after all. The Tsar saved his former ally from extinction, and even Napoleon had a certain interest in the existence of a buffer state between the opposing parties.

Prussia was now reduced to about half of its former size. It had lost the territories west of the Elbe — they now became part of the new kingdom of 'Westphalia' — and its most recent Polish acquisitions. These became the French-ruled duchy of Warsaw, in a personal union with the kingdom of Saxony, and a 'free city' of Danzig. In addition, Prussia was forced to pay an undisclosed sum in war contributions: the evacuation of the occupied provinces was made contingent upon the payment of these sums. Hardenberg had to step aside. As a European or even a German major power, Prussia was finished, it had become a third-rate power. First it was the late absolutist Austria, then the old feudal Empire, and now Prussia, the model state of enlightened absolutism, the youngest, most modern and dynamic major power in eighteenth-century Europe, the strongest German military state, crushed under the fist of the man who had brought the Revolution to its conclusion and then tamed it: Napoleon.

Napoleon and the Tsar concluded a treaty of friendship and established a partnership, fragile though it was, to control Europe. Napoleon gave the Tsar a free hand with respect to Finland and, to a lesser extent, with Balkan Christians. The Tsar had intended to join the fight against England.

Napoleon's Empire seemed to have reached its zenith. He appeared finally to have established direct or indirect control over western, central and southern Europe. Germany seemed to have firmly integrated into the French system, and only Austria retained semi-independence. The empire of Charlemagne appeared to have been resurrected under French hegemony and Europe seemed to be uniting. The confiscation and removal to Paris of major art treasures from the conquered countries was a symbol of the new Empire. Russia had become a partner in the Empire, and this partnership was reinforced at the meeting between Napoleon and the Tsar in Erfurt in September 1808, where they formed an alliance against England, the Spanish uprising and a possible Austrian secession. England's options on the continent were limited. Even so, the Empire's position was not completely stable. England remained a constant and unresolved threat, and the Russian alliance was of a temporary nature. Storms were brewing in Scandinavia, the eastern Mediterranean and in Poland. The tsardom could not be incorporated into the front against England, and when Russia finally declared war on England, she did not go through with it. The Empire still meant foreign rule and repression and incited resistance in the developing nations — the popular uprising in Spain was the first sign of the unrest and it committed large sections of French troops over a long period.

How did the Germans and the German states fit into this Empire? They were all subject to the imperial economic system. This meant that, first of all, they all had to comply with the Continental Blockade, the economic embargo against England, which Napoleon had imposed in 1806 and intensified in 1807. England was to be cut off from her supplies of raw materials and her export markets on the continent. Imports into and exports from England were prohibited — even on neutral ships. Compared with a traditional war, where only the combatants are involved, this was a step towards bringing war into the civilian area, a step towards total war. It was thus both revolutionary and modern, a step towards the ultimate mobilisation of all the means to a political end. The immediate result of the blockade was an outbreak of smuggling on a massive scale, via the North Sea and the Baltic, Denmark and Sweden, Heligoland — captured by the British in 1808 — Bremen, Hamburg and Lübeck and as far south as Frankfurt and Leipzig. Most of the goods that found their way on to the continent and into Germany were of British colonial origin.

The logic of economic warfare dictated close co-operation, especially between those countries with coastlines and France, the hegemonial power. When more and more breaches began to weaken the embargo, and when resistance escalated, Napoleon was driven further down the road of direct intervention and annexation. In view of the widespread network of corruption, control was only effective when French troops were sent in. Following measures taken against Spain and Portugal, and against central Italy, which were designed to break resistance to the blockade, Napoleon annexed Holland and the German coast as far as Lübeck in 1810. His drive for victory in the trade war against England ultimately led him into the Russian débâcle. In the same year, Napoleon altered the rules of his blockade, replacing the import ban with a duty of between forty and fifty per cent. Police surveillance and penalties were considerably increased. On 18–19 October 1810, for instance, French troops were sent to Frankfurt, where they confiscated great stores of English goods and burned them. Yet smuggling continued to flourish. For instance, again in 1810, some three to four hundred wagons carrying goods from the British colonies rolled through Freiburg daily. The Prussian administration confiscated the goods, but returned them for payment of a heavy fine. This brought them in about 12 million taler between 1810 and 1812, which went to finance the reform of the army.

In addition to the Continental Blockade there was also the 'Continental System' which put an especially great strain on the German territories. The French territories were closed to German exports, thanks to high customs tariffs. The same applied to Holland and Italy, where the French had a monopoly. Germany, on the other hand, was wide open to French exports. Furthermore, German merchants were subject to outrageous customs duties, which naturally benefited the French economy. The system served French economic interests first and foremost, and sabotaged the economic unity of the continent. Even worse, it undermined the solidarity of the empire by provoking the self-interests of the satellite states.

The economic consequences were ambivalent. On the one hand, it was principally north Germany which lost its markets for cereals, wood and linen, a situation which led eventually to crises. Goods in general became considerably more expensive (especially, of course, goods from the colonies) and there were many business failures which intensified the difficulties caused by the war. On the other hand, a boom was experienced in many trades, especially in the textile sector, in the Rhineland and in Saxony, now that there was no English competition. Despite high cotton prices, the number of mule spindles in Saxony increased twenty-fold to 256,000 between 1806 and 1815.

The territories on the left bank of the Rhine profited by their incorporation into the French economic sector. In Germany, the situation as a whole was less severe than in France, since prices of English goods were lower. Yet this did not result in a predominance of French goods. German exports to France even increased, despite the tariff barriers, and there was a positive growth in trade with eastern Europe. Leipzig gained even more importance as the largest trading centre. In addition to the collapses, there were large capital gains in these high-risk times. However, the most critical effect of all was politico-psychological. Everyone was effected by the controls and the harassment, and these were clearly seen to be the effects of French economic policy, as were the economic situation as a whole and the standard of living. Scarcity and price increases were most instrumental in arousing a growing bitterness against French rule, a feeling which, especially in the Confederation of the Rhine, replaced initial pro-French sentiments or feelings of indifference. Thus it was French imperial economic policy, combined with the military and taxation policies, which eventually began to win support for slogans about emancipation.

The 'Third Germany', outside Austria and what remained of Prussia, and, of course, excluding the now French-controlled territories on the left bank of the Rhine, was organised as the Confederation of the Rhine. Even the northern and central German states had had to join it, making it effectively a Rhine–Danube–Elbe confederation. In addition to the old states of the north and centre, the enlarged — and thus new — states of the south, and a collection of the remnant of dwarf territories (which owed their continued existence primarily to personal alliances), the Confederation also included the new Napoleonic artificial states. These were: the grand duchy of Würzburg; the grand duchy of Frankfurt, which was to be passed on to Napoleon's stepson after the death of its grand duke, the former Imperial Chancellor Dalberg; the kingdom of Westphalia, consisting of Hesse–Kassel, Brunswick, the Prussian territories west of the Elbe and large parts of Hanover, whose capital was Kassel, and which Napoleon handed over to his brother Jerome; and the grand duchy of Berg. Berg had initially been ruled by Napoleon's brother-in-law, Murat, and then, following the latter's 'transfer' to Naples, by a nephew who was still a minor, with a French *commissaire* as regent. These were the real satellite states. Even the southern German dynasties were tied to Napoleon's family through a series of marriages. It is not worth outlining here the numerous territorial changes in this period. Suffice it to say that the constant changes in state allegiance and rule, pushed through by bureaucratic appropriation in the form of sequestration orders, remained a formative experience for many Germans.

The Confederation of the Rhine was, on the one hand, a loose federation of German states. Attempts to impose a tighter organisation upon it, with an overall administration on the lines of a federal state — as Dalberg, the foreign ministry in Paris and at times even Napoleon himself tried to do — foundered as early as 1807–08 as a result of opposition from Bavaria and Württemberg, who saw this as a threat to their newly acquired sovereignty. Napoleon saw no point in risking unrest when he could carry through his imperial goals in other ways, and his aversion to any specifically German organisation was growing. The Confederation of the Rhine was, on the other hand, primarily the instrument of French domination. Napoleon, from a military and foreign policy point of view, was the de facto sovereign ruler of the Confederation. Decisions about war and peace, proposed alliances or arms build-ups, were all his. In this respect, this was no confederation of states, but a protectorate. Its states were used as military deployment zones against potential enemies. They had to provide — and this was the crux — a fixed quota of soldiers for the imperial army. In 1806, the figure was 63,000, and in 1808 it was 119,000 (out of a population of about 14.6 million and with a French army numbering 200,000). Even Bavaria and Württemberg had to maintain enormous armies as the price of their independence, stretching their resources to the breaking-point. Their military obligations were continually being pushed to the limit in all the new wars; and the states also had to stump up the considerable costs of provisioning the French armies during wars and often for long periods afterwards.

The states of the Confederation of the Rhine were firmly integrated into the Continental System and the Continental Blockade. They had to maintain law and order among their subjects for the Emperor. Furthermore, Westphalia and also Berg, to a degree, had to supply the newly created French civil and military aristocracy of merit with large country estates from the demesnes of the dispossessed sovereigns, which meant forgoing a large part of their normal revenue. This compelled them to impose maximum rates of taxation in the service of the Napoleonic Empire. In this respect, the Confederation of the Rhine was primarily a system of exploitation and repression, and no amount of detachment from the older nationalistic historiography could change that fact.

Another integral part of this system was the attempt to push through internal reforms, extending the task begun by the revolution (the dissolution of the feudal system of rank) which Napoleon had consolidated. For France this had a threefold function, though one primarily of power politics. It meant that the administration, laws and constitution would be harmonised, bringing them into line with France, in order to cement and secure the unity of the Empire. The reforms were designed to make the states more effective and to mobilise all their forces for the benefit of the French Empire. They were also eventually intended to make the system more attractive and therefore more stable. So this was to be a conquest of hearts and minds: 'What nation would want to return to the arbitrary rule of Prussia, once it has tasted the benefits of a wise and liberal administration?' 'The people of Germany require equality as citizens of a state and liberal ideas' — this was Napoleon's programme, and it was precisely the new Napoleonic states which were to be the models for the others. Modernisation and the consolidation of power were two sides of the same coin, but when a conflict arose, it was the consolidation of power which took precedence — in Westphalia the featherbedding of the new aristocracy was more important than the emancipation of the peasants. Power politics and Napoleon's drive for reform joined forces with the self-interest of the new states of the Confederation of the Rhine and set the wave of major reforms in motion. Napoleon had struck a good bargain with the princes; by allowing them to absorb the smaller territories and thereby extend their sovereignty, he had turned them into revolutionaries. The Emperor's ideas for reform corresponded to a large extent with their own *raison d'état*.

The states of the Confederation of the Rhine (and by no means only those ruled by members of Napoleon's family or his own administration) were, in addition to their formal obligations, under constant pressure from Napoleon in numerous ways. The French ambassador was the focus of power in all the capital cities. The Emperor's desires, demands, and his veto, could affect any issue of internal politics, even new appointments, and could only be evaded with great difficulty. Many orders were issued over the heads of the confederated states, as, for instance, when Stein was ostracised in 1808. Faced with a growing crisis in the Empire, the Emperor drew in the reins, and he did so more sharply in the north than the south. Any dissenting opinion, let alone opposition, was suppressed, and censorship intensified. Since the Spanish episode, Napoleon had feared any rumblings of resistance or a liberation movement. Supporters of freedom or nationality were hunted down with growing hatred; he began to be suspicious of anything German and would fight it. His system degenerated into a frequently authoritarian despotism. The governments remained loyal to Napoleon, even when the popular mood eventually changed; anything else would have been political suicide. Yet, around 1812, covert criticism and a debate about a change in European relations were on the increase everywhere.

The territories on the left bank of the Rhine had become part of France. It was here that the great administrative, legal and social reforms had made their greatest strides. However, total integration could not be achieved. In spite of all the new freedoms and talk of prosperity, the system of rule never lost its character of foreign domination. It was the French who ruled. The people of the Rhineland and the Palatinate were not really equal; they were to become Frenchmen. The language of the administration and the law courts was French, and the movement towards standardisation was even creeping into the education system. After the Spanish uprising of 1808, police surveillance and repression had been stepped up. This was the case everywhere throughout the

Empire, but it was intensified here by the mistrust of the non-French section of the population and any possible links they might have with the other bank of the Rhine.

Prussia did not have to join the Confederation of the Rhine after the Peace of Tilsit, but it was largely subject to Napoleon's will, primarily due to the war contributions imposed upon it. Napoleon had initially demanded 154.5 million francs, whereas Prussia had counted on only 20 million. Napoleon knew that these sums could not be raised, especially as the state revenues were mostly spoken for to cover the costs of the occupation, but he wanted to keep the occupying forces in situ for as long as possible. This was so that he could use his bases on the Oder and Vistula to maintain pressure on the Russian ally he still distrusted. As long as Napoleon could keep Prussia firmly within a military and financial vice, he could quell its aspirations to political independence. Initially, in 1807–08, the leading Prussian minister, Stein, advocated a policy of compliance and coexistence, thus hoping to get the country back on its feet. Napoleon protracted the negotiations about contributions and withdrawals by constantly changing and adding to his demands. This aggravated Stein, and under the influence of the Spanish uprising, which seemed to have given a fillip to those who sought to resist Napoleon in Europe, Stein joined the political opposition in August 1808. He now shared the belief of the military reformers that a coalition with France under any sort of tolerable conditions was impossible, and therefore the only option left was war — in alliance with Austria and with the help of a popular uprising. The task in hand was to prepare for war.

Scharnhorst and Gneisenau, as well as other military men, called for a popular uprising in the whole of (north) Germany under the banner of peasant emancipation, a constitution and the dethronement and dispossession of the enemy. However, these could by no stretch of the imagination be called the politics of the Prussian leadership. A letter from Stein dated 15 August 1808, in which such measures were referred to, fell into the hands of the French police. Napoleon had it published in his government newspaper and used it to force the Prussian negotiators to sign the Treaty of Paris on 8 September 1808. A payment of 140 million francs was demanded (to be reduced two months later after the Tsar had interceded), to be paid in thirty monthly instalments. The occupied territories were to be evacuated, but the fortresses on the Oder and the military routes to them were to remain occupied by 10,000 men, the costs of such occupation to be borne by the Prussian state. If the payments were delayed, Napoleon threatened military reoccupation; Prussia had to provide an auxilliary corps in the eventuality of a war, and the strength of its army was reduced to 4,000 men. Prior to withdrawing some of his troops to Spain or before the Tsar could intervene, Napoleon had pushed through this treaty of submission under the most favourable conditions to himself. When the Tsar reconsolidated the partnership with Napoleon in Erfurt, the dream of the 'patriots' of a war of liberation evaporated, for the time being at least.

This particular Prussian crisis ended with the dismissal of Stein on 24 November 1808. A reactionary opposition and the king's annoyance at the self-importance of the patriots were instrumental, as was Stein's own ineptness. However, in the last analysis, it was a consequence of the reasoning that now, and especially after Erfurt, the only political option open to Prussia was coexistence with Napoleon, and a more humble existence at that.

This came as a terrible piece of bad luck for the Prussian reformers, since Stein had been their soul and their driving force. With him out of the way, their cause was fading.

On 16 December, Napoleon had Stein outlawed, pronounced 'the name of Stein' an enemy of France, confiscated his property and threatened him with arrest, even the firing squad, if he should be found. This action, which was not covered by any law in force between the states or in any of the German sovereign states, was the direct result of Napoleon's fear of a conspiracy, but it also showed his instinctive recognition of a dangerous opponent. Warned by the French ambassador, Stein was able to escape to Bohemia. The outlawing of Stein enraged his contemporaries, and it contributed in no small way to his elevation to a key position in German and pan-European resistance to Napoleon in the years which followed. Stein had become a symbol.

The remaining half of Prussia had to take over the entire debt of the old state and renounce all claims in the ceded territories. It had been bled dry by war and occupation — the costs of occupation are said to have amounted to 216 million francs — and was plunged further into deep economic crisis thanks to the Continental Blockade, which cut off its agricultural exports to England. The estates were in enormous debt, severely limiting state credit resources. Payment of the tribute to France was an intolerable burden under these circumstances, and, to make matters worse, the transfer of the agreed sums represented a quite insoluble problem. Foreign loans were illusory; the mortgaging of the demesnes, compulsory loans, the issuing of interest-bearing bills of exchange — insofar as these existed at all — were not enough. As early as 1808–09, Prussia fell quite substantially behind in in its payments, and the breathing-space which Napoleon had allowed *de facto* during the Austrian war was soon over. Negotiations over the postponement of repayments etc. broke down completely. Napoleon, deeply suspicious in view of the Prussian army reforms then in progress, aggressively insisted on payment in accordance with the agreement. The government had already resolved to enter into talks on the secession of Silesia, but the king refused. In June 1810, Hardenberg, who had been unable to become Stein's successor in 1808 owing to Napoleon's dissent, was appointed State Chancellor. He pledged to bring the crisis under control with a package of financial and political measures. Hardenberg's policies toward Napoleon were guided in the long term by the hope of a collapse of the Napoleonic system, but for the present they were directed more realistically toward mere survival, subservience to the Empire and, wherever possible, the exploitation of favourable opportunities. They were certainly not geared to heroic resistance, nor towards emancipation. It was the old-fashioned foreign policy of a diplomat, one of *raison d'état*, not that of a revolutionary nationalist. This became very significant later on, during the war and the reorganisation of Germany after the fall of the Emperor. Under pressure from Napoleon between 1810 and 1812, even the king had slumped into a sort of apathy, a condition only intensified by the death of his eminent and energetic wife, Queen Louise, whom Rauch's memorial immortalised even further than Prussian legend.

It remains astonishing that, even under Hardenberg, the interest and principal on the payments to France never rose above the level reached in 1808–09. Growing tensions between France and Russia and the incorporation of Prussia into the anti-Russian front pushed the issue of reparations somewhat into the background. French pressure still remained the onerous reality. Prussia, heavily damaged by the Continental Blockade, was still bled dry financially; in military terms, it remained under the control of the French troops at the Oder and the heavily armed forces of the Confederation of the Rhine.

Then there was Austria. It had forfeited its standing as a major European power, but still retained relative independence. After 1805, in an attempt to preserve this independence, it swung to and fro between accommodation and resistance. In 1807, after Tilsit, it seemed totally isolated and had to join the Continental Blockade in the Mediterranean. Napoleon's actions in Spain in 1808 now seemed like concrete proof that it was impossible for the old powers to reach an understanding with the Napoleonic Empire. Austria lived under the constant fear that it would be its turn next. Even Metternich, the ambassador in Paris, abandoned his policy of accommodation and came to the conclusion that resistance was the only alternative to imminent destruction. The final decision to go to war was made in Vienna that autumn. The Austrians believed that Napoleon had been weakened by the Spanish resistance and by internal opposition in France, and that Russia, committed in Finland and at the mouth of the Danube, was not prepared for a war against them.

A new factor then entered the equation: the concept of a nationalist war, a war of the people. The leading Austrian minister since 1805 had been the south German Imperial Count, Philip Stadion. A conservative devotee of the old Reich, Stadion wanted to base the state more firmly on the idea of nationhood. He tried, particularly in 1808, to mobilise a new patriotism through the press, to make affairs of state the affair of the people. He thus made 'freedom' his battle-cry. Moreover, Austria's war was to become a nationalist pan-German war for emancipation and a rebirth of the Reich. The intention was to unleash revolts in the German states, principally in the north — 'the people themselves must become our allies' — in order to carry hesitant governments along in their wake. Gentz and Friedrich Schlegel became the official publicists of this cause, as did Adam Müller and Kleist in the north. The winter of 1808–09 saw Austria embroiled in a frenzy of patriotic German sentiment which even seized the Kaiser. The call to arms by the supreme commander, Archduke Karl, was addressed to the people of Germany, to Austria's German brothers (implicitly excluding the princes of the Confederation of the Rhine, who were not free), and called for emancipation. These were the tones of revolutionary nationalism. The Austrians were counting on old imperial sympathies and support for the fallen dynasties (in Brunswick and Hesse–Kassel, for instance). They were also counting on volunteer corps and help from Prussian patriots, who were adept at drumming up support for popular uprisings and winning over the regular troops to the people's cause.

The whole enterprise failed. It was based on a misreading of the Austrian, the German and the international situation, though certainly Napoleon's good luck on the battlefield tipped the scales as well. Neither Stadion nor anyone else was capable of unleashing a nationalist war in Austria. The new *Landwehr* (militia) was only a defensive force; the war continued, led by the state and fought by the regular army. This army was not able to make best use of surprise tactics, nor could it concentrate its forces in order to smash its opponents one by one.

The war began with defeats and Napoleon's capture of Vienna. The Austrian victory in Aspern, though it boosted their morale as the first outright victory over Napoleon on the battlefield, remained an isolated incident; the war was finally lost with Napoleon's victory at Wagram. Hopes to internationalise the war came to nothing. England refused to provide direct assistance, nor would Prussia enter on Austria's side — the king's caution won the day against the insistence of the 'war party' of Scharnhorst and

Gneisenau. Nor was any agreement reached with Russia. Stadion had misjudged the forces of the Austrian body politic as well as the European situation as a whole. The uprisings in territories outside Austria, like the mobilisation of troops by the Prussian Major Schill, the Westphalian Colonel Dörnberg in Kassel and the Duke of Brunswick, remained isolated incidents. Those taking part in the revolt in Hesse, in part just unarmed peasants, dispersed in the initial battles outside Kassel. The mass of the Westphalian troops remained loyal to the new king. There were no Austrian successes to whip up enthusiasm for the revolts and an English landing in the north failed to materialise. The primary cause for these defeats, however, was the fact that these sporadic outbursts of popular revolt found no universal echo in the population as a whole, at least none that would encourage them to active resistance. In fact, the forces of emancipation sometimes encountered passive resistance by the people. The pressure from Napoleon and the violation of sacred, directly experienced traditions were not yet so great as to drive the people — whom years of absolutism, feudalism and a bureau-cratic regime had lulled into passivity — into a revolutionary partisan and guerrilla war.

This leaves only one astonishing incident to report — the popular revolt in Tyrol. After the region had become Bavarian in 1805, it was ruled by the Rhenish-Confederate–Bavarian bureacracy. The feudal constitution was abolished; new taxes and conscription violated the old legislation; even the name of Tyrol was abolished and the Tyrol Castle auctioned off. The Prince-Bishops of Trient and Chur were expelled from the country and religious worship fell under state control. Such anti-clerical and extremely bureaucratic measures by the occupying power encountered fierce opposi-tion from forces demanding the reinstatement of old rights, religious and dynastic loyalties and the tradition of a free peasantry. Tyrol's proximity to Austria, which had systematically orchestrated the Tyrolean peasants' revolt, and the mountainous terrain which was ideally suited to a guerrilla war, were contributing factors. It took only five days to liberate the country; the peasants, led by Andreas Hofer and others, won four victories over the French and Bavarians at Mount Isel. This was a notable event even in the eyes of contemporaries; a people's revolt and war of emancipation fuelled by conservative regionalism were hardly the sort of revolutionary nationalist and democratic movements which one might expect in the age of revolution.

Such movements, and particularly their adherents who died for the cause (Major Schill was shot dead, and Andreas Hofer was killed in Mantua), were to be imprinted deep in the memory of the nationalist and liberation movements of the nineteenth cen-tury as the first martyrs to the cause. Although they had revolted in the name of their old dynasties and not for the cause of Germany against Napoleon, their place was nevertheless secure in the gallery of myths and legends. They had acquired a stature similar to the bookseller Palm, who was executed at the behest of Napoleon in 1806 for distributing the pamphlet *Germany in its Period of Deep Humiliation*. Uhland's song about the 'Good Comrade' was written at the time that they were laying down their lives. This song has accompanied war and death in war in Germany for more than 150 years.

The war ended with the peace settlement of Schönbrunn, in which Austria had once again to cede large territories, in particular the south-western provinces of Villach right up to Croatia and Istria, then Salzburg, Berchtesgaden and the Innviertel, as well as a substantial part of its Polish territories, in addition to having to pay enormous war reparations. Though he could have demanded even larger territories or even the dissolution of Austria, Napoleon calculated that this would have created an unmanageable vacuum. This might have promoted competition among the princes of the Confederation of the Rhine and left Russia even more alienated than before.

If one calls to mind the series of huge defeats suffered by the anti-Napoleonic powers from Austerlitz through Jena and Friedland to Wagram, it will be obvious how inept the powers of old Europe were in coming to terms with the revolutionary policies of the heir to the French Revolution, how no fully committed coalition could be formed, and how the individual powers were smashed individually, one after another. It was thought that the conqueror could be tamed by appeasement and by appeals to his reason and common sense. An alternative policy practised was that of continuing to act politically as individual states in the calm waters of seemingly normal power conflicts of a traditional kind, and not pulling the chestnuts out of the fire for other powers who were 'coincidentally' also opposed to Napoleon. All these options were considered or acted upon. This explains the disjointed actions and the weaknesses of all the coalitions, as well as the acts of collaboration and appeasement.

In all this, two factors are significant for the march of German history. First, Austria's attempt to place itself at the head of the fight for national liberation reaffirmed its standing, at a time of incipient nationalism, as a German power based on old imperial patriotism, and to a certain degree gave it a modern image. It continued to be influential until 1848, when the Paulskirche (the Frankfurt National Assembly) elected as Imperial Administrator (*Reichsverweser*) Archduke Johann of Austria, who had played a major part in organising the war and the Tyrolean uprising. A part of the 'better', German tradition of Austria seemed to have been established, one to which Metternich's pan-German opponents could adhere in the following decades. Secondly, the feeble attempt to found an Austrian polity, via a war of liberation, on the alliance between government and nation, collapsed with the end of the war and was never renewed. The appeal which the militaristic state of Prussia began to have for the Germans in the nineteenth century, by dint of its great reforms and those who supported them, namely its model civil service, had no Austrian counterpart. This has become a vital factor in the history of the nationalist issue.

The Austrian policy of resistance had failed, and the state was seriously weakened. Metternich, who now became the chief minister and who would remain so for forty years, came to the obvious conclusion. The only possible policy was an easing of tension, one of actual collaboration with France. This was Austria's only hope of surviving relatively unimpaired and independent, until such time as a new European order came about in which Austria could rebuild her strength and regain her freedom to act. In foreign policy, Austria had an advantage over Prussia, for on 1 February 1810 Napoleon married the daughter of the Austrian Emperor. The son of the Revolution used the archaic, pre-revolutionary political weapon of marriage to obtain the dynastic legitimacy of old Europe, which would guarantee him and his empire greater security and an existence beyond his own lifetime. Since he had been unable to marry the Tsar's sister, he took the Emperor's daughter instead. Metternich — a realist, not a legitimist — had used all his diplomatic skill to push this marriage through, for though it was without direct 'compensations', it was a guarantee of Austria's existence. And he succeeded in evading both a pro-French engagement against Russia — in Poland or in the Balkans — and any anti-French agreement with Russia.

The climax of Napoleonic rule over Germany and the continent and the onset of its demise came when the fragile partnership between France and Russia fell apart, an outcome which had been eagerly awaited by Napoleon's opponents, the committed patriots as much as the diplomats playing a waiting game. The manifold tensions were swelling into a flood-tide. These were, in part, caused by Turkey, Sweden and its new crown prince Bernadotte, as well as by the Polish problem, the failure of the proposed marriage to the Tsar's sister, French annexation of the North Sea states and Oldenburg which was linked by blood ties to the Tsar, and above all by the Continental Blockade. The Napoleonic system needed successes to stabilise itself in the face of mounting crises. In the final analysis, the Tsar, as a potential ally of the English, remained the latent threat to the Napoleonic system. Napoleon's drive for an economic victory over England forced him into a confrontation with Russia, and the Tsar had to realise that, in the final reckoning, no lasting arrangement was possible with the revolutionary who had turned existing European relations on their head.

In this situation, both German powers had to choose between an alliance with Russia or with France, since neutrality was impossible in view of Napoleon's position of strength. The decision rested initially with Austria. Metternich rejected an alliance with Russia. He was not convinced either of Russia's commitment and loyalty to the alliance, or of the chances that a new coalition would have of achieving victory. In any case, Metternich considered Prussia's position so precarious and threatened that he wanted to avoid any closer ties. He succeeded in avoiding a full alliance with France, which would have made Austria into a satellite. Austria's sole obligation was to provide a relatively autonomous and primarily 'observational' auxiliary corps — a symbolic presence, so to speak — in case Napoleon should triumph (and was able to signal Austrian 'passivity' to the Russians). In exchange, Metternich was assured of territorial compensations (in case of a disintegration or a territorial 'displacement' of Prussia: should the need arise, Silesia was available!).

In Prussia, the 'patriots' demanded a union with Russia — since Napoleon, as they saw it, even if he were victorious, would destroy Prussia. They began with some vigour (and English assistance) to rearm in secret. In August 1811, Gneisenau again suggested a popular revolt in north Germany. He was seeking to arouse the nation's enthusiasm and readiness to make sacrifices, as well as its total resistance. He thus intended to make citizens' rights, elections and access to official positions, as well as inheritance and land acquisition, contingent upon active participation in the struggle. In response to the king's cool remark that this was 'good poetry', he said something that was at once odd and yet characteristic for one of the most senior military men: 'The security of the throne is founded on poetry — on the lifting of hearts.' When straightforward alliances with England and Austria proved impossible, Hardenberg initially offered Napoleon an alliance which would have rid Prussia of its military and financial strait-jacket, and which even included the prospect of territorial compensations. Napoleon, however, demanded total integration (*Anschluss*), the provision of troops and the right of passage for his armies through Prussian territory, with no compensations. Hardenberg felt that this would mean the abdication of Prussia's sovereignty and was now in favour of an alliance with Russia. For the king, with one eye on Austria and Russia, and the French troops standing by to march in, the risk was too great. On 24 February, Prussia acceded to Napoleon's demands. Prussia had to provide an auxiliary corps of 20,000 men, becoming the deployment zone and transit territory for the *Grande Armée* and even having to stump up enormous sums to keep the force supplied. Prussia had already been forced into rearmament some time before. In 1812, Napoleon once again had the whole of Germany subject to his will.

Many of the patriots gave notice in the face of this 'defeatism' of the king and the majority of the establishment. About 500 officers, almost a quarter, resigned their commissions. Boyen and Clausewitz went to Russia. This was a radical switch of allegiance, from loyalty to the king to loyalty to an abstraction — fatherland and nation. Their obvious self-interest defined their sense of duty. Gneisenau went to England; officially, he was on leave. The head of the Prussian police, Justus Gruner, went to work for the Russians and started to form a spying and sabotage organisation from Prague, which would simultaneously serve to mobilise active resistance inside Napoleonic Germany. He was arrested by the Austrian police in August 1812, before his organisation was able to have any real effect.

But what of public opinion? What was the German people's attitude to Napoleon? In the first place, there was a large circle of supporters and admirers of Napoleon and the Confederation of the Rhine, a pro-French 'party', so to speak, and not only in the states of the Confederation, but even in Austria and Prussia. It was these supporters who had set the tone in Berlin, not only before 1806, but even during the period of occupation and at the time of Stein's dismissal in 1807–08. There was a peculiar admixture of anti-Austrian and anti-English sentiments, combined with a Berlin enlightenment. The two great Germans of the era, Goethe and Hegel, were admirers of Napoleon and his greatness in 1805–06 and the following years. For them, Napoleon was the Spirit of the World (*Weltgeist*) on horseback, the man of the present and the future, and others thought the same. For some, he represented progress, the cultured *Zeitgeist*, freedom; he was the mortal enemy of feudalism and the *ancien régime*, as the Bavarian J. Christoph von Aretin saw him. For others, he was the saviour who had emerged from chaos, the tamer of the Revolution who had preserved its achievements. Or he was the unifier of Europe, the protagonist of the true balance of power. Indeed (and here we see his own propaganda working) he was the bringer of peace, according to Niklas Vogt and Johannes von Müller, in any event, the prevailing tone one was of hope and expectation. In the first few years after 1806, the Confederation of the Rhine even had a whole publicity machine which spoke of it as the embodiment of the progressive ideal. The argumentation was in part pre-nationalist and particularist, in part supra-national, European and cosmopolitan, and in part quintessentially German and in the old Reich tradition. According to Dalberg, for instance, the Confederation of the Rhine should represent German national unity in the universalistic new empire of Charlemagne. These were the kind of motives which led many important men to offer their services to Napoleon or the states of the Confederation of the Rhine. Then there were the realists, whether markedly particularist or not, for whom co-operation with Napoleon was the only possibility, whether they identified themselves fully with his system or not, and whether or not they supported or distanced themselves from the incipient nationalist feeling. Support for the Confederation of the Rhine and nationalist feeling were not contradictory. On the margins there were, of course, the opportunists, those who sought to turn intimacy with the powerful to their own advantage — like a number of Prussian reactionaries who were prepared to co-operate with the French simply to be rid of

Stein. In the occupied and exploited territories, moreover, poverty and everyday worries precluded any thoughts of resistance.

The majority of the people were long-suffering and passive. In the beginning, there was a clear anti-Austrian and pro-French mood in Bavaria, for instance, and in other parts of southern Germany. The Confederation of the Rhine agreements were signed in just this sort of prevailing atmosphere. The reorganisation met with broad agreement. In the artificially created states of north-west Germany, the fervour of liberation and a new euphoria were elicited but soon faded. The levying of troops, the heavy tax burden and especially the Continental Blockade, as well as violent measures by the police and the occupying forces, the absence or delay of social reforms and an onerous bureaucracy, all contributed to the sharp rise in discontent with French rule. This was already in evidence by 1810; it was quite strong by 1812, though it produced precious little active resistance and little in the way of a nationalist spirit. In 1813, Napoleon could still take for granted the loyalty of the subjects in the Confederation of the Rhine, though there was a form of passive resistance, especially in the north-west, where the number of desertions and tax boycotts increased.

The developments in the annexed territories on the left bank of the Rhine are both interesting and ambivalent. On the one hand, the sweeping modernisation measures met with approval, and the growth within the French economic sphere could only reinforce such approbation. Affiliation to a great empire seemed to offer more stability and security than was the case in the other Germany at that time, and the people were, of course, gradually becoming accustomed to being ruled by a power which seemed to be there to stay. On the other hand, especially after 1808, there was a growing feeling of oppression and a dwindling consensus, generated by army recruitment and taxation policies, the national egotism and arrogance of the French, the unavoidable taint of 'foreign rule'. The Emperor's anti-clerical politics, or his appropriation of church power to serve his own interests, along with press censorship and a dictatorship of opinion, were all contributing factors.

The intellectual elite also demonstrated this ambivalence, but in their case it was of a more political nature. Their attraction on the one hand by the progress toward freedom and modernity in the territories under French law—at times, in fact, they were ready to believe that a unity of nations and a peaceful empire were on the horizon—was opposed by a republican distaste of tyranny. As modernists and nationalists, they rejected foreign rule in favour of the new 'fatherland'. They projected the romantic rediscovery of a national identity, German history and culture which had a particular resonance in the territories of the Rhine. The Jacobin from Coblenz, Joseph Görres, became Napoleon's most decisive opponent and an advocate of a nationalist democracy which was romantic in tone, while the progressive poet of the Vormärz, Heinrich Heine, born in Düsseldorf in 1797, retained a positive impression of Napoleon throughout his life.

At the other end of the scale were Napoleon's most decided opponents. They opposed the man of violence, the amoral despot, traits which had become more obvious in his nature since the murder of the Duc d'Enghien. They were opposed to the man who had destroyed Europe, its balance of power and its peaceful order. Their most notable representative was Friedrich Gentz. A Kantian and a supporter of the English conservative reformer and enemy of the French Revolution, Edmund Burke, he later became secretary to Metternich. More important and of more consequence in the long term than this moral and European opposition was that of the 'patriots' even though they take up the themes of the farmer. For the decisive difference is that the resistance to Napoleon, the desire for the independence of one's own country and its 'liberation' grows into a nationalistic patriotism. This means first of all that the state is founded on the politically organised and active *Volk*, i.e. the nation; and secondly that this nation is no longer understood as a particularist one, such as Prussia or Austria, but rather *gesamtdeutsch*, to include all of Germany.

The old provincial patriotism becomes a nationalist German patriotism and spawns the German nationalist movement. It was precisely the opposition to world dictatorship which mobilised the nationalist movement into a political and revolutionary movement. The patriots were mostly civil servants (*Beamten*), army officers and educated men, and the movement was centred in Prussia after 1806, later gaining ground in Austria. This core was soon joined by philosophers, journalists and writers.

The reformers and the patriots were not, of course, one and the same. General Yorck, for instance, was a Prussian patriot and an enemy of the reformers; Theodor von Schön started out primarily as a reformer without any great foreign policy interests; and Hardenberg's policies steered clear of 'patriotic' sentiments. In general, however, the striving for inner renewal and for emancipation from dictatorship and foreign rule became one and the same thing. A new nationalist ideology was born. It was propagated and publicised primarily by the philosopher Fichte, beginning with his Berlin 'Addresses to the German Nation' of 1806–07, and by the publicist Ernst Moritz Arndt, son of a serf from Rügen. Both Fichte and Arndt took the prepolitical ideas of cultural and popular German nationhood and politicised them by linking them to the democratic nationalist tendencies of the French Revolution. These ideas will be discussed later in more detail as part of a review of the nationalist movement.

The desire for nationhood and national statehood now became paramount, and the nation was to be based on the people. A way of thinking was turned into a practical goal, and both Fichte and Arndt developed a sort of nationalist Messianism, with collectivist-socialist ideas, but motivated above all by an imperial sense of mission. This intellectual extremism won influence among the educated classes and young people, initially in Prussia. Idealistic philosophy and nationalistic patriotism converged. Arndt became the prophet of the crusade against Napoleon, the enemy and demon of the world. In 1808–09, the movement played an important role among journalists working in Berlin (writers such as Kleist and Adam Müller, for instance) and in Vienna (Schlegel and Gentz). The romantic preoccupation with the identity of the Germans, their history and culture—as found in the writings of Arnim, Brentano, the Schlegels, the Grimms, and Görres—also fed into this movement. In the case of Görres, the incipient nationalist opposition helped, as well; in 1813, he became, after Arndt, the most effective publicist of the democratic-nationalist cause. The journalists, philosophers and practical reformers surrounding Stein and Scharnhorst were soon joined by the first of the semi-secret organisations of the emergent nationalist opposition. In Königsberg, the much-discussed and overemphasised 'League of Virtue' (the 'Society for Morality and Science' as it was actually called) was one of the first such societies. In fact, this germ of the patriotic movement was more effective on a rhetorical than on a practical level. In Berlin in 1811, Friesen and Jahn founded a German Association for Liberation, Inner Renewal and the Ultimate Unification of the German People. By 1812, it had eighty members in Berlin, as well as seven branch organisations in Prussia and four more elsewhere, and a wide range of contacts. The gymnastic associations started by Jahn, which were democratic and nationalist in outlook, based on the *Volk* and national traditions and directed towards liberation, were part of this movement. Then there were the beginnings of the German student association (*Burschenschaft*). In its original form, it was an umbrella organisation of all German students, dedicated to the German *Volk* and fatherland, and committed to Germanness in word and deed. This phenomenon caught on in Prussia and beyond, especially among students, in Jena, Heidelberg and Landshut. Even among the ruling elites in the states of the Confederation of the Rhine — in the court of the Bavarian Crown Prince Ludwig, for instance — there were strong nationalist-patriotic, anti-Napoleonic stirrings.

The importance of these movements should not be overestimated. They were clearly minority organisations which flourished solely among the bourgeois-aristocratic and educated elite, especially its younger members. In Prussia, its adherents included civil servants and officials in the reform movement. However, by virtue of their position in the Prussian state and through the *émigré* Stein, they had a certain political influence. In 1813, their spokesmen were the loudest voices at a period when the masses were largely silent and the Napoleonic system was being discredited. In its limited way, this movement played a significant historical role in 1813, even if the consequences were quite different from those of 1815. In hindsight, however, this can be seen as the beginning of the nationalist movement which was to become so critical in German history.

2. The Great Reforms

The era of Napoleonic rule in Germany was also the era of the great reforms, in Prussia as well as in the states of the Confederation of the Rhine. It was at this time that the foundations of the modern state and the modern society in Germany were laid; the success and the failure of the reforms had a determining effect on the history of the Germans up until 1848, or indeed into the 1860s. German history of this period is a story with diverging narratives, with the separate developments in Prussia, Austria and southern Germany the result of the variant dramas of reform enacted in the different territories.

In the first instance, these reforms were responses to an impetus from outside, to the French Revolution, and to the Napoleonic challenge and consequent geographical reorganisation of the German world. The world of the *ancien régime* had fallen apart; it had not kept pace with the new and revolutionary political realities of power. The demands made upon a state had changed. To survive, to remain efficient and competitive, a state would have to come to terms with these new demands; it would have to renew itself. But what necessitated the reforms was not merely the iron dictates of power politics, the successes of the Revolution and the new demands imposed in its wake; it was also, and almost inseparably, the new norms. The new ideas of a civil society, grounded on civil liberties and equality under the law, had taken away the legitimacy from the feudal system of estates. These new norms, however one felt about the Revolution, also found recognition and resonance in Germany, even in broad circles of the ruling establishment. The force of these principles, Hardenberg claimed in his Riga Memorandum of 1807, 'is so great and they are so universally acknowledged that the state which does not embrace them must either be forced to accept them or await its downfall.' It was now no longer possible to govern against the prevailing currents of the time, a belief shared by almost all leading politicians, even those who only identified with them half-heartedly. What was needed, therefore, was renewal — the situation itself and the new modified norms demanded it. The pressure for modernisation from outside now began to mobilise the desire for modernisation from within and gave it its real momentum and tenacity: reforms undertaken in the period of absolutism and the Enlightenment were taken as reference points. The task now was to give them a more modern thrust, to bring them up to date, thus transforming them in the process. The reforms were referred to as a revolution from above, a revolution 'in the best sense of the word'. According to Hardenberg, the reforms were 'democratic principles under a monarchic government', a revolutionising of existing relations within a framework of order and evolution and under the authority of a monarchic-bureaucratic state.

The revolution from above would abolish the old order of society which was no longer equal to the new demands made upon it and was irrelevant to the new norms; it would modernise the state and society. First, it would concentrate and intensify the power and effectiveness of the state; it would make it more rational and effective against all forms of feudal and particularist rule, and it would establish for the first time its sovereign power within its own borders, right down to the last inhabitant. Secondly, it would unify its separate territories into a single, integrated state. And finally, in place of the society of feudal estates, it would bring about a society of citizens with equal rights and emancipate the individual from feudal-corporative bonds (and state tutelage) so that all might work in the interest of society as a whole. Subjects would now become citizens, and the divide between state and society, government and people would be bridged. The French had become a political nation; this is what gave them their strength. Equality of citizenship and the participation of citizens in political decisions, these were the two elements of this programme, even though they did not necessarily belong together. Participation of the nation, of the people in the workings of the state, could only come about when the society based on estates became a society of enfranchised citizens — in this sense, there was an obvious tension between the socio-political objectives and what it was possible to achieve.

The supporters of revolutionary reform were not the masses, not a bourgeois society, but the *Beamten* (civil servants). They were the protagonists of modernity — to whom both the feudal order of estates and the absolutist-dynastic order were equally anathema. They felt themselves opposed to all particularist interests; they were the *Allgemeiner Stand* (the general estate), in service to the law, reason and the common good, the true *raison d'état*. They wanted to create a new society of enfranchised citizens and a new state. Bureaucratic rule would replace absolutist and feudal rule, and only within this framework — another element of tension — could there be any real participation of the nation in political life.

(a) The Prussian Reforms

It is worth looking at Prussian reforms in some detail, since they serve as an example of the problems of reconstruction that were generally prevalent at that time. In order to outline what is specific to them and what distinguishes them from others, we will attempt to define the basic terms, the motives and tendencies common to these reforms.

(1) All continuities aside, one brute fact predates the reforms: the catastrophe of 1806, the collapse of old Prussia. All reforms stand in the shadow of the financial crisis threatening the very existence of the state: the raising of the contributions. Prussia, unlike the territories in the south and west which were consolidating a new state into which a number of new territories were to be integrated, was fighting for its survival. It had to rebuild a state which had been defeated and sliced in two, and which was still bleeding from its wounds.

(2) Nevertheless, the reforms did bear the stamp of the Prussian legacy, of absolutism and enlightenment, especially of their late phases. In Prussia, absolutism and centralisation were already entrenched, and the multiplicity of particularist powers and orders, still flourishing in the territories of the south and west, had long since been levelled out. Hence, it had less of a need to catch up where absolutism was concerned. Prussia's problem was the inflexibility of its absolutist system — what critical commentators of the time referred to as the machine state — which was much more pronounced there than elsewhere. At the time of Frederick the Great, Prussia had been one of the classic lands of reforms, a progressive country. The impetus of the enlightened reform programme had kept it moving, but it had got stuck in first gear. No form of social modernisation had been achieved; feudal autonomy remained intact. The *Allgemeines Landrecht* (the Prussian legal code dating from 1794) was typical of this ambivalence. It had put onto the agenda the concept of a state bound by a system of laws and a society of enfranchised citizens under the state, while at the same time entrenching the regional order based on estates and giving it a legal basis. Reforms were planned in many areas, like the abolition of serfdom, or were carried through, like the emancipation of the domain peasants (we are speaking here of the preliminary reforms). But they lacked energy and inner cohesion and the muscle to force them through across the entire social order. The inherited order was strong, the effectiveness of the state limited. The reformers certainly advanced their standing in this period of preliminary reforms, but they still did not have the say; the question of who wielded the real power in the state was still a contest being fought out between the monarchy, the nobility and the bureaucracy.

(3) The Prussian reform movement was deeply influenced by philosophy; it was an idealistic and moralistic movement. This went beyond rhetoric, tone or superstructure, it also characterised its concrete goals and gave it its high standing. No matter how critical and sober we have learned to become when faced with the many idealising distortions of Prussian–German historical legend, this idealistic-metapolitical ethos retains its kernel of truth. The reform was no longer guided, as it was elsewhere, by the spirit of the Enlightenment. It had, so to speak, put the Enlightenment behind it and now stood on a base of Kantian philosophy. The human being is more than an agent, a cog in a machine; he is also an end in himself — autonomous, self-defining, independent. He is more than someone who obeys orders and merely follows tradition — he does things by himself, guided by his own inner voice, his own reason and will. His actions are directed beyond enlightened self-interest and the utilitarian and welfare ethic of the Enlightenment,

towards the good, towards his duty. This Kantian ethos was the rock on which the reform programme was built; it was propagated by idealist philosophy (especially by Fichte), by the educational theories of Pestalozzi, and by the whole German idea of education (which will be discussed later). In the realm of political ideas and morality, reform centres on autonomy and responsibility; it seeks a *neuer Mensch*, a 'reborn', a 'refined' human being. This new man was not only the goal of the reforms; he was needed to carry them out. In this respect, it was much more than an institutional reform; it was, in the widest sense, an educational reform. One of the significant concrete consequences of this initiative is the political concept of civil liberties. Freedom is not only the freedom of the individual from the state and feudal-corporative powers, the freedom to develop his own abilities (this is the concept of freedom specific to Napoleonic reform). Rather, to have freedom is to have a 'share', to be able to participate as a citizen in the workings of the state. This is far from being the sovereignty of the people. It is not democratic self- or co-determination, but is much more an attempt to turn the subject into a citizen, to make the business of the state his business, to have as the basis of the state the independent and free citizen, the people, the nation. The people should no longer be merely the object of bureaucratic patronage, the 'state knows better' syndrome. The whole has been thought out much more from the point of view of the state than from that of the individual, more in terms of duties than of rights; this is the peculiarly idealistic concept of freedom as the *Freiheit zum Staat* (the freedom to take part in the formation of a state). This is the root of Stein's idea of political education, which has it that a common spirit will only be forged by a participating citizenry. This philosophical-political idea of freedom is characteristic of the Prussian reform. Idealism's turn against the ideas of the Enlightenment led the Prussian reformers to adopt a certain distance from the French and Rhenish confederate models and was one of the factors which led some to look to England as an example. There is also a historical aspect at work here. This involves the attempt, with Burke, to fasten onto old traditions, or, as in the case of the anti-absolutist Stein, to hark back to the theories and institutions of old Europe, to estates, intermediary powers and separation of powers.

(4) In addition to the influence of philosophers on their activities, many reformers were impressed by the liberal economic theory of Adam Smith, whose principal advocate had been Professor Kraus of Königsberg: the conviction that competition and the unfettered economic activity of the individual are the real engines of increasing productivity, that the vigorous pursuit of individual self-interest works for the benefit of all. Nowhere did the idea of the liberation of economic energies play as strong a role as in Prussia.

(5) Unlike the situation in the states of the Confederation of the Rhine, the Prussian reforms were always directed towards liberation. What was, in fact, a military and foreign political objective was the force behind all reforms as well as the fundamental ideas of pedagogic nationalism. It was this which gave the reforms their patriotic, nationalistic tone, which developed very quickly from a strain of specifically Prussian particularism into a strain of German nationalism.

The Prussian reforms are referred to in the plural, since they were a series of partial reforms, some implemented simultaneously, others consecutively. They certainly were not developed nor did they proceed according to an overall plan, but were, in their conception and their goals, an integrated whole. The renewal of the separate sectors were part of an overall process; they were to form the constituent parts of a coherent new state and society. Gneisenau put it in a nutshell when he referred to the 'triple alliance' of weapons, science and constitution, of which the liberation of the peasants was also part. One can speak of priorities in the reform agenda, the highest of which was the reform of government and administration. Earlier reforms had come to grief owing to the impotence of the state and a governmental structure which was in part chaotic, in part autocratic. The organisation of a rational administration and the concentration of public power with this administration would establish the dominance of the civil service (*Beamtentum*). This was the real soul of the state, the champion of reasonable opinion, of law, and of the common good, of progress and modernity. The next priority was social and economic emancipation and mobilisation, the creation of a new modern society of free property-owners, with equal rights as far as was possible, out of which a political nation could be formed. And then the consitution: this would cement and consolidate the dominance of the administration, while at the same time binding it by statute; it would safeguard the basic rights of citizens and guarantee their participation in public affairs, in the process of which the state and the administration would be strengthened and legitimised. The organisation of the administration and the emancipation of society were the first tasks, the constitution the last; participation was to be more a consequence than an instrument of modernisation. Here was an inherent source of conflict within the reforms.

Prussian reform, as elsewhere, was a reform of the bureaucracy. The reform wing within the civil service and the officer corps held temporary sway over the aristocracy, as well as over the faction of pro-restoration bureaucrats, and was successful in influencing the monarchy. There were different tendencies within the reform party, and two major positions were advanced under the names of the two first ministers. Stein as a first minister initiated the Prussian reforms in 1807 and 1808. Hardenberg, following a caretaker government, became State Chancellor in 1810. He remained in this position until his death in 1822 and continued the reforms until they finally broke down in 1819–20. Stein's period of office was marked by his leanings towards the old system of estates, the tradition of the Imperial Knights and a harking back to old imperial institutions. He was anti-absolutist, anti-state, mistrustful of the all-regulating centralist state and bureaucracy, and in favour of decentralisation and collegial government. Stein was a conservative reformer, inasmuch as he tried to use traditions, estates and the existing corporate bodies as a basis, and inasmuch as he distanced himself from excessive economic liberalism. But at the same time he was modern, in that he championed the participation of citizens in public affairs. He was more concerned with the citizen's role in the state than the citizen's role in the economy. He was a moralist who tried to incorporate ideas of self-reliance, education and the nation into his practical measures.

Hardenberg, who lived like an eighteenth-century *grand seigneur*, was first and foremost a statist. He wanted a strong state and a tightly organised and centralised administration. He was a liberal individualist who was concerned with the unshackling of economic energies within society. Committed to equality of opportunity, Hardenberg believed in the freedom to develop one's abilities to the full, in respect for property and an equal system of laws and taxes. He was more concerned with civic, economic and individual freedom than with political freedom, less concerned with philosophy, with moral forces, with *Volk* and nation and their participation in the state. He was more a realist and a rationalist, more strongly inclined towards French models. In this sense he was more modern, authoritarian, more radical and dynamic, certainly more pragmatic and less tied to principles. One could go on, but such simple polarisations are deceptive. In truth, we are dealing with mere differences of emphasis within a reform 'party'. It is correct to speak of the Stein–Hardenberg reforms, and by this it is meant not only that they were active at the same time, but also that they shared motives and objectives.

One of the first main areas of reform, therefore, was the modernisation of government and administration. Since the reforms as a whole were a matter for the administration, its own internal reform had a high priority and was part and parcel of the whole structural reorganisation and changes in the distribution of power within the state. Just as in the late absolutist period, no unified state had yet been formed — there were only states, provinces and territories governed by His Majesty. There was also no unified government, rather a confusion of partly specialised, partly provincial *Oberbehörden* (regional authorities). There was no common system of organisation or information, with no overall view over such things as finances. Besides the ministers, there was the king's cabinet, his personal advisers and councillors, with whose help in the main he would make the real decisions. This anarchic, irrational and, at the same time, autocratic system had long been the subject of protest from the senior bureaucrats. Stein lost his ministerial position in 1806 as a result of this protest, but at the onset of the reform era in 1807 this system was gone. The cabinet system eventually disappeared — the last remaining cabinet minister, Beyme, was removed, even though he was a reformer himself. In place of the former *Oberbehörden*, a ministry was set up, organised along departmental lines, which — without interference from the *Nebenbehörden* (subsidiary authorities) — was directly responsible to the king. This went beyond being simply a more rational organisation. It was a system whereby the previous autocracy was replaced by a twin leadership of bureaucracy and monarchy, in which ministers occupied a strong position and even predominated during the reform era. The king now had to work alongside his ministers and could only govern through them; an autocratic authoritarian state was turned into a bureaucratic one. This represented an extraordinary power gain by the senior bureaucracy, which also managed to edge out the third power block in the state, the feudal aristocracy.

The ministry was, as Stein wanted it, a collegiate body without a first minister raised above the rest. This was to change in 1810 when Hardenberg took office. He assumed the position of State Chancellor, thus controlling access to the monarch. In Stein's plans, a critical role was played by the establishment of a *Staatsrat* (Council of State) which consisted of current and former ministers, heads of departments, as well as the princes and persons appointed by the king. It was intended as a legislative body and one which laid down the principles of administration, exercising supreme control over governmental business and over the administration with decision-making powers — a sort of surrogate parliament, firmly in the hands of the bureaucracy. It constituted a counterbalance against any possible relapse into absolutist, autocratic despotism and the influence on the king of feudal and military circles and court favourites. The *Staatsrat* thus constituted an important stage on the way to the desired objective of a constitutional state under the rule of law. However, the implementation of such an ambitious project was doubtful. For a start, the task of putting the ministers and departmental heads on an equal footing was a very thorny problem indeed. In 1808, the establishment of this Council of State was, in fact, suspended, and in 1810 Hardenberg delayed it further, downgrading it to the role of an advisory committee.

The administration, as well as the government, was the subject of reform. In the course of the modernisation process of integration after 1807, the whole state was referred to as Prussia. The country was divided into largely artificial administrative districts (*Regierungsbezirke*), at the head of the administration of which were district governments. These were subordinate to the *Ministerium* (state government) and subdivided on a departmental basis. These governments — and this was something specific to Prussian reform — were not placed under the control of an all-powerful prefect on the French model. They were organised instead on a collegiate basis under a president, who was *primus inter pares*; discussion and consensus, Stein's ethos, were the stamp of the Prussian bureaucracy. These governments satisfied a persistent demand of the reformers — the separation of administration and justice. In exchange for a fee, a legal right of appeal was granted over which the administration itself would decide. The stage was not reached where the judiciary exercised control over the administration, because (thus went the dialectic of the reforms) this would have given the more conservative judiciary of the time the power to stonewall the reform initiatives of the administration.

The central problem of Prussian administrative organisation, in fact of the state constitution itself, remained the organisation of the lower tier, the *Kreise* (literally, circles). This was to enable state power to penetrate into the countryside. After numerous preliminary drafts, Hardenberg ordered a far-reaching reorganisation under the so-called *Gendarmerie-Edikt* of 30 July 1812. The *Kreise* became a unified administrative unit which was placed under state control and which encompassed peasant villages, domains, *Gutsbezirke* and small towns. A *Gutsbezirk* was an administrative unit comprising a large number of estates (not incorporated in a parish). A *Kreisdirektor* appointed by the state was to take the place of the *Landrat* appointed by the nobility, i.e. the replacement of a feudal *Kreis* administration by a bureaucratic one. This *Kreisdirektor* had a position similar to that of a prefect: supervisory and directorial powers over all local authorities. An autonomous regional police force (*Gendarmerie*) was created which was to make the policing rights of the private estate-owners largely superfluous. The patrimonial jurisdiction of the private estate-owners was also replaced by the state judiciary. Alongside the *Kreisdirektor* there were six *Kreis* deputies, appointed by an electoral college made up in equal parts by peasants, townsmen and landowners. Together with the director and the judge, these would make up the *Kreis* administration and would be competent to pass resolutions on all important matters, especially questions of finance. In this respect, the system was one in which administration, representation and justice were in a curious way amalgamated and combined, thus partially fulfilling Stein's concept of the participation of the citizenry in the administration.

This *Kreis* reform, one of the most radical reforms against the aristocracy, failed. There was a fierce outburst of protest from the aristocratic opposition, and the measures were suspended in 1814 when they were barely under way. In 1816, a decree was issued which stated that the district magistrate would be selected as a general rule — which meant in the east — from a list of three estate-owners proposed by the *Kreisstände* (*Kreis* assembly). This led to the long-term consolidation of the powerful position of the Junkers at local level — in conflict with both the bureaucratic state and the incipient bourgeois–peasant society in the countryside.

Finally, there was local government reform. Coming chronologically after the liberation of the peasants, the second large-scale reform measure was Stein's Municipal Ordinance of 19 November 1808. This provided for the reorganisation of municipal self-administration — the measure which has since been most closely associated in liberal Germany with the name of Stein. Above all, this was the clearest expression of Stein's idea of reform, of bringing together state and society, state and nation, of founding the polity on the freedom of the citizenry and their participation in public affairs. What self-administration meant, in effect, was being part of and on a level within the constitution of the state as a whole, the construction of the state from the bottom upward, the build-up of co-determination and autonomy in the smaller spheres, where it was possible to keep an overview. These were the roots of something like a democracy. Here, on the one hand, Stein's old-style European mistrust of the centralised state and of the crippling domination of the all-regulating bureaucracy found expression. Self-administration was a counterbalance and a corrective against the bureaucratisation of life by the absolutist modern state. On the other hand, we see expressed Stein's vision of the future, his penchant for political education. Self-administration as a means of co-determination was to awaken an interest in public affairs and encourage active involvement in them. As Stein put it, 'We must train the nation to conduct its own affairs, so that it may grow out of its childhood state.'

According to Johann Gottfried Frey, Stein's colleague and the real author of the Municipal Ordinance, 'Participation in public affairs' 'stimulates interest in the common good and encourages public service, which in turn creates the national spirit.' The individual should thus be elevated ('ennobled') above his own passivity and his own interests and private egoism, and this would eventually lead to a strengthening of the state. Behind this philosophy lay the conviction, which owed much to the old European idea of estates and was kept alive by the English model, that the political order was not grounded on the simple opposition of state and individual, but rather on a wealth of intermediary forces, based in the local administrations. Added now to what were considered the determining forces of the state — monarchy, aristocracy, bureaucracy — was a new one: the citizenry. In this respect, the programme of self-administration was just as closely linked to the reform of state, administration and constitution as it was to the emancipation of civil society.

It is curious that Stein's reorganisation of communal self-administration started in the east of Germany, which had few actual cities. What cities there were were completely under the control of the state administration, and such self-administration as did exist was devoid of meaning. The judiciary, for instance, frequently made up their numbers from retired military men. Stein's concept (and rhetoric) of returning to old traditions was not very realistic, since the old orders and the vestiges of them which still remained were based on legal immunities and particularist interests, on petrified guilds and corporations, on privileges and nepotism. They were unmodern and hostile to progress.

In this respect, it was indeed a new order. On the one hand, the Municipal Ordinance cleared away the vestiges of the particularist system of estates. Special rights for regions and individual towns were abandoned, and there was now a unified state-wide municipal constitution. The residual particularist sovereign powers of the cities over the judiciary and policing were surrendered to the state. The cities were placed under the overall supervision of the state; they could no longer be little republics, states within a state. In this sense, the reform completed the work of absolutism. However, what was new and decisive was the creation of communal autonomy, the liberation of the cities from state tutelage, intervention and encroachment by the military, and they were given sole charge of their affairs. Above all, this involved the right to determine taxes and expenditure. Matters of policing were also returned to the hands of the cities, as a duty they were to perform for the state. Moreover, this new autonomy was now based on a new internal structure of cities, not a corporate system of estates. The inhabitants were no longer divided according to their estate at birth, into *Grossbürger* and *Kleinbürger* — (upper middle and lower middle class). They no longer voted in corporations, but in districts, and their representatives had a free mandate which was no longer subordinate to directives from above.

Nevertheless, differences remained. Not every city-dweller was a citizen; citizenship was to remain a special right based on civic pride and civic consciousness and had to be applied for. Though it was no longer tied to birth and membership of a guild, citizenship was now contingent upon length of residence, on home ownership, or the practice of a trade. Stein's mistrust of the civil servants and the educated professions played a role in this; they seemed to him too far removed from the practical definition of the 'normal' citizen. As a general rule, these classes were bundled into the category of *Schutzver-wandten* (protected citizens), who were city-dwellers without the right to citizenship. Those without property, soldiers and Jews also belonged to this class. In this sense, vestiges of the feudal social order remained in place, while at the same time a new class system was being created. A low-level census was taken to determine the right to vote which included the lower middle class. However, eligibility for political office was usually confined to property-owners. It was basically self-evident at that time that participation was confined to the middle classes, property-owners and/or the 'educated classes'. Municipal self-government was based on the principle of the separation of powers. The municipal council and the *Magistrat* (its elected executive) were composed of paid members elected for twelve years and unpaid members elected for six years, professional administrators within the community and honorary members. Dislike for the bureaucracy and the fear of creating a new communal bureaucracy also played a role here. When commissions were appointed — to deal with poverty, for instance — they consisted of representatives of the citizenry and *Magistrat*. The municipality was headed by a mayor, who, like the *Magistrate* (executive councillors), had to be endorsed by the state.

Involvement in self-administration was a duty — 'the people are not allowed, they are *ordered* to govern themselves' — and the citizens had not demanded this right. This was the paradox of the revolution from above. For this reason, there was great difficulty in putting the new measures into effect. In many cases, officials were re-elected who would otherwise have been pensioned off; in Königsberg, Frey, who had devised the measures, was defeated. Perhaps the apparatus of communal constitutionalism was too much for the small Prussian cities to swallow, but in the medium and long term they became the models to emulate. In Prussia, the city came to be regarded as the home of increasing freedom and participatory government.

Admittedly, reform remained fragmented and its actual intention unfulfilled. Reform began with the cities, since the opposition from established interests was small there, or at least surmountable. However, reform was also to be extended to the rural districts. The strict separation of city and country, which was one of the structural principles of absolutist as well as feudal Prussia, was to be overcome. But communal reform in the country never got beyond the stage of initial drafts. It had been meant to replace the feudal supremacy of the *Gutsherren* and *Grundherren*, even over the peasant villages, with a workable self-government at village level.*

Communal reform sank in the mire during the battle for *Kreis* reform and a constitution, defeated by the revitalisation of the old aristocracy. This is the tragic reverse side of the successful Municipal Ordinance: it reinforced the distinction between town and country as a basic fact of nineteenth-century Prussian history.

The second large area of reform was the reform of society, which first and foremost meant reform of the agrarian constitution — what historians call the 'liberation of the peasants'. This was a process which was taking place at different stages all over Europe and caused the dissolution of the old, feudal, seigneurial and co-operative agrarian structure. The peasants were to be freed from levies, services and duties, which hitherto they had been bound to render to the landlords. They were to achieve personal freedom, full property rights to land, and the freedom to offer their manpower to whomever they wished. In this way it was not only labour but the land itself which would be liberated from previous non-economic, non-material, personal ties. At the same time the peasants were to be liberated from co-operative obligations — the communal possession of fields and woodlands and the *Flurzwang*, the obligation to conform to the rules governing an open-field system. They were to become free individuals. The liberation of the peasants was no partial reform, for 'land' was the dominant economic and social reality; it was a great and fundamental reform of society as a whole which opened the way for the bourgeois era. For this reason it needs more careful analysis. The implementation of these measures in Prussia is of particular importance for German history, since it was in Prussia that the old social order was first radically broken up. It was in the east, in a region dominated by *Gutsherrschaft*, that reform had a deeper impact than anywhere else, and the new social order on the land became so crucially important for power relations in Prussia and Germany as a whole.

By about 1800 the Prussian agrarian constitution (and, for that matter, the agrarian constitution in general), with its feudal foundations and its mercantile and absolutist flavour, was considered out of date by the civil service, the educated public, the agricultural 'experts', even by a section of the aristocracy. It was considered by Schön to be 'barbaric' and a 'remnant of a dark era'. Reform was on the agenda, for which there were different reasons and motives. Politically, the enlightened absolutist bureaucracy wanted to extend the arm of the state right down to the humblest subject, eradicating all feudal intermediary powers. The liberation of the peasants was an episode in the battle fought by the bureaucracy against the aristocracy. Morally, in the spirit of the humanitarian enlightenment and Kant's ethical rigorism, the human rights and human

---

*TRANSLATOR'S NOTE: *Gutsherren* and *Grundherren* refer to two different forms of landowners. The *Gutsherren* were the lords of the private estates, equivalent in England to the lords of the manor. They had ultimate power over their *Gut* (estate) and the way in which it was farmed, within the context of a particularist state. The *Grundherren* were landowners who did not hold ultimate power over their *Grund*, and who would lease out their land to peasants in numerous holdings. The peasants under *Grundherrschaft* enjoyed a more economic independence than the peasants under *Gutsherrschaft*.

dignity of the peasant were to be recognised; he should no longer be society's slave and a beast of burden, but should be liberated from his brutal and indolent condition. Serfdom had become morally repellent.

But there was something else. In the late eighteenth century, from Rousseau to Justus Möser, the peasant had been re-evaluated and idealised, so his emancipation acquired a historical justification as well as one based on natural right. The peasant, from Möser to Arndt and Baron vom Stein, harking back to 'old Germanic' times, is the core of the nation. As a freeman and property-owner he is the true backbone of a liberated polity. There are clearly anti-aristocratic overtones here. The farm of a Junker in Mecklenburg, where the peasants had been 'laid flat' by the lords of the manor, was, in Stein's vituperative phrase in 1802, like the 'den of a beast of prey' in the wilderness. Not only should the peasant be allowed to live as a human being; he should also become a full citizen. Only on the basis of peasant freedom could state and society be 'ennobled' and 'made moral', and therein lay the pathos of the reform.

From an economic standpoint, questions were raised by physiocrats and cameralists as to whether the agrarian constitution was 'expedient' for the 'welfare of the land', casting doubt on what had hitherto been self-evident. The economic liberalism of Adam Smith, which had had an extraordinary influence through Kant's pupil Kraus in Königsberg, especially on those studying to become civil servants, taught that the unfettered pursuit of self-interest was the only 'rational landlord'. This meant that only the free owner of his own land and labour was productive and effective and could increase his productivity. According to this theory, compulsory labour was slow, poor, and uneconomic in comparison to free wage-labour. Every innovation to increase productivity, for instance the summer cultivation of 'fallow land', foundered on the fixing of duties and services and on the *Flurzwang*. The aristocratic privilege granted on the estates of the Imperial Knights blocked the influx of necessary credit, *Bauernschutz* (protective measures for peasants) hindered the creation of rational production units, and the duty of the *Herr* to provide welfare for his serfs prevented the establishment of a more rational system of labour. In this sense, it was necessary not only to liberate the peasants, but to liberate the landowners from obligations outside the realm of economics and to create free labourers. England, the most progressive agrarian country of the age when the large landowners were finally in total control, was economically the great example to all. The emancipation of the peasants ought eventually to improve their welfare as well as the state's tax yield. 'Freedom and property', 'rational agriculture' — these were the slogans of a bureaucracy influenced by absolutism, enlightenment and early liberalism. Modernisation, not only of the land but of society, was the central issue of the programme of reforms.

Not only did the norms change, but the relationships had changed as well. Large-scale agriculture was commercialised and geared towards profitability. The tenants on the large estates were now members of the middle class. A flourishing trade in land severed the patriarchal ties between aristocratic families and tenants, and brought in buyers from the middle class — via special authorisations — into the ranks of the knights; sovereign rights now became purchasable. The majority of aristocratic families lost their land base. Levies formerly rendered in kind were now paid in money, which on the domains also applied to services. The growth in population made *Gesindezwangsdienst* (compulsory servitude) and the ban on migration less important, but the growing landless underclass presented a new problem. The large landowners' (*Bauernschutz*), interests in rationalisation and modernisation clashed with those of the peasantry, and the landlord's obligation to provide for tenant welfare (*Fürsorgepflicht*), with the practice of exemption from leases for the nobility on estates and the exclusion of the merchant class from the land. The aristocracy, in a sort of united front, responded by imposing even more services and obligations on their tenants, driven by the prospect of increased profits. In short, the tide of economic and social change was forced up against the legal barriers of the system and thus eroded them. Admittedly, at first only a small percentage of the landed gentry were prepared to give up privileges, like compulsory services or *dominium directum*, in exchange for complete freedom to expand; the majority were pre-capitalist in mentality. Investments were a loss, whereas compulsory services cost them nothing.

The greatest advocates of liberation for the peasants were the reformist civil servants, not the peasants themselves. There had been various outbreaks of unrest since the French Revolution and the promulgation of the *Allgemeines Landrecht* in 1794, especially in Saxony and Silesia. But they were directed more against abuses and increased oppression by the nobility than against the system itself, or else they took the announcements of reform as an immediate encouragement to carry them out. There were instances of peasants in central and western Germany who actually rejected emancipation, as it meant they would no longer receive seigneurial concessions. The peasants were not interested in modernisation. Reform was for the most part something the peasants had imposed upon them, not something gained by their own efforts. They had been excluded for too long from the historical arena of movements for social change.

Prior to 1806, there had only been 'preliminary reforms' as part of the general trend for reform in Prussia. These principally involved the liberation of the peasants on the state-controlled domains (though in East Prussia this amounted to 55% of the peasants, if only 7% in Silesia). This was finally completed in 1807, if for no other reason than that the peasants were a financial burden on the state at a time of war. The quite varied legal and property arrangements pertaining to peasants, which was just as much the case in Prussia east of the Elbe as in the rest of Germany, made it advisable to implement the reforms gradually, province by province. The situation in Silesia, in East Prussia or in Brandenburg could not be lumped together (and even today we must get away from the idea that the territory east of the Elbe was unified). The liberation of the 'private peasants' did not, however, make great strides, which was no surprise considering the power of the nobility. It was only with the collapse in 1806–07 that the situation changed. First, the state laboured under a huge financial burden and had to make every effort to increase income and productivity — miracles were expected, even in the short term, from the liberation of the individual within the economy. Second, the hour had come at last for the reformist civil servants, like Theodor von Schön. This is where the personality factor in German history takes on such importance, especially in the person of Stein and in his appointment as chief minister. He had the freedom and the ability to govern, and as a non-Prussian was sufficiently distanced from the eastern agrarian system. He implemented the draft presented to him of the first stages of the emancipation, not just for isolated provinces, but for the whole of the remaining Prussian state, and he did this without consulting the nobility. A radical reform of society was only possible if it was implemented unswervingly from above. On 9 October 1807, ten days after he took over office, he issued the famous October Edict, the fanfare for the coming reforms.

Three aspects of the edict are particularly important. (1) 'On Martinmas in 1810 all forms of subordination on landed estates will cease in all of our states. After Martinmas in 1810, there will be only free persons.' For the peasants with more favourable proprietorial rights, this came into effect earlier. The peasants were personally free, free to move away or to marry; compulsory domestic service to the lord by the children of peasants was abolished. With this freedom, the peasant now became for the first time a genuine subject with legal rights, with the right to own property and take an active part in the economy. The question of the ownership of land and compulsory services, which went with land tenancy, was not yet resolved, but the prospect of emancipation on these points was promised as part of the reform programme.

(2) The edict introduced the 'freedom to dispose of land'. Everyone, whether nobleman, commoner or peasant, could buy and sell land, could divide up land freely or take out a mortgage. This was effectively the end of the *Bauernschutz,* which Stein had wanted largely preserved for the time being, but which the edict and subsequent decrees greatly restricted. Confiscation of peasant land was now possible, even if it required state authorisation; even small peasant holdings were taken by the estates.

(3) Finally, all occupations were open to everyone. 'Every nobleman is permitted, without in any way disadvantaging his estate, to practise a common trade.' Peasants were no longer restricted to peasant occupations, the commoners were no longer restricted to common occupations. Freedom of movement, free disposibility of land, free choice of occupation — all these dissolved the estate-based, immobile society in which social position was determined by birth. One could advance merely on the strength of one's determination, talent, performance and mobility. Society as a result became more competitive and career-orientated. The equality of its members before the law was now, at least in principle, a reality. With this pillar of the modern economy in place (the abolition of the legally enshrined privilege of birth) a new class-forming principle — the economic inequality of property — was generated. Since commercial achievement still depended on opportunities based on property, true equality of opportunity did yet not exist. Out of this competitive and career-orientated society the class society was born, though it would still retain a residue of the estate-based feudal social system.

Integral parts of the new society inaugurated by the October Edict were, besides personal freedom, the mobility of money and land, the proposed free labour market and the freedom of competition. In short, the legal framework was being established for a transition to the modern market society. These aspects in particular made this first act in the emancipation of the peasants a social revolution from above.

The continuation of the reform, the granting of property rights and the abolition of services, proved to be a problem, as could be expected. The reformers were, of course, not united as a group, acting together on the basis of a fixed plan. The individual reformers put the emphasis on different aspects and pursued different aims, based on their own individual interests. These might be economic and fiscal interests, such as an efficient agriculture; or political and social ones, such as a strong peasantry; or they could be more favourably disposed towards the nobility and the landed gentry, others towards the peasants and the middle classes, and there were many other intermediate tactical positions. The majority of the nobility, the Junkers, bitterly opposed reform. There was, on the one hand, an ideological opposition, for which Junker Friedrich August von der Marwitz became the spokesman and symbolic figure, in the spirit of the growing romantic conservatism. The line they took was that the transition from personal (seigneurial) bonds to material contractual ones would leave the peasants fettered to anonymous capital and usurers ('the creditor was a far harder master than the former private estate-owner'). The peasants, they maintained, would also find themselves in the shackles of the modern bureaucracy, for the state would want to move on from here to control more and more aspects of social life. Reform would thus lead to an 'alienated' existence.

On the other hand, opposition was even greater and more widespread from vested interests: 'Rather three more lost battles of Auerstedt than an October Edict.' This is how Schön characterised this group, who were defending the status quo out of pure self-interest and wanted to make every 'concession' contingent on large compensation, especially the freedom to turn peasants off their land. The opposition from the nobility could be easily and swiftly organised through the *Landschaften*, the credit institutes of the knights, through the remaining regional estate bodies and through close personal and family ties. These vested interests were naturally represented in the government and the civil service. The reform had to reckon with the resistance of the hitherto most powerful class in Prussia.

It was felt, in the unanimous legal opinion of contemporaries, that the abolition of *dominium directum* for the *Gutsherren* and compulsory services (not, however, the edict's elimination of the restriction on personal freedom) was an infringement of existing property rights, a form of dispossession. Feudal seigneurship was understood as a system of property rights. While creating a state under the rule of law, Prussia had guaranteed property rights in the *Allgemeines Landrecht* of 1794. This basic principle of the bourgeois world view was thus first used to protect feudal rights. Dispossession was only possible with compensation, and compensation consequently became a central issue. Such compensation could hardly, in the prevailing opinion of contemporaries, be fixed at an equal rate across the board even for the short term, but rather had to be calculated separately in each individual case. Among the factors to be taken into consideration were the rights and obligations of those affected, including the welfare duties (*Fürsorgepflicht*) of the lords towards peasants who had got into difficulties, the so-called *Präbenden*. This prevented a quick and simple solution. The revolution from above was contingent on the legality of these proceedings.

Clearly, compensation was an elastic concept. One of the officials implementing the reforms was of the opinion that many peasants did not need to pay any compensation, since their landlords were being relieved of considerable burdens. Others felt that the *dominium directum* of the landlords was worth little or nothing at all and, therefore, the proposal that compensation should be set at a quarter the value of the peasant's land was far too high. Equally at issue was whether compensation should be paid in money (as was the case with the peasants on the estates) or in land. The other problem, at least in the eyes of the reformers who saw things in economic terms, was how to supply the estates with a labour force once compulsory service had been abolished. Indeed, how could one prevent the estates from being weakened, making them economic, rational and productive, in order to maintain their position in the national economy as the most important production units for ensuring a viable market and supply? In other words, how to emphasise economic efficiency as well as the social reorganisation of agrarian society.

In view of these problems and the balance of power, reform proceeded in low gear; concessions to the nobility dictated the pace and the 'price' of reform. The longer the reforms were delayed, the more the nobility, which in 1807 had been heavily discredited politically and economically, gained strength. Reform became more difficult.

The state did a lot for the landed gentry. It shored up the debt-laden estates against the bankruptcy threatened by the collapse in price of agricultural produce. In 1810, the state issued a decree on servitude, the *Gesindeordnung*, which, though it represented progress in comparison with the *Allgemeines Landrecht*, seemed conservative in comparison with the line taken by the October Edict. It fixed in law the rights of the master towards his servants, such as the right to administer corporal punishment and a ban on resistance. These landowners were treated sympathetically by provincial and district administrations — in Silesia, for instance — even when they attempted to stall the emancipation and to thwart further reform. Only in 1811 was the second crucial stage of the reforms undertaken, the so-called Regulation Edict for the so-called *Lassiten*, the peasants on the private estates with few property rights. Compulsory labour services and *dominum directum* with their concomitant expenditure, as well as the welfare duties of the *Gutsherren* landowners, were to be abolished. In compensation for this, the peasants would hand over a portion of their land to the landlord, one-third in the case of those with better property rights, a half for those whose rights were fewer. Levels of compensation now had to be calculated, a process which it was then estimated would take four years. At the end of this period, all 'freed hands' would be granted the right to own property.

How compensation was to be paid, and how much, were matters which were hotly disputed by those involved, and this dispute still continues among historians. Monetary compensation — which the peasants on the domains were required to pay, and which many knights would have preferred to see practised everywhere — remained the exception (by request and mutual consent). The peasants' poverty and the state's wretched financial situation — the latter was in no position even to subsidise the peasants' payments, let alone take them over — put paid to such a solution. The introduction of a ceiling on debt for peasant smallholdings (25%) — a kind of safety-net for the peasants who were still unfamiliar with the workings of the market, in stark contrast to the economic liberalism in force elsewhere — and the shortage of credit prevented the peasants from raising capital. A section of the politically powerful Junker class also favoured compensation in land, since financial compensation was fraught with risks. The development stages of the edict show that the terms of compensation, as planned by the civil service, were originally more favourable to the peasants. The first draft was prepared by Scharnweber, one of the administrators in the reform movement. It proposed first of all to guarantee possession and then work out levels of compensation, rather than having a fixed system of compensation. Hardenberg gave in on many points to demands from the opposition and from the assembly of notables appointed by him. He saw the agrarian reform as an integral part of the reforms as a whole, as a part of an overall campaign by the state against the nobility, as well as part of the 1811–12 plan to place *Kreis* administrations under state control and reform taxation. This minimised the significance of the regulation for him, and he reckoned with the power and influence of the Junkers on the king. Hardenberg too wanted the emancipation of the peasants and the abolition of feudal rights. He also wanted a liberal meritocracy, though more for reasons of productivity and tax revenues. He favoured capitalist agriculture, a system of credit and a simplification of the land-parcelling system. The socio-political objective of creating the broadest possible strata of independent middle-income and wealthy peasantry, which the group of reform officials around Stein were striving for, interested him less, at least in the event of conflict. Though he had the leader of the aristocratic opposition arrested, Hardenberg still felt he could, nay must, make some significant concessions to the nobility in the final drafting of the edict. Nevertheless, its primary objective was to liberate the peasants, not to pacify the nobility, and it provoked fierce anger from the aristocratic opposition.

The regulation of the peasants' position which this edict had set in motion had to be postponed because of the war. In 1816, it was 'clarified' by a 'declaration' in which the peasants' position was actually made worse. The *Bauernschutz* was removed while the regulation was in progress. The minor peasantry who did not even own draught cattle were excluded from the regulation, as were those farmsteads which had only been created and entered on the land register after 1763, a bad year for the peasantry as a whole. The expectation that four years would be enough to carry through the regulation was abandoned. People resigned themselves to the fact that the newly established special authorities, the 'General Commissions', would take a long time to become effective. The newly energised forces of restoration, the escalating resistance of the Junkers who saw 'Jacobin' ideas in every reform, a certain degree of opportunism and disinterest on the part of Hardenberg, and the concern of the more strongly economically orientated councillors about productivity and scarcity of labour for the large estates were all instrumental in the deterioration. However, despite the charge that has usually been levelled against the new measures ever since, it seems questionable as to whether the small farmsteads could have survived a regulation involving the cession of land, the loss of seigneurial welfare provision and the *Bauernschutz*, and continued to be viable. In the last analysis, such a 'regulation' might also have worked to the advantage of the major landowners, or it might have created a new land problem, namely the hunger of the smallholders for more land, as happened later in Russia. Even Stein, who was more kindly disposed towards the peasants, directed his attention to the more comfortably off among the peasantry, not to the smallholders. For the reformers, the symbol of a new agrarian society was not the humble cottage, but the house. But we will be discussing this later.

It was in 1821, then, that the 'redemption' (*Ablösung*) of the peasants was enacted, which granted them property rights beyond mere usufruct, which could also be bequeathed. This applied not only to the peasants under the *Grundherrschaft*, of whom there were many in the east as well, but also to a considerable and frequently predominant section of the peasants on the estates (about 60% in Prussia and Brandenburg, about 47% in Pomerania). Compulsory services were rendered in land or money, and other dues in cash instalments. Finally, agrarian reform was finally supplemented by the introduction of separation, the dividing up of common land (of *Gemeinheiten* or *Allmenden*) consisting mainly of pastures and woodland (and the

Weiderecht (grazing rights) to manorial as well as to peasant land), the removal of the *Flurzwang*, the amalgamation of smallholdings, the evacuation of farms, and the beginnings of a *Flurbereinigung* (land reparcelling). The co-operative agrarian constitution was dismantled at the same time as the seigneurial agrarian constitution. In the view of liberal economists, it was an obstacle to intensive land use and any attempt to raise productivity.

In the newly acquired or re-acquired provinces of Posen, Westphalia and the Rhine Province, the Napoleonic laws remained in force after 1815 (especially the abolition of personal servitude). Further measures fell into line more or less with the state-wide regulations. In Posen, partly because of the temporarily reinstated *Bauernschutz*, the peasants got a better deal than anywhere else, since the nobility there was Polish. In the province of Saxony the liberation was only just beginning; in Swedish Pomerania, where there were hardly any peasants left, further measures were not implemented.

The concrete effects of the emancipation of the peasants will be discussed in detail later. What can be said now is that Prussia (ignoring the territories on the left bank of the Rhine) showed the way forward after the dissolution of the feudal agrarian system in Germany. It was the first German state to push through the modern idea of property against a thousand-year-old tradition. As a direct result it gained hugely in power and, indirectly, became one of the major winners in the reform. This also meant that the economic methods of individualistic capitalism triumphed on the land, giving rise to 'agrarian capitalism' and the improvement in productivity which accompanied it. As far as the relationship between the peasants and the nobility was concerned, the reform slowed down — in good part since it had been so early in coming about. Resistance from the nobility was too strong, and the position of the reformers was weak, since they had no social constituency to back them up. Moreover, the politico-economic belief of the reformers that 'land would make its way to the best landlord', and the belief in free competition in the agricultural sector, were stronger than the socio-political national interest in having a strong peasant class at the expense of the large landowners. That this dogma was only valid when there existed something approaching equality of opportunity in the market was not, or not sufficiently, considered.

As is so often the case, the social consequences of the new 'freedom' had been given little thought and developed a dynamic of their own aside from whatever was planned or intended. One alternative, which might have decisively reduced the political power of the nobility in relation to the bureaucracy, would have been to have Junkers without estates, like the seigneurial nobility in old Germany. This, however was unrealistic not only in 1816 and 1821, but even as early as 1807. Nevertheless, unlike the more progressive England, Prussia did not become a country made up entirely of large landed estates (*Grossgrundbesitz*). Much more important than the fixing of a system of compensation was the fact that the reforms ceased to move forward. Important privileges held by the landed gentry remained in place — patrimonial jurisdiction, policing, patronage of churches and schools, hunting rights and tax exemptions — despite the best intentions of Stein and Hardenberg. The plan to reduce aristocratic power and dominance at a local and regional political level failed, as did the attempt to put the *Kreis* administrations under state control and to dissociate the nobility from the state. This removed the basis for a peasant self-administration at communal level. The reform ended with a compromise between bureaucracy and nobility. In Prussia, a free peasant class was created; but the power of the knights' estates was reconsolidated economically as well as politically within a more modern system.

The liberation of the peasants was, to a large extent, if not exclusively, given direction by the ideas of economic liberalism. This was particularly characteristic of the reforms in Prussia as a whole. A principal aim of all reformers was the unshackling of all the productive, individual forces, and Hardenberg in particular was an energetic advocate of this policy. It was directed against feudal and corporative restrictions on property and other forms of activity, as well as against absolutist-bureaucratic forms of control and regulation of economic life. These were to be replaced by new freedoms, and the removal of restrictions on any one who had ability. Each man would be free to find his own role in economic life and to fulfil it to the best of his abilities. An integral part of this freedom was competition, which entailed the removal of all restrictions on competition. The freedom to compete was seen as an instrument and a basic requirement to spur on the individual to the highest achievements while producing maximum profit for the benefit of all. Progress was necessary, and it was only possible through freedom, but freedom — so went the prevailing opinion — produced nothing else but progress. The state's task then was — precisely in its own interest — to set the economy free and to set the parameters of this freedom. This was the function of the reforms. After the liberation of the peasants, the freedom to choose where to live and what occupation to follow, and the free disposability of land, the second major step in this direction was the introduction of the freedom to practise a trade, as announced in Hardenberg's Trades Edict (*Gewerbeedikt*) of 20 October 1810. Monopolies and privileges were abolished. Everyone was free, on obtaining a trading licence, to practise a trade without first having to obtain proof of competence or a concession, and without first having to obtain permission from a guild. There was no longer a distinction between town and country. From 1811 onwards, every tradesman was allowed to employ apprentices and journeymen; the guild changed from an association, membership in which was compulsory, into a private club. Only a few trades remained — such as pharmacist and chimney-sweep — for which certificates were still required, in the interests of public safety.

The freedom to practise a trade was a measure which was imposed upon the urban middle class and was carried through against a flood of protests and prophesies of doom — towns deserted or swamped with the rural proletariat, botched workmanship, swindling and general moral decay. The effect of this on the towns was at first slighter than had been anticipated. The effect on the countryside, however, was great, a fact which was for a long time ignored. It was envisaged that the smallholder and landless classes would derive their existence, or at least subsidiary income, from rural crafts. But in the medium and long term, the freedom to practise a trade gained in general a quite crucial significance for the restructuring and modernisation of society and industrialisation. It became — like marital freedom — the showpiece of liberal social policy in Prussia, in contrast to the conservative course being followed in the south German provinces.

The tax system and tax reform stood at the intersection of the state constitution and the social constitution and their reform. The financial problem — raising the contribution — was the central political issue during the reform period. Hardenberg's accession and early years in office were totally dominated by it. To summarise Hardenberg's measures: he succeeded in steering the state through the financial crises of tax increases, the sale of the large estates, the transfer of church property to secular ownership, the growing debt and, in particular, compulsory loans and various other dubious measures, without bankrupting the state or causing paper money inflation.

The financial crisis caused Hardenberg to attempt large-scale, general tax reform. This reform had three aims: (1) the unification of taxes, to be applied to the whole state, all the provinces, and to town and country alike; (2) the simplification of the system by replacing numerous separate taxes by a smaller number of easy-to-administer major taxes; and (3) equal treatment of all citizens under tax legislation, which meant the dismantling of the taxation privileges of the aristocracy. In this respect, the tax reform was closely related to reform of state and society.

The tax reform was, however, only successful in a piecemeal way, and in many important aspects it failed. Excise duties — which previously had only existed in the towns — were extended to cover the rural areas, and reduced to a small number of main articles. In response to the protests, however, the government modified its proposals in 1811, and the system only came into final effect in 1819. A trade tax was introduced to replace the numerous previous levies; it was equal for urban and rural areas, and for all classes, and was progressively graded according to the size of the business. Plans for the reform of the *Grundsteuer* (a tax on landed property), which meant in practice taxing the nobility at the same rate, failed; on this issue the government retreated in the face of opposition from the Junkers. In 1811–12, following pressure from individual provinces, a one-time income tax was introduced — on a graduated scale down to 5% — as well as a one-time wealth tax based on the principle of self-assessment. There was resistance to this, not only from the nobility and the landowning classes, who were unwilling to pay taxes, but also against the intrusion of the state and public bodies into the private sphere — something which has become second nature to modern citizens of the tax state but which was then quite revolutionary. In 1820, income tax was replaced by a class tax, something in between income tax and a poll tax. Each person was categorised into a social class and then had to pay a fixed rate accordingly. However, the towns were able to retain a system of indirect taxation, grain tax and slaughter tax, and many of them did so. In this respect, neither a uniform and integrated system of taxation nor tax equality were achieved. The poor were, relatively speaking, more heavily burdened by the system of consumption tax and class tax than their more well-to-do compatriots.

A central and characteristic piece of Prussian reform was the reform of the army. There had always been interaction between the socio-political constitution and the military constitution, but this measure was especially important in the emergent modern state, since compulsory national service represented the greatest encroachment of the state hitherto upon the freedom of the individual. It was also the impetus for movements advocating national integration and democracy, for compulsory national service was after all a democratic principle. This is especially true of Prussia, which as a military state became in a specific sense the country which was most responsible for Germany's fate.

The Prussian reform was all about liberation. This is why the reform of the army played such a decisive role, even given the catastrophic state of affairs. Senior officers formed a nucleus of staunch reformers. They included many without the traditional Prussian background who were from other states and services and from common families, like Grolman and Gneisenau; Scharnhorst was a peasant's son from Hanover. They were part of the military reorganisation commission, along with Clausewitz and Boyen — the only reformers with the traditional background of the Prussian aristocrat — which the king set up in 1807. Scharnhorst was the leading figure, in close association with Stein, who succeeded time and again in winning over the hesitant king. The reform was triggered by the experiences of 1806. The army had failed; they had been no match for the French owing to their poor internal organisation. The Prussian army was like a machine — immutable, and with no initiative or independence allowed to the individual combatants and combat units, in contrast to the tactical role of the French infantrymen and soldiers of the line. In the Prussian army, privileged officers and soldiers were objects without a will, subjected to a harsh system of orders and punishments; a third of them were foreign mercenaries. It was an army which constituted a state within a state, a quasi-professional army with its own institutions — police, church, courts — isolated from civilian society. Furthermore its special status and exclusive mentality was hated, feared and despised by civilian society. Contrast with this the French army of the Revolution — no longer subjects, but citizens, full of self-motivation, fighting spirit and patriotic enthusiasm. Universal conscription, introduced in 1792–93, had not only created an inexhaustible supply of reserves, but had brought about the unity of nation and army: the French military was the people in uniform. A new modern army needed a new spirit, a new organisation, a new military and political constitution. The central idea of the army reformers was that the army should be built on the strengths of the nation, on patriotic motivation. The army's special status within society had to be abolished. This, however, meant reforming the relationship between state and subject. This, according to Scharnhorst, meant 'the government forging an alliance with the nation', and 'the nation being injected with a feeling of independence'. Subjects must be made into citizens, free, independent, refined, with equal rights. Prussia must base itself, Gneisenau pointed out, on 'the triple alliance of arms, science and constitution'. Consequently, liberation of the peasants, abolition of estate privileges, self-administration and education reform were all part of the context of military reform. All these things were interrelated, and reform of the army, which was so pressing, would lead the way. Other reforms would follow in its wake.

Concretely, the army reform had three goals:

1) The reform of the internal structure of the army and its relationship to society. The army should be based on a new image of mankind, which respected the honour and human dignity of the soldier; a vision more in line with the new sense of civilian justice. The draconian system of punishments within the old army and corporal punishment were, for the most part, abolished. The abolition of flogging — 'freedom of the back', as Gneisenau called it — and a greater emphasis on 'self-motivation' were to make the army more attractive to the ordinary citizen.

2) The reform of the officer corps: seventeen generals, fifty high-ranking and 141 junior officers were purged. Even more important, an officer's career was now open to commoners and former prerogatives of the aristocracy were removed. Knowledge, education, and practical ability: performance and examinations were what counted now. Noble birth was no longer the qualification for military service, or for a commission.

The enlightened monarch is well aware [Gneisenau wrote in a newspaper article in 1808] that all energies must be roused and must be channelled into the areas in which they will be most effective. Birth must have no monopoly on merit. If too many rights are preserved for the privileged few, a host of energies lie sleeping in the lap of the nation, undeveloped, and the soaring wings of genius are crippled by repressive conditions. While an empire dies in weakness and ignominy, there is perhaps a Caesar tilling the soil in some wretched little village somewhere, an Epaminondas scraping an existence from the products of his labour. Let us open the doors to genius wherever it may be found. Let us open the triumphal gates to the commoner, the gates which until now prejudice has closed to all but the nobility. The new era needs more than old titles and parchment deeds, it needs new action, new energy.

Naturally, the opening up of the officer corps to commoners provoked opposition from the conservative nobility. Yorck caricatured the open-door policy, saying that there was an obsession that no God-fearing and talented swineherd be left unconsidered. He believed that officer status would provide cosmopolitans, intellectuals and social climbers with a new route to wealth and position. He even put it to Prince Wilhelm: 'If your Royal Majesty takes away my own and my children's rights' — the monopoly on officers' commissions, which provided for the nobility — 'on what are Your Majesty's own rights based?' But the king wavered no longer on this decision. The consequences were not as dramatic as had been anticipated, since, true to the ideas of self-administration and *esprit de corps*, the officer corps of a regiment had the right to choose candidates from among the certified officer cadets. This was a sort of co-option into the real officer corps. Former officers had an important say in this, and so old aristocratic standards were preserved. Moreover, aristocratic officer cadet schools remained, against the reformers' wishes, though their intake was reduced. For the time being anyway, there were enough officers from the old corps. The old officer corps continued to function despite the purge, though it was now squeezed by limitations on military spending — it was impossible to create a new one in such a short time. Like admission, promotion would also be decided on the basis of merit, as opposed to family pedigree, which would nevertheless still be the deciding factor in the higher ranks. Military academies were now expected to provide a better education for officers. There would be Courts of Honour which, by instilling a new idealistic and reformist code of honour, aimed to create a new type of officer. Though the impact of this on the officer corps as it then existed was limited.

3) The prerogatives of military justice, which were such an anathema to civilian society, since they also applied in cases where civilians were involved, were reduced, though the offence of slander, which was of such great emotional importance for the relationship between the military and civilians, was retained.

Other reforms were designed to improve the efficiency of the army. Mobility was improved by a new internal organisation, the promotion of the new tactic of the 'little war', and an increase in small groups of mobile infantry. The multiple military administrations were streamlined: in 1809, the War Ministry, one of whose departments acted as a high command, was set up. Though the ministry lacked ministers until the appointment of Boyen in 1814 — Scharnhorst was the man in charge — and though heads of departments still had direct access to the king, and though the king retained supreme command, the placing of the ministry between king and army was nonetheless the start of a constitutionalisation of the monarchy.

The Alpha and Omega of military reform was universal conscription. 'All inhabitants of the state are born to defend it' was the 'simple maxim which everyone could understand'. Only then, so went the idealism of the time, would military service become an honour and a duty one was glad to perform; only then could the army be built on patriotism. The old system of privileged and non-privileged subjects, whereby the former could pay for a replacement to do their service for them, which had reflected the status-based social order and the absolutist economic and tax system, was to go. The whole nation was now liable for military service. This was both a new 'ethical principle', as well as an unprecedented (and cheaper) way to exploit fully the military reserves. A series of plans and experiments was implemented, including the so-called 'Krümper system' — early retirement and new intake — which swelled the numbers of trained soldiers beyond the limit of 42,000 imposed by Napoleon. But universal conscription was never introduced. The king hesitated both for reasons of foreign policy, as well as for considerations of a more general political nature, and the political leadership could not reach agreement.

On the one side, there was the conservative, traditionalist aristocratic opposition, for whom a militia and universal conscription, the arming of the nation, contravened aristocratic prerogatives and the authority of the standing army. It was all part of the revolutionary nonsense about freedom and equality. On the other side, there was the opposition of the professional and educated classes. Niebuhr, though certainly a reformer, found the idea 'in itself so corrupting, that only the body, and not the intellect, is counted, and that the educated and the vulgar alike are to be prized only for their physical prowess'. It was, Niebuhr stated, a monstrous invention of fanatics and 'ignorant captains. Farewell culture, farewell finances.' Vincke spoke of the 'graveyard of culture, science, commerce and trades', of freedom and of happiness, and Altenstein echoed this. But the more affluent of the middle classes and the peasants felt similarly. The pre-revolutionary enlightened repugnance for the inhuman, unproductive and the unbourgeois army was prevalent here, as was the modern concern that the new ethos of equality would destroy individual freedoms. The French and south German solution of mediation between bourgeois and soldier favoured the former: one could buy a replacement. The reformers rejected this, considering that it would rob the army of true moral energy and intelligence, of the right ideas. They wanted to reduce the seriousness of the problem by shortening the length of service for the educated and propertied classes. So the decision was postponed. The dreams and schemes of the military patriots between 1808 and 1812, Gneisenau's especially, the revolutionary nationalist ideas of a people's war and insurrection, never met with the king's approval; it was all 'poetry'.

Only when war came along did the reformers get their chance. On 9 February 1813 all exemptions from military service were abolished and universal conscription was introduced. The educated and wealthier sections of the citizenry could also choose to arm themselves and join their own independent units. In March, the *Landwehr* (militia) was formed. Manned by those with no prior service experience and non-conscripts, it was established for the defence of the homeland and as reserve to the army in the field. District committees organised recruitment; educated *Bürger* could be elected as officers. This was the army in which the philosophy of the reformers, the fusion of *Volk* and army, was most strongly manifest. With its motto 'With God for King and Fatherland', it was deeply embedded in the memory of the Germans for a century to come.

Finally, there was the *Landsturm*, a total mobilisation of fifteen- to sixty-year-olds, a guerrilla militia recruited from amongst the *Volk*. With no formal uniform, it had elected officers and was geared to a scorched-earth strategy. Naturally, the nobility and the municipalities had the gravest reservations about such a revolutionary nationalist, Jacobinist egalitarian army of institutionalised patriotic enthusiasm. Total mobilisation was abandoned as early as July, and what remained of the *Landsturm* was subjected to a rigid and hierarchic discipline. Although actual universal conscription (which was very unpopular) was removed from the agenda in May 1814, it was reintroduced in September as part of a general armed forces statute under the direction of the war minister, Boyen. This was astonishing, but there were larger political considerations involved. The king, who had been hesitating hitherto, wanted to create a new, larger and relatively cheap army to strengthen Prussia's hand at the peace negotiations. Boyen used the opportunity to steer through his reform. All who were eligible (twenty years or over) were obliged to serve. In principle, they would do three years in the regular army and then two years in the reserve. They would then become part of the *Landwehr* (those up to the age of thirty-two in the first call-up, those up to thirty-nine in the second call-up), along with those over twenty years with no prior military service. In the event of an enemy invasion, they would serve in the *Landsturm* until their fiftieth year.

The centrepiece of this concept was the *Landwehr* — the *Volk* in arms. From a military point of view, it served as the reserve of the regular army. But the *Landwehr* had an independent organisation, with its own units (at district level), its own exercises and its own officers. It was not intended to be a military special unit, but would be part of the *Volk*, a sector of civilian life supported by the lively participation and patriotism of all classes. Because the regular army (referred to then as the *Linie*) was more militaristic, more isolated and more feudalistic, the *Landwehr* was intended as an independent institution which would encourage the virtues of civic pride and soldierly honour. The educated and wealthy had the option of a voluntary period of service lasting only one year, after which they had the option of becoming officers in the *Landwehr*. This was the Prussian compromise between the military and the individualistic upper middle class. In the last analysis, it was not primarily a privilege of the wealthy, but of those with an education, which was very soon to mean an education certificate and proof of attendance at particular schools. Military status, school attendance and social class were thereby linked in the uniquely Prussian and later Prussian-German manner.

What was new was that the mass of soldiers were no longer career soldiers; service in the armed forces became a transitional stage in the life of the individual. Through compulsory military service, everyone was now drawn into a direct relationship to the state. After 1815, however, the reorganisation of the military constitution and in particular its civilian political centrepiece, the *Landwehr*, sank into the reactionary mire.

What, then, were the effects of reform on the army between 1813 and 1815? They were, in fact, threefold and contradictory. First, the army was adapted to suit the new type of warfare. It was on the whole better led, with general staff officers playing an important role for the first time. The army also had better reserves at its disposal than before. Without the reform, Prussia would never have been able to assemble 280,000 men. Second, the bulk of the army were not 'inspired'; desertion and non-compliance with the call-up were certainly not rare. The bulk of the officer corps was in the old-fashioned, conservative mould: royalists, not patriotic nationalists. The townspeople strongly resisted universal conscription, and the reformers spoke of the 'egoism of the *Bürger*', but there were even desertions from the *Landwehr*. Finally, patriotic enthusiasm for a fight for liberation and freedom nonetheless took a special hold on the educated classes and the youth, extending to the *Landwehr* and the army in the field as well. Arndt's *Catechism for the German Landwehr Soldier* had a wide readership. The war acquired something of the character of a nationalist and people's war, even though Arndt's expectations that it would destroy the caste mentality of the army and its function as the instrument of tyrants were unfulfilled, as was his demand that nationalist goals should take precedence over military discipline. However, it was the experience of the war as a nationalist uprising which made the educated classes and the youth hope that the German situation was about to change. For those in the reactionary camp, this was frightening. They wanted to shepherd such revolutionary energies back into the safe fold of the established and hierarchical order.

In retrospect, one might have said the reform failed because the military constitution had not been based on the militia. Furthermore, the educated classes received special privileges, the *Linie* remained the king's army, and the military monarchy stayed intact and, if anything, was strengthened by the militarisation of the nation. These are only half-truths, unhistorical and unjust. Reform could only live in the soil in which it was planted, and this meant the kingdom, the nobility and an existing officer corps, a middle class that was unsympathetic to the military, the need for a strong army. The reform was a beginning. It sought to modernise the army and base it on the new forces active in the nation; it wanted to give the military spirit a new vigour and make it a part of the nation. This meant mobilising the nation and placing the army under a constitution. There was to be a new allegiance besides loyalty to the monarch, and yet not in conflict with it: an allegiance to the state and the nation, loyalty to the fatherland. This was the element within the reform which the conservatives feared, the spark of democratic con-stitutionalism that could produce a more egalitarian and participatory society and lead to a restructuring of the state.

The approach was ambivalent. The removal of the aristocratic exclusivity of the army could not be carried out at one stroke, and a parallel modernisation of state and society certainly could not. Naturally enough, the modern military constitution was still bound to the monarchic, authoritarian order. The legitimation of the military on a democratic nationalist basis, and the democratic 'militarisation' of the nation, might have had democratising as well as militarising effects. They may have become detached from one another, which was not the intention of the reform. The new military could have turned its back on bourgeois democracy, or caused the militarisation of society, to an even greater degree than had been achieved by the Jacobins or Napoleon. But the way was open: the reform had its sights on the future. It opened up possibilities for development, and the *Landwehr*, in particular, was an institution of the future; it offered a chance for change. It was, despite all idealistic and visionary expectations, a timely compromise between the existing Prussian monarchy and the incipient bourgeois nation.

Another key area was the great educational reform which also had its beginnings in the period of late absolutism. The whole Enlightenment debate about improving education spread to the administration itself. The public called upon the state to take up this cause, and the state answered the call, giving rise to the so-called *Staatspädagogik* (state education). This was designed to provide citizens with state-run education in order to 'improve' them. The result was to be higher productivity, a higher tax yield, greater efficiency, greater loyalty, less criminality and better-educated administrators. Schools were to be useful, primarily secular rather than religious. They were to harmonise with the state's purpose and with the estate-based social order. However, the question of which form of education was expedient for which estate led to the question of social mobility. The paths of advancement were to be opened to those with talent. For instance, gifted pupils from a 'humbler' background were to be exempted from military service. Freedom through education was a maxim which was to hold true, at least for an exceptional few. Education triggered a change in society based on birth and property. Another factor here was the desire to assert the sovereignty of the state. The endless particularist, local, feudal and corporate schools were to be turned into state schools. At least they were to come under state supervision, which meant state control over their organisation, finances, curriculum, examinations and teaching staff. A systematic and unified school system was to be formed from the existing multiple systems. There would also be new administrative and inspection bodies for the emerging schools. The church's hold on schools would be relaxed or reinterpreted as a duty it would perform on the state's behalf. By exercising control over the schools, the state was seeking to establish a more direct relationship with its citzens.

Generally, by the late eighteenth century, the universities had ossified and fallen into decay. They were trapped in a corporative guild mentality, with privileges based on their corporate status and patronage. Learning and education were more often than not scholastic, pedantic and, at best, encyclopaedic. The student body, which included many unsuitable individuals, lived in many cases in a loutish 'hooligan' subculture, a state of moral decay which manifested itself in riots and the terrorising of the general public. One of the few exceptions was Göttingen.

As far as the discovery of new truths and their discussion was concerned, the academies and societies, journals and salons were of more interest than the universities. It is no coincidence that Lessing and Winckelmann were among the universities' severest critics. Reform of the universities was one of the priorities of the time. It aimed to abolish the many minor universities, convert some universities into *Fachhochschulen* (colleges of further education) and bring about the state regulation of education. This was to be accomplished together with a rational reorganisation and state appropriation of the chaotic particularist structure of universities, in order to modernise them into effective institutions.

This was the problem faced by almost all German provinces at the turn of the century. It is quite surprising to note that there was still quite a lot of life in the bureaucratic reforms of the late Enlightenment period, even during the turbulent period of Napoleonic domination. In Prussia, however, reform was even further advanced.

In the opinion of the reformers, the renewal of state and society required a new outlook, a renewal of the individual human being. And this called for a new form of education. In this respect, education and science became burning issues. They were closely bound up with peasant emancipation, universal conscription and a constitution. At the same time, a new concept of education and knowledge had come to the fore, one based on idealism and neo-humanism. This was a crucial moment in the history of the reform period, and in the development of the German mind, and thus calls for a more detailed analysis.

Fichte, taking Kant as his reference point, developed the most articulate version of the idealistic theory. He saw man as self-motivated. Creating his own self and fashioning his own world, man is autonomous, free, mature. Fichte felt education was about self-definition, not about learning how to adapt oneself to fit into the traditional world. Education was not about being 'trained' to do what is useful, nor primarily about imparting certain knowledge and skills. It was about arousing 'inner strengths', spontaneity and abstract insight, so that, even in unforeseen situations, the individual would choose to do what is right for himself of his own free will. For Fichte, therefore, education was not primarily a matter of content, but of form. It was not related to profession or estate: it was something 'universal'. Indeed, as the republican Fichte would have it, it was essentially national, the education of the entire *Volk*. For this reason, the ideas of Pestalozzi were adopted. He had come upon the idea of self-motivation by his own route and developed a workable form of popular education from it. He was to become the spiritual father of German educational reform.

Then there were the ideas of neo-humanism, nurtured in the soil of German classicism, and which, thanks especially to Wilhelm von Humboldt, had an effect on the Prussian reform. The neo-humanist idea of education turned against the ideals of the Enlightenment, which had been easily trivialised, ideas of comprehensibility and usefulness, welfare and happiness. Central to this new concept was individualism. Education was seen as the all-round, harmonious development of individual aptitudes — from within and by appropriation of the world outside — into something whole and unique, the personality. The key ideas were individuality, universality, totality (wholeness). Education would encourage the individual to develop *Humanität*, the concept of humanity. This form of education was to be something apart from mere academic education. It was to be a lifelong, unending process, which becomes an end in itself, one of the highest values. The term 'self-cultivation' could also be used to describe it.

This form of education was elevated above the world of practical realities, work, the economy, wage-earning. It became something esoteric. Education was to be distinguished from training. It was not seen as the uninterrupted development of an unspoiled nature. Rather it was an education which fulfils itself through the medium of culture and books. In the assimilation of alien genius and its works, one's own spirit would be awakened and educated.

Integral to this was the theory of classicism, newly developed by Schiller, the idea that art has a fundamental and moral significance for life itself. Art became a part of education, and this conviction spawned the idea, which was so important for the mentality of the educated class, of the poet as a spiritual guide.

The ideal of a perfected *Humanität* was — and this is the new twist — said to be the Greeks. The Romans had suppressed the individual, the Christians had suppressed the natural, and modern man had sunk into over-specialisation and utilitarianism. The Greeks had not only founded western culture, they had also embodied the ideal of a fully developed, all-round individual. Discourse with this great nation in all its facets, according to Friedrich August Wolf, would exercise all our 'intellectual, moral and aesthetic energies'. It was largely thanks to Humboldt that the study of Greek acquired a new significance. He considered language to be the form in which human beings assimilate the external world, so an analytic understanding of such a sophisticated language would develop the individual's own linguistic competence. It was not just *what* the Greeks thought, but *how* they thought, that was critical. Humboldt went on to state: 'It is no less useless for the carpenter to have learned Greek than it is for the scholar to make tables.'

The idea of an all-round, formal education provided a bridge to link the apparently esoteric neo-humanists with those who championed the idealistic cause of self-motivation and the programme of popular education devised by Fichte and Pestalozzi. The neo-humanists, Humboldt and Süvern, would also become the fathers of the new *Volksschule* (providing elementary schooling).

The concept of *Wissenschaft* (academic study, scholarship, science) was fundamental to this new philosophy. It had originated in a series of German universities, primarily among scholars of idealistic philosophy and classical philology. It found its ultimate expression in the debates about the founding of the University of Berlin. *Wissenschaft* was defined as (1) something incomplete in itself, 'something not yet quite found and never entirely discoverable' (Humboldt). The business of *Wissenschaft* was to seek and find new truths and knowledge, i.e. research. The communication of such knowledge was not a question of passing on something already given, but of productive, 'independent' reflection on principles. (2) *Wissenschaft* is a whole. The study of any academic subject was to be prefaced by reflection on the world in its entirety and on life, its meaning and synthesis and on norms of action. In practice, this meant philosophy and the classical humanities. Research and reflection on totality would distinguish *Wissenschaft* from mere 'trades'. (3) *Wissenschaft* is primarily something pursued for its own sake; its practical use, its relevance, is secondary. The search for truth for its own sake leads to the most important and useful knowledge, and therefore, in the last analysis, also serves society. Science is to the universities as research is to teaching. It is precisely this scholarly research freed from pragmatic considerations and reflection on the totality which provide education as well as good training. Only then will the students be at the stage where they do not learn pre-packaged knowledge, but form their own understanding, their own independent judgment and individuality. Only then will students 'acquire the skill, the freedom and the power which are necessary to adopt a profession from one's own inclination, and for its own sake, and not simply to make a living by it.' Education and training through pure *Wissenschaft* were what was important. This was a new ethos, 'a normative basic attitude to life' (Schelsky) which aimed at objectivity in dealing with the world, and acting in accordance with ideas. 'Solitude and freedom' (Humboldt) from the compulsions of state and society, from the constraints of social background and future prospects, were therefore considered vital for the universities.

Education, and education through *Wissenschaft*, was the new ideal. Two aspects of this should be emphasised here. First, education took on the character of a faith, a secular religion — hence its extraordinary status. This religious aspect was heightened even further by the worship of Hellenism. Universities and *Gymnasia* (secondary schools) became quasi-temples; philosophers and philologists took on the aura of priests and spiritual leaders. The grace of the intellect replaced the grace of God, while the word of the Greeks was more important than God's. The religion of the Greeks supplanted the old stock-in-trade of cross and sin, salvation and the world beyond, replacing it with a belief in this world, in dignity, beauty and the perfection of man. In the real world, however, and under the influence of idealism, this non-Christian tendency of the new religion of education was clothed in a mantle of Christianity. This form of education also had its contemplative, aesthetic and starkly individualistic traits. The freedom which it offered was a spiritual, inner freedom, beyond political and social realities.

Today, such freedom is often discredited as an 'escape into the inner life'. That reproach is narrow-minded. Such freedom beyond politics has value, in that it provides a corrective against the domination of politics and society, which were becoming ends in themselves beyond the needs of human beings. In no sense did the spokesmen and supporters of this movement retreat from political life. On the contrary, they saw this metapolitical education as providing the strongest impetus towards a new era of political thought.

It is an astonishing fact that this concept of education originated and established itself around 1800. Neither the major forces of the eighteenth century (feudality, absolutism and municipal citizenry, enlightenment, philosophy and natural science) nor the rise of industrial society in the nineteenth century seem to fit in with it. It seems almost like an autonomous development. In terms of intellectual history, it is significant that the new philosophy was no longer grounded in physics and mathematics, but in history, language and culture. As far as religious history was concerned, the new concept of education offered an answer to the crisis of Christianity and the crisis of the Enlightenment.

Most important of all are the social background and social consequences. The impetus for the new education emerged from the small social class consisting of the educated, the civil servants and the liberal professions. Since a strong commercial bourgeoisie was absent, this was the only class besides the nobility which could justifiably stake a claim to leadership. In the more sophisticated social and cultural environment, it gradually took upon itself the function of an intelligentsia outside of the church. The objective of the new education was a new society. Turning its face against the old world of the estates and aristocracy, it sought to promote talent and achievement as the keys to social status, not birth. Education was the true qualification, the new and genuine certificate of nobility, and Greek was the new badge of bourgeois refinement, replacing the French culture of court and nobility. Education should be general and formal, education for its own sake, not training for a career. This implied that education was to release people from their existing social constraints, liberate them from the tyranny of family background and land, from being 'trained' for a particular profession, which in practice was almost exclusively bound up with one's station at birth. It would emancipate people from 'roles' ordained by the estate they owned or from narrow, specialised professional roles. The curious distancing of this new educational ethos from the world of work gave it a liberating air. Education makes free — this was to become the rule rather than the exception. It would mobilise society and turn it into a merito-cracy. Education and freedom to choose one's occupation were very closely interrelated. To put it another way, a form of education would be introduced which taught the individual to think and act for himself. It would replace authority and tradition with reflection and self-motivation, and would thus change society. The new education, in Humboldt's view, was to be an all-round education of the whole person, 'for the commonest wage-labourer and the man with the finest education must be tuned in the same way, so that the former will not slide into brutality and the latter become sentimental, chimerical and eccentric'. Education was to be something for everyone, a truly national education.

In this respect, the idea of education arising from neo-humanism and idealism was not the privilege of the silver-spoon class, not a harking back to a supposedly 'more democratic' line of the Enlightenment. Its true significance was moral and political. It sought to lay the foundations for a free society of enfranchised citizens and eventually a bourgeois constitutional state.

This idea of education was by no means egalitarian, however. Its objective was to create a new meritocratic elite, as well as a new ruling class which identified itself with the interests of the state, the rule of those with a philosophical and scientific education. Although education would be opened up to the lower orders, the academically schooled civil servants still stood at the top of the educational hierarchy. The bourgeois merito-cratic elite was distinguished by intellectual activity directed to no specific purpose, an almost ascetic devotion to education removed from practical reality and direct use. This was a social ideal which was curiously at odds with civic-bourgeois values. It was founded on knowledge and intellect, not on property and work, success and practical diligence.

Education was something which went on outside of economic life, work and govern-ment; such a distancing was inherent in it. Set against the society based on estates, this was a modern concept. But at the same time, it was related to the pre-industrial and pre-capitalist society of Germany at that time. It has been of lasting consequence for the history of Germany that this idea took root in German life at the beginning of the century, before the rise of industry, technology, commerce and the bourgeoisie. Conflict clearly existed between the idea of a society built on talent and achievement and the idea of an educated elite. The adoption of the Greek ideal of *Humanität* was, despite everything, patently an ideal for higher education. What sort of education an individual would receive was still very much dependent on that person's social background. The prerequisites of such a non-vocational education were good schools, a cultivated lifestyle and the opportunity for leisure; only then was it possible to despise 'vocational study'. This was the social problem at the heart of the debate on the future of education.

Lastly, the new programme for education was a matter for the state. Only the state had sufficient power to release the education system from the crippling influence of the corporation system and particularism, and to liberate it from the constraints of immediate objectives and from society's emphasis on the utility of education. Humboldt's early idea that society could correct itself on the basis of its own internal organisation was inadequate. Education was linked to freedom, but the state was the agent and the guarantor of freedom and modernity. What was required, then, was that the state be given sovereignty in matters of education and culture. This was based on the idealistic assumption that the state would act as guardian and promoter of education and science for their own sake, safeguarding their freedom without intervening in their internal affairs. The advocates of the new concept of education and science would pro-pose to the state what kind of curriculum and educational standards were required, and the state would then put these into practice. The provision of education and science was seen as a fundamental objective of the state, for this would be the soil of freedom and morality in which the state could thrive and renew itself and ultimately grow stronger. It was in the state's own interest to make the objectives of freedom and education its own. State and education were dependent on one another. The state served education and in the final reckoning, education served the true, free and rational state. These were, of course, idealistic assumptions in which the realities of power were obscured. Yet seen in their real context they were not so eccentric. It was the state alone which could put reforms into practice, and the reformers in the civil service were preparing themselves to refashion the state in their own image. However, when education and science become the business of the state, they are then subjected to shifting tides of power within the state. In addition to their idealistic purpose, schools themselves now acquired the function of preserving the existing power structure, and this became the central problem for educational policy in this century.

The idea of an educational elite and state organisation of education called for an effective examination system. Examinations were required as proof of educational performance — that is the other side of the bourgeois-humanist idea of education. Since then, examinations in Germany have become a crucial factor in determining an individual's path in life, and, therefore, in the stratification of society. The link between education, examinations, military rank and even social status was to become a specific German reality. These consequences will be discussed later in greater detail.

To return to the Prussian reforms, these ideas were not exclusive to Prussia, but nowhere else did they come together and prevail as completely. It remains astonishing how the advocates of the new ideas, the professors and neo-humanists, worked together with the reformers of the civil service. The utopian, high-flown ideas of renewing humanity and the nation through education were not, of course, taken over in this form. Stein was convinced that a person's life and circumstances were more important to his education than was the school, and he felt that the state should not be erected upon the school. However, he considered that the state should support the new idea of education as a means of encouraging independence and nurturing creative faculties, rather than being a 'training ground' for useful occupations and the instilling of passive obedience. Stein felt that the state should promote education as a means of building a public spirit, because this is what the state needed. Humboldt, Süvern and Nicolovius became ministerial officials, with Schleiermacher as one of the most influential advisers. A link was maintained between administration and *Wissenschaft*; the new ideas were made into basic principles of administration and had a marked influence on the rebuilding of a modern education system.

The *Gymnasium* (secondary school) was reconstructed on the basis of the neo-humanist programme. The old *Lateinschulen* (Latin schools) were institutions governed by rote learning and the stick. They were both overcrowded and financially insecure, with no adequate final examinations and an atmosphere hostile to intellectual stimulation. The Latin schools were subsequently abolished or reorganised. Before the reform there were sixty Latin schools in East Prussia. By 1818, there were twelve grammar schools. In Prussia as a whole (which had almost doubled in size), the approximately 400 Latin schools of 1750 had been replaced by ninety-one *Gymnasia* in 1816. These *Gymnasia* were given a more stable organisation and financial base. In 1810, a state examination for new *Gymnasium* teachers was instituted, which was intended to liberate them from feudal and communal patronage. Teachers thus moved into a more direct bond with the state, since the state now decided their suitability for employment through an examination. A new profession with its own standards and career structure was created, that of 'philologist' as distinct from theologian — another piece in the emancipation of the school from the church. Teachers' examinations, model curricula and, in 1812, the first regulation for the *Abitur* — the university entrance examination which, while not yet compulsory for every entrant to the university, was certainly obligatory for those who wanted to become teachers — standardised the requirements of the new school.

At the level of the *Volksschule*, the construction of a 'blanket' network of consolidated schools made it possible, for the first time, to introduce compulsory school education for the population as a whole. The process of teaching itself was reformed by the introduction of Enlightenment teaching methods, with even more emphasis on those first devised by Pestalozzi. The major reform was the introduction of a new education for teachers within 'ordinary schools', and through newly founded or revamped 'seminars', which Pestalozzi pupils, or teachers whom the state had sent out to Pestalozzi for instruction, could attend.

The teaching profession had consisted hitherto of people from all (indeed, frequently marginal) walks of life, untrained and often poorly educated. It was now to be turned into a systematically trained profession of specialists in which reformist enthusiasm about the renewal and transformation of the individual would find its place. In fact, in the short period between 1807 and 1813, the *Volksschulen* changed very little and very slowly. But what was important was that the terms of the new system to come had been set, and were beginning to be implemented.

The educational reformers worked on the basis of a distinction between elementary and higher education. Basically, they wanted a two-tier system of schooling, the *Gymnasium* and *Volksschule*, and only these two. The large number of intermediate types of school were to disappear. Considered to be below standard and geared merely to practicalities, they were thus an obstacle to the construction of a unified national school system. However, the separation between the two school systems was not quite so rigid. In Humboldt's plan, the 'commoners' should also attend *Gymnasia*, which would offer an equivalent education, though one with a greater bias towards mathematics and natural sciences, with a shorter period of schooling, and no *Abitur*. This was to be an education which would prepare them for 'the outside world'. In this respect, the higher educational level was not yet the exclusive preserve of a narrow social stratum. It was also taken for granted that urban *Volksschulen* would have a more socially heterogeneous intake than village ones. But, above all, *Volksschulen* and *Gymnasia* were self-contained, but nonetheless complementary levels of schooling within a unified national school system. Süvern had established this central piece of reform in 1819, in the draft of a general legislation for schools. The education system should not — and could not — abolish social divisions, so access to the higher level of education was not equal. However, the new system could provide a counterbalance, and promote and extend equality of opportunity for talented pupils, thus enabling a more free and mobile society to develop in the long term.

Higher education also had an emancipatory character. It offered a general humanist education beyond the realm of the occupational world for a society of the future, while at the same time providing an education for state employees, whose task it would be to create such a society. The civil servants were thus to be the vanguard of the new bourgeoisie.

As has already been indicated, educational reform also included the organisation of a fully operational school administration and a schools inspectorate. It was initially administered from a special section within the Ministry of the Interior (and the Police!) concerned with education and culture, but after 1817, a separate ministry was created for the purpose. A controversial arrangement, it was nevertheless compatible with the traditional proximity of the individual spheres, and with the considerable exchange of personnel between the ministries. Practically all enlightened schoolmasters and school administrators, especially in the *Volksschulen*, were theologians. The newly inaugurated municipal self-administration was actually granted only a limited right of co-administration in the higher level of schooling. Headmasters were appointed by the state and had a strong position; these expert appointees were to be given precedence over any local participation in decision-making. There was an attempt to balance out the bureaucracy at the head of the administration by appointing advisory commissions (*Deputationen*) consisting partly of paid members and partly of honorary members. They were there to add their expertise and institutionalise criticism and the impulse for reform.

Finally, there was the reform of the universities. In 1807, Prussia had lost not only its western German and Franconian universities, but also its main university in Halle. This prompted the idea of building a new university. It is still astonishing to consider that this defeated state which had been cut in half and financially bled dry, and whose main concern was sheer survival, should not only set about reorganising its finances, the military and the state, but at the same time found a new university. As the king, not normally noted for his philosophical utterances, explained in 1807: 'The state must replace by intellectual power what it has lost physically.' Humboldt and others put the matter in terms of foreign and national policy. The university was 'one of the best means by which Prussia could gain the respect and attention of Germany', thus asserting its claims to leadership in the field of 'true Enlightenment' and 'the cultivation of the intellect'. These were referred to later as moral conquests. This was, of course, how the establishment circles in the Prussian military and administrative state saw it, and was characteristic of the 'spirit' of this reform.

In 1810, the new university was finally founded in Berlin, a location chosen primarily for practical and financial reasons. It was not a large institution at first. It had three professors each in theology and law, six professors of medicine and twelve of philosophy, with a student body of 250. But this was a new type of university, clearly inspired — as far as institutions were concerned — by the new ideas, and it became the model to follow for the rest of the century.

(1) No *Fachhochschulen* (colleges of further education) were formed, and the university held firm as the place where all branches of knowledge would come together under one roof. The practical sciences, however, (such as building, forestry, mining technology, and even a part of the old cameralism) were excluded. The unifying centre was now to be the 'philosophy faculty', which meant primarily the study of philosophy and the ancients. This faculty was the purest embodiment of the new ideas. It was the thread which tied together all the other educational faculties. The centre of the new world view, it was the transmitter of meaning to the new secular institution.

(2) The professors now had to submit to the new imperative of research and Socratic teaching, combined with philosophical reflection upon the whole range of thought.

(3) A new motivation was demanded of the students: they should study out of curiosity and interest instead of using the university as a step up the career ladder or a ticket to gentrification. 'Vocational study' became a term of opprobrium. Study was liberal, not organised around a curriculum or a fixed number of years of study, as in schools. The pursuit of knowledge, in an open dialogue with the lecturers and through independent work (for the first time students were given free access to the libraries) was their sole duty. At the centre of this universe stood the individual and science. Communal structures on an older or newer model, as in the cloister or the English college, did not develop. What was important was the intellect, the pursuit of knowledge, rather than other, perhaps more vital or 'marketable', abilities.

(4) The university was a state institution; the state organised, financed and supervised it. The idea of furnishing the university with the means to support itself independently, or of running it as some sort of association of free intellects, failed on both financial and political grounds. The concept of further education institutions independent of the state was outside the terms of the debate on educational policy; the state monopoly was firmly in place. This also meant that the church no longer set the terms of reference, since the universities were now secular institutions. In addition to the administration of the university's external affairs, the state dominated the staff. Since the professors were state officials, the state appointed them. For Humboldt, this was the sole guarantee of freedom and of competing against the guild ethos and nepotism. Since the state was, in effect, the client, it influenced teaching through state-controlled examinations.

(5) The traditional corporate rights and rights to autonomy were remoulded into a modern form of self-administration. The university was to have the right to decide on its own internal affairs, research and teaching. It would decide on academic performance and had the right to arrange lectures. It would also have a joint say in the appointment of new teaching staff. It was within this climate of co-operation and antagonism between state and self-administration that the new university grew up. It quickly became the model for the other German universities.

One of the central problems of the reform as a whole, which eventually determined its fate, was the problem of the constitution. In the initial stages, all the reformers and all the reforms aimed at establishing a constitution, a situation in which the governed took part in the formation of the general political will through their representatives. This was designed to integrate the state, abolish the separation between state and society, government and nation, and thereby strengthen the state. The memoranda and debates of the reformers were full of it. In the case of Stein, his dislike of bureaucracy and centralisation was as significant a factor as his idea of the nation educating itself through participation in its own affairs. The real purpose of the system of self-administration was to act as the first tier of a representative system for the whole state. Whereas Stein was quite happy to take old European estate-based ideas as a reference point, others were more statist in thought. They were less concerned with traditions and pedagogic nationalism, though they also wanted a representative constitution, in order to bind the people to the administration and strengthen the state. All shared the same idea of a graded system of representative organs which would build upwards from the lower levels to a national representative body. After 1808, with the king's consent, the government repeatedly announced the introduction of such a system, 'to ensure the effective participation of the nation in legislation'. An important stimulus for this was the financial crisis — the question of credit and debts, the sale of domains, forced loans and taxation. Without the participation of the country's representatives, these were all very difficult to regulate. The question of the constitution was always tied to a continuation of large-scale social reforms and very much depended on the particular situation at any one time. For this reason, there was no unified and targeted plan for a constitution, only a succession of different experiments.

One of these was the attempt to 'bring the administrative bodies into closer contact' with the nation. This was to be done by assigning to each district administration representatives with full voting rights and a salary, a procedure which had its precedents in the old estate-based order. Stein wanted an elected civil service as well as a career civil service, state and communal administration acting in combination in collegiate organs. The more bureaucratically disposed of the reformers saw this rather as an outlet for anti-bureaucratic sentiments. The experiment, which was really only carried out in Königsberg, failed and was abandoned in 1812; but ideas like this, as we have seen, did have a role to play in the reform of the *Kreis* administration.

Secondly, there was an attempt to reactivate or to create regional or provincial estates. Without them, the financial and taxation questions — the collection of the contributions had been shifted to the provinces — seemed impossible to resolve. In East Prussia, the experiment of 1808, whereby both bourgeois and peasant were recruited, seemed to be working. These committees, however, later proved to be bastions of Junker opposition against such reforms as the admittance of peasants and the imposition of an income tax. The majority of reform administrators in 1810 saw these estate bodies as a barrier to the reforms; they were in favour of deferring the constitutional question. Hardenberg took a different line. Stein had plans drawn up for convening a Reichstag in the autumn of 1808. There were times when he, along with other convinced reformers, wanted the Treaty of Submission to France — a fundamental question of foreign policy — placed before parliament for its decision.

After Stein's removal from office, such plans were postponed until Hardenberg took them up again. In February 1811, he summoned a provisional 'Assembly of Notables'. He hoped to mobilise the 'nationalism' of a state-wide assembly against the provincialism of the old organs of government. He wanted to nationalise provincial debts, thus creating a common national interest. It was Hardenberg's way of appealing to national solidarity. The assembly members were to think of themselves as citizens of a state in which equality of responsibility as well as equality under the law would have to apply. In the provinces, they would have to build and nurture confidence in the government.

These policies were only partially successful. The assembly would only advise on preset subjects and only on the procedures for government bills. In Hardenberg's eyes, the assembly was no more than the representative of regional and estate-based interests and did not work for the 'common cause'. He could not, however, escape its scruples and eventually learned to get along with it. When the Assembly of Notables was dissolved in September 1811, a new 'interim' National Representative Assembly was announced. The old estates now rose up in opposition to the political activities of the Assembly of

Notables, claiming that constitutional and financial reform could only have an effect through agreements with the individual provincial estates. The chief spokesman for the estates was the Junker Friedrich August von der Marwitz of Brandenburg. He and his colleagues were the defenders of the 'old law' and the autonomy of the old regions. In their view, Hardenberg's policies broke the law and violated the sanctity of contracts and property rights. Such policies would lead to the break-up of the state and wreak havoc on the land.

The Junkers protested at the downgrading of estates and the mobilisation of land for the benefits of Jews and capitalists ('Final Objection of the Estates of the *Kreis* of Lebus'). In appeals to the king, they even forecast the introduction of a right of dissent. Hardenberg had two of their spokesmen, Marwitz and Finckenstein, arrested and imprisoned in a fortress for five weeks, without protest from the rest of the aristocracy. The majority of Junkers were far less interested in conservative principles than in selfishly defending their own privileges.

In April 1812, the new interim National Assembly sat to draw up measures to deal with debts and state credit. The assembly members had a 'free mandate' and were no longer obliged to carry out the directives issued by the electorate. This was intended to unshackle them from particularist interests. The assembly, however, was still divided into nobility, commons and peasants, and the principle of civic representation in the modern state was as yet hard to distinguish from the estate-based model. In many preliminary drafts, there were impure versions of the representative process. Stein, for instance, wanted to prevent the peasant or middle-class landowners from electing men from other estates, lawyers for example. This would have gone against his intention of bringing practical qualities to the fore, though it was taken for granted then that ownership of property and land were prerequisites of the right to vote. The powers of the assembly remained unclear, and Hardenberg was unable to use it as a vehicle to push through his policies, since it was dead set against the system of organisation into *Kreise*.

Hardenberg simply decided to bypass the assembly in the drafting of his major statutes. Nevertheless, the president, along with a few of Hardenberg's closest allies, formulated a sort of constitutional statute regarding the election and the competence of a future National Assembly. Before the assembly was dissolved in 1815, Hardenberg had persuaded the king to issue a decree on 22 May 1815 which promised a constitution and proposed that in September a *Landtag* (state representative assembly) would be convened, based on provincial estates. This never happened, however. The dissolution of the interim assembly before any clear successor was found for it proved fateful for the constitution question.

There was clearly a good deal of tactical manoeuvering, especially in the realm of financial policy, in Hardenberg's constitutional policies. He certainly did not want a parliament to whom the government was in any way answerable. His idea of a constitution fitted neatly into his bureaucratic statism and was, therefore, limited in this respect. Hardenberg, however, was after much more than a Napoleonic sham constitutionalism. After 1789, it seemed to him impossible to govern without the participation of the upper and middle strata of the nation. He wanted a representative body which would advise and support the government, supervise the administration and ensure that it had a higher profile in public life. It would reinforce the integration of the greater state against the separatist mentality of the regions.

For Hardenberg, even the old ploy of recourse to the provinces had a modern flavour. He wanted new provinces and new provincial bodies which would limit the prerogatives of the nobility, avert an anti-Prussian opposition, hold the provinces together and integrate them into the greater state. In this respect, his promises to create a National Assembly and constitution in 1810 and 1815 were absolutely serious. But the reform of state and society took precedence chronologically and materially over the constitution.

Hardenberg's fight with the opposition covered all the key areas of reform — taxation, agrarian reform and the *Kreisordnung* (local government ordinance) and thus, by implication, the constitution. Whatever Hardenberg's motives and intentions, there was a tragic dialectic of the reform. The constitution presupposed a bourgeois society within a greater state, no longer particularist or based on estates. But this society first had to be created. It was a society of the future. The way to such a society and to the participation of the nation in its politics seemed to lie in a bureaucratic dictatorship by educational means. Policies of modernisation could not be advanced by the representatives of the old society; they were more likely to hinder them. However, for reasons of financial and national policy, it was not possible to manage without them. This was the dilemma. The new polices relied on the old pillars of society, even though they were about to deprive them of their privileges. The reality of a society controlled by the estates meant that every representative body used its power and influence to block the continued progress of reform and the dismantling of aristocratic privileges, while attempting to preserve particularist special rights, thus blocking agrarian, tax, district and communal reform. For this reason, the experiments with representative organs were short-term and limited; the economy and adminstration would first have to be reformed.

When the reformers realised that a representative system did not necessarily work to the benefit of reform, it lost much of its interest for them. But the financial crisis was unmanageable without assistance from the estates and this lent more weight to the forces of conservatism and restoration forces, particularly in the provinces. Since there was so much experimentation and many matters were left pending, most radical measures were avoided. This provided the opposition with the opportunity to weaken the reforms in a long-drawn-out series of conflicts, or to put a stop to them altogether. To put it another way, reform was an attempt by the bureaucracy to gain the upper hand over the feudal system and to transform it into a state run by bureaucrats in short, to modernise society.

The nobility was, however, still a very influential section of society. Although the reform envisaged the participation of the nobility in key political decisions, it would have been very difficult to implement. The modernity of these socio-political and state-political objectives conflicted with modern constitutional politics. That is why no final decisions were made before 1815.

(b) The Reforms in the Confederation of the Rhine

During the Napoleonic era, the states of the Confederation of the Rhine had, like Prussia, embarked on an accelerated process of modernisation of state and society; this was the period of the great reforms. As in Prussia, there were special conditions at work which gave a specific stamp to what was a general problem of the time. First, there was Napoleon's direct influence. He wanted to consolidate the internal relations and cohesion of his empire by bringing to bear upon it the achievements of the French Revolution, as watered down by his monarchic rule, in order to strengthen his hand both financially and militarily. In the event of conflict, the immediate interests of power and exploitation — such as providing the French military aristocracy with country estates from the domains of the conquered German provinces, especially Westphalia — clearly took precedence over all reforms dedicated to inaugurating new freedoms. This was not only a contradiction, but a clear dividing-line.

In addition to pressure from outside, there was also an internal impetus for reform. Unlike Prussia, the southern and western German states were 'new'. Now that they had become secularised and mediatised, they were forced to create a state out of a multitude of sovereign territories with their own quite distinct political, legal and religious traditions, to integrate core territory and newly acquired territory into a single state. Baden had quadrupled in size, Württemberg had doubled; the new state of Bavaria embraced about eighty previously independent territories.

The southern German states were given denominational parity. The inhabitants of Baden, despite its Protestant ruling dynasty, were two-thirds Catholic. The new states had revolutionised the map and now had to fill it up with people. At the same time, they had to concentrate state power and establish state sovereignty against the confusion of feudal, clerical, communal and corporate privileges and immunities. The new states had ground to make up in terms of centralising and bureaucratising reforms to even reach the levels of the late absolutist period. Only now was a relationship emerging between the territorial fragments of the old Empire and the modern bureaucratic state. This was their only chance of surviving in the harsh climate of international politics, the only way to raise taxes and recruit soldiers. Financial pressure also played an important role in these states, even though they did not have the persistent threat of catastrophe hanging over them, as did Prussia.

Nevertheless, debt was growing everywhere. In Württemberg between 1806 and 1819 it rose from 15 to 22 million gulden; in Baden (before 1818) from 8 to 18 million; and in Bavaria the debt in 1811 had climbed to 118 million gulden. Everywhere the figure for debt was far higher than the figure for annual state income. The problem of integration, of reshaping the expanded territory to form a state, was now scarcely capable of being resolved by extending the legal and administrative system of the core territories over into the new territories. This would have unleashed violent resistance. What was needed was a complete reorganisation, a break with what already existed, rather than letting the new state grow 'organically'. Precisely for this reason, the reforms in the Confederation of the Rhine were of a rational and constructive nature. This is why they were pushed through with an almost ruthless energy. The states were new and in this sense revolutionary, and so were Napoleon's claims. Now all the established powers began to feel the chill from the sharp winds of revolutionary change.

The spirit of these reforms was first that of enlightened absolutism, which had not yet lost its impetus here, where it had not been able to establish itself fully, where it had not yet reached the paralysis of absolutism in its completed state, and enlightened convictions were still fresh and secure from the doubts which prevailed elsewhere. The philosophy of the Prussian reforms, influenced by Kant and the early idealists, with its anti-absolutist and anti-rationalist, its modern and traditionalist trends, was not on the agenda here, where there was simply no call for it. There was a belief in rational planning and analysis, in *raison d'état* and the common welfare. These reforms were full of an optimism in the ability to effect change, a spirit that was truly of the eighteenth century. What was actually more modern about the reforms in the states of the Confederation of the Rhine was their willingness to take on board the ideas of 1789, tempered by authoritarian requirements. This translated itself into the concept of founding the new state on the emancipation of equal and free individuals and property-owners in a society of enfranchised citizens. Such ideas were expressed differently by various reform administrators; they were clearly at odds with the bureaucratic and absolutist ends and means of the reforms. Various strands here were actually interwoven, such as the state's assertion of its supremacy over the *ancien régime* and the establishment of a society of enfranchised citizens. For the average citizen, there was a little equality here and a little freedom there, all of which were part of the dialectic of reform. Should conflict arise, precedence would be given to the authoritarian centralisation of society, in short, the statist-bureaucratic aspect would outweigh the liberal modernisation of society and the activation of the nation to encourage it to participate in the workings of the state. The social achievements of the revolution were to remain within the bounds of the modernised power structure.

The reforms in the southern and western German states were also reforms of the bureaucracy. As such they constituted a stage in the power struggle between bureaucracy and feudality. Middle-class administrators, many of them later ennobled, had a special role to play in this. So did outsiders, such as the citizens of the Palatinate in Bavaria and the French in the states ruled by Napoleon. The newcomers were the main movers and shakers who toppled the old order. However, in contrast to the situation in Prussia, the reformers often had to first build up the nucleus of an effective bureaucracy, or at least adapt what they had to the greater scale of the new task.

The first major step in all the reforms was the organisation of a unified and effective administration and the establishment of state sovereignty by means of this administration. New administrative districts were formed everywhere. Although similar in geographical size, they were artificial in relation to many old regional districts. Two intermediate administrative tiers were created between the *Gemeinden* (parishes) and the ministries, corresponding to the *Kreise* and *Regierungsbezirke* (districts) in Prussia. In Baden, the leaders of the district administrations were known as *Kreisdirektoren*. In Bavaria, they were *Generalkommissare*, and in Württemberg, *Landvögte* (governers of royal provinces). The administration was unified. Competing administrative bodies were abolished and powers were rationally and clearly delimited. The administration was tightly organised and hierarchical, each post having a clear responsibility and being bound by certain specific directives. The *Mittelbehörden* (intermediate authorities) were run by relatively independent administrators with the power of French prefects; the lower *Behörden* were merely executive bodies. There were no collegiate bodies as in Prussia; one person was always in charge to take the ultimate bureaucratic and administrative decisions. The estate-based corporate self-administration in the communities was abolished, and local government was brought under state control. Mayors were appointed by the state.

This administration had a wide range of powers. It had discarded the whole hierarchy of feudal and clerical, communal and corporate administrative bodies, as well as the various territorial special administrations and powers, privileges and immunities. These were replaced by a unified system of state control and supervision of all matters which were considered public — marriage, immigration, the right of citizenship, trades, schools, welfare, church and taxes, etc. From this plethora of ancient territories and areas under a common jurisdiction there emerged a modern, centralist and unified state. Now as never before, the state directly intervened in all spheres of life, and it did so at an administrative level. It was a devastatingly new experience for every subject.

There was a corresponding requirement for the establishment and standardisation of efficient administrative bodies which would take charge of schools and churches, tolls and taxes; new measures were also needed to modernise them. In Bavaria, for example, the new tax administration was in charge of the new assessment system for land tax, and therefore of the huge task of land measurement. For the first time, the unity of the state as a customs union was established. The school system was reorganised while being placed under state control, though the impetus and energy behind this reform was not so great as in Prussia. The socio-political function of education was for the most part interpreted in late-Enlightenment terms. An idealistic, neo-humanist concept of education was becoming noticeable in some areas, such as in the Bavarian secondary school reform. The reorganisation of some universities — Heidelberg, Würzburg, Landshut — was a modernising reform, though it stopped short of achieving Humboldt's dream of establishing a new concept of 'scientific' knowledge.

The military constitution followed the French model and adopted the guidelines of the eighteenth century. These included conscription and long terms of service, and the opportunity for the educated middle classes to buy themselves out, principally by the system of proxies. Unlike the Prussian situation, however, no significant initiatives towards an overall military reform emerged from this system and its administrators.

Another feature of these reforms was most evident in Bavaria. The rights and obligations of the upholders of the new state, the civil servants (*Beamten*), were laid down in detail in advance, including education, examinations and salary. This occurred in Bavaria in 1805 through the so-called 'Service Code of Practice', which, in the administrative state, was of primary significance to the basic law.

Part of the reform of the administration was aimed at a rational reorganisation of the various law courts and their instances. Judiciary and administration were separated from one another, at least in the upper and central *Behörden*, where the judiciary became 'independent'. Judges now had security of tenure and were obliged to rule according to law. This became the norm, whether written or unwritten, within the new state under the rule of law. In some provinces, the law was standardised and reformed, in particular by the adoption of the *Code Napoléon* (as in Westphalia and Berg) or a modified version of it (as in Baden and Frankfurt). In other provinces — Bavaria, for instance — it remained unchanged. However, the reform of the criminal law in Bavaria, through the introduction of a new standardised statute book, was epoch-making.

The state had exerted full sovereignty through the administration and legislature. Through bureaucratic rule, it had managed to unify both territory and population. A league of subject states under a unified system of law came into existence. Submission to the unified bureaucratic-authoritarian state was combined with the abolition of corporate estate-based freedoms and privileges. This also entailed the liberation or emancipation of the individual from corporate estate-based ties and particularist powers.

When an authoritarian state assumes control over all aspects of public life, a good deal of individual freedom is released. The reason for this, and the reason that the situation in the Confederation of the Rhine was more than the mere replacement of one form of rule by another, is that the new state and legal order adopted by the reformist members of the Confederation kept the actions of the state in line with laws and legal procedures. At least in principle, the equality of subjects before the law, equality of taxation, equal access to public office and the guarantee of security and property were to apply to everyone.

Reform of the administration involved reform of the government. As in Prussia, the jumble of administrative bodies at the higher level, whose responsibilities were not clearly defined, was replaced by ministries organised into separate departments with clearly outlined responsibilities. No collegiate governments were created. In Bavaria and Baden, it would be more accurate to speak of the ministerial absolutism of Montgelas and Reitzenstein. The new organisation of government produced a change in the relationship between government and monarch. The cabinet system was abolished and the role of unaccountable advisers to the monarch was significantly curtailed. It was the usual practice for monarch and minister to work in combination. A 'countersignature' procedure operated in the issuing of laws and decrees, with the exception of absolutist Württemberg. The state was rationalised. Out of the system of principalities, a sort of entailed state (*Fideikommiss*), there emerged a modern state. In finance and property matters — once again with the exception of Württemberg — a distinction was made between dynasty and state. Effectively, the state had now gained the upper hand over the princes, with the monarch as a functionary of the monarchy. The noticeably more bourgeois lifestyle adopted by the monarch at this time was a parallel phenomenon to the shift in the constitution.

The reforms of the religious and church constitution were quite important. All states now contained citizens with a variety of religious affiliations. In Baden and Württemberg, large Roman Catholic populations were now living under Protestant monarchs (and a Protestant civil service). In Baden, this actually amounted to two-thirds of the population. In Bavaria, Protestants from free imperial cities and from Franconia moved into a state with a Catholic tradition. Everywhere tolerance was the order of the day. In many cases, this meant equality under the law, parity between denominations with regard to access to public office, freedom of settlement and the establishment of Protestant churches in Catholic cities like Munich, and Catholic ones in Protestant cities. The conversion of deeply Protestant Old Württemburg and staunchly Catholic Old Bavaria into modern states with denominational parity is a particularly good example. In line with the idea of the sovereignty of the state (and in the spirit of late absolutism), the state favoured the practice of taking church-run institutions like schools, grammar schools and universities, or charity and welfare institutions, under its own control, even if much of this, as with the *Volksschulen*, remained more a programme than a reality. Besides the introduction of the principle of parity, the state now set the limits of the church's sovereignty. The churches, which were still the major influence on social cohesion and peace, would now have to fall into line with the principles of the new state. The supervision of churches was tightened up everywhere and the state's sovereign rights were enforced more intensively. The prerogatives of the clergy were abolished as part of the general move towards equality under the law. The state began to have a major influence on clerical appointments, especially in the selection of bishops in the Catholic church. Clerics could now appeal to the state against decisions taken by the church. As far as marriage was concerned, a civil code of marriage was introduced alongside the church ceremony. This was intended principally for mixed marriages, particularly for dealing with the questions of the religious denomination of the children and divorce. Training of the clergy was now a matter for the state; church finances were now state-regulated; church ordinances required official approval. In short, the church no longer governed itself. Instead it was governed by the state via an independent church administration and a minister in charge of church affairs. The state wanted the church to serve its own purposes, even on matters of interest to the church alone. The church was an institution of popular education, the clergy were 'religious teachers of the *Volk*' or 'officers of morality'. In effect they had become state officials.

In the interests of peace, radical denominational positions — mysticism and fanaticism, as they were referred to — were to be shut out. In Bavaria, and to a certain degree in Württemberg, this went hand in hand with the fight during the latter years of the Enlightenment against 'abuses', such as pilgrimages, processions and rogation gatherings. The state decided on the number and time of masses and processions. It banned the ringing of bells during storms, the erection of cribs at Christmas and preaching about miracles. In Württemberg, priests were subject to codes regulating beard- and hairstyles. The king introduced a new liturgy to combat the 'plague' of pietism. It was a mixture of rationalism and orthodoxy which no longer featured the devil. In short, the church was brought to heel politically under an authoritarian, enlightened *raison d'état* as an instrument for the creation of a uniform state society.

What was of greatest importance, however, was the forward march of secularisation. In 1803, the old territories under clerical rule had been secularised by the new states, which took over not only their sovereignty rights, but also church property. At the same time, the states were empowered to secularise — i.e. nationalise — the wealth of all religious institutions which were not self-governing under the Kaiser, but which had still been subordinated to the territorial states. This affected the monasteries primarily and also the clerical foundations. The motives for this move were to be found in the acute financial crises in the states, in the desire for political integration and in the anti-monastic spirit of the late Enlightenment period. There was strong feeling against the unproductive wealth of the mortmain, and anti-clerical hostility to the 'obstacles to culture' and to monks *per se*.

Nowhere was this internal state secularisation carried through so radically as in Bavaria, with the exception of the territory on the left bank of the Rhine. Elsewhere, it was tackled more cautiously, as in Württemberg, for instance, since the dynasty there was Protestant. As early as 1803, all the monasteries in Bavaria — which had owned more than half the land, and controlled 56% of the farms — were broken up, nationalised and sold off. Their libraries and art treasures were confiscated. The storming of the monasteries and the demise of the old clerical institutions are things which are deeply engraved in the consciousness of the Bavarian people. Secularisation had crucial consequences for the state, for society and for the church itself. The demise of the monasteries removed the strongest bastions of pre-modern, non-state power in the south and west. This enabled the state to establish full sovereignty and to begin to constitute itself in its modern form. The abolition of all autonomous institutions with their own rights, levies, immunities and privileges, those intermediary powers between subject and state, strengthened the hand of state in the battle against feudalism. The church had been a part of the feudal-particularist order, and the modern state, which wanted this order superseded, had to secularise. The princes were so greedy for land and property that they violated the old law and caused a revolution, thus legitimising the modern state from the viewpoint of world history.

What were the consequences of this for the church? The state now had to spend money to secure the buildings, equipment and personnel of the churches. The church then became (and has remained ever since) a recipient of state funds. But at the same time, the state was able to emerge from the feudal system and disengage itself from the secular power structure which enabled it to become once again a purely spiritual institution. Secularisation marked the beginning of a new spiritualisation of the church. Release from feudalism also meant that the higher offices of the church were no longer the preserve of the nobility, and the cathedral chapter no longer a foster home for the younger sons of the nobility. From then on, the clergy became more egalitarian and middle-class, though this did not happen overnight. Finally, secularisation led to a large-scale restructuring of property relations, and this had important social consequences. Monastery buildings and land (with the exception of woodland), as well as any cottage industries they might support, were sold off. In Bavaria, many of the buyers were members of the petty bourgeoisie and tradesmen, as well as some who were directly dependent on the monasteries for their living. The land was parcelled off. A redistribution in favour of the urban middle class and those with considerable capital did not occur. The peasants were now under the direct domination of the state.

The state made only limited and short-term gains from these sales. The estates were thrown quickly onto the market and in many cases sold off below their true value. Only the extensive woodlands owned by the monasteries remained state property in the long term. In the terriories on the left bank of the Rhine, the situation was different. There, the urban bourgeoisie benefited from the sale of the estates. This prompted speculation and accumulation on a large scale, owing to the large profits to be made. To be sure, here too the land was passed on to peasants or a newly emerging peasant-bourgeois landowner class through resale.

While the territories, communities, corporations, institutions and groups were being integrated into a new order in the new monarchist-bureaucratic state, the nobility as well as the church constituted a particular problem. The nobility lost a whole series of privileges, including their monopoly on certain public offices and army commissions and the right to be tried in special courts. In Bavaria and Baden, however, the nobility, senior administrators and the educated classes as a group retained a certain special status. In principle, the aristocracy was also included in the universal obligation to pay taxes, though, in practice, there were limitations. The estates which had been mediatised in Bavaria and Württemberg were compensated for this new burden. Seigneurial jurisdiction and local police sovereignty were abolished in some states. In others, such as Bavaria, they remained in force and were subject only to state supervision. Wherever legal privileges were not abolished, they were converted into property titles valid under private law. Certainly, the nobility was never completely subject to the principle of equality before the law.

The mediatisation of the nobility, which had been self-governing under the Kaiser and the Imperial Knights, produced a new problem with the nobility in the south.

The pre-1806 Reich constitution and subsequent Napoleonic constitution for the Confederation of the Rhine guaranteed them certain special privileges, from which the landed gentry profited indirectly. For this reason, the process of streamlining the nobility to fit into a modern society of enfranchised citizens was delayed.

All of this was part of the delay in the implementation of the great social reforms. Napoleon had planned to transform feudal society into a society of free property-owners, which meant primarily the removal of *Grundherrschaft*. This was what the new law, the *Code Napoléon*, meant in a socio-political sense. However, the abolition of feudal rights and revenues was, according to the property guarantee built into the code, subject to compensation. The rights of those who had undergone mediatisation were expressly guaranteed; the French military nobility, for example, was not allowed to incur any loss of seigneurial income as a result of reform. In this sense, Napoleon's policies towards the aristocracy had prevented any comprehensive reform of society. Then there was the problem of distinguishing between two sorts of claims by the gentry, claims which were valid under private law and those validated by the public legal code. To this was added the difficulty of bringing the endless, quirky local by-laws under a unified system of control. The principles of the planned agrarian reform were interpreted restrictively. It was carried through in single stages, but in practice the laws did not work. In the grand duchy of Berg, for example, all titles to property which were not valid exclusively under private law were abolished in the autumn of 1811 without compensation. Because of opposition from the nobility and then the war, however, this remained true only on paper. Serfdom was abolished wherever it had not already been eradicated, but this was of no great significance in the west and the south. Levies were more precisely fixed and co-ordinated, and on the whole peasants were now able to convert their tenancy duties into monetary payments. This did not apply, however, to the *Adelsbauern* in Bavaria, who constituted about a quarter of all peasants. The arrangement was contingent on an agreement being reached which the peasants were unable to finance, nor could the state assist them through credit, and it could not renounce its revenues as landlord of the domains. The liberation of the peasants never got beyond the first couple of hurdles.

Nevertheless, this did not result in any increase in the economic and political power of the nobility, as it had in Prussia, since the south and west were dominated by landowners who received rent from tenants. It was only in the regions on the left bank of the Rhine where the liberation of the peasants, abolition of most levies without compensation and reform of land rents had any real success. Even there, however, financial pressure from the gentry was replaced by the pressure of taxation from the state.

In the reformist states of the Confederation of the Rhine, the idea of a constitution eventually played a role. Existing corporate bodies were abolished. There was also a plan for a system of national representation. Put forward by Montgelas in 1796, its underlying conviction was that, in addition to administrative and authoritarian integration, a new national spirit had to be created, a partnership between nation and state. Reforming legislators such as Anselm Feuerbach emphasised, with good reason, that the legal transformation of society and the establishment of civil liberties required, in the last analysis, a constitutional monarchy and the participation of the citizenry in legislation. However, such ideas soon took a back seat among influential politicians.

Only two constitutions were actually established, one for Westphalia, drawn up in Paris in 1807, and the Bavarian constitution of 1808. These proposed a national representation, elected by a small section of voters whose eligibility was contingent upon payment of taxes rather than membership of a particular estate, as previously. In Bavaria, however, the king was to have a hand in appointing electors. The assembly would decide only on laws and the budget, as laid down by the government. The core of monarchic sovereignty, which determined state action and the fixing of laws, was unaffected. In this respect, a sort of sham constitutionalism was the result. Personal security, property, rule of law, equality before the law, and the independence of the judiciary — the *de facto* foundations of the new constitutional states — were guaranteed. But these constitutions did not work; the Westphalian chamber was summoned only twice, the Bavarian one never. The problem was basically similar to the one which Prussia had faced. Those eligible to vote — *de facto* — largely the nobility — were opponents of a modernising social and taxation reform. The constitution presupposed a comfortably-off and educated middle class which did not yet exist. Reform seemed possible only in a bureaucratic sense, not constitutionally, so long as the *Volk* were still organised and still thought along estate lines.

The reforms as a whole prevailed over the lifeless and paralysed *ancien régime* and replaced it with a modern, centralist, secular and bureaucratic state. The reforms meant that, for the first time, the individual experienced the direct influence of the state; they established the enormous power of the modern state to control lives. It was the administration which held the state together and which sought to regulate communal life in a thoroughly authoritarian and patrician manner, and it succeeded. Under pressure from Napoleon, and partly also at their own behest, the states of the Confederation of the Rhine also developed aspects of a police state; a tendency towards state omnipotence was unmistakable.

Yet this state, though authoritarian, was also liberating. It emancipated the individual from corporate ties and also from corporate liberties, and it did away with the particularisation of society and its endless inequalities. By subordinating everyone to the state, it made everyone the same and brought about an increase in civic, individual and, initially, personal freedom. It was part of the dialectic of reform that the rise of the bureaucratic-authoritarian reformist state liberated the individual, however much it subordinated him to its own rule. The modern state was rationalised, becoming a state under the rule of law in which security, property and equality before the law were guaranteed, at least in principle. Society did not undergo a revolution. The principle of equality before the law had only a relative value (it was more a slogan than a reality). But the society based on estates and its hierarchy was made significantly more open, even though the autocratic oligarchy still remained powerful, and the bureaucracy rose to become the ruling class in the country for quite a time. This was still a transition stage in which a society based on equality and the oligarchical structures of rule of an older and a newer variety still overlaid one another. The modernisation of society had only just begun.

The differences between the states in the Confederation of the Rhine should be examined further at this point. Three areas have to be distinguished here. The central and north German states remained almost unaffected by the reforms. In Saxony and both Mecklenburgs, the pre-revolutionary order of state and society carried on as before. In the smaller states of northern and central Germany, the reforms remained modest. Then there were the artificially created Napoleonic states of 'Westphalia' and Berg and, in a certain sense, Frankfurt. They were to become 'model' states of uncompromising reforms. The French achievements, the reorganisation of the system of justice and law, played a special role. But these reforms broadly failed, or remained mere rhetoric. These states, of course, were under foreign rule, and the French Emperor could intervene on any matter he wished. French was the state language. The contribution, military obligations and enormously increased tax burdens were bleeding the country dry. A major part of the domains was handed over to the French military aristocracy, driving states such as Westphalia to the brink of bankruptcy and halting the process of the liberation of the peasants. Not only was the promise of a liberal state under the rule of law left unfulfilled, it was acutely at odds with the system of foreign exploitation. Indeed, Westphalia, with its censorship, political police and the power monopoly held by the administration, seemed to be heading towards the dictatorship of a lawless state. In Berg, the climate was somewhat more moderate and well-meaning, but there also the dilemma could not be resolved. Finally, the demise of these states between 1813 and 1815 meant that the reform initiatives which had taken place had little continued effect.

Ultimately, the true *loci* of reform in the Confederation of the Rhine were the southern German states. The reforms there had a lasting effect. In Bavaria, the fate of reform over this whole period was interlinked with the fate of the leading minister, Montgelas (and his assistant, Zentner). There, the reform was the most uniform and emerged out of one mould, driven forward with the utmost vigour. It even reached a certain fever pitch, culminating in a state of bureaucratic, statist over-centralisation. In Baden, the thoughtful Brauer and the stormy figure of Reitzenstein, as well as Gagern and Marschall in Nassau, were, on the whole, successful in pushing through reform. Württemberg was a special case. Here the new king, Friedrich, was a driving force behind the reforms. They were absolutist, aimed at independent rule by the monarch, and nothing short of violent against the estates and nobility, popular forces and liberal ideas.

A special role was played by the territories on the left bank of the Rhine, which from 1801 to 1814 were cut off from the rest of the German states and belonged to France. Here, a particularly old-fashioned, pre-absolutist, estate-based feudalism had continued to exist. Consequently, it was here that reform was most radical, and the upheaval most acutely felt. Church and nobility were dispossessed. The tight, rational and effective French administrative system was introduced. Above all there was the French legal system which was based on the freedom of the individual and property, social mobility and equality before the law, and, in addition, courts with a jury and public oral hearings. This legal revolution, combined with the boom in the French war economy, had smoothed the way for the rise of a bourgeois, property-owning society, and the removal of economic restrictions. In terms of social policy, the Rhenish territories were well ahead of the rest of Germany.

For quite some time, the reforms in the states of the Confederation of the Rhine were overshadowed by those in Prussia. They were seen as the products of foreign rule or as merely the products of Enlightenment rationalism, and not as 'organic' reforms. Today, there are those who champion the Rhenish reforms in this debate, precisely because they were more strongly influenced by the Enlightenment and the (domesticated) ideas of 1789. Both these points of view are ideological, and they are better left aside. Both types of reform, within the framework of the reform period as a whole, were independent and of equal importance. Both had a specific modernity, though of a different hue. The reforms in the Confederation of the Rhine, as compared with the Prussian reforms, were more statist-orientated. The idea of mobilising popular forces, of the participation of the nation, which in Prussia had had a determining influence on military and educational reform, self-administration and the planning of the constitution, played no important role here. The state, not the state and nation, took centre stage. The reforms in the states of the Confederation of the Rhine, unlike those in Prussia, were not so definitively set on a liberal course of economic and socio-political liberation of the individual and of competition. The most important social reform, agrarian reform, never got beyond the initial stages. The reforms in the Confederation of the Rhine, on the other hand, were, in theory at least, more bent on superseding the society of estates, and followed the revolutionary principle of equality. However, history looks not only at intentions, ideas and objectives, but also at results and effects. That is how the geography and status of reform is determined.

In southern Germany, the reform period established a tradition which had repercussions for the whole century. The state had been the agent and driving force of modernisation. It was this that led initially to an extraordinary strengthening of the monarchy — a fact that is often ignored. Following the end of absolutism, the monarchy had managed to ride out the storms of the revolution. Under the patronage of the new Caesar, Napoleon, it had adapted itself to the more modern environment and had gained sufficient legitimacy, authority and prestige, particularly in the eyes of public opinion, to sustain it in a new bourgeois century. As far as the upwardly mobile middle class and the liberal forces were concerned, the state and the monarchy — despite vestiges of feudalism and the authoritarian structure — offered a partnership through which to maintain the momentum of the reforms. This had a significant influence on south German liberalism. At the same time the reforms imbued the bourgeois movement, as well as a part of the bureaucracy, with the spirit of the French law and the French idea of a society of free and equal property ownership. The fact that the south German states acquired constitutions after 1815 was in no way due to the earlier reforms, but it gave them a new and modified character afterwards. The delay in agrarian reform had made superfluous the kind of vigorous restoration and modernisation of the aristocratic power base that occurred in Prussia, and had therefore, in the long term, not been so detrimental to the process of transition to a more bourgeois society based on equality before the law and freedom. The result of the reforms was therefore different from its ideas and its original character. The south experienced the political and constitutional modernity of the early constitutions, while Prussia experienced the socio-economic modernity of a liberal, economically driven society. Owing to a lack of private landed nobility in the south, it had been able to develop a much stronger bourgeois society over a long period.

(c) Austria: A Brief View
During this decade, Austria did not experience a great wave of reform, a revolution from above, in the way that Prussia and the south and west German states of the

Confederation of the Rhine did. This is of great significance for the way German history progressed.

There are a number of reasons for this. First, Austria in the late eighteenth century, especially under Joseph II, had been the country most committed to the enlightened reforms of absolutism. These included the abolition of serfdom, freedom for the sons of peasants to choose their own occupations, the opportunity — even for the middle class — to purchase aristocratic estates, tolerance, integration of the church into the state, general education, modernisation of the judiciary, centralisation and bureaucratisation of the administration. However, the reformers had not had an easy time implementing the reforms; they were too numerous and the pace was hectic. The reform had provoked fierce resistance, and a good part of it petered out or was blocked. Austria remained less centralised and old-fashioned, a conglomerate of empires in the hands of the dynasty. There was no unified constitution for government, while concessions made to the interests of the higher nobility remained an essential feature of the system. Revolutionary events and a Jacobin conspiracy had instilled in the Emperor and other leading ministers a lasting fear of revolution, causing them to equate reform with revolution and making them cling stubbornly to absolutism. The Emperor was against any liberation of the forces within society, against any accommodation with new social movements. He sought to exercise the state's authority with an even firmer hand. In Austria, furthermore, there was not the same necessity for reform as existed in the other German states. It did not face as great a threat to its existence as did Prussia, nor was there a necessity to integrate a fragmented territorial area. It did not even need to catch up on or complete the process of absolutism in the state's assertion of its sovereignty. Neither the feudal nor the bureaucratic-absolutist structures were in such disarray as elsewhere; the arrangement between absolutism and feudalism was more efficient. Even a permanent financial crisis had failed to mobilise sufficient pressure for reform. Finally, there was no pressure group of civil servants and senior officers, whose modernist convictions and *raison d'état* turned them into spokesmen for the common good and who sought to push the reforms through to completion.

A whole series of late absolutist and Josephist reforms was carried through to completion, especially in the legal sphere. There was a new code of civil procedure, a new criminal law, and above all a new civil law, the *Allgemeines Bürgerliches Gesetzbuch* (Common Civil Code) of 1811, one of the last great codifications of natural law. The fundamental rights to freedom and property, including equality under private law and the autonomy of private law relations under the state, were now fixed, though only in principle; they were not presented in explicit form for application to social and economic relations. This heralded a society of free and equal property-owners, based on achievement and talent, and not one in which the state made all the decisions. The judiciary and the administration were separated, at least as far as the middle tier was concerned. Municipal administration was taken under state control and the primary school system was extended further, though, in contrast to the Prussian Pestalozzi-based ideal, this schooling was geared towards the creation of obedient subjects, to useful knowledge and church-dominated religion. Church policy remained Josephist and statist, but the laws were interpreted very much more favourably towards the churches and religious orders.

On the question of major issues, however, reform stagnated. No progress was made in the liberation of the peasants. The abolition of duties and services proceeded no further, nor did reform of the economy and taxation. The nobility, with the exception of Hungary, was not exempted from paying taxes, although it continued to receive preferential treatment. A chaotic constitution remained in place in which the integration of policy lay solely in the hands of the Emperor. The problem of imperial unity and regional autonomy was kept off the agenda, and bureaucratic institutions were no longer opposed to the aristocracy, but even fought on their behalf.

In 1805, Philip Stadion, chief minister from 1805 to 1809, promised to involve all classes of the population and all nationalities in the rebuilding of the state. He was aiming at the continuation of peasant emancipation, a more open state bureaucracy and the revitalisation of representative bodies from the nobility and estates in those countries and provinces which had their own national identity — a degree of federalisation. However, this was clearly limited by the authoritarian norms, and remained reform-conservative and patriotic-nationalist theory (just as the reform plans of Stadion's adversaries, absolutism in the Confederation of the Rhine mould with a contemporary sprinkling of individual freedom, could not be carried through). The approach had some similarity to that of Prussia, but there was no internal renewal, since the forces whose aim this was were too weak. Such ideas only became concrete in the military sphere, which Archduke Karl reorganised with the help of his brother, Archduke Johann (the *Reichsverweser* (Regent) in 1848!).

There was to be no separation of army and society, and the defence of the fatherland was to involve everyone. Exemption from military service was to be further restricted and the period of service limited. Military punishment and training were to be made more humane. Above all, there was to be a militia in addition to the standing army, to be raised and financed by the regions. It would train at home and on Sundays.

The *Landwehr* was popular and successful. It was one of the first forms of universal conscription, though somewhat crude and with many exceptions, especially for town-dwellers. But this was no more than an episode and had no further consequences for politics or the public consciousness. The patriotic tide of 1808–09 ebbed away. When the Peace of Schönbrunn was concluded, the Viennese population embraced one another with great enthusiasm. Defeat brought to an end attempts at a larger universal reform. Domestic politics concentrated solely on the financial crisis in the state, on the huge debts which the losses of territory and the lost wars had only served to multiply. It also focused on the growing inflation which resulted from the failure of the state leadership to raise sufficient revenues or to make adequate cuts in its expenditure, seeking its salvation in the issuing of paper money. In 1811, this financial crisis led to a sort of state bankruptcy, a depreciation of paper money to a fifth of its former value. But there was no attempt to use reform initiatives to bring about stability. The war of 1813 was financed once again — despite promises to the contrary — primarily with paper money. In 1817, when a quasi-independent issuing bank was set up, paper money underwent another steep depreciation. Administrators, wage-earners and others who received a fixed income were hardest hit by inflation, and it was the tax-paying farmers and tradesmen who lost most by the subsequent deflation. The domestic climate was dominated by unrest and the crises which this situation provoked. The psychological consequence was a growing loss of faith in the government on the part of the *Volk*. Under these circumstances, the state and government continued to have very little room for manoeuvre, both in domestic as well as in foreign policy.

3. The Great War and a Difficult Peace

In late May 1812, following a magnificent congress of princes in Dresden, Napoleon ordered the *Grande Armée* to march. The army consisted of more than 600,000 men, nearly a third of them Germans. His campaign against Russia ended in the defeat of his army, an outcome which nobody had expected, not even his adversary, which had reckoned on a longer struggle. The advance came to nothing, faced with the defensive tactics of the Russians and without a decisive battle. Disease decimated Napoleon's army. The Tsar, bolstered by the nationalist and religious resistance of the Russian people, refused a peace settlement. The burning of Moscow and the terrible winter forced Napoleon to retreat. Cold and hunger, skirmishes and yet more disease added to the existing problems. Perhaps 100,000 men (excluding the Austrian and the Prussian corps) — ill-equipped, sick, wounded and scattered — reached the Polish and East Prussian borders again in late 1812.

The Tsar now decided, against the wishes of the majority of his generals, to continue with the war. The Russian defensive war had turned into a war not only to re-establish the balance of power, but also to liberate Europe from a criminal tyrant. German emigrants like Arndt and Gruner formed a German–Russian legion and began distributing war propaganda.

While the Prussian king and his government, still conscious of their weakness, were cautiously devising tactics, the commander of the Prussian Auxiliary Corps, General Yorck, concluded a pact with the commander of the Russian army. This was the Convention of Tauroggen, signed on 30 December 1812. The Prussian corps was neutralised in East Prussia, and therefore broke away from the French alliance. The way to East Prussia was now open to the Russians. The convention was concluded without the knowledge of the king — and with a corresponding reservation. When the king declared it invalid and dismissed Yorck, the latter stuck to his guns and declared that he would lead his troops against Napoleon, contrary to the king's will. This was an amazing development. Here was a general serving the militaristic state of Prussia (motto: *Obedience*), in no sense well disposed to the reform movement, who took it upon himself to act independently, indeed claimed the right to disobey. He was putting patriotic and nationalist legitimacy higher than dynastic and military authority; in doing so, he changed the course of a small part of history. Tauroggen subsequently acquired a mythical significance in both liberal and conservative nationalist tradition before 1933, and indeed until the early days of the GDR. It became a symbol of Prussian (German)–Russian unity, as well as a symbol of the right of dissent. In East Prussia, Stein organised a Provincial Assembly, which (once more in opposition to its royal sovereign) assembled troops and declared war on France.

The Prussian king hesitated and negotiated first with Napoleon, then with Austria and, of course, with Russia. Court and government entered unoccupied Breslau on 22 January 1813 and began to arm themselves. After long-drawn-out negotiations, Prussia concluded an alliance with Russia on 26–27 February on the basis that Prussia would cede to Russia a part of the Polish territories it previously held, for which it would receive territorial compensation from Germany. King and government were under a certain pressure from the patriots; they were anti-Napoleon and pro-Russian and demanded a liberation struggle. They now had a determining influence on public opinion, especially the educated classes. There were anti-French demonstrations and even the possibility of a spontaneous uprising. Despite his hesitation, his diplomatic anxiety and his dislike of the patriots' enthusiasm, the king was pressured into supporting a patriotic liberation struggle. As E. Kehr so correctly put it — in a reversal of the Prussian legend: everyone, everyone shouted for the king to come, until the king came.

On 10 March, the king founded the new order of the Iron Cross, and on the 16th he declared war. On the 17th the famous rallying call was issued, 'To My People'. In this, the king reminded them of the earlier struggles of oppressed peoples for their liberation and appealed to the people's willingness to make sacrifices in the decisive battle for independence, for king, fatherland and honour. It was to be a patriotic war, a people's war, and this was something completely new. Associations of volunteers were formed; conscription was made universal and all exemptions were lifted. It became everyone's duty to defend the fatherland, this fatherland which guaranteed security, protection for property and 'civil liberties protected by the law'. Whoever tried to dodge his duty would have to reckon with considerable restrictions upon his basic rights as a citizen. In this sense, the volunteering was not quite so voluntary. We know that the *Freikorps* consisted entirely of city-dwellers, but the educated youth in no way dominated — they made up 12% — only in the Lützow Rifles did they constitute about a third. However, it was the educated youth who answered the call for volunteers, and these formations (10% of the armed forces at the outset and over 12.5%, or 20,000, at the end) were what gave this war its special character.

Volunteers from other German states also served in the Lützow Rifles. They swore allegiance, not to the king, but to the fatherland. For the most part, the *Landwehr* was assembled without resistance, but it lacked equipment and leadership. Discipline was poor for quite some time, and the fighting strength low. The spirit of sacrifice among the citizens was considerable: 6.5 million thalers were collected in the impoverished countryside: 'I gave gold for iron' became the motto. In Prussia, then, the war — leaving aside the exaggeration of later legend — had aspects of a popular uprising, even if one were to judge it with critical sobriety; the people appeared to perceive it as their war. Prussian-German patriotism forced its way into the public mind, and the war songs of Körner and Schenckendorf, Eichendorff and Rückert became popular. *Leyer und Schwerdt* by Theodor Körner (a Saxon in the Lützow Rifles) was the definitive war book: 'It is not a war of the kind the kings know about, it is a crusade, 'tis a holy war.' This reflected the mood among the educated and the young, at least. Ernst Moritz Arndt above all was one of many whose writings (such as *Catechism for the German Landwehr Man*) popularised this spirit and who more than anyone else propagated the struggle as a pan-German, nationalist struggle: '[We are] not Bavarians, not Hanoverians, not

Holsteiners — neither Austrians, Prussians, Swabians, nor Westphalians, all who may call themselves German, [are] not against one another — [we are] Germans for Germans.'

However, there were no such 'German uprisings' for the present outside the free provinces of Prussia. The population of the states of the Confederation of the Rhine remained for the most part loyal to the system or simply passive. In Westphalia, Berg and the coastal regions, people refused to pay taxes. There were desertions and isolated incidents of unrest, especially as Napoleon had new troops assembled, but these were swiftly put down, sometimes with the help of the civil guards. In south Germany, everything remained quiet. Napoleon had nothing serious to fear in the territories controlled by him. A popular insurrection was planned in the Alpine regions from a base in Vienna — from Carinthia, across Tyrol and up to Switzerland — and the preparations for this were well under way. But Metternich, who did not want to see his cabinet policies disturbed, had the instigators arrested or put out of harm's way. Preparations were halted.

The war had a peculiar ambiguity. For the patriots, who now had public opinion behind them in Prussia, it was a war of the people and the nations, a German uprising, a crusade against tyranny. It was about emancipation and freedom. Stein spoke about the people needing to break free of their shackles; he wanted to organise 'armed masses' behind Napoleon's back. He regarded the princes who had joined forces with Napoleon as usurpers; they were 'totally indifferent' and had no claim on their rule being restored. The fatherland was to be found where 'honour and independence' resided. Arndt wrote: 'When princes do and demand something which is opposed to the fatherland, or when they behave as though this is what they wish to do, their subjects are then no longer bound by their oath.' This was the tone of the nationalist revolution.

The aim of emancipation was to create an independent, united and strong Germany under the leadership of Austria and Prussia, to bring happiness and freedom to the German nation. These were certainly the ideas behind it, but at the same time the war was one fought by monarchs and governments, states and powers. It was a war about dynastic rights and claims, power interests and a balance of power, about the restoration of stability. It was not just about a new age of freedom and the nation. In Prussian politics, in which the patriots in the government and the army had a strong hand, and in Russian politics, both elements played a part — this is where the Tsar's ideas for liberation ran parallel to the concept of Stein and many of his advisers. The Proclamation of Kalisch was presented at the Russian headquarters on 25 March. In it, Kutusow, the Russian supreme commander, gave notice of the war aims of the allies, a typical manifestation of this line of thought. The aim of the war was to restore law, freedom, the independence of the princes and peoples of Germany and Europe, the dissolution of the Confederation of the Rhine and the restoration of a rejuvenated united empire with a constitution 'based on the inherent spirit of the German people'.

The princes, the people, indeed every single person, was called upon to leave the Confederation of the Rhine; the princes who stayed loyal to Napoleon were threatened with the loss of their thrones. The liberation of oppressed peoples and the restoration of dethroned princes, as well as the continued existence of the individual states, the nation, legitimacy and the interest of the state, stood side by side, equal in importance. The Tsar styled himself as a liberator. His actions were, of course, bound up with the power interests of Russia. These included compensation for Prussia for the territories seized by the Napoleonic princes, and a federal constitution for Germany which gave it order and limited its potential strength. As the leading power in Europe, Russia was to act as the guarantor of this new order. No politician could have predicted how the Russian power interests and Russian ideology of liberation — especially considering the Tsar's unpredictability — would develop.

The prospects for the allied powers were initially not very favourable. The allies were too weak on their own to throw the still-powerful Napoleon on to the ropes. In the spring of 1813, he had assembled a new Franco-Rhenish confederate army. In May, he triumphed over his adversaries, Grossgörschen and Bautzen, driving them out of Saxony and back to Silesia. He did not take advantage of this favourable position, but offered an armistice instead. Napoleon wanted to consolidate his army and at the same time break apart the coalition of his adversaries by reaching an agreement with Austria or Russia, while sacrificing Poland. All the enemies of Napoleon throughout Europe, Prussia, Russia and above all Napoleon's major and lasting adversary, England, as well as Sweden, Spain and Portugal formed a great coalition.

Everything hinged on Austria. Both Napoleon and the coalition powers were relying on it. Metternich tried delaying tactics; like the Emperor, he was in no mood to fight a war. He did not want to stake everything on one card, at least not right now. He did not want to go to war before rearmament was completed and he did want to keep Austria's strength in reserve by keeping the war distant from his own soil. In addition, Metternich had no desire to break the treaty with France, not only because the Emperor's daughter was Napoleon's wife, but also because Austria's whole existence rested on the 'sanctity' of treaties. He did not want Austria to become a mere appendage of the existing coalition. His aim was to dictate the terms of the war. It would not be a people's war, not a revolutionary nationalist war of patriots and emancipators, and certainly not a crusade. It would be a war of states to restore the balance of power in Europe, a legitimate order and stability, a war fought by politicians and diplomats with rational and clearly limited goals. A people's uprising in the Alps or the dethronement of the princes of the Confederation of the Rhine did not fit into this plan. The revolutionary nationalist elements had to be rechannelled. Only this would serve the security and power interests of the dynastic, artificial state of Austria. For this reason, agreement about the aims of the war and the new peacetime order were more important than victory. The important thing was to prevent new revolutions from occurring, and — even more important than this — to prevent Russia from achieving hegemony over Europe, to restrict the ambitions of Russia in Greater Poland and to stop Prussia becoming a satellite of Russia. Since France was to continue to provide a strong counterbalance, it should therefore be spared. In contrast to most of Napoleon's adversaries, Metternich had long since felt that the best and most stable solution was to have a Napoleonic empire confined to France and accommodated into the European order of states, thus protecting France and Europe from further revolutions. Finally, neither in Germany nor in Italy should a national state be allowed to develop which could break up the supranational state of Austria or the balance of power in Europe. In Italy, Austria ought to become the leading power, a primarily European one, not Germanic. In Germany, Austria should forgo territorial positions as well as south German hegemony. Prussia, with its claims to a north German hegemony and protectorate, should be firmly checked, and should be integrated into an internal balance of powers in Germany, a federal order which would consolidate the whole.

The way in which Metternich gradually managed to sever his ties with Napoleon, and pass via neutrality and mediation to the coalition while simultaneously persuading the coalition powers (in principle at least) to abide by his war aims, has always been considered a masterpiece of diplomacy. Because Prussia was in a coalition with England, despite the fact that the latter continued to lay claim to Hanover, it had to forego a quasi-revolutionary reorganisation of north Germany. Following an agreement with the coalition (the Convention of Reichenbach, 27 June 1813), Austria initially attempted to negotiate with Napoleon on the basis of a programme which was, even for Metternich, minimal, and to which the coalition powers were not bound. Napoleon was to renounce his domination of Poland, give up Illyria and the Hanseatic towns and his occupation of the Prussian fortresses and agree to the expansion of Prussia in the east. Napoleon, as the coalition powers had expected, refused *de facto*. In a famous nine-hour discussion in Dresden, he confessed to Metternich that he could go before his people as the son of the Revolution, as a non-legitimate monarch, but not as a defeated man. After this, and as agreed, Austria entered the war on 11 August. On 9 September, the Treaty of Teplitz called for the restoration of the European balance of power as it had been in 1805 as one of the aims of the war. As far as Germany was concerned, the most important points of the treaty were independence for the German states, the restoration of the territorial order of states (of 1803) in north-west Germany, and the Rhine as the German frontier.

A weakened Austria — remaining, as it were, in reserve — became the central power in the coalition, and Metternich became its quasi-prime minister. He had finally turned a people's war into a war of the major powers. The aim of the war was not emancipation, freedom, or even national unity; it was order and the restoration of a balance of power. This was possible, of course, because, in the last analysis, Russia and Prussia were also anti-revolutionary powers.

The 500,000 men of the three armies of the alliance now once again confronted 440,000 of Napoleon's men. By employing skilful tactics of delay and flexibility, the alliance managed to steal the initiative from Napoleon. Once its armies were brought together, it threatened his line of retreat. In the 'Battle of the Nations' at Leipzig (16–19 October) Napoleon was decisively defeated. He was able to beat a retreat, but following the loss of about a third of his army, he had to withdraw to beyond the Rhine.

Before Napoleon's might had been smashed, Metternich had concluded a treaty with Bavaria in Ried on 8 October, which was to be of the utmost significance for the future of Germany. Bavaria joined the coalition, and in return Austria guaranteed to preserve Bavaria's current territorial possessions (with the option of exchanges) and sovereignty. This meant that the Napoleonic order of territories and states, in the south anyway, was firmly established in principle. The dissolution of the states of the Confederation of the Rhine — on the basis of the right of conquest — was just as much off the agenda as a return to the conditions of the old Empire. The medium-sized states from the old Empire which had been broken up, and which had subsequently been reorganised under a Napoleonic protectorate, became part of the post-Napoleonic new German order of states. The later resolution of the German question along the lines of alliances between states was prejudiced by the sovereignty guarantee. That is why this treaty was later heavily attacked by German nationalist historians, who viewed it as a major misfortune of German history for which Metternich was to blame. It is certainly questionable whether the coalition actually required Bavaria and the other south German states to join it so urgently, and whether the logic of events would not have brought about their entry into the coalition under a much narrower range of conditions. But Metternich had other reasons for his actions. Prussia had rejected a common strategy with Austria in the south and pursued its own interests. In this sense Austria's strategy was also a reaction to Prussian ambitions. Above all, this guarantee for Bavaria was in line with the fundamental conception of Metternich's politics. Metternich wanted stability, and the abandonment of Napoleon's territorial reorganisation would have brought about a chaos of old and new claims. He wanted to end the centuries-old competition between Bavaria and Austria, and to make Bavaria an ally of Austria in any dispute with, for example, Prussia. A strong Bavaria was to secure the federal equilibrium in Germany under the indirect patronage of Austria.

The Treaty of Ried, which Prussia and Russia also joined in November, was followed by similar treaties with Württemberg and the other states of the Confederation of the Rhine. Stein's plan to subordinate these states under the 'central administration', established for the conquered territories under his chairmanship, did not materialise. Indeed, these treaties had built into them restrictions on sovereignty for the benefit of a future German confederation, though this changed nothing of fundamental importance for the path which was already being followed. The true Napoleonic states were dissolved and restored to their former rulers. In the case of Saxony, Berg, Frankfurt, parts of Westphalia and the territory on the left bank of the Rhine, they were brought under the central administration. Stein hoped that this would at least give him a lever which he could then use to force the individual states into a unified national structure.

After the victory over Napoleon, the question arose as to whether the war should be continued. In the interests of the balance of power, Metternich wanted a peace settlement on the basis of the Rhine border; the claims of the partners to the alliance should not be augmented, nor should the war be total. The hawks, on the other hand, wanted the complete liberation of Europe and the fall of Napoleon. The proponents of this plan included Stein and a large part of the Prussian army, the Blücher's general staff, including Gneisenau — the nest of Jacobins, as it was called in the king's circles — as well as the vociferous nationalist publicity machine. Arndt wrote one of his most effective pamphlets, *The Rhine: Germany's River, not Germany's Border*, and Görres turned his new newspaper, the *Rheinischer Merkur*, into a campaigning organ against Napoleon.

There was no response to a peace offer from Metternich. Then, in the new year of 1814, the allies crossed the Rhine. However, the rifts within the coalition remained. The hawks — the majority of Prussian generals and the Tsar — wanted a quick and decisive offensive against Paris. Metternich and the doves wanted a slow war strategy and negotiations. There were additional disputes concerning the internal reorganization of France. Metternich would have preferred to keep Napoleon; the Tsar wanted to put in Crown Prince Carl Johan of Sweden, the former Marshal Bernadotte. So the war dragged on despite the superiority of the allies; the atmosphere was pervaded by threats of independent initiatives or separate peace settlements. Finally, the British foreign minister, Castlereagh, in conjunction with Metternich, succeeded in establishing a common political strategy for the coalition. The allies renewed their partnership. France was to be reduced to its 1792 borders and was to give up all its spheres of influence in the Netherlands, Germany, Switzerland and Italy. England had managed to force home its major territorial objective, the independence of the enlarged Netherlands, just as Austria had succeeded in exerting its dominance in upper and central Italy and in forcing through the federal organisation of Germany.

The allies committed themselves to upholding the peaceful order for at least twenty years. But a corresponding offer of peace from Napoleon was rejected once again; the son of the Revolution could not give up the conquests of that same Revolution. Metternich's attempt to bring the war to an end before a 'final victory' had failed, but the war was diplomatically contained. Only now, at the end of March, was Paris taken; Napoleon had to abdicate. The Peace of Paris on 30 May 1814 allowed France to continue to exist within its 1792 borders. It was a peace based on appeasement — as if it could be anything else — a peace dictated by the victor under pre-democratic conditions, with no immediate pressure from the public. The conquered peoples also had to to be included in the new balance of power.

The reorganisation of Europe after twenty-five revolutionary years of disruption and war was the task of the Congress of Vienna. This was a bizarre assembly of monarchs, ministers, diplomats, aristocrats, men of letters and adventurers. It has entered the public consciousness as a series of intrigues and love affairs, lavish balls and parties — 'the Congress dances' — in which the European aristocracy celebrated itself and the end of the threat to their world.

The Congress itself did not conduct the negotiations. The business was dealt with in meetings between the four major victorious powers and France, and in numerous individual negotiations. The task was to create, some felt to re-create, a stable and lasting European order which could be accepted in principle by all parties, and a new internationally acceptable legal code. The general desire was for an order which achieved balance, an order based not on the freedom and self-determination of peoples, but on the legitimacy of dynasties and states. This did not mean the restoration of pre-revolutionary conditions — the great changes in the order of states were irreversible facts — but the legitimation in international law of those states which had earned a claim to continued political existence. This was now to be done through the international community of states.

These were the terms of reference within which the different powers sought to enable their opposing interests to prevail, through conflict or compromise. What this meant, above all, was the establishment of fixed borders and the apportionment of land based on a 'head count', in order to confirm old dominions or install new ones. Today, one may find this obsession with the acquisition of territory either amazing or repugnant. But at the time this was certainly not confined to princes; it was a general practice, the classic way of securing or acquiring power.

The reorganisation of Germany was inextricably bound up with the reorganisation of Europe and the interests of the major European powers. England and Austria were the true promoters of the policy of equilibrium because it suited their interests. What this really meant was the containment of Russia, the curbing of the independence of France and the consolidation of a European centre which was to be as independent from the west as it was from the east. This entailed Austria having the dominant position in Italy — the security of Europe would have to be defended at the Po if necessary. It also involved pacification, as well as the inclusion of Prussia in a German federation which

Austria and Prussia would jointly lead. Both powers had already safeguarded their own particular interests in the treaties of war. Russia wanted to reinforce the strong position it had in Europe by extending its presence in Poland, indeed by establishing a Polish kingdom under the Tsar. Russia had already received a number of pledges from its partners on this issue. At the same time, it was pressing for a strong position for its special ally, Prussia. Prussia was, after all, the least satiated of the constituent members. If it wanted to continue playing the role of a first-rank power, it would have to press for expansion. For Prussia in particular, the internal organisation of Germany was a security problem of the first order. Prussia had entered the war early and unconditionally, and could hardly claim to possess binding pledges of peace. Furthermore, it lacked the power to exert pressure on its alliance partners.

The major problem of the territorial reorganisation of Germany, as with the German and European distribution of power, was the problem of Prussia's east–west shift. Russia laid claim to the large chunk of Polish territories which had been Prussia's reward on the last two occasions when Poland was partitioned. Prussia had to receive compensation in exchange. It was forced to expand its territory further into Germany, though the details of this were not yet fixed. The restoration of British rule in Hanover limited any expansion in the north-west. Prussia now wanted to annex Saxony, which had not freed itself from Napoleon and was, in this sense, a conquered territory. Since Saxony was a neighbouring country with a similar structure, Prussia could have formed an integrated state with it. Prussia would thus have been relieved of the burden of opposition to Poland and Russia and could have secured and extended its position and power in Germany, perhaps even its hegemonial ambitions. If necessary, the Saxon royal palace could be moved westwards.

The idea of ruling Alsace soon came to grief when Britain objected that the new France would not want to be burdened with such a handicap. The Polish–Saxon question became the question on which the fate of the Congress hinged in the winter of 1814–15. Metternich and Castlereagh wanted to block the Polish ambitions of the Tsar — his territorial demands and the establishment of a Polish kingdom. They managed to draw Prussia on to their side. After long hesitation and with all kinds of provisos, they were prepared to hand over the whole of Saxony to Prussia. But the Tsar would not budge an inch, and Hardenberg had to withdraw from the anti-Russian block at the behest of his king. After this, the offer of Saxony was enfeebled and Metternich reverted to dynastic arguments. Now, by defending the existence of Saxony, he became once again the protector of the medium-sized states. Prussia threatened to take matters into its own hands, even to declare war. Austria, England and France forged a secret alliance on 3 January 1815. Prussia was forced to compromise, especially as the Tsar, who saw his Polish claims secured, no longer provided it with full support.

The largest section of Poland, so-called Congress Poland, fell to Russia and was to be ruled as a kingdom in individual union with the Tsarist empire. Following small concessions by the Tsar, Prussia received the 'Grand Duchy of Posen' and a few territories which had been attached to West Prussia, including Thorn. The burden of the partitions of Poland has been an important influence on German politics ever since. Prussia was pushed further towards Germany, while Saxony was divided. Prussia received about a half of its territory, containing two-fifths of the population. Additional compensation for Prussia came in the form of the Rhineland as far as the

Saar and the Nahe. Prussia now extended as far as the Rhine and took over the burden of defending German central Europe on its western border.

Originally, Prussia had only wanted to take on such a commitment in the west in union with Austria. When Austria withdrew, it initially favoured other compensations, Ansbach for example, but this proved to be unrealistic. England, in view of the military weakness of the Netherlands, wanted Prussia's engagement at the Rhine, and Austria saw this as a relief. The expansion of Prussia as far as the Rhine is one of the most fundamental facts in German history, one of the bases for the foundation of the Reich of 1866–71. With the addition of the Rhine Province, the artificial splitting of Prussia into eastern and western territories was reinforced, and was even more sharply emphasised than before. This became the strongest driving force behind Prussian power politics; eventually it became important to eradicate this split. Prussia's role as Germany's guardian power at her western frontiers — together with the split in half — led to the situation in which Prussia's own security was inextricably linked to its position in Germany. Her striving for hegemony in the north, at least, was for this reason almost a necessity. When the *Kleindeutschen* (literally, Lesser Germans, i.e. those who favoured a confederation of German states that excluded Austria) spoke later of 'Prussia's mission' to protect and therefore unite Germany, one has to acknowledge that, strategically and geopolitically, Prussia had been forced into this 'mission'. Finally, this defensive task had provided a new stability and legitimacy to Prussian militarism. At the same time, the addition of the Rhine Province had made Prussia the strongest German economic power and further emphasised its peculiar modernity. The country's internal structure was also shaped by the decision of 1815.

The many other conflicts over the final territorial organisation of Germany need not be dealt with in detail. Austria eventually gave up her former Dutch and upper-German territories, and, after much to-ing and fro-ing, she also abandoned the idea of building a new position in the central section of the Rhine (Mainz and the Palatinate). She withdrew as a power in the south and west and concentrated on the German south-east, where she won back Tyrol and gained Salzburg. She extended her position of power in Europe in Italy at the expense of her German power base. Since then, Austria was less a German power than Prussia was, and this was to have far-reaching consequences for the national history of the Germans. As compensation, principally for Tyrol and Salzburg, Bavaria was given Ansbach and Bayreuth, Würzburg and Aschaffenburg, as well as the region of the Palatinate on the left bank of the Rhine. Bavaria's ambition to become the ruling power in south Germany, between Austria and Prussia, through acquiring Frankfurt and Mainz, Heidelberg and Mannheim and parts of Württemberg, came to nothing as a result of resistance from her south German competitors and the major German powers. Mainz was allocated to Hesse–Darmstadt, and Frankfurt was made into a free city like the three Hanseatic cities. Hanover acquired East Frisia, so that the whole of the North Sea coast was *de facto* under an English protectorate. Lauenburg as a German duchy went to the Danish king, while Prussia acquired Swedish Pomerania, including Rügen; Luxemburg became a German grand duchy subject to the Dutch king. The mediatisation of the knights and the highest ranks of the nobility was not reversed. Most of the remaining small states, in the area of central Germany and Thuringia, in Nassau, in Waldeck and Lippe, stayed intact. Anomalies like the Oldenburg area of Birkenfeld in Hunsrück and several others were newly created for reasons of compensation. On the whole, however, the large-scale revision of the German map carried out in the age of revolution and conquest, above all the founding of the medium-sized states in south Germany, was consolidated. The territorial pattern of Germany drawn up at that time would remain until 1945, if one ignores the Prussian annexations of 1864–66.

Besides the territorial questions, the question of a national German organisation was also of decisive significance. There was a relatively general consensus that Germany as a whole would have to be given some form of centralised state organisation. The European powers wanted to see the state consolidated. A power vacuum would have provoked constant intervention and disturbed the peace. Prussia and Austria, in the interests of simple power and equilibrium, favoured institutionalised control of the small and medium-sized states. To add to this, there was the German feeling of solidarity, tradition and the memory of the old Empire, as well as the new national consciousness. The nation was a basic fact of communal life, and in particular a basic political fact, having the right to unity, self-determination and independent development. This conviction was disseminated through the patriotic writings and experiences of the uprising and liberation, and considerably influenced the people's expectations. Arndt and Görres were only the most prominent representatives of a widespread publishing operation. At the suggestion of Arndt, German societies were formed, particularly in the Middle Rhine region, which wanted to instil the 'spirit' of 1813 into a national and constitutional new German order. The gymnastics clubs and the beginnings of the students' associations (*Burschenschaften*) have already been mentioned. These trends also affected the daily activities of politicians. They influenced Stein and the Prussian patriots, and scarcely anyone was able to ignore them totally. Declarations of war and the treaties between the allied powers had promised a reorganisation of Greater Germany.

How could the multiplicity of German states and the unity of Germany be reconciled? One section of the patriots, including Arndt and Jahn, Gruner and Gneisenau and many others wanted to see power removed from the princes of the Confederation of the Rhine. What they wanted was the creation of a nation-state, if possible under Prussian leadership, for only Prussian politics seemed to be open to patriotic nationalist ideas. The Prussian and the national interest appeared to coincide, in their eyes at least. Outside Prussia, in the south-west or in Karl August von Weimar's circle, such opinions were also prevalent. However, they were still in a minority. No concrete ideas had been formulated concerning methods and goals, and these opinions played scarcely any part in the major decisions.

A nation-state had no chance of success in 1815. The European powers hardly favoured such a solution. They felt that instead of pacifying the forces in Germany within a balanced system, it would simply bind them together, making them more dynamic and constituting a danger to the rest of Europe. This solution was not even favoured by the large and medium-sized German states, nor even by the masses. Nevertheless, the idea of a united Germany was not without effect. When it became obvious that it was unrealisable, people like Stein, Arndt and Görres, and even Humboldt to a certain extent, turned it into the more realistic concept of a strong federal state. Hardenberg utilised the concept, its advocates and its resonance in his Prussian policy.

The regionalists, mainly in the south and west, as well the victims of mediatisation and the princelings, the opponents of the absolutism of the Confederation of the Rhine, and even Austrians and supporters of Stein favoured a restoration of the old German Empire and of the Habsburg Empire in Austria. Theirs was a combination of traditional Reich patriotism and a new nationalism. However, the old Reich was in ruins, dead; it could not easily be renewed in reality nor even in spirit. The medium-sized states were against it. Prussia felt that a monarchy with power would be unbearable, while one without power would be useless. Compromise solutions, like making Prussia into a German or north German federal martial state within the Confederation under the Austrian Emperor, proved to be unrealistic. A new empire foundered on the rocks of Prussian–Austrian dualism. Finally, and this was the main reason, Metternich and the Emperor decided, after some hesitation, to oppose such a restoration. The Empire would burden Austria with the unending conflict between imperial power and particularist states, and with the opposition of the medium-sized states, and would therefore be damaging. The problem of German dualism was not to be solved by the creation of such an empire. Austrian rule of Germany could only be achieved indirectly and through the quasi-natural alliance of the medium-sized states, certainly not by creating an empire.

To be sure, and this was an important consequence, Austria disappointed many nationalist expectations by its choice and forfeited the reputation it had regained in Greater Germany in the nationalist consciousness. Nevertheless, a version of this idea more in line with *Realpolitik*, involving a combination of federal state and empire, was taken up again in 1815 by Stein, the mediatised powers and the princelings, and played a significant role at the Congress.

One possibility which remained was federalism, whether along the lines of a confederation of states or more like a federal state. However, any such organisation would first have to solve three problems. It would first have to determine what was to be the position of both German major powers in relation to the other states and to one another, i.e. the problem of hegemony and dualism. Secondly, it would have to define the relationship between the confederation and the individual states, the division of sovereignty, the distribution of authority and the construction of an effective federal ruling body. It would have to deal with the problems of appointing a head of the confederation and a government and establishing a legal system and legislation. This would determine whether the new structure was to be more like a federal state or more of a confederation of states. Finally, there was the question of a constitution. No one considered the restoration of absolutism. Reformers and patriotic-nationalist movements wanted constitutions. 'By granting the people its small share in its own government,' Görres stated, 'one may anticipate the sort of lively participation in the welfare of all which is absolutely necessary if Germany is to continue to exist.' The bourgeois-constitutionalists wanted basic rights. Statist reformers and even conservatives wanted constitutions in order to integrate and strengthen the state or to buy off social movements through concessions. There was also the particular problem of the nobility — the mediatised imperial nobility as well as the aristocratic opposition who were fighting against the bureaucratic and authoritarian reform states. A constitution would have to ensure the co-operation of the nobility or integrate it into the state. The modern bourgeois-constitutionalist and the traditional property-based aristocratic elements contained in all such demands for a constitution often existed undifferentiated side-by-side. A constitution could be liberal or conservative, and it could be interpreted in a statist or estate-based sense, and for this reason the call could be taken up by all sides. Reference was usually made to corporate constitutions, either provincial or state-wide in nature. The European powers also supported a constitution. European constitutions modelled on that of Great Britain, the new French *Charte* of 1814, and the constitutional plans of the Tsar, all played an important role.

The outcome of the Vienna negotiations was the loosely integrated 'German Confederation' (*Deutscher Bund*). But initially there were other, apparently realistic, alternatives. It is worth selecting a few from the multitude of plans and ideas. Stein had been proposing a whole series of plans for a constitution from 1812 onwards and had been sounding out their chances of being realised. His search for a solution is clearly illustrative of the difficulties of the 'German question'. In November 1812, for example, Stein had considered dividing Germany into two spheres of hegemony, while in August 1813 he was looking at the organization of the 'Third Germany' as a 'Reich' linked by individual union to the Austrian Emperor and tied to Prussia by firm and long-term treaties. Humboldt attempted to reconcile the idea of a nation-state with the reality of the German community of states and the interests of Prussia in maintaining an equal status with Austria; he thereby developed intermediate forms between a confederation of states and a federal state. Hardenberg adopted many of these ideas.

This gave rise to the joint draft constitution drawn up by Prussia and Austria in October 1814. Germany was to be divided into districts (*Kreise*), a throwback to the old Reich constitution, to be headed by Austria, Prussia, Hanover, Bavaria and Württemberg. The Council of Heads of Districts (*Kreisoberen*) was to be the executive organ of the confederation which, assisted by an Austrian *directoire*, was responsible for legislation together with a council of princes and municipal authorities. There was also to be a supreme federal court. The authority of the confederation extended over a broad sphere. It included not only military and foreign policy, but also 'all matters relating to internal welfare', primarily the economy and law. The individual states would retain sovereignty with regard to taxation only. The confederation was to lay down the framework for the constitutions of the individual states and, as was agreed later, was to guarantee the co-operation of the *Landständen* (state parliaments or assemblies) in legislation and taxation, as well as the right to impeach a minister. The mediatised powers (and even the nobility to an extent) were guaranteed special rights and a privileged position in the *Landständen*. Hardenberg had even wanted to give them a seat and a vote on the council of princelings and municipalities, and this was proposed again at a later stage. The federal court was to be responsible for ensuring that constitutional norms were adhered to, and for protecting the special rights of those who had undergone mediatisation. Prussia and Austria were excluded. They were not fully subordinated to the federal constitution and were to be allowed to conduct an independent foreign policy. Neither they nor their territories were members of the confederation.

The planned confederation was based firstly on the supremacy of the five large and medium-sized powers, primarily the kingdoms, and the separation of their spheres of influence. Secondly, it was founded on the dual hegemony of Prussia and Austria in both the confederation and the executive, where they had two votes each, the three others having only one. Of course, the extra vote only helped when they were in agreement. Thirdly, the confederation was based on the restriction of the sovereignty of the medium-sized and small states by the federal organs on the one hand, and on the other by the newly created internal counter-forces — the estates and the mediatised powers — which were protected by the federal court.

These measures would have led to a 'quiet mediatisation' of the states of the Confederation of the Rhine and a strengthening of the confederation as well as of the hegemonial powers. On this basis, a compromise had been found between a federal state and a confederation of states, with a functional executive, a legislature with sufficient responsibilities and a supreme court. There were to be no representative bodies at national level. This was a source of irritation to the supporters of the national and constitutional movement, though hardly surprising under the circumstances. It is worth remembering that Austria and Prussia agreed on this compromise. Hardenberg, the reformer, agreed with Metternich, the restorationist. At this juncture, in the interests of stability, Metternich wanted to link the individual states to Austria and Prussia. He was thus appeasing Prussia and committing it to co-operation with Austria, thereby restraining its ambitions to rule Germany or north Germany. Prussia still depended on consensus with Austria, since it was unable to rally the support of the medium-sized states to its cause.

These plans failed. Bavaria and Württemberg scarcely disagreed with the hegemony of the kingdoms, but they fought vehemently against any limitations on their sovereignty and against Prussian–Austrian hegemony. Austria, Prussia and Hanover were, in fact, willing to make significant concessions, but they held firm to the idea of a functional federal organisation which was not too weak *vis-à-vis* the sovereignty of the individual states, and to the federal guarantee of constitutions. They even considered finalising the confederation without the south German kingdoms, if necessary for the short term. In this they were supported by the Tsar.

Then came opposition from quite another quarter, the 'non-royal Germany' which Stein had organised with journalistic help from Görres. These states campaigned for equality among the members of the confederation. Only then would they be prepared to renounce sovereignty, and they campaigned once again for a new form of empire. The crisis over Saxony now intervened to destroy the consensus between Austria and Prussia. Metternich performed a *volte-face* to join those who supported the idea of a confederation of states, seeking a compromise in which the full internal and external sovereignty of the medium-sized states would be preserved as far as possible. He wanted to do without the institutional hegemony of the German superpowers altogether, since this would only lead to conflict. Instead they would be allowed to use their greater power only indirectly.

Prussia was unable to push through a solution more along the lines of a federal state against the south German states and Austria. It was still dependent on Austria and had no choice but to switch, albeit hesitantly, to solutions based more around a confederation of states. Only a minimal federal structure was now being considered. Even so, negotiations appeared to have reached an impasse. Metternich did not want to use diplomatic pressure or issue ultimatums to quell south German resistance. That would not have squared with the politics of consensus and equilibrium which he was pursuing in Germany. At one time, Metternich had used the return of Napoleon and a new outbreak of war to persuade all the participants to a minimal settlement and agree on a framework which might later be elaborated on. Prussia took this as a basis for future development, while the south German governments saw it as the ultimate concession.

On 8 June 1815, the *Deutsche Bundesakte* (Act of German Confederation) was finally passed. The indissoluble confederation consisted of thirty-nine (later forty-one) sovereign states and cities. Prussia and Austria's attachment to the Confederation only involved membership of the regions which had formerly belonged to the Empire. The kings of England, Denmark and the Netherlands were members, as they belonged to the German landed nobility. The major powers had renounced the *directoire* (and, hence, workable executive), as well as the division into districts and the military constitution which was based on it. They did without a common church constitution, a federal guarantee for the constitutions of the individual states, and finally, at the instigation of Bavaria, the federal court. Indeed, they ruled in the end that the important resolutions concerning fundamental laws and institutions of the confederation, questions of religion and the affairs of individual states could only be settled by a unanimous vote, and not with the customary two-thirds majority.

The sole organ of the confederation was the *Bundesversammlung* (Federal Assembly), soon to be called the *Bundestag*, a congress of ambassadors in which the larger states received, in the highest instance, four out of sixty-nine votes. Within this body there was a smaller council with seventeen votes, of which the eleven larger states held one each. This body would draft proposals, and these would be passed by a simple majority. The confederation was to take all necessary measures for the internal and external security of Germany. This is how its purpose was defined, and it was limited to this. Equality of religious denominations, relative freedom of movement and the freedom to acquire land regardless of which state one belonged to were guaranteed to all subjects as a fundamental right. Those who had experienced mediatisation were also granted certain prerogatives. On the subject of constitutions it was stated: 'All states in the confederation will have a *Landständische Verfassung*' (i.e. a corporate state constitution).

The *Bund* was still a relatively weak federation with little power to act. It was a confederation of states with some elements of a federal state, but without an executive, a judiciary and *Verfassungsschutz* (office responsible for the defence of the constitution), and with minimal competences. The sovereignty of the individual states and their claim to equal rights had been affirmed. A tighter federal organisation, which had seemed possible at first, had come to grief when the Prussian–Austrian consensus fell apart and Metternich gave in to resistance from the south German kingdoms.

The German Confederation was a denial of the moderate form of a national federal state, which the nationalist movement, as well as Prussia and a number of small states, had wanted to see. Stein expressed their disappointment, saying that the Confederation did not meet the expectations of the nation, the scale of their ambitions, their suffering and their vigour. They saw in it neither a guarantee of their civic and political freedom, nor of their external security in the event of war.

It is certainly inappropriate and anachronistic to measure the sovereignty policies of the south German governments and princes, or Metternich's policy of equilibrium and stability, by the yardstick of nationalist standards. It is equally incorrect to condemn them. A nation-state, founded on the self-determination of the nation, was impossible at this time. For half a century, the Confederation was instrumental in bringing a peaceful order to Germany and Europe. It had enabled the German states to live in peace with one another, while at the same time neutralising and softening their influence in Europe, ensuring that they were not a burden on Europe. Indirectly benefiting from the power situation in Europe, it had secured the German borders against pressure from outside, acting as a stabilising factor. Nevertheless, the Confederation did not represent freedom or national unity. It was a barrier against any liberal-nationalist movement of the future, a victory for the restoration of the particularist states. This is precisely why it was the background for both German revolutions, in 1848 and in 1866–71. With the benefit of hindsight, the outcome of the founding negotiations — the loose confederation of 1815 — was perhaps a misfortune for German history.

The question could be asked whether a tighter federation, as was originally on the agenda, a federation which allowed more room for common policies, would have given rise to a different, less disruptive, more liberal pan-German development. We do not know. It is questionable whether the five-power domination would have worked and whether the unity of the major powers would have lasted, whether the political will of the emerging nation would not have turned against the dynastic order of federal states, or whether it might have been able to reshape it. One might ask whether, for the people who came from the regionalist and estate-based old Empire, the national federal state was not something untimely. The modern particularist state, despite all the bureaucracy, was still something the individual could see and comprehend, a necessary transition phase on the way to the modern state. It could be that the particularist and egoistic rationale of sovereignty of the south German princes created a very timely phase of development, despite their intentions. A cunning logic may have been at work here. It is worth considering, though the truth will never be known.

We now return to high politics and to the peace treaty. While the Congress was still negotiating — and this is still a part of folk memory — the news came in March 1815 that Napoleon had landed again in France. This restored the unity of the four victorious powers. All overtures from Napoleon were rejected. War was declared again and ended in the summer with the decisive Anglo-Prussian victory at Waterloo. Napoleon's last attempt had failed.

This new situation rekindled hopes and endeavours for a radical revision of the new order. Germany, 'which of all of them had made the most valiant efforts and had suffered the greatest hardship, was outwitted and sacrificed by them all'. This was how Joseph Görres's *Rheinischer Merkur* put it in its edition of 1–2 July 1815. Nothing had been 'safely concluded'. The 'Reich' had been offered no security against France, 'where all borders lay open', nor even against Russia, 'which in Poland had driven the mightiest wedge deep into German territory', nor against England, 'which had devoured all the coasts from the Elbe to the Scheldt'. These were the protests of incipient German nationalism.

The Congress of Vienna had incurred the nationalists' wrath because freedom and the German people had played no part in the negotiations. Instead of a new Reich, they argued, the delegates had come up with only the disappointing German Confederation. In the interests of his own Prussian policies (and as a means of putting pressure on the medium-sized states), Hardenberg had given the Prussian and the pro-Prussian patriots (Arndt, Gruner and Niebuhr) a free hand in their propaganda campaign. In a sharply worded pamphlet, Arndt wrote that England was 'the little shopkeeper who rules our seas and rivers, and who, given the chance, would turn the whole of Germany into an English warehouse'. He went on to state that the German princes had prevented the rise of a new mighty 'Germania'. Austria had, in Arndt's view, renounced its former occupation, that of leading and protecting Germany; the people were not there for the princes, who were superfluous, when the people had no more need of them. Europe, he thought, would not lose its balance if Germany and Italy were to become united and mighty empires. It was now up to Prussia to 'use its strength to build and preserve honour, power and harmony'.

With regard to Germany's organisation on a national level, such rumblings remained vague and ineffectual. The effects were more concrete on a demand for a revision of the borders with France, which would at the same time strengthen Prussia's pursuit of a nationalist policy. The talk was of Alsace and Lorraine in the spirit of an old imperial patriotism, as well as of the new concepts of the *Volk* and of nationality based on language. Görres even demanded the restoration of the 'Burgundy legacy', old possessions, 'before they are wrenched from us by force and deception'.

The patriotic moralising of the war led in some quarters to the idea of punishing the French, striving for absolute security led to the idea of large-scale annexation. These ideas were voiced not only by a handful of journalists, but even by princes and politicians, especially from the imperial nobility, in Württemberg, Hanover, the Netherlands and Austria (for example, Stadion and Archduke Karl). Even Hardenberg demanded that France surrender the fortified strip along her east coast from Belgium to Italy, though this was for reasons of power politics and security.

Practically nothing came of all this. The recent restoration of the Bourbons had quickly improved France's position again. In the interests of reconciliation, balance, and French internal stability, neither Britain nor Russia wanted any significant weakening of France. Furthermore, Metternich did not want any 'nationalist' movement springing up, like that of the Prussian 'Jacobins'. He wanted no new conflicts which could lead to the break-up of the pentarchy in arguments over new 'spoils'. Hardenberg had to give way. In the armistice and occupation negotiations, Blücher and Gneisenau, the leaders of the Prussian army in France, tried to implement such a policy. They attempted to create a *fait accompli*, to play off the army (and even the king) against the government and diplomats, and they took it right to the brink of insubordination. Castlereagh, Metternich and the Tsar considered this army a potential revolutionary force. In the end, however, Hardenberg won through against the politicising generals. In the second Peace of Paris, despite a few boundary changes (Landau and Saarbrücken), the new German–French border was left as it was.

The Congress phase concluded with the signing of two international treaties. First, the alliance of the four victorious major powers, the so-called Quadruple Alliance, was renewed. It was to secure Europe against new attacks by the French and safeguard the Peace of Paris. It also proposed European conferences to clear up international questions which still needed to be resolved. Secondly, the European powers — with the exception of the Pope, the Sultan, and even, strictly speaking, England — concluded the famous/infamous Holy Alliance. Driven by religious motives and influences, the Tsar had wanted to make a major declaration heralding the arrival of a new spirit in politics, beyond cabinet diplomacy and Machiavellian power-broking, a new era of fraternity among princes and peoples. They were, he said, a single family, one nation, in which the monarchs would rule over their peoples in a fatherly, Christian and peaceful spirit. Metternich had 'edited' the draft of this speech. He had erased the prophetic tone, the condemnation of earlier times, the heralding of a fundamental change in attitudes, talk of a unified Christian nation. Instead he had placed the emphasis on the fraternity of monarchs instead of that of the people. A proclamation about a crusade and a new era was transformed into a declaration of the end of the revolutionary period and a return to the normal path of history. The role of the universal community (whose protector would have been the Tsar) was taken over by the major powers. Metternich used Christian theocratic formulae to win the Tsar over to his own way of thinking. The Holy Alliance was not an instrument of the *Realpolitik* of the European powers, but rather a symbol of the conservative, anti-revolutionary restoration and the politics of stability.

Looking at the reorganisation of Europe as a whole, three things stand out. First, there was a new constellation of the major powers. The real victor in the era following the collapse of French hegemony was Britain. Its power on land and sea was reinforced by the European equilibrium, yet it was at the same time the power which guaranteed this equilibrium. Britain had her continental buffer states and controlled the European market for goods.

Russia had a stronger position than ever before in Europe, with the lion's share of Poland, plus Finland and its border at the mouth of the Danube. Russia had not, however, been able to achieve actual hegemony of the continent. This was one successful aspect of the Anglo-Austrian containment.

France was restored as a major power, though restricted in its freedom of action. Because of its internal structure, Austria was not a strong power in itself, although it was making its presence felt in Poland (Galicia) and now dominated Italy. Nevertheless, Austria still had considerable political muscle. It would always hold the balance when any European coalition was formed because it had checked the expansion of Russia in Europe and Prussia in Germany without actually inciting the enmity of either of these powers. Austria depended to a considerable degree on the system of equilibrium which stabilised its influence as well as its supra-national organisation. Prussia had strengthened its position in Germany, but had not achieved its real objectives. Owing to its geography, it was not saturated territorially in the long term. As a European power, it was practically in the second rank, forever in the shadow of Russia and Austria.

So, then, a second characteristic of the European reorganisation was that the new order, like that of the German Confederation, was an order of restoration, a bastion of princes and states against the liberal and nationalist movements, against the right to self-determination of nations. The existing power structure of states, indeed the legitimacy of the dynasties, seemed to be cemented in international law. Every change since then clashed with the European system. The liberal and nationalist protests of the nineteenth and twentieth centuries against the Vienna settlement were well founded.

Ultimately, however, and in contrast to this, the third essential feature of the reorganisation was that both its task and its outcome was the creation of stability. After the revolutionising of all European relations, the European order was to be restored by treaties and obligations, by recognition and consensus. This was what the new legitimacy was all about. It was about taming the uncontrolled dynamism of single-state power and imperialistic claims, as well as the modern nationalist and revolutionary movements and their messianic ideologies. This peaceful order reduced conflicts. It became something which was taken for granted in Europe — in all its reorganisations. It achieved a relative longevity, right up to the Italian and German wars of unity, or indeed, in a certain sense, up to 1914. For this reason, it has fascinated all who have sought to assess it ever since. Peace settlements in the age of nationalism and democracy have been on the whole less rational, less reconciliatory, less fair and less stable.

It is in the nature of great historical phenomena that what we like and what we dislike about them are both inherent characteristics; they will not grant our wish to find all positive elements on the same side: freedom and peace do not fit together exactly. This is constitutes their greatness, and also their tragedy.

II

Life, Work, Business

1. Population

In 1800 the population of the German territories was some 30 million. The area in question was the Reich as it existed in 1871, excluding Alsace–Lorraine but including the Austrian territories in the German Confederation, of which Bohemia and Moravia also formed part. By 1816, after the Napoleonic wars, it had not grown substantially, but stood at around 32.7 million. By 1865 it had risen to over 52 million. Thus, in this period, for the duration of the German Confederation, it rose by 60%, corresponding to an average German growth of 0.94%. Of course, such averages are not very informative. As Table 1 shows, the population increase was very uneven. Within Prussia the strongest population growth (80–120%) was in the agrarian, landlord-dominated eastern provinces and in the predominantly commercial regions of the Rhine Province and the province of Saxony. In the rest of Germany, growth was above average (80–100%) in the agricultural state of Mecklenburg, in the trade-orientated kingdom of Saxony, and in the commercial centres of the Rhine–Main region and the province of Saxony, though in this last case the fact is obscured by the statistics covering the entire land area of their respective states.

In north-western and southern Germany population growth was in some areas substantially below the German average of 60%. It was lowest in the Austrian Alpine regions, being virtually stagnant in Salzburg and Tyrol.

In addition to the regional difference there was also a temporal one. In the first twenty-five years of the period 1816–65, the population grew much faster than in the second twenty-five years. Population density, however, was another matter. In spite of the strong population growth, nowhere did population densities reach those of today (with the exception of Berlin, of course). Furthermore, it is striking that the extremely vigorous growth rate in the agricultural areas of Mecklenburg and Prussia starts from an extremely low level. Even Tyrol and Vorarlberg, with its great expanses of uninhabitable, barren land, were initially more densely populated! The old trading and cottage-industry regions and areas of partible inheritance (*Realteilungsgebiete*) of Saxony, Bohemia, Upper Silesia, south-west Germany, the urban regions around Vienna, Trieste and, of course, in the Rhineland were at least relatively 'densely' populated.

Table 1: Population of the states of the German Confederation (000)

		1816	1865	growth 1816–65 %	annual growth rate %
Kingdom of Prussia (incl. West Prussia, East Prussia, Posen, Hohenzollern) of which:		10,400	19,445	87	1.3
West Prussia	not in	571	1,261	121	1.6
East Prussia	the German	886	1,775	100	1.4
Posen	Confederation	820	1,532	87	1.3
Kingdom of Prussia, to the extent included in the German Confederation (incl. Hohenzollern, Prussian in 1849)		8,093	14,785	83	1.2
of which: Berlin		198	646	226	2.4
Brandenburg (excl. Berlin)		1,086	1,992	83	1.2
Pomerania		683	1,442	111	1.5
Silesia		1,942	3,532	82	1.2
Province of Saxony		1,197	2,053	72	1.1
Westphalia		1066	1,676	57	0.9
Rhine Province		1,871	3,379	81	1.2
Schleswig–Holstein (Schleswig not in the German Confederation)		681	1,017	49	0.8
Hamburg		146	269	84	1.2
Mecklenburg–Schwerin		308	555	80	1.2
Hanover		1,328	1,928	45	0.7
Oldenburg		220	302	37	0.6
Brunswick		225	295	31	0.5
Electorate of Hesse (Hesse–Kassel)		568	754	33	0.6
Grand Duchy of Hesse (Hesse–Darmstadt)		622	854	37	0.6
Nassau		299	466	56	0.9
Thuringian states		700	1,037	48	0.8
Saxony		1,193	2,354	97	1.4
Baden		1,006	1,429	42	0.7
Württemberg		1,410	1,752	24	0.4
Bavaria (incl. Palatinate)		3,560	4,815	35	0.6
Luxemburg/Limburg (to the extent incl. in the German Confederation)		254	395	56	0.9
Other federal territories excluding Austria		543	817	51	0.8
German Confederation excluding Austria		21,156	33,824	60	0.9
Austrian kingdom, where part of the German Confederation		9,290	13,865	49	0.8
of which: Alpine regions		4,291	°5,870	37	0.6
of which: Lower Austria (incl. Vienna)		1,045	°1,900	82	1.2
Upper Austria					

(incl. Salzburg)	760	°880	15	0.3
Tyrol and Vorarlberg	726	°875	21	0.4
Styria (incl. South Styria)	765	°1,115	46	0.8
Coastal areas (only Trieste and Görz district)	158	°290	84	1.2
Carinthia and Krain	642	°810	26	0.5
of which: Sudetenland	4,853	°7,485	54	0.9
of which: Bohemia	3,163	°5,015	59	0.9
Moravia and Silesia	1,690	°2,470	46	0.8
of which: Duchy of Auschwitz (under Galician administration)	335	(510; unproved, estimated)		
German Confederation total	30,446	47,689	57	0.9
German Confederation and parts of Prussia not included in the German Confederation	32,723	52,257	60	0.94

° approximate figure.

There is a clear element of time in the population density linked to population growth. Taking statistical data for the three years, 1816, 1840 and 1865, Table 2 shows that population density increased in Prussia from 38 through 54 to 71 inhabitants per square kilometre; in the Prussian federal territories, from 44 through 62 to 80 in the German Federation excluding Austria, from 49 through 65 to 78; and in the Austrian federal territories from 47 through 60 to 71; while the regional differentiation was maintained. In the industrialised and trading regions — in Saxony, Bohemia, Upper Silesia, the Danube basin, Baden, Württemberg and the lower Rhine — it was particularly high, while in the north German plateau, right up to the River Weser and in the Alpine regions, it was markedly lower than average, with the exception of Schleswig–Holstein.

The period under review is the high point of the demographic revolution — the astonishing fundamental fact that was the motivating force of European and German history from the mid-18th into the early 20th century. This revolution was caused by a change in the reproduction habits of the population as a whole, in the 'mode of reproduction'. In the old world, marriage was tied to work and nutrition, to 'position'. Only some of those capable of reproduction actually married, while the others were forced into celibacy by legal and economic constraints and by the constitution of the military. In view of the sanctions against cohabitation, ability to reproduce was greatly diminished. To this should be added the relatively high age at marriage, between the mid- and late twenties, thus shortening the reproductive phase. When a marriage was contracted, there was no limit set on the number of children, and so the number of births was high.

On the other hand, there was a high mortality rate, especially of infants, children and youths, from one-third to one-half. All the same, there was usually a slight excess of births over deaths, but periodic crises, epidemics, wars and starvation due to harvest failures led to great decreases in the population level, and in the long term restored the balance between the population level and the margin of nutrition.

Table 2: Selected population densities (inhabitants per square kilometre)

	1816	1840	1865
Kingdom of Prussia (incl. West Prussia, East Prussia, Posen, Hohenzollern)	38	54	71
of which: West Prussia	22	36	49
East Prussia	24	38	48
Posen	28	43	53
Kingdom of Prussia, to the extent within the German Confederation (incl. Hohenzollern, which was part of Prussia in 1849)	44	62	80
of which: Berlin	3,100	5,200	10,200
Brandenburg (excl. Berlin)	27	38	50
Pomerania	23	35	48
Silesia	48	71	88
Province of Saxony	47	65	81
Westphalia	53	68	83
Rhine Province	69	96	125
Mecklenburg–Schwerin	23	38	42
Brunswick	61	72	80
Thuringian states	57	72	84
Saxony	80	114	157
Baden	67	86	95
Württemburg	72	84	90
Bavaria	47	58	63
German Confederation excluding Austria	49	65	78
Austrian Empire, to the extent within the German Confederation	47	60	71
of which: Alpine regions	38	45	53
of which: Lower Austria (incl. Vienna)	53	71	96
Upper Austria (incl. Salzburg)	40	45	46
Tyrol and Vorarlberg	26	30	31
Styria (incl. South Styria)	34	43	49
Coastland (only Trieste and Gorz)	102	142	186
Carinthia and Krain	32	38	40
of which: Sudetenland	61	79	93
of which: Bohemia	60	80	96
Moravia and Silesia	61	78	89

By comparison, in a large number of European regions, e.g. Venetia, Lombardy, Tuscany, Upper Alsace, French and Belgian Flanders, and in the English industrial regions, the population density around 1816 was over 150.

This situation changed in western and central Europe from the late 18th century onwards, as is demonstrated statistically in a now permanently high excess of births over deaths. There were two reasons for this situation. One is that, especially in the late 18th century, there were slight variations in mortality, attributable to climate, immunisation, greater robustness due to improved nutrition, improvements in personal hygiene, smallpox vaccinations, the absence of major epidemics (the last plague appeared in 1709–11, and the cholera of the 19th century was more limited in its effect) and a reduction in the ravages of war.

Even slight decreases in mortality had a powerful effect on the population level. For instance, in Bohemia mortality decreased from 33.3 per thousand (1784–1814) to 29.4 (1815–38). This increased the excess of births over deaths by a third. Within the period in question, the death rate settled down after 1815, which is the date from which continuous statistics are available, with marked temporal and especially regional variations; at the end of the period under review it was no lower overall than after 1815.

Table 3: Live births, deaths, excess of births over deaths per year in 25-year averages (per 1,000)

	1816–40			1841–65		
	L.births	Deaths	Excess	L.births	Deaths	Excess
Prussia total	39.4	27.5	11.9	38.0	26.0	12.0
West Prussia	46.0	32.4	13.6	44.4	32.5	11.9
Berlin	33.6	30.6	3.0	33.4	27.3	6.1
Rhine Province	35.2	24.6	10.6	34.5	23.9	10.6
Westphalia	35.2	25.7	9.5	34.0	24.4	9.6
Mecklenburg–Schwerin	37.3	20.2	17.1	33.9	21.9	12.0
Grand Duchy of Hesse (Darmstadt)	(no data)			32.6	22.9	9.7
	(from 1827)					
Saxony	38.8	28.3	10.5	39.4	27.8	11.6
	(from 1826)					
Bavaria	33.8	27.7	6.1	34.2	28.0	6.2
Austria, incl. Galicia, Bukovina	(from 1819)					
Dalmatia	28.7	30.1	8.6	37.7	31.5	6.2

Depending on the years and periods chosen, one might discern a tendency towards a slight decrease, as in the 25-year averages, for example, if one stressed a 'low' around 1860 and attributed the renewed rise in the curve in the 1860s to 'special' circumstances; but whatever the case, there was no marked, let alone dramatic, decrease. The great advances in medicine had not yet borne fruit. Life expectancy remained relatively constant right into the 1860s, i.e. during the period from 1816 to 1860, staying around 24.7 in East and West Prussia, around 29.8 in the Rhine Province, and around 31.3 years in Westphalia. No marked increase can be confirmed until the 1870s; then it was 35.6 for men, 38.5 for women.

In addition to the regional differences, and linked to them, there were age-specific and social differences. For instance, mortality among 10–14-year-olds dropped from approximately 1845 onwards, but not that of the older population. In the upper and middle classes, life expectancy was somewhat higher overall, especially as a result of better nutrition, and child mortality tended, if anything, to decrease. In a sample from north-west Germany it decreased between 1800 and 1850 from 25% to 12.3% for children up to 15 years of age. In general, though, infant (and toddler) mortality did not diminish, oscillating between 28% and 33% in Bavaria from 1820 to 1870 between 23% and 25% in Austria from 1800 to 1870, remaining around 26% in Saxony, and oscillating between 17% and 21% in Prussia. It was highest among illegitimate and foster children, and among the lower classes — where the number of working mothers was greatest, and where poor nutrition or malnutrition was common. In Erfurt, for example, in 1848–69, at 30.5%, it was twice as high among the poor as in the middle classes, and four times as high as among the upper classes.

More important than the changes in 'normal' mortality was the steeper decline compared with earlier times in 'crisis' mortality. Cholera, hunger years and influenza epidemics were no longer catastrophic in their effects, and population numbers stabilised.

If the high excess of births over deaths is not explainable by falling mortality rates, it is more attributable to the rise in the birth rate. The birth rate and excess births over deaths did not, of course, develop uniformly. There were great variations due to differing strengths of representation among the age groups, and to changes in the economic climate. Roughly speaking, they were high until 1830, and then tailed off. In 1847–49 there was another marked dive, and subsequently in 1849–51 and from 1857 onwards the figures rose again, of course to a slightly lower level than at the beginning of the century. The excess births over deaths during the period under review averaged 9 per thousand in Germany, 12 per thousand in Prussia, being concentrated in the early phase to 1830 and the period after the 1850s.

Of far greater interest than these variations are the regional variations, the great number of excess births in the Prussian north-east and in the trading regions, and the small number in the other regions.

This leads us to the causes of this situation. A large excess of births over deaths is caused by an increase in marriages or a decrease in the age at marriage in the relevant regions. Approval of marriages is most important here. Wherever, as in Prussia, no official permission from the authorities was required by the community, nor a ration certificate (*Nahrungsnachweis*), and where the twelve-year military service no longer applied, there were more marriages. In the south and north-west, community marriage restrictions were partly maintained, and in part reintroduced. The rise in population brought about a great debate, in which Malthus's pessimistic assumption that the population grows in geometric progression, while food production grows only arithmetically, played an important part. Those of a more conservative disposition attempted to counter the danger of 'propagation of the rabble'. 'From the family of each honourable master craftsman who employs a number of journeymen, feeds them and keeps them on the ethical straight and narrow, a number of small families is to emerge, with each journeyman marrying his wench and becoming the sire of a new breed destined to starve and suffer.' Thus did General Yorck fulminate against the reforms. And that was almost uniformly the mood in the communities of the representatives of the old tied order. For people holding this opinion, marriage and residence restrictions were the natural means of dealing with the situation (e.g. Hanover 1827, Baden 1831 and 1851, Württemberg 1833 and 1852, Bavaria 1808, 1825 and 1834).

Table 4: Birth rate, mortality rate, excess births over deaths in
selected 5-year averages (per 1,000)

	1821–25			1841–45			1861–65		
	b.	d.	ex.	b.	d.	ex.	b.	d.	ex.
Prussia overall	41.38	25.06	16.32	38.28	26.06	12.22	39.54	25.80	13.74
West Prussia	50.44	27.46	22.98	44.58	28.56	16.02	45.24	29.74	15.50
Berlin	33.62	27.20	6.42	32.28	24.54	7.74	36.40	27.72	8.68
Rhine Province	35.54	22.10	13.44	36.02	24.64	11.38	35.10	23.46	11.64
Westphalia	35.80	22.88	12.92	34.88	25.22	9.66	35.26	24.82	10.44
Mecklenburg–Schwerin	36.66	17.30	19.36	33.28	21.60	11.68	31.26	21.54	9.72
Grand Duchy of Hesse (Darmstadt)	(no data)			35.40	23.66	11.74	33.62	23.76	9.86
	(1827–31)								
Saxony	40.08	28.38	11.70	39.10	28.76	10.34	40.22	27.80	12.42
Bavaria (incl. Palatinate)	(1827–31) 33.26	26.40	6.66	34.36	28.20	6.16	36.20	28.94	7.26
Austria (that part incl. in the Reich, i.e. incl. Galicia, Bukovina, Dalmatia)	39.78	26.84	12.94	39.16	29.55	9.61	38.19	29.38	8.81

For Comparison

	Birth rate	Death rate	Excess
Federal Republic 1979	9.5	11.6	–2.1
GDR 1977	13.5	13.4	0.1
Austria 1979	11.5	12.3	–0.8

Although the level of illegitimacy (usually a child born to a woman in her late twenties) under such laws was twice that of other regions, it was quite compatible with a low overall birth rate. Excess births over deaths on the right bank of the Rhine — in Bavaria for example — were (1816–55) 5.4 per thousand, less than half the level in Prussia. The opponents of such restrictions were led by their support of the Enlightenment and Christian family ethics to consider children as something to be treasured. This attitude prevailed in Prussia; the great statisticians Hoffmann and Dieterici favoured liberal social policies and rejected state intervention by bureaucratic means. Experience east of the Elbe, where population growth went hand in hand with increased production, appeared clearly to contradict the pessimism of the Malthusians.

Job creation and new workplaces were the other reason for the rise in marriages and thus the excess births over deaths. East of the Elbe, so-called land development brought about a huge increase in jobs, thus providing the economic circumstances for the founding of families. The births came from the various groups of agricultural workers, the lower classes, and the younger sons of peasants. They actually sustained this growth, increasing it by two to three and a half times their numbers in the population.

At first, in the pre-1840 period, this growth was absorbed by the countryside. In the trading regions, as previously in the cottage-industry regions in the late 18th century, the old peasant-guild marriage restriction was lifted from those who found a 'position', the social control of honour no longer applied to the lower classes, and the control of parents over their children weakened. The possibility of entering into a marriage which had previously been denied, increased greatly. In the administrative region of Münster, for example, a region where property passed undivided to a single heritor (*Anerbengebiet*), characterised by small and middle-sized farms without much trade, whose inhabitants thus had few opportunities to found a family, the birth rate until 1870 was approximately 30 per thousand (as compared with around 40–44 per thousand in Prussia). There were few illegitimate children, proportionately fewer women who marry, and the age at marriage was higher, whereas in the neighbouring trading districts of Minden and Arnsberg it was around 37–40 per thousand. Of course, an increase in marriages always involves a combination of the contingencies of marital rights, economics and rights of inheritance; therefore, for example, marriage restrictions had less effect in the *Realteilungsländer* of Hesse–Darmstadt and Nassau than in Bavaria. The analysis of regional differences shows the significance of socio-economic conditions.

Furthermore, marriages and births involved class-specific differences. In the north-west German sample referred to above, there was a slight decrease in child numbers. The number of children in marriages contracted among the administrative classes and public employees before 1825 was 6.4, in those contracted before 1849 it was 5.1, and in those before 1874 it was 4.4. Employers and craftsmen followed this trend, after a time-lag of some 25 years. There was also a decrease among peasants, i.e., 1750–99, 7.11; 1800–1849, 6.3; 1850–74, 5.5.

The first indications of deliberate birth control among the educated classes may be established from the gap in years between the first and last child. Age at marriage (according to the same sources) increased among educated men from 32 to 33 years, among women from 22 to 25; for employers and craftsmen the increase was around three years, for farmers around four years, for small farmers just under three years. The age of upper-class women at marriage also increased; before 1800, 34% were under 20, from 1825 to 1874, only 9.3%; that of peasant women increased from 22.7 before 1800 to 25.1 after 1850; that of the lower classes was markedly higher overall.

The lower rate of growth between 1840 and 1865 is only in small part attributable to the slightly lower number of births (and marriages); more important here is the second factor that influences the population level besides births and deaths, namely the balance of immigration and emigration, which in these years meant a population decrease through emigration. In Mecklenburg, for instance, in spite of a large excess of births over deaths, the population level was virtually stagnant. This will be dealt with below. The above-average growth of the urban and industrial regions was due mainly to an influx of population from other regions.

Table 5: Average proportion of illegitimate births out of the total number of births, 1830–69 (%)

Territories without marriage restrictions

Prussia	7.5
of which: Westphalia (1841–69)	3.2
of which: Rhine Province (1841–69)	3.6

Territories with marriage restrictions

Hanover	9.7
Württemberg	13.2
Baden	15.2
Austria	15.6
Bavaria	21.1

Two factors arising from these population movements must be stressed because they are of particular importance to the overall history. Firstly, the society was a society of young people: a third of the population on average was aged under 15, and only 5–8% were over 61; here the regional variations mirror the differences in excess births over deaths and the gains from immigration. From this too the potential workforce by estimating the number of working women can be calculated at about 45% of the population. Secondly, the 'centre of gravity' of the German states shifted. In 1815 Prussia had barely two-sevenths and Austria had a good two-sevenths of the population, as did the five large states of the Confederation. Prussia overall had somewhat fewer than the number of inhabitants in the medium-sized and small states, while the Habsburg Empire had about twice its numbers. By 1865 the population of that part of Prussia included within the Confederation already exceeded Austria's population by around 1 million, and that of the five larger medium-sized states by 2.5 million, and, including all of its provinces, was 0.75 million stronger than the medium-sized and small states of Germany. After the border changes of 1866 almost two-thirds of the inhabitants of the Reich of 1871 lived in Prussia, and its population had also increased in relation to that of Europe, with 24 million, compared with 23.2 million in England and 37.4 million in France in 1867.

One last theme in the history of the population during the century is that of the great migrations, primarily internal migration, which in the period under review mainly meant urbanisation. Around 1800–1815 just over 10% of Germans lived in communities of over 5,000 inhabitants (these may with reasonable certainty be termed 'cities', in spite of the *Ackerbürger* — city-dwellers who farmed smallholdings); 5% of whom lived in cities of up to 20,000, 3.8% in cities of up to 100,000 and 2% in 'large cities' of over

100,000 inhabitants. The rest lived in the country and in small cities of less than 5,000 inhabitants. Of 1,016 Prussian cities in 1800, 400 had less than 1,000, and a further 500 had less than 3,000 inhabitants. In the German Reich in 1870, 11.2% lived in cities of between 5,000 and 10,000, 7.74% in cities of between 10,000 and 100,000, 4.8% in cities of above 100,000, and overall 23.7% in cities with more than 5,000 inhabitants; 63.9% lived in communities of less than 2,000 inhabitants (in 1852, the figure in Prussia was 67.3%). In the Alpine regions 20.7% (1869) and in the Sudeten territories 5.9% lived in places with over 5,000 inhabitants. In Prussia the urban population had more than doubled from 3 million to 6.3 million. Differences between the original situation in the regions and how they developed, and the growth of individual towns are shown in Tables 7 and 8. Important as they were, the high growth rates of the smaller cities should not be considered in isolation; in the cities the starting level was, of course, much higher, and even in Berlin 1.8% represented 3,000 more people around 1800, while in 1850 3.5% represented almost 15,000. In the Vormärz, urbanisation was relatively slow, population growth taking place predominantly in the country.

Table 6a: Proportion of the total population aged under 14 (%)

	1822	1840	1864
East Prussia	38.5	34.6	37.1
West Prussia	38.4	35.8	38.8
Posen	40.7	36.7	36.7
Whole north-east	39.2	35.7	37.1
Rhine Province	35.7	34.7	35.1
City of Berlin	25.1	25.6	28.3
Prussia total	36.1	34.5	35.8
Baden	. . .	(29.7)	(29.4)
Württemberg (Age limit 15 years; hence estimated figures)	(29.5)	(29.4)	(27.0)
Saxony	(30.2)	(29.7)	(30.3)
Bavaria	29.6 (1834)	28.6	28.3

Table 6b: Proportion of population aged over 60 (%)

	1822	1840	1864
East Prussia	6.0	5.9	5.4
West Prussia	5.4	4.9	5.0
Posen	5.1	4.3	4.8
Whole north-east	5.5	5.1	5.1
Rhine Province	6.8	6.5	6.4
Prussia overall	6.2	6.1	6.1
Berlin	6.1	5.2	4.9
Baden	. . .	. . .	7.0
Württemberg	. . .	. . .	. . .
Saxony	6.1	6.8	6.7 (1871)
Bavaria	. . .	. . .	9.4 (1871)

Table 7: Proportion of inhabitants in communities of over 5,000 inhabitants (%)

	1815		1870	
Saxony	15.0		26.1	
Prussia	13.3		21.5	
Württemberg	11.4		14.3	
Baden	11.0		17.1	
Bavaria	9.7		12.1	
Later German Reich	9.5		23.7	
Austrian Alpine regions				
including Vienna	10.9	(1816)	20.7	(1869)
excluding Vienna	5.7		8.5	(1869)
Austrian Sudeten				
territories	4.1		5.9	(1869)

However, the urban population was barely capable of maintaining its numbers, owing to unhygienic conditions, so urban growth derived mainly from immigration, predominantly from the surrounding countryside. This was particularly true of capital cities, royal seats and administrative seats like Berlin and Vienna, Munich, Stuttgart and Dresden, in some of the traditional trading centres (Breslau, Cologne, Leipzig, Magdeburg) and the middle-sized and small cities of the early high-density trading regions — Krefeld, Eberfeld, Barmen, Aix-la-Chapelle. It also applied to the old cities and small towns on the Rhine and the Ruhr (Dortmund, Düsseldorf, Duisburg) and, for example, to Chemnitz in Saxony. Wherever early industrialisation took place in the countryside, for example in the Sudeten territories, there was correspondingly less urbanisation.

While population growth decreased after the mid-century, the process of urbanisation intensified. Industrialisation took root, as did improved transport networks, and the 'filling up' of the countryside right to the limit of the margin of nutrition. Immigration into cities was still provided for the most part by emigrants from nearby and proximate regions. The migration from Silesian to east German migration to Berlin is something of an exception.

For people in the modern professions too, migration gradually became inevitable, their mobility increased greatly, and they migrated over great distances, though they are of course not of statistical significance.

There are various types of cities and of urban growth. The old administrative and market cities became railway junctions and centres of industry, or, like the ports and trading centres, were involved in the rise of the transport and service sectors (Hanover, Mannheim, Nuremberg, Königsberg and Hamburg in additon to those previously mentioned). The old textile and trading cities continued to grow. Whole new cities emerged in the Ruhr, and the older cities — Essen, Dortmund and Duisburg — grew phenomenally. To the three German 'large' cities of over 100,000 inhabitants, Berlin, Vienna and Hamburg, eight new ones were added by 1870 — Breslau, Dresden, Munich, Prague, Cologne, Königsberg and Magdeburg. An element in the growth of the cities in the 1850s and above all the 1860s, after 'defortification' — the pulling down of the city walls — consisted in their integration with suburbs, which themselves expanded and 'urbanised'. Part of urban expansion was due to incorporations (especially in the 1860s), the increase in population density in the 'suburbs', leading to incorporation into the cities and renewed growth; therefore the urban areas expanded as well. Territorial boundaries and political considerations, the fear of excessively large cities and excessively powerful administrations in some places kept cities from growing into each other that would otherwise have done so. Examples are Altona in Holstein and Harburg in Hanover from Hamburg, and Charlottenburg, Spandau and Schöneberg from Berlin.

Table 8: Population of German cities (000)

	1800	Avge. annual growth in % 1800– 1850/51–	1850/51	Avge. annual growth in % 1850–70 1860/61	1860/61	Avge. annual growth in % 1860/61– 1870/71	1870/71	Avge. annual growth 1850/51– 1870/71
Aix-la-Chapelle	27	1.5	53[7]	1.4	60	2.1	74	1.9
Altona	23[1]	0.9	32[8]	2.7	53[9]	4.9	74	3.4
Augsburg	26	0.8	39	1.4	45	1.3	51	1.4
Barmen	16	2.0	36	2.5	46	4.9	74	3.7
Berlin	172	1.8	419	2.7	548	4.2	826	3.5
Bremen	40	0.6	53	2.4	67	2.2	83	2.3
Breslau	60	1.3	114	2.5	146	3.6	208	3.1
Brünn (Brno)	26[2]						74	1.9
Chemnitz	11[3]	2.6	34	2.8	45	4.2	68	3.5
Cologne	50	1.7	97	2.2	121	0.6	129	1.4
Danzig	41	0.7	58	1.9	70	2.4	89	2.2
Dortmund	4	2.0	11	7.6	23	6.7	44	7.2
Dresden	60	1.0	97	2.8	128	3.3	177	3.1
Düsseldorf	10	2.0	27	4.3	41	5.3	69	4.8
Duisburg	4	1.6	9	3.8	13	9.1	31	6.4
Elberfeld	19[4]	2.3	47	1.4	54	2.8	71	2.1
Essen	4	1.6	9	8.9	21	9.5	52	9.2
Frankfurt/M.	48	2.3	65	1.6	76	1.8	91	1.7
Graz	31	0.6	55		84	2.1		
Hamburg	130	1.2	175	1.3	200	3.8	290	2.6
Hanover	18	0.6	29	9.4	71	2.2	88	5.7
Kiel	7	1.0	16		32	3.5		
Königsberg	55[5]	1.3	73	2.7	95	1.6	112	2.2
Krefeld	8[6]	0.6	40[7]	2.3	48	1.7	57	2.0
Leipzig	30	3.4	63	2.2	78	3.2	107	2.7
Magdeburg	23	1.5	52	2.6	67	4.5	104	3.5
Mannheim	19	0.5	24[7]	2.8	30[9]	4.0	46[2,9,11]	
Munich	40	1.9	107[7]	3.6	148	1.3	169	2.6
Nuremberg	30	1.2	54	1.6	63	2.8	83	2.2
Prague	75	0.9	118	2.8	143[10]	0.7	157	1.4
Stettin	18	1.8	44	2.8	58	2.2	72	2.5
Stuttgart	18	1.9	47[7]	2.2	56	5.9	92	3.8
Trieste	29	2.1	83				123	2.0
Vienna	249	1.2	444	1.0	476[10]	4.4	834	3.2

[1]1809 [2]1815 [3]1806 [4]1810 [5]1802 [6]1804
[7]1852 [8]1845 [9]1864 [10]1857 [11]1875

In addition to internal migration, there was emigration. In the first half of the century the emigration rate was highest in the German south-west. Overpopulation, crises of pauperism and alienation from one's social group at home were the important causes, resulting from acute general (1816–17, 1846–48) or private crises. To this should be added the appeal of the destination countries, especially of the United States, which was nourished both by vague expectations and by reports from those who had already emigrated, so that a pull-effect acted in tandem with the push-effect. Emigration on conscientious grounds, as in the case of Württemberg pietists or Silesian 'Old Lutherans', and on political grounds, in the case of victims of the reaction like Karl Follen, Franz Lieber or Friedrich List, and 'forty-eighters' like Karl Schurz, was at a relatively low level in quantitative terms, important though it was for the consciousness of the Germans and of the Americans.

Table 9: Emigration

	From regions of the German Reich of 1871	From the Austrian part of the German Confederation (figures very uncertain)
1820–29	50,000	14,000
1830–39	210,000	8,000
1840–49	480,000	?
1850–59	1,161,000	28,000
1860–69	782,000	42,000

From the end of the 1840s the rate of emigration rose considerably, owing to population pressure. The proportion of south-west Germans dropped (29% in 1845–49, 17% in 1860–64), that of the west Germans and, especially from the 1860s onwards, of the north-east Germans, where the land could no longer absorb the second wave of population growth, increased (in 1871–75: 396,000 from the north-east, 154,000 from the north-west, 256,000 from the south-west, and 194,000 from other regions). The great majority continued to emigrate to the United States during these decades. There was much concerned debate on the subject of these emigrants, and a great deal of sentimental obfuscation, in the collective memory and in mythology, of the great poverty which had set it off: at that time the 'uncle from America' became a figure in popular folklore.

2. Family, Gender, Generations

Relations between the sexes and the generations, and the family institution are historical facts, in spite of their bases in the natural world. They have changed radically in the modern period, first in 18th-century England. In the period of German history under review this revolutionary transformation first took place among the bourgeoisie: the emergence of the modern family unit. Its history is not well researched, and for that reason the story is somewhat sketchy, but it is worthwhile telling because it is relatively unknown.

A few basic conditions of the old world remain valid throughout the period. These are the high birth rates and high child mortality (with a third to a quarter dying before coming of age), and also higher mortality among married couples. The average marriage lasted twenty years (1800); death shortened the lifelong bond of marriage just as divorce does today. Families were fragile, death an ever-present fear and occurrence, orphans and second marriages (stepmothers and stepfathers) quite normal. The tradition of marriage at a relatively late age, towards the end of a man's twenties, one to two years younger for women, was maintained, and even increased slightly. Therefore, the period of effective fertility was restricted to fifteen to twenty years, and the number of children was correspondingly limited. A woman gave birth every two to three years. Finally, marriage was tied to independence, to a job and a house, and was therefore delayed; this is as true of the bourgeoisie as it is of the workers — a period of saving preceded marriage.

On this basis, various types of family in the 19th century can be distinguished according to whether they were traditional or modern, and by social class. Firstly, there is the traditional family type that continued, with certain modifications, among the peasants and petty bourgeoisie. The received opinion that the pre-modern family was an extended family with three generations and unmarried siblings must be qualified. The average household contained no more than five members, but this average is deceptive, for everyone was a member of smaller or larger families at some stage during his lifetime. The norm in the old world was the household built around a single couple. Children left home early to become apprentices and to work, at fourteen years of age, not only among the lower orders, but also among craftsmen and peasants. Of course, the numbers of people ejected from their homes were greater among the poor and lower class, and they left home earlier. Nor was remarriage as inevitable in the cities as it was in the countryside. Among the peasants, and occasionally also among urban craftsmen, grandparents several times widowed or unmarried sisters lived in the family.

Grown-up children (heirs and their siblings) lived in the families of farmers with medium-sized or small land holdings.They were denied independence, though the heirs continued to wait for it. Above all, though, farmhands, journeymen and apprentices, in other words servants, were part of the family as domestic and social community. The family was integrated into the system of 'house' rules. This family was both a social and productive community; beyond the house as institution it was also part of the community, part too of the political community. It was also a social security institution, a safety-net for illness and old age — in short, it had manifold functions, not restricted to the private as opposed to the public domain. In the period under review, for peasants and the majority of craftsmen (and small merchants), the old unity of home and business was maintained. Of course, here too one can observe the signs of a concentration on the nuclear family: the expulsion of the old and unmarried in the cities and in the *Realteilungsgebieten*, the gradual movement of journeymen and later of apprentices out of the craftsmen's domestic communities, and the separation of master and servants among the big farmers.

The peasants' and craftsmen's families had little 'privacy' from the outside world, but were 'open', to the neighbours' gaze, to their fellow guildsmen, to the priest. Family life was subject to social control in all its aspects — from the state of the laundry to proper relations between husband and wife — a situation that still obtains in villages in the form of trial by gossip, 'rough music' (*Katzenmusik*) and charivari. A man was unable to separate his roles of paterfamilias, citizen, churchgoer, producer and consumer; that situation was to persist, even once the legal bond between citizenship and fatherhood was long severed. It was only with the loosening of social control in the big towns that the family gained privacy and self-containment and assumed the new 'bourgeois', individualist family mentality.

From the late 18th century onwards, the choice of marriage partner was no longer made by parents, even among peasants and craftsmen. The children's choice and the parental right to advise and veto were complementary. Romantic love, individual passion and inclinations were not particularly important in these circles as a motive for marriage. Industriousness, property, the means to support a family and the ability to tolerate each other's company were decisive. A decision to 'look for a wife' was often the beginning. Seen in this light, for example, the number of marriages to older women in 1800 was still high (25–30% in the places investigated), and only decreased slowly towards the mid-century. Love comes not before but with marriage — that was the old-fashioned view. In the country, the old forms of encounter between the sexes persisted: spinning-room and festival, nocturnal visits to girls' rooms (*Kiltgang*) and fraternities, in which choice, fixed ritualisation of roles and social control by one's peers were interwoven. Naturally they were attacked as loutish and immoral by church and bureaucracy, who no longer understood archaic practices, and were finally deprived of their power by schools, geographical mobility and industry.

The aim of marriage was the management of life at a given social level by mutual help and the division of labour, child-rearing, and the satisfaction of sexual urges. Marriage was taken for granted in life, beyond all dogmas, rights and doubts. Even the unmarried, widow or widower, bachelor or spinster, remained within its orbit, at least among the better-off. It was religiously sanctioned, by notice of intended marriage, blessing, entry in the parish register and family prayers. It was through marriage that a person took part in the bestowal of Christian meaning upon life among men. Marriage was predicated not on a 'feeling' (love), but was a social and self-evident 'office'. Relations between members of the family were not particularly warm or emotional, but tended to be cool, distant, and characterised by 'mutual regard', less variable and spontaneous, in fact stiff and wooden in modern eyes. Older men did not know how many children they had had, or even how many miscarriages and still-births their wives had suffered. The 'replacement' of a marriage partner after his or her death was therefore no major emotional problem. Of course, this emotional aridity, conditioned by the contingencies of death and need, and the conservative behaviour of the family and its members, had been overlaid since Luther's time with the doctrine of an unromantic but cheerful love between marriage partners, of the idyll, the 'cheer' and 'sweetness' of marriage, and this process continued to operate, simultaneously absorbing modern subjective love and institutionalising it. In the towns emotional bonding also developed among the petty bourgeoisie from about 1800 onwards. The mode of address between marriage partners changed to the familiar *Du*, if not to the uniform use of Christian names.

Gender roles and work were, of course, strictly divided between man and woman. The life of women was characterised in the first instance by their family status as girl, wife and mother, widow. In the countryside, women were still distinguished in the mid-century by traditional dress, which they continued to wear longer than the men. Domestic affairs were the exclusive domain of the wife. She was responsible for the poultry, the vegetable patch and milk production. That was where she worked, it was her 'calling'. But relations between the sexes were completely patriarchal; male-paternal authority was unalterable and impressed upon each child, supported and countenanced by all social forces. The husband made all the significant decisions and determined the family's relations with the outside world; he was the 'head' of the family, she was a 'tool', and humility and obedience were considered its virtues. Of course, the situation reported in certain regions of France, where a peasant valued the life of his cow higher than that of his wife, did not obtain in Germany. And having her own sphere of work did give the wife a certain *de facto* independence.

Relations with children were unsentimental, short, strict, distant and determined by discipline and obedience, work and the rod. The peasants' resistance to schools derived from their claim to authority over their children against that of the state. Around 1800, the children of the petty bourgeoisie and the peasants still addressed their parents in the third-person *Er*, around 1850 very frequently in the formal second-person plural forms, *Ihr* and *Sie*.

Of course, the new 'bourgeois' family life gained ground — beginning with the urban middle class — in the traditional spheres as well: the sense of parental responsibility for children, e.g. for school and professional education, increased.

The traditional family did not, in fact, provide any individual privacy for its members; everything took place communally and in a few rooms. Bourgeois morality made slow progress with its criticism of parents and children, youths and farmhands sleeping in close proximity.

This contrasts with the 'modern' family, which emerged in England, developing in Germany among the educated bourgeoisie from the late 18th century onwards, and then taken up by the aristocracy. It came to predominate during the 19th century. Firstly, production and work in the modern family are kept separate from the home. This tendency increased during our period with the decrease in production for domestic use, especially among bourgeois families. Technological 'advances' in the home — lacquered floorboards, kerosene, even gas lighting — relieved women of some of the burdens of housework. The family became a community of consumers. This would appear to be of little importance to those not active in real production, but in conjunction with the modernisation of society, the social status of a person was henceforth determined outside the family, outside birth and estate, and was individually attained.

Next, the modern family clearly became the 'nuclear' family of parents and children, with clearly defined boundaries. Ties with the extended family were loosened. This is indicated, for example, by the greater diversity of Christian names. Further, the family became 'private', closed to the outside world, to the public, social and economic domain, and inaccessible to social control. It drew a boundary between itself and the rest of the community; it limned an interior space of its own. Ceremonies and festivals, for example, lost their public character, and became family events. This happened to weddings, baptisms and funerals, and to the celebration of Christmas, which only became a specifically family occasion in the early 19th century. On the other hand, this new 'private' family gained in importance as a social unit at the expense of the peer-group, i.e. contemporaries, members of the same social class, fellow professionals, fellow churchgoers, and members of one's community. Social intercourse and friendship were introduced into the family, and a new family culture emerged. The simultaneous and clearly compensatory development of a new division between male and female society, gentlemen's social evenings and ladies' tea parties, the after-dinner withdrawal of the ladies from the smoking and card-playing men; the club and the table for regulars at the inn (*Stammtisch*) are further expressions of this compensatory mechanism.

Marriage was, in principle, based on personal choice, not primarily on property, work, and the struggle to survive, but in personalised love, which, of course, was possible only for an 'upper' class with fewer material cares. The element of romantic love was part of this. The couple's encounter was considered to have a quality of destiny, inevitability, uniqueness: love at first sight, being made for each other, the absolute importance of this love, indeed the immaculacy of the loved one, or the idea of the grand passion, of erotic attraction. These ideas had their source in novels, not in reality, but they gave wings to the imagination and changed reality. General opinion, of course, held that such loves and passions were transitory, and that marriage must rather be founded on empathy, on a partnership of compatible sensibilities. But this was also something new. The purpose of marriage was no longer that of an 'office', assistance, the fulfilment of social roles, but was now to be based on the shockingly new concepts of 'self-fulfillment' and personal, individual happiness.

Of course, traditional elements, conventions and interests and a parental right of veto or delay entered into the practicalities of the marriage contract. Freedom to encounter and make each other's acquaintance was restricted by custom and by class-specific social behaviour. Love and class status therefore rarely came into conflict. In any case, girls were excluded from taking direct initiatives, and an excessive number of proposals refused led to an unacceptable decrease in the chances of marriage. But the consciousness did prevail (especially among girls) that a marriage must be founded on 'love' and mutual affinity. Marriage rested on a personal, subjective decision, no longer on something 'objective' — parents, circumstances, God — that, as it were, assigned one person to another.

Such a marriage, personalised and emotional, had a new style, despite the gap between the ideal and its realisation. Where distance had prevailed, there was now warmth; where there had been fixed roles, there was now informality and spontaneity. Now the informal mode of address *Du* and the use of Christian names became the norm.

The displacement of the experience of death is also characteristic. Death was no longer experienced primarily as the death we all face, not even, as in the primal Christian experience, as 'my death' in respect of judgment and salvation, but as the death of another, 'your death', the death of a loved one, of the irreplaceable family member. In the process, the accent shifted from the dying or dead person to the mourners, from public to private, from acceptance of what is natural and decreed by God to the experience of a devastating blow, to the sorrow of abandonment, from ritual to a grief beyond formulation. The old, pious custom of dying in front of the family ceased (as did those demonstrations of justice, the public executions, after 1830). It was not judgment or resurrection, nor primarily the world's remembrance of the representative of an 'office', but the memory of the family, departing and 'meeting again' in heaven, as was still believed, that became the content of a new eschatology. The new culture of the cemetery as a romantic ensemble of individualised family tombs and engraved tombstones of great longevity, before which the family members would gather in remembrance now and again, was new, and even agnostics adopted these practices.

The aspect of individualised and emotional partnership first remained within the framework of traditional patriarchalism — indeed, by a curious dialectic, renewed and reinforced it. First, around 1800, the bourgeois wife gained some freedom. Like the classical, romantic ideal, sensibility displays modern traits compared with, say, the strictly paternalistic German Enlightenment represented by Campe. The wife became a partner to a greater degree; consideration towards her became a new virtue; she assumed a more important role within the household and in society. Patriarchal attitudes declined, and that too determined the pattern of lives and of reality. Women were relieved of economic burdens, had more leisure, were better educated, became parties to conversation, not beasts of burden and mothers, but persons. The Romantics stressed the individuality of woman, and in their mockery of the prosaic Schiller and his ideal of the orderly housewife, tended towards a mystical (and unreal) deification of woman.

After 1815 the style changed. The emphasis placed on education and breeding as the basis for understanding and partnership also made the differences more acute, because the education of men for professional and political life was and remained different from that of girls. Reflection upon the polarity of the sexes in partnership led to a new ideology. Women were more highly valued, and were considered 'delicate', but different from men, and thus subordinate to them in a new sense. The opinion was that woman lives 'inwardly', for others, for the family, not reaching out into the world. She does not have man's 'cold' rationality, being naïve and unreflective. Inwardness and warmth are to be found in the home, and she thus must conform to the standards of being home-loving, industrious, hygienic, yet gentle, adaptable, yielding, peaceable.

Wilhelm von Humboldt, one of the presiding spirits of the age, was astonished at the humble 'Yes, my lord' attitude of his daughter Gabriele during and after her marriage. Such attitudes were strengthened by the new articulation of roles due to economic developments. With the break up of the combined workplace and home, the husband turned into provider and money-earner, while the wife concentrated on the 'family'. During the phase of greatest industrialisation that developed into the opposition between the struggle to survive and the ideal of 'home sweet home' (*das traute Heim*), it became the wife's role to provide compensation for the daily grind. Thus, after the radical change around 1800, a new patriarchalism emerged after 1815.

This new patriarchalism was accompanied by the process of the 'feminisation of woman', so typical of the 19th century. In the educated upper classes, in which the women and young girls were to a greater degree relieved by servants of the duties of housework and the full burden of child care, a female leisure culture emerged. Music, culture and science were specially reworked and popularised for women (as the 'bluestocking' was still an object of terror). Especially after 1815, middle and higher girls' schools sprang up, a result of the new drive for education and of the idea of a specifically feminine education. The elements of this new culture became status symbols and ornaments, the piano-playing 'refined daughter' (*höhere Tochter*) being one of its better-known products. There was a concomitant characteristic tightening of all the rules of ladylike conduct, for work and leisure activities, the prohibition on travelling alone, on carrying burdens oneself, and even on walking quickly, on working, unless it was at one of the obligatory 'handicrafts' without a real purpose. To this can be added over-refinement. Women were tender, weak, delicate, nervous, feeble and especially prone to headaches. Because they were viewed thus, some or many indeed became so.

The conservative Riehl criticised this as 'hyperfemininity' (*Überweiblichkeit*), as an externalised and exaggerated differentiation of the sexes, and considered the philistinism of men at the alehouse to be the equivalent of the women at their tea. Relief from the need to work and the disappearance of a stabilising role beside the nuclear family, as it existed among the aristocracy, peasants, craftsmen, workers and the Protestant clergy, were the reasons for such Victorian features in the lives of women in the family. Of course, that was a tendency, not the whole of bourgeois reality. Housekeeping, child rearing, scarcity of means, and mutual dependence limited their effectiveness. Since the men left home for their occupations, the women's role in decision-making and influence over their children became more extensive, thereby increasing their independence, and thus reality went a step ahead of theory. There was also the reverse side of patriarchalism, the henpecked husband, as immortalised in Wilhelm Busch's characteristic contemporary satires. All in all, henceforward the new paternalism of 'Victorian' marriage was conspicuous. However, the revolution in marital and family relations that modernised the family was of far greater historical importance.

The other great change in internal relations within the family was that of the relationship with children. Indifference, distance or strictness were replaced by emotional relations, warmth and concern for the children. Children became the object of spontaneous affection, pleasure, and relaxation. The success of Rousseau's appeal to the mothers of the upper classes to breast-feed their own children was a start, as was the end of swaddling clothes. Child-rearing became the first concern of women relieved of the burden of work. Praise, encouragement and love more than punishment determined the style of child-rearing, with the cane largely banished from the educated classes. There was more liberalism, children were treated with sympathy and understanding. Critics at the beginning of the century speak of a new 'besottedness' of mothers for their children.

Children were now allowed to address their parents in more intimate forms (*Du, Mama, Papa*). Grief at the death of a child now flowed from a new experience of its irreplaceability. There was a huge expansion of literature, games and clothes specifically intended for children. Doctor Hoffmann's *Der Struwwelpeter* is a classic example. In 1840 Fröbel established the first kindergarten, the practical application of a new concern for children to an institution, especially where the family was not of itself sufficient. Children were given such new, sentimental epithets as sweet, simple, innocent and were compared with angels. The story of Jesus and the little children became a major new theme in religious life. Concern for health and breeding and the 'civilisation' of a human being, the transformation of breeding into a moral issue separated the child's world from the world of adults (also distinguished by sexuality). The 'discovery' of childhood or the renewed attention given to it and the new parental control of children were manifested in the new concept of the well-bred child. To the toddler phase (until six years) were added the new phases of childhood and youth, in which the children were no longer treated as little adults, but as members of a unique age group. Children's desires, choices of career and marriage partner were taken into consideration. Parents, especially fathers, paid more attention to their children during festivities, walks, games, food, instruction.

This attitude towards children was not without tension. With the freedom came increased concern, care and more breeding, control and authority. From this tension between individual freedom and authoritarian care there emerged the acute father–son conflict of the end of the century. The situation of children also changed objectively. The family, which was no longer a community of producers, became not merely a community of consumers, but an educational community as well. The social status of children was won outside the family on the basis of its education. That placed quite new demands upon the family, which had to bear the increasing economic burden of education, thus simultaneously investing greater moral and emotional expectations. In the process, gender differences became more acute. The education of sons was more important than the dowries of daughters, which took second place. In the numerous instances in which a conflict arose, the daughter had to stand down, often sacrificing a chance to marry, thus leading to an increase in the number of unmarried middle-class women.

Marriage as an emotional partnership and affection for children, privacy and an increasing intensity in family relations were reflected in the Biedermeier family culture. This was the image of a new and more intensified togetherness of the family — all seated at a round table — playing music together, walking, playing together, the father present and in empathy (at ease in his dressing-gown or nightgown) with the children. In this family culture, social gatherings, from the taking of tea to house balls, took on the complexion of social relations between families. The cheerful family and domestic happiness were the ideal. A visual document of this inward, warm family is provided by the idyllic paintings of Ludwig Richter. The extraordinary popularity of these paintings shows the extent to which this painted ideal corresponded to people's notions of happiness, and to an extent even to reality.

After 1850 that changed, of course. Fathers became more serious and strict; they no longer exclaimed and wept with their little ones, for such expressions of feeling had become 'unmanly'. The characteristic dressing-gown or nightgown was replaced by a dark suit. The element of spontaneity, prepared with such care and pedantry, in education too, went into decline. Family sociability was forced out by more conventional and formal representational sociability; the division, which had already been customary in the houses of the great and good, of the cigar-smoking or card-playing men from the 'ladies', became the norm for evening social gatherings.

The new attitude to children spread from the economically less-burdened educated classes to the middle classes and the respectable workers. Responsibility, more maternal care, prioritisation of the child over self-assertion in the life struggle, and greater interest in education became increasingly manifest despite the stricter, more distanced, authoritarian and partly brutal style of upbringing of these classes, characterised by needs and work.

Another distinguishing feature of the new bourgeois family was the development of privacy within the family. The nuclear family was clearly separate from the previously ubiquitous domestic servants. The members of the family, parents, husband, wife and children, were accorded more privacy. Children's bedrooms, study (for gentlemen), drawing-room (for ladies), the corridor that made it unnecessary to walk through other rooms, were characteristic developments, and they were gladly taken up by the petty bourgeoisie wherever possible.

One final element of the bourgeois family is something that is actually just outside it, and known to everyone from literature, legend, or oral history, but on which historians are usually silent: the domestic servants, or classically the 'servant girl'. In a certain sense, servants were nothing new, and they have been mentioned here in the context of the extended family; but they must now also be considered in connection with the new bourgeois nuclear family, no longer a community of production and representation but a community of consumers and of education. What was new about it was the servant girl in place of the maid, the domestic servant in place of a farmhand. The running of the household, lifestyle and even child education among a broad class extending right into the mid-ranking bourgeoisie were in the hands of such servants. In 1871, in Berlin 17.3% of all households had domestic servants, in Hamburg 21.6% and in Bremen 24%. By 1882, every fourth teacher's household (inclusive of the mass of poorly paid elementary school teachers), and in the mid-century the better-off craftsmen and shopkeepers had servant girls. During the Vormärz, domestic servants comprised 10–14% of the population in the more affluent cities — approximately 25% of them were men, coachmen etc. — 45.3% of the population of the old city of Vienna in 1822–25, and 25% in 1869. In the smaller or poorer cities, they represented 4–9%, and 5–9% around 1870. But this decrease was, above all, due to the proportionate decrease in households with two or more servants. Urban masters and girls from the country, bourgeois children and nannies, the 'madame' and her maid — these became very important, life-shaping social relationships; and a certain 'embourgeoisement' of the country, of the small folk, the respectable workers, of their culinary and eating habits, housekeeping, code of behaviour, fantasies, occurred through the medium of these 'servant girls' (and, incidentally, the books they read) and their marriages. Of course, the family was more sealed off in its privacy than in earlier times, but the continued existence of one (and occasionally two) stranger(s) in the home created a special closeness. Of course, it was a matter of giving orders and obeying orders, hiring and firing without notice. Scant wages, unlimited working hours, little freedom or leisure time, separate meals in the kitchen and small, narrow bedrooms were the norm. And yet there was also a great deal of paternalism, the assurance of being provided for during the years of service, teaching and education, a sense of belonging with the master and his family (sometimes into old age), co-operation and trust (in rearing the children), a relationship that was identical neither with the old 'master–servant' relationship nor with the new employment relations. The lives of women freed from the burden of work (though not unemployed) depended on this 'institution'. In the bourgeois family, the 'lesser duties' were delegated, and the children grew up in an atmosphere of being served and giving orders.

At this point, mention should be made of the beginnings of women's emancipation, for it was a revolutionary side-effect of the new bourgeois family constitution. Around 1800, women assumed a leading role in the Berlin and Vienna salons, with equal rights and acknowledged intellectual claims. There was talk of emancipated women, even if an 'excess' (of learning, say) was frowned upon. From the 1820s onwards, the cult of singers and actresses, those exceptional women who did live independent lives, was of particular importance, and from the 1830s the number of female writers rose enormously. Women found a new, quasi-public field of activity in charitable, welfare, educational and church societies, and the new bourgeois female occupation of deaconess came into being. The concept of female emancipation, the oppression of women and how to eradicate it, which originated in France, became a theme in the 1840s, as in the work of George Sand, to which the 'Young Germany' movement added a critique of marriage in the name of free love. Women like the pastor's daughter Luise Aston walked about in men's clothes, smoked cigars and advocated (admittedly modest) feminist goals. Real problems developed. In the cities, unmarried women without occupations were no longer supported by their families, became isolated, and looked for an occupation. The most important female bourgeois profession emerged in connection with the education of girls, which was to mould the later women's movement: the profession of teacher. In 1848–49, Louise Otto-Peters (incidentally the wife of a democratic journalist and German Catholic) was the first to found a public women's movement with the first women's journal (1849–52). In 1865 the Allgemeine Deutsche Frauenverein, the German Women's Society, was founded at the First German women's conference. Education and the 'emancipation of labour' — i.e. equal work opportunities for women — were the modest demands. True partnership and greater independence through education were advocated on the one hand; propagation of the qualities considered typically feminine, and welfare and education for professional life outside the home, on the other. In 1865–66, the ideologically more conservative, practically-orientated Verein zur Förderung der Erwerbstätigkeit des weiblichen Geschlechts (Society for the Advancement of Employment for the Female Sex), a breeding-ground for all social work, was founded in Berlin. These beginnings of the women's movement were modest, but in fifty to a hundred years they would transform society and the world more than any other movement.

It was true of all family types that divorce, although permissible under state law, and, in the case of Protestants, under church law, remained uncommon. The family was still a stable institution. External forces and the internalisation of the marriage ethic held in check the caprices and susceptibilites of subjectivity that had been spawned by emotional individualism and 'romantic' love. The family was a matter of course, not yet a matter of concern.

The third family 'type' is that of the very varied lower classes. In the 'old' world, which lasted right into the Vormärz, there were legal and economic impediments to the founding of families. After 1815, official permission to marry was made considerably more difficult to obtain by the authorities in some territories. On the other hand, the foundation of a 'household' or family was not tied to inheritance, property, or taking over a business, a 'settled position', as it was among peasants and craftsmen; and because the family was not the basis for the organisation of labour, this class increasingly included incomplete families.

Rural cottage industries at first, and later the great expansion of jobs for agricultural labourers, created new opportunities for family life, extending the old type of the day labourer's and home-owning day-labourer's family. At first, children did not just represent more mouths to feed, but also more producers. In these classes, the parents had hardly any influence on their children's choice of marriage partner — the person to be married was no longer at home, or the father was dead — and property and housekeeping skills were of little importance to the men. The choice of marriage partner was thus more individualised, and often quicker and less considered too, with sexual attraction and the overcoming of isolation playing an important part (although the well-paid textile worker was always a 'good match'). But in this environment determined by needs and work, hunger and constriction, there was as little room for the individualised culture of feeling, for self-discovery and fulfilment, or even privacy — those typical products of education and relief from the burden of labour — as there was for the traditional peasant-craftsman's division of labour and gender roles. Work in the fields and especially outworking at home made the sexes equal, because both had to contribute to their keep. The community of producers turned into a community of wage-earners. The children were sent away even earlier than among the peasants. The maxim 'to keep many of them as necessary' did not apply here (only in the cottage textile industry was the situation different). Offspring had to find employment and status outside the home.

Relations within the family were harsh — 'crude' as the contemporary bourgeois observers put it. There were patriarchal and tyrannical men, often brutal with wife and children (alcohol consumption was a significant factor here), and subordinate women. The children were brutalised into obedience by frequent beatings, interspersed with neglect. The situation was similar in the pre- and early industrial lower classes of the towns. In the country, of course, a degree of social control was still exercised by the church, the authorities, the ruling class and the neighbours — in brief, the village. It was industrialisation that greatly increased the numbers of and opportunities for founding families.

Whereas similar conditions to those just described prevailed among the unskilled workers, as with the wife or older children having to earn money (these could be described as 'needy families'), among the skilled workers the tendency developed towards a 'respectable' worker's family. Self-assertion, and the drive to education and social improvement on the one hand, and church and bourgeois influences on the other, led to the assumption of the family values of the 'decent' petty bourgeoisie, to concern for the children, and the restriction of obligatory work and brutality, or indifference. Wherever possible, the women were supposed to look after the children. Other modern features, such as a sense of the individual rights of family members, besides that of the man and father, e.g of the daughter's right to money earned by herself, naturally took longest to penetrate.

This is where the question of women's and children's work arises. Both were taken for granted in the pre-industrial rural and urban worlds, and neither was considered a problem: that was just how it was. The 'auxiliary' family members were statistically and in reality still a significant entity during the period under review. This work pattern continued in women's 'paid employment'. In 1848, just over a quarter of women were in paid employment, 50% as domestic servants and farmhands, the rest as day-labourers and workers in home and factory; 36% of the industrial workers in Saxony (1846) and 30% in Baden (1840) were women. In the factories, they worked for half a man's wage, but that was still more than in the hidden unemployment of rural pauperism. Unfortunately, the later statistics do not distinguish between married and unmarried women, and those with children. There are good grounds for surmising (against prevailing opinion) that girls entered industrial and waged work, but generally left after marriage and the birth of a child or children, and only returned to work for brief periods in times of need. (In Germany in 1907, 7–10% of married women and widows were in paid employment.)

Mothers worked irregularly and sporadically, mostly in the textile industry, and probably less in the cities than in the country. In a sense, the family situation determined the division of labour, as in the pre-industrial world, labour being divided into earning the daily bread, bringing up the children and providing for the family.

The children of the traditional lower classes (like those of the peasants) had to contribute to their keep by working. That is the reason for rural resistance to schooling. Pauperism worsened the situation of children. In addition to hunger and work, begging and vagrancy increased. This mass misery was was the background to the 'other', sometimes not quite so bad, mass misery, of the child factory workers, especially in the textile factories, and also the background to the mentality of parents, employers and public opinion, which had a positive, uncritical attitude to children's work. A six- to eight-hour day was 'normal'. The figures are not particularly high in absolute terms (and conceal the work of children in the countryside). The proportion of children among the small minority of factory workers in the 1830s and 1840s was, to be sure, high (17% of workers in Chemnitz in 1840), even if the conditions were never like those of early industrial Britain. The first child protection laws, passed in 1839 in Prussia, were tightened up in the 1850s and were relatively effective, after the setting up of a factory inspectorate. In 1853 factory work was forbidden for children under 12 years, and restricted to six hours for 12–14 year olds. Child labour did not disappear, especially in cottage industries, but declined considerably and was really at the margin of the social question.

In the case of the traditional lower class, especially in the massive poverty of so-called 'pauperism' and the emerging proletariat, it is necessary to consider not only the family, but its enforced absence, as a way of life. This is especially true of the regions with marriage restrictions, partible inheritance and urban poverty. Riehl speaks directly of the absence of families among the fourth estate. In the towns, where life without marriage and unrecognized marriages were always more common than in the country because economic and social existence were not so dependent on marriage and household, there were opportunities for young workers to live without families, by renting a place to sleep, as boarders or simply renting a bed — the latter were called *Schlafgänger* ('bunkers'). Elsewhere in the countryside nomadic labour had caused significant changes to families.

One symptom of this was the increase in the numbers of illegitimate children. The steepness of this rise and its uneven distribution are significant. The figures vary for different areas, mainly because of differences in marriage legislation and the extension of the margin of food production and of jobs. The general rise, and the reduction in sexual abstinence lying behind it, was connected to the loosening of family, community, church and other traditional controls which was caused by the loss of property, increased impoverishment and the transition to cottage industry. To this was added increased mobility and anonymity in the towns, in which a man who had made a girl pregnant found it easier to leave his 'duties' unfulfilled, while the girl was more isolated and less stable. That this was an 'urgent problem' is probably also demonstrated by the fact that the age of unmarried mothers was relatively high, around the mid-twenties. Several illegitimate children were a great exception. Mortality was particularly high among children born to unmarried mothers. Among peasants the mother was usually supported, but among craftsmen and in the lower classes she might easily go under, unless she managed to find a husband. Illegitimate daughters almost routinely gave birth to illegitimate children.

Table 10: Illegitimate births (%)

	Berlin	Prussia	Saxony	Bavaria	Later German Reich
1816–20	18.3	7.1			
1826–30	15.3	6.7	11.9	19.6	
1836–40	15.4	7.0	14.0	20.6	
1846–50	14.7	7.3	15.1	20.5	11.1
1856–60	14.7	8.0	15.5	22.8	12.1
1866–70	14.5	8.4	14.4	19.4	11.0

Around 1750, the percentage of illegitimate births in the largest cities was between 4% and 7%, but by 1800 it was significantly higher. In Styria and Salzburg in 1850, it was as high as 25–26%.

The history of sexuality plays an important role in the history of the family, the sexes and the generations. Around 1800 in Germany there was considerable sexual permissiveness outside marriage in court and aristocratic circles, and among the lower classes. In the old world of guilds and small communities the custom and ethics of respectability were dominant, especially in the sexual domain. Control was strict and sexual 'freedom' or 'self-fulfilment' were of no significance, marriage not being grounded in sexuality. We do not know the extent to which sexuality was emotionalised and emphasised in the new 'bourgeois' family, but many things suggest it was. The romantic concept of love attempted to dissolve the dualism of friendship and sensuality in an erotic marriage. But Wilhelm von Humboldt, for example, whose marriage was held up as an ideal to the educated classes of the century, was an habitué of brothels, and for him, as for the old upper classes, love and sexuality were still distinct. The revolutionising of the sensibility of the family, the discovery of love and partnership also 'desensualised' the image of woman in manners and in public discourse. From the late 18th century onwards, the bourgeoisie was united in a furious battle against aristocratic libertinism. This morality had intensified to Victorian proportions by the mid-century. A contemporary opined that it was now (1830) impossible to boast of one's erotic adventures — as one had a few decades ago — indeed, one was ashamed to be accused of them in public.

The 'purity ideal' of the fraternities from 1815 onwards was extremely effective. The paramours of Metternich and Hardenberg and the mistresses of the princes had become intolerable to the bourgeoisie by 1850. Mistrust of Goethe, the irritation of such people as Börne and Menzel at his relation to sensuality, the fact that Wieland and Kotzebue were considered 'lascivious' around 1850, enthusiasm for Schiller's pure idealism, all point in the same direction. The norms became stricter; open libertinism disappeared. Sexuality was tied to marriage, became taboo in conversation, and was suppressed wherever possible; society became prudish.

This prudishness often prevented girls from being sexually enlightened before marriage. It was precisely the idealisation of woman and concentration on the family that forced through these new ethics. Woman was kept strictly separate from sexuality with its negative connotations. Even sublimated expressions of passion by women in private love-letters to their husbands or bridegrooms were considered ill-mannered, even repugnant, according to a letter-writing primer written before 1837.

One of the few exceptions was the emergence of female nurses. Until the 1830s and 1840s it was quite impossible for female nurses to work in male hospitals, and it took the deaconesses and orders to change these attitudes. Boys' first experience of sexuality was invested with fear and shame, and this was intensified by the curious obsession of pedagogues and doctors in their struggle against the 'vice' of masturbation. Of course, a certain double standard was at work here. Honour, i.e. the social existence of woman, was predicated on premarital chastity and marital fidelity, while it was more pardonable for a man to flout these norms. Of course there were in this world of the *'haute bourgeoisie'* also 'relationships' between men and girls who were their social 'inferiors', and the twilight world of prostitution. But unlike France, say, where the family ethic and liaisons were quite compatible, 'Victorian' attitudes and behaviour became characteristic and predominant. The Social Democrats of the end of the century were still beholden to these norms of respectability when they disputed the existence of Marx's illegitimate son. Bourgeois middle-class morality triumphed over the hedonism of the aristocracy and the lower classes, without being attributable, as in Britain, to an evangelical revivalist movement.

Things were different in the country, as ever, and overweening sexuality was still caught, as it were, within the peasant order of things, premarital conception being frequent and legitimised through custom. The lower classes conformed least to the general norms. Premarital conception and illegitimate births increased considerably, as has been shown. There was a release of sexuality, surely less from the imaginary desire to be 'free' than from the relaxation of social controls.

The question of the causes for the emergence of the modern family is very complex. Certainly, economic changes played an important part. The disappearance of the household as a production unit released, as it were, domestic intimacy and emotional ties. Capitalist production and the cottage industries and factories loosened the social order and relaxed control, rendering young people more independent and sexually less restricted, less self-denying. The individualist market economy and profession-orientated society increased concern for children and education, and word of the new family ideal was spread by reading. But the modern family emerged in Germany, as in Britain, before capitalism and industrialisation, and precisely not among capitalism's supporters and victims.

The change in mentality had other roots unique to itself. These included the individualisation and moralisation of religion, the collapse of belief in sin and Satan, the release and cultivation of naturalness and feelings in literature, a new humanitarianism with regard to children, the disappearance of passive sufferance of the world and the search for happiness in this world (not in the other). These tendencies and themes substantially contributed to the emergence of the modern family of bourgeois education. It remains astonishing and unprecedented in world history that a social system should be created which allowed itself the luxury of acknowledging individual autonomy, privacy and self-expression as values, thus eroding and undermining a society based on commitment and distance, authority and sanctity, through which it maintained its identity, stability and non-alienation. However, in the period under review, social discipline, of children, of women, of the lower classes, was so ingrained through custom or so impressed upon people by the new morality that social cohesion did not suffer.

The development of family life was accompanied, though not always simultaneously, by a corresponding development of family rights and ideology. The jurisprudence of the late Enlightenment individualised the family by interpreting it as a contract. One had the option of serving notice, i.e. divorce. The rights of wife and child were defined against the patriarchy of the husband (e.g. he alone could represent his wife in court). These rights, which the state claimed to protect, gained in importance. Simultaneously, the family was no longer bound by the rules of the homes; indeed, the legal and political, public nature of the 'home', with the paterfamilias as its chosen representative in the matter of 'public rights and duties, was disappearing. The law individualised and privatised the family, which was placed outside the jurisdiction of the state, being opposed to it as 'private' state and society, but in such a manner that it was precisely the state that protected its privacy. The liberal development of law, which stressed property, rights of inheritance and contracts, further developed that individualisation, especially in the field of property rights. The romantics also individualised marriage as a union of souls, but located it outside the law, making of it an interior state, not a social institution.

This was unrealistic, to say the least. Hegel correctly formulated the bourgeois view of marriage: marriage is a relationship grounded in subjective inwardness, but is 'ethical', i.e. is an institution. Divorce was made considerably more difficult by the Prussian restoration of the 1840s. Everywhere the family was raised to the level of the highest and ultimate value of bourgeois life, glorified in song and in the language of religion, and considered quasi-holy. In 1775, German dictionaries contained five compound words which included the word 'family' (*Familie*); by 1862, they recorded ninety such composites. Conservatives and liberals were not to be outdone. According to the Enlightenment liberal Rotteck in 1837, the family is the 'foundation of states and of everything most precious in human and bourgeois life (and) happiness'. The state was therefore not to 'interfere with the shrine of happiness'; public education was acceptable because it was taken for granted that it would not be used against the family. The family was publicly revered, precisely because it was the bastion of private existence. In the tension between the life-struggle and the 'home sweet home' ideal, the significance of the family increased. Living within the family and working for the family became a part of the meaning of life; hopes transcending one's own life were directed towards the children; they and the persistence in the memory of the family of one's own life became a significant component of bourgeois immortality, increasingly so with the further demise of Christian eschatology. This is precisely what gave both the family and the individual stability and identity in politics and the economy.

3. Everyday Life

Even the basic circumstances and habits of everyday life are historically conditioned, and these changed substantially, especially during the period under review. One cannot, of course, succumb to that defensible and charming curiosity for all things nostalgic or antiquarian, and must be confined to highlighting what was common and what was new in the everyday life of the various social classes.

First, there was the situation in the home. Three things are true of all classes. (1) The family sphere of production was separated from the sphere of consumption and life. This process was only in its initial stages among the peasants, but was already completed among the craftsmen, not to mention the other classes. Homes became autonomous domains separate from the workplace. Thus, a part of life, of the vital functions and immediate social relations, was domesticated and made private. (2) The family, long accustomed to living in its own house, or in its own shack, slowly but increasingly ceased to do so; in the large cities, and later to some extent in the middle-sized cities, homes were rented, and the rented apartment came to predominate (by 1800, in Berlin only one-third of households owned their own homes). Tenancy in Germany, by contrast with England, for example, became a constitutive, and finally a predominant trait of modern urban life. As far as one can see, this was due primarily to planning regulations, and still more to land rights and credit practices. Tenancy was by no means a condition unique to the workers, and they were joined by some of the bourgeoisie, officials and the educated classes, those who would later be considered employees (*Angestellte*), i.e. those dependent on changing employments.

While at first it was usual to rent an apartment in a house occupied by its owner, in the 1860s blocks of flats built for rental came into existence. A new force emerged — a new class, the rentiers (and their agents, the caretakers), more real and more inevitable than many of the other, more often discussed forms of 'class domination', because land in the cities was scarce. 'House rules' daily made palpable the existence of these new masters, and also demonstrated how necessary and difficult it was to organise co-operation and consideration between people who had previously been independent but were now living in houses with shared corridors, cellars, floors and toilets. The choice between accepting a rent rise or being given notice to quit became a threatening dilemma, hanging like a cloud above the head of the tenant with his everyday cares.

Tenants were also more mobile within the same city, compared with landlords and with tenants in times of rent control. Evictions, changes of workplace and changes in the family situation, made changes of home, compulsorily or by choice, into a fact of urban life. In the liberal society of the century, the 'production' of homes was a matter neither for public authorities nor for patriarchal forces; even at the end of our period it was scarcely dealt with by co-operatives, but by the market and the individual property-owner as a matter of capital investment. Land was thus exploited to the utmost. (3) Finally, technical and industrial advances also affected living conditions, gradually making life easier. Solid fuel briquettes were used for heating, linoleum was easy to clean; the efficient stove, usually in place of open fires, was used for cooking. The rapeseed oil lamp, the kerosene lamp and gaslight replaced candles and tallow lamps (with their accessories, candle snuffers), which were the norm until the mid-century. Safety matches were used for lighting fires and lamps (think of poor Paulinchen in *Struwwelpeter*), not to mention other 'gadgets' that made housekeeping easier. Bathrooms were very rare before the middle of the century, toilets in apartment buildings were frequently shared, and were situated on the stairs. The decisive hygienic improvement, that of the water-closet, only came into general use in the 1860s.

Homes are specific to class. Bourgeois homes became the model for all later developments. Concomitant with the development of family privacy we find from the late 18th century onwards there is a separation of the 'private domain' from that of the domestic servants (hence the bell in the living-room). The old-style all-purpose rooms for everyone's use were divided into separate living spaces, especially the sleeping and living areas. The bed in the 18th-century salon disappeared from centre stage, acquiring an intimate space of its own. Among the better-off, each family member was given a separate room. Nurseries came into existence (for sleeping, playing and living combined), and rooms were separated by corridors.

Rooms of a social, representational character were largely forced out of existence during the first half of the century, and were of little significance. Among the entrepreneurs of the wealthier middle-classes, the villa emerged, certainly impressive, but with the private domain fenced off with walls or hedges. The style of bourgeois homes until 1830, and still an influence through to the 1850s, was the Biedermeier, the last unified style of the century. It was simple, solid, durable, practical and functional, enliveningly and imaginatively detailed. The furnishings were typically pleasant, cosy and comfortable. Draped and pleated curtains screened the family from the world outside. The writing-desk, a new item of general furniture, served for writing letters and for contact beyond one's immediate surroundings. The sofa and oval table to one side of the room became the focal point; work-tables and sewing-tables were used for women's work. The glass cabinet displayed precious, and rarely used, porcelain, glass and silver. The bird-cage, floral-patterned upholstery, flowers, engravings and pictures, statuettes and bric-à-brac and bookcases, where there was a large amount of wall space, determined the atmosphere and were characteristic of the style.

After 1830, this style slowly went into decline, and after 1850, at first in the homes of the grand bourgeoisie, the development occurred that led into the *Gründerzeit*. Increased plushness was now the mode. There were thick carpets, floor-to-ceiling curtains. Walls were adorned with massive mirrors and a plethora of paintings — landscapes, histories, genre pictures above all, and soon prints as well. There were tall, massive bookcases and glass cabinets, padding and stuffing, all in dark, heavy colours, all to create a feeling of luxury, and a strong oriental influence in the form of Persian rugs, divans, new plants, and paintings of the Orient. The Biedermeier style was forced out by the neo-rococo and eventually the German renaissance styles. Spaces of a purely social, representational character began to flourish again, and the previous sociability of friends and families was formalised into 'at homes' and the formal 'returning' of visits.

Both earlier and later bourgeois life determined the style, not in its details but certainly in its character, above all of the 'living-room' with sofa, chairs and table; the petty bourgeois *Gute Stube*, the parlour, used only on Sundays, was an early manifestation of this trend.

In the countryside, traditional peasant ways of life persisted, and only among the rich farmers did embourgeoisement extend as far as having a *Gute Stube*. In the mid-century there were also special rooms for farmhands. In general, the farmhands lived in miserable conditions, in attics and stables. And with the expansion of the rural lower classes and their impoverishment, these miserable living conditions worsened. The farm labourers often lived squeezed together near the animals in fairly primitive, dark, unhygienic shacks with one common room and one bedroom.

Scarcity of space and sparse furnishings also characterised the homes of the urban lower classes during the period of pauperism, especially in the infamous and exceptionally dreadful slums in Berlin and Vienna, where several families lived in one large room. With the advent of industrialisation, accommodation became even more of a problem, and the accommodation 'question' became part of the social question. For the workers, and for the working underclasses, there were various types of accommodation. In the old cities, there were flats in attics, cellars and outhouses in the city centre, which still contained a mixture of social classes. There was also housing near the factories in new urban districts and the suburbs and in industrial villages. In the large cities, especially in the east, apartment buildings were very densely populated, most of all in Berlin in the notorious tenement blocks which had up to six storeys and six courtyards containing perhaps a hundred small apartments. In the Ruhr region, and in the west and south-west, people were more dispersed, in districts which lacked old town centres, and in industrial conglomerations. Since the bourgeoisie was weak here, there was no mixed housing and very little house-building.

In addition to old property, like the huts of the miners in the Ruhr, there were cottages, terraces of two and four houses, each with a little stable in the garden for small animals, and an attic (frequently used for *Schlafgänger*), which came into existence predominantly during the construction of worker's colonies in the 1860s. This met social needs and responded to the interests of entrepreneurs in having a 'core personnel', an aristocracy of the workforce. But overall, the rented apartment came to predominate outside the cities as well. Flats were cramped and overpopulated, usually with one (at best two) rooms and a bedroom with a shared toilet. They were expensive for what they were, especially the small ones; in the case of the Berlin tenement buildings, this was due to the high ground rents and the enormous mortgages that the owners had taken out. Flats were scarce, for economic and psychological reasons, and the market for them was over-subscribed.

One important consequence of their price and scarcity was the widespread practice of subletting and renting out places to sleep, especially from the 1860s onwards. That became the norm for workers aged between twenty and thirty or thirty-five, whose tenants subsidised the cost of their accommodation. In the few cases in which we know more than the lack of space and the price, i.e. concerning furnishings, such as among factory workers in Esslingen, an astonishing (and probably widespread) fact emerges. The living-room furniture — sofa, chair, table, mirror, picture — was the centrepiece of any marriage; these were the items for which money had been saved up during the previous years, at a time when workers received the highest pay of their working lives. Thus the ideal of the skilled artisan had percolated through to the workers. These groups were basically no different from each other, and they only differed according to their greater or lesser means. With the 'normal' impoverishment of the workers, upon reaching old age, the difference naturally became more acute.

As new types of accommodation and industrialisation moved in step with urbanisation, one of the great living environments of human beings, soon to become the typically modern one — the city — changed fundamentally, both in appearance and character. Right into the first third of the century, most German cities still maintained an old-world, almost medieval character, with ramparts and ditches, walls and gates, with little old houses and a few big ones, with gardens, fields and barns within the town precincts, with crooked alleys, grass on the frequently recobbled streets, and sandy open squares. The countryside began right outside the city gate. By night, this gate was locked and was only opened upon payment of a toll; the night watchman was part of the city's night life.

In Berlin, the first pavements were laid in the 1820s. In 1837 the first attempts were made with asphalt, and from the late 1820s onwards gas lighting was introduced in the large cities, at first for winter nights. Early on, the cemeteries were placed outside the vicinity of the church and city centre, suburbs came into being, usually growing out of old villages on the outskirts, but still separate from the city, and soon thereafter came the first factories. The city expanded, becoming more densely populated, and simultaneously grew upwards, into the sky. Little by little, and increasingly from the mid-century onwards, the cities were defortified as walls and gates were pulled down, and the steep bank in front of the wall, previously kept free for the line of fire, was built up and old houses were replaced by newer and larger ones, all in the name of expansion and transport requirements.

It was a prolonged process, with many observers complaining of the opposition between the old and the new, the unfinished and wild aspect of the new cityscapes (only Berlin was considered completely 'modernised' by 1840). The streets were still empty in the evenings and nightlife did not yet exist. Most royal capitals and 'large' cities, with the exception of Berlin and Leipzig, Vienna and perhaps Hamburg, were considered 'boring' or 'barren' by their visitors. More important still was the fact that roughly in the first half of the century, dwellings, production centres, offices and trading areas were still in relative proximity. The city was still a pedestrian zone (cabs were rare, coaches a luxury). Therefore, tenements and mansions stood side by side along with the homes of the intermediate social strata. Early apartment blocks included flats for the upper classes, the *haute bourgeoisie* and the middle classes, as well as modest (roof and outhouse) apartments above the caretaker's basement flat. The social strata still lived together here. Gradually, though not everywhere nor uniformly, a social stratification emerged in the 1860s, first in the new urban districts which had once been on the city's outer limits, and in the suburbs, around the factories, into *haut bourgeois*, bourgeois, and proletarian districts, and into the industrialised eastern and northern suburbs and the more 'refined' west ends of the larger towns. In western Berlin, the smart suburb of Potsdam was developed, while in the south-west lay the so-called *Geheimratsviertel* (Privy Counsellors' Quarter); in Hamburg the first Villa Quarter emerged in Wandsbek in 1865. The beginnings of a city were laid down in central shopping streets. Urban transport, however, in the shape of the horse-drawn tram, was still infrequent and poorly appointed.

As stated, factories and the construction of apartment buildings, changed and determined the appearance and character of the cities, especially of the large cities, supplanting the aristocratic and ecclesiastical aspects and the homes of wealthy merchants and craftsmen. Two other forces were of decisive significance in this transformation. One was the railway. New centres of commerce, factories and stores sprang up in its vicinity, and poorer residential areas sprang up alongside the track. The great terminuses and the railway stations became the new city gates. At first stations were divided into large reception areas for the crowds of people, salons, waiting rooms for certain groups (for example, ladies), and the operational areas with their long, covered platforms. Stations became new city centres, the focus of squares and streets, to which hotels and other magnificent buildings were added, and then the less 'beautiful', new or restructured station district. Within the city, the railway tracks became dividing-lines. They had to be negotiated by the installation of bridges, level crossings and underpasses. Areas 'on the wrong side of the tracks' emerged, where districts were cut off and no building development took place. Also, before the imposing banks and handsome department stores were opened in Germany, 19th-century towns were characterised by the great expansion in public buildings, state and local government offices and institutions. These were testimony to the universal processes of functional differentiation and the bureaucratisation of life. Government buildings, inland revenue and customs offices, post offices and expanded town halls were built. Schools, especially *Gymnasia*, and universities and clinics were constructed. Courthouses, 'palaces of justice' appropriate to the bourgeois ideal of the state under the rule of law, were erected, with huge entrance halls and wide corridors, because justice had become middle-class and was administered in public. The other important appurtenances to the new state-bourgeois culture industry, museums, theatres and concert halls, also put in an appearance.

Of the palaces of commerce, the most important were the stock exchanges in the large squares, and then the first arcades, streets full of covered shops in transition from markets to department stores. Such buildings, the surrounding parks and the squares that they formed, put their stamp on certain parts of the (new) city centres.

The expansion of the towns brought about by the new construction projects and by the growth and greater population density of the cities was largely autonomous and unplanned. It was connected mainly with land rights and with the limited sphere of competence of the communities and of the state, and finally with the fact that the public building sector was limited, by contrast with that of later times. Railway construction and house-building were in private hands and were left to market forces. The great reforms of the early part of the century liberalised not only the agrarian constitution, but also land rights in the cities. Urban land was, in principle, freed from obligations to landlords and co-operatives, from the multiple layers of partial and frequently inalienable rights of use and disposal. They became unified, freely-disposible, individual property. Only now was it possible really to view land or ground as goods, to mortgage it, to integrate it completely into the market and into economic circulation, to mobilise it.

The upturn in the property market and in specialist mortgage banks were both consequences of this development. This new order of land rights on the basis of individual property affected planning legislation. *Dominium directum* and building obligations, facts of 18th-century life, disappeared, while planning departments and planning permission had not yet developed. Legal ordinances which provided for planning intervention by the authorities in the common interest were restricted in the liberal formulations of the first half of the century to the mere circumvention of danger. The freedom to build was basically upheld with only secondary restrictions. Of course, the number of these building ordinances increased during the period under review, becoming more exhaustive and, compared with the start of the century (though not with the present day!), more restrictive.

The laws concerning fire safety and minimum distances between neighbouring buildings were supplemented by health regulations during the second third of the century. The first norms relating to heights and distances within a single building were also introduced. Yet what was enforceable in respect of the relationship between neighbouring property-owners could not be extended during the period under review distances between buildings owned by the same landlord (to protect the interests of tenants). In general, the position of landlords remained very strong in the face of community complaints and attacks. Market conditions, scarcity of land, limitations to the potential for increasing rents due to the limitations on mass incomes, made it necessary for apartment buildings to exploit all the available land surface.

One step in the direction of planning arose from the fact that the communities were responsible for paving and maintenance of roads and for street-lighting. Once the importance of public health facilties was realised, a matter of equal importance to all, rich and poor, and one impossible to regulate on an individual basis, these communities also assumed responsibility for the resulting sewerage systems and improved water supplies. Mains water was provided in Vienna in 1803, in Hamburg in 1848 and in Berlin in 1852. The town centre of Hamburg got its sewerage system in 1842. Berlin, Danzig, Breslau, Frankfurt and Munich got their sewerage and drainage systems in the 1860s. Public health care and local government administration of services emerged for the first time.

There were no development charges for the landowners to pay, and in part the cities had to buy the land for the streets from its owners. One of the results was the construction of very large buildings. All the same, the communities had a regulatory influence through road-building and the provision of water and sewerage systems, which also caused some restructuring of the old cities. It did much to change the relationship between individual property and the common weal, market forces and community planning. To that one might add special conditions that promoted and even required planning, for example, the remodelling of cities or their reconstruction after catastrophes, and, much more frequently, the defortification of cities and the building up of the previously open areas in front of city walls.

The reconstruction of Hamburg after the great fire of 1842 took as its starting-point the technical, engineered planning of wider streets and of a modern sewerage system, to which Semper's designs for the interpenetrating spaces of the Alster were added, all on the basis of a normative building ordinance that enforced unity and sacrificed mere profit in this reconstructed area. Where the architectural genius of someone like Semper was lacking, the design was a geometrical, rectangular, symmetric pattern, as in the plans for Bremerhaven and in most examples of defortification. Of course, there were variations. To an extent, parks or boulevards (arterial roads) were laid down, with free-standing houses in a 'pastoral' style, built at first under low-demand conditions, as in Munich at the Maximiliansplatz or on the Sonnen street. The geometrical patterns predominated, the high-density, rectangular buildings, as in Munich's Maxvorstadt district. At the beginning of the century, in Munich a relatively large amount of planning went into the first expansions, but that was to prove to be incidental to the life of the centralist administration, and it ended in 1818 with the fall of Montgelas and the reintroduction of urban autonomy. Only a monarch was able thoroughly to plan and execute magnificent one-off streets: the land had to be in a single person's hands, and for the most part monumental state edifices were constructed. The Ludwigstrasse and the Maximilianstrasse in Munich are the classic examples. Indeed, the Maximilianstrasse, with its changing widths, forum-like widening, boulevards, parks, memorials and its orientation towards the Isar embankment and the Maximilianeum, was a direct attempt to escape from the tyranny of the urban grid. However, the bourgeois property developers could not be made to adhere to the 'Maximilian style' and its grandiose façades.

When Vienna was defortified in 1857, the bare hillock between the town centre and the suburbs was subjected to planned construction (between 1859 and 1865), without impinging on existing property. This was when the famous Ringstrasse was built. It is 57m wide and 4km long, and had parallel paths for goods vehicles and pedestrians. A ring road was built in Cologne between the city walls and the outlying suburbs but it was originally intended as a street of smart villas.

As a final example, the urban plan for Berlin was completed in 1862 by the engineer James Hobrecht, who was renowned for his sewerage systems. He merely laid down the framework of the rectangular, grid-like road and sewerage network, deep into the surrounding open country, and left untouched a building ordinance that permitted the building of five- and six-storey blocks of flats with miniscule rear courtyards (only enough room to turn a fire hose). The ideal of the surveyors, and of the communities who had to keep road costs down and therefore wanted a high town profile, was rectangular blocks, and the construction of these was permitted according to the then prevalent concept of rights from an individualistic, economic viewpoint. The 'cityscape' was more or less ignored in this plan, which took as its starting-point public health, transport, and individual property.

A few words will suffice on the social history of costume. The trend in male clothing, among the upper classes at first, was towards a bourgeois look: a simple, practical, 'natural', inconspicuous appearance. The English fashion was heavily influential. Hair stayed short and unpowdered. Trousers replaced aristocratic knee-breeches even in court circles, the deep-pocketed frock coat was worn, and the fancy waistcoat, the only variable and decorative item, became the norm. On more ceremonial occasions the correct attire was top-hat and tails, boots, stiff collar and the modern broad tie. Apart from the waistcoat, male dress was dark grey until 1848, after a few lapses into colour. The opinion of the English dandy Beau Brummel that inconspicuousness and a certain relaxed quality constitute true elegance, and that only the cut and the seat determine the quality of clothing, became sartorial gospel.

Certain groups attempted to manifest their opposition by deviations from 'normal' dress. The idea defended above all by Jahn of a 'traditional' German national costume was thrown out by the Carlsbad agreements, but politics played an important role in beard fashions. For instance, until 1848 a democratic, oppositional quality was invested in the beard, but from the 1850s onwards the democratic beard was clipped at court and thus converted into the Vandyke beard of Napoleon III, and into the 'emperor's' sideboards of Franz Joseph and Wilhelm of Prussia, thus becoming fashionable on many fronts. Bourgeois costume separated aristocrats and bourgeois from the peasant and urban masses, and the work-jacket was a class feature. It was an ideal garment for the lower classes. In the countryside, at least among men, (ceremonial) folk costume went into decline, though it was gradually revived by romantic artifice, especially in the Alpine regions.

Female fashion, for all its changes, was determined after the disappearance around the 1830s of the Empire style with its decolletages and exposed ankles, by wraps which covered the entire body, whether to stress slimness or ampleness. The crinoline, which reached its apotheosis in the mid-century, stressed motherhood and, one might say, (in France) the legitimacy of the wife compared with the illegitimacy of the mistress. To this could be added, at least until the mid-century, the artfully arranged curls, halfway down the face and on each side of straight hair smoothed from a central parting and with hair piled up at the back. The wide variety of bonnets and hats were decorated, like the dresses, with ribbons and lace — this was the great age of the milliners — and another universal novelty accessory was introduced, the shawl. Paris continued to set the trend for ladies' fashions. Mass production went into operation in the 1850s, first in men's clothing, later in women's clothing, leading, at first only among the bourgeoisie, to a certain democratisation of luxury.

Everyday life was still determined by a greater extent than ever before and even more than in the century to come, by the full-time occupations of the overriding majority, including the bourgeoisie. Free time, leisure, pleasure and sociability played a small part in daily life. For the simple people (and the petty bourgeoisie) social events included fairs; in the Rhineland the carnival was revived. These festivities featured shooting and skittles, card games and dances. There were inns selling beer, and wine-lodges providing wine — customarily only in the wine-growing regions — beer cellars and dance halls. The 'educated' upper classes held parties, such as masked balls, public or private, in competition with the traditional court balls. They featured dancing, especially the waltz. *Herrengesellschaft*, male social gatherings in the open air, with food and drink, the 'promenade concert', visits to the coffee-house and cake-shop, and communal, private or public dinner parties, with the expanding custom of after-dinner speeches and toasts, were also popular forms of entertainment. It was not uncharacteristic of the social style and operation of the *haute bourgeoisie* in the 1840s that the various factions of the Frankfurt National Assembly were formed in cafés and inns and took their names from them. In the home, chess and card games then became the specific forms of aesthetic, Biedermeier-style amusement. The livelier forms included party games, *tableaux vivants*, theatre, and impromptu poetry readings, as well as other forms of amateur theatricals and music recitals and home concerts. 'Artistic' pursuits such as water-colour painting, making silhouettes, or writing poetry (and diaries) were important. Intellectual conversation and discussions were important among the intelligentsia. From the 1830s, artists and men of letters tended to prefer to frequent the homes of the bourgeoisie, rather than court circles. The club, a very important and novel form of bourgeois and petty bourgeois communal life and of leisure culture will be discussed again later, as will the role of art, music and literature.

Travel was a completely new element of leisure culture, because it only grew with the emergence of railways and the improved postal service. New aspects were added to the 'educational' or 'grand' tour — visits to fairs, exhibitions and congresses. The upper classes especially would spend holidays at spa resorts. These sophisticated European great spa towns had avenues, assembly rooms, foyers, theatres and casinos. People travelled to Baden-Baden or Wiesbaden (which had 30,000 visitors each in 1850), to Homburg or Carlsbad, Ems or Kissingen, or to new spa towns like Neuenahr, which was developed by a public company in 1857. Then, around the mid-century, the (usually short) summer holiday trip of the middle classes came into being, born of the post-Romantic bourgeois relationship with nature. The development of seaside and mountain resorts began here. The first Baedeker guide to Germany was published in 1842. In 1863–64, the first guided tour from Germany to the Orient took place. The Austrian Alpine Club was founded in 1862, its German equivalent following not long after.

The change in the economy and work, in society and mentality, also wrought deep changes to the vital, even quasi-natural, field of nutrition, of eating and drinking. The predominance of self-sufficient farming, normal at least in rural and semi-rural regions, went substantially into decline with urbanisation and the dissolution of the production unit of the 'whole household'. Admittedly, around 1860, self-sufficiency continued to play an important role in the countryside. Two-thirds of all loaves are believed to have been baked at home; animals and even kitchen gardens were kept in the rural industrial regions, with the grocery trade still predominantly a trade in 'colonial goods'. All the same, trade, with buying and selling, came to predominate. This released the problem of domestic provision from the year's slow rhythm, and turned it into a weekly matter. The provision of needs by means of purchase and money enabled quicker exchange, and trading improved the supply of goods. Certainly, seasonal and local products still predominated (compared with present-day conditions), but trade fundamentally changed the function of certain products.

Rice, for instance, originally a luxury item or a treat, from 1850 onwards became a staple for mass consumption (rice soup). Honey, once an everyday item, became rare as a result of an increase in the sugar supply. Liebig's Meat Extract and the first meat and sausage factories signalled the emergence of industrial food production within our period.

Shop-bought foodstuffs loosened the deep-rooted traditionalism of eating habits (and the associated disparity between everyday foods and those consumed only on feast-days), especially with the decline of the class morality which categorised foods as either everyday or luxury items. Urbanisation, jobs outside the home and the factories, changed the place and time at which meals were consumed. Snacks between meals went into decline in the towns, partly with the increased popularity of coffee. In *haute bourgeoise* and middle-class circles, cake shops and especially coffee-houses and cafés were on the rise, in which people chatted to each other and read newspapers, especially in the cities. This was particularly true of Berlin (the Kranzler coffee-house is one example) and above all in Vienna, where there were seventy-five coffee-houses in the 1840s.

The mid-century saw the rise of the restaurant, a place where, without requiring a cook of one's own, one could afford the luxury of an excellent meal, quickly prepared and consumed in pleasant surroundings. The occasional soup kitchen was provided for the impoverished masses (Leipzig, 1849), and rations and canteens were provided in the factories (Krupp, 1860). Otherwise, a bowl of stew carried in a lunchbox was greedily wolfed down during the factory mealbreak. Mealtimes were shortened everywhere in the towns. Yet, astonishingly, in post-1850 Germany, old habits reasserted themselves, despite factory canteens and packed lunches and the tendency of the smart set to eat late at night. Luncheon once again became the main meal of the day, according to petty-bourgeois custom.

Around 1800, the modernisation of culinary practices and, above all, economic and technical changes, in the form of a refined bourgeois cuisine somewhere between that of the peasantry and the aristocracy, as well as table manners and elegant tableware (crockery and cutlery), were already established among the upper and upper middle classes. There was a strong French influence on cookery, though English customs were influential in meat cookery. Nevertheless, there were still extreme variations between simple, everyday fare and luxury, festive foods. The variety of foods consumed also included the strongly regionalised and traditional peasant fare, and the food consumed by the lower classes. The two great innovations — coffee and potatoes — were already widespread. In all classes, though with regional differences, potatoes and bread tended to replace pulses, soup, porridge and puréed vegetables, and coffee was supplemented in north and central Germany by bread or bread-and-butter (sometimes with cheese or sausage).

In other respects, nutrition history is, at first, class-specific. The lower classes, in both city and country, barely survived, and were constantly hungry and malnourished. The terrible stories of the 'hungry forties', of starvation and hunger, are legion. Potatoes and cabbage, groats, pulses and soup were the principal forms of nourishment. Carbohydrates, with little fat or protein, and boiled meat every now and again (roasts were for the aristocracy and bourgeoisie), or herrings in the coastal areas then became the norm. They were monotonous fare.

There then emerged — surely the product of a curious imitative trend — a surrogate form of coffee, chicory coffee, and schnapps, the consumption of which increased hugely with the rise of potato distilleries and cheap production, especially in the 1830s. Schnapps became simultaneously the national drink and a social problem, perhaps as a kind of lively reaction against the monotony of diet and work. The popularity of sweets is known from the cottage textile industry, and is a similar phenomenon. Hunger and malnutrition were largely overcome in the 1850s, with the end of pauperism and a rise in real wages. Now sugar consumption (2.4kg per head in 1840, 7.3kg per head in 1873) and meat consumption also increased. It was 13.6kg in 1816, 20kg in 1830–40. The average was inflated by the greater amount consumed by the middle classes. In 1873 it was as high as 29.5kg per head. Meat consumption now shifted towards the consumption of pork, which was cheaper. There was higher consumption of fats, bread and noodles, a shift from carbohydrates to fats and from vegetable to animal protein. Bourgeois cuisine in its simpler manifestations — schnitzels, cutlets and goulash — was now adopted by a wider range of classes. The bourgeois cookbooks (Henriette Davidis's book in 1845, Katharina von Prato's in 1858) were republished almost annually and were bestsellers in their day.

To be sure, these were mere tendencies right up to the end of the period under review, and the working man's fare scarcely compared with bourgeois, or even with a balanced, diet. There were many constraints. The worker's family still had to spend 50–80% of wages on nutrition (58% on staple foods in 1858). The tradition of heavy, rural, plain fare (*Hausmannskost*) was maintained, and working-class wives were only partly trained in and capable of assimilating the mysteries of bourgeois cuisine. In peasant and worker households, the husband was entitled to more and better food than the other family members. Yet what remains decisive is the transformation of traditional rural and lower-class fare into that of the urban bourgeoisie, with the slow convergence of a previously pronounced divide. The history of tobacco, the increasing popularity of the cigarillo and cigar among men, shows similar tendencies.

In a period of low life expectancy and high mortality rates, especially among infants and children, not only was death more ubiquitous than it is today, but the common human occurrence of falling sick was more of a threat, more associated with dying and death. In spite of many improvements, the colossal advance that came about with the advent of scientific medicine did not bear fruit until after this period. To the 'individual' illnesses should be added the great national diseases and epidemics. The plague was no longer a danger. Smallpox, with an estimated 600,000 cases per year and 75,000 fatalities at the beginning of the century, was brought decisively under control by means of vaccination, including compulsory vaccination and revaccination (Bavaria 1807, Württemberg 1818, Prussia 1816 and 1834). However, a cholera epidemic broke out in 1831, causing the death of 63.1% of those infected in Berlin, and repeated epidemics decimated parts of Germany during the subsequent decades. Typhoid was also of significance, especially in the hungry years before 1848. Venereal diseases, especially syphilis, were still nationally widespread, though at lower levels than in France (from 2.2

to 3.8% in the Prussian army, 4.9% in the large cities). This was a fact of life that neither prohibitions, licences nor the inspection of brothels and prostitutes could eradicate. In the port of Hamburg, the number of brothels grew from 100 to 150 between 1840 and 1870. Consumption, or tuberculosis, was to become the great national disease of the century, especially in its latter half. Virchow estimated in 1860 that 15–18% of all fatalities were attributable to it.

The primary healers were doctors. During the first decades of the century, state control of courses of study, examinations and admissions led to quite distinct classes of medical doctor: Qualified doctors (with degrees), surgeons, surgeons (second class), who were trained as as in a trade, and the less-qualified rural practitioners. The only clear distinction drawn by 1800 was that between the above-mentioned categories and the less respectable types of healers. These classes grew into a unified, academically trained medical profession around mid-century (1852 in Prussia). There was only partial freedom of practice. Elsewhere there was restricted admission to a district (until 1865 in Bavaria), and in Nassau doctors had quasi-civil-servant status.

Medical officers and district health officers existed everywhere. They also supervised the pharmacies. In 1827, 48% of doctors were in public service, and 36% in 1842. The state regulated fees and required doctors (using police coercion, if necessary!) to treat the poor. A large medical reform movement agitated for the unification of the medical profession, for independence and autonomy, and against state control. Medical societies and the medical press were of great importance to this professionalisation. At the same time, doctors emerged out of the old class divisions and were completely integrated into new, upper-middle-class society.

The increase in the numbers of doctors was barely proportional to the population. There was one doctor per 2,955 inhabitants of Prussia in 1825, and one per 3,268 inhabitants in 1864. However, in the district of Gumbinnen the ratio was 1:10,011 and 1:9,931, in Berlin by contrast 1:1,153 and 1:1,251 respectively, while in the Cologne district it was 1:2,900 in 1817 and 1:2,150 in 1842, and in the town of Cologne 1:1,140 and 1:1,041 respectively. Originally, the doctors mainly served the upper classes. In around 1800, ordinary people did not visit the doctor, but relied on quacks. Within the cities, that had changed by the 1860s, thanks to the doctors who provided free treatment for the poor (*Armenärzte*). In the country, the use of doctors for treating illnesses was by no means taken for granted. In the 1850s one doctor from the administrative district of Cloppenburg estimated that hardly a fifth of the sick visited the doctor — still less children and the aged. In the administrative district of Cologne only 20% of all those deceased had been provided with medical help in the period in 1820–24. All the same, the dissemination of medical information, medical question-and-answer booklets, handbooks, popular education in periodicals such as *Die Gartenlaube* and illustrated magazines and calendars, all increased, causing folk remedies to suffer a decline. Quacks (*Kurpfuscher*, as they are now called) came under attack. However, in 1869, on the instigation of liberal doctors who did not want the sole right to treat patients nor state supervision of such treatment, the 'ban on quacks' (*Pfuschverbot*) was struck from the trading regulations of the North German Bund.

The doctor was a general practitioner, and the emphasis was on house calls, not office hours. During the 1840s, in bourgeois circles, a discretionary payment was still made in some regions at each New Year: a relict of the estate mentality. The new achievements and aids to diagnosis such as auscultation, percussion, precise case histories, accurate temperature-taking and stethoscopes did not enter into common practice to any considerable degree until the second half of the century. Scientific medicine did not yet contribute significantly to therapy; indeed, science maintained a lofty disdain for practical treatment and had little influence, even though its students, the younger doctors, were better able to make diagnoses. Blood-letting, sweating, poultices, diets, laxatives remained important.

Practitioners stressed the significance of the individual case and of the overall constitution of the patient, asserting that medicine was an 'art'. Medicine was long to remain at the mercy of the doctrine of the pathology of humours, which described sickness as a disturbance of the 'vital juices'. Progress in the fight against ill-health was based more on the systematisation of experience and on the recommendation of a sensible way of life, on the care of infants and of women in childbed, on 'the art of prolonging life' (as Doctor Hufeland's bestseller of 1797 was called), than on the new scientific advances. Echoing Rousseau and the Romantics, natural health cures were developed along with scientific ones. These consisted of treatment at spas, coastal and mountain resorts, the latter against tuberculosis, hydrotherapies of the kind developed and popularised by the farmer Priessnitz and the pastor Kneipp, and gymnastics such as those of the Leipzig doctor Schreber. At the start of the century, 'animal magnetism' (Mesmerism) and hypnosis, the seances of doctors Jung-Stilling or Justinus Kerner, were an important phenomenon. 'Romantic' doctors made much of the 'soul', the unconscious and the psychosomatic component of illness (Carus, Feuchtersleben). The homeopathy of Samuel Hahnemann only achieved popularity in Germany after its success in the United States. This is an early example of a 'movement' that wished to reform life on the basis of a medical doctrine.

Besides the increasing professionalism of doctors, the emergence of the modern hospital was an important factor in the treatment of the sick. The old hospital had united the poor, the aged, the infirm and the sick in a kind of social asylum, and it would be hard to talk of treatment of the sick *per se*. It was not until around 1800 that specialised, public institutions were created for in-patient treatment of the physically ill. The underlying cause was a changed mentality, a different view of illness and also a new philanthropism. The collapse of the urban hospitals and foundations, and the rationalist and revolutionary secularisation and centralisation of welfare, especially in the Napoleonic region, on the one hand, and the demands of the professors of medicine for scientific investigations at the sickbed ('in no way is the maternity hospital there to serve the needs of expectant mothers', in the words of a Göttingen gynaecologist) and the state interest in good medical training, on the other, led to the establishment of 'general', usually urban, hospitals (e.g. Vienna in 1784, Munich in 1813–18), to the university clinics, to the public maternity wards and later to specialist children's hospitals (in 1830 in Berlin, in 1837 in Vienna). In addition, there were the hospitals founded by humanitarian, and usually denominational groups (such as the Catholic Bürgerhospital in Bonn in 1840). In 1822, in Prussia there were 155 public hospitals, and in 1855 there were 684; this meant that the ratio of hospitals to population dropped from 1:75,000 to 1:25,000. From the 1850s onwards, they were provided with gas, lighting and water-closets. In the course of the decades, there was an upward 'socialisation'. Where previously it had been the destitute whose families were incapable of nursing them who entered nursing homes, they were later joined by educated and wealthy patients, attracted by famous doctors. Additionally, there was the upgrading of nursing conditions, previously dismal, by nuns of the religious orders (the Sisters of Mercy and the Order of St Vincent de Paul, beginning with the mother house in Munich in 1832) and the deaconesses' movement, which began in 1836 in Kaiserswerth. By 1864 there were thirty-two mother houses with 1,600 deaconesses. These were augmented from the 1850s by a small number of lay nurses.

Treatment of the mentally ill underwent similar changes. In place of the prisons and madhouses for social deviants, anti-social individuals and the insane, special asylums and sanatoria were built on the French model, in which attempts were made to influence the patients, now respected as human beings and considered from a medical and psychological perspective, without chains or brutality. The great institutions were state-run. Bayreuth (established 1850), Siegburg or Illenau in Baden (established 1842) were particularly famous. In the 1840s small private institutions like that in Bonn, where Robert Schumann ended his days, emerged. Institutions for deaf-mutes and the blind (schools) have a similar history.

The state had assumed a kind of overall responsibility for all these areas (including the pharmacies). There was a medical administration, and in a transition from the late absolutist medical police to the public health policies of the 20th century, a specialised 'health service' emerged during the 19th century. After the publication of the monumental works of the later Enlightenment, *A System of Complete Medical Supervision* by J. P. Franck (1779–88) and *Medicine* (1817–19), there was a theory concerning the social and political preconditions for good health and bad, and a project existed for carrying out the state's duty to improve public health by force or persuasion. Unfortunately, this attitude contradicted the liberal ideas of the century concerning the role of the state.

Virchow stressed the social causes of illness in his investigations of typhus in Upper Silesia, and demanded state aid. This became the 'medical reform' movement of 1848, which asserted that medicine was a 'social science', that the doctor was the 'natural advocate of the poor', and that there was a right to health, for which the state was responsible. From the 1860s, public health care was a central issue. Lorenz Stein included in his work on public administration (1867) an entire volume dedicated to the health service and the duty of society to provide the conditions necessary for health, irrespective of the wealth of the individual. To these may be added the great achievements in hygiene and public health, the provision of clean water and the installation of sewerage systems in the towns. Max von Pettenkofer, a physio-chemist in Munich, became the founder of modern medicine and modern health care, and of the corresponding laws (1858 and 1867 in Bavaria), with his investigations into the cholera epidemic. New water mains were laid in 1840 in Vienna, in 1848 in Hamburg, and in 1852 in Berlin, but it was not until the 1860s and 1870s that the cities were provided with 'clean' water, sewerage systems and the introduction of regulated waste disposal (the Berlin Riesenfelder in 1870). Later, the smaller cities followed suit (Danzig in 1869). Finally, observation of cases of trichonosis in the 1860s led to obligatory meat inspections and to the installation of municipal slaughterhouses. This also changed the function of the city councils. They took over the new public duties, carrying out social functions that required high levels of taxation, in spite of liberal principles. This led to the new health policies, introduced by the medical reformers of 1848, such as Salomon Neumann, a Berlin town councillor from 1853. The public was gradually made aware of the connection between poverty and sickness by way of the public health issue.

4. Agriculture and Rural Society

We now turn to the large sectors of the economy and their corresponding social groups.

During the period under review, and also after the industrialisation that grew apace after the 1840s, Germany remained a predominantly agricultural country. Though the economic, social, political and cultural dynamism came from the cities and was confined largely to the bourgeoisie and administrators, rural conditions determined the way in which socio-economic modernisation came about, and how the political order developed. This is especially true, of course, of the pre- and early industrial phase which lasted until the mid-century. The old world was agrarian, the overall economy dependent on agriculture, with power relations and living conditions, indeed systems of norms, developing within the framework of and based upon agricultural society. Its development was therefore of decisive significance to the overall history of the period.

This development was substantially determined by four factors. These were: the agricultural situation; technical and economic advances; social developments on the basis of peasant emancipation, power and property relations, and population growth; and finally the mentality of the rural population. All of these factors are intertwined and determine the real history in their interaction.

Firstly, we shall consider the economic events and crises. The period around 1800 was a prosperous one, especially for north Germany, with grain prices rising (between 1730–40 and 1800–1810, and especially from 1790, by 110%) as a result of population growth and exports to England, without wages or commercial products becoming substantially higher. As a result, the value of property increased by 100% between 1780–90 and 1803 alone, and that reflected income expectations. Of course, these high prices led to considerable debt. Political events and the Continental Blockade triggered off a rapid fall in prices, but by 1812 they seemed to have recovered.

Then the first great agricultural crisis occurred. From 1817, grain prices collapsed due to good harvests and the introduction of the English tariffs on corn. In 1825, they were only 28% of their 1817 level in the ports. It was a crisis of over-production (and secondarily of under-consumption). Land prices fell by 25% in Silesia, 33% in Holstein, and by more than in eastern Germany. Here, the property market collapsed completely for a while, owing to the surplus supply of properties. Some businesses went bankrupt — peasants whose *Ablösung* (redemption) was in the form of rent payments (up to 50% in the East Friesian marshes), and the overdrawn, overvalued and export-dependent big businesses. War damages, compensation and the general shortage of capital made the crisis more acute. In East Prussia, for example, some 40% of the manors were compulsorily auctioned or sold, and elsewhere the figure was higher still.

The crisis brought the estates of the aristocracy into circulation. From the end of the 1820s, when debts and land prices were down, sales increased due to the growth in population, as did exports. Later, after the English tariffs were dropped, a new economic climate came into being, which was to last into the 1870s. Production and land prices rose considerably, especially between 1830 and 1860. In Prussia, for instance, rents, as an indication of land prices, rose from 19 thalers per hectare in 1849 to 31 in 1869, while land prices are estimated to have risen three- to fourfold from the end of the 1820s to 1870.

This boom resulted in renewed overvaluation, the incurring of huge debts, and frequent changes of ownership of properties. In East Prussia, for example, each large estate changed hands an average of 2.14 times between 1835 and 1864, only in 37.4% of cases by inheritance, in 60.2% by sale, and in 5.1% by bankruptcy. Throughout Prussia, the number of changes of ownership of properties from sales was almost twice that from inheritance. In other words, the mobility of real property remained an important factor.

The peasants also profited from the rise in ground prices and later also in product prices. A final feature in this connection is the fact that production costs (wages and non-agricultural production) were relatively stable, hardly dropping at all during periods of falling prices, and hardly increasing during periods of rising prices. Thus, in that respect, incomes were dependent above all on product prices.

It must, of course, be assumed, especially for the first half of the century, that the long-term economic and price trends were overlaid by short-term, quite considerable trends, depending year by year upon the harvest, but also on the period between successive harvests. This was still of considerable importance for individual businesses, compared with the later 'stabilisation' of prices. Small and indebted businesses were particularly badly hit.

The economic climate was of great importance to peasant emancipation, inasmuch as the periods between calculating peasants' payments influenced the size of *Ablösungen*, just as the economic climate influenced the maximum burden of payment sustainable by the peasants. The results of the various reforms in Germany were thus largely dependent on their timing.

There was also another kind of agricultural crisis. The German economy in general and people's livelihoods, especially those of the poor, depended on the harvest, and in good measure also on regional harvests. Poor harvests led to considerably increased prices, which were advantageous only to those producers with considerable market share. They also led to famine. In view of the lack of national and international transport networks, and of a free trade policy (when prices increased elsewhere, the borders were frequently closed), such failed harvests could hardly be compensated. Periodic famines were part of the fabric of people's lives, right up until early industrialisation, and their effects were much more far-reaching than any industrial crisis since then. In 1816–17 and 1845–47, Germany (like the rest of Europe) was affected by such crises. There were failed harvests, especially the potato blight of 1845–46, which, especially in 1845–47, intensified mass poverty to a terrible degree. These events are part of the social preamble to the 1848 revolution.

The modernisation of agriculture, which one might describe as rationalisation, intensification and economisation, is intimately connected with these crises and economic circumstances. Of course, this development has several causes. They were, above all, the increase in demand due to population growth and the release of productive forces resulting from the agricultural reforms, as well as a new trend towards rationalism in ideas and attitudes, and a succession of changes in the institutional structure. The latter factors will be discussed first.

Albert Thaer, originally a physician in the Enlightenment tradition resident in Celle, was impressed by the agricultural revolution in England and its great achievements. In 1806, the Prussian regime summoned him to Möglin, where he established a model and experimental farm and an agricultural college. Later, when a counsellor-of-state and professor, he wanted to put agriculture on a scientific footing and develop it. His book, *Principles of Rational Agriculture* (1809–12), became the classic work of a new academic discipline — the study of agriculture. It was concerned primarily with overcoming a tradition of mere farm labour by means of the systematisation and quantification of experience, and by experimentation, in order to supersede merely 'imitative' agriculture and develop an 'art' of farming, applying laws and finally determining 'scientific' laws, which would lead to practical activity with a scientific basis, such as crop rotation, the systematic breeding of animals, and soil science. Secondly, in the spirit of Adam Smith, Thaer was concerned with agricultural economics, and agricultural business administration. 'Agriculture is a trade that has the purpose of making a profit or obtaining money by means of the production of vegetable and animal substances. The more sustained this profit, the more completely is this purpose fulfilled.' This was the new capitalist attitude to the economy, with its new norms: income, profitability, maximisation of profits, convertibility and accountability. There was a distinction between gross and net profits, bookkeeping, and the calculation of market opportunities. These were the logical consequences for agricultural business science. Being a farmer was no longer, like being a peasant or landowner, a given estate and inheritance, but a profession that could be chosen.

All this constituted intense provocation to traditional attitudes, and it is no coincidence that the theoretician of aristocratic opposition, Adam Müller, gave literary expression to the resistance which was then widespread. Agriculture, he claimed, was actually a duty to the state and the community. If it were guided by the economic criteria of providing for its survival, it would be 'completely stripped of its dignity and incorporated into the great mechanism of industry' ('into the universal factory of urban life', and into the market place as a 'wage-labourer'). Without the mainly inherited relationship between property and landowner, the landowner would become 'the representative of the productivity of his fields'. What was important in agriculture was not the 'brilliant coup' of a year's yield, but the 'century's yield'. Expressed thus, this was certainly ideological, but corresponded to a widely held conviction (throughout Europe!). Agriculture was held to be neither business and calculation, nor 'factory-like industrial agriculture', but a moral obligation, God's ordinance, tradition, and therefore also the first object of the state economy. Hegel — certainly progressive as far as these matters were concerned — had said that nature, rather than industry or reason, was the important thing for a farmer, and even Thaer spoke of the moral preconditions for agriculture — peace of mind, a love of creation, and an ability to get to know the ways of nature.

All the same, in the 19th century the spirit of rationalisation of agriculture, though certainly a frequently interrupted and incomplete process, made great advances. Agricultural science developed. On the empirical basis of keeping exact books at his estate, Johann Heinrich von Thünen, a student of Thaer's, worked out mathematical formulae for the different influences of distance from the factory gate on the profitability of various goods (location theory). Later, Justus von Liebig put agricultural science on the firm basis of the modern quantification and causal explanation of the natural sciences.

The effects of fertiliser and soil exhaustion were still unexplained at that time. Just as the biologists believed in a 'life force', people believed in a 'soil force' (*Bodenkraft*) in the humus. In *Organic Chemistry in its Application to Agricultural Chemistry and Physiology* (1840), Liebig analysed plant metabolism in relation to soil and air, nitrogen and minerals, and explained soil exhaustion and the possibility of mineral 'replacement'. This was more than a revolution in analytical method, for it also destroyed the concept of the generative power of the earth and the 'law' of diminishing land yields. It made possible an increase in yields which had hitherto been unimaginable. Agriculture attained a degree of emancipation from nature, the farmer no longer 'followed' nature: but was in a position to refashion it, to organise its forces. In place of the millenium-old unconscious 'over-exploitation' of resources, the 'self-conscious mastery of the farmer over his fields' was now to begin. The farmer became a kind of chemical producer, farming became technology (not art), and the earth a sort of laboratory.

In concrete terms, agriculture became less dependent on organic fertilisers, which were difficult to obtain, because inorganic materials could replace them. Liebig's mind, so critical of tradition, his academic bias and errors and his technical failures naturally entangled him and his doctrine in an extended dispute with the guild of agricultural experts, who were no longer Romantics.

The new discovery was only put to practical use with the successful production of artificial fertilisers in 1862. It is hardly necessary to mention the revolutionary expansion of the margin of food production that resulted, for it is so well known.

The academic and technical rationalisation of agriculture was spurred on by the agricultural colleges, academics and university faculties. These were Weihenstephan, near Munich (1803), Möglin (1806), Hohenheim near Stuttgart (1818), Idstein in Nassau (1818), Darmstadt (1823), Jena (1826), Tharandt in Saxony (1829), Eldena near Greifswald (1835), Regenwalde in Eastern Pomerania (1842), Proskau in Silesia (1842), Poppelsdorf near Bonn (1847), Weende near Göttingen (1851) and Waldau near Königsberg (1858), with their experimental farms, manuals and handbooks of practical farming written by their lecturers (Johann Burger in Austria, Johann Nepomuk Schwerz in south-west Germany, Max Schönleutner for Bavaria, and Johann Gottlieb Koppe).

Medium-grade, more practically-orientated agricultural schools for peasants, of a very different standard and quality, only emerged decades later. In 1857, there were nineteen in Prussia and equal number in the rest of Germany. A technical literature emerged, specifically geared to the peasantry. These included textbooks for holiday courses, pamphlets, peasant novels, almanacs and weeklies. The slow march of modernisation can be judged from their contents and size of circulation. Certainly, rational, technical and modern business-orientated agriculture did not simply replace traditional agriculture. 'Scientific' insights provoked reservations and communication problems. The subsistence ethic of old-style farming and the idea of an economy not determined by market and growth, but by mutual aid and 'morals', was just as important to the peasants as the traditions of conspicuous consumption and the priority of social status and its life-forms over business requirements among the property-owning aristocracy. In short, in no sense did all farmers embrace capitalist and technical farming methods, as was the case, to some degree, in other countries where tenant farming was practised. The modernisation could be termed lengthy and erratic.

A final element in this connection is the rapid development of agricultural associations, beginning in the late 18th century. There were fifteen such associations in Prussia in 1820, and 361 in 1852. The states encouraged the founding of these associations wherever they could, and spurred on the organization of central agricultural associations (firstly in 1809, in Bavaria). Prussia favoured organisation on a district administrative and provincial level, and in 1842 gathered the provincial organisations, that swung between free associations and semi-state bodies into the *Landesöko-nomiekollegium* (College of Land Economy). In 1837, the first pan-German association of German farmers was founded, whose congresses were to be of considerable importance (3,307 participants in Königsberg in 1863). All the associations were designed to further agricultural progress by the dissemination of knowledge and innovatory methods, exhibitions, periodicals, prices and advice, and also by the organisation of the new agricultural festivals. The Munich *Oktoberfest* (first held in 1810–11) was to become the most famous of them.

Beyond this, the central organisations represented agricultural interests to the governments, who called upon them as experts and specialists. These associations were normally run by officials, property-owners and 'friends of agriculture'. However, the idea took decades to catch on, and associations owed their slowly increasing support mainly to the wealthier peasants, whom they helped to lead out of their geographical and spiritual isolation. In 1860, there were 'only' 9,556 farmers out of a total of 21,352 members of the 'Agricultural Asociation' (*Landwirtschaftlicher Verein*) in Bavaria. The (short-lived) political associations appeared only in 1848. This situation changed at the end of the period under review. In 1862, Baron von Schorlemer-Alst founded the Christian (Catholic) Westphalian Farmer's Association, which was no longer primarily concerned with technical progress, but with representing economic and political interests, with co-operation and self-help, and with the stabilisation of a 'moral' consciousness of Christianity and landed estates. Other Catholic regions followed the example.

Through the colleges, experimental farms and associations, as well as the prevention of fatal catastrophes — such as flooding by using technical innovations such as hydraulic engineering to dam rivers, and the prevention of livestock diseases by health controls — and indirectly through the schools, the state encouraged the modernisation of agriculture. This end was also served by the taxation policy. Land was revalued on the basis of quality and yield, a process partly carried out during the Vormärz, and partly in the 1850s and 1860s. It greatly encouraged rational and economic thinking among those affected.

One important prerequisite for modernisation was the credit institution. During the modernisation process, investment capital for innovations (acquisition of livestock, machinery and buildings, and for making paths, etc.) became increasingly significant. The embourgeoisement of life and its increasing subordination to a legal code led to a price being placed on inheritance, and the introduction of the dowry and the *Altenteil* (a part of the farm reserved for the farmer when he handed the estate over to his son). The amounts increased with increasing land prices. This absorption of agriculture into the capitalist financial and legal system increased the importance of capital, even without investment. Everywhere mortgages and credits were reorganised by means of state laws, usually in the spirit of economic liberalism. There were favourable credit opportunities for large landowners in the frequently state-privileged rural areas (*Landschaften*), which had come into being during the 18th century and continued to be founded during the 19th century.

For the peasants, by contrast, things looked bad. For this reason, usury and *Hofschlächterei*, the destruction of estates by means of directed loans, were widespread in the regions populated by peasants with small and medium-sized holdings. It was not until peasant obligations to landowners were converted into monetary terms in the 1830s that some mortgage banks were created, initially in some of the medium-sized states (such as Cassel in 1832) and from 1850 onwards almost everywhere else, giving not only credit for the 'redemptions' (*Ablösungen*), but also general credits to the peasants. Finally, in 1848, Friedrich Wilhelm Raiffeisen, moved by the poverty of the years 1846–47, began to found and encourage the growth of village savings and lending banks on a co-operative basis. These first spread quickly in the small farm districts of western Germany, where part of the trade in goods was thus transferred to the village. Co-operation and self-help were the liberal (and the Christian) aim, which, in opposition to the conservative nightmare of the domination of monetary forces in the country, was intended to secure the freedom and effectiveness of the peasants in what was still a patriarchal era.

In this process of rationalisation and modernisation of agriculture, large landowners were economically and institutionally privileged by education and initiative. Indeed, it was the eastern German estates which took on board Thaer's profitability programme and were quickest to adapt to agrarian capitalism. Of course, their outlook still remained a more traditional estate-orientated attitude towards agriculture, which thus became an ideology. The peasants were much slower to follow this path into modern capitalist and rationalist agriculture, and the process was by no means completed by the end of our period.

When examining the economic reality, we must keep in mind that all statements about 'German agriculture' are inadequate abstractions, because they stretch from the eastern Germany manorial estates, over a farm in lower Bavaria on in the marsh, to a poor mountain or forest peasant, or a vintager in the Palatinate. Though, admittedly, they are abstractions without which we cannot manage.

The history of 19th-century agriculture is marked by a colossal advance in production and productivity. The proportion of farmed land (and compared with woodland and, above all, with the barren and untillable land, moorland, heath and scrub, which were often inseparable from the common pasturage) and especially of field crops (as compared with meadowland and pasture) once again increased tremendously. Fallow or almost fallow land was brought under the plough. This is especially true of the more sparsely populated east, where one may speak of a new 'land development'. Additionally, the old three-field system, in which a third of the fields lay fallow (and similarly the four- and five-field systems), was slowly abandoned. An improved three-field agricultural system which utilised the fallow by planting it with leaf vegetables, the alternation every several years of ploughed fields with pastureland (so-called alternating farming) and finally crop rotation (cereal and leaf) had considerably diminished the amount of fallow land by the mid-century. The break-up of the commons and the withdrawal of grazing rights (which had included the communal use of fallow land for pasture), i.e. individual use of the land, considerably facilitated and encouraged the transition to the new systems.

A few figures will suffice on this subject (for all their uncertainty). In 1800 there were approximately 18 million hectares of arable land in Germany (excluding Austria), of which more than 4 million were fallow, in other words 13–14 million hectares of arable land in actual use. By mid-century one may assume a figure of 25 million hectares, i.e. almost double the previous figure. Even if the fallow had not yet quite disappeared by then, it may be assumed to have done so by 1870. Seven million hectares of new arable land derived from the cultivation and intensification of what was previously commonage and 'untillable' land. The ratio of meadowland to arable land changed from 1:1.6 in 1800 to 1:2.3 by 1878. In Prussia arable land increased by 94% between 1816 and 1864 (or 7 million hectares), of which 6.5 million hectares were in the provinces east of the Elbe. Here the share of land in agricultural use increased from 26.5% to 51.4% (indeed, in Pomerania it increased from 15.5% to 52.3%), and the proportion of untillable land dropped from 40.3% to 7.1%. Overall, of course, the amount of land in agricultural use increased, from 55% around 1800 to 75%. In Austria the arable land surface rose from 8.7 million hectares at the end of the 18th century to 10.1 million hectares by the mid-19th century, a rise of some 16%. Fallow still accounted for 25% in 1830–50, but only 14.5% in 1870.

Besides the expansion of usable and arable land, an important aspect of the intensified and increased agricultural production was the sharp rise in the share of overall production occupied by so-called leaf vegetables, which made more effective use of the land, potatoes, sugar-beet, clover etc., while the proportion of grain decreased (from three-quarters at the start of the century to half of overall production in 1883), in spite of the fact that more grain was in cultivation for use as animal fodder. It was the abolition of laws ensuring grazing rights and the cultivation of fallow land that made these changes possible in the first place. Fallow land was also used for the 'new' crops. In Prussia the proportion of root crops in arable farming rose from 5.2% in 1816 to 13.2% by 1861; in Germany from 2.3% in 1800 to 11%; in Austria from 8.1% to 12.3% between 1830–50 and 1868–73. According to Henning, potato cultivation rose from 300,000 in 1800 to 1.4 million hectares around 1850, to over 3 million hectares at the end of the century, and to a proportion of 10% in Prussia by the mid-century. The calorific value of potatoes harvested from 1 hectare was 3.6 times that of grain (the so-called grain equivalent), and by that criterion, the proportion of root crops in overall production rose still further from perhaps 3% to 24% (29.9% in 1883), in Austria from 7.7% in 1783 to 18.4% in 1869.

The potato brought about a revolutionary change in the nutritional basis of the growing population — indeed, it was what enabled the mass of the rural and urban poor to survive — and it is characteristic that the great hunger of 1846 was triggered off by potato blight; it was one of the preconditions of the industrial revolution. Potato consumption rose much faster than the population, especially as from the 1860s the potato was also used to feed pigs, the poor man's meat. The second important new product was sugar-beet, which has a 6% sugar content, and was profitable once again — after the Napoleonic period — from the 1830s onwards. Sugar-beet production in Germany (excluding Austria) increased from 1,000 tons in 1836–37 to 12,100 tons in 1840–41, from 49,300 tons in 1850–51 to 244,100 tons in 1870–71, from 1.4kg per inhabitant in 1850 to 13.0kg in 1880. In Austria, development was similar (from 1,232 to 90,863 in the period from 1831–35 to 1865–69). In certain regions, sugar-beet cultivation and the sugar industry gained a key role as a secondary agricultural industry, in part on a co-operative basis. It was labour-intensive, yielded considerable profits and at the same time supported the breeding of livestock with its by-products.

Clover was planted everywhere, increasing the production of livestock (in sheds). Indirectly, through the resulting increase in the amount of available animal manure, it also increased other agricultural production by increasing the yields of other plants (in crop rotation).

Eventually, the change in production over an expanded area gave a better yield. Machines could not yet replace human or animal power, but traditional implements like the plough and the harrow were substantially improved and supplemented by a new tool, the cultivator. The ploughs, for example, cut deeper, up to 25cm instead of the previous 10cm; the 'progressive' scythe replaced the sickle outside the smallholding regions, and machine production of farming implements brought the new models quickly into use. After the Great Exhibition in London, practicable threshing machines and reapers also came into use. Large agricultural machine factories were established, like the one in Lanz in 1859, which by 1860 produced fifty types of machinery. Before artificial fertilisers came onto the scene at the end of the 1860s, the quantity of natural fertilisers was doubled by the increase in livestock numbers. Eventually, the number of workers employed in agriculture increased (by around 20% by 1850), as did output per head, even on a per hectare basis, by around 65% by 1850. Between 1790 and 1850, productivity in Austria increased by 20.7%, and again by 16.9% by 1869. Although the agricultural sector as a whole was overmanned, at least until 1860, there was still chronic under-employment in some areas, owing to the lack of other work. The increase in yield per hectare can be attributed to these factors, as Table 11 shows. It must be borne in mind here that this average increase was achieved even though large areas of marginal land were put under the plough. If the three significant factors — the increase in per hectare yield, the expansion of areas under cultivation and the shift in production (to the potato) — are taken together, it can be seen that, in terms of grain values, vegetable production increased threefold between 1780–1800 and 1870–75, and twofold by the mid-century. It was especially in the decades following the mid-century that the factors mentioned had their greatest effect.

Table 11a: Estimated yields (100kg per hectare)

	(German Reich of 1871)		
	1800	1848–52	1870–75
Rye	9	10.7	12.7
Wheat	10.3	12.3	15
Barley	8.1	11.2	13
Oats	6.8	10.9	13
Potatoes	80		90
Clover etc.	30		40

The estimates are somewhat lower for Austria, but the trend is the same.

Table 11b: Total yields (million tons)

	1800	1870–75	Increase (%)
Bread cereals	5.3	9.8	85
Forage cereals	3.9	8.2	110
Potatoes	2.2	28.0	1,173
Forage plants	1.0	6.5	550

Around 1800, approximately 50.8% of vegetable production was used for human consumption, 31% for fodder, 17.6% for sowing; in 1883 the ratio was 30.4–49.2–11.9.

Table 12a: Increase in livestock numbers (millions):

German Reich within the 1871 borders

	1800	1870–75	Increase (%)
Sheep°	16.2	25	54
Cattle	10	16.8	68
Horses	2.7	3.6	33
Pigs	3.8	7.1	87

Austria

	1800	1837	1850	1857	1869
Sheep	4.7		7.5 (+59.5%)	5.02	(–33.1%)
Cattle	5.9		7.4 (+25.4%)	7.4	(–)
Horses		1.04	1.20 (+15.4%)	1.4 (+16.6%)	
Pigs		2.9		3.4 (+17.2%)	

° The actual wool producers, the Merinos, increased by 600%.

Table 12b: Output

	1800	1818	1835	1869	1870–75	%
Weight at slaughter						
of cattle (kg)	100		160		190	+90
of pigs (kg)	40		50		75	+87.5
Milk output per						
cow° (litres)	6/700		900		1150	+75
in Austria		900		950		+5.5
Wool per sheep and						
year (kg)	0.75–1				2	+100
in Austria (kg)	1				1.20	+20

° There was a significant difference between 'normal' farms and specialist milk-producing businesses (between 600 and 1,500 litres around 1800).

Table 12c: Index figures for livestock production (1872 = 100)

	1816	1840	1864
Meat production	27.2	53.5	99.8
Milk production	41.7	65.3	94.2
Wool production	32.4	76.5	108.8

Part of the increase in agricultural production was accounted for by an expansion in animal husbandry, despite the decrease in pasturage. The essential factors at work here included an increased cultivation of crops for fodder, the transition to trough-feeding (the pig was converted from a grazing animal into a penned animal), systematic breeding and the introduction of more productive strains, and the fact that more animals were produced to be sold at market, no longer primarily for subsistence farming and manure production. The numbers of animals, especially of pigs, increased after 1830 (until then animals lost in the war had to replaced), and grew out of proportion to population growth. Only sheep numbers diminished after 1860, as a result of overseas wool imports. At the same time, animal output improved, especially in what had originally been less-developed regions, as well as in Prussia. In addition, the time it took to rear cattle for meat production shortened. If the increase in livestock numbers and yields is taken together, it can be assumed that animal production doubled by 1850, with a threefold increase by 1870–75. Thus, here also, there was a disproportionate increase in production compared with population growth.

In overall terms, then, agriculture was able to support the increase in population, and was now in a position to provide food more efficiently, which in more precise terms meant the disappearance of chronic under-provision. While it must be assumed that, for the period before 1850, the staple diet of large parts of the population consisted of potatoes and cabbage, the situation improved thereafter. Meat consumption per head rose from below 20kg to nearly 30kg between 1850 and 1870 (other estimates give a figure of around 37kg), which is, of course, an appreciable increase, even though such averages mask a very variegated pattern throughout the different social classes. There was also an increase in the consumption of butter and milk per head of population.

The increase in production in the east and north was greater overall than in the south and west. Firstly, these regions had more reserve stocks; and secondly, it was in these regions alone that the process of peasant emancipation had been thoroughly implemented. Economic activity had been liberated from corporate and feudal bondage, while at the same time the new liberalised marriage laws in Prussia had given rise to a disproportionate increase in population, which meant more workers and more mouths to feed. In the south, commonage and land protection rights — impediments to the new productivity — were abolished later, as was the tithe, which was another deterrent to change and growth. In the densely populated *Realteilungsgebiete* (multiple-inheritance regions), e.g. in Württemberg, increases in productivity were slight. In Austria the rise in productivity was generally slower, even after 1850, when the capital raised from *Ablösungen* was pumped into the mechanisation and intensification of farming on the large estates.

However fascinating the rural classes and the interplay of the relationships of power and the brute facts of deprivation and poverty, it is extremely important that attention be paid to this enormous economic development, which benefited the rural population as it did society as a whole. Successful growth did not, of course, abolish the inequalities in the rural economy, which will be dealt with presently, but it did cushion them. It was the big landowners, clearly, who reaped the greatest rewards from increased growth, and not the peasants with medium-sized and small holdings. The opportunities for powerful farming businesses to profit from expansion were greater in every respect, but the disproportionate increase in land prices for peasant holdings does demonstrate that the peasants had a share in the new (relative) prosperity.

Taken as a whole, the rise in productivity meant increased income levels for independent farmers, especially as they could now get better prices for their produce, while their costs remained relatively stable (or even fell). Of course, feudal duties, *Ablösung* and mortgage payments, nibbled away at incomes considerably, and it was only in the two decades after 1850, when the redemption procedure was better worked out and the terms were more favourable, that there was an overall improvement in income levels. The very small farms were an exception to this rule, and the fact that the rise in income was not uniform, but varied according to region and the individual concerned (the sizes of businesses varied, as did the type of soil, the competence of the farmer and the transport facilities at his disposal) should not be ignored.

With regard to the growth in production, one might also add the rider that it was not terribly great compared with that of later times, or with other agricultural areas under capital-intensive cultivation — indeed it was slight. Certainly, the increase in working productivity per head was moderate, the capital invested in agriculture less than one might have expected. The capital transfer from *Ablösungen* was only partly invested in modernisation; expenditure on consumption and inheritance disputes over highly priced properties, as well as the better returns on monies invested in railways and industry diminished investment in agriculture, and even did something to siphon money — in the case of compensated landowners, for instance — away from agriculture. Certainly, the growth in the south and west was less than in the east, and, one would guess, less among the peasants than among the large landowners. It is therefore debatable whether one should speak here, as in the case of late 18th-century England, of an 'agricultural revolution', or only of an (essentially slow) advance in productivity. This is a question of differing perspectives. For German agricultural society, which was unable for social, psychological and political reasons to participate in a phase of bourgeois-capitalist, industrialised agriculture (which would have been the model of high-speed growth), the extent of this growth, and not the fact that it lagged behind other growth rates, is nevertheless the decisive factor.

A brief word about woodland will be instructive. Here too, in the forests owned by the state and the nobility, scientific and economic timber management had asserted itself. Primarily during this period, the many fairly wild deciduous forests, all long-lived, were transformed into short-lived, more orderly and profitable coniferous forests.

A final aspect of modernisation was the integration into capitalist relationships and institutions, to which reference has already been made, and into the marketplace. Farms slowly but increasingly became market-orientated. This was true, in the first instance, of large estates, but also increasingly for the more prosperous peasants, although their market quota rarely rose above 40%. It was also true of the conurbations, where the new sales opportunities gave rise to new market products, such as milk, vegetables, eggs and bridles (for the carriage trade). Between 1830 and 1850 the number of chickens in the industrial regions of the Rhine and Westphalia rose from 12 to 80–100 per farm. Overall, one may assume a doubling of the market quota by 1870. Of course, integration into the market was a slow process and also depended on the gradual improvement in communications by rail and road. By the end of the period under review, the majority of farms were not specialised, but were all-round operations with a high proportion of production for their own consumption. The subsistence ethic continued to play an important role, and rational, economically motivated farm management progressed slowly.

One example of economic and rational modernisation which significantly affected behaviour and institutions was the introduction of insurance. With thatched roofs and open hearths, fire was an ever-present risk, in addition to hail and pests. Until then, all disasters were viewed as acts of God which had to be suffered, with assistance from one's overlords and the state. From the 1820s and 1830s, the great fire insurance companies, and later the hail and livestock disease insurance companies, came into existence, greatly encouraged or even organised by the state. The risks were quantified. Resistance from the pious, in Pomerania for instance, who claimed that this was depriving God of His 'rod of punishment', could not halt this secular process.

Of course, if one compares German agriculture with that of England, and with the judgment that Marx formulated on the basis of the English example concerning the role of agriculture in the industrialised capitalist economy, or even with conservative fears, then German agriculture was only partially integrated into bourgeois-industrial capitalism. Tenant farming was not especially important, nor were mortgages or the capitalist-monopolist organisation of sales and traffic routes so dominant that they made agriculture subservient to 'monetary forces' and the towns.

Table 13a: Land lost and gained by the peasants in Prussia (hectares)

Losses through compensation	400,000–580,000
Losses through confiscation (expropriation of peasants' land) (Estimates of confiscations of smallholdings appear to have been included in the maximum figures)	300,000–500,000
Losses through sales to smallholdings	323,000–325,000
Losses through sales to estates etc.	117,100–175,000
Total loss	1,140,000/1,580,000
Land gained from reparcelling	600,000–630,000
Net loss	510,000–980,000
Acceptable estimate: loss	700,000

This was 8.2% of the peasant farmland of 1816.

According to previous estimates, the number of farms only decreased by 1.99%; according to more recent calculations by GDR historians for Brandenburg, Saxony and Pomerania, by contrast, it was 4–8%, and around 8-2–22% for the big farms. In any event, the number of smallholdings increased sharply, by between 73% and 216% (Pomerania) according to the GDR historians, and their proportion of the land surface by 126% (by 1867) in Brandenburg.

Although agriculture became a 'rational business' in a capitalist market economy, and although its overall economic significance decreased during the course of industrialisation, its importance, as conceived by the farmers themselves, as well as by the ruling class was quite different and far more traditional. The idea of the fundamental, primary, extra-economic significance of agriculture persisted — as it did in England and in the United States, an aristocratic nation and a nation of farmers respectively — and its political and social importance was greater than its (far from small) economic importance. This was also one of the reasons for the strength of the rural, non-bourgeois, military-aristocratic power structure and political culture in Germany, especially in Prussia.

Social relations in the countryside, stratification and class structure are closely linked to the implementation and consequences of peasant emancipation. This is especially true of Prussia east of the Elbe, which will be dealt with first, in view of its importance to subsequent German history. Here the reform had initially triggered off a great wave of land redistribution, as Tables 13a and 13b are intended to show, in spite of the high degree of uncertainty associated with nearly all of the figures, which are based in part on dubious statistics, in part on estimates (e.g. of the extent of commonage before the reform).

Table 13b: Land gained by the large landowners in Prussia (hectares)

By compensation	400,000–580,000
By confiscation	300,000–500,000
By purchase	117,000–175,000
Overall gain	817,000–1,255,000
Acceptable estimate: gains	1,000,000
Gain from the reparcelling of 4.237 million hectares of commonage (1.636 million *more* than the original share of approx. 48% of land in use by noble landowners)	3,670,000
Net gain	4,670,000

According to another estimate, some 5% of private lands and 25% of the overall cultivable surface of the land owned by peasants and of the lower peasant classes were transferred to the large landowners. Some portion of the estates must have gone into the enormous increase in smallholdings and their surface areas, but is not shown here.

The peasants lost a great deal of land, although this loss is smaller than one might expect on the basis of a conventional, superficial knowledge of the matter. The demesne peasants and the 'free' peasants were not affected; the peasants subject to 'redemption' gave up very little land in compensation (only 0.375 hectares on average); though this was in fact the majority of peasants. The *Lassbauern* (leaseholding peasants) who had been subjected to regulation were much more greatly affected; they surrendered an average of 5.5 hectares, some 32.4% of all land to which the regulations applied. Somewhat less land was given up by the private owner than was envisaged in 1811–16, in part because farmers only required as much land as they had capital available for sensible use, and also because financial settlements could be reached in lieu of the expropriation of lands. But the loss of peasant lands was aggravated by the fact that instead of receiving some 52% of the commonage, they only received 14%, with the landowners receiving the lion's share, and also by the fact that redistribution drove the peasants from the better to the poorer land.

Besides land expropriations, financial compensation played a great, and for many peasants a pre-eminent role, even in Prussia. For the *Regulierungsbauern* (peasants who were subordinated to *Regulation*) it averaged 39 thalers, and for the *Ablösungsbauern* it averaged 36 thalers; one would estimate at least 642 million marks (excluding interest) for the whole of Prussia, and it was probably more. That placed a considerable burden upon the emancipated peasants and considerably augmented the productive and expansionist power of the large landowners, and greatly eased the reduction of debts, land purchases, investments (and of course speculation), increased consumption, and incomes from rents. A rough estimate of the restructuring of incomes (including the changing burden of taxation) would show the aristocracy losing perhaps 10–20%, if one excludes from feudal incomes the compensation resulting from the peasant emancipation (feudal quota), but that was vastly compensated by their great initial advantages. For the landowners disposed of land, of credit and — with the exception of the agrarian crisis of the 1820s — money, and (even at this late date) feudal obligations, thus having an enormous head start. The peasants, at least until the mid-century, were unable to improve their disposable income. But the gain in freedom and in opportunities to enjoy their own share of economic success was of incomparably greater significance.

Table 14: Relative proportions of the various sizes of property (from large landed estates to the smallest smallholdings) in Prussia in 1855

(a) of the total surface of cultivable lands (%)

	over 150 hectares	150–75 hectares	75–1.25 hectares	75–1.25 hectares
East Prussia	34.3	63.8	3.4	0.5
West Prussia	53.1	43.1	3.1	0.7
Posen	56.0	38.4	5.1	0.6
Brandenburg	48.9	45.2	4.7	1.2
Pomerania	61.8	33.7	3.7	0.8
Silesia	51.9	33.8	11.9	2.3
Saxony	28.1	57.2	11.6	3.2
Westphalia	16.6	65.0	14.8	3.5
Rhine Province	21.8	40.9	27.0	10.3
Whole of Prussia	42.87	45.70	9.01	2.42

(b) of the number of properties (%)

Whole of Prussia	0.86	19.54	28.83	50.77

In 1869, the division of land between the estates and the landowning farming communities, was as follows:

Whole of Prussia	38	56
Eastern provinces	45	49

The increase in land owned by the landowners was one of the main results of the reform, and thus eastern Germany became — predominantly in some provinces, but decisively in any case — landowner's and not peasant land. On the other hand, however — and this is the second main result — the peasants with medium-sized holdings who could provide draught animals, and were thus capable of surviving independently, held their own. They made sacrifices, but were not themselves sacrificed to the reform, and were partly able to compensate for these sacrifices by increased production.

With regard to the peasants with small holdings and without draught animals, the landowner had the opportunity of continuing to demand services or to withdraw holdings or to buy them up, to choose between land and labour, depending on demand, capital, and economic conditions. In spite of the increased number of holdings and of land, in part from peasant bequests to younger sons, the small-scale peasants were in the main forced to become agricultural labourers. They were the most unfortunate victims of land reform and, as a class, were the basis of the gain in socio-economic power of the landowners. This was the third main result of the reform.

The implementation of the reform — that is, the calculation of duties, land to be ceded, services, and land redistribution, which was the function of the special 'General Commissions' — was a protracted process that unfolded at different speeds for individual groups and for individual provinces. It triggered off countless conflicts (over 5,000 court cases) and by 1848 had largely destroyed the credibility of a bureaucracy that regulated the social and economic conditions of life to an extreme degree. The peasant uprisings of 1848, including those in Prussia, and above all in Silesia, resulted from delays in the reform, vestigial feudal laws, and the exclusion of certain groups from the reform.

The revolution of 1848 completed the process of peasant emancipation in Prussia, as it did in the rest of Germany, and even the reaction helped to bring about its long-overdue end, though partly on tactical grounds. One last law passed in 1850 made *Regulierung* and *Ablösung* possible for all, and under better conditions, no longer primarily in land, but in rents, which were financed and subsidised by a state-owned mortgage bank. By 1865, and substantially by 1860, the *Ablösung* of 12,706 peasants with draught animals, and 624,914 *Kleinstellenbesitzer*, or smallholders (78% of the peasants liable to feudal services), was complete. With that, peasant emancipation was achieved.

In socio-historical terms, the result of the reform was the development of a new three-tiered class structure in the countryside, consisting of owners of large estates, peasant farmers and agricultural labourers. This class structure was overlaid and intensified by the political power structure. Landowners and agricultural labourers deserve closer study.

The landed gentry benefited from the reform, and they reinforced their economic power and thus their position in the battle against the bourgeoisie for class domination, a battle which continued throughout the century. It seems doubtful to me that the Junkers would have been politically subordinated to the bureaucracy if they had profited less from the peasant emancipation and improvements in production. It is precisely the economically threatened classes that fight for power; even the landless aristocracy (the majority) held power in the officer corps and in the civil service. And the idea of breaking up large estates and the economic base of the Junkers was quite illusory even to the most pro-peasant reformers — a historical impossibility.

In principle, the 'feudal' lords of the manor turned into landowners and agricultural entrepreneurs, from an estate constituted by birth to a class constituted by property. This is most clearly seen from the embourgeoisement of the lords of the manor. Crises and poor economic circumstances, over-indebtedness and excessive consumption, auctions and sales, also made property more movable. Descent from and ascent into the landowning class became a significant phenomenon, especially in the first half of the century. It is estimated that more than two-thirds of the properties changed hands through auctions or sales between the 1820s and the 1870s. By the mid-century, almost half of the manors were in the hands of the bourgeoisie (43.1% of the 12,339 manors in 1856; 64% in 1880), if not the *latifundia* of over 5,000 hectares. That led to an embourgeoisement of the whole new class with respect to their business and farming methods; in addition, a quarter of the large estates were not even owned by the aristocracy.

Conversely, in the area of standards and conduct, the newcomers assumed aristocratic traditions. The aristocracy attempted, at least until 1848, to keep the bourgeoisie out of the political institutions — district assemblies and state parliaments. They were integrated, and to a certain degree were also accepted, very slowly, and some were later knighted. The rich bourgeois's love of land and of the aristocratic country lifestyle is a pan-European phenomenon, and not at all extraordinary. In Prussia, however, it did not generally lead to an amalgamation of the upper classes, especially as the younger sons of the aristocracy did not become bourgeois as in England. On the contrary, the caste-like separation and segregation of the Junkers from the bourgeoisie continued for the most part unchanged, even though bourgeois owners of manors were accepted.

Yet the new agricultural entrepreneurs were still '*Ritter*' (knights). There were residual feudal privileges, especially in the area of public and state sovereignty. These included the right to hunt on peasant land, an economically important, but above all a symbolic right of the ruling classes that made the power structure all but palpable. Additionally, there was tax exemption for some (about 50%) of the estates, and this tax exemption was supplemented by a taxation policy, and in the countryside by a system of 'class taxation', which was very soft on the upper classes — only 20% of taxes collected were paid by the owners of some 50% of property.

In addition, the knights had local jurisdiction, so-called 'patrimonial jurisdiction', and control of the local police. Admittedly, this privilege began to carry less weight as it became too expensive to employ legal experts, and the state took control. All the same, in 1837 a third of the population was still subject to such courts, and was thus not autonomous. Besides the 'patronage' of school and church, i.e. primarily the right to choose who to employ, there was the dominant position of the lords of the manor in the unreformed constitution of village communities. They continued to exercise power locally, and the choice of mayor was theirs. Peasant villages outside the jurisdiction of the manors remained weak, and no functioning autonomous peasant government could develop in or from them. Stein's idea of extending local autonomous government along the lines of municipal government to the countryside did not come to fruition, partly because that would have made the peasants independent. After all, the lords controlled the *Kreis* administrations.

After the *Gendarmerieedikt* (police edict) had been passed, Hardenberg had attempted to restrict this power, to assign to them only one-third of the votes in the *Kreistage* (*Kreis* assemblies), but especially to turn the post of *Landrat* (head) of the district administration into a state-appointed office, where previously it had been chosen from three candidates presented by the entrenched aristocracy and of their own political stripe. The attempt failed decisively in 1821. The *Kreisordnungen* (*Kreis* government ordinances) of the various provinces (1825–28) guaranteed the lords an overwhelming majority in the *Kreis* assemblies, and the associated right to recommend a candidate for the post of head of the district administration. The government attempted by means of a whole series of measures to reinforce the power of the *Rittergutbesitzer*, under Friedrich Wilhelm IV, for instance, by restricting land mobility and divisibility, or by fixing income levels in an attempt to bring back or create from scratch new aristocratic rights. Only in Posen, and after the 1831 rising, was the Polish aristocracy stripped of its control of the local police and its right to choose the *Landrat*.

To this extent, reform, which also aimed at making the peasants into state citizens through several levels of self-administration, failed. A good deal of legal, administrative and political power remained in the hands of the aristocracy. It was still a frequent occurrence for a lord to thrash someone who did not obey orders, or who did something of which he did not approve. Independence, money, and greater faith in the process of law would have been needed for the injured party to take his case to court. This power, especially over the *Kreis* assembly and police, entailed considerable economic advantages, for instance from road-building, with the granting of countless licences and concessions, and increased even further the initial advantages of the large landowners. It established the social control of the landowners over the peasants, the village craftsmen and, of course, the agricultural labourers. Feudal and capitalist superiority and the corresponding profit opportunities went in league.

Of course, the relationship between former (and new) 'lords' and the rest of the countryfolk should not be seen merely from the viewpoint of conflict and the exercising of power. Traditionally, the lords were respected, and their leadership role was more or less taken for granted. This was true in the case of agricultural progress, in the agricultural organisations, in their activities as employers and clients, and in negotiations with central government on behalf of local interests, since these educated representatives were capable of acting in public life. In the east, however, this social superiority was achieved through a naked power relationship which intensified the situation, and changed it. Before 1848, but even into the 1860s, this power structure maintained the opposition between the peasantry and the aristocracy. In the long term, of course, it reinforced the authority and dominance of the Junkers. Independent attitudes, which were able to develop among the 'free' peasantry of the north-west and south, were held back in the east.

The 1848 revolution abolished some of the the residual feudal privileges, for example hunting rights and patrimonial jurisdiction, and transitionally — until 1856 — seigneurial policing. The liberal government planned to reform the local government on the lines of the *Rhenish* model, which was intended to release the villages and *Kreise* from seigneurial authority, and in 1850 the bureaucratic reactionary government attempted such a defeudalisation of local government in the countryside, although with more plutocratic elements. Even this fell victim to the renewed reaction, and a reversion to the situtation of the Vormärz. Exemption from *Grundsteuer* (a landed property-tax) was not abolished, and was only achieved during the liberal New Era of 1860–61 with the wholesale creation of new peers. Whereas the position of the aristocracy was strong everywhere in the countryside because the reforms had stagnated, social power of the aristocracy in the countryside thereafter became restricted to Prussia east of the Elbe.

Economic success, political privilege, social power, capitalist methods, traditional proximity to the seat of power and the king, and a traditional (anti-bureaucratic) consciousness helped the landed gentry, including its bourgeois class equals, as well as the landless aristocracy, equals by birth, to continue to claim political leadership with every expectation of success. As a result of reform, the aristocracy lost 'ground' to the bourgeoisie, but retained its claims to power and withstood the bureacratic challenge of reform.

Of course, when studied at close range, the landed aristocracy east of the Elbe looks much less homogeneous and much more differentiated. There was a broad spectrum ranging from the highest nobility to the ordinary Junkers, people holding diplomatic or other offices of state (such as Bismarck) and 'simple' farmers, people with and without connections at court, Silesian magnates and owners of latifundia who played a part in the history of industrialisation, wealthy owners of large or of several estates and poor '*Krautjunkers*', rational farmers and traditional status- and consumption-orientated aristocrats, capitalist entrepreneurs and patriarchal lords of the manor. There were also the mass of intermediate patriarchal types, ranging between cultivated and uncultivated, refined and coarse 'lords', between conventional and unconventional types, between conservatives and (especially in East Prussia) liberals, between the orthodox, the pietists and the atheists. Not only do a healthy lust for power and profits, but also an ethos of duty, service and rights, and even a powerful strain of resistance to Hitler, originate from this world. This world contained not only the brutal or stupid overlord, the feudalist, capitalist exploiter or caste-conscious despiser of the bourgeois plebeians, as depicted unforgettably in polemic and satire, but also Stechlin and other characters as sketched by Fontane, who was certainly critically distanced. The refined and estimable qualities of an old ruling order were also part of the picture. Historical judgments, frequently obsessed by the struggle for economic success and for social and political power, are apt to become one-sided, and with the passage from history of this class stratum, its way of life may well recover its discreet charm.

Success, privileges, power, anti-bourgeois and non-bourgeois attitudes, all questions of caste, are of overwhelming significance to German history in the 19th and 20th centuries, and the reactionary and robust aspects of the majority of this class outweigh the considerable counter-images and all the nuances that fairer characterisations provide.

Besides the landed gentry and the peasants, the third great class in the countryside is that of the agricultural labourers. This class was not, as the Social-Liberal interpretation of the history of the 19th century assumed, a product of the reform; around 1800, a considerable proportion of the 'sub-peasant' strata, landless peasants and owners of smallholdings with a second occupation, already existed. But the situation was now aggravated. Again, there were various groups in this class. A rough-and-ready typology might run as follows: the *Eigenkätner* who tended a plot of land, (garden and potato patch) and who also had to earn money by day-labouring and second jobs; the *Instleute* who tended estate land (three to eight acres of wheat, one acre of potatoes, forage for one cow), worked full-time for the estate, for which they usually received perquisites or market shares, and their families were also obliged to perform seasonal work; the day-labourers, lodgers and hirelings, without land of their own, or fixed duties, often without their own homes, were completely subject to the vagaries of the labour climate. Finally, there were the farmhands, usually unmarried, on estates and farms, some just passing through, others resident for a lifetime. The *Instleute* were best off, at least during the Vormärz, in that their lives were relatively secure and to an extent less miserable than before the reform. However, landowners still baulked at building homes and accommodation for seasonal and 'pure' agricultural labourers. Their position had, of course, changed by the mid-century. The provision of land was reduced to gardens and potato patches; the shares in the harvest were replaced by payment in kind; and finally, though with regional variations, payment in coin took the place of remuneration in kind.

The position of the *Eigenkätner* and day-labourers was significantly worsened by the reforms. Whereas until then the commonage and pastures allowed the small and sub-peasant classes to keep cows, pigs, or goats (and also use the wood), this precondition for existence fell away after the division of the commonage to the benefit of the peasants and the lords of the manor. The poor woman of the fairy tale lost an important prerequisite for life, not only in the east, and the village community was no longer prepared to support her. The division of the commons, it was said, turned the peasants into aristocrats and the other villagers into beggars. The enormous importance of timber theft in the criminal records of the 1840s is a classic indication of this position.

Table 15: Payment in kind/payment in currency (%)

	1849	1873
East Prussia	89.2:10.8	86.5:13.5
Brandenburg	76.2:23.8	71.7:28.3
Province of Saxony	35.6:64.4	18.0:82.0
Silesia		17.5:82.5
Pomerania		80.2:19.8

Table 16: Average yearly population growth by social class in rural East Prussia 1805–67 (%)

Landed proprietors	1.4
Farmers	0.3
Eigenkätner	2.1
Instleute, day labourers	1.6
Village tradesmen	1.9
Farmhands	0.5

These sub-peasant classes multiplied at an extraordinary rate, varying according to social group, but out of proportion to the peasants. They were the main source of population growth in the countryside east of the Elbe. Whereas the number of positions available for peasants remained roughly constant between 1805 and 1867, that of the people on the estates increased by a factor of 2½, and that of the villagers (*Eigenkätner* and craftsmen) rose to 3½ times its former level. There were three principal reasons. The Prussian marriage laws placed no restrictions on marriages and the founding of families. Secondly, there was a demand for workers, required by the estates, especially for land cultivation and intensified farming (potatoes); in other words, the increase in land, margin of food production and work for some decades created new 'positions', new opportunities for subsistence, and absorbed the population growth, and even immigration. And, finally, the small peasants without draught animals who did not qualify for regulation, as well as some of the younger peasants' sons, descended into these classes, before migration and the flight to the towns.

After the 1840s, in spite of the huge increase in food production, the population pressure was palpable, poverty in the countryside, which in times of poor harvests was transformed into catastrophic distress, became a predominant feature, especially, of course, in the outworker regions (such as the weavers in Silesia), though not only there. A surplus labour pool and under-employment were the economic indicators of this crisis. Fritz Reuter depicted the crushing poverty outside Prussia in Mecklenburg, where conditions were extremely feudal (though not uniquely so), in his *Kein Hüsung* ('Nowhere to live'), and there are countless objective reports from the hungry years before 1848 of the landless masses on or below the poverty line. Population numbers and opportunities for work had fallen out of step. Railway construction, which at first had attracted armies of workers, only gave provisional relief. It was only with industrialisation and migration to the towns in the 1850s and 1860s (and emigration from the 1870s onward) that the situation changed.

It is, of course, a naïve myth that the formation of a rural proletariat was an avoidable error of a 'liberal' or feudal policy without any vision or concern for the social consequences. In reality, this proletariat already existed before the reform, and it developed in all the agricultural systems of Europe. It was the demographic revolution under conditions of overall economic stagnation that led to this process. It has to be said that neither a pro-peasant agricultural reform and policy by the middle classes nor one that attempted to protect agriculture from the freedom and mobility of the market would have greatly influenced this result.

As for the peasants, it was difficult for them, unused to market forces as they were, to become independent during the agricultural crisis. They were burdened with obligations fixed at a time of high prices, but they held their own. After 1850, these pressures persisted, but incomes improved slightly. Though the majority of the peasant enterprises in the east were small and not wealthy (under eight hectares, with soil of modest quality), an intra-village, intra-peasant differentiation into larger and smaller peasant farms came into being after the dissolution of the opposition to their masters that had determined their lives.

Things developed differently in the part of Germany west of the Elbe and outside Prussia. There were special cases, positive and negative. Mecklenburg, where there was not much emancipation, passed regulations (1824 in Strelitz, and only in 1862 in Schwerin) which were wholly in the interest of the Junkers. In Schleswig–Holstein, where an early and far-reaching reform had taken place (especially in 1805), the great development in the economic farm management and the favourable economic circumstances led to results favourable to the peasants, and to a socially balanced agrarian structure. In the regions on the left bank of the Rhine, the revolutionary dissolution of seigneurial rights, and an *Ablösung* (redemption) that favoured the peasants, continued. In the regions on the right bank of the Rhine and in Westphalia, Prussia took over the *Ablösung*, which had been introduced but had run out of steam, and implemented it following the Prussian example of 1821. In the large number of other German states where villeinage had been abolished but the dissolution of seigneurial rights and duties had not taken place, peasant emancipation was considerably delayed after 1815. Anti-French reaction (in Hanover and the Electorate of Hesse) and an old-fashioned style of government (Saxony), reform 'fatigue' and timorousness (Austria) were all involved. In southern Germany, and in part in the central German states, the legal and political reinforcement of the aristocracy was of particular importance. Just like Napoleon before them, the Congress of Vienna and German federal law placed the 'mediatised' princes, their property and rights, under special guarantee and in certain respects placed them outside the jurisdiction of individual states; the interests of the other landlords were conjoined with theirs. The upper chambers of the constitutional states gave the landlords an opportunity to block the laws on agricultural reform or to give them a pro-aristocratic complexion. The Prussian reformers knew very well why they wanted first to reform society and only then to introduce representative bodies.

The treasury, a beneficiary of the redistributions that had occurred, and epecially of secularisation, took a considerable interest during this lean period in the incomes of the landed gentry from state property, especially as they were independent of parliamentary approval. Therefore, the treasury was also a retarding factor at the time. After all, the landed gentry had hardly any economic interest in reform, as represented by the profitability of labour under free market conditions. They were patriarchal landlords, economically backward, and concerned with 'historic' rights. Only in the wake of the July revolution was the *Ablösungsgesetzgebung* (legislation concerning *Ablösungen*) once again enforced almost everywhere. In Saxony (1832) and the Electorate of Hesse (1831) it took place with the help of the mortgage banks. The reforms in Saxony and Hanover were particularly 'successful', under the leadership of the liberal-conservative Johann Stüve (1831–33); here a strong middle class was enabled to retrench without the transfer of a large amount of property.

In general, however, the process of peasant emancipation was very halting, even in the Electorate of Hesse. Owing to the bewildering multitude of rights and duties, attempts were made to implement the particular complexes of problems bit by bit, in partial reforms. The question of the legal nature of particular achievements could lead to an avalanche of court cases. The transfer of the peasants from state — and in some cases, from church — landownership proceeded considerably more quickly than that of the 'private' peasants or even of the 'subjects' of the mediatised princes. Where the *Ablösung* was voluntary, it often did not function. The legislation proved impracticable, or could not be put into practice within a reasonable time-span, so they were implemented extremely slowly. In Bavaria and Austria, the *Ablösung* of the *Privatbauern* (peasants living in independent peasant communities) was not even considered during the Vormärz; and this was also true of the *robot* — a form of labour services — in the eastern regions of Austria under the rule of the landed aristocracy). The uneven and slow pace of change increased the divide between expectation and reality; indeed it appeared that vestigial feudal rights were being deliberately preserved. Feudal hunting privileges persisted almost everywhere outside the west, which had been revolutionised by Napoleon. Peasants were obliged to deliver messages, to help during the hunt, and — especially unpopular — to work on the roads. These rights persisted particularly in Austria and Bavaria, with patrimonial jurisdiction, seigneurial policing, patronage of church and school, and control of the community and district administrations. The entry of the bourgeoisie into the 'ruling classes' was forbidden by law in the *Grundherrschaft* regions during the Vormärz.

Peasant emancipation was thus not a Jacobin revolution, even in the *Grund-herrschaft* regions, but a generally hesitant reform. Its main supporters were, first of all, the bureaucracy, which wanted to assert once and for all the sovereignty of the state over the aristocracy (and especially the mediatised aristocracy). Besides (and sometimes before) the bureaucracy came the entry of the bourgeois-liberal parliamentary majorities into the constitutional states. For the liberals, what was important was not so much an interest in rational agriculture — Friedrich List was one of the few to argue for the reform on economic grounds — nor a general emancipatory interest in equality, but above all a conviction of the importance to a liberal state of secure landownership, especially for the peasants. The peasants, though by no means the sub-peasant classes, were 'kings of freedom', according to a kind of liberal romanticising of the peasants. The peasants themselves were not the real initiators and promoters; but the post-1830 uprisings, which were simply protests rather than conceived projects, and the potential 'agricultural revolution', did exert an influence on the reform.

In the south (from Austria as far north as Baden and Nassau) the delay in carrying through the reforms finally led to the peasant revolution in the spring of 1848. In the south-west the political consciousness of the peasants had become more pronounced owing to the Napoleonic influence on the territories and estates conquered by the French and the absence of closed feudal districts. For a short while, revolution overtook reform. The response of the new liberal governments was to carry out general emancipation, and *Grundentlastung* (a compensation procedure whereby the peasant was required to cede a portion of his newly acquired land to his former landlord), and to redeem and abolish the public rights of the aristocracy in favour of the peasants. In Bavaria and Württemberg, part of the cost of this *Ablösung* was met by the state itself. In Austria, the state met one-third of the costs, while another third was written off (i.e. had to be met by the landlords). State redemption banks (*Ablösungsbanken*) were everywhere.

Nevertheless, defeudalisation in the south appeared somewhat 'delayed' compared with defeudalisation in Prussia, which was an integral part of the 1848 revolution. But this had its advantages. The reforms in the backward provinces were faster, more comprehensive, and far more beneficial to the peasants than would have been possible four decades previously. The political power of the aristocracy in the countryside now came to an end (this was not the case in Prussia) nor was it later reinstated. *Gutso-brigkeit*, the authority conferred on the landowners, and *Exemtion*, exemption from taxation or jurisdiction of land, no longer applied to villages in Austria after 1849, while in Hanover the *Landgemeindeordnung*, (local — i.e. county — ordinances) passed in 1852, broke the dominance of the aristocracy.

As a rule, the peasants did not give back a portion of land as compensation but instead paid the landowner a sum of money, usually in the form of an annuity. Henning estimates the total amount of *Ablösung* monies for Germany (including Prussia but excluding Austria) at 4.5 billion marks. Statistical calculations place it much lower, of course, at 1.5 billion. In the south and south-west, a large proportion of this money went to the treasury. The aristocracy themselves profited to very varying degrees. For example, the mediatised princes in Württemberg received an average of 394,000 gulden; the knights of the ancient orders, 55,460; and the aristocratic freeholders 24,280 gulden. The Thurn und Taxises on the other hand received 5.4 million, the Hohenlohes in Württemberg 4.4 million, the Oettingen-Wallersteins 2.8 million, and the Fürstenbergs 2.3 million gulden (and the proportions were much the same for the magnates of Austria). The aristocracy had to accept various losses on its revenues. These figures give no indication, however, of the varying degrees of success the reforms had for the peasants in places such as Hanover.

Table 17: Losses in feudal revenues % (estimated value of earlier revenues minus compensation)

Hanover	0
Baden	5–15
Brunswick, Electorate of Hesse	15
Hesse–Darmstadt	14–16
Saxony	17
Bavaria and Prussia	10–20
Nassau	20–28
Württemberg	47–48
(after further compensation for the aristocracy in 1865)	35
Austria (minimum estimate)	30–35

Both before and during the *Ablösung*, most of the common land (with few exceptions) was distributed among the peasants and came under general property law, where it became freely divisible, taxable and mortgageable. This was also the case in Prussia. In law, the principle of the division of the inheritance and of financial settlements to those heirs who yield their portion of the land (the so-called *weichende Erben*) etc. became the norm. In the *Anerbengebiete* (regions of impartible inheritance), the old customs were retained — and in Hanover were explicitly made into law — but even here heirs could be bought out with the resulting burden of debt on the property.

The lords of the manor lost their civic and jurisdictional functions as an autonomous ruling class. However, they retained their primary and secondary enterprises such as the breweries (which were negligible in proportion) and developed them to an extent, especially in the case of woodland. They also used the option of leasing their land.

On the whole, the lords of the manor did not expand their enterprises to the same extent as the squires in the east. Only a small proportion of the total financial compensation was put back into the land (with a certain exception in Bohemia). Most of it went into paying off debts or into buying state bonds or shares in the railway. Only in exceptional cases was it invested in industry, as in the case of the Hohenlohe-Öhringen family, who invested in the industry of Upper Silesia. The aristocracy lived partly off the land and from their subsidiary enterprises and partly on income earned from capital. A few, at least, would with time have to seek income from work in bourgeois occupations. In spite of the loss of their public functions, the proximity to the court and the pre-eminence they had inherited in the senior ranks of the army and the civil service as well as in the diplomatic corps (though this now depended on passing examinations and on competence) remained a privilege of their class. This was also true of their involvement in politics beyond the level of the first chamber. Just as important was the opportunity the landed aristocracy had to develop into a regional and rural elite separate from the farming community, churches, associations or parliamentary representation, and to combine the superiority they had in education, wealth, and power with the new-found trust of the country-dwellers — with whom they shared opposition to the city — and use it for the public good. These were ways in which the aristocracy of south and west Germany, who were less domineering and power-conscious — though less successful than their east German counterparts — played a role in the leadership of the country or, in Austria's case, maintained a dominant position. All in all, the aristocracy succeeded in retaining their families, property and rank, by both formal and informal means, through disinheritance, or forbidding marriages or by sanctions, such as those against 'bourgeois' marriages.

The peasants were on the whole better off, especially after 1848. Admittedly, the burden of taxation did increase overall, to the extent where those peasants whose lands had not been redeemed suffered for a time during the Vormärz. There were also the financial burdens of the mortgages and the cost of maintaining the land once it had been redeemed. But after 1850 disposable incomes increased, even despite rising agricultural prices; if the reforms were favourable, the *Ablösung* payments could be deducted from taxes; and public works, such as building paths or regulating streams, benefitted the peasants themselves. The constitutions of the communities developed and strengthened peasant self-rule in the villages (the so-called 'despotism of the peasants' with which the Bavarian nobility was confronted after 1848).

Of course, the relationship between the peasants and the nobility and the various forms of emancipation were not the primary determining factor in the peasants' situation and destiny. The differences in agrarian structure and the variations in the size of farm and quality of the soil were of increasing importance. This is clear from a comparison between the large and medium-sized farms in areas of the north-west where the custom of a principal heir persisted (the *Anerbengebiete*), where 45% of the land was owned by the large farmers. A similar situation persisted in old Bavaria, and can be determined by comparing the small peasants in the *Realteilung* (partible inheritance) regions in the south-west, in Hesse and the Rhine province, where 80% of all farms were of less than 5 hectares, and only accounted for a third of the overall surface area. There were obvious differences between those who farmed good land and the poorer peasants who farmed the soil of the coastal moorlands, heathlands, woods and mountains of the same region; or between those who were dependent upon the market (such as wine-growers) and those who were self-sufficient.

The growth in population, the shortage of land, of work and of credit were also important factors. In the areas where the *Realteilung* system persisted, such as the

Electorate and the Grand Duchy of Hesse, parts of Thuringia, the Rhineland, the Palatinate, Baden, Württemberg, and Franconia, poverty increased among the smaller farmers and other dependent trades during the Vormärz. The pressure of population grew, despite attempts to restrict marriage, and farming was barely able to create new jobs. The cottage industries underwent a crisis; industry as such still did not exist. In the poorer mountain areas, the rural economy was combined with subsidiary work — forestry, charcoal-burning, iron and metal manufacturing, salt-works, and home 'industries', such as making bowls, toys or clocks. List has described the meagre existence of those in the regions where estates had been fragmented or 'pulverised', and where there was not enough fodder or straw available to make it worthwhile to keep livestock. 'The majority of farmers, [who] spend their lives farming and eating potatoes', fell into a rut, unproductive and underemployed. Underemployment and poverty were commonplace. This was the rural pauperism of the 1840s and of the old Germany. In the Electorate of Hesse, a third of the population was impoverished; in Spessart, the mountain peasants survived on a gruel of bread and water, thickened with a little milk for breakfast, and potatoes with sour milk for lunch, and ate the broth again for supper. As List wrote in 1844 of south-west Germany, 'Potatoes with no salt, soup with black bread, oatmeal porridge, here and there black dumplings. Those who are better off are lucky to see a modest piece of meat on the table even once a week, and most of them only know of roasts from hearsay.'

This gradual process of impoverishment exhausted, and even outweighed any benefits the *Grundentlastung* might have had for the smaller farmers, at least before 1848. The boundaries between the poverty of the small farmers and the poverty of other trades — manual labourers, home-workers, day-labourers, all hard hit by the division of common land, as well as the loss of grazing land and wood — were not well marked. In the west and the south too, the numbers of day-labourers increased, although many still had their huts and their gardens. Since peasant children frequently worked for periods as farmhands, the gulf between farmhands and peasants was narrower than in the east. In the south and west, wood-thieving and poaching was common even among the children. Even the smallholder cultivating his potatoes no longer had any straw and came to depend on the forest for bedding material. The memory of the old rights of commonage gave rise to an anarchic rebelliousness against the new-fangled bureaucratic state, embodied in the forest warden, and hence the poacher became a folk-hero of the common people. He became mythologised in song and legend, especially in the Alpine lands. Only after the 1850s, when emigration was beginning to accelerate and industrialisation, increased sale of farm products, greater productivity overall, and better communications, were all starting to have an effect, could pauperism be defeated.

Even though the shared opposition to their masters (and to the state), and the shared poverty, had a unifying effect, hints of a class structure within the village were plain to see. As Büchner discovered, the opposition was not between 'hovel' and 'palace'. Even the smallest farmers had their own homes, and in cases of conflict, as on occasion in 1848, the community of home-owners turned against that of the hovel-dwellers.

Before 1850 the peasants only had a limited share in productivity and the opportunities afforded by the market, and even this depended on the size and location of their land. Nevertheless, whereas in 1800 a farm became viable (depending on the quality of its soil) when it consisted of only 4 hectares of land in the west and 8 in the east, by 1850 farms of 2 to 3 hectares were considered viable, thanks to potato farming. After 1850 the large and medium-sized farmers had an ever-increasing share in growth. The differences between villagers and peasants became more sharply defined, based on the size of their farms. Wages for agricultural workers and farmhands, almost completely static until 1850 owing to surplus supply, rose by 50–100% up to 200 thalers per year as a result of industrial competition. They still averaged 20% below the wages of industrial workers. Even outside Prussia, certain rules governing the *Gesindeordnungen* (Servants' Ordinances) made it difficult to change employer, forbade the formation of any associations and permitted unlimited working hours. This ensured the low social status of farmhands and agricultural workers. Living conditions even among the farmers were generally pitiful.

In spite of all the progress (and beyond mere statistics), one must not forget how difficult and desolate life was, how hard the families worked, the isolation from city life, the long distances which had to be travelled to the notary, the courts or the doctor (a fact reflected in the death rate), not only for the small farmers, but even for the medium-sized farmers, notwithstanding the small fortune their land might be worth.

The social contradictions and tensions of life on the land (in both east and west), between masters and peasants, the larger and smaller farmers, the landed and the landless, are all eclipsed by two areas of common interest which were decisive after 1848. These were the economic interests of farming for both large and small producers (and here, both nobility and peasants worked in tandem), and, still more fundamental, the common interests of the country people as opposed to the world of the city. The interests of the soil included those who were not farmers. Village craftsmen, for example, identified themselves more closely with other villagers than with urban craftsmen: they were really peasants practising a trade.

This leads to the last aspect of the peasant mentality, the decisive factor in existence and behaviour, in importance for surpassing physical conditions, economic climate, the different forms of production and the position of the peasants within the structure of rule and class. It is the poverty factor, which has been very thoroughly covered by the anthropologist Jeggle.

As was the case for everyone outside the upper classes in older societies, peasant life was determined primarily by immediate and crushing poverty. In the case of the larger farmers, poverty was merely an imminent threat. Life was determined by the fight to survive, and survival could only be ensured through work. Life was work. It meant cultivating the land in order to survive and to enable one's family to survive. The peasant was dependent on nature, which provided for all his basic needs (something which hard work and industriousness were not able to guarantee). And yet, nature was also hostile. It was foreign, strange and uncontrollable. Accepting the rule and inexorability of nature was an essential part of life. The field, the beasts and his tools were man's immediate environment and they determined his life. The peasant's feelings, thoughts and actions were therefore more closely linked together and more consistent than those of the more mobile city-dwellers. The one thing specific to the peasant was the possession of land, of fields, and these formed the basis of peasant existence. All the peasant's thoughts and deeds revolved around the soil. Property, large or small, determined the fate of the individual or his social position. First and foremost, that meant inherited property. Inheritance and property were security against poverty, against misfortune, against the possibility of falling out of nature's favour. And added to work and property were the house and the family — that was only natural. Without them a person was nothing. To be unmarried was to be a social outcast, for in old age one became a burden on others and on the community. House and family were the primary units of work and production. They were the main insurance against poverty, sickness and old age. The family were part of the property. They belonged to the house, for the house gave the family its name. Marriage was the marriage of property and the marriage of workforce. It was a way of acquiring land and of providing for old age. Even an outburst of purely sexual passion could be harnessed and put to use through the illegitimate children it might produce. Whether male or female, child, adult or grandparent (the three generations lived together), life was determined by position within the family. One's family of origin was just as important as the immediate family, and this included the more distant relatives in the villages, who made up a dense network of communication and control. The family into which one was born determined inheritance and the circles into which one could marry. It was more important than individual ability. To a much greater extent than in the city it determined social standing and social destiny. Family determined social class.

This relationship between work, property and family was deeply embedded into the workings of the village. The task of the village, a community which was to some extent still based on common need, was to provide the basic necessities of life. These were a well and a bakery, woodland and livestock, a school, a midwife and a fire brigade. It also provided fences, paths and boundaries which both joined and separated. Comprehensible, practical, commonplace and inevitable, saturated with different sympathies and antipathies — the village community was certainly not harmonious or happy, not by a long chalk, nor was it a society determined by contract, delegation or anonymity. Everyone knew everyone else, and there was nowhere else to go. Despite and because of these tensions, the village was the world. It was the world in which one lived, separated from the larger world outside.

Peasant life in the village was surrounded by and steeped in religion. Faith in God, prayer, processions and the all-pervading influence of Catholicism existed to counter the strangeness and uncontrollability of nature. The church represented the sensual dimension of life. Through the Sabbath and the various festivals of the community, it also came to represent a dimension of life outside work. The pastor and the priest (the latter so strange because of his celibacy) came to represent something which was different in the village, the 'other', even if it was still accepted. One's adherence to Catholicism or Protestantism, even if only by custom or convention, thus became as important as the agricultural structure of the region or one's economic and social status.

Property, the purchase and amalgamation of property and the division of inheritance were the basic categories of life. Relationships, especially between close relatives, were ambivalent. A farmer would plough with his brother but still try to stop him from gaining the advantage in the division of inheritance. Life was spent between co-operation, for which one was dependent on the family and the neighbourhood, and competition for inheritance and dowries among siblings. Life was a struggle for dominance between the generations. There was the desire to disempower one's parents but to be 'well' treated by one's own children (i.e. given enough to cover one's own needs). There was conflict between the generations. When should the 'young' be allowed to marry; when should the old 'hand over'? Conflict and court cases over care of the elderly were typical of this.

Relationships were not particularly personal or individual, nor were they particularly loving. They were filled with latent distrust, marked by cheating and the fear of being cheated, but overlaid with ritual formalities and customs. Custom, what is done and what has always been done, was carefully monitored by the village, and left a lasting mark on behaviour. This encouraged behaviour which was conservative, non-individualist, unsentimental, and matter-of-fact. Custom, the family and property would limit any deviation from the norm. Differences in market position (or in taxation) did not differentiate people as much as in the cities. At best, only the criminal showed any strong individuality. This static aspect of the village, the aversion to innovators, activists and organisers, went hand in hand with particularism. The farm, the village and the interests of the peasants stood at the centre of their world; they were not interested in ideas, principles, or generalities. This accounts for the intelligentsia's violent criticism of the backwoods mentality of the peasants, who could not see beyond their own church steeple.

These proprietary attitudes caused much suffering among the poor, the unemployed, the illegitimate, and even the old. The village as an entity regarded them all as a potential threat to its provisions for food and accommodation, and tried to deflect as much responsibility for them as possible. Orphans, for example, were handed over to whoever demanded the least money for maintaining them. Everyday life was filled with such social harshness. All the same, in spite of acute tensions within the village, these values and norms were accepted by those who had little or no property, unless, that is, they moved on. The sense of belonging, encouraged and strengthened by various ties and dependencies, and various privileges afforded to the better off, often outweighed or bridged the divisions between the classes, and from the outside (and in comparison to outside) it appeared as though the country folk were reacting as a unit.

Admittedly, there were strong group-specific differences in the peasant mentality, as it has been described here. The complex systems of the inheritance, ownership and division of property in areas where there was a single heir had a different (though no more harmonious) structure as already stated. Wilhelm Heinrich Riehl, a contemporary, described, for example, the isolated farmers of the heathlands as rigid and backward, cut off from the rest of the world. The poorer peasants in the forests, on the other hand, were men 'of heart and fist', whose lives were coarser and livelier, perhaps even more 'moral', than those of the rich, landowning peasants, those heartless misers and surly rural proletariat who made short shrift of each other. In parts of central and south-west Germany, in the mid-Rhineland for example, the boundaries between city and country were more fluid, and the rural mentality was much less marked.

Experiences of the outside world started to have a greater effect on village and peasant life during the course of the century. The changes and advances in economy and technology gradually altered farming behaviour (albeit unevenly). It did not (yet) alter the underlying psyche at all. The overturning of territorial laws and legal systems revitalised power relations and legitimacy. Military service, school and the press brought a piece of the outside world to the village. The dissolution of the feudal system — due to outside forces — once again altered the village, and at the same time made it more independent. Bureaucracy and 'the state' made themselves increasingly felt in different areas of people's lives, in the administration of state justice, in the many trials, the tax demands, and the regulation and sequestration of land (for roads or railways, for example). On the other hand, with regard to river control and the expansion of communications, the state was indirectly beneficial. The 'common good' was perhaps not only the good of the government or the state, and administration was more than just control. People rebelled in the old tradition against duties and sacrifices to an anonymous 'authority', beyond the horizons of their own immediate interests. Yet they also wanted to share in the advantages it offered. The harder they struggled against the world of the state, the more they became entangled in it. As the village was their whole world, the liberal institutions and resurgeance of self-government in the villages took root in the west and south-west. Peasants were proud of their local authority and community politics became their whole experience of politics in general. In some areas, such as the Palatinate or Thuringia, the fabric of religious life began to crumble — the pastor was turned away, for example, if he turned up without an appointment. In general, after the middle of the century (and not only in the opinion of nostalgic romantics) customs, dress and folk art went into decline. But where the ties of community and neighbour were weakened, 'modern' innovations, such as the voluntary fire brigade and choral societies of the 1850s and 1860s strengthened them once more.

In spite of such experiences and new modes of behaviour, the power of custom and tradition and the parochialism of interests remained dominant throughout the period. The farmers and the people of the land did not regard themselves as producers, but as a 'class' with their own values and norms, as opposed to the people in the city, whether bourgeois, worker, intellectual, or civil servant. Herein lay their obstinacy. And they were much less individualised and differentiated, less abstract and rational, less specialised, but incomparably more parochial than the city folk. In this sense (a purely pre-political and apolitical one) they were old-fashioned and conservative.

Here the question of the political outlook and orientation of the peasants arises, and its significance for German political history. Admittedly, there was opposition to the feudal system of landownership, as well as to the authoritarian bureaucratic system. This caused the peasant unrest and subsequent full-scale peasant revolution of 1848. There was something democratic, emancipatory and egalitarian in all of this. Yet these words are misleading. The radical agitation of the townsfolk in Hesse in the 1830s encountered a wall of rejection from the peasants. The demands of the peasants were not abstract or theoretical. They were concrete and directed against their tormentors, against local officials, and against unjust situations. For example, they would engage in lengthy arguments, based on the old laws, about the woods, or about the achievements of their overlords. Or they would argue in biblical fundamentalist terms. Of course, the 1848 uprising was directed against the whole feudal system, and even in part against the redemption procedure, but this time without recourse to the old laws. In this lay its great proximity to democracy. Yet in economic and social terms, the demands were conservative, since there was no capitalist economy with increased production or competition. It was a moralist economy based on a fair minimum for all. For this reason, the peasants were anti-Jewish and essentially anti-urban.

Politically, they stood for the village community, and the autonomy of the community — under a king. Liberal or democratic slogans — for citizens' rights, constitution, nation — left them unmoved. They did not stand for any emancipatory social policy for any one class; they stood for specific interests. In some ways, they could not be classified as leftist or rightist. It was due to this and to the quick fulfilment of their demands, that they lost their common ground with the democrats in 1848. Riehl described the peasants as the 'great conservative force' of the time, saying they had stopped before the thrones and thereby saved them. He said that they were conservative not for theoretical reasons, but out of instinct and custom. They were opposed to both the bureaucratic and liberal levelling of society according to abstract principles. On the other hand, Marx and Engels considered the peasants conservative because of their parochial narrowness. Certainly, the peasants were anti-feudal and anti-state, mistrustful of authority and bureaucracy, with the exception, of course, of the distant king, a sacred symbol. They stood in latent opposition to every establishment, and there was always something populist in their conservatism. But the opposition to the capitalist, industrialist and intellectual world of the city, and their rationalist anti-clericalism, was fundamental. The peasants were not a party (nor did they form one), and they barely allowed themselves to be drawn into politics over an extended period. But they were a latent conservative force. The conservatives, particularists, the patriots, the orthodox, Catholics, royalists, in short the anti-liberals, found their strength and support on the land in the 1860s.

Certainly, there were areas which were liberal — in central Germany and in parts of south-west Germany for example. Here conservatism crumbled. There was also the split between the different religious denominations, where Protestant peasants voted liberal in opposition to a 'Catholic' party. Or there were other differences, such as that of the Palatinate and old Bavaria. Liberal landowners were putting down roots, and the structure of conservatism itself was provocatively feudal-authoritarian. All these factors played their part. In the constitutional conflict of Prussia, the liberals intermittently gained majorities over large areas east of the Elbe, admittedly not in the third class, but certainly in the second class of voters (large and medium-sized farmers). All the same, these were rather special conditions, and liberalism was unable to command great masses of 'natural supporters' in the rural areas. This considerably diminished its chances in Germany since even by 1871 society was still predominantly rural. The radical democratic potential that existed among the peasants, in spite of their conservative way of life, could not be mobilised. There was no urban bourgeoisie conservative enough to provoke a left-wing protest among the peasants, as had been the case in Scandinavia and Switzerland. And also, as a result of the several decades elapsing between secularisation and peasant emancipation, there was no massive peasant anticlericalism, as there had been in France, which could turn into a general atmosphere of irreligiousness. Neither was there the same tradition of those who had emerged victorious from the revolution. In spite of class tensions in the country after the end of the feudal agrarian constitution, the countryside itself was, in fact, more of a stabilising factor when it came to a system of values, ways of life, religion and politics, compared with the mobilising tendencies of the city. Any mobilising effects technology or the economy might have had on the countryside were counteracted by the social order, the mentality and political orientation found there.

5. Industrialisation

The greatest achievement of 19th-century Germany, and the factor which determined the whole fate of the epoch, was, of course, here as elsewhere, industrial revolution. It was a technological revolution in the ways and means of production; it was a capitalist revolution in the economy, machinery, the factory, the market and growth; and it was a revolution in all the social, political and mental consequences of these aspects. Technology was no longer limited and conditioned by nature. It was no longer tied to producing imitations or models of nature. It could produce something new, something which had not been seen before, such as machine tools and engines. Coal and iron, themselves products of human activity, came to replace wood, which hitherto had been the main raw material. Through the steam-engine, coal came to replace the natural sources of energy — man and beast, wind and water. Procedures such as exact measurement far exceeded man's natural capabilities. The old ways of working were abandoned, and old-fashioned 'skill' became (for a short period) irrelevant.

Invention was no longer a chance occurrence. It was planned, based on quantification and systematic and methodical procedure. It was based on science. Man became the master of nature. Work was replaced by mechanical forces, which, once produced, could be deployed anywhere and at will. And this technology was used not just in production, but also in the transport system. In production, the factory became the place where work tools could be combined with motors and engines, and where division and co-operation in working procedures could be organised. At the same time, a system of economy came into force which was no longer simply directed towards nourishment and livelihood, but towards the maximisation of profit, and which turned everything into money and property, into capital. And because capital was abstract, i.e. fungible, its multiplication was unlimited, which set its dynamics in motion. This form of economy was rational, calculable, it quantified everything, it was impersonal, totally objective. In a model environment it related to an anonymous, unknown market. Whoever did business in this way was in competition with other economic factors — not in harmonious solidarity, or in the protected, isolated, economic spheres particular to each. Indeed, it was this competition that brought the modern market into being.

The type of economy, which we call capitalist, came into force in the 19th century. After its emergence in banking and trade, it appeared in manufacturing. The driving force behind this type of economy was the mechanisation of production. It was both these aspects, mechanisation on the one hand, and capitalism, market and competition on the other, which made innovation and progress into a new, decisive criterion for production. It was all of this which finally brought about the 'leap' into the modern economy and the growth of the gross national product, a self-sustaining growth. It was this which brought about the predominance of industry over agriculture and other sectors of the economy. From the viewpoint of economic theory, these factors may be linked in very different and more rigorous ways. That is not at issue here. The important thing here is that they are all interdependent. Industrialisation in the context of this book means the transformation of production, the revolution of industry and the preconditions for these developments, as well as the parallel phenomena and the effects of the new production techniques on German society.

What exactly were the preconditions for industrialisation in Germany? Of course, some of the European heritage which formed part of these preconditions — rationality and science, the legal system and the structure of life in the city — was already at work here. There was the same curiosity and the same ambition to master nature, the same asceticism and work ethic. What was important was what was specific to Germany. Germany had iron, and although it had not yet been exploited, it had coal. There were the old areas of trade such as the Bergisches Land where metalworking was practised and Wuppertal with its textile trade, to name but two. But these were still crafts, still cottage industries. They were orientated towards export, and a high proportion of the population was involved in the trade. There was a whole reservoir of trained workers. There were the mining, steelmaking and metalworking regions, dispersed far and wide, especially in the hill regions, where ore, wood, coal and water power were all available. There was a well-developed work and professional ethic and a social discipline rooted in religion. Science and schools were held in high regard by society. And in the long term, the Protestant desanctification of the world had created an environment which was favourable to the innovatory potential of the technicians and entrepreneurs.

Enlightened absolutism separated official interests from self-interest. It increased bureaucratic rationality, which was a prerequisite for continuous, calculated business activity, and managed to break through the old order of the guilds, which with their countless regulations were inimical to innovation. The aristocracy, where it controlled access to minerals, forests, a workforce, money and power, helped to found enterprises. The growth in population increased the available workforce and encouraged individuals to develop their potential. Germany was in no way comparable with a developing country of today, because it already had an infrastructure, capital and a reasonable standard of living.

The factors which inhibited industrialisation were far greater in comparison with England. Geographically, commerce with Germany was difficult, and it did not represent a coherent market. There was a shortage of raw materials, of wool and of known and accessible sources of coal. Germany had remained backward in terms of trade, and without the stimulating effect of colonial expansion, had been pushed out of the world economy. It was a favourite setting for wars and the devastation wars could wreak. It was not integrated politically, or in terms of taxation or customs duties, not even within the large states. Division of labour and the integration of the market economy had barely begun. The marked divisions between the classes, poor mobility and a guild mentality made the guiding principles of society the maintenance of the status quo and security, considerably restricting initiative, innovation and freedom of activity. Entrepreneurship was not highly prized, and the new breed of man had difficulty in obtaining startup capital. The aristocracy and the landowners had the most prestige. Even existing businesses were orientated towards preservation and tradition, not expansion and profit. They revolved around security, not risk. Saving, not investment, was the prevailing ethos. Competition was socially decried in a moralistic and harmonious concept of the economy. The rationalising and innovative effects of the price mechanism were therefore weakened. The princelings and the aristocracy, together with the guild mentality, had caused the stagnation of the old trading and industrial cities and had driven new trade out of the towns. Feudalism and taxes had diminished mass purchasing power, while the consumption of luxury goods and military expenditure did little to encourage growth.

Huge variations in the distribution of wealth restricted demand for standardised industrial goods. Poverty, low demand and the lack of industry all operated to create a vicious circle. Nowhere was full production capacity ever exploited, the workforces hardly ever fully employed.

The first steps towards mechanisation were taken during the last decade of the 18th century. The first mechanical cotton-spinning mill was opened in Ratingen in 1784, and the first Arkwright steam-operated spinning-jenny was imported in 1794. In 1785, the first steam-engine was used in mining in Bergbau (Mansfeld). After 1794, coke-fired blast furnaces, iron casting and steam-engines were introduced into the Upper Silesian mining region. The Prussian mining officials and the magnates who held the mining rights and who had introduced their feudal employment regulations into industrial mining were the innovators here. But overall these were marginal achievements that neither signified nor introduced a technological revolution. The economic climate, export and population growth in some areas encouraged a certain boom, but the drive towards technological innovation which might have resulted from this was absorbed by the excess workforce.

In this context, too, the Napoleonic era created a new situation. On the one hand, the reforms in part created and in part improved the basic conditions for industrialisation. State sovereignty and state citizenship were asserted over feudal and particularist forces. The centralist bureaucratic state was one which was rational and calculable. The new legal systems were geared towards the freedom and security of property. They dissolved (at least in principle) the society based on class. The freedom to chose one's abode and one's occupation helped create a mobile society which was geared towards occupation and performance. Property, mobility, legal security and a limiting of state activity were, however, preconditions for the emergence of a market economy. Certainly, there were differences. In the regions on the left bank of the Rhine, French law and French institutions fostered the development of industry. Prussia had a liberal and more progressive economic and social policy (despite certain important exceptions). The other states had a more conservative course in social and economic policy.

However, even more important were the contrasts with the pre-reform period. The emancipation of the peasants had heralded the revolution in agriculture. This ensured the subsistence of the population during the period of intense industrialisation. Indeed, it evened out the balance of commerce, which in turn gradually strengthened demand and freed the workforce potential for future industry. The redistribution of territories brought together the smaller areas under larger ones. The newly discovered truth that all loyalties and affiliations were essentially fickle changed attitudes and expectations and, in the long run, eroded traditionalism. This was directly true of economic behaviour. The main experience was one of constant flux in the political, politico-economic and economic situations of the Napoleonic era. Ownership and economic opportunities were fiercely risky: a sudden rise due to unusual opportunities (the Continental Blockade, for example) might soon be followed by an equally unexpected collapse, or both could happen simultaneously. This helped mobilise attitudes and the willingness to take risks.

On the other hand, there were fundamental disadvantages. Wars and devastation, unproductive expenditure, the appalling way in which Napoleon sucked the economy dry — all led to general economic recession. There was a fall in purchasing power, blockages in production, lower returns, lack of capital, indeed general impoverishment. The overwhelming stagnation in trade throughout this period only served to increase the gap between German and English industry and technology. Where there were any machines, they were out of date by 1815.

When the Continental Blockade ended, the German market was defenceless against the overpowering pressure of extremely cheap English exports. This brought much of industry into crisis and slowed down development. Finally, the Continental Blockade and the subsequent competition from England substantially changed the regional economic structure of Germany. The regions on the left bank of the Rhine shared the economic climate of the French economic empire. The north-east German and part of the Silesian textile trades, however, could not survive the loss of the export markets or the fall in purchasing power. Only now did eastern Germany become a predominantly agricultural country. Only now did the contrast between a trading western and central Germany and the agricultural east become a basic fact of German history. From this point of view, the Continental Blockade was of the utmost importance for the subsequent history of Germany.

These difficulties persisted after 1815, and new ones arose. The distance between England and its junior competitor, Germany, increased still further. The German export markets had largely fallen to England, which simultaneously increased the levies on German grain imports. Investment costs of machinery — insignificant at the beginning of industrialisation — had greatly increased. This restricted any propensity to invest, as did the low level of demand. The Germans bought second-hand, old-fashioned machinery, and this ensured that the English retained the advantage. Demand within Germany, especially during the agricultural crisis, was throttled. Debtor states followed policies of deflation — there was no inflation or monetary expansion to encourage new enterprise. Workforce potential still exceeded demand. The redistribution of territories had not led to a common customs zone or a common market within Germany, and the incentive for industrial mass production was therefore limited.

Finally, Germany was, technologically speaking, a developing country. So it was not only English machinery which was required, but also initially English mechanics. The English attempted to impede such 'exports'. But the Germans circumvented this. English foremen and mechanics, who had to be handled with extreme care, as they held the monopoly, played an exceptional role in the early history of German industry (and in the education of German mechanics). Some of them became large-scale industrialists, such as Mulvany on the Ruhr or Douglas and Thomas in Austria.

In spite of all these restrictions, industrialisation began to make itself felt during the mid-1830s, and by 1850 was in full swing. Before the individual sectors in which this process took place are examined, consideration must first be given to the role of the state. In the past, it has frequently been exaggerated. If one compares it with present-day developing countries, it is immediately apparent that the state in Germany neither created nor initiated industrialisation. It did not encourage it at any cost. It tolerated it, created the basic conditions it needed, and encouraged it indirectly, and even unintentionally, by somewhat limited measures. These included the development (for both economic and military reasons) of the communications networks, i.e. the roads, canals, rivers, and later on the railways. Undoubtedly, by far the most important was the creation of a wider customs territory (and with it, a wider economic territory), and the establishment of a German customs union, or Zollverein, in 1834. This will be discussed later.

Then there was the old-fashioned system of taxation, which was for the most part a burden on consumption and on land. Even the Prussian personal and class taxes, a crude precursor of income tax, greatly spared (even if unintentionally) any income from industry or trade. Direct state investments were rare. The *Preussische Seehandlung* was a famous exception. It was a bank and and holding company, which, under the leadership of its president, Rother, helped to found and fund industrial development projects (such as the first Prussian mechanical worsted mill in Wüste-Giesdorf or the Egells engineering works in Berlin) on a non-profit basis. It was not always successful. The state-run mining administrations in the West Prussian provinces, in the Saar region and in Bavaria also tried to encourage technological progress.

The most extensive network of state measures was manifested in what we refer to as commercial and industrial sponsorship. Encouraging private initiative and releasing economic forces became the political imperative for a group of reformers in Prussia. (They included senior civil servants like Kunth and Beuth, some heads of provincial administrators and, in Baden, the *Staatsrat* Nebenius, as well as the journalist Friedrich List.) They argued for the liberation of entrepreneurial spirit, for the importance of taking risks, by overcoming traditionalism, and indolence and by promoting mobility, productivity and competition. They wanted people to be 'educated for industry' and to use machines. Machines would be able to counteract the economic hardship which was a result of the growth in population and even bring about progress. There was a reaction against the rising sentimental traditionalism. As Beuth put it, no more could 'a humane general, out of an aversion for gunpowder, win battles with bows and arrows' than could 'fantasies about the domestic bliss of the cottage spinner and poetry about the spinning-room slow the march of progress or set limits on the spirit of invention.' The civil servants wanted to modernise the economy, and that often meant liberalising society after the model of the marketplace of individuals (as in Prussia), or founding the state on a constitution (as in Baden, for example), because they saw political participation as an important motive for productivity.

Education was the key to this commercial sponsorship. 'Only the educated person is able to overcome the force of sloth in himself and find pleasure in activity'; thus, according to Kunth in 1816, only 'education' would help in the competition with other industrialised countries, such as England. And in 1824 Beuth said, 'Where science is not introduced into commerce, commerce is not on a secure footing, and there is no progress.' The development of technical education, business schools, polytechnics and technical colleges was therefore at least one area of state support for commerce, even if it was not the main one. It will be discussed in another context. These measures only had any real effect after the 1850s and 1860s. Only then was technology made completely 'scientific'. Only then did technical advances become dependent on science and schooling. Krupp and Siemens were great, but self-taught, inventors and innovators. Only now, with the process of industrialisation at full throttle, did science and the educational system become significant factors in the development of industry. Only now did general secondary education make any noteworthy contribution to the education of skilled workers and apprentices. Technical education did play a part in early industrialisation, but did not have the importance that its supporters attributed to it.

Besides the educational structures, the state sponsorship of commerce extended to organising trips abroad for young technicians and civil servants, especially to England

and even to the United States. Industrial exhibitions (with new machinery often smuggled out of England) were periodically organised and prizes were awarded. For example, Egells, who was a fitter, was sent to England by Beuth and later received English lathes from him for his engineering works. Borsig, later to become a locomotive-builder, a pupil at the Berlin *Gewerbeinstitut* (Institute for the Trades), was his foreman. Everywhere, civil servants were founding associations for the 'promotion of industriousness in trade'; these were polytechnic associations, following the Anglo-French model, which could inform and instruct, encourage projects, hand out scholarships, promote progress and self-help, and forge ties between craftsmen, factory-owners, technicians, theoreticians and practitioners. Such semi-state-run associations were of great importance for the achievement of technological progress.

By the 1820s and 1830s, the publication divisions of larger associations, of polytechnic institutes and of independent bodies had produced a considerable body of technical journals to disseminate the advances made in technology. By 1856, there were more than thirty such journals. From state activity and private initiative, a community of technicians and persons interested in technology, a kind of technological movement, emerged, which kept people informed of what was new. It even occasionally assumed the function of a technological lobby. Added to this was the professionalisation of the role of the technologists ('parvenus' somewhere between scholars, artists, businessmen and industrialists). This could be seen in the founding of the Austrian Architectural and Engineering Association in 1846 and of the Association of German Engineers in 1856. Professional interests, the striving for social acceptance, the regulation of technological norms and of patent laws, the belief in technical training and the recognition of the technical culture and its 'mission', were all uniquely integrated here.

Table 18: The cotton industry

	1800	1828	1830	1850
Spindles				
within later Reich	22,000		436,000	940,000
in Austria (incl.		435,000		1,346,000
Lombardy)				

Production in	1815	Average 1844–1848
later Reich		
(tonnes)	1,963	11,615

growth of 491.7%

Production per	1815	1849
spindle	5.1 kg	17.1 kg

Spindles per factory	1841
e.g. in Bohemia	5,571
in Lower Austria	9,788

Finally, the establishment of a chamber of commerce and industry must be mentioned here as examples of the state's organisation efforts. They were French organisations situated on the Rhine, partly state-run, and representative of various interests. They were organisations of 'self-government' and state advisory bodies, functioning as integrating bodies for businessmen and entrepreneurs, who, through them, developed mutual trade and a mutual consciousness and thereby grew into a new class. From the 1830s, the arrangement was adopted in other provinces and territories. In 1861, they amalgamated to form the Deutscher Handelstag. The new force, the 'Economy', had found its representative in an organisation which was state run.

As has already been said, the state created the basic conditions for industrialisation, whilst industrialisation itself was an autonomous process. As it proceeded very differently in the various sectors, we must first look at a few of these, during the first phase of industrialisation up until 1850. In England, the country where industry originated, the textile sector was perhaps the classic one, in which the first machine tools were used in conjunction with the new engines, where production was organised within the factories and enormous growth rates appeared. In Germany, something similar happened in the cotton-spinning sector. The number of spinning-jennies multiplied quickly, irrespective of any crises, and the industry was converted from hand-spinning to water and then to steam power, mainly in the 1830s.

Mechanisation was relatively simple and greatly affected prices. This drove it on. Usually, the factories were very small. In Prussia, it was said that if a farmer or a miller was getting too comfortable, he would build himself a spinning-mill. But large factories were sprouting up in Augsburg, Mönchen-Gladbach and Rheydt, in Saxony, Bohemia and in the Vienna basin. Within the Zollverein, consumption of raw cotton increased almost eightfold between 1830 and 1850. Only 25–30% of this, however, was home-produced. Overall, German production in 1850, was a quarter, or at most a third, of French output. As for England, there was simply no comparison. The mechanisation of spinning had not yet spread to weaving. The number of looms rose, in the regions of the later German Reich, from 35,000 around 1800 to 150,000 in 1846 (a rise of 328.6%). Production increased still further, from 1,800 tonnes to 31,000 (a rise of 1,627.8%). Other statistics give a figure of 39,000 tonnes. This meant that productivity per loom rose from 51kg to 206kg (a 303% increase). Yet in Prussia in 1846 only 3.79% of the looms (2.2% in the later Reich) were mechanical.

In the wool-spinning industry, the process of mechanisation, and the transition from workshop to factory was much slower. In 1835, only 30% of production was mechanised, in 1850, it was about 50%. This was because consumption and sales were increasing only slowly. Wool-weaving was still mainly a cottage industry. Around 1850, only some 6% of looms were mechanical. In Moravia, in 1841 some 12.3% of looms were mechanised. In Moravia and Bohemia by the 1830s large enterprises existed which controlled the whole of wool production.

As for the linen industry, it was hardly mechanised at all. In 1850 only 5% of spinning production was mechanised, and only 3% of weaving in 1855. It remained a cottage industry, and underwent a near-fatal crisis from the pressure of competition from cotton and from England. Prices in 1840–50 were still 57% of the prices of 1800–10, and it was this, and not mechanisation, which was the cause of the terrible poverty of the weavers during the 1840s. Throughout the whole textile industry, the amount of hand-weaving in cottage industry was still on the increase. In 1800, there were some 315,000 weavers in Germany. By 1846–47, there were 520,000 full-time and 50,000 part-time weavers. This was an increase of 67.6%, which was a rise from 3.3% to 3.8% of all those in employment. This shows how cheap labour and also cheap production techniques, as well as the continued dominance of England, was inhibiting mechanisation and industrialisation.

The second area of interest is the mining industry and the foundry industries. In the iron industry, rapid technological modernisation and accelerated growth was manifested from the late 1820s. The first technological innovation, which emerged from England, was the puddle process for manufacturing wrought iron. This cost only one-seventh of the time and labour required by the old refining technique. From the 1820s, the process became widespread throughout the west (in 1824, the Rasselstein–Neuwied puddling furnace operated at Hoesch near Düren). In 1842 39% of iron bars, and in 1847 70%, were manufactured by the puddle process.

From the 1830s modern rolling mills emerged, used mainly for rolling railway tracks (Rasselstein 1835). All these factories also processed large quantities of imported crude iron. In 1841 a new process for cheaper steel manufacture was developed. Krupp was able to manufacture a two-tonne steel block by means of the new process, and thus scored one of the very rare industrial successes for Germany at the 1851 Great Exhibition in London. Because the new processes no longer depended on wood, but on hard coal, the foundries moved into the regions where there were favourable transport connections to the coal-mining regions or direct access to the mining regions themselves, for instance from the Eifel to Eschweiler.

The other technological innovation, the considerably more powerful coke-fired blast-furnaces, only came to the fore in the 1830s and 1840s. In 1837 90.5%, and in 1850 75.2%, of iron was produced using charcoal, though by 1853 the figure was only 37.2%. All the same, as in the puddling process, the old technologies overlapped for a considerable period. Again, this forced the foundries to move to the coal regions or to sites with favourable transport connections. The foundries in the mountains, in the Austrian Alpine regions, in the Eifel and in Hunsrück were no longer productive, and the first large foundries were built in the Ruhr (in 1847–49, the Friedrich Wilhelm Foundry at Mülheim). The puddling process and coke-fired blast-furnaces led to the first concentrations of iron industry on the Rhine — Stumm on the Saar (1840) and Hoesch at Eschweiler (1846). Iron production increased enormously. Production doubled between 1823 and 1837, and rose by another 35% by 1847 (from 85 to 175 to 230 thousand tonnes). It slowed down because the old techniques and production centres still persisted, and even stepped up their production owing to increased demand. Between 1837 and 1850, more than 12.66% of pig-iron was manufactured with charcoal, and more than 17.28% of wrought iron. In the part of Austria that belonged to the Confederation, iron production more than doubled (from 55,000 tonnes to 119,500 tonnes per year) between 1823–27 and 1843–47. Between 1819 and 1847 production increased almost three-and-a-half-fold throughout the whole of Austria. In the Alpine regions, however, the puddling process and the coke-fired blast-furnaces were only introduced to a very small extent, and by 1850 they had fallen a long way behind. This was due especially to the unfavourable transport conditions. A considerable amount of the demand, which was increasing by leaps and bounds, was covered by imports, which adversely affected technical progress. Between 1837 and 1844, imports of iron and steel, including finished products, increased tenfold.

Coal-mining was encouraged by two factors, economically, by the increase in demand of the iron producers, and technologically by the transition to deep mining (the first deep mine shaft was constructed by Haniel in 1839), and with the aid of steam turbines. In 1840, there were 174 steam turbines of 5,400 horse power in operation in Prussia. By 1849, there were 332 with 13,200 horse power. In the 1840s, scores of deep coal shafts were dug, first on the left bank of the lower Rhine and later in the Ruhr area. Essen became part of the coal-mining areas, and coking developed. Duisburg became the centre for shipping coal. The coal traders Haniel and Stinnes were at the forefront of progress. (Hard) coal production in the later Reich area slowly rose by 50% from 1815 to 1830–34, and again by 50% until 1835–39. By 1845–49, it had risen by 110%. In Austria (which was not really comparable, because the figure includes brown coal) production had risen by 100% in 1830–34, while between 1830 and 1850 hard coal production increased by 440%.

Taking the mining and foundry industries together, the number of workers had nearly trebled by 1848. Production methods and output were, however, still backward compared with England and Belgium. Above all, it was the boom in demand from railway construction which first boosted iron and then coal production, and led to the introduction of new technologies. The rates of growth and the technical advances were indications of the transition to industrialisation. It was no longer the textile industry which led the way, but, for both technological and economic reasons, the mining and iron industries.

As for engineering, the stories of individual entrepreneurs are of greater significance than any statistically demonstrable growth. When a topographic survey was made of Bavaria, at Napoleon's behest, the requisite instruments were lacking, since they had hitherto been imported from England. Joseph Utzschneider, with the military technician Reichenbach and the optician Fraunhofer, founded two 'institutes' in Munich for the construction of measuring instruments using scientific-mathematical principles. It was the beginning of precision engineering in Germany. Reichenbach created a miracle of contemporary technology in the 1820s, a salt-water pipe from Berchtesgaden to Reichenhall. This carried the extracted salt to an area which was richer in wood, and its hydraulic engines pumped the salt water up to a height of nearly 400 metres.

Friedrich König developed the first modern printing-press (1810–14) in England, because he could not find the necessary capital in Germany. In 1817, he set up his printing-press factory in a deconsecrated Premonstratensian abbey near Würzburg. This was consolidated after many years, but only after journal and dictionary publishers such as Cotta and Brockhaus took over the new technology for the mass market. Friedrich Harkort, perhaps the most famous of the early entrepreneurs, and a supporter of both industry and 'social' policies, opened his 'mechanical workshops' in 1819 in the castle of Wetter in the Ruhr. He built steam-engines and textile machines, and added puddling and rolling mills to the factory. He failed, admittedly, in business terms, and had to leave the company in 1832 with considerable debts.

The stories of these and other entrepreneurs emphasise the extraordinary difficulties they faced. The work was performed using English machines and English mechanics. The workers had to get used to the discipline of using machinery in the work environment and the intensity of factory work, and this was a slow process. The employer had to organise orders, sales, transport, inventory, and management, and was hard pushed to keep to delivery schedules because of breakdowns or lack of materials. In addition, resistance to mechanisation was still strong. König, for example, said of the installation of the first mechanical printing-press in Augsburg: 'The editor-in-chief was a cautious man, and able to hide his feelings, but the assistant editor declared that he would rather write under the open skies than under one roof with a steam-engine; the copy-boy quit, saying he valued his life too highly. Cautious people no longer ventured down that street. Cotta gave instructions for a painstaking examination, so that there would be no danger of any explosion, and so that we could give sincere assurances that the steam-engine was the most innocent and harmless little thing in the world.' During their first years, the existence of these enterprises were under constant threat.

From the 1830s, steam and textile machinery, and above all the railway, spurred on the engineering industry. In 1846–47 there were 423 engineering works employing 12,518 workers within the Zollverein. The most famous of these were in locomotive and railway construction. They included August Borsig and Schwartzkopff in Berlin, Henschel in Kassel, Egerstorff in Hanover, Hartmann in Chemnitz, Kessler in Esslingen and Karlsruhe, Maffei and Kraus in Munich, Clett in Nuremberg, Schichau in Elbing, and the engineering works in Augsburg. The first German locomotive was built in 1839. By 1842–43, 15.5% of the 245 locomotives were manufactured in Germany, and by 1851, 62.6% out of 1,084. Borsig, the largest factory of this type, built its 500th locomotive in 1854.

The gas industry is also worthy of mention. Gas lighting was introduced to Hanover in 1826. It reached Berlin in 1829 and Dresden in 1836. In 1850, there were over thirty-five gasworks (using the slogan 'bright streets, well-lit home'). Factories could now work nights, and the dependence on natural time, on day and night, decreased significantly. The chemical industries of the 1840s, which manufactured soda, chlorine and sulphuric acid for the textile industry, and the secondary agricultural industries (brickworks, breweries, mills, and the sugar and spirit factories) all made increasing use of engineering.

The railways were probably the most important sector for forcing the pace of industrialisation. It is hardly an exaggeration to state that the 'transport revolution' in Germany (as opposed to in England, where the reverse was true) preceeded the industrial revolution. Around 1800, transport conditions in Germany were totally inadequate. Complaints about the wretched, miserable streets, the slowness of the mail coaches and vans, about the entrepreneurs, the workers, the innkeepers, and the authorities who made money from them, and about the border posts, were legion.

Before the start of railway construction, there were two important developments. Firstly, there was the development of the waterways, canals and rivers during these decades. Most famous of these was the diversion of the upper Rhine from the 1820s onward, primarily in the interest of agriculture and of those who lived along the banks. This was the work of the Baden planning official Tulla who based it on precise scientific calculations. He became the 'tamer' of the wild Rhine, and parts of the Danube and the Isar were similarly regulated. The harnessing of the wild waters made them into waterways, freed from the river's natural course. In 1832, the width of the Rhine at the Binger (Felsen) Loch was extended from 9 to 23–30 metres. Smaller rivers, such as the Ruhr and the Lippe, were also made navigable, and canals were built, like the famous Ludwigskanal, which connected the Main River with the Danube. Around 1800, primarily in Prussia, around 490 km of canal and 670 km of river had been made navigable in Germany. In 1850, there were 3,528 km of artificial waterways.

There was a concomitant revolution in the means of transportation. In place of rowing, sailing and propelling boats upstream by means of man and beast, came the steam boat, scientifically constructed from iron, using first a paddle-wheel, and later a propeller. In 1816, the first such (English) steamer arrived in Cologne. In 1826, the Prussian Rhine Steamship Company was established, and steady traffic started from Rotterdam to Cologne, extending to Mainz in 1827. In Vienna, the Danube Steamship Company was founded in 1829. Similar ships ran on the Elbe, the Weser and the Oder. After passenger travel had been revolutionised, the steam packets and barges followed suit with the local goods traffic. In 1841, Camphausen founded a company for this purpose in Cologne. The dissolution of the power of the seamens' guilds was tied in with the replacement of manual work through machines via capitalist businesses and joint stock companies. The traditional legal constraints (duties, trading rights, haulage monopolies, etc.) and borders made this transport development considerably more difficult, and only in 1831 was freedom of passage granted along the Rhine. The new transport conditions created new centres. The new town of Duisburg-Ruhrort became one of the largest ports in Europe, with its own shipyard, even before the development of the Ruhr region. Cologne returned to former prominence, and on the middle Rhine, Mainz was toppled from its position by Mannheim (with a new harbour in 1840) and the Bavarian town of Ludwigshafen. Even Berlin became part of a network of waterways in 1830. Goods traffic for 1850 was estimated at 900 million km–tonnes in Germany (it was already 700 million in 1835), while in Austria — which used a different measurement — it was 263,000 tonnes in 1850, having been as little as 2,000 tonnes in 1835.

The other development which preceeded the railways was the construction of stone-paved roads and avenues. For military reasons, Napoleon had been a great supporter of these, as the avenues of poplars on the left bank of the Rhine, and to an extent on the right bank, still bear witness. After 1815, road-building continued, especially in Prussia, where in addition to agricultural interests there were also significant military, political and strategic considerations in the struggle for the Zollverein. In 1816, there were 3,836 km of roads there, and by 1843, 12,817 km. Things were similar in other states. The establishment of the Zollverein in 1834 and the construction of the railways (which also required feeder routes) spurred on road-building even more. In 1850, there were some 53,000 km of road in what became the Reich, most of it in the west (16,689 km in Prussia in 1852). In all of Austria, there were 89,833 km of state and district roads in 1850, and 96,212 km in 1859 (excluding Lombardy).

Finally, there was the railway, the alliance of the artificial iron route — i.e. the rails and a new means of propulsion — the steam-engine and the locomotive. Whereas in England it had been developed as a result of a huge demand for transport, in Germany it actually created such a demand. Entrepreneurs such as Harkort and Camphausen lobbied for railway construction, as did Friedrich List, newly returned from the United States (in 1833 he wrote a pamphlet entitled *Concerning a railway system for Saxony as the basis of a general German railway system and in particular concerning the laying of a railway from Leipzig to Dresden*). List explained the economic advantages of cheap, quick and regular mass transport — division of labour, choice of residence, a larger market — and proposed a new, practical model. He proposed publicity among the populace to win them over, the election of a committee which would calculate the costs and profitability and negotiate concessions or guarantees with the government, the foundation of a company and the provision of shares for subscription. This became the procedure almost everywhere. In 1835, the first 6-km stretch of railway between Nuremberg and

Fürth was opened. This site was chosen for its favourable geographic and economic conditions. At night, people still journeyed by horse, thanks to the anti-railway protestors — the Greens of their day. Begun in 1837, the Leipzig–Dresden route including the first German railway tunnel, was completed in 1839, as was Berlin–Potsdam in 1838, Berlin–Anhalt in 1841 and Berlin–Stettin in 1842. In 1836, the construction of the Austrian *Nordbahn* (Northern Railway) was begun, under the auspices of the Viennese Rothschilds. It ran first from Vienna to Brünn. Later, it was supplemented by the Southern Railway (*Südbahn*) to Trieste. The crossing of the Alps led to a number of important technical advances. In the west, in 1837, Camphausen started on the construction of the Cologne–Aix-la-Chapelle–Antwerp line, where he was soon joined by Mevissen and Hansemann. In 1847, the Cologne–Minden (Hanover–Berlin) line was completed; in 1843, the Elberfeld-Dortmund line; and in the south, in 1839, the Munich–Augsburg line; and the Upper Rhine railway from Mannheim to Basel, was completed in 1838. In 1840, there were 468 km of railways in Germany, and in 1850, there were 5,859 km, while in Austria there were 473 km in 1841, but only 1,357 in 1850. The Prussian network grew by 20% per year in the 1840s, and investment capital (that is the value of capital stock at par) rose from 23.03 million marks in 1840 to 435.79 million marks in 1849. In the area which was to become Germany, it rose from 58.8 million marks to 850.5 million.

This accelerated expansion is manifest in the average annual growth rates of the output of the German railways. Between 1841 and 1849, this measured 65.5% for km–tonnes and 31.0% for passenger–km. In 1850, it measured 302.7 million km–tonnes and 782.7 passenger–km in the area which was later Germany, and 1,441 million tons of freight and 6.5 million passengers in Austria.

The majority of railways were privately owned by their shareholders. All the same, the state dispensed concessions and was thus able to influence the running of the lines. The cities of Mannheim and Heidelberg, for example, were 'punished' for their opposition to the Upper Rhine railway by building the line through Mannheim–Friedrichsfeld, an artificial town between them. The state facilitated the necessary land dispossessions and guaranteed interest payments, and was thus able to assume rights of supervision, which was not the case in the United States. Indirect financing by the state was quite considerable. Owing partly to private initiative and the profits private businesses expected, and partly to the sovereignty of the particularist states, there was no railway 'system' as such, from a national economic, or pan-German point of view. Baden even used a different track gauge to the other territories, right into the 1850s. In 1842, Prussia produced a kind of general plan. Of course, 'developmental railways', such as the *Ostbahn* to West and East Prussia, could not be constructed by private means, and a state loan was required. For this reason it was necessary, after much deliberation, to summon the *Vereinigte Provinzialstände* (United Diet) in 1847, and this led to the revolution. State supervision also shaped the unique character of the business, the uniformity and grading of personnel, which, as one Englishman observed, was a 'form of supervision not quite appropriate to the nature of trade and transport'.

The railway asserted itself despite great resistance from the interests of haulage companies and canal-owners, and in the face of fear and mistrust (and superstition) of the 'fire-belching monsters'. It was claimed that fire from the locomotives would set fire to fields and woods, that the noise would send herds of cattle into a frenzy and make homes uninhabitable. It had to assert itself against nostalgia for the unhurried pace of life, like that of Friedrich William III: 'Everything is supposed to rush headlong, and calm and comfort will suffer. I can't imagine any great joy in getting from Berlin to Potsdam a couple of hours earlier, but time is the great instructor.' The railway could hardly have been built in a completely democratic system. On the other hand, great hopes and expectations did exist to counter these feelings, as well as a new feeling of optimism. The railways which connect spaces and diminish distances would bind Germany together, it was believed. They represented 'change, dedicated to the unity of Germany'. The rails were 'marriage ties and wedding rings'. They would encourage the free exchange of ideas, and even have a democratising effect, for rich and poor, regardless of class divisions, could move equally and at equal speeds. The railway was the most powerful and exciting symbol of the new age.

In the short term, the most important effect of railway construction was the enormous impulse given to the demand for engines, tracks, iron and coal. Even if much was at first satisfied by imports, it still drove on the modernisation and expansion of German industry. In the medium and long term, the most important consequences of the transport revolution were the colossal expansion of the volume of transport and the cheapening of the cost of transport. But, above all, it meant that raw materials and energy, ore and coal could be available for use in production plants anywhere, independent of natural conditions. Only now was the supremacy of coal possible. Only now, with the widespread use of the steam-engine, was it possible to concentrate production in large businesses, and have regional and local division of labour. Only now, was the mechanisation of the iron and steel industries, and the concentration of factories at railway junctions made possible. The railway increased the mobility of labour and further enabled its concentration. It made sales from industry decisively cheaper. It created a German and a European market, thus enabling mass production and competition, and therefore fostered even greater technological innovation.

Finally, the communication revolution of the century was that of the transmission of news by telegraph. The electrical telegraphs (Gaus and Weber, 1833), the needle telegraph and the morse system (1837) and industrial application in a developed communications technology (Werner Siemens, 1847) were the stages of its development. In 1847, the first public telegraph line came into being (Bremen to Vegesack). Within a few years, all the centres were connected to each other — along the railway and under the aegis of the postal service. Now the rest of the world became real. And only now, when all news became simultaneous, was there a functioning national and international market.

The Rhine province became the leading region. It had traditionally been a trading region, rich in raw materials, with a transport network and liberal trade laws. Upper Silesia and the Austrian Alpine regions fell behind in the mining and metal industries. The textile industry had many centres, with Saxony the most concentrated. The heavy engineering industry settled at the railway junctions.

If an industrial revolution signifies not only engines and factories, but also commercialisation and the adoption of capitalist economic methods and markets, then a brief survey must be made of the 'tertiary sector'. Firstly, the banks, in addition to their usual functions of exchange and personal credit, were court and state banks, pre-industrial, and largely tied to the Jewish bankers who served the princely courts. They financed the wars and satisfied the princes' and the state's financial requirements by arranging loans. The House of Rothschild, which rose during the time of Napoleon, and with headquarters in Frankfurt, Vienna, Paris, London and Naples, is the most famous of such enterprises, an international monetary force the likes of which had been unknown since the Fuggers. They financed Metternich's restoration policy, and were ennobled in Vienna in 1822. But apart from them there was a string of other important finance houses. They were of little importance in the early phase of industrialisation compared with individual private bankers, such as Salomon Oppenheim and Abraham Schaaffhausen in Cologne or Schaezler in Augsburg, who (co-)financed enterprises with credits and loans. The opportunities for these banks were of course limited, and insurance, shipping and railways were more attractive than industrial concerns. Savings banks, credit institutions of the petty bourgeoisie, were founded during this period, but were not yet of any economic significance. Insurance, with its rationalisation of risk and relief from the uncertainties of destiny, was more modern, and expanded rapidly from the 1820s onwards, against the pre-eminence of British companies. In 1819–21 Ernst Wilhelm Arnoldi founded the first great German fire insurance company, and in 1827 added a life insurance company, the Gotha company, still known to all Germans today. It was a mutual insurance company, that is to say, with a co-operative basis. In 1825, Hansemann founded the Aix-la-Chapelle (and Munich) fire insurance company, and many others were added in the 1830s and 1840s — against hail, livestock diseases, shipping disasters, and finally for the provision of reinsurance — they were also important institutions for the accumulation of capital.

The organisation and practice of wholesale and export trade was also modernised. The same was true of maritime shipping. Regular traffic was introduced, although the steamboats did not yet have the upper hand over new, large and fast sailing ships. Shipping companies were gradually organised into joint stock companies (HAPAG in 1847, North-German Lloyd in 1857). In the port towns, the constant increase in export trade had its effect. After a long period of stagnation, Hamburg returned to prominence as the port receiving imports from England. Bremen received tobacco imports and was the port of departure for emigrants. When it was threatened with exclusion from sea trade by the increase in size of ships, it founded Bremerhaven in 1827; Geeste- (or Weser) münde in 1847, and Wilhelmshaven in 1853, were new (and competitive) harbours for Hanover and Prussia. It was not until after 1850 that the bulk of passenger shipping and foreign trade moved, once and for all, from the Baltic to the North Sea ports.

Before summarising, a brief look is required at the sources of capital which financed early industrialisation. Capital did not flow into industrialisation to any great extent from agriculture, from the colonies, or from foreign trade. All the same, Germany was not as short of capital as was earlier believed. Firstly, there were the *Ablösung* payments. Government bonds did not pay a great deal in the 1830s and 1840s, and so capital was not quite so scarce. Fixed interest securities were doing well in agriculture, and there were no problems with securities in the railways. Some capital was invested abroad. All the same, capital backing was fairly thin, compared with England or France. And, more importantly, the available capital was not secured in industry. The profits and risks were too variable, the credit system could not adapt to it, and the entrepreneurs were hesitant of accepting foreign capital, which greatly hindered expansion and modernisation. The modern form of capital organisation, the joint stock company, was not favourably viewed in government circles outside of the left bank of the Rhine. These were much more in favour of personal responsibility (in accordance with old economic practices), supervision of the partners, and unlimited liability, and in no way wished to endanger the credit requirements of state and agriculture. Only the steamboats and the railways urgently demanded joint stock companies. The Prussian law on stocks and shares of 1843 certainly facilitated their foundation up to a point, but by no means gave them *carte blanche*. Finally, there was foreign capital and credit from private bankers. But industry was for the greater part self-financing. First of all, the capital of the entrepreneurs (frequently merchants, such as coal and wool merchants), their families and friends was invested, the profits of which were in turn invested, though these were very variable, owing to the high risks involved. The level of investment required in the textile and engineering industries was still relatively low, while in the iron, steel and coal industries (especially after technological modernisation) it was extraordinarily high.

Thus mechanisation, the founding of factories or transition to new technologies, the demise of hand-spinning, the modernisation of the mining and foundry industries, and the development of engineering, did not form part of one single continuous process. It accelerated and intensified from the mid-1830s and early 1840s onwards. The number and horse power of steam-engines increased, especially in the mining and foundry industries, and in textiles and milling. From 1840 to 1850, the horse power of machinery rose from 40,000 to 260,000 in Germany, and from 20,000 to 100,000 in Austria (compared with 1,290,000 in England in 1850, and 1,680,000 in the United States). In 1845–46, within the Zollverein, excluding railways and ships, there were 1,318 steamboats with 26,192 horse power. In Prussia between 1836 and 1847 the number rose from 423 to 1,139. In 1841, there were 608 engines of 11,641 horse power in Prussia, of which 21.3% were in the textiles sector, and 64.1% in the mining, foundry and engineering sectors of industry. In Austria, in the same year, there were 223 engines of 2,798 horse power, of which 49% were in the textiles sector, and only 24.3% were in the mining and metals sectors. The number of patents filed in Prussia rose between 1822–37 and 1838–48 from 17 to 59 per year. Factory sizes increased, e.g. in Baden from 18 employees in 1809 to 50.7 in 1850, with a marked jump from 1833.

It is difficult to determine exact numbers of employees, owing to the unreliability of early statistics, and because there was no precise definition of the word 'factory'. In 1846–47, excluding mining and steel manufacture, and excluding textiles, where no differences are indicated between home or cottage industries and industries run on a factory basis, 13,600 factories with some 170,000 workers were recorded within the Zollverein, representing about 1.1% of those in employment. The total number of craftsmen and industrial workers in the German states (excluding Austria) increased disproportionately to the population between 1800 and 1846. Around 1800, its share of those in work was at least 16% (of an estimated 45% in employment) to 19.7% in 1846–48. In the process, the proportion of craftsmen decreased from 75% in 1800 to 68.4% in 1846–48, while the number of those employed in large-scale industry increased from 1.8% to 6.8%. If one then adds the figures for those employed in spinning and in the transport sector (and make adjustments for certain statistical errors), it can be said that in 1800 20%, and in 1850 some 25%, of those in work were employed in crafts and industry. These figures are estimates, as there were no reliable statistics before 1846. In the whole Federation (*Bundesgebiet*), around 60% of the total number of workers were employed in agriculture, 25% were employed in trade, and 15% were employed in the service sector and other types of employment or were unemployed (pensioners, day-labourers, farmhands, those receiving poverty relief, etc.). In Prussia, as in all the German states (excluding Austria), the percentage of those employed in agriculture was a few (1–3) points lower, and that of workers in the trade and service sectors correspondingly higher.

In Austria, for which there are no reliable figures, the level of industrialisation was markedly lower. Assuming a level of employment of 54.8%, only 19.6% of those in employment were in the commercial sector, even as late as 1869. In Prussia, incipient industrialisation, mainly around Berlin, was mirrored in the growth in the number of factory workers from 2.5% in 1822 to 4.2 % in 1846. The number of miners rose from 0.6% to 1.1% of the male population above fourteen years of age. In Saxony alone, the most heavily-industrialised country, conditions had already changed. Here, by 1848, 63.9% were in the commercial sector, and only 25.1% were in agriculture.

Table 19: Workers employed in crafts and industry in the later Reich,[1] c.1800 and 1846–48 (estimates)

Worker group	Number of workers			
	c.1800		1846–48	
	absolute (1,000)	%	absolute (1,000)	%
Crafts	1,230	75.0	2,000	68.4
Textiles[2]	340	20.7	570	19.5
Coal, iron & steel[1]	40	2.4	155	5.3
Major industry[3]	30[4]	1.8[4]	200	6.8
Total	1,640	99.9	2,925	100.0

[1]Within 1870 boundaries (excluding Alsace-Lorraine).
[2]Excluding spinners and those employed in mechanical spinning mills.
[3]Excluding large concerns in textiles and coal, iron and steel.
[4]Figures estimated according to figures in Prussia.

Table 20: Coal-mining in the Ruhr

	1850	1860	1870
Number of mines	198	277	215
Hard coal extraction in (000 tonnes)	1,961	4,274	11,571
Workers	12,741	28,657	50,749
Workers per mine	64	103	236
Extraction per worker (tonnes)	154	149	228
Extraction per mine (tonnes)	9,904	15,437	53,819

Table 21: Iron production in Prussia (000 tonnes)

	Charcoal-based	Coke-based
1850	95	33
1855	123	158
1860	96	399
1866	54	756

The question of total economic growth is also difficult to answer given the lack of reliable numbers. The total production of the trade and agricultural sectors, as well as the industrial sector, has to be included here. Production in the trade sector, as in the agricultural sector, grew at a faster rate than that of population growth. Estimates for industrial production between 1800 and 1815 and 1850 suggest a six- or sevenfold increase. Total growth in the 1830s and 1840s could hardly have been greater than half a percent annually per capita, and probably actually decreased in the 1840s. Neither did investment per capita increase. That the profits from growth were not evenly distributed is understandable given that there was poverty on a massive scale. Per capita growth was — despite pauperism and population growth — positive, but it was not large.

Industry's share in the overall economy was still very small. Germany was still an agricultural country, to judge from the population distribution and the number of those in employment and production. The *Verlagssystem* (a system of sub-contracting within cottage industry) was still the dominant form of production in commerce, besides the crafts. Indeed, it increased with overpopulation and under-employment on the land, and with the drop in prices of half-finished goods. Even in the 1840s, only about 18% of German exports were finished goods. This demonstrates the economic backwardness of Germany. Old and new technologies existed side by side in industry. In general, new machines did not replace old ones, but simply expanded production. The moderate and uneven growth and the great variations in profits and scarcity of capital all reduced willingness to invest and encouraged the economy's tendency to stagnate. Working conditions (of which more later) still had marked paternalistic and uneconomic aspects. The upturn of the 1840s ended in the great crisis of 1846–47. This was an industrial recession, but even more so a crisis in agriculture, bringing famine in its wake. It showed to what extent the overall economy was still determined by the agricultural sector. Commercial turnover diminished. Growth stagnated. Both old and new entrepreneurs were threatened with economic collapse. There was no question yet of the great leap into industrial production and self-sustaining growth. But — and this is just as important — the decisive institutional, technological and structural innovations were in existence, and the foundations of growth and of large-scale industrialisation had been laid.

After 1850, Germany entered a phase of large-scale industrialisation, and joined the ranks of the advanced industrialised nations. Coal, the new universal raw material, and the classic technologies of machine tools and powered engines, as well as the new types of machinery, such as the carding machine and the steam-hammer, become the basis for production. Germany reached the stage of accelerated and permanent growth. Industry became a leading rather than a marginal sector of the economy, and the factory, workers and industrial cities became the new pioneers of society.

The mining and iron industries were now at the forefront. Hard coal demand increased between 1850 and 1869 from 5.5 to 26.3 million tonnes, and the demand in brown coal increased from 1.5 to 7.6 million tonnes. In Austria, it increased from 540,000 and 340,000 tonnes (respectively) to 3.5 and 3.1 million tonnes. The rise was most marked in the Ruhr; the transition to deep mining and the discovery of Ruhr coal were reflected in these figures. Between 1860 and 1870, the growth rate in mining was 170%. Although only temporary, the 45% rise in the price of coal between 1852 and 1856 was a boom to the drilling of new mine shafts. The industrial concentration and the increase in productivity in the 1860s can be seen from Table 20. By 1870, 71% of all coal-mining was done by the mines which had a production of over 100,000 tonnes. Mining output, especially the mining of iron ore, which had a brief boom, increased fourfold during the two decades. Pig-iron production in Germany increased from 184,000 (1845–49) to 1,012,000 (1865–69) tonnes, or from 222,000 (1850) to 1,413,000 tonnes (1869), more or less a sevenfold increase. In Austria, it increased from 130,000 (1848) to 405,112 tonnes (1865). The growth rate in iron production overall was around 10% per annum (and still higher in the 1850s). According to the figures, metal ore production increased fivefold. Steel production in what became the Reich increased from 196,900 tonnes in 1850 to 1,068,000 tonnes in 1869, a growth rate of 9.3%.

Changes were even faster in the industry of the Ruhr. In the area of Dortmund, pig-iron production increased thirty-five-fold between 1851 and 1871. Here, almost twice as much was mined during 1871 as in the whole of Germany in 1843. Reprocessing, rolling and steel production also increased considerably. Coal usurped the pre-eminence of wood as a fuel. In 1842, in Prussia, 82% of iron was still extracted using charcoal. By 1862, this was down to 12.3%. In 1849, only 32 out of 247 blast furnaces were using coke. Blast-furnace productivity increased sevenfold from 720 to over 5,000 tonnes between 1850 and 1870. At the same time, iron production began using coal. In this way, a new region of concentrated heavy industry was formed, the Ruhrgebiet. This had by no means been a predominantly commercial region hitherto, but was henceforth one of the great European industrial conurbations. 57 coke-fired furnaces were installed here between 1851 and 1857, more than the total number previously installed throughout the whole Zollverein. The great ironworks were founded mainly during the 1850s. It was in the iron and steel industries that the size of the foundries increased, in line with the rationalisation of production. In 1853, the Borbeck foundry in Essen became the largest of its day, with three blast-furnaces, 252 horse-power, 450 employees, and an output of 19,800 tonnes. By 1870, twelve foundries were larger. The Horder foundry had three times its output. Nevertheless, the ten largest entrepreneurs only accounted for 35.9% of pig-iron production in 1871.

Elsewhere, mechanisation and growth did not take such a dramatic upturn, but the signs were clear enough. In the textile industry, mechanised cotton-spinning, using new machinery, expanded considerably. The proportion of yarn imports decreased from 70% (1836–40) to 52.6% (1851–55) to 22% (1867–69), although overall demand increased considerably. Demand in cotton rose overall from 17,100 to 64,000 tonnes. The number of spindles rose in Germany 940,000 (1850) to 2,519,000 (1867), and in Austria from 1,346,000 to only 1,400,000, owing to the loss of northern Italy. Linen production was gradually mechanised (5% in 1850, 10% in 1861). Bielefeld became the new industrial centre for the trade. The mechanisation of wool-spinning was virtually completed (over

50% by 1861). But the linen industry went into sharp decline compared with the fast-expanding cotton industry. The woollen industry stabilised at one-third of textile production. The weaving industry continued to expand, both in terms of looms and of productivity (e.g. cotton production rose between 1840 and 1861 from 220kg to 385kg per loom). But mechanisation was a slow process. Only one-third of all looms in the cotton and woollen industries were mechanised by 1870. Compared with England and with the coal, iron and steel industries, modernisation was slower. Old methods persisted alongside new ones. The old cottage and home industries still accounted for one-third of production right into the 1880s. In the fully mechanised factories, of course, the number of spindles and looms increased, together with the number of employees. And after the introduction of the sewing machine, a new small and cottage industry sprang up in ready-to-wear clothing.

The engineering industry developed quickly in the wake of industrialisation. Metalworking increased fourfold (and, of course, continued to do so). Borsig, which built its 500th locomotive in 1854, was building its 1,000th by 1858. The average factory size increased eightfold betwen 1849 and 1871 — the workshop became a factory. Three-fifths of businesses were medium-sized, i.e. 50–400 workers, employing 53% of the workers. Besides the transport and communications centres and capital cities, the regions of heavy industry — the Ruhr and Bohemia — became engineering centres. The steam-engine began to be used in traditional trades, such as food processing and ironworking. The gas industry continued to grow, from 35 gasworks in 1850 to 340 in 1869; and the metal tube industry followed in its wake. The electrical industry was foreshadowed by the telegraph industry (Siemens and Halske, 1847), which in turn led to the spin-off cable and rubber industries.

The chemical industry, on the one hand, increased production of the chemicals necessary for the textile industry and, on the other hand, discovered the benzine ring and developed organic chemistry. This led to the new and later so famous scientifically based chemical factories. These included Bayer's aniline dye factories in Barmen in 1861–63, the Hoechst factory in 1863, and the Baden aniline and soda factory in Mannheim in 1865. The only branch of industry to remain untouched by mechanisation, in spite of the invention of cement, was the construction industry.

Overall, the growth in heavy, primary and capital goods industries during these decades was disproportionate to the growth in consumer goods, light (and small-scale) industries. An index for overall mechanisation is the total available horse power. It was estimated at 260,000 in Germany in 1850. In 1860, it was 850,000, and in 1870 2,480,000. In Austria, it rose from 100,000 horse power in 1850, to 330,000 in 1860, to 800,000 in 1870. As another indication, the number of patents filed in Prussia rose from 59 (1838–48) to 74 (1848–70) per annum.

This high pace of industrialisation was first and foremost spurred on by the pace of railway construction, which made use of coal and engines and made coal available everywhere. The German railway network expanded from 5,856 km in 1850 to 18,876 km in 1870, while the Austrian network expanded from 135 km to 3,698 km in 1865. The increase in production can be gauged from the figures for passenger and goods traffic on German and Austrian railways. Passenger-kilometers increased in Germany from 782.7 million in 1856 to 3,533.8 million in 1869. During the same period, the number of passengers on Austrian railways increased from 6.5 to 16.8 million. Goods traffic in Germany increased from 302.7 million tonne-km to 5,502.4 milion. And in Austria, it rose from 1,142 to 17,194 million tonnes (though it should be remembered that Austria employed a different standard of measurement). Railways accounted for the greatest proportion of investment (15–25%), and company dividends increased from 5% in the 1840s to 7.5% in the 1860s. Of course, state influence also increased; in 1843, some 43% of railways were state-owned.

The gross national product would have approximately doubled between 1850 and 1870 (with 1913 as the index number, from 9.5 to 18.8%) — although other calculations show only a 50% increase. By 1873, there was an annual growth rate of some 2.3%. In per capita terms, that is still in excess of 1% per annum. At the same time, overall industrial production, especially in the key modern industries, grew even faster. (Net) investment compared with overall production rose considerably, from 7–9% in the 1850s to over 10% in the 1860s, and in the boom years of 1860 and 1863 to 13% and 14%. Investments in agriculture dropped from two-thirds during the 1820s, to one-third and even a quarter during the 1850s and 1860s. The share in industry and transport rose to a good two-fifths (21% in industry, 15–25% for transport). The rest was accounted for mainly by housing. Exports roughly tripled, and as is typical for an industrialised country, imports of raw materials and exports of finished products increased heavily. The proportion of those employed in agriculture fell slowly and continually, while that for trade and industry, and for transport and services, rose correspondingly. In 1850, the appropriate ratios would have been about 60:25:15. In the 1860s (1861–71) it was around 51:28:21 (in the area of the German Reich), while in Austria it was still around 67:20:13 in 1869. Of course, those employed in commerce were predominantly craftsmen who worked in small businesses, but the proportion of craftsmen was on the decline and would soon be overshadowed by the rise of industry. The distribution of the net domestic product shifted commensurately. In 1850 the distribution was 47% in agriculture, 21% in industry and crafts, 1% in transport, and 7% in trade, while in 1870 the ratios were 40:28:2:8 (the rest being taken up by the service industries). Thus the trend continued: Germany was on its way to becoming an industrialised nation.

By 1870, Germany had overcome its industrial backwardness compared with the western European countries, and had gone some way to catching up with France and Belgium. The latecomer's handicap now also brought some advantages with it. It was able to take on board advanced innovations in technology and business practice, and it could handle half-finished goods and capital goods and could develop larger types of business. Less rural capital and labour were invested in the traditional trades, so Germany could count on a state better disposed towards industry, and yet compensate for disadvantages due to competition by reducing wages.

This process of industrialisation was stimulated and accelerated by a combination of factors. Firstly, there was the cumulative effect of the technological and economic development of the 1840s, especially in railway construction. Efficient distribution was achieved thanks to the new transport conditions. Inefficient production methods fell prey to competition, and even cheap labour and increasing demand could not sustain them. Price competition, against which there were a great number of reservations in Germany, became the norm in a functioning market, and forced modernisation; crises, such as that of 1857, helped to clear out dead wood. Transport and increasing demand led to the exploitation of new sources of raw material, like Ruhr coal. Industrialisation kept creating new demand — the textile industry, for example, required machines and chemicals — and was a stimulus to the further progress of industrialisation. Finally, industrialisation did not lead, as feared, to the loss of jobs, but to a redistribution and increase, enabling them to absorb population growth and the labour force released in the countryside. Pauperism was overcome, the standard of living improved — low as it was among the emergent proletariat — and purchasing power increased far beyond population growth. Examples are the consumption of textiles, or the use of the machines and chemicals now required by agriculture. A cycle of increased demand, higher production levels, greater profits, greater investments and more disposable income was created, and this was intensified at each stage.

Changes in the legal framework were also driving factors. They had hitherto inhibited competition, the market and industrial-capitalist production. Now, civil law was divested of certain agrarian, traditional and corporative features; capital goods, industry and individual enterprise became more important. The General German Trade Law Handbook of 1861 testifies to this trend — as does the liberal application of the Prussian Shares Law of 1843. Although a franchise was still required, the founding of new firms and the expansion of existing firms in the form of limited liability joint stock companies (*Aktiengesellschaften*) was made significantly easier. A redrafting of mining law, especially in Prussia, was part of these changes to the structure. Even where there was no state ownership, as in the Saar and Upper Silesia, the *Direktionsprinzip* (state management principle) applied until 1851, at least in the west. This meant that the state controlled the management of companies and management policy and fixed prices and wages. Certain innovations, like the transition to deep mining, were impeded by this arrangement but the most important consequence was that capital investment remained unattractive. From 1851, mining law was liberalised, and company management, increased profit and risks were left to the owners' discretion, although legal guidelines on safety, the common welfare and the social rights of miners were retained. As a general rule, bureacratic practice did not hold industry back, even in states without a legal guarantee of free trading. In another sense, the policy of customs union in the Zollverein — standardisation of currency (Zollverein thalers in 1857, the Austrian florin in 1858) and free trade agreements of the 1860s, which enabled foreign trade to flourish and increased pressure of competition, helped industry to develop. Finally, the extraordinary increase of currency in circulation was another economic stimulus. The Prussian Bank increased its note circulation from 18.36 million thalers in 1850 to 103.26 thalers in 1870. For the regions of Germany excluding Austria the figures are 30.8 and 284.7, constituting almost a tenfold increase; if coins are included, the figures increased from 372.6 to 864.8 million thalers, from 43.1 to 100 index points. Interest on credit was therefore relatively low, slightly above 3%. The reasons for the increase in the money supply are extremely complicated, but were triggered off by the increase in the quantity of gold in the world following the discovery of gold in California.

One other condition for the huge expansion which took place independent of state or institutional control was the so-called financing revolution, the creation of a new type of bank. Private wealth — in trade and industry — and traditional methods no longer sufficed to finance expensive capital goods in industry. Deposit banks were founded on a shareholding system. This broadened the clientèle to include also small investors and property-owners, and capital was accumulated and mobilised, thus 'democratising' the money market. These banks catered to a totally new type of business, long-term investment in industry, the foundation of joint-stock companies, the sale of shares on the market, and credit-financing of enterprises. The model for this came from France — the famous Crédit Mobilier — and from Belgium, and was quickly adopted by Germany.

The traditional private bankers had their part to play in this new development. In 1848, the Schaaffhausen Banking Society was saved from bankruptcy by the flotation of shares — supported by the liberal März government in Berlin. In 1835, as a result of the more favourable legal situation in Hesse, Mevissen founded the Darmstadt Bank for Trade and Industry; in 1856, the Berlin Trading Company was formed; and finally, in 1856, the Discount Society was established. In 1855, the Austrian Credit Institution for Trade and Commerce was founded under Rothschild's aegis. All these merchant banks operated across local and regional boundaries. By 1857, over 200 million thalers were invested in banks (compared with some 140 million in railways). These credit banks generated money. They enabled the financing of the economic upturn and the organisation of the joint-stock companies that supported it. It was precisely due, on the one hand, to the predominance of capital-intensive heavy industry and the railway sector in industrialisation and investment, and, on the other, to the lack of extensive private wealth that the joint-stock company became the prototype for industrialisation. The founding of the Cologne Mining Company in 1849 by Mevissen was the start of the great wave of industrial company launches. By 1853, there were eight joint-stock companies in the Ruhr. Whereas 123 enterprises with a total capital of 225 million thalers had been founded in Prussia during the years leading up to 1850, between 1851 and 1870 there were 295, with a total capital of 802 million thalers.

Institutional reforms and industrial successes finally liberated the drive to produce, make profits and compete. The precept of the old world, ensuring survival, had not been abandoned under the new conditions, because something hitherto almost unknown had come onto the scene — growth. Individual enrichment was not simply at other people's expense, but was drawn from the wealth created by growth. This changed economic ethics. Of course, although industrialisation was a prolonged process, more than a 'revolution' followed by a 'launch', the actual peak of industrialisation, between 1850 and 1873, was relatively brief. The mentality, the soul of the people, could hardly adapt that quickly to the profound changes of the industrial era; it was the very speed of these changes which unleashed resistance against this 'new' world, the despair created when people whose mentality is old-fashioned try to live in an era of progress. This was to prove of great importance to later German history.

The pace of industrialisation, growth and the increases in the standard of living were by no means uniform. This must be made very clear, and it is the reason why reference has been made to individual sectors. Social classes were not always equally affected, and this was even truer of the different branches of business; there were always losers, victims, people left behind.

Because progress created permanent, dynamic change, an element of unrest, uncertainty and tension accompanied it. Nor was development regionally uniform. The advantage which the west and north had over the south and east, or, more precisely, the predominance of west and central Germany, has already been mentioned, and the south-west could be added to the list. Silesia, for example, began to fall behind in terms of its communications networks.

More important from the political point of view was Austria's failure to keep in step; in spite of many parallels, its growth rates, at least until 1867, were not comparable with those of the states in the Zollverein. They were not sufficient to develop an industrial economy. An expanded and mechanised textile industry remained the leading sector here, but obsolete technology (charcoal-firing) still played an extraordinarily important role in spite of the increase in coal and iron consumption and production. This 'backwardness' was based on a lack of raw materials, especially coal, on the state's miserable economic plight and consequent deflationary policies accompanied by high rates of interest, on the protectionist barriers against outside competition and the pressure for change which competition brought to bear, as well as on a certain backwardness of the entrepreneurial classes which had socio-cultural roots. A comparison between the later German Reich and Austria (Table 22) shows the economic disparity. This does not mean that economic growth or economic requirements made it necessary for the Reich to be founded, for growth took place without it, nor does it offer a simple explanation for the fact that Prussia founded the Reich; but it was surely a very significant precondition.

Table 22: Economic comparison between Austria and the German Reich of 1871

		Austria	Germany excluding Austria
Pig-iron production (000t)	1850	155	210
	1870	279	1,261
Hard coal production (000t)	1850	665 (1851)	5,500
	1870	3,759	26,398
Steam engine capacity (000 HP)	1850	100	260
	1870	800	2,480
Railways (km)	1850	1,357	5,856
	1870	6,112	18,876
Cotton spindles (000)	1850	1,346	940
	1870	1,500	2,600

Besides the social, sectoral and regional variations, there were also temporal ones. Industrialisation, transregional markets, growth and the new network of foreign trade changed economic climates. Recessions and crises gained in importance, becoming a new factor in determining the fate of society as a whole. They no longer took a huge toll of human life like the agricultural crises and famines hitherto, but still threatened the existence of the individual and the stability of society. These new crises, no longer 'naturally' created and difficult to explain, were of great importance to human experience. While short-term cycles of crises are observable in the 1830s and 1840s, with the recession of 1846-49 overlaid by the agrarian hunger crisis, in 1850 an unprecedented boom occurred, followed in 1857 by a world economic crisis, with price falls and the collapse of established as well as speculative enterprises, accompanied by a sharp decline in investment and growth. There then followed a new economic upturn that lasted through the 1860s until 1873.

On the whole, industrialisation in Germany must be considered to have been positive in its effects. Not only did it change society and the countryside, and finally the world, in a manner unprecedented since the settlement of the nomads of the early Stone Age, it created the modern world we live in. It solved the problems of population growth, under-employment and pauperism in a stagnating economy, and abolished dependency on the natural conditions of agriculture, and finally hunger. It created huge improvements in production and both short- and long-term improvements in living standards. However, in terms of social inequality, it can be assumed that it did not change the relative levels of income. Between 1815 and 1873 the statistical distribution of wealth was on the order of 77% to 23% for entrepreneurs and workers respectively. On the other hand, new problems arose, in the form of interrupted growth and new crises, such as urbanisation, 'alienation', new under-classes, proletariat and proletarian misery, new injustices and new masters and, eventually, class warfare. This will be outlined in greater detail later.

Entrepreneurs are needed for industrialisation. The spirit of enterprise and initiative were preconditions for industrialisation. Entrepreneurs drove it forward. As a class, they were also its product. The organisation of business (capital, raw materials, machinery, workers, production and working processes, sales), the making of decisions, the introduction of innovations, the taking on of risks, those were the functions of entrepreneurs in the period under consideration. Unlike the craftsmen, they were primarily market- and profit-orientated, dedicated to the rational organisation and supervised profitability of their businesses. They originated from various social and professional groups. A fair proportion, indeed the majority in the mining, ironworking, and textile sectors, came from old trading families. In the iron industry there were Stumm, Wendel, Krupp, Hoesch, Poensgen and Schöller. This was particularly true of *Verleger* (those who contracted out work under the *Verlagssystem*) who had been the true 'entrepreneurial' type of the pre-industrial era, and those solely engaged in buying and selling in the relevant sectors, such as wool or coal merchants (Mannesmann, Stinnes, Haniel). Sometimes their forebears had been middle-ranking traders in these sectors, such as the father of the great industrialist Hermann von Beckerath who had been a master ribbon-maker with six to eight journeymen under him.

In heavy industry and engineering, the founding fathers tended to originate from the ironworkers and woodworkers (Dinnendahl, Egels, Borsig, Henschel, König). Aristocrats, like the Bohemian industrialists and the Upper Silesian magnates were an exception; but whoever 'happened' to have exploitable mineral reserves was able to participate. During the phase of peak industrialisation, people from the middle ranks of the new industry, like the technician Mulvany or the chief railways inspector, Louis Baare, were able to become entrepreneurs.

Finally, there were the sons of men who worked in other agricultural, middle-class and educated professions. There was the artillery officer, Siemens, son of a tenant farmer; the pastor's son Hansemann and Röchling, a doctor's son. Among the educated classes, of course, disdain for 'trade' made access more difficult; the father of the director of the German Bank, Georg von Siemens, a state official, used to call the latter 'my son, the travelling salesman'. Hardly any entrepreneurs came from the ranks of the lower classes or the upper working classes — with the exception of fitters — for here the barriers to adavancement in a technical or sales capacity were too strong.

All the same, the Cologne industrialist and president of the chamber of commerce Johann Jacob Langen, had been an elementary school teacher, but his was an exceptional case. It was more likely for the rise to take place over three generations. Merchants played a central role in major industry, for example in the Ruhr. Here, there was also the 'businessman' type, active in several enterprises, for example the Rhine merchants, Camphausen and Mevissen, who founded and ran steamship and railway companies, insurance companies and banks, oil refineries and mines.

Craftsmen probably predominated in small industry; but the usual development here was not the conversion of a craftsman's business into a factory, but rather the foundation of factories from scratch after a long time spent as a journeyman. In spite of the effective exclusion of the lower classes, the new 'profession' was comparatively open to talented parvenus, independent of family background. In this sense, entrepreneurs were the spokesmen for new values, a new society, a new mentality. After the mid-century, the self-made men of industry were joined by their heirs, who became the majority.

The training of entrepreneurs during the period under review was substantially practical and empirical. Training was largely in commerce and was rarely technical. The school leaving certificate (*Abitur*), before the rise of high schools, was a rarity, while there was an increase in those who possessed a 'one-year certificate' (*das Einjährige*). After 1830 it is possible to speak of 'higher education' in this context, but academic study was only of any importance in mining and, from the 1860s onwards, in chemistry.

Significant in terms of origins were the proportionally high numbers of Protestants in this class, especially in the west with its Catholic majority or in the multi-denominational Palatinate, and even in Austria. In the Catholic imperial cities and dioceses, it was not the native citizens, but emigré Protestants who founded industries, in Cologne for instance. Occasionally, reservations about founding factories on deconsecrated church land constituted a factor, but above all it appears to have been the different mental disposition characteristic of Protestants which explains why they took to technology, industry and capitalism. They possessed a certain spiritual asceticism, with a strong emphasis on work, scholarship and performance, planning and saving, and a distaste for the simpler pleasures of life, like playing cards. Protestant restlessness combined with an ethos which held poverty to be scandalous, and wealth the basis of honour. This outlook only developed among the Protestant community during the 18th century, with the emergence of civil servants and the educated classes from the world of the estates. German Catholics shared a distaste for the active dynamism of the new economic culture, despised ambition and mobility, liberalism and 'materialism'. The Catholic social environment encouraged neither economic and commercial nor technical activity. Life in the ecclesiastical states may have helped to encourage this viewpoint. The proportion of Jews was high in the textile sector, in the Upper Silesian coal trade, and in certain branches of industry in Austria; here the historically-determined concentration on trade and the economic mentality of a minority without equal rights were the most important factors.

The early entrepreneurs were, for the most part, individual entrepreneurs, full or part-owners (with family capital or partners), who also managed their enterprises. Only in the great mining industries, the foundries and the chemical industry, which were organised as joint stock companies, were the founders and entrepreneurs distinguished, in principle anyway, from the owners.

For this reason, the above-mentioned entrepreneurs with diverse interests who founded and managed many and various companies, the talented stock exchange speculators like Mevissen and Hansemann, or at the end of the period the legendary 'king of the railways', Stroussberg, were able to join the ranks of those industrialists who were tied to one factory or line of business (such as Krupp or Stumm). But even the great public mining and steelmaking companies were usually controlled by an inner circle of businessmen and entrepreneurial families. In the small and medium-sized businesses that predominated before 1870, the entrepreneur managed the company himself, collaborating, supervising and issuing orders. Only with increasing company size and diversity were jobs delegated and shared and the technical and sales aspects separated. Managements emerged. Kocka has calculated that at Siemens there was one so-called 'official', including the foremen, to every ten to fifteen workers in the years 1855–67. The railway system developed into a bureaucratic monolith.

For the early period, before the end of the 1850s, one may speak of a certain paternalism amongst the management of businesses that were not excessively large, a sort of 'social policy' — support for the aged and infirm, provision of accommodation and a Christmas bonus for those long employed in the company. The pre-industrial ethic, and the interest in having a 'fixed' labour force, initially served to hold in check the hire-and-fire mentality motivated purely by profit. However, the boom-and-slump cycle forced management into a corresponding cycle of dismissals and re-hirings.

The impulse inspiring the entrepreneurs was in the first instance determined by a specific work and professional ethic: hard, thorough work without let-up, in which a man proves his worth and finds his life fulfilled; work as happiness, duty, God's decree; work also as a rational way of spending one's time, as opposed to every kind of activity which wastes time. To that one might add as being equally decisive the will to succeed, expand, make profits, innovate, and in consequence the courage to take risks. Decisiveness, drive, courage, an 'indefatigable mind for business' these were the characteristics demanded of entrepreneurs. Innovation, not preservation; profit, not simply keeping oneself fed; investment, not pleasure; work, not leisure — these were the norms which made the entrepreneurs specifically modern.

The will to succeed was expressed in the unbridled pleasure taken in making money, uninhibited by any scruples. Later, after the mid-century, the relentless pursuit of private gain and advantage became paramount, overcoming traditional scruples. The desire to make money in the form of speculation became distinct from work, the separation of private virtue and impersonal, abstract business maxims became paramount, and financial success was also justified as being something beyond mere self-interest. It was expressed as a 'service' to higher ends, to the enterprise, which, as it were, took on a life of its own (and was linked to the family); and it was indeed — after the decline of the strong religious ties which had forged the race of entrepreneurs in the first half of the century — in a very subjective application of Adam Smith, a contribution to improving human relations and the progress of culture. The entrepreneur's bourgeois sense of honour was inextricably bound up with money and possessions. Part of this was his credit rating, based on moral virtues, hard work and thrift. Bankruptcy was seen as the result of incompetence or inferiority, and entailed a loss of honour. Together with property, status in the community and, above all, independence from others were seen as part of the trappings of success. Success was experienced as an extraordinary privilege, compared with the rewards gained from being a state official; it was experienced as a new freedom.

Lifestyle, family and household followed business fortunes. Expenditure during the Vormärz tended to be slight, modest and bourgeois, and all 'appearances' were avoided. The family was something beyond the mere nuclear family, it was a central institution, extending into business, a focal point of existence. The other focal point during the Vormärz was to a large degree still the church. The culture of the educated classes was slow to penetrate these households. The theatre was generally taboo, but music had its part to play. The middle-class culture of associations and clubs gave a different and more refined dimension to life. Entrepreneurs, businessmen and bankers began to consider themselves as middle-class notables. Through their mutual distrust of officialdom and the world of the educated classes — only the pastors were accorded due respect — the economic and educated middle class slowly began to mix. Distaste for the old elite, for example in the Rhineland, included contempt for army officers and the aristocracy whose exclusivity and the irrational pre-eminence they accorded to 'birth', their lack of bourgeois virtues, their idleness and pretensiousness were all condemned. Unlike the aristocracy, the economic bourgeoisie fostered the dignity of of productive labour, and now claimed to be the elite of a new and improved era in world history. Titles, palaces, marriage into the aristocracy would all have contradicted their sense of their own worth. Their sons were kept away from military service as far as possible. They also tended to cut themselves off from the lower classes whom they often despised, though there were increasing examples of marriage of the new men into other classes.

These attitudes gradually changed from the 1850s onwards. Rage against the aristocracy and a conscious attempt to distance themselves from it remained a strong element in the psyche of the industrialists. The big entrepreneurs increasingly vied with the old upper classes, in the ways familiar from the English example. The patrician villa with its large reception rooms, coaches and fine clothing, riding and hunting were adopted. In the 1860s a sort of *jeunesse dorée* emerged in large industrial towns. Krupp held court on his estate and entertained like an aristocrat. However — and this is the crucial point — he refused a title; aristocracy and industry did not go together.

There was nevertheless a simultaneous striving for recognition by the old ruling classes and endeavours were made to enter it. The striving for titles, titles conferred on distinguished businessmen and membership of privy councils, and ennoblement or the entry of sons into distinguished regiments, were obtained at the price of adopting conformist pro-government postures; a 'feudalisation of the bourgeoisie' had begun. In the administrative district of Düsseldorf in 1861, the leading businessmen included four privy councillors and thirty-six leading members of business associations and fifty holders of honours. Between 1850 and 1870, the same business community boasted five ennoblements, but the number of refusals due to 'anti-government attitudes' was greater. Aristocracy and bourgeoisie, conservative and progressive literary figures poked fun at the new breed of bourgeois. The larger and more significant sector of entrepreneurs, however, still being added to by upward mobility, held on to their bourgeois anti-feudal norms. Some, like August Thyssen, kept to a simple lifestyle. Krupp was a role model for the bourgeois, anti-feudal attitude like that of *Die Gartenlaube*. He saw the aristocracy as incompetent, immoral, arrogant, capricious and reactionary, the entrepreneur on the other hand as hard-working, enlightened and nationalist.

An almost parallel development occurred in political orientation. During the Vormärz, the entrepreneurs were liberals opposed to feudal privileges and favouring a constitution. When a bill was presented, in 1843, providing for the stripping of noble titles as punishment, the entrepreneurs in the Rhenish *Landtag* were in uproar against the idea of turning the bourgeoisie into a 'colony of aristocratic criminals'. Simultaneously, they inveighed against supervision by 'ignorant' bureaucrats on matters of politics and economic policy — the bureaucrats, for their part, considering the interests and level of understanding of the entrepreneurs to be only the 'restricted understanding of subordinates (*Untertanen*)'. An example of this was the prolonged opposition of the bureaucrats to the setting up of joint stock companies. Specific demands of the entrepreneurs merged with the general demands of the bourgeoisie. It was self-evident on Christian and humanitarian grounds that entrepreneurs were also obliged to serve the public interest. The Rhenish entrepreneurs were very mindful of the dangers of pauperism, of the polarisation between the 'monied aristocracy' and those without property. They attempted to counter this danger, for example by campaigning for a constitution and free associations.

The appointment of Karl Marx to the *Rheinische Zeitung*, the newspaper which represented opposition to industry, was no coincidence. During the revolution, the entrepreneurs were in the camp that favoured a constitution and a liberal legal system. They wanted to force through the demands of the liberals and stabilise a renewed government as a force for order against the threat of upheaval. During the period of peak industrialisation, the politico-economic conflicts between entrepreneurs and governments decreased with the enactment of liberal legislation. Economic interests could be voiced in their own organisations (in 1860 in the Prussian Congress of Trade and Industry, in 1861 in the German Congress of Trade and Industry, in 1858 the society for the mining industry in the central mining authority region, Dortmund, in 1852 the Association of Iron and Steel Trades for the territories in the Zollverein). Some entrepreneurs renounced political principles which did not 'square with the commercial bottom line', but the great majority remained liberals. In the Prussian constitutional conflict, they were opposed to an increase in military spending and against breaches of the constitution, and were thus on the side of the opposition. It was not until the gulf opened between radical, 'doctrinaire' opposition and the search for a realistic compromise that the entrepreneurs found themselves on the side of the pragmatic, more conservative liberals. Of course, the entrepreneurs hardly engaged in active politics. For instance, only 8% were members of the Prussian *Landtag* in 1866. It was difficult for them to find time for this, and it was the educated men, better versed in rhetoric, who retained the leading liberal positions.

6. Crafts

Pre-industrial trade, which, with the exception of manufacturing and mining, was organised on a small-business basis — it was crafts-based. From the social point of view, crafts and small trade were the basic elements of the 'old middle class', and essentially, in spite of the rural crafts and domestic craft industries in the countryside, they formed the basis of the 'old' urban middle-class world, of the old urban *Bürger*. In the 19th century craft workers were frequently included in the newly invented sociological category of the 'petty bourgeoisie'. How did crafts develop in the age of modernisation, industrialisation and liberalism?

Let us look first at the statistics. The crafts sector, like the trades in general, expanded out of proportion to the population from the 1830s onwards. This disproportionate increase only tailed off towards the end of the period under review. Certainly, industry and the factory workforce expanded even more quickly, so that the proportion of crafts to trades as a whole dropped slightly; industry began to take the place of crafts in commercial production. But the rise of industry, statistically speaking, did not take place at the expense of the crafts sector, at least not at first. Of course, there were various reasons for this disproportionate growth, and it took place in various phases. For the 1830s and especially the 1840s it would be fair to speak of overmanning in the crafts sector under conditions of economic stagnation. The rise in numbers of workers was not due to 'growth', but to increased 'immigration', to an expanding population when labour requirements were falling and at a time of economic stagnation. Overmanning corresponded to underemployment, income cuts (approximately 25%) and poverty. Between one-quarter and one-half of the artisan population lived on or below the poverty line, and the majority did not pay trade taxes. Many, in the cities and in Berlin for example, were dependent on charity. There was a leap in the number of master craftsmen who could not afford to employ any journeymen. The weavers, clothiers and stocking-makers, poor folk with barely enough to survive and victims of the later mechanisation of the textile industry, greatly increased in numbers (in Saxony, for example, the numbers of clothiers doubled between 1836 and 1849, while the numbers of stocking-makers and weavers quadrupled). This was all part of the pre-industrial return to cheap labour. In short, the crafts industry was not an economic growth sector during these years, but, like the lower classes in the countryside, was much more threatened by pauperism, the mass impoverishment resulting from the widening gulf between population growth and a stagnant economy. After 1848, industry absorbed the under-employed immigrants; growth based on the economy began for the first time, and the initial crisis seemed to have been overcome.

Table 23: Craft workers within the borders of the later German Reich (estimates)

	1800 absolute	Index	1846–47 absolute	Index
Total	1,230,000	100	2,000,000	163
Masters	820,000	100	1,070,000	130
Assistants	410,000	100	930,000	227

	1800 %	1846–47 %
Proportion of craftsmen among the employed	12.0	13.4
Proportion of craftsmen in the total population	17.0	16.0

Of course, this statistical growth must be interpreted in several different ways. Firstly, there is overall growth, and after 1830 the number of journeymen and trainees increased far more quickly than that of the master craftsmen (with the exception of the crisis years of the 1840s). While on average every third master craftsman had a journeyman in about 1800, and every second master craftsman had a journeyman in about 1816–19, by 1861 there were already more journeymen than master craftsmen, in spite of a certain number of 'defections' to industry. These ratios varied greatly, of course, by geography and by sector. In the countryside, in the west and the south-west, in the food and clothing sectors, there were more masters than journeymen, while in Berlin and in Saxony, in the construction, wood and metal sectors, the number of journeymen (per business) was much higher. In general, the extremes (i.e., the numbers of masters without journeymen at one end of the scale, and the large-scale craft workshops at the other) increased, though this trend is obscured by the averages. One important social consequence of this development was that a journeyman could no longer expect, as was the rule heretofore, to become a master, which fact, together with pauperisation, explains a good deal of the radicalism of the journeymen during the 1840s. Thenceforth, growth varied regionally. In Prussia, especially in the east, it was especially high, owing to the high rate of population growth, perhaps because of the lack of restrictions on trading, and because at first there were proportionally far fewer craftsmen than in the south and west. In the large towns, outside the centres of heavy industry, the economic growth rate was higher, while in Bavaria, by contrast, it was lower than the population growth rate. The relative proportions of rural and urban artisans stayed approximately equal between 1805 and 1850.

Table 24: Development of crafts in Prussia

Year	Population (millions)	Masters	Craft Workers Assistants	Total	Masters and assistants as % of pop.
1801	10.0	c. 330,000	c. 110,000	440,000	4.4
1816	10.4	258,830	145,459	404,289	3.8
1831	13.0	334,346	187,565	521,911	3.9
1837	14.1	375,097	244,875	619,972	4.3
1840	14.9	396,016	280,089	676,105	4.5
1843	15.5	408,825	311,458	720,283	4.6
1846	15.9	457,400	384,800	842,200	5.3
1849	16.3	535,232	407,141	942,373	5.7
1858	17.7	545,034	507,198	1,052,232	5.9
1861	18.4	534,556	558,321	1,092,877	5.9

Table 25: Index figures for the development of crafts in Prussia, 1816–46

Year	Population	Masters	Assistants and apprentices
1816	100	100	100
1819	106	100	98
1831	126	124	123
1843	146	151	205
1846	156	170	256

Table 26: Shift in the distribution of persons employed in individual crafts sectors in Prussia, 1816–46 (%)

	Masters		Assistants		Combined	
	1816	1846	1816	1846	1816	1846
Clothing sector	45.5	45.5	40.9	31.1	43.8	38.9
Metalworking sector	17.7	16.7	17.0	15.3	17.4	16.1
Woodworking sector	14.4	18.9	10.8	13.9	13.1	16.6
Food sector	13.2	11.4	8.4	7.1	11.4	9.4
Construction sector	7.4	6.2	20.8	30.8	12.4	17.5

Table 27: Numbers of masters and assistants within the populations of individual states, 1846–49 (%)

	Masters	Assistants
Prussia		
Eastern provinces	2.4	4.2
Central provinces	3.3	7.0
Western provinces	4.0	6.4
Silesia	2.7	5.2
Hesse–Nassau	3.8	6.1
Thuringia	1.9	3.6
Kingdom of Saxony	3.6	8.4
Baden	4.5	7.0
Bavaria	3.4	7.0

Finally, there were sectoral differences. The large-scale crafts sectors, which provided food, clothing and accommodation, expanded slightly; in other words, their proportion remained relatively stable. Trades such as those of builder, joiner and locksmith underwent an expansion after 1850, while the cottage textile industry went into decline at the end of the period. Certain crafts, such as those of soapmaker or candlemaker, almost completely disappeared, while others — glaziers, coopers, rope-makers, tanners, wood-turners, wheelwrights — went substantially into decline, especially after 1850, driven out by industry. Others again, like the shoemakers — whose numbers continued to increase, though by less than the growth of crafts as a whole — changed their function and became predominantly repairers. Crafts did not succumb to industry as anticipated by the prophets of the mid-century — Marx and the conservatives — but survived, though greatly displaced and transformed, and the victims of this change suffered a great deal of hardship. The stable and expanding crafts sectors also accepted factory products, such as half-finished goods, but, astonishingly, they were able to hold their own on this new basis.

Table 28: Numbers of craftsmen by region

Region	Craftsmen (000)
Saxony	133
Baden	130
Württemberg	94
Hesse–Kassel	75
Hesse–Darmstadt	74
Bavaria	72
Rhineland	70
Westphalia	66
Lower Saxony	63
Palatinate	59
Silesia	58
Hesse–Nassau	52
Pomerania	52
East Prussia	41
Germany	59

The mode of production remained traditional and static. There was no capital-intensive modernisation, and productivity did not increase. Products were made for local sale and, where appropriate, were made to order. It was not until the emergence of department stores for clothes and furniture that the situation changed. Complaints about the new form of competition from these department stores cannot disguise the fact that they increased the number of orders for products. In addition to production, as stated, there were repairs and, in part, direct sales. Economic modernisation was also provided by the credit co-operatives, the *Vorschussvereine*, founded by the liberal-democrat Hermann Schulze-Delitzsch, which took care of purchases, sales, and credits, and expanded from the 1850s onwards.

As far as changes in income are concerned, attempts to ascertain an average income, outside of the crisis periods of the 1840s, are problematic. There were major variations depending on region and trade sector, company size and home ownership. Craftsmen in the agricultural and building sectors were generally well off. An investigation in

Göttingen showed an increase between the years of 1829 and 1861 of the upper income bracket from 7.3% to 10.6%, and that of the lower income bracket from 17.6% to 34.1%, with a decrease of the middle bracket from 75.1% to 55.3%. It might be concluded that a relative impoverishment had taken place. In general, however, there is no simple answer to the question of whether the soil in which crafts had flourished had turned barren.

What was the economic, commercial and political structure which the crafts sector needed in order to continued to exist and develop? At the beginning of the period under review, crafts were organised into guilds, those multi-functional associations that encompassed and regulated the economy and life, with their characteristic tradition of 'reputability', which afforded a social identity and a closed shop, excluding competition and outsiders. Crafts were also pursued outside the guilds, with the approval or even the encouragement of the ruling classes, and large-scale industry was beginning to emerge, especially in the countryside. *Gewerbefreiheit*, the freedom to pursue a trade, was introduced into the French regions and in Prussia (1810) during the reform period. The guilds lost all control of admission to a trade, to demarcations and the training of apprentices. After 1815, this was also the case in the old Prussia of 1807 (excluding Posen, Saxony and Western Pomerania), in the Rhineland and in parts of Westphalia, as well as in the Palatinate and in Nassau. In 1845, the freedom of trade was introduced generally throughout Prussia, of course with certain modifications. In certain sectors, such as building, proof of competence was required. Elsewhere, in north Germany, the old guild regulations continued to operate, or, as in the south and in Austria, were reformed by state concessions and the exclusion of industry, without introducing the freedom of trade. The autonomy or monopoly of the guilds was universally restricted by state control, and the old political power of the guilds in the community became a thing of the past.

Both the freedom of trade and industry were seen as the true enemy of the craftsmen, a total threat to their present and future existence. In reality, of course, the effects of the freedom of trade were much less dramatic, and the differences between the areas in which it was valid and those where the guild regulations applied were not very great. The numbers of branches, the level of competition, and of poverty, developed more or less independently of these differences. The territories without freedom of trade legalised non-guild crafts, but in the territories with freedom of trade the more informal influence of the guilds on management, training practices and behaviour continued to operate. Population growth and economic stagnation were, therefore, more important to the fate of crafts than differences in policies regarding the trades.

Whether as a result of the freedom of trade or of a relaxation of the guild monopoly, the security and assured welfare of the master guildsmen disappeared. Of course, in the south, owing to high employment in the craft industry, there was a quasi-natural limit to growth and the danger of pauperisation, while in Prussia both were primarily a consequence of the freedom of trade. In Prussia, the free movement of craftsmen into industry also facilitated the process of industrialisation.

The conservative governments of the period after 1848–49 attempted to respond to the craftsmen's protest, to restrict freedom of trade, and to further the interests of the guilds, in order to exploit the politico-economic conservatism of the crafts industry. For instance, in Prussia in 1849, the requirement of a 'proof of competence' was introduced almost everywhere, and matters concerning apprentices and examinations were placed in the hands of the guilds. In Hanover, Nassau and Baden, the freedom of trade was not introduced. However, this policy failed. Overmanning and under-employment did not cease. The problem of the craftsmen was not to be solved in this way, especially in view of the rise of industry. From the end of the 1850s (Austria in 1859) almost all states finally came down in favour of freedom to trade. The liberal version of a crafts policy — progress through competition and self-help through co-operatives — now gained acceptance in the wider political arena, and also among some of the craftsmen.

The mentality of craftsmen, their behaviour and value system was rooted in tradition and formed by the guild ethos of reputability. They lived in their environment, proud of their 'vocation' that was anything but a mere 'job', proud of its customs, of its corporate connections. They had internalised the 'honour' of their estate — a phenomenon unknown today. Ambition, the desire to better oneself and innovation were disdained in the interests of solidarity and security. A sense of what 'became' them, and what did not (e.g. riding in a carriage), gave them an 'old-world' quality. Willingness to work, thrift, reputability, a dry and rigid, slightly authoritarian sense of justice and morals, a sense of family that was at times slightly sentimentalised, all these were characteristic. The worlds of work, home and family were still in close proximity; for that reason, craftsmen had an integral sense of their own identity and were not yet alienated. Of course, they fought tooth and nail against anything unfamiliar and new, against innovation and progress, rooted as they were in the particularist interests of their community and their own locale, which extended no further than the parish boundaries.

These are precisely the qualities which were maliciously dubbed 'Biedermeier' or even 'philistine' (or 'petty bourgeois'). Part and parcel of this, though clearly only up until 1848, when they could be afforded, were the small-town comforts, such as the morning and evening tipples. This also entailed a predominantly static economic ethic. Why should they make more of an effort than was necessary to survive? Why take risks, strike out in new directions, stake capital, exploit opportunities, transform working conditions, engage in and suffer from competition, exploit debts and change forms of training? Restiveness and dynamism were not the artisan's primary attributes — although change represented a grave threat to them. People were opposed to unrestricted marriage, immigration, the withdrawal of tariffs, the parity of town and country. More than in any other occupation, once a craftsman had decided upon a trade, he stuck with it, even though industry and the market drastically diminished its chances, as in the rural textile trade. The weavers wanted to remain weavers.

Yet modernisation was having a liberating effect even in this sphere. Economic and family reasons led to the demise of the patriarchal master craftsman's household, beginning in the cities. The journeymen moved out, and this represented a fundamental change in lifestyle for them, an end of the old obeisance to authority and corporation. The craftsmen, and not only the restless journeymen, took part in literary and intellectual life, in the nation's political and religious issues. Schiller was especially popular among them; and outside the guilds and estates, they entered the new associations organised by the bourgeoisie — the choral, gymnastic and shooting societies, the musical and dramatic societies and foundations. Hardship and competition, the growing power of the marketplace and of financial connections also led — at first in economic behaviour — to the emergence of individualistic instead of corporative norms, and gradually eroded the life of the guilds and the guild mentality.

The artisans' sense of historical time, which also determined their political outlook, centred round the threat brought about by change. The collapse of the world of the guilds and towns, the eruption of competition due to the new population surplus and to industry, the loss of security, and the possibility of falling into the proletariat, were all feared. This is clearly shown from the hardship suffered by the quasi-proletarian single and small craftsmen and journeymen in the crisis of the 1840s. The positive features can be viewed in retrospect and are confirmed by statistics. They are self-assertion and growth, restructuring and differentiation, which made a small and belated impact. And if one bears in mind that intelligent socialist and conservative observers had been prophesying the decline, and even the fall, of crafts through the onset of industry, this sense of threat is the more understandable. It was impossible, or at least difficult, to protest against the real cause of the pauperism of the 1840s, namely population growth and a stagnant economy, for these were such abstract quantities. The protest had identifiable targets, primarily industry and the freedom of trade. There were also other bones of contention, such as restrictions on the guilds, freedom to settle, citizen's rights and unrestricted marriage in the cities; opposition to the bureaucracy was particularly strong, for it was the bureaucracy which operated in such an abstract, rational, general manner and was forcing through a modern society against the particularist, secure world of the craftsmen. The craftsmen constantly protested against freedom of trade, which already existed in Prussia and appeared to be imminent elsewhere. This, for them, was the real evil, the root of all ills, the principle of the anonymous and deregulated market, of unrestricted egotistical competition, of the fight of one against all. This would be a world in which social status was not determined by personal 'honour' acquired through work, but by success in the market-place; for the craftsmen this spelt the end of morality. This was the reason for the moral tone of their protest. In contrast to the new developments, what they wanted was guaranteed 'sustenance', legislation to regulate production and sales, the prohibition of rural competition, of peddling and progressive taxation of factories. The reply of the Prussian bureaucracy, which was to have fascinating consequences over the next thirty-eight years, was that the purpose of trade was to serve the public, not the reverse, and that every restriction impeded innovation and growth and ultimately damaged the interests of the craftsmen themselves.

This could not set the craftsmen's minds at rest. References to the absurdities of guild demarcations — no joiner was allowed to use nails, but carpenters were — only added to their embitterment. The officials apportioned most of the blame for the decline of crafts to the individual and his 'indolence', and neglected the structural problem. The other evil from the craftsmen's point of view was that there were too many factories, English and German (that, in terms of the national economy, there were in fact too few, was beyond their ability to comprehend). This combined with the protest against the 'rich' factory owners and capitalists — in the declining rural textile crafts, for example, but also elsewhere — and with the protest against the state, which favoured factories and did not prevent competition from imports. And it was by no means only the craftsmen directly affected by the crises who protested: they all had their say, even those, like the builders, who were well off.

The journeymen once again intensified this protest during the crisis of the 1840s; they wanted to be craftsmen, to become master craftsmen, and could barely do this under acceptable conditions. They were threatened with the lifelong wage-dependency of the factory. They had to fight side-by-side with their masters, and also against them and the guild monopolies, against police controls and harassment, which directly affected their working conditions. They were for tradition, not progess. Some of them were uprooted from their areas of origin, without being able to put down roots in a new environment. For this reason, they were particularly receptive to the enlightened, radical democratic, early socialist critique of society, and were the real source of the social unrest in the Vormärz.

In the spring of 1848, there were uprisings in central Germany and in the Rhineland, of which the craftsmen were the main instigators, rebelling against factories and machines, and in some places also steamships and railways. In Solingen, for instance, they fought against the 'low-quality' machine-made steel products, which competed against hand-forged quality scissors. In Krefeld the weavers succeeded in abolishing large-scale production; they wanted to work at their looms independently, and in voluntary association — they felt that nobody should have more than four looms.

Elsewhere, artisans demanded restrictions on factory production (or steamship travel) and price stabilisation. Craftsmen everywhere in Germany, in assemblies, and through petitions and societies, demanded a return to the old trade regulations. The strength of the traditional mentality is shown most clearly by the fact that the journeymen, who, independent of the masters and more radical than they were, held their own 'revolutionary parliament', and were in complete agreement with their masters on this matter. All were opposed to the prospect of losing their class status and citizenship through pauperism, the growth of industry and rampant competition. Such protectionist demands, however, were accompanied by liberal-democratic and social ones, including progressive taxation and free education, job creation schemes and social welfare payments by the state. It was the journeymen who voiced these more radical demands. They rebelled against the arbitrariness of capital and fought for the dignity of labour, for the right to work and make a living. However, they were against any 'communist' system, and in favour of the free blossoming of talent and achievement; they opposed the guild monopoly and were in favour of guaranteed provision: they wanted the best of two conflicting worlds.

Overall, then, the craftsmen were politically ambivalent. They were on the side of the people, against the 'lords and masters', who were the scourge of the little man, against the bureaucracy, the aristocracy and the rich. They belonged to the opposition, liberal or democratic, they were for people's rights, participation, constitution. They were, and behaved like, *Bürger*. Yet in terms of social and economic policy, they were conservative. They were against liberalism, and for a tightly governed order that protected them from capitalism and the proletariat. Although during the Vormärz the liberals, and especially the elected representatives, were by no means promoters of the freedom of trade, the Frankfurt National Assembly at Paulskirche demonstrated that in the final analysis they had to side with the principle of individual economic freedoms, competition and the overcoming of the crisis by modernisation, and so they spoke for the interests of the entrepreneurs and large-scale merchants. Contradictions in economic and social policy stood parallel to constitutional and national political contradictions. This was the source of the latent tension between crafts, petty bourgeoisie and liberalism, and it was part of the tragedy of the German revolution, a consequence of the fact that it occurred during the death-throes of the pre-industrial world.

Like the governments after the revolution, the conservatives attempted to exploit opposition between crafts and the liberals, to mobilise trade for its own interests with a 'popular conservative' trade policy. In the 1860s, some of the conservative support in the towns certainly came from the trade sector. Some of those who protested against the freedom to trade became involved in the formation of Catholic parties. Spokesmen for organised crafts, especially in north Germany, tended to emphasise their opposition to the liberals. But there was no question of a unified attitude among craftsmen. Large sections of the craftsmen in the Protestant areas were indeed liberal, for reasons unconnected with trade policy. They had overcome the crisis of pauperism; some sectors among the craftsmen had held their own and contributed to the improvement in the economic situation; and so liberal concepts of self-help, technical modernisation and association won support, even among those affected. Craftsmen were not conservative in the way that the peasants were; they were too urban, too bourgeois, too little distanced from the 'spirit of the age'. Alternatively, while among peasants the roles of 'professional' and bourgeois were almost identical, they began to separate out among the craftsmen, and political and socio-economic orientations could pursue different paths.

The radical opposition of the journeymen declined after the revolution, although their number practically exceeded that of the master craftsmen. Transition to a (specialist) factory workforce, together with the first stirrings of the workers' movement and the relative consolidation of crafts, alleviated the problem, even when, in the 1860s, the government stopped clamping down on the slightest rumbling of unrest among the journeymen, as it had done formerly.

7. The Lower Classes, Factories, Industrial Workers, Social Problems

Below the craftsmen and farmers, the educated classes, the businessmen and officials in the old order, there existed a mass of people so heterogeneous that they can only be formally grouped together as an underclass. They continued to exist within the increasingly bourgeois society and, later, within early industrial society. These people lived outside the accepted orders, they were 'the estate without status'. They included dependent workers living by their labours, most of them without fixed incomes, without wealth and, above all, without any property worthy of the name. In rural areas those who owned land lived in huts or cottages, while those living in the old cities were denied citizens' rights because of their lack of property and lived in, or on the fringes of, destitution (the 'estate of the poor'). In rural areas, this mass consisted of agricultural workers ranging from crofters to boarders with no home of their own. There were also home-workers engaged in rural industries such as textiles and related areas. In the towns they were the servants, day-labourers and workers in transport and manufacturing, the factory and casual workers — all non-citizens.

In addition, especially in the cities, there were the poor in the old sense of the word: the unemployed, those living on poor relief, beggars, vagabonds, the work-shy, the disabled and the social misfits. Soldiers, petty officials and lowly clerks were borderline cases. Lastly came those whose status, expectations, ownership of property or job description placed them outside these categories: the smallholders, manual workers and apprentices who could be sucked towards, and occasionally below, the poverty line in times of crisis, and would then be indistinguishable from the true underclass in terms of living standards: those under direct threat of 'pauperisation' or 'proletarisation'.

Members of these social strata were either born into them because their parents were from the same background, or else dropped into them, either through circumstances beyond their control, as in the case of disinherited sons, or apprentices who failed to find a job as a master, or through their own fault, as in the case of drop-outs and the work-shy. These last groups gave rise to the view, especially prevalent in Protestantism, that poverty was a result of indolence and evil, the antidote to which was education and coercion.

The poor have always been with us, but by about 1800, they constituted a substantial community which had been on the increase throughout the 18th century. Mention has been made above of rural classes below the farmers, some of them 'proto-industrial' home-workers. In the cities, this was an even more striking phenomenon. In 1811 in Frankfurt-on-Main, only one-third of the male population enjoyed citizen's rights (the figure for 1723 had been three-quarters!). The corresponding figure for Hamburg was under a half. In 1816 in Bremen, 54.1% of all wage-earners were manual workers or in service; counting apprentices and trainees, the figure was 64.7%. Thus, in its first half at least, the 19th century was typified by a disproportionate growth of the lower classes, the number of dependent workers, and poverty.

From about 1830 onwards poverty became a mass phenomenon, a collective rather than an individual fate, and a new term entered the currency: pauperism. Industry was not to blame; the culprit was population growth coupled with stagnating economies with frozen or proportionally lower labour demands. In the 1840s, distress was at its greatest where there was no industry; after 1850, the crisis of pauperism rapidly abated when industrialisation created new jobs. Liberalisation of marriage rules, new opportunities offered by the expansion of agriculture and home-working and changes in customs and outlook meant that members of the traditional lower classes and previously 'superfluous' sections of the population could now consider earlier establishment of a family, where previously such a step would frequently have been entirely impossible.

As illustrated above in the case of the relationship between farmers and agricultural labour in the east, it was the lower classes that were reinforced by the growth in population. Smallholders east of the Elbe were forced into the underclass and the subpeasant class lost a sizeable amount of its social insurance once common land was abolished. The numbers below the poverty line grew at first in the towns and *Realteilungsgebiete*. Thereafter, as employment tailed off with the intensification of agriculture and home-working, the process spread still further; the surplus from the middle classes (artisans and farmers) also dropped below the line. For the destitute who owned nothing to pay for their passage, emigration offered no escape. In Prussia in the year 1846, 45% of males over fourteen were dependent manual workers, the majority of them living a poor and insecure existence, and 10–15% lived a proletarian-like existence. The Prussian statistician Dieterici estimated that 50–60% of the population lived precariously or in need, and that in times of crisis they existed in misery and fear of their lives. A very strict interpretation must put at least one-third of the population in the category of proto-proletariat proletariat. In the mid-1840s, a further acute crisis deepened the existing structural crisis. The failure of potato and cereal crops between 1845 and 1847 and price increases approaching 100% were exacerbated by an industrial and economic recession and resulted in famine and misery on an even greater scale. The affected groups were chiefly urban day-labourers, although skilled workers and craftsmen also suffered: there was two-thirds unemployment in Solingen and Pforzheim, while in Berlin only 5% still paid taxes. The number of city-dwellers so poor they could no longer afford accommodation rose during the 1840s to around 5–6%. In Hamburg, the figure was around 10–12%; in Cologne it reached 25% for a time; while in Bavaria it reached 33% in places. It is a universal fact that such conditions lead to rises in criminality and prostitution. At a rough approximation, jobs would have been available for 80% of the workforce (about 45% of the population). This mismatch did not result in mass unemployment (that was impossible) but rather to widespread under-employment and/or wage cuts to below subsistence level. The construction of roads and railways required mass labour for a time — especially from the rural population — and in fact at first drew its labour resources exclusively from agriculture, but it could not provide long-term contracts or employment.

In general, rather than cutting the number of jobs, industry had the opposite effect. However it was responsible for pressurising certain trades, exacting some victims, and eliminating certain jobs; the bargees and tugboat men on the Rhine spring to mind. The advancing misery that afflicted so many is distressingly exemplified by the plight of home-working handloom weavers and spinners in Silesia and their protests in 1844 — other food riots and revolts occurred in the 1840s — and was highlighted by the ensuing journalistic and literary debate and the shock felt both at the time and thereafter. The old-fashioned home-working methods came under dual pressure from competing industrially produced and imported goods on the one hand, and a surplus of labour on the other.

Faced with increasing inability to compete and an endangered market for their products, workers reacted, not by changing jobs or switching to new methods, but by boosting their productivity through longer working hours, the use of more family (child) labour and accepting cuts in wages and earnings that approached 40%; the net result was to intensify the financial pressures that threatened them. In Silesia there was a further factor in the incomplete reform of agriculture: the cottage weavers were still labouring under the financial yoke of feudal dues. The position of the weavers was bleak, and the middlemen and manufacturers, the 'capitalists' upon whom they were dependent, were seen as symbolic of their position. One of them, the *nouveau riche* Zwanziger, fell victim to mob rule. Furniture, clothing, coaches, stocks, business papers and an ancient estate were destroyed by a crowd of 300 weavers, but no one was attacked and there was no instance of arson. The army put down the 'rebellion' and heavy penalties were imposed, but the outbreak of frustration made a lasting impression on the public, and not only among radicals such as Heinrich Heine, whose poem we include here, but also notably, among conservatives.

Song of the Silesian Weavers

No tears in their sombre eyes,
They sit at the loom and bare their teeth:
Germany, we are weaving your shroud,
We are weaving into it
The threefold curse
We are weaving, we are weaving!

A curse on the God
To whom we prayed in the winter's cold and in time of famine;
We have hoped and waited in vain,
He has mocked and fooled and deluded us —
We are weaving, we are weaving!

A curse on the King, the King of the Rich
Whom our wretchedness could not soften,
Who has extorted our last penny from us,
And has had us shot like dogs
We are weaving, we are weaving!

A curse on our false Fatherland
Where only disgrace and shame flourish
Where every flower is soon broken
Where putrefaction and decay refresh the worm —
We are weaving, we are weaving!

The shuttle flies, the loom creaks
We are weaving busily day and night
Old Germany, we are weaving your shroud,
We are weaving into it the threefold curse
We are weaving, we are weaving!

Heinrich Heine, *Selected Verse*, translated by Peter Branscombe (Penguin Classics, 1986).

After 1845, food riots became increasingly frequent, for example in Berlin, where the 'potato revolution' took place on 21 April 1847, or in Upper Silesia, where 80,000 fell sick with typhus, of whom 16,000 died. Protests of this kind were put down by military force in all cases. However, reports and subsequent studies — e.g. those undertaken by Virchow — directed public attention to the scale of pauperism.

Life for the lower classes was conditioned primarily by three main factors. The first of these was naturally the economic situation and standard of living. The true growth of the economy is not known with any accuracy, and neither is the distribution of that growth and the development of living standards. There are therefore a number of open questions, for instance whether the position of the underclasses grew significantly worse — ignoring famines — whether poverty came to be felt more keenly, and whether inequality increased with respect to the (modest) standards enjoyed by members of slightly higher social strata. It is likely that the situation was worse at the end of the 18th century, but the sheer scale of poverty was something new. Attempts have been made to determine income in these groups by compiling data on wages and prices among factory and craft workers. With food prices rising at the turn of the century, wages were at their lowest in real terms; there was great fluctuation up to 1817, followed by an improvement during the 1820s and 1830s when food prices began to fall. Wages then dropped during the 1840s, reaching their lowest point in 1847, though this was still above the level for 1800. For most of the first half of the century, wages were generally insufficient to keep a family of five above subsistence level, and would at times be insufficient to feed such a family. Admittedly, data of this kind can do no more than illustrate a trend. Local variation in wages was as great as variation between different occupations and positions; even then, the cost of living in particularist economies was far from uniform. Pay for hand-spinners and linen weavers working in the old ways was particularly poor. For craftsmen in construction it was quite good, while for factory workers it was better than for unskilled manual labour. Often there was a certain degree of self-sufficiency — vegetable plots, goats, cattle or pigs — though the exact degree is unknown. In rural areas payment in kind accounted for a considerable proportion of income. The majority of the members of the underclasses were not simply wage-earners; in the pre-industrial world work was undertaken by the whole family, and the whole family were co-earners. The amount of charity given to individuals by church or private benefactors cannot be estimated. For these reasons, the means at a family's disposal were more than just the wage earned by an individual; a family could not live on a single wage. For a good proportion of the underclass, opportunities for work were precarious; weekly pay therefore reveals nothing about annual wages. Under such conditions, the concept of unemployment is virtually meaningless. The situation was typified by irregular working as well as chronic under-employment. Overall, however, it is possible to say that most of the underclass laboured around the fringes of a poverty line that was in any case pitched very low. Between two-thirds and four-fifths of income had to be spent on food in such households. Standards of nourishment matched standards of accommodation as already described; they were of the poorest.

Insecurity was the second hallmark of the existence led by many sections of the lower classes. Their employment and incomes were insecure, as was their outlook at any time of crisis, both general and personal — especially during illness, old age or on the death of members of the family, especially that of the mother or father. Saving for emergencies was out of the question because of the income situation. The hand-to-mouth existence of the underclass, and the fact that the extent of that class made them far more vulnerable to crises by comparison with former times, was as much a new experience for them as it was for their contemporaries. An element of this experience was the general hopelessness of ever breaking out of that particular stratum. Their social position became a collective fate.

Thirdly, with pauperism the existence of the underclasses gained a new moral quality. Despite living by the rules of the traditional social order, albeit on its edge, they fell out of that scheme when agricultural, occupational, legal and family structures underwent change at the same time as their numbers were on the increase. The old society crumbled, and having no access to status, land or guild organisation, the lower

Table 29: Weekly wages in various trade sectors for the period 1840–49 (in 1873 marks)

Trade/profession	Weekly wage in marks	Location/region
Crafts		
Masons	10.17	Rostock
Stone-masons	11.58	Schopfheim/Baden
Carpenters	12.24	average of Hamburg and Rostock
Smiths and Fitters	7.20	Wüttemberg
Joiners	7.20	Wüttemberg
Tailors	6.00	Schopfheim/Baden
Average of craftsmen (excluding building trades)	7.72	Baden
Textile trade		
Spinning		
Hand-spinning in:		
Flax	0.75	no location given
Worsted	1.05	various locations
Machine spinning in:		
Cotton	7.80	Wüttemberg
Male workers	6.86	Steinen/Baden
Female workers	4.98	Steinen/Baden
Wool	7.50	Wüttemberg
Hand-weaving in:		
Linen	2.00	Silesia
Cotton	6.78	Württemberg
Carding-wool	7.30	Württemberg and Chemnitz
Worsted	10.50	Sachsen
Mining		
Coal	11.10	Saarland
Iron-ore	8.16	Left bank of the Rhine
Copper-ore	7.20	Mansfeld
'Factories'		
Agate-button factory		
Mechanics	28.83	Baden
Machinists	8.24	Baden
Women	4.98	Baden
Machine Factory		
Piece-work	14.25	no location given
Wage-labour	7.90	no location given
Iron foundry	8.22	Essen (Krupp)
Chemical works	9.01	Hamburg
Paper factory		
Male workers	6.86	Freiburg/Baden
Female workers	4.12	Freiburg/Baden

Table 30: Incomes of selected groups of employees in the territory of the later German Reich for 1810–49

Year	Nominal income		Cost of living index (1913 = 100)	Real income index (1913 = 100)
	absolute in marks	index (1913 = 100)		
1810	278	26	45	58
1811	275	25	44	57
1812	288	27	51	53
1813	277	26	51	51
1814	279	26	50	52
1815	281	26	54	48
1816	283	26	67	39
1817	284	26	95	27
1818	289	27	66	41
1819	290	27	51	53
1820	293	27	42	64
1821	287	27	46	59
1822	287	27	48	56
1823	287	27	44	61
1824	288	27	40	68
1825	284	26	44	59
1826	284	26	39	67
1827	285	26	40	65
1828	286	26	49	53
1829	287	27	46	59
1830	288	27	51	53
1831	292	27	50	54
1832	293	27	50	54
1833	294	27	50	56
1834	295	27	48	59
1835	296	27	46	59
1836	297	27	49	55
1837	301	28	48	58
1838	301	28	53	53
1839	303	28	54	52
1840	303	28	49	57
1841	304	28	47	60
1842	305	28	50	56
1843	305	28	59	47
1844	306	28	57	49
1845	307	28	57	49
1846	313	29	63	46
1847	311	29	61	48
1848	312	29	47	62
1849	310	29	44	66

classes were the first to break away. Socially they became stateless and uprooted (especially in the cities). Old standards were no longer valid or else were no longer observed. Contemporary accounts describe the process as moral decline and psychological dissolution, whereas radical thinkers absorbed it into the concept of alienation. In security, the vanishing hope of anything worthwhile and the state of economic flux led to disenchantment with the future, dissipation of means, and the decline of personal forward planning and energy directed at self-advancement, the work ethic and discipline. The effect of the decline of the home — firstly through its invasion by home-working, then the closure of the master's household to his apprentices — was one of demoralisation. There was enormous peer pressure in the journeymen's hostels with 'disreputable elements' setting the tone. Increasing alcoholism also had its roots here. The release from tradition, at once both disembodiment and liberation, joined forces with need and overwhelmed morals in its wake (and not only by 'middle-class' moral standards). At the same time, the subjective experience was one of disintegration, isolation, social statelessness, insecurity and helplessness.

It must be said that, despite these common characteristics, the underclasses were not at all uniform. Objectively speaking, there were enormous differences between country-folk and city-dwellers, as there were between journeymen and labourers or domestic servants. Factory workers, for example, were far better off than poor labourers in a village. Smallholders, boarders and farmhands would occasionally have been at an advantage over urban lower classes in terms of security of their social position and conditions under which they lived. Subjectively, the variations, and even divisions, were far sharper. People commonly thought of themselves as belonging to either their village or their city and, beyond that, to their region. However deplorable the situation at home, it was always felt to be better than elsewhere. They also regarded themselves as members of their occupation or business, or even as belonging to their employers or masters in the case of servants. They lived in households or businesses, not in communities. There was no sense of belonging together, no political consciousness or sense of class. Prevailing traditional attitudes to the social hierarchy dictated that subordination and compliance were taken for granted — norms and beliefs which still bore heavy Christian hallmarks. For individuals who were keen to get ahead, the liberal concept of finding a solution to social problems through education was greatly enlightening. Social criticism and its revolutionary slogans were the domain of bourgeois intellectuals, and later of journeymen who had travelled abroad, not of the lower classes.

It is an established fact that these underclasses developed into the industrial working classes as industrialisation advanced. Before describing that process, some comments are appropriate on the new organisational unit in industrial labour, the factory. The factory was the centre of all new production, all of which was determined by the use of machinery, division of labour and co-operation. Factories revolutionised the relationship of humans to time. The pre-industrial world was timed by the natural clock; the hour of the day, the seasons of the year, weather and 'natural' tasks such as harvesting, milking or the tending of charcoal ovens all gave structure and rhythm to the passage of time. Units of measuring area were even thought of in terms of time: the *Tagewerk* (the amount of land that could be ploughed in a day). The quality of time was obvious; it could be directly perceived. Days could be long or short according to the job in hand; interpersonal contact took place within that same temporal framework, so that work and life were barely separated. Time was not yet money, and time was wasted (in the sense in which that expression is understood today). The church divided the day by the ringing of bells and the year by the celebration of feasts, divisions that were reflected in the alternation of work, rest and play. In agriculture and crafts, time requirements were flexible. In the *Verlagssystem* and the home-working system much time was passed in waiting, fetching and carrying. The work itself could be irregular in duration, might be required quickly, or could even be of unstipulated length — provided it was all completed. Swapping between craft, household and agricultural tasks, especially at harvest time, was also an element of this flexibility. In short, it was necessary to switch between many tasks, and between periods of work and idleness — the 'blue Monday' (skipping work on Monday) was symbolic of this.

Throughout the early modern age clocks became increasingly widespread, and the 18th century saw rationalistic attempts at limiting the number of feast-days, both phenomena being signs of change. However, it was the machine that redefined time. Machinery ran regularly and demanded division and synchronisation of labour; manufacturers bought and paid for that labour by units of time. Time became technical, industrial, regular and abstract; it was not primarily lived but measured. The new concept of time demanded that the labour supply be punctual, continuous and regular, with breaks being limited and fixed. Time at work became something quite different from time for living. Time was rationalised — in factories (and similarly in another modern institution, the school) it was measured by clocks and signals. Time became money. Such new time discipline — the discipline that spread throughout the world via the factory, the office and the school — changed mankind. It created the peculiar dynamism of industrial man which can be felt in any developing country today. Time in its new guise also brought in its wake the peculiarly modern split between work and life. At this point both criticism and nostalgia set in — a picture of a world in which time was fulfilled, where there was none of the gnawing anxiety felt by modern man in his constant race against time, and his concern for making use of all that is available.

The early stages of industrialisation and the early factories themselves showed signs of conflict where the new norms of timekeeping were concerned. People had difficulty adjusting from the earlier natural clock and maintaining discipline. Reluctantly, workers had to obey fixed hours of work and regular workloads. The pressures of the new practices were keenly felt, not least because they were seen as being in opposition to nature. The free choice of days off had to be abandoned because days had to be worked in uninterrupted sequence. In the interests of rational organisation, it was necessary to put an end to many common practices among early factory workers, such as taking holidays when enough money was saved for a few days off, or returning home at harvest time. This was assisted by strict factory regulations which aimed at achieving discipline through instructions, inspections and penalties, by the issuing of contracts of employment to eliminate absenteeism, and lastly by pay structures which sought to achieve continuity of employment through low wages and incentive payments. Diligence and punctuality (as well as early rising) were all elements of education in the work ethic. Manufacturers and factories pushed through the new principles in the face of resistance and with many difficulties, because they had to be assimilated by workers from an earlier age.

The struggle for reduced working hours and remuneration of overtime was only possible thereafter.

The problem of motivation and the transformation it underwent were closely related to reorientation to a new concept of time, though not identical to it. Among newcomers to factory work, especially the unskilled, the early stages of industrialisation came at a time when indolence, lethargy, lack of inclination to effort and learning, and a lax attitude to the work ethic were rife. Because needs were modest and unchanging, it was difficult to make wage incentives effective with the whole of a workforce. New forms of motivation and discipline only succeeded after the rise of pauperism and the removal of rural reserve holdings on the one hand, and after adjustment to new standards of industrial performance and the relative rise of individual ambition on the other, even though there was further expression of the old, non-performance-orientated outlook — for instance in the high rate of mobility among sections of the working class.

Many pages of discourse in other places have outlined the division and simultaneous synchronisation of labour implied by factory methods. The individual's contribution is remote from the product, the sum of all the processes, and it is said that the removal of the worker from the visible object, the final product, means a loss of satisfaction, an 'alienation' in the worker–work–product relationship. The content of work is not the transformation of raw materials, but the supply and control of machinery. Concentration, alertness and an ability to execute repetitive actions regularly therefore become important virtues. Overall, in the concrete historical context of 19th-century Germany, machines did not reduce the physical load on the worker, and manual work remained or was shifted elsewhere. Machines both replaced and created work simultaneously. A new type of work, and a new relationship between the worker and the production process and the product itself, was certainly created thereby, but for the period under scrutiny there is too little concrete information about the development of that relationship or how it was experiened.

Conditions varied widely. 'Monotonous' textile mills — though home-working in that industry can scarcely have been much different — contrasted with machinery plants where the end product would have been plain for virtually all to see, and where many worked alongside each other on numerous processes and various products. Between these two examples were any number of other industries. While they were not crafts in the strictest sense, mining and smelting still required enormous skill and confronted workers with highly changeable conditions. All in all, it was the later rise of heavy industry and the increased specialisation demanded by rapid industrialisation from the 1860s onwards that finally established new working practices as shared experience. Dehumanisation of factory work and its organisation around machinery was, to be sure, an early development. It made the average unskilled or semi-skilled worker immediately dispensable. The dispensability of labour and the depersonalisation of work were a new reality, a new experience.

This brings the argument around to the social reality of early factory organisation. It was not only machine-centred work that was responsible for the degree of impersonality, anonymity and abstraction at the workplace (before the development of new social relations); the scale of production and division of labour also affected relations in this way. It was not possible to duplicate the atmosphere of the working household in the factory, and the larger the business, the more that possibility diminished. Looking at mining during its transition to large-scale industry, there are obvious signs of the growing distance between management and workers.

Other aspects of the factory as a social institution were the nature of power within it, and its hierarchical structure. Control naturally existed in rural and commercial 'household' businesses, but power now assumed a different character because work was separated from life and labour from the means of production, besides which workers no longer worked on their own premises with their own materials and tools. It became more modern, more formal and colder. Patriarchal authority was superseded by purely economic and legal powers of determination. A factory was not a living community demanding input from the whole person and offering a — liberating — element of community; the worker essentially became a factor in production, a 'unit of labour'. Formally, employment rested on a free contract between worker and employer, which could be terminated at will. Under prevailing economic and legal conditions, as has been illustrated a hundred times, the employer was in the superior position — except in the case of skilled craftsmen who were in short supply during the early stages of industrialisation and were consequently greatly prized and sought after. Thus it was the employer who fixed terms of contract, work and wages. Workers were not parties to a contract, but more in the position of subordinates. Instructions and orders, harsh conditions and the threat of punishment secured obedience — but at the cost of the workers' silent opposition to the new patterns and division of labour, and also their probable dissatisfaction with pay and hours. The practice of reaction to market fluctuation by ordering immediate lay-offs might have incurred indignation, but the threat of dismissal, together with pay cuts, was the surest way of securing compliance.

In larger concerns, where personal relationships were a thing of the past, work and factory regulations set out the duties of employees, bureaucratically rationalising responsibility for the issuing of instructions. One spoke of 'positions' and 'functions' rather than 'people', thereby formalising the organisation — hesitantly at first, and only gradually. At the same time, there was the rise of in-house hierarchies in medium-sized firms in which the owner had no hand in the day-to-day running of the business, at least not by himself. Workshop chiefs, craftsmen and foremen (at the top of a hierarchy extending down to skilled and unskilled labour) enforced regulations and controlled working efficiency. In large companies, it was often the lower end of the hierarchy where friction was at its greatest, for example in the relationship between shift leaders and miners in the coal industry. Financial incentives were employed to enforce order, discipline and efficiency — all ideas that were new and alien and not taken for granted at all. To these ends, weekly payment was introduced along with piecework (brought in during the 1840s) and long-term contracts aimed at reducing absenteeism and enabling better selection of personnel.

Overall it was this objectification and depersonalisation of employment, the dissolution of 'moral bonds' between employers and workers, that brought about the new experience of 'exploitation' and infringements of human dignity, and would lead to protest and social unrest in factories and businesses.

However, because of the absence of a fixed social order in Germany, unlike England where it was taken for granted, the businessman not only had to organise a firm economically and rationally, but also had to pay a certain amount of attention to the 'social' aspect. Patriarchalism overlay the control of factories in Germany. This was partly due to the traditional valid social norms, rooted in agriculture, crafts and the state.

Entrepreneurship and a simple hire-and-fire mentality were not fully accepted, nor were class struggle, exploitation and the rapid accumulation of wealth; in the face of threatening social revolution, these tendencies gained strength. Fear of revolution and society's moral expectations led to the classification of industrial conflict and working conditions as non-rational and non-economic. In compensation, the entrepreneur, the self-made man, could morally legitimise following the patriarchal example and discharge a duty to provide a degree of welfare. Besides this was the Christian ethic of love of one's fellow man. Disciplining workers to the new patterns of working reinforced the entrepreneur's sense of being educator and guardian of his workforce.

Patriarchalism stemmed partly from new rational and functional considerations. Disregarding tradition, many entrepreneurs were concerned to secure a core of workers — the lack of which had posed such a problem in the early stages of industrialisation — and in given situations, to mobilise the loyalty and fidelity of the workforce as a means to achievement unconstrained by contractual obligations or demands for compliance. Workers would thus be tied to their company, thereby receiving additional motivation. The old traditional patriarchalism and this new functional strain alternated during the early stages of industrialisation and subsequent industrial expansion, whereby religious, ethical and reforming goals also played a role. The result was a defined industrial social policy. There were, for instance, relief funds for sickness, invalidity, dependants of deceased workers and funerals — sometimes also savings funds — either wholly or partially subsidised by businesses. Some were newly formed, others were absorbed from craft, mining or iron industry traditions and were therefore in the nature of works funds which, naturally, only benefited long-serving members of a company. Where such funds were jointly administered by the workers, they essentially amounted to a workers' representative body within the firm.

The first tentative steps towards the building of industrial dwellings began after 1850. This initiative became more pressing with housing shortages and the deterioration of living conditions, at which point joint rent and work contracts became the norm, followed by the establishment of company stores and canteens. Besides these institutions there were emergency support — usually for the elderly — Christmas bonuses (partly paid for out of wages kept back for the purpose), sometimes even dividends on profits, as well as benefits for long-serving members of staff. Occasionally, as at Siemens, there was even discussion of business matters and employees' wishes at company meetings, personal contact with 'all diligent workers', the extension of periods of notice or restrained policy regarding dismissals during economic slumps. In extreme cases — as at Krupps — the provision of 'welfare' extended to paternalistic control of a worker's private affairs.

Whatever the motives or aims may have been, these measures naturally bound a worker to a firm, and largely benefited a privileged group of the skilled or the long-serving. Company policies typically took the patriarchal approach of acting unilaterally on the behalf of others; they aimed to achieve more or less ambitious targets for the workers, but made no attempt to enlist their assistance. A third new group of 'patrons' emerged among entrepreneurs of the 1860s; they aimed to educate workers through voluntary work and association, sometimes through funds or, in isolated instances, through workers' delegations.

Social policies of this kind and voluntary welfare work extending beyond contractual requirements are all part of the history of the structure of the German factory, but one should in no way imagine it was idyllic. Welfare work was the ideal, and in specialised cases was very widespread, but it was by no means the rule. While living and working conditions in the early industrial age were tough, welfare was very restricted in the amount (and the extent) of relief it could provide. Competition limited its financial latitude as soon as demands took a toll on costs, which forced redundancies in reaction to downturns in markets. Once the lack of qualified labour had been overcome and a core had been formed, the 1850s and 1860s saw a growing tendency to elasticity and the application of hire-and-fire practices. The transition from weekly to hourly pay in many businesses is an indication of this. With labour in plentiful supply, individual companies found it more important to make economical use of workers, or else dismiss them, rather than retaining them when it was uneconomical to do so. From the 1860s onwards, larger, flourishing businesses needing a specialised workforce exploited social measures in order to 'win the minds of the workforce', though at the same time this failed to check the spread of an opposing proletarian class-consciousness in the long term.

In focusing our attention now on the factory workforce, comprising an expanding social group, it is first of all necessary to contradict the false impression of the uniformity of this new stratum. Its enormous variation is by far its most striking feature, a variation that is both objective, in terms of its true structure, and subjective, in terms of its identity and the prevalent attitudes towards it. There were diffferences in origin and education, between old hands and newcomers, between natives and immigrants from near and far. Geographical and dialect differences had an impact, natives enjoying better positions and greater prestige; there were those with rights as local people and those with no citizens' rights or rights to assistance; there were the superior townsfolk and the country folk. There were also craftsmen and the rest. In paper factories, for instance, the former worked in their own space and were the only workers entitled to wear aprons. Even guild demarcations were transferred to the factory. Coppersmiths, for instance, ranked higher than blacksmiths. In the mining industry, before the liberal reforms, the legally privileged rated above the newcomers. In short, great importance continued to be attached to where one came from and who one was. There were also differences between the sexes. Factories with a female or mixed workforce ranked lower than those that were exclusively male. Some elements of these differences were gradually eliminated, although the vertical differences between occupations were constantly being revised. The machine both levelled and differentiated work to almost the same extent.

In the early stages of industrialisation, workers with craft training had great freedom of choice which was subsequently limited and even completely lost with the advance of mechanisation. Differentiation between functions was and remained the decisive point, that is, in effect, a horizontal differentiation between those with training (even if that meant only in the use of machinery) and those with none. Besides these skilled and unskilled workers there were the semi-skilled, those who were versed in procedures on specific machines.

There were highly differentiated pay scales, anything up to six or eight among as few as thirty workers. Specialists started at rates four to five times as much as the unskilled. In Baden in 1848, pay differentials were extreme. Earnings for women compared to specialists (mechanics) were in a ratio of 1:11.5. Within the male workforce, the differential could be as high as 1:2.5; taking masters and mechanics into account, the figure rose to 1:5. At Krupps in 1845, the corresponding differential was 1:5; in 1855 it was 1:6.6. Taking an overall view of the regional 'workforce', the pay differential between a thatcher in the Black Forest and the highest-paid factory worker was 1:50.

Naturally, most wages fall within the lower ranges of the scale, and the tendency is for the margin to decrease; the numerically superior lower group and the smaller upper group converged in the central group, which then became the more numerous. This was typical of the homogenisation that occurred and gradually distinguished the workforce from management staff. The 'factory specialists', the semi-skilled workers, increased in numbers as a group between the skilled and unskilled as manufacturing processes were increasingly broken down; the unskilled grew in numbers too, not through the absorption of 'trained' workers but through the integration of new labour. However, the essential difference remained between skilled — both in the craft and factory sense — and unskilled/semi-skilled workers, and this difference was very real to the workers themselves and determined their view of society. The sense of common dependence, similar situations and the sense of community within a class and consequent feelings of solidarity were slow to develop.

At least until the middle of the century, miners (and also to a certain extent, foundry-workers) represented a special case. They were an 'order' enjoying state privileges and having ancient rights and rules, similar in organisation to the guilds. They were often under state administration — as in Prussia at the time of the so-called *Direktionsprinzip* — or even under its control and tutelage. They were 'subjects', but welfare and other provisions gave them privileges similar to those of civil servants, as a result of which their relationship to the authorities was characterised by obedience, trust and a sense of group importance. Their jobs were protected, their reasonable pay was subject to state regulation, and the state, along with their traditional trade associations, covered them against the risks of their work and everyday lives. Their cottages were mostly provided with some land; they were distinguished from the mass of other 'workers', including the 'new' landless mineworkers, by their position as well as by their strong sense of identity. This situation remained unchanged until the liberalisation of mining law — which occurred in Prussia in 1851 — the shift to organisation on private sector lines, and then the technical and economic transition to large-scale mining which made the miners into proletarians and brought them further (but not fully) into line with workers in industry. It was then that the mineworkers protested against and opposed codes of discipline brought in by the kind of 'new' factory policies discussed above, even though they tended to be directed at newcomers and semi-skilled workers in the industry.

Once industrialisation was fully into its stride, the 'rise' of the factory workforce began. Only then did it become the dominant element (though not the majority) in the 'manual working classes', and at the same time the divide between it and the truly 'poor' widened still further. Because the available statistics do not differentiate enough, it is only possible to guess at this group's absolute and proportional scale. Within the territory of the German Reich, this group numbered slightly fewer than 1.8 million (not counting a small number of businessmen and salaried staff) in 1873, or less than 10% of all wage-earners. If home-workers, transport workers, workers in agriculture, servants, and apprentices (some of whom would admittedly progress to being self-employed) are included, a very rough estimate puts the proportion of the underclass, or of dependent wage-earners engaged in manual work, at around 55%. However, as well as typifying the trend of development, factory workers now came to dominate the lower classes themselves because other classes lacked a voice. Thus it was that ownership of the means of production became such an important debating point.

Factory workers tended to originate in one of four social groups according to level of education and/or father's occupation. The first group included the craftsmen, mainly apprentices and above all those employed in the wood, metal and machinery industries, some but by no means all of whom continued to learn their trade under new factory conditions. Subjectively, it was often difficult to make the switch to the factory and abandon a promised expectation of independence; objectively it was often a great relief and offered greater security. The self-employed were slower to take up factory employment as independence tended to act as a brake to mobility. The second group consisted of home-workers, especially in textiles; on the one hand women and children, on the other the less capable who were unable to compete with machines by faster production of finer or more specialised work of their own. The 'craft' prestige of home-produced goods nevertheless persisted thanks to the bad reputation of the factories. As well as the textile, cutlery, tobacco and sugar industries, certain other crafts — shoemaking, tailoring, joinery — went through a pre-industrial stage when many were employed in home-work. Thirdly, there was a large group of agricultural workers, day-labourers and farmers' sons whose transition from a pre-industrial existence to factory work was the most abrupt of all. Krupp recruited most of his workforce from this surplus rural population, and the same was true of heavy industry in the Ruhr. Finally, there were those who were constantly being absorbed into new industries from mining and the iron industry. Railway construction and road-building brought occasional relief from the impoverished existence of agricultural and home-workers.

Geographically, workers were chiefly drawn from the urban or rural region in which their factories were situated, or its immediate surroundings. This was especially true of unskilled labour, which was available in abundance. Only in isolated cases did factories draw their workforces from more distant sources, almost exclusively from urban areas and from the sought-after ranks of skilled workers. Migrants seeking work in the cities were generally more willing to take risks, more capable of adjustment, better qualified and more successful than those who migrated to rural industrial centres, whether the latter moved from the country or the city. Rural migrants largely represented the unskilled workforce. Frequently, they were seasonal workers or migrants who worked only periodically in the factories. Factory work replaced former part-time occupations or else served as a means of marking time, one which admittedly often became a permanent position.

The main reasons for taking on work in industry lay in the collapse of traditional means of support and the transformation of traditional branches of the economy. Necessity was thus a more powerful motive than taking advantage of worthwhile jobs and opportunities for mobility, factors which only entered into the choices made by skilled or trained workers. Ownership of land was an obstacle to mobility and tied people to their land and their craft or home-working occupations. There were more than a few cases of factories being set up in rural areas where labour was available in greater abundance than in town. Finally, southern Germans were handicapped by local laws concerning settlement and entitlements, which as well as proving an obstacle to the mobilisation of the underclasses as factory labour, simultaneously restricted marriage.

The frequently encountered fierce hostility to outsiders was a psychological result of this situation, which only declined after 1850, though before the relaxation of restrictions on marriage and entitlements to citizens' rights. Early branches of industry sometimes acted as recruitment pools for others — the textile workforce, for instance, was a source for many other groups of workers. Craft training still remained an important element, however, with crafts acting as the training ground for the factories. Obviously, the transition to factory work, when accompanied by migration from the country to the town, created substantial human problems of uprooting and adjustment.

Mobility and the ebb and flow of factory workers are closely linked with the migration that took place on a gigantic scale during industrialisation. This migration was far greater than is suggested by figures for the spread of urbanisation; however, the variations were also great, and motivations differed. One category consisted of the 'opportunistic' migrants, who took advantage of economic and labour market trends both locally and over longer distances. The kind of skilled workers who were in the greatest demand (for instance, metalworkers in the machinery industry) were most likely to take part in this kind of migration. In addition, there were those who undertook temporary work, the demand for which started in the early days of industrialisation and persisted with the rise of new industries. This kind of employment was neither truly economically stable, nor a socially acknowledged alternative to agricultural or home-work or the routines of a day-labourer; rather it was seasonal or part-time work that could not be pursued during seasons of peak labour demand in agriculture or when stability was necessary for a time. From the 1850s or 1860s onwards, partly as a result of the situation just described, there came a kind of drifting mobility. This was the lot of those with few qualifications, those who were due for redundancy, those from rural backgrounds who felt the 'shock' of factory life, the young, or those that preferred an ever-changing way of life. In certain groups, there was quite irrational fluctuation. Unmarried people aged between twenty and thirty-five constituted one such group, while on the other hand it could be a lifelong situation for some workers without family or property. 'Floating' workers became part of the new urban industrial reality; between 1844 and 1853, 73% of all workers at the machine factory in Augsburg left the factory within a year of starting work, and in other places the figure was between one-third and a half. Despite high rates of fluctuation, a solid core was formed among older, married (and especially qualified) workers, many of them with years of service in the same company; equilibrium gradually developed between constantly and irregularly filled jobs, between the permanent and the floating workers.

The next points to be examined are workers' living standards and conditions. In the early stages of industrialisation, it is possible to say, overall, that factory workers enjoyed slightly more security and a higher income than other members of the 'manual' labour classes, especially home-workers and ordinary 'manual' labourers (day-labours). This applied particularly to skilled labour, though only to a minimal extent to textile workers, whose prospects were subject to extreme fluctuation. The difficulties of pinning down the true significance of real wages have already been discussed. Of course, disregarding industries in rural areas as well as casual and seasonal workers, there is a steady rise in the significance of wages as the basis of a worker's existence that corresponds to increases in urbanisation, landlessness among workers and decreases in the importance of child labour and, above all, of working married women and mothers. If one excludes

Table 31: Income of workers in industry and crafts in the territory
of the later German Reich for 1850–70

Year	Nominal income		Cost of living index (1913 = 100)	Index of real income (1913 = 100)
	absolute in marks	Index (1913 = 100)		
1850	313	29	45	64
1851	323	30	52	58
1852	305	28	62	45
1853	320	30	57	53
1854	338	31	70	44
1855	348	32	75	43
1856	357	33	63	52
1857	385	36	63	57
1858	387	36	56	64
1859	386	36	58	66
1860	396	37	62	60
1861	400	37	67	55
1862	400	37	65	57
1863	413	38	62	61
1864	414	38	63	60
1865	414	38	60	63
1866	434	40	62	65
1867	445	41	71	58
1868	457	42	68	62
1869	480	44	66	67
1870	487	45	69	65

the highly varied employment in Württemberg and similar regions; the workers lose the
additional meagre support provided by the pre-industrial rural village family. From the
late 1850s onwards (apart from the depression of 1847) rapid industrialisation brought
ever higher real wages; by 1871 the index reached 69 (in 1855 it had stood at 43), and
savings were on the increase. 'Pre-industrial' pressure from home-working, female and
child labour and the demands of competition from England were no longer a burden on
wages; with the onset of expansion and favourable trends, demand for labour grew and
pauperism began to tail off.

Wages in industry varied not only according to qualifications but also according to
the industry concerned. Construction and metalworking were in the mid-range.
Wages were highest in mining, printing and machinery, while in textiles and
woodworking they were lowest. For the individual, there was a typical 'earning curve'
that varied according to age. Low income during training or apprenticeship was
followed by a time of peak earning that varied by occupation between the mid- and
late twenties until the age of about forty or fifty-five, after which pay decreased,
partly because of poorer performance on piecework and less overtime, and partly
because of being transferred to other wage structures, such as daily payment.

Table 32: Wages in mining 1850–70 (in marks)

Year	Coal mining in the Ruhr		Total for mining and salt-works	
	Net annual wages (estimated)	Net wages per shift (individual mines)	Worker's cash wages cash wages	Work income of all parties
1850	334	—	439	457
1851	406	—	477	496
1852	376	—	460	478
1853	366	1.72	445	463
1854	436	1.78	534	555
1855	490	1.99	555	577
1856	568	2.27	580	603
1857	559	2.27	619	644
1858	552	2.50	616	641
1859	479	1.82	545	567
1860	493	1.77	554	576
1861	457	2.03	523	544
1862	520	1.93	563	586
1863	550	2.05	612	636
1864	611	2.18	641	667
1865	702	2.33	667	694
1866	647	2.32	687	714
1867	682	2.37	698	726
1868	748	2.46	720	749
1869	829	2.54	735	764
1870	793	2.76	767	798

Due to different assumptions about the number of shifts performed annually, the wages cannot be compared directly.

Relating the curve to life and family cycles there was, first, a period of relatively 'good' income for men and women before marriage, with low outlays; secondly, a drop in income and a rise in outlays after establishment of a family and when bringing up children; and thirdly, a relatively typical period of poverty in old age. Overall, it was not so much absolute wage levels that mattered as much as the length of the period during which pay was at its highest. If the high-earning phase outlasted the growth of a family, it was possible to accumulate a modest amount of wealth in the form of property and take a step up the social ladder (either personally or through one's offspring). Up to about 1870, earnings were still largely related to individual (and far from standardised) training.

Working conditions were as hard as living conditions were shabby, though they were certainly not as bad as in early industrial England, as depicted in horrific contemporary reports, and definitely better than the misery of pauperism that was essentially a pre-industrial phenomenon. Of course, any assessment depends on changing criteria. Life expectancy and working conditions grew in proportion to the improvements that came

Table 33: Average wages of workers in the engineering works in Esslingen, 1848–70

Year	Number of workers	Nominal wages		Cost of living 1848 = 100	Real wages	
		Marks	1848 = 100		1848 = 100	Marks
1848	491	467	100	100	100	467
1849	382	533	114	89	128	598
1950	283	491	105	88	119	556
1851	328	561	120	100	120	560
1852	420	620	133	117	114	532
1853	512	617	132	129	102	476
1854	642	640	137	133	103	481
1855	645	685	147	143	103	481
1856	823	681	146	142	103	481
1857	1076	726	155	140	111	518
1858	1065	715	153	136	113	528
1859	1120	699	150	131	115	537
1860	713	670	143	111	129	602
1861	753	667	143	124	115	537
1862	947	700	150	139	108	504
1863	919	733	157	132	119	556
1864	920	708	152	125	122	570
1865	847	731	157	136	115	537
1866	958	735	157	157	100	467
1867	1038	759	163	160	102	476
1868	1157	775	166	151	110	514
1869	1117	763	163	144	113	528
1870	1211	798	171	147	116	542

about. Even so, 'hard' and 'shabby' remain relevant terms to use in describing relative situations. The notorious 'truck system' — a pre-industrial practice entailing payment with overpriced and unnecessary goods — was widespread in western Germany before 1848, especially in payments to home-workers; it must be said that most industrialists rejected it, and after 1848 it vanished entirely (it was banned in Prussia in 1849). Hours were generally 12–14 per day (including 1½–2 hours' break); in 1870, one estimate puts the average six-day working week at 78 hours. As factories increased in number and size, the lack of transport led to growth in the length of journeys to work.

Noise, dust, cramped conditions, bad light and the risk of accident and disease were common at the workplace. Long hours and minimal safety precautions were responsible for the rising number of industrial accidents. The threat of starvation and the breadline had been left behind — the rise in meat consumption has already been highlighted — although it cannot be overstressed that standards varied greatly, for instance, between the skilled and the unskilled; however, 65–70% of income went to food (figures for Saxony, 1857: food 65%, clothing 10%, accommodation, heating and lighting 17%, leaving 5%; comparative figures for the middle classes: food 55%, clothing 18%, accommodation, heating and lighting 17%, leaving 10%). Living conditions were still humble and modest, and very different from all bourgeois standards. The increase in the factory workforce and the growth of cities was reflected in massive rent increases, and also in the fact that living in rented accommodation was the basic way of life; the percentage of workers owning their own houses dropped sharply.

Workers lived under different and poorer conditions than craftsmen and farmers. In absolute terms, their position had improved, but compared with the middle classes and after adopting more 'normal' standards of consumption, the working household still laboured on the brink of poverty.

The most important element conditioning life for many at that time was lifelong insecurity, not, of course, measured by the standards of today's welfare state, but rather by those of pre-industrial and bourgeois society. Sickness in the family, incapacity, old age, or death of the breadwinner were the kind of blows to a worker's livelihood that were difficult to absorb. Involuntary short- or long-term loss of work, either through economic changes or poorer individual productivity, were equally threatening.

Whereas in the old days there had been extended families or resources from the land or savings as a safety-net in times of need, these were now either negligible or non-existent. Before marriage, when earnings were high, it was possible to save, and this was what the determined worker would do, but later on the opportunity for saving diminished steadily; savings and items of value were only sufficient to cover the needs of a certain number and scale of emergencies. Insecurity remained a conditioning factor in a worker's existence, and in some ways became even more acute, despite pay rises and the eradication of pauperism. Besides this, there was the psychological and emotional problem of being uprooted from an old, fixed rural or urban order and the transfer to a new existence — especially in migration between the country and the city — where there was no possibility of forming a new social *Heimat* ('homeland'). There was lack of integration, the separation of bourgeois from traditional forms of life, the sense of being set apart in the town and the different society that grew up both symbolically and concretely in working-class streets and districts in the 1860s.

The experience and outward signs of displacement from old, familial, rural and small-town commercial surroundings continued in the case of the underclasses, as did their psychological and moral proletarisation. Proof of this is provided by the role of drink and the tavern, however much they may have become social focal points. It was a long time before new bonds were able to develop in the worker's new socio-cultural milieu. On the other hand, it must be pointed out that at least among skilled and semi-skilled workers, and those that established families, traditional bourgeois values with Christian trappings were strong: the craving for 'respectability', and values in education, achievement and work. The group that had not become fully accepted had a basic wish to become bourgeois. A typical sign of this is the proliferation of workers' associations in the 1850s and 1860s.

It is difficult to assess the extent to which a worker's existence was dependent on fate, and how hard it was to change that existence. Similarly, it is difficult to say whether the individual was, objectively speaking, tied to his position in society and whether he therefore sensed that position to be hopeless. Overall, the opportunity for accumulation of wealth had vanished, power structures in the factories had become entrenched, and upward mobility into the middle classes was minimal. Lack of education and capital were both virtually insuperable obstacles. Personal accounts and views that have been passed down indicate that a worker's lot was immutable, and also that the labour movement was gradually gaining ground and both expressing and forming opinions among workers.

Admittedly, this is a one-sided view. If one takes into account the great variation among the workforce and adjacent groups, and then also tries to combine a number of criteria to determine social status (occupation, income, wealth, prestige), then the amount of mobility both within the working environment (from fitter to foreman) and outside (sons becoming engine-drivers) is greater than commonly supposed. Among textile and machinery workers in Esslingen, where both groups were studied extensively, the mobility rate was high, calculated at 40–50%, which admittedly was due to a particularly favourable social structure. Elsewhere in the Ruhr, in large cities with little diversification, the corresponding figures are lower. It appears to be a distortion to define the workforce as both a reservoir of 'drop-outs' and the breeding-ground of upwardly-mobile elements. However, at least for the period up to 1870, mobility — in a gradual and limited form — was far more common than has hitherto been acknowledged.

The worker's position with regard to a firm's power structure was one of isolation and vulnerability; only when his labour was in demand did his position become stronger. Freedom of contract in the period under discussion here was generally coupled with a legal ban on workers' combinations (trade unions). The worker's position thus remained weak. The authorities and courts differed in their application of the laws, depending on time and place; after the period of reaction there was general toleration of workers' combinations (and even a certain amount of strike action). However, for a worker to pursue in court the numerous points of dispute that could arise out of employment was *de facto* impossible.

Overall, after 1850 the consciousness of factory workers became increasingly uniform. This occurred despite the persistence of old differences and the rise of new ones, despite the line drawn between skilled and unskilled, and despite traditional guild practices, all of which surfaced repeatedly. Journeymen in particular made increasing use of the term 'worker' when referring to themselves, a term which contained a new element of pride. The sense of a common way of life and shared experiences, especially isolation from management, the state and bourgeois urban society grew ever clearer. In this period — without reference to the emergent labour movement — it still seems inappropriate to describe the formation of this group feeling and identity as 'class-consciousness'. This will become apparent later, when the workers' political outlook is examined.

During the Vormärz, the phenomenon of mass poverty and pauperism was the cause of widespread discussion of what later came to be termed the social question. Factory workers and the industrial proletariat were important elements in that discussion, and not always clearly differentiated. In a wider framework, the factory system and capitalist economy also attracted attention. Although they far from dominated the situation during the Vormärz, factory workers and industry remained a burning topic for all interested observers. The consciousness of coming developments was alert and expectant, fed both by theoretical and analytical interest in society, and by an awareness of current events and debates in France and England. Lorenz Stein's epoch-making book of 1842, *A History of Social Movements in France from 1789 to the Present Day*, and, equally importantly, Friedrich Engels's *Condition of the English Working Classes* (1845), determined a great deal of the attention and debate devoted in Germany to social conditions in western Europe. The phenomenon of poverty, the growth of the working classes, their absence from the pigeon-holes and restrictions of the traditional order, and the emergence of the 'proletariat' (the term *Proletair* first spread through Germany in the writings of the Catholic philosopher Franz von Baader) were all powerful enough to displace old standards that had regarded poverty, for instance, as natural and God-given; the new view employed the metaphor of disease within society.

Besides this, and again with regard to western Europe, there was a consciousness that underclasses and workers posed a threat to the balance, order and continued existence of bourgeois society and the state, especially when misery and dissatisfaction provided room for the expansion of communist thinking. In short, debate was coloured by fears of revolution and the collapse of society. Observers and commentators gave their accounts of the vulnerability, helplessness and lawlessness (*Vogelfreiheit*, in Baader's phrase) of the emergent proletariat, and examined the position of the rich who grew richer while the poor grew poorer. In addition to their objective accounts, nearly all these writers laid great stress on the deterioration of morality, psychological decay, and a new reaction, rebelliousness and envy which the proletariat faced with the expanding gap between themselves and the rich. The problem of alienation — of mindless, mechanical and stupefying work on dislocated, mechanised production — had been common currency since Hegel. In 1830, his pupil Gans questioned whether emancipation from corporate entities would lead to the despotism of the factory, and List later spoke of the 'abasement' of the working classes.

Explanations were always numerous, varying according to the individual's powers of observation and political stance. There was a broad range of assumed causes: population growth and/or a static number of job vacancies; the laws on emancipation which encompassed freedom for farmers and freedom of trade. Others blamed the decorporatisation of society through individualism and the principle of competition, and the modern rule of law which was based upon it, as well as the mobilisation of people, land and values. The liberation of self-interests and the breaking of personal social contacts, the depersonalisation and economisation of labour, displacement and disorientation, the unleashed power of money, the formation of an aristocracy purely on the basis of wealth and capitalist factory production (low wages, exploitation and over-production) were all given as reasons for the malaise. Factories and machines themselves were occasionally held to blame. On the other hand, it was claimed that there was a lack of industriousness and of economic and rational activity, that there was too much (or too little) education, and that religion had declined. There was a tendency among conservatives to blame the bourgeoisie, while the butt of liberals was failure of the state or feudal relations. Of course, it was possible to contrast the 'good old days' with the dreadful new conditions. Formerly, even the poorest would have had their place in a fixed, hierarchical and harmonious order — community as opposed to society, as it was later described. However, the more serious debate took the irrevocability of the technological and economic transformation as its starting-point.

The most important features of this topic are the proposals for mastering the situation, beginning with the 'bourgeois', non-revolutionary solutions to the challenge of the proletariat; the revolutionary theories of the labour movement will be examined later. There were general and politico-economic formulae, such as the promotion of migration, or — from conservative quarters — curbing the population growth, increasing freedom of movement and freedom of trade. On the progressive side, there were proposals to expand and develop industry, whose growth alone, according to some like Bruno Hildebrand, could solve the crisis, or the 'de-restriction' of labour, competition, and individual opportunity for mobility — in short, the self-correcting powers of a modern economy. More important in the context of this book, however, social reform was seen as the specific solution. In the 1840s, bourgeois social reform and social policy first attained its position as one of the century's dominant themes. Common to all points of view — after the failure of previous systems of poor relief in the face of the new problem — was the need for the de-proletarisation of the proletariat, (re-)instatement of citizenship, the integration of workers into society — above all by the return of lost means of social insurance and, in some cases, property — and the revitalisation of moral codes and values and their institutional framework.

Assuming all this, priorities and considerations varied; possibilities ranged from establishment of institutions to education in moral convictions. State measures, charitable and paternalistic efforts by bourgeois society, self-help and organisation by the workers were all favoured depending on individual standpoints. Insurance, educational schemes and unions were further proposals, as was some kind of rebuilding of society according to its former orders with obligatory corporations, or a reorganisation of society on the basis of free association. There was discussion of state measures for 'organisation of work', such as banning child labour, the truck system and other practices, fixing of a maximum working week (73 hours) and even of a minimum wage, profit-sharing and an embryonic type of co-determination (by the liberal Robert Mohl), or state work-creation programmes. Lorenz Stein, who viewed the problem in the language of class struggle, believed that only a 'social kingdom' could mediate between bourgeoisie and proletariat and exercise justice; the conservative Hermann Wagener also believed that only state and government could represent the interests of the worker.

Conservatives and liberals were far from cleanly divided when it came to the solutions they proposed. Calls for and rejections of state intervention were equally numerous among both groups, and occasionally very similar proposals emerged from the opposing sides. Even so, typical 'social conservative' solutions can be differentiated from typical 'social liberal' ones. As already pointed out, social conservatives, both Catholic and Protestant, maintained a romantic, anti-liberal understanding of society as developed by, for example, Adam Müller and Franz von Baader. 'Liberalism' was the cause of society's problems. It loosened bonds and was itself unbound; it automatically broke up society and promoted beliefs of individual autonomy and freedom which were mere self-deception and would only lead to renewed despotism and slavery, while its (covert) atheism liberated self-interest. It thus became incumbent upon the state either to reverse the liberation of bourgeois society with its principles of merit and class, or at least to restrain it, while reinforcing or preserving agrarian and craft society.

However, this identification with a vanishing world naturally had its utopian elements. Even in this model, the reality of social problems demanded different solutions. To this end there was, on the one hand, preservation, restoration and intensification of religion through new workers' associations and institutions. Religion (and the banishment of 'religious distress', as it was called by Johann Hinrich Wichern, founder of the *Innere Mission*) was at the centre of de-proletarisation and humanisation. Besides this there were, of course, more general social and moral patterns for moral education. The workers should be filled once more with the ethos of 'service' (as Wagener put it), and, in the words of Wilhelm Heinrich Riehl, they should be strengthened through 'decency' and 'diligence', protected from the 'desire for change' and differentiated from the 'estate of those without status', 'society's dross', and made to attain a true standing within society, not outside it.

Another solution, almost always linked with the above, was corporative organisation of the workforce. Franz von Baader, for example, wished to see obligatory corporations under the leadership of clergymen, who would also represent the workers with seats and votes in the *Landtage*. Similar ideas were promoted by the true founder of 'social Catholicism', Franz Joseph Buss, an elected parliamentary representative for Baden. Slowly and hesitantly, but with increasing commitment from Baader, Buss and Wichern, Ketteler, Victor Aimé Huber and Hermann Wagener, this was followed by demands for corrective measures to be implemented by the state, and for a social policy, chiefly aimed at protection for the worker, and occasionally demands for a certain amount of state power over material living conditions and pay, though the economics of the latter were usually unclear. The Protestant conservative Huber even championed 'production co-operatives', aimed at making 'workers without property' into 'working owners'. In all instances where the conservatives and clerics promoted state measures and self-help, they broke the charitable, patriarchal and purely religious pre-industrial social mould and began to show signs of 'modernity'.

The liberals start with modern freedom and mobility, the freeing of society and the individual from state and corporative ties and prevailing market and economic conditions, from industry and the progress of industrialisation. They had a threefold approach to the solution of society's problems and 'de-proletarisation'. The first element was education. Education would qualify the individual for a life of work and increase productivity, open the way to social mobility, and lead to rational ordering of life and the home, to self-awareness and independence instead of the subservience of the feudal authoritarian tradition, and would allow insight into social and economic realities to challenge the utopian demagogy of the communists. According to the most important social-liberal of the Vormärz, the businessman Friedrich Harkort, these ends would have to be achieved by state measures, especially the improvement of schools for the lower classes and the direction of education towards greater reality and independence.

It was not only a bourgeois belief that education led to freedom, it was also that of all thinking apprentices and workers. Self-help was also to form part of their reforms; this did not mean renewed organisation of 'labour', but organisation of workers to help themselves through savings banks, welfare, insurance and co-operative societies from the cradle to the grave, and educational institutions as well. The state, or preferably the citizens, should provide assistance towards self-help and organisation. Harkort and Schulze-Delitzsch were proponents of this scheme which struck a chord among the workers early on and became the liberals' weapon in opposing the socialist labour movement. The scheme rarely, and only after 1860, embraced the formation of the trade unions that aimed at realising the potential equality between labour and capital.

Finally, both liberal and conservative programmes included the build-up of social and reforming activities in bourgeois circles, with the establishment of church and humanitarian institutions and societies on varying scales, and the rallying of all who were interested in social reform to discuss, propagate and encourage. An early example of such an institution was the *Verein zur Beförderung der Arbeitsamkeit* (Society for the Promotion of Diligence), founded in Aix-la-Chapelle by David Hansemann and active between 1825 and 1833, which established savings banks that rewarded savers with dividends. The Centralverein für das Wohl der arbeitenden Klassen (Society for the Welfare of the Working Classes) was established in Prussia in 1845 under royal patronage; branches were formed all over Prussia, and it was the first bourgeois organisation aimed at social reform. Results of practical social reform were, for instance, changes in the nature of poor relief. Job allocation took the place of welfare activities; in the 'Eberfeld System' of 1853, for example, the 'poor' were obliged to accept any work they were offered.

Finally, there is the relationship between the state and the social question. The state was, of course, responsible for setting numerous conditions, including legislation on the setting up of professional practices, marriage, freedom to choose one's occupation, taxation, formation of societies and regulation of rural workers. Road and railway construction were typical instances of state impact on labour markets. In general, however, it must be said that the state made no direct intervention in the condition of the working classes, paupers and the factory workforce; liberal maxims of non-intervention held sway, and the condition of society was left at the mercy of forces inherent within itself and conflicts between the classes.

In the mining industry in the Rhineland and Westphalia, the state played an active role in shaping society through regulation of pay and conditions, the treasury and job security. However, when the mining law was liberalised between 1851 and 1865, the state withdrew. Moderation in this sense had unforeseen consequences. The Prussian state, for instance, was only able to react as a force of law when unrest grew out of the social crisis in the 1840s, using a combination of the army, the police and the judiciary.

There were exceptions to this moderation, and these are of interest in this examination of the early history of state social policy. In Prussia in the middle of the century, liberal economic and social policy was impinged upon largely by the Christian–conservative–patriarchal concept of the state. As early as 1817, Hardenberg began a famous survey of child labour in factories, because 'upbringing of factory workers was taking precedence over the upbringing of citizens and human beings', and because lack of variety in the factory was, in fact, making people incapable of adjusting to changing conditions, thus laying them wide open to the depths of poverty whenever there was a stagnation in the economy. However, in the case of child labour, state intervention was rejected because of resistance from companies and, above all, parents. In the interests of making compulsory schooling a reality, the Minister of Education and Culture attempted to limit child labour by law, but he failed in the attempt, which brought about his administration's *de facto* abandonment of restrictions on child labour. In 1837, Schuchard, a factory-owner from Barm promoted a reopening of this debate in the provincial *Landtag* for the Rhineland, thereby provoking a great deal of public discussion besides. Because of fears about the supply of conscripts, the proposals also drew decisive support from the military authorities; in 1839 a 'regulatory measure' prohibited labour for those under nine years of age, and fixed a maximum working day for those over nine (ten hours, including breaks). The terms contained many rules to cover exceptions, and it was difficult to enforce without inspections. Even so, a principle had been established for the beginnings of a state labour protection policy.

In 1853, in the interests of social stability rather than with exclusive regard to schooling and conscription, the minimum working age was fixed at twelve, with a six-hour working day for the under-fourteen's; the introduction of a state factory inspectorate provided an instrument for the implementation of protective measures. For technical and economic reasons, child labour had also been reduced in the meantime (between 1846 and 1858, figures fell from 31,064 to 12,592). Certain other German states followed with their own similar measures: Baden 1840–62, Bavaria 1840–54, Saxony 1861–65 (where children under fourteen were restricted to working a ten-hour day in any factory employing more than twenty people), and Austria, whose first feeble attempts at limiting working hours came in 1859. The reform of the Prussian trade regulations in 1845 and 1849, which were aimed at consolidating the position of crafts, also brought certain stipulations of social policy. The truck system was outlawed (as in Saxony), and provisions were introduced to nullify contracts for Sunday working, and to introduce obligatory support funds at local level to which employers could be forced to contribute. Workers were allocated places on the local trade councils, and some regulations were introduced to enforce health and safety measures. In the laws governing mining, a weakened form of the old welfare provisions was carried over in nearly all the new liberal restructurings; with liberalisation of the mining laws (1851–65), insurance under control of the *Knappschaften* (miners' guilds) was reorganised as an obligatory self-governing institution for all. Other German states were, in general, more restrained in their reforms.

The ban on workers' combinations for the purposes of industrial disputes was a central problem of employment. It had been introduced as a formal measure in Prussia in 1845. The forces of reaction fought against every conceivable revolutionary stirring, directing themselves against any organisation, society or body that was capable of taking action, particularly among workers. The *Gesindeordnung* (Servants' Ordinance) of 1854 reinforced the ban on workers' combinations for agricultural workers, though the courts put a restrained interpretation on the provisions of these laws. By 1865, punishments had been ordered in only twenty-six cases (far fewer than the 'real' number of infringements). In the 1860s, the liberal-democratic Progressive Party took up the cause in Prussia. In accordance with both liberal economic doctrine and industry's demand for workers, 'all obstacles to the natural process of pay structuring' should be abolished. Social-liberals now held the optimistic belief that through striking and uniting, workers could improve their lot. Furthermore, liberals were fighting to make amends for the inevitable rift that had developed between themselves and the workforce after their rejection of the right of association. In conservative circles, Wagener and Bismarck had tackled the problem positively, attempting to win workers' support for the monarchy, to organise them into corporations and to stave off the bourgeoisie. The war of 1866 delayed legislation, and finally in 1869 freedom of organisation (with grave reservations on the subject of use of pressure and force) won a place in the statute book. In other German states, repressive federal policies to counter crafts apprentices' leagues were also applied to 'workers'; in 1847 there was an outright ban on such associations in Hanover, as there was in 1852 in Austria. But by 1861, freedom of organisation was granted in Saxony, followed by the Thuringian states, Baden and Württemberg in 1862, and Austria in 1870.

8. The Problem of Minorities: The Jews

How a society deals with minorities, and how minorities develop within it, will reveal much about that society. The problems of national minorities and of Christian religious minorities that arose during the first two-thirds of the 19th century will be examined elsewhere; the Jews are of immediate interest here. Hitler's extermination programme makes it impossible to ignore the significance of the Jews as a group, even in a history of early and mid-19th-century Germany.

In the old world, Jews had lived as an individual group, a particular community of faith, law, culture, a 'nation' outside but alongside the orders of society, one which was tolerated but treated as alien in the eyes of the law. Its members were restricted both in their choice of occupation and their rights of abode, and isolated by their peculiar attributes in a medieval, ghetto-like way. The rise of individual aristocratic financiers and the privileged and educated Jews who gathered in their entourage, in Berlin or Vienna for instance, did nothing to alter these conditions.

Through Lessing and Dohm, the German Enlightenment placed the themes of tolerance, 'improvement of Jews as citizens', 'emancipation', bestowal of equal rights and recognition as citizens on the agenda. This agenda included the liberation of individual Jews from their bonds within the Jewish collective. The condition of the Jews was seen as intolerable, both for themselves and for Christians and society at large. The humanity of the Jews was promoted above their Jewishness, and their peculiarities were explained as a product of their traditions. Emancipation was aimed at the eventual removal of these peculiarities and the integration of Jews as citizens. The state was regarded as leader and defender of the process. Resistance from both traditional Christian and Jewish quarters was directed against the absorption of the Jews into society, the dissolution of their special closed order, and the abolition of their essentially medieval circumstances.

The French Revolution brought the complete legal emancipation of the Jews at a stroke. This was introduced in the regions west of the Rhine, the Napoleonic satellite states of western and northern Germany, and in Frankfurt under Dalberg. Thus two patterns of emancipation were current in Germany. The first was the French model, with immediate bestowal of liberties, emancipation at a stroke. The second, and more widespread, was the piecemeal process that would be accompanied by gradual surmounting of prejudice among Gentiles and, above all, by corrective education of the Jews themselves. Its progress would be measured in terms of the advance of education, and the 'improvement' of the Jews, and as a model it was almost wholly in tune with enlightened concepts of the bureaucratic state's function as educator. Welfare and protection were conjoined under the principle that the effect of a damaging group — the Jews — could only be reversed slowly, a sudden leap from subjugation to liberty being unsettling to the order of society. Emancipation was thus the domain of the bureaucrat and an affair of state; adherents to this model had no faith in society's integrating power. In the Confederation of the Rhine, integration of the new states also led to a clutch of new laws concerning the Jews, aimed at unifying the endless variety of ordinances in force at the time. However, when it came to emancipation, their restraint was extraordinary.

In Prussia, matters were different. As early as 1808, the *Städteordnungen* (municipal ordinances) granted the Jews certain rights of citizenship. An edict of 1812, promoted by Humboldt and Hardenberg in the spirit of the Prussian reform, established equal citizens' rights for Jews, including the abolition of special courts. The Jews were thus granted citizens' rights, freedom of movement and choice of occupation, marriage and the acquisition of land, the only preconditions being the adoption of a surname and the German language. However, one important exclusion remained, and that was access to state office, apart from teaching posts, which Jews were allowed to hold — but this exclusion was to be eliminated later. The provision of civil liberties applied only to the commercial community to begin with. In 1812, the enabling legislation was only applied to the limited territory of the Prussian state, so it affected only a small number of Jews.

In the face of the tendency towards piecemeal measures and education as described earlier, Humboldt established the basis of emancipation, dependent upon equal rights and equal obligations for its justice and effectiveness. Any reservations would provide fuel for the opposing flame of segregation. At the Congress of Vienna, Metternich, Hardenberg and Humboldt led the Prussian and Austrian attempts to bring about emancipation of the Jews within the German Confederation, but this move ended in failure. It stemmed from the realisation that only a relatively uniform solution for all Germany could overcome the obstacles in individual countries. Not even a guarantee of the former — Napoleonic — laws could be put through against opposition, especially by the city-states; they immediately repealed the reforms. The first stage of emancipation was at an end.

All previous efforts were thwarted during the post-Vienna restoration era. After 1815 emancipation was first publicly criticised, and this became a factor in the political and spiritual processes.

Besides the traditional antipathy towards the Jews, a new kind of hostility sprang up and joined forces with certain tendencies within the radical new democratic nationalism. There was xenophobia and a crisis of identity in 'Christian-Teutonic' circles, whose leading lights included the professors Rühs and Fries and elements of the early German student associations (*Burschenschaften*). Their attitude were as typical as the antisemitic outbursts among peasants and the petty bourgeoisie in 1819, which were at one and the same time a kind of revolt of the old against the new, another face of social change in crisis, as well as an expression of dissatisfaction with government.

These movements, fuelled by popular wrath, hung like a 'sword of Damocles' over the progress of emancipation. In Prussia, the edict was not extended to include the 'new' provinces; in the most important of these, Posen, restrictions still applied to choice of occupation, ownership of land and freedom of movement; a naturalisation process was not brought in until 1833, and then only on an individual basis. Exclusion from state office was extensively stage-managed by the administration and applied to provincial *Landtage* and communal positions, while available opportunities in schools and universities were abolished. Instead of equality of entitlements, it was the division between Jews and Christians that was emphasized. The bureaucratic liberal social policy at least offered better opportunities for Jews than they enjoyed in the south. Nevertheless, in 1846, 36.7% of Jews in Prussia were denied civil rights and lived in a kind of closed community, especially in Posen. Attempts had been made to form a new corporation of the Jews as an element of the policy of the 'Christian state' which would have resulted in their *de facto* isolation from the rest of society, but they ended in failure before 1848; their own unanimous protest also prevented their exclusion from military service. The Prussian Jew Laws of 1847 became a conservative-liberal compromise; there was continued exclusion of Jews from positions of authority, but there were still many exceptions, as in the case of Posen.

In the south, emancipation came to a dead stop for a long time because officials linked the process to educational progress, the 'improvement' of the Jews, and aimed legislation and administrative practice at 'correction' of the Jews. Besides this, the dominant conservative social policy was of only limited liberation of society, if any. Citizens' rights were dependent on the pursuit of an appropriate occupation, but communal and state rights were not granted to Jews. As a precondition for true state citizenship, the *Landtag* in Baden demanded the cessation of a range of religious customs, which, it was said, amounted to rejection of 'nationality'. The liberals also put more faith in the education model, besides which there was fear of the anger of the populace, and an enlightened anti-Judaism directed against the fossilised, fanatical, anti-social and bigoted Jewish nation; the typical early liberal demands for complete integration of the Jews as an equal group within liberal German society was also a factor.

Emancipation faced a range of obstacles at this time. In Prussia, it was the concept of the Christian state; in the south and northern Germany outside Prussia there were the economic and security interests of the agrarian and artisan population. In Hanover, Saxony and Mecklenburg there were a number of very outmoded limitations. Marriage and freedom of movement were heavily restricted, for example in Bavaria, Austria and Frankfurt. In Prague, the ghetto was still in existence, and even in liberal Baden there were no local rights for Jews. Only in the Electorate of Hesse was emancipation further advanced.

Despite all the obstacles and reversals and the many variations, there was overall improvement in legal entitlements for a growing number of Jews, with the abolition of restrictions on earning, admission to schooling and rights of abode. In the 1840s, the liberals, the majority of the educated and propertied classes and a considerable proportion of the nobility began lending more solid support to full unconditional emancipation. Yet universal liberation and the end of discriminatory differentiation, freedom as citizens and equality before the law — that is to say, true emancipation in terms of equality of entitlement — did not follow until 1848. During the revolutionary phase, the principles were almost uncontested both in the Frankfurt National Assembly as well as in the *Landtage* of the revolutionary period.

Certainly, in 1848 there were anti-Jewish excesses in the countryside in the southwest, in Hamburg, the east and south-east (Prague), social unrest which had been brewing in the ranks of the farmers and small traders; such movements were of a traditional pre-modern, even medieval kind. For the political and civil world they were an anachronism. The forces of reaction again attempted reversals and administrative limitations as a means of achieving revisions — the withdrawal of the oath for instance, which barred the office of judge to all but Christians — but the foundation of the emancipation was unshakable. Liberalisation was on the march. Government no longer disputed the process after the New Era, and the granting of freedom was a principle that was set above educational measures, successful or otherwise, just as it was considered of greater importance than public opinion. Jews were granted legal equality in Württemberg in 1861–64, in Bavaria in 1861, in Baden in 1862, in Austria in 1867, and in the North German Confederation in 1869.

The uneven progress of emancipation and the parallel courses followed by various processes naturally created ever-renewed tensions and did not bode well for its success. How did the Jews of Germany and their relationship with the Germans develop? Embourgeoisement and assimilation are two concepts that are helpful in describing events.

There were 270,000 Jews in 1820 living in what later became the Reich, over half of whom lived in Prussia. Of this latter group, 40% lived in Posen and a further 20% in West Prussia and Upper Silesia. Within the parts of Austria belonging to the Confederation (including Prague and Bohemia) there were 85,000. In 1850 the corresponding figures were 400,000 and 130,000; the former reached 512,000 in 1871, the latter just over 200,000 in 1869. These figures represent 1.25% of the population of the Reich, and 1.5% of the population of the parts of Austria belonging to the Confederation. South and west German Jews emigrated to America in large numbers up until just after the middle of the century. It was not until after the mid-point of the century that the flood of migration to urbanised areas began, especially into the large cities (Berlin 1837: 5,645, 1866: 36,000; Cologne 615–3,172; Frankfurt 3,300–7,600; Vienna 2,873 and (1869) 40,230). In 1880 in the old Jewish centres of Posen, Fürth and Frankfurt, over 10% of the population were Jewish, in Vienna (1869) 6.1%, in Prague (1857) 10.7%, in Beuthen, Mannheim, Breslau and Mainz (1880), over 5%, in Berlin 4.8%; in Munich, Dresden and Hanover, Jewish communities were only just beginning to form.

Table 34: Jewish social structure within the borders of the later Reich (%)

	1848	1871–74
Secure bourgeoisie (upper and middle classes)	15–33	60
Petty bourgeoisie and those on minimal incomes	40–25	35–15
Poor, marginal and non-bourgeois livelihoods	40–50	5–25

For 1848, the first figures apply to the Prussian situation and the second set to the Bavarian (the situation in Württemburg was similar). There was also a similar tendency in Austria, but the number of poor Jews in the eastern end of the monarchy was very high, once the Jews had been granted freedom of movement.

In 1815, the Jews of Germany could be separated into three typical social classes. Firstly, there were the rural Jews, primarily in the south-west and south, living as pedlars, and on proceeds from the finance and cattle trades; in the east, there were similar groups, but also a second type: traders and home-workers both in the countryside and in cities. The third type was the urban Jews, dealers and money-lenders, most of them poor. The number of rich, educated 'bourgeois' Jews — the circles around the financiers to the princes or the bankers like the Rothschilds — was very small.

The phenomenon that can be identified during these decades was the decline of pauperism among Jews and the rise of many to the economic and intellectual upper or upper middle classes, especially after the 1840s. The process generally favoured large cities, whereas the provinces and the east lagged some way behind. Upward mobility among Jews was entirely different from the escape from pauperism made by the population at large. Some insight into the centuries-old economic ethic and practice is helpful in identifying the reasons for this — pressure of achievement, adjustment and an ability to innovate, and capitalist economic practices free of guilds. The Jewish family structure may also have played its part, enabling many small capital sums to be pooled and put at the disposal of the mobile individual. Among bourgeois Jews, where the internal social structure differed from that of the Gentiles, trading and finance remained dominant (involving over 50% of wage-earners in 1870).

Jews were widely active in industry, especially the growing ready-to-wear clothing industry, and thereafter in the textile industry in general, as well as in food and printing. This kind of mobility was related to access to education. The proportion of Jewish pupils attending grammar schools (*Gymnasia*) rose from 5.9% in 1852 to 8.4% in 1866, even though they represented only 1.34% of the population at the very most. Among university students the proportion was even higher; in Vienna and Prague in 1872–73 11.6% of university students were Jewish. Access to academic professions was barred for a long time by law, not so much for doctors — Jews had been allowed to study medicine since the late 18th century — but certainly for jurists and teachers. There had been Jewish lecturers (on an unsalaried basis) since 1814, who were joined by untenured professors in the 1850s and 1860s; full professorships were still the exception — apart from Jews who had been baptised — the first instance being in 1858.

As the Jews of Germany rose increasingly to the ranks of the bourgeoisie, they also permeated the national culture and assumed certain of its elements. Around 1800, there was still only a small number of Jews who craved the enlightenment, education and cultural conviviality of the Gentiles, however much this small group may have pioneered later developments. The walls of the ghettos fell and the power of tradition diminished. Schooling and society brought the Jews into the modern world. Even among the dwindling number of Jews retaining the old traditions, there was evidence of the cultural affinity with Germany. In Posen in 1848, the Jews supported the Germans against the Poles.

Assimilation became the goal of the majority of the upper and middle classes. Baptism was not the key. It was not (to use Heine's term) the 'entrance ticket' to European culture, though it did serve to help Jews gain access to state office and professorships; in 1848 in Prussia, only 1.5% of Jews were baptised, and before 1840 there were even fewer. More important was the existence of consciously liberal and national 'German citizens of the Jewish faith'. Gabriel Riesser, a member of the Frankfurt National Assembly who advocated emancipation for the Jews, was strongly representative of those in favour of the German liberal example, as were the writer Berthold Auerbach and the journalist Julius Rodenberg. The Jews were also now taking an increasingly active part in German cultural life.

The process of assimilation was directed at values and codes of behaviour among the middle classes. This implied a break with Jewish tradition. Historically, theirs was a complete way of life, a society of their own, and therefore more than a religion or even a 'creed'. The division between the temporal and the spiritual (religious) was transferred from the Christian tradition. This smacked of secularisation, and the separation of life and faith caused a crisis. However, for many Jews assimilation brought freedom from the socio-cultural ghetto. For the majority of middle-class Jews, the answer to the problem of the split came in the form of the reform movement, the so-called *Reformjudentum*, the attempt at renewal on the basis of 'pure' religion interpreted on Kantian lines, the severance of social structures and the repudiation of the medieval Jewish outlook and a Jewish 'nationality'. The *Wissenschaft des Judentums* ('Science of Judaism' movement), the systematisation of orthodox Jewish tradition, was then in its early stages and was the other side of the split. Middle-class Jews saw their faith interpreted in liberal philosophical terms and saw it becoming a special province, a denomination within a superstructure of national and bourgeois culture.

Jewish political outlook was affected by these prevailing conditions. During the Vormärz, the majority professed no particular political loyalty; if anything, attitudes ranged from conservative to 'wait and see' — Toury estimates that only one-third of all Jews were liberals. After 1848, and especially after the end of the 1850s, liberalism grew among the Jewish community. For the period up through the 1870s, one could speak of a common path of Jews and liberals; equal rights and the defeat of the old order were on the liberal agenda and gave the demands of the Jewish community a universal element. However, Jews who had become assimilated were not politically active as Jews but as citizens and Germans. Among politically active German Jews, the proportion of left-wingers, radicals and, eventually, socialists, had always been substantially higher, from Heine through to Lassalle. In the years before 1848, one-third were radical and 12% 'socialist'. Of course, this was largely the result of legal and social discrimination against the Jews. The break that these activists made with their Jewish traditions and with their social status as elements of the intelligentsia led to the acuteness of their criticisms and their near-utopian demands for emancipation.

The uneven but advancing emancipation and assimilation eroded isolation and alienation between Germans and Jews, but only up to a certain point. Around 1800, social intercourse was on the increase among the educated. The salons of Rahel Levin, Henriette Hertz and Fanny Arnstein in Berlin and Vienna are well-known as venues not only for Jewish-German contact, but also for contact between the middle classes and the nobility, and civilians and the military, in an atmosphere of reforming officialdom and on the basis of equal rights. In the upper and educated classes before the 1840s, and thereafter throughout the bourgeoisie, a broad band of social contact can be identified that was growing continually, especially through associations and in communal organisations. This was certainly true of large and medium-sized cities, which were the true ground on which assimilation occurred. Besides this, military service had had an integrating effect. At the same time, especially in personal relationships, distance was generally preserved by both sides, as was the sense of the difference between the two cultures. Richard Wagner, admittedly not a completely trustworthy witness on the subject, was not entirely unrepresentative when he said that in 1848 he fought with his fellow liberals and radicals for the abstract concept of Jewishness and its emancipation, rather than on behalf of particular Jews. Mixed marriages were infrequent and often led to disownment by the Jewish family.

There was no end to the historical, political, socio-economic, 'national' or religious criteria or prejudices, or the sense of dealing with 'aliens'; Gentiles kept their distance from Jews, thereby binding the latter more closely together and creating further segregation. In the quest for the early history of antisemitism that came later, any number of anti-Jewish accounts have been collected from the Vormärz and Nachmärz periods. There was a great aversion to radical Jewish journalists and, after about 1850, the typical city sophisticate; furthermore, satires against bourgeois capitalism, the *nouveau riche* and money-orientation — for example in the newspaper *Fliegende Blätter* — largely availed of Jewish stereotypes. Because the Jews did not lack modernity — the modernity of the city, capitalism and an intelligentsia critical of tradition — the society in which they lived, which itself had not got to grips with that modernity, kept its distance, harboured negative, critical sentiments, and tended to exaggerate the significance of a group which, though having a high profile, was itself small.

Thus the old atmosphere prevailed. It is no coincidence that the anti-heroes in middle-class novels such as *Soll und Haben* (Debit and Credit) and *Hungerpastor* (Hunger Pastor) were Jews, even though neither Raabe nor the convinced (and pro-emancipation) liberal Freytag were antisemitic. Even so, this was not the real issue; the attainment of equal rights and 'fraternity' were of greater significance. The anti-Jewish protests that accompanied the unrest early in 1848, and were an amalgam of economic and social protest with xenophobic and religious elements, appeared old-fashioned, passé and disagreeable; they did nothing to upset the process of rapprochement between Germans and Jews. *Die Gartenlaube*, the popular organ of the middle classes, and Eugenie Marlitt, its star authoress, wrote in the spirit of liberal emancipation, characterising the Jews as part of German society and culture. At the beginning of the 1860s, the Jews seemed well on the way to achieving their niche within that framework — despite the obvious tensions — and this was the view of the majority, both in bourgeois and in Jewish circles.

9. Bourgeois Society

Society in 19th-century Germany was descended from the old society based on the estate system. Following its emergence in the 18th century, bourgeois society developed throughout the first half of the 19th century and the formative phase of revolution. The implications of the process were threefold.

Firstly, the inequality of the old system, enshrined in state law, changed — slowly and with the trappings of the estate system — into the legal equality of a civilian society. Secondly, modern principles of merit and occupation superseded birth as the determinant of social status. Thirdly, there was the typical 19th-century development of class within German society. Stratification of society became dependent on the individual's property, economic power and position in the production process, as well as other, differently determined elements of social prestige. Economic and social change, socio-cultural developments, state measures and specific political trends were all decisive factors of equal importance in the process. The initial impetus came from political and national developments, with the economic and social process gradually assuming an importance of its own.

As demonstrated earlier, bourgeois society essentially arose during the Reform Era. Even then, however, a substantial residue from the estate system endured. This was at its most obvious in the case of the nobility, which was destined to endure as an estate both politically and socially. During the reforms, the privileges enjoyed by the nobility were greatly curtailed, since the principle of legal equality for all citizens was intended to replace the inequalities of the former system. As landowners, officers or officials, the nobility now had to compete on equal terms and, in fact, submit to bourgeois demands for achievement and education. State administration and justice exerted pressure on feudal power in the countryside, and simultaneous and direct intervention by the state on behalf of those still bound to servitude gradually loosened the grip of the aristocracy on their partial stake in the hierarchy. Elements of their former rights and privileges remained, and were even strengthened between 1815 and 1848. Above all — in nearly all cases — a nobleman retained 'patrimonial jurisdiction'. Besides this, he would have his own courts of law, thus being exempt from the usual lower courts. With the introduction of representative bodies — upper parliamentary chambers in constitutional states, and, in Prussia, the *Kreis* assemblies and provincial *Landtage* and later the Herrenhaus (the upper chamber after 1856) — the nobility received new privileges, and even a new function.

Further laws governing social status also applied. For example, there were the Prussian marriage laws. Marriage into the lower classes was subject to royal assent, which was often withheld; the curious institute of the 'left-handed marriage' (morganatic marriage) was supposed to preserve parts of the nobility as an estate. In criminal law, the honour of the nobility was assessed differently from that of other members of society and the defence of honour by duelling was *de facto* permitted. In civil law, nobles were privileged in being allowed to designate their estates as entails, thus protecting a family seat from division and heavy mortgaging. After 1840, Friedrich Wilhelm IV even attempted to bestow new privileges on the nobility within the new 'class' of titled bourgeois estate-owners. That the loss of nobility, and hence the entry into the bourgeoisie, was supposed to represent a form of criminal punishment, provoked outraged protest among the middle classes in the Rhineland. Lastly, there were the educational establishments that were either wholly or chiefly the preserve of the nobility, such as the Prussian cadet academies or the Pagerie in Bavaria.

In the south the system of privileges accorded to the mediatised *Standesherren* had taken effect on the position of the aristocracy as a whole. Before 1803, these princes and lords had been answerable only to the Reich. The Confederation of the Rhine and the Congress of Vienna secured them a special position both with respect to the new states and their old lands, as a kind of lower aristocracy with citizens' rights. Up to 1848, the bureaucrats' reforming attack on the Prussian nobility continued until halted by a restoration of the aristocracy, at least at the highest levels of the state and government. In southern Germany, on the other hand, the bureaucracy maintained anti-feudal attitudes that were, however, blocked by existing laws and the concentration of power which maintained the position of the nobility until 1848. It was not until 1848, and then the 1860s, that the bulk of privileges were abolished, including some of the most offensive.

Even ignoring privileges and after their withdrawal, the nobility continued to retain their special status, and they continued to dominate certain areas. One reason for this was the practical preference exercised by the state and its political proximity to the ruling classes. These aspects will be examined later. In the upper reaches of the officer corps, and among the independent executive, status was earned on merit, though education and career combined with the 'alloted' status of birth, inheritance, marriage and social connections. In Prussia, particularly in the eastern provinces, the nobility largely retained top administrative posts at *Kreis* level, and in general remained in the 'political estate' whose members typically held senior administrative and ministerial offices. In Austria and Hanover a similar position obtained, but elsewhere too the aristocracy stood a greater chance of securing political office than their bourgeois counterparts, a fact that was conditioned by Germany's monarchical system.

The thirty-four princes (as at 1818) and their courts stood firmly in the aristocratic tradition and secured the nobility's leading position. They determined court administrative posts and courtly society and the class that was deemed acceptable at court — the core of which was, of course, the nobility. Social hierarchies in the royal capitals were determined by these facts. Indeed, for every member of society throughout the land, the monarchy maintained the profile of aristocratic values and positions by the award of orders, titles and honours. Besides this, however, after the revolution had come to naught, it was only natural — and comparisons with Britain give this a very concrete form — that the nobility's traditional social preferment should continue in new forms, even under the new dictates of bourgeois society.

Education, property, responsibilities in public affairs and the bureaucracy, access of the nobility to the nobility, the combination of official functions with social intercourse and remuneration commensurate with living standards, reputation and sophistication all served to secure for the nobility a continuing and disproportionate share of the public life, chiefly in the domain they had made their own, the diplomatic service. In other cases, the nobility assumed a new function as a regional agricultural elite able to win voluntary concessions from peasants (once compensation of the nobility through return of lands had been concluded). This tended to happen when local official functions had been lost or — as in the case of Prussia's Catholic nobility — when the aristocracy had no particular link with state powers. Despite heavy sacrifices of political function in the bureaucratic and later the constitutional state, the nobility remained the favoured source of the political leadership even after the revolution — and a further phase of development in the 1860s — had increased equality of opportunity. Their position was maintained or re-established at the core of national and regional political elites even under the new conditions.

It could be suggested that the reaction of most nobles to the loss of former political functions was expressed in rejection of politics as a career and a concentration on professional pursuits such as agriculture or the new urban occupations. Other available options were withdrawal into private life as a rural lord of the manor or, less frequently, into more refined circles. There can be no doubt that some felt forced onto the defensive by the rise of the bourgeoisie. However, in terms of German history, the aristocracy retained their decisive impact on the reorganising political elite and its own claims to power.

The aristocracy was by no means a homogeneous unit. There was great differentiation, and its make-up varied widely both in terms of origins and of social and economic position. Mediatised princes, for instance, had an exalted position and were equal by birth with the ruling families. There were knights and freeholding nobility, formerly answerable only to the Reich, major and minor ranks such as counts, barons and baronets down to the many Prussian Junkers whose names were prefixed by a *von*. There were nobles who had held titles since time immemorial, those who were first honoured after the Middle Ages and the recently titled nobility. There were noble landowners and many noble officers and officials, the very rich (such as the Silesian magnates and the high-ranking nobility of southern Germany). The comfortably off and the poor completed the picture of nobility at the time. After the demise of the former welfare institutions in the Catholic Reich, youngest sons constituted the dispossessed nobility, although connections with the 'family seat' were maintained for some length of time. The most important differences in the period under examination here were those between higher and lower nobility, the landowners and those who had been landless for generations, the old hereditary and the newly honoured aristocracy, some of them responsible for sharp social divisions, especially in Vienna and Austria. With the rise of the modern bureau-cratic state there came a levelling of the nobility and a certain amount of unity vis-à-vis the bourgeois world, despite intermarriage and the conferment of titles on the bourgeoisie. The political, economic and social privileges enjoyed by the nobility as a whole also rubbed off on its poorer sections, including disinherited children.

Socially, the nobility were basically relatively exclusive, despite connections with senior officials and large landowners from bourgeois circles. Among students, feudal and bourgeois fraternities existed separately. Contact was sought and found principally among one's own kind. In many respects, the nobility had without doubt absorbed many features of bourgeois existence, in terms of clothing, family morals, rules of civilised behaviour, education and participation in culture, and above all within the economy. More important, however, were the old values and ways of life retained in the bourgeois age as a partial barrier against the spread of bourgeois values. Most obvious among these were ideals of the refined or the aristocratic and the culture of the country seat, even where the economic basis of the aristocracy had been removed by political measures. On the estates, for instance, the patriarchal behaviour of the lord as against the bourgeois tenant was a typical model.

Thus the aristocracy continued as a way of life and a political elite. As early as 1815, the reforms restricting inheritance of titles to eldest sons and introducing the conferment of peerages on rising members of other classes, which had been much discussed at the turn of the century, were no longer an issue. The aristocracy did not abandon its younger sons and — basically — remained a closed shop. The liberals in the Frankfurt National Assembly wanted the abolition of privileges, but not of the aristocracy itself or the system of titles. In the bourgeois age, an aristocrat's existence was attractive to rising members of the middle classes, just as it was in England. This fact was exploited by the monarchy, in line with time-honoured tradition. By creating new peers, the regime attempted to maintain and even extrapolate the pre-eminence of the aristocracy and the gradient of social prestige. Attainment of seniority in the administration was regularly attended by conferment of a title, and on this basis an official bourgeois aristocracy endured throughout the 19th century.

Outside the upper reaches of government the practice of conferment of titles differed from state to state. In Bavaria or Württemberg, for instance, many more were elevated to the aristocracy than had been in Prussia during the Vormärz, and in the states of southern Germany, life peerages tended to be more commonly bestowed than hereditary honours. Between 1807 and 1848 in Prussia, 95 officers, 82 civil servants, 50 landowners, 10 merchants and 4 others (a total of 241 people) were raised to the peerage, peak periods coming after 1815 and after 1840.

All in all, the majority of the nobility actually descended from that estate, but the newly honoured formed a not insignificant group to refresh the traditional nobility without throwing open its doors to all and sundry. Though hesitant to accept the newcomers, the old nobility eventually did so. Sons of the new peers were soon absorbed into the old aristocratic ways, both socially and in terms of outlook, and they were permitted to marry within their new social grouping. The trend was generally the same with regard to intermarriage between the nobility and the bourgeoisie. After reform of the minor nobility in Prussia, there were more marriages between aristocrats and the middle classes than in southern Germany; bourgeois civil servants in particular were able to marry the daughters of the former nobility. In short, opportunities existed for integrating limited numbers of bourgeois elements into the elite on the basis of merit or property, and advantage was taken of such opportunities.

Despite privileges and social segregation, and even though the majority of the nobility belonged to the ranks of the conservatives, one should not overlook the substantial section of the aristocracy that supported liberalism, and even bourgeois liberalism rather than the purely aristocratic 'Whig' liberalism (of which the Bavarian Prince Oettingen-Wallerstein was a typical representative). Besides the Junkers, the strong liberal grouping of eastern Prussian nobility, mention should be made — both representatively and symbolically — of one of the most popular of the leading 1848 liberals, Heinrich von Gagern, as well as Rudolf von Bennigsen, the authoritative leader of the Nationalverein and later of the National Liberal Party. The aristocracy thus entered liberal German politics as they had entered British politics, as neither a dominant nor an insignificant force but very characteristic.

The two remaining 'political estates', the civil service and the military, especially the officers, were in a special position, and will be examined here in connection with state organisation. The civil servants with their academic backgrounds had forced the estate and corporative system into submission; they were selected on the basis of democratic principles of education and merit rather than on feudal criteria such as birth and connections. As a result of their own system of legal privileges, they had themselves evolved into an estate and this accorded not only with their self-assessment but also that of the rest of society. At the time, many even believed that the gulf between civil servants and the rest of the population was wider than that between aristocrats and non-aristocrats. Along with the upper strata of the educated middle classes, civil servants had been extracted from the old order towards the end of the *ancien régime*. Their list of privileges grew and elevated them above the general citizenry. Like the nobility, they had their own courts of law. In matters of honour they had their own codes of punishment; marriage to members of the nobility was rarely, if ever, disallowed; they enjoyed partial exemption from taxation, and a special system of individual and voting rights.

Examinations and titles were the mark and proof of special entitlements for both the civil service and the educated classes — serving as their nobiliary prefix; ranks and, occasionally, uniforms highlighted this fact. The social hierarchy of prestige placed the civil servant below the nobleman and the officer, but far above the businessman or engineer. This again accorded with civil servants' own assessment of their status. They attained their rank through their proximity to power and education, not through property, and that rank was much higher than any earned through bourgeois wealth. In the period under discussion in this book, or at least during the Vormärz, wealth and income did not yet determine social status. Although recruits could enter this group from below — if one considers it to contain more than merely administrators and jurists — in practice, selection tended to be made from academic circles. This will be discussed later when looking at the nature of universities. In the upper reaches of the administration there was an occasional tendency to rely on the nobility, but anti-aristocratic feelings were typical of the period, as a popular protest against privileges of birth and in favour of achievement. Overall, at least during the Vormärz, the civil service was typified by its relative isolation both from the bourgeoisie and the nobility. Only after the revolution did that isolation become less sharply defined when certain legal privileges were suspended.

The state regulation of education, examinations, and the practice and establishment of the professions meant that the members of the liberal professions — doctors, pharmacists, lawyers and notaries — almost had a legal status of their own. The privileges of education were theirs, if not the privileges of office. The typical social group that may be termed academics — with common standards, common identity and isolation from non-academics — was a product of Germany's educational tradition and the role of that tradition within society and the state. Here was a case of education determining social status and stratification.

Together with civil servants and Protestant clergymen, this group represented the 'educated bourgeoisie' as opposed to the 'property-owning bourgeoisie'.

Finally, and very importantly, another group attained a quasi-estate position within the order of German society by means of the third political estate, the military, and its rules concerning eligibility for a commission. Elsewhere, we will address how in Prussia, certain educational qualifications enabled partial exemption from military service ('*das Einjährige*'); the same level of education also qualified one to serve as an officer in the *Landwehr* (the militia) and the reserves. In southern Germany, the educated or propertied classes could be exempt from all military service if they were able to appoint a replacement; such solutions accorded certain special rights to this class. In many ways, the upper middle class in a certain sense only came about through the military organisation, the new breed of officer and the educational requirements necessary to obtain commissions (the legal and social opportunity to become an active officer was also a means of social climbing). Military rank and university degrees, as well as the officers' legal and political privileges and their proximity to the nobility, impacted the social hierarchy so as to divide those eligible for service as officers from the lower middle classes, farmers and all dependent workers and labourers and to introduce a pre-modern, non-bourgeois and anti-egalitarian element into emerging bourgeois society.

Thus the emerging bourgeois economic society was developing into the political estates of the aristocracy, civil service and army, the educated middle classes and the classes discussed earlier — industrial and commercial entrepreneurs (the monied commercial and property-owning classes, or bourgeoisie), the craftsmen and merchants, peasants, industrial workers and other 'underclasses'. Growth occurred in sub-groups such as the educated public servants, entrepreneurs and — at a lower level — college teaching staff; differentiation between the social groupings of the old estate system increased, and the underclasses grew. At the same time, economic changes, population growth and rising mobility replaced the former system outside the political domain despite the retention of elements typical of the estate system, some old, some new. The emerging society, a modern economy, was built on a complex system of occupations and achievement. Liberal social reform had idealised concepts of merit and equality of opportunity — a free rein for the capable and the talented. Instead, property, economic power, position in the production process and ownership of the means of production — as well as a home — became more important for the individual's social status and the stratification of society, and formed new social groupings to which the individual was assigned by social origin, which itself was largely the determinant of educational opportunity and property, and not that of merit, occupation or acquisition. Social strata supplied the foundation for transformation into social classes, and society assumed a class structure, particularly during the phase of rapid industrialisation.

Naturally, any subdivision of a society into groups, strata, 'estates' or 'classes' encounters difficulties and limitations. It would be wrong to ignore such factors as ways of life, economic situation, life-expectancy, social consciousness, educational conditions, traditions and values. As well as self-assessment of social status, the judgments of others are important; political functions (and probably many other elements) also enter the equation. All must be correctly combined and evaluated, and the many marginal and transitional groups and the inner differences of the larger groups must be clearly distinguished. Models built around a single or very few criteria usually fail the acid test of reality; one need only think of the opposition between home-owners and tenants within the middle-class environment. The concept of class must be used only when it is freed of its current trivialisation and given a more complex and differentiated significance.

Strict divisions of social groups according to estates vanished during this era. They were replaced by divisions — no longer based on estates — and demarcations shaped and determined by economics (property and income), education, social prestige and mindset, all of which tended to entrench themselves anew. The strata existed both in overlap and in parallel.

This was also an age typified by a high degree of social mobility, simultaneous with transition to the bourgeois society. The collapse of occupational structure, the formation of a new rural order, particularly among smallholders and the younger sons of peasants, rural and urban mobility, the decline of home-working and the rise of secondary and later tertiary industries were all characteristic of the process. The scarcity of data makes it harder to define the extent to which there was access to upward mobility, and what opportunities were available to members of the lower classes and industrial and agricultural workers. Mobility was, without doubt, less extensive than in a country such as the United States with its egalitarian principles, but it was far from minimal, even though progress was unlikely to be made in leaps and bounds. Closer examination reveals mobility by small steps, for instance from skilled worker to craftsman, or gradual advance (or regression) over three or more generations. It is important to bear in mind intermediate groups such as teachers, craftsmen, railway staff or petty officials. Obstacles were daunting because the structure of Germany's emergent meritocracy was so closely linked to education and qualifications, and career decisions affecting later status were generally taken during the early stages of training. Because scholarships were few in number, and also because families could ill afford to give up the earning potential of the younger generation, education was largely dependent upon parents' means, as well as upon the prevailing negative attitude towards education to be found in agricultural and working circles. Generally speaking, immediate earnings and security were viewed more positively than the delays and risks implicit in an uncertain 'educated' career. For those with their roots in lower rural and working classes, these were the objective and subjective arguments against upward mobility.

During the crisis of pauperism the likelihood of achieving mobility was slimmer than during rapid industrialisation. On the other hand, among the lower-middle strata of society, the families of skilled workers, craftsmen and petty officials, there was greater likelihood of upward mobility, if only by small steps or over three generations.

The social groupings and classes in Germany were fairly rigidly compartmentalised, a tendency that was reinforced by the sense of distance and attempts at dissociation, group solidarity — that is often reported — and combinations of economic status, education, political rights and the views nurtured by traditions and professions. Such demarcation was most typical of northern Germany, where the line between dialect and standard language was much more sharply defined, and eastern Germany and Prussia, where the feudal and military legacy was greater and the authoritarian nature of the bureaucracy more striking. More liberated forms of social intercourse led to less decisive demarcation.

In addition to social friction, there were other forms of conflict, such as those between Catholics, orthodox-pietistic and liberal Protestants, Jews, non-denominational and secularised groups. Besides this, German particularism had a lasting impact on the social fabric and views of certain groups; for this reason, numerous different and opposing social 'milieus' endured, transcending economic and class boundaries. In some cases, denominational and regional differences were more important than social and class conflicts.

One of the most profound political and social problems of 19th-century German history was how these relatively adverse milieus should develop into single large classes, and how a single, relatively homogeneous nation with a single identity, a German society, could emerge. Of course, there were also factors at work which facilitated integration. The condition of the industrial working class and the rising labour movement went some way towards uniting the working classes. Opposition to the aristocracy, liberalism in politics and formation of leagues and associations created the upper and lower levels of the urban bourgeoisie and then (around 1848) a single entity out of the two. Groupings valid throughout urban Germany — if not the entire country — were the product of, on the one hand, mobility and emergent class-consciousness among workers, and, on the other, the bonds of university education, cultural awareness and liberal national ideals among the middle classes.

Among the dominant social contrasts — that is to say, ignoring those of a regional, religious and political nature — the city–country contrast still commanded a central position. The migration of surplus rural population to the cities made no difference whatever, while the gradual trickle of urban ideas and ways of life into the country — economic rationalisation, bureaucracy and political platforms — had only a marginal impact in the country. Admittedly, the power of this contrast was latent rather than overt.

The second important social contrast was the gap between the middle classes and the nobility. It was most keenly felt by the middle classes and was instrumental in advancing their integration. Bourgeois literature and other publications such as the journal *Die Gartenlaube* were filled with attacks on and criticisms of the privileges and exclusivity of the aristocracy, their precedence within the officer corps and senior administrative positions, their exemption from the demands of work and achievement, and their pretensions and way of life. All of which motivated the opposition in this age of conflict.

During both the Vormärz and Nachmärz the consciousness arose that liberalism was a 'bourgeois' movement that could claim to represent the real strength of society: work, achievement and progress. The middle and upper reaches of the bourgeoisie were united in that belief, which was also a rallying-point for most of the petty bourgeoisie. A kind of class identity began to crystallise, a sense of advancement and an increasing entitlement to claims to be the true nation. That sense was the embodiment of a gradual fusion of the educated and propertied middle classes under the banner of liberalism during the Nachmärz, a time when social contact between the two groups was also growing. Within the bourgeoisie itself, there was a complex interplay of tension and unity. Tension existed between propertied and educated sectors, but also between those same elements and the lower-middle classes. At the same time, the majority felt that officialdom was patronising and arrogant; yet it was precisely those officials who, together with the academics, were in the vanguard of liberalism, speaking for the people as a nation of independent citizens. Politics bridged the social divides; the same was also true of Catholicism and, to a certain extent, even of conservatism.

The third main, but vague and hazy division was drawn between the middle and the lower classes. It has already been said that the lower classes were far from uniform. However, there was still a clear divide between the condition of the poor and the dependent on the one hand, and, on the other, typically middle-class features such as home-ownership, independence and security. During the crisis of pauperism of the Vormärz, this divide was temporarily obliterated by the line between the 'little people' and the 'monied and titled (and educated) patricians'. In the long term, however, and especially at the height of industrialisation, the line between even the most modestly secure middle classes and the dependent workers and lower classes became increasingly well defined, despite being bridged both politically and religiously before the breakthrough of the socialist labour movement. Ways of life, standards and goals differentiated the groups very clearly, even on adjacent margins of the two strata where there was no great difference in wealth.

At the same time, the fourth great contrast was forming, especially within the middle classes: that of polite society and the little people. The educated, now joined by the industrialists, contrasted with the 'Volk'. The opposition between those with servants and those without was a matter of central psychological significance, since this was precisely the line that differentiated portions of the 'middle middle class' and, within it, whole occupations such as craftsmen and shopkeepers.

Social mobility, social groupings and their contrasts and relationships are not the only features requiring consideration when examining the emergence of the complete bourgeois society which was occurring at this time. The specific contrast between bourgeois society and the old order was that it was a society of individuals. The advance of the individual and individuality itself was characteristic. The process was accompanied by the watchwords of the conservatives and liberals: fragmentation of society, liberation of the individual from the yoke. In the old world, people were bound to households, corporate bodies, guilds, the village collective, the local master, the neighbourhood, one's birthplace, a church community or a region: one's immediate world. Families counted for more than individuals. A corporate body such as a guild embraced a person's entire life outside home and church and — without attempting here to specify how — combined his interests with those of other guild members. Their values were collective rather than individualistic and were typical of the group itself, orientated in a 'particularist' sense rather than towards outside society.

The church was the place which gave meaning to life, an institution to which one belonged from birth, and which subverted the Christian emphasis on the individual. 'Culture' was tied to social functions, especially the church and the court, rather than a reality that confronted and shaped the individual. It was a world in which intitiatives and aims, even consciousness, were largely prescribed. Customs and traditions rather than individual reflection tended to provide the basis for belief and behaviour through the medium of images and symbols by providing models. Normally the individual's identity coincided with that of his group and he lived in conformity with that group. Social structures had the character of prescribed and all-embracing communities. The structure of society was static, and personal roles were fixed and were not varied enough to lead to tension and thereby to the growth of individuality. A person's subjectivity was restricted from the start by bonds of this nature, and the same was true of the value of that subjectivity.

As the late 18th century progressed, life became increasingly less bound by these restrictions. Existence was no longer determined by tradition and status at birth; instead there was the possibility of 'self-determination' and the attainment of 'personal status' through achievement and education. The individual confronted a world of immutable ties with demands for room for freedom of action, self-fulfilment, the setting of targets and application of mental faculties. A person could become self-supporting and break out of the solid and restrictive mould of his social origins which had previously been the sole point of reference.

This process of individualisation had its beginnings among the educated upper-middle class of society in the 18th century. Its effects permeated through to the nobility and finally, by degrees, to the rest of society. An attempt to describe this process was made in the survey of family history. The causes and motivation of the process were many, and included religious and intellectual ones, such as pietism, the first steps towards secularism and the Enlightenment. Political and socio-historical events added their influence, as did the rise of the bourgeoisie from outside the original system of 'estates', supported by the increasingly bureaucratic state. Finally, and generally later, economic change introduced new practices to agriculture and commerce that gnawed away at old traditional and corporative systems. The politics of the bureaucratic reforms, the increasing pressure of economic (and social) changes, the spread of new ideas and the education of society which provided a new authority which competed with that of the home and which confronted tradition with reflection, increasing mobility, the rise of the movers and shakers into the traditional realms of society: corporative society lost ground on all fronts, and individualism was the beneficiary.

The gradual replacement of rural control and collective structures gave the process of individualisation a very concrete quality, as did the release of the underclasses from both their obligations and their security and the crisis within the guild system; the process now became a mass phenomenon. The individual was far from a mere invention of enlightened liberal theory; social roles and a new position made the individual more than just a concept to be opposed to 'state' or 'society'. A century ago, personality and behaviour were far more dependent on tradition and social position than they are in today's western civilisation with its standards of liberty, urbanisation, change, and criticism of tradition. But in comparison to the traditional world, there is a tangible loosening of the prescribed social obligations, an increasing individuality of personality and lifestyle, of career and consciousness. The modern relationship of individual and community/society gains against the traditional one. At all social levels old-fashioned collective honour is replaced by the principle of individual, personal honour.

One important consequence of individualisation deserves mention here. In breaking free from limited social structures of background and tradition and the ever-present standards and values, the individual began to feel a certain sense of isolation, that has often been described as uprooting or alienation, and, in a more concrete sense in the earliest stages of the process, as a breach between the generations. Points of reference lost their former clarity, which led to the relatively rapid formation of new and specifically modern ones. Large, abstract groups became the focus for the individual — humanity or nation, the enlightened or the educated, the like-minded. They offered a sense of belonging, a degree of certainty and an opportunity for identification, but in return they claimed the loyalty of the individual. Admittedly, these groups no longer existed in solid fact; rather they were represented by ideas or principles. The new-style orientation around and identification with large secular groups and ideals had an impact on what the author would term 'political faith'. That faith, whether liberal, nationalist or socialist, had a hitherto unprecedented effect on the individual's equilibrium.

Individualisation proceeded in tandem with the increased significance of culture and its popularisation. Arts and sciences were freed from their functions within the old order of society, thus basically becoming accessible to all. Interpretation of life and the world became the province of the layman, the public, rather than the exclusive domain of the church. The meaning and conduct of life and society became cultural debating points, at once a means of individualisation and an expression of individuality. In the traditional order, standards had had a tangible and symbolic quality; now they existed as the stimulus to reflection for the self-reliant individual. This accounted for the extraordinary importance of the medium of thought, that is to say language and literary culture.

The new enlightened bourgeois faith in education, advancement and the transformation (and transformability) of the world was a further component of the process of individualisation, which could now also aim at emancipation from an authoritarian state and demand the cooperation of all citizens on behalf of the public good.

In terms of social organisation, the implications of increased individualisation were likewise serious. In the old order, individuals were organised into corporations, membership of which was decided by birth and estate; these bodies impinged in an intangible way on all aspects of life, but determined their members' rights and status. In time, as has been said, society was decorporatised, and new types of organisation took over to fill the vacuum. These associations or societies were voluntary collectives, consisting of individuals who were at liberty to come and go, independent of their members' legal status and having no effect on that status. They set their own goals, goals that were of a specific nature, unlike those of the guilds, for instance, which had been handed down and affected the whole of life. By the mid-19th century, after modest beginnings late in the 18th, associations and clubs gained the power to shape society and determine the life and activities of the individual. The century became the century of the association (*Verein*), and practically everyone was in some way — and often in many ways — connected with their work. Even in a traditional institution like the church, with its official institutional nature, the associations thrived. And the state, membership of which was compulsory, promoted free association for public ends. The self-appointed aims of clubs and associations ranged from companionship to education, from 'service' to art and science, and encompassed ideals such as public service and social change and improvement. They were styled as 'casinos', 'resources', reading circles and museum associations. Freemasonry, scientific, artistic and musical societies were also established. Professional and trade bodies, partly or wholly political associations, *Burschenschaften* (students' associations), choral societies and sports associations, welfare groups and workers' associations can largely be traced back to this period. They were the expression of a new need felt by the individual for which the old world had had no room, a need for self-awareness through discussion and communal activity. Individualisation and free association of the individual: each implied the other. Quasi-natural structures were replaced by an order based on the freedom of the self-reliant person: in short, on association. Because the membership of a society lacked the element of compulsion contained in corporations, the former allowed greater liberty to the individual.

Clubs and associations were of crucial significance to the new structure, differentiation and integration of society. Their original stance was against the estates. It was usual, indeed universal, for membership to be accepted not by virtue of birth or status but by merit and education. The 'purely human' took precedence over boundaries of status. Bodies of this kind sought to bring together their members from every stratum of society. Specifically, they were against segregation of the aristocracy, whom they demanded should, first of all, accept values of education and humanity — the bourgeois code of values — and, secondly, join the essentially bourgeois movement they represented. Around 1800 the clubs and societies grouped together officialdom, academics and aristocracy to form the new upper stratum of early 19th-century society. Even though the partial co-operation between middle classes and nobility became strained after 1815 when the aristocracy regained some of its former standing, clubs and associations had by then played a substantial part in its embourgeoisement.

More importantly, however, societies, clubs and asociations were a means of imparting solid form to a mass of people from every imaginable walk of life and binding them to create a non-abstract body, a symbiosis that was achieved through exchange of experience. *Burschenschaften* — the generic term for student organisations, many of which had their roots in the ancient traditions of yeomanry — professed precisely these ideas. Anti-aristocratic and community tendencies were joined by a new elitism. Differences in education replaced former estate divisions, a 'natural' expression of the need for group homogeneity in social intercourse. Especially after 1815, general educational and social societies such as the Museum, Casino, Harmonie and Ressource associations became differentiated in terms of the typical background of their membership; they are divided up according to education, wealth and lifestyle. At the same time, societies that were more 'democratic' in nature, especially the sports associations and (male) choral societies (with the exception of church organisations) retained their popular liberal character and transcended all social strata, the whole nation. In short, isolation and integration existed in parallel.

Liberal moves against the corporative and authoritarian order had been accompanied and promoted by the model of the association which they now applied to the solution of social problems. As has been demonstrated, their concept was founded upon associations — including workers' associations — as the cure for society's afflictions. Association would grant a degree of self-help to those who had nothing, and it would guarantee true liberty; these were the two strengths of a liberal society. By association, the proletariat would lose their proletarian features to be absorbed into the bourgeois order. That attempt was destined to evoke articulate opposition to integration into a liberal society and associations eventually became the organisational vehicle for the new classes which were struggling against the bourgeoisie. Thus during the mid-19th century associations, societies and clubs promoted parallel tendencies: differentiation of the bourgeoisie, integration of the nation as a whole, and the formation of a workers' class.

A second product of modern society was the process of specialisation; this was at once a cause and an effect of the development of association. Early societies and clubs often had several aims — nature study and industry, culture, commerce and morality. Life's generality was their domain. An opposition was constructed between the universality of life and the world and the particularism of the traditional order, as well as the new specialisations in modern working surroundings, the latter a feature that was identified in its earliest stages. The one-dimensionality of training, work and prosaic occupations was contrasted with the diversity of education and a freely directed culture; to put it another way, humanity was set against bourgeois existence and the alienation of work. Here, then, are the origins of the separate cultural world that formed an important element of educated life. Culture was both individual and universal — even the simple members of a choral society could bask in the reflected glory of a 'higher' sphere. Typical of early bourgeois culture of this kind was the dilettante, the amateur, the collector and connoisseur, students of nature, art and history, the informed layman.

The first reversal occurred at this point. The more one identified with 'culture', the sooner it could appear to be replaced by life itself. Cultural life became the 'domain' of a certain type of 19th-century bourgeois, alongside work and political activity. Free time became dedicated to education and abandonment to culture and the serious and direct practice of its constituent elements. Because culture existed for its own sake, its connections with the rest of life could be severed, thereby allowing the two to exist side by side. Human activity thus became splintered, and societies and associations typify this. After 1815, 'cultural societies' were increasingly separated from the mainstream of developments and concentrated on their own field. That did not — yet — imply that life itself was compartmentalised or one-sided; the individual could follow a variety of interests under a number of umbrellas and become integrated into each of them. The autonomy of culture highlighted by this fact had a complementary and compensatory significance. The power of the achievement principle and the *vita activa* of economy and politics contrasted with a modern form of *vita contemplativa*, the independence and freedom of direction of culture; such was the nature of the compound in which it provided nourishment for life.

After overcoming the particularism of the old order and its universal standards, bourgeois society (and therefore the modern world) began to specialise and differentiate, and not only with regard to the 'autonomisation' of culture. Demands and aims became more numerous, more complex and more differentiated, as did economic and business interests. The process of specialisation mimicked society itself and may be traced most accurately in the proliferation of associations and societies which subdivided or were founded anew, until by the middle of the century there was an association for practically every interest group. Despite this, larger educational, social and choral societies preserved general, non-specialised trends within society until well into the second half of the century. De-particularisation and specialisation continued as two opposing but complementary processes throughout the period. Opportunities and roles for the individual expanded and became more differentiated without endangering integration or identity.

Finally, associations and societies reflected the new relationship that was emerging between the individual and the state. They implied a private and autonomous sphere of activity free from state interference. Freedom accorded the individual was transferred to joint, and initially unpolitical, activities. Since they provided a semi-public arena for discussion of public matters, societies soon contained a political element. Societies with public-spirited objectives could not escape having an impact on public affairs; thus the line between state and voluntary activity became blurred and a citizen's initiative in public affairs gains importance through the activities of the societies.

Another development was that of the society that had true political aims. To begin with, the state and the societies were perceived as collaborative and complementary partners. The state promoted agricultural and commercial bodies, and the same was true of societies in other fields of interest: history, education, reform, philanthropy, etc. All were intended to fulfil tasks that could not be undertaken by the bureaucracy. Bureaucratic liberalism and the state in its reforming and educational intentions both took advantage of the existence of clubs and associations; self-organisation was intended to boost the capacity of state institutions. By replacing the corporation and the traditional order, the state became the ally of the modern individual and his organisations and promoted the cause of freedom. It must be said that from 1819 at the latest — the end of the age of reform — public organisations were restricted to the non-political, since it was felt that demands for co-determination within state politics should be thwarted. Political societies were banned, and societies were excluded from politics. To quote Karl von Ibell, a *Staatsrat* in Nassau in 1819, 'It is not only senseless but also unlawful for private persons to think themselves, either individually or in league with others, competent to take a hand in Germany's affairs of state.'

Strict party bans were implemented, although in the case of clubs and societies there was alternation between freeze and thaw. One consequence of this was de-politicisation of the societies; but at the same time it also gave rise to the kind of crypto-politicisation seen in the choral societies and sports associations, and in the 1840s in the reading circles, casino and citizens groups, and even in doctors', teachers', apprentices' and workers' associations. With the revolution and after the reactionary interlude of the 1850s, the process culminated in the establishment of the modern system of parties and political organisations during the 1860s.

Thus civil society developed as a society which was strongly divided and differentiated by occupation and class. It also retained a number of trappings from the old order but was essentially a society of the individual and of societies and organisations.

III

Restoration and Vormärz, 1815–48

1. The End of the Reforms:
Constitutions and Restoration

The problem of the five-year period after 1815 was whether and to what extent the reforms of the Napoleonic era would be continued or at least consolidated, or whether they would be brought to an end, or even revoked. This problem focused particularly on the question of whether the individual states would be given a constitution. The period ended in division, only the south German states becoming constitutional states, but not Prussia and certainly not Austria. However, for Germany as a whole it would be true to say that 'restoration' became the dominant principle of the epoch and brought the reform era to an end.

The constitutional question had its own history in the individual states and groups of states. However, political decisions of such magnitude as the introduction of a constitution naturally affected the interests of all powers, and especially the larger ones, which were dependent on the balance of power in Europe as well as in Germany as a whole. They were all part of the discussion about constitutions which had been taking place in Europe since the French *Charte* of 1814.

The Tsar primarily kept this discussion moving until 1818 with his 'gratification' programme to introduce representative constitutions, not only in Poland, but everywhere else as well. The German Confederation was bound by the decree — which the Congress of Vienna had practically nullified — that all states within the Confederation 'would have *landständische Verfassungen*' (constitutions including a corporately constituted state parliament). The question initially was whether the Confederation derived any authority from this. Metternich did not want to be steamrollered by a development which seemed to have a momentum of its own; the Confederation or the major states were to set out a framework. In 1816, Saxe–Weimar wanted a guarantee of its new constitution from the Confederation; the estates of Lippe wanted any new constitution banned; whereas Württemberg wanted a decision on constitutional principles. Metternich tried to persuade Prussia and the south German kingdoms of the merits of his idea of having 'estates' in the provinces and an advisory privy council (*Staatsrat*) at the centre, which suited supranational Austria very well. But this fell on deaf ears at first. The south German states did not want a regulation which applied to the whole Confederation, and certainly not one on old estate lines, and although the Bundestag (Confederate Assembly) finally (25 May 1819) disclaimed competence, the mere possibility was grounds enough for them to go their own ways.

Prussia also set off on a solo course, and Austria was in danger of isolating itself in terms of constitutional policy, and so intensified its pressure on Prussia and the other states. In a much-discussed document published in 1819 and entitled 'Concerning the difference between *landständische* and representative constitutions' Metternich's secretary Gentz developed the thesis that only constitutions based on old estate lines were in keeping with the Federal Act, and that the members of estate-based assemblies represented only their own estates, and not the people as a whole. The radicalisation of the *Burschenschaften*, the student associations, and the assassination of Kotzebue changed the political climate, and in 1819 Metternich succeeded in winning over Prussia and in putting a stop to the movements for a constitution. This will be outlined presently, after discussion of the developments in south Germany and Prussia.

The south German territories gave themselves constitutions between 1818 and 1820. Nassau acquired a constitution as early as 1814, as did a number of small states, the principal one among them being Saxe–Weimar (1816). More crucial examples, however, were Bavaria, Baden, Württemberg and Hesse–Darmstadt. Considering what had happened during the era of the Confederation of the Rhine, the rapid adoption of constitutions was surprising. There were a number of complex reasons for this. (1) There was the main problem of these states, namely that of integration. In 1815, territorial changes had occurred again. Once pressure from Napoleon had abated and the state of war ended, the 'mediatised' sovereigns, the rulers formally possessing the right to autonomy under the Kaiser (*reichsunmittelbar*), demanded, if not reinstatement, then at least autonomy and special rights. The constitution offered a way of consolidating the 'new' states. In addition to administrative integration, it offered the unifying structure of parliamentary representation, turning administrative unity into national unity, a unity of citizenship under the state. It was only by dint of a constitution that natives of Baden–Baden, Durlach, Breisgau or the inhabitants of the Palatinate became one unified *Volk* of Baden; only with the help of a constitution was the Bavarian king able to exert his dominion over Ansbach and Bayreuth, Würzburg and Bamberg. Once the mediatised sovereigns were given a part in the political process by granting them a seat in the upper chambers, they were integrated. However, what was even more urgently required was middle-class representation by means of a second chamber, as a counterbalance against the aristocracy. (2) In concrete terms, what was needed was active and effective representation for taxpayers in order to stabilise debts and safeguard state credit. The drain on finances became a driving force for constitutional policies. (3) Of course, expectations based on the political ideas of the time had a role to play, since these were also getting an airing in the governing establishment. The bureaucracy wanted a constitution in order to bind the monarchy to laws and institutions; the aristocracy wanted to safeguard old rights; whereas the civilian population sought modern representation and a share in the political process. In spite of the general weakness of this civilian population, constitutional movements started up in Hesse–Darmstadt and, along more old-fashioned lines, in Württemberg, with publicity, petitions and assemblies, which brought a certain pressure to bear on the government. (4) Particularism, of all things, was an engine for the constitution: the desire was to pre-empt a ruling by the Confederation, and therefore in 1818, the political offensive for a constitution intensified (that is, if we ignore Württemberg). (5) Finally, the individual states themselves had their own particular reasons, in accordance with their own respective *raison d'état*.

In Bavaria, a constitution had been discussed in 1814–15, but nothing had been done about it. The question was reopened only after the fall of the all-powerful minister Montgelas in February 1817 — the result of the combined promptings of General Wrede, the Crown Prince and the permanent secretary (*Ministerialdirektor*) Zentner. A constitution was billed, and enacted on 26 May 1818, which became a sort of model for south Germany. Aside from the more general points of view, there were two in particular which played a part here: the desire to revise political concessions made to the church in a concordat with the help of a constitution; and the wish to enhance the case for Bavaria in its dispute with Baden about the region of the Electorate of the Palatinate on the right bank of the Rhine. In Baden, a constitution was promulgated on 22 August 1818. This was also intended to bolster claims to the region of the Electorate of the Palatinate on the right bank of the Rhine, as well as to safeguard the succession of a collateral line and the indivisibility of the territory, this time against Bavarian claims.

The situation in Württemberg was unusual. A lengthy 'fight for a constitution' ensued, in which the monarchy, though absolutist, was modernistic and opposed feudalism and the old middle-class estates. The latter defended the traditional constitution based on estates and privileges, referring to it as the 'old law'. Sandwiched between them was a small group of constitutional liberals. A variety of coalitions was formed here. In 1817, the king had even tried to sanction a draft constitution against the estates by means of a plebiscite, but this failed. Finally, on 29 September 1819, a compromise was struck between the monarchic statism of the government and the old estate-based forces in the provinces. The constitution here was a constitutional contract; the old relationship between king and estates was taken on board, but was reinterpreted in a modern constitutional sense. In 1820, finally, another constitution was enacted (though never actually formalised), this time in Hesse–Darmstadt, on the basis of an agreement between the monarch and the estates. The south German territories succeeded, astonishingly enough, in pushing through their constitutional policy even against Metternich. The substance of these constitutions will be discussed later. First let us turn to Prussia.

In Prussia, the constitution failed. This was of epoch-making significance for 19th-century German history, though this could not have been foreseen in 1815. The situation in Prussia after 1815 was characterised by three basic facts. (1) The Prussia of 1815 was a new state consisting partly of regained territories, and other completely new territories covering a wide area, with their own, quite varied political, legal and social constitutions, whether they were traditional, or had been completely remodelled by the reforms of the Napoleonic era. These component provinces included the Rhineland, Westphalia, Saxony, Swedish Pomerania and Posen. Two-fifths of the population were Catholics, almost a fifth were Poles, and the state was divided geographically as well as structurally into a western and an eastern half. In 1817 the *Oberpräsidenten* (heads of provincial administration) spoke of 'our . . . colourful, new and diversely composed state' which was not held together by any natural force or instinct. This state — from Memel to Aix-la-Chapelle — was actually faced for the first time, and to a greater extent than all the south German states, with the problem of integration, and this at a time when the pressure of war and imperium had subsided. The heterogeneous nature of this state was both a stimulus and an impediment to all initiatives for reform. (2) The reform of the old states and the old society was incomplete; the takeover of public powers by the state across the board and the development of a bourgeois society and a constitutional state based on the participation of its citizens were still to be achieved. The reform movement, spurred on by war and victory, appeared to be strong; the 'State Chancellor' and important ministers, the vast majority of the *Oberpräsidenten* and the majority of the *Regierungspräsidenten* (chief administrators of the governmental districts) and the ministerial bureaucrats counted themselves as supporters. (3) On the other hand the opponents of reform, the supporters of the old estates, the feudalists and the bureaucratic absolutists, had gained ground and were now making their voices heard in court circles and in the centres of power. The king's brother-in-law (and commander of the Garde de Corps in 1816), Duke Karl of Mecklenburg, the Prince Wittgenstein (Minister of Police until 1818 and then Minister of the Royal Household) and a whole series of other ministers were the spokesmen for this 'party'. Opponents of reform had been rallying around the Crown Prince since 1817. Since war and the pressure from abroad had fallen away, this so-called 'restoration' gained in strength. The king, Friedrich Wilhelm III, upright and not very independent, had sat by while the reform policies had gone ahead, and now he was quick to fall under the sway of their opponents. Naturally enough, the aristocratic resistance in the country hardened itself against all these new-fangled reforms.

Nevertheless, after 1815 a number of reforms continued to be implemented. Reform of the administration was paramount, in addition to the reforms of finance and taxation, education and trades, which were described earlier. Before a constitution could be considered, the new regions were to be given a unified organisation and integrated into the state. These consisted of new, artificial administrative districts (*Regierungsbezirke*), and new administrative units, the provinces (*Provinzen*), each headed by an *Oberpräsident*. This system had originally been devised in 1807, but had remained on paper. The *Oberpräsidenten* were not a middle tier, they were commissars and representatives of the central government in the province. They were very independent and also became representatives of their province at central government level.

The provinces were more than decentralised administrative units; they gained a relative independence, becoming quasi-federal units within the Prussian state. The citizens grew together as Rhinelanders, Westphalians or citizens of Brandenburg and merged into the Prussian state. At the centre, the *Staatsrat* (privy council), planned in Stein's time, was finally established in 1817 as a body in which proposed legislation could be debated. It consisted of state ministers, princes, army generals and persons nominated by the king, a 'parliament' of senior administrators and aristocrats, which held in check the potential autocracy of the monarch, represented by his non-legally-binding but still influential council, within the structures of a bureaucratic state under rule of law — in other words, a sort of a surrogate constitution.

One of the successes of the reform party was that in 1818 it managed to delay the introduction of the Prussian legal code into the Rhineland until an overall reform had taken place — which meant, however, for an indefinite period. The reformist administrators did not want to surrender the liberal and modern elements of French law, and this meant that the goal of a legal integration of the state as a whole had to take a back seat.

Other reforms were revised by conservatives or simply ran out of steam. The liberation of the peasants continued, but the regulations of 1816 involving the transfer of land from peasant owners with limited rights, and the exclusion of the lowest orders, only benefited the noble landowners. The reform of the *Kreise* in the eastern provinces was abandoned in 1815, reform of the rural parishes in 1820. The *Landrat* (head of the administration of a rural *Kreis*) in the eastern territories remained a loyal representative of the landowners. He was appointed by the king, who was allowed to choose from three candidates. The rural parish remained under the control of the Junkers. The state's extension of its control into the countryside had run up against the feudal power structure. As a result, the integration policy of the reformers also failed, this time due to opposition from conservative forces. The administrative constitution of Prussia was split along the boundary between its eastern and western sections.

Nevertheless, and despite such setbacks, the crucial issue, on which the fate of the reforms hinged in the long term, was the constitutional question. The reformers, Stein as well as Hardenberg, had their sights set ultimately on a representative constitution, which since its announcement in 1810 had been a central theme in Prussian politics, its star still shining through all the various, and not very successful, experiments. Hardenberg took matters to the stage where the king, in a decree of 22 May 1815, promised a written constitution and 'representation of the people', which would, however, only be in an indirect form, via *Provinzialständen* (provincial diets), and which could only debate legislation and taxation. Nevertheless, the constitution was to give a firmer basis to 'civil liberties' and produce an administration founded on order and reason; it was to safeguard and complete the modernisation programme of the reformers by allowing the nation to participate. But this was precisely the problem inherent in founding a constitution. Prussian society was not homogeneous; it contained territorial and particularist special interests, as well as being traditionalist and in part still based on estates. For this reason, even the reformist administrators were doubtful as to whether national representation would better safeguard and promote the unity of the state and protect the maxims of freedom and reason, or whether the state might best be run by the state civil service (*Beamtentum*).

The hopes invested in a constitution were quite varied. Most of the nobility wanted the old regional estates with their feudal bias restored. They required autonomy for the regions, federalisation of the state as a whole and feudal participation in decision-making. But the peasants and the bourgeoisie, even in the less modernised areas, turned against this, and demanded their ultimate right to have a say in government, commensurate with their status. In other words, they demanded parity. The Poles of Posen hoped for some form of national autonomy.

In the western territories, where the modern property-owning society was already more prominent, the bourgeoisie wanted safeguards on individual freedom, on property, and legal equality through participation in the political process. Middle-class publicists campaigned directly for a liberal constitution. Johann Benzenberg, a Rhinelander, made demands for a constitution in two pamphlets written in 1815–16; in Westphalia there were Arnold Mallinckrodt and many others. Matters came to a head in the Rhineland in 1817–18 with a series of petitions. In February 1818, Joseph Görres and a deputation from the Rhineland handed Hardenberg a petition written by him and containing many signatures, and shortly afterwards demanded in a pamphlet that Prussia put itself at the head of the constitutional states in Germany.

All these demands differed in their fine print, some more traditional, others more modern, but there was no mistaking their overall bourgeois, constitutional slant. If one looks at the state and its social forces as a whole, however, the various constitutional aspirations were distinctly antagonistic to one another.

In July 1815, the existing national representation system, which of course consisted only of representatives of the old provinces, was dissolved. The reorganisation of the administration and the integration of the new provinces took precedence over the constitutional question. There were good reasons for this. Furthermore, the constitution itself was linked in the minds of its planners to the idea of *Provinzialstände* — participation was to be built from the bottom upwards. The greater state, so it seemed, was in need of decentralisation. The feudal party, particularist and based on the old estates, demanded concessions. Yet the next two years, when a constitution became a universal political objective, and when in Prussia, in Germany and in the whole of Europe, it might still have been possible, nothing was done. Only after the administrative reform had been concluded did Hardenberg convene a commission in 1817 to discuss the constitution; however, because of their divergent points of view their work came to nothing. Then, in 1819, Hardenberg himself and the newly appointed minister for estate affairs, Wilhelm von Humboldt, tried, a little more decisively this time, to get things moving. Both their memoranda — advocating a graded system of representation, discussion of laws and the safeguarding of fundamental rights — were put before a new commission in the autumn, of whom a majority were still in favour of a constitution.

A crisis now arose in the ministry as Humboldt became Hardenberg's rival. He and other ministers opposed the State Chancellor system and wanted it replaced by a ministry which operated collegially. In the autumn of 1819 this opposition also turned against the new anti-revolutionary federal laws, the Carlsbad Decrees; it wanted to restrict their validity to two years. Hardenberg, in a clear attempt to make room for his constitutional policy, had been a firm supporter of these decrees and had ensured their implementation. In the autumn of 1819, for instance, he had given the police notice to arrest Görres for publishing the pamphlet *Germany and the Revolution*, thereby forcing him into exile. He was able to accuse his opponents in the ministry of making common cause with the revolution.

Added to this there was the conflict between the War Minister, Hermann von Boyen, and the restoration party, which was very influential at the court. This concerned the special position accorded to the *Landwehr* (the militia). To the reactionaries, it was in competition with the real army, an army of the nation rather than the king's army, an army of potential revolutionaries, unreliable, without *esprit de corps* and without 'honour' — the quintessential artifice of feudalistic militarism. The reformers, with their liberal ambitions for making the army into a more bourgeois institution and their democratic idea of turning the army into the *Volk* in arms, were now being called Jacobins. The reactionaries raised objections on military grounds — the standard of training of the *Landwehr* and its organisational links with the *Linie* (the regular army) left a lot to be desired — and won over the king, against the views of Boyen, who was both Minister for War and a general. When the king demanded certain changes in the organisation of the

Landwehr, Boyen resigned. The actual reason for Boyen's resignation was certainly less important than he made out. However, what was decisive was that he had lost the confidence that he would be able to bring the military under a constitution. From a political point of view, the *Landwehr*, without the backing of a constitution, was very much up in the air.

Humboldt and Beyme, the other opposing ministers, were dismissed on 31 December 1819. This was a victory for Hardenberg, but it was a Pyrrhic victory, for now the opponents of the constitution and reform finally had a majority in the government. The dismissal of Humboldt marked the end of the reform era in Prussia. Of course, the question might be asked as to whether Prussia towards the end of 1819 — as a great power feeling the pressure from Metternich and the Tsar and their hardened policies of reaction in quite another way from any of the small German states — could still actually 'afford' a constitution. We do not know; but it would in any case have been extraordinarily difficult. And certainly the opponents of reform and the constitution in the circle around the king had grown stronger and stronger. The reformers had their backs to the wall. The radical nationalist movement of the *Burschenschaften* had actually heightened reservations among some reformers about the constitution. Fear of misuse of the constitution increased generally, and this in itself became a weapon against the constitution. But the brute fact remains that it was the split between the reform ministers which destroyed the last small chance for a constitution.

Hardenberg actually managed to build another safeguard into the constitution in the form of a law concerning the state debt (17 January 1820): new debts could only be incurred with the co-operation and guarantee of *Reichsstände* (estates of the Empire). This became a central pillar of Prussian policy in the Vormärz, but it changed nothing directly. Hardenberg's attempts to salvage a sort of minimal constitution in 1820 failed. The climate was dominated by the fear of demagogues and the romantic notions of restoration of the monarchy held by the Crown Prince's party. There could be no compromise between monarchy and democracy. Hardenberg himself was considered a democrat and even a Jacobin. In June 1821, the formation of a national representative assembly was finally destroyed. Hardenberg's death in November 1822 brought this phase of constitutional politics to its ultimate end. Only the provinces acquired 'estate-based' constitutions in 1823–24. These 'assemblies of the estates', were strongly feudal in character and had few powers. This was a conservative-statist compromise solution, which changed nothing of importance. Until 1848, Prussia remained a state without a constitution, a fact which became fundamental to the course of German history.

A new force entered the pan-German debate about constitution and restoration, namely the radical nationalist movement of the *Burschenschaften*. At its source were the hopes and expectations of 1813, especially those of the younger generation, and the deep-seated disappointment of 1815. This was a manifestation of popular nationalism dedicated to freedom, and it was an understandable reaction to the reorganisation which followed the Congress of Vienna, characterised by the confederation of states and particularism, legitimism, bureaucracy, even despotism. This new generation was seeking an inner 'ethical' justification of the political order, and somewhere along the line it wanted to identify itself with such an order.

This was precisely what it could not do. The defeated hopes culminated in protest. Three organised groups voiced this nationalist and liberationist protest. First there were the gymnastic societies (*Turner*), founded by Jahn and Friesen before 1813. Their didactic and moralistic notions of physical education and the nurturing of a spirit of community were linked to political objectives from the start. Behind their anarchy and all their crude and noisy posturing, their language and mannerisms, their beards and hairstyles, behind all their 'hyper-Germanness', their Germanic drapery and Teutonic xenophobia, they had the dual purpose of binding the nation together into a strong unit and creating a democratic and egalitarian society, no longer divided along estate lines. The gymnastic societies were not a life-reforming sect, but the prototype of a political party. After the disappointments of 1815, they captured the hearts and minds of a whole generation of school and university students. They were a movement which cut across German inter-state borders, a state within a state; the word *Turnstaat* entered the vocabulary. However, the unsettling and mischievous nature of this organisation stirred up a great deal of controversy and aroused considerable public mistrust.

Secondly, the period after 1814 spawned a number of German societies in the Rhine–Main region, among them the so-called Hoffmann League. These nationalist organisations agitating in the cause of freedom and drafting petitions for constitutions were soon forced underground.

The third and most important of these organised groups were the *Burschenschaften*, the real linch-pin of this political youth movement. The first, the original *Burschenschaft*, was founded in Jena on 12 June 1815, and other universities quickly followed suit. The idea of the *Burschenschaft* was of a society embracing all the *ehrlich und wehrlich* (honourable and militant) students of a university. It was an organisation seeking to reform student life, to rid it of the crude, authoritarian, anti-educational student ethos of the old world, and to conduct a civilising crusade for the cultivation of the inner self, bringing to the fore the new idealistic ethos, the new spirit of friendship and community, the concept of an internalised 'honour'. The *Burschenschaft* was 'democratic', in so far as it ignored class background, and it was 'nationalist', opposed to the provincialism of the old *Landsmannschaften* (provincial associations), as well as to the cosmopolitanism of the student 'orders' of the late 18th century.

The *Burschenschaften* were German, pan-German — and in the spirit of 1815 this was bound up with a Christian identity (unbaptised Jews were for the most part excluded). This nationalist orientation was closely bound up with the liberal idea of freedom. 'Honour, Freedom and Fatherland' was their slogan. The black, red and gold of the Lützow Volunteer Corps which were soon held to be 'the' old imperial colours became the symbolic colours of the new movement. Irrespective of state boundaries, this student movement turned into a community based on pan-German consciousness and experience, a 'student state', which, as it were, in its own sphere pre-empted the national state it so deeply desired.

Admittedly, the *Burschenschaften* movement was actually mainly confined to the Protestant regions; more than one-fifth of students had hardly any connection with it. But it was precisely the politically active students who did take part. A series of university lecturers and professors and leading intellectuals such as Luden, Fries, Oken and Steffens, Arndt, Schleiermacher, Hegewisch and Karl Theodor Welcker also supported it.

On 18–19 October 1817 the *Burschenschaften* held a large nationalist rally at the Wartburg, on the tercentenary of the Reformation and in commemoration of the battle of Leipzig in 1813. The celebration was held to mark the liberation of the fatherland from foreign tyranny, of the liberation of *Innerlichkeit* (the inner person) and emancipation of the spirit from Roman Catholicism and papal tyranny and outward shows of devoutness. This curious blend of nationalist and Protestant sentiment was typical of the time. The rally was attended by five hundred students from at least eleven universities. The speakers included the professors Oken and Fries. The student memorial address, moderate in tone, recalled nationalist hopes and disappointments.

The rally was a new form of political event. Independent of any authority, a 'private' gathering was turned into a public demonstration. It allowed supporters to bask in momentary glory and the vigour of a tangible community, and it was a provocation to opponents. It evoked a public response and became a manifestation of power. This was a new form of politics. On the evening of the first day of the rally, Jahn's radical school students organised a burning of 'un-German', reactionary books — those of Karl Ludwig von Haller and Kotzebue, the Prussian Police Laws of Schmalz and the *Code Napoléon*, for instance — as well as the burning of the corporal's baton and tufts, the symbols of the standing army.

Metternich and the conservatives responded immediately. They saw it not as a bit of youthful high jinks, but as a revolutionary action against the state, though, for the moment at least, one which had had little success. The Grand Duke of Weimar, ruler of the Wartburg as well as the University of Jena, maintained a benevolent policy of 'wait and see' with regard to this student movement. On 18 October 1818 the *Allgemeine Deutsche Burschenschaft* was founded as an umbrella organisation of German students; it was to be dedicated to the role of German youth in relation to the 'nascent unity of the German *Volk*'. In the 'Wartburg Rally Declarations', the student Riemann summarised the movement's aims: national unity and constitutional freedom, a constitution and a national representative system to combat the particularist and police state and rid society of its feudal vestiges. On these points there was unity. French revolutionary ideas of liberty, equality and fraternity, of democracy and aggressive rationalism were combined — in a not always compatible mixture — with romantic notions of an organic community, Christianity, medieval imperialism and passionate enthusiasm. The past was searched for reference points from which to criticise the present and for justifications of goals for the future. Despite all its contradictions, the *Burschenschaft* was the first movement in Germany dedicated to a political faith. The member identified himself personally with the cause of the nation, and dedicated himself to it in his deeds and self-sacrifice. In this sense it manifested a specific and new form of radicalism.

A radical wing now formed within the *Burschenschaft*. It was known in Jena as the 'Old Germans', and in Giesen as the League of 'Blacks', whose central core were the 'Absolutes', led by the private lecturer and jurist Karl Follen. On the one hand, the goals became more radical. They now consisted of national democracy and a unitarian republic, direct elections, plebiscites, *volonté générale* and tight centralisation of religion, with all the churches combined into a national church. These were manifestations of the totalitarian Jacobin tendencies. Above all else, it was their ideas of how to achieve these ends which made them more radical. The end justified the means. In their view, the cause of German unity must be advanced through direct action and, where necessary, through violence and tyrannicide. A new guiding principle took hold, developed primarily by the philosopher Jakob Fries, the notion of conviction. A conviction was a subjective belief, a freely acquired internalisation of a moral truth based on feeling. This kind of conviction was absolute, and in comparison with it any other professed belief was reprehensible, the object of contempt and hatred. Such a conviction, emotional and voluntaristic, was not really threatened by arguments — it was affected only by states of mind and changes thereof. To change convictions constituted an act of treason. One's duty was to be true to one's own convictions.

Finally, such conviction demanded action and justified it; the absolute conviction demanded the absolute deed. The greatest deed was one committed out of a sense of conviction; the person committing the act was considered to be someone acting from conviction, and in an extreme case a martyr to his conviction. Everywhere, Karl Follen contested, where an ethical necessity obtains, any means are justified for those who are convinced of it. Here we have, twenty-five years after the Reign of Terror instigated by Robespierre, a new philosophy born of the ethical rigour of subjectivism, one which justified violence and terror.

Metternich regarded the *Burschenschaften* as the vanguard of a revolutionary movement. In order to counter it, he wanted to restrict the freedom of the universities at the Congress of Aix-la-Chapelle in 1818, in collaboration with Russian government circles. This failed at first, resistance from Humboldt and Hardenberg being a major contributing factor. On 23 March 1819 Karl Ludwig Sand murdered the writer August von Kotzebue in Mannheim. Kotzebue was known to have provided the Russian government with reports about German universities and their Jacobin tendencies. He was an accomplice of the planned repression, and in his magazine he had mocked the ideals of the *Burschenschaft* movement; otherwise he was a successful and prolific writer. He had been called, among other things, 'a German bluebottle living in Weimar who never stops leaving stains and filth everywhere' and a 'rascal of the revolution'; he was an insignificant figure, though nevertheless a suitable target for a demonstrative terrorist act.

Kotzebue's assassin was twenty-three years old, from Wunsiedel, the home town of Jean Paul, in the Ansbach Fichtel mountains. He had become a *Zwangsbayer* (forced Bavarian), a volunteer in 1814, and was a theology student in Erlangen and Jena, where he fell under the influence of Follen. He was awkward, not very bright, emotional and fanatical. A note which he had on him at the time justified the murder. 'Death to August von Kotzebue, the most dastardly seducer, bent on the complete corruption of our *Volk*.' The murder was designed to 'stir up' popular feeling, the 'glorious human endeavour to do God's will'. The assassin identified himself with the Gospel, and his convictions required that he commit murder, as well as sacrificing his own life. A few weeks later the chemist Karl Loening, who was closely connected with the 'Blacks', murdered Karl von Ibell, the chief administrator of Nassau. Both Sand and Loening were certainly loners, and the vast majority of the *Burschenschaften* wanted nothing to do with such actions, but it would be a mistake to underestimate the radicalism of the *Burschenschaften* by considering these two as merely pathological cases. This radicalism did have revolutionary traits and had the potential within it for the sort of terrorist direct action which has been witnessed in more recent history.

The public reacted in a curious, ambivalent and confused way. The liberals and intellectuals chose to be sophisticated about it, attributing altruistic motives to the assailant; Görres related the action to the 'existing despotism'. Martin de Wette, professor of theology at Berlin University, wrote (though this was in a letter to Sand's mother): 'The error is offset by the purity of the conviction; he considered it right, and in this sense he did right; this action carried out by this pure and pious young man, with such belief, such faith, is a beautiful symbol of the times.'

This must have been a shock to the ruling powers. Sand was condemned to death; he accepted his execution solemnly, as a martyr and a hero; the crowd sobbed and dipped hankerchiefs in his blood and tried to retrieve pieces of the scaffold or locks of his hair which had been cut off. Flowers and weeping willows were brought to the place of execution for a long time afterwards. The executioner, a democrat from the Palatinate, built a summerhouse from the scaffold in a Heidelberg vineyard, where the *Burschenschaft* held secret meetings. They were in Sand's scaffold as guests of his executioner.

Metternich tried to use the assassinations for his own purposes. The *Burschenschaften*, as far as he was concerned, were only a part of the treacherous revolutionary movement in Europe, whose seedbed was the university and the free press. He considered them a threat to internal security and to the monarchy, as well as to the principle of a confederation of states — in short, a threat to order. It was the Confederation's responsibility to protect the status quo. Metternich now wanted to mobilise the Confederation against the 'demagogic subversives'. When this plan ran into difficulties, Metternich first sought the support of Prussia and the other major powers in secret negotiations. Prussia stepped in against some of the 'demagogues' in July. Jahn, Arndt and the Welcker brothers in Bonn were arrested, Schleiermacher's sermons were placed under surveillance. The king was anxious, and Metternich wanted to bolster his own consitutional policies by taking a hard line against the radicals. At the end of July, in Teplitz, Metternich managed to persuade the king to co-operate with him. The plan was put to the ministers of the larger German states for them to vote on at a conference held in Carlsbad (6–31 August). Under pressure from the major powers, and in a very dubious procedure, the 'Carlsbad Decrees' were rushed through the Bundestag on 20 September. Delegates showed their approval by singing an Ambrosian hymn of praise.

This procedure was not the only thing which gave the impression that this was virtually a federalist *coup d'état*. The nature of the Confederation had been changed. In the fight against the radical movement, the sovereignty of the individual states had been reduced, and that of the Confederation enhanced. It was becoming a powerful reactionary institution, in addition to the elements within it of a state confederation and of a federal state. The decrees may be grouped into four categories, as follows. (1) Any university lecturer who disseminated 'teachings hostile to the public order or undermined the principles of the existing state institutions' was to be dismissed. The *Burschenschaft* was banned; 'continued community and communication between the universities' was 'absolutely forbidden'. Former members were excluded from public office. Anyone wanting to change universities had first to obtain a certificate of good conduct. A supervisory commissioner was appointed to each university. (2) A press law subjected all newspapers, periodicals and pamphlets to advance censorship and all books to censorship on publication; the ban on an individual edition could be extended to the publication as a whole, and the editors could be stopped from carrying on their work. The Bundestag itself could impose bans, even at the request of an individual federal state. (3) A central commission was set up in Mainz to investigate 'revolutionary subversion', a sort of fledgling federal executive with the combined role of defender of the constitution and a secret police. (4) Finally, the executive powers were consolidated against unruly member states, or those threatened by revolutionary tendencies.

At the same time, Metternich tried to put a stop to the movement in favour of a constitution. He wanted to make the theses of Gentz — that every constitution based on popular representation, public proceedings, accountability of ministers, the right to petition etc. was revolutionary, and that the 'estates' could only represent particular corporate bodies — into a constitutional norm in the Confederation. He won over the Prussian king on most points, and the Bavarian king seemed prepared to withdraw the constitution. But this attempt failed owing to opposition from Württemberg and from Bavaria, represented by the Foreign Minister. 'The contest has begun, it must be continued.' The argument was that — whether they were wise or unwise — the constitutions existed and must therefore be abided by. Metternich abandoned his counter-revolutionary *coup d'état* and the abolition of the constitutions, despite pressure from the governments of Nassau and Baden. The fact that they existed, he felt, provided a measure of stability and order, and this should take precedence over all doctrine and any tendency to bring them all into line. There should, however, be no constitution negotiated and agreed between the monarch and the provincial representative assembly. At the Vienna conferences, at which the regulations for the implementation of the federal acts were laid down, it was ruled on the one hand that existing constitutions could only be altered in a constitutionally appropriate manner, and on the other hand the 'monarchic principle' was defined as the norm. The whole of state power must remain concentrated in the supreme head of state, and the princes should only be obliged to work together with the estates in the case of certain defined rights. This restrictive ruling blocked any wider interpretation of constitutions. For this reason, and since Prussia had not been won over to the camp of constitutional states, the restoration policies of Metternich and the German Confederation were able to live with this result. In terms of overall policy, the constitutionalisation of Germany was retarded.

The Carlsbad Decrees were implemented in the individual states with varying degrees of enthusiasm. In Bavaria, Württemberg and Saxe–Weimar the mood was casual and reluctant; in Austria, Baden, Nassau, and especially in Prussia they were implemented with great vigour. 'Demagogues' were ordered to be 'hunted down'; suspicious professors were — like Arndt — suspended or, in the case of Fries, Oken or de Wette, dismissed, though they soon found other professorships elsewhere. The *Burschenschaft* members, especially in Prussia, were severely persecuted, expelled, some even imprisoned for a number of years, though pardons were later issued which enabled them to continue their studies and to enter public office, as was the case with the later conservative professors Leo and Stahl. Censorship, especially in Austria and Prussia, was tightened. Anything detrimental to the principles of religion and morality and the dignity and security of the states, or which showed revolutionary movements in a favourable light, or might provoke displeasure, was to fall under the knife of censorship. Fichte's *Addresses to the German Nation* was not allowed to be reprinted, and Schleiermacher's sermons continued to closely monitored. Gymnastics, knee-bending and beam exercises were banned, as they were clearly a danger to the security of the state.

Despite the comprehensive hearings it held, the investigation commission was not very effective. In 1827, it compiled a report, in which such prominent figures as Fichte, Schleiermacher and Arndt were named as intellectual founders of the movement, and Stein, Gneisenau and even Hardenberg as its sympathisers and accomplices, because their conservatism was anti-Prussian. Yet the lengthiness of investigations bore no relation to what came out of them. In so far as the public paid attention at all, the commission was the butt of everyone's jokes.

The Carlsbad Decrees were renewed in 1824, and officially remained in force until 1848. They mark the 1820s, and in a broader sense the time until 1848, as the era of restoration. Metternich and the conservatives were no fools; they felt their cause was under threat. The radical movements seemed to confirm their assumption that there was a simple choice between order and anarchy and no 'middle line', that the situation could not be kept peaceful by liberal tolerance, by separating the assassins and the extremists from the rest of the 'movement'. One had to be uncompromising in the early stages. For it was not only about fending off the revolution, that would have been more or less normal; but it was about using preventive measures to nip the very ideas behind the movements in the bud.

These policies were founded on fear of dangers which were already in the past. There is no sense in speculating on how the German situation might have developed without the *Burschenschaften* and the terrorism; suffice it to say that the upsurge in radical movements raised the tenor of the restoration to its highest.

The restoration did not work well because the state and the Confederation did not have sufficient means to enforce totalitarianism. There were too many differences of opinion within the establishment, between the ministers and the civil servants, and even among the individual states. The federalist structure meant that enough gaps were left in the system of censorship to ensure that what was published elsewhere managed to filter across the borders.

The states also had their own priorities. In the course of time the energy and impetus of the policies of Carlsbad waned. The *Burschenschaften* continued to exist secretly, and by about 1830 were once again operating relatively openly. In short, the restoration was not the whole story, but it had made its mark on this period to lasting effect. The political system entrenched itself and intensified its character as authoritarian rule by civil servants, a system of tutelage and control. It may be only a slight exaggeration to say that it became a police state.

The exercise of power became a system of repression. At any rate, this is how all those who were becoming politically aware experienced it. The fact that all free movements were suffocated and suppressed meant that no political life, no public life and accountability could come about, no large-scale objectives and no concrete tasks could be undertaken, and there was no free interplay of different forces. These were the tendencies of the time, but they were repressed. As contemporary critics had been remarking since the 1830s, the situation gave rise to a sort of pathological condition in Germany. German life was turned in upon itself, into Biedermeier philistinism, into 'cosiness', sometimes into indolence and resignation, or into crank religions, science, the empire of thought, history and apolitical attitudes. Those who found the situation unacceptable were provoked into taking action, and it made them bitter and full of hatred. Opposition was forced underground and into protest, unless it compromised with the system. This gave rise to a peculiar form of intellectualism, one which was idealistic, anticipatory, utopian and abstract, but which at all events was incapable of relating to the real situation. The German obsession with theories and the penchant for absolutes intensified. In this climate the radicalism of the intelligentsia thrived and became one of the curious long-term side-effects of the repressive restoration.

Between 1819 and 1848 (only up to 1830 in fact) Germany was far from being one huge prison, even in a political sense, and it was certainly not a revolutionary volcano. There were enough outlets, sufficient interplay between progressives and recalcitrants in the political life of the individual states. The modern movements of liberalism and nationalism emerged in this period. However, the general system of restoration intensified the natural political and social conflicts and was a serious obstacle to the formation of pragmatic elements within German political culture.

2. The Great Movements

The 19th century was the age of the great political movements — liberalism, nationalism, socialism as well as conservatism — out of which the typically modern form of the political parties developed. Politics ceased to be the exclusive concern of court and government, of estate-based and ecclesiastical institutions, from which the ordinary citizen was excluded. Society itself became political, became articulate in different ways and sought to influence political decisions. These movements were certainly bound up with vested interests, and they were always concerned with concrete circumstances and measures, but they were guided by ideas. The political battle was primarily — and even in the minds of contemporaries — a conflict between different concepts of how the state and society should look. However, in the 19th century these ideas were no longer simply philosophical theories, derived from nature or reason; they were moulded by historical experiences and tried to interpret them. The new experiences of history — experiences of upheaval, change, movements, as well as the open question of the future — were now characteristic of political ideas. The outlines of the future were simultaneously images of the past and interpretations of the present.

(a) Liberalism

The first great movement, the true party of movement and progress, was liberalism. It transformed the socio-political landscape in Germany and everywhere in Europe, but at the same time the difficulties it faced and the defeats it suffered demonstrate one of the central problems in modern German history — the problem of democracy in Germany. 'Liberal' — a word first coined for the supporters of the Spanish constitution of 1812 — is a term which extends beyond the political arena, for it can also refer to the church, the economy and interpersonal relationships. These boundaries were particularly fluid in the 19th century. This book is concerned primarily with the political movement, and with an attempt to define its basic principles.

In a quite general 'metapolitical' sense, liberalism is about autonomy, the self-legislation of the individual and of reason. It is the legacy of the Enlightenment, in Germany especially the legacy of Kant. Autonomy is a reaction against things as they are, mere traditions which are required to justify themselves in the forum of critical reason and in accordance with the criteria of the free self-determination of human beings. Autonomy in the 19th century involved a rejection of the traditional bonds of estates and corporations, as well as of bureaucratic, seigneurial tutelage of the individual. Autonomy, therefore, signifies emancipation. It was characteristic of liberalism that it launched its attack on two fronts, against the feudal-corporate society, as well as against the authoritarian state. At the centre of this world-view is the individual and the development of his potential and talents, whence derives the meaning and the purpose of the state and society. Of course, autonomy and freedom of the individual are not meant in an anti-state, anarchistic sense; they aim, again under Kant's influence, for freedom within the law — not so much freedom from the state, but freedom within it and the freedom to form a state. This is a typical German variation on the liberal theme.

Lastly, freedom and autonomy are directed in a dual sense to the future. They aim to change the world in an unspecified way and place reality under the primacy of imperatives, norms and ideals. They also spring from a characteristic anthropological optimism, on the premise that everyone wishes to develop his own freedom and can use it rationally, that more freedom means more happiness. The future is progress towards freedom and reason. This, beyond any demonstrable proofs, is the true faith of liberalism.

Continental and therefore also German liberalism stands firmly in the tradition of 18th-century Anglo-Saxon ideas, movements and institutions. Yet in a very specific sense it is primarily the inheritor and representative of the ideas of the French Revolution, the ideas of 1789. This means two things: limits should be placed on the actions of the state and the methods used to carry these out, and the freedom of the individual should be safeguarded from the omnipotence of the state. This implies human and civil rights, separation of powers and a state under the rule of law. On the other hand, it is about the possession of state power itself; the nation wants to determine its own fate and to govern itself — this is the principle of popular sovereignty — or it wants at least to participate in its own government. Government is only legitimate with the consent of the governed. Besides the singularly liberal principle — protection of the individual from the excesses of the state — there is the democratic principle, which has as its focal point the demand for majority rule.

The liberal and the democratic principle are by no means identical, neither logically nor historically. Tensions and contradictions exist between individual liberties and the rights of the majority. For instance, are the Jesuits to be expelled because the majority wishes it, or does one defend their civil and minority rights? This was to become one of the major problems of the late century. But it was true of early liberalism, in Germany especially, that there was an inherent and inseparable link between the two constitutional principles, precisely because there was a desire to avoid the logical consequences of pure popular sovereignty and pure majority rule. There were those who put more emphasis on the liberal principle and others who stressed the democratic principle, but both self-evidently belonged to the one large movement, which was bent on changing existing conditions.

This was all to do with the fact that liberalism was a post-revolutionary movement. The trauma of the whole of the first half of the 19th century had been the transformation of the revolution into totalitarian democracy, dictatorship and the Jacobin terror, into mob rule of demagogues and then into military despotism. Unlike the conservatives, the liberals did not see the events of 1793 as a logical consequence of the revolution. Freedom and law and a constitution with separation of powers had to be given greater protection against the dangers of radical majority rule; checks and balances had to be built in to limit equality and popular sovereignty. But revolution since then retained something sinister — it was unplannable, an accident — better, in the liberals' view, to have reform and evolution. The rise of freedom stands in the shadows of terror; this diminishes its élan and makes it cautious.

Liberalism was, of course, primarily a movement of the rising bourgeoisie. Reason, autonomy, individual freedom, freedom and security for property, equality before the law and protection of rights — the central core of basic rights, opposition to the all-powerful police state and to the feudal society — these were all bourgeois principles, bourgeois interests. The individual was now to derive his social status not from his background and blood, but from the strength of his talent and achievement, education and property. The state should not tell him what to do — and this could only happen when he himself had a say in the running of the state. The bourgeois class was, as Sieyès said, nothing, yet it was now staking its claim to be everything, a general estate.

The historical preconditions which moulded the fate of liberalism in Germany were not the result of a swiftly emerging merchant middle class. Nor were the aristocracy significantly involved as in England. Liberalism in Germany emerged within a society which was still old-fashioned, in which the mass of the people lived traditionally and unpolitically in the world of the estates and particularism as subject peoples. Liberalism was the cause of a narrow sector of the population, namely the educated elite and the bourgeoisie whose interest in public affairs had emerged in the late 18th century. The ideas of this class were well in advance of the social and political reality of the German states and the associations. Its powerful opponents were the feudal system and the absolutist state.

Liberal protest potential was weaker than in France. There was no pre-revolutionary situation, and protest was difficult to mobilise because the abuses were not so great. The state of enlightened absolutism had made a start in reforming the feudal as well as the absolutist system. The Catholic church, less absolutist and more moderate on the whole, was experienced as a less oppressive institution than in France; aggressive anti-clericalism, which in the Romance countries had aroused emotions and mobilised the masses in the cause of liberalism, was still lacking in Germany. Certainly the 'small-state mentality' and the 'minor princedoms' aroused the bitterness of the new educated class, but on the other hand the small states, easily comprehensible and with their rulers near at hand, consolidated traditional ties. The possibility of moving from one German state to another — the fate of the German intelligentsia from Schiller to Görres to the Göttingen Seven — diminished the oppression of authority, as did the competition between individual states for good administration and good universities. The fact that things were different everywhere in Germany, that everyone had different experiences, that there was no centre, made it difficult for the liberals to find common ground beyond pure theory, and contributed to their diversity.

Finally, the problem of German particularism burdened the liberals with the task of simultaneously achieving freedom and unity, with a consequent tragic dilemma. Under these given historical conditions the liberals had a hard time of it. Certainly, the territorial reorganisation had mobilised old loyalties, and revolution and reforms had set people thinking — but it was a long time before this took effect.

The peculiar relationship of the liberals with the state is particularly significant. They wanted to supercede the authoritarian state, but the state itself, especially in the Napoleonic era, was also a reforming state, which was turning its back on the structures of the feudal society of estates and had taken up the cause of the emancipation of the citizens from this order. It had begun to rationalise state rule and bring it under the rule of law. This revolution from above fitted in to a significant degree with liberal objectives. The state was capable of correcting itself; it was an agent of modernity, of progress, indeed of freedom. This was the Janus-face of the bureaucratic authoritarian state in Germany. In the liberals' struggle against the feudal society of the estates, the state was for them, weak as they were, a potential ally.

The liberals were somewhat timid; in the German political and social climate of the time, they could not be self-confident and aggressive. They were experiencing the continuity of state reforms, and this explains their ambivalence towards the state. They saw co-operation with the state as a way of reforming society, and the reform of the state even from within, building in their own objectives along the way, as a possibility one which was not as unrealistic as it might have seemed later. Eventually, they came to have other things in common, such as opposition to church orthodoxy, a concern that social-revolutionary chaos was brewing, and an eventual attempt to solve the national question, not against the wishes of the existing states, but to work with them in finding a solution. It is obvious that this policy had the inherent danger of accommodation with the enemy and the sacrifice of other liberal goals merely to come to some form of arrangement with the conservatives, but it did not by any means have to be so.

On the other hand, of course, liberals were fiercely opposed to the authoritarian system, with its control, censorship, persecution, rigid adherence to the status quo and monopoly rule by the monarchy. In the last analysis, was it not up to the society to liberate itself, instead of being set free by state officials? This vacillation between co-operation and confrontation, both of which were legitimate political possibilities, became the quintessential problem for German liberalism.

Furthermore, German liberalism had initially and for a long time afterwards sought direction to a great extent from ideas, theories and principles. There was something doctrinaire about it, and it lacked pragmatism. The liberals saw politics to a large extent in moral and spiritual terms. Freedom for the *Volk* was closely bound up with education. What brought the liberals together in the first place was a common conviction and world-view; only then did they draw up concrete political objectives. So long as they were politically impotent, and had no significant influence on political decisions, this could hardly be otherwise. And only ideas, only a political faith could break down the old social reality and bind together the different interests and opposing factions.

Of course, this was a part of the German mentality, shaped by its religious and intellectual history. Luther had connected conscience to books and their scholarly interpretation, which was practised primarily at the universities. This continued throughout the period of secularisation. Doctrinaire teaching, theory and its professorial and quasi-professorial interpretation continued to be a crucial feature of German as well as of political culture. Luther had also imprinted upon the German consciousness the sharp distinction between the two realms of the spiritual and the temporal, the internal and the external, between freedom and compulsion, ethos and politics, and this dualism persisted in the secular sphere. Kant, one of the spiritual fathers of liberalism, had imprinted this concept even more sharply. Freedom belongs to the realm of the mind and the imperative, and contrasts with the reality of the socio-political world. This gave German political thought and action its philosophical, unpragmatic aspect, making relationship with reality into a problem.

Nineteenth-century liberalism, especially in Germany, was also shaped by the great intellectual movements of the early decades of the century, namely Romanticism and historicism. These constituted a new intellectual basis for freedom. Besides the rationalism rooted in natural law, and the individualistic justification, freedom was now given an historical justification, not based on French models, but derived from old Germanic and German traditions. These emphasized co-operative self-organisation and the preoccupation with the *Volk*. They took the existing estate-based representations and estate-based freedoms as norms, and attempted to give them a liberal interpretation. This might easily have given a conservative tinge to liberal ideas, but at the same time they legitimised their own aims through an appeal for historical progress; this was the progressive twist. The alliance with the new movements of the time, Romanticism and historicism, also strengthened liberalism.

'German liberalism' in the first half of the century was a multiform, almost protean movement with conflicting tendencies and blurred boundaries, but the task of the historian writing for those to come is to find a common theme running through all the numerous anecdotes, figures and opinions, and delineate basic outlines. This species of liberalism was first and foremost a political movement, which aimed at transforming the state and creating a constitutional state under the rule of law. We take this so much for granted nowadays that we need to take a close look at the historical significance of this demand. Power relations were to become relations based on law, power was to be rationalised, and the state made into a system of codified rights. Rule would not be by persons, but by norms: this was what the demand for a constitution meant first of all. It is, in fact, the constitution that makes up the unity of the state, the common will formed from the mass of individual wills. In the ideal case, sovereignty within the state would rest neither with the monarch nor with the *Volk*, nor with the parliament (nor all of these combined); it would, in fact, rest with the constitution. This constitution would have to be a written one — a piece of paper, as Friedrich Wilhelm IV said with contempt — only then is it stable and demonstrable, and only then does it become, in fact, law.

Where does the constitution come from? It is something, as a citizen of Baden said to his grand duke in 1848, which is not 'given' but 'taken'. It is, in actual fact, the representatives of the nation, formed into a 'national assembly', who produce the constitution. A constitution which is given by the monarch, one which he 'imposes', is not a true constitution, for in this instance, should any dispute arise about its interpretation, the monarch remains the master of the constitution. In view of the power situation as it stood, the early liberals were concerned essentially with gaining agreement on a constitution thrashed out between the monarch and the 'estates' (representatives of the *Volk*); this would also be a genuine 'constitution', since it contained a provision for some kind of popular sovereignty, which the moderate liberals considered indispensible.

An essential part of any real constitution is a list of basic rights, since the constitution exists to facilitate and safeguard the free development of the individual. Basic rights are something more than a guarantee of already existing rights, and they are more than a programmatic declaration. What they represent is a dynamic and concrete transformation of the relations between the individual, the society and the state, which not only guarantee rights to the individual, but also define and limit the actions of the administration and the judiciary, indeed legislation itself. The principle was new: from this point on, the individual's own sphere of freedom — and these days it has to be said explicitly: the private sphere beyond all politics — was to be in principle unlimited; it could only be restricted by laws. Until then the principle was: what is not permitted is forbidden ('It is permitted to walk on this path,' was quoted ironically in the Vormärz). The new principle was to be: what is not forbidden is permitted. There is a powerful difference between the two.

From among the many liberal demands for basic rights, four will be examined in particular, because of their significance and the problems inherent in them. The first of these was the right to freedom of expression. The conservatives felt that there should simply be a freedom to express the truth; the liberals pleaded for the additional freedom to express error and untruth, for nobody, in their view, should have the monopoly on truth, which only emerges in the process of discussing conflicting and even misguided opinions. This is something which liberalism has imprinted firmly in our consciousness. Behind this lay the optimistic assumption that rational truth would win through against prejudice and error, empty phrases and seductive rhetoric, stupidity and uneducated opinion, and this provided the impetus for improving popular education. Freedom of expression, however, was more than an individual right; it aimed at forming public opinion and specifically freedom of the press. It was the cornerstone of any free order.

The second basic freedom was the right to associate freely. This was so important because the association (*Verein*) was the new social form — as opposed to estate and corporation as well as bureaucratic tutelage — with the help of which the liberals were confident they could solve the essential political, social, economic and cultural problems of the time. Freedom to associate was a central pillar of liberalism.

Thirdly, there was — and this is central to bourgeois society — the freedom (and security) of individual property, education, inheritance, and the way in which property was used, free from the restrictions of state interference as well as corporative restrictions. The right to property was to become an unrestricted right, and property was to be freely disposable. All property was to have an equal status under the law — land, capital, moveable property; property would be a mobile commodity, and where it was not, it would be made so. This amounted to the desire to create a society of property-owners — but the property guarantee should also guarantee any already existing inequalities of property-ownership; nobody had any doubts about this. Otherwise, however, economic freedoms were not part of the canon of liberal ideas of what constituted basic rights. People were to have the freedom to choose their own occupations, but not the right to practise them freely, i.e. free trade and freedom of residence were to be limited by the rights of communities.

Finally, in addition to the rights to various freedoms, there was the principle of legal equality, the equal applicability of laws to everyone and equality of everyone before the law. Everyone would have equal access to public office, would be obliged to pay taxes and also to do military service. In the view of the liberals, it was only when such legal equality was enshrined that equality of opportunity would come with it, thus making real freedom possible. The social question would later shake the foundations of this belief in the intrinsic link between legal equality and freedom, but this only emerged slowly. The demand for equality was, of course, limited by the political situation in these decades. The right to vote was not a basic right; it was taken absolutely for granted at this time that property took precedence over everything else.

The second fundamental ingredient of a 'real' constitution was the separation of powers. A constitution was to be a 'mixed' constitution; it was there to limit and control the power of the executive; it was to install a system of checks and balances in order to avert any misuse of monarchic as well as democratic power. This was meant both in the classic sense of the independence of the courts and the separation of the legislature from the executive; but also, concretely and historically, it meant that, since there was no actual republic as in the United States or in France in 1793, there should be representation for the states and the *Volk*, alongside the monarchic and authoritarian government. Participation of the nation in government was the democratic aspect of the separation of powers. Separation of powers and the provision of some form of popular sovereignty, whatever their theoretical justification, essentially belonged together.

The nation, therefore, was to play a part in the activity of the state, in legislation above all, though this participation would be not in the form of the plebiscite, direct democracy, but through representation. The representation of the *Volk* by an educated elite, it was felt, would be a pillar of reasoned opinion, which would ensure that decisions were kept free from the capricious influence of the somewhat immature masses, would guard against total folly and guarantee stability against any possible revolution. Representation was not conceived along the lines of the old estates. The members of the assembly would not represent their own group of voters and be duty-bound to serve their interests, but they would — in theory at least — carry a 'free' mandate, one which was 'not tied to commissions and directives'; they would be representatives of the entire *Volk*. Parliament should not represent any individual interests, but should aim to serve the well-being of the whole of society. It should also not be divided up into parties, who would represent 'particular' interests. Parties were seen in a bad light. Even the Liberals did not consider themselves to be a party; they were not a faction, but the representatives of the whole *Volk* — in so far as they were not 'led astray' by those in authority, by demagogues, or by the clerics. The liberals represented, as Paul Pfizer put it, that which 'the whole of the people in their own rational interest wants or must want'(!). The ideal scenario was that options would be discussed and the best solution reached on the strength of the persuasiveness of rational arguments. The liberal idea of the parliament was, originally at least, anti-pluralist.

The concrete question was then, firstly, whether the parliament was to have one or two chambers. In England, as in the early German forms of the constitution, there was an upper house, which represented the old, privileged classes, principally the nobility. One section of the liberals accepted this; even in the American republic there was a senate. Two chambers were appropriate to the system of checks and balances; an upper house, they felt, would be a stabilising factor, being less at the mercy of wavering popular opinion. Friedrich Christoph Dahlmann was of the opinion that with an upper chamber the social fact of large-scale wealth and large-scale landownership could be better fitted into the structure of the state; the ultimate objective would be to give it a more middle-class composition, and perhaps limit its powers to a certain degree. The more democratically inclined liberals would have preferred to do away with the upper chamber in principle, but then seek to establish the principle of checks and balances by procedural regulations within the *Volkskammer* (people's chamber).

The people's chamber was the elected representative of the people. The question of the right to vote became one of the issues which changed the course of liberalism. The liberals, in accordance with the modern principle of representation, did not want to have elections based around the estates, and they wanted to do away with the vestiges of such an 'electoral system' — special rights for the nobility and clerics, differentiation between city and country. The early liberals were, however — as one would expect — against universal suffrage. The mass of the *Volk* were still, as far as they were concerned, uneducated and incapable of making judgments; they paid no attention to the common good and were too embroiled in particularist interests. Dependent workers were felt to be subject to others, while those without property were felt to be guided by envy and egotism; only independence and property gave one freedom, and only an education gave one the ability to speak responsibly for the common good. Education and property: these were the prerequisites for the political prerogative, to be allowed — and to be able — to vote. And since the bourgeoisie considered themselves to be the 'general estate', representing the true interest of all, there was no need for them to have any bad conscience about this definition of the right to vote. Universal suffrage was felt to be an issue for the revolutionaries and the demagogues, and, just as importantly in the mid-century, an issue for the reactionaries in the government and the clergy. The masses, it was felt, would have no resistance against demagogues and against pressure from those with power.

The radical-democratic wing of the liberals turned away from this elitist political conception in the 1840s, and history left such attitudes by the wayside on its forward march. To modern thinking, this attitude seems like pure ideology, the anxiety of the property-owning middle class with regard to the rising masses. This view was voiced often enough by contemporaries who considered that the way should not be left open for those without property to make decisions on the taxation of property. Such judgments are historically unjustified. The idea of a nation of independent property-owners was not yet, in fact, unrealistic, and one section of the liberals put serious emphasis on the link between improved popular education and an extension of the right to vote. But leaving all this aside, the liberals' anxieties were not unfounded. Napoleon III had based his Caesar-like rule on universal suffrage, but in Germany Bismarck used it as a stick to beat the liberals with. Two things which are so precious to modern society, the constitutional state under the rule of law and universal suffrage, were not part of the same programme, and for quite a time actually conflicted with one another. In Europe as a whole, the extension of the right to vote was a long time in coming, and there were to be many hold-ups along the way.

The right to vote was to be worked out according to a franchise, to landownership, to the payment of taxes, or to a position as a civil servant (*Beamte*). Indirect elections were considered preferable. The interposition of 'electors' was intended to encourage the selection of sensible representatives. It was taken for granted that these should be middle-class notables who represented the *Volk*. There were to be no professional politicians, and without the 'diet' system the only people who could take seats in the assembly were those who were available to do so because they were wealthy or could take time off from their posts as civil servants or because — as in the case of a lawyer — they could combine profession with mandate.

The role of the representative body of the people was first — in accordance with the principle of separation of powers — to participate in the legislative process. Every law was to require its approval. Even where this was recognised, as in the first German constitutions, this demand came in three parts. (1) There had to be a definition of a law. Parliament wanted to have responsibility for every general norm which related to freedom and property, as in the sphere of basic rights, a movement against the other form of state action — against decrees and emergency decrees, which rested solely in the hands of the government. The battle over the definition of law was a battle about the competence and power of the parliament. (2) Parliament also wanted the budget to be passed in the form of a parliamentary bill, and to have the right to approve taxation policy — a central constituent of parliamentary participation — extended to include the right to approve specific expenditure. (3) Parliament wanted not only to approve or reject laws, but also to be able to propose them. The liberals demanded the right to initiate laws.

The other role of the parliament in liberal theory was to monitor government. Since the monarch could not be brought to account and was in this respect 'not responsible', this demand focused on the 'accountability' of ministers. This meant that they had to answer for the actions of the monarch (or else they would have to pack their bags). They were to act within the framework and the spirit of the constitution, and were to justify their actions before parliament and, therefore, before the public, since the liberals made it a central point of their platform to make parliamentary proceedings public. Parliament was to have the right to impeach government ministers if they violated the constitution (*Ministeranklage*). This was another example of the liberal tendency to carry over political ideas into the sphere of judicial institutions and processes.

All this is linked to the central problem of early liberal constitutional theory and the relationship between goverment and parliament. The liberals started from the premise that the two were in opposition, in a sort of equilibrium, the so-called theory of dualism. The goverment did not have to secure the confidence of parliament, nor was parliament there to legitimise the government or to participate in its formation. It was also part of the theory that parliament did not exist in order to govern or make political decisions. Parliament was a sort of an advocate for the nation and the constitution; it was there to supervise the goverment, to ensure that it protected the constitution and civil rights, and ensure that it passed rational laws.

The goverment, any government, is always under suspicion of misuse of power, that it may act in an authoritarian way, or violate the rights of the people. Parliament's natural posture is one of mistrust, supervision and latent opposition. This sense of its own role, this behavioural norm, has been deeply imprinted (and one could say with disastrous consequences) on the German party political and parliamentary system for a whole century. It is a theory which has come under a lot of criticism today on the grounds of inconsistency, and the liberals have been accused of lacking the will to power. But unfortunately it is a historical legacy, that of a tradition of absolutism as well as of the dualism within the estates, a reflection of reality under the early constitutions in which government and the houses of parliament really were in opposition to each another in a form of institutionalised dualism.

There is clearly more to it than this, however. There is also a remnant of old-fashioned theories about separation of powers — analogous to the relationship between the President and Congress in the United States — and a piece of metapolitical ideology. It was customary to draw parallels between the dualism of the goverment and parliament and the balance of order and freedom, stability and change, unity and plurality.

Finally, the idealistic theory that true sovereignty should lie with the constitution obscured the problems of dualism. The question of how any conflict between the two bodies should be settled was only given a vague answer; the main preoccupation was keeping a lid on the issue of power and sovereignty. The two institutions were expected to be forced to compromise and seek a harmonious solution to temporary conflicts. The government, so went one optimistic assumption, would take heed of the debates in parliament and of public and enlightened opinion even without any institutional pressure being brought to bear. For this to happen, of course — and the majority wanted this — the actual predominance of the governments in the early constitutional system would have to be dismantled, the legislative rights of the parliament strengthened, and limits placed on the right of the monarch to dissolve parliament. Parliament's ultimate weapon, the impeachment of ministers, would have to be fully developed. The more radical dualists, like Karl Rotteck for example, believed that in the event of a lasting conflict, the monarch would have no choice but to appeal to the *Volk* through new elections.

Like the other liberals, Rotteck still considered the monarch to be the head of the executive. The French liberal view that the king ruled but did not govern had no support in Germany. The parliamentary model of a government backed by the confidence of parliament was only developed later, in 1845, by Robert von Mohl (according to the procedure worked out by the expert on constitutional law, Heinrich Zachariae) as the only realistic solution. The concept was influenced by the English example with many 'conservative' provisos. Yet leaving aside all such theories, the nuances were fluid. Even in England, the parliamentary system of government did not arise out of theories and political platforms, but emerged through a multitude of small power shifts and precedents, one of which was the opportunity to impeach ministers. The liberals might have placed their trust in the imminent dynamic development of a 'dualistic' constitution. In 1848, '*de facto*' parliamentarianism suddenly become a *fait accompli*.

Two vital areas were integral to the liberal idea of the constitutional state under the rule of law, which would truly consolidate a constitution and give it a living force. The first of these was the liberal reform of the judiciary. This consisted of assertion of state judicial sovereignty, the safeguarding of the independence of judges, the safeguarding of the rights of the accused, the conclusive separation of judiciary and administration, and judicial control of the administration. It would finally take shape under Mohl as a fully developed adminstrative law with a separate judicial system which safeguarded and fixed the rights of 'servants of the state'. Reform of court proceedings was another aspect of this development: public, oral proceedings with the participation of laymen through the introduction of jury trials. This was not simply something dreamed up by legal experts; in 1848, it was one of the three basic demands for which people risked their lives. Laymen were to give the law a 'popular' basis, and since they would take responsibility for political and press matters, they would cut down the influence of the authoritarian judicial bureaucracy. Behind all this lay the deep conviction of the liberals that they could bring about and guarantee freedom by means of law and justice, i.e. liberal law and liberal justice.

The extension of self-government was just as important as judicial reform. It was to act as a corrective to the authoritarian and bureaucratic administration, manifesting as it did the right to freedom and participation and another form of the separation of powers. It was a typical belief of German liberals, one which was directed against French centralism, that a liberal constitution was only possible and could only endure if it were part of a liberal administration and self-government. This had led some to give the administrative question a peculiar precedence over the decisive constitution issue.

Liberalism was first and foremost a constitutional movement. This is something that we must understand despite our preoccupation with social questions. Of course, the transformation of the state could not be separated from the transformation of society, nor could the emancipation from authoritarian tutelage be separated from emancipation from the ties of estate and corporation. The issue was also the establishment of a bourgeois society of individual freedom and equality before the law, and the liberal concept of law was also a transformation of society. The residue of the feudal order and feudal privileges were to be swept aside, the liberation of the peasants was to be pushed through and completed, and the freedom of property ownership was to be established where it was still restricted. Trade and transport were to be made easier, and bourgeois work was to be developed and based on education and achievement. Liberalism, from a social point of view, was also a force for modernisation. The majority of liberals believed in social and economic progress, the progression of society towards a more bourgeois form.

The majority, however, regarded the new economic forces, industry, capitalism, the principle of market forces and competition in a very ambivalent light, indeed with a certain amount of anxiety. They envisaged a threat to social stability, the loss of a secure social order, pauperism getting out of control and a sharp polarisation of classes. The majority of liberals — especially in south Germany — were not, like Friedrich List, in favour of forced industrial growth, but for the protection of the little people against too much *laissez-faire* policy and against absolute freedom of trade. For the most part, they were also against free trade and the dismantling of all state regulations. Mohl, among others, even wanted restrictions on the freedom to marry and advocated forced emigration. In short, the liberals were not true supporters of a capitalist, industrialised, competitive market economy, and most did not even support uncompromising economic liberalism. They were not even spokesmen for the emergent economic bourgeoisie, however much this group, the Rhenish entrepreneurs for instance, felt themselves to be liberals as a matter of course.

This is another explanation for why constitutional south Germany remained sociopolitically more conservative than Prussia. The liberals' image of society was preindustrial, geared not to growth and dynamism but to stability and the status quo, not to competition and conflict, but to harmony between different forces and interests. The liberal ideal was of a society composed of many independent individuals, propertyowners, craftsmen and farmers, an almost classless society of citizens, in which talent and achievement as well as background and inheritance balanced one another out. Gall rightly said that the liberal ideal was not the society of industrial and commercial England, but the more harmonious society of Switzerland. The true *Volk*, for such liberals, was the broad class of the financially independent and the mass of the middle classes — they did not want an antagonistic society — and they hoped that society would develop in this direction, and that such a state of widespread prosperity could be achieved and stabilised by political means.

These liberals were certainly not egalitarians. Anxiety about the propertyless, uneducated masses, the underclasses, remained a preoccupation in liberal thought. Here we see a dualism within German liberalism, which soon came to the surface in

1848. It was expressed firstly in liberal ambivalence towards modernity. The liberals were all for a bourgeois meritocracy, but distanced themselves from industry and the market. Something had to give in the long run, and the traditionalist elements in their idea of society caved in before the inevitability of modernity. In the last analysis, the liberals had to support trade freedom and freedom of residence. On the other hand, they did not want to tie themselves down to concrete social interests, but felt that they had the common interests (that of the property-owners or potential property-owners) at heart. They spoke for such interests, only in so far as they could be extended to the generality, but they lacked a firm anchorage in social and economic interests. A serious discrepancy always existed between their political aims, which were broadly supported, and the economic interests of their supporters.

There were many strands within German liberalism. It was a differentiated movement, groupings within it differing according to their foundation, what priorities they set, their choice of means, whether they favoured a more radical or a more moderate opposition, a politics of small steps or of major confrontation — and there were many cross-overs between these different strands. One can distinguish between two major strands. One is the form of liberalism for which Karl Rotteck was the classical spokesman. This was in the Enlightenment tradition, the tradition of natural law and reason and norms set according to 'what should be', of individualism — taking its models from French liberalism — thoroughly dualistic; for them the much-vaunted popular sovereignty was an element of the dualistic construction of the state, but it also had a strongly egalitarian tone, opposed to the feudal order of privileges or plutocratic tendencies. On the other hand there was Friedrich Christoph Dahlmann (*Politics, on the Basis and the Scale of the Given Conditions*, 1835), who attempted to change the liberal programme from one founded on normative-rational law to a constitution based on historical realism. The problem is not that of finding the constitution which is in itself (*an sich*) the best, but of finding a good one, suited to the given circumstances in the country and history. This form of liberalism took its cue from the evolutionary development of England, with its aristocratic upper-middle-class parliamentarianism. It was less egalitarian and — alongside liberal individualism — was more concerned with the question of how the state could best function. It was more moderate and somewhat more conservative, setting its sights on a gradual transformation of what already existed. There were also many cross-overs here — it was possible to provide a historical basis for Rotteck's claims, as Karl Theodor Welcker did, or supply the Dahlmannesque idea of the state with more strongly parliamentarian or more strongly egalitarian aspects.

Liberalism had initially developed at an especially brisk pace in the constitutional states of the south and west; here it had a forum in the *Landtage*, which broadcast its ideas to the public. In numerous proclamations about the constitutional national law, liberal theory developed and became more sophisticated. The fifteen-volume *Staatslexikon* by the Freiburg professors Rotteck and Welcker (from 1834 onwards) became the book that every educated liberal household in south Germany had on its shelves. Even in the Rhineland a centre of liberalism had formed early, concerned mainly — under the leadership of civil lawyers — with a vehement defence of French law, whose achievements were put almost on a par with a liberal constitution. In the 1830s a specifically upper-middle-class liberalism of wealthy entrepreneurs developed here — whose spokesmen were men like Mevissen and Beckerath, Camphausen and Hansemann. In Westphalia a man like Friedrich Harkort was typical of this. Austria and the old Prussian provinces stood back; they lacked the unifying voice of state-wide *Landtage*, and the restoration reacted more strongly with censorship and police presence. But even in Prussia an independent liberalism developed out of municipal self-administration and in the universities and many of the provincial *Landtage*. The spokesmen for this everywhere were first of all the educated classes: professors, academics, especially civil servants; then the middle-class professions specifically suited to political involvement started to have their say, lawyers and journalists as well, while the nobility also played a key role in the leading groups of liberals; something of the nature of German Whigs came into being. These circles had — in a society which was still very hierarchical — a recognised and elevated social status; they were — predominantly by virtue of their education, cosmopolitanism and contacts — most strongly involved in supraregional issues relating to the whole state and national questions. In the Rhineland, as mentioned, there were also the wealthy entrepreneurs. But this is a somewhat one-dimensional picture. The literary-publicistic and intellectual movement for freedom soon grew into a general movement of the middle classes. The 'grassroots' in the communities also included the middle-class *Bürger* — craftsmen, businessmen, restaurant-owners. In the 1830s and 1840s the social basis of liberalism expanded more and more. Through associations and festivals, through elections and parliamentary debates and — despite censorship — through the channels of the press it grew into a middle-class, even a mass movement.

Related to this there was another shift. Liberalism as a middle-class political movement broke away from the liberalism of the reformist state officials, to which it had originally been closely connected, with which it had been all but identical. Modernisation of the state and society from above, and modernisation through participation and self-determination of the society, took separate paths. Society did not want to be liberated; it wanted to liberate itself. The bureaucracy wanted to have the prestige of being a modernising force, especially when the pressure of the 'social question' was beginning to take effect. The complaint that the bureaucratic caste was too domineering and obsessed with drawing up regulations became a common one; the politics of restoration demanded its tribute also from those *Beamten* who remained liberal. The liberal movement finally put their weight behind the precedence of the constitution over the administration. The conflict between state and society could not be settled simply by installing a liberal civil service (*Beamtenschaft*). This did not mean that the liberals wanted radical curbs on the activity of the state — for example, by taking schools or churches out of state hands — but they wanted to put the bureaucracy under parliamentary supervision and place it on a civil basis. It was possible to work together with bureaucratic liberalism, but this was no longer enough.

(b) Nationalism

The other great movement of the century, before socialism, was the national movement, or — let's be uninhibited about it — nationalism. The catastrophes of the 20th century have made us wary on this point. But it is not fair to look at nationalism, which has dominated German as well as European history for 150 years, and today is the real organising force in the whole world, primarily from the point of view of Hitler or of the self-destruction of Europe; such a perspective precludes any deeper insight.

We speak of nationalism, where the nation is the major collective group, to which the individual feels he belongs first and foremost, where allegiance to the nation and loyalty to it are at the top of the agenda of allegiances and loyalties, and the nation becomes a supreme spiritual value. The primary supra-personal context is the nation, not estate and not religious denomination, not region and not family lineage (or allegiance to a dynasty), nor is it class, nor political ideology. Also the individual is not — as in the philosophy of the Enlightenment — primarily a member of the human race and a citizen of the world, but a member of his nation; primacy is given not to the equality of the universal species, but the plurality of individuals grouped within nations. The individual finds his supraindividual identity in his identification with the nation, its historical-cultural legacy as well as its political existence, and in this lies the identity of the nation with itself. For the individual the nation is the space wherein he locates, where he has come from and where he is going to; the nation transcends the world of daily notions to constitute something primal and something still to come. Life acquires a part of its meaning through the nation. And the nation is not a self-evident thing, it is a dynamic principle, which triggers actions and emotions. In the epoch of political faiths, the nation acquired something like a religious character: religious values were attached to it — eternity and a future fulfilled, sacredness, fraternity, sacrifice and martyrdom. The religious element was secularised in the national principle; the secular element was made sacred.

The consciousness of being German and belonging to the German nation was there very early, but this was more of a naïve sense of a self-evident truth, the place where one finds comparison with others. In the second half of the 18th century there emerged in the educated classes the reflected consciousness of a 'national culture' — directed against the pre-eminence of the French; one becomes conscious of one's context and of the national character of a shared German culture; the idea of the 'national theatre' was characteristic of this. The aesthetic-historical understanding of cultural phenomena, which developed in the study of Greek civilisation and culture, made use of nationalist categories of thought: it was felt that this was the only way to comprehend what makes a culture tick, to understand the spirit of a culture. Culture was seen, therefore, as something which always has a national character; but all this was entirely, and in classical literature even more so, a product of cosmopolitan, humanistic education.

A new epoch in the intellectual history of nationalism was marked by Herder. First, language gained a completely new meaning. It was now seen as the system by which the human being appropriated and interpreted the world, the formative influence *per se* on human beings. For this reason linguistic differences between peoples were a central factor of life. Secondly, the place to look for the *Volk* was not primarily in the 'higher' culture of elites, but in the elementary pre-intellectual forms of life and in the forms of self-expression of simple people. The *Volk* was not primarily a category of the intellect, but a fact of life. Finally, the singular and particular, the distinctive quality, was prized and took precedence over what was general and universal. Humanity, it was held, exists only in terms of peoples; with their different voices the latter are diverse expressions of the one divine order. Every *Volk* has a specific contribution to make to the development of humanity, which is their 'mission'; and every individual develops his own humanity in proportion as he develops his own nationality. This is the humane idealism which yields and informs this form of nationalism. Romanticism intensified this preoccupation with what was individual and particular, what was unique, the preoccupation with the past and with origins, with the elementary essence of the *Volk*, the unconscious 'spirit of the *Volk*', and extended and refined it. The Germans were to be recognised as a *Volk* by virtue of language, particular forms of life and self-expression, and history, and this perception was of central importance. The task now was not only to establish a national identity, but to desire it, to grasp it, to maintain it, and develop it further.

The fact that the nation became a central value firstly for the educated class had an important socio-historical background. As has already been stated, the old world was breaking up. Home and status, the traditional ties, the particularist (local, estate-based) groups, the fabric of personal relationships, the 'community' and the clear presence of norms and meaning of traditions were all disappearing. It was the age of the individual who now wanted emancipation and the right to determine his own conduct, to individualise himself. He entered into the emergent commercial and market society, and joined large, anonymous groups with their rational and abstract structures. The individual became simultaneously more self-reliant, and yet more isolated and less immediately connected. Each person became dependent on others who were alien to him. Groups, loyalties and norms were no longer tangible presences. Self-evident truths were on the retreat; religion was less important for defining the values of the inner world, it was no longer the chief provider of social cohesion, and only in a limited sense could it help to discover life's true meaning. The new bonds of individualised, deep friendships were not enough. For this reason, the *neuer Mensch* (a reborn human being) spent more time than ever before in reflection and discussion, i.e. living through the medium of language and culture. In the new communications society, language and culture acquired a new significance. It was only through them that an educated man could discover his identity. The sense of a shared identity with others, which hitherto had been provided by tradition, had to be newly defined. This was why the nation, rooted in a shared language and culture, now took on such importance; it was the nation which truly integrated these 'unintegrated' individuals within an objectified and pluralistic society and gave them an identity. The preoccupation with the nation answered an inner need. This explains why the most mobile groups within society, the intellectuals and the student youth, swore allegiance to the nation and finally became devotees of the new faith of nationhood.

Historically speaking, the modern form of nationalism in Germany also had a quite different and eminently political origin in the French Revolution. In 1789, the inhabitants of the provinces of the French king had formed themselves, over and above all regional, estate-based and religious differences, into a people within one state (*Staatsvolk*). They had formed themselves into one nation and wanted self-determination, to be the subject, not the object of the political will. The people, in the process of staking a claim to sovereignty, became a nation. Here the nation was seen as a political reality, based on will and on political decision. It existed within the state, but only the nation itself could legitimise the state and its rulers. The nation was a group of self-determining people within a state (*Staatsvolk*) or the masses desirous of establishing a state. In the liberal tradition, the right to self-determination of peoples is a consequence of this situation, and it is the basic right of the individual to decide on his own nationality, hence the definition of the nation as a 'daily plebiscite' (Ernest

Renan). Jacobin, radical nationalism, on the other hand, developed totalitarian traits. The collective will of the nation had to be asserted even by the use of force against individuals and minorities; the nation was one and indivisible, egalitarian and homogeneous, and in its name one opposed dissent, pluralism, federalism or autonomous institutions like the church. One became militant. The idea of the nation gave the majority principle a new and powerful thrust. This nationalism finally turned outwards aggressively, messianically and imperialistically. Napoleon himself was the son of nationalist-Jacobin democracy.

Two different types of nation derived from this forked root of nationalism. Firstly, there was the nation-state, the product of a subjective and common will, of a contract, and consequently firmly rooted in law (nationality is synonymous with citizenship). It was born in the present and directed towards the future, taking its bearings from the idea of sovereignty. On the other hand, the cultural nation (*Kulturnation*) and *Volksnation*, objectively present through language and a shared heritage, and thus taking precedence over the individual, had fluid, open frontiers, *Volk* being a more open concept than state.

The French citizens of Alsace belonged to the first category, because they wanted to be citizens of the French state; the Germans belonged to the second category, because they were by virtue of language, culture and history members of the German *Volk*. One can only form a nation when one already feels oneself to be a nation. These two types refused any attempt to be geographically divided between western Europe on the one hand, and central and eastern Europe on the other. In reality, they overlapped one another; it was evident that even the French nation of 1789 or the nation of the plebiscite based itself on a shared language, culture and history. Nevertheless, peoples who have no state or who are divided between states are those who seek to define themselves, first and foremost, according to language, culture and history, according to the *Volksnation*. This was the case with the Germans.

It had been Napoleon's rule which had politicised the romanticised sense of nationhood and national consciousness of the Germans; it was experienced by many and for a long period as foreign rule, as oppression and exploitation, an attempt to impose uniformity on Europe. Resistance to Napoleon became a patriotic resistance, and was based less and less on separate territorial platforms and on individual states, becoming instead a united German chorus. The years between 1806 and 1813 were the years which gave birth to the nationalist movement, first and foremost among the intellectual elite. The educated cosmopolitans of the late 18th century swung to nationalism in considerable numbers under the pressure of events and experiences; the pro-Napoleon stance of Goethe or Hegel was untypical.

Joseph Görres, a Rhenish Jacobin, cosmopolitan and francophile, had felt let down by Parisian imperialism, and turned his gaze romantically to medieval Germany. In 1813, he became the leading publicist for national liberation, unity and a constitution. Johann Gottlieb Fichte turned from Jacobinism to become a revolutionary nationalist prophet and propagandist. He spoke of Germany's calling. The Germans were an *Urvolk*, uncorrupted by Roman and Latin influences. They should lead the way to a new and more perfect world order which would supersede the era of mechanistic division, the era of the French. It was Fichte's belief that Germany held the blueprint for the new, more complete human being — the issue was still the development of the human species, but, as far as Fichte was concerned, Germany should stand in the vanguard of such development. Here, nation and state became closely linked. Education and culture would be the tasks of the state; since these are national preoccupations, the state must be a national state. Only when the nation-state and the *Kulturnation* became identical would the life of each human being be justified and fulfilled in the supra-individual community, which now became a key element in idealist ethics. In the real world, this gave rise to the revolutionary nationalist appeal for the mobilisation of all forces and energies within the nation — this was the only way in which liberation, indeed 'salvation', was possible. Fichte's works contain elements of anti-individualist, potentially totalitarian Jacobin nationalism. Only within the state, so the thesis went, can a person find his humanity. The citizen takes priority over the human being, the state over the individual; the state should be the 'tyrant who enforces Germanness', since what is objective must be forced home and developed against the false consciousness of separate individuals. In bringing the concept of 'community' firmly into the political arena, Fichte gave an extra irrational and emotional dimension to Jacobin collectivist nationalism.

Ernst Moritz Arndt, who came from a family of serfs from Swedish-ruled Western Pomerania, became the major publicist of this Prussian-influenced democratic-nationalist patriotism. Friedrich Jahn, the 'father of the gymnastic associations', coined and developed the concept of *Deutsches Volkstum* (the character of the German *Volk*), which eventually became very influential in the future, even beyond the German borders. There were also people from other traditions and with other aims in mind, who became the champions of the new nationalist movement. There was, for example, Stein, with his imperial patriotism based on the estates and the order of knights; there was Humboldt, spokesman for the classical, neo-humanist educational system, and originally a staunch anti-statist and individualistic liberal. Then there was Schleiermacher, the great idealistic theologian and philosopher; he transferred the pietistic ideas of sacrifice, fraternity and community to the *Volk* and the fatherland and saw the *Volk* as God's creation ('loyalty to the *Volk* is loyalty to God'). He wanted to turn the state from a legal into an ethical ('moral') reality, and this would be achieved, as he saw it, when the state was not simply an institution of rule and order, but a nation, a community of those who lived in it. The quality of nationhood legitimises the state, he claimed. Only within the state does this supra-individual community of the nation exist, in which the life of an individual acquires its true meaning.

This early phase of German nationalism was imbued with anti-French sentiment, which was sometimes taken to extreme lengths, as for example in Heinrich von Kleist's *Hermannsschlacht* and *Katechismus*. There were anti-southern European, anti-Latin, anti-Roman prejudices, notably in the outpourings of the maniacally pro-Teutonic Jahn and his followers, a harking back to old Germanic freedom (against all world domination and all despotism). There were signs of a belief in a messianic role and national hubris; Stein and Arndt particularly hated the princes and their particularist rule, who were regarded as allies of despots and enemies of the nation. The nationalist movement — shaped by the situation in which it had been born — had its sights set on a dual objective from the very beginning, that of emancipation from foreign rule and self-determination for the nation within its borders: freedom from without and freedom within. Both were legitimate aspirations, yet, as is known, they were by no means identical. The burden of this dual problem and its concomitant tensions has left its imprint on the history and the tragedy of the German nationalist movement for more than a century.

All the different tendencies outlined above came to a head in the 'national uprising' and the nationalist fervour, at least among a major part of the educated classes in 1813. The Germans, as the patriotic sermons would have it, were 'a sacred people', the 'heart of our continent', and in their battle against the despots they were fulfilling God's mission; a sacrifice for the nation would be a Christian sacrifice. To be a *Volk*, explained Arndt, was 'the religion of our time'. Nationhood was given a religious consecration — it was sanctified; and on this basis the new departure was felt as something ecstatic, stylised as a new solidarity and a new community. Even a normally reserved man like Humboldt remarked that in millions of people the feeling was alive that Germany constituted a whole, and that this rested not merely on 'shared customs, language and literature, but on the memory of rights and freedoms jointly enjoyed, glory jointly won, and danger jointly overcome, on the memory of a more intimate bond, which held our fathers together and lives on now only in the longing of their grandsons.'

In 1815, the situation changed and the nationalist movement took on a different character. Certainly, on the one hand, nationalist enthusiasm continued to be charged with emotive calls for freedom and the ingredients of a religious faith. The early history of the *Burschenschaften* before the Wartburg rally, up to the incidents concerning Sand and Follen, bore witness to this. The other side of this coin was the disappointment felt by precisely the younger generation which has been referred to elsewhere. 'Where is the Germany', was the question Heinrich Steffens put to a soldier returning home, 'for which we have been summoned to fight? It lives in our hearts. Show us where we shall find it, or we shall be forced to look for it ourselves.' Friedrich Rückert composed lines about Barbarossa sinking into another hundred-year sleep; hitherto the legend of Kyffhäuser had been the anthem of the nationalist movement. On the other hand, there were unmistakable signs that the intensity of the nationalist movement of the opening phase — hatred of the French and of despots, messianic faith and an odour of sanctity, the prophetic tone and 'Teutomania' — had significantly fallen away. Events were developing along a different line.

The years after 1815 were marked by an intensification of cultural and historical national consciousness. This was spurred on by Romanticism and a blossoming of the arts. Language, custom and law, fairy tales and legends, literature (the national epic) and history (and the historical origins especially) of the Germans, the Middle Ages and early history became the central preoccupations of the time. There was a search for the spirit and the essence of the nation, which, it was felt, were the foundation of all historical experiences and institutions. A true German artistic style was sought, one which was felt to be best expressed in the Gothic or 'rounded arch style'. There was also a search for the specifically German expression of the true universal power of Europe, that of religion, the church and piety. For the Protestants, Luther and Germanness were practically synonymous. In short, the nation became the key to understanding the culture and the history of one's own world, one's identity, and this led to the demand, that what is national should be preserved and maintained; it must be remembered, developed, liberated and intensified. One must be true to the national character. Tradition, it was felt, must be recalled and set down in books, periodicals and collections, in works of art and historical paintings, restored buildings and — typical of this century — in statues of the great men of the nation, such as Dürer, Gutenberg and Schiller, Beethoven and Mozart, Goethe, Boniface, Luther, Arminius and many more to whom 'national' monuments were erected with the support of all Germans.

Anniversaries of the great Germans were commemorated. The 'Valhalla Enterprise', in which memorials to the great men of the nation were to be assembled, was planned in 1810 by Ludwig, Crown Prince and later King of Bavaria. It was eventually completed in 1842, a true memorial to the spirit of the age. Thus was the nation was made aware of its collective heritage.

Even new buildings were to conform to the idea of the national style, and music for its part acquired nationalist overtones. Operas, such as Weber's *Der Freischütz* for example, were to be national operas. Through schools and readers, ballads and historical novels, through folkloric memorials and anniversary celebrations, songs and choirs, this historico-cultural national consciousness spread out across a wide spectrum of the *Volk*. At the same time, it gained a foothold in the establishment. The two leading monarchs of the Vormärz, Ludwig I of Bavaria and Friedrich Wilhelm IV of Prussia, who had both grown up in the era of Napoleon, were, unlike their fathers, filled with this new spirit and proclaimed it openly. The 'Valhalla Enterprise' and the Kelheimer Hall of Liberation in Bavaria, and the Cologne Cathedral Festival of 1842 in Prussia, which celebrated the completion of the cathedral, were examples of this new feeling.

Politically, of course, this strand of the nationalist movement, at least in the eyes of the monarchs and establishment circles within the individual states, was aimed at preserving the status quo of the German Confederation and confined itself to the moral sphere. It was about restoring German 'harmony', princes and bloodlines, not the unity of the Germans, it was about 'shared emotion', not shared institutions, but it was not to remain so for long.

In 1815, it was not yet clear whether the *Kulturnation* and *Volksnation* would automatically produce a *Staatsnation* and a nation-state. Goethe, for one, wanted nothing to do with any such state organisation, and the historian and diplomat B. G. Niebuhr was only one of many who saw the Germans as analagous with the ancient Greeks in that they were a close cultural community which did not require unity within the state.

In actual fact, the Germans were really less of a nation than their western neighbours. They were particularised, lacking effective common institutions like a cabinet, parliament and parties, an overall judiciary and administration. They were a community of very varied experiences. German society was still very heterogeneous, and was divided into countryfolk and townsfolk, the educated strata, Protestants and Catholics, and also (to a certain extent) estates and classes. Each of these still inhabited quite different worlds and cultures.

Nor was this the only obstacle to the formation of a nation: there were other counterforces everywhere. There was an old and a new universalism, which defended the peaceful order in Europe and the confederate structure of Germany against outbreaks of nationalist egotism, and there was an old and new statism, which saw the state (and not the nation) as the true and historically legitimised principle of political order. Beyond all else, however, there was the reality of the German territories, the individual states, deeply anchored in the consciousness of the *Volk*. The separatist mentality — that one was a Hanoverian or Württemberger — was still strong. It went beyond establishment circles in the individual states, the dynasty and a large part of the nobility, the bureaucracy and the church. It was deeply instilled in the *Volk*. Particularism — as the nationalists polemically and negatively characterised this counterforce — was not simply confined to the old and now modernised claim for full sovereignty, but something much more 'rooted in the soil'. Indeed, as will be outlined later, it was none other than the south German states who succeeded, even after the Napoleonic territorial revolution, in forging a new particularist consciousness, a new loyalty, by means of administration and constitution, history and dynasty. This had modernised the old particularism. Even the liberals, with the help of a 'constitutional patriotism', boosted particularist loyalty. There were some — they were, of course, exceptions — who began to celebrate the small state as the repository of culture, peaceful order and liberal values as against the national unified state.

Nevertheless, the nationalist movement became a dominant political force in Germany before 1848, one with the avowed aim of creating a national state. The basis for this, first and foremost, was that in these decades a new and intensive communications society developed in the German linguistic and cultural realm. The unified school system, the common experience of the new *Gymnasium* education, the lively contact between universities, professors and students alike — only Austria differed in this respect — the enormous increase in the production of magazines and books throughout the German-speaking market, scientific and professional conferences, the network of clubs and associations and the multi-regional festivals, together with the mobility of the educated classes, including intra-German emigration, all created a realm of shared experiences, problems and attitudes.

From 1830 onwards, at the latest, this became a political factor. The problems, whether social, political or economic, were now similar, and so were the conflicts. Political events in individual states — the Hanoverian *coup d'état* and the protest of the Göttingen Seven, or the arrest of the Archbishop of Cologne in 1837 — were events whose impact was felt throughout the German-speaking world. The radical movements of the 1830s and 1840s, especially in the German south-west, spread across state borders. They were self-evidently an all-German phenomenon; the Hambach festival of 1832 was so indisputably nationalist as well as liberal-democratic, for instance, showing that these two tendencies were inseparable. The other political 'parties' also underwent a similar development.

The romantic ideal of the *Kulturnation* and the liberal ideal of the *Staatsnation* began to fuse. The historico-cultural sense of a national community led the majority of those who were of this frame of mind to look towards the political unity of the nation in one state, as if this were a matter of course. The linguistic and cultural community, the *Volk*, ought, they felt, to be identical with the state. For the liberals the idea of 1789, that the nation was the true political subject and that the state had to become a national state, became in turn self-evident. Nationhood stopped being a pre-political entity and became a political demand. Nationalism and liberalism in Germany did not only go hand in hand, they were in fact identical. The fact that there were pre-nationalist liberals (like Kant) and conservative nationalists (like the friend of the Prussian king, Joseph von Radowitz), and that between the great objectives, between unity and freedom, there were tensions and conflicts, was secondary to this essential point. Liberalism and nationalism were both interested in autonomy and self-determination. They turned their backs on the dynastic, particularist, authoritarian state. Theirs were progressive, almost 'leftist' tendencies; they were the parties of movement. In the states with constitutions and where struggles for a constitution had been fought from time to time — in the 1820s for example — liberal goals might have been more in the forefront of activity as well as of theory. Institutions and circumstances offered concrete opportunities for this possibility, but nationalist aims were also part of this trend, though for the time being they were less vociferous. Their impact grew right up into the 1830s, a period in which they found considerable public support.

Added to this, as it were, self-evident politicisation of romantic cultural nationalism, the nationalisation of constitutional and democratic liberalism, were demands for a German nation-state, whose motivations and *raison d'être* were different. This was partly due to the turn against the small state (which extended from the petty principalities to the medium-sized kingdoms). Small states, the majority of the liberal nationalists felt, were a breeding-ground for narrowmindedness, stifled imagination, pettiness, vanity and intrigue, and led to moral deprivation; they rotted away character. Without the power and independence of a large nation, dignity and self-reliance were unable to flourish; without major challenges, no sophisticated public life could thrive as it did, for example, in England. Paul Pfizer spoke of an overstretching of resources, an 'expenditure exceeding the resources of the provinces, as though a standard had been set which deliberately took no account of the limited resources, and the state apparatus had taken on the scale of huge empires.'

As nationalism had developed before 1815 in the fight against Napoleon, so the liberals of the Vormärz sharpened their teeth in the fight against the 'particularism' of the individual states and their federal merger, the German Confederation. The appeal to the German nation was a powerful weapon against the legitimacy of the princes and the fortuitousness of their territorial rule, a counter-legitimation. The familiar conflicts over freedom and a constitution merged into the national problem. Political activity and reform within the individual states had reached their limit, a fact which was particularly clear after 1830, since it was the German Confederation which blocked any changes within the individual states, and which propped up anti-liberal governments.

Under such circumstances, every issue concerning freedom was an issue about the national reorganisation of Germany. Freedom required unity, and it went without saying that unity could only be brought about and maintained through representation through the nation and, therefore, through freedom.

The complex of problems which the dual objective of freedom and unity entailed surfaced at regular intervals. The radical liberal Johann Wirth said at the Hambach rally in 1832 that should there be any threat from France, the unity issue would have to take precedence. Karl Rotteck, on the other hand, considering the hypothetical case of a conflict of objectives, made a plea for freedom on an individual state basis and was therefore opposed to unity through restoration of the monarchy. 'Rather freedom without unity than unity without freedom' was the essence of the case for liberal particularism.

There were others who, so to speak, put the goal of freedom first. Paul Pfizer, in his *Correspondence between Two Germans*, shed a very clear light on the problem of this conflict of goals. The first correspondent would rather have seen 'the most cruel despot as the ruler of Germany' than have 'the most perfect constitutions without any national unity for the individual small states.' But these were, on the whole, extreme and purely theoretical conclusions. In principle, all liberal-nationalists wanted to avert any either/or scenario emerging between the goals of unity and freedom. Both aims were inextricably linked.

Alongside criticism of the small state and the link between the issues of freedom and unity, there was criticism of the German Confederation for failing to take any steps on all 'practical' questions, which required co-ordination from the centre, like the system of tariffs, the monetary and transport systems, or at least specific areas of law. In fact, an economic justification for the demand for a nation-state only slowly gathered momentum. Friedrich List, who saw the fragmentation of Germany and of the German economy as one of the main causes of economic misery and delayed industrialisation, and who supported the nation-state as a means of overcoming pauperism and increasing productivity, was something of a lone wolf in this respect.

Finally, foreign policy issues played an important role in the nationalist movement. Demands for power and expansion were only isolated voices (e.g. Friedrich von Gagern in 1826) in the predominantly ethical-idealistic national movement before 1848. However, surprisingly, in 1848 there arose a chorus of such demands. The question of security and of frontiers led to a snowballing rise of nationalism after 1830. This will be discussed presently.

The form of nationalism which strove for political unity began as more of a yearning and an intellectual conviction than a concrete political programme which took into account the real possibilities and difficulties involved in forming a national state. The problem of Austro-Prussian dualism continued to be ignored. As the head of the restoration and as a supra-national empire, Austria was losing some of its popular reponse, just as Prussia was as a militaristic, bureaucratic, authoritarian state. Pfizer, a liberal from Württemberg, outlined the dilemma in 1831 in his *Correspondence between Two Germans* and came down firmly on the side of what he saw as the only realistic option, namely Prussian, *kleindeutsch* ('small German', i.e. excluding Austria) unification, which would have only assigned Austria a place in a confederation under international law. A number of north German liberals, like the Saxon Karl Biedermann (1843), who contrasted contemporary Prussia with the ideal Prussia of reason and reform, thought along the same lines. On the whole, however, the questions about how the power conflict between Prussia and Austria could be resolved, how Austria's supra-national empire could become part of a nation-state, indeed how to heal the discrepancy between *Volksnation* and the historic state in central Europe, as well as whether in the last analysis the nation-state was the 'correct' form of political organisation in this instance, were left unanswered or pushed aside. The fact that Austria was German and that Germany included Austria, that it extended from the Etsch to the Belt, was something which the nationalists as a whole, and the great majority of their spokesmen, simply took for granted.

The question of the organisation of a future nation-state remained relatively open. It was once again self-evident to the vast majority that this Germany would be a federalist state, a federation of German *Stämme* (ethnic groups) and provinces (or 'cantons'). The idea of a centralised state, the one and indivisible republic, had practically no part to play in the nationalist movement. The setting up of a national parliament at the level of the German Confederation, as Karl Theodor Welcker demanded at the outset in 1831, was probably the only concrete concept of how to move closer to the creation of a national state which the whole movement could agree upon.

There was also the other huge problem implicit in the formation of the German nation and national state, namely the question of frontiers, especially of that area where historical territory and linguistic and ethnic identity did not overlap: the question of who should belong to Germany. It remained unresolved for a long time. The nationalist movement was anchored in its romantic and liberal idealism, in a humane ethos of justice and freedom. It did not consider the nation as an end in itself. Nationalism was internationalist and the nationalists were an 'international'. Every nation had the right to self-determination — on this there was solidarity. Only a Europe of individual nations, it was optimistically believed, would be a peaceful Europe. The Germans and other Europeans were enthusiatic supporters of the liberation struggle of the Greeks in the 1820s; much of their own suppressed nationalistic yearnings were transferred into this pro-hellenism. This feeling — whether the tone was neo-humanist or Christian — existed far beyond the liberal nationalist camp.

Then, after 1830–31 it was the Poles, so many of whom had to emigrate westwards following the suppression of their own uprising, who became the pioneers and martyrs of the nationalist and liberal cause of freedom. Polish enthusiasm and sympathy with the Polish cause were characteristic symptoms of liberal nationalism in Germany. This was surprising, considering that this was the time when there were rumblings of the forthcoming conflict between Poland and Germany. The Prussian government had tried after 1815 to integrate Prussia's Polish subjects into the Prussian state within the 'grand duchy' of Posen by offering concessions and guarantees of their separate nationality. But sympathies with the rising of 1830–31 provoked a sharp reaction: Prussia sensed a threat to its statehood. A new *Oberpräsident*, Edward von Flottwell, went on the offensive against the spokesmen for the Polish cause, the nobility and clerics. His policies, he explained, would benefit the bourgeoisie and the peasantry alike, but they would also abolish Polish 'special rights' and move towards assimilation and Germanisation. The land owned by emigrants (and also some secularised former monasteries) was auctioned off and fell into German hands. German was declared the single official language, if not the sole language of the schools. Even though after 1840 Friedrich Wilhelm IV set a course more towards reconciliation, the fight of the nationalities had started in earnest. In the meantime, however, this was a matter for the government and the administration. It was not yet dominant in the minds of Germans, even in the neighbouring areas, and it remained confined to the one region. The German nationalist movement remained unaffected by it, and continued to be pro-Polish. The nationalist aspirations of the non-German peoples of the Habsburg Empire also provoked no nationalist German response; the growing potential for conflict remained for the most part hidden.

French nationalism and the German–Danish conflict were a different matter. Both significantly influenced German nationalism and intensified it. The anti-French character of German nationalism which had originated in the Napoleonic era had significantly decreased in the early liberalist period and the nascent radicalist era. France was seen as the land of the Enlightenment and, after 1830, as the land of the liberal civil constitution. The turning-point here, following initial irritation over French ambitions in Belgium in 1830 and over Luxemburg, was the Rhine crisis of 1840. The French public, disappointed by the diplomatic defeat in the Orient, suddenly demanded the Rhine frontier with great vehemence. A powerful wave of patriotic excitement spread across broad strata of the German population. Nikolaus Becker's *Rheinlied*, 'They shall not have it, the free German Rhine', immediately became immensely popular. It was estimated that there were between seventy and two hundred different arrangements of it. From the flood of other lyrics written on this subject, those which have lasted are the 'Guardhouse on the Rhine' (*Die Wacht am Rhein*) and the German national anthem of Hoffmann von Fallersleben. Nationalist patriotism once again had a new external enemy to focus upon, and once again acquired an anti-French tenor which it was to retain for a hundred years. The sensation of being under threat gave rise to a new experience of emotional solidarity. Even conservative governments and princes joined this upsurge of nationalist feeling. The internationalism of the left in particular began to waver; it was, of all things, the French left who were the spokesmen of this aggressive nationalism, and a potential split opened up between staunch liberal and the nationalist demands.

It was then that the conflict broke out over Schleswig–Holstein, intensifying German nationalism and turning it outward. At first this was a regional issue, and it requires some background.

Provincial patriotism in Schleswig–Holstein was based along the old estate lines and early constitutionalism, but it took on a nationalist flavour after 1830. As early as 1830, Uwe Jens Lornssen, the *Landvogt* (provincial governor) of Sylt and former member of the *Burschenschaft*, demanded a joint representative constitution for the two duchies and restriction of the ties with Denmark to a mere personal union. He did not find the popular support for these sentiments that he had hoped for, and had to go into exile; the government approved only separate provincial estates. Representatives from these estates did, however, band loosely together in the mid-1830s, as did the representatives of the Danes in Schleswig, whose radical wing wanted to incorporate Schleswig within Denmark (Eider Danes). The nationalist issue had thus grown out of the old-fashioned issue of provincial autonomy within a dynastic unified state.

The conflict intensified — once again along old-fashioned lines — owing to a problem of succession to the throne. The Danish king, who had reigned since 1839, had no children, and nor did his brother and heir apparent. The rule of female succession applied in Denmark, but in Holstein only a male heir could claim the throne; in Schleswig the issue was disputed. The king and government attempted to integrate Schleswig more firmly into the Danish state and enhance the status of the Danish language there. A new German nationalist movement voiced its opposition to these measures. While offering support to the claims to the throne of the Duke of Augustenburg, its supporters demanded the inseparable union of Schleswig with Holstein — 'indivisible forever', in the phrase used in a treaty of 1460. Schleswig was to remain a German province. This demand was also directed against the Danish minority in north Schleswig, whose legal claim to national self-determination was rejected: the right to self-determination was only upheld for the whole province, which was historically — though not entirely ethnically — German.

This was a change of perspective in the interests of their own nationality. Petitions and demonstrations, a constitutional appeal by the Holsteiners to the German Confederation, and demands by the Schleswigers to be part of this, intensified the conflict. In Kiel since 1840, the historian Johann Gustav Droysen became the most effective spokesman of the movement, alongside Georg Beseler and Karl Samwer.

After 1844, this movement began to find support throughout Germany. Its demands became pan-German demands. *Landtage*, universities and other assemblies and associations took up their cause, and this gave a further boost to the nationalist movement. Once again, a patriotic song 'Schleswig–Holstein Surrounded by the Sea' (1844) became a German nationalist 'battle-cry'. The All-German Song Festival of 1845 and the second Germanists' Congress of 1847 in Lübeck took place very much against the background of the Schleswig–Holstein question and the nationalism to which it had contributed a new fervour.

Finally, it is worth taking a look at the major supporters of the nationalist movement and its structure. For the most part, the structure reflected those of liberal, middle-class public life in which the nationalist movement made its voice heard, at first in a pre-political and crypto-political way. The early *Landtage* were liberal, but hardly nationalist forums. Nationalism found its expression in public support for the liberation struggles of the Greeks and the Poles. Later, when more political insight had been gained, nationalism was expressed through science, literature, publications, pan-German congresses, academic and professional associations, folklore associations — mainly glee-clubs — and later in the gymnastic associations. All of these provided a popular basis for nationalist support. There were also festivals which combined folklore with politics, and societies for the erection of national monuments. Common traditions, forms of expression and tasks — these form the basis of the increasingly political form of nationalism.

The social basis was thus quite similar to that of the liberals, extending from the educated classes and young people across broad swathes of the old and new middle classes, though it was, of course, less pronounced among the peasantry and in the lower classes.

One nationalist recruiting-ground deserves special mention. It consisted, paradoxically, of regionalists in the opposition who had no desire to put down roots in the new states. If they were no longer able simply to call themselves Rhinelanders, or citizens of the Palatinate, Franconians or Osnabrückers, but now had to be Prussians, Bavarians or Hanoverians, then they would rather be Germans. The regionalist opposition to the new particularist states did the rising nationalist movement more than a few favours.

(c) Conservatism

The third major political force of the first half of the century was, as everywhere else in Europe, conservatism. We live now in a society which takes the liberal-democratic transformation of state and society for granted; it is therefore difficult to come to terms with 19th-century conservatism, and not to consign its supporters to the scrapheap of history as hopeless reactionaries, because in doing so we cut out part of the story and ignore the fact that conservatism — the political right — managed to assert itself as a political force through all the great changes which took place.

Just as liberalism was the embodiment of the ideals of 1789, so conservatism was their true opponent. The naïve traditionalism which puts continuity and preservation above all politics became impossible once the Revolution had raised autonomy and the transformation of the future to the level of a political programme, once the Enlightenment had relativised and revolutionised all traditional justifications, once socio-economic developments had abolished the traditional relationships of production.

Traditionalism was given a new intellectual basis and became a theory grounded on the new experiences. This was the birth of modern conservatism.

The first signs of this phenomenon occurred in the late 18th-century critique of the Enlightenment, as manifested in the works of Justus Möser for instance, to whom we will refer in the context of historicism. However, what was decisive for the development of the conservative idea was the experience of the Revolution, and the adoption of the great western European theories of the opponents of the Revolution: Edmund Burke, Joseph de Maistre and Louis de Bonald. A periodical, published by Chateaubriand in 1815, *Le Conservateur*, gave the movement its name.

The movement was supported by a broad sector of opinion, who after twenty-five years of incessant changes, upheavals and wars, yearned for peace and quiet: 'When everything is tottering . . . where the whole of social existence is at the mercy of the winds and waves, this is the time, when we need to take a grip, to provide an anchorage for those who are searching, where those who have lost their way can take refuge' (Metternich). The Revolution was the spark that ignited conservative thinking, and it was central to it.

This signifies two things. The Revolution was seen not as an event but as a principle whose effects continued to increase after 1789 and came to threaten the world as it was. All revolutions, it was felt, have this in common; they are parts of one and the same process. The French Revolution had clearly demonstrated that the liberal beginnings of 1789 had given birth only to terror, dictatorship and military despotism; the demands for freedom were followed, after demands for equality, by the suppression of freedom and by chaos. This was seen not as chance, but an inherent necessity, a logical consequence. This extremist view postulates that between revolution and order there is only an either/or situation, there is no third path, no middle way. It was the line of attack used against the liberals. The claim was that basic rights, separation of powers, constitution all lead to the radicalisation of popular rule, democracy, anarchy and socialism, 'the battle of the want-to-haves against the haves' (Metternich). The liberals, so the argument went, have no leg to stand on when faced with this either/or situation. It is they, however, who are the true threat, because by their attempts at mediation they conceal from themselves and others the inescapable logic of the situation. They must be nipped in the bud.

The major conservative ideas consist of order, stability and preservation. Freedom is never the starting-point, but order; it keeps chaos at bay, it alone makes 'true' freedom possible; freedom can only be a finishing-point. Behind this is the anthropological premise, which runs totally counter to the major theme of the Enlightenment, that human beings are not good, but finite and sinful. Freedom unleashes its destructive forces in spite of the good intentions of its friends; what they need are institutions to maintain order. What is required at this juncture is not the emotional charge of movement, but stability.

The only way to maintain order and stability is through authority. In the ideological civil war, in which heads roll in the name of reason; as de Maistre concluded (as Hobbes had done earlier), there must be an authority for the sake of peace as well as to hold society together, which can maintain rule away from the heat of the battle of opinions and factions. Law and the legal process are too weak for this, something only the liberal illusionists fail to recognise. Their favourite weapon, discussion, can give no basis for authority, can make no final decisions (faced with the question, Christ or Barabbas, the liberals would form a committee, mocked Donoso Cortés). The majority always vacillates in the end; it is unstable, and the idea that it will act 'rationally' is nothing more than an adventurous hope. 'Authority, not majority' was the battle-cry of the Prussian conservatives in the mid-century. Authority must be singular they felt; state power cannot be divided up, as this will only lead to a permanent conflict between the heterogeneous elements within society. The true authority, then, is held to be that of the monarch. This is justified — and this is the conservatives' next slogan — by the principle of legitimacy. What makes power legitimate is age, continuity and legal recognition; in the case of the monarchy, this means birth and inheritance.

The traditionalistic legitimists fall back on God. He installs kings and dynasties and keeps them there; thus the old expression of humility, 'By the Grace of God', becomes a tenet of state theology. The king has a royal pedigree, and therefore he reigns. Of course, it is easy to prove that all power is based on usurpation — but here the principle of the lapsed claim applies. God, by allowing continuity, legitimises rule; justice grows out of injustice 'like flowers out of a dung heap' (Ernst Ludwig von Gerlach). In the real world of politics a part is also played by the argument of effectiveness. In other words, anyone who receives enough popular support to rule and maintain order acquires automatic legitimacy. This holds equally true for Napoleon or the President of the United States.

Authority and legitimacy, unlike under enlightened absolutism, are strengthened by religion, by the bond between throne and altar. This is not a specifically German idea, it also lies at the heart of French and English conservatism. 'When heaven is revolutionised, the earth can never remain peaceful', thought Heine. For the conservatives, this meant that in order to ensure that the earth remains peaceful, one should never revolutionise heaven. The virtues of the conservative Christian tradition, worship, reverence and humility, loyalty and obedience, are part of the bedrock of the conservative world. And since the conservatives defended the religious tradition against attacks and emasculations from secular, anti-ecclesiastical rationalists and from liberals, they gained the support of an enormous sector of the masses.

The conservatives wanted to preserve and develop, not make and remake. They believed that the revolutionaries were self-deluding. Those who were bent on progress believed that they could make or plan almost everything, that they could perfect the world or put it to rights. For the conservatives this was hubris, it was utopia. It was their view that one had to make the best of things as they were — this was the conservative appeal to realism. And part of this was a profound scepticism with regard to the promises of progress, which, they felt, at best only replaced unintentionally a known evil with a new and unknown one. After Burke, the one-sided concentration on the present and future was replaced by an emphasis on tradition, on the past and things that have evolved. For the conservatives, a nation was not the sum of its present citizens, as the democrats would have it; it was a community which includes those who live today, the dead and those to come — this is a central theme of conservatism. What has evolved historically is valuable — it should not be simply leapfrogged. New things can only develop 'organically' out of what has evolved before. If there is doubt, the historically given takes precedence; time has no calling to be a legislator.

Part of this attachment to tradition is the insistence that concrete existence is manifold, varied and individual, and that this in itself is a value. The progressives, they felt,
wanted to place everything under universal laws of nature or reason, under abstract
principles; they wanted to level things out. For the conservatives, one must not do away
with what is unique and particular in the name of abstract freedom and equality; instead
one should preserve it. This provides the bedrock of genuine freedoms, as opposed to
an egalitarian freedom before the law, which actually only leaves individuals at the
mercy of the state's supreme power. Indeed, to the Conservative mind, man is not the
abstract construction of enlightened philosophers, not simply autonomy and reason, but
an historical, a social being.

The conservatives came out against the individualism of the liberals, calling it
'atomistic'. State and society are not constructs derived from the individual; the whole
takes precedence over the parts, and is more than the sum of its parts. Man does not
live as an isolated individual, but in combinations and corporations, in families and occupations: this is where his real existence lies. This cannot be ignored, and should not be
broken up. The liberation of the individual, emancipation, is not a sensible programme;
more individual freedom does not bring more happiness, only more ultimate alienation.
Society should not be individualistic, it should be corporative, estate-based, tied.
Implicit in this is that it should also be unequal and hierarchically structured. There
should be tutelage and patriarchal provision, as against the unshackled autonomy of
equal and isolated individuals.

The conservatives countered the liberals' claim to universality with a sharp
ideological critique. The prime 'movers' in society, they explained, are the urban middle
class, the capitalists, and especially the intelligentsia, the 'educated proletariat' of professors, men of letters and civil servants. The liberals spoke of a 'state ruled by reason',
but it was they alone who would rule; in no sense were they speaking for the *Volk* as
they were claiming to do. The *Volk* did not want constitutions or any other forms of
'world improvement', but peace and welfare. This, in the conservatives' view, was what
they should have; but since the *Volk* was liable to be led astray, it also needed to be protected. The attack on liberalism as the ideology of the bourgeoisie and the intelligentsia
was a powerful weapon for the conservatives, and it was no coincidence that it was a
conservative, Bismarck, who introduced universal suffrage as a weapon against the
urban middle class.

The priorities all forms of conservatism shared were order and authority, status quo,
tradition and bonds. These were the categories which Metternich, the restoration
incarnate, believed in and acted upon. The governmental wing of the conservatives,
which was bureaucratic and statist, and frequently a late absolutist exponent of the
authoritarian state, contented itself with this.

However, a new element, a new key offensive took over among the bulk of conservatives, namely opposition to the absolutist state. The conservatives, like the
liberals, trace their origins to opposition to the modern and modernising state of
absolutism and against bureaucratic reform. They were a party of opposition.
Absolutism was rationalistic and atomistic; it wanted an abstract levelling of its subjects, and it swept aside old particularist and corporative intermediary powers and
centralised, bureaucratised and rationalised personal rule. It turned monarchs and
their servants into servants of the abstract state. The modern state, so the theory

went, sought omnipotence. It had expanded its objectives, its responsibility and its capacities further and further and was becoming despotic. This was the root of the peculiar parallel drawn by the conservatives between the modern authoritarian state and democracy, absolutism from above and below. When the state placed itself and society under the norm of the revolution from above, this was the signal for the conservatives to go into opposition.

The conservatives, like the liberals, wanted a limitation of state power, safeguards on 'freedom' by means of the law. But this was quite a different species of demand than that of the liberals. Corporative, estate-based and regional associations and institutions of self-administration were to be used to limit power and rights already earned. Freedom was seen not as a right, but as a privilege; it was not the fanfare of the new, but the preservation of that which existed already; freedom was not a singular thing, it was the sum of all concrete freedoms. For the conservatives, then, freedom was not related to the claim to equal rights and opportunity, but was freedom within the terms of the inequalities ordained by God. The estate-based federal order of inequalities, as they would have it, protected freedom from the over-powerful bureaucratic state. The emancipation of the peasants from patriarchalism, Friedrich von der Marwitz felt, creates no genuine freedom, it only multiplies the power of the emancipated bureaucracy and leaves human beings alienated in a world grown colder.

This was the school of thought which incorporated what might be called romantic conservatism. The great minds behind this school of thought were Friedrich Schlegel and Adam Müller (*The Elements of Statecraft*, 1810, or *On the Necessity for a Theological Basis for Political Science and the Affairs of State*, 1819), both prolific writers and publicists. Müller railed against 'the principle of representation by headcount or the pocket' or the 'chimera of a sovereign *Volk*', to which all inherited experience, institutions and rights were to be subordinated. The state, he felt, is not based on contracts, it is not a 'machine' and not an 'insurance institution', but 'an organic totality', the 'spiritual union of the entire internal and external life of the nation', of the generations 'in an emotional and living whole', consisting of dependencies, rights and duties. In his writings, he reserves his fiercest attacks for economic liberalism, the free market and competition, the separation of capital and labour, and the imposition of economic efficiency on agriculture. Property was defined by him in very romantic terms as something non-material, personal, as 'an extension of the limbs'. In 1837, the Catholic philosopher Franz von Baader then extended this criticism to the new social problem of the proletariat. Joseph Görres, in his long development from Jacobin and nationalist democrat, from his emigration from Strassbourg in 1819 to his becoming a professor of history in Munich in 1827, eventually became one of the figureheads of Catholic-romantic conservatism. The Munich periodical *Eos* in Munich (published until 1832) gave expression to this particular circle. All of these romantic conservatives argued historically and theologically, and, influenced by fashionable nostalgia, they saw the Middle Ages as the ideal of the harmonious unity of state, estate, society and religion; on such was the focus of their dreams and desires.

On the other hand, the conservatism of the estate-based anti-absolutist school drew much of its basis from the theories of the Swiss, Karl Ludwig von Haller, as expressed in his *Restoration of Political Science, or The Theory of the Natural, Sociable Condition, as Opposed to the Chimera of the Artificial Bourgeois Condition* (1816–34). Haller, unromantic and more of a rationalist of the 'natural order' school, developed the thesis of the patrimonial state, in opposition to modern theories of contract and sovereignty. The state was a construct composed of property-owning families. Power corresponded to property, and all public power was based on property, on private law and contract. The sovereign (*Landesherr*) is the greatest of these property-owners, and is the fundamental owner of the state, the *paterfamilias*; the state is his *patrimonium* (heritage). He is answerable to no one except God, but his power is limited by contract and law, and by the property and autonomy of others. All modern bonds between the state and the subject — like the obligation to pay taxes, to do military service and attend school — are repugnant, signs of the state's presumptuousness, because they break through the property pyramid. There are no objective relationships, only personal ones.

This is a peculiar throwback — though one which is logical and well thought out — to a feudal order, and excludes all modernisation. Power is justified by mere property ownership and ultimately by God's will. This curious thesis had a powerful impact primarily on the nobility east of the Elbe. It justified, of course, the manors and their public rights as well as providing a backing for the regionalist and traditional estate-based opposition to the bureaucracy, to the absolutist and anti-feudal tradition of the Prussian state and, above all, its tendencies towards liberal modernity, against Frederick the Great and against Baron vom Stein. It provided a more Christian slant to the naturalistic theories of power propounded by Haller and interpreted contracts as 'moral and spiritual' bonds, more in line with romantic conservatism.

Prussian conservatives, in Berlin especially, formed themselves into circles and factions; the circle around the Prussian Crown Prince, later Friedrich Wilhelm IV, including the brothers Leopold and Ernst Ludwig von Gerlach, was the most influential group among these Prussian 'high conservatives'. In 1831, they and others founded the *Berliner Politisches Wochenblatt*, the leading organ of German conservatism throughout the 1830s.

The conservatives as a whole were not only opponents of liberalism, but also opponents of nationalism. Nationalism was against tradition and legitimacy, against historical states and monarchies — basically, they felt, it was an invention of the intellectuals. Even in Bismarck's time, Ernst Ludwig von Gerlach spoke of 'the stealing of crowns and the whole wretched business of nationalities'. Nationalism was seen as revolutionary. Furthermore, the conservatives were defending not only regionalism and federalism, but also the universalism of a European order based on law and peace and extending beyond every national state organisation. They sensed the explosive potential of rising nationalism.

Conservative analyses and ideas are interesting in that they underline in a clear-sighted way the problems and dangers of modernity — bureaucracy and alienation, the loss of tradition and identity, the dialectic of freedom and equality, emancipation and anarchy, parliament and '*Volk*', the market and morality. In much of what they said they pre-empted the socialist critique of bourgeois society. It is also obvious that these ideas were based on massive vested interests.

The conservatives took more pains than anyone else to present the totality of their values and ideas with a claim to universal validity, and for this reason they can be accused of propounding an ideology. The case against them is as follows. Conservatives were those who had an interest in the status quo. The majority of the nobility were busy defending their privileges by supporting the monarchy, though only in so far as they could bind it to family background and aristocratic influence, the retinue of vassals, and a section of the bureaucracy. Conservatives were those who believed in order, were frightened of revolution and were opportunists. However, there were others who were under threat, or felt themselves to be under threat. These were the pious, who were frightened of the secularising tendencies of liberalism, and the particularists, who did not want to have a national state. Some sections of the old estates were also potential conservatives. They were the peasants and craftsmen, who with modernisation and the coming of the market system and the break-up of traditions found themselves in economic, social and psychological difficulties. There were also the orthodox Protestants, who felt threatened by the liberal transformation of religion. From 1827 onwards Hengstenberg's *Evangelische Kirchenzeitung*, became the leading organ of north German conservatism. This was the reason why, in the long run, the conservatives also gained a popular power base. But before 1848, since conservatives still retained influential positions, this was still fairly irrelevant.

It is interesting to note that even in these early days there was a conservative intelligentsia. In Prussia, for instance, they provided the Junkers with the ideal backing they needed to hold their ground against the eloquent liberals, in the confidence of having an intellectual integrity of their own. Karl Mannheim has explained this phenomenon psychologically. The modern intelligentsia has no fixed position socially, it is 'free-floating', existing in a heightened subjectivity without the support of fundamental origins and orders. It lives, futuristically, for something, but not out of something, and it is therefore in danger of being a stranger in the world, alienated even from itself, and suffering as a consequence. In such a situation, what is objective and solid — order, something which provides a home — acquires a special power of attraction.

A similar situation existed in our own century with the order offered by communist theory. The conversion of so many romantic subjectivists to the 'objectivity' of Catholicism in the first decades of the century is a classic indication of this. This also created the situation in which clever intellectuals became the leading voices of conservatism. There was also another motive: the modern romantic intellectuals were (and are) ambivalent and have a tendency to change their posture according to the particular situation. It is a question, as Friedrich Gentz explained, of equilibrium; if this is upset, then the tendency which has been forced down must be pushed to the extreme, and so it was, against the *Zeitgeist*, with the conservative position.

3. The State and the States

The state in Germany in the first half of the century was first and foremost a bureaucratic authoritarian state. Of course, leaving aside the free cities, it is certainly true that the state was a monarchy. The monarchical principle was certainly in force; sovereignty and the final say lay with the monarch. He appointed and dismissed ministers and senior state officials, he was commander-in-chief of the army, he convened and dissolved estate assemblies and had the final say on legislation and policy guidelines.

Where there was no constitution, his legal position and power were naturally stronger than in the constitutional states. Yet everywhere the sovereign was no longer simply an absolutist ruler. His reign was no longer primarily dynastic and patriarchal, and it was no longer legitimised by tradition and religion alone, but was functional. He was an instrument of the state, the bearer of the monarchic principle, a working sovereign.

The style had changed. Certainly autocratic tendencies were in evidence, in the reign of Ludwig I of Bavaria, for instance, and there was the very personal style of rule of, say, Friedrich Wilhelm IV of Prussia; but these were the exceptions, and there was no comparison with 18th-century regimes. The monarch, as a general rule, had a fixed income accounted for in the budget (the 'civil list', in the constitutional states). He could not be forced to act, but could only take positive action with the consent of other state bodies. Of course, there was still a 'court', but on the whole the monarchs, and their families, became more bourgeois and adapted to the general constraints and conventions of society.

The nobility, as a ruling estate, had, of course, not been emasculated by a revolution — the hitherto *reichsunmittelbare Standesherren* retained a sort of limited power, especially in the south-west. The nobility still retained quite a strong influence in court circles, in the senior ranks of the military and the bureaucracy, in the estate-based assemblies, and in the countryside. However, since the reforms they had been incorporated into the structure of the modern state, unlike under the pre-revolutionary system, which had been distinctly feudalistic. In short, the state was no longer simply a princes' and aristocrats' state, but first and foremost a bureaucratic authoritarian state.

The state of 1815 could certainly not be measured by the standards applied today to a welfare state which also ensures some distribution of wealth. The state's share of the national income was comparably small, about 4.9% in Prussia in 1850; today it stands at 37%. But, historically speaking, there was still a lot more state control, more than ever before. The state, by asserting its own sovereignty over the feudal and corporative powers, placing the judiciary and local administration under state control — at least in principle — and concentrating power, gained in importance.

The state, in turn, extended itself, by imposing more judicial order upon life and submitting itself to laws and to directives which had something akin to the force of law, whereby interpretation and the regulation of conflicts took on greater importance. Of course, the state wanted to grant more freedom to society, and to resolve conflict as much as possible by itself, without resorting to the former 'police' methods. It no longer wanted to be the sole provider of 'happiness', welfare and social security. But this called for an active strategy of liberation and demanded that the new freedoms be protected, contained and controlled.

The liberation of the peasants was implemented under the aegis of the state; self-government was monitored; trade freedoms were extended or limited. The state took on new tasks or new tasks accrued to it. These included education and culture, expansion of the transport network and the sponsorship of trades, the consequences of social change and its pace — in other words, anything that fell within the domain of social policy. Indeed, the state began, with more purpose than ever before, to plan or direct future developments. Put in another way, the state now burdened the citizen with three of the great obligations of modern man: the universal obligation to pay taxes, compulsory school attendance, and obligatory military service. This gave it more power and made its influence inescapable. And what is astonishing by today's standards is that all this was achieved without any substantial increase in staffing. As the state extended its reach, so the character of state rule changed. In comparison with former times, it become more impersonal and more objective, more rational and more effective. Even where fewer things were standardised, standardisation was more intensive. The state became an apparatus, an institution — in short, a bureaucracy.

Those who ran the state were, therefore, primarily the bureaucrats, the *Beamtentum* (civil service). The *Beamten* were no longer simply servants of the monarch, they were servants of the state. As servants they were not only an executive organ, but the senior levels among them, paradoxically, played a significant role in determining the will and the decisions of the state. The *Beamten* saw themselves as the 'general estate' (*allgemeiner Stand*), as representatives of the universal, of the public interest, as against all the particularist self-interests. They regarded themselves as advocates of the objective truth, even of reason — as indeed they were, up to a certain point.

The role devised for the civil servants in the early modern state was now intensified and modernised. They were tied to no particular place, but were mobile and replace-able. Their reports had to have a new level of supra-regional applicability, and be readable at central office level, capable of being checked, and able to stand up in court. They lived in the world of systematic order and logic, the world of principles and rational reflection, which they had learned at the university. This elevated them above the world of particularist traditions. They lived, not on their background, but through their jobs. The civil servant found his identity in his occupation, his activity and achievement, his intelligence and his insight — in this he was quite modern — and in his place in the hierarchy of the state service. The civil servant did not inhabit the familiar little world of local everyday life, but the big abstract world of the state, the merciless world of hard law.

From the late 18th century onwards, the civil servants had been more than admin-istrators: they were the activists who wanted to centralise and rationalise, to break down the old world with its particularist eccentricities. They wanted change, to create more prosperity and more power. As they saw it, the world should stop wanting to stand still. They wanted to abolish the feudal corporative system or at least 'bring it under state control'; they wanted to prohibit all arbitrary rule and bring about equality for all citizens before the law.

The more conservative among them wanted to replace feudal disorder by rational and hierarchical order. They considered that the state should provide this order, and in the period under review this conviction was shared by all. The reformist wing of the *Beamtentum* sought to create freedom through this union of state and law, a freedom not primarily achieved by means of a constitution, but by means of administration. This, then, was their materialist ethos. It involved holding in check any possible capricious-ness of a monarch within the quasi-legal system of specialised bureaucratic knowledge, and likewise with noble claims to privilege based on birth. The civil servants considered themselves to be a new aristocracy of intelligence, expert knowledge and achievement to counter the old feudal world, but also to control the new commercial entrepreneurial bourgeoisie, as well as 'demagogic' and popular movements. With regard to the *Volk*, the civil servants affected a well-meaning paternalism. Their new role and new self-con-fidence gave rise to the 'virtues' of the civil servants: competence and effectiveness, rationality and objectivity, loyalty and a sense of duty, responsibility and self-reliance. Of course, in their everyday life the civil servants were no different from anyone else — the reality hardly squared with such an ideal; but these were the standards they tried to live up to, and these are what this study is concerned with.

In the period of late absolutism and of the great reforms, the civil service was restructured in accordance with these criteria. The abuses which had become endemic in the *ancien régime*, corruption and civil servants getting bogged down in local affairs, dependence on subsidiary income and fees, lack of interest, indolence and egoism — the 'mercenary spirit', as Stein called it — were, for the most part, swept aside. The civil service was made more professional. Entrance to it, education and examinations, career structure, salary and legal status, official activity and discipline, were all made subjecct to legal and universally applicable norms. The employment status of a civil servant differed from a contract drawn up under civil law; a civil servant was defined as a public employee subject to a public legal code; since the famous Bavarian 'code of practice' of 1805, laws for the conduct of civil servants sprang up everywhere. In Prussia, the *Allgemeines Landrecht* of 1794 had drawn up rules on some of these questions. The civil servants, therefore, were no longer subject only to the individual will of the sovereign (or his acts of mercy); they were now bound by law.

Entrance examinations now became the standard, and there was a course of study for entry into the higher offices. In the long term, this gave rise to the so-called monopoly of jurists, i.e. the demand for legal training, with the exception of the specialist civil servants for building, the church, schools and medical matters. For the late absolutist centralisers as well as for the neo-humanist reformers, the study of law was the epitome of an all-round formal education; for the liberals it was the precondition for the civil servants to abide by the norms of the future state under the rule of law. The older tradition of an education including finance and the science of policy (i.e. administration), already discredited by the supporters of economic liberalism, did not survive. Attempts, in Württemberg for instance, to make the study of political science or political economy the prerequisite of a career as a state official did not succeed. There was, however, an attempt — with different emphases in individual states — to integrate these spheres into studies or preparation for the job.

It is fashionable today to criticise the predominance of legal training as formalistic or even authoritarian — but what is much more astonishing is to observe what legally trained civil servants actually achieved in the fields of economic and transport policy, social or education policy; this deflates the criticism at once. Graduation from university was followed — in Prussia this was almost more important — by internal administrative training, a period of unpaid apprenticeship. This was a long haul, especially as there was always a surplus of candidates, and in Prussia after the 1830s it lasted for more than ten years. The examinations were made harder; the Bavarian system — differentiation between examination grades up to two decimal places — emphasised the achievement principle and was designed to give an equal chance to all talented candidates. In Prussia, the period as a trainee operated as a social and political filter: it aimed at deterring and excluding the impoverished and those with dubious backgrounds. More important, however, was the official assessment of a candidate, and how he fitted in to the civil service; employment, when finally obtained, almost had an element of co-option about it.

The civil servants won a privileged status. Salaries were, with the exception of the top levels, rather modest. A *Regierungspräsident*, the chief administrator of a district (*Regierungsbezirk*), in Prussia in 1849 earned 7,000–10,500 marks a year. A *Vortragender Ministerialrat* (head of a government) depending on length of service, earned between 6,000 and 9,000, a *Regierungsrat*, a senior civil servant, 2,400–4,800. Middle-ranking officials earned 1,050–3,000 marks, junior officials 540–900, and if they served in the ministry, up to 1,350 marks. Police inspectors and secretaries earned five times as much as ordinary policemen in 1845, *Regierungsräte* eight times as much, and *Vortragende Räte* fifteen times as much. By 1870 this had levelled off a little; the figures were respectively 3.3 times, six times and ten times as much. But the civil servants were guaranteed a regular salary, a pension including widow's and orphan's pension, and through a promotion system based partly on age and partly on achievement, they had a fixed career structure. Before the bourgeois society had properly established itself, the civil servants, as the *Staatsstand* (estate of the state), were elevated to a rank above peasants and the urban middle class by a series of special rights and concessions (courts of jurisdiction, protection of honour, military status, exemption from specific communal duties and obligations, 'civil uniforms' and titles). The civil servant lived according to the ethos of duty and service, which set him apart from the rest of the bourgeoisie and its private moral code.

As educated servants of the state, the civil servants had a position of high prestige. In the hierarchy of values which was specific to Germany, this compensated for their low salaries, and a state like Prussia supplemented this prestige by awarding honours and titles.

The state civil service was rigidly and hierarchically structured. Discipline, authority, powers and the authority of superiors (reinforced by the principle of seniority) were rigidly defined. Official assessment, *Conduitenlisten*, promotion and replacement were means to ensure this. The obligation to abide by laws and directives became self-evident. Disciplining was, so to speak, the other side of the coin to privilege, but as well as loyalty to the monarch, the government and their superiors, they had a corresponding duty to act independently, to take personal responsibility, to have their own views on what constituted the common good and the state interest. This was something that was expected of them.

However, there was an element of conflict between the two duties for the 'political state official'. The civil servants could not — for the most part — be dismissed, which was the basis of a certain independence, and, in law and in practice, they were also citizens; this provided the basis for the phenomenon so characteristic of the German Vormärz, that of the oppositional civil servants. Certainly, at the time of the restoration, discipline was tight. Official warnings, non-promotion and replacement — if necessary combined with a reduction in salary — the threat of early retirement or with disciplinary measures, up to and including dismissal, were strong weapons in government's armoury. Yet there were sufficient checks and balances to avert the creation of a politically uniform civil service. Discrimination due to political views remained an exception — even the courts were united on this point. Many of the liberal reformist civil servants had held high positions for decades, which also prevented the service being filled up with conservatives. Certainly the nature of recruitment and the promotion system did encourage people to toe the government line, not so much in the judiciary, but certainly among the administrative officials. The political and social movements did much to moderate the original reformist liberalism. The ideal of reforms from above and firm order within came into conflict with the new demands for reform from below, and with threats to this ordered system from without. However, 1848 showed that liberalism had outlasted a good part of the civil service, that in fact there were a number of younger civil servants active on behalf of the left. Only after the revolution were the reins pulled in tighter everywhere. Before 1848, the civil service was, strangely enough, relatively pluralistic in spite of the conservative governments they served.

An important question is that of the social background of the civil servants. It was in fact varied. The study of law and the period as an unpaid trainee excluded the lower classes for the most part. Of course, there were social climbers from the petty bourgeoisie, but the non-aristocratic civil servants were predominantly from educated bourgeois backgrounds or sons of civil servants; it was a form of self-recruitment. Primarily, however, a large proportion of the aristocracy became civil servants.

The aristocracy's share in the excercise of state power now went significantly beyond the posts they held within the community. Now that they had jobs as civil servants, they could acquire the corresponding status and privileges. At the same time, the high-ranking civil servants were frequently ennobled (between 1790 and 1806 in Prussia 212 people were raised to the nobility, among them 68 civil servants; between 1807 and 1848 there were 241, of whom 82 were civil servants). The sons of these ennobled state officials frequently entered state service, so that in fact there was a kind of symbiosis at work in the civil ruling class. In Prussia in 1820, 75% of the members of the *Regierung-spräsidia* and *Oberpräsidia* (the district and provincial administrative offices) were from non-aristocratic backgrounds, and 25% from the nobility. After 1825, the reactionary atmosphere increased the percentage of nobility in these positions, and in 1848 the ratio was 68% to 32%. The senior jobs were occupied by a much greater percentage of old nobility, and after 1825 this increased to an extraordinary extent. Among *Regierungspräsidenten* and *Vizepräsidenten* the ratio in 1840 was 8 non-aristocratic civil servants to 20 from the nobility (though this included ennobled *Bürger*), and in the case of ministers, only a quarter were non-aristocratic. The single exception was the judiciary, which had a higher proportion of non-aristocratic officials. Among the presidents of the *Oberlandesgerichte* (provincial high courts and courts of appeal) and their representatives, 29 were non-aristocratic, and 19 from the nobility. If one adds ennobled non-aristocratic officials to the total, 60% of all presidential posts were occupied by non-aristocratic officials in 1835.

In the country, the situation was quite different. The majority of *Landräte* (heads of the *Kreis* administration), who were proposed by the aristocrat-dominated *Kreistagen* (*Kreis* assemblies), were from the nobility. In 1818 they accounted for 74%, and by 1848 the figure was still 72%. Prussia and Posen had a non-aristocratic share somewhat above the average; in the Rhineland 45% to 50% were from the non-aristocracy. In south Germany the proportion of people from a non-aristocratic background was greater not only at the level of councillor, but also amongst ministers. However, in Bavaria between 1806 and 1848 the majority of *Regierungspräsidenten* were still noblemen.

In Austria, the *Dienstadel* (nobility whose titles derived from being in the king's service) predominated, the higher ranks being occupied mainly by the old nobility. Even if 'the nobility' within the civil service was in no sense uniformly conservative, such figures are, however, an indicator of embourgeoisement, aristocratic privilege, or a non-aristocratic/aristocratic symbiosis in the German states during those decades.

Three things should be noted on the subject of the state civil service. Firstly, the number of higher officials was small, and, despite mounting tasks and a growing population in the Vormärz, these numbers did not grow, for reasons of economy. In Prussia in 1825, they totalled around 1,600. The number of *Räte* (councillors) fluctuated between 915 (1820) and 835 (1848), and the real enforcement body, the gendarmes, numbered a little more than 1,300. Secondly, the higher officials, the *Räte*, were closely connected to the academic professions through university and education, as members of the educated class. One section of this class, the professors, *Gymnasium* teachers and pastors, had a status commensurate with that of civil servants, though they were in general less subject to state discipline. The other academic professions, doctors for example, were subject to more or less overt state supervision. Finally, besides the higher officials there were the often overlooked but evidently larger number of middle-ranking and lower-ranking officials, the *Subalternbeamten*, who had a variety of ranks and class backgrounds and who enjoyed a measure of privilege, but were subject to stricter discipline and had less independence.

The activities and powers of officialdom now came in for increasing criticism; 'bureaucracy' was soon to become a battle-cry. As early as 1820, Friedrich List wrote, with reference to the notorious Württemburg 'pen-pushers', of 'a world of officials, cut off from the people, spread out across the whole province, and concentrated within the ministries, knowing nothing of the needs of the people and the conditions of middle-class life . . . bogged down in endless formalities . . . rebuffing any influence from ordinary citizens, as if this might be a danger to the state'. (List paid for this criticism with a trial and banishment.)

Stein also complained of the book-taught, salaried 'pen-pushers' having no contact with reality and no interest or property. Theodor von Schön, though an *Oberpräsident* himself, continued such criticism at the beginning of the 1840s, which was now of a general nature. The key words were tutelage, narrowmindedness, absorption of the whole of public life by the state, obsession with drawing up regulations for the church and schools, trade and railways, self-administration and social questions. Critics spoke of soullessly mechanistic, high-handed, arrogant, know-it-alls with a brusque, authoritarian manner. They argued that there were too many officials, they were too expensive, and they were dispensable. Conservatives and liberals, Catholics and Protestants, rich and poor, nobility, middle class and peasants all agreed on this. The social crisis of the 1840s and the political stagnation, the conflict in which the state officials found themselves with the middle-class and popular movements within society, their conflict in effect with progress, all intensified the criticism. Wherever there were strong regional loyalties, as in the Rhineland, this was soon combined with criticism of the bureaucracy. In the decade before the revolution, the prestige of the bureaucracy plummeted significantly. Lothar Bucher — a radical in 1848 — claimed that the major motive for the revolution had been 'to finally get these overbearing state officials out of our hair', and there were many others who felt the same. Of course, Prussia was especially important, as it was the 'model country' of bureaucracy, but the criticism was widespread and particularly massive in south Germany.

The conservatives, on the other hand, wanted to bolster the autonomy of feudal estates, while the Catholics, for their part, wanted autonomy for the church and religious organisations; but it was the proposals of the liberals which were to acquire particular importance. They wanted a 'popular' administration, which meant strengthening parliamentary control on the one hand, and on the other hand more self-administration — down as far as the level of *Kreise* and *Bezirke* (districts). Self-administration — whose tendencies towards professionalisation were overlooked — was considered to be a counter-measure against the bureaucracy. It would both safe-guard a free constitution while actually becoming its founding element.

The conservatives wanted greater independence of the civil servants from the central administration, and more freedom of action. They also wanted the administration to be put under judicial control, and to no longer be self-policing, but under the control of courts — ultimately, in fact, of administrative courts. These were to mediate between the ideal of the state under the rule of law, and the actual reality of the bureaucracy.

The radicals went even further: they spoke of the 'self-organisation of the *Volk*'. Instead of professional civil servants, they wanted elected ones, a demand which in 1848 they were quick to slap down on the table.

Below the state bureaucracy there were self-administration structures, though they varied greatly in format. In Prussia, at first, the rural parishes and rural districts remained under the control of the landed aristocracy and the *Landrat* who answered to them. In the old provinces of the east, Stein's municipal ordinance was slowly taking hold. A revised municipal ordinance of 1831 which reinforced state supervision and the position of the *Magistrate* in relation to the town councillors, attached voting rights more rigidly to the possession of property, and separated the officials further from the town citizenry. This ordinance only applied in Saxony west of the Elbe, in Posen and in Westphalia. The provinces which were exempted — a unique example of Prussian decentralisation and liberalism — remained under the old ordinance. As an example of how little integration there was, the Rhinelanders retained the French communal con-stitution. They had wanted to have a modern, unified local authority for city and country and therefore agreed to accept state-appointed mayors. Only in 1845 were district councils (*Gemeinderäte*) elected, and the right granted to propose candidates for the office of mayor. At the same time, there was a right to vote, in which the voters were divided into three classes according to a scheme which was adopted from Baden. The few who contributed the first third of all tax revenue formed the first of three voting classes.

In terms of overall policy, three phenomena are important. (1) The state was moving, in a modern spirit of socio-economic liberalism, towards becoming a 'community of its inhabitants'. Every inhabitant was to become a citizen of the state without having to acquire any specific right of citizenship, and there was to be no restriction on immigra-tion; basically these changes were the direct result of the introduction of the freedom to marry and the freedom of trade. In 1842 — though this was not yet absolute — assistance for the poor, the central problem of this period, was no longer tied to place of origin but to place of residence. (2) For the conservative government, self-administration was limit-ed to the local sphere, and any attempt by municipal committees to extend it beyond this was forbidden. Municipal self-administration, safely contained within the authoritarian administrative state, was intended to fend off demands for a constitution. (3) This plan failed because the municipal institutions became the forum and the arena of incipient liberalism in Prussia.

In other regions with a feudal structure of large farms, such as in Mecklenburg, most of Hanover, the eastern territories of Austria, and, to a lesser extent, in the regions of the large landed estates of the south and south-west, the rural communal constitution was still controlled for the most part by the nobility.

The situation was different in the cities and towns of the south and south-west, in the 'individualised' country, as Wilhelm Heinrich Riehl called it, in contrast to the centralised territory. Here, the modern bureaucratic and centralising state had made deep inroads into the particularised, traditionalist and static old world, into the guild structure, civil rights, and the network of personal relationships, which until then had secured a certain way of life and community.

Under the Confederation of the Rhine, the cities had been taken under state control. They had lost their autonomy, privileges and their right to seal themselves off against all 'newcomers' from outside. Certainly, this centralisation had its limitations. A single authority in Munich was unable to cope with about 9,800 guilds; the social fabric of city-dwellers and their resistance could not be effectively overcome by mere orders from above. Governments were faced with the necessity of decentralisation and compromise with the interests of the citizens of the towns. This meant self-administration, without abandoning the policy of the integration of all states, equality before the law, and general civil and individual freedoms, and without re-establishing the old form of particularist-traditionalist self-government for the cities.

In the Rhineland, reform and liberal progress, unlike in the originally powerless cities of the north-east, clashed with the municipalities' aspirations for autonomy. In south Germany after 1815, municipal self-administration and communal elections were introduced in varying degrees. The traditional urban oligarchies adapted to their new roles. After 1830, a similar system was introduced in the Electorate of Hesse, Saxony and Hanover, as well as in Baden, where it was extended in a liberal-constitutional sense.

Where city and state came into conflict was over the freedoms to settle, to marry and to trade, and acquisition of the right of citizenship. The cities resisted immigration, for selfish reasons certainly, but they were defending their own patch and their self-determination. The state represented the interests of all; it was modernising, centralising and bureaucratic. After 1815, the cities won back many powers of this kind. For instance, they were able to refuse to accept someone on the grounds of his 'bad reputation' or 'inability' to support a family. In the 1820s the state bureaucracy had taken such decisions upon itself or, as in the case of the guild examinations, had controlled them. After 1830, a number of states, including Bavaria and Württemberg, gave way again to the municipalities in the interests of general stability. The poor law and poor relief, however, around which the conflict centred, broke down under the onslaught of pauperism. Liberal self-administration against authoritarian bureaucracy, illiberal particularism of the communities against the mobile society and the modernising tendencies of the bureaucracy, all overlapped in a peculiar fashion. The cities were politically liberal and socially conservative.

The second pillar of state power alongside the bureaucracy, though less prominent during these decades, was the military. Three areas are of significance. Firstly, there was Prussia, where universal conscription was retained but no longer enforced. Prussia spent 38% to 43% of its budget on defence, but finances were tight; this meant that the army could no longer accommodate the growing number of those eligible for military service, and there was no external threat at this time. The consequence was a large degree of unfairness with regard to military obligations. In 1837, there was a switch to the system of a two-year period of service, but this did not change the situation in the long run. The regular army, the *Linie*, did not become, as the reformers had envisaged, the army of the *Volk* and the citizenry. The recruitment of more non-aristocratic personnel into the officer corps and the new system of officer training, apart from the general staff, were brought to a halt. The officer corps became more feudal and more exclusive, shielded from the new spirit of the times. Indeed, it became staunchly royalist, and the same applied to the non-commissioned officers and soldiers, who had to do a 25% longer period of service. The army was a profession, at a remove from civilian life, it was a state within a state, the personal bodyguard of the king, its commander-in-chief, who exercised his authority directly through his close contact with the senior officers. In the event of a state of emergency, all the power lay with the military. The *Landwehr*, which the reformers believed would reconcile the nation and the army, remained a stepchild of politics. Its officers had less military training, and they were not the educated men whom Hermann von Boyen had in mind. They lacked bourgeois self-confidence, and Boyen's second period of office after 1840 brought no change in this. The army, built on the revolutionary democratic principle of universal conscription, became a tool in the hands of the pre-constitutional monarchy, and came into conflict with the nation, which was on the road to liberalism. Military suppression of social unrest and harmless demonstrations in the 1840s intensified this conflict into a deep repugnance for the army. Certainly the nation was not militarised, and the military did not have a critical influence on the government. The army had no externally directed aspirations of a Greater Prussian or nationalist variety; the reforms were brought to a halt, but not retracted; the question of the relationship betwen army, nation and state was not yet finally resolved.

Secondly, in the medium-sized states, the armies, in light of the external political situation, the neutralised ambition for power and to the financial situation, were small. It often seemed that the only justification for an army was to fulfil the obligation to the Confederation. Under parliamentary pressure, many defence spending cuts were made. For instance, Bavaria and Baden spent only 20% to 26% of their budgets on the military. Conscription was reduced as a result of the many exemptions; eventually lots were drawn, and in some cases only a sixth of those obliged to serve were really drafted. It was even possible, by paying to get someone to take one's place (a 'stand-in'); this opportunity, was taken advantage of by, on average, a quarter of those whose names were selected in the draw. The officer corps, initially dominated by the nobility, received a much greater non-aristocratic intake, especially in the 1840s, from the pupils of the frequently very good cadet schools. For the higher nobility, only the most senior ranks were attractive, and it was there that they and the princes played an important role. The army, officers and soldiers alike, were loyal and royalist (this was due to the fact that the liberal bourgeoisie bought themselves out, indeed rejected a military career altogether). Some, as in the case of the Prussian officer corps, saw themselves as the *avant-garde* of the counter-revolution. Even in the states with constitutions, the armies remained armies of the monarch, whose allegiance was not to the constitution, but only to him. In Austria, there was a similar system. Conscription had been in force much longer there, and the senior ranks were entirely the preserve of the nobility. 'Breeding', social class and contacts were frequently more important than achievement and ability. But the army, despite the dire financial situation, was also proportionately larger, and had more clout politically and socially.

Finally, there was the Liberal position, which Karl von Rotteck summarised very clearly in 1816. There was no doubt, in his view, that powerful armies and a universal obligation to perform military service were necessary for the defence of the country, but the nation should not become the army. On the contrary, the soldiers should become *Bürger*. Universal conscription, he argued, would lead to the total militarisation of the *Volk*; the standing army would assist despotism and breed arrogance towards the people; it would spell death to intellect and culture. The sole guarantee of freedom would be a national militia, organised at community level, and training only briefly. Bourgeois civilians, who disdained the military, clung to the illusion of a national militia. The liberals, in fact, had no idea of how to conduct the defence of a large modern state. Their mistrust of the army was the source of the ambivalence of some liberals towards Prussia, which was now a military state.

What were the tasks and the problems facing the state during these decades, besides mere self-preservation? It should be emphasised that the state was not aiming to extend its power base. The external political situation and the structure of the German Confederation prevented this. The state was to provide order and maintain that order — this gave it a defensive aspect during these decades. The state was to exercise the rationalist, bureaucratic system of rule and administration — the school state, the tax state, the judicial state — and was to counter feudal and particularist forces by bringing about unity and an integrated structure. This caused the old powers to rebel.

The new problem, a legacy of territorial revision, was that of regionalism. The 'new' territories, in particular, developed a certain strain of anti-centralist regionalism, born of their special sense of their old territorial identity. This was particularly true of the Catholic Franconians and above all the Protestants in Bavaria, the Catholic Westphalians and the original inhabitants of Posen in Prussia. Those who felt most strongly on this subject were the inhabitants of Rhenish Hesse, the population of the Rhenish Palatinate and the Rhinelanders subject to French law and French institutions and traditions, who were cut off from their newly integrated states. The problem of regionalism was a central problem of the time, and the final integration into the new states was a long process, with many hitches along the way. In fact, in some cases it was never completed. Furthermore, the state, whether actively or reactively, had to steer its way through the socio-economic transition, tackle the problems of the organisation of agriculture, the trade system and transport. This meant getting involved in the bitter conflicts arising out of social upheaval.

The state, bureaucratic and bent on unification, now had to take on independence movements initiated by the Catholic church. These were another consequence of the territorial revision which had upset the balance of denominations within different states and had introduced parity for religious denominations. In so doing, it created a new arena of conflict.

Finally, the state had to take on the bourgeois constitutional movement and its conservative opponents, which became the major political problem of the time. The outcome of this, as already indicated, were the policies of restoration, a rearguard action against politically progressive forces. We will be looking more closely at the varied structure of the important states and groups of states, but first let us look at the two leading states, Prussia and Austria.

(a) Prussia

Prussia was, above all, the classic modern administrative state of the Vormärz, not a constitutional state like the south German states, yet not autocratic or run along old estate lines like some of the north German territories. It was not an old-fashioned conglomerate of states like Austria, having put the vestiges of particularist feudalism behind it. Prussia was certainly an authoritarian state, its chief preoccupation being the maintenance of order, but it was not a state ruled by caprice or the police. The state civil service was the nucleus of this state.

At least at first, Prussia had an excellent organisational structure; it was rationally and efficiently run — the regulations for the management of the budget and debt repayment (1818–22) and its policy of rigorous economy are indicative of this. Prussia was seen as a state founded on intelligence and insight instead of crusty tradition, it was seen as progressive and modern, and so it was no surprise that Hegel championed it. For this reason, Prussia was held in high esteem in Germany and in Europe. It was a state which had taken on board at least part of the bourgeois achievements, its actions were bound by law and legal procedures, and it had provided significant guarantees for property and freedom, as well as for the independence of the judiciary.

Prussia was still not 'a state under the rule of law' (*Rechtsstaat*). It still issued emergency measures and cabinet decrees on grounds of state security. Judicial control of the administration did not apply in all matters, especially not police matters, and the reins were tightened during the period of the Vormärz. Yet when all was said and done, Prussia was a state legitimised by law and a state with civil rights. This is why any violation of these basic legal principles, such as the 'arrest' of the Archbishop of Cologne in 1837, caused such a sensation.

The state civil service at the beginning of the reform period considered itself to be a general estate, the guarantor of civil freedom and legal equality and the representatives of the true interests of the nation as well as of the state. In 1817–18, the Prussian *Oberpräsidenten* declared that Prussia, heterogeneous as it was, could only be held together by the 'spirit'. The administration sought to represent and to direct the 'power of the public spirit', and any fight against this public spirit would be useless and would lead to hostility between the government and the people. This was the legacy of reform.

To put it another way, the civil servants considered themselves to be just as much the representatives of the adminstration as of the administered, as the true mediators between society and state, guardians of society and defenders of the general good and a sensible future against particularist self-interest. An opponent like Metternich saw Prussia as the 'head of that sinister league of the educated proletariat', the professors, civil servants and men of letters, who had their sights set on the *Vernunftstaat* (a state founded on reason). The administration was firstly a surrogate for the prospective constitution, and was at the same time the nucleus of the actual constitution of Prussia. Paradoxically, it was the state servants who participated in forming the will of the state — they were 'shareholders' of power.

A series of institutions and regulations reinforced the quasi-constitutional character of the administration. First of all, there were the *Oberpräsidenten*. Prussia, as we have already seen, was faced with the problem of integrating new territories with quite diverse legal, political, social and religious traditions, diverse nationalities even, in the east and in the west. The problem of the south German states of 1806 had taken on a totally new dimension, and its solution was no longer made easier through external pressure and war.

Under these circumstances, new provinces were formed. With the exception of Silesia and East Prussia, these were new or their boundaries had been redrawn. They had special integration problems, though they were less heterogeneous and more manageable. Prussia sought to solve the problem of integration and regionalism not by means of federalism, but through decentralisation. The province was run by the *Oberpräsident*, not as a middle tier between the ministry and district governments, but as commissar of the central administration in his province. He had a few direct powers, such as the ability to convene *Landtage* and some authority over the church, *Gymnasia*, health care and road-building. Primarily, however, he was there to control and co-ordinate the district governments (he himself was also president of one such government). His role was to bring 'unity, life and activity' to the administration. The post was not important to administration; it had more of a political significance.

The *Oberpräsidenten*, politically relatively independent in relation to the ministers, became trustees and representatives of the province. Their desire to become more like ministers of the provinces was blocked, but their positions assured them sufficient flexibility between the interests of the centre and the regions, between a provincial consciousness and a slow process of growth into the state as a whole. It was left very much to the incumbent to tailor the post to his own requirements — even after it was given a more formal structure in 1825. As a general rule, the *Oberpräsidenten* continued the tradition of reform which in (East and West) Prussia had been started by Theodor von Schön, and in Westphalia by Ludwig von Vincke, and in other provinces.

The second peculiar feature was that the district governments, which in the new and artificially created districts took care of the bulk of business, were not hierarchically organised as a prefecture, but as collegiate bodies. Collegiate discussion and decision-making was intended to ensure an absence of partisanship and secure legality, liberality, unity of the administration and a fair settlement of conflicts. Indeed, the government, which had to tailor laws and decrees to heterogeneous reality, was obliged to be independent and to dispute illegal directives issued by ministries. It was also its function to contribute to the debate on laws relating to the whole state. In this sense, the governments were also there to mediate between the whole state and the regional interests of society, and despite the administrative hierarchy, they provided a network of independent and participatory administrative authorities. This was still the case when, in 1825, the position of the *Präsidenten* was strengthened, and a certain division of labour was introduced, and when the administration of indirect taxes, the central tax offices (*Oberfinanzdirektionen*), was devolved to the regions.

Finally, in Berlin the *Staatsrat* (privy council) was established. It was composed of princes, ministers and senior civil servants, and functioned as a sort of parliament of experts and civil servants, with responsibility for discussing important prospective legislation. Although the monarch was not bound to take notice of its reports, no law was issued if there was an explicit vote against it by this forum. The king could refuse to give his consent, refuse to dot the i's, as he put it ironically, but on each positive step he took he was obliged to conform to institutional practices and standard pro-cedures. The *Staatsministerium* also functioned as a collegiate body once the office of Chancellor had been abolished after the death of Hardenberg.

On the whole, this administration was in a very unique sense one which was based on discussion, initiatives, inquiries, plans, reports and critical separate votes. Criticisms of the reports, or anti-reports, were passed between ministries and governments, and to the *Landräte* even outside of official channels. They all presented their astonishingly independent and liberal views and learned from each other. There was a broad spectrum of opinion, a permanent quasi-parliament of relatively independent chambers, though this was, of course, not public, nor, owing to the long-drawn-out and cumber-some procedures, was it very effective. In principle, an administration of this type provided some of what the reformers had expected from a national representative body, without the fear of the restrictions imposed on social reform by the estate-based particularist forces. But in the long term this was not enough. The failure to create a constitution, as the king had promised, became a decisive factor in the end, as will be seen presently.

If one were to ask what the administration actually did, one would see the Janus face of Prussia. On the one hand, reforms were carried out, though some were slowed down or slightly revised. This meant primarily the release of the economy and society from its traditional strait-jacket. The administration had held firm to freedom of trade against all protests and had accepted unpopularity and social crises in the interest of creating a free society in the future and economic growth. This included the preservation of freedom to marry and freedom of residence, the mobility of society, as well as a free-trade cus-toms policy, and the creation of the Zollverein, which counted as the single great success of Prussia in these decades.

Industrialisation was fostered through technical education, development projects, regulation of mining and foundry works, and extension of the transport system. Liberation of the peasants continued, despite all the conservative restrictions. In spite of many reservations against the formation of joint stock companies, the aim of these poli-cies was to break up the old society of estates, and to make the transition to a bourgeios society of property and achievement, competition and growth, the market and the class structure. Even the schools policy, despite considerable resistance from the head office, was pushed at least halfway — no more, no less — along the road of reform.

However, the state officials, faced with both a growth in population and economic stagnation, could no longer cope with the social problems, which the modernising social policies had done much to foster. The new free society overtook reform by the civil servants. Aid measures — crisis aid, emergency food measures and tax cuts, the begin-nings of worker protection (reduction of child labour), new regulations on help for the poor, control of journeyman craftsmen, draconian disciplinary measures for railway workers and social clauses imposed on railway entrepreneurs — did not solve the problems, nor did a return to the practice of calling in the military to put down riots.

The other side of the coin, despite such policies of reform, was Prussia as the classic state of the restoration. The anti-reform 'party', the party of state conservative bureaucracy and feudal interests, had taken a firm hold in court circles and was gaining the upper hand in the government, especially in the Interior and Justice Ministries; the reformist civil servants were fenced in and forced onto the defensive.

The general course was that of restoration of the former status quo. It included, to start with, the restoration of the special status and power of the nobility. The liberation of the peasants after 1816 had favoured the nobility. The patrimonial courts and the lords' own private police force were retained, and the rural parishes in the east remained under the rule of the knights. The *Kreistage* were practically the knights' own private bastions of power. The *Landrat*, nominated by them, remained an exponent of patriarchal, feudal rule in the countryside. The small number of gendarmes, about 1,300 for the entire state, ensured that the state still had to rely on the old channels of authority and power. The role of the nobility in the *Provinzialstände* will be discussed later. For the most part, the nobility retained their tax privileges, and the fact that the *Landrat* was the assessor of taxes also did them a few favours. Credits and moratoria eased their economic situation. They still dominated the officer corps, and their share of the higher civil service posts rose again slightly. The government had a conscious policy of consolidating the position of the nobility and elevating it above the middle class. Special jurisdiction and separate norms with regard to matters of marriage and honour, among other things, were intended to secure their exclusive position.

The consequences of the new mobile society were to be contained. Non-aristocratic lords of the manor were excluded by any number of special measures from posts in the estate-based assemblies and as *Landräte*. Otherwise — especially in the *Landtage* in the *Kreise* and *Provinzen* — the separation of the estates was constantly reinforced. No one was allowed to represent another estate, and the civil servants and educated classes, even if they now had the status of landowners, were effectively excluded. In the Rhineland, where the forced re-establishment and preferential treatment for the nobility was particularly artificial, this led to long-running protests. After 1840 at the latest, such protest was common amongst the middle class and peasants. This policy had, on the whole, given an even sharper edge to the conflicts between the estates than in south Germany; the policies of the reformist civil servants, which were aimed at creating a bourgeois society, ran aground here.

Another aspect of the restoration was the suppression of political movements, a policy advanced by the Carlsbad Decrees. This was the case everywhere, it is true, but the ban on opposition and criticism as a policy was particularly severe and rigorous. Censorship was draconian before 1842. It extended to books over twenty pages long and university publications. The punishments for 'demagogues' — professors and students — were more severe. The emergency measures for the protection of the state put critical limitations, as far as the middle class perceived it, on the standardisation of law and justice within the state. The pressure to conform and the severe disciplinary code imposed on civil servants — through promotion and replacement, reprimand and suspicion, right up to dismissal, the ultimate disciplinary sanction — was very considerable.

These policies were only moderately successful. Censorship was unable seriously to restrict opposition literature and publications. There were several loopholes and protected areas in the vast German communications network. Examples are the Hegelian philosophy championed by the Minister for Education and Culture, Altenstein, as well as the rationalist theology and the new liberal theology. The courts, moreover, could and did contradict state directives. The plurality of the administration, with its separate departments, provinces and districts, the principle of life tenure, the prestige and independence of the reformist state officials prevented any conservative, restoration levelling process being carried out. The liberal-reformist wing survived, and in 1848 civil servants comprised the largest section of the liberal members of parliament. However, the boundaries were clearly drawn. The civil service was more heavily split, and the liberal section had to keep an eye over their shoulders and act with reserve.

The attempt to impose conformity of opinion and discipline led to the alienation of those who were not state-tenured (*nichtbeamteten*), originally the intelligentsia in state employment. Civil servants were no longer the representatives of the educated public, but fell into conflict with them; the state lost some of its moral authority. The reformers had wanted to generate a 'patriotic state of mind', but the civil servants were supposed to keep this out. The civil servants lost their role as the pioneers of reason and the commonweal in relation to the movements of the civil society, and this could hardly be otherwise; but their incorporation into the system of the restoration, even if they were utterly opposed to it, only accelerated this process.

As a 'replacement' for the deferred and impeded constitution the government set up *Provinziallandtage* or *Provinzialstände* in 1823–24. This was a compromise between the different concepts of a constitution proposed by the constitutionalists, those who wanted a bureaucratic constitution or others who favoured one along the lines of the old estates. Prussia was not to become a unified state, but one composed of provinces, each having its own separate constitution. 'Integration' extended across the largely new and artificially created provinces. The beginnings of an 'inner-Prussian regionalism' (Faber), decentralised or federal, were taken a stage further by these new assemblies at the level of the province. There was no harking back to the old estates, despite the wishes of the conservatives, because they had gone into decline, were regionally fragmented, and did not contain a sufficient proportion of peasants and *Bürger*.

New estates were necessary, but it was up to the state civil service to create them, and they were still to be separate estates of *Adel* (nobility), *Städter* (city-dwellers), and *Bauern* (peasants or smallholders). Deputies had to belong to the estate from which they were elected, and were to represent solely the interests of their particular estate, rather than the people as a whole. Long-term ownership of land was a precondition for election, and civil servants and the educated classes who were not landowners were excluded.

In the east, the ratio between the noblemen (i.e. the Junkers), townsmen and peasants was about 3:2:1 (in East and West Prussia the peasant contingent was greater), in the west, it was 1:1:1. In addition, there were hereditary members like the mediatised princes (*Standesherren*) (in Westphalia in 1827 they were 15.5%, in the Rhine province 6.3%). This appeared to politically crystallise the estates in society. In the Rhine province, the estate system had to be artificially created. The 4% of the land that belonged to the nobility accounted for one-third of the seats in the *Landtag*: the circumstances in the west were becoming like those in the east. The predominance of the nobility — stronger even than in the constitutional states with their 'upper houses' — was for the most part assured. There was certainly no imperative mandate, and the plenum could take majority decisions beyond estate divisions — this was an element of constitutional representation.

The provincial *Landtage* had limited powers. They only took decisions on a few minor matters relating to the province. Otherwise they were advisory committees, especially concerning state-wide legislation. The whole system was, in this sense, a concession to the estate-based restoration party, but the monarchic, bureaucratic decision-making structure was not altered by this. Paradoxically, it was precisely this narrow competence to take decisions, namely the competence to advise on state-wide issues, which prevented the provinces from developing separately from one another. This is how the federal idea based on old estate lines had expected things to work out, and it led to these insignificant *Landtage* finding a new role to play in state-wide politics. At first, of course, they were for the most part pro-estate, conservative, particularist and narrowly provincial. But in the long term, they became forums for state-wide politics and forums for liberal opposition in the western provinces, especially in the Rhineland, and then in East and West Prussia, where a large part of the nobility was of a liberal frame of mind, and later also in Saxony. They now functioned, again in opposition to the bureaucracy which had been tamed by the restoration, as the advocates of interests relating to society as a whole, outside of the strait-jacket of the estates.

Prussia never got its constitution. The administration, which might have functioned as a quasi-constitution, good as it was, failed it in the end. Legislation stagnated, and the great renewal of the *Allgemeines Landrecht* was abandoned in the 1840s. The integration between west and east and all the areas with their distinctive legal codes and various trade or municipal structures, even between city and country, in fact, did not progress any further. Constitutions for the *Kreise* and provinces were deliberately redrafted in different ways. No balance was achieved between nobility and bourgeoisie, precisely because of the restoration of the nobility. Integration remained solely a matter for the state civil service, and this meant that up until 1848, Prussia would remain very much a *Beamtenstaat* (state run by civil servants).

Neither integration nor the other tasks facing the state could be dealt with in this situation. Under the sign of the restoration, the *Beamtenstaat* lost the confidence of civil society, which was now asserting its independence, while social problems were getting out of hand. The state came into conflict with society, a conflict which the state itself had initiated. Authority and modernity, the key elements of the revolution from above, were moving in different directions. Modernisation policies were confined to particular areas. The bureaucratic state was becoming involved in the bitterest conflicts, even with the church.

The advances of the reform era, so it appeared, were being dismantled. Even south Germany, despite all its restrictions, was becoming more middle-class. A new Main River boundary was discernible on the political map of Germany. Or was all this only a momentary retrograde step in the path of a reforming state towards a modern industrial and bourgeois society, one geared to education and achievement, and to a 'sensible' balance between state and society? This was the question raised in 1848.

(b) Austria

Now for the other major state, like Prussia a leading power of the restoration, a state without a constitution, but nevertheless quite different. Austria was not a state like the others, it was an old European dynastic empire, a *Kaisertum*, an 'aggregate of many state organisations, which were themselves kingdoms' (Hegel), a number of different fatherlands. Certainly, the state as a whole extended further than the simple link formed by the overall ruling dynasty. The territorial links, the shared historical experiences and a series of overall authorities and institutions helped to forge the concept of a state among the ruling class and the bureaucracy. Austria was not only a common destiny but also the state framework, within which only the peaceful existence and coexistence of its territories and peoples was possible. It was significant that the greater state was predominantly in the hands of Germans. In 1835, they held 60% of the leading administrative state jobs, and on the basis of their quasi-hegemonial position they were the element which held the empire together.

The major problem facing this empire was the relationship between the greater state and the territories. The centralistic experiments of Joseph II had failed. Metternich wanted to keep the administrative centre independent from the various regions, but to decentralise the administration from above. However, this did not happen either. The problem remained unsolved, and it grew more complex, for alongside the historical territories, and within them, different ethnic groupings were forming, different nationalities. There were Germans and Czechs in Bohemia, and Magyars in Hungary, and non-Magyars, the latter amounting to over 45% of the population there. They made conflicting claims against one another to the greater state and to the historical territories.

The problem of the nationalities became the major problem of the century for the monarchy, until its downfall. This nationalities problem, however, stood at odds with the advance of liberalism in this century, no matter how much liberalism and nationalism belonged together. For Austria's problem was not the liberal problem of individual *versus* state, but the problem of nationality *versus* state. Popular rule was no answer to this, when the elements of such rule did not actually exist. The Austrians were not one *Volk* and did want to become one. A parliament, a state-wide representation, took on a quite different character when it represented not one people, but a variety of many different peoples. The liberal recipe of the parliament was unsuited to this Austrian problem, and could only lead to disintegration and fragmentation within the state.

The liberals only really recognised this problem from 1848 onwards; whereas for Metternich it was something he had long been aware of, and it strengthened him in his rejection of any liberal constitution for a single state or on a state-wide basis, which he saw as a threat to Austria's existence by releasing nationalist feelings. In this sense, then, Austria, more than the other German states, was engaged in a rearguard action against the two fundamental currents of the epoch, against nationalism and liberalism, and the rigour with which Metternich placed the state on this particular offensive once again seriously restricted the opportunities for compromise, as well as the possibilities for modernisation.

The other routes to modernisation of state and society, such as an absolutist, bureaucratic revolution from above, or a consistent policy of reform, were also left uncharted. The risk seemed too great, and the counterforces, nobility and regionalism, appeared to be too strong. Fear of revolution dominated everything. Metternich's principled policy rejected any middle way. Emperor Franz I was insecure and autocratic, indecisive and lacking in verve.

The preservation of the status quo, stability, was the dominant principle. Any innovation was seen as fundamentally evil, and the government sank more and more into a general paralysis, in which it could neither plan nor do anything. The great problems were left to fester, were put off or circumvented by stopgap measures.

The constitution of government was old-fashioned and ineffective. There were a multitude of partly state-wide, partly territorial *Hofstellen* (court bodies) with overlapping responsibilities, but there was no modern bureaucratically organised ministry clearly divided up into departments; the co-ordination of government business was barely institutionalised, as a 'conference of ministers' could not afford this. So there was no government to lead the state. In addition, the central nucleus of absolutism was still in place. The monarch had not been incorporated into the state; he did not govern on the basis of consultation with his ministers, but through his cabinet. Emperor Franz I preferred to take everything upon himself, but he became bogged down in the day-to-day trivia of administration, and lacked any great political will.

Yet it was now fundamentally impossible to govern in an absolutist fashion. The Austrian system of government consisted of absolutism, bureaucracy and a total lack of systematic order. Even Metternich was not the real power-broker in Austria. Although he had the title of State Chancellor from 1821 onwards, he had real influence only on foreign policy. There was a great deal of power rivalry, and much intrigue between the ministers, which was deliberately encouraged by the Emperor. After 1826, the Bohemian Count Kolowrat was Metternich's most important rival, and a significant role was played by factions within the court and personal conflicts within the Emperor's family. In this atmosphere, no decisions could be taken, and attempts at change failed.

When Franz I died in 1835, the problem worsened. His son and heir, Ferdinand I, was feeble-minded, but Metternich, fearing that the legitimate line of succession to the throne would be destroyed, rejected other solutions or a regency, and so what the country now had was an absolute monarchy with a monarch incapable of doing anything. Actual power was devolved to a State Council (*Staatskonferenz*), in which Metternich and Kolowrat and the changeable court factions vetoed each other's policies constantly. Anarchy spread through the centres of power — and this was in a system which considered the fight against social and democratic anarchy to have the highest priority. Of course, the state machine chugged on, but it was more a case of it being administered rather than governed, and the pressing problems remained unresolved.

Below the government there was the administration which, like everywhere else, was becoming more powerful. Many administrative measures were enacted, and there were a number of decrees, authoritarian and centralist in tenor, since there was no particular call for self-administration and independent initiatives from the citizens. The administration was not bad, not unjust, nor especially corrupt, but because of the mountain of work it had to do and the pettiness of its daily activity, it was endlessly slow and ineffective. The bureaucratic state did more to irritate its citizens than benefit them. Control and centralisation of decisions strangled any initiatives the bureaucracy might have devised; decision-making was smothered by internal conflicts, and the shelving of tasks was often a way of getting one's own way in these funds. Josephists of the statist Enlightenment persuasion and feudal-conservative or clerical anti-Josephists frequently obstructed one another.

The nobility dominated the highest jobs. They had, in fact, increased their influence in the restoration era. Between 1830 and 1848 only 10% to 30% of senior positions were in the hands of the middle class. A number of down-at-heel aristocrats and *Dienstadel* (nobility whose titles derive from being in the king's service) had forced their way into the middle ranks, since contacts were very important for entry into the service and improved career prospects. This added to the internal tensions.

The predominance of the nobility boosted a certain anti-bourgeois stance in the bureaucracy. Of course, the Austrian bureaucracy had also played a modernising role. Judicial reforms were now carried through, and the legal system was thereby placed under the aegis of the state, or put under state supervision, made more professional and modernised. The forcing through of obligatory school attendance was a matter for the administration, and it was they who decided what should happen in disputes between peasants and nobility. It was through the administration that the state, slowly and gradually — and most emphatically in the formerly French or Bavarian provinces — nosed its way into the autonomous sovereignties, and in this way facilitated the transition from a feudal to a civil society.

Clearly, before the revolution, Austrian society retained a markedly feudal character. The nobility, as already indicated, retained possession of the higher positions, retained their privileges, retained their public function in the legal system and the local administration, and retained the services and duties of the dependent peasants, especially on the private estates. The government left agrarian reform to stagnate, although among the lords of the manor there was an increasing tendency to move over to a free labour system. The nobility was very numerous and was constantly increasing by the creation of new titles. Of course, the ancient aristocracy was strictly separated from the officer nobility and the ennobled civil servants, but the conflict between nobility and bourgeoisie was bitter. The cities remained heavily corporative and guild-dominated. Economic and trade policy was partly protectionist, partly undecided, but in any case was far from liberal, even though it sought to promote the expansion of trade, industry and transport. Nevertheless, socio-economic development, commerce, industry and railways, the emergence of a bourgeoisie and mass poverty slowly began to transform society, against the resistence of the politically entrenched estate-based order.

The central problem facing the state was to put the financial system back on an even keel; but in the circumstances described above, this problem could not be solved. In spite of the many attempts, there never was a fundamental reform of the old-fashioned taxation system, and economic policy did not effectively increase the tax base. State expenditure consistently topped state income by a wide margin, and the state had to live with a growing deficit. It was forced to borrow more and more, and worsening conditions led to ever-expanding debt-repayment schemes, and thence to diminished expenditure on investment. State debts tripled in the period up to the 1840s. The Austrian state, even more than other states, was becoming dependent on high finance to bail it out, through the Rothschild Bank, for example, and was therefore also at the mercy of changes in the economic performance of the banks. This aggravated the economic crisis in the 1840s, while providing the populist opposition with the ammunition they needed in their battle against the absolutist monarchy and Jewish banking capital. Wages were cut, as was expenditure on the army. Austrian policy as a major power moved into a critical phase, when any possible mobilisation of the army would have brought the country to the brink of financial collapse. Even an outstanding expert like the later Finance Minister Baron von Kübeck was unable to solve the structural problem. The system, embroiled as it was in a survival crisis, appeared incapable of reform.

When one thinks of the Austria of this period, one thinks of the 'Metternichian system'. Austria was the classic country of restoration. The top priorities were law and order and the status quo, the blocking of any political movement, or even any possibilities of forming one. There were, it has to be said, provincial representative bodies in many territories, but they were along old estate lines, dominated by the nobility and clergy, and they were dependent on the government. They could express their wishes, but they had to approve the taxes demanded by the governments. Friedrich Christoph Dahlmann said of them that they 'could do even less for freedom than a painted supper could for hunger'. Under the Carlsbad Decrees, the universities were purged, the famous philosopher and theologian Bernhard Bolzano being one of the victims. State control was tightened, and it became impossible in practice to study at an university in another German state. Even the schools, especially the secondary schools, were placed under tight state supervision. They had a conservative curriculum forced upon them, and were cut off from new ideas.

The most important instrument for the maintenance of the status quo was the police. All signs of life, all associations, all forms of social gathering, no matter how harmless, were put under surveillance, and liberal use was made of informers and denunciations. Suspicion was all-pervasive. The correspondence of, say, foreign ambassadors, senior officials, even the members of the imperial family, was constantly checked. Most infamous of all was the system of censorship, which was devised and perfected by the chief of police, Josef Sedlnitzky. Censorship was preventive, and it extended to everything printed in Austria. It even affected belles-lettres. The theatre suffered very badly, it being the practice to cut out particular passages. Even such an unrevolutionary writer as Franz Grillparzer was constantly getting into difficulties, since the mistakes and absurdities of this policy were legion. Schiller's dramas were 'cleaned up', and a dedication by Beethoven to the Polish composer Chopin was banned from publication.

Clearly, the terrible stories circulated as part of the liberal, *kleindeutsch* (Little German, i.e. excluding Austria), anti-Catholic, 'black' legend of the 'graveyard calm' in Austria during these decades must be put in perspective. Firstly, the system was not perfect and therefore not totalitarian. There were conflicts within the establishment, and, in practice, censorship was not uniformly rigorous. Astute writers developed an indirect style and played a cat-and-mouse game with the authorities. Even Austria could not be entirely shielded from publications emanating from other German territories. For instance, Metternich needed the liberal-conservative *Allgemeine Zeitung* in Augsburg to help him on foreign policy matters, and therefore had to tolerate it coming into the country. The educated could also get special permission to read forbidden foreign literature, and there was a widespread smuggling network, run jointly by readers, booksellers and publishers. Austrian journalism of the 1840s was widely read in Austria. Secondly, intellectual literary life flourished; the romantic intellectuals formed their own circles, modern medicine and modern oriental studies at the universities, for example, were able to develop; and the great dramatists — Grillparzer, Raimund and Nestroy — were figures well known to the public, and their plays did not convey the impression of originating from a stifling, paralysing atmosphere.

Political thought and oppositional opinion was, for the time being, the preserve of a narrow class. The mass of the *Volk* and the majority of the urban middle class still lived in a patriarchal and unpolitical climate of tradition. At the beginning of the 1830s critics spoke of the superficiality of the Austrians, and especially of the Viennese: 'What of the constitution? What of the administration? The word in Vienna is entertainment.' This was clearly a result of Metternich's policies. He wanted to divert society into the non-political and private sphere, into an entertainment culture. The great cultural zenith of the Austrian Biedermeier era from Schubert to Stifter was not the product of Metternich's suppression policies, but the system had indirectly encouraged it.

Nevertheless, and beyond all of this, the impact of the police and censorship was extraordinary. It had put a stop to all forms of public political life and every opportunity for the society to articulate itself. It gave birth to the archetypal 'whinger', who carped about everything, without being able to offer an alternative position of his own. In the long run, it alienated the educated classes, and then the broader middle class, even many of a conservative persuasion, from the state. All those who perhaps only took offence to isolated measures were forced in the long run into a collective though only half-articulated opposition against this police system. The policy of bans and prohibition sparked off criticism and protest. It finally isolated Austria from the rest of Germany, although Austria was never a 'spiritually foreign land' with respect to the other German territories, as the *Kleindeutschen* later claimed.

The system of the restoration was not closed and compact; there were tensions and rifts within it. In the narrow government circles there were, as we have said, personal conflicts and conflicts of policy, e.g. as to whether the domestic problem or Austria's European policy should take precedence, or concerning economic problems. Relations with the church were difficult. Metternich wanted an alliance with the church as a conservative power, and was therefore anxious to avoid conflicts — indeed, he himself ordered the banishing of the Ziller Valley Protestants from the Tyrol in 1837, contrary to all ideas of enlightened tolerance.

Against this there were the supporters of the Josephist tradition in the bureaucracy, nobility and dynasty. To them Metternich was the advocate of ultramontane reaction, and they held firm to the rights of the state church. It was precisely for this reason, however, that the church also remained reserved towards the system. Even among the nobility opposition developed against the system, against the regiment of bureaucrats, against centralism on a regionalist ticket, and, as regards economic policy, against the close ties between the government and financial capital, or against expensive transport projects. One section of the nobility — in Lower Austria in 1844, for example — set its face against the conservative government by supporting agrarian reforms. They felt that the modern, capitalist agrarian system required a free labour system in order to flourish, and the passive resistance of the peasants also pointed to this. Out of a sense of the general untenability of current power relations in the state, a moderate aristocratic reformist liberalism was born (Montecuccoli, Doblhoff, Schmerling) in the Upper and Lower Austrian estates. In 1841, the Baron von Andrian-Werburg, in a pamphlet entitled *Austria and its Future*, demanded true representative estates and their incorporation into a state-wide assembly, in addition to a strong self-administration, liberalisation of the judiciary, education and the press, and the modernisation of the economy and finance. Everywhere else there was progress, whereas Austria had stiffened into a lifeless mummy. Similar sentiments were voiced in a pamphlet written by two tutors to the royal family just before the revolution. Metternich, it said, should give back to Austria the thirty years that had been lost. The vigorous middle-class opposition to absolutism and bureaucracy jumped on the bandwagon, railing against 'obscurantism' and inefficiency, and against the privileges of the nobility — in short, against the whole system.

In Vienna, the Lower Austrian Trade Association (1839), the Association of Writers' and Artists' Concordia (1840) and the 'Legal and Political Readers' Association' (1843) became centres of criticism and the movement for reform. Count Auerspberg used the pseudonym Anastasius Grün to publish *Spaziergänge eines Wiener Poeten* (Walks of a Viennese Poet), which was heavily critical of the time in which it was written, and in the 1840s more and more critiques of the system were published (by Franz Schuselka, Anton Gross-Hoffinger and Joseph Tuvora, among others), giving a great fillip to the smuggling trade in Austria.

The opposition intensified. By the mid-1840s, Andrian was considered by many to be passé and too moderate. Among students and the craft workers threatened by pauperism there were considerable rumblings of radicalism. Nevertheless, all this opposition was for the time being confined to the urban and bourgeois environment, especially in Vienna.

The development of the nationalist questions, which took on such vital importance for the Austrians as well as for all Germans, deserves examination. There was the irredentist nationalism of the individual nations, the Italians and the Poles, who had had their own ruling class and a long independent history, but were now internally divided. In 1815, it was perhaps not yet a certainty that Italy would become a political nation; the regionalist movements were still very strong, and the incipient Italian nationalist movement had diverse aims. However, Austrian politics had not yet tested out the possibilities of compromise. The Austrian administration was in no sense bad, but the Italians, mainly the bourgeoisie and nobility, were united in their opposition to 'foreign rule'. After the first stirrings of revolution around 1820, the Italians were not very active, but were potentially endeavouring to sever their ties with Austria. The Poles wanted their own state again. In 1846, a revolution in Galicia and Cracow foundered following the uprising of the peasants in Ruthenia (45% of the population), who cut down the Polish landowners by the hundred, filled with mistrust of their promises of liberation and retaining confidence in the distant Emperor. For the time being, this defused the threat of the Polish nationalist movement for the state as a whole. Cracow, which had been independent until then, was now annexed by Austria.

Hungary was an autonomous state under the dynasty and wanted to remain so. It was not integrated into the greater state. In 1846, the Hungarian territories only contributed 36% of the taxes one might have expected them to pay, considering their proportion in the overall population. Hungary was a country with an aristocratic system along old estate lines and a feudal social order. The autonomy of the aristocratic estates prevented any reform of power relations across the whole state, as well as of the internal structures, and Metternich did not want any reform which offered constitutional powers. A liberal-nationalist movement sprung up out of the old opposition of the estates and the countryside; indeed, it grew into a democratic, nationalist movement, turning its back emphatically on Vienna and all that came out of it. State-wide reform was no longer possible. In Hungary itself, a staunchly Magyar nationalism developed, which now turned — through language laws, for instance — against the non-Magyar nationalities.

Finally, there was the nationalism of the emerging Slav nations, the southern Slavs and — most important of all — the Czechs. Bohemia had a *Landtag* dominated by the nobility, which sought to defend and extend the rights and autonomy of the country against Vienna and its rulers. This was a form of the old territorial patriotism, which united Germans and Czechs. The majority of the nobility wanted to be neither Czech nor German, but Bohemian. In the 1840s the demands from the estates became more vehement, and at the same time more modern, i.e. they were given a new liberal and constitutional interpretation. The estates felt themselves to be the advocates of liberal freedom. Alongside this, a Czech nationalism sprung up, initially in the form of a romantic, cultural nationalism, which the Austrian government and the Germans also supported — Prague was, of course, a strongly German city. In 1818, the Bohemian National Museum was founded, and in 1830 the Committee for the Preservation of the Czech Language and Literature. In the 1830s this movement gradually became more politicised; the head of the museum and the historiographer of the estates, Franz Palacký (who wrote a *History of Bohemia* (beginning in 1836), first printed in German) was their leading spokesman. There were calls for emancipation from the Germans and a demand for equal rights with the Germans, clearly still within the framework of the Habsburg Empire. The journalist Karel Havlíček, a democratic nationalist, organised a 'repeal' movement on the Irish model in the 1840s against Vienna, which some Germans also joined at first, but this old form of territorial patriotism soon nationalised itself. The Czechs opposed the Viennese government because it was centralist, bureaucratic and absolutist, but also because, like the greater state, it was German. They wanted autonomy for their country, a constitution and national autonomy at the same time.

The Germans in Austria were also very conscious of the national identity of the Germans as a whole, and censorship could do nothing against this. But, for the time being, there were no political repercussions. No one had thought of breaking up multinational Austria in favour of creating a German national state. It was taken for granted that the German and Bohemian territories were part of the German Confederation. And within Austria itself it seemed self-evident that the Germans, the only nation with an educated middle class, would also play the leading role under liberal auspices. They were not unsympathetic to the separatist demands of the Italians and Poles, and to the movement for autonomy among the Hungarians, but these were distant and did not affect the current situation. They supported the cultural, nationalist aspirations of the Slavs, but no one expected any political consequences to arise from this. The idea that the 'sovereign *Volk* of Slovakian broom-makers or the Galician schnapps farmers' might play an historic political role was considered a joke. What the consequences of a liberal constitution would be for the supranational state of Austria, and what consequences the formation of a new German national state would have, were not yet clear in anyone's mind. Only a few people, like Franz Schuselka, expressed doubts about the continued existence of a multinational state.

(c) The Constitutional States of the South

The south German states also initially bore the stamp of monarchic and bureaucratic authoritarianism. The bulk of reform legislation had been implemented. The state had grown stronger through a thorough reorganisation of administration and the legal system, and by placing an increasing number of areas of life under legal restrictions. Regulation, mobility and centralisation gave a unified spirit to the administration, and the unified nature of the new states themselves became more pronounced. Despite regionalist opposition (in the Palatinate and in Rhenish Hesse this was bound up with the defence of French institutions), and despite the special status of the mediatised sovereign states, the new states were successfully integrated.

The constitutions and the common experience of constitutional life were major contributing factors to the voluntary nature of this integration, an integration 'from below'. A constitutional patriotism sprung up in the individual states, which was most pronounced in Baden. The governments also did their bit in generating a new territorial patriotism, for instance by harking back to the integral history of the regions, and of Bavaria, Baden and Württemberg. This now became the vogue. One example of this was the 'Hall of Fame' of the great Bavarians in Munich. These manifestations proved most successful. However, the *Beamtenstaat* (civil servants' state) was at the same time a source of increasing tension between state and people.

In terms of social and economic policy, the south German states tended to be conservative. The reforms which aimed at establishing a bourgeois society were not repealed, but they were hardly pursued. The nobility retained a leading position through the court, the upper houses of the parliaments and by holding a least a part of the most senior administrative positions. There was no genuine 'restoration' of the nobility as there had been in Prussia, but the privileges the aristocracy still retained in local administration and in the courts — and in some cases also in the taxation system — survived more or less intact.

Grundentlastung and peasant liberation hardly progressed on any further. The corporative, guild-orientated organisation of trades underwent only a very cautious reform; freedom of marriage and the rights generally granted to citizens of municipalities remained restricted, or were actually cut back even further. Unlike the situation in Prussia, policies were not firmly targeted at mobilisation and modernisation, the creation of markets and competition, nor were they even aimed at industrialisation (although Karl Friedrich Nebenius, the man who actually drew up the constitution in Baden, and who was a *Staatsrat* and later a minister, claimed that 'the constitution and the machine' were the progressive symbols of the era).

Policies aimed mainly at stability and mere survival. They were more protectionist, and from the 1830s onwards anxiety about pauperism reinforced this conservative line. The characteristic schism and chiastic pattern within German society developed, in which south Germany had a progressive constitutional system and a conservative social policy, whereas in Prussia there was a progressive economic system, and to some extent even a progressive social system, alongside a conservative, outmoded political structure. Certainly, the objective development — railways, commerce, industry — gradually undermined conservative social policy, even in south Germany.

The striking fact for contemporaries, and the most important fact for future German history, was the advent of the constitution and the development of a parliamentary life. The south German constitutions, despite their many differences, were basically all of a piece. These constitutions showed — and this is easily overlooked — that the lessons of the Napoleonic era had been learned. They became the basic laws of the state, defining the state as unified and indivisible, and defining its objective, abstract, and depersonalised sovereignty within and without. The princes were now incorporated into the state, obliged to abide by its constitution and its laws. A prince was no longer the sovereign owner of his state, but its instrument. He could not make arbitrary decisions about the state and the constitution. State sovereignty took precedence over monarchic sovereignty, and the servants of the princes became servants of the state. The prince became the head of state. His power was actually above that of the constitution, but he became the bearer of the power of the state and was bound to the predetermined purpose of the state, which he could no longer define or change himself. The absolutist, dynastic state was formally replaced by the bureaucratic, monarchic authoritarian state. Certainly, the monarch remained the master of the state's dealings, of the executive and the initiative. He was not a constitutional body like the others, but superior to all. He was the creator of the constitution, not its creation. Thus, the monarch could place himself above the constitution in times of conflict. But it did not come to this *de facto*. Self-restraint won out.

The constitution thus gave the state a new structure. Just as important, and in terms of the future even more important, was, of course, its liberal and constitutional content. The constitution introduced representation of the people — the corporate diet, the *Landtag*, the chambers of parliament — and made legislation and taxation contingent upon the participation of this representation. A dualism of monarchic government and *Landtag* was characteristic of these early constitutions. The new parliamentary representation was modern, inasmuch as every one of its members had a free mandate, as spokesman for the whole people, not as the delegate of a particular group. Nevertheless, these bodies in some cases still retained vestiges of feudalism. A society of state citizens with equal rights beyond the old estate boundaries did not yet really exist.

In view of the social as well as politically strong position of the nobility and the special rights of the mediatised powers, an upper house was inaugurated everywhere. These upper houses were essentially composed of aristocrats, and membership was hereditary, though Baden also elected members. It also included persons nominated by the monarch, among whom were senior civil servants and military personnel, and in some cases representatives of the churches and the universities (the great leader of the liberals in Baden, Karl Rotteck, was for a long time a member of the upper house as the representative of the University of Freiburg). In this way the nobility helped to shape the will of the state, and their old rights and freedoms were carried over into the form of constitutionalism.

The lower chambers also, the real 'houses of commons', were in some cases still assembled according to estate-based principles. In Bavaria, for example, the lower nobility and the clergy constituted an eighth of the members, the cities a quarter, the country a half — the estates were, so to speak, transformed into voting classes. In Baden, the members of parliament represented, in a simple and modern sense, the cities and authorities, the cities taking slight precedence by virtue of a sort of 'constituency' structure. The right to vote was restricted and worked out according to a census, for which the prerequisite was the ownership of land and/or a predetermined level of tax payment. In Baden the civil servants, so-called *Urwähler*, were also correspondingly privileged. Eligibility for political office was indirect: primary voters chose electors, who in turn elected the members of parliament. In Baden and Württemberg, about 15% to 17% of the inhabitants (including women and children) were able to vote, in Bavaria, which had conservative voting rights, only municipal councillors (*Gemeinderäte*) and judges voted, i.e. no more than 6% of the taxpayers.

The parliamentary chambers met very infrequently, but regularly, 'periodically'. Only the monarch could convene them, adjourn the meetings or dissolve them. The chambers helped to shape legislation. Every law — and this meant every regulation concerning freedom or property — required their consent; without this no law could be implemented. This also applied to the authorisation of taxes. On the other hand, the chambers — except in Württemberg — did not have the official right to decide on state expenditure or to draw up the budget, although it was put before them for their information and approval when taxes were being authorised.

The chambers did not have the right to propose laws themselves ('initiation of laws'). However, they had the 'right to petition' and could forward complaints and requests, though these might also relate to legislation or other general political questions. They had no influence over the formation of a government or its continuation in office — this was the exclusive business of the monarch. The constitutions laid down the 'responsibility' of ministers. This meant that acts of the monarch were only possible with the countersignature of a minister, and that the minister was publicly accountable for the actions of the government. Yet, should there be abuses, the chambers were not able to take any action under state law. In some regions there was the opportunity for impeachment of ministers before a state court, but this only applied in the case of violation of the constitution.

Finally, the constitutions included a catalogue of basic rights which guaranteed the freedom of the person, of conscience, of opinion, the freedom to choose an occupation, the freedom of property, and equality before the law. In principle, the individual was accorded a freedom beyond the state, and the basic rights contained the initial signs of a movement to transform the older society of privileges into a society of enfranchised citizens with equal rights. Of course, these were no more than initial signs.

The constitutions were for the most part compromises between the old order and new principles, between the crown and the government on the one hand, and the *Landesvertretung* and *Volksvertretung* (provincial representation and popular representation) on the other, between the nobility and incipient bourgeois society. It was on this basis that the beginnings of constitutional life in Germany developed.

The *Landtage*, above all, the 'popular assemblies' (*Volksvertretungen*) the lower chambers, will be examined first. In spite of the fact that in some cases they were almost estate-based in composition, they were able to develop into genuine representative bodies of the citizens of the *Volk*. It was taken for granted by the bourgeois and peasant voters that its members should be notables, and this was also accepted in principle by the mass of those ineligible to vote. When the masses were allowed to vote in 1848, they still elected notables. Furthermore, the incipient new bourgeois society — anti-feudal and no longer divided into estates — was a hierarchically structured society, and this structure was, for the time being anyway, accepted. The members of parliament came from the educated and property-owning classes, not primarily from industry and commerce, but more likely from rural and trades circles, and from the academically educated civil service. In 1819 in Bavaria 49% of the members of parliament were civil servants (including professors and mayors); in Württemburg between 1833 and 1838 the figure was 50%; in Baden in 1834 the house had 32 civil servants (3 of whom were priests), 22 rural mayors, i.e. farmers or tradesmen with the functions of a civil servant, 3 restaurant owners, 11 businessmen and factory-owners, 3 lawyers, 1 doctor and 1 chemist; in 1846 there were only 24 civil servants, but 9 lawyers.

The civil servants were literate and articulate and could understand the matters discussed in the *Landtage*; they considered themselves to be the 'general estate'. They were in some cases conservative and on the side of the government, but in other cases they were liberal — the real spokesmen of liberalism, in fact. Since an independent and politically educated middle class had only just begun to develop, the representatives had the confidence of broad classes of voters — they were, as it were, predestined to be representatives of the *Volk*. In 'governmental' as well as in 'oppositional' houses the civil servants played an equally significant role. It remained one of the peculiarities of early parliamentarianism in Germany that the servants of the government simultaneously constituted the nucleus of opposition to these governments.

The members of parliament were independent; they were individuals who voted diversely; only slowly did stronger bands of political opinion form themselves, pro-government and opposition — precursors of the later parties. In Württemberg in the 1830s for instance, a loose constituency organisation had begun to form on both sides — but there were still the floaters, the members who voted individually from issue to issue. The chambers remained more of a forum for discussion, in which majorities formed at any one time; staunchly pro-government or liberal chambers, though they certainly existed, were not the norm.

The predominantly aristocratic upper chambers did not simply 'toe the government line'; there were, of course, 'government men', but the strongest voice was the old feudal resistance against the bureaucratic government and its socially levelling tendencies. Should the governments, for example, want to push agrarian reform through the lower chamber, they would frequently encounter opposition from the upper chamber. They contained — as in Württemburg — a strong Catholic opposition to the government, and there were also liberal opposition groups. In Bavaria, for example, especially in the 1830s and 1840s, liberal-conservative *Reichsräte*, who were not subject to pressure to vote with the government, formed a genuine opposition from time to time. But, for the most part, the upper chambers were likely to support the status quo, to take the government's side, or were at least more likely to get in the way of the progressive ambitions of the lower chambers.

The main question was whether and how the constitutional compromise would function, how the relationship between the government and the *Landtag* would work itself out, whether this dualism would lead to a manageable, working partnership or to a delicate equilibrium, whether it would at least lead to a stabilisation between state and society, as the inaugurators of the constitution had hoped, or whether, on the contrary, it would give rise to more and more tensions and conflicts, or even to a stalemate. The question was whether there could finally be a gradual transition to a parliamentary system.

This depended primarily on how the two sides understood their roles and the instruments of power at their disposal. The governments wanted to use the constitutions and chambers to integrate the state and give it financial stability, to pacify their subjects and keep them happy. In this, the representative chambers were to become a sort of assistant body to the state. The centre of gravity of the state was to remain with the monarch and the government. The constitution was an extreme concession, a means of keeping the peace; in principle, the states wanted to give it a restrictive interpretation.

The liberals, on the other hand, wanted to set a process in motion whereby they would have an independent say in political decision-making. They saw themselves as 'partners to a contract' with the governments; they wanted to extend the rights of parliament, give a broader interpretation to the constitution and develop it further. These were opposing positions. The powers the government had at its disposal were strong. It could prorogue a *Landtag* — which anyway only convened at lengthy intervals (in Bavaria every two or three years), and for a few weeks at a time — whenever they wished, or even dissolve it. They could apply the pressure of the state apparatus to influence elections. They could take disciplinary measures against members of parliament whom they did not like — there was no secure form of 'immunity' from this — and they could deny the civil servants under them the necessary leave to attend at the assembly, a practice they could also extend to municipal civil servants. Friedrich List, for example, was refused entry to the house in Württemberg three times, on the last occasion with the chamber's consent, until he was forced into exile. The monarch was the master of the executive — and the government was the central initiator of laws within the state.

Faced with this, the options available to a parliamentary opposition were limited. Its strongest weapon was to reject the taxes — the government depended on them in this respect. Opposition participation in other matters of legislation was of less importance at a time when the government, if it needed to, could get by without new laws or could fall back upon decrees. Impeachment of ministers — since there was no fully worked out constitutional jurisdiction — was a blunt instrument. Nevertheless, parliament was not powerless.

The government wanted, though in a controlled and limited manner, to modernise and integrate, implement laws and balance the books; it wanted to contain public opinion and civil movements, which were gaining in influence, within the structures of the state. It did not want lasting conflicts, but stability, and one section of the senior bureaucracy also wanted reforms. The liberals attempted to abolish feudal structures through compromise with the government, to control the direction of social change and move forward step by step. There was a basis here for some form of agreement. Of course, the constitutions generally proved themselves to be a sort of armistice, within which the fundamental conflicts continued to simmer. But the history of early German parliamentarianism began with successive phases of harsh confrontation, repression and opposition on the one hand, limited co-operation and partial liberal successes on the other. Two examples will illustrate this more clearly.

The first example is provided by Baden, the classic province of early liberalism and constitutional development in its early stages, in which all conflicts were dealt with quite thoroughly and analysed in the process. Already the first meetings of the chambers produced serious conflicts. The liberals strove for the right to initiate laws, which they did not have, by means of petitions. They demanded press freedom and *Grundentlastung*, and also judicial and administrative reform. The government wanted them to draw up an urgently required financial bill, but they did not deliver. They used the right to approve taxes in order to make cutbacks in military expenditure, and this meant also pushing through parliament's right to set a budget. Finally, the *Landtag* demanded that the government revoke a revised aristocratic edict drawn up under pressure from the German Confederation, which they had promulgated six days before parliament had convened. The government promptly sent the *Landtag* packing by 'adjourning' it. The idea which had been bandied about during this dispute of revoking the constitution by a *coup d'état* failed in the end, owing to Metternich's opposition, who regarded such a move as a threat to order and legitimacy. The conflict concerning the nobility ended with a compromise, since the government and the lower chamber had a common interest in limiting the rights of the mediatised princes, and in asserting state sovereignty over the Confederation. The aristocratic edict did not come into force and was replaced by individual agreements which brought the rights of the mediatised princes in the long run — and with compensation — under state control.

Between 1820 and 1822, the government temporarily took a softer line and relaxed the censorship laws. But when the *Landtag* refused funds for the military budget in 1822 — and under constitutional law this meant that they were seeking to extend their right to approve taxes into a full right to set a budget — the government steeled itself for a confrontation. It sought, stretching the bounds of legality to their limits, to reduce the influence of the chambers, and continued to draw up the budget without their consent. The government finally dissolved the *Landtag* and exerted so much pressure during the election that a huge governmental majority was achieved. The period between election and budgets was lengthened; the opposition, under the leadership of the great parliamentarian Johann Adam von Itzstein, took a stronger line and became more radical.

In 1830, Grand Duke Leopold entered the government — a succession to the throne at this time frequently enough had political significance. He left the conservative ministry in 1831, partly under pressure from the movements of 1830, and handed over the Ministry for the Interior to Ludwig Winter, a reformist civil servant, who had been a member of the opposition in the chamber. This was the only instance in the Vormärz of a member of parliament becoming a minister. The elections for the *Landtag* in March 1831 were no longer influenced by the government and produced a strong liberal majority; some form of co-operation between government and parliament seemed to be in the offing. The lengthening of the period between budgets was reversed; a law on *Ablösung* (the redemption of peasant feudal obligations) and a law concerning municipal self-administration were drawn up, and also finally — when the chamber threatened to reject the budget — a press law, which removed censorship completely, at least for the reporting of issues in Baden.

This tore a loophole in the censorship laws of the German Confederation. The liberal Rotteck declared that the Confederation treaty had only been concluded between the princes, and that for the people only the eternal law of common sense and 'the constitution of our land' applied. Finally, the liberal Welcker proposed that the government should work in Frankfurt 'for the organic development of the German Confederation' and the formation of a national representative assembly. The government, however, refused even to discuss this proposal, and the matter was put out for a commitee to stew over. This showed the insurmountable boundaries of such policies. The Bundestag declared the press law to be a violation of the Confederation; the grand duke was pressured to remove it once again by means of a decree. Protests at Freiburg University ended with Rotteck and Welcker being forced into retirement.

The question of extending the constitution of the individual states had come up against the restoration policy of the Confederation. Without an all-German solution, the liberals could make no gains even in the individual states. Freedom was contingent upon unity, and liberal policies could only be carried out at national level, The all-German, national solution to the constitutional problem gained precedence. The same problem also arose in Württemberg. When the majority of the chamber, at the behest of Paul Pfizer, declared the reactionary decrees of the Confederation of June 1832 to be incompatible with the state constitution, the government dissolved the *Landtag*. The government of Baden became conservative once again; even the liberal minister Winter and his successor, the great administrator Nebenius, could do nothing to change this. A split opened up between the liberals in the civil service and the liberals in the chamber. In 1841, the house declared government actions — censorship, police measures, refusal of leave — unconstitutional. The grand duke promptly prorogued the parliament, but the delegates declared this adjournment unconstitutional, whereupon the sovereign dissolved it.

In the election of 1843 the liberals were victorious again. The ministers refused to take part in the negotiations, and the chamber expressed its disapproval in the first example of a vote of no confidence in the history of German parliamentarianism. In terms of constitutional law, this had no significance, but it was of great political significance. All extensions of a parliament's competence, as for example in England, have emerged from such acts and cases of precedence. The Grand Duke of Baden dismissed the leading minister, Baron Friedrich von Blittersdorf, soon afterwards, in 1843. In 1846, following another election victory by the liberals, a moderate liberal official, the Minister for the Interior Johann Baptist Bekk, became leading minister. A tolerable spirit of co-operation now developed between the government and the majority in the chamber; they both clung to one another in the face of politicised Catholicism and the radical democratic left. The possibility now emerged of a continuous extension of constitutional life. However, the uneven path of constitutional history in Baden, and the sobering realisation that liberal civil servants could just as well put non-liberal policies into practice, put this in jeopardy.

Our second example of the development of German parliamentarianism is provided by Bavaria. Here, also, constitutional life began with fierce conflicts. There were legal petitions from the chambers of parliament, cuts in military expenditure as a result of parliament's refusal to approve taxation, and a demand that the army swear an oath of allegiance to the constitution, in order to remove it from the unlimited sovereignty of the monarch. Liberal members of parliament were refused leave of various kinds, but after 1825 the situation appeared to calm down. The new king, Ludwig I, appeared to want a new political situation, one which was more liberally inclined and less dominated by the statist attitudes of enlightened absolutism, a regime which would be more 'popular' (*volkstümlich*) and thus more in tune with the spirit of the times.

Some form of collaboration was in the offing between liberal government officials and the leader of the liberal wing in the chamber, Ignaz von Rudhart, but hopes of this were dashed by the revolution. The king was quick to turn away from his liberal leanings after the shock of the July Revolution and the Hambach Festival of 1832. He now wanted autocratic rule for himself, and the spirit of this rule was to be conservative. An early indication of this was the appointment of the conservative and pro-clerical Edward von Schenk as Minister for Education and the Interior (1828). In 1831, Schenk issued a severe decree of censorship of the press, for which he was heavily attacked in a stormy *Landtag* debate and even threatened with impeachment. Following this, the king dismissed him after a formal period of notice. The decree was reversed. Not in legal, but in political terms it was an instance of parliament bringing about a minister's downfall, another signal for the extension of the constitution and a strengthening of parliament. Even a conservative, like Württemberg's Minister for the Interior, Johannes von Schlayer, said in the 1830s that a minister who did not have the confidence of the chambers of parliament would have to resign sooner or later; his solution was to create a government party.

The Bavarian incident remained an isolated case, however. The liberals did not want any kind of press law, and certainly did not want to enter into any coalition government by way of compromises.The king and his government had just as little interest in the long run in co-operation and concessions. Various conflicts, for example on expenditure cuts, whereby the money saved was then used for the king's many architectural projects, and with regard to military budget, aggravated tensions. After 1837, following the rule of the moderate conservative (or liberal) Prince Oettingen-Wallerstein, the administration of Karl von Abel steered an expressly anti-liberal and Catholic-clerical course. This phase did not end in structural or great political changes; in fact, the dénouement came — and this was characteristic of politics at the time — in the form of an almost accidental series of events. Through his relationship with the dancer Lola Montez, the king got into trouble with the Catholic-conservative circles. He sent the protesting professors into early retirement, and he dismissed the government, but the two succeeding *lolamontane* governments, as they were nicknamed, were unable to continue effective co-operation with the chambers, in view of public outrage over the affair, even among the liberal masses. In early 1848, Bavaria found itself embroiled in a governmental, even a state, crisis.

The outcome of this constitutional development deserves closer scrutiny. The *Landtag* was the forum and academy of German liberalism, in which programmes and critical analyses crystallised and different liberal factions and schools of thought forged their own separate identities. It was through the *Landtag* that liberalism graduated from a mere idea to a political party, and, with the help of the public support it gained there, eventually became a 'popular' movement.

The liberals learned how to be an opposition; they gained experience of conflict. All the important issues converged in the constitutional questions regarding the stature and role of the parliament and government respectively. In this sense, every dispute had something fundamental about it, and every issue took on the dimension of a world problem — despite the small-state arena in which all this was played out.

The incongruity of this situation demonstrates one of the peculiarities of German parliamentary life in its infancy. There is a deeply ingrained tendency towards the doctrinaire, towards the politics of dogmatism in German political culture, and this is especially true of the opposition's role. The liberals interpreted their experience in the light of their theory of dualism, and used this to confirm their sense of themselves. For them, the adversarial relationship between government and popular assembly was the central factor. The liberals held firm to the role they felt was ordained for them, that of an opposition, the defenders of the people's rights, the dissenters holding the government in check. They staked no claim to being the party of government.

As a general rule, the government and the parliament were not players on the same stage, neither had they been able to come to some form of balanced arrangement. The constitutions had not provided the basis for consensus, but for conflict. They had not relaxed the tensions between the bureaucratic, monarchic state and the incipient bourgeois society — they had in fact aggravated them. Restriction and repression by the government and corresponding obstruction from the opposition had become the set postures. Whenever any concrete question regarding legislation or the approval of taxes became a constitutional issue, the constitution proved itself to be a stopgap. The liberal idea of implementing only a moderate form of the constitution — initiation of laws, the right to draw up a budget, the accountability of ministers — and to use this as a platform on which to build a liberal state and a liberal society, with freedom of the press, a free judicial system, self-administration and liberation of the peasants — failed. Constitutional life, after a period almost thirty years, sank into stagnation and disappointment. Even in the constitutional states, the pressure of censorship and police oppression had impeded the development of a free public life. Everyday politics became a catalogue of half-concessions and half-retractions, which had a polarising effect on the opposing camps, each retrenching their positions. Constitutionalism, as the liberals must have seen it, had regressed into a form of sham constitutionalism. Compromises or some form of accommodation with the government did not seem to pay off in the long run; even in the 1840s the moderate claims of the liberals and the defensive policies of the governmental bureaucracy no longer seemed to to be able to find common ground. The result was conflict, stagnation and disappointment, which pleased nobody and prepared the ground, politically speaking, for revolution, not only in Austria and Prussia, but also in the constitutional states, leaving aside for the moment the social unrest.

(d) The Smaller States

Finally, we take a look at the other medium-sized and small states in north and central Germany. The first decisive point to note here is that, in principle, no new or significantly enlarged states came into being. In this sense, the problem of integration, which elsewhere had given momentum to modernising reforms and constitutions, was not an issue here. The four *Freie Städte* (free cities) re-established their estate-based and patrician constitutions. In both Mecklenburgs the old estate-based constitution had survived intact, and they remained the classic territories of Junker rule, providing fuel for sporadic revolutionary anti-feudalism in north Germany, of which Johann Heinrich Voss and Fritz Reuter were the leading spokesmen in German literature.

Saxony remained, like the old Reussian and Anhalt small states, a state with an order of old estates retaining their aristocratic privileges. Even in Hanover, whose king resided far away in London, the nobility held sway, although its regional assemblies were combined in a *Landtag*, and supplemented by representatives of the municipal authorities (*städtische Magistrate*). In 1829, peasants were also granted representational rights. Then there were those states which reverted to an autocratic, bureaucratic absolutism, of which the most significant was the Electorate of Hesse, where the returning Elector, now the archetypal man of the *ancien régime*, reintroduced the old ways and revoked all the measures and reforms implemented in the Franco-Westphalian era. He even took the absolutely illegal measure of annulling the private legal transactions of those who had bought domains, and so in effect dispossessed them.

The case of Holstein is interesting. The knights here defended themselves against the statist, centralist tendencies of the Danish king, such as the abolition of tax privileges, and they fought against the integration of the duchy of Schleswig (which had numerous links with Holstein, and certainly did not belong to the German Confederation) into the Danish state. They demanded a constitution along estate lines. It was an old-fashioned and regionalist constitution, a form of liberty graded according to estates, but it also contained some elements of modern, early-constitutional representation. One reformist section of the knights, for which Fritz Reventlow was the spokesman, wanted to develop the estate-based representative system into a constitutional form. The historian Friedrich Christoph Dahlmann, secretary of the order of knights from 1815, and the *Kieler Blätter* (1815) advanced this idea of reshaping the constitution by force of argument and propaganda. The middle class, originally opposed to the estates, got involved in the large-scale campaign of petitions organised by the constitutional movement. Of course, the Danish king, for the time being at least, would have nothing to do with any constitution, whether on old estate lines or in a more modern form. The appeal by the knights to the German Confederation fell on deaf ears (1823), and the unrest ended for the time being in a status quo.

4. German and European Politics

(a) The German Confederation

At the Congress of Vienna Germany was finally organised into a confederation of sovereign individual states — a German Confederation, in fact. The Act of Confederation (*Bundesakte*) had been agreed upon under the pressure of a deadline, so that much was left to later regulation and reorganisation, which was just how Metternich had wanted it.

Decisions on what political form the Confederation should have were made in the first few years after 1815. Firstly, the Confederation remained a very loose conglomeration of individual states, whose sovereignty was left untouched, so far as this was possible. The Confederation — against the aspirations of the public and of some governments — remained inactive on the most important issues in which it might have become actively involved. No agreements or regulations were drawn up on questions of the economy — trade, transport, the monetary system — nor on questions of law or church policy. The attempt by subjects of the Elector in Hesse to take their case for illegal dispossession to the Confederation, was, after initial hesitation, sharply rebuffed on Metternich's insistence.

On the subject of *landständische Verfassungen*, the Confederation remained for all intents and purposes silent. The Confederation did not become the sort of institution that might have advanced things a stage further, nor did it wish to do so. This was the single great disappointment which the nation experienced. There was no, or scarcely no, agreement even as to what sort of minimal institutional framework this 'Confederation' might require; an arbitration decree for the settling of inter-state disputes was practically the only bill which was enacted. With regard to questions of whether or how the Confederation was to intervene in the internal affairs of the individual states and concerning the organisation in case of war, agreement was only reached in 1821, and this only after much arduous discussion. It was always the sovereignty of the individual states which stood in the way of any regulations across the board.

Then, in the wake of the restoration, the Carlsbad Decrees and the Vienna Final Act (*Wiener Schlussakte*), the Confederation became active as an instrument of all-German policy. At the same time, it also became more unified, or, as the Bavarian minister Maximilian von Lerchenfeld remarked, less like a confederation of states, and more like a federal state. This was paradoxical. For in its attempts to safeguard dynastic legitimacy and territorial sovereignty against the liberal-democratic movement, and to protect the state-confederate order against the nationalist movement, it actually reduced the sovereignty of the member states and strengthened its own hand at the centre. If there was any unity, it was only to be found in the reactionary chorus against the unity of the nation. The Confederation initiated clampdowns, restricted constitutional sovereignty decisively, and claimed the right to intervene and take action against its constituent states if they could (or would) no longer toe the general line.

Of course, the actual power of the Confederation with regard to all these matters remained smaller than Metternich had wished. The various constitutions and different systems within the Confederation remained in place — another of the consequences of federalism. But this was not the point, and this brings us to the second major disappointment of contemporary politics, the fact that the Confederation was nothing more than an instrument of restoration. It was a tool of Metternich's system, of opposition to the liberal and nationalist spirit of the time. The Confederation embodied the federalism of the restoration and the status quo, the federalism of the governments, one which was entirely opposed to the federalism of the nation. Outside establishment circles, the Confederation was totally discredited. The rallying cry of those who were politically active, of the opposition, was *Bundesstaat* (federal state). This became the watchword of hope, the watchword of the future.

In terms of power politics, the Confederation was characterised at first by the dualism of Austria–Prussia, their latent competition and by their actual dual hegemony. Militarily and in terms of foreign policy, the Confederation relied on this dualism for its security and continued existence. This was one of the major reasons why there was no real centre of power within the Confederation. However, it was because this dualism had been muted that it was able to survive. If the Confederation had been more effective as a unit, Prussia would have been provoked into pursuing its ambitions of domination or into attempting to force out Austria. This was why Austria was not interested in strengthening the Confederation, and since Prussia had failed on this count in Vienna, it had abandoned any ambitions of this kind. Prussia was not now bent on strengthening or activating the Confederation; its principal aim was to hold Austria in check. Metternich, on the other hand, wanted the Confederation to provide a buttress against the forces of change. Since Austria had no direct and realistic hegemonic ambitions in Germany, and was content with the loose confederate structure, it was not really in conflict with the medium-sized and small states, whereas Prussia was under constant suspicion of harbouring hegemonic ambitions or of leaning towards a federal state structure.

Metternich saw quite clearly that the compromise between the two major powers was essentially what held the Confederation together and enabled it to function. This suited him perfectly in that no institutional safeguards existed, but were something which had to be negotiated diplomatically at all times, thus allowing him, where necessary, to play off the medium and small states against Prussia. He was thus able to establish his influence on these states. As a general rule, however, everything which happened in the Confederation was subject to prior agreement between Austria and Prussia, and since in Prussia the restoration was also firmly in place, one can speak of a co-operation between the major powers and of their relative unity.

The medium-sized and small states, the 'Third Germany', also attempted to band together as an independent force, in order to counterbalance the prevailing dualism as well as the predominance of the major powers, or even to overcome it. This is called the 'German triad', and until 1866 it played a significant role in the development of Germany. There were clearly different and ultimately conflicting versions of such a triadic idea. There was the federalistic triad, the joining together of the medium-sized and small 'pure German' states into a confederation within the Confederation, in order at least to maintain their relative independence. This idea had been mooted by the publicists Vogt and Murhard, as well as by the Württemberg minister, Karl von Wangenheim.

Then there was the hegemonic triad, a combined grouping of the 'Third Germany' under the leadership of one or two of the strongest medium-sized states. This was then confined, on the basis of various theories regarding the differences between north and south, to Germany south of the Main. The Bavarian publicist Johann Christoph von Aretin had advocated the idea of a Bavarian-led south Germany in 1815 in the magazine *Alemannia*. In 1820, a confidante of the King of Württemberg published a *Manuscript from South Germany* under a pseudonym, which called for the 'pure German' ethnic groups of the south to come together under the leadership of Bavaria and Württemberg.

Liberal circles devised their own constitutional triad idea, according to which south Germany, as the land of liberalism and constitutions, would act as a counterbalance to the two major powers; however, the first initiatory moves along these lines quickly came to nothing. The first substantive versions of this scheme took concrete shape in the policy put forward after about 1817 by the Bavarian Bundestag delegate Johann Adam von Aretin and his equivalent in Württemberg, Wangenheim. They attempted to set the 'Third Germany' on an oppositional course against the hegemonic powers, and to use the federal constitution to bring this about. The defence preparations worked out by Austria and Prussia, which emphasised their pre-eminence, ran aground against this obstacle. The idea was to combine the military forces of the 'Third Germany' in a purely German federal army. A restructuring of the military only came about in 1821–22. The medium-sized and small states provided four of the ten army corps, but there was little unified strategy in any sense.

Any such triadic policy was doomed to fail. Aretin wanted a Bavarian hegemony, Wangenheim a true federation, and attempts at forming a south German customs union, for example, came to grief on this point. When, however, Wangenheim also mobilised opposition against the Mainz commission of inquiry in 1822, the major powers, with backing from the conservative governments, had him dismissed, along with two other delegates, an event referred to as the 'purging' of the Bundestag. Against the background of the restoration, it was futile to try and wage a political campaign against the major powers, to which the majority of all states owed allegiance. The delegates were now strictly obliged to abide by the directives of the governments, and no more triadic policies were put forward in the Confederation until 1848.

For the remainder of the period German politics were based on the majority consensus of the restoration, to which any governments who strayed from the line were shepherded back, by prior agreement between Prussia and Austria. There were numerous rifts in this consensus, principally regarding the customs issue and the Zollverein policy, or in 1830 when an attempt was made to forge a common military policy for Prussia and south Germany, which led to the fall of the Prussian foreign minister Count Bernstorff. On the whole, however, it was a workable co-operation. The dualism — leaving aside the customs issue — was kept under wraps.

(b) The Zollverein

The single outstanding event in all-German politics of these decades was the founding of the German Zollverein. In terms of the development of a German national economy, as well as in the history of the formation of a national state and of the struggle for domination between Prussia and Austria, it marked the beginning of a new era. Economic developments were moving in the direction of a division of labour and an increasing integration of different spheres of the economy; markets were expanding. International competition and the existence of self-contained national economies in France and Great Britain forced the Germans to band together to form their own. Customs boundaries were impediments and made no sense. Economic progress was contingent upon a unified economic territory, which meant a unified system of tariffs, transport and currency. There were also sound economic reasons for moving towards national unity. Friedrich List, who had been a professor in Tübingen as a young man, had been one of the first to campaign for such ideas. But the principal actors in this drama were not looking so far ahead, and they took their cue from another quarter.

At the Congress of Vienna it had been the opposition from Bavaria, anxious about its sovereignty, which had prevented the Confederation from achieving a unified customs policy. The discussions which were proposed ended in stalemate, at first because of the political and economic particularism of the individual states. The separate German territories were in fact at different stages of economic development and were still too heterogeneous.

It was Prussia which made the first moves towards resolving this question. Prussia, because of the separation of its two western provinces from the core territory in the east (and a 7,500-km customs boundary with many enclaves and exclaves), had a vital interest in a larger customs territory. In 1818, Prussia enacted a new customs bill, designed to rationalise the toll system, to integrate the state in terms of customs policy, and to force the enclaves and small states surrounded by Prussia to join the Prussian system. To prevent smuggling, the bill demanded high tolls for cross-border transit, and — something rare until then — it was strictly enforced. Such a rigorous unilateral move on Prussia's part raised eyebrows everywhere, and incited bitterness and protest. It was felt to be particularist. The German Association for Trade and Commerce (Deutscher Handels- und Gewerbeverein), one of the first pan-German assocations, principally of south and central German entrepreneurs under the leadership of its 'consultant' Friedrich List, organised a large-scale petition movement for a common customs union, and took its case to the Confederation and to governments — who were, of course, wary of such democratic and 'inter-state' initiatives.

A series of governments did, however, turn against Prussia's unilateral policy. Since a unified customs policy for the whole of the Confederation was clearly encountering obstacles, the Württemberg Bundestag delegate Wangenheim, who was in contact with

List, devised the plan of a triadic solution to customs policy. This involved the amalgamation of the medium-sized and small states, i.e. the 'pure' German and, for the time being, primarily the south German states. A number of Bavarian politicians also added their voices to this cause. In May 1820, Württemberg, Baden, Bavaria, Hesse–Darmstadt and the majority of the Thuringian states concluded a preliminary customs treaty. But the long negotiations between these states, which lasted from 1820 to 1825, failed, firstly owing to the conflict between the free-trade-orientated Baden and Bavaria, which favoured a protectionist customs policy, and, secondly, because Bavaria in the last analysis did not want a triadic solution which gave equal rights to all, even if this was confined only to customs policy. It wanted either a Bavarian hegemony or the retention of full sovereignty — anything else would have meant an unacceptable loss of power on Bavaria's part. Neither the Confederation nor the south German states seemed to be ready for a common customs policy.

Prussia, in fact, conducted what amounted to a customs war against the Anhalt principalities in 1819–20. This it was forced to end in 1821–22; and, principally with the help of free movement granted to shipping on the Elbe, a huge smuggling zone came into existence — Anhalt imported seven times as much per head as Prussia. However, on the whole, central Germany remained locked in a sort of positional warfare on customs policy, which did not do a great deal for the popularity of Prussia at this time.

Influential Prussian politicians, including the head of German and customs affairs in the foreign ministry, Albrecht Eichhorn, and above all Friedrich von Motz, originally from the Electorate of Hesse, *Oberpräsident* of the province of Saxony and Finance Minister since 1825, drew up far-reaching proposals. They sought in the long term to create a separate confederation with regard to customs policy, at least for north and central Germany, in which Prussia, as the strongest economic power, would naturally be at the head. For Motz, one of the few political thinkers of this time (Heinrich von Treitschke called him a 'statesman in a cabinet of businessmen'), this clearly had wider political implications for the German-speaking territory. He was convinced that the small states were incapable of solving the political problems of the time, and that there-fore, and quite unromantically, Germany needed to join together into a large and strong state. Austria, he felt, was riven internally and too embroiled in European affairs to solve the German question, so Austria should split off from Germany and Prussia should bring it together. Customs unification would then be the first step towards state unification. As Motz put it in 1829, 'If it is a fact of political science that tariffs are only the result of political division between different states, it must also be true that unification of these states in a customs and trading union should likewise lead to a unification within one and the same political system.'

At the same time Motz, like many other liberal reformist civil servants of the res-toration era, was convinced that an economic policy geared to the interests of bourgeois society would in the last analysis make the enactment of a constitution compatible with the interests of the state. Customs policy was also constitution policy. This was, however, only one point of view and was not necessarily shared by everyone. Of more pressing importance to Prussia was the necessity of bringing together the two halves of the state. This particularist interest of Prussia began to find common cause with those forces seeking national economic unity. What was ultimately important in Prussian political circles was that the new economic order would be based on free trade, at least in principle. The state officials were followers of Adam Smith; they believed in the international division of labour, and saw competition as the spur to economic progress. The economy and geography of the country — agrarian exports and the west, central German, and Silesian industrial and trading regions — seemed to provide good conditions for free trade.

At the end of the 1820s Prussia intensified its customs policy. A new customs war forced Anhalt to join its customs territory in 1828, but the Electorate of Hesse and Hanover, which separated the western provinces from the rest of the state, were not to be won over. The strategy of moving forward 'from border to border' ended in a cul-de-sac. The solution to the Prussian problem of integration pointed to the need for a larger all-German framework. Again in 1828, Prussia concluded a customs treaty with Hesse–Darmstadt. In terms of customs policy, this was a 'leap' over the Main boundary, which was intended to encourage the neighbouring states to follow suit. Prussia had guaranteed Hesse extraordinarily favourable conditions financially, and had put its own customs administration at Hesse's disposal, all of which was designed to make the Prussian system attractive.

The non-Prussian states felt threatened. Austria, tied to its own separate economic policy, was clearly in no position to develop its own counter-measures in terms of customs policy, and Metternich could not press forward with all guns blazing against his greatest allies in his restoration policy. But the states most strongly affected, Hanover, the Electorate of Hesse, Nassau, also Saxony, some of the Thuringian states, Brunswick and Bremen, formed a central German commercial union, with the benevolent assistance of France and Austria. High transit tolls on Prussia's west–east trading traffic and the obligation not to join any part of its toll system, marked this union as the product of simple negation. The existence of this union led Prussia and Hesse–Darmstadt, likewise in 1828, to join the newly created system covering Bavaria and Württemberg, even though it had little prospect of expansion or, indeed, any notable success. Prussia succeeded, with the help of its road-building policies, in winning over two of the Thuringian states, thus building a bridge across to south Germany. In 1829 a trade treaty was signed between the Prussian and the south German customs system, which envisaged the abolition of tariffs and the two systems moving closer and closer together.

The central German union fell apart. In 1831, the Electorate of Hesse joined the Prussian system, which meant that Prussia had finally forged the link it had been seeking with the western provinces. In March 1833, the Prussia–Hesse system and the Bavaria–Württemberg system finally joined together to form a joint organisation, for which the name Deutscher Zollverein (German Customs Union) was adopted. Prussia had, in turn, made considerable concessions with regard to the distribution of revenues, which was a significant factor in bringing about the merger. Bavaria, for example, was able to raise its toll revenues by 100%; Prussia, on the other hand, raised them by only 25%. Saxony and the Thuringian states joined shortly afterwards. On New Year's Eve 1834, the toll restrictions were abandoned and the Zollverein came into being. In 1835–36 Baden, Nassau and Frankfurt joined, and in 1841 the agreements were renewed for a further twelve years. By 1842, 28 of the 39 states in the Confederation belonged to the Zollverein. The north German flatland states, Hanover, Brunswick and Oldenburg, collaborated in a 'tax union' organised along similar lines.

The Zollverein was not concluded by the governments out of 'nationalist' interests, nor even for political motives. The guiding factors were particularist, and in good part fiscal interests. But the Zollverein broke through the German system installed by the Congress of Vienna in 1815, of this there is no doubt. Metternich remarked with sharp insight that the Zollverein was 'a state within a state'; it made possible or affirmed the 'preponderance' of Prussia and destabilised the German situation, promoting, as he put it, the 'highly dangerous idea of German unity'. Certainly, the Zollverein did combine the idea of an objective national amalgamation and Prussian hegemony, and was a precursor of the later *kleindeutsch* nation-state. Objectively speaking, the Zollverein would inevitably promote the formation of such a national state. It provided everyone with an alternative model of a workable federation. However, the old idea of the historians, that the Zollverein led inevitably to the foundation of the *kleindeutsches Reich*, is not tenable. Modern experiences with the European Community have taught us differently. Prussia remained, like the medium-sized states and like Austria, a staunch supporter and defender of the state confederate structure of Germany, of the sovereignty of the individual states, and for the time being opposed to all movements seeking a unified national state. This might seem out of place, even contradictory, alongside its commitment to *kleindeutsch* economic unity, but politically speaking this was its major objective.

Since Austria remained outside the union as a strong federal power, the members of the union were apparently always opposed to a merger with Austria. This was what secured its own sovereignty and the confederate state structure of Germany. Even the Zollverein itself was organised along the lines of a confederation of states. The highest body was a congress of delegates, and every member had a right to a veto and the opportunity to walk out, should they wish to do so. Notwithstanding all careful assurances about equality, there was no doubt that Prussia, as the strongest economic power, had a hegemonic position. In the long run, Prussia, by threatening to leave the union, was in a better position to force the others to accede to its wishes than vice versa; however, for the time being the union was not so riven with conflicts.

(c) Germany in Europe

In retrospect, German history in the period from 1815 to 1848 seems to have been dominated by internal developments, and in the arena of foreign policy there was a strange calm, considering that up until then Germany's fate had been so bound up with the shifts of power and allegiance within Europe. On the contrary, in no way were international relations unimportant in these decades. They were responsible for the long-lasting peace and security which the restoration had brought into foreign policy and for the standstill in Austro-Prussian dualism.

As the centres of power slowly shifted, the positions which the two major powers adopted in the struggle to resolve the German question between 1848 and 1866 were inseparable from their international allegiances. Finally, foreign policy became interwoven with internal developments. Foreign policy, the arcane art of governments and diplomats, began to become a matter for the people. In the 1820s the Germans were ardent supporters of the Greek struggle for independence; after 1830–31 German liberals felt likewise about the Poles, to such an extent that sympathy for the Poles was practically a symbol of liberalism. In 1847–48, German liberals supported Swiss liberal democrats in their fight for a separate confederation. Obviously, in

Germany, where nothing much was happening, this provided an outlet for German aspirations for freedom and unity, but it was also an example of the genuine internationalism of the liberal and nationalist movements, a belief in the solidarity of nations in their struggles for freedom. At the same time, and in contrast to this, certain foreign policy issues, like the French insistence on the Rhine frontier in 1840 and Danish endeavours to incorporate Schleswig, aroused great public excitement. These were no longer simply matters for cabinets.

The German Confederation was involved in European politics through the activities of the major European powers, Austria and Prussia, whose influence extended beyond the territory of the Confederation, as well as through the personal ties of German territories with Britain, Denmark and the Netherlands. However, as a Confederation it played no active role in foreign policy, completely forgoing its own diplomacy and alliance policies. Its importance in European terms consisted in the fact that the internal German equilibrium neutralised any possible power ambitions of the Germans. In this sense it contributed to peaceful relations in Europe. The policies of the two German major powers and the interest of Europe as a whole in the stability of central Europe sufficed to secure its existence.

Since Prussia, the weakest of the major European states, followed Austria on most things, active German foreign policy in these decades was the concern of Austria and the policies of Metternich. His policies were guided by three principles. Firstly, there was a strong ideological impulse to preserve the conservative order in Europe and to recreate solidarity between the powers, who were to join forces to combat any possible revolution. Secondly, Austrian policy was directed at stability and equilibruim, seeking to hold ambition in check through collective security. Metternich loved to portray himself in any concrete issue as the doctor of the revolution and as the guarantor of a secure European order. The third factor guiding policy was, of course, Austrian *raison d'état*. Every revolution threatened the existence of this supranational dynastic empire, and every change in the power situation weakened the position of Austria, which as the stabilising influence, despite its structural weakness, laid claim to a disproportional measure of power and was entirely saturated territorially. Metternich's chief aim was to maintain a balance between these objectives, as tensions were always mounting. A few key stages in the development of foreign policy deserve examination.

A peace alliance was formed in 1815 out of the war alliance between the four major powers, which was intended to protect the European order from revolutionary threats and threats of war, especially from France. Regular conferences between the major powers, in which France also took part after 1818, were to guarantee peace and collective security. The predominance and the solidarity of the major powers, of the European Areopagus, were intended to guarantee the peaceful order in Europe.

The true defenders of the status quo in power politics at this time were Austria and England, who sought to prevent Russia achieving a hegemony in Europe, setting their faces against the politics of the Tsar, which were volatile and difficult to interpret. The Tsar apparently aimed at transforming the human sphere in a moral and mystical sense. He seemed to consider himself as the patron of the progressive party and the umpire of Europe. However, this balance of interests could not hold up in the long run, even under the most European-minded of English politicians, the staunchly conservative foreign minister, Castlereagh (until 1822).

England's priority was to maintain the balance of power, and not the restoration or even a conservative legitimacy. It wanted concrete solutions to concrete questions, but did not want to be led into pursuing 'the politics of principle'. It did not want the conferences to become institutionalised, nor did it want any form of league of nations or the major powers taking on a role as some kind of world police force. With regard to the parliament and the public, it did not want governments to pursue policies which were contrary to the will of the people. It wanted to hold in check its opponent on the world stage, Russia, and in this sense it did not set much store by the establishment of solidarity between the major powers. The more the objective of keeping France under control became untenable, the more isolationist the English public became.

Metternich — in the face of Russian predominance — wanted to maintain a community of interests with England, but as a continental and conservative politician, and as a neighbour of Russia, he must have been anxious to restrain the disturbing policies of the Tsar within a realistic conservatism, in a true solidarity of monarchic governments. There was no mistaking that for him the primary long-term objective, in contrast to that of the English, was the fight against the revolution, which was to be uncompromising and organised on an international basis, wherever it reared its head.

Equilibrium and restoration, therefore, were not one and the same thing. For this reason, the large-scale political activity of the European congresses between 1818 and 1822, at Aix-la-Chapelle, Troppau, Laibach and Verona, came to an end. The main issue now was what line the major powers would take with regard to the outbreaks of revolution in southern Europe — in Spain, Portugal and in some of the Italian states. The burning issue was 'intervention'. Should the major powers adopt a collective strategy against the revolution, or should they engage one particular power to do the job for them, or should they give the closest and most interested power free reign to take whatever measures it deemed fit? In 1820, in Troppau, Metternich succeeded in winning over the Tsar to his own strategy and in commiting him to a policy of intervention, though not collective intervention, in which Russia would play its part in, say, Naples or in Spain, in a way which would have been unacceptable to Britain. Thereafter, England's role at the conferences was only that of an observer. In Verona in 1822 it was decided that France should intervene in Spain, but England eventually rejected this policy. The new foreign minister, George Canning, turned his back on the system of Metternich, gave recognition to the revolutionary states of South America, and resolved to do his best to help the bourgeois nationalist movements and the independence of the smaller countries of Europe. These were England's new clientèle.

Then came the eastern question, which was to play a key role in political life in this century, and was to change the course of ideological foreign policy more emphatically than any other issue. In the Danube principalities, the core territories of what would later become Rumania, and in Greece, there was an uprising against Turkish rule. Metternich did not want any reorganisation of the Balkans, because, in his view, this would have shaken the Habsburg empire and extended Russia's influence. Even the non-Christian Sultan, he felt, was protected by the principle of legitimacy. England, fearing a Russian protectorate, placed herself on the side of the Greeks, and switched — in opposition to the restoration — to the liberal policy of intervention. Russia, initially held back by Metternich, switched from the legitimacy policy to a Russian nationalist policy after Nicholas I had succeeded to the throne (1825), and surprisingly joined forces with the western powers in favour of military intervention. Greek independence was thus assured. Metternich's politics of principle came to grief on this issue. Once he had lost the indirect support of Britain, and, in fact, now that he was, at least periodically, at loggerheads with Russia, his informal leadership role in Europe became a thing of the past.

The Paris July Revolution of 1830 unleashed another crisis, one which was to have a great effect on the German powers. Not only had revolution reared its head again in one of the major countries of Europe, but, more significantly, it had sparked off revolutionary unrest across the whole continent. The Belgian revolution gave Belgium independence from the kingdom of the United Netherlands, and there were disturbances in central Italy. In Poland, in the autumn, there was a huge uprising against Tsarist rule. The territorial order of 1815 and the balance of power seemed to be under threat. A planned intervention by the — conservative — eastern powers against the revolution in France was withdrawn once a realistic assessment had been made as to the strength of forces and the risks involved. There was talk for a while of intervention on the side of the Dutch king, since the Belgian question impinged directly on German-Prussian security interests, but England, who did not see an independent Belgium as in any way a threat to her security, opposed any intervention. France threatened to go to war should this occur; Austria, militarily and financially weak, was committed in Italy; Russia was busy dealing with the Polish rising, and the German powers, likewise, were not totally free to act.

The European crises created a log-jam on all sides. The eastern powers could not intervene in the west, nor the western powers in Poland, nor France in Italy. Thoughts of war continued to play a part in negotiations over the independence of Belgium in the winter of 1830–31, when France introduced the idea of compensation from Belgium or of a French pretender to the throne, but this had no hope of succeeding against the united front of England and the eastern powers. As a result, Belgium was founded with help from the German powers. They could do nothing to stop the formation of the new Belgian state, but they were able to prevent the emergence of a French-dominated Belgium or a Belgian republic, and they were also able to put Belgian neutrality on a firm international footing. Metternich's system had suffered a serious defeat, but the defeat had been contained. The final settlement was delayed, however, until 1839, for only then did the Dutch king renounce his opposition. The greater part of Luxemburg which belonged to the Confederation fell to Belgium, and in return the Dutch province of Limburg became part of the German Confederation.

Despite the agreement over Belgium, the conservative eastern powers banded closer together. Prussia had seen the Polish rising as a threat to her own territorial existence, and by deploying an 'observation' corps had cut off the rebels in the Russian part of Poland from any conceivable support, thus helping Russia. In brief, the heirs to the partition of Poland now formed a united bloc to serve their own power interests — that was made clear anew. The old pentarchy was replaced by a new dualism. The three eastern powers stood in opposition to the 'liberal' western powers, even though the common interest in peace and stability kept this opposition under control. In 1833, a new formal agreement was reached between Austria and Russia on what measures to take against the revolution and — this was the burning issue — about the preservation or, if necessary, even the division of Turkey; Prussia went along with the agreement. This represented a strengthening, so to speak, of the Holy Alliance, and Russian power interests were, as it were, shepherded into the fold of the conservative powers of Europe.

A new eastern crisis once again changed the constellation of powers in 1839. Mehemet Ali, the half-sovereign ruler of Egypt, threatened to invade Turkey. He was supported in this by France. England, as well as Russia and Austria, for a variety of reasons, committed themselves to protecting Turkey. Metternich succeeded in bringing about a settlement between England and Russia and committing them to a collective strategy. The four powers forced Egypt to withdraw, and France suffered a heavy diplomatic defeat. This now elicited, as mentioned before, a peculiar and thoroughly modern response from the public. The country had seen its 'national pride' wounded. The government threatened to go to war and started to arm, while at the same time the site of conflict shifted. France demanded the revision of the treaties of 1815 and the Rhine border. The German powers united around a military plan of action, which also included Austria's interests in Italy. But French policy failed. The leading minister, Thiers, had to resign. France had to give in, and even Metternich worked for mediation.

The Turkish crisis was resolved by a new Straits Convention between the major powers. It now emerged that the west and east were not in fact standing face to face as fixed blocs, but that their spheres of interest overlapped. France's prestige policies and economic conflicts led to tensions with England, the balance of power was more important than ideological boundary lines. In the 1840s, the French government, stirred by anxiety about the revolution, moved closer to Austria. The unrest in Galicia and Cracow in 1846 once again cemented the solidarity of the eastern powers.

Metternich never succeeded in either taming the revolution or the egoism of the major powers. He suffered a series of defeats, but managed to contain the damage and remained, until 1848, one of the crucial figures in the European power game. However, the power situation had now changed. Austria's creeping loss of power was clear to anyone who took a closer look. Since it no longer had the safeguard of harmony of interests with England, however indirect these were, its potential independence from Russia grew. Whether the community of conservative interests could keep the lid on the power conflicts which had ensued with regard to the situation in the Balkans and the East became very uncertain after the ferment of the 1820s and 1830s.

5. The Effects of the July Revolution

It was the French July Revolution of 1830 which got things moving in Germany. Certainly, the 'European Revolution' was not a single, unified event, much less a conspiracy, as the conservatives would have had it, but there were shared European features, and similarities between the conflicts. The revolution in Paris immediately became a paradigm, and its events reverberated throughout Europe. It was felt to be an epoch-making event and the expression of a general crisis; it appeared that a stabilisation of the European order through restoration would not hold in the long run. This filled the conservatives with fear and concern, and the liberals with hope and expectation, giving them a new self-confidence, while the protests and uprisings spread. The revolution encompassed part of Italy, Belgium and the Russian-ruled part of Poland, in other words the countries bordering on Germany. Liberal Germans took a great interest in the fate of the Poles, and their initial enthusiasm and later sympathy for them provided the impetus for their own movement.

In particularist Germany, the revolution initially sparked off movements and changes in a succession of individual states. These have their individual histories, but are also interconnected. Basically, they show how the authority of the prevailing system had been brought into question since 1830.

Firstly, constitutional movements had sprung up in some of the pre-constitutional states of northern and central Germany, a second phase of constitutionalisation in Germany. In Brunswick, the young Duke Karl, in a sort of *coup d'état* in 1827, had abolished the estate-based system of participation in government, which had recently been inaugurated by his guardian. Hanover appealed to the Bundestag, but without success. The duke ruled, as the historian Treitschke put it, 'with complete princely irresponsibility', and the aristocracy, officialdom and the bourgeoisie were united in their opposition to him. In September 1830, there were disturbances in the capital, which were mixed, as elsewhere, with elements of social protest by craftsmen, workers and young people. When the duke declined to summon the estates, the castle was set on fire the next day. The duke fled, a citizens' militia maintained law and order, and a committee of the *Landtag* took *de facto* charge of government, declaring the duke unfit to govern; in other words, it deposed him. His attempt to return was thwarted by both the citizens' militia and the regular army, and his brother was named regent.

The revolutionary show of force had come from 'the *Volk*', but the aristocratic-bourgeois establishment, still in its old rut of estate-based resistance to the overthrow of the monarchy, was happy to turn the uprising to its own ends. The conflict ended in 1832, after a corresponding peasant uprising, with a general agreement on a constitution and increased representation of the middle classes and the peasantry, simultaneously heralding the modernisation of the feudal structure of Brunswick society.

Similar events took place in the Electorate of Hesse. Here too, normal opposition was intensified by despotic and absolutist rule and the mishandling of the economy by the sovereign. The Elector, Wilhelm II, also offended the new bourgeois sensibilities by cohabiting with his mistress. In 1830, there were citizens' assemblies in Kassel, Hanau and Fulda which demanded a *Landtag* and formed *Bürgergarden* (civil guards). There were also workers' protests and revolts.

A social protest movement also spread through large parts of the country. The people's rage was directed against the burdens of taxation and feudal duties, bureaucracy, the police regime and corruption. Before the formation of the Zollverein, tariff barriers and customs duties were also causes of unrest, and the customs houses on the border with Hesse–Darmstadt were frequently stormed. The citizenry of Kassel exploited the situation to declare that a constitution was required in order to avert the threat of a 'war waged by the poor against the rich'. The government intervened and convened a *Landtag*. The monarch moved his court to Hanau, on account of his mistress. The *Landtag* demanded that he return to Kassel without the lady in question, and hinted that residence elsewhere would be tantamount to abdication and that he would be stripped of the right to rule. The heir to the throne was designated co-regent and instructed to govern.

In 1831, the government agreed upon a constitution with the *Landtag*. Sylvester Jordan, a liberal lecturer in constitutional law, played a prominent role in drafting it. It was the most liberal constitution of its day. It laid down a unicameral parliamentary system with a middle-class and peasant majority, relatively democratic voting rights, an obligation on civil servants and the army to swear an oath to the constitution and on the monarch to give a similar pledge, and the right of the chamber to initiate legislation, to decide on the budget, to endorse 'emergency decrees' and to impeach ministers. It guaranteed basic rights, a judicial constitution, the rights of officials, and even of the *Bürgergarde*. At the same time, of course, the constitution was dualistic in the traditional sense. The monarch retained control of the executive, and it was for him to convene the *Landtag* and to dissolve it.

In Saxony too, where an old feudal system continued to limp along incompetently, there were disturbances in the summer of 1830. Both Lutheran and anti-Catholic elements were instrumental in the unrest, and social tensions and craftsmen's and workers' protests against factories and factory-owners, the police and the ossified municipal administration, which extended from the cities right down to the textile villages also played a part.

The established bourgeoisie allied itself with this movement, formed civil guards and demanded a reform of the old-fashioned estate-based system. This was also desired by a section of the high-ranking civil service. The despised ministry was replaced by a reformist ministry under Bernhard von Lindenau. Under pressure from new disturbances in 1831, the government managed with difficulty to get the old estate-based *Landtag* to assent to a constitution. This constitution was more conservative than that of the Electorate of Hesse, a compromise between the estate-based and the representative types. The aristocracy retained a strong position in both the upper and lower houses. In addition to cities and villages, industry too had a special position in the lower house; the government position was strong, and budgets and legislation which had been approved by the king and the upper house could only be overturned by the lower house with a two-thirds majority. But, overall, state and society underwent a moderately progressive reform from then on, as in the case of municipal and local government. In 1832, the *Ablösung* (redemption) of peasant obligations on the land began with the help of a state bank, and in 1843 tax exemption for the nobility was abolished.

Finally, there was the case of Hanover. Here, protest was directed not against the king, who ruled in London, but against the old estate-based feudal system which was in complete command, and against the chief minister, Count Münster. Disturbances and uprisings took place in south Hanover in the winter of 1830–31. In Göttingen the rebels, led by three *Privatdozenten* (lecturers), took power in January, before the uprising was quelled by the military. It took half the armed forces of the entire territory to accomplish this. Despite its victory, the government attempted to reach a compromise. Münster was dismissed, and negotiations were initiated with the *Landtag*, which now contained more liberals from the cities., on the subject of a constitution. The constitution arrived in 1833, though relics of the old estate-based system were retained. Taxes were reduced, and above all the *Ablösung* of the peasants was finally set in motion (1831–32), thanks primarily to Johann Stüve, an Osnabrück liberal of the old school.

With the entry of these four states into the circle of constitutional states, the arena of public political life in Germany was expanded. The national communications network also grew tighter.

In south Germany, the July Revolution initially intensified liberal opposition and its struggle to establish constitutions in the individual states. Although public disturbances only took place in Upper Hesse, being directed against taxation, tariffs, and feudalism, opposition grew more vehement everywhere, and was ever more clearly manifested in elections and petition movements. In Baden and Bavaria, the liberals formed a majority in the lower house, and were able, as already described, to force through important liberal demands. The police system was relaxed for the time being, and a great deal of change seemed under way. Then the governments stepped in with severe counter-measures, and liberal policies everywhere ran aground on the recalcitrant structure of the German Confederation, with the opposition between government and houses of parliament growing harsher. The dissolution and prorogation of *Landtage* was back in fashion, and in Nassau the opposition walked out after the budget was passed.

Another phenomenon, one which was new and more important in the long run, was extra-parliamentary opposition across the boundaries of the individual states. This extended from the *Burschenschaften* and particularly their radical wing, *Germania*, and the secret, revolutionary *Burschenschaft* congresses of 1831–32, through extensive journalistic activity to a general popular and middle-class movement of liberal-nationalist protest. A multitude of events was organised. These included collections of addresses and signatures, 'banquets' with local representatives, orations and toasts, a multitude of festivals, revolutionary, press and Polish festivals, all with a latent tendency to civil disobedience and general rebelliousness. The participants extended from the intellectual *avant-garde* to the wine- and beer-drinking and occasionally philistine alehouse politicians and anti-government polemicists. There were Polish festivals in Munich in December 1830, in which the 'Marseillaise' was sung and which ended in clashes with the military. The tone became more radical. In addition to calls for basic rights and participation in government, there were more emphatic demands for democracy and popular sovereignty, and there was opposition to the princes and particularist states. The rebels did not demand reform in the spirit of existing constitutions and the transformation of the prevailing state of affairs, instead their objective was a genuine new order. They wanted to move forward not by compromise, but by pressure from the people and direct action. The whole movement had broad grassroots support from both the petty bourgeoisie and the peasants, and from the lower orders in general.

The whole movement initially came to a climax in 1832 in the Hambach festival. Two journalists, Johann Wirth from Munich and Philipp Siebenpfeiffer from the Palatinate, who were acquainted with censorship from bitter experience, began a press campaign against the princes and governments in Germany and specifically in the Palatinate. Here French law, a liberal judiciary and hitherto less stringent censorship laws offered more protection.

The delegates to the Palatinate assembly, such as the lawyer Friedrich Schüler, were to a man more radical than the 'customary' parliamentary opposition. In February 1832, they founded the *Vaterlandsverein* (Society of the Fatherland) in support of a free press, which was soon renamed the *Press- und Vaterlandsverein* (Press and Fatherland Society). It rapidly built up a network of 116 branches with 5,000 members, extending from south-western to southern and central Germany, ignoring state boundaries. It formed the prototype of a political party, which aimed at mobilising the power of the intellect and of public opinion against the power of the princes, for the 'rebirth of Germany' and its democratic reorganisation. By March, this society, together with the journals of its main founders, *Westbote* and *Deutsche Tribüne*, was already banned, but the campaign continued with increased publicity.

In April, people were invited to attend a great 'peace-loving, beautiful' festival in the ruins of Hambach Castle near Neustadt (Wirth referred to it as a 'national German festival') 'to fight to shake off the shackles of internal and external power'. The Palatinate district government finally allowed the festival to take place. On 27 May 20,000–30,000 people assembled, making it the largest mass event in Germany before 1848. The participants came primarily from the Palatinate, where the crisis caused by a poor harvest, famine and tariff disputes played an important part for craftsmen and peasants, who carried a black flag with the inscription 'Wine-growers must mourn' — with others from Hesse, Frankfurt, Baden, and a few from the Prussian Rhine province and other territories. There were around 300 members of the *Burschenschaft* movement, predominantly from Heidelberg. Poles and Frenchmen also attended.

The festival began with a ceremonial procession in which the black, red and gold banner of the *Burschenschaft* movement featured prominently. There were about twenty speeches. Siebenpfeiffer called for a celebration of the day when 'the princes exchange the colourful ermine of feudal rule for the manly toga of German national dignity, when German women are no more the dutiful maidservants of their male masters, but free female comrades of free citizens, who let their sons and daughters drink of the milk of freedom before they can properly speak, when young German maidens see the most worthy youth as he in whose breast most powerfully beats the love of the Fatherland, where the civil servant and the warrior no longer decorate themselves with the insignia of master and lord, but with their national costume, the day when a common German fatherland will arise that greets all its sons as citizens'.

Such was the democratic pathos of the period. But it must be made clear that the festival was, for the time in which it was held, an 'act of political representation' (Ernst Rudolf Huber), as distinct from debate or conspiracy. The idea and the movement were emerging into the open, and thus becoming a public force. The tone of the festival was one of national democracy, no longer *Teutsch*, or *Ur*-German, as in 1817, but western and enlightened. It advocated rule by the people as opposed to monarchism, and it repudiated any half-measures. As Wirth put it, 'There will be no salvation for the Fatherland until the princes are toppled.' The goal was a 'United Free States of Germany'. The festival supporters distanced themselves from liberalism and from the *juste milieu* of moderation. The existing constitutions were considered inadequate to protect the rights of the people, hence the cry 'Down with the constitution and pseudo-constitutions'. Revolution was only one step away: 'If the free press is annihilated, laws flouted and all human development stunted, then there is no longer any choice . . . then the fight is one of self-defence, in which all means are justified, and the most incisive are the best, for they bring a just cause most quickly to its end.' Or there was talk of a 'lawful revolution'. An indivisible component of this liberal-republican ideal was the demand for a national state and a confederation of nations. In the event of a threat from France, Wirth called for the cause of unity to take precedence provisionally over freedom, while Karl-Heinz Brüggemann hinted at the possibility that Alsace might become

German and Wallonia French, but there was a general belief in the international solidarity of liberated nations, in a nationalist 'International'.

On the following day, 500 'loyalists' were chosen to discuss what measures should be taken against 'the tyranny of the national assembly'. The proposal that they should become a permanent fixture, in other words a revolutionary committee, was rejected. They had no competency to elect representatives of the nation. The jibe of the radicals, to the effect that the revolution in Germany foundered on the question of competence, is a cheap one. The attitude of the 'loyalists' was realistic and showed a loyalty to the democratic rule of law, which had brought them together in the first place. Despite the radical rhetoric, the majority of festival-goers and speakers were not revolutionary; nobody had a political strategy, and the 'critical mass' for revolution had not yet been reached. This was more of a radical-liberal protest than the start of a revolution.

The Hambach festival was followed by a whole sequence of other, smaller festivals from Baden right down to Franconia and the Electorate of Hesse. There was a mini-revolution in the Coburg enclave of Lichtenberg, on the Middle Rhine, during the planting of a 'freedom tree', which was put down by Prussian troops. But the leading liberals from Karl Rotteck to Heinrich von Gagern distanced themselves from this whole movement. 'None of the excellent popular representatives could be heard above the furious clamour of the demagogues', to quote a newspaper controlled by Rotteck.

The reaction of the regimes was direct and decisive. The Bavarian government attempted to 'pacify' the Palatinate and punish the initiators by means of internment (the so-called *Strafbayern*), and by declaring a temporary state of emergency. Most of the participants were able to escape, however.

The reaction of the German Confederation was more important. Metternich did not want to let this opportunity slip through his hands: 'Properly used, this festival might become a festival for the good.' He also felt that in order to maintain order, every means available to the state must be used against the whole movement, against freedom of the press, of association and of public assembly, and that liberal constitutional tendencies must also be curbed. The Prussian government was in full agreement with this line, and the governments of the constitutional states, unsettled by the quasi-revolutionary tendencies, had to go along with it.

A federal law of 5 July 1832 increased censorship and again prohibited all political societies (or those under another name which served political purposes), assemblies, festivals and speeches. In short, it cemented the unconditional ban on the restoration on political parties and public political activity. The individual states followed suit with bans of their own. Baden had to withdraw its liberal press legislation, though in practice the degree of repression varied.

Another law, the Six Articles of 28 June 1832, was just as significant. The Confederation did not interfere, as originally planned, with the constitutional sovereignty of the individual territories, but it supplied a standard 'interpretation' of the constitution within the framework of the basic laws of the Confederation. Petitions from *Landtage* which were in breach of the 'monarchical principle' were forbidden. So was rejection of a budget if it were necessary for the performance of the 'federal duties' of a government. Acceptance of the budget on condition that some other concessions be granted was deemed to constitute a refusal. Freedom of speech in the parliaments and the freedom to report on them were restricted. A judicial interpretation of the federal constitution was ruled out; a commission was to supervise parliaments in future.

The governments retained a powerful weapon to use against the parliaments, in that they could define what was 'incompatible with federal law'. Constitutional progress in a particular territory was henceforth blocked by the Confederation; for the liberal movement, this meant that change and progress were only possible on a national level, and only by means of a new all-German constitution. The only road to freedom was through national unity.

Of course, the unrest could not be quelled that easily. In 1833 there were fresh demonstrations in the Palatinate on the anniversary of the Hambach festival, and shortly afterwards Siebenpfeiffer and Wirth had an opportunity to expand at length on their political ideas before a jury and distribute pamphlets. They were, in fact, pronounced not guilty, to the delight of the opposition. The jury had shown itself to be a bastion of freedom. On 3 April 1833, a small group of revolutionaries, predominantly intellectuals, attempted to take control of the city of Frankfurt by surprise (this became known as the 'storming of the guards in Frankfurt'). They wanted to give the signal for a broad-based popular uprising, occupy the Bundestag building, arrest the delegates and establish a central revolutionary power. They succeeded in capturing the guard positions, but the whole operation foundered, and not merely because it had been poorly prepared and its intentions revealed too early. The people of Frankfurt remained curious but calm; not even the released prisoners took advantage of their freedom. The revolutionaries lacked the ultimate coup; revolution as the conspiracy of a handful of the initiated did not work. Frankfurt was not Paris, nor was it the centre of political power in Germany.

The Confederation reacted with new and even more severe counter-measures. A new central authority for political investigations was set up. By 1842 it had conducted 2,000 investigations, drawn up a list of suspects and refugees, and had compiled reports on underground activities. Prussia took an especially hard line against the *Burschen-schaften*, membership of which was considered high treason. For such treasonable activities, the state imposed 39 death sentences and 165 life or lengthy prison sentences. These were meant as a deterrent, and the punishments were later moderated by amnesties, but it was a hard fate to bear for some of the politically active youth. Even Fritz Reuter, whom one could hardly call a radical, reported on it in *Ut mine Festung-stid* (Low German for 'During my time at the fortress').

The shock effect of these measures can easily be imagined. The attempt by the German major powers to restrict the constitutions even further failed this time owing to resistance from the constitutional states. The so-called Sixty Articles of June 1834 remained secret. They did not constitute a federal law, but they did bind the governments to abide by them. On questions of the right to draw up a budget, on refusal to approve taxation, the granting of leave to civil servants, supervision of the universities and on censorship (they wanted to get away from positions 'blackened' by censorship, which had had such a provocative effect) there was once again unanimous backing for a quite severe course of restrictions and suppression. However, suppression of public opinion and the muzzling of the *Landtage* could not be carried out in the long run given the pluralistic order of German states, especially after 1840.

A final flurry of south-west German unrest broke out in Hesse. This was associated with the name of Georg Büchner. Büchner, a medical student, had founded a 'Society for Human Rights' in 1833 in Giessen, the traditional home of the radical *Bursch-enschaft* and of the Giessen 'Blacks' of 1817–19. In 1834, together with the clergyman Friedrich Ludwig Weidig, he wrote the *Hessischer Landbote* (The Hessian Courier), which was distributed as a pamphlet in two editions. This was the first great manifesto of social revolution. In 1833 he had said: 'If there is anything which will assist us in these times, it is force. Young people are reproached for their use of force, but do we not find ourselves in an eternal state of violence?'

The pamphlet was directed against exploitation by the princes — described as traitors, greedy torturers of human beings and slave-drivers — and against the aristocrats, the governments and their tyranny. It also railed against bourgeois-liberal moderation and its ideals of legality. *Landtage* and constitutions were described as futile and contemptuous, nothing but façades. 'What are our electoral laws? Nothing but violations of the civil and human rights of the majority of Germans.' It called for Germany to rise up as a 'free state of the people', as a republic, for social emancipation and true equality. There were appeals to the poor and to the lower classes, especially in the countryside: 'Peace to the hovels! War on the palaces!' This was the new slogan and the new social dividing-line, which must have been a source of unending consternation to those of the bourgeoisie and peasants who had neither hovels nor palaces, but homes. All of this was supported by statistical data about the unjust distribution of levies, and the whole was formulated in a powerful, biblical-sounding language. A network of conspirators, lecturers, students, academics and craftsmen from Marburg, Giessen and Frankfurt were the purveyors of such revolutionary propaganda, but in April 1835 their cover was blown by the police. Some of the leading figures, like Büchner, were able to flee; others, like Weidig, were arrested. During the long interrogations in prison the latter took his own life, thereby becoming a martyr of the popular opposition.

Part of the great radical-liberal protest wave of the 1830s was a new direction in literature. A significant part of literary output became political, turning its back on the domination of aesthetics. These writers were not interested in the timeless quality of literature, nor in introspection; they wanted a literature that was tendentious and critical, receptive to the *Zeitgeist*, progressive and dedicated to emancipation. The novel, travel writing, essays, and even drama were all infused with this new spirit.

Ludwig Börne and Heinrich Heine were the pioneers of this new mode of writing. After they had moved to Paris following the July Revolution, though thoroughly hostile to one another's work, they launched increasingly vehement attacks on the political and social, the ecclesiastical and intellectual environment in Germany, attacking it for its 'backwardness'. Heine above all had a great effect. He was a brilliant, sharp-sighted, ironic, witty, world-weary, an ambivalent and unpredictable writer, a republican emancipator, railing against the monarchy and nobility, the church and particularism, liberals and the *haute bourgeoisie*, the lower middle class and philistines. He had an almost desperate love-hate relationship with Germany and his fellow Germans. In 1834, a group of young writers emerged who took Heine as their model and were soon referred to as the 'Junges Deutschland' (Young Germany). They were Ludolf Wienbarg, Karl Gutzkow (*Wally the Doubter*), Heinrich Laube (*The Young Europe*) and Theodor Mundt. They were full of the emotions of youth, and flouted tradition and convention, religion and church-inspired morality. They championed the emancipation of women and the hedonistic 'emancipation of the flesh'. They stressed material needs, a Bohemian, unbounded subjectivity, and were fervent supporters of the Enlightenment. They took great pleasure in provoking the ruling powers and flouting custom and tradition. In December 1835, the Bundestag banned the writings of *Junges Deutschland* on charges of blasphemy and immorality, even including Heine.

The literary and political significance of these writers has frequently been overestimated both then and later. They were too full of theory, confused and selfish, and not serious enough, as Friedrich Engels remarked, and the group soon fell apart. Nevertheless, it had a mobilising and politicising influence on the reading public and on public opinion, and, in a metapolitical sense, it had intensified critical reflection on the prevailing conditions, as the Young Hegelian critique of Christianity did in the late 1830s.

Heine and Börne were the first true political émigrés, before the disturbances and clampdowns of the 1830s drove political refugees abroad. In exile, centres of the radical liberal movement were formed whose influence was broadcast back to the homeland. The genuine political émigrés, writers and intellectuals, were accompanied by journeyman craftsmen and trainee salesmen, for whom a period spent abroad was, so to speak, customary. In the 1830s and 1840s they became politicised. Convivial German associations grew into political organisations, incipient political cells. A brief look at this phenomenon will suffice here.

In Paris a German People's Association (*Volksverein*) was formed, initially as a branch of the Fatherland Association (*Vaterlandsverein*). In 1834, this gave rise to the 'League of Outlaws' (*Bund der Geächteten*). In Switzerland, a section of Mazzini's Secret Society of Young Europe (*Geheimbund des Jungen Europa*) was formed, consisting principally of craftsman's associations and *Burschenschaften*, and calling itself *Junges Deutschland* (not to be confused with the aforementioned group of writers). Some of its supporters had to flee to Paris, where they contributed to the split within the 'League of Outlaws', and the formation of the 'League of the Just', from which the first socialist organisations then developed. Brussels and London also played a part in this, and the names of 390 activists were known to the investigating authorities in Frankfurt alone. Emigration at that time was an international phenomenon, and for this reason German émigrés were determinedly internationalist. The majority of them were democratic and egalitarian — radicals, in fact — so it was not surprising that here in the advanced industrial nations, and under the influence of western European radicalism, socialism took its first steps. The émigrés had left, but they maintained very close ties with Germany through personal contacts and journalism. The police and governments, to their great chagrin, had a very hard time of it keeping watch on their activities in Germany.

When one considers this phase of development as a whole, it remains a quite astonishing phenomenon that Prussia, and likewise Austria, remained almost unaffected by the upheavals of the July Revolution, although Prussia came face to face with the Belgian revolution at the Rhine and the Polish revolution in Posen. There was no new large-scale outcry for a constitution, nor any mass social protest movement; a few disturbances by craftsmen and workers, in Aix-la-Chapelle or Berlin for example, were swiftly contained. The authoritarian leadership in Prussia was able to hold true to its maxim of the 'limited *Untertanen* (subjects) mentality' in practice. It was, in fact, a quite different conflict, old-fashioned and modern at the same time, namely the conflict between church and state (described elsewhere), which really shook the rafters in Prussia.

In this decade, a staunchly reactionary movement as regards constitutional policy began to assert itself in two individual states — in those very states, in fact, which had gone over to the constitutional system after 1830. This had repercussions throughout the whole of Germany.

The first of these was the Electorate of Hesse, which became a territory permanently plagued by constitutional conflicts. For one thing, the new regent was no less reactionary and despotic than his father; a misalliance and family conflicts fuelled the disdain of the bourgeois world. Secondly, it was precisely the constitution, so advanced in its liberalism, which, because it held firm to the dualistic system, aggravated the conflicts. In May 1832 Ludwig Hassenpflug took over the reigns of the government in Hesse; he was the brother-in-law of the brothers Grimm, staunchly state-conservative and anti-parliamentarian, and he was possessed of a quite autocratic self-confidence. He was religiously orthodox and anti-liberal to boot and became one of the most hated figures of the reactionary camp.

When the government enacted federal law in the form of the Six Articles after the Hambach festival, the spokesman for the Liberals, Sylvester Jordan, called for the right to impeach ministers. The monarch dissolved the *Landtag*, and the committee of representatives from the estates, who were to take over in this instance, got rid of Hassenpflug, saying that he had remained in his position without the express directive of the *Landtag*. This was not against the letter of the constitution, but it was certainly against its spirit. The government attempted to refuse Jordan permission to carry out his duties as a member of the assembly with the help of the code for officials (*Beamtenrecht*); the *Landtag* was dissolved several more times, and the ministerial prosecution hearing ended with the acquittal of Hassenpflug. The rights of the parliament which were guaranteed in the constitution against the issuing of decrees by the government could not be invoked, because no time limits or procedures had been laid down, which might have tied the hands of an indignant government. The regent did, in fact, dismiss the self-confident Hassenpflug in 1837, and for a time a *modus vivendi* seemed to emerge, but the government remained reactionary and was forever in dispute, whether latent or actual, with the house. The sense of 'rights' having been violated became deeply engrained in the consciousness of the liberals of the Vormärz through their experiences during the constitutional battles in the Electorate of Hesse.

The other state to experience a reactionary movement was Hanover. In 1837, the union with England came to an end because of the varied line of succession. Ernst August, Duke of Cumberland, a staunch High Tory, became King of Hanover. In 1833, he enforced a rule with regard to the constitution that it should be subject to the consent of all heirs to the throne, as it was at the time of the entailed estate and in pre-absolutist times, and he wanted to give back to the dynasty the domains which had been taken into state ownership. At his coronation he refused to swear the oath to the constitution, prorogued the *Landtag*, and on the 1 November declared the constitution invalid. This was a royal *coup d'état*. The oath that civil servants had sworn to the constitution he declared void.

On 18 November, seven professors from Göttingen University — Jacob and Wilhelm Grimm, Dahlmann, Gervinus, Ewald, Albrecht and Weber — declared that they were sticking by their oath as civil servants and that they would not take part in any elections or other activities which were against what they saw as a valid constitution. No corresponding declaration came from the universities as a whole; some professors, and not only the conservatives and opportunists amongst them, claimed that their *Wissenschaft* (science, scholarship) gave them the right to make constitutional judgments; they wanted to draw a strict line between *Wissenschaft* and politics. The Göttingen Seven, however, insisted on the intrinsic link between truth and justice.

The issue became public knowledge more or less immediately. The seven protestors were dismissed from their chairs without notice, and three of them were exiled. All this evoked an unprecedentedly massive response from broad sections of the German-speaking public. It was experienced as a national issue. The seven became the martyrs and heroes of liberalism. In one fell swoop, so to speak, the professors were having their finest hour on the political stage, and this time the audience was the German public. Through constant airing in the Frankfurt National Assembly, this issue was to dominate the ensuing decades. For the first time resistance had not come from radicals, writers, the youth or the 'little people', but from a pillar of the bourgeois establishment.

Dahlmann stated the liberal case in his apologia. In 1831, he had sharply rebuked the Göttingen revolution, saying that people should not be judged by their motives, no matter how worthy, but by the means they use to achieve these ends — and only lawful means, not force, could justify ends. But now things had changed. This was not a case of a revolution fought in the name of natural law or popular sovereignty, but resistance against a *coup d'état*, taken up in the name of the law. It was a 'protest of conscience'. In the opinion of Ernst Rudolf Huber, the Göttingen Seven were not revolutionaries opposing the state, but 'defenders of the true state against monarchic caprice'. 'When I take up the weapons of the law to combat the whims of the mortal king in contravention of existing laws, I am fighting for the immortal king, namely the will of the government practised in accordance with the law.' This strain of reformist liberalism in defence of the state under the rule of law (*Rechtsstaat*) was what gave even the moderate and often apolitical academics the clear guideline they needed to stand up and fight.

The Hanoverian opposition appealed to the Confederation against the *coup d'état*. Even constitutional states, like Baden and Bavaria, called upon it to intervene, but the majority were persuaded by Metternich to reject this course. The Confederation had thus *de facto* sanctioned the *coup d'état*. In 1840, in Hanover a new constitution was enacted, which this time restricted the powers of the parliament and abolished the principle of ministerial accountability, but it was less reactionary than one might have expected after the events of 1837 and considering the king's political persuasion. This was most likely due to the wave of public protest.

6. The Formation and Restructuring of the German Political Parties

The year 1840 may be taken as a convenient historical milestone marking the approximate time of formation of the modern German political parties. Political ideas gave birth to political movements, free groups of people sharing a particular political belief, within an emerging politicised public, whose activities were centred around political institutions, *Landtage* and elections, and who, in rudimentary form at least, had an overall conception of how they wanted state and society to be.

The old opposition between the forces of change and preservation, which had been in place since the revolution, expanded into a five-party system, which would then shape German history for the next hundred years. It consisted of Conservatives, Catholics, Liberals, Democrats and Socialists. It is astounding that all this came to pass during the new phase of repression in the German Confederation of the 1830s. But the emergence of a political public and the wide spectrum of views within it could not be held back. Censorship, as we have already indicated, was not absolute, even though authors, publishers and booksellers felt intimidated and their existence threatened, and even though it did prevent a climate of freedom from emerging.

The same happened to the bans on associations and assemblies. German pluralism, the fact of emigration and the contacts across national boundaries, the flourishing 'surrogate public' of science, universities, art and literature, of apolitical journalism and the church had all managed to survive under the proto-totalitarian system of the restoration. The communications network grew tighter, and there was a massive growth in publishing. Literature remained political and critical of the contemporary milieu. In the 1840s a great wave of political poetry was written, which was also popular and had a broad impact. It was liberal, nationalist, radical and critical of society, a new force of primarily oppositional politicisation. There was a form of crypto-politics everywhere, which frequently turned into real politics. In short, the public sphere grew larger and larger, and the public was growing ever more political, though the threat of new clamp-downs and bans was ever-present. People were arrested every day; the left retreated underground or fled into exile; and there was never an atmosphere of free public discussion.

This was the climate in which the political parties formed. It was typical of these times that parties forged their identity through magazines, newspapers and compilations. The *Berlin Political Weekly* of the High Conservatives (1831–41) and the *Historical and Political Magazine* of the state-conservative Leopold Ranke (1832–36), the *Historical and Political Journal* (after 1838) of the Catholics, the *Halle Almanacs* (1838–43), and the *Rheinische Zeitung* as the organ of radicalism joined the numerous liberal publications, of which we need only mention once again the *Staatslexikon* (1834–43) by Karl Rotteck and Karl Theodor Welcker, which can accurately be said to have contributed to the formation of a political party.

There is another surprising aspect to the formation of the parties. In German tradition, party politics and the party system had a somewhat negative connotation. The parties were something apart which pursued their own separatist interests, not the interest of the common weal. If the Liberals basically identified themselves with the people, they also directed themselves against other parties, the pro-government parties, the clericals and the demagogues. In 1842, Georg Herwegh, in a famous poetic feud with Ferdinand Freiligrath, sang the praises of the party, but what he was referring to was partisanship, engaging oneself in the cause of freedom and progress, the party of the future against that of the past, the party which would eventually represent the whole of the people. But as early as 1830 Baron vom Stein had considered the 'splitting up into parties' as better than the division of society into estates, and Heinrich von Gagern declared in 1837 that 'party rule' was an essential feature of a free society. In the 1840s, parties and the party system became the subject of political theory, difficult though it was for the Liberals to recognise the pluralism of parties. The German parties were not private coteries, not simply interest groups, nor mere participants in the battle for power, for they hardly had any share in power, and as yet they were not 'organised'. They saw themselves as parties of ideas, representing a particular world-view or belief, and this is what they were. Underlying them was a metapolitical philosophy, a secular theology. This was the legacy of the university and the faculties within it, philosophy and theology, and the legacy of German pluralism. It was a consequence of the special role played by the educated classes in German society at this stage, and the fact that they had avoided taking on any substantial political reponsibility. This formative phase of the German parties had long-lasting repercussions for German history. The political profession of faith remained a characteristically German phenomenon. The parties tended towards doctrinaire views, and political conflicts were easily prone to turn into fights about fundamental convictions.

The emergence of a party system changed the relationship between state and society. The Liberal picture — of the state and the Conservatives on the one side, society and the Liberals on the other — became blurred. Instead, there was now a plurality of ideas and interests within society. Parties became intermediary organs between society and state; they articulated the views and the will of forces within society, and sought to make them count.

One should not allow oneself to be deceived. In the context of the 1830s there has been considerable mention of radical movements, for these were new. But they were in no sense the predominant socio-political force. On the 'right', as one began to refer to it, of the German party system, stood the Conservatives. Mention has already been made of the authoritarian-statist and bureaucratic Conservatives, and about the romantic, estate-orientated wing, about their fight against liberal individualism and the omnipotent state, against bureaucracy and absolutism, as well as democracy and the constitution, against emancipatory freedom and levelling equality. This form of, primarily Prussian, High Conservatism was now transformed and modernised by the right-wing philosopher Friedrich Julius Stahl. Any self-respecting party in Germany needed its philosopher, and the Conservatives were no exception.

Stahl, a baptised Jew from Bavaria, formerly a member of a *Burschenschaft*, and a pupil of Schelling, was called to Berlin in 1840 to plough back the 'seeds of discord' sown by Hegelian philosophy. This little man with an intellectual disposition, a thinker of high stature, became the spiritual leader of the Prussian Junkers, one of the semi-official theoreticians of the Prussian state, and for a time an adviser to the king. Stahl was also, of course, a dyed-in-the-wool conservative. He stressed the 'preordained order beyond the human will' as opposed to the desire to change and perfect the human species, bonds as against individualistic emancipation and self-alienation, the power of tradition as against the promises of the future. Beyond this he campaigned for the 'Christian state'. The state, in his view, can (and ought) not to be based on the autonomy of the human individual and on profane norms and institutions, but on Christian ones. Politics should be a Christian politics. Luther's separation of the two realms was pushed into the background, despite Stahl's profession of Lutheran orthodoxy. The state should ensure, for example through the marriage laws, that the polity remains Christian. The state should not issue orders to the church, and it should not separate itself from it;

rather it is in its very nature integrally linked to it, for the two exist in a symbiotic relationship. This became the ideal of Prussian policy under Friedrich Wilhelm IV.

But of greater importance to the future of conservatism were Stahl's ideas concerning the constitution (e.g. in *The Monarchical Principle*, 1845). In the first place, Stahl freed conservatism from its rejection of the modern state. The state, as he saw it, was not a quasi-private, estate-based and particularist structure of power and property. Instead it was the single undivided polity, which all forms of public power serve; it was a modern state. From this, Stahl developed his second principle, that rights and freedoms should not be guaranteed by means of contracts or patriarchal inclination, but by a 'constitution', and the 'nation' should have a part in shaping and safeguarding the public code of law through representatives. In Stahl's view, conservatives also must eventually come round to acknowledging this fundamentally 'new form of the state'. Stahl was tireless in emphasising the estate-based roots of the parliament, using the example of England. However, Stahl's third point was that this constitution would not be that of the liberals or of the 'west', nor one based on popular sovereignty and the division of powers or the rule of parliament; it would instead be a 'monarchical constitution'. The monarch, for him, was the shaping influence and controlling power within the state. Parliament would not be allowed to participate in shaping the policy of the state; its competence would be restricted. It would take part in determining legislation and taxation, and it would be allowed to impeach ministers, should they violate the constitution, but it would be nothing more than the guardian and guarantor of popular freedoms and rights, and of the constitution itself. This interpretation was also directed towards limiting the independence of the throne, whether it be absolutist or bureaucratic, or in alliance with the middle class, ensuring that it remained bound by convention and aristocratic interests. The king was not to break ranks with the aristocratic world. This theory formed the basis of the conservatives' own version of the constitution, which they now put forward in the fight against the liberals, and it contributed to their growth into a party.

Besides this, there were two other new developments, though less important. The standard conservatives (*Normalkonservativen*) were opposed to the nationalist movement and were supporters of the German Confederation and of the understanding between Prussia and Austria. But there were moves to form a new nationalist German conservatism of Prussian stamp. Joseph von Radowitz, the friend and adviser of Friedrich Wilhelm IV, and before the revolution military plenipotentiary in Frankfurt, then an ambassador, developed the thesis that in order to safeguard the monarchy and the state, it was necessary to take on board the 'idea of nationality'. This was, in his view, 'the most powerful force of the present time', and was the only basis on which the existing political order could be maintained. In concrete terms, he was thinking (in 1847–48) along the lines of a federal reform implemented by the governments, but what is more crucial here was that the former adversaries, conservatism and nationalism, seemed to moving closer together. Finally, Victor Aimé Huber, a son of Therese Forster, who was based in Berlin after 1843, put forward the first firm programme for a social-conservatism in pamphlets and journals. He advocated a state-controlled social-policy and a system of co-operatives which would turn propertyless workers into working property-owners. Huber remained an outsider for the time being, but through Hermann Wagener his ideas influenced Bismarck's social policy, and he was to become the father of the small but ever-present wing of German conservatism concerned with social policy.

The second movement in the developing German party spectrum, and the first to break the tension between inertia and dynamism, was the political Catholic movement. Catholicism's formation into a united political force — unlike Protestantism — in fact a party, is a fundamental feature of modern German history, the importance of which cannot be overestimated. After the revolution, the Catholic church evolved a relationship of permanent tension between itself and the modern state, which will be discussed in the context of the history of religion. The unquestioned link between church and state had vanished with the revolution and ensuing secularisation. The church called for liberation from the state's many powers of control and intervention and demanded state-protected powers over society, especially the two 'mixed' institutions that had such a determining effect on life, school and marriage. Conflicts raged over this issue. Under the old order, their settlement would have been a matter for established authorities such as government and the bishops. Now that political decision-making was no longer the sole province of state bodies, where the citizens, the *Volk*, the public came into question, the party of Catholicism gained political headway. This was all the more true because church demands were not directed merely at the authoritarian and secular state, but equally at liberalism and its ideas of autonomy of the individual and his liberation from authorities and corporative bonds. It also opposed liberalism's belief in reason, its critique of tradition and dogma, and its aversion to the Catholic clergy and the ties with the Pope. Essentially, the Catholics were opposed to one of the dominant features of bourgeois society, indeed of the very age. All these factors increased the inevitability of a coalition outside the church hierarchy and the formation of a general and, if necessary, political movement.

Initially after 1815, the newly-evolved political demands of the church were represented by only a handful of bodies and journals. By the 1830s, small groups of expressly Catholic delegates began to join forces in the *Landtage* of southern Germany. In the lower houses of the constitutional states and the provincial *Landtage* in Catholic regions of Prussia, the aristocracy allied themselves with the clergy to form both defensive and offensive opposition to the bureaucratic state and anti-clerical liberalism. The church was moving ever closer to an ultramontane stance. One implication of this was that the majority of the Catholic community were increasingly bound to the church as well as being mobilised and organised. A whole range of means was employed to encourage activity by the layman and strengthen the congregation's links with the clergy; there were church circulars, pilgrimages, to the Holy Coat of Treves for instance, and, especially in the 1840s, Catholic societies. The political demands of the church gained their resonance and mass basis from this kind of activity. In the age of the mass movement, Catholicism rose to become a political power.

The formation of an actual Catholic party which pursued issues beyond specific church politics had to wait until 1838, however. The 'Cologne Incident' of 1837 suddenly put church affairs at the centre of general politics; the arrest of the Archbishop of Cologne at the height of the dispute with the Prussian state about mixed marriages provoked a thunderous public response. The incident transcended regional boundaries and became the first political experience to be felt by German Catholicism as a whole. And it united the movement. It had an additional polarising effect on the whole of political life. Links between Protestant and Catholic conservatives as reflected in the *Berliner Politisches Wochenblatt* were dissolved; most liberals and those on the left joined forces to oppose Catholicism, and the loudest voices were now proclaiming anti-clericalism instead of the usual protest against the bureaucracy and the omnipotence of the state. That was a highly consequential decision. Catholicism now became a political movement. In his fierce and brilliant polemic *Athanasius*, written in 1838, Joseph Görres first put the relationship between one's denomination and one's party on the agenda. Because of the free relationship between church and state, and because political parties were a feature of modern constitutional states, Görres believed the denominations required counterparts in the party system. The faith was politicised, the party denominationalised. The question of the constitutional framework within which the church might achieve freedom and self-determination remained unanswered.

In 1838 Görres and his friends, especially Karl Ernst Jarcke, recently of the *Berliner Politisches Wochenblatt*, founded the *Historisch-Politische Blätter für das katholische Deutschland* in Munich. The publication achieved continuity and helped mould the party. The conservative wing of political Catholicism grouped around it. Drawing on reserves of Christian and Catholic convictions, the group evolved a conservative political theology that owed a debt to French traditionalists and political romanticism. They emphasised order, tradition, authority and man's status as custodian rather than creator, his transience and the unattainability of happiness. Revolution was a typically modern secular 'sin' that destroyed order in the name of progress, atomised community in favour of the individual, and replaced experience with theoretical construct. To them the liberals were the heirs of the revolution, sweeping man along in a wake of continuous renewal without reference to actuality; liberalism aimed to uproot man with pledges of emancipation and deny him his liberty. The bureaucratic and authoritarian state as embodied by Prussia was simply another facet of the degenerate spirit of the modern age; Jacobinism from above was as bad as that from below. According to them, however, the true root of the modern malaise was the Reformation, whose subjectivism spawned Enlightenment, absolutism, revolution and social upheaval. They applied theological interpretations to political problems and contrasts. Eve's encounter with the serpent was viewed as the scene of the first discussion on 'human rights'. They described the deepening crisis of the age in eschatological terms and foresaw a clash between Catholicism and atheistic socialist democracy; they believed that liberalism and Protestantism, the occupiers of the 'centre', were powerless and would not endure. Thus there was essentially no link with conservative Protestants. They invoked faith as a binding and decisive treatment for the maladies of the age and advocated formation of a new 'higher' medieval order of monarchy, estates and corporate society. These were the terms of the debate among conservative intellectuals, but they had an impact on the other leading Catholic groups, the aristocracy and the clergy; this state of affairs reflected the pre-modern outlook that was retained by the majority of adherents to the Catholic faith, such as the peasants and small-town craftsmen.

Within Catholicism, a liberal grouping stood in parallel with this conservative core. The theology of liberal democracy — equality and liberty for God's children, the alliance of church and people, and the pledge to improve the world — had made no great impression on conditions in Germany; their most brilliant representative, Abbé Lamennais, had been forced to resign from the church. The hardening of the church line against the rationalism professed by its liberal elements proved too contradictory for the theoretically-minded Germans. However, the Catholic movement was in favour of liberty and emancipation; the struggle for freedom among the Catholic Belgians, Irish and Poles was followed with great interest in Germany. A pragmatic combination of liberalism and Catholicism evolved. Liberal demands for freedom of association, assembly and the press, limitation of state power, self-government, the rule of law and a constitution were also raised by the Catholics, not only because they offered potential assistance to church policies, but also because they were readily justifiable from the natural laws that formed an important element of Catholic thought. The citizens of the Rhineland with their Catholic and anti-Prussian outlook and constitutional aims, were natural liberals. The metapolitical bases and conclusions of liberalism — rationalism and individualism, the abolition of ties and norms — were of no interest, however. Typical proponents of this pragmatic liberal view were two jurists from the Rhineland, August Reichensperger and his slightly more conservative brother Peter, who held central positions in the political Catholic movement from 1848 until the foundation of the Reich; in 1848 their views were shared by the majority of Catholics.

A final marginal development was the growth of social Catholicism with its foundation of political theology emphasising the dissociation of Christianity from wealth and competition, and the Christian call for solidarity and justice. They believed that division of labour and a free economy would establish an opposition between labour and capital and that unbridled competition would nourish self-interest among the strong at the expense of solidarity and morality. They also argued that liberal freedom in a decorporatised society meant the demise of true liberty for the workers. Adam Müller and Franz von Baader (*On the Present Disparity between the Propertyless or Proletarian Class and the Propertied Class in Society*, 1835) were among the many who wrote in this spirit of Catholic romantic social criticism.

Franz Joseph Buss, professor at Freiburg and a *Landtag* deputy, continued the pursuit, but did not stop at simple criticisms of industry and liberalism, or the call for religion and charity as the only real cure; he also advocated associative or corporative organisation of the workers, education, limitation of property ownership and job protection by the state. In broken-down form it sounds unremarkable, but in its sum it provided the inspiration for social Catholicism in the form that was promoted by Bishop Ketteler after 1848. It must be said that it was easier for Catholics to voice their criticisms on this subject, since they held a smaller stake in the capitalist industrial system than the Protestants, even falling victim to it in some cases. They also remained firm in their support of an agrarian and craft society as an ideal, to which industrial workers were some kind of exception. Adolf Kolping's founding of the Apprentices' Societies in 1845 was one concrete answer to social questions of the 1840s to come from Catholic quarters; they were intended to provide moral, pastoral, familial and professional support to overcome the apprentices' 'lack of status'. At the same time, the programme that set the tone for Catholic socialist policy for the next hundred years was spreading; its demands included de-proletarianisation of the proletariat and property for all.

In its relationship to the national movement, political Catholicism found itself in a curious situation. The traditional patriotism and romanticism of the old Reich bore all the hallmarks of Catholicism, whereas the new nationalism was strongly

Protestant. The Catholics were at odds with the nationalists who saw a contradiction between an international faith and national loyalty. To quote the *Historisch-Politische Blätter*, if that was to be the alternative, then there was 'a vastly more profound bond' between a Catholic German and a Catholic negro than there was between the latter and a German atheist. This was a simple means of guarding against overestimating the importance of nationality. However, it is not at all true to say that the Catholics stood outside the nationalist movement. They were, one might say, natural federalists, the majority of them both fiercely anti-Prussian and instinctively and emotionally supporters of Greater Germany.

The crucial point is that the conservative and liberal elements lying at the core of political Catholicism showed no tendency to go their separate ways, but rather put their joint stamp on the Catholic party. Their shared principal aim, the defence of church interests, was so elementary that it bound together the opposing forces. Both socially and in its political ideals, the Catholic party was a congregational party. There was another element to be taken into account too. The Catholic movement was anti-establishment, opposing both the bureaucracy and the comparatively narrow stratum of the educated and propertied liberal middle classes; its support came above all from the simple folk organised by the church: peasants and the 'little people'. The conservative or liberal orientation around the traditional elites was alien to the movement. This — transcending all ideals and programmes — was the truly democratic, populist element of the Catholic party make-up. In time the party therefore had to modify its role to represent the interests of its followers, but that time was yet to come.

Of course, it was not imperative that there be a Catholic party founded on the basis of political Catholicism. The Frankfurt National Assembly did not include a Catholic 'party', and even as late as 1870 there was still an amount of to-ing and fro-ing in terms of organisation. But political Catholicism became one of the most striking realities of the German situation. Overall, it actually functioned with reasonable continuity as a party. To begin with the number of representatives was small and, especially in 1848, the Conservatives and Liberals won a share of the Catholic vote. Its indirect effects, organisation of societies and petitions for instance, should also be taken into account; in 1848, Catholicism was still exercising a great influence on voting.

The age-old opposition in German history, the opposition of faiths, regained a place of central importance in German life through the formation of the party; it had always had the effect of intensifying regional, social and political splits, as well as those between city and country and tradition and modernity. The confrontation between Catholicism and Protestantism led to further segmentation of a society that already lacked homogeneity. Germany's special feature was that political Catholicism broke through the classic opposition of conservatism and liberalism; it provided a legitimate secular opposing force and both the Protestant Conservatives and the Liberals made efforts to intensify that opposition. The triangular relationship weakened Liberal aims of gaining power and a majority and, at least temporarily, integrating society; a further effect was to push them further towards the conservatism of state. Especially in the wake of the failure of the Greater German approach, popular forces in Germany became so entrenched in their opposition to each other that none of them was capable of forming a government. This placed an additional burden of delay on the transition to a parliamentary system, and is another element of the tragedy of recent German history.

Around 1840, just when the radicals were becoming established, liberalism slid towards the 'middle ground' and became just another party among many; this was a difficult period, and overall, until 1848, a sense of belonging to the 'opposition' prevailed. At the same time, liberalism became a popular movement, rather than the literary and press movement that it had been previously. And lastly, as a complication to its many existing facets, its individualism and the permanent state of flux so typical of liberalism with its open frontiers and, to one who craves a system, often inexplicable amalgam of motives and aims, it still eventually split into a left and a right wing.

The left wing embraced liberalism in its classic southern German form as typified by Rotteck, with its tradition of enlightened laws of reason and nature with overtones of the French example. The individualists and rationalists of the left wanted to uphold basic rights in the face of the state and historical laws such as those of feudalism and corporatism. The left called for expansion of the constitutional system; dogmatists wished to emphasise the role of the people's representative body as an opposition, while others wanted to expand its responsibilities and therefore its importance. The theory of dualism as described earlier was a fixed element, but the equilibrium between crown and parliament was to be maintained by greater application of parliamentary pressure. These aims were more expressly directed at a parliamentary system than is commonly supposed among historians. They demanded that regardless of the interpretation put on laws of state, after any election government should, and must go along with the majority view of the assembly. Their keenest and most effective weapon was the rejection of taxes. Lastly, the identity of the people with the citizenry was a firmly held conviction; there was deep mistrust of any upper stratum of the bourgeoisie. The political community was to comprise medium-sized and small property-owners alike, all of whom should be granted membership; equality and liberty were not regarded as incompatible.

The 'right wing', typified for example by Dahlmann, did not employ natural laws in their arguments, but history. They were more oriented towards English than French models. Their collective thought was more linked to concepts of state. Instead of the supposed opposition of the individual and the state or liberty and the state, they proposed reconciliation; neither did they accept elementary distrust of the state. To them the individual was not the one true reality, and social groupings were not merely the sum of their individual members linked or divided by personal interest. There existed realities beyond the individual, and one of them was the state; the Göttingen revolutionary of 1831, Heinrich Ahrens, made proposals along these lines in his 'organic' theory of state (1850). According to Dahlmann, 'The state is neither an invention of necessity nor one of cunning, . . . it is not a . . . contract, or a necessary evil but a fundamental order, a necessity . . ., the state is not something held in common among people but a physically and spiritually unified being.' The right wing believed that the state aimed at the general common interest above and beyond the sum of individual interests. Faced by the state, the individual not only had rights which he was unconditionally entitled to assert, but also duties. The pathos of resistance was joined by the ethos of obligations; basic rights were coupled with basic duties; the public interest was as important as individual rights. In the ideal model, the contradiction between the claims of the individual and the state was avoided by establishing the state as guarantor of rights and guardian of liberty. This was no deification of the state because the aims of individuality, humanity and liberty were not relinquished, but for this very reason the state had to be effective; the old liberal isolation from state vanished in this context. The tone was clearly different from that of the left wing and had its impact elsewhere too, for instance during the debate on basic rights in 1848. Another element was the emotional opposition to radical calls for political mobilisation of all and sundry directed at simple emancipation, as well as a rejection of tap-room politics and the spouting of political platitudes. Right-wing attitudes to the constitution were more strongly in favour of participation in the state than defence of liberties under attack from government; and within the overall liberal belief in sovereignty of the constitution, separation of powers was viewed as more important than the sovereignty of the people. To put it more concretely, the governing capabilities of the state should not be neglected; government had to be strong, and, by means of a right of veto, the monarch should retain a certain amount of power over parliament. The desired system was not strictly parliamentary, but a dualist constitution — although the theoretical divide between the two actually grew slimmer, and even broke down in right-wing liberal thought. Egalitarian tendencies among the radicals were firmly rejected — indeed, a potential conflict was perceived between equality and liberty; de Tocqueville's book on America, in which this very problem was tackled, was well known in Germany in the 1840s. Equality was a condition for liberty, but it tended to restrict, even destroy it; these liberals were awake enough to realise that egalitarian democracy tended towards totalitarianism. Liberty was supported, but with reservations; by contrast with the left-wingers, there was a fear of the masses — 'the uneducated and unpropertied rabble', as Dahlmann called them. The right wing was firmly anti-revolutionary — revolution was a curse; their faith was invested in gradual evolutionary restructuring of conditions; their watchword was pragmatic, not doctrinaire. Conflict and radical means were less important than compromise and consensus for the achievement of liberal aims.

It was again the southern German members of parliament, and in general the academics, that initially set the tone for the right wing. They were joined by an independent new element representing bourgeois liberalism among entrepreneurs in the Rhineland, such as Beckerath, Camphausen, Hansemann and Mevissen, who also led the opposition in the Rhenish provincial *Landtag*. They had less time for theory, but at the same time were keenly power-conscious and self-confident; they were more fiercely opposed to bureaucratic strangulation of the economy and more aware of the class character of the emergent new society, and demanded that leadership ('the gravitational force of state', to use Hansemann's words of 1830) should be ceded to their stratum. Suffrage was to be restricted, but parliament itself should be strong. A not insignificant aristocratic element was also present among their ranks, and these may be characterised as the German 'Whigs'. In a very self-confident fashion and eager to reform, they combined with the upper-middle classes to oppose bureaucratic absolutism. The British model acted as their proof that a parliamentary system, a determining role for the aristocracy and a 'fair order' could coexist. Sections of the East and West Prussian nobility (Rudolf von Auerswald), the Westphalian (Baron von Vincke), the Austrian (Anton von Schmerling) and the southern and south-western aristocracy (Prince zu Leiningen and Baron von Gagern) were typical of this group. In this way the liberals were more than just a 'bourgeois' party.

Despite the distinctions between wings and directions, liberalism possessed natural coherence. It advocated opposition to the existing order, the fight for a constitutional state and a national state; all these were concrete and pressing aims held in common by all liberals.

The popular basis of liberalism had spread considerably. Societies and educational groups, choral and gymnastic festivals, shooting matches, monuments and much of the burgeoning political poetry of the 1840s all contributed to a public life in the atmosphere and spirit of the liberal national movement. The movement grew to encompass all Germany and outstripped the ever-increasing literary and press output. The pseudo-public arenas of the arts and sciences provided the first platform. Since 1822 the natural scientists and the doctors had held their conferences; in 1837 they were joined by the philologists and pedagogues. In 1847, Lübeck hosted the all-Germany choral festival. Meetings of the 'Germanists' in 1846 and 1847 were particularly political — 'Germanists' came from all walks of life, but especially the legal profession, and the term covered everyone with an interest in German history; Heinrich von Treitschke described them as intellectual *Landtage*. Politicians were also forging closer links with the movement. Ever since the early 1840s, southern, western and central German liberals had been meeting at the estate in Hallgarten belonging to Johann Itzstein, a representative at the Baden assembly, and radicals such as Friedrich Hecker and Gustav von Struve were also among those present; the most gifted liberals from the south and west travelled north, and *vice versa* — all of which was cause for celebration. In 1846–47, the *Deutsche Zeitung* was founded in Heidelberg; those from the south-west — Friedrich Bassermann, Heinrich von Gagern, Georg Gottfried Gervinus, Ludwig Häusser, Karl Mathy, Karl Mittermaier — were the prime movers, but northern liberals — including Georg Beseler, Georg Waitz and Johann Gustar Droysen to name but a few — were also contributors. The paper aimed to cover the whole of Germany and also the whole of liberalism, despite a preponderance of the right-wing liberals. In October 1847, leading liberals of all factions — 'the rich and the intelligent' — met in Heppenheim and discussed a common programme. They demanded a state based on law and a constitution, the settlement of outstanding land compensation, and measures to combat poverty and need, all of which were admittedly couched in vague and tactically rhetorical terms. They further demanded the establishment of a German federal state with a unified government and unified parliament on the basis of the German Confederation or, if necessary, the Zollverein. Although the liberals did not support the revolution, they confronted the prevailing state of affairs and demanded a new order.

We have already examined the radical tendencies of the 1830s. Although the shared sense of 'opposition' still prevailed, as did the sense of personal belonging, the emergence (around 1840) of democratic radicalism on party lines from within the movement could not be overlooked. This is shown in sharp relief if one stops to examine their theories of constitution and society. The unity of ideas from 1789 dissolved. In the first place, the liberal principle of limitation of state authority and separation of powers lost ground to the democratic principle of sovereignty of the people and the power of the majority. Sovereignty was one and indivisible and was in the hands of the people; anything else was semi-absolutism. Thus the 'republic' was the only true people's state, contrasting with every form of monarchy however great the restrictions imposed upon it. The constitutional ideal was parliamentary strength without too many checks and balances; some advocated additional provisions for direct democracy. The stress on sovereignty of the people is linked with a second and similar stress on the principle of equality. The radicals' view of 'natural inequalities' — in liberal terminology the product of talent and achievement, namely education and ownership — was that they were a result of existing power relations. They had no desire to do away with inequalities but wanted to limit them by regulation of taxation and inheritance and free entry to educational institutions. Equality was a precondition for liberty; forced to choose between the two, they would pick equality, but in contrast with the liberals they did not believe freedom to be jeopardised thereby. It might also be added that the liberals drew their support from the ranks of the financially independent, whereas the radicals drew theirs exclusively from the 'little people', the dependent and the downtrodden. The differences between the two strands were embodied in their stance on voting rights. The radicals were against the application of any assessments or class restrictions on the right to vote, and in favour of free universal suffrage; the nation as a whole was to be the bearer of democracy.

Radical aims were accompanied by radical means. The radicals opposed compromise and were basically against evolution; they were in favour of conflict and action and, in the extreme case, even revolution. Thus they were not merely opposed to the prevailing system and its supporters, but also the educated and propertied bourgeoisie, the *juste milieu*, the constitutional liberals with their great expectations of parliament and constitution. They were the 'whole' opposed to the 'halves'.

Politically, socially and, indeed, regionally, radicalism comprised two components. The first of these was a radical intelligentsia. At the end of the 1830s, Left and Young Hegelianism were rising to become a force both in the formation of political ideas and in journalistic circles. The Young Hegelians turned against what they saw as Hegel's philosophy of conciliation and his justification of reality. The point was to use the 'weapon' of the absolute critique and the 'terror of reason' (Arnold Ruge) to attack reality and rob it of its legitimation, freeing the individual to be himself through radical thought penetrating to the root of the matter. From its beginnings in David Strauss's and Ludwig Feuerbach's critiques of religion, and a general philosophical discussion on the age, it led to revolutionary critiques of state and society. Here were the beginnings of the theory of 'actualisation'; it was imperative to transform theory into practice, the critique into the act, and the thought into physical force. The theory became a great subject of debate. Revolution, both political and social, was legitimised as a historical imperative because the 'idea' developed in that age had to become reality. In 1838, Arnold Ruge together with Ernst Theodor Echtermeyer founded the main organ of this movement, the *Hallesche Jahrbücher für deutsche Wissenschaft und Kunst*; the Prussians were its leading contributors, since for a time Prussia represented all that was progressive. After 1841 it appeared as the *Deutsche Jahrbücher* in Leipzig, and for a short time after 1843 it was published in Paris as the *Deutsch-französische Jahrbücher*. It was a rallying-point for radical intellecuals such as Bruno Bauer and Karl Marx. In a 'self-critique' of 1843, Ruge made the classic and decisive formulation of the rejection of liberalism by radical democrats and revolutionaries. Other intellectuals were associated with these circles, while others again were thinking in a similar direction. Foremost among them was Julius Fröbel, nephew of the kindergarten pioneer. There was a feeling of belonging to the *avant-garde* and possessing the 'true' consciousness and ability to interpret the present and the future. The formation of a revolutionary intelligentsia that existed without contact with the social reality of the time and claimed to represent a social and political force was truly an odd phenomenon. The self-assurance of the 'perfected philosophy' justified the absoluteness of the demands of revolutionary policy. However, assertions about the nature of reality which fired the imagination of many of the intellectually motivated younger generation themselves became a constituent of that reality.

Far simpler to grasp and more accessible to all, was the political poetry of the 1840s. It too attained a certain spiritual political power, and its main exponents became followers of national-democratic and social-critical radicalism. Hoffmann von Fallersleben was one poet with some sympathy for those tendencies; in 1841 he published his *Unpolitische Lieder* (Apolitical Songs) and promptly lost his university post. Ferdinand Freiligrath was a more fervent supporter; his *Glaubensbekenntnis* (Confession of Faith) and *Ça ira* dating from 1844 and 1846 were written in exile and lay bare the emotions of a trumpeter of the revolution. Georg Herwegh wrote in similar vein in 1841 in his work *Lieder eines Lebendigen* (Songs of a Living Man), which had been through two impressions by 1843. He had been in Switzerland since 1839; on his accession to the throne, Friedrich Wilhelm IV summoned him for an audience amid great public interest, but then exiled him, after which he settled in Paris. There were also any number of other minor poets.

The *Rheinische Zeitung* was a further important and idiosyncratic publishing experiment. Its founders and publishers were bourgeois entrepreneurs, such as Ludolf Camphausen and Gustav Mevissen, and jurists; radical intellectuals, Karl Marx and his circle, formed the editorial staff. The paper appeared between October 1842 and 31 March 1843; tolerated by the Prussian state at first, it was later banned; as an organ of radical criticism levelled at German and Prussian affairs, the bourgeoisie and the *juste milieu*, it was a success. A collection of mostly short-lived radical papers and a range of literature published in exile also found a readership in Germany; the *Literarisches Comptoir* published in Switzerland by Julius Fröbel carried over a hundred radical publications between 1840 and 1845. Emigrés also formed the natural nucleus of the radical party.

Alongisde the intellectual *avant-garde* wing, there were also populist radicals. The extent of radical opinion in the south-west has already been demonstrated; in poor rural areas and emerging industrial centres as well as larger cities, agitation found an attentive radical audience. In politically-minded Baden — where French and Swiss influences had left their mark — Friedrich Hecker and Gustav Struve, lawyers, journalists and members of the *Landtag*, began to shape a radical movement through public meetings, speeches and societies. They were typical of the 'men of the people' at that time. Populism of this nature also existed in Saxony; with his countless educational, press and society activities, Robert Blum stood at the head of the regional movement. During the 1840s, the two religious opposition groups, the Protestant *Lichtfreunde* (Friends of Light) and the German Catholics, maintained numerous links with the emerging democratic movement. Both were anti-establishment factions of religious origins, but motivated by enlightenment principles and Christian values of freedom, equality and fraternity, as well as by ideas of democracy and nationhood; it must be said that their significance was greatly overestimated at the time.

Johann Jacoby in Königsberg, Heinrich Simon in Breslau and Gottfried Kinkel in Bonn also numbered among the radical democrats resident in Germany in the mid-1840s; many maintained contact through correspondence and visits. On 12 September 1847 the Baden radicals met at a mass meeting in Offenburg and proclaimed a programme that may be loosely termed the radical party manifesto. Besides general opposition aims shared with the liberals, the programme called for a people's militia, equal voting rights and educational opportunities, progressive income tax and an end to the 'disparity between rich and poor'; thus it was a distinct counter-programme to that of the liberals.

The socialist movement and party had their beginnings in the decade leading up to 1848; because of their later significance as one of the decisive forces of the age, the modest beginnings are worthy of particular attention. It was shown earlier that the scale of the crisis of mass poverty, pauperism and other social problems became central features of the discussion on the future of society and state that was concerned with society's basis in markets and competition, the loosening of corporate and personal bonds, division of labour, the status of labour as a commodity, and proletarisation as a collective fate. Other themes running through the debate were the state of progress in Germany when compared with conditions in England and France and especially the social theories being developed in those two countries, and how to tackle the dual problem of industry and factory labour. Socialist theories provided an approach to the solution of these questions. The workers were the focus of designs for the reordering of society; the theories were conceived for and with regard to the workers. The term 'labour movement' is used to describe the united efforts of workers in industry and commerce to improve their social conditions. It does not necessarily imply socialism. But the socialist movement became an element of the labour movement; the origins of the latter in Germany bore the decisive impression left by the former.

Initially it was not the German underclasses themselves, nor the emerging industrial proletariat, that provided the foundation of socialism and the labour movement. The lower classes were excluded from political life, and the vaguest hint of insurrection was subject to police repression; they had no common consciousness or experiences. They still did not represent a 'class'; for many years the socialist idea of an industrial proletariat completely failed to capture the reality of the poor masses of Germany. The socialist movement consisted of the odd combination of radical intellectuals in league with craft apprentices, the most mobile and aware element of the working classes; both groups drew on their experiences of the capitalist industrial system in the rest of western Europe where early socialist ideas were most virulent. Freedom of thought and speech were more common outside Germany, and both were important preconditions. The emergence of the socialist movement on foreign soil had other effects on its origins; the early history of the new party was played out in the strange surroundings of expatriate life. Days spent in debate of theories, new theories and disputes about theories, conspiracy and intrigue, splits and new formations are almost unreal by any normal social standards.

Socialism originated in democratic egalitarian radicalism. The tradition of the French Revolution and the Enlightenment, belief in reason, inner happiness, well-being and progress were shared by all socialists. Revolution meant a complete transformation, the remaking of the world, the actualisation of reason and theory; revolution also meant action by the people in league against tradition and authority to achieve emancipation, human rights — liberty, equality, fraternity — and self-determination. The socialists — opposed to everything conservative, feudal or monarchic — sensed themselves to be the heirs and defenders of the great liberal democratic emancipation movement. Like the radicals, however, they directed themselves against the liberals of the *juste milieu*, the emergent educated and propertied bourgeoisie and bourgeois 'privilege'; they attached central importance to equality as a precondition for liberty. They also embraced an almost Jacobin tradition, emphasising the importance of the 'little people', the dependent and the uneducated. However, the socialists went further than the radicals in attacking all private property, and especially ownership of the means of production; they called for a society of restricted ownership and common property. Though actually standing in the political tradition of liberalism, the socialists thus set up the latter as their enemy. The socialists also specifically rejected the individualism and self-interest of the liberals, and their curbing of the power of the state. There was a curious proximity between socialists and conservatives in their criticisms of the liberals and bourgeois society; their anti-capitalist aims, on the other hand, won different allies and opponents. However, by contrast with the conservatives, even the early socialists stood firmly in the age of the industrial revolution despite many corporative aims that were common with the traditional order; regression was not their aim.

Thus, the socialists were neither Luddites nor nostalgics, but futuristic. They had no time for protection of the status or this or that profession; they were universal, wanting no less than a new society. Thought and deed, unity and loyalty were all determined by these aims, and thus arose a movement in the modern sense.

The artisans' associations abroad were becoming increasingly political and radical, whereas initially they had been only a potential revolutionary force. In 1836–37, out of the radical Bund der Geächteten (League of Outlaws), a splinter group was formed, the Bund der Gerechten (League of the Just), with parallel organisations in Switzerland and London; these were the first socialist organisations. Karl Schapper and, above all, Wilhelm Weitling were the leading figures. Weitling, a tailor's apprentice, was the only non-intellectual of the founding generation, living in Paris (1835–41) and Switzerland (1841 onwards); his books (*Humanity, How It Is and How It Should Be*, 1838; *Guarantees of Harmony and Freedom*, 1842; *The Gospel of a Poor Sinner*, 1845) also helped make him the most influential representative of early German socialism. A popular philosopher, eccentric, religious, sectarian (Jesus as communist), full of the need for happiness and redemption — reverting to secularism — yet on the other hand rationalistic, Weitling followed the early French socialists who applied critiques of inequality and organisation of property to the new reality of industrial capitalism and developed new utopian orders for society that transcended property and competition. Weitling's critique of society has its naïve elements: property and money were to be abolished as they were the root of evil; they would be replaced by a type of communism of equality that organised work and the fulfilment of needs; equality and liberty would be kept in equilibrium by applying communal measures. Weitling's thoughts were directed at the craftsman rather than industrial labour, and his idea of solidarity through community contains many elements of craft tradition; this in its turn added to his popularity among expatriate artisans. But utopia aside, his vision embraced revolution, overthrow and struggle; in his view it was necessary to progress from political to social revolution, and to replace liberal freedom of exploitation and enslavement with equality. Weitling's secular religion of redemption lived on within the future labour movement, but his form of socialism was ousted by other theories. Moses Hess, the 'Communist Rabbi', and Karl Grün, a journalist and writer long active in the Rhineland, advocated 'True' Socialism (*Socialism and Communism*, 1845); it was still the mere theoretical product of intellectuals. On the basis of an analysis of society founded on economics, abolition of property was, after all, in the scornful words of Marx, a consequence of using the correct argument. However, this approach won a great deal of support among intellectuals and journalists of the left.

The socialist theory developed by Marx and Engels first savaged these and other competing theories, then established itself in Germany. Karl Marx was born in Treves in 1818 of Jewish parents; though he was baptised, the *de facto* non-emancipation of the Jews affected him greatly, as did general anti-Prussian sentiments prevalent in the Rhineland — besides Görres and Heine, Marx was the third great enemy of Prussia to spring from the vicinity of the Rhine during this century. He was a Left Hegelian, took a doctorate in philosophy, and edited the *Rheinische Zeitung* from 1842–43; after the paper was banned he settled as an exile in Paris. His preoccupation with early French socialists and the economy of Britain were the starting-points for his conversion to socialism. In 1845 he travelled to Brussels, and after the revolution he finally moved to London. In 1844 he became acquainted with Friedrich Engels, the son of a factory-owner. Engels, born in Barmen in 1820, was critical of his pietistic bourgeois family background, and had, as a young man, been an adherent of Moses Hess; from 1842 to 1844 he lived in Manchester, where he developed his critique of the British economy and wrote his epoch-making book *The Condition of the English Working Classes* (1845). Marx and Engels worked closely together in Brussels after 1845 when they published their joint works *Die Heilige Familie* (The Holy Family) and *Die Deutsche Ideologie* (The German Ideology), which dealt with other current theories as well as acting as expositions of their own evolving ideas. In London, they became members of the League of the Just, which was restyled as the League of Communists in 1847. In February 1848, the programme that they had developed, the 'Communist Manifesto', was published in London.

Marx's social theory will be the subject of a later chapter; here it will be sufficient to sketch the early history of that theory. In taking a philosophical supposition rather than an economic or sociological analysis as his point of departure, Marx adhered to the methods of the Young Hegelians. He aimed to capture the present in a system of thought and criticise reality for its contradictions, outdatedness and 'untruth', since reality no longer accorded with the current stage of development of the world spirit. The reality had to be actualised, however, and reality thus became revolution. Revolution required a vehicle, supplied, in Marx's terms, by the proletariat. The problem afflicting the age was the modern industrial society; the bourgeoisie, however, did not want to be involved in the search for a solution. This brings in Marx's humanist approach that called for an end to alienation of the individual — the 'impossibility of being oneself' which had reached its peak under the capitalist system. The proletariat was the very element of humanity that was the most alienated; the person was identical with the unit of labour and became a mere adjunct to the machine because of division of tasks in manufacturing. In the wages system, labour became a commodity; according to the *Dialektik*, the proletariat was the only force capable of conquering alienation, and it was the general estate that held the key to the fate of humanity, since the human being can only realise himself — in 'totality' — within society. Abolition (*Aufhebung*) of alienation meant abolition of proletarian existence and the class society and was possible only through a revolution of the proletariat — this was the means that Marx employed to link the philosophical and speculative critique to the actual needs of society and the origin of the political and social programme. After 1844 Marx and Engels allied the concept of alienation ever more closely with their analyses of the relation between labour and capital. They explained the historical 'necessity' of proletarian revolution and the classless society as a development of capitalism — through crisis, concentration and decline — and the 'laws' of the class struggle. All of this, with a particular focus on the needs of the moment, flowed into the *Communist Manifesto*. All history is the history of the class struggle; and this includes the struggle over the state, since the state is nothing more than an instrument of class rule. According to the theory's eschatological pathos, history progresses towards victory of the proletariat in their clash with the capitalists, and an eventual communist society. The immediate concern to ensure victory was to cultivate class-consciousness among the proletariat. At the same time, however, the bougeois democratic revolution represented progress and would provide the necessary basis for a socialist revolution; it would therefore have to be supported. The theory contained the prognosis, the programme and the call for action all in one. Future decades were destined to ring to the exhortations' 'The proletarians have nothing to lose but their chains. They have a world to win.' — 'Workers of the world, unite!' It must be said that the manifesto was far in advance of the conditions prevailing in Germany in 1848. It was still not clear whether Marx would have a lasting impact on the German labour movement. But the socialists were ready to embrace his concept — to them it was more scientific, more realistic, more unified, had a stronger basis in economics and history, and showed the most promise. By contrast with France and other Romance countries, the legacy of early socialism, such as Proudhon's co-operative anarchy, had entirely lost its impact.

Socialist and communist ideas — as yet undifferentiated — and revolutionary rhetoric held a significant place in the minds of members of the organisations set up by exiled artisans, workers and intellectuals (which were too numerous to be mentioned individually here). At first they embraced utopian ideals, then competing theories, until at last Marx was posed to overthrow Weitling. At the same time it would be wrong to ignore the many reforming aims that were developing on the basis of craft traditions; the coexistence of revolution and reform, which later becomes so characteristic of the labour movement, was already present in this early phase. Organisations had a very pronounced integrating power; socialism became an element of the shared way of life through the repertoire of communal songs and the use of symbols. One feature was highly noteworthy: the dream cherished by these workers was international and applicable to all mankind. Their organisations, however, even in international centres, were still national in character, and this affected their life. In terms of future developments, this was an important feature.

Within Germany the outlook was different. There was no actual labour movement; uncoordinated and isolated spontaneous activity was occasionally directed at machinery, individual factories or their owners. Pre-industrial unrest such as the Silesian weavers' uprising was as uncommon as other forms of social protests, food riots and wage struggles. By the 1840s, events surrounding the exile communities began to take effect on German conditions. Socialist intelligentsia met here and there — such as the circle of communists in Cologne inspired by Moses Hess and centred around two doctors, d'Ester and Gottschalk; workers' educational societies grew up under bourgeois patronage and occasionally contained elements who voiced demands that outstripped the bourgeois concept of emancipation and, especially in Berlin, used the groups to establish contact with other radicals. Modest centres sprang up, especially in western and northern Germany, and there was a certain amount of propaganda besides. Overall, however, the socialists consisted mainly of intellectuals; the impact of their theories was practically indiscernible among apprentices and workers. The socialists now had a party, but for the time being, did not constitute a force, and as the labour movement took up its position on the political scene in 1848, it was far from the Bund der Kommunisten.

7. Vormärz

Throughout the 1840s, while there was a great deal of continuity in the developments in most of the German states, a new political constellation was rising in Prussia. Events in Prussia provoked great attention — among contemporaries as much as among later students of history — and especially because Prussia's status as one of the two most powerful German states was indispensable to the solution of the German problem.

When Friedrich Wilhelm IV succeeded to the throne in 1840, the event was, in typical contemporary fashion, seen as an hour of hope. He was said to be imaginative and open-minded, kind, and occasionally brilliant; he opposed the authoritarian bureaucracy that had predominated during his father's reign, as well as its fossilisation. He also opposed the absolutist Prussian tradition of Frederick the Great and the Hegelian concept of a new Prussia based on an officialdom comprising the intelligentsia and aimed towards the transfiguration of the state; he was open to romantic national ideas and believed in reconciliation rather than conflict. His first act as king was to resolve conflict and heal old wounds: amnesty was granted to political detainees, and political investigations within the Confederation were limited. Arndt and Jahn, the 1819 demagogues, were rehabilitated, and three of the Göttingen Seven were called to Prussia. Initially at least, censorship was applied less strictly, and the conflict with the Catholic church was settled. There was a review of the *de facto* policy of Germanisation applied to the Poles in Posen, and Boyen, the former Minister of War during the reform era, was reinstated in 1841; the Ministries of the Interior and Legislation were placed in the hands of new moderates. Because the new king wished for popularity and to live in harmony with 'his people', he sought public support, often employing glittering, though not always substantial, rhetoric that captured the spirit and ideas of the time. The *Dombaufest* in Cologne in September 1842 was a typical instance, when the project of completing the unfinished Cologne Cathedral was begun. The popular movement calling for the completion of the great work of construction drew support from Catholic, liberal and nationalist circles, and the king managed to transform the celebration into a festival of integration, and at the same time to counter the Hambach festival, by rallying all groups as well as their press support. The event was as much intended to celebrate the new harmony between state and church, and the peace among the denominations, as was as the harmony between king, state and people, especially the Prussians and the Rhinelanders. Lastly — against the background of Rhine romanticism and the French threat to the Rhineland in 1840 — it was intended to celebrate the unity of the German people and their leaders, the German nation. The cathedral, the work of 'a German sense of brotherhood', was symbolic of German unity. The king's speech was a source of intense irritation to the leaders of the restoration, Metternich and the Tsar; he deceived many of his contemporaries and possibly even himself about his relationship to the times in which he was living. Contradictions and ambiguity abounded, leading to a reign that Treitschke characterised as 'a long string of misunderstandings'. In fact the king's main influence came from romantic conservatism; he believed in the divine right of kings, the patriarchal ethos, the ordering of society according to estates and a Christian state; he was quite unresponsive to bourgeois society and desires for a constitutional society and was unable to reconcile the Prussian restoration with the dawning new age. In general the cabinet was drawn from traditional conservatives and, despite claims that it was a kind of political royal bodyguard, was essentially without a leader. The king's friends and advisers, the Gerlach brothers, General Radowitz and Stahl (known among themselves as the 'camarilla' in 1848) possessed decisive non-governmental influence and were convinced conservatives. Policies of the 'Christian state' were especially applied in the case of the Ministry of Education and Culture. Albrecht Eichhorn, the new minister, had been an old colleague of the reformers (and one of the architects of the Zollverein) but was now committed to the new line; religious conviction and anti-revolutionary conservatism were the new recruitment criteria for schools, universities or the church, although notable figures such as Friedrich Wilhelm Schelling or Stahl were exceptions; Hoffmann von Fallersleben was dismissed and, in 1847, so was Adolf Diesterweg, the well-known seminary head who had enjoyed the protection of the courts for some time. Rationalism, Hegelian idealism, emancipation from tradition and its bonds, modernity — all were rejected; the move was bound to be taken as moral restraint among sensitive educated liberals and would help to mobilise them against the 'system'.

The key issue in Prussian politics surrounded the constitution that had remained an unfulfilled promise since the reform era. Public reminders of the fact could not have escaped the notice of the king. As early as 1840, the provincial *Landtage* of East and West Prussia — the majority of the aristocracy were liberals — passed a motion to send a memorandum to the king indicating the earlier pledge for the introduction of a full constitution. The king's answer contained a rejection of 'state laws enshrined in parchment' that, as he often said later, came between God, the king and the people. Theodor von Schön, the *Oberpräsident* and still a committed reformer as well as having personal connections with the king, renewed the demand in an anonymous internal publication entitled *Woher und wohin?* (Whence and Whither?) that appeared in an edition of thirty-two copies. The king would not relent, and when Schön's piece was leaked to the public in 1842, he was promptly dismissed. In February 1841, Johann

Jacoby, a doctor from Königsberg and a supporter of radical liberalism claimed in a pamphlet entitled *Vier Fragen, beantwortet von einem Ostpreussen* (Four Questions Answered by an East Prussian) that the pledge of 1815 unequivocally established the people's right to a constitution and a true people's assembly instead of provincial bodies based on the estates. Prussia had the pamphlet banned by the Bundestag, but this merely boosted its effect, and two courts acquitted its author of *lèse-majesté* and high treason.

The king naturally could not ignore the question of the constitution any longer. He felt a certain amount of responsibility toward the earlier promises. Also, the state required loans; because loans required the approval of a full state parliament, the planned apparatus was set in motion. A first experiment ended in failure in 1842 when 'Joint Committees' consisting of selected delegates from the provincial *Landtage* met; they were to advise, apparently in a purely technical capacity, on matters of transportation — the extension of a railway network to serve the whole country. They declared themselves in favour, but state finances would be necessary for the project, and only the *Reichstände* were competent to take the decision. The original function of the provincial *Landtage* had been to block a full state constitution, but now, in 1845, with the exception of those in Pomerania and Brandenburg, they became the initiators and bearers of demands for *Reichstände* and a constitution; a significant proportion of the aristocracy had lent their voice to the bourgeois demands. The *Landtage* began to take up other affairs of state. In 1841 and 1843, for instance, nearly all of them called for freedom of the press; again in 1843, the Rhenish *Landtag* threw out an essentially progressive penal code because it contained varying punishments dependent on social status, and even cited loss of noble status as a form of punishment. After lengthy machinations, and against the judgment of Metternich and the Tsar, the king founded the *Vereinigter Landtage* (United Diet) in February 1847; it consisted of all members of the provincial *Landtage*. The king regarded it as the finishing touch to the traditional regional structure of the Prussian state; for the public and the determined reactionaries however, it was neither one thing nor another, just an anachronistic concession. The body was scheduled to meet neither regularly nor 'periodically', but whenever convened by the king. The extent of its powers was to decide on taxation and loans — except in time of war — to legislate but only at the discretion of the government, and always taking into account the divisions of social status; a single 'Joint Committee' was to meet regularly to collaborate on legislation. Although the liberals did not regard these measures as fulfilling the promise of a constitution, they accepted the new institutions with the aim of using them as a lever to achieve a true constitution.

In April the United Diet met in Berlin. It consisted of 70 lords, 237 knights, 182 urban and 124 rural representatives, all of them landowners and very few of them, as in constitutional Germany, civil servants or members of the educated middle classes. However, the majority of the delegates no longer viewed themselves as traditional provincial members, but as deputies of the Prussian people, and for this reason they were now divided according to political direction. Proceedings swiftly turned to the basic issue of the constitution. The government wanted the state to act as guarantor for agricultural credit institutions who were to finance the *Ablösung* (redemption) of the peasants, as well as for a loan for the construction of the railway from Berlin to Königsberg which was proving impossible to finance from the private sector. There was no objection to the financial provisions, but a two-thirds majority led by East Prussians and Rhinelanders refused to approve the measures unless the assembly was guaranteed to meet regularly and the ominous Joint Committee was abolished. Hansemann's famous comment (*in Gelddingen hört die Gemütlichkeit auf*, loosely translated as '*in money matters geniality has its limits*') has become proverbial. The government was not prepared to grant the assembly even this minimum of constitutional validity of *Reichstände*. Instead the king abandoned work on the railway and closed the assembly at the end of June. Despite all suspicions and in the face of unbending opposition from a minority, the majority elected a new Joint Committee. However, the king's half-hearted attempt at an interim solution had broken down and was symbolically overtaken by the modern world in the shape of a railway. At the same time, monarchic reasons of state had lost their validity and the opposition had been provided with a fulcrum for the assertion of their principles. Even in the province of Prussia — where, in the east at least, an almost feudal system was still in place whose provincial institutions still bore the typical hallmarks of an estate-centred organisation embracing the aims of the restoration — the aristocracy and the urban and rural middle classes had combined to form an opposition representing the country and the nation. But even their moderate demands had no outcome. Through his estate-based experiment and his repeated refusals to honour an earlier pledge, the king fuelled the flame of the movement rather than dousing it. The conflict surrounding the constitution smouldered on and temperatures continued to rise until the revolution in the following March.

Throughout the 1840s, tensions and unrest were mounting all over Germany. In the constitutional states, sporadic disputes broke out between governments and their councils of deputies on the subject of a restrictive or an evolutionary interpretation of the respective constitutions. In the fields of justice, self-determination and agrarian reform, the liberals' chief policy areas, business proceeded at a snail's pace. The constitution had failed to find a working balance, and the sense of frustration and stagnation was growing. Opposition was vociferous, even in Metternich's Austria. Censorship and party bans were still in force and provoked growing anger and resistance despite, or perhaps because of, being extensively undermined. The parties representing the movements (and the Catholic opposition) were growing in self-confidence; they had stockpiled their human resources and were beginning to organise and co-ordinate nationally on programmes and strategies. This was as true of the liberals as it was of the radicals. Despite the many obstacles, the public debate gained intensity, additional national communication and volume. The impact of the work of the exiles was beginning to take effect on radicals and socialists. Through associations and clubs, festivals and congresses, monuments, poetry and the press, the national movement spread metapolitically, emotionally and existentially; frontier disputes with France and Denmark boosted the wave that was already building. Above all, there arose the call for unification, a national organisation of all Germans to replace the moribund German Confederation that had no function except as an instrument of repression. To achieve the evolution of the constitution at home, it was necessary to look outwards to the rest of Germany and smash the strictures imposed by the Confederation. Economic and social needs also indicated the correctness of this course. The desire for nationhood was an aim that far surpassed all such considerations — it was the political bedrock. The murmurs crystallised into demands, such as the demand for a national parliament. Finally as a separate issue, there was increasing social unrest in the transition from the old society to the new. There were delays in providing debt relief (*Grundent-lastung*) for the peasants; crafts were under threat, and the small traders were feeling the pinch of the market and industry. Pauperism was still a problem and the population was growing without the prospect of a corresponding growth in the number of jobs. Then there were the lower classes, many without jobs or homes, facing proletarianisation. Finally there was the problem of starvation that had swept the whole of the — still markedly agrarian — economy in 1846–47. These worries differed distinctly from those of the liberal *Bürger*, whose predominant interest was politics, but the two fields intersected; social unrest was at once the background and the substance of political protest, the former intensifying the latter and providing its drive. Overall, a threefold crisis — the constitutional, the national and the social — was approaching its culmination.

Taking an overall view of the decades after 1815, the initial most striking phenomenon is the rise of the middle classes. A whole middle-class culture evolved, embracing science, education and the arts. Typical standards and ways of life arose among the middle classes at home, at work and in their social life, and they gained a particular economic function within the emerging capitalist framework. The old traditions of the *Bürger's* existence became integrated with the new middle-class, *bürgerlich* world. In its turn, it affected the adjacent strata of society, the aristocracy, the farmers and respectable elements of the lower classes. The outcome of voting in 1848 confirmed the nation's acceptance of the new arrival. Middle-class existence was questioned, but not by the *haute bourgeoisie*, the upper middle classes. Its critics came from the ordinary middle classes, the many independent workers distinguished from each other by their education and property; besides these there were the critical intelligentsia, small in number but important both politically and socially. Though they were not dominant, the middle classes were arbiters of styles and trends, and they set the tone through their values and standards of autonomy and individuality, achievement and competition, wealth and work, talent and education, debate and public life, privacy and liberty, as well as their new way of giving meaning and pleasure to life — the association. The middle classes rose to a leading position in society despite the continued existence of feudalism and the numerical weight of the lower classes and countryfok. As their base of support grew, so there was proportional increase in their claims to political joint supremacy — if not complete supremacy — against the aristocracy and the military, bureaucracy and monarchic autocracy, and the same was true of their demands for state and society to be organised on their own terms. The middle classes wanted the fulfilment of the pledges made during the reform era.

The second phenomenon of those three decades was the state itself. It had limited modernisation and opposed the political claims of the middle classes — and that was the sum of its achievements, despite all the pushing and shoving that had occurred over that period. The behaviour of the state was dictated by a fear of revolution, and other risks of days gone by; it mobilised defences against each and every movement and every stage of the evolution of the middle classes. Metternich and the forces of reaction were not the only ones to blame. The police, censorship, repression, internment and exile had been suffered by all political and youthful thinkers of the age. But there was yet another force at work: the constant tutelage of the bureaucracy and the dogma of the 'limited faculties of the subjects'. Bureaucracy was responsible for half-hearted concessions, retractions, delays, denials and resistance to the 'spirit' of constitution. The German Confederation had consolidated the system and stood in the way of all development.

The whole policy rebounded on itself. There was no free public, political or institutional life which allowed development of interests, opinions or activity on the part of individuals or groups, still less the evolution of responsibilities. This was doubtless also the source of the energy that fed scientific and artistic culture as well as motivating the cosy Biedermeier culture. It also nourished private inward reflection, as much as the philistine attitudes of the German world and the compartmentalisation of life. This naturally occurred elsewhere under quite different political conditions, but it was especially pronounced in Germany. It also led to the doctrinaire approach and lack of pragmatism displayed by the opposition in the newly emerging political system. It explained the intelligentsia's inclination to radicalism and the problems of coming to terms with reality. Within German life, basic consensus and agreement were largely lacking.

Disappointment was reflected in resignation and dissatisfaction, criticism and opposition, protest or, in isolated cases, resistance, but above all in a desire for change. Beneath the shadow of bans, the middle-class movements established their crypto-political and semi-political ground. Their spokesmen no longer invoked reason or the law, neither did they see themselves as the *avant-garde*; they spoke on behalf of all of society. For this reason, the pressure of stagnation and conflict intensified in proportion to the number of demands made. It was all taking too long. Revolution was only favoured among the radical intellectuals. Liberals regarded revolution as disaster — their thoughts were on the violence and incalculable negative results. Everyone, however, wanted and expected change — fundamental change. Around this time Dahlmann published his histories of the French and English revolutions; his intent was purely political. A signal came when the short civil war in Switzerland in the autumn of 1847, the '*Sonderbundskrieg*', ended in victory for the democratic and radical cantons over the Catholic conservatives, and plans for Austrian intervention failed, mainly because of resistance from England. 'Lord Firebrand' had conquered 'Prince Midnight', and the victory blazed a trail for 'light and the law', even in Germany. Such was the prevailing atmosphere. Although revolution was not inevitable — least of all in the spring of 1848 — the 'critical mass' had been prepared. All that was required was a jolt to set it off.

It must be said that, following in the path of middle-class demands — though partly overcome by the shared opposition to the establishment — the pluralism of society and politics increased. The rise of the middle classes released the non-middle classes, who raised quite different demands conditioned by their social condition. The atmosphere of the 1840s was typified by this dualism, which was repeated in the tensions between liberalism and radicalism. These were the burdens to be overcome in the dawn of the state based on freedom, citizenry and constitution.

IV

Faith and Knowledge; Education and Art

1. Religion, Church, De-Christianisation

Nineteenth-century Germany was still an age marked by Christianity and the church. Their force in people's lives, thoughts and behaviour went without saying. For the state, society and culture they were also of crucial importance. Questions as to life's meaning or the meaning of 'truth' were purely religious matters. It is true that since the eighteenth century there has been a general shift towards secularisation, which has led to the relative decline of Christianity in the 20th century, where active Christians are a minority and religion and the church are relegated to a small and distinct area of life. But it would be wrong as a result to regard the 19th century as merely a prelude to this process. The 19th century was alive with the fight over Christianity and modernity, but in this fight, Christianity asserted and adapted itself and was renewed, even gaining in power and authority. The churches and religion were not simply relics of the past embedded in the 19th century; they were rather both products of it and forces which shaped its history.

At the turn of the century, the *Volk*, the vast majority of people, lived without questioning the teachings of Christianity and the church. These teachings influenced every aspect of family life, people's jobs and their standing in the community and were passed on through tradition and the catechism. The churches — half-enlightened, half-traditional — were not flourishing. The parish priests were not particularly well educated — many country priests were farmers as well — and few of them were filled with any religious fervour. The Catholic monasteries were attracting fewer and fewer people. Despite the opposition of tradition and Enlightenment with the church, much of religious life was often conventional and superficial by any normal, human standard. The state and the bureaucracy kept their distance, preferring to spoon-feed the churches and treat them like children. They saw the churches as channels for education, as a means of instilling morality and obedience, or for propagating useful things, just like bee-keeping or potato-farming. In Catholic regions, the state wanted to reform the churches, to secularise them and bring them under its control. The churches were not a very powerful force, neither were they are particularly vital or attractive one. Classicism and the Enlightenment held sway among the educated classes; the church and religion were not highly valued, for the *Zeitgeist*, the spirit of the age, was against them. We will discuss the 'religion of education' (*Bildungsreligion*) in Germany, as found, for example, in Goethe and Schiller, on the margins of and even beyond Christianity. Schleiermacher addressed his talks on religion to its 'scorners' rather than the believers — even if it was the 'educated' among them — and this is typical of the time.

And yet barely a decade and a half later, the situation had changed dramatically. Once more, the *Zeitgeist* was religious. Once more, religion was a fundamental part of the nation's psyche. It influenced the way people looked at their world, at life and their environment. All this had been brought about by several factors. The enormous upheavals wrought by twenty-five years of revolution and war could not be overcome by many people stoically or with 'Enlightenment'. Instead, they turned back to the old ideals, whereby the fate of an individual was determined by God's will. At first, the French Revolution had been greeted with enthusiasm in Germany as a means to free mankind. But once it had broken away from religion and then turned against it, it had led to countless atrocities under the Jacobins, where people were always being executed in the name of some new reason or other. Jacobin rule had led to continual chaos and confusion, to military despotism and endless wars. It had led to Napoleon's quest to conquer the world. The promise of freedom and reason free of religion had ended in a hideous débâcle. And was the Enlightenment not the very foundation of the Revolution? Should the Enlightenment's rejection of religion not be carefully examined? The intellectual movements of the day turned their attentions to these problems. The culture of classicism had a religious parallel — in the figures of Hamann, Jung-Stilling, Lavater and Claudius — which was not without influence. The opposition to the abstract rationalism, utilitarianism and moralism of the Enlightenment grew in strength. Romanticism was a cry against man's fixation for rationality and against the isolation which comes with complete autonomy. It was a cry against the 'heathen' religion of classicism. Romanticism turned back to the pre-rational and the non-rational, to the unconscious and the secret. It turned from the unholy present back to origins and tradition. It rejected rootlessness and alienation in favour of the ideals of common bonds and societies which stretched far beyond the individual. Romanticism rejected pure concepts in favour of symbols. It embraced a world which was familiar. It turned to the Middle Ages, to what was infinite and transcendent. And when Schleiermacher defined religion as a feeling of absolute dependency, then his definition was a purely Romantic one. The intellectuals of Romanticism had had their fill of the subjectivism of the Enlightenment. And they began to look for the comfort of a shelter, for a sense of security which would cushion and protect them, for something which was objective and independent of them. All this gave religion a new meaning. The philosophy of idealism saw itself both as the triumph over the Enlightenment and the reinterpretation and revitalisation of the Christian religion. The relationship between the mortal and the immortal became a central issue for philosophical thought and for a religious interpretation of life. There were also political changes: in strong contrast to the French Revolution, the reformers in Prussia saw their task as a religious one and wanted to see a society and a state founded in the rebirth of religion. The nationalist movement which was then forming was defiantly anti-Napoleon and ran contrary to the nationalism of the French Revolution. Because of this, it had a strong religious (and predominantly Protestant) streak. This was also true of the wars of liberation and the revolutionary student fraternities (*Burschenschaften*) of the following years, right up until the festival of the Wartburg and the figures of Karl Ludwig Sand and Karl Follen.

The return to religion had two aspects. The one which has perhaps been most emphasised was that it corresponded to the general spirit of the restoration. It was conservative in the widest sense. It was anti-revolutionary, opposed to the autocracy of reason and subjectivity, of the will of man and his abilities. It emphasised man's limits and his mortality. It stressed the lasting and inviolable order of the world, which would safeguard peace and continuity, the divine will, common bonds and tradition, the home and the hearth. It favoured such values as reverence and respect, piety, fidelity and obedience — all conservative values. It is not untypical that those Romantics who were so despairing of subjectivism should have been attracted to Catholicism. Catholicism was a less subjective, less rational, less sceptical form of Christianity with its rigid institutions, its symbolism and its rituals. The string of conversions among the Romantics, of Protestants such as Friedrich Schlegel, Zacharias Werner, Adam Müller, Franz Overbeck, and sceptical Catholics such as Clemens Brentano or Joseph Görres were indicative of this. In addition, the period was conservative in a strictly political sense. The state wanted an alliance between 'throne and altar'. This ran contrary to the anti-church stance of the Enlightenment, of enlightened absolutism, and of the period of the Confederation of the Rhine. Religion took on an important political function: the churches were regarded as the necessary pillars of authority. For only they could legitimate the power of the state, and only they (so it was believed) could prevent blatant struggle for power and its abuse.'Wenn man den Himmel revolutioniert, kann die Erde nicht ruhig bleiben,' said Heine. (If there is revolution in heaven, the earth cannot stand still.) This became the credo for the politicians of the restoration, from the rationalist Metternich to the pious King Friedrich Wilhelm IV of Prussia. Religion had to be preserved. It is characteristic of the political climate of the restoration in 1815 that the European powers should form a 'Holy Alliance' under which Christian principles should be called upon as the foundations and safeguards of social order and international law against revolution and war. 'Throne and altar' was not a slogan peculiar to Germany. It was common throughout Europe and had been heard first in England and then in France. Only in 1815 did it become a theme for the history of Germany. Of course, the plurality of denominations, as well as both the latent and acute tensions between church and state, made a close alliance impossible for any length of time. But it must be remembered that the revitalisation of religion after 1815 was by no means purely a result of political manipulation — it was a phenomenon in its own right.

It was said that there were two aspects to the return to religion: firstly, renewal and reform; but liberalisation, modernisation and even the legacies of the Enlightenment played their part. A new liberalism in religion stood alongside the aforementioned conservatism. This will be discussed later. Both in its conservative and liberal aspects, the re-evaluation and revitalisation of religion brought with it internal debate on tradition and the problem of opening up and reorganising the church: people fought against the modernists and even against a path of compromise. In contrast to the Protestants, the overall tendency for German Catholicism was to reject liberalism and the modern, to cut out any influences of the Enlightenment and centre itself around the two pillars of tradition and authority.

There was one further aspect to the return to religion which must be mentioned. At first, the contemplation of Christianity and its values was peaceful and unaffected by denominational barriers. But by reaching back to general religious truths, denominational truths were highlighted, which in turn led to a war of polemic between the different denominations, and this pervaded every aspect of public life throughout the middle third of the century. Should the Reformation, in its revolt against authority, be regarded as the source of all revolution, as the Catholics believed? Or was the Reformation in actual fact counter-revolutionary, with revolutions only occurring in Catholic countries, as the Protestant conservatives claimed? Or was the Reformation the principle of reasoned reform and non-violent evolution which Hegel and the liberals believed it to be? Such questions disguised many kinds of political, historical and denominational issues, and debates of this nature were commonplace.

(a) Catholicism

The history of the different denominations must now be considered: first of all the development of Catholicism.

As has been seen, the Catholic church in Germany was perhaps the one most affected by the enormous changes which followed the Revolution and the Napoleonic reforms. Its close ties with the political order of the old Reich and the social and economic constitution of the *ancien régime* crumbled. The church lost its share of power and a large part of its estates and incomes. It can be said that the church was effectively de-feudalised. This had important consequences for the 19th century. Firstly, the Catholic church, whose spiritual character had for so long been accompanied and at times even been eclipsed by its power and property, reverted to a purely religious institution; questions of authority were now exclusively questions of religious authority. The secularisation of ecclesiastical rule and church estates may have signified the dispossession of the church, but it also meant its liberation: it was the basis for a re-spiritualisation of the church which would be felt throughout the whole of the 19th century. The first, immediate consequence of de-feudalisation was that the church was no longer a church for the nobility. Cathedral chapter and episcopates no longer provided for the younger sons of the nobility. The clergy became 'bourgeois' (though it would not be until after the middle of the century that bishops from the nobility would become an exception, and they would never disppear completely). The church was following the general trend of the 19th century towards a bourgeois society, and towards a greater social equality. The new bishops were not, however, simply the bourgeois, less wordly successors of the older ones. They had (and this is the third consequence of secularisation) even less power and importance, while the Pope and the curia gained in power and authority. The old episcopalism (the belief that the church should be governed by bishops) was replaced by the new 'papalism', the centralism of Rome and the absolutism of the Pope. The Catholic church became less a church of bishops and more the church of a single Pope, less a regional-national church and more one of international importance and stature. The process was a very complicated one in Europe. It was not only the increasing power of Rome and the Pope which played a part, but the 'democratic' opposition of the lower clergy and laymen against the 'aristocracy' of the bishops. Most influential of all was the church's determination to maintain a powerful, independent and international force in the face of the modern, powerful state. The rise of the papacy in the 19th century was (apart from the ultramontanist movement which will be discussed in a moment) a result of the rise of the modern state at the beginning of the century. The Catholic church developed an altogether different relationship to the state now that it no longer had direct or indirect access to power. It now confronted the state without its feudal, estate or corporative rights. It was also confronted with a new form of state: a state whose sovereignty was extensive, a state with a bureaucracy and later on a parliament and a constitution, a state of denominational parity and tolerance. The old ties with the rulers and the territorial state had disappeared, and as a result, the church could no longer remain unaffected by the territorial shambles of the Third Germany.

In order to consider the inner development of Catholicism, there must first follow a discussion of the history of theology and ideas of the time. It would be foolish to dismiss these areas as esoteric. Apart from being important in their own right, it must not be forgotten that they are not without wider implications. So, for example, it may be seen, that through the catechism and through the instruction of clergy, the current ideas in theology were able to shape the mentality of the common people.

There are three trends to consider after 1815. Firstly, there was the continuing 'enlightenment' of Catholicism, which had an impact on every generation up until 1840: this involved loosening the dogmatic, juridical and ritualistic aspects of the church. People rejected the old, ornate acts of piety such as pilgrimages. There was opposition to the mendicant orders, and a new rational and Christian humanity was preached. There was reform of the church service, even to the extent of having a German mass. Heinrich Ignaz von Wessenberg is one example of the Catholic enlightenment. A product of the feudal church — he was vicar-general in Constance from 1802, he had been a prebendary since 1792, but was not ordained until 1812 — he educated a whole generation of enlightened, well-educated and worldly priests in his own seminary in Meersburg, and they were to be of great importance for south-west Germany up until 1848.

Secondly, there were attempts to reconcile Catholicism with the prevailing tendencies of the time and thereby revitalise it. Georg Hermes, professor of theology in Bonn from 1819, tried to explain the Catholic faith on the basis of a psychological interpretation of Kantian philosophy and thus reconcile science with faith. The Viennese theologian Anton Günther made a similar attempt using the philosophy of Hegel. Both had a considerable number of students, Hermes having almost a complete monopoly on theological training in the Rhineland. Both were placed on the Index (Hermes in 1835, Günther in 1857), and their teachings were suppressed.

Attempts to revitalise Catholicism in conjunction with the main trends in German culture, with classicism and *Empfindsamkeit* (the age of sentimentalism) and especially with Romanticism, as well as other attempts to overcome the division between German culture and Catholicism, had more lasting effects. An example of this can be seen in the efforts — modelled on those of the circle around Princess Gallitzin in Münster — of Johann Michael Sailer, professor and later Bishop of Landshut, to introduce the spirit of Pestalozzi and Goethe's *Bildung* (development or education) into Catholicism, to internalise faith and lead the church to *edler Einfalt* (noble simplicity). This would help bring about and develop a new, pious humanity and intimacy which had almost been worn out by dogma, institution and authority; the central issues of the Enlightenment were thereby simply swept under the carpet. Sailer made a profound and lasting impression, particularly in Bavaria on Ludwig I and his advisers. In Vienna, the priest Clemens Maria Hofbauer gathered round him a group of intellectuals (his popularity with the *Volk* is another matter) who despised the Enlightenment, but who were well disposed to Romanticism. In this way the case of Romanticism against the Enlightenment took on a Catholic tone, and the conversion of Friedrich Schlegel illustrates this. The process led to a type of Late Romanticism in Munich in 1826, when the old Bavarian University was re-established in that city. The audacity of the Enlightenment and the dualism of faith and knowledge would be overcome by a new Catholic and Romantic science. Joseph Görres, who has already been mentioned, a Jacobin in Coblenz back in the 1790s and a Romantic in Heidelberg, who had returned to Catholicism in 1821, and all his circle were examples of this; as was the short-lived journal *Eos* (1823–32), the philosopher Franz von Baader and Johann Ringseis, a medical doctor. There seemed to be an effort to make Munich the intellectual centre of German Catholicism, rather than Vienna. It can thus be seen that Catholicism was closely connected with contemporary education and intellectual development.

Finally, from a theological point of view: there was the school at Tübingen and its journal the *Theologische Quartalsschrift*. The church historian Johann Adam Möhler used the term 'organism' in its early historicist meaning. The church was not merely a body of dogma and legal institutions, but a living organism, a closely interwoven, evolving system. Behind every single detail and all the debris of past tradition there stood a unifying principle, a 'spirit', a view of life. Behind all the dogma there was real existential, anthropological substance. If only people would stop reducing man to mere reason as the Enlightenment did, and instead take his desires and feelings into account, then they would be able to grasp this substance. The church was not to be regarded as an historical institution, but as something which could grow and develop. It was the sum of many isolated parts. Here was the true meaning of 'Catholic'. In history, even truth could develop and grow, in a way similar to what Hegel had described. It was from these postulates that Möhler defined anew the contrast between Catholicism and Protestantism in his book *Symbolik* (Symbolism) and tried to show that Protestantism started from a pessimistic view of man. He also tried to prove that Protestant liberalism and criticism of the Bible was an inevitable consequence of Luther's criticism of tradition. It is interesting to note that while the Catholic opponents of the group in Tübingen saw these approaches as a 'Protestantisation' of Catholicism, the search for origins and the attempt to define historically the underlying idea of Protestantism only served to sharpen the contrast between the denominations which rose out of pan-Christian Romanticism. The huge literary and journalistic uproar which greeted the publication of the book was an indication both of the climate of the period and the style of debate between the denominations, and it showed the enormous importance of such debate to the period. The aim of the second key representative of this school, Johann Baptist Hirscher, was to establish a fresh approach to ethics. He rejected casuistry, the authoritarian standardised approach to problems and the cool formulae of an ethical system based on specific prescriptions. In their place, as a spiritual follower of Pascal, he sought to understand ethics through a single, unifying principle. He endeavoured to link ethics to the subjectiveness of man and his potential to do good; that emphasis was rather unorthodox for this particular school of thought, and for this reason Hirscher ran into conflict with the strengthening orthodoxy. As a result, he never became a bishop as had previously been expected. The relative liberality and plurality which first characterised the school were effectively suppressed in its 'second' generation. Its Catholicism became harsher, more aggressive and more pointedly anti-rational: Ignaz Döllinger, who represented the old-style Catholicism in the debate surrounding the dogma of infallibility, was, in his early years, the outstanding intellectual talent of the movement.

However large an influence these movements of regeneration may have been for the educated classes for even decades afterwards, they were not of any lasting importance for the large mass of Catholics or for the Catholic church as a whole. What was important, however, was the emergence of the so-called ultramontanist movement, a harsh and polemical rejection of the age. The aim of the supporters of the movement was that Catholicism should finally learn to assert itself in what was felt to be a hostile period and environment. Up until then the church had been shaped by the necessity to defend itself against the relentless attacks of its enemies: the modern state, modern society, liberalism, and the spirit of the age. From now on, the church was going to have to concentrate on itself and reject any compromise with the outside world and the *Zeitgeist*. It would have to reject any ties from outside. All wordly concerns, politics and society, culture and science above all, were to be looked at in the light of Catholicism. They would have to judged by how well they conformed with Catholic teaching. This is what was meant by Catholic 'integralism'. People looked to the past and tried to re-establish the spirit and form of the Counter-Reformation and its scholasticism. The Catholic church would have to be united and unified if this were to happen. There could be no room for pluralism or individual differences. And for this reason, the church had to have rigid hierarchy and strong discipline. Furthermore, it would have to have a centre. Here was the change. The church became strictly orientated around Rome, hence the name 'ultramontanism' (literally, 'on the other side of the mountains' — as Rome was from Germany). To be more precise, it became strictly orientated around the now absolute authority of the Pope. The church had become a church of priests in a new sense. The clergy were organised into a strict hierarchy, and their authority was crucial.

The movement started out in Mainz. Its driving forces were the Bishop of Mainz, Colmar, and his leading advisers, Liebermann and Räss (later Bishop of Strasbourg). These men were from Alsace, and they had been deeply shocked by the Revolution in the 1790s. From 1821, the movement centred itself around the journal *Der Katholik*. The movement rejected, as has been said, the general spirit of the age. It opposed the state with unusual bitterness and implacability for the way it interfered with and controlled the church, and in the way it pushed the church out of the public domain, as for example, in the schools. It despised the state for the way it tried to diminish the influence of the church, and for its egalitarianism and profaneness. More importantly, ultramontanism was initially a movement within the church itself. It was a movement against those who wanted to modernise the church, whether wholly or even partly, and against those who compromised or deviated from it. It rejected those members of the clergy who fraternised with the state, the episcopalists, the supporters of a national church and the opponents of Rome as the church's centre. Ultramontanism rejected the opponents of papal absolutism, the opponents of discipline and hierarchy, those who opposed a neo-scholastic theology, a casuistic morality and the Roman forms of religious devotion. Above all, it rejected all Catholics who were not ultramontanists — and at that point that meant the majority of the church. It can be seen in one of the main themes of the 1820s and 1830s: the fight against the universities. Ultramontanists wanted Catholic priests to be educated in closed seminaries rather than 'modernistic' universities, which they boycotted as a result of their objection to state influence, the 'worldly' atmosphere and unsuitable theologians. At the very least, they demanded that these institutions be controlled from Rome. It caused a great deal of conflict throughout the 1820s.

After the 1840s, the ultramontanist movement, with help from Rome, gradually took hold of the church in Germany. Its influence was stronger in some places than in others. In Marburg and Giessen, for example, whole faculties were shut down, while in Bonn and Munich, the period of 'drying out' lasted much longer, even over a period of many years. The theologians at the universities were particularly closely watched by the guardians of orthodoxy and, where necessary, were denounced to Rome. The Jesuit seminary for priests in Rome, the Collegium Germanicum, which had been reopened in 1824, was instrumental in this. The 'Germanics' who were educated there, were seen as absolutely loyal to Rome and were given leading roles. From 1840 onwards, the episcopal sees began to be filled by the supporters of the movement, from Mainz to Cologne, Eichstätt and Munich, and even as far as Breslau. In the theological faculties they also became more prominent. As the predominance of Rome and the scope of her authority increased, so discipline, hierarchy and control within the church strengthened. With the orientation to Rome as the new 'headquarters' of the church and the emergence of a pro-absolutist and ultramontanist 'party', the old episcopalism and independence of bishops, indeed the whole character of a 'national' church and all its institutions, soon disappeared. Hirscher's idea of introducing synods into the dioceses in 1848, for example, was defeated by the general opposition of the ultramontanists to the measure, which they saw as a step towards 'democratisation'. Similarly, an idea, aired at the the first conference of bishops in 1848, to establish a national synod and an Archbishop of Germany was dropped because Rome disapproved. Obedience to the church, to Rome and to the Pope became the primary virtue for a Catholic. The status of the Pope increased, and after being expelled from Rome in 1848 by the revolution, he came to be regarded almost as a martyr, an opinion strengthened by the fact that the independence of the church and even the very existence of the Papal States seemed threatened. This opinion was officially sanctioned by the Vatican Council of 1870 when it introduced the dogma of infallibility. Theology became founded on the stringency of its dogma. Form, institutions and codes came to dominate the church, while its 'spirit' diminished.

As the church was transformed by the ultramontanist movement, so the religious practices within the church changed. The modern ones and those of the Catholic Enlightenment were consciously replaced by older ones which bore the stamp of the baroque and the Counter-Reformation. They had a more southern, more Latin flavour to them. Examples of this were the exuberant revival of the cult of the Virgin Mary and the tenet of the Immaculate Conception. These were accompanied by new cults and saint worship, such as the cults of Joseph and the Sacred Heart, and the reappraisal of phenomena such as miracles and stigmata. Pilgrimages, acts of penance, missions, strict and formal acts of conspicuous piety and devotion (such as eternal prayer), brotherhoods, religious orders and a new sentimentalisation and emotionalisation of religion and piety were once again common practice. The monasteries and the religious orders were revived and their numbers swelled. In Bavaria in 1825, there were 27 monasteries. In 1837 this number had grown to 83. During the following years it grew to 160 in 1848, until finally, in 1864, there were 441 monasteries throughout Bavaria. The monasteries held great influence in areas such as schooling and nursing. The upsurge was fundamental to the revival of Catholicism. Above all, old orders such as the Jesuits and the Redemptorists, which for so long had barely been permitted in Germany, were now given special encouragement. Casuistry and general, authoritative statements were applied to the confession box and to morality as a whole. The topic of the church was given priority in sermons. Acts of devotion became more demonstrative — even displays of loyalty to the church and to the Pope and the suppression of individual opinion. The displays became more material, more ostentatious and, as a result, more superficial. Spectacles of mass piety dominated public festivals and gatherings, in strong contrast to the Enlightenment, which preferred the personal and the individual. One famous example of this was the exhibition of the Holy Garment in Trier in 1844. Even for the Catholics of the time, this was extraordinary: 1.1 million pilgrims travelled from all over the country, at a time where there were still very few railways. For fifty-nine days there were huge processions with crosses and flags. The sick were healed, and the news spread fast and furious: this was Christ's 'inspection' of the faithful. It was a demonstration against the spirit of an age which had been corrupted by science.

The pilgrimage gave rise to the vociferous separatist and oppositonal movement of the 'German Catholics', who have been much discussed. Johannes Ronge was a priest from Silesia who had run into conflict with the church over the enforced resignation of the enlightened Josephinist Prince-Bishop of Breslau. Ronge attacked Arnoldi, the Bishop of Trier, accusing him of encouraging superstition and vice in allowing the pilgrimage, which he saw as idolatry. The affair excited enormous interest, and Ronge was excommunicated. There was a strong movement of appeal for Ronge. Coins and goblets bearing his image even appeared, and 'German Catholic' congregations were formed. Germans wanted to be led to God in their own way. They wanted to destroy the hypocrisy of the clerics and the Jesuits and purify religion. They wanted to reconcile mankind through love and freedom in the spirit of the age. They were defiantly pro-Enlightenment and anti-Rome. They were influenced by Protestantism — around two-fifths of their members were Protestants. The radicals and the liberals set great store by this movement. They hoped it would undermine the Church of Rome, the harbour for reactionism, and reconcile the nation and religion in a national church (according to Gervinius), or reconcile religion and democracy (according to Robert Blum). But despite a great deal of sensation and hope, despite publicity and parliamentary debates, the movement remained nothing more than a sect, and in 1848 numbered no more than 60,000. In the end, it actually strengthened ultramontanism and loyalty to the church, because of its radicalism, which forced many anti-clerical and anti-ultramontanist Catholics to side with the official church.

The ultramontanisation of Church and religion was accompanied by a mobilisation of the masses, of the *Volk*. Paradoxically, the church, which was so opposed to everything that was new and modern, was itself using the most modern methods. It used the people's support, organised it and created a democratic-plebiscite basis for the new Catholicism, despite the overall clericalisation of the church and the large role the clergy played in many organisations. An extensive church press network soon grew up during the 1830s and 1840s, in the manner of the aforementioned journal *Der Katholik*. Sunday newspapers appeared, almanacs, periodic tracts, etc. (Catholic dailies only appeared after 1848). Catholic organisations also began to appear during the 1840s. In Bonn in 1844, for example, the *Borromäusverein* or Borromeo Society, which was named after a saint of the Counter-Reformation, was founded to distribute books for Catholic people. In 1845, the charitable nursing organisations, the *Vincenzvereine* (Societies of St Vincent), and the *Kolpingsche Gesellenvereine* (Kolping Brotherhood) were founded, and in 1849 the *Bonifatiusverein* (Boniface Society) for the Catholics of the diaspora, which produced propaganda for a return to Catholicism. After that, many different sorts of societies were set up for many different groups — for craftsmen, farmers, workers, young people — and for specific areas of the church — missions, the defence of the church, etc. 'Association Catholicism' (*Verbandskatholizismus*) had arrived. In 1848, there was the first general assembly of the new *Piusvereine* (Pius Societies), the 'spiritual parliament of the Catholic people', and after that, all these societies and associations met regularly at the large all-German Catholic conferences.

The arrival of ultramontanism meant that (particularly in education) secular, non-Catholic movements in culture, society and politics had to be guarded against. International as it was, the Catholic church, at least in Germany, resisted any attempts to make it a national church. The efforts of Catholic Romanticism, for example, to give official recognition to a specifically German form of Catholicism, as opposed to its Latin form, or to combine Catholicism with the nationalist movement, were regarded as heretical. To have too much contact with Protestants, or to display a piety which was either too ethical or too spiritualised, were similarly denounced as heresy. Even an assembly of Catholic scholars that Döllinger wanted to convene in Munich in 1863 ran into difficulties because the ultramontanists were opposed to any degree of independence. As a result, there was a certain hardening, even a nervous aggressiveness towards anything which was not Catholic. It also led to a certain degree of sectarianisation of everyday social life, where the 'Casino' societies became the social centres for the Catholic middle classes.

Catholic teachings were at odds with the rest of the modern world. In an encyclical in 1864, the Pope drew up a list of eighty failings of the age, and these were appendixed in a 'Syllabus of Errors'. They included freedom of religion, freedom of opinion and freedom of science; civil marriage, state church and state schools; liberalism and free-masonry; sovereignty of the people and democracy, universal suffrage and sovereignty of the nation; socialism and capitalism — in fact anything which might connect the Pope with progress, liberalism or modern civilisation. It was a concise and powerful declaration of war against the modern world. Opposition to everything that was modern became the criterion of orthodoxy. Of course, in the form it took, it resembled more an exaggeration on the part of Rome, even if it did concisely convey the intentions of the ultramontanist movement. The German Catholic Conference of 1865, for example, tried to soften the tone, by declaring that (one is tempted to add 'of course') only anti-Catholic liberalism was intended, not a Catholic-based, constitutional liberalism; neither did it mean concepts of freedom in general. In Germany, the Syllabus played more of a role in Protestant-liberal polemics than in the day-to-day workings of Catholicism.

There were still reservations about the ultramontanist movement, however. There were still some vicars-general and professors of theology among the clergy, who were either anti-ultramontanist or simply non-ultramontanist. The dogma of infallibility, which had been developed during the 1860s — the crowning glory, so to speak, of the papalistic-ultramontanist movement — met with widespread antipathy, for which Döllinger provided a scholarly basis. Even the majority of bishops could not support it, for a variety of reasons, some objective, some opportunistic. The aversion of (educated) German Catholics to the Jesuits had been slow to disappear. The clergy of Baden found little support with the Catholic middle classes during the *Kulturkampf* of the 1850s. And the reform-Catholicism of the romantics was still prominent among the educated classes. Certainly, Catholics had much closer ties with the modern world and its culture than many priests and supporters of the Syllabus would have wished, especially if they were not involved in the institutional side of the church. And Catholics in Austria — who were, of course, in the majority and still in the Josephinist tradition — were less affected by the new style of devotion in the church. This is particularly true among the educated middle classes, in the large cities and in the Sudetenland. In the areas of the later Reich where Catholics were in the minority (and even in Bavaria), the influence was greater. But the church and its clergy had become strongly ultramontane; the opponents of ultramontanism were on the defensive, and they were fighting a losing battle. The educated Catholics of the age suffered a great deal and were faced with agonising conflicts, for they could never fully go along with the church. As a result, there was bitterness and resignation, silence and self-denial. They were forced to adapt. They were forced to shut out the problems between the church and modernity and were not allowed the liberty to ask any questions.

Among the lower middle classes and the peasants, there was a certain amount of anti-clerical feeling, and a certain hostility to many of the manifestations of the new style of church. But there was also a feeling of loyalty towards the church, which had been instilled by tradition and which was now stronger; the women felt it more than the men. People adapted to the church and the trends within it. The feeling (and the fact) that the Catholic faith and the Catholic church were under threat from the state and from liberalism, and the need for unity in the face of a hostile world, were not without success. For this reason, there was no 'modernistic' opposition within the Catholic church and, on the whole, no de-Christianisation or diminuation of church power. There are no definite statistics on church attendance, but in comparison with German Protestants and with certain rural and urban areas in France, the number of people who fell away from the church and the degree to which religious ties were weakened, was slight. At most, it could be seen in the proletarianised lower classes, who were breaking away from traditional ties. An indication of the strength of church ties can be seen at the height of the *Kulturkampf*, when three-quarters of Catholic voters supported the Catholic party. It is also significant that it was mainly workers born into Protestant families who organised and supported the decidedly un-Christian movement for social democracy. It may be assumed that for the majority of its followers the Catholic faith was far more than just a small part of their lives; rather it was central to the very balance of their lives.

Despite whatever criticisms Catholics today may have against the rise of ultramontanism and the development of a 'ghetto church' in the face of a hostile world, and despite whatever difficulty modern man (or a Protestant author) may have in understanding the anti-modern and un-modern stance of ultramontane Catholicism, the extent to which it succeeded in asserting itself in both church and milieu, and in faith and organisation, must be taken into account. It was the successful self-assertion of a minority against the political and social establishment, and against the dominant trends of the time. The fight for freedom and emancipation of political Catholicism was based on the process of revitalisation of the Catholic church, which, paradoxically, was certainly not primarily an emancipatory process in itself. Certainly, ultramontanism served only to heighten the differences between the denominations, which were already weighing on German society, just as it served to fire the anti-Catholicism of both religious and non-religious Protestants. But it must be remembered that the anti-Catholicism of the *kleindeutsche* liberal nationalists was prevalent throughout the whole of the 19th century in Germany, no matter what form Catholicism took.

The development of Catholicism, both in the church and in the faith of the people, was not determined by forces within Catholicism alone. Perhaps the most decisive factor was the relationship between the state and the church. This can be see in the phenomenon of the *Kulturkampf*. How did this relationship develop?

The overall trend of the 19th century was to separate church and state: to free the state from the church, and the church from the state. But it did not prove easy to dissolve the traditional ties between the two powers. It was far more than just a legal problem, for the ties were deeply embedded, socially, politically, metapolitically and morally. A force such as the church, which held power over life itself, interacted directly with political constitution and social order. The two could not be isolated from one another. The church could hardly be totally divorced from politics. The state laid claims to authority in spiritual issues, the church to authority in worldly issues. The state saw its task in ensuring peace and law among its citizens (and that, of course, meant among church members, and between church members and the clergy) and in ensuring parity and tolerance between the different denominations. The church, on the other hand, not only demanded independence from the state, but wanted to take an active part in public life. The church's claim on control over the form of society, of the public, went up against the state's claim on issues of sovereignty, law and peace.

The conflict between the two sides flared up first of all on the issues where these claims overlapped — marriage and education. In the modern state, mixed denominational marriages and marriages where partners did not always heed the judgment of the church, (particularly in cases of divorce) turned to the state for legal settlement. The 'civil' marriage took its place alongside church marriage, even if it was only an option at first. And it was in the early part of the 19th century that the school was to become an independent social force, as will be discussed later. The interest of the state in educating a person to be a citizen ran into conflict with the interest of the church in educating a person to be a Christian. The traditional church as educator came up against the modern state as organiser. Or, from a different point of view, the fight for the schools was an inevitable result of the increased schooling of society. The conflict between state and church also flared up on another issue — the issue of church autonomy. To what extent should it be subject to and part of the state after the demise of absolutism? At question here was the authority of the church within the state and the authority of the state within the church: the state had banned all direct official communication between the bishops and Rome; all church (and papal) rulings had to receive state approval (the *placet*); there was strong state influence in the election of bishops and other church offices; clergymen had the right to appeal to state jurisdiction against the decisions of their superiors; the state alone could authorise orders and monasteries; and the state had a say in the training of the clergy. Behind all this was a fundamental question: to what extent did the church, which held a decisive moral and social power over a large mass of people, owe obedience and unconditional loyalty to the state? There were other issues as well: the excessive bureaucratic power the state had held over the church during the late Enlightenment and the period of the Confederation of the Rhine; state interference to reform what were considered 'abuses' within the church; the use of the church and religion for reasons of state; and the education of the people to a unified society of the state. After 1815, such issues receded, but both in the memories of those who had been affected, and in the general trend of the bureaucracy, they were still virulent. In short, the themes for the great conflict of the 19th century had been set.

The dissolution of the old Reich and the old church with it had led to a situation where the demarcation of the dioceses bore no relation to the new political boundaries, and where 'old' dioceses stood empty because the old ways of electing bishops were no longer applicable. The financial provision of the church was also no longer guaranteed. After 1815, these problems had to be resolved. According to the Congress of Vienna, it was not the German Confederation which would be responsible for this, but each respective state. But because the Catholic church came under the jurisdiction of the Pope, a foreign power, any such resolution could only come about through an international agreement between the state and the Roman curia — a concordat. The reigning bureaucracy in the German states was unwilling to surrender any rights to the church (a legacy, perhaps, from the period of church sovereignty). It wanted, moreover, to consolidate its existing rights and achieve a sovereignty of its own by bringing the organisation of the church into line with politics. It would do this by replacing the old dioceses, which bore no relation to any political boundaries, with new dioceses organised within state borders. These problems led to sharp conflicts in the south of Germany. After long negotiations, which had been made all the more difficult by the fact that they supported the enlightened vicar-general of Constance, Heinrich Ignaz von Wessenberg, while Rome was demanding his resignation, the south-western states (which, it must be noted, had Protestant monarchs and civil servants) finally reached a compromise in 1821: Wessenberg would be dropped and his old diocese dissolved; five new dioceses would be formed from it — Freiburg, Rottenburg, Mainz, Limburg and Fulda. In the election of bishops, the state had the right of veto, even in the nominating process. The first bishops were, on the whole, amicable to the state. With the help of new ordinances, the state's power over the church was secure.

In Bavaria, Montgelas negotiated a concordat in 1817 — in part to restrain Catholic opposition to the new state. Here, too, the old dioceses were redrawn to fit the new state borders. The king nominated the bishops, who had to swear an oath to the state. The church was generously financed, and its administrative and disciplinary powers were guaranteed. A general clause saw to it that the state would guarantee the privileges and rights claimed by the church under canon law. That led to a storm of protest, not only among Protestants but also among Catholics opposed to Rome, for it in effect subjected state legislation and administration (over marriage, censorship, tolerance, parity) to control by the church. The government sought to revoke this subjugation of its power by introducing at the constitutional level a law pertaining to religion; this led to a sharp conflict with the bishops and the church, which was formally ended — if not entirely resolved — with a compromise in 1821, which allowed the state to keep its position of strength. Despite the passionate rhetoric, the conflicts in the south-western states progressed harmlessly relative to those that would come later. This was primarily because the ultramontanist movement was not yet dominant, and because the bulk of the public was not as involved as they would become later, and because the compromises had been made with a clergy that was in no way opposed to the state.

Even in Austria a similar compromise was reached, though without a concordat. The 'state-ecclesiastical' tradition of enlightened Josephism endured, and so did state supervision of the church. The Jesuits —the symbol of the subjugation of the spirit and a real bogey for many Austrians — were not tolerated. But open conflicts were avoided. To safeguard his policy of restoration, Metternich — himself a rationalist of the 18th century — sought to bring the church, as a force for order and education, to the aid of the state. State policy slowly began to take on clericalist features; the most extreme example came in 1837, when Protestants were banished from the Ziller valley — in fundamental violation of the law, even in Austria. The event produced wild outrage in Germany. Because, however, the state did not fully bow to the desires of the church — because it remained 'Josephist' — the church kept its reservations.

In Prussia, in contrast to both the Catholic and Protestant parts of the south, the relationship between the church and state was good. The state, Protestant by tradition and in its ruling classes, now had to contend with the Catholics who made up two-fifths of the whole population (including the Poles). It was therefore concerned to maintain a good relationship with the Catholic church and integrate its various groups, particularly in the area around the Rhine and in Westphalia, where the population had a well-developed consciousness of its separate identity. The year 1821 saw the first agreements on the division of the dioceses, on the state's right of veto in the election of bishops, on the supervisory rights of the state, and on the substantial financial support the state would offer the Catholic church (even in comparison with that of the Protestant church).

The relationship, which began so peacefully, was shattered by the argument over 'mixed' marriages. Such marriages were growing in number, owing to the slight increase in intercourse between denominations, and because the decision to marry was becoming an increasingly personal one. In the Catholic regions in the west, marriages between Protestant officers and civil servants and the Catholic daughters of the middle classes and aristocracy played a significant role. The state regarded marriage for the middle classes as a legal matter of parity and tolerance — in the civil law of these regions, the sons followed the denomination of the father, the daughters the denomination of the mother. After the 1820s, however, in general all children adopted the denomination of the father. As things stood, this favoured the Protestants, and the Catholics of the Rhineland and Westphalia saw it as an invasion of Protestantism and the Protestantisation of Catholic families. In the Catholic church, a 'mixed' marriage was only possible with special dispensation which ensured that the children would be brought up as Catholics. The Protestants saw this as 'proselytisation' and demanded that the state 'protect' the Catholic brides' freedom of conscience from the pressures of the Catholic church. The contradiction between the state norm and the church norm was reconciled at first by a so-called 'mild practice' on the part of the church: the priests would marry mixed couples and give them their blessing (marriage was, after all, both religious and symbolic), even without the required promise on the education of the children. But in the 1820s, when ultramontanism was beginning to grow in strength, and the tensions between the Catholic middle classes in the west and the civil servants in Prussia were mounting, the practice became more problematic. At first, a (secret) compromise was reached between the government and the bishops in 1834, which gave a very generous interpretation to the Pope's instructions on the subject, issued in the form of a papal brief: if the bride indicated her intention that at least some of the children would be brought up as Catholics, then the marriage would receive the blessing of the Catholic church. The agreement was rejected, however, after much indecision, by the new Archbishop of Cologne, Clemens August von Droste zu Vischering. It also became public when it was revoked — from his deathbed — by the Bishop of Trier. The archbishop, a conservative and an ultramontanist, had, at the instigation of the Prussian government, been appointed in 1835, to the astonishment of the clergy and against the wishes of the majority of the cathedral chapter. The ensuing arguments intensified after Rome's condemnation of the theologian Hermes (mentioned above), when the new archbishop — also against the will of the cathedral chapter — barred all prospective priests from attending the state-run faculty of theology in Bonn, in order to maintain his own authority there. They also intensified because the Catholic middle classes of the Rhine were opposed to the Protestant character of the Prussian state and the discrmination of Catholics which this entailed.

The issue became the subject of great journalistic debate: first of all in 1835, in the *Articles on the History of the Church in 19th-Century Germany*, the so-called 'Red Book', which served as a firebrand to set off all the explosive material that had built up. The public was now getting involved in the conflict between two traditional, established institutions, and this was a new phenomenon. On both sides, the strategies aimed at conflict won out. The archbishop, with the zealous support of the ultramontanists, rejected both a return to the agreement and calls for his resignation. The government, on the other hand, ordered his suspension from office in November 1837 and, under threat of coercion, he was forced to leave the region. This was referred to as his 'arrest', and it all became known as the 'Cologne Incident'. The government claimed that the archbishop had put himself in the wrong through his ambiguous confirmation to uphold the agreement when he had neither the support of his cathedral chapter nor that of Catholicism in general. But his 'arrest', without the judgment of a court, was politically motivated and contravened both the legal principles of the age and the basic order of Prussia. It was seen, therefore, as 'legal' despotism and put both the state and the government in the wrong. The Pope and bishops took issue with the state in the sharpest tones, and the conflict spread to the east. In 1839, the Archbishop of Posen was 'arrested', and in turn the Pope forced the resignation of the Bishop of Breslau, who was well disposed towards the government. Not since 1815 had public opinion been aroused to such an extent. In

January 1838, Joseph Görres published his *Athanasius* (four editions by April of the same year), in which he popularised, simplified, emphasised and polarised with great rhetorical feeling the concrete legal issues involved, and transformed them into a matter of principle between the church and state, between Catholicism and Protestantism. The book it was a charter for political Catholicism. In 1838, over 300 leaflets appeared on the topic. Even the Pope and the government entered the forum of public debate with 'white papers', a revolutionary event. Most but not all Protestant conservatives and liberals sided with the state. Any common ground between Catholic and Protestant conservatives crumbled. Catholicism began to form its own party. It was — understandably, given the circumstances of its formation — strongly anti-Prussian; that is the most important consequence of the crisis for the subsequent history of Germany. When Friedrich Wilhelm IV came to the throne in 1840, with his politics of a 'Christian state' and the free association of church and state, the conflict was laid aside. The state backed down on the fundamental issues, such as mixed marriages, and the bishops' right of veto in the appointment of chairs in the faculties of theology. A Catholic 'department' was set up in the ministry of education and the arts. The state saved face through the suspension of the Archbishop of Cologne, and a coadjutor, Geissel, one of the leading and most important ultramontanists, took over his duties. On 4 September 1842 a festival was held to celebrate the resumption of work on Cologne Cathedral. It was a celebration of the Rhine and of Prussia, of Germany and the monarchy, and of the German people. It was a celebration of state representation and integration, and also a celebration of the church. It was, finally, a festival to celebrate the reconciliation between church and state.

Under the influence of both ultramontanism and liberalism during the 1830s, the Catholic church's demand for independence from the authoritarian state with its claim to an ever-increasing role in society, and in marriage and education in particular, steadily grew. At the same time, the church gradually cut itself off from Protestantism as well as the new liberal culture. As a result, new conflicts developed in areas outside Prussia. In Baden and in Württemberg, the old bones of contention (independence of the church, mixed marriages and the sanction of religious orders) were felt more sharply, to which came new ones such as authority over the seminaries. Government and liberals moved closer together against the 'clerical' party. Faced with this opposition, the anti-ultramontanist Catholics, who had been in the majority at first, were crushed. The atmosphere in Baden during the 1840s could be described as one of latent *Kulturkampf*. From 1837 in Bavaria, on the other hand, Karl von Abel's ministry followed a more 'clerical' course: monasteries and religious orders were supported, bonuses were given in jobs for faithfulness to the church, schools became religious, and there was discrimination against Protestants. In 1839, the King of Bavaria decreed that any soldier, whether Catholic or Protestant, could be ordered to attend mass, and that any soldier, whether Catholic or Protestant, had to kneel before the Holy Sacrament, even in processions (the so-called *Kniebeugungserlass*, or Decree of Genuflection). It was only after prolonged and heated arguments throughout Germany, and widespread journalistic debate, that the king was reluctantly forced to revoke this unconstitutional decree. What the Cologne Incident had been for the Catholics, the Decree of Genuflection was for the Protestants. Both were indicative of the new climate of increased interdenominational tension. There was a great deal of opposition to Bavaria's new 'clerical' course, by no means limited to the liberals and the Protestants — in the *Adelskammer* (House of Nobles), for example, or in the figure of the Crown Prince. In a move very out of step with the times, the king's affair with Lola Montez led to the replacement of the ultramontane ('Jesuit') regiment by a *lolamontane* one, as the citizens of Munich mockingly called it.

The role of Catholicism in the revolution of 1848 will be discussed later. It is sufficient to point out here that the church placed itself within the realm of liberal constitutional policy and achieved a whole string of its constitutional demands by compromising with the liberals and with the aid of a strong popular movement. The church was independent and administered its own affairs. The state could only monitor this within the framework of general rather than specific church laws. Jesuits could not be banned. The churches were equal before the law. There was no privileged (quasi-state) church, and no one could be forced to behave or act according to the dictates of the church. This meant, for example, that civil marriage was now possible. One of the basic demands of the liberals was that all aspects of schooling except religious instruction be supervised by the state. Private (i.e. Catholic) schools could, however, be set up, and they would be financed by the local authorities. In this way, Catholics could expect Catholic schools if there were a Catholic majority. The constitution never came into force, but it demonstrated just what could be achieved through compromise. The Prussian constitution which did come into force had similar results and became known to Catholics as 'the Magna Carta of religious freedom'.

Governments during the period of reaction sought the support of the church in their effort to re-establish the conservative order. They tended to back down on the old issues — they allowed the church a leading role in the schools, and they favoured church activities and insitutions such as missions, monasteries and religious orders. This was most apparent in Austria. Centralist neo-absolutism tended to lean towards the ultramontane church and away from liberalism, federalism and nationalism of nations and peoples. 'Josephism', or the system of state church which had dominated up until then, was dropped. The church became an autonomous body, and the clergy were now subject to the disciplinary powers of the bishops and the Pope. The church became the chief influence in education, even down to the appointment of teachers. A concordat in 1855 cemented this position in law. It declared Catholicism as the state religion and awarded church law an almost public status. Even in the eyes of the state, Catholics were subject to canon law concerning marriage. Church censorship and the disciplinary decisions of the church had to be executed by the state. On the whole, the policy failed, because the Catholic clergy and the Catholic nobility in the non-German regions favoured their own national interests and were therefore anti-centralist. It failed in the German regions as well, because clericalisation aroused such resistance that it brought about the end of the reaction. Franz Grillparzer bitterly claimed that it was this sort of Catholicism which was responsible for Austria's poverty and backwardness. 'Give us two hundred years of Protestant education, and we will be the world's leading people. As it is, our only talents are music and the concordat.' The battle against the concordat, a type of *Kulturkampf* on its own, became the central theme for German liberalism in Austria. In 1861, when the monarchy had turned to a constitutional system, the predominance of Catholicism was broken by a Protestant charter. Policies during the 1860s were dominated by the attempt to move away from the concordat and reach a compromise with the liberals. This continued right up until 1870, when, after the fall of the papal state, the government declared the dissolution of the concordat.

In Baden, the relationship between the state and the church developed differently — though with similar tendencies. There, the Catholic church — very consciously — continued to fight against what remained of the state church during the 1850s. The Archbishop of Freiburg, Hermann von Vicari, outlawed the customary requiem masses for the Protestant grand duke, and he locked up any priest who disobeyed. He appointed his own nominees to offices without first obtaining state consent, he ignored government directives, and he forbade any state involvement in theological or seminary examinations. The state appointed a church commissioner, the bishop excommunicated the civil servants involved, and the state had some priests arrested. The town councillors of Freiburg, most of them Catholic, gave the 'banished' (so medieval was the vocabulary of the time) mayor the freedom of the city and expelled the Jesuits. The people remained calm — contrary to the expectation of the archbishop. But the rest of Germany took a lively interest. Prussia took on the role of protector of Protestantism and the modern state. In 1854, the archbishop was arrested, and in 1855, after a short truce, a concordat was drawn up between the curia and the government, whereby the latter would surrender its rights to a state church, Catholics would come under ecclesiastical jurisdiction, and the state would be obliged to encourage the professors of Freiburg to follow Catholic teaching. The liberals and the lower house were indignant and rejected the agreement. The grand duke revoked the agreement (which had not been ratified) and passed a similar law which did not contain the offending conditions but which — just as important for the liberals, who were so keen on theory — was made on his own sovereignty. Only gradually did the situation calm down. From 1866, a new *Kulturkampf* smouldered. 'Cultural' examinations, a peculiar invention of the anti-Catholic liberals, were made compulsory for Catholic priests, and consequently, because of anti-Prussian feeling and opposition to liberal economics, the church won the support of the masses. In Württemberg, the situation was similar, although more moderate. All in all, as a result of the co-operation, the conflicts and the tensions between the church and the state throughout the 1850s, the contrast between a liberal and a 'clerical' party developed into a fundamental conflict of politics.

Once again, the situation in Prussia was very different. Here, the reaction also tried to prop up its system through the schools and by favouring the church. But the conservatives here were emphatically Protestant, and their differences with the Catholic church could not simply be swept under the carpet. There were restrictions in the numbers of missions, in the activities of the Jesuits, and in the numbers of students sent to Rome to study, and these became the main points of friction which kept the Catholic church at a distance. For the time being at least, there were no seeds of *Kulturkampf* in Prussia at the end of the reaction, and liberalism was once again on the rise.

Political Catholicism in Germany and the political orientation of German Catholics arose as a result of revitalisation and of tensions between church and state, church and modern society, and church and liberalism. But the phenomenon was also closely linked with the history of the political parties in Germany during the different periods. This has already been discussed and will be discussed again later.

(b) Protestantism

Just as important in the history of 19th-century Germany as the conspicuous self-assertion of Catholicism *en bloc*, its transformation by ultramontanism, and the growth of a Catholic party, was the much less visible development of Protestantism and its own division between conservatives and liberals, its own confrontation with the modern, and its role in the process of de-Christianisation. It was not only the German *Geist* and German *Bildung* which were deeply affected by the developments and conflicts within theology, but also the political parties and, in fact, the whole mentality of the Protestant population. This was in strong contrast to Catholicism, and to Protestantism outside Germany, e.g. Anglo-Saxon Protestantism. Ideas, theories, political agendas within Germany had an altogether theological flavour. Arguments had something of the theological battle about them. Both liberalism and conservatism had their own definite theological and religious bases. The role played by the sons of priests and by former theology students in the intellectual and political history of 19th-century Germany was a substantial one. In the Protestant churches moreover, the history of congregations and devotion, even of the Christianity of the people, is connected to the history of theology as a whole.

Around 1800, the church, in both its theology and the faith of the people, was influenced by three different movements: the Enlightenment, orthodoxy and pietism. The first, the Enlightenment, was perhaps the dominant one, and in Germany it was a Christian movement, initiated and supported by theologians. It was characterised by the attempt to reconcile reason with divine revelation, to interpret divine revelation on the basis of reason. Fundamental to it was the Lutheran principle that truth must come from within. This meant that individual conscience was bound to intellectual truthfulness, and that truth should come first, even if it ran contrary to tradition and authority, to the 'letter' of biblical scripture, or the 'papacy of the letter', as Lessing described it. A Christian should make personal decisions within the framework of critical examination or general critique. In its enlightened form, Christianity became a religion of reason and of creation. It became a humane ethos based on reason and nature. Piety and morality ranked above any dogma. Secondly, there was the old orthodoxy, which stood in contrast to the Enlightenment. It retained those elements of divine revelation and traditional dogma which could not be explained through reason. There was also a new orthodoxy, 'supranaturalism', which sought to re-establish 'supranatural' elements of divine revelation through rationalistic (and Kantian) arguments. Finally, there was pietism, 'the quiet in the land', the undogmatic religion of a pious heart, of deep feeling, of the direct experience of sin and repentance, and of pious works in charity and calling.

After 1815 situation changed, and new forces came into play which were to have a lasting effect throughout the rest of the century. Enlightenment and rationalism continued their hold on the universities. In this way they influenced a whole generation of priests and, through the priests, the common people, despite the fact that both the Enlightenment and rationalism had been discredited by the leading minds of the age. Halle, with an average of 800 theology students, was a leading light in rationalism up until the 1830s under the leadership of the professors Julius Wegscheider and Wilhelm Gesenius. The rationalist Heinrich Paulus played a significant role in Heidelberg, where there were only fifty students of theology. The Christian religion should, it was believed, be explained through the moral nature of man. Miracles and dogma were reinterpreted through reason — as an extreme example, Christ's resurrection was explained by saying that Christ had only appeared to be dead. The traditional teachings of sin, justification and grace, so repugnant to modern man and the modern citizen, lost their moral severity. Calm and reasoned order, clarity, practical morality in the face of the mortality of man, this was the new tone of religion. And, in contrast to the 18th century, it was adopted on a popular basis. The enlightened devotion in the folk and Bible tales of Johann Peter Hebel, a Church Councillor, provides one of the most beautiful examples of this in a work that has entered into our literary canon. Another is Heinrich Zschokke's devotional work *Stunden der Andacht* (Hours of Devotion), published in eight volumes between 1808 and 1815, which is perhaps less original and lightly sentimentalised, but equally effective; it was reissued many times up until the middle of the century. The Enlightenment's critical rejection of miracles and dogma, of orthodoxy and pietism, became virulent among the urban middle classes during the 1840s, when its support in the universities was dying out, and this eventually fed into the process of de-Christianisation.

On the other side of the church, the former enemies, orthodoxy and pietism, had come together as the representatives of 'positive' religion, as it has been called since Schleiermacher. They were now the new conservative wing. They rejected the way the Enlightenment reduced Christianity to generalities and reason. They rejected any idealistic and liberal reinterpretation of religion and any compromise with the modern. In a history of religious faith, the movement can be regarded as a 'revivalist' movement. As the pietist tradition was revived, so the Protestant faith became based on feeling, on the direct, personal experience of divine intervention in a person's life, and central to it was the profound Christian experience of sin and rebirth which could not be argued away by any liberals and rationalists. Of course, the experience would take place and be felt in many different ways, through examining one's conscience, through telling people about one's conversion (or rebirth), through 'salvation', through cultivating one's 'inner' life and interpreting every small detail as the product of divine will. The pietists insisted that naked theory and naked intellectualism would fill the heart with consternation. This led to a certain schematism in their piety, and, in turn, to the peculiar self-righteousness and self-satisfaction of the pietists, who 'peddled' their piety, and expressed it unctuously at every opportunity. For an outsider, this could sometimes prove unpleasant, obtrusive, tactless and even embarrassing. Added to the new revivalist pietism there was a new fundamentalism in the interpretation of the Bible. The Bible was the basis for life — not as a testimony to God's works, but as his Word, spoken by him directly to his people, and which they had to take literally. The new theology saw the word of the Bible as God's revelation, as the rationalists and the liberals had done, and it claimed that the writers of the Bible had been directly inspired by God. The new 'born-again' pietism which took the word of the Bible as its basis cut itself off from reason, which it saw as an instrument of man's hybris and the devil, for it was precisely those elements which defied reason that characterised the revelation of God for its followers and theologians. The new piety also cut itself off from culture and the 'world' — its followers regarded them as temptations — and it rejected the modern. For this reason, the more extreme forms of the new pietism were marked by narrowness and bigotry, as its opponents pointed out. This piety was not realised merely by a pious life for its own sake, it was realised in activity, in practice, in 'works of love'. The Christianity of feeling was also the Christianity of deeds and the community. In this way orthodoxy and pietism came together. One adopted a piety based on feeling and direct experience, while the other adopted the dogmas and formulae, although the division was by no means so clear-cut. Some pietists, for example, were opposed to the state or compulsory church, and formed their own communities and convents. The neo-orthodox theology, on the other hand, systematised the experience of sin, rebirth and salvation and the fundamental 'facts of salvation' (in contrast to the mono-poly of facts held by science, and nonetheless in line with the 19th century's new-found faith in facts). The beliefs of the Reformation almost took on the same character of divine revelation accorded to the Bible. Both the faith and form of the Reformation should last for eternity. Luther became the father of the faith, the father of objectivity and a figure of unconditional authority. Any subjectivism on his part, any freedom in the interpretation of Bible texts, any hint of freedom of conscience or the individuality of faith, in short, anything which might connect his name to the modern world, was revoked, even denied.

The movement was by no means simply a relic of earlier times, as the modernists would like to regard it, or a combination of traditional and conservative forces. It was, in fact, completely new, even modern, within the context of the 19th century itself. It com-pletely reshaped the 19th-century view of religion and the meaning of life. It brought religion once again onto the agenda of the age, revived it, and attracted new converts. It established a new force. If it was conservatism at all, it was a new conservatism.

The movement had several centres throughout Germany. Most important was, per-haps, the area to the east of the Elbe: the pietistic nobility in Pomerania, the Thaddens, the Puttkamers, the Kleist-Retzows, with their prayers held in the manor house. Every-one is 'brother' or 'sister'; that plays an important role in the story of Bismarck's betrothal. Next came Berlin: the nobility such as the Gerlach brothers, or civil servants such as Georg Nicolovius or Moritz August von Bethmann-Hollweg. There were the professors, such as August Neander and Friedrich Tholuck, or the circle around the Crown Prince Friedrich Wilhelm, from which the idea of the Christianisation of the state (the 'Christian state') orginated. After that followed the area of the Lower Rhine and the Bergisches Land, which was less well integrated into the church as a whole, and the Wuppertal in particular (the town of Barmen was labelled 'der fruchtbarste Ort im Reiche Gottes' — the most fertile area in God's kingdom). Here, there were industrialists alongside crafts-men and peasants — ascetic, charitable and capitalist at the same time, as the young Friedrich Engels observed. And finally, there were the old pietistic regions of Württem-berg, with the lower middle classes and farmers, shut off from the rest of the world, from science and worldliness; shut off, too, from the hypocrites and learned men, stubborn and brooding in their own communities, waiting for the future kingdom of God. But outside these areas, which were influenced by pietism, the new revivalist devotion and theology had a lasting effect on the conservative parts of the church and even among the educated classes. The movement captured the imagination of both the rural and urban lower middle classes up until the middle of the century. The large mission festivals equalled in size and importance the liberal-democratic 'festivals'. In its common opposition to ratio-nalistic liberalism, the new political conservatism had gained popular support. The theolo-gical leader of the new orthodoxy was Professor Ernst Wilhelm Hengstenberg from Berlin, who was able to form a church party from the supporters of the 'positive' religion by means of the newspaper, the *Evangelische Kirchenzeitung*, which he had edited since 1827. And although he was unable to drive the rationalists from the universities, he was able, through the use of very 'worldly' methods, to ensure his new party a strong position in the Prussian church after 1840. In Bavaria, the conservative theologians in Erlangen played a similar role.

One of the great achievements of revivalism and the form of devotion it inspired were important organisations and 'works' of practical Christianity: the Bible and missionary societies, and the institutions and establishments which would later be part of the *Innere Mission* (Inner Mission). These included refuges and the schools for the poor, which had been born out of the poverty of war, and as a result of the fact that Pestalozzi's ideas on education were now adopted and used in the Christian religion — examples are those established by Christian Heinrich Zeller in Beuggen, Johannes Falke in Weimar and Elias von der Recke in the Düssel valley; the Amalie Sieveking poorhouses and nursing homes in Hamburg; the asylums, prison societies, youth organisations, orphanages, hospitals and deaconess homes, which had been founded first in Kaiserswerth in 1833 by Theodor Fliedner (and were the first places within the church to allow women an active role); Wichern's *Rauhes Haus*, or 'Rough House', founded in 1833 for the education of neglected children; and many others such as those in Neuendettelsau, founded in 1854 by Wilhelm Löhe, and Bethel, founded by Friedrich von Bodel-schwingh in 1865. What was important here was that the activity was not initiated and organised from above, through the church, but that it developed freely, in the form of societies, and that these societies were able to break through an institutional and traditional force such as the church, even its anti-liberal wing, and unleash the strong participation of laymen. It is true that even the liberal Protestant middle classes took part in the activity later on, often very generously, but it was the new revivalist movement which was there first and started it all. The first great non-pietist, non-revivalist organisation of German Protestantism must be mentioned here, the Gustav Adolf Society, founded in 1832 for the support of the Protestant diaspora.

In opposition to this movement stood liberal Protestantism, as it had developed out of the idealistic reinterpretation of Christianity. Fichte and, above all, Hegel wanted to use philosophy to interpret the truth of Protestant Christianity and make it comprehensible to a post-Englightenment and post-Kantian age. Hegel had a particularly large influence over his theology students, even those in the church, up until the 1840s. In this brief survey, it is sufficient to mention the original idealist theologian, Friedrich Daniel Schleiermacher, the greatest Protestant theologian since Luther, and the father of liberal Protestantism.

Schleiermacher introduced the problem of reason into theology. Modern-day conscience, the centre of the Protestant faith, was inextricably bound up with enlighten-ed, critical reasoning. It tested every religious authority, the Bible for example, by the modern interpretation of truth, for only then could a faith based on conscience and freedom truly exist: reason had to be recognised, for the sake of faith. But reason was more than just a means of a critical examination of religious truth. Reason, the mind and humanity all had a religious dimension, which made philosophical analysis necessary; to use the categories of idealism, in being finite they referred to the infinite. The Christian religion was tied to what is naturally human, to the sense of the infinite. In contrast to the Enlightenment's practice of eliminating everything which ran contrary to reason and of reducing Christianity to morality, idealism endea-voured to take in every aspect of Christianity and reinterpret it; it did not seek to reduce the religious aspect of man's existence to mere morality. Man was also feeling and imagination (a Romantic idea); he was a totality, an individual, who developed and strove for perfection. To be a Christian was more than simply knowing what was decent and wanting what was virtuous, it was completely transforming one's existence with a new knowledge of oneself. Schleiermacher started from the assumption that there were no hard and fast rules or dogma, and that rules laid down in past times had no validity in the present; instead every age must seek out its own explanations, and every age must find its own words to interpret existence and pass on its meaning. Not rationalism alone but also an historicism based in the present became the leading interpretative principle of theology — Schleiermacher saw it as the norm for the Christian faith, for a faith 'in the strength of the mind'. Christianity had to be interpreted both anthropologically and existentially in terms of the present, without falling back onto morality or general declarations. Schleiermacher started in the category of feeling: religion was the feeling of *schlechthinnige Abhängigkeit*, or absolute dependency on the infinite, and the Christian religion interpreted this as a father–child relationship. Any such interpretation was the task of theology, and theology as a science, in combination with natural reason. For from the beginning there was a single issue: that of examining religion (and not only religion, but the feeling of piety) scientifically, and to investigate its relation to reality. Theology, in other words, was the interpretation of a faith and the confrontation of that faith with the reason and humanity of the age. For this was part of it: the Christian faith and the church should not be isolated from life, restricted to morality or a final 'meaning'. Rather, the 'children of the age' should be able to take their questions there, and 'truly and honestly' belong to it — the church as an opportunity for the public to reflect on the meaning of life. For this reason, faith and the church had to have a lively and active relationship with 'culture' and national life. They should not cut themselves off from them. The task for 19th-century 'scientific' philosophical theology, then, was to establish a correlation between Christianity, reason and humanity. In 1821, when Schleiermacher reformulated his agenda, the emphasis had changed: no longer did theology have to defend itself against those educated people who scoffed at religion. The new enemy were the superstitious and the *Übergläubige*, the sanctimonious and those who believed too literally. The fear now was that Christianity would conjoin with barbarism, and science with scepticism.

Schleiermacher's other qualities are less important — they were merely a product of the age: his typically romantic style of expression; his rejection of harshness, violence, the crises and inevitable suffering caused by inhumanity; and his reinterpretation of salvation. His faith was a worldly and a cultural one, for which the world was a revelation of the glory of God, for which mankind was fulfilled in culture and in the progress of culture. Such was the main trend of liberal Protestantism in the 19th century. The ethos of truthfulness and conscience and the ethos of rationality demanded freedom from dogma and the letter. People's consciousness of their own time and their own humanity demanded that they constantly reassess the old interpretations of Christianity in the light of their own experience, rather than accept as absolute the old forms and formulae of the 1st and the 16th centuries. In this way liberal Protestantism followed in the footsteps of idealism and rationalism. It was receptive to the philosophies and central ideas of the age, for the Christian 'solution' to the 'deeper' questions of the age could only be expressed in contemporary language, and it was for this reason that Protestant theologians became eclectic and free. There was a clear difference between the truly liberal theology of Schleiermacher and his 'left-wing' school, whose central theme was the scientific nature of theology and whose aim was to reconcile science and philosophy, and the 'mediatory' theology (*Vermittlungstheologie*) of the school of the 'right', which was more concerned with reconciling theology and culture than criticising dogma and the Bible. And it was here, in the field of mediatory theology, that 'cultural' Protestantism — as it was called by its critics — arose. Cultural Protestantism tried to establish a balance and harmony between the world and the Christian faith, without any sharp dialectical tension. It attempted to strike a balance above all between Christianity and culture, classical humanity, science and modernity, between divine revelation and the development of man. The main mediatory theologians were Karl Immanuel Nitzsch, Isaak August Dorner and, perhaps the most radical, Richard Rothe. Rothe taught that with the increased moralisation of the state and culture, the church as an institution would become superfluous. There was an increased spiritualisation and subjectivisation of religion, and one example of this was the typically modern critique of the (by then obsolete) legal interpretation of the *Rechtfertigungslehre* (doctrine of justification, or compensation through a third party). The doctrine was the centrepiece of Protestantism, and when people rejected it, the rigour of its existential content went overboard with it. There was a new emphasis on conscience and a new strength of conviction against all forms of — Protestant — clericalism, against the church as an institution, and even the religiosity of the masses, which could endanger the freedom and spirituality of the individual. For this reason, people differentiated sharply between authentic Christianity and an objectifying and clerical church. In reaction to the 'positive' Christians, Luther was modernised and came to be regarded as the father of the spirit, of freedom and of modern culture. The church was now a place where people could reflect upon the meaning of life in public, in view of a tradition where one could, after all, just as well preach on Goethe as on St Paul. Nevertheless, behind the less extreme efforts, and behind the new faith in harmony and culture, there was a decisive seriousness. There was, namely, the will to combine both modernity and Christianity and establish Rothe's *'unbewusste Christentum der Gebildeten'* ('unconscious Christianity of the educated classes') — which was by no means a modern discovery. Liberal Protestantism allowed the middle classes to reconcile the Protestant faith with the new interest in science and philosophy with a clear conscience; and at the same time it allowed them to relate the central tenet of humanity and a civilised society, and all the problems it entailed, to theological reflection and Christian tradition. People learned that secularisation and Christianity need not be mutually exclusive. The 'modernity' of liberal Protestantism gave the secularisation of modern society its strong Protestant flavour. Of course, all this concerned only the educated classes, for it had been their problem to start with, and that was true even of Schleiermacher. The attempt to satisfy modern reason, modern ethics and modern culture remained a difficult problem, and the existential reinterpretation of Christian teachings was still very complicated. The mass of people who were falling away from the church and the Christian faith, and the mass of people now fired by rationalism, could not be reached in this way. The less sophisticated and anti-rational 'positive' Christians had more success in this area.

The scientifically radical branch of liberal theology was historical-critical theology. This examined the origin of biblical writings using historical and philological methods and was concerned with the discrepancy between modern consciousness and biblical accounts, starting with the question of miracles. And it was particularly concerned with the way biblical writers would interpret events, and the relationship between the actual course of events and the writer's account of them. The consequences of this sort of criticism for all Bible-based doctrine were fundamental. Born during the Enlightenment, the theme dominated the 1830s. Wilhelm Vatke wrote his historical-critical book *The Religion of the Old Testament* in 1835. Ferdinand Christian Baur used Hegel's approach of understanding the objective process of an event historically, beyond the boundaries of an individual. In this way he founded the history of dogma. He responded to modern society's question on the nature of Christianity by exploring its history, and showed how the writings of the New Testament could be explained through the situation and groupings of the first Christians, and in particular through the conflict between Judaism and Paulinism. The historical authenticity of the writings of St John, a favourite of the idealists, was brought into question; the resurrection was only comprehensible as a sign of the belief in resurrection, and was explained as the certain victory of truth even in death. Baur, in fact, posed all the decisive questions of the new theology. But the true man of the age, who won the most popular support, was another Hegelian, David Friedrich Strauss, whose book *The Life of Jesus*, written in 1835, was one of the most influential books of the 19th century. The life of Jesus was, like the nature of Christianity, a matter of interest first for the Enlightenment and would be discussed continually throughout the rest of the 19th century. Strauss examined the contradictions between the different gospels and within each gospel, notwithstanding the question of miracles, and in doing so he called into question their reliability. Their stories were, he claimed, the product of an imagination which remembered and transfigured facts and was strongly influenced by a sense of community and Jewish tradition. In as far as Strauss demonstrated the 'mythical' and 'ahistorical' elements of biblical writings to an unprecedented extent, the book had the effect of an earthquake. What was left was a human Jesus, who became an object of faith after his death for his followers and their writings. Jesus was not the orthodox Christ, but neither was he the virtuous sage of the Enlightenment or Schleiermacher's sinless ideal man. Christ, as perceived by the church, could not be equated with the historical Jesus, and this became a topic of great debate for subsequent theologians. The book released a great deal of polemic — fifty different works were written on the subject by 1840. In the history of the dissolution of institutional Christianity, and in the numbers of educated and, soon afterwards, not so educated citizens who fell away from the church, the book proved to be one of the most decisive turning-points before Darwin. In a later edition of the book, in 1864, Strauss again tried to portray Jesus, in contrast to Jews and Greeks, and to priests and those who believed in miracles, as the ideal personality of an intellectual morality. It was typical for a liberalism which touched on religion, but it was no longer epoch-making, and neither was his theory that an historical examination of dogmatism would demonstrate its irreversible dissolution into a common humanity.

For the laymen and theologians of the time, the decisive factor from the 1830s onwards, was that the battle for Christianity was no longer fought systematically or philosophically, but with the weapons of the 'positive' sciences — on an historical and philological basis. The problem between faith and understanding was replaced by the problem between faith and history. Although Strauss was no longer a party to theological discussions, the themes he had raised remained the dominant ones for the scientific work of theologians during the latter part of the century and the effect such work had on public life.

In their continual confrontations with the 'positive' Christians, the liberals also formed a 'party', and anyone who was at least partly educated became involved. Every adolescent from the educated classes was faced with the conflict between the meaning of life and the interpretation of the world. German Protestantism, it may be said, splintered into two new denominations, and political liberalism consumed much of the energy and emotions of liberalism within the church.

One point must be emphasised. For everyone, for the rationalists, the positive Christians and the liberals, for the return to reformatory dogma as well as for the new philosophical-historical interpretation of religion, the separate consciousness of each denomination was strengthened. The irenic 'evangelicals' became 'Protestant' once more, whether orthodox liberal or anti-authoritarian liberal, but in both cases anti-Catholic and anti-Rome. The anniversary of the Reformation in 1817 had partly irenic overtones, and in 1830 the anniversary of the Augsburg Confession was decidedly 'Protestant'. The distinctly anti-'Roman' Gustav Adolf Society for the Protestants of the diaspora was founded in 1832. And Bismarck, who was neither orthodox nor liberal, born in 1815, would still associate Catholicism with the Inquisition and the Gunpowder Plot when he was young.

As was the case with Catholicism, the influence of Protestantism during the period under review is difficult (and statistically impossible) to gauge. The emergent proletariat and part of the educated upper classes fell away from the church during the latter part of the century, and there were other signs of a growing indifference. Nevertheless, it can be said that the majority of Protestants maintained their religiosity, although it was not as strong as within the Catholic population or the Protestants of the Anglo-Saxon countries. It was, however, stronger than in France. Faith in God and immortality and the validity of Christian ethics endured even in the face of a slackening of church ties. Custom and convention, baptism and confirmation, marriage and burials all played their part, despite the fact that a certain distance displayed towards the church and religion soon became socially acceptable. The mothers of the Social Democratic leaders of 1900 were almost all still active in the church. The sense of belonging within Protestantism and Protestant culture and the depth of feeling against the Catholics were all strong enough among the educated classes to cover any substantial losses in numbers. The non-Christians felt 'Protestant' in their opposition to Catholicism.

The relationship between church and state must be examined, for it was a relationship which was suspected of reinforcing authority and subservience. The state not only held supervisory rights over the Protestant church authorities — as it did over the Catholic church — but the sovereign was the highest bishop in the church (*Summepiskopat*), and through an administrative body he even had a say in internal church matters. During the 18th century, the church administration became part of the state administration within Germany; and during the Napoleonic era, the integration, unity and sovereignty of the state were served by the way in which the state reorganised the established churches, out of what had been a mere shambles, and by deploying the military when a new hymn-book was introduced in Württemberg to counter obstinate pietists. The state ruled over the church and generally ensured tolerance between the different denominations. The priests were, in fact, state civil servants. The trend of the 19th century towards autonomy, independence and self-administration among both the liberals and the conservatives provoked a strong reaction against this bureaucratically absolutist system. The church should be independent in 'internal' matters, and it was here that conflicts flared up.

There were corresponding trends within the reform in Prussia. Stein, old-fashioned in his beliefs but with overtones of Enlightenment, saw Christianity as a means of 'ennobling mankind' and aimed at a 'reawakening of religious sense'. Other reformers agreed, even the king and the nationalist-revolutionary *Tugendbund* (League of Virtue) and it was for this reason that they were all opposed to a church as a type of spiritual police, equipped to give orders. It was the state's role to set the church free, even to teach it to be independent. But in some regions, most notably Prussia, that problem was overshadowed by another one: the problem of the 'union' between the Lutheran and Reformed (Calvinist) parts of the church, which until then had represented two different areas within Protestantism. It was a phenomenon of the period. People wanted to irenically resolve the conflicts between dogmas — brought about by fruitless theological debate — faith and practice were what mattered. The Enlightenment, pietism, revivalism and idealistic theology all pointed in the same direction, if for different reasons. The union also corresponded to the state's need for integration and calm. In Baden, the Palatinate, Nassau and the two Hesses similar unions came about as a result of the co-operation between state and and the individual communities. And in Prussia the king made the union there his personal concern. In 1817, on the tercentenary of the Reformation, he proclaimed one such independent union, and it received overwhelmingly positive support — over 200 leaflets were printed on the subject. The matter was complicated by the fact that the king wanted to introduce a new, archaic, high-church liturgy which would prefer ritual to (prosaic and intellectual) sermon. Considerable opposition arose to the measure and to similar measures imposed from above. But the king managed to push through his liturgy, and with it the union, by means of indirect force such as disciplinary action against Schleiermacher, for example, or by appointing his own nominees to certain offices. Only the Calvinists in the Rhineland and the Bergisches Land and some of the orthodox and pietist Lutherans in Silesia offered any resistance. The state countered the opposition between 1830 and 1834 by suspending and arresting various officials, and by having the army occupy the churches. It was only in 1837 that the opponents were even allowed to emigrate, and more than a thousand of them sang chorales as they sailed on boats through Berlin on their way to America. It was the final culmination of statism and the authority of the state over the church. Friedrich Wilhelm IV resolved the conflict in 1842–47, when it became legally possible to leave the established church and to form free churches. The policy of the reform period, of using the state — the only power in a position to do so — to reform the church and make it more independent, was caught up in its own dialectic.

The issue of the relationship between the state and the church was inextricably bound up with the issue of the internal organisation of the church. Would a church organised on a hierarchical, authoritarian basis, with consistories and superintendents appointed from above, be preferable; or one with a democratic constitution, presbyteries and synods, as in the traditional reformed church of the western provinces? The idea of a constitution with synods was analogous to the political constitution, and it was this which sealed its fate. The tentative steps towards reform — such as the advisory provincial synods — were not pursued after the 1820s. Bureaucratic and state principles dominated, principles of hierarchy and of bishops; there was a general superintendent in every province. There was no free movement of theologians or church members; there was no representation or participation. There was only calm and subordination. It was only in the western provinces that presbyteries, synods and laymen were given a more substantial role. The movement for a general synod for the whole state was rejected.

During the 1840s, the theme became more topical, primarily because church politics were given high priority by the devoutly Christian King Friedrich Wilhelm IV. But the problem was also now closely linked to the position of the church 'parties'. The liberals adhered strictly to Schleiermacher's idea of the 'invisibility' of the true church, and this diminished the significance of any institutions. On the other hand, they defended the real church as an institution and a community, against anti-institutionalism and the extremes of individualism, so long as it remained a society, a free church for the community, which could develop and in which the theologians would play a subordinate role. The church should not be spoon-fed by the state, nor by orthodox pastors, and yet neither should it be dominated by an unenlightened, traditionalistic or pietistic majority of the church members. Freedom of conviction should be maintained, among clergy as well as among laymen, and this meant a certain plurality. The consequence of these contradictory demands was a 'constitutional' compromise: relative autonomy within the community; synods, co-operative bodies, and the protection of individual freedom from majorities; and freedom from the state, but only to the extent that the state could still guarantee freedom within the church. In opposition to this stood the 'positive' and the orthodox Christians. They were gradually developing a concept of the church as a sacred and objective institution, in which tradition and duty, church power and church authority — hierarchy and episcopate, rather than the individual members of the community — would play the decisive role. It can be regarded almost as 'Catholicisation'. The old pietist emphasis on the role of the layman lessened. The church should be tied to Christianity and all its formulae as God-given law, not as merely as some badge to be worn, as the liberals seemed to regard it. The church should act as protector of the faith, against the disintegration of the modern world, and it was for this reason that it should not simply be left in the hands of a lay congregation which could adapt to the modern world all too quickly and easily. The ideal church would be a hierarchical confessional church. The conservatives may have supported autonomy from the state, but only for as long as it was determined by a rationalistic bureaucracy, and they preferred monarchical authority over the church to liberals and synods.

Within the state leadership there were conflicting positions and principles. Most of the bureaucracy was — at least until 1840 — enlightened and liberal when it came to religion; or they were at least tolerant, and supported the pluralistic unity of a quasi-state church, while rejecting the pietists and revivalists and the attacks of the orthodox on the freedom of university theology. With the arrival of a new king, conservative forces grew in strength after 1840. In view of an increasing radicalism in politics and an anti-church stance, any slackening in the faith of the church was seen as the first steps towards revolution. Liberalism within the church was treated with suspicion. The state combated the lack of faith with increasingly conservative policies in church, education and administration, as well as with other measures, such as making divorce more difficult. But even the conservative leadership came into conflict with the conservatives in the church, owing to the fact that they supported the 'union' for political reasons, while the orthodox increasingly stressed the old differences between the various groups of

Protestants. The king himself pursued the ideal of an autonomous church, free from the state, while recognising the fact that the church would have to be organised into episcopates. The issue of the constitution of the church could not be divorced from the issue of the constitution in general. A victory for the principle of synods in the church would have serious consequences for the state as a whole — and for the time being that was the stumbling-block for any sort of reform.

In 1846, Friederich Wilhelm IV appointed a general synod to discuss the constitution and the issue of a new statement of confession. Against the wishes of the liberals, he did not allow any positions within the synod to be elected, but appointed about half of its members from the ranks of non-theological notabilities from the moderates in church politics, so that the 'positive' Christians were in the minority. The attempt to tie the church to an orthodox, historical interpretation of the faith was defeated. The liberals maintained their position within the church, and the principle of tolerance within the church was to continue. On the question of the constitution, a compromise was reached between rights of election and appointment by the state — but in fact the predominantly authoritarian constitution already in existence remained in force.

In other German states as well, no liberal church constitution was introduced during the Vormärz. The character of the various churches varied enormously, of course. The Lutheran churches in the north of Germany and the church in Bavaria remained or became extremely conservative, while the churches in central and south-west Germany were more liberal, even rationalistic.

One other movement to capture the imagination of the people of the time must also be mentioned: the *Lichtfreunde* (Friends of Light). In opposition to the established church and the conservative church policies of the Prussian government in particular, this movement grew out of a circle of rationalistic clergymen, mainly from Berlin, who supported a progressively undogmatic and 'free' Christianity. The government reacted against the movement by suspending and punishing its supporters and by bringing in the police. This only served to increase the predominantly rationalistic and democratic support of the movement within the urban and lower middle classes. The municipal authorities in Berlin demanded a free church constitution, free parishes and free elections of clergy, and it was only in 1847, when leaving the church and the formation of free 'religious societies' were legalised, that the problem was solved. The church was no longer unquestioningly regarded as a determining force in people's public lives. Unity between the Catholic population and the established church dissolved, and in time this called the sovereign's authority over the church into question.

The 1848 revolution led to the defeat of liberal reforms and the reinforcement of a conservative and statist church policy. The period of reaction was characterised by an alliance between its governments and the new orthodoxy. It was precisely in those states with an emphatically Lutheran orthodoxy, and where a stridently hierarchical ideology of church and duty developed (as August Vilmar put it, 'Wenn ich das Wort Synode höre, ist mir, als wenn der Teufel an mir vorüberstiege' — 'When I hear the word synod, it is as though the devil himself had just walked past.'), that any attempt at constitutional reform was blocked — the forms and formulae of the old high church were reintroduced; Lutherans and members of the Reformed church sharply divided; liberal pastors and professors persecuted; the church became strongly clerical; and a pastoral orthodoxy established itself against any liberalism within the community. This was certainly the case in Mecklenburg, the Electorate of Hesse and Bavaria, and even parts of Saxony. In Prussia, however, the desired re-sectarianisation and disciplining of the universities was defeated, despite the presence of an orthodox church hierarchy. With the New Era, any encouragement of orthodoxy had vanished. Conservative policy provoked resistance — people's resistance to new statements of confession, etc., — in Hanover, and in Baden, where the protest led to the fall of the conservative church hierarchy in 1861 and to the decree of a new liberal church constitution. From the mid-1860s onwards, the church was constitutionally reorganised into synods in other states as well. The political and constitutional compromise between monarchical state and liberal middle classes spread to the church.

Out of the developments in Baden grew an organised movement among the liberals to join together against reactionism within the church. It was a movement, they claimed, 'to keep Christianity alive, the Christianity which the German people need to carry out its duties, . . . in the spirit of Protestant truthfulness and freedom'. It was a movement for liberal church constitutions and one which aimed to reconcile science, Christianity and culture — the *Deutscher Protestantenverein* (German Protestant Society) 1863–65, sidekick of the *Nationalverein*, in which many liberal leaders, such as Ludwig Häusser, Johann Kaspar Bluntschli and Rudolf von Bennigsen, played an important role.

The significance of the conflicting trends within Protestantism, and the significance of Protestantism and politics for the political orientation of its supporters, must now be considered. Prussian reform had a religious basis. The division between religion and politics, or the the Lutheran ideal of submitting to obedience, were not the decisive factors, but it was out of the Lutheran ethos of work and duty that the demand for political freedom and freedom for the state came. For Hegel, the Reformation had established the consciousness of 'freedom', and since then the Protestant state had concerned itself with how it would incorporate that freedom into the world (in the concept of free obedience). And even Schleiermacher, without the same concern for the metaphysics of the state, used a Protestant and theological basis for his early liberalism, which went beyond any concept of natural rights. These were the first signs of a political theology of liberal reform which is often forgotten. On the other hand there was orthodoxy and revivalism. Revolution was a 'sin', a deed of the devil, as were the principles of human rights and sovereignty of the people; they were examples of mankind's desire for autonomy — for they all had their roots in man's presumptuousness in believing that he could bring about justice in the world through his own efforts. Whoever wanted to base a state on the will of mankind stood in defiance of God's order — indeed, in defiance of God himself. If anthropological pessimism (i.e. the belief that man was essentially and totally evil) were to have any currency, then a humane order could not be brought about through humanity, reason or the will of the individual, but through authority and existing institutions. And that would only be possible if there were a supreme, inviolable order, and a piety which regarded the already existing order as God-given. The sanctity of law and order could only exist in a state whose authority was entrusted by God and not by a majority; only a state such as that and the revelation of Christ would stand fast against chaos and the un-freedom of socialism and democracy. And on the conservative principle that there was no middle ground, but only an 'either/or' situation, liberalism, liberal constitutions and liberal reform tumbled after such an indictment of democracy.

This, at any rate, was how Friedrich Julius Stahl defined the mutual dependence between the conservative party and 'positive' theology. Church and political conservatism were one and the same; they helped and supported one another. Revolution, reason and scepticism were all opposed to legitimacy, the kingdom of God and faith. It was for this reason that the state and all its institutions had to be Christian; and it was on this basis that the neo-orthodox Protestants formed an alliance in 1840 with the authoritarian state. The idea of western European and American political reformed theology, that power was evil and had to be controlled, and that it was precisely the institutional framework of a constitution that could stem human malice, played no part in conservative political theology.

Out of this amalgamation of politics and theology arose the orthodox and pietistic resistance to the revolution of 1848, which was regarded as a sin, disobedience, a falling away from God, but also as a cry for self-help and emancipation, a cry for human rights and the independence of reason. It was this mood which dominated the newspapers and sermons of the positive Christians, and to a lesser extent, the first all-German Congress of Churches in Wittenberg in 1848. In 1849, a day of thanksgiving, prayer and penance was declared to commemorate the overcoming of the revolution, and Friedrich Wilhelm IV completed the 'task' of the counter-revolution 'in the name of the Lord'. But the picture so often painted here is one-sided. The liberals of the revolution were by no means anti-church; in fact, they argued from a Christian and Protestant viewpoint. They wanted, as was shown in Karl Bernhard Hundeshagen's widely read book *German Protestantism* (1847), to dissolve the alliance between church and police state once and for all, and combine political freedom with a popular church, as had been achieved in the Anglo-Saxon countries and in Switzerland. In the Frankfurt National Assembly, Karl Biedermann also gave theological reasons for these liberal demands. Like many other church congressmen, the mediatory theologian Isaak August Dorner defended — against Stahl — the revolution in Schleswig–Holstein, in which Lutheran pastors played a leading role. Obedience was required only as long as the authorities acted according to the constitution, otherwise the right of resistance was permissible. The Bavarian Lutheran Adolf Harless deplored the 'appearance of temerity' in the revolution, but affirmed his support of a constitutional state. Moritz August von Bethmann-Hollweg, who was a moderate conservative both in politics and in the church, rejected the constant emphasis by various governments on the 'sanctity of law', for the 'sanctity of limits in the law', and for constitutions. The funeral ceremony for those who had fallen in March in Berlin was naturally a religious one, and people sang the hymn 'Jesus meine Zuversicht' (Jesus, My Trust). Even the democrats still thought, as the Friends of Light had done during the Vormärz, along religious lines. The rationalist Rudolf Dulon, for example, described the revolution as the 'work of the Lord', and claimed that only democracy would further the kingdom of God. Any radically anti-Christian prophecies, however, were few and far between, such as the prophecy that the Day of Judgement for the monarchy and hierarchy would soon come, and that, according to Heine, it was only the symbol of the cross which was delaying it. Wherever there were murmurings against religion (rather than against the clergy), they only served to damage the cause of radical democracy, and in fact proved to be of benefit to the conservatives. On the whole, Protestantism was certainly no great force or powerful supporter of the revolution, but, in contrast to the vociferousness of the conservative church establishment, neither was it a decisive factor in mobilising the masses in counter-revolution.

The preferential treatment given to the 'pious' Christians did nothing to strengthen the conservative front during the period of reaction. In fact, it only served to heighten the reserve of the lower and educated classes towards the official church. A new parish liberalism among the middle classes arose to counteract the pastoral orthodoxy and the powers of the church. The Protestant Society was the expression of a coalition of ecclesiastical and political liberals in response to the political and ecclesiastical bloc of the conservatives. With the New Era, the system of political clericalism came to an end in Prussia. The governing body of the church, the church assembly, tried, for example, to stem the conservative attempts to turn political conflicts into religious ones such as the demand to abolish the intercession for the provincial assembly from the common prayer. This made the battle between the parties all the more bitter and poisonous. And the distinction between politics and the Gospel became even sharper. This was the opinion (a very Lutheran opinion) of the conservative Bismarck, and it brought him into conflict with his traditional conservative friends. But where the circumstances were different, so were the consequences. The orthodox Lutherans in Erlangen, for example, could not readily comprehend Stahl's idea of a 'Christian state' within Catholic Bavaria. And for this reason, they changed their conception of history and the people within the state, to the extent that Harless could be both constitutional and *grossdeutsch* (an advocate of the unification of Germany including Austria) and Hofmann both progressive and *kleindeutsch* (an advocate of the unification of Germany without Austria). Thus it can be seen that the parallels between left and right in the church and left and right in politics do not always hold, and such cross-overs were not uncommon.

This was closely connected to the second main problem. During the period under review, German Protestantism had an altogether remarkable and conflicting relationship with nationalism. During the first stages of their development and throughout the Wars of Liberation, patriotism and nationalism were profoundly Christian. The French Revolution had raised the nation to a sacred position: people died for the Fatherland, and altars were consecrated in its name. But there was another nationalism which ran counter to this and fought against foreign oppression. Idealism had brought the idea of the state, through the concept of a nation, into the field of morality — this was, I believe, a response to man's social emergence from the world of estates and tradition. Idealism interpreted culture and nation as 'higher' and 'moral' communities, stretching beyond the individual, and saw service to the community as an ethical and Christian duty. Christian concepts such as revelation, rebirth, resurrection and salvation took on a secular, politico-ethical and nationalist meaning. Propagandists of the new nationalism saw themselves in a religious light. 'To be one people, to have one feeling for one issue and to come together under the bloody sword of revenge, that is the religion of the age,' said Arndt. 'Loyalty to the people is loyalty to God,' claimed Schleiermacher. War against the tyrant, war for the Fatherland and, moreover, war for the people, the German people, was 'holy war'. Among the wealth of 'patriotic' sermons, there was much talk of the national spirit and national tradition, and of the German people as God's people. 'Our Germany is our own Jerusalem'; Germans were 'purified . . . in the blood of our own people . . . a new race, a holy people'.

This enthusiasm for both nation and Christianity — symbolised in Prussia by the Iron Cross — ebbed somewhat after 1815. It was only in the nationalist-democratic, Christian-German phenomenon of the *Burschenschaft* and the festival at the Wartburg, which celebrated both the Reformation and the battle of Leipzig, and only in the radicalism of Karl Follen, who believed that religious, popular and nationalist-democratic striving were all one, and in the demand for a national Christian religion outside the boundaries of denomination, that it lived on. Christianity and Protestantism in the cultural and liberal nationalism of 'normal' Protestants during the Vormärz were naturally tied up with Germanic and German tradition, with both liberal and moderate Protestants emphasising the ties between the ideas of nation, German-ness and (Protestant) Christianity. It was even claimed that the Gustav Adolf Society was there to 'serve the great holy construct of the unification of the whole of Germany'. The new orthodoxy protested vehemently and anxiously against the 'idolisation' of the nation, or *Nationalitätenschwindel*. It supported the state and the existing laws. When the majority of the pastors in Schleswig–Holstein regarded the 'national' revolution as legitimate and Christian, the conservatives, with Stahl at their head, turned their efforts against them and thereafter underlined the distance between Christianity and the will of the nation. Like the old Prussian conservatism, central German Protestantism was neither *kleindeutsch* nor nationalistic. And it was perhaps because of this that there was no feeling of identity between Protestantism and national liberalism, as much as *kleindeutsch* liberalism believed itself to be the true heir of liberal Protestantism. And it was for this reason that the any radical nationalisation of German Protestantism only began after 1871.

Finally, the relationship of Protestantism to the social question must now be considered. Johann Hinrich Wichern, whose starting-points were revivalism and the great charitable organisations of the Vormärz, was the first to tackle the issue and provide an answer in a moving speech at the Church Congress in 1848 where he outlined an agenda for the *Innere Mission*. The social welfare work of the free societies, in conjunction with the church, would confront the real problem caused by the revolution: pauperism and proletarianisation. The church should once again become — in a very real and modern way — a church for everyone, and that meant for the poor in the cities as well. This was a very traditional point of view: social poverty was not economic, but was to be interpreted as 'religious and moral poverty' and a matter of sin. The solution would be welfare which was highly paternalistic, and the ideal would be an old-fashioned society based on estates. But next to the individual, Wichern saw a whole society; he saw not only individual poverty and brotherly love, but general injustices and the need for general measures. It would fall to the state to take these measures, and all for one aim: to bring back the people to the Christian faith. In itself, this was a new approach in overcoming the conflict between the church and the world of the poor and the workers on the basis of practical social work. But Wichern placed himself squarely on the side of the conservative counter-revolution. With his 'Christian socialism' he may have been able to introduce a socio-political element into the conservative party, one which could easily associate itself with its anti-liberalism, but the *Innere Mission* became a concern for the establishment, even if more revivalist and orthodox, and it clearly distanced itself from the world of the educated. It also became a means of preserving the paternalistic style of existing social hierarchy, and this made it all the more difficult for the new, proletarianised masses to identify with the church. The church retained its pre-industrial and bourgeois structures, and in the debate on modern science and culture, the church retained its influence on the middle classes. In contrast to England, social Christianity in Germany certainly wielded considerable influence, although that influence was not political.

The other 'father' of Christian social conservatism, Victor Aimé Huber, thought along more concrete, more institutional lines. He recognised the problem of a new class and its right to a consciousness of its own. He wanted co-operatives so that he could turn workers without property into working property owners: During the 1840s and 1850s he remained an outsider both from the conservatives and from the Protestants, but he was not without influence: much of his way of thinking along with many of his ideas found their way into Bismarck's social policy by way of Hermann Wagener.

(c) The path towards de-Christianisation; the meaning of life

At the beginning of the period under review can be seen a unique phenomenon, which ran between the Enlightenment and liberalism, revivalism and pietism: it was the German *Bildungsreligion*, or religion of education, the religion of classicism, which stood outside the boundaries of any church, on the very edges of Christianity and was a phenomenon of the educated upper classes and thus of the history of ideas, but which nevertheless influenced a whole approach to the debate between Christianity and modernity for 125 years. Man, according to the new belief, would come to his true self, by 'educating' himself and developing his individual personality. And he could do this through the world of culture, through art, science and history. Culture should not be taken for granted. It was a duty, a moral imperative which had to be appropriated and then developed. Within this framework belonged the idolisation, the cult, even, of Genius, which had been a part of German *Bildung* since the period of the *Sturm und Drang*, and which celebrated the greatness of man, and his divinity. There was also a pantheistic view of nature and the world, a faith in the immanence of the divine in the world, which was to be worshipped in all its forms. It can be called a religion, because it was concerned with 'ultimate things', and it was concerned with those problems which ultimately concerned mankind, but which hitherto had been regarded as 'holy' and the 'kingdom of God'. The new humanity meant a non-Christian form of human life and contrasted in many ways with the Christian interpretation of life. What was important here were not the Enlightenment's rationalist objections to traditional Christianity and its teachings, but the re-evalutation of life's values. This *Bildungsreligion* was widespread and took on many different forms, and lay a very different emphasis on life than the Christian elements. It embraced the new enthusiasm for Ancient Greece of Winckelmann and the neo-humanists, an aesthetic view of life, where, for the first time, antiquity as opposed to Christianity was regarded as the normative means of revealing both divine and human nature. It also embraced the *Sturm und Drang*, with its vitalistic criticism of Christianity's denial of this world, in favour of the real world and the world of the senses. It embraced Schiller's aesthetic exploration of Kantian ethics; the old Christian interpretation of the relationship between human action and divine rule, with its concepts of fatherly providence, requital and miracles, was dissolved. What was now important was the relationship between necessity and universal aims, and also an idealistic teleology, tragic guilt and fate. The world of the ideal became the 'sacrament' through which man attained godliness. Only for the unnumbered masses could religion alone solve life's real conflict, the conflict between duty and inclination; the true solution, however, was art — for art did not of itself turn what was moral into what was good, but made it beautiful.

Goethe was the first determined non-Christian in Germany to have any influence on the German history of education and ideas. He dismissed the traditional religious definition of the meaning of life and simply swept aside any questions arising from this which could not be answered. His view of life, of nature and the world, started from within. He examined the 'soul', the inner life, which had hitherto been so closely bound to Christianity, in all its complexity and profundity — but he examined it with profane eyes; he freed it from religion. And he expanded the contents of this life beyond Christianity's restrictions and brought them out into the world of the 'heathen'. A pantheist, he cut out all the traditional elements of the view of God, his personality and morality; for him, the divine became a creative force, whose power could only be felt by man, never fully comprehended. The enlightened and Christian concept of 'providence', he secularised into the concept of fate and, in doing so, aimed to tie the incomprehensible with the inner law of an individual and the ultimate perfection of human striving. He reduced guilt to mere inadequacy and error, and conscience seemed to dwindle from its previously dominant role in life. Goethe redefined life's meaning and goal: no longer was it the aim in life to fulfil rules laid down by God and morality, to fulfil duty and brotherly love, but to develop in every way individual personality, to seek, strive and create — the new aim in life was useful activity. Life was fulfilled in the present, not in eternity. Nature, Art and Eros (reconciliation in the final part of *Faust*) achieved the rank of the final and the absolute. Christianity was deposed: it retained its importance, of course, but it ceased to be the key to life. If it were to be respected within its own limits (of church and upbringing) by those who did not attend church, it would have to lose its obtrusiveness and surrender its exclusive right to dominate life. There was more to life than the 'revelation' in the Bible. What Goethe's life and work made clear to the 19th-century intellectual was that the humanity of the individual and of others at its best was no longer a Christian humanity, as had been accepted until then — and it was here that it proved truly revolutionary.

The philosophy of idealism attempted to combine elements of the *Bildungsreligion* with (once again) elements of Christianity. In doing so, it would cut back Goethe's heathenism, reconcile immanence and transcendence, 'christen' the new humanity and interpret Christian teachings in the light of that humanity. Of course, some of the central teachings of Christianity, such as the doctrines of grace and justification, were scandalous when judged by the dominant pathos and ethical rigorousness of the freedom and autonomy of man: why should the guilt of an individual be accepted by another? And as a result, Christianity's central view of man as a creature of sin had to be considerably altered.

In some ways, Romanticism managed, as has already been pointed out, in contrast to the rationalism of 'heathen' classicism, to bring about a return to Christianity. But it also brought about a curious expansion of an undefined and secular 'religiosity'. The poetic became religious, and the religious poetic. Art, especially, and even individual feelings, such as love in the works of Novalis, took on a religious character. According to Novalis, absolute love was religion, the Self and the not-Self as Thou — that was the 'Amen of the universe'.

And so it continued: personality and *Bildung*, art and culture, the worldliness of heathen classicism, the concept of autonomy with its rigorous idealism, the feeling of eternal longing, the 'depth' and creative force of art; all this, once it had distanced itself from Christianity, took on a religious or quasi-religious aspect.

Even in the field of politics a similar religiosity developed, that which I have called political faith; and while it sometimes equalled the Christian faith in importance, at others it even took its place. At the Hambach festival, for example, it was not mere rhetoric when the founding of the Fatherland and the rebirth of the German character was described as 'holy work'. And in the *Hessischer Landbote* (The Hessian Courier) of Georg Büchner and Friedrich Weidig, the tone of social justice, equality and brotherhood was, aside from the conscious use of biblical language, clearly religious. National and social democracy took on the dimension of enthusiasm of political faith — they were the promise of salvation, and they made great demands on life and death. The religion of politics took its place next to the religion of culture.

On the other hand, the problem of 'the death of God' appeared, alongside the *Weltschmerz* and the new radical and rationalistic tendencies. It was a problem of the loss of faith in God, no matter what form that faith took, and it brought with it the gnawing pain of nihilism. Büchner's *Danton* was a prime example of this. In the history of education and in the statements of sensitive young people, and especially those of poets, of the sons of priests and theology students, the crisis in religion, the doubts towards Christianity, indeed the rejection of Christianity, or the compromises which disguised a new distance towards it, could all be seen to grow.

A new stage towards de-Christianisation which also occurred during the 1830s was the emergence of the movement of *Junges Deutschland*. What was formulated here was not a rationalistic or political protest, but a vitalistic uprising against traditional, church-inspired ethos. It was an uprising for the emancipation of the flesh, of pleasure, a hedonistic revolt against the 'mummification' of life and nature (Gutzkow in his preface to *Wally the Doubter*), a revolt which attacked Christianity and the priests using traditional morality, while the politically progressive Ludwig Börne still propagated the cliché of Goethe being 'immoral'. All the motives and elements for a rejection of Christianity, of church and religion can be found in the works of Heinrich Heine during the 1830s and 1840s, before his reconversion to religion: the elements of rationalism and relativism, of heathenism, Saint-Simonism, all the worldly, sensuous, nihilistic and political elements were clearly there. Priests and religion were regarded as the cement for a damnable status quo, the enemies of freedom and emancipation. In Heine's work, Christianity is merely the object of irony and fun. He was to become one of the great promoters of de-Christianisation and would have a great influence on the minds and thoughts of the young generation during the 1840s.

Yet another stage, and one which this time would mark a new epoch, was the Young Hegelian criticism of religion, which accompanied D. F. Strauss's *Life of Jesus*. The 'facts' of salvation in the Bible were myths; the statements about Christ were to be applied to the whole of mankind; and Christianity could only be understood as a type of humanism. The Young Hegelians turned against idealism, and as idealism regarded itself as a reinterpretation of Christianity, this was a turn against Christianity itself. Suddenly, Christianity was denounced (in irritable and apodeictic polemics) as out of date, damaging and even inhumane. Behind it all stood, of course, political opposition to the conservative state, a state which, particularly around 1840, saw itself as a Christian one. Bruno Bauer was the first to predict the end and the destruction of religion as a consequence of Hegel, and he even planned a journal for atheism and for the mortality of man. Hegelianism was atheism; God was self-awareness without God. In 1841 he declared in *Das entdeckte Christentum* (Christianity Exposed) that religion was unnatural, obsessed with suffering, a hell of misanthropy, the curse of the world and the destruction of self-awareness. God was the 'provost of hell', and the theologian was guided by nothing more than 'filthy fear', was inhuman, was Satan. Theology should be neither humanised, nor anthropologised, but destroyed and the world de-Christianised.

It was not Bauer, however, who was to be most influential, but Ludwig Feuerbach in his book *Das Wesen des Christentums* (The Essence of Christianity, 1841). The book provoked a wave of enthusiasm among young people (Marx and Engels said: 'We are all Feuerbachians at the present time'), and in 1845 there followed a further book, *Das Wesen der Religion* (The Essence of Religion). Feuerbach's starting-point was that the real was that which escaped or defied understanding; it was the material, the sensual, the non-spiritual. What was immaterial, imagined and thought was not, as the philosophers and the theologians claimed, real, but unreal. The theory was a revolt against Hegel, who had reduced everything to 'intellect' and the 'spirit', and who had subjugated everything to the tyranny of abstraction. In terms of life, this meant that only everything of this world was real, only man in his real world. What was important was man's free development within his world and the improvement of it. This was a polemical rejection of Christian faith in God and of Hegelian metaphysics of the spirit, both of which had deceived man of his self and the improvement of his world. 'Wherever life in heaven is the truth, life on earth is a lie.' God was the intolerable enemy of the free development of man. What was important was to reverse the situation. From 'candidates for the other world', people had to become 'students of this world'. Culture and progress were hindered by the expectations of the other world. This was also true of death: 'Instead of placing the other world above in heaven, we should place it above our graves in our own world, namely in the historical future of man.' Religion was thereby invalidated, but also explained, for it was part of man's history. Religion came from man's basic need, his basic feeling (and feelings belonged to the world of the senses), to relate to himself. Religion was a product of man, in which he reified opinions of himself and his desire for something outside of him. According to this way of thinking, because religious ideas corresponded to human desires, these desires were the original source of the religious ideas; as religion was a source of comfort, religion must stem from man's need for comfort. God was a projection of man; or, to be more precise, statements about God were not lies or madness, but statements about man himself, and here was the new development: they were statements on man as a 'species', on mankind, as opposed to man the individual. Religion corresponded to an early stage in the history of man. But it had become damaging and illusory. Man had become the slave of his product, a stranger to himself, untrue to his own, physical self and in his duty to the world around him. Religion made man obsessed within his own limited individuality, isolated him from and put him into conflict with the rest of his species, and it was this element of Christianity which was rejected so indignantly. The history of religion showed, by way of Christianity and Protestantism, a gradual anthropologisation. Man was once again becoming the centre of man's life. In the modern world, men had appropriated the human content of the Christian religion for themselves, before any philosophy had, and transferred it to their scientific, aesthetic, political, social and economic interests, for it was in these areas that they found meaning, final certainties and absolutes, and it was these areas which were important to them. Christianity as a religion concerned with the other world was relegated to Sunday; it stood in irreconcilable conflict with the modern world. What was important now was to recognise religion as anthropology, and to translate and raise religion into a science. Man is a god to man, and in the 'pious' atheist Feuerbach he inherited all the divine characteristics, such as justice and love. In the species of man, man was freed from his limitations, his heart was redeemed, his conscience comforted, he became perfect and immortal, and the species of man could be seen in a real and concrete way, in the relationship between Self and Other. Here was God. From here, all love and friendship was transfigured. Work took the place of prayer, earth the place of heaven, and politics took the place of religion. It was surely this mixture of science and sermonising, of realism and a lightly sentimentalised philosophy of love, of the pathos of progress, of work and of history, as well as the emphasis on soul and feeling, that contributed to the overwhelming success of the theory.

Marx based his criticism of religion on Feuerbach's theories, but he also expanded, changed and radicalised them. Certainly, religion, as a system of alienation, had to be abolished for the sake of this world and for the sake of happiness; the world had to be de-sacralised; and Wilhelm Weitling's recourse to a biblically communist Jesus was sarcastically rejected by Marx as 'lovesick drivel' (*Liebessabbelei*). But (and this was more marked than in Feuerbach, and a legacy of the Enlightenment), religion had to be quashed, because it was scientifically out of date. Faith in science accompanied faith in happiness; science became the new measure, even in the search for meaning and happiness. The path of science was the path of truth, of freedom and humanity; reason took the place of religion. Religion for Marx was not only psychologically but also sociologically the product of man: it was an ideology, the expression, mask and mystification of certain relationships of production, class, power and dependency. Religion was simultaneously the expression of real misery in the world, a protest against that misery and also its deflection into a different world. In this way religion made misery and authority legitimate and hindered any necessary or possible change. Religion was thus the 'opium of the people', and the social principles of Christianity were nothing more than an apologia for the existing injustices in the world. Furthermore, any critical exposing of religion would not be an end in itself, but would help make change in the world possible. Only when 'comfort' had been destroyed would 'misery' become unbearable and real change begin. But religion could only be destroyed through a revolutionary change in the reality which gave birth to it, and not through a genetic explanation or anthropological reinterpretation of religion. Only when there was no more need for comfort or for sanction, because the conditions for them were no longer there, would religion disappear. Religion could not be quashed through some philosophy of Self-Thou, but through revolution and socialism. The fight against religion was a fight against a world where religion was still needed. Criticism of religion was criticism of politics. The rejection of religion was absolute and total, just as man's demand to be his own master was absolute and total, that man has only himself to thank, that he create and redeem himself; for that reason, there can be no God. Marx stayed with this theory, even when he later emphasised man's dependency on others, on the species and (reluctantly) on nature; mankind created itself. The goal was absolute, as was the battle for that goal. God was only an obstacle. It was here that the quasi-eschatological messianism of Marx's atheism, of Marx's doctrine, was founded, the prospect of perfecting society, the new world of socialism, the promise of ultimate meaning for the individual. The earth and mankind, these were the ultimate, and any concern for 'private' fate and 'private' salvation was pure egoism. Scientific socialism took the place of religion, answered its questions, became faith, hope and charity, and made 'secondary' issues such as the individual, death and guilt, inequality in talent and fate disappear. Thence the radicalism of the battle. The new man who would bring about the new society was necessarily an atheist, and a militant one, even if he did speak tactically of the freedom of religion; he would free the world and his fellow men from the spectre of religion. Socialism would annihilate Christianity. Alongside the new religions of culture and science, and the religion of politics, appeared a new phenomenon, which has been an integral part of history ever since: social religion, which saw the meaning of life in the production of a new society and a new man.

In a history like this one, which is more concerned with the effects of such ideas on contemporary society, the figure of Feuerbach was, at first, more important than Marx. But Marx was more important in the long term because the workers' movement adopted his criticism of religion. The workers' movement grew up in a radical democratic milieu, which had been shaped by rationalism and by the conviction in the conflict between science and religious faith, and later during the 1850s by pervasive scientific ('vulgar') materialism. The movement's experience with Christians and the churches had been a negative one, for the latter were conservative and preached humility and submission. Their social milieu was provincial and rural, or the milieu of the educated middle classes. The church on the whole was alien to the way of life of the proletariat, and liberal theology was occupied with different problems and seemed to be unconcerned on the issue. The church appeared idealistic, and it may have been for this reason, that the proletariat became 'material-istic'. Marx's doctrine of revolution was an 'ultimate' faith, and it was from its atheism that it drew its vital strength. Finally, in contrast to England, the alliance between socialism and atheism in Germany can be traced back to the fact that here it was the Marxist version of socialism which had been adopted.

Feuerbach and radical rationalism shaped the central years of the 19th century. In 1848, an explicit hatred of religion became evident, even among the lower classes, owing to the part played by rationalistic teachers in elementary schools, and there were, in addition to this, signs of a certain indifference. But, as has been said, the self-evidence and resolute defence of Christianity remained almost untouched. After 1840, the philosophy of totality declined as a doctrine, a doctrine of nature and history, of the world and of life, and of the meaning of the world and life — the philosophy that theology had always preserved, in whatever form. The 'positive' sciences, the empirical sciences, slowly took its place. It was these which became more important, even prominent, in interpreting life. The natural sciences, with their insights into the nature of matter, the earth's expanse, causality, the earth's history, the structure and development of life, had gradually and inexorably undermined the traditional religious assumptions in the picture of the world and the perspective of life, which the Enlightenment and idealism had preserved. These assumptions were no longer self-evident, even where there was no express opposition, and they began to fade into the background. The historicisation of the world through the arts resulted in the fact that people started to regard the Bible (even outside the field of Bible criticism) in historical terms and in terms of its historical figures. They saw it as merely one of many historical phenomena, even though such a viewpoint was balanced out by theories among the majority of historians that Christianity was the culmination of the history of the world. The affinity of the spirit to God, the special position man occupied in the universe, and man's freedom, became imperceptibly uncertain, as did any ideas of divine providence and the meaningful concepts of revelation and eternity. For many scientists, science itself became a religion ('Science has become our religion,' said Rudolf Virchow in 1865, and the early history of such ideas will be discussed later), because science 'revealed' truths about the world and about life and exposed them to the light of day. And it was for this reason that not only the results but also the process of discovery had a distinctly religious flavour.

For the middle classes, two distinctive figures and movements were important in the process of de-Christianisation between Feuerbach and Nietzsche, that is to say during the 1850s and 1860s. First of all, there was Schopenhauer, the first important philosopher to see himself as an atheist. His philosophy of life won widespread support after 1850, especially with those whose religious interpretation of life had collapsed under the weight of Feuerbach and the materialists, but who could not accept the new options offered them. Religion, for Schopenhauer, was a branch of metaphysics for the people, which no longer had any validity for the intellectual, but was merely tolerated. Its claim to be a theology was dismissed (theology itself was described as 'metaphysics based on a chronic lack of intelligence'), and it seemed that many people thought like that. Schopenhauer also wiped out idealism's claim that it was a science: science, according to Kant, was nothing more than empirical science; 'metaphysical need' could only be satisfied through a free interpretation of existence. What made Schopenhauer different was this: in contrast to the optimism of culture and progress in idealism, and in contrast to science and empiricism, and to all ideas of 'meaning', Schopenhauer was a pessimist. At the root of all being was an unconscious and blind will to live. Man's goal was to free himself from the compulsion and will of this self-ness (*Selbstheit*), while recognising and sympathising with it. The highest agent of liberation was art. The goal for an ascetic victory over self-ness was a sort of quietistic nirvana. A sharp individualism was required, a rejection of state and society, of the majority and the general. What was important here was not so much the arguments and theories, but the character and the feeling. It was an individualistic, irrational-istic and atheistic 'doctrine', but also fundamentally an idealistic one, which dealt with the reason for the world and the goal of life. It did not destroy the content of cultural existence, as Feuerbach and the materialists had done, but it solved the puzzle of the world and thereby took on the character of a religion. Here was an answer to religious nihilism, after the demise of idealistic philosophy, to *Weltschmerz* and pessimism, to political resignation and the 'shock' of materialism, and it was an answer which could also join forces with the existing religion of art. Schopenhauer had his own 'congregation', a key phenomenon in the history of the dissolution of religion among the middle classes. The academic popular philosopher Eduard von Hartmann spread Schopenhauer's philosophy; Wilhelm Busch, Wilhelm Raabe and many others were deeply influenced by it; and Richard Wagner gained his view of life, his poetry and his religion of art from it. It was art which adopted the function of salvation. It salvaged the seed of religion (that is to say, the theory of the world as mere appearance) and thereby humanised mankind. The beautiful and the holy, the pathos of heroism and the mysticism of salvation were all combined in this profane and pessimistic way. Art was a sacrament, Bayreuth (from 1876) a place for pilgrimage. All this was present in a remarkable, perhaps compensatory reaction to the robust ethos of work, success, money and power, and to the positivism of the time.

And so on the edge of the natural sciences, and partly also from within their ranks, a scientistic popular movement developed from around the middle of the century, one which drew its 'ideological' and sceptical conclusions from the growth of science and from 'materialism', or 'vulgar materialism' as it was later described. Already Feuerbach had been the first person in Germany to use 'materialstic' arguments in his attack on idealism. His saying 'Man is what he eats', taken out of its very difficult original context, achieved the status of a popular slogan. But it was only after 1850 that a popularisation of materialism, coloured by science, could begin. Jakob Moleschott, a physiologist, who lost his lectureship in Heidelberg as a result of the reaction in 1854, proclaimed that chemistry was the supreme science, that man was the product of physical influences, consciousness a function of the brain, thinking a physical movement connected with calcium phosphate, and that man could better himself through taking better care of his brain. Karl Vogt, also a physiologist and a member of the Frankfurt National Assembly in 1848, inveighed against the idea of a 'soul', and claimed that thought was connected to the brain in the same way that bile was connected to liver, and that the soul was connected to the brain in the same way that urine was to the kidney (*Blind Faith and Science*, 1854). Ludwig Büchner, a doctor and brother of the writer Georg Büchner, wrote the popular 'bible' of such simplistic materialism in his bestseller *Strength and Matter* in 1855. Love and hate, magnanimity and murder were all necessary consequences of reactions of substances within the brain; there were no 'immaterial' motors. This was aimed not only at church theology, but also at the basic Christian assumptions of non-ecclesiastical culture: the acceptance of the existence of God and the existence of the soul. As a result followed a naturalisation of life, universal determinism and a rejection of all normative ethics. This form of materialism appealed to the pathos of undogmatic, empirical research, was optimistic and held faith in progress. There was no support among these people for Schopenhauer's pessimism, Georg Büchner's nihilism, or for the hero of Turgenev's *Fathers and Sons*.

From the 1850s, scientists and the public became involved in the debates between the materialists and those who were more religiously orientated over the creation, the soul and the freedom of will, and the overwhelming response to Darwin within Germany can only be explained as a result of this situation. Darwin once again revolutionised the relationship between Christianity and general consciousness. Without making any claims to a whole interpretation of the world, and without any great polemic, Darwin made the story of creation, as well as the concepts of creation, creator and immortality, unnecessary ('The old God has nowhere to live,' said David Friedrich

Strauss), and swept aside the fundamentally Christian doctrine of man's special position within the world. The zoologist Ernst Haeckel, who had been in Jena since 1865, became the spokesman for Darwinian doctrine and its 'ideological' consequences for Germany during the late 1860s. Of course, the debates within the natural sciences before Darwinism cannot be judged by its extremes. Neither the materialists nor the religious idealists were in the majority. But what was prominent was a very conscious agnosticism, to use the classic description, a silent adoration of the unexplorable (or unexplored).

To such explicit rejection of Christianity, to the gradual displacement of Christian truths through science, there belonged a change in the way and atmosphere of life, particularly after the middle of the century. Feuerbach had seen it as the practical removal of Christianity's power and the severing of workdays from Sunday. The fundamental element of modern life was now the importance this world, the belief in man, who created himself and the world around him, including the absolute, and everything which had meaning. The realities of this world took on a religious character, became substitute or quasi-religions, became the objects of 'worship', of a secular faith. The religion of art, from classicism through to Wagner, and later the religion of science, science as religion, have already been mentioned, as has the religion or cult of the personality, of education and of culture. The political faith of the liberals, the democrats, the socialists, and, in the middle years of the century, the political faith of the nationalists, was gaining in importance. The opinion often expressed by the liberal-nationalists in 1870, that there was nothing more to live for, because national unity had been achieved, was an example of such faith. And finally, as has already been mentioned, there were two great private myths of the middle classes: the myths of the meaning of life and of immortality. On the one hand these were the family, and occasionally (more in theory than in practice) the sanctification of personal love, which would become almost holy. And on the other hand there was work and, especially in the big businesses, the factory. Work and the family (the same age-old duties) were the realities of life, of 'morality'. They became something which made life worth living, gave it meaning, and something which could stand firm in the face of death. The value placed upon work far exceeded, either explicitly or implicitly, the value placed on private life. Work served the progress of mankind. It was more than individual hard work, more than just earning a livelihood: the belief in the progress of mankind and of culture became the new secular religion. This lifestyle did not grow up in opposition to Christianity, but alongside it and within it. Compared with the new areas of modern life, Christianity became boring. It did not pose any of life's important questions, or even answer them. It retreated into the background of Sunday. Or, far removed from the resolute rejection of Christianity and far removed from atheism, agnosticism arose and became not untypical among the educated classes throughout the second half of the century. It provided an insight into the evasion of transcendence, into Christianity's inability to answer the questions of the modern world, the turning away from a desire for and possibility of a meaningful wholeness. The issue of the legitimacy of morality and the validity of Christian values, a topic discussed by Nietzsche, was already beginning to make itself felt. And resolute non-Christians stood at the edges — especially the intellectuals who had weathered the various writings which reflected on the critique of religion, most with a little less rejoicing than Feuerbach and Marx, perhaps, but who now calmly accepted the stoical burden of existence in a godless world, or who now concerned themselves solely with culture and progress. In comparison with the situation in England or in France, it can be seen that Germans did not attribute the same importance to religion in both private and public life as people did in England, neither did they yet openly reject religion as vehemently as people did in France.

There were a number of variations and combinations of these positions. In literature, for example, Gottfried Keller and Theodor Storm were firmly non-Christian, with composure or with torment, as was Paul Heyse, in a more aesthetic and bourgeois manner. Neither Friedrich Hebbel nor Wilhelm Raabe was religious, yet neither were they connected with the irreligiousness of the advocates of 'this' world. And then there was Gustav Freytag, who accepted Christian teaching as part of the national and cultural tradition. Even a man of the Prussian establishment such as Moltke declared his faith in a 'free-thinking' rational and ethical view of the world (with many social-Darwinist traits). Paul de Lagarde and Franz Overbeck were representative of a theologically influenced, rationalist-ethical or historicist rejection of Christianity; Jacob Burckhardt of a quiet atheism of an historian and art lover. Alongside the materialism of the 1850s stood the powerful and independant continuation of the religion of classicism, in its more Kantian moralistic form, and the adoration of genius. The liberal-nationalist Schiller festival of 1859, which was extremely popular and had a strong idealistic flavour, was an example of this, and belongs in the history of secular religion in Germany. The aged David Friedrich Strauss, with his bestseller *The Old and the New Faith* of 1872 (scorned by Nietzsche), represented a part of the *Bildungsreligion* at the end of the period under review: the demise of the Christian faith and of any form of transcendence beyond this world; the middle classes' faith in education; the cult of genius; the celebration of humanity; the ideals of culture; and traditional, even if somewhat secularised ethics — it represented all these things in a religious form. The 'new faith' was a type of post-Christian or non-Christian religion for the average citizen. It was only Nietzsche's anti-Christianity which would add a new dimension.

2. Education: School and University

Nineteenth-century Germany became a land of schools. Alongside compulsory military service and compulsory taxation, compulsory education became one of the basic duties for the modern citizen. It was the state which had established this duty. It organised the schools, thereby intervening in the life of the individual and a person's journey through life, as it had never done before. The state became the school state. The fight for the schools became a new and important area of debate for the political and social forces of the time. School became an issue for politics, and school policy became a new phenomenon of the 19th century. School produced a new grouping of youth. It influenced a person's chances in life and shaped society according to career structure and class. Society became a school society, eventually even a schooled society, and the revolutionary aspects of this process must be kept in mind, especially in considering other developing countries. The history of schooling can no longer be regarded as an esoteric subject, but as central to modern history, and this was particularly true of Germany, for the new developments made themselves strongly felt here at a particularly early stage.

In the 'old' world, education was primarily a matter of home and estate. The individual grew into his world by dealing directly with it and with those around him. Behaviour was dictated by tradition, practised through concrete examples and methodic learning, not through abstraction or reflection. It was the church and oral tradition which helped the individual to find his place in the world. At most, schools were merely back-up institutions for the home as a whole. But the demographic, social and economic changes of the period around 1800, the expansion and rationalisation of the power of the state, the demand for emancipation of the citizen, and the 'discovery' of man's autonomy dissolved this world. The 'new' man was no longer tied to background and social status. He had discovered his own 'personal' status. His behaviour was dictated from within. He planned his own actions, shaped his own world, and acted on abstraction and reflection. For this, he needed new knowledge, new abilities, and the education of life could not provide them. He needed professional education — the school. This was the background for the educational reforms of the Napoleonic era, which have already been discussed, and the background for the revolution in education during the 19th century.

If one turns to the history of schooling and education after 1815, one must first of all talk about Prussia, the model state in educational reform, which was far ahead of the majority of other German states by two or three decades. The great upheaval was discussed above. But with the end of the era of reform, around 1819 say, school reform also began to stagnate. What had already been introduced was implemented, but what had yet to be introduced was abandoned, and the process of reform remained incomplete. The consequences of this were manifold.

Firstly, the idea of a unified system of national education was no longer possible — that is, a system where each stage at school was connected with the next, and where general education and equal opportunities could be negotiated within the reality of social differences. Johann Wilhelm Süvern, a councillor of state, failed in his attempt to introduce a law which would enable this to happen, and as a result lost his position. The different stages at school now became independent types of school specific to different classes in society. It was now the aim of state policy to develop *Volksschulen* (elementary, and later also *Mittelschulen*, or middle schools) and *Gelehrtenschulen* (classical schools) that were separated from each other, based on class lines. *Volksschulen* and *Gymnasium* (secondary school) developed in different ways and totally independent from each other. This was clear even from the organisation of the different departments responsible for the schools: the *Volksschulen* came under the jurisidiction of the government, while the secondary schools were the responsibility of the *Oberpräsident*. The failure of this concept of reform for the school system was first and foremost a consequence of a conservative reaction in school policy. The conservatives countered the idea of equal education, which was fundamental to Süvern's bill by stressing the inequalities between people, their social backgrounds and their varying opportunities; and the educational demands of the individual were subordinated to the needs and demands of society as a whole and the employment system. Education for a job became more important than a general education, and the need for a stable society became more important than creating social mobility through school. The political and social consequences of the reform were to be cut back, and both the reforms and the schools de-politicised. The failure of Süvern's bill was also due to other factors more important than the conservative reaction; it also failed owing to pressures resulting from specific issues. The bishops, for example, fought against the diminution of church authority, and the state could not afford to run into conflict with the church after 1815. The question of the financing of schools also proved difficult: should it be the responsibility of the state, the parishes, the parents or the landowners? It is true that the interests of the Junkers proved to be an important factor. But the main point was that the parishes could not afford the financial burden of the reforms, and any other form of financial distribution would be impossible. The reforms were simply not possible at the present level of national income or of public finances. Last but not least, the interests of the parents and their sympathy for education were not based on progressive notions of reform. Because of their realistic job expectations, they favoured the different types of school, and even further delimitation. School reform presupposed a mobile society, which had not yet been achieved. School reflected rather than created the different structures within society, and whatever influence it may have had will be discussed later.

The abandonment of the reforms therefore meant that school policy retreated from the centre of politics. There was nobody like Süvern, who in 1817 described school reform as 'the most important gamble of all which, if not now, then later will reap rewards all the more bountiful'. Neither was anyone else like Hermann von Boyen, who in 1819, as War Minister no less, saw the employment of 'every possible and available means' to improve elementary schools as the principle measure against demagogic and revolutionary threat. School became just one department among many others.

Furthermore, conservative tendencies became stronger in the debate concerning school policy, quite independently of the failure of Süvern's bill. The reformers were now on the defensive. To educate people to be autonomous, to think for themselves, to criticise tradition and authority and to reason independently was regarded by the conservatives as dangerous and unrealistic. Rather than emphasise the dangers of too much material and formal education (of 'over-education' and the 'under-education' which accompanied it), the limitations of education in general were underlined. It was the fear of the mobilising, perhaps even revolutionising consequences of school which fired the conservatives. Any such conservative tendencies did not, however, dominate the reality of school. The provincial and district administrations continued to develop the school system on the basis of the reforms, despite ideological conflicts. The reforms and their institutions developed their own dynamics. But the conservative programme of the restoration which was gradually finding its way into the head offices of almost all the states was the one which set the boundaries, and it was for this reason that there were some restrictions and changes in direction. Politics were gradually seeping into the schools. The development of the schools was now shaped by modernisation and by controlling the consequences of modernisation, by activating forces for the community and making sure these forces were not political.

After the separation of the different types of school, the *Gymnasium* or secondary school gained in precedence and preference. It was closely or even directly connected to the state, competitive and modern, and it had high prestige. It was better and more extensively cultivated than other schools. The interests of the intellectuals in education, which during the Enlightenment had concentrated on the education of the people, now shifted to higher education, to the school of the intellectuals and the school of their children. Even the reformers who strove for a society where education was universal had to assume that it would be the civil servants who would bring about that society; the education of the servants of the state who were really an instrument for the common goal could quite easily become a priority in view of that goal. In the long term, then, the coupling of higher education and state office, no matter how legitimate, had in fact a socially conservative aspect.

The more important types of school must now be considered.

(a) The *Gymnasium*

The *humanistisches Gymnasium* (secondary school with an emphasis on Latin and Greek) was the standard school of higher education in 19th-century Germany. Although at a somewhat slower rate than in Prussia, and with a few specific exceptions, it became accepted throughout the whole of Germany. In Bavaria, this sort of secondary school had been established during the Napoleonic era under Friedrich Immanuel Niethammer (1808) and then under Friedrich Thiersch in 1829, while it was not until 1850 that it would be established in Württemberg, where the old humanist schools still dominated. Austria alone remained unaffected by neo-humanism, and the older types of school, which had been deeply influenced by the religious orders during the restoration, continued to exist; post-humanist considerations then increased in importance in 1849–50, when the *Gymnasium* became subject to modern reforms; there was a new emphasis on versatility and on the natural sciences as opposed to the old languages, and a new acceptance of the lower schools as schools for the middle classes. Nevertheless, the developments in Prussia are on the whole prototypical.

It has been shown how the new *Gymnasia* had been picked out from the mass of the old type of Latin schools. In 1818, there were 91 *Gymnasia* throughout Prussia. The numbers grew to 118 in 1848 and 145 in 1864. The numbers of pupils also increased significantly, though not steadily, by 73% between 1816 and 1846, and the number of teachers grew correspondingly by 69%, in contrast to the elementary schools. In 1822 there were 14,826 *Gymnasium* pupils; in 1846, 26,816, and in 1864, 44,114 (and in addition to this, there were 16,491 pupils at *Realgymnasia* secondary schools with an emphasis on modern languages, maths and science). The teacher/pupil ratio was favourable and hardly worsened (in 1864, it was 1:20). The *Gymnasium* was fundamentally a state school and no longer an independent establishment of class and community. The foundation and maintenance of the schools, their syllabuses, exams and supervision, as well as the examinations and appointments of the teachers, were matters for the state. The teachers were civil servants. The towns contributed to the financing of the schools, especially through construction, but their influence, and the influence of the administrations and of the school deputations, was severely limited and neutralised through the fact that it was the state which nominated the directors. This particular type of school was no longer the primary concern of the parish, and certainly not the concern of the parents. In this way they were free from local pressure and from patronage, but also stood out from the society around them. The state guaranteed the financing of the schools. The school fees may have covered only up to half the costs, but the teachers were no longer forced to scrape a living as they had before. The state also played the dominant role in the administration of the schools. Not only the old inefficiency but also the new experimentation of single schools, which had been one of the main characteristics of the period of reform, were now subject to strict norms laid down by head office. Schools were gradually bureaucratised. The compulsory *Abitur* (school-leaving examination) in its final form (regularised in Prussia in 1834), the syllabuses, the compulsory reports and supervision were all used as instruments of standardisation. There may not have been any way of 'bringing the schools into line' in the conservative-liberal administration — Catholic and Protestant schools and schools in large and small towns all retained their different characteristics, and directors could make their own mark on the 'spirit' of their schools, but it was the character of state school which prevailed.

This had considerable consequences. The *Gymnasium* laid down general and universal standards, ways of thinking and rules, as opposed to regional, denominational and class differences and details. It educated an all-German citizenry. It formed a 'nation', and to this extent it was modern. In fact, because the education at a *Gymnasium* was similar throughout the whole of Germany, its contribution to the development of an all-German national consciousness among the middle classes cannot be underestimated. On the other hand, Prussia's role as promoter of the new education helped considerably to establish and maintain the *kleindeutsch* identificaton of Prussia's 'vocation' with German education and the trust in the liberal modernity of the state.

The *Gymnasium* was the school of the new humanism. The old languages, classical subject-matter and formal education were clearly given precedence. There were various changes as time progressed, and differences from state to state — a greater encyclopaedic all-round education, or a greater concentration on the classical languages, on Latin for example — but that is not important here. In Prussia in 1837, the weekly timetable for a course of nine years was divided into 280 unit-hours of lessons (the figures in brackets represent the division of hours in the ten-year course of 1812): Latin 86 (76), Greek 42 (50), Mathematics 33 (60), German 22 (44), History and Geography 24 (30), Religion 18 (20), Sciences 16 (20), Drawing and Calligraphy 13 (18), French 12 (0), Philosophy 4 (0), Singing 10 (0). After the 1840s, the subject of German freed itself from the predominance of antiquity, concentrated more on medieval and classical literature, and came to be seen, like national history, as a national duty. School was becoming nationalistic. Nevertheless, the predominance of classical antiquity, the identification with the idealism of the Greeks and the old literary-philosophical flavour remained intact.

The continued survival of neo-humanism was surprising enough, for the emergent middle classes, like the old ruling classes, were more the supporters of a realistic, practical education, and the conservatives sensed in the idealisation of the Greeks, perhaps not unjustifiably, a certain republicanism and paganism. Friedrich Wilhelm IV wanted to generate a 'better' way of thinking through the *Gymnasium*: Christianity as opposed to scepticism, history and realities as opposed to theories and doctrine. But such aspirations were in vain: the *Gymnasium* held fast, and even during the period of reaction it survived unscathed in the slipstream of various conflicts. There were several reasons for this. Firstly, it was due to the fact that since the period of reform there had been a strong neo-humanist lobby which occupied the decisive positions and was supported by the universities, the educated public and the civil servants, and even by ministers such as Altenstein, the Prussian Minister of Education and the Arts. Once its prestige and the irrefutibility of antiquity and the classical studies had been established, the new *Gymnasium* took on a greater aspect of political neutrality and became a refuge for freedom. Secondly, school policy tried to check and absorb any 'republican tendencies': political and topical discussions were banned, the duty of loyalty was tightened, and religious instruction was given greater importance. The leading ministry official, Johannes Schulze, emphasised the scientific character of the school, encyclopaedic knowledge, intellectual ability, memory and formal schooling to such an extent that the other idea behind it, the idea of moral and political regeneration, faded into the background. More important was a third factor. Classical studies, the 'mother' of the *Gymnasium*, grew from a central and philosophically influenced science of the ideal humanity of the ancients to a sum of many positivist single sciences of an historical or philological nature. It represented specialised knowledge rather than education. Textual philology no longer educated a person to be a 'shaper of mankind' but a grammatical specialist. Formal linguistic schooling and philological techniques repressed the 'spirit' which had been so important to the neo-humanists: the *Gymnasium* had become a school for grammar and ancient languages. The brilliance of its humanistic-universalistic elements, its critical and republican zest in the face of a feudal and authoritarian world, which were the founding ideas of the school, faded. What was true, good and beautiful dissolved into trivial rhetoric. There was a final reason for the continued survival of the *Gymnasium*. In 1810, the rediscovery of Greek antiquity and the founding of a new school had been revolutionary. But within the context of the new intellectual climate, the school as an institution became part of tradition. Antiquity could become a protector against the *Zeitgeist* and the future, as a means of turning away from the present. If the natural sciences claimed to be able to free mankind, then humanism could no longer be plagued by the reproaches of the conservatives. The anti-class and anti-aristocratic idea of a meritocratic elite which was one of the founding ideas of the *Gymnasium* lost its revolutionary aspect after the nobility and the conservatives had come to accept the *Gymnasium*. They could now defend it as a school for an elite minority within the existing social order. The *Gymnasium* as a school for the intellectuals was, however, a good school. It was on this basis that German science developed so remarkably, and it was through this that the existence of the *Gymnasium* was guaranteed. Thus it can be seen that what had seemed politically and socially impossible had now become possible: the humanistic *Gymnasium* remained the standard school in German higher education.

The *Gymnasium* was a school aimed more at the theoretical side of learning and knowledge and had very little communal life, as compared, for example, with the English public schools. It had very little spontaneity, initiative or joy in life, and this became more pronounced the longer the *Gymnasium* was established. Duty, accuracy, drills, super-vision and discipline, as well as a pronounced seriousness, dominated the atmosphere. This was part of a more general conservative process of 'stiffening', as Johannes Schulze envisaged it, but it was also simply an expression of the bourgeois concepts of order, achievement and authority which can be found throughout the whole of Europe during the period, and especially in France. From the middle of the 1830s, however, the *Gymnasium* was hampered by complaints of expecting too much and putting too much strain on its pupils.

Before the social significance of the *Gymnasium* is considered, its political effect must be looked at. At first, the *Gymnasium* had been progressive and had had a mobilising effect. One of the fundamental ideas behind it was to produce a world which was based on independence and autonomy, on the self-development of the individual, on rationality and science, achievements and education. These were the ideals of a bourgeois world which fought against a world of tradition and authority based on class and inheritance, and they were to have considerable, and not always expected or even conscious, consequences in the shaping of the state and society. The *Gymnasium* was the school of the liberal middle classes of 1848 and of the liberal nationalists during the 1860s; it was the school of a new elite. The conservative and stabilising elements which were to become more prominent in later years stood in direct opposition to this: elements which aimed to reduce political influence in the schools and even assimilate the schools into an authoritarian state, and also to dissociate them from the *Zeitgeist* and from modernity, and form an elite. This had little to do with classical humanism, however, for the secondary schools of liberal England and the schools of republican France were no less classically orientated than German schools.

There was a further element: the values promoted by the *Gymnasium* stood outside the world of work and economy, of technology and industry, and outside the world of science. Education was restricted to literary and historical culture. This emphasis did nothing to hinder the meteoric rise of science and industry — in fact the great men of science had been pupils at a *Gymnasium* and usually defended it. It did, however, sharpen the contrast between two different cultures in the world, the conflict between 'spirit' and economy (or 'materialism' in the eyes of the humanists) — capital, profit and business — and the distance of the world of education to the realities and the practical world. It only served to accentuate arrogance and disapproval. It was here that an ideology of 'inner values' would later grow and spread after 1870, in contrast to the political and social world. The dividing-line among the German middle classes between education for the civil service or self-employment and economic, capitalist and technological employment was decisively deepened.

During the first few decades of the 19th century, the new humanism was clearly a motivating force behind the schools, the teachers and the pupils. Bismarck claimed that he left his school, like every other pupil of a Prussian *Gymnasium*, a pantheist and (theoretically at least) a republican. Riehl had told how Greece became a 'second homeland' for every pupil during his time at a *Gymnasium* in Prussia, and how every pupil saw in Greece a model for their own nation and period. But for a substantial number of students, the ideas of the new humanism must have remained utopian, lost in the trials and tribulations of learning a language. From the middle of the century, the volume of critical voices increased. The original idea of unity behind education faded in the face of increasing specialisation of subjects. Nietzsche sharply criticised the pedantry of the philologists, saying that the spirit of the *Gymnasium* had been lost. It is true that as a basis for life, education at a *Gymnasium* was far from contemptible, for it remained a form of humanism. And the sceptics who philistinely dismissed the *Gymnasium* perhaps overestimated its relevance and ignored the actual normality, which sets in when something originally seen as a departure from the norm becomes part of an institution. The motivating force of an ideal of life faded, however, to literature and an established education, or even to something antiquarian and museum-like, something which was merely rhetorical and formal.

As has already been mentioned, the *Gymnasium* teachers and philologists played an important role in the history of the school. The teachers consolidated their position as a professional group by establishing professional standards and career models. They defended the uniqueness of the *Gymnasium*; they defended the superiority of the neo-humanist spirit against the demands of industry and economy for greater 'realism'; and they defended the elitist character of the school for a few against an expansion which would provide more equality and social mobility. The idea of the 'community' of the school system was of no importance to them: as philologists they felt they had nothing in common with other teachers, at the elementary schools for example. They felt they had more in common with the academically educated civil servants. For both objective and career-related reasons, therefore, they became the champions of the *Gymnasium*'s uniqueness and even came to resemble a kind of pressure group. Their evolution naturally reveals the educational changes in the *Gymnasium* — from their origins as out of the first all-round teachers of the first standardised exams, they became the teachers of specialised subjects of the middle years of the 19th century.

From its inception, the *Gymnasium* was the school of the future elite, of the gifted on the one hand, and of those destined for state-appointed careers on the other. Even in the material it taught, literature and the ancient languages, it was exclusive. In a period of poverty and hard work, that which was of no practical use, which was far removed from reality, gained a quasi-aristocratic flavour when isolated from the hardship of everyday life. It was this which was the basis of the high standards of the *Gymnasium*, and to denounce the sincerity of the aims behind it would be egalitarian nonsense. What is important here is the question of where the pupils of a school for the elite were drawn from; of how, why and when a school which was anti-estate became a school based on class.

Firstly, the *Gymnasium* did not only require intellectual talent, it also required motivation and the financial means of the parents in the form of school fees: in 1864 in Prussia the fees were between 19 and 90 marks, an average of 48 marks per annum, (the income of an elementary school teacher in the city was something under 750 marks). It also meant that the son would have to be supported financially, and he would be unable to contribute to the family's income. The quasi-aristocratic educational goal therefore favoured only those who could afford it. In short, the *Gymnasium* was first and foremost a school for the sons of the upper classes. Of course, that was certainly not a result of the restoration. The fact that the school was directly connected to the division of society, was a result of the level of economic resources — any comparison with other European countries points to that fact — and anything else was simply not possible. The social characteristics of the *Gymnasium* were, however, still not so clear-cut.

Here the *Berechtigungswesen* (a system for establishing qualifications) peculiar to Prussia and Germany must be taken into account, because it was to play a decisive role in the relationship between education and social status. It must be remembered that in Prussia the conflict between universal conscription and bourgeois individualism had been resolved by reducing the period of military service for the 'educated' classes to one year. This was directly linked to the length (and success) of a pupil's attendance at a 'higher' school. (In 1818, it specified *Immatrikulation* — matriculation; from then to 1822, it required *Abitur*; up until 1831, six months' *Untertertia* or fourth form; in 1859, it was the whole of the fourth year; and until 1868, six months' *Untersekunda* or fifth form.) In an idiom that speaks volumes, the degree necessary to obtain the reduction in military service itself became known as '*das Einjährige*' (the one-year). In addition to this, there were many other conditions for entry into the middle careers within the civil service and other careers under state control which were tied to various school examinations (chemists, the building profession, etc.). Certificates of education became more important than actual achievement in the basis for careers and social status. Thus school became the allocator of social opportunity, and it was primarily the middle classes which were defined according to their educational qualifications. The system also spread to other states where the military was structured differently.

The system of qualifications was now centred around the *Gymnasium*, because it was the only type of school which had nationwide standards. Along with the *Abitur*, which according to the neo-humanist ideal was the only true final examination, it created a string of alternative examinations. This was to have important consequences for the social composition of the *Gymnasium*. The children of the skilled and commercial middle classes and the children of the potential social climbers attended the *Gymnasium* (and in the smaller cities the *Pro-Gymnasium*) with no intention of following the neo-humanist course of education right through to the *Abitur*. The requirement of Greek proved to be no barrier, because special dispensations were available. Particularly in the first few years (up until the *Quarta* or third year), and even after then, the *Gymnasia* may not have been *Gesamtschulen* (or 'comprehensives'), but urban *Bürgerschulen*. In any case, they were certainly not 'aristocratic' in their restrictiveness. The proportion of pupils (all boys) undergoing compulsory education at secondary schools in Prussia rose from 1.7% in 1828 to 3.6% in 1864, and in Berlin from 13.2% to 16.6% (excluding private secondary schools, which were attended by an additional 11.4% and 7.5% respectively). Of course, in the cities the proportion was generally higher than in the rural areas. The proportion of those attending *Gymnasium* was growing, and the proportion of pupils in non-compulsory education at secondary schools grew from 9.7% in 1828 to 17.8% in 1864, and in Berlin (including private schools) from 21.8% to 26.2% in 1837 and then back down to 21.9%. In other words, between 6% and 6.8% of those aged from 14 to 19 attended a secondary school. In Berlin, between 3% and 4.4% of one particular age group made it through to the matriculation exams, while between 1.4% and 1.9% made it through to the *Abitur*. These figures are important, if one considers the small proportion of people within the educated and upper classes. Figures at a string of western German *Gymnasia*, for the period up until 1848, showed that 36% of pupils came from the middle middle classes and 43% from the lower middle classes. In short, it can be seen that the schools were relatively open to the urban lower middle classes. The situation was similar for the students who passed their *Abitur*. The number of students in this category was small. Of every 10,000 male inhabitants in Prussia in 1830, only 2 went into the sixth form. In 1846, 1.5 in every 10,000 made it into the sixth form, and in 1864 the figure was 2.3 for every 10,000. On the whole, about one-fifth of pupils who attended secondary school made it to the *Abitur*. In absolute figures that meant: 590 in 1820; 405 in 1830–31; 956 in 1835; 1,659 in 1855; and 1,803 in 1863. Socially speaking, almost a half of them came from the (lower) middle class (in Berlin, 17–25% were civil servants, 21–35% were skilled manual labourers and businessmen, and 5–10% came from the lower classes). But elsewhere the figure was only one-third. What was noticeable was the high proportion of children of white-collar workers — minor civil servants and elementary school teachers, and the relatively small proportion of children of skilled workers and tradesmen. The children of the managing classes were virtually absent. Differences in career were more important here than any differences in income, status or class. The peasants and lower classes were excluded altogether from these areas. In short, both the *Gymnasium* and, to a lesser extent, the *Abitur* acted as a barrier and a sluice-gate for social mobility. Admittance to a *Gymnasium* corresponded to the desires of the parents, a desire to climb the social ladder on the one hand, and a desire differentiate themselves from the lower classes. The high school fees signified not only the privileges of the prosperous, but were also a symbol of the willingness to make sacrifices. Social diversification according to a person's education was not an invention of the ruling classes, neither was it a matter of concern for them alone, but corresponded to a fundamental, non-egalitarian tendency among all social climbers and middle classes towards that sort of differentiation. The state tried to counteract the 'inflation in education' and the 'common man's addiction for study', in order to preserve the system of employment as well as the politico-social status quo. It attempted to make 'breaking out' of a particular social class more difficult by raising the school fees in the lower schools, but this achieved only middling results. It was not until the end of the period under review, during the 1860s, with the strengthening of the *Volksschulen* and *Realschulen*, that social mixing at the *Gymnasia* became less common, and the number of early school-leavers dropped.

Within the upper classes, the *Gymnasium* brought about the conformity of the nobility to the new norms. The nobility was forced out of private education and into the new schools, with the exception, of course, of the cadet schools, where principally the sons of the poorer nobility were prepared for a career as officers. The reforms here foundered on the strength of the reactionary opposition. On the other hand, there were also the middle classes of business, employers and big merchants who were alienated from the schools — the dividing-line between education and business proved difficult to cross. The social prestige of the *Gymnasium*, in actual fact, only served to increase the distance between the civil servants and employment in the world of business.

Even if one takes into account the social openness of the *Gymnasium* and its function as a sluice-gate for social mobility, and at the same time recognises its legitimacy as an elite organisation, it cannot be overlooked that both the *Gymnasia* and the universities only served to emphasise and reinforce class differences through the division of people into educated, partly educated and uneducated (the '*Volk*') groups. Education as a concept of social status signified not only the possibility of social mobility, but was also a clear demarcation point. The educated were now the upper classes. The gulf between education and the people deepened. This was a result not only of the value placed on the new education, but also of much more fundamental social changes: proletarianisation, urbanisation and the social diversification between various parts of the city, as well as the expansion of the educated classes, who could thus more and more live among themselves. This phenomenon was stronger in the north, where dialect created a social gap, than in the south. The division between the educated and uneducated classes became a fact of life in Germany as in the rest of Europe. The liberal belief in the omnipotence of education, the belief that education was emancipation, that it offered equal opportunities irrespective of background or property, that it had the ability to resolve social problems, beliefs which were shared by every section of the population, still tended to cover up this tension for the time being.

The social history of the *Gymnasium* was also closely connected with the history of the 'middle' schools, or those schools which prepared their pupils for practical jobs.

The neo-humanist bureaucracy did not want secondary schools to be orientated around practical or 'useful' education. The middle *Bürgerschulen* would fulfil those aims and needs, and, with the exception of the trade schools, these were left to the municipal authorities. A whole range of every possible kind of school soon grew up, including middle schools and non-humanist secondary schools. As long as these schools were not allowed to dispense the aspired qualifications, they could not compete with the attractiveness of the lower and middle stages of the *Gymnasia*. The townspeople, the provincial classes and the school reformers attempted during the Vormärz to push through *Realschulen* and a realistic programme of education, in the form of secondary schools, in opposition to the neo-humanist establishments. Justus Liebig described the humanist monopoly *versus* the 'realistic' forms of education as the battle of the 'soap-boilers against gas lighting'. The school civil servants were, however, opposed to the school 'of materialism'. And even the future manual workers should not become slaves to the 'material view of the world' (Johannes Schulze). The school, it was claimed, would lead to revolution and democracy by generating educational demands it could not fulfil. It would not be until the 1850s that the state would give in to the arguments of the 'realists' and the demands of the trading middle classes — a way also of relieving the *Gymnasia* of the 'wrong' pupils. It was in this way that the administration finally became involved in the slow process of state regulation of secondary schools other than the *Gymnasia*, through the introduction of examinations and qualifications. In 1859 in Prussia, the *Realgymnasium* (the *Realschule* 'of the 1st order', a secondary school with an emphasis on modern languages, maths and science) became institutionally established: a secondary school with a course of nine years, ending in the *Abitur*, but with no general qualification for university entrance, and predominantly directed at technical and construction careers and a career as an officer. The same type of school without a sixth form was called a *Realschule*. Finally, there was the *Oberrealschule* (a *Realschule* of the 2nd order), a school with a course of nine years, but without Latin, and there was also a corresponding school without a sixth form and with lesser qualifications. What was important was that the state was excluding new forms of secondary schools from the wide range of municipal schools and that the main one, the *Realgymnasium*, would remain a Latin school. Once again, it was not industry, technology or business which shaped the new form of school, but the civil servants. This meant that the norms of the system of qualifications, of admittance to state offices, remained of primary importance, and it was for this reason that the school remained a Latin school. Central to the theory of education at the new schools was the idea that people should not be educated for a specific career, but that they should receive a general and formal education for active life. The old *Gymnasium* placed very great pressure on pupils to strive for a higher rung on the social ladder, and this was favoured especially by the teachers. The goal was to make pupils more academic, and apart from its prestige, Latin offered a wider range of opportunities. Even those citizens who campaigned against the academic schools still favoured higher academic qualifications and greater prestige and wanted to be different from the great mass of people. With school fees and the requirement of Latin, this type of school retained its exclusive element and therefore appealed to the parents' desire for social differentiation. The state would not, however, allow the pre-eminence of the *humanistisches Gymnasium* to be challenged. From now on, the *Gymnasium* would be able to concentrate, for both pedagogical and socio-political reasons, on the *Abitur* and thereby reduce the number of pupils who left school early. The *Realgymnasium* became a school for children of businessmen. The number of pupils at the *Realgymnasium* remained lower, however, than the number at the *humanistisches Gymnasium* (in Prussia in 1864, there were 44,114 *Gymnasium* pupils, as compared with only 16,491 at 49 *Realgymnasia*).

Apart from the new state-regulated schools, there remained a small number without any qualifications, who offered one or two foreign languages, and it was from these that the new types of state-recognised and state-regulated *Mittelschule* or *Realschule* were formed after 1870. A large number of children from the urban middle classes, who would formerly have attended the lower stages of the *Gymnasium* or the *Bürgerschulen*, now attended the newly fully developed, diversified and comparatively improved form of municipal *Volksschule*. Whether this impaired mobility, as some people think, was of no importance. Nevertheless, it would not be until the end of the period under review that there would be a diversified, tripartite school system, where the schools were not completely interchangeable. Indeed, it was the *Realschulen* and *Mittelschulen* which strengthened social differentiation, especially of the middle classes.

(b) The *Volksschule*

If the *Gymnasium* was the school of the educated minority and of a small number of the urban middle classes, then the school of the large majority was the *Volksschule*. Victor Cousin, who would later become the French Minister for Education, remarked in 1831 that Prussia was the 'great land of barracks and schools'. In fact, the school system in Prussia was model and leader for most of the other German states and during the latter part of the 19th century became the focus of international attention. As has already been said, what was particularly important for the history of the Prussian education system was that expansion and restriction existed side by side. Expansion was silent and largely outside the discussions on domestic affairs, but continued inexorably with decisive consequences. The administration pushed through the reforms all over Germany, often against the will of the community, for the schools were considered too expensive by the citizens. So-called 'winter schools' in rural areas became schools all year round. The school administration forced people to comply with the obligation to go to school — often against the will of the parents, who relied on the assistance and labour of their children, both on the land and in the cities; against the will of the factory-owners who relied on child labour; and even against the will of other parts of the administration which shied away from any such 'intrusion' into economic freedom. It was the state which was the driving force behind the measure. While in Prussia in 1816 60% of all those who were legally obliged to go to school atually did so, in 1846 the figure was already 82% (95% in Saxony and 70% even in backward Posen) and by 1864 it had reached 93% (94.3% of all boys). The number of 'factory children', which was still high during the 1830s in the industrial cities, had fallen substantially by 1839–40. In Cologne in 1827, for example, there were 2,130 of these children, but this dropped to nil in 1844. The rate of illiteracy among the recruits — although the figures vary widely and were not always based on reliable standards — stood between 2.1% and 2.5% in advanced provinces such as Brandenburg and Westphalia in 1841, 7.1% in the Rhenish province, between 12.3% and 15.3% in Pomerania and Prussia, and 41% in Posen. That gave an overall average of 9%. By 1868, that figure had fallen to just 4% — 18% in Posen, 7% in Bavaria in 1865, 1% in Saxony, between 13% and 24% in Lower Austria in the 1850s, and between 34% and 40% in Bohemia. In Prussia, it was estimated that 20% of the population above the age of ten in 1850 were illiterate, while by 1871 the figure was between 12% and 13%. Most of those were among the old people; there were more women than men who were illiterate; and the rate was higher in the rural regions and in the east than in the urban regions and the west. These estimates applied more or less to other German states, although the provinces of the Sudetenland, the Alpine province and the two parts of Mecklenburg lagged somewhat behind. Compared with England and France, these figures must be seen as a great success: in England in 1861, around 30% of the people were illiterate, and in France in 1866, 24% of military recruits.

The *Volksschule* became the school for the majority of people. Private education and private schools declined, and only in the cities did they still play a role — in 1864, 8.5% of education was private education (in Berlin in 1820, 39.5% of pupils went to private schools, in 1828 the figure was still as high as 15.2%), and some of these schools were the forerunners of the *Gymnasia*. Feudal relationships were retained only in part — in school patrons and the position of the landowner on school committees. The control over policy within schools and outside policy, as well as regional supervision, remained in the hands of the state administration. Indeed, it was intensified, and it therefore became bureaucratic. Despite the power of the state over the schools, however, institutionally they remained schools for the community. The community carried 75% of the costs on average, and in addition to this the parents had to pay school fees (in rural regions this was 1.9 marks on average, and in the cities 4.3 marks). The community also paid for the poor. The state contribution was very small and only increased in 1830 for the poor schools, as a form of compensation. In actual fact, however, the rural communities had very little say in the running of the schools, apart from their contribution to teachers' pay, and it was only within the framework of the urban self-administration that they had any powers of participation. The state had to force penny-pinching magistrates and city councillors to invest in schools, especially schools for the poor, and it was only towards the middle of the century that the cities accepted responsibility for all the schools.

The *Volksschule* was a denominational school. Mixed schools were rare (apart from in Nassau) and were repressed. This was taken for granted outside the larger cities and other areas where there was a certain amount of mixing between denominations, and where mixed education became the established norm. The school was connected to the church in other ways as well; for example, teaching posts were closely tied to the lower positions within the church (verger, sexton or organist). The clergyman would often be entrusted with local and regional supervision of the schools and sat on the school committees, and the church had very specific supervisory powers in religious education, which was still unquestioningly considered a subject of central importance. The school may have been worldly and an institution of the state, but it was still closely tied to the church.

Teaching in the schools centred around religion and the acquisition of elementary cultural techniques. There was very little concern for 'realistic' subjects such as geography or natural history. Also included in the timetable were formal subjects such as languages and mathematics, as lessons for abstract reflection. On the whole, of course, achievement, discipline and order were most important. Theoretically, the *Volksschule* was influenced by neo-humanism and concerned itself with reason. 'Industrial' schools which educated a pupil for specific employment through work were disappearing, and school was becoming separated from the practical world of work and craftmanship.

Perhaps most important of all — apart from the enforcement of compulsory education — was the fact that new teachers were coming into the schools, teachers who had studied for two or three years at a teacher-training college, had passed state examinations, were exempt from military service, and who were armed with a basic supply of knowledge and methods and filled with a new awareness of themselves and their jobs. It was a new profession, created by the state, and one which was replacing the old teacher-craftsman. The real achievement of the Prussian state was the founding or reorganisation of 35 different teacher-training colleges during the Vormärz (64 by 1872) and a special college for teachers in Berlin in 1832 (there were 1,500 trainee teachers in 1828 and 2,000 by 1845). These colleges were boarding colleges for financial reasons, and were usually set up in small towns, for political and moral reasons. A sense of duty to the state and to the church and upstanding social behaviour were inculcated there. Through conferences and associations and through various journals the administration was able to organise a continual and extensive training for these teachers.

Finally, the vast differences and obvious failings of this system of schooling must be considered. The urban schools — municipal, parish, elementary and poor schools — were more differentiated and on a different level to the village schools. During the 1840s in Berlin they consisted of four classes. Not until 1864 would there be an average of 3.6 classes and 3.5 teachers in Prussia, and 73 children to one teacher. The *Volksschulen* in the (large) cities ceased to be schools for the poor after the 1850s. They gradually became schools consisting of eight classes and with different 'streams'. They received a greater proportion of communal taxes and eventually abolished school fees. They took the place of the *Bürgerschulen* of the middle bourgeoisie. In Berlin in 1830, only 30% of pupils attended the *Volksschulen*, or poor schools as they then were; by 1865, it was the vast majority. The lower middle classes turned to these new improved schools. After 1850, this improvement proved very important — it was not simply a case of driving potential 'climbers' to the *Volksschule* and away from the schools that were supposed to lead to further education. In rural regions, the school usuallly consisted of a single class (an average of 1.1 teacher per school in 1864), and they were often overcrowded — statistics varied between 54 and 70 pupils per teacher in 1816, to 90 in 1848, and down to 83 in 1864. The degree of success of such teaching was therefore often questionable. The rate of expansion of the school system and of the number of teachers, however, did not keep pace with the number of pupils. Between 1816 and 1846, for example, the number of schools rose by 18%, and the number of teachers by 40%, but the number of pupils by 108%. Teacher training, despite the colleges, often lacked a great deal (owing to the lack of previous educational background), and there were many teachers who were only 'half-educated'. Lessons were therefore similarly 'half-educated'. One of the primary reasons for this was the miserable pay — it was below that of a skilled labourer or a policeman, and in rural areas not much above the pay of day-labourers (in 1864, the average pay in rural regions was 483 marks and 864 marks in the cities). On the land, some of the wages were paid in kind and this led to much friction between the teachers and their payers or 'debtors'. Many teachers were forced to take second jobs — in the church, in agriculture, or (as was the case in the cities) in private tuition. During the 1850, the number of trained teachers fell below demand. The quality of the schools was dependent on the quality of the teachers.

But no matter how much one may criticise the poverty and failings of these schools — either from the standpoint of the ideals of the time or by the standards of a later age — the new and important thing was that they continued to exist at all and that they expanded even further.

What significance did politics have for the *Volksschule*? Since the beginning of the 1820s, starting in Prussia, the conservative ideology of schooling had begun to creep into the ministry; there was criticism of the modern school and the excess of formal and material education, which it was believed would lead to autonomy, scepticism and intellectuality, false expectations of equality and revolutionary unrest. To counteract this, the conservatives demanded that school restrict itself more and more to simple knowledge and ready facts (instead of reflection), to fewer subjects and to teachings which were more concrete. It should turn once again to respect for tradition and authority (as well as inequality), to feeling and loyalty, to being satisfied with one's lot; it emphasised assimilation into society and demanded a markedly conservative interpretation of religious education. The school was not there to improve social mobility, but to stabilise it. The target for criticism was teacher training. The teacher who had been 'corrupted', only half-educated or even 'mis-educated' in the city and was alienated from the reality of village life became the object for criticism. The teacher-training colleges would have to be freed from the excess of science and reflection and from inessential elements and brought (back) to a level which was pure and where traditional crafts were taught. In contrast to the philosophy of restricting education, there stood the liberal philosophy of expanding it, of continuing the reforms. The liberals believed in a better education, in an intellectual one. Education was one of the conditions for freedom, and it was naïvely taken for granted that freedom was a necessary consequence of education. Education would be the key to solving social problems: it would make man more productive, it would enable him to help himself, understand laws, and it would make him immune to (communist) demagogy. This was the argument, at least, of Friedrich Harkort, a politician and businessman, during the 1840s. The merchant Gustav Mevissen from the Rhineland and the pedagogue Adolf Diesterweg held similar views. In the *Landtag*, for example, people argued for better schools, for a more general and more scientific teacher training, for higher wages for teachers, and almost everywhere the liberals and the teachers argued for the 'emancipation' of the schools from the church and from church supervision. In practice, there were clearly contradictory movements: movements to restrict educational demands, to keep 'the poor' in their place and the schools cheap. All this played an important role in the liberal and bourgeois town administrations during the Vormärz.

Even the educated councillors resented any *Volksschule* teacher who tried to cross the dividing-lines. They were more interested in the middle and secondary schools.

The conservative movement was slowly becoming more prominent in the ministry. Special decrees halted and set the boundaries of education more clearly. Staff policy followed along similar lines. Church influence was increased. Nevertheless, the success of such policy was not overwhelming before 1848. The conservatives shied away from bureaucratic centralism. Regional and provincial civil servants remained set on their course of reform, and the pluralism of the administrations continued. In the churches, especially in the Protestant churches, the old supporters of the Enlightenment and new liberals still outnumbered the orthodox on the topic of schools. In the teacher-training colleges, in journalism, in textbooks, a whole new pedagogical establishment developed in the tradition of the reform, and even conservative pedagogues could not ignore it. School policy in the cities remained relatively independent from the state. An idealistic rationalist and liberal pedagogue Diesterweg was beginning to make a name for himself. He became director of the training college in Moers in 1822–23, founder of the leading pedagogical journal of the time, and father of the teaching associations; and then in 1832, he was appointed by the state as director of the college in Berlin. It was typical of the situation of the time. Only in 1847 would he be forced out of office, and even then still under the protection of the Prussian courts. In the area of staff policy, the conservative position became stronger, and after 1840 the new minister, Albrecht Eichhorn, adopted a much harder line against the teacher-training colleges and 'sceptical' teachers. But the policy did not extend beyond individual measures. On the whole, the basis of reform, once it had been introduced, continued to exert an influence through its own momentum and through the majority of civil servants, whatever changes in ideology or policy there may have been. Rationality, productivity, modernisation, to find and use new forces — these were the aims of a state which wanted to found itself on intelligence. A better school, so the reformist civil servants believed, could overcome the revolution, and it was for this reason that the schools must be improved still further. In short, the state needed the modern school, for with it, it could revolutionise society.

The process took place throughout the whole of Germany, but at different times. With the exception of the old-fashioned states of Mecklenburg and Hanover, and with the exception of Austria, which had stopped at the niveau of the late Enlightenment and where there was no teacher training, the *Volksschule* developed in the same way throughout the whole of Germany. Everywhere there were similar conflicts concerning school policy, which were at their most heated in the two parts of Hesse and in Bavaria, but less so in central Germany and Baden, owing to the liberalism in the church. Indeed, Bavaria broke off the process of progress as early as the late 1830s.

The *Volksschule* had two main effects up until 1848. First of all, teachers became elements of unrest and opposition. They were new people, charged with civilising society and spreading humanity. Their wages, however, and their social status were pitiful — they were addressed informally and were barely allowed to marry a peasant girl. They were watched over and disciplined by the state, but had none of the privileges of civil servants. They were socially mobile, but would never be allowed to become integrated into society. They were the champions of the new education, but were still subject to the traditional authority and power of the church. They were stuck between the poor and the state. These discrepancies created unrest among them (and not only in authoritarian Germany) — Riehl said it 'made one feel uncomfortable in one's own skin'; it created the desire to 'rebuild society'. This can be seen all too clearly in the history of the teaching associations. They first appeared as societies for further training (often founded by the state), but soon became convivial societies against the social isolation of the teachers. After 1840, they became political: they would represent the interests of the teachers and then the demands of progressive school policy for autonomy, development and emancipation from the church. In fact, they soon became the representatives of liberal-democratic opposition in general.

Secondly, the *Volksschule*, although far from perfect, had changed the conscious-ness of the people. The teacher became a new authority in the village, alongside and in opposition to the priest, and alongside and in opposition to tradition. The competition between the different ways of interpreting the world and different ways of behaving gave rise to a critical stance towards tradition, which would often spread to political and social institutions. In addition to this, the school, through teaching people to read, had brought the real and the concrete into conflict with the *Zeitgeist*, had mobilised thoughts and ways of thinking. Even an inadequate school was a revolutionising and modernising factor, at least as long as it was not integrated into the new society, through nationalism, for example, or its effects were not neutralised in some other way.

After 1848, the conservatives made a renewed attempt to push through their policies. The policy on the *Volksschule* was central to the restoration in the fight against revolution. Ferdinand Stiehl, a *Geheimrat* (privy counsellor) in Prussia, with his *Regulativen* (regulations) of 1854 came to symbolise this policy, which could be found in various forms all over Germany. School and teacher-training colleges would be restricted once again to a simple craftsman's level, to simple cultural techniques, religion and rote memory, to traditional truths, order and assimilation into the norm. Reliability became more important than intellectuality and usefulness. It is true that the policies may have contained partly justifiable criticism of the excessive (and even extravagant) intellectuality of progressive pedagogues and their alienation from reality, but it was primarily an expression of reactionism in school policy, and an admission that the conservative policy of the Vormärz had failed. For this reason, it became the target for all the anger of the liberals. The effect of the policy must not, however, be over-estimated. Stiehl's regulations had no relevance for the municipal schools, where diversification and expansion continued apace. Even in the teacher-training colleges, the policy actually guaranteed a minimal competency for teachers and saved the colleges themselves. Another result of the school policy of the restoration was, finally, an improvement in the position of the teacher. If the salaries of the teachers increased more than three-and-a-half-fold between 1816 and 1878, and if the minimum wages in rural areas gradually came up to the national average, then it was a consequence of the policy of restoration. In 1872, the regulations (a *ritardando* in the history of the school, to use Spranger's phrase) were lifted. The *Kulturkampf* shattered the conservative union of throne and altar, brought the issue of church and school into the foreground, and made freer development possible once more.

Teachers had survived these times without becoming agents of the authoritarian state. During the 1860s they were just as liberal, just as religious and just as conservative as any other profession. In some cases, of course, denominational ties did become more prominent, but that was not simply a result of the authoritarian measures, but a reaction against the anti-clericalism of the liberals. The teachers slowly became more integrated into society, and even became people of some importance in the villages. *Volksschule* pedagogy became a solid, and yet also narrow and rigid formalism for experts in the school of Johann Friedrich Herbart, and this also affected the inner life of the schools. Any possible political implications for the school were at last subdued in an unpolitical professionalisation — not in a school of underlings, but in a developing school of individual learning, of knowledge and ability, of duty, authority and restricted happiness. National integration and military and industrial requirements afforded a new legitimacy to competitive schools. From 1866, a journalist's witticism made the rounds that it had been the Prussian schoolmaster who had won the battle at Königgrätz. It is impossible to assess such statements, but a formal primary education certainly played a part in increasing the military capabilities of the soldiers and the productive capacity of industry. Social mobility may not have favoured the *Volksschule*, but that was more due to economic opportunities within society and the motivation of the parents. The *Volksschule* was not so much a barrier to social mobility, but simply there, like the rest of society. It was not peculiar to Germany or to Prussia that the *Volksschule* was a school for the masses, for the lower classes, which centred around loyalty to society and the hierarchy; it was instead a European phenomenon, in an age when both the liberal and conservative forms of state were bourgeois. Even the German *Volksschule* could not immunise its pupils against the rise of social democracy, just as it could not influence the political 'socialisation' of Catholics or prevent the decline of Protestant religiosity. Here, too, both life and society proved too strong.

It was not primarily the school which trained people for a job. The place for that was the home and the workplace itself, and the methods there were not theoretical reflection, but active participation. Craftsmanship provided the training for industry. In addition to this, there were Sunday schools which also (and later only) taught purely practical and worldly subjects. Then came evening schools; these were schools of further education, often only part-time schools, which sprang up everywhere under different names. They were voluntary (except in Baden in 1834), trained their pupils in a craft, and were greatly expanded after the middle of the century — Prussia had 232 in 1855; Württemberg 70 in 1846, and 155 in 1871; Bavaria had 30 in 1866; and Baden 44 in 1873. There also arose, in the course of state sponsorship of commerce during the period of reform, a small but important sector of 'polytechnic' or technical colleges such as the one- or two-year provincial trade schools in Prussia (30 in 1869) and the *Gewerbeinstitut* (Institute for the Trades) in Berlin (which consisted of three classes by 1826); and then after 1850, the *Einjähriges* degree and other institutions, in Saxony and Bavaria for example, which prepared pupils for entrance into further technical institutions (colleges or universities) on the one hand, and produced 'modern' craftsmen and technical staff for the process of industrialisation on the other.

Finally, girls' education must be considered. Throughout Germany, the *Volksschulen* included both boys and girls. Both sexes also attended the *Landschulen*. The legacy of

Pestalozzi was important here. The middle and secondary schools, however, in so far as they were open to everyone, were almost always for boys. In accordance with the bourgeois interpretation of the role of women (home and children, sentimentality and a specific female intellectuality), there had been a separate concept of girls' education since the 18th century. Middle and secondary schools for girls or 'young ladies' (*Töchterschulen*) grew up in the cities, where training was predominantly practical, with only a few literary and musical subjects. They were for the most part private, and when Catholic, came under the direction of the religious orders. Occasionally they were communal and only rarely had any contact with existing *Gymnasia*. By the end of the period under review, there was a fully developed system of *Töchterschulen*. The first directors and teachers were men, a fact which did not long escape a well-meaning bureaucracy. By 1837 there was an examination for women teachers in Prussia, and things were similar in the rest of Germany by the middle of the century. As a result, private female teacher-training colleges sprang up, which trained women for these schools. After that, more and more women teachers went into the *Volksschulen* — in Prussia, this was more true in Catholic areas than in Protestant ones. Although it was at first still peripheral, by 1872 the job of the woman teacher had come to be regarded as a profession. Women teachers, especially in the *Töchterschulen*, then went on to become of the utmost importance in the history of women.

(c) The University

For the history and ascent of the sciences in Germany, the university of 19th-century Germany was of the utmost importance. As a new type of university, it would also become a much-admired model for the rest of the world — for neighbouring states, for Europe as a whole, for Japan and for America. The university and science stand alongside music as two of the great achievements which brought recognition to Germany throughout the world during the 19th century. The modern university also shaped the history of education, of bourgeois society and politics within Germany itself, perhaps more so than elsewhere, because it had long been academically trained civil servants and citizens (rather than the commercial middle classes) who had brought about political and social change, and also because modernisation had always been particularly closely tied to science and scientific education. On the whole, the universities had been of pioneering importance for the German consciousness and life in society and state since the Reformation. The consciences of Lutheran priests had always centred around the knowledge and theology of scholars; the early form of the modern state can be traced back to the universities as institutions of knowledge and conscience; and offices in both church and state were always closely connected to scholarship. It was for these reasons that the territorial states had their own universities, and it was for these reasons that the civil servants received a university education. The new class of the late 18th century, the bourgeoisie, who were responsible for modernisation in Germany, were the class of those who had been educated at university. University therefore had a particularly important role to play in both public and private life — in contrast to both England and France. This tradition — renewed for the 19th century, on a secular basis, by the reforms — becomes definitive.

The university reform in Prussia, which, with the founding of the University of Berlin, created a new type of university, has already been mentioned. The new type soon established itself throughout the rest of Germany, following the idea and organisation of the university in Berlin. Breslau in Prussia, which had partly inherited the university of Frankfurt/Oder, was organised along the same lines, and in 1818 the university of the Rhineland was re-established in Bonn. The universities in Würzburg, Heidelberg and Landshut (where the university of old Bavaria had moved from Ingolstadt, which then relocated to Munich in 1825–26) reorganised themselves along similar lines. These universities soon achieved a high prestige — after 1815, about 40% of all students studied at the four large universities of Berlin, Breslau, Bonn and Landshut/ Munich, and their reputation and example persuaded other universities to follow. Only Austria retained its old institutions up until 1850 and Thun's reform of universities and colleges. It is astounding how something which was founded by philosophers before industrialisation could not only survive a whole century of industry and technology, of democratisation and mass activity, but also develop within it and even help shape that century. The aim here is to emphasise that part of the history of the university which is important to the history of Germany in general, as well as to the history of science and the social history of education. It will be shown that the history of the university is closely tied to social structure, to the relationship of the state to society, and to the attitude towards life in general.

As has already been said, the new university, both as an idea and as an institution, was based on the new concept of *Wissenschaft* (science, scholarship). Science was an end in itself, beyond any practical considerations, and it concentrated on the search and discovery of new truths, on research. Such a concept lasted through until the 1840s and was the driving force behind research and the rise of science. It was also the driving force behind the rise of the German universities — from institutions of peripheral importance to those of international stature, attracting students and researchers from all over the world. Professors were coming to a new understanding of their role, shaped by the new ethos and the new imperative of research. The exploration of the unknown, the discovery of the new, the constant striving towards the truth and the expansion of knowledge — these became the highest moral duties of man, the highest form of his existence; they became almost holy, something which would grant him a share of immortality. They became the dominating passion which would bring an ascetic discipline into other areas of his life. Method — the core of all research — became an inner attitude, which shaped behaviour and expectations, as well as standards and careers. For given the indivisibility of teaching and research, only a good researcher would be a good teacher — that was the primacy of research. Research became a profession; there was a council of researchers who laid down strict criteria, supported them and kept an informal check on them. The criteria for choosing staff were perhaps an indication of the importance of this. No longer were local considerations, popularity or unpopularity among colleagues, social, rhetorical, literary or teaching skills of primary consideration in making appointments to posts; what was important was the originality of research and its results. And that would not have to be proved simply in front of the members of a faculty, but in front of the national and international scientific public, in journals or at congresses. Careers could be made not only by carrying on the fruitful work of previous generation, or by fitting in with the current thought of the time, but also by challenging established opinion and authority, by risking conflict. This proved favourable to innovation in scholarship. Even entrance into an academic career (through *Habilitation* — the post-doctoral qualification as a university lecturer) became more difficult — where previously the process had been somewhat casual, new standards were introduced and the age of *Habilitation* arose.

All this was boosted by a string of institutional and political measures and conditions, and any results in research were given a reward. Firstly, there were *Privatdozenten* (outside lecturers) and the *Extraordinarius* (associate lecturer or reader) — young people who were unpaid, or who were paid a small sum if they were a little older, and only rarely in receipt of state grants or prizes, who 'served' research and had to 'scrape by', driven on by the hope of a professorship. This introduced an hierarchical air into the scholarly republic of the university, a differentiation between the 'haves' and 'have-nots' which would eventually lead to problems. More important, however, for the period under review was the fact that competition stimulated productivity. In 1796, the ratio between professors and other lecturers was 100:37, while in 1864, it was 100:90 (40 of these were associate lecturers). The Prussian government supported the development against the wishes of the faculties. The conditions drove the younger people to the front line of research. Freed from established authority, specialisation was one of their big chances to assert themselves, and it was for this reason that in the natural sciences, and in medicine in particular, completely new subjects were appearing. By means of its staff policy, the state was able to contribute greatly to pushing through the new performance criteria. The state could disagree with the suggestions of the faculties in the appointment of professors, and it often did so, not primarily for any political reasons, but because it wanted to encourage new directions and sponsor productive, promising and outstanding new researchers, instead of the interests of a particular school or guild; neither did it want to foster an organisation of cliques. The opinion of the scholarly community as a whole, and not merely of local luminaries, would be important. Alexander von Humboldt's recommendation, for example, proved decisive in bringing the twenty-four-year-old Justus Liebig from his studies in Paris to a professorial chair in Giessen. Many of the important innovators, such as the mathematician Carl Gustav Jacobi, the physiologists Johannes Evangelista Purkinje and Johannes Müller and the clinician Lukas Schönlein, were more or less imposed on the faculties concerned. In this way the state was encouraging the growth of research. Eminent scholars such as Liebig, for example, were therefore in support of state influence in the appointment of professors. The conflicts between ministries and universities which arose here eventually led to the introduction of standards of scholarship at the professorial level as well — so such conflicts gradually subsided after 1850. German federalism also helped foster the great variety, ambition and competition between the different states and the different universities, the mobility and competition of their scholars, their motivation and productivity, and the importance which they attributed to the respect of their scientific colleagues outside their immediate locale. Even the common conservatism of the governments could not frustrate these developments. Opposition or exiled professors, especially during the Vormärz, were able to find a new domain elsewhere, and not just the Göttingen Seven. Johann Lukas Schönlein, a modernist, who had been driven out of Würzburg by the conservative Johann Nepomuk Ringseis, went to Berlin in 1840 via Zurich. Lorenz Oken lost his chair because of his sympathies for the student fraternities, but was able to go to Munich in 1827. When he ran into difficulties again in 1832, he was 'merely' posted to Erlangen, and later he went to Zurich. And Virchow 'atoned for' his participation in the revolution in a professorship in Würzburg, and was only later to return to Berlin.

The position of the new sciences in society also played an important role in their rise in the new universities. University and science held a particular attraction for the talented of Germany, and this was connected to the socio-political structure of the community. Partly because of the fact that entrance to the leading positions within society (such as administration, military and politics) was still severely limited through the *de facto* remains of the rights of the nobility, and partly because there was still no 'career' in politics as such, discrimination of the middle classes could be to some extent compensated by scientific achievements and positions within the universities. State office and a way of life dedicated to theory were equal on the scale of social prestige. Careers in science therefore held a particular attraction as opposed to leading positions in the economy, even when those positions were not dependent on capital. The rise of science was therefore helped by authoritarian and feudal elements within the structure of society. Modern science was also a gathering-place for those talents who, plagued by doubts, had turned away from the theological tradition of the middle classes — people such as the sons of clergy and social climbers.

Alongside the appointment of staff at the universities, the founding of institutes and teaching departments also proved to be important for research at the universities, and this tied in with the indivisibility of teaching and research. In 1820 in Berlin for example, there were 7 institutes of medicine and 3 institutes of theology and philosophy. By 1850, these figures were 10 and 8 respectively, and in 1870, 16 and 11. Liebig's institute for chemistry in Giessen marked a new era in the development of chemistry, just as Johannes Müller's did in Berlin in physiology. The teaching departments of mathematics and physical sciences (in Königsberg in 1835–36, in Halle in 1839, in Göttingen in 1850, and in Heidelberg, Giessen and Berlin) later gave rise to experimental physics. Teaching departments and institutes were the institutions of training in research — the most gifted students gathered together here as the pupils of a 'master' and grew to become the scholars of the future.

What part did the university play as an institution of training and education? One of the founding ideas of neo-humanism — education for all through science and through philosophical and humanist reflection — had only a limited effect. The universities remained primarily institutions for training civil servants and those who would occupy other jobs related to the state. The classical 'career' faculties of medicine, law and theology were still in the majority, and they were still centred around career and practice, as were their exams. Only during Hegel's time, under the influence of some outstanding individuals, could the faculty of philosophy fulfil the central and integrating role intended for it. Philosophy was losing its function as a subject which could lead and unite. The sciences of man (philology and history) were becoming noticeably more specialised. There no longer seemed to be any relationship to a whole; there was no unified, humanist picture of the world. The scientification of the humanities — which could no longer be pursued by non-professionals — meant that the humanities lost their educating function for students of career-orientated subjects. The faculty education, with its neo-humanist ideals, gradually became a faculty for training of teachers and scientists. Study at university could no longer be organised around the participation in research. Nevertheless, through the great university teachers who had been brought up in the tradition of an idealistic concept of education, the original idea was able to be maintained — law students received a philosophical and historical education; medical and science students were trained in philosophical reflection; and theology students were schooled in philology and history. The Prussian administration of justice, for example, insisted that a university education should be a general one, in contrast to a period of traineeship which was based on practical experience, and it is often forgotten, that it was civil servants who had received that sort of general education who built up the modern administrative state.

Wissenschaft had now become the norm for study at university. Intelligence in scholarship was what counted, and scholarly study was held in the highest regard. The steep rise in the number of doctorates was a symptom of this. The university departments thrived on the notion that everyone at some point should be able to take part (no matter how modestly) in the process of research. The new position of *Wissenschaft* in the universities, its rigorousness and high standards drove the dilettante and the 'layman', the college ideal of a gentleman of worldliness, rhetoric and wide knowledge, out of the universities. The university was neither a school (where students came to take courses) nor a college (where students lived and studied in close proximity with their instructors). Studies should be 'free', with no agenda and no curricula. It should be left to the individual to determine the length of his studies and how he would divide his time. The aim of the university as such was not to create general patterns for life; it was centred around the individual, a person's inner motivation, and his 'solitariness', around individual life and around scholarship. Education at a university concentrated on the encounter between the individual and scholarship, and the requirement to live for *Wissenschaft* was the main driving force behind it. There were two consequences of this. Firstly, as the university was neither school nor college, the mobility of the students was high. They were not tied to their 'own' university, but to a national profession, to the scholarly community and to universities in general. For this reason, the universities weakened the traditions which were particular to them, and became national, *gesamtdeutsch*; they tended towards the homogeneity of a national society — that was their characteristically modern function. Secondly, it led to an educational deficit within the universities: there was now a deep rift in perceptions regarding the required inner motivation, between the interest in scholarship and the reality of looking and being prepared for a job, between 'solitariness' and the need to live within a society. The encounter with *Wissenschaft* was not a sufficient educational force, at least not for everyone. This area — outside the reach of the institution of the university and its neo-humanist ideal — was covered by the student associations which also shaped university life. Precisely for this reason, the student associations were the real communities of student life.

Even after the *Burschenschaften* (student fraternities) had reformed student life, there was still a student subculture, in which, after the initial idealism, drinking and fencing once more found a place, and where the fraternities' concept of honour once more came to the fore and even became a symbol of status. Feudal patterns and norms were handed down in the 'aristocratic' duelling corps at the university, although these did not play any significant role for the middle-class students until the 1860s. Alongside these there grew up other new groups during the 1850s: sports, choral and regional associations and the first explicitly Christian groups. Politically, liberal-nationalist tendencies, both moderate and radical, dominated throughout the period under review. The associations adopted the estate-based, pre-bourgeois conventions which were seeping back into the world of the middle classes alongside modernity and *Wissenschaft*. And they also served to counter the bourgeois ideals of achievement and qualifications, because they enabled the use of personal connections to reach privileged positions.

The aim of the university was to create a new educational elite, and here the number and social make-up of students were important. In the area which would later constitute the German Reich the numbers rose from circa 6,000 in 1800 to circa 9,000 between 1816 and 1825, then to just over 16,000 in 1830. They fell again and hovered around 12,000 between 1835 and 1860, and then rose again in 1865 to 13,500. In Austria in 1851 there were 3,500 students in the German universities, of whom 2,100 were German, and in 1865 there was a total of 5,081, of whom 2,900 were German. During the Vormärz the figures were somewhat higher, although they varied enormously and are not, it would seem, really comparable with the figures of other countries in 1830, there were 8,243 students at university, in 1840, 9,060, and in 1844, 6,544, of whom at least 60% were German. Around 1830, there was therefore a certain amount of over-subscription, especially among the law and theology students, but this then fell drastically owing to poor career prospects and counter-measures undertaken by the state. In 1830, 0.05% of the population was at university, in 1850, 0.035%. Between 1851 and 1855 1% of the male population between 18 and 22 attended university, while between 1840 and 1870 the total figure was 1.2%. As a percentage of the population as a whole, these figures showed a decrease. The number of available academic positions, the demand in the church, the bureaucracy and the number of 'free' jobs had not increased. Only towards the end of the period did the growth in the population, industry and the economy and the growth of the state have any discernible effect on the academic market, and then only in the faculties of philosophy, i.e. among teachers and scientists. In 1830, 27% of students studied Protestant theology, 11% Catholic, 28% studied law, 15% medicine, and 19% in the faculty of philosophy. In 1860–61, these figures were 21%, 10%, 20%, 17% and 31% respectively.

The social background of the students will now be considered, and the problem of equal opportunity. In the eyes of the ideal university, talent in itself was independent of social background. The notion, however, of pure education presupposed good schools and the possibility of leisure. Only then could a career-orientated course of study be dismissed. For the most part, the students therefore came from families with an academic education (50% in 1860), and also from the nobility (as much as 12.5%) and from the wealthy middle classes (circa 14%) — these figures are based on small samples and merely indicate the proportions and the trends. In a bourgeois period where resources were scarce, where there were a limited number of academic places, and where the parents' main concern was their children's livelihood, these figures were not particularly surprising and cannot be seen as a reason for anachronistic, egalitarian indignation. What was surprising, however, was the number of social climbers: 25–30% came from the lower middle classes, were sons of craftsmen, small businessmen, minor civil servants and schoolteachers, and in Württemberg this figure was 44%. After the middle of the century, and especially after the number of students increased, the proportion from the nobility and the educated classes decreased (the latter to 39% in 1870), while the proportion from the propertied classes grew (32%, including the nobility), and the number of social climbers fell slightly (a little below 31%), while the proportion of children of minor civil servants and schoolteachers increased. Although these figures say little about the opportunities for the children of these classes, in comparison to western Europe they proved quite considerable. The university may have been as little an institution for equal opportunity as the *Gymnasium*, especially for the children of peasants, workers and the lower classes; and the state specifically sought to hinder social climbers for fear of an academic proletariat during times of overcrowding, but the university was not simply a barrier for social mobility, but also a sluice-gate. The opportunities for talent and achievement were not sacrificed to maintaining the social status of the upper middle classes, and it was the faculties of theology and philosophy and, towards the end of the period, the faculty of medicine which attracted the social climbers. The university teachers themselves were an indication of this: 60% came from the educated classes after the middle of the century, 20–25% from the middle classes, and perhaps 10% from the lower classes. Talent could rise here, even through the hardship of the years spent as *Privatdozent* (outside lecturer), by means of grants and subsidies. At least as interesting as the figures of mobility was the fact that the white-collar workers — minor civil servants, teachers and academics — were more inclined to train their sons to be craftsmen and businessmen than to follow in their footsteps. It was the difference in career that was more important than any differences in class, status or income, as had been the case with the *Abitur*. There were now two different cultures: education and civil service *versus* economy, trade and craftsmanship.

In reality, university education had the effect of forming a new class and a new elite. It created social barriers, a normal phenomenon which fitted in with the desire for social differentiation. The idea of science and of a scientific education rightfully contained an elitist and meritocratic element. In a society which was strictly divided into a class- and estate-based system, this could, of course, lead to a situation where university study *per se* determined whether a person belonged to the upper classes, and this interested students both among the social climbers and the sons of the established upper classes. In this way the educational claims of the universities favoured and strengthened the special standing of the academics in Germany. It also emphasised the difference between the 'intellectual' and the non-intellectual, between the business and the educated middle classes, as can be seen in the length of time in which the graduates of the *Realgymnasium* were shut out of university study. Academic qualification eclipsed, modified and established the social strata — thence the distinctive system of examination, qualifications and title which formed the basis of social organisation and of a person's journey through life. In order to establish education in place of birthright, examinations would be required, and the nobility had been submitted to this new passion of the middle classes since the period of reform. From the civil service the practice was transferred to jobs connected to the state, and then to many other areas of employment. The coupling of educational degree and military status (in the form of the *Einjähriges*) has already been discussed. The connection between education, examination and qualifications for office became rooted deep within the social structure and mentality of Germany. Examinations became symbols of status and titles. Competence in exams came to replace experience of life and success in career. Despite the general embour-geoisement of society, the university only served to change and strengthen the old estate-based and the new class-based differences and hierarchies of German life.

State and administration wanted to consolidate and develop the new universities still further after the initial phases of reform. The financial framework remained limited but stable, and only after the 1840s did the budgets grow and the universities expand. Between 1820 and 1870 in Berlin, for example, the budget increased threefold. The lion's share of this went to the teaching departments and the institutes — their budget increased tenfold, and if in 1820 it was still only one-sixth of the total salaries, by 1870 it was higher. This was a clear indication of the growth of medicine and the natural sciences in particular. In Baden, most of the new budget was ploughed into chemistry after 1850. Alongside the old-fashioned task of the state in sponsoring education and cul-ture, there was now a conscious encouragement of economic growth, and a determined effort to overcome economic crises in areas such as agriculture. The number of university staff increased slowly: in 1796, there had been 650 posts of professor, an average of 20 per university, and many of these were scrapped. In 1864, there were 725 posts, an average of 30 per university, and this figure gave a very clear indication of the rate of growth. But in view of the scarcity of state finances, and in view of conservative mistrust towards the intelligentsia in science as well as the professors, it was quite astonishing — was this a liberal sector for state activity?

There was, of course, a trend in the opposite direction. Wherever the growth and expansion of the universities became a social and political threat, the state would intervene. The expectation that the state would remain neutral towards the political consequences of science, that it would give in to the unreasonable demands of the professors, and that the universities could simply educate civil servants as they saw fit, proved illusory in a pre-pluralist, authoritarian and bureaucratic state. In the first few years after the founding of the university in Berlin, Humboldt's successor Friedrich Schuckmann, a conservative bureaucrat, pulled the reins of state control more tightly over statutes and practice — the service the university owed the state was more impor-tant than the service the state owed the university. The politicians of the restoration harboured the not totally unfounded fear that the university would become a separate state within the state. As has already been seen, the states attempted to discipline both students and lecturers, and also to persecute demagogues and members of the student fraternities under the Carlsbad Decrees. They tried to neutralise science, banish politics from the universities by way of decisions affecting staff, examinations or similar measures. In short, the states aimed to meet the 'dangerous' philosophy of the state with 'positive' state rights. During the 1830s, the number of students was reduced by various methods out of fear of an academic proletariat. In Prussia, for example, philosophy lessons would be brought in line with the state by favouring the followers of Hegel. Many such examples fill the histories of the universities written by liberal professors, and while it is not the aim here to play down an authoritarian practice, it should be noted that such policy was unsuccessful on the whole, apart from in the Austria of Metternich, and it remained nothing more than an interlude.

On the whole, the Ministries for Education and the Arts, as part of the legacy of reform and as the opponents of domestic and police affairs, protected the moderate freedom of the university. Altenstein, the Prussian Minister for Education and the

Arts until 1840, was a supporter of Hegel, and the interest in tolerance in church politics proved to be of benefit for theological and scientific pluralism. The strong competition between the different German states meant that people were able to skirt around the restoration: professors who had been exiled from certain areas could easily find employment elsewhere. It was already too late when Friedrich Wilhelm IV prepared to do battle against the 'seeds of discord' of Hegelian philosophy in 1840 in Berlin, and the newcomers Schelling and Stahl were nonetheless intellectuals of some stature. Even Young Hegelian *Privatdozenten* (outside lecturers) in Prussia who propagated atheism were simply transferred from the faculty of theology to the faculty of philosophy, to their eternal annoyance. Thus, despite an authoritarian state, despite a general line of conservatism, and despite specific anti-liberal measures, the spirit of middle-class opposition (liberal-nationalist rather than radical-democratic) maintained its hold on the academic establishment.

Even the period of reaction during the 1850s, in contrast to the school system, brought about very little change apart from the emigration of active revolutionaries. Virchow was punished for his democratic activities with only a few years in exile, before returning in triumph to Berlin. After the 1860s even university policy was once again moderately liberal. Occasionally, as in Baden, the conflicts were even reversed. When the government took action against a faculty, it was in order to appoint liberal or Jewish scholars. This moderate liberality of the states had its limits, of course, and not only against political radicals. In Protestant states such as Prussia, things were difficult for Catholics, and unchristened Jews were not allowed to take up office in a university right up until the 1860s. This was not merely a matter of the state — but part of a social system in the universities that was simply taken for granted. On the whole, then, the relationship between university and the state was not one of constant tension — in fact, it was rather good. The benevolently authoritarian, objective and partly unpolitical state administration significantly fostered the rise and growth of the universities. In the shadow of areas more closely connected with power, the universities were able to develop more steadily and calmly. Of course, the state did not emphasise the aspect of freedom in the notion of a university, but simply saw it as a part of culture. The state thought it was finished with the political consequences.

Despite the emphasis on science, despite its solitariness and freedom and despite its distance from society — or perhaps because of it — the university also played an important role in the politics of the period. The political professor became a new, leading figure for middle-class society during the Vormärz and the revolution, and the radical *Privatdozent* played an almost comparable role for the radicals. As has already been seen, it was the state which allowed this figure into the university. Certainly, there were many unpolitical professors, and those who attempted to separate strictly politics and science, but what was more interesting and more noticeable were those who were active in politics, in journalism and in parliament, and who included not only historians, economists and the teachers of constitutional law. Despite a prominent conservative and Catholic wing, the liberal and nationalist professor became representative between 1840 and 1870 — from the Göttingen Seven, the heroes of the Vormärz, to the professors of the Frankfurt National Assembly and those of the New Era and of the *Nationalverein* and the *Reformverein*, of the Prussian parliament of conflict. The political parties and political public life were unimaginable without these professors.

And the value of science, as well as the legal autonomy of the universities, made it possible that even in the so-called authoritarian states the professors — who were, after all, civil servants — were leaders of the opposition.

There was one further aspect of all this. The universities were *de facto* if not *de jure* national institutions. Professors and students could swap between universities and cities. Scientific congresses and organisations established a nationwide specialist public, such as the assembly of German natural scientists and doctors from 1822, of philologists from 1839, of Germanists (law historians and linguists) from 1846; and all these crossed over the territorial and denominational boundaries. The new cultural studies developed the concept of national spirit and of nation. And it was for this reason that the universities played an important part in the growth and development of the nationalist movement — professors and students were its supporters and champions. The importance of the universities within and for the nationalist movement proved favourable to the *kleindeutsch* supporters. It was the Prussian university and the role of Prussia in the university system that strengthened the attractiveness and significance of Prussia. Prussia, the state of the university, of education and science, the state of freedom and intellect, was a point of reference with which people could survive the traces and periods of reactionism within Prussia, for it embodied the rudiments of liberalisation. In this way the universities established the belief in the 'German vocation' of Prussia.

The nationalist flavour of the universities did not, however, detract from the factual internationalism of science — at least not until 1870. And the international stature of German scholarship, of philology and philosophy, and then of history and the natural sciences, and the attractiveness of the German universities for foreign students, from east, south-east and northern Europe and from America, visibly increased in these decades.

Apart from its educational function, the university as the home of science had a twofold and contradictory relationship to life and society. Firstly, there was the distance. Solitariness and freedom, science as an end in itself, made it resemble a cloister, and from this developed the idea of an ivory tower. The new notion of *Wissenschaft* and the university — no matter how modern it may have appeared in relation to a world dominated by an estate-based system — stood in an exclusive realm outside of economy and work, of practical efficiency, economic success and property. The university was pre-industrial, a matter purely for civil servants and scholars. The practical world, and in particular the world of technology and economics, was totally distinct from the world of the university and its concerns. To this extent, the university certainly contributed to the division between theoretical and practical culture, between 'higher' and 'lower' areas. Out of this 'distance from everyday life' grew the criticism that the universities were unpractical, had no connection with life, that they were in no position to 'appreciate social conditions' (Diesterweg), that they encouraged 'theoretical speculation' (Biedermann), and so the eternal counterpoint continued right through until Nietzsche.

On the other hand, the attractiveness of the universities extended far beyond the political. It was central to the way and meaning of life of bourgeois society. It was more important than literature and journalism, than a free intelligentsia and the bohemian world, it was more important than political debate and often even more than the churches — it had a central role. The great transformations, crises and conflicts which have determined German intellectual history, such as the historical and philosophical transformation of Christianity, the historicist and scientific transformation of the conception of the world, the belief and disbelief in progress, the development of nationalism, the discovery of society, the cultural and political controversies — all these centred around discussions in the universities. The sciences formed the different interpretations of the world, and the university, despite the decline in the disciplines, produced the cornerstones for these interpretations, and this would become even more important in the *Kulturkämpf* and the controversies of political ideologies. Thus the university was not merely one province in the intellectual household of Germany, it was a central authority. The knowledge of the sciences and the conscience of those who took action and suffered — these things were part of the same context. Both the established conception of the world and that of the subculture, the old and the new, certainly existed before the new science and outside of it, but they entered into a connection with the university as both proponent and opponent.

It was also in this context that the professors became a new middle-class elite. They had been trained both socially and morally to work hard and succeed. Of modest and middle-class lifestyle, they were hardly men of the world. They were often quarrelsome and dogmatic, caught up in the different theoretical arguments of the time, but not as comical as in the 18th century, being less alienated. They stood in a tradition, developed it further, and yet at the same time they were the representatives of modernity. They were full of faith in science which would provide the key to divine and natural order and ennoble mankind. Indeed, science was one of the highest goals of man. This provided an heroic dimension to their quiet, civil-service existences; it provided them with a mission. In their little provincial towns they could therefore explore new worlds and distant cultures, without setting foot inside foreign countries. Until the latter half of the century, they continued to incorporate their own actions into a whole philosophy of the world, and they could still maintain an overview of the whole of their subject, as well as other related subjects, despite increasing specialisation and despite the growing trend towards 'positivism' and the empirical. Within the typical university town in Germany, professors had a socially elevated position. They belonged among the leaders not only of middle-class society, but of the people as a whole. This also helped to explain their political role.

(d) Technical education
Finally, we must consider a special form of university: the *Technische Hochschulen* (technological colleges and institutes), which were as important for the development of technology as they were typical of the division between two cultures. In the late 18th century, technical education had been attached to technical and military academies such as the famous *Bergakademie* (mining academy) in Freiberg. The founding in Paris of the *École Polytechnique* had marked a new era in education. It had been set up to train civil and military planning and construction officers with a grounding in science, and it became the model for all future technical education. Neo-humanist reform had reserved the 'pure' sciences for the universities, shut out the technical subjects, and established the universities' aversion to the 'necessary arts' and to 'polytechnics or whatever one wants to call the material schools of thought' (Friedrich Creuzer, 1830); and it had been the same neo-humanist reform which

dismissed the idea that these had a place in science or in higher education. Separate institutions began to spring up as a result, 'universities of working life' or 'academies' as their champions euphemistically called them. In 1806, on the initiative of the estates, especially the aristocratic entrepreneurs, a 'Polytechnical Institute' was founded in Prague, a place of higher education in technology and science for industry; and in 1815, there was the 'Polytechnical Institute' in Vienna for the 'industrious common estates in the useful arts and technical services', an institute for 'the important class of higher [i.e. non-manual] industrialists and tradesmen'. Pupils of the *École Polytechnique* in Tulla founded a school for construction engineers in Karlsruhe, refusing to establish it in the university at Heidelberg, and the architect Friedrich Weinbrenner founded a school of civil engineering. In 1825, the two joined together and now included a department for mechanical engineering and a trade school. First of all Vienna and then Karlsruhe led the field. They offered the full spectrum of technical subjects with a mathematical-scientific basis and the driving forces were theory and scientific curiosity. Other schools began to spring up elsewhere — in Dresden in 1822, in Stuttgart in 1825, in Munich in 1833 (with branch establishments in Augsburg and Nuremberg), in Kassel in 1830, Hanover in 1831, Brunswick in 1835 and Darmstadt in 1836. They were still not *Hochschulen* as such, as the schools in Vienna and Karlsruhe were to a degree, but scientific technical colleges (*Fachschulen*) for skilled manual workers and industrialists, foremen and engineers, apprentices who had passed their final examinations at school and pupils from the *Realschulen*. The entrance age was usually seventeen. In Berlin, the *Bauakademie* (School of Architecture) had been in existence since 1799, for training civil servants in construction fields (both architects and civil engineers) on a scientific basis. Peter Beuth founded the *Gewerbeinstitut* in 1822 for training 'civil' (actually, mechanical) engineers. To start with, the pupils were taken from the *Volksschulen* at the ages of between twelve and sixteen, but later they came from the trade schools; it was really more on the level of a trade school, and was far behind the *Bauakademie* in the technical training it provided. The aim was to produce skilled manual workers, foremen and industrialists — August Borsig was only one famous example — as well as the teachers for the future technical trade schools (the famous chemist Friedrich Wöhler was a teacher at the trade school in Berlin).

From the middle of the century, there was a gradual process of scientification in the institutions and their subjects. The Austrian Ferdinand Redtenbacher who had been in Karlsruhe since 1840, was the first person to place mechanical engineering on a scientific, mathematical and theoretical basis. In 1844, he provided rules for constructing the great turbine of St Blasien which had been developed by chance, and he had been able to calculate its efficiency. Redtenbacher had managed to combine teaching with research and design. Karl Karlmarsch had a similar effect in Hanover from 1837 with his outline for mechanical technology, Gustav Zeuner in Dresden with his theory of the steam-engine, and Franz Reuleaux in Berlin. In addition to this was the influence of the Swiss Federal Polytechnical College in Zurich. Requirements for admission were laid down more clearly — pupils had to pass the final examinations of a *Realgymnasium*, and after 1860 the structure of a university was gradually introduced. The polytechnics became — around the 1860s — technical universities, and the training of foremen and mechanics was made distinct from the training of engineers, which now had a scientific basis. This was an important development which would have great significance for the second phase of the industrialisation of Germany and its success. The professionalisation and organisation of the career of engineer, which has already been mentioned in connection with industrialisation, was one of the consequences of this development. In 1840, there were 757 students at technical institutions (within the borders of the Reich of 1870), 1,180 in 1850–51, 2,020 in 1865–66 and over 5,000 in 1872–73. In Vienna, Prague, Brünn and Graz in 1850 there were 1,028 German students.

The relationship between the technical colleges and universities, and the role of the former in higher education, remained precarious and controversial. The battle between the established 'humanists' and the up-and-coming realists for the *Gymnasia*, and for the *Realgymnasia* and *Oberrealschulen* was once again repeated. The 'humanists' suspected technical education of intellectual impoverishment, of the rejection of idealism, of materialism, one-sidedness and the loss of freedom, soul and intellect. In the case of the middle schools, they talked of 'plumbing academies', and of 'utilitarian junk-schools', while the supporters of technology argued that living standards would be raised and output increased, and that only progress would bring about a new flowering of art and science, of humanity and intimacy. They sought to counter the accusation of one-sidedness with a subsidiary course in humanities, but they could not achieve equal status. The gulf between two cultures remained — between a humanist culture and a technical and economic one. Even the new prestige of science was not able to benefit the 'other' culture.

3. The Sciences

(a) Natural sciences and medicine

One of the most significant events on the world stage in the 19th century was the rise of the sciences to become a major force which transformed all aspects of life. The world was revolutionised by the sciences, and the Germans had their own specific part to play in this historical development, so that any account of German history of this period must consign a central place to the rise of science and its transforming effect upon the world.

It was in the 'exact' sciences, the natural sciences, where this process was most emphatic, and where it made the most lasting impact on public consciousness. Natural sciences, in the fields of technology and medicine, brought about more fundamental changes to the world in which we live than ever before. The revolution in natural sciences during the 19th century had a much more far-reaching impact than the first revolution brought about by Kepler, Galileo and Newton.

Around 1800 Germany had been left behind in the field of natural sciences and medicine. All the important developments in modern scientific methods — experiment, measurement, mathematical analysis, the maturation of classical mechanics (of both mass points and the heavens) with the help of mathematical analysis, the developments in optics, electrical theory, chemical analysis, electro-chemistry and atomic theory, in pathological anatomy and the beginnings of physiology, and more precise methods of diagnosing illness — were taking place in western Europe. It was here that Laplace and Lagrange, Volta and Faraday, Lavoisier, Priestley and Cavendish made their mark. None of this work was done in Germany, although it is true that Germany began to take an active interest in these developments from the late 18th century onwards — we know this from Goethe, for instance. Academic institutions began to put money into research in the natural sciences, collections and observatories came into being. The Vienna General Hospital, the Mining Academy in Freiberg, research in the fields of mathematics and astronomy in Göttingen had an international reputation, but these were exceptions. The practice of exact sciences was still a dilettantish business. The only two German contributions to the exciting new developments in electrical theory: Johann Wilhelm Ritter's discovery of ultra-violet light, which he did not pursue any further, and Georg Simon Ohm's discovery of the law of electrical resistance (1826), which took its name from him, had something accidental about them, and, like Ernst Chladni's foundation of experimental acoustics at the beginning of the century, or the anatomist Franz Joseph Gall's pioneering work on the brain, they remained isolated discoveries. There were, of course, outsiders in scientific research later, but they were soon shepherded into the fold of professional research, and their numbers quickly dropped. Gregor Mendel, a monk and plant-breeder, who discovered the genetic laws of inheritance in the 1860s, and whose results were ignored for quite a time, remained outside the scientific establishment and was regarded as old-fashioned and a 'dilettante'.

The three most important, indeed seminal figures in German natural science of the early decades of the century made their names as individuals initially, rather than as representatives of a general development. One of these was the mathematical genius of the first half of the century, Carl Friedrich Gauss in Göttingen, who was equally prominent as a physicist, astronomer and geodesist. He calculated the refraction of light and a new method for plotting the course of any heavenly body, such as comets, located the magnetic South Pole, and (among much else) made a decisive contribution to furthering our understanding of geomagnetism and the system of units of measurement in physics. Another was Joseph Fraunhofer, who rose from being a craftsmen to being one of the first to give a mathematical foundation to the construction of optical instruments, discovered the Fraunhofer lines (the basis of spectral analysis) in the course of experiments on the refraction of light, and calculated the wavelengths of the colours in the spectrum. Then there was Alexander von Humboldt, the most famous of all, an empirical geographer also concerned with measurements and experimentation, a 'modern' scientific researcher and at the same time a classical polymath, a 'natural scientist' beyond all specialisation. He rose to become a central figure in scientific research after writing up the results of his field research in Latin America (1799–1804), which proved enormously fruitful in all fields of geographical research, and, from his base in Paris (until 1827), he became the most respected international representative in the field of natural science and many of its branches, not only geography. In his four-volume work, *Cosmos* (1845–58), written in old age, he attempted to describe the various phenomena in their relation to the whole of the natural world, a work which 'was both stimulating in its vivid use of language and a delight to the mind'. This represented a final encyclopaedic endeavour in the spirit of classicism, and it was translated into all the major languages of the world, although it has to be said that against a background of ever-increasing specialisation it soon became outdated.

The development of the natural and medical sciences in Germany was over-shadowed for two or three decades by the so-called natural philosophy of Hegel and Schelling, and the romantic natural scientists like Oken, Steffens and Hofmann. It was not long before this fell into disrepute for being unscientific, speculative and fantastic. Heat was seen by this school of thought as 'matter reconstituting itself in its formless, fluid state, the triumph of its abstract homogeneity over any definite properties specific to it' (Hegel). Catarrh was considered to be a regression to the condition of a mollusc (Hofmann). Analogies were drawn between plants, buds and gouty deposits, as well as between polarised elements like liver and spleen, iron and mercury, and hence one was advised to take iron to combat ailments of the spleen. Such 'diagnoses' strike one as an anthology of absurdity.

Underlying this was a holistic approach to nature. Nature was perceived as a unified whole, a system having the quality of an organism, in which all the different elements interrelated, all expressing a basic 'life-force', all working together in a purposeful and teleological process of development. Non-living matter was considered to have the potential to live — it represented a preliminary stage in the development of the 'spirit'. In this sense special attention was given to the chemical, magnetic and electrical 'forces' present in inorganic forms. The tendency was towards a 'speculative' understanding of natural reality with the help of philosophical categories like identity and polarity, development and improvement and specific categories of organic life: irritability, sensibility and reproduction. The magic powers at work in this speculation were intuition and analogy; the central preoccupation was with the process by which 'forces' changed themselves into various manifestations. Induction, experiment and mathematical interpretation, on the other hand, were scorned.

One particular form of this natural philosophy was romantic medicine. The legacy of the 18th century survived in this; manifestations included the beginnings of comparative anatomy, physiology and the classification of illnesses through diagnosis and description, and the traditional variety of theories concerning the 'nature' of illness: the disruption of mechanical processes, breakdown or friction, tightening or slackening. Specifically romantic were the fashionable theories about illness: illness as an imbalance of humours (humoral pathology), as a particular form of parasitic existence (animism), as too much or too little 'irritability' of the muscles, sensibility of the nerves, stimulation and reaction to stimuli (and it was no surprise therefore that the discovery of animal electricity by Galvani aroused particular interest). The assumption that there was such a thing as a 'life-force' was a specifically romantic notion, and hence the preoccupation with the disposition and constitution of the person who was sick, and therapy was conceived in terms of strengthening the 'life-spirits' and life-forces. A central preoccupation was the relationship between the body and the soul. The fashionable pre-romantic therapy of magnetism devised by Franz Anton Mesmer achieved greater popularity as a form of suggestion therapy; and as a corollary to this, the romantic penchant for occult phenomena, the interest in spiritism, clairvoyance and necromancy became vogue again — as illustrated, for example, in the work of the celebrated Swabian doctor Justinus Kerner, or the work of Gotthilf

Heinrich von Schubert, who explored the 'dark side' of nature. There was also an enormous interest in mental illnesses. The brain anatomist Gall attempted to locate specific abilities in the brain, crudely formulated for example, as social aptitude, a tendency to steal, or an especially pious disposition. One of his followers developed the fashionable theory of phrenology, in which certain things were inferred about the mind and character from specific shapes of the skull. The celebrated 'romantic doctor' of this period, Carl Gustav Carus, took a special interest in the development of the soul and a theory of facial expressions. The most striking manifestations of romantic medicine were to be found in the theories of Catholic physicians like the renowned professors Johann Ringseis in Munich and Karl Windischmann in Bonn. The seat of illness was seen in the last analysis as the soul: sinful, infected by lust and greed, enslaved by a disordered love of unimportant things, and ultimately 'misguided'. This condition was to be treated by using the natural healing powers of the sick person, also magnetism, exorcism and the powers of grace administered by the church. Healing and salvation (cleansing of sins) were closely bound up; the doctor was regarded as a kind of priest, exercising control over divine forces. The Protestant Johann Christian August Heinroth preached a similar creed, though in a more prudent form. Finally, a somewhat different approach, though still born of a similar, partly Romantic, partly pre-Romantic spirit, came from Samuel Hahnemann, the founder of homeopathy, who interpreted illness as a dulling of the life-forces, treating illnesses with 'similar', analogously working medicaments in small doses, and adjusting the specific mixture of medicaments to the constitution of the sick person, i.e. to each individual case. He became the figurehead of the first of the modern health sects, which, through a combination of his own stridency and resistance from the establishment, had to enjoy its first great success in the United States.

There are two features of what appears to us such an alien and alienating phenomenon which remain important today. Firstly, a decisive force behind this approach was a resistance to incursions from incipient radical empiricism that were not themselves empiricaly justified. This was seen as a general assault from what was referred to as mechanism and materialism: the atomisation of nature, the tendency towards determinism, the 'mechanistic' interpretation of life, the complete 'objectification' of human beings into the object of natural scientific medicine, the isolation of the individual illness from the whole of the sick person. This assault was to be rebuffed by appeals to the old certainties: life, the soul, the spirit (and God), at any rate the question of the unity of nature, the search for what was referred to later as a 'vitalistic theory of life', for the origins of illness in the nervous system and in the soul (and this was only possible by dealing in the categories of the theory of sin). For all the extravagance of these ideas, a specific problem was laid bare here. Secondly, this philosophy is significant — Thomas S. Kuhn emphasised this — for a whole series of 'modern' developments: the electromagnetic theory of Oerstedt and Faraday, for instance, or for the discovery of the law of the conservation of energy, for the discoveries of comparative morphology and embryology (the study of mammals and their development), for the beginnings of the theory of evolution, as well as for the precise understanding of illnesses like tuberculosis (by Johann Lukas Schönlein).

Even though we are attempting to do justice to antiquated figures of the past, and the naïve faith in unambiguous progress is lost to us, and even though a modicum of

Romantic speculation still subsists in modern discoveries, we must nevertheless admit that, in view of medicine's achievements in shifting the boundary between life and death, illness and health, and doubling our lifespan, the historical process we have been considering is a story of progress. It is, therefore, true to say that this philosophical science was an impediment to the progress of scientific development, and despite the points where they overlapped, the response of the exact sciences to this philosophy was one of revolt. Liebig referred to it as a criminal scandal, 'the plague of our century. A man, who in the condition of madness, murders another man is locked away, whereas we allow natural philosophy to educate our doctors and to instil in them its own peculiar form of madness, which allows them, with conscience clear and principles intact, to kill thousands.' The revolt against natural philosophy was an important factor in the triumphal march of the modern exact sciences in Germany.

Let us turn our attention first to medicine and the life sciences, because it was in these fields and in chemistry where the first historic breakthrough in the new science took place. Medicine was now to be grounded solely on factual evidence, exact observation, measurement and experiment, and more particularly, therefore, on the actual natural scientific disciplines of physiology and anatomy. It was the development of physiology which revolutionised medicine from the 1820s onwards: research was conducted into the cell as the basic unit of life (by the zoologist Theodor Schwann and the botanist Matthias Jacob Schleiden), its structure and development (cell division). Karl Ernst von Baer discovered the mammalian ovum in 1827, which led to physiological research into fertilisation, the development of the embryo and comparative embryology. Only now, for example, was the old theory of preformation (the belief that Eve carried all future human beings in a minute preformed state in her ovaries) scientifically disproved once and for all. Johannes Müller, in Berlin especially, was the first master of this new science; his *Handbook of Physiology* (1834–40) became the 'standard educational work for everyone' (Virchow). He, together with his followers — Virchow, Henle, Helmholtz, Du Bois-Reymond and many others — founded physiology in all its branches: physiology of the circulation, breathing, metabolism, of the sense organs, muscles, nerves and ovaries. It was only at the end of the 1830s that the phenomenon of menstruation was understood and no longer interpreted as a consequence of the Fall or the effects of cultural conditions, change of moon, an excess of blood, or as a process of decontamination or fermentation, or as a sort of 'moulting'. The animal experiment now became the indispensable basis of all research: in 1849, for example, to name just one among many, a physiologist, Arnold Berthold, implanted into castrated male chickens testicles from other cockerels and discovered their effect on the secondary sexual characteristics, and thereby something of the process of hormonal secretion. Max Schulze gave a new basis to the theory of cells in 1861 (the discovery of 'protoplasm'). By the end of the period, the physiologist Karl Ludwig had become the most internationally renowned in his field and responsible for creating a number of schools, having co-ordinated the development of research and pushed it forward in various directions. At the same time anatomy made new discoveries with the aid of the microscope and new staining techniques, which led to the investigation of tissue: histology. Pathology, especially as practised by Virchow, was given a strict basis in microscopic observation, as well as physical and chemical analysis, and it was to become the key to the understanding of illnesses.

Rudolf Virchow founded cellular pathology in 1858 and took the first important step by stating that the carriers of life and illness are cells, not the blood or nerves. He described illness as the life of cells under altered, abnormal conditions, and research into illnesses would now concentrate on research into cells. For the first time, therefore, illness had been localised, and the observable object, the cell, rather than the cause of the illness, was now the focus of interest. The life of the cell was explained causally, as having mechanical, physiological and chemical causes in the same way as organisms, life and illness. The vitalistic assumptions, like the existence of a 'life-force', had now apparently been pushed aside. One might speak of a 'change of paradigm'; endeavours to find the ontological 'nature' of illness or the purposes and the 'expediency' of organic processes were no longer of interest.

The second revolution in the field of medicine after the founding of cellular pathology was the development of serology and bacteriology, which in their application to combat illnesses brought about a real historical change. This began around the mid-century with research by Pasteur into spoilage and fermentation, and the results of Ignaz Semmelweis's research (in 1844) into puerperal fever and infection, a discovery which was ignored initially owing to opposition from other medics and the lack of an adequate theory. It was only at the end of the 1860s that antisepsis and disinfection finally established themselves on the basis of procedures inaugurated by the English doctor Joseph Lister; until that time, 50% of surgical patients suffered from 'hospital fever', and one-third of all leg amputees died of it in 1858, for example.

Physiology, anatomy and pathology brought about a revolution in medicine, and at the end of our period a new field of study, that of scientific hygiene (through Max von Pettenkoffer), came into being. Discoveries were immediately disseminated, and they were no longer so accidental; since the same problems were being worked on everywhere, solutions were always just around the corner, and hence the unprecedented flood of discoveries. The results and methods obtained would be put to immediate use in the clinics. Johann Lukas Schönlein (active in Würzburg in 1817–18, then in Zurich, and from 1839 onwards in Berlin) was one of the first modern clinicians. He was the first to carry through exact observation and measurement of the processes of illness, took the microscope to the sick-bed, initiated chemical analysis, the control of illnesses by the pathologist and the systematic use of the new techniques of percussion and auscultation. In the same way the clinician Joseph Skoda and the anatomist and pathologist Karl Rokitansky, active in Vienna from the 1830s onwards, revolutionised the clinic through drawing up exact protocols of illness and conducting anatomical and pathological examinations. Surgery also developed — firstly in Heidelberg, and then in Berlin — from being a craft to being a science. New techniques and instruments were developed: the stethoscope in 1819, narcotics in 1846 in the USA, the ophthalmoscope (pioneered by Helmholtz) in 1850. In 1851 the regular measurement of fever was instigated, and in 1852 the fever curve was devised; injections came into use in 1853–55, the laryngoscope in 1858, the stomach pump in 1867, and the end of the 1860s saw the beginnings of blood transfusion. The classical branches became more specialised: pediatrics, ophthalmology, otolaryngology, dentistry.

The new scientific medicine slowly became the basis of medical training. Initially it had a transforming effect primarily on diagnoses, less so on therapy. The Viennese hospital director Dietel had this to say in 1845: 'Just as our ancestors were more concerned with the success of their cures, we are more concerned with the success of our researches. Medicine is a science, not an art.' It was attitudes like this which led initially to a widespread scepticism with regard to therapy; the old methods and medicines were scorned because there was no scientific basis for them, but there were no new ones as yet. In this sense the coming together of medical research and practice was a slow process. The journals which were started up in the 1840s played an important role in bringing together researchers, clinicians and practitioners: e.g. *Archive for Physiological Medicine* (1842), *Archive for Pathological Anatomy, Physiology and Clinical Medicine* (1847), and *Journal of Rational Medicine* (1842). Resistance to modern medicine came from the old 'schools' — the vitalists and the like — who contested that the whole constitution of the human being was of more importance than the localisation practised by the cellular pathologists. Practitioners were sceptical also about doctors who gave diagnoses without therapy. One practitioner in 1843 claimed that the understanding of how a person is cured is outside the bounds of human knowledge, and he categorised illnesses according to the medicines that were known to cure them. There were disputes, intolerance and conflicts of interest, even in the new schools, and savage debates frequently broke out, like the opposition of the Viennese clinic director to Semmelweis, or that of the great Virchow against the founder of bacteriology, the country doctor Robert Koch, in the 1870s. Up until the 1860s, the new medicine had, in most cases, won the battle against scepticism and opposition.

Medical advances in Germany were accompanied by advances in chemistry, especially the founding of organic chemistry ('the dawn of a new day', as Liebig called it) by Justus Liebig, primarily through his analysis of nutrition in plants, animals and humans, and Friedrich Wöhler (through the synthesis of urea in 1828–31). Liebig, who was professor in Giessen at the age of twenty-four, led the way for others with his teaching and research laboratory, and new schools formed around him. He was one of the first to bring radical changes to the field of practical chemistry, by his application of chemistry to agriculture (1840) as described above. From the mid-century onwards the development of chemistry in Germany moved forward at an unstoppable rate, and important contributions were made to the basic founding principles of modern chemistry, to molecular and atomic theory. These included the discovery of spectral analysis for identifying chemical elements (by Robert Bunsen, together with the physicist Gustav Robert Kirchhoff in 1859), August Kekulé's proof of the quadrivalency of carbon (1857) and his construction of the benzene ring (1869), Lothar Meyer's contributions to the 'periodic table of the elements' (1864–70), which was simultaneously being developed by Dmitri Mendeleev, the development of physical chemistry, physiological chemistry, nutritional chemistry, the technologically and economically revolutionary aniline dye chemistry (by August Wilhelm von Hofmann), to mention only a few symbolic points of reference.

We turn now to physics. In the second third of the century, Germans were playing a full part in modern scientific developments: i.e. the application of classical analytic and mathematical models and methods to explain the workings of new and newly developed fields, such as heat, light and electricity, and the attempt to interpret them in a unified way. We must mention here the discovery of the law of the conservation of energy by the long overlooked doctor, Robert Mayer (1842), by Joule (1843) and Helmholtz (1847), all independently of one another. Energy was acknowledged as a single unified principle present in various manifestations; the conversion of energies, movement and heat, was expressed in quantative terms and proved in all areas of nature. Such general propositions as this were not particularly common at this time. Mayer's and Helmholtz's treatises were not taken up into the *Annals of Physics*; with a view to the unified front against natural philosophy, they were considered too speculative. Bitter conflicts erupted also between a physics formalised in terms of classical mathematics — at this time, therefore, mechanics — and the slowly evolving discipline of experimental physics, which detected in the old mathematics the taint of anti-empiricism, *a priori* reasoning, even philosophy, and these conflicts took a long time to sort out. From the late 1840s onwards physics in Germany advanced at a breathtaking speed. Rudolf Clausius in 1850 formulated the Second Law of Thermodynamics, and hence the principle of entropy — heat cannot be totally converted back into work. In 1856–57 he and August Karl Krönig developed the kinetic theory of gases (heat as the result of the movement of molecules). Kirchhoff discovered the laws relating to the resistance of electrical conductive systems and pushed thermodynamics and spectral analysis further. In 1856 Wilhelm Weber calculated the speed of light using electrical data; in the second half of the century Hermann Helmholtz, originally a physiologist, became the leading figure in German natural science through his great discoveries and theories in all major areas of physics. Astronomy would also play its part in the breathtaking rise of exact sciences in Germany, through the development of new techniques of observation and measurement, through the application of new mathematical laws, and through new discoveries and hypotheses, like those concerning sun-spots, and, finally, about how the world is constructed.

It was from research in the field of physics ultimately that the 'applied', strictly mathematicised technical sciences developed from the mid-century onwards, principally the study of mechanical engineering (pioneered by Ferdinand Redtenbacher in Karlsruhe).

The methodological principles and achievements of the century had their effect on all the exact sciences mentioned. The experiment was central to all of them; its use was extended beyond physics primarily to chemistry and physiology, and it became irrevocable, systematised, repeatable and quantified. Quantification was advanced primarily with the aid of a revolutionary measuring technique. This made it possible to observe phenomena imperceptible to the natural senses, even with the aid of intensifying instruments, like the telescope or the microscope, but could only be perceived indirectly by other means — such as thermic or chemical ones — ultra-violet light being one example. Physics thus developed into an abstract science. Finally, research concerned itself with questions which arose from the interpretation of observations and the problem of squaring them with others. The hypothesis and the practical experiment, or the empirical inquiry for which these are the starting-point, were now part of the same reciprocal process, from which arose the great theories, models and laws.

Lastly, we should mention the descriptive natural sciences, particularly geology, botany and zoology, the last two developing by way of the methods of comparative morphology and, as already indicated, comparative physiology and embryology to become a general biology. These sciences were strictly and exclusively founded upon empirical principles, in accordance with the positivist conception of science characteristic of this century. The most significant feature of these sciences was that they became 'historically based'. Geology became firstly the historical study of the earth, which saw the geological strata as the outcome of an evolution, which was interpreted in various ways. The newly developed and systematised study of the fossil remains of plant and animal matter, palaeontology, became an important subsidiary science in the search to determine the chronology of the earth's history. Palaeontology and the comparative biological sciences joined forces in a new study of natural history, an inquiry into how life developed (e.g. Ernst Haeckel, *General Morphology of Organisms* (1866), written before his conversion to Darwin's theories) and from an early date spawned very diverse theories of evolution. In 1860, a year after *The Origin of Species* was published, Darwin's book was translated into German, and in the late 1860s it was widely discussed inside and outside scientific circles. These new interpretations of the history and origins of the earth and of life made things very difficult for the old biblical story of creation; indeed, even in circles where this story was interpreted metaphorically, the Christian doctrine of creation itself was being severely tested. It was only with the real breakthrough of 'Darwinism' from the late 1860s onwards that the foundations of the Christian doctrine of creation, which had traditionally been taken for granted, even though symbolically interpreted, were radically shaken.

We must add a comment here about mathematics, which, of course is neither a natural science nor an experimental science, though modern natural science is unimaginable without it. The period we are covering witnesses the golden age of mathematics, even, and especially, in Germany. Besides the greatest mathematical genius of the century, Carl Friedrich Gauss, who was eminent in all fields of mathematics, there was also a whole corps of highly important mathematicians. For laymen and in the interests of a general history, there were perhaps three things which are important. New and important fields and methods were developed: set theory (Bernhard Bolzano and Moritz Cantor), the theory of functions (in the work of Bernhard Riemann), the calculation of probability. Mathematics went beyond the boundaries of 'natural' imagination, of 'natural' reality, and constructed non-Euclidian geometries (Gauss, first of all, who did not, however, publish his findings, and after the Russian Lobachevski and the Hungarian János Bólyai there was the schoolteacher Hermann Grassmann in 1844 and Bernhard Riemann in 1854), spaces with n, i.e. more than three, dimensions. These developments and similar advances in number theory, together with the logical analysis of axioms and the ever-increasing demands on the strictness of proofs, finally led to questions about the logical-epistemological principles of mathematics (questions about the nature of numbers, for example). Mathematical thought was understood more and more as a construction, and less and less as a representation. Thus was to have important consequences for the overall shaping of 19th-century thought.

A significant factor in the rise of the new natural sciences in Germany was the growth in the production of scientific journals. They acted as a mouthpiece for the new sciences and contributed to their rapid ascent, as they could act much quicker than could academic discourses and correspondence, which past centuries had relied on, to make the results of research known internationally; they were thus extremely effective in generating common knowledge of the state of research and what new research was being undertaken. A similar factor was the setting up of specialist societies and congresses, the first of which (1822) was the 'Congress of German Natural Scientists and Doctors' — inaugurated by the natural philosopher, Lorenz Oken — a forum originally still grounded in the Romantic belief in the unity of nature, and marked by a tone of national unity. This annual congress split — after 1828 — into sections, of which there were nineteen natural scientific and fourteen medical in 1866, and from the 1840s onwards specialist societies were set up for the individual disciplines, and the process of specialisation and strict imposition of scientific criteria continued apace.

In terms of historical development as a whole, there are two issues of particular interest. The first is the question of nationality and internationality. Of course, the history of the exact sciences is international; the part played by the English and the French, the Scandinavians, Italians and Russians in the achievements of the century is obvious. Scientists thought of themselves as an international community dedicated to research. Nevertheless, around 1800, Germany was lagging behind in the fields of natural sciences and medicine, and it was only around mid-century that it took on a leading, indeed dominant role. Germany's standing in the world in this century was based on this fact, alongside its dominant position in music, philosophy, the university and the arts. This is not to be overly patriotic, but there does seem to be a great deal of truth in it, and it deserves an explanation. The accompanying tables (following J. Ben David) attempt to quantify this phenomenon.

Table 35a: Number of Germans and those of other nations involved in vital discoveries in the field of physiology

	Germans	Other nations
1805–14	4	16
1815–24	18	29
1825–34	41	30
1835–44	63	43
1845–54	105	39
1855–64	156	57
1865–69	89	11

Table 35b: Number of Germans, as compared with French and English, involved in discoveries in the study of heat, electricity, magnetism and optics

	Germans	French/English
1806–15	26	75
1816–25	34	175
1826–35	64	125
1836–45	108	206
1846–55	189	269
1856–65	231	201
1866–70	136	91

(After 1836 Germany had a larger share than any other nation.)

Table 35c: Number of Germans, as compared with French and English, involved in medical discoveries

	Germans	French/English
1800–09	5	22
1810–19	6	41
1820–29	12	45
1839–39	25	46
1840–49	28	40
1850–59	32	37
1860–69	33	29

(After 1830 the Germans had a higher share than any other nation.)

The facts themselves do largely support the subjective view. Until 1830 it was the general rule that talented and curious young minds gravitated to Paris; but from then on they came, in ever-increasing numbers (American students, for example) to Germany, to Berlin.

What were the reasons for this? The development of the natural sciences in Germany was institutionally based, it took place within the universities, not in academies, societies, private laboratories, as was the case in England, and not within new research institutes, as in Paris. Natural sciences blossomed in professional circles, not in elite circles of intellectuals and dilettantes; the growth was not generated by the new requirements of technical and industrial society or in the medical field, and it did not take place against the background of a scientistic movement within society, which (the followers of Bacon, Condillac or Comte were a good example) expected that the development of natural science to bring with it welfare, freedom and rationality. Natural science in Germany was university-based; it developed within and spread out from the universities. This was surprising, since the university on the Humboldt model did not appear in itself to be an especially favourable environment for the development of natural science. The reformist university had been set up by humanists, philosophers and philologists; its central concern, unlike in the 18th century, was no longer nature, but culture, and so the education it provided had a spiritual and literary character. The new idea of 'pure' science was not concerned primarily with experience and experiment; it was more synthetic than analytical, more universal than specialist. The new ideal of the professor, who was to have an original and comprehensive overview of his discipline, was not taken from the field of the natural sciences. It might have been expected that in the early founding era of universities the denigration of 'vocational study' would have driven the natural sciences onto the defensive — which would have been the complete reverse of the development in Napoleonic France. However, these sciences, which the universities had traditionally left alone and at best tolerated, appropriated the new ideas of science as an end in itself, of the primacy of research, of the new imperative of research, of the new role of the professor — of which we have already spoken. Moreover, both the institutional set-up of the university and the university policy exercised by the state were highly beneficial to the natural sciences.

The extraordinary rise of the natural sciences in Germany can be attributed to many different causes, including the priority given to achievement in research, the encouragement to young people to make their names in the field of research, to specialise, even to found new disciplines. To add to this, departments and institutes were good breeding-grounds for research, and disciplines were professionalised with regard to their standards and career structure; there was more competition between academics and between universities within the individual states themselves, as well as between the states in the confederation. Appointment practices by the governments, whose job it was to carry through these norms, were another factor; the universities had prestige and exerted a pull on talented young people, and one should not forget that the natural sciences were more attractive to Protestants than to Catholics. Once the new *Wissenschaft* ethic was adopted as part and parcel of of the new university set-up, it gave a tremendous boost to the natural sciences, even though this had not been foreseen at the outset; and then from the 1830s onwards the successes in this field were sufficient to clothe it in prestige. The brief reign of natural philosophy no doubt also acted as a provocation, and gave a particular energy and intensity to the modern 'exact' sciences, as they rose in 'opposition' to it, but this was only a secondary and temporary stimulus. External stimuli and motivations, like the demands of technology, and utilitarian movements which wanted to harness science to serve the goals of happiness and progress, were of no importance as the century progressed, with the single exception of agricultural chemistry in the mid-century. The prospect of a revolution in production and the removal of hunger crises influenced science policy and gave a fillip to the institutional development of chemistry.

The other question is how modern natural science saw itself and its effect on how people looked at the world. The natural sciences developed in Germany as a revolt against classical idealist philosophy, against speculation, the construction of (all-embracing) systems, against *a priori* reasoning, teleology, the vitalistic question of whether elements, species, illnesses and bodily organs behave in accordance with a fixed purpose. Natural science toppled them all from their thrones. The universal idea of a unity of knowledge also seemed illusory, even misguided. The new ethos of research, and also the driving force behind it, was specialisation and analysis, not synthesis. Natural science in this century retained an anti-philosophical trait, a symptom of the circumstances of its rise to prominence. Nevertheless, natural science did give rise to a reflected understanding of its significance in the world. Firstly, among research scientists there arose an enthusiastic sense of the new and unprecedented power of science. They were full of the excitement of modernity, the emancipation from old doctrines and authorities; they believed in progress (even as far as dreaming of putting an end to all illnesses). As early as 1822 the assembly of natural scientists was given the high-sounding title 'Council for a Future Age'. In 1826 the word was that the present age had scaled heights never before experienced in history. The fashionable rhetoric was about the 'temple of science' and the natural scientist as 'priest'. After the mid-century, science was taking on more and more of the attributes of a religion. Virchow made this explicit in 1860 when he said that the sciences were 'taking the place of the church' and its 'transcendental aspirations'. In 1865 he said that 'science has become a religion for us'. Some scientists wanted to make natural science the basis of a world-view. Science, as they saw it, would not only liberate mankind from the supremacy of nature and bring with it prosperity, health and welfare, but it would also make people and society freer, truer and more moral. Virchow — and he was only one of many — spoke of the 'republican' consequences of the growth of science and declared the scientific ethic, free-thinking and the result of his own scientific researches (the structure of the organism as a system of equal cells) to be a model for politics and society. Hence, natural scientists were seen as 'priests of freedom', and it was the 'true religious devotion of science', which gave their work legitimacy. Medicine, it was said on another occasion, is a 'social science', and politics nothing more than 'medicine on a broader scale'. Emil Du Bois-Reymond, though this was admittedly not until the 1870s, agreed with Comte in declaring that the age of natural science was the end-goal of history. What God could only imagine, man could now put into practice; with his knowledge he now had the power to master nature, and the world would no longer be a vale of tears, but the true home of mankind. It has already been outlined, with reference to the movement away from the Christian interpretation of the world, that an important part was played by the natural sciences in loosening the hold of the traditional Christian version of how life originated and what it means, as well as the way in which the vulgar materialists turned against the Christian religion. However, there were a number of natural scientists in the 1850s and 1860s who sought to defend Christian doctrine and its assumptions of the existence of God and the soul, creation and immortality. This was essentially a battle fought between materialists and idealists. Generally speaking, however, the prevailing view among natural scientists was one of scepticism, an agnosticism which gladly acknowledged the limits of science. This view insisted on the importance of personal experience and declared that the ultimate questions could not be solved scientifically, and they contented themselves with the familiar retort *ignoramus et ignorabimus* ('we do not know and we shall not know'). This also applied, in theory, to Virchow and Du Bois-Reymond, in spite of all their mould-breaking theses. It was not only a question of religion, but of how free-will (and therefore ethics) was possible in a causally determined world.

This was why philosophers like Hermann Lotze (*Mikrokosmos*, 1856–64) or Gustav Theodor Fechner (*Elements of Psychophysics*, 1860) had great success. They were attempting to distinguish between the 'material' and the 'ideal' sides of the world and to relate them to one another, while giving the sciences which lay outside of the two 'isms' their legitimate place. Neo-Kantian philosophy, finally, supplied a theory of the natural sciences as well as of personal ethics, which took the sting out of the 'scientific' battle for whose world view should dominate.

The contribution of natural science to education in Germany, to the predominant figures through which the culture's meanings were transmitted, was clearly limited. Unlike the situation in the 18th century, education during the first half of the century was humanistic, under the influence of classicism (despite Goethe) and idealism, and predominantly based on the historically orientated humanities and philosophy. This also applied, of course, to the education received by the natural scientists themselves. Natural science only made its way slowly (back) into the general curriculum. Humboldt's *Cosmos*, Liebig's 'Letters on Chemistry' in the *Allgemeine Zeitung* (1840), newspaper articles on the advances being made by natural science, the interest shown by primary schoolteachers and by a number of associations in natural history, and the setting up of museums of natural history: these were all stages in the new popularisation of science.

However, the new mathematical base of science and its abstraction set limits on this, as did the dominance of the humanistic grammar schools; the gap between the 'two cultures' had certainly not yet been bridged. In terms of reshaping the picture people had of the world, an interpretation of human life and one which loosened the grip of Christianity, the natural sciences were as important as the historical humanities. An ideology of progress grounded in natural science failed, nevertheless, to conquer the high ground in bourgeois Germany, unlike positivism in France. It was only in Marxism, especially in Engels's works and then later in the German workers' movement, where fragments of an ideology can be found, like the belief in the historical laws at work within society, and the belief in evolution and progress, which were derived in a distinctly vulgarised form from the results and methods of natural science. But all this went on outside the realm of science.

(b) The revolution in historicism and the evolution of the humanities

An integral part of the *Wissenschaft* phenomenon in the 19th century, separate from the natural sciences but ranking alongside them in value and effect, was the development in the humanities, the so-called *Geisteswissenschaften* (literally, 'intellectual sciences'). They became — before sociology and psychology gained ground — the actual experience-based sciences, dealing with man as an intellectual, social and cultural being. They took over centre-stage from philosophy, and they were, in fact, primarily historical sciences. They provided the setting for one of the greatest intellectual revolutions of the modern era, which would change human existence, perhaps not as dramatically as did the one enacted by the natural sciences, but no less decisively. Hence, it would be insufficient to place this development within the history of science alone — it belongs also to the history of politics and society, part and parcel of a whole new way of life and way of looking at life. We call this revolution *historicism* — an ambiguous and controversial, but nonetheless characteristic, term.

Historicism was, firstly, a new method for approaching the question: what do we know about the past? It brings to light the peculiarity and the profound otherness of the past, its 'individuality', its 'development', its mutal dependence, and its use of the critique of sources and the tools of 'interpretation'. Historicism, secondly, evidenced a growing preoccupation with the past, with history; it sought to interpret the world as history, as the outcome of history as it has moved on through various stages. The world, it said, is not a system, it is history. Man, his works and institutions, forms of life and values, indeed his truths, are bound to historical time; they exist in a constant temporal process of 'becoming' and change; they have become what they are, and they are becoming something else, they have an origin and are developing, they change and can be changed. In the course of a process, which was started then and continues today, more and more of that which was considered outside time, as 'natural' and permanent, has been recognised as historically determined. Reality, even in the sphere of practical action and human relations, was no longer regarded as something fixed, as a given, but as something caught up in the flux of time, of history. The condition of man and his institutions at one given moment in the present is defined by its history, by where it has come from: to understand the present, we must know something of its history, and, similarly, if we want to know what the future holds, we must consult history. Historicism came in two forms, progressive/futurist and traditionalist, depending on whether the stress was put on origins and *Gewordensein* (the state of having become) or on the future and changeability, but there were, of course, many intermediate forms. Integral to these new perceptions of the world as history was the dismantling of what we may regard as a traditional and venerable paradigm for dealing with the past: the '*historia magistra vitae*', the idea of learning from past history, from which were taken exemplary, applicable situations and examples of good, bad, intelligent and foolish forms of behaviour. This was based, however, on the premise that one situation could be compared with or equivalent to another, and this idea lost its validity, since to perceive the world as history one must also recognise the profound peculiarity (*Unterschiedenheit*) of present and past, indeed of the many different pasts. The old idea, finally, was that there was just simply history, and only the history of something (of the church, of the town, etc.). It was only in the late 18th century that the experience and concept of 'history' in itself came into being, which as the great flux of time in motion marked out the space in which supra-individual memory and expectation exist.

Another integral part of the 'historicist' view of the past, fundamentally as a condition and impetus, was the historical perception of the human world and present; it was this which was the revolutionary new element extending far beyond the scientific sphere. The new outlook on the world — and this is the third meaning of historicism — involved the creation of radically new values and norms. By consulting history we establish the norms of our collective, especially political actions, the meaning and purpose of our actions and institutions. It is not God, or nature, or reason, who are now and ever shall be the legislators, who tell us what we should do. It is history which assumes this role (even if history is in league with God, nature or reason in a variety of ways). History serves to justify norms; we can no longer justify the aims of our actions without referring to history. This is, once again, something new, another factor which marks out the 19th century especially as the century of history. To put this another way: if mankind needs history to come to an understanding of itself, then this means, in a normative sense, that one needs history in order to achieve one's individual and collective identity. If a group of people wants to see itself as a nation, for example, and yet find themselves in a world where regional, denominational and estate-based convictions, which traditionally told them how to act or defined their political orientation, are breaking down, then they need to refer back to history. This is how the revolutionaries justified their aims. They consulted history in the form of a philosophy of history which would certify, indeed legitimise, their 'rational' blueprint for a better world by confirming their belief in 'progress' as the law of history. In the same way the conservatives defended tradition, the past carrying on into the present, against those who scorn and seek to have done with it, against the *tabula rasa* creed of the futurists, with its 'frightening' terroristic and bureaucratic consequences. Then, there were the reformist liberals, the true historicists, who attempted to find a compromise between the limiting force of the past on human activity, the 'tendentiousness' of history and man's freedom of action.

The roots of historicism as a general phenomenon were diverse, but these began to converge at the beginning of the century. An outline of the most important of these will have to suffice here. Firstly, there was the discovery or at least the greater stress put on individuality, the singularity and uniqueness of particular phenomena, which are more than mere 'instances' of a general principle (*das Allgemeine*), and hence there was a move to unseat this sovereign 'general principle' exemplified by natural law or reason. In order to recognise the individuality of things, so the argument went, one must understand how they have developed, and attempt to understand them on their own terms (and not on the assumptions of the present time, understood as valid for all time). This signalled a move away from the Enlightenment, which saw the world primarily as a system and not as history. Nature, reason and the *Allgemeines* (general principle) were its supreme yardsticks; it tried and convicted the past in the courts of the present and believed the nature of individual human beings to be homogeneous. The European culture of feeling had already countered this, putting the stress on sensitivity, on the subjectivity and individuality of human beings, and on the non-rational and hence non-general aspects of their make-up. It was German classicism and neo-humanism, with their artistic ideal and their ideal of the cultivation of personality, which had been slowly working the clay for the new categories of individuality and development. Humanity, to which man aspires, is not a process whereby the common human attributes emerge from the bud and bloom as rationality and morality, reason and virtue and 'usefulness', but the development of the particular individual aptitudes into a harmonious totality of all the 'spiritual energies', including emotional and aesthetic ones. The human being thus develops by appropriating the cultural legacy of the past, for this is the only way of overcoming the one-dimensionality and alienation which Rousseau saw in the civilised world. This ideal gives a special status to the attempt to understand past 'culture', while at the same time providing a new category to help us understand past reality in its definition of individuality as a 'totality' and as a 'harmonic development' of aptitudes and possibilities. One should add to this the fruit of the artistic theory of the 18th century, the principle of 'inner form': the idea that a work of art is not a sum of individual parts, but is organised around a central element, a core, which has first to be deciphered. It is a universe, in which all parts work in unison or, as the contemporaries put it metaphorically, (though in a manner which we nowadays find irritating): it is an 'organism', or the 'expression' of an 'inner self'. This led someone like Winckelmann to search for the 'spirit' of the artist as it manifests itself in the work of art, and for the meaning of each separate epoch in art. This was the discovery of what we call artistic style.

Other concrete historical developments were now viewed in this light — a constitution, a social system, a culture. It became the key for unlocking the past. Historical phenomena began to be regarded as 'expressions' of an underlying creative 'spirit'; only by understanding this spirit would the 'meaning' of each expression become clear. This was the process of understanding, which became the basic method of all sciences concerned with the manifestations of the human spirit, i.e. the *Geisteswissenschaften* (arts and humanities). At the same time, this implied that the phenomena of the human world could only be understood in terms of the reciprocal relationship of all the separate parts of a 'culture' (art and religion, art and society, etc.), and hence the crux of the matter was that the whole of a culture could only be apprehended in terms of the interdependence of its constituent parts. This approach to understanding first made it possible to make the cohesion of the human cultural world — the interaction of individual persons, society and culture — an object of knowledge. From a methodological standpoint, this was another example of the move away from the Enlightenment. The latter explained historical processes as resulting from one single cause or a number of them working side by side, from the insights and passions of individual actors and, as it were, external initiatives: a constitution, for example, was seen as the work of the person granting the constitution, and as arising from a simple chain of causes. The opponents of this view spoke of an infinite series of causes, they looked for 'inner' causes (an *Anlage* (innate ability or predisposition), the immanent logic of a beginning) as opposed to external ones; they were concerned that an element of freedom not be lost in the process of causation, concerned with the reciprocal, interdependent relationship between all the elements of a whole, and they sought to understand processes, which could neither simply be explained causally nor teleologically. This was the meaning of the philosophical category referred to as '*Entwicklung*' (development). Each individual thing cannot be separated from its genesis, its development, and '*Entwicklung*', once again, was a concept directed against the Enlightenment, which only took into account activity which is planned and directed towards a purpose, or the accidentality of an individual passion.

Included in this interpretative schema were many assumptions which to us appear strange and irrational: assumptions about the organism and the organic evolution of the 'germ' and the innate tendency, about reality as an expression of an 'inner self', a spirit, about the inexhaustability and incomprehensibility of the individual thing — *individuum est ineffabile* was Goethe's phrase. It would be useful to see these things as ciphers for contemporary problems which the Enlightenment had not solved, and for new solutions to problems. This moral-aesthetic and yet historical theory of individuality and development (*Entwicklung*) had yet to shake off the norms of classical *Humanität*, though in a revised version. But the approach to the Greek model was different, for it involved an attempt to understand the Greek culture in all its different aspects, the Greek man in the totality of his world. This was the origin of the study of classical antiquity.

If we look at how individuality and development (*Entwicklung*) evolved as norms in the interpretation of the present and the past, a figure of the utmost importance is Johann Gottfried Herder. His interpretation was different. For him the fundamental category was the 'life' of contemplation and sensibility; the multiplicity and individuality of the world and all its forms, peoples, languages, epochs — and not its uniformity — was the main thing, the true manifestation of God. Individuality, in his view, was not an aesthetic norm, the central tenet of aristocratic education, but something elemental and vital, a primary reality; and he put the stress not on what has already become (the work of art and the state of culture), but on the process of becoming. The theme of the connection between epochs and cultures was developed further by the contention that it is the *Völker* who are the subjects in the historical drama. History is not primarily moved on by planned activity directed towards a purpose, but by a collective unconscious active within the *Völker*, from which cultural and social conditions 'quietly' emerge. The thesis expounded by Justus Möser was political in nature and aimed to bring about change in social institutions. It opposed the razing of tradition by the Enlightenment, with its levelling and regimental tendencies and its general principles laying claim to universal validity, and turned its gaze instead to the history of fatherlands, seeking to justify traditional political and legal structures as expressions of a particular 'regional common sense', while at the same time, and more strongly than Herder, emphasising the reality of the collective, the communities as they are and as they have evolved, as opposed to the Enlightenment construction of the world which had the 'isolated' individual as its starting-point. Burke also, in his attack on the French Revolution, declared that every society was determined by its own tradition, thereby striking a powerful chord in Europe as well as in Germany.

Wilhelm von Humboldt made an attempt to bring together the new belief in the irreducibility and sovereign right of the individual and the classical belief that *Humanität* was a normative concept. Individuality and events should (and can only) be understood as parts and manifestations of the one totality of mankind. Idealistically, the dynamic historical forces, which bring about the unity of epochs, were considered to be intellectual ideas — these were, so to speak, the code for understanding how the dynamic historical forces relate. Humboldt then took on Kant's great intellectual challenge to discern how it is at all possible for living man to know anything about past reality, how he can interpret what has gone before — in other words, the theory of historical hermeneutics.

It was the early Romantics who brought these developments full-circle. The decisive *Weltprinzip* (principle of the world) was now the individual — in opposition even to the normative ideal of classicism. Individuality was now explicitly seen as infinite, and — in the spirit of the Romantic revolt against a rationalised, civilised, institutionalised and, in an objective and normative sense, stabilised world — individuality was seen as determined by the force of the individual and collective unconscious, which was the major revolutionary discovery of Romanticism. Early Romanticism, especially, showed itself to be always receptive to anything characteristically individual, especially if this was foreign, and it was obsessed with the new ability to interpret how things are and how they will be — foreign works of art, religions and cultures. Individuality was no longer bound, in a general and objective sense, to the ideals of classicism: all individuality was put on the same level, and what made it so attractive was precisely this diversity. At the same time, the emphasis was shifting, as it had in Herder's ideas, from what has already become to the actual process of becoming. 'History' was no longer bound to an aim, whereas Herder still connected the celebrated multifacetedness of mankind with the norm of *Humanität*. In place of presence and longevity, which for classicism were the leading categories of time, Romanticism preferred more subjective notions like longing and memory.

A second root of historicism, this time originating from within the *Wissenschaft* movement itself, was the development of the critique of sources, which had grown up in the 17th and 18th centuries in historical study of the church and the law, and philological criticism of literary texts, particularly of the Bible.

The third root of historicism was, paradoxically, the Enlightenment, especially for the philosophy of history which the Enlightenment founded. The Enlightenment had released the world from the history of divine creation and salvation; it had taken profane history seriously and sought to take man as the starting-point in any interpretation of history and see it as the work of man (for example, it even viewed theology in a profane sense as a history of schools of thought developed by man). The Enlightenment also consulted the past to demonstrate the superiority of the present over the 'dark' ages, and to put the past in the dock, but at the same time it interpreted the past from the perspective of progress, in order to validate the future and to justify its own avowed objective of a world governed by reason.

It was the category of progress, which first opened up the temporal dimension and gave scope to secular change, as well as reinforcing the continuity of past, present and future as true elements of history, while asking the question of world history, the history of man, its meaning and its goal. By applying a critical perspective to the interpretation the past, delving deeper into it so as to discern the direction in which history was moving, legitimacy was found for the positive shift towards the future. Interest in the future generated a new interest in the past, which articulated itself as a philosophy of history. In this 'history of progress', culture and society now took their place as the central areas of human life as against the established world, the church and the state; and in the process of applying a critical and relativising perspective to the interpretation of one's own established world, cultures from beyond the European continent were brought into the picture, and, therefore, the variety and diversity of historical worlds and the inquiry into the particular conditions which go to make up the characteristic elements of such a world received new impetus. Finally, since Rousseau, human history was seen in terms of decadence rather than progress, while at the same time there was harboured a secret hope of finding in this a point which signalled a change for the better.

More important than the humanistic and aesthetic moves to understand individuality and the interrelation and evolution of cultures and peoples, more decisive also than the Enlightenment preoccupation with the philosophy of history, was the fourth root of the revolution taking place in man's understanding of time and history. This new experience of reality coincided with the age of upheaval around 1800, the sense that the world was undergoing accelerated and fundamental change, that things which had seemed permanent were breaking down, and the sense of a new rift between past and present. It was no longer taken for granted that old customs would continue to apply in the present. Tradition was under siege. The pace of change was breathtaking: the reforms of enlightened absolutism, its attempts to give a new rational shape to public life, its institutions and system of laws; the great revolution, its failed attempt to win longevity for its new order, the discrepancy between its plans and intentions and what resulted from them; the great upheavals and reforms in the wake of the revolution; also, however, the changes in working and public life brought about by economisation and division of labour, bureaucratisation and the beginnings of technical reorganisation; the change in behaviour in people themselves, whose actions were no longer guided by tradition, but directed from within, from inner reflection; the mobilisation of society and its norms. People witnessed these things and thought: there is a strange intangible 'power', time, history, controlling us, something beyond our will and that of anybody else. Those who sought to preserve tradition had to defend and justify it, and so the conservatives, instead of talking about tradition as something self-evident, natural, divinely ordained, began to argue historically. Those who sought revolution now called upon history, since the various revolutionary parties sought justification of their ends in reason, in whose name they bashed heads and hacked them off. Those who favoured the reformist approach — between tradition and revolution — wanted to avoid the revolutionary breach between the present and the past, feeling that this would only plunge them into a bottomless pit of instability and the loss of identity. They began to support their arguments in historical terms. The categories of individuality, integrity and development were supplemented by the central experience of the acceleration of time as a process of change. The term 'history', which became as it were the subject of the changes taking place in the world, was symptomatic of this. The new focus on history was an attempt to build new bridges between the past and the present.

This was the situation in which historicism had its genesis. Before moving on to look at the rise of the historical sciences themselves and their effects on life, reference must be made to the two great intellectual movements of the 19th century, which eventually forced home the revolution of historicism: Romanticism and idealism.

In early Romanticism, the pathos of the unhappy consciousness confronted with an alienated and hostile world, 'homesickness' and nostalgia was of paramount significance. This had a double effect on the new preoccupation with history. Firstly, a new ideal world was discovered, the (late German) Middle Ages. This was seen as an integral world, sensuously and sensibly structured, but also, and unlike the Greek world, rich in mystery, with its eyes raised towards the trancendental sphere. The second effect was a turn to history in search of an earlier period, an origin prior to all alienating objective notions, a youthful age close to God as opposed to our own age, long in the tooth and far from God, a world full of endless possibilities, in which that which was in the process of becoming came to dominate over what had already become. The early, primal ages were considered — in an aesthetic and nostalgic sense — as a charmed realm in the past. This grew stronger in the later, more recent Romanticism. The religion of art in early Romanticism, in which works of art — those from one's own culture and those from foreign cultures — were regarded as the seat of truth, was replaced by a religion of the past and of history. The preoccupation with origins and antiquity turned into a preoccupation with myths, with the 'dark', irrational powers of the unconscious — night, death, sexuality, fate beyond all will — and with religion. They explored beyond the classical map of clear and humane antiquity, to chart more archaic and religious paths, the dark and wild, mythical territories, a process which Goethe condemned as a barbarisation, an orientalising and romanticising of the Greek world. A dual experience provided the impetus for this: the experience of the flow and breaches of time, and that of the overwhelming and elemental power of the past. All seeds of the future, so it seemed, were present in the primal age, and this led some Romantics to a quasi-religious glorification of antiquity and origins. This feeling (prior to all knowledge) of the interconnection of present and past reaches its peak in this relation to origin, because that is where the proximity to the eternal lies. From this intuitive standpoint historical study is no longer seen as an aid in building the future, a method for understanding the present or for understanding the nature of individuality, but a form of ancestor worship. Hence, the new fascination in history was not so much the freely acting individualities, not works of art and the cultural framework, works and institutions, but the coming and going of generations, the collective individualities of the *Volk*, and — typically Romantic — unconscious growth. The *Volk* moved on to take up a central place in history, an manifestation of unconscious nature, which gives rise to language and customs, law and poetry, and much more. This was the root of the idea of the creative, upright, poetic *Volksgeist* (folk spirit). The fascination for the *Volk* had religious overtones: by seeking the the origins of one's own *Volk*, one could locate oneself in the stream of time, whose course is directed towards God. The truth of our being, the source of our identity was to be found, according to this thesis, in the *Volk*. This also represented a rejection of the arbitrariness of the will and the accidentality of external impulses. It was a peculiar (and thoroughly ideological) belief in an 'inner necessity', which is the distinguishing feature of the 'true' development, the 'unfolding' of an original innate tendency, an essential core. This was also the origin of the antiquarian aspect of Romantic *Wissenschaft*, the sense for the quiet and the small things of the world, the reverence for antiquity, for the insignificant.

It is easy to scoff at such Romantic metaphysics, and to point to the harvest incipient nationalism reaped from all this. However, one should not forget that this corresponded on the one hand, to a fundamental feeling of the age. On the other hand, it should also be seen that behind what to us have become foreign categories of thought there were very real problems of historical knowledge — collective mentality, the unconscious realm, the progress of human cultural and social products towards an independent existence, which, in turn, influence men, to mention only a few.

Finally, there is German idealism. We must content ourselves here with a brief sketch of the important role played by Hegel in this major revolution in thought. (1) For Hegel, history is the locus of truth, since truth is not something permanent but has its existence in a course of events; the Being of the world consists in a process of Becoming (*das Sein der Welt ist Werden*). History is a process of exegesis, Being manifesting itself in the course of time. History has a direction, a goal: it is 'progress towards the consciousness of freedom', the history of freedom. This is a legacy of the philosophy of history begun during the Enlightenment, and of classicism with its norm of *Humanität*. Hegel rejects the Romantic claim that history can be broken down into a network of individualities or into an undirected stream of life. However, history is not an ancilliary process of the self-affirmation of the normative truth of Reason, it is not the path of *Geist* ('spirit' or 'mind') through a number of stages, of which the present one is of no basic importance. Rather, one can only speak with conviction of the present or the actuality of the human world in historical terms, and this actuality can only be recognised in the course of the historical process: history is the key to knowledge, and the present is defined by its location in the historical process. And since the Being of the world is defined in the works of Hegel as spirit, it is spirit which is inseparable from history, from time. Hegel was the first philosopher to replace the sovereignty of 'nature' in the exegesis of the world and life with the sovereignty of 'history'.

(2) Hegel left the model of organic development (germ and innate tendency, which unfold from within) behind. This model was a reaction against the explanation of phenomena in terms of a single or a few precisely discernable causes. Hegel accepted the infinity of conditions, but saw this as a confirmation of the universal inter-dependence of human social reality and its process. The world is a structure of relations, which cannot be explained by reference to substances (essences, germs etc.) nor by taking biology as a model. His notion of 'development' is objective, socio-intellectual, and in his works consciousness and the will of agents, the objective logic of institutions, supra-individual tendencies and external challenges (challenge and response) play a crucial role in explaining historical processes. His system incorporates — with the help of the famous dialectic — the leaps, breaches and contradictions inherent in reality.

(3) Hegel was the first to conceptualise human reality in all its social and institutional systems (language, law, society, state, religion) as well as in the systems of human works (art, science or technology) as systems created by man, which exercise power over man; he termed these as manifestations of the 'objective spirit' and analysed them. Such systems are neither simply products of the actions of individuals, nor the manifestations of an unconscious current of life. Man is shaped by them, for example through institution-alised role expectations — popes create the papacy, certainly, but the papacy also fashions its popes — and the objective tasks which they are set up to solve. Hegel, in his analyses, shows how everything that is individual is fitted into the overall scheme of the objective

spirit, and how the individual person and the formation of collectives are related. Individuality is not only aesthetic self-perfection, the development of talents and the appropriation of the essential things in the world (*Weltgehalten*), nor is it simply the unconscious coming to life, but it is also present in institutions and consciousness, and so the notion of individuality can also be allied to institutions, social groups and social realities.

(4) Individuality, apprehended and extended in this more realistic form, is not, however, presented as an absolute, and cannot be understood simply by looking at its own particular genesis, but is defined only within the context of the world and its place in world history. The relation of the individual to God is not 'unmediated', but mediated through the course of world history.

What Hegel was actually doing was attempting to understand an epoch, a series of events or phenomena (art or philosophy, for example) in terms of a guiding principle or tendency, which he called, using metaphysical terms and the language of idealism, 'spirit' or 'idea', and sought to discover this in institutions and actions. At the same time, all historical reality was seen as a stage in a dialectical development operating in world history, and yet he attempted to give every reality its rightful place, thus eschewing any moral condemnation of the past (the Middle Ages, for example) or any nostalgic glorification. Finally, Hegel did not content himself with an interpretative description of that which has been (and how it has been), rather he sought to explain why it was so. For this reason, his form of historicism was an idealistic, philosophically contructive historicism, which qualified experience with speculation: hence his preoccupation with central ideas; his self-confident distinction between what is essential, necessary and merely accidental; his dislike of anything concrete, for the mere presentation of the facts of the past — how it really was; and his disdain for the 'swamp' of mere facts, for the empirical approach. He endeavoured therefore to build a complete construct of the past, in which only the stages of what was clearly a hidden rationality and necessity were given value, so as to arrive at a true understanding; and hence his hybrid claim to be able to understand world history from the standpoint of its constructed unity and its anticipated goal. Hegel did not become a historian, but remained a philosopher of history, and the historical sciences took up arms against that tendency; they wanted to free themselves of it. As a result, Hegel's idealism died with him. For our purposes, however, it is more important to acknowledge Hegel's positive contribution to the foundation of historicism and the *Geisteswissenschaften* (the humanities). The important discoveries of individuality, of the unconscious life and the community, and the worship of the past, were supplemented by his own historical conceptualisation of institutions, of the 'objective spirit', the self-awareness of 'ideas' and 'tendencies', the interrelationship between the particular and the general, the particular event or phenomenon and the world-historical context. He took the classical theme of history, namely state and society, and found modern historical categories to explain it. The triumphal march of historicism would have been unthinkable without Hegel, as would much in the works of Marx and many developments in the empirical sciences which branched off from philosophy.

Having charted the origins and the components of historicism, from which the rise of the historically orientated humanities derived, a brief summary of the latter will suffice.

It began with the emergence of the study of classical antiquity. Classical philology, the study of the classical texts, developed in the wake of classicism and neo-humanism, under the influence of the new ideas of individuality, the work of art and culture, to become an historical science. Friedrich August Wolf, building on the work done by Christian Gottlob Heyne in Göttingen, was the real founder of this new science of antiquity or archaeology, which struck out beyond antiquarian interests, the mastering of ancient tongues, understanding texts, formal schooling, rhetoric or admiring works of art, to find new aesthetic and ethical goals. It sought to encourage the most comprehensive knowledge of Greek and Roman man in his own world and in all its aspects, so that those who studied it might chart a course towards their own humanity. Knowledge of the world of antiquity no longer had the merely subsidiary function of helping to explain the texts under study, it now had a value in itself. Passion and enthusiasm for the Greek world, rational scepticism and criticism, the new aesthetics of inner form, the interrelationship of individual and world, all provided a framework for a new interpretation of antiquity, and especially the Greek world. The critical tools developed during the Enlightenment were used to achieve an understanding of how things developed, e.g. in reconstructing the genesis of the *Iliad*, and shortly afterwards Schleiermacher worked out the order in which the Platonic dialogues were written. Wolf and Schleiermacher then became the founders and first theoreticians of the new philological methodology of interpretation: hermeneutics. Of course, the task of a thoroughgoing historicisation of the Greek world was crucially hindered by the exemplary status of the Greeks. The Romantics (Friedrich Creuzer and, in a more historical and methodological manner, Karl Otfried Müller and Friedrich Gottlieb Welcker) attempted to uncover the symbolic world, the mythology, the 'dark side', the origins of the Greek world, the pre-Homeric, oriental world and the history of the early tribes. August Boeckh went further towards presenting a broader picture of the Greek world, the 'prosaic' world of the Greeks: *The Athenian National Budget* (1817) depicted the Greek world, outside of the aesthetic and religious sphere, as the merely political realm. This was a piece of social and economic history, adhering to the classical and Romantic dictum of seeking the 'totality', the unity of a past age of mankind. At the same time, the world of antiquity was perceived as less ideal and no longer static, but historical, it was now seen as something which had experienced development. As a result of this, the primary question was no longer: what did this author think? or what was the 'significance' of this institution, or of this belief? The question now was: how did this or that come about?

Besides the historically orientated study of antiquity and its special form, material philology, and as a counterforce to it, rationalist and critical textual philology developed. Gottfried Herrmann, August Immanuel Bekker and Karl Lachmann were its main representatives, and it flourished with the help of major internationally recognised 'standard' editions. After the mid-century 'positivism' came to the fore: the concentration on materials and problems of detail, specialisation and a turning away from philosophical reflection and all-embracing syntheses. The emphasis on the scientific approach drove out the method of presenting a culture in order to extract lessons from it. Texts and materials now became central; a notion like *Geist* ('spirit' or 'mind') seemed too vague, too speculative — it was not sober enough. Classical philology was thus transformed into an historical and critical science of antiquity. This began to lead the way internationally, in part by means of the great dictionaries.

Historians, philologists from other branches of knowledge, representatives from the field of biblical studies and the new revolutionary theologians all passed through this 'school'.

Other philologies developed out of a combination of exact critical methods with Romantic-idealistic feeling. There was *Germanistik* (German studies), which began with the work of the Brothers Grimm, principally Jacob Grimm; this was an historical science, but with no fixed agenda or tasks, a form of 'ancestor worship', whose aim was to achieve an understanding of the life of a *Volk*, or ethnic group, in all its aspects, language and poetry, mythology, laws and customs and how they all fitted together. What in Herder and the Romantics had merely been a stimulus was carried through concretely, methodically, empirically and clearly in the course of a single lifetime with infinite perseverence and passionate devotion. So, following the quintessentially Romantic work on grammatical gender, the principle of the feminine and masculine 'world' in language, there came the *German Grammar* (1819–37), a history of German intellectual and cultural life and the German outlook on the world; then the *German Mythology* (1835), the books of ancient law and wisdom, and the epoch-making *German Dictionary* (1854–). Karl Lachmann, a philologist, founded German literary studies, firstly of the Middle Ages. Then along came Romance philology (Friedrich Diez) as the study of intellect and culture, language, literature and folk life from an 'historical point of view', and later English, Slavic and ancient oriental philology. Lastly, comparative linguistics was founded by Franz Bopp, who — beginning in 1816 — through his study of Sanskrit discovered how the Indo-European languages were related, and developed the concept of the 'internal structure', the 'organism' of a language; also important in this field was Rasmus Kristian Rask (1818). Humboldt's linguistic theory — that language is not only a system of signs, 'ergon', but the life of the spirit, 'energeia', the storehouse and product of man's view of the world, self-consciousness and experience — was the major philosophical achievement of the new science.

Besides linguistics and philology, the second grouping of new historical sciences to be established was, astonishingly enough, jurisprudence. Jurisprudence was inseparable from the law in its practical social application. New ideas about and research into the law had a direct practical political significance. Neo-humanism and Kantian idealist philosophy were the first to breathe new life into jurisprudence. Taking the Kantian critique of knowledge and idealist philosophy as a basis, it was to be reconstructed as a systematic science: a logical and systematic organisation of the material of law, with its own intrinsic intellectual context and a new relation to the whole of knowledge. This idea of an inner totality was a leitmotif of a new science for the major legal minds at the beginning of the century — jurisprudence as a philosophically based intellectual science. But of more epoch-making significance was the turning away from the idea of rational and natural law dominant in the 18th century, the switch to an historical outlook on law. Like historicism as a whole, this had a variety of roots. One of these — and this is often overlooked — was a revolutionary one. Rational law and its codification by the authoritarian state produced a fixed canon of law — secure against self-rectification and further development through scholarship and the administration of justice; it was an expression of the state's legal tutelage of the citizenry and omnipotent control over the future, once Kant's critique had limited the claims of natural law to validity. By giving the law a firm base in history, the law was renewed. To this came the discovery that the law was not something outside of history, but something historically created, having empirical and concrete causes, the product of a culture. One concrete example of this was the confusion of different legal norms obtaining in Germany — both in theory and in practice — something which could not be clarified by a return to abstract and deductive natural law, but only by breaking it down into its constituent parts in the process of a historical critique, and by taking Roman law as a reference point. Any interpretation of law had to start from the premise that law was historical in nature; the present was determined by history. The meaning of words and expressions could no longer be defined philosophically, as when a new language for science was being developed, but historically, according to what the Romans had meant by them. As early as the 1790s, for example, Gustav Hugo had set about founding a new discipline, that of legal history. Then the Romantics began to interpret law as the product of a collective unconscious, a *Volksgeist* (folk spirit) in the process of 'organic development'. It must be made clear that the reference to the historical nature of law also pointed to its inseparability from its social context.

The founder and spokesman of the new 'historical school' was Friedrich Karl von Savigny. In his *Law of Property* (1803) he first separated out the various stages in the development of Roman law, which until then had all been lumped together, and distinguished the Roman law of antiquity from its later transformations, carrying this process further in his subsequent major work, *History of the Roman Law in the Middle Ages* (1815–).

This historical approach took on a more polemical character during the Wars of Liberation. It was raised well beyond the debate about a new scientific approach to play its part in the general political scene, and initially acquired a more conservative slant. In 1814, the Heidelberg jurist Anton Thibaut published a pamphlet entitled *Concerning the Necessity for a Common Civic Code of Law for Germany*. A reorganisation of legal life, especially after the Napoleonic legal reforms, was very much on the agenda. Thibaut demanded the establishment of a national code of law to replace the traditional particularist law and the foreign, French law. Articulating one of the deep liberal convictions of the century, he insisted that the law should not be a dead tradition, but a living property, and that it should be progressive, opposing reactionary elements, and serve the cause of national integration. Thibaut rebelled against the omnipotence of the authoritarian legislators and the codification of the natural law. In view of the evident state of emergency, he advocated an 'organic' reconstruction of law, and in this regard was a staunch supporter of freedom for legislators, an example of progressive and reformist historicism.

Savigny countered this with a pamphlet which would become equally famous: *On Legislation and Science: Our Age's Vocation* (1814). He denounced the arrogance of the Enlightenment, indeed any doctrine advocating that it is the role of a legislator to set and make laws; he opposed codification and state dominance. The law, in his view, was something to be left alone, something rooted in the continuity of habit, custom and practice, which were subject to an organic process of development; it was something living, something which has grown, original, ancient, venerable, something nurtured in the *Volk* and emerging from the common beliefs of the *Volk*, from a feeling of inner necessity 'which excludes all ideas of an accidental and arbitrary genesis'. Law was not a set of statutes, but a tradition, and the *Volk*, as a counterforce against renewal, was identified with tradition. However — and this was an extraordinary idea — the people were not represented in the persons of the jurists; the academics and the judges were now given the responsibility of preserving the law and enabling it to develop organically, neither the state nor the people directly, but the legal profession themselves, were given the task of 'purifying' custom. Tradition, another astounding idea, was now synonymous with Roman law. Savigny was thus putting his weight behind the common European tradition of Roman law, in order to counter the idea of a future German national legal code. Here, historicism overlapped with traditionalism: science (and the new praxis it had shaped for itself) should not take its cue from traditional law, but from old Roman law, which had first to be rediscovered. This was the basis of a renewed systematic jurisprudence, and hence the confused 'popular' (*volkstümlich*) legal tradition was to be purified at its source. For the non-Romantic, indeed classicist Savigny, the fact that Roman law was normative and possessed a formal perfection played a significant part. The swing to conservatism was clear and the overcoming of natural law seemed to lead to a sort of quietism. This encouraged the view that organic development only applied to the past, that there was no place any more for the autonomy of the individual, or the idea that it was the 'calling' of every new era to inaugurate reforms and redevelopments. This was a very controversial point. Hegel felt that if one took away from a civilised nation the capacity to devise a code of law, this was one of the greatest insults one could visit upon it. For him the state took priority over the 'people'; and Dahlmann put it more simply, in a manner typical of liberals who adopted an historical approach: 'If the roof collapses over my head, it is my calling to mend it.' Despite these political implications, and despite the classicist-normative views held by Savigny and the concomitant obligation to adhere to an absolute value system, the effect of his programme was decisive. Only by consulting history, according to the arguments espoused in his *Journal of Historical Jurisprudence* (1815–), could one arrive at a true understanding of ones own situation. The 'historical school' sought with ever-growing tenacity to find an historical justification for legal dogmatism.

Alongside Savigny's *Romanistik* was a second branch of this historical school, *Germanistik*, founded by Karl Friedrich Eichhorn with his *History of the German State and Law* (1808–), which was elevated from its basis in antiquity to the rank of a science. It was here that the emotive preoccupation with one's own past, with the nation, took hold. This gave rise to a major scientific, political and public dispute: a fight between the *Germanisten* (of whom Georg Beseler was a typical representative) and the *Romanisten*. The Roman influence, the foreign, Romance law and its adoption, so the argument went, had been a national catastrophe for the Germans, something they must put behind them. *Volksrecht* (the law of the people) was played off against *Juristenrecht* (law by the jurists), and there was an attempt made to argue in terms which the the people understood, by referring, for example, to co-operative institutions. The Romantic harking back to the *Volksgeist* merged here with democratic nationalist and right-wing politics. Otto von Gierke's *Law of Co-operatives* (1868–1913) and his fight against the *Bürgerliches Gesetzbuch* (Civil Code) in 1900 were examples of this trend continuing later.

Despite its moves to become more historically based, jurisprudence remained a systematic science, and the more one investigates the past from a historical standpoint, the more questionable becomes the idea of continuity, the possibility of establishing a systematic relationship to history. The mid-century was dominated by 'concept-based jurisprudence', and a 'positivist' approach. Savigny's pupil, Georg Friedrich Puchta, ignoring the social context of law (analysed by Eduard Gans, a follower of Hegel, in his *Law of Inheritance in World-Historical Development* (1824–35)), gave a strict conceptual basis to law — the problems of legal accuracy and justice — treating law as a logical system. Following the collapse of a religious and metaphysical justification and legitimation of law, the archetypal modern problem, how *'das Sollen'* (what ought to be) can be squared with socio-historical reality, a case was made for the autonomy of jurisprudence based on the Kantian critique — it deals only in the separate sphere of law and seeks to find, in the logical sense, a 'correct law'. This accorded with the constitutional system, the political balance between the crown and the citizenry: the job of the law was to neutralise conflicts. The state was actually, leaving aside the fact of power, a state under the rule of law; conflicts were to be settled by means of official rulings, and it was the role of jurisprudence to preserve such a balance. The other central component of this discipline — the principle of private autonomy, as of the partner in a contract — was in tune with bourgeois liberalism. It was anti-estate and opposed professional distinctions, and represented in this regard a move towards equality. It was also *de facto* pro-capitalist, supported free competition, and was therefore in tune with the newly emerging class division. The systematic development of liberal procedural law and commercial law (codified in the commercial code of 1861), which had a pioneering role in the development of the modern economic society, count as particular achievements of this branch of study; instances where the priority of the formal principle was contravened occured only at the margins — the authoritarian *Gesinderecht* (law relating to servants), for example, and the beginnings of the 'welfare state'. At the same time, however, jurisprudence, and hence the education of jurists, remained under the guidance of the humanistic idea of education, of Kant, neo-humanism or idealism, and so it was not surprising that this shaped the outlook of jurists. From the end of the 1850s onwards, doubts were raised about the implicit presuppositions of this discipline, Kantian ethics and the overly positivist 'idea' of law, which seemed to amount to an optimistic metaphysics of history, and philosophical realists launched a critique of concept-based jurisprudence, questioning how much of it was nothing more than logical fantasy. In his work *The Battle for Law* (1872), Rudolf von Ihering sought to explain law as the expression of interests, grounded in real causes, purposes and uses. Similar doubts later provided the impetus for the founding of legal positivism.

We shall now return to historicism and turn finally — after looking at the study of antiquity, philology and historical jurisprudence — to so-called 'normal' history, the foundation of modern historical studies, and the eventual transformation of the writing of history into a relatively strict discipline. At the head of this 'revolution' was Barthold Georg Niebuhr, state official and diplomat, born of peasant stock in Holstein, with his lectures on Roman history (1810 in Berlin, published in book form in 1811). He was the first to make the historical and critical method — the systematic gathering and critical examination of all sources, the 'eternal war of criticism against all tradition', i.e. the historical source texts — compulsory when engaging with history. In this sense he was interested in depicting 'genuine history', eschewing the principles of aesthetic (re)construction and philosophical reflection, which had been dominant in historical writing until then. He made use of the critical methods of the

Enlightenment, while at the same time going beyond them. He was not only interested in a negative critique of sources, but felt that by subjecting them to a thorough analysis one might break through to the 'genuine' material, the verifiable facts. His claim, typical of historicism, was that the researcher can assume that the history of a *Volk* shows a continuous development, and that he can plot back from what he knows to what he does not know, from the effect to the cause, from later expert witnesses, from legal formulae and customs, to arrive at a past anterior to all written tradition. This was not only a methodological principle but testified to a growing interest in the material facts themselves: Niebuhr was not concerned with the aesthetic literary reality of a past age, but — predating the philosophical rehabilitation of state and institution by Hegel — with the socio-political world, with the constitutional and agrarian history of the Romans, who before their entrance onto the world historical stage were, of course, a peasant people. The pre-classical and pre-Romantic traditional concern with the state, the law and institutions joined forces with the emerging new discipline.

The other founder of the new discipline was Leopold von Ranke, and since he, unlike Niebuhr, was not only a researcher but also a major historical writer, his influence was much more decisive. He combined the critical method, the Romantic preoccupation with the past and the new categories of interpretation of historicism, and applied them to a study of political history. A brief summary must suffice here. Ranke began as a theologian, and then set himself the task of uncovering the workings of God in history. He approached the past from a Romantic and religious standpoint. His concern, unlike that of the classicist and neo-humanist Humboldt, was to extend and perfect his own personality by coming to an understanding of a past individuality, and, unlike Hegel, he was not attempting to interpret the past in terms of consciousness or the regulative idea of a totality of mankind. He was much more concerned with immersing himself in the flow of life and time in order to awaken a 'feeling for the existence' of a particular past age. The religious sentiment on which this approach to the past is based — something barely comprehensible to us today — led Ranke to two of the fundamental principles of historical studies, which since then, even if they are now given a quite different (and no longer theological) justification, define the scientific approach to the past. (1) The individual, the singular, the particular in history is an absolute — even the major institutions and life systems, the state, the church, the law, the *Volk* are in this sense individualities; they cannot be regarded as stages of a totality, of mankind, of the development of spirit, progress in the consciousness of freedom, the self-perfection of man. 'Every epoch has an immediate relationship to God'; it is more than a prologue, an expression of the world-historical law, it is something peculiar to itself. For Ranke, then, only God gives context (and meaning) to history, and historical phenomena are 'sacred hieroglyphs'; but we can only discern this structure through religious reverence — it remains unknowable to us. Finite humanity does not possess a plan of the whole, a plan of *Weltgeschichte* (world history). (2) The second consequence is the postulate and posture of objectivity: the dream of 'extinguishing one's ego' and of only allowing the grand realities of the past to speak, the firm resolve only to determine 'how it really was'. This is directed against the moralising, all-knowing and pedagogical tendencies of the Enlightenment approach to history, and all that descended from it, against the tendency to use critical history to put the past on trial, and turn the historian into a state prosecutor and judge (or even a legislator); against the poeticised and transfigured 'fairy-tale' past of the Romantics, against the 'construction' of the past in terms of an idea of world history, a logic of spirit in the works of Hegel; against the hijacking of the past for political ends. Reality is the important thing, and not constructions or any opinions of our own. Every past reality has an equal right, and each should be interpreted on its own merits (and not in terms of whatever clever thesis we might invent to explain it). If this is the case, then calm, loving research and representation — *sine ira et studio* — is what is called for. Ranke's love of reality was not an example of positivism. He wanted to comprehend the intricate nexus of relations between individual human actions and the spatial-temporal constellation, the particular 'stages' (*Momente*) of development, and with the overall scheme of things, the tendencies and necessities (which he considered more important than the scope for freedom of action), and he attempted to find internal dynamic principles beyond the mass of facts, which, being a true son of the philosophy of his time, he called tendencies, ideas or 'manifestations of the spirit' (*Realgeistiges*). In the light of these, the past, he felt, would become more transparent.

Ranke's central interest was reserved for politics, the state and the individual states, the church and the institutions. He felt that history was not the history of cultures or peoples, but the history of states, of nation-states. Ranke therefore applied the new method of interpreting source texts, material works and institutions to the study of political action. This was to be interpreted in terms of motives, general tendencies and all those unconscious things which are 'taken as read'. *Realpolitik* and *raison d'état*, power interests and power constellations, equilibrium and hegemony played a leading part in his work. Politically, he was old-fashioned, moderate, state-conservative, and pre-nationalist, remaining true to universalist principles. He wrote works on German, French, English and Serbian history, i.e. European history.

Ranke's postulate of objectivity was heavily contested. Johann Gustav Droysen called this point of view 'eunuch-like'. Nationalist and liberal historians gave a new legitimacy to the conscious tendency, and although Ranke did not delude himself with the belief that an historian could be totally objective, there was a certain contradiction between this postulate and his conservative convictions, which also coloured his works. Nevertheless, Ranke personified one line of historicism, the objectifying strain; even his opponents could not escape the methodological imperative of his demand for objectivity. He turned the historical method, study and critique of sources into a recognised norm, and major political history into a science.

Besides the figure of Ranke, there are two phenomena worth mentioning from the decades of the Vormärz, when public interest in history grew even further. Firstly, the older, pre-scientific or rather pre-historicist forms of historical writing survived. Friedrich Christoph Schlosser wrote a work in the moralising tradition of the Enlightenment, pedagogic, influenced by the 18th century as well as by Kant; this was his extraordinarily successful world history (first published in 1811). This was history as ammunition for the political battle fought by the early liberals, and a similar, though less philosophical and less erudite approach could be found in Karl Rotteck's universal history, which became very influential in southern Germany. More historicist in approach, but still methodologically naïve, was the great liberal figure, Friedrich Christoph Dahlmann, who felt that history should serve the demands of the day, but at the same time placed the emphasis on political action, knowledge, historical understanding of the facts and what has 'become'. Other members of the pre-critical school were the Romantic and nationalist Friedrich von Raumer with his *History of the Hohenstaufen and Their Age* (1823–25) and the high-conservative and discredited Hegelian Heinrich Leo, who attempted to write a universal cultural history.

Study of the Middle Ages, on the other hand, emerged from romantic and patriotic motives. In 1819, the Baron vom Stein founded the Society for Old German History, which collected and published the sources for historical study of the Middle Ages in its massive compilation, the *Monumenta Germaniae Historica*. Georg Heinrich Pertz and Johann Friedrich Böhmer were the real pioneers of scholarly investigation into the Middle Ages, which grew out of a fashionable enthusiasm for this period and a sort of historical 'homesickness', and there was at the same time a surge of interest almost everywhere in regional history and the history of the states, feeding on the general growth in historical interest and its organisation into historical associations.

Historical scholarship and historical writing rose by mid-century (between 1840 and 1870) to become a leading, if not *the* intellectual force — a large, rapidly established discipline, which attracted many followers and engaged a large number of important academics, researchers and historical writers, who were leading lights in the intellectual and cultural sphere, as well as in constitutional, nationalist and denominational politics. All the major disputes of the time were conducted using historical arguments, were accompanied by historical controversies, and were led by politically active historians. The important political journals of the day also had an historical slant; the name of the leading Catholic journal, *Historical and Political Journal*, testifies to this. Historical writings and journalism not only reflected what Germans were thinking politically, but frequently pushed them in a particular political direction. This will be discussed often enough in the later account of political events and tendencies.

If, instead of taking the historians as representatives of a particular party, we look at their field of study as a whole, three major points stand out. (1) The contemplative, objectifying and universal approach of Ranke waned, although he had given a tremendous boost to historicist interpretation of the world and had put the study of history on a more scientific footing. He had simply gone out of fashion. On the one hand, particularly in medieval studies, a scientific positivism developed, grounded in the critique of sources and the establishment of facts, which was noticeable for its methodological rigour and growing specialisation. Research became more important than presenting the facts. The major forces in this movement were people like Georg Waitz, or the Institute for the Study of Austrian History in Vienna, founded in 1854 and soon to achieve high renown, and which gave particular support to the so-called historical ancilliary studies, the whole apparatus enabling people to read and understand old — principally medieval — handwriting and documents, and in particular to develop the techniques for determining whether they are genuine or not.

(2) Historical studies were once again becoming more political, without sacrificing any of their scholarly rigour; they became 'engaged'. Those aspects of the vast complex of historicism whose aim it was to consult history to seek justifications for man's actions, gained the upper hand. History was concerned with consolidating man's identity and legitimising his goals, serving freedom and emancipation, progress and, above all, the formation of the nation and its unity. It looked into the past, its own as well as that of European man as a whole, seeking out the great binding tendency which would justify

the here and now and would be the right one to carry into the future. The romantic and contemplative traits disappeared, and with them the universality. Johann Gustav Droysen, still a follower of Hegel, achieved early fame through his *History of Alexander the Great* (1833) and his discovery of what has since been called *Hellenism* (1836–53). A right-of-centre Liberal politician in the Frankfurt National Assembly, he was to be the great theoretician of historicism in its anti-Rankean form, soon to become the dominant school among the *Kleindeutschen* (those favouring the unification of the German states with the exclusion of Austria). From an analysis of interpretation as the fundamental procedure of historians he extracted the notion that all historical knowledge was subjectively derived and related to the present, no matter how much it is corrected by applying an objective method. He also attempted to justify the historian in taking sides, once again from the standpoint of history as a process of development, which only the historian can call upon. Behind such theory (and the historical writings based upon it) were a number of idealistic basic assumptions: that the world and its history can be understood as a meaningful process, i.e. typically as an organic process; that man despite all supra-individual necessities, all causal determinations, is a free being, free to act, free to set goals and purposes; that history is about values and norms, which are to be institutionalised into objective systems, like family and work, church and state, and that it is in fact about 'moral powers', as Droysen called them; that in this sense spirit (*Geist*) is the leading category of history; that the age and the development come together in ideas and tendencies, which have a determining influence on people, on their interests and needs. Wickedness and evil are not excluded from this schema; the past has a meaning. In contrast to Romantic history and Ranke's position, which was influenced by it, 'spirit' and 'will' and the intentions of acting individuals were given more emphasis, whereas 'nature', 'unconscious' becoming and supra-individual necessities moved into the background. The view that it is 'men' who make history, which until then was not a common belief among historicists, now started to gain ground. Politics was the central feature of such history, as it had been in the works of Ranke, and special emphasis was placed on the internal structure of the state and the relationships between states as powers. Another theory which began to gain ground slowly was that of the 'primacy of foreign policy', the theory that external political forces controlled the internal political situation. Next in line to politics was the church and, embedded in both of them, ideas. The spheres of culture, of social life, which had previously been of such importance, were marginalised, especially as they had branched off into separate disciplines.

The dominant group among such historians was liberal-nationalist and *kleindeutsch*. They were liberals, but theirs was a moderate liberalism, opposed to feudalism and absolutism, bourgeois, they were in favour of liberty — for a sphere which was free from state interference but also concerned about their voice in the state. They were against revolution, egalitarian democracy and majority rule, favouring bourgeois constitutional monarchy and the separation of powers, and firmly behind the state and the idea of its precedence over society. The state for them was practically an article of faith, and they placed great trust in it — understandably so, given the history — as a guarantor and agent of justice, liberty and culture, confident that it could reconcile law, morality and power to achieve the right balance. In short, they were driven by a certain idealised notion of the state grounded in a spiritual notion of power. This liberalism was 'Protestant', anti-Catholic and anti-clerical, justifying the individualism and the culture of the 19th century and the secular state of the Reformation. They also championed the work and professional ethic as the means to human self-fulfilment, an idea which had its origins in the Reformation. These historians were nationalistic, seeking not only the cultural, but the political unification of the nation. This was needed to secure the existence of the German nation within Europe against external threats, and bring German history full-circle. These historians were *kleindeutsch*; they believed unification was only possible through Prussia, whose historical task and calling this was. Droysen, in his history of Prussia, had the singularly absurd notion of examining concrete political events since the late Middle Ages to find evidence to support this thesis, going back as far as the establishment of a Hohenzollern regiment in the Mark Brandenburg. Alongside Droysen, we should mention the historian Heinrich von Sybel, who was also the true founder of the *Historische Zeitschrift* (1859), a journal rooted in the ideas of this 'school' but soon to become the mouthpiece for German historiography as a whole. Finally, we come to the greatest of these political historians, Theodor Mommsen, who was an eminent research academic as well as an eminent historical writer. In the 1860s, he had a more strongly defined liberal political stance, while maintaining a greater critical distance in the academic sphere (although he did place the theme of the fall of the Roman republic and the rise of Caesar firmly within the context of the contemporary ambivalence displayed by liberalism, Bonapartism and Bismarck.). Indeed, he was altogether more modern in his interpretations thanks to his well-defined sense of the important role of the masses, even in political history. Historians of different political persuasions now practised the new methodology: *grossdeutsch* (demanding pan-German unification), federalist, particularist, Austrian, often (but not always) more conservative and staunchly Catholic. The clash between Julius Ficker of Innsbruck and Heinrich von Sybel on how medieval imperial policy should be interpreted fanned the flames of the debate between the *grossdeutsch* and *kleindeutsch* camps. The peculiar tension which existed between political commitment and research (critical in its methodology, with a broad scope and great intensity, 'positivist' even, and certainly objective) had a decisive impact on this period and the decades to come.

Finally, (3) the concentration on political history and the exclusion of independent cultural philologists from the 'academy' of the humanities led to a separate branch of cultural history developing alongside mainstream political history. This embraced the history of society, the realms of work, the economy and daily life and/or the history of thought, of the arts, of 'high' culture. In the work of Johannes Scherr, who emigrated to Switzerland, cultural history operated as a democratic history in opposition to the established forces. In Gustav Freytag's popular *Pictures from the German Past* (1859), it sought to present a liberal history of the citizen, of employment and everyday life. In the work of Wilhelm Heinrich Riehl, the founder of folklore studies, it represented a reform-conservative popular history of the old estates in particular: the peasants and the artisans. A quite different approach, though on the same rank as Ranke or Mommsen, was displayed in the cultural history of the Swiss writer, Jacob Burckhardt (*Renaissance Culture in Italy*, 1859–60), which turned its back on politics altogether and attempted to visualise the people of a certain epoch by painting a portrait of the life they lived, in all its diversity. It was a work which was not without influence in Germany. Nevertheless, cultural history remained on the sidelines of scientific inquiry until the founding of the Reich in 1871.

Within the short period of the early decades of the century, a comprehensive system of humanities had grown up and generated a range of disciplines based on historical principles. The development of art history must not be overlooked — once again deeply influenced by Hegel, and yet leaving him behind (Karl Schnaase). Nor should we forget the development of geography as one of the humanities, in the form of cultural geography (Carl Ritter). All areas of culture, which were once the terrain of enthusiasts and dilettantes, now became the object of scholarly attention, distinguished by a sense of history, a grasp and understanding of sources and a capacity to place them in their historical context. This growth in the sciences was a uniquely German achievement which was 'broadcast' across the globe, to eastern, northern and southern Europe, to the Anglo-Saxon world, and even, to a degree, to France.

We now take a brief glance at the sciences of the future: the social sciences of economics and sociology. Classical economics, the theory of the liberal capitalist economic system, was primarily developed and refined in England (Adam Smith and David Ricardo); the Germans took it up, and only developed it slightly. In Germany, the seed fell on somewhat stony ground — a national economy was far from becoming a reality, and in a culture of financiers and merchants, the role of the state occupied more attention. Karl Friedrich Rau brought the two strands together and proceeded to divide the discipline into economics, political economy and the econonics of finance. Others tried to restate the classical doctrine in ethical and idealistic terms, seeking to objectify the concept of value as use value, with the aid, for example, of a hierarchy of needs (Friedrich Benedict Wilhelm von Hermann, 1832; Hermann Heinrich Gossen with his two laws, 1854; and Hans von Mangoldt). These attempts also marked the first steps along the road towards the later theory of marginal utility. Of greater importance, however, were three outsiders who only later found a place in the mainstream. First, there was the landowner Johann Heinrich von Thünen, who, by separating out the factors at work in a concrete economic system, defined the concept of the local differential in ground rents (in terms of communications) and the principle of marginal production in *The Isolated State in Relation to Agriculture and Economics* (1826, 1830, 1863). Then there was the writer, professor, journalist and politician Friedrich List, whom we encountered in connection with the Zollverein, the building of the railways and the liberalism of the Vormärz. List showed that every economy was also dependent on social and political factors, that it was national, and that the normative validity of general laws should be qualified in this light. The assumptions of the classical economists about the international division of labour were, in his view, unrealistic (and, moreover, an expression of England's dominance in the international economy). He also emphasised the importance of productive forces in contrast to the classical concentration on production. There were consequences here for the political economy: the state should develop productive forces and should shield a nascent industrial system from developed ones by instituting protective tariffs. This was clearly the economic theory of a developing nation, and it was to be right in the thick of the 19th-century controversy surrounding protective tariffs and free trade. Finally, there was the landowner Carl von Rodbertus, who has a well-deserved place in the history of socialist theories. In investigating the value of labour, he discovered, analogously to Marx, the theory of surplus value, the theory of the diminishing wage quota and the indentification of economic crises as crises of under-consumption. He remained firmly committed to state socialist measures and sceptical about the revolution of the proletariat, and so remained an outsider in the new socialist movement.

Around the middle of the century, the direct effects of historicism were beginning to be felt in economic circles. The first, or older, historical school was made up of Wilhelm Roscher, Bruno Hildebrand and — of a higher intellectual order — Karl Knies (*Political Economy from the Standpoint of Historical Method*, 1853). According to their thesis, there was no economic theory which could claim validity in every age, nor were there any universal economic norms; economic institutions and measures were contingent upon a certain situation and were more or less appropriate to that situation. The economy was not a fact of 'nature' which could be taken out and subjected to abstract and deductive analysis, but a cultural fact which could only be understood through an inductive process which treats it as an individuality in the context of non-economic, i.e. historical, social, political and national conditions. The individualistic classical model of self-interest, of Robinson Crusoe alone on his island, of the *homo oeconomicus*, was insufficient; the motivations for economic activity were many, including ethical ones. Hence, economics was a moral science. Economic history, the development of 'economic stages' (e.g. economies based on payment in kind, on cash, on credit) and historical comparisons were fundamental to it. Admittedly, at first, all this remained little more than a programme and a polemic; a truly historically informed economics did not develop until the 1870s.

Before we list the leading German economists, we must turn our attention to the development of an autonomous social science. In the traditional thought of the old world, reflections on 'society', on people's social relationships and social institutions, came under the auspices of philosophy, politics, law and ethics. The double-edged revolution — double-edged in that it was a democratic and industrial revolution — changed all that, with its elimination of an essentially static, estate-based society and the development of a dynamic bourgeois society, with its characteristic forces of change, movement and process. The social norms of tradition and religion lost their power to unite; the doctrine of natural law fell apart, since in the name of opposing interpretations of natural law, people were chopping each other's heads off left, right and centre. This gave rise to the tendency to derive the norms of social activity and the legitimation of institutions, if not from history, then from the laws governing the structure and motive forces in society. Society now became the object of special scientific and methodological interest, which ultimately gave rise to the establishment of sociology. Germany was not in the vanguard of this movement, partly because it was not yet at the centre of the revolutionary upheavals, and partly because historicism offered an alternative answer to these challenges. Nevertheless, some very effective, albeit very specialised, innovations were developed here. Once again, and yet in a new way, philosophy took the leading role. In Hegel's system, the analysis of bourgeois society, the 'system of needs' (*System der Bedürfnisse*) was central, based on the adoption of English economics and the whole revolutionary experience of the age. Society — located between the individual and the state — was *de facto* dynamic and modern. The fate of liberty was played out in society. Hegel was the first to set out, within the framework of his system, an elaborate theory of society and its meaning for the whole of the human world; all the social theorists of the century were then obliged to address these problems. For example, they were implicit in the works of the early historicists, who, like August Boeckh, for example, cast an eye over the whole of the human world; they were explicit and ideological in the romantically conservative theory of, say, Adam Müller, which has been referred to elsewhere. Finally — and this is something which is often forgotten — the doctrine of public law in the first half of the century was still an all-embracing political science, whose leading exponents (Robert von Mohl was one) incorporated an analysis of politics and society in their works. Towards the close of our period Otto von Gierke appears on the scene with his theory of co-operatives, Lorenz von Stein with his theory of administration, and Rudolf von Gneist with his theory of self-determination; all these were instrumental in extending the legal tradition with the help of social science.

An indigenous social science began in Germany under Hegel's influence, with Lorenz von Stein. In 1856, he wrote *The Theory of Society* (the second volume of his *System of Political Science*). 'The Concept of Society and the Laws of Social Movement', the title given to the introduction to the new edition of a work written in his youth (1842), which in 1850 appeared under the new title, *History of the Social Movements in France*, was the first example of German sociology. Stein's starting-point was the social determination of political change, the interfusion of social being and consciousness (*Sein und Bewusstsein*) and the separation of state and society. He analysed the structure and intrinsic processes of the modern acquisitive society, based on property and labour. He also analysed the various forms of rule, the separation of capital and labour, the separation of the property-owning class from the class without property, and the struggle of both classes to gain control of the state. He diagnosed the threat to liberty and the individual posed by a society left to its own devices and guided by self-interest and egoism alone. Faced with the two alternatives in such a society, social revolution or social reform, he called for the state of social reform ('the social kingdom'), the social state which would steer a course through crises, harness capital to the principle of labour, and would realise and guarantee real personal freedom for all. In his later *magnum opus*, the *Theory of Administration* (1865–84), he was one of the first to conceptualise the state of modern subsistence provision (*Daseinsvorsorge*), and he used a wealth of detail to back up his thesis.

Alongside Stein, Wilhelm Heinrich Riehl appeared on the scene after 1850. His first work, *The Bourgeois Society* (1851), was, from an intellectual and structural point of view, incomparably weaker. It was broad, essayistic, plaintive and wheedling, and had a more conservative slant, in that the picture he painted was of a pre-industrial society — of peasants and lower middle classes. But he did enjoy a certain literary success, and he did have a sharp eye for the weaknesses of liberals and their blindness to reality, as manifest in their concentration solely on the constitution and the political sphere; a sharp eye, too, for the regional diversity of the German society and its historical roots. His researches and his writings marked the beginning of the peculiarly German discipline of a social scientific ethnology — German folklore (*Volkskunde*).

Admittedly, these were experiments which did not at first lead to the development of a social science. The end of a philosophy preoccupied with the 'whole'; the jurist's turn to positivism and that of historians to the primacy of politics, state and nation — or to culture; their successful defence against a positivist scientific sociology based on laws, like that of Comte, which had fallen under suspicion of being materialist; the shift of historically informed economics to look at social questions and lastly, the general atmosphere in Germany, where priority was given to the national state, the constitution, the church, and the conservation of human cultural values — all these factors played their part in putting back the development of a new, original and independent social science in Germany by several decades.

Lastly, the name of Karl Marx must be entered into the history of national economics and the new sociology. Clearly, Marx was more than just an academic economist and sociologist. He was also a philosopher, a prophet, a revolutionary and founder of the socialist workers' movement. In the 19th century, the only other figure who could claim to be of such central importance to German history was Bismarck. It was not only the effects Marx wrought which justify placing him within the history of science, knowledge and theory, but also the claims which he made, and the vision he had of himself. However, this is not the place to go into Marx's economic and sociological theories in any great detail. Brief pointers and reminders will have to suffice.

Marx proffered a simultaneously sociological and economic analysis of the capitalist system, its structure and mechanism, its dynamic and its development, and examined the fate which guided contemporary man and his foreseeable future. His central sociological insight was that the character of modern society was antagonistic. It was governed not by an hidden harmony among competing individuals, but, on the contrary, an opposition — by the class struggle between the employers and the workers — this conflict made up the fundamental problem of society and its dynamic. Society was based on inequality and the exploitation of the weaker members of society, not on equality before the law, but on the inherent advantage possessed by the owners of the means of production, an advantage which increased over time. As a result, classes and the class struggle were the central features of society. Indeed, so central were they that society was polarised into two basic classes which put their stamp on society, obliterating the other intermediary classes, or compelling them to face up to a critical 'either/or' situation. Hence, the struggle for political power was purely an expression of social conflicts, i.e. class conflicts. Behind this analytical description lay the insight that people have created social institutions and social relationships, and have set social processes in motion which now exert power over them, that people are the products of a society which they themselves have created. It is well known that Marx developed this insight into the social determination of man into the discipline known as historical materialism. Social being determines individual consciousness. The sphere of production was the economic and social 'base' on which all other human realities — state and justice, religion and morality, culture, etc., i.e. the 'superstructure' — were ultimately dependent, although not in a straightforward or direct sense. In spite of this emphasis — and in part precisely because of it — this type of sociological analysis is aimed at the 'totality' of social conditions, at society as a whole, in contrast to the isolation of individual spheres and facts. This kind of sociology inherited the mantle of philosophy and its attempt to embrace the 'whole', rather than the more modest individual sciences. To conclude: the situation of the individual was interpreted from the standpoint of 'alienation', which had been adopted from the idealist philosophers. It became a sort of universal key. The exploited wage-labourer and the employer forced into competition could no longer 'be themselves' (*bei sich selbst sein*). Bereft of property and under the heel of the division of labour, they were alienated both from their labour and the products of their labour. Indeed, they moved in a world in which, under the rule of capital and the 'cash nexus' (*Geldnexus*), everything — love, art and natural needs — became a 'commodity'. Behind this concept lay the peculiarly romantic, eschatalogical idea — as in all protests against industrial societies based on the division of labour and the pressure to achieve — that mankind has an innate tendency and desire to seek universality and totality.

Given such an interpretation of the social structure of modern society and the fate of the individual within it, it became a matter of the utmost importance, economically, to grasp the nature and the functions of the capitalist economic system. Capitalism was based on the desire for profit of the owners of the means of production, which was finally set free with the rule of money and fungible, anonymous capital. It was also based on the division between the owners of the means of production and the workers, a division which grew in importance with the rise of industry and the factory. From an economic standpoint, it is significant that Marx, who was influenced by Ricardo, but took an opposite line to him, defined profit (*Gewinn*) not as a matter of subjective description which would bring it into the category of morality, but as a systemic necessity. The 'value' (*Wert*) or, more precisely, the 'exchange value' (*Tauschwert*) of a thing corresponded to the average ('socially necessary') number of labour hours invested in its production (the labour theory of value) the 'wage' (*Lohn*) corresponded to the value of the commodity, in this case 'labour' (*Arbeitskraft*), i.e. the necessary goods required for the subsistence of the worker. The value of a product in the market-place, however, was considerably higher than the value of the labour invested in it — that is the famous notion of 'surplus value' (*Mehrwert*) which found its way back into the pockets of the employer. This was the economic crux of exploitation. Here the internal dynamic of the capitalist process, which Marx empha-sised so strongly in opposition to his predecessors, took over. The employer existed in a state of competition — which Marx described as anarchic; he had to accumulate and invest his profits to satisfy the laws of subsistence and maximisation of profits. Such an economy was informed by growth and the constant 'revolutionising' of the means of production. For Marx, this gave rise to a double-sided thesis on the 'concentration' of wealth in an ever-decreasing social class and the 'pauperisation' (*Verelendung*) of the masses, or, to put it more precisely, the proletarianisation of the intermediate classes and the impoverishment of the proletariat. Marx draws these conclusions because he assumes that there would always be an industrial 'reserve army' of unemployed, partly because of population surpluses, and partly because of the reduction in available jobs by technological innovation. What is more, this economic dynamic would inevitably lead to constant and ever-worsening crises, owing partly to the fact of anarchic competition, and partly to the lack of parity between growing production and available purchasing power (under-consumption). Marx interpreted contemporary experience as systemic necessity. Finally, the mechanisation of production — the consequence of competition and increased pro-ductivity — led to an overall narrowing of the profit margin (*Profitrate*), for, according to Marx, profit is not based on 'constant' invested capital, but on the 'variable' capital of the wage fund (*Lohnfond*), which in turn increases concentration, pauperisation and the susceptibility to crisis. In other words, the employers persistently revolutionised the means of production, thereby landing themselves in a situation which conflicted with what Marx called the 'relations of production', and which we might — to put it briefly — call the organisation of property and the distribution of income, resulting in an aggravation of class antagonisms. Marx then applied the results of his socio-economic analysis to a philosophy of history. The capitalist system generated the forces and relationships which would lead to its own destruction, and — eventually — to proletarian revolution, since they would now constitute the overwhelming majority in society. This represents an application and accentuation of the dialectic: the contradictions inherent in reality which here come to the surface would intensify and finally cancel one another out. Marx's sketch of the future remained singularly undefined: it entailed the abolition of private ownership of the means of production — which was, as it were, the magic key to the future — production would become 'communal', and the class system and alienation would come to an end.

Once again, this is not the place to examine or criticise the validity of Marx's economic and sociological arguments. Methodologically, these arguments have taught us to perceive and interpret phenomena more clearly — even if they do not demonstrate a logical consistency, nor have been vindicated by reality. In any case, the analysis of dynamic development and its contradictions, and the recognition of parallels between the development of productive forces, the relations of production, class formation and class struggle, belong among Marx's most important methodological achievements and innovations. The transformation of insights into reality by means of a very German radical intellectualism — the remnants of Hegelian claims to comprehend the 'whole', of the dialectic, of the mythology of alienation — and by means of a peculiar messianic belief in progress are unmistakable, as is the fact that Marx's politically eschatalogical will, his mould-breaking and unqualified value judgments gave him a shrewder understanding of the economic and social phenomena of the industrial, capitalist, bourgeois world than that of any of his contemporaries or his predecessors — the English economists, the early French socialists, or the German Hegelian philosophers.

To conclude this chapter, we will take one more look at philosophy, which claimed to be the one fundamental and universal science among all sciences — and whose scientific character has been thrown into doubt by the empirical sciences of our own age, either suspecting it of being coloured by ideology or confining it to the level of scientific and ethical theory. This is not the place to give a concise historical sketch of philosophy, either as a science or an expression of ideology, but we cannot ignore the strange paradox, which was so peculiar to Germany and had a lasting effect on its history: the dominance of philosophy in German intellectual life during the first third of the century, and its collapse thereafter. Note the parallels that can be drawn here with what has been said earlier concerning the history of religion.

During the first four decades of the century, under the impact of Kant, philosophy had a determining influence on scholarship and the universities, the intellectual climate and the direction of intellectual discourse in a way which has no precedent in other ages or other societies. In this period, philosophy was not only the *primus inter pares*, but the leading intellectual force which could claim, with justification and with common consent, to have the capacity to grasp the 'whole' and to make meaning intelligible or create new meaning. What is more, it was recognised as such by the other sciences, if not without a certain relutance. One only has to consider Hegel to get an idea of the widespread influence and domination philosophy enjoyed. This was effectively a philosophy of the Prussian state, and even the opponents of this or other philosophies, even non-philosophers active in the sciences, in literature and in public political life, came under its spell. Every intellectually-minded youth was attracted to this philosophy and moulded by it during these decades, even if at the end of this process he turned his back on it. Philosophy had a real impact, which is a truly remarkable fact, considering its enormous complexity, its esoteric language and modes of thought, and especially considering the absolute alienation experienced by any reader who has approached these works since then without the benefit of a specialist education. We are referring in particular to the philosophy of 'German idealism', the philosophy of Fichte, Schelling and Hegel. Initially, it centred in Jena and then in Berlin, where, from 1806 to 1814 Fichte, from 1818 to 1831 Hegel, and from 1841 Schelling in his conservative 'positivist' old age, were all active. Yet the impact of their work was felt far beyond the confines of Berlin. Why the century in its infancy should have produced such a concentration of great philosophies and great philosophers is not entirely clear. Such an accumulation of talents is, naturally, a fortuitous event, as was the appearance of a genius like Kant, whose 'Copernican' revolution in thought sparked an explosion in philosophical thought throughout the German-speaking realm. Along with the more general explanations for this, three specifically German factors come into play. Firstly, there was a marked theological orientation in general philosophical thinking in the Protestant realm, which, ever since the Reformation, had gone hand in hand with the rise of the universities, and the enduring bond between knowledge (*Wissen*) and conscience (*Gewissen*). This persisted in the religious character of free secular thought. Modern thought in Germany did not coexist or conflict with theology, but dwelled in the long shadows cast by the problems it had set, by the 'totality' it had laid claim to. In short, philosophy was the heir to theology's throne. Secondly, philosophy also functioned as a substitute for practical engagement in the public sphere, or as a substitute for revolution and the instigation of piecemeal reform and large-scale economic activity. The fondness for theory also had a compensatory function. It is no coincidence that the great philosophy, had its roots in the decade of north German peace (1795–1805), though in no sense apolitical, it was a self-contained phenonemon which only revealed its true political import later. Certainly, the rise of philosophy went hand in hand with the development of a specifically German idea of education, self-development and the cultivation of the personality through an appropriation of the world of external phenomena, beyond the utilitarian ethic of professional, economic or political praxis. Philosophy fitted in here, with its claims to 'totality', and hence its high status in the reformed scholarly institutions, the new universities. Philosophy was no longer a preparatory course but the epitome of all knowledge. The great philosophers, unlike those in the early modern period, in western Europe or in the late 19th century, were university people, tenured professors, and this was the basis of their effectiveness.

The layman must be careful not to mistake the content of idealist philosophy for a speculative tangle of concepts or for mere ideology — a risk inherent today in both brief and extensive expositions, since the problems and concepts of metaphysics have become so foreign to our way of thinking. He must be careful, too, not to miss the point that philosophy set out to analyse and understand reality. We owe it to these writers to make an effort to read as it were with their eyes, as difficult as this may be for us.

Idealist philosophy can be approached through the history of philosophy. It began with Kant and his critical definition of the possibilities and limits of knowledge in opposition to the old conceptual rationalism and empiricism. It had its roots in his 'transcendental' revelation, i.e. the insight that consciousness, with its forms and categories of perception, shapes the objects of our perception and understanding and the connection between them, and in his new critical foundation for human liberty and his rejection of the contemporary moral philosophies which were geared to utilitarianism. It was grounded, too, in his theory of aesthetic perception and organic nature. The idealists tried to solve certain fundamental problems (like the 'thing in itself' — *das Ding an sich* — that is, the reality which lies beyond our cognition, or like the unity of the multifarious 'properties' of the subject). They set aside the element of realism found in Kant and sought to show the unity of thought and liberty in the subject. They thought they could show, through analysis of the evident yet unrecognised conditions of experience, that, in the last analysis, thought takes itself as subject, and that our natural realism, which experiences the self and the world in the opposition of subject and object, is itself conditioned, and that 'truth' lies behind (or before) this division. Fichte had understood the world of objects as the 'setting' (*Setzung*) of the self (subjective idealism); Hegel, on the other hand, had understood it as being of the same order of being (*Seinsart*) as 'consciousness', as Spirit (*Geist*) (objective idealism). In his *Phenomenology of Spirit* (1807) he regarded the experience of 'consciousness' — in the process of a theoretical and practical discourse with the world — as the experience of itself in the course of many stages, which correspond, to a certain extent, to the historical stages which man passes through in his relationships to the world. Kant's critical delimitation of knowledge, and philosophy in particular, led, paradoxically, to a new and universal claim to knowledge made by a new metaphysics. Moreover, while for Kant the process by which natural science and mathematics arrive at a knowledge of the world remained his point of departure and central problem, indeed, remained his model of knowledge, and for him the foundation of morality and freedom (a problem which was thrown into sharp relief by the shock of Rousseau's critique of culture and society), the world of history, society and culture, and hence the sciences which concerned themselves with these, now took centre-stage. The idealistic interpretation of the relationship between the self and the world was displaced by the importance of the realm of objects.

This all may seem somewhat complicated. If, instead of starting with the problem of 'franscendental philosophy' (i.e. how knowledge and experience, how the world as an object of consciousness and experience, is possible), we take a more general look at the intellectual situation of the time, Hegel's philosophy, probably the most important and influential philosophy of that time, can be seen as a courageous attempt to resolve the conflicts and contradictions facing his contemporaries in their relationship to the world and in the multiplicity and contrasting nature of the various interpretations of life and the world which were then open to them. And Hegel himself clearly understood his 'system' in this way — as did his followers and his opponents. Hegel's primary concern was the contrast between the objectivity of reality, of the substantial power of the outside world, and the subjectivity of man, of his *Innerlichkeit* (inwardness) which stood in direct contrast both critically and morally to that reality — *Sollen* (what should be) stood in direct contrast to *Sein* (what is or was), was alienated within the world, suffered in the conflict and despaired of any resolution. What concerned Hegel and his system was the rupture between the self and the world, between finiteness and infiniteness, the split between the public and the private, between religion and politics, the disintegration of the world into the small and everyday and the vast and universal. Hegel's attempt to reconcile this must be seen in all its complexity. On the one hand, there was Hegel's desire to penetrate and understand the 'real' reality in all its forms; the fascination and pathos with which he sought to contrast reality with the arbitrariness of an enlightened, moralising and romantic subjectivity and all its pretensions; and the way in which he sought to contrast the substantiality of the world with the empty abstractions of subjectivity. He sought to rely on and face up to reality, and to take seriously its harshness and impenetrability. Hegel's system was the most powerful example of the conflict between of western theory (calm contemplation and penetrating insight) and the rashness of practice and its claims to priority, which never get beyond the arbitrariness of one's own will.. And it was for this reason that Hegel was the first philosopher to bring modern realities such as state and society, revolution and economy, isolation, the demise of religion, collective and institutional power, the emancipation of art and politics and the connection between absolute freedom and the terror of Jacobin rule into the realm of philosophy. On the other hand, however, was Hegel's realisation of how important subjectivity and its contradictions really were. There was an acceptance of negation: no one before Hegel had been able to penetrate and express to the same degree the modern experience of reality and of the self — the analysis of the 'unhappy consciousness', of 'alienation', of reflection, which for him were a huge leap from the objectivist naïvety of earlier viewpoints, as well as a strong characteristic of the modern world. Hegel's metaphors were still full of the modern intellectual, aesthetic, post-revolutionary and post-religious conflicts between man and the world. These two points of view are reconciled, much more than his critics realised, because Hegel's 'system' did not resolve them abstractly and once and for all by simply declaring them identical or achieve a permanent solution by a forced reconciliation; rather he resolved them gradually, in increasingly complicated stages which took into account the concrete world and man's historical experience of the world and its harsh irreconcilabilities; the self-complacency of objectivity and that of subjectivity cancel each other out. This empirical abundance, this worldliness, keeps the system of reconciliation and mediation from sinking into the mystical night in which all cats are grey. Certainly, at the end of it all (but no one can speak of the end who has not travelled the path) there was 'synthesis' as a higher stage of objectivity mediated through subjectivity, and there was his statement that everything real was rational and everything rational was real, a statement which has caused much controversy and can only be understood if one reads the word 'real' in its emphatically philosophical sense as the 'substantial' — that which corresponds directly to its concept — as opposed to the accidental, the decrepit, and to 'idle existence' — although the difference between substantial and accidental then becomes the issue.

Hegel's philosphy of spirit was the first great philosophy to raise the modern and revolutionary experience of change as a fundamental and lasting process to a central position in thought. The being of the world, of spirit, was movement, development, history — but it was not something which was merely added to a static 'substance', it was the very nature of being itself. The remembrance of history was therefore the indispensable path to true 'absolute knowledge'. Of course, it was no aimless movement, no 'empty' change, but one with a definite direction, a development and unfolding of the spirit using the terminology of idealism, and it was the philosopher who knew the goal: progress in the knowledge of freedom, which meant a world where man could be and was himself, for only that was freedom. The way in which this movement progressed, and the method with which reason analysed, described and understood it, was called dialectics.

Every object, every phenomenon, every concept could only be conceived of in its relationship to others — there was no substance (as in earlier philosophy) to which relations were added, but both object and relationship exist from the very beginning. There were tensions, contrasts and contradictions within these relationships which drove reality and thought forward. It is true that this model, if seen in terms of the eternal triad of thesis, antithesis and synthesis, could revert to an empty schematicism with which anything could be proved; but the potential for an analysis of human experience and of the world of history and culture — in short, that which Hegel called objective spirit — could not be overlooked. Added to the connection between movement and dialectic was the system in which Hegel related everything to the whole. Every phenomenon could only be recognised within the general view of the world and its movement — truth was the 'whole' — and all partial truths, those with which finite knowledge was primarily concerned, were to that extent untrue, and any contradiction could only be resolved by looking to the whole. It was this which constituted the hybris of such a demand, the holism which made the 'whole' the sole criterion of truth and guaranteed its irrefutibility; but it also constituted the scope and energy of the system, a system which incorporated everything in one truly philosophical whole.

Finally, Hegel's system, in accordance with its ideals and its comprehension of a moving reality, provided an answer to three central problems of the age. Hegel was the universal philosopher, the philosopher who sought to resolve the great problems of his age from a single starting-point. Hegel's philosophy sought to close the gap between faith and knowledge. It was philosophical theology, the dissolution of Christian values into a rational conception of being and the world and of self-determination. In this way the Enlightenment's moralistic restriction of Christianity could be cast off in two different ways — the first, by turning Christianity into a metaphysical doctrine of reconciliation (like philosophy), and the second — following the trend of all German intellectual movement since classicism — by expanding morality from the simple individual and social morality of Kant and the Enlightenment to a whole ethics of culture and community, in which the participation in the intellectual process of world history, in the workings of the intellect and of education, in the great institutions and communities of life (such as the state and later the nation) became a moral duty for the citizen. Thus, Hegel sought to mediate between society and the individual (without sacrificing the individual, although later critics claimed he had done so), between individual, society and the state, between revolution and tradition, past and future, progress and stability, and between law and individual freedom. This is not the place to recount or contribute to the endless debate which has raged since Hegel's death over his political philosophy. Hegel may well have placed the state as a 'system of morality', as a state of a rational bureaucracy at the very centre of his political philosophy, but that did not mean that he was a forerunner or a supporter of later authoritarian ideologies (and certainly not of a nation-state ideology) or totalitarianism. Neither was he the court philosopher of the restoration or period of reaction in Prussia, although he was certainly no champion of democratic or liberal revolution and progressiveness. Throughout his life he was driven as much by the ideals of freedom and emancipation of the French Revolution as by the knowledge that they had reverted to dictatorship and the Terror; he was fully aware of the new alienated and antagonistic class system, and of the danger this new system might hold for freedom, and he was sceptical about its ability for self-determination. All these were very real reasons for his very realistic thinking about the modern state. He sought to fight against the dangers both revolution and restoration by advocating freedom as the essence of the law. But once again, what he offered was reconciliation of contemporary conflicts. In a unique way, Hegel's philosophy was a philosophy of completion and of fulfilment: of the consensus of philosophy with the progress of history, the progress of the world spirit and its goal — a goal which was the *Zu-Sich-Selbst-Kommen* ('the coming to a knowledge of one's self') of God; the progress in the knowledge of freedom. It was a philosophy filled with the knowledge that the goal could be achieved through philosophy and that the way of the world had meaning. Hegelian philosophy was both the philosophy of the crisis of modernity (of alienation and conflict) and the attempt to resolve it. It was the synthesis of the universal knowledge of reason with the modern conditions in the world; and it was the 'putting to rest' (*Zur-Ruhe-Stellen*) of the universal movement of the spirit. Herein lay its enormous attraction: not to be just anywhere, but at the peak of history and of time, and to be able to express the age and the results of history in thought. This particular feeling and the growing disquiet about what would come afterwards characterised the intellectual situation at the time of and immediately following Hegel's death in 1831.

After Hegel's death, his followers split into the 'Young Hegelians' and the 'Old Hegelians' (the 'Left' and 'Right' Hegelians), and this was to shape intellectual debate during the 1830s and early 1840s. What was important for history in general was the collapse of the Hegelian or, more generally, idealistic philosophy of a 'system' and 'mediation', as well as the break of contemporary consciousness with philosophy as an universal science which determined a person's interpretation of life and the world. It came primarily from the 'Young Hegelian' revolt against the 'system' and the 'whole', against the identity of reason and reality, the specificity of individual and the generality of concept and idea. It was a revolt in the name of 'real', sensory, material and existential reality, in the name of a reality which no longer stood in the light of freedom but in the shadow of alienation, which could no longer be reconciled or mediated, but was seen as contradictory and disunited, and which first Feuerbach and then Marx turned on its head. It was the revolt of unrest against the strain of placation, of practice against theory, and of change in the world against its (mere) interpretation. Hegel's attempt to comprehend history gave way to extravagance and intellectuality in contemporary thought, and the influence of the past on the present was replaced by the new importance attributed to the future: future and progress were the new norm, the highest authority of spirit — indeed, spirit became future itself. In place of the traditional religio-philosophical view of eternity were new substitute eternities, and reality and the world of the present disintegrated into contradictions. Hegel's great syntheses which had been so important for his time were dissolved. Indeed, it was precisely these which the opposition objected to so vehemently: the synthesis, for example, of Christian faith and philosophical and secular knowledge (David Friedrich Strauss, Feuerbach and their supporters have already been mentioned); or the synthesis of the bureaucratic state of reason and the fundamental principle of freedom within reason, the synthesis of a state and a bourgeois society based on acquisition, which Marx exploded, and the synthesis of history and a present which was a culmination of that history. Thus, part of the new philosophy became a philosophy of revolution.

Even if the explicit criticism of Hegel is ignored, it is easy to detect a rejection of the issues and problems, the trends and intentions of Hegelian philosophy within the political, religious, 'educated' and scientific thinking of the time — the turn to what was real and concrete, to the future and the individual, the turn against religion, the existing state and the supposed opportunism of reconciliation. History and art usurped philosophy. Less conspicuous than the intellectual debate of the young philosophers, perhaps, but a lot more effective was the decline of philosophy and the rise of the separate sciences, their passion for facts and reality, and their claim that it was they and not some philosophical system which could determine and explain the truth of the world. Empirical science laid claim to the legacy of philosophy and became an important part of intellectual life; along with the new critique of religion, politics and society and its advocates; along with the interest of the liberals in the social, economic and political world, and the resulting turn from philosophy to more concrete goals; and along with the aesthetic and emotional response to the feeling that philosophy had failed to offer any lasting solution to the contradictions of life.

Traditional philosophy lived on, however, in the popularity of Arthur Schopenhauer's irrationally pessimistic interpretation of life — but it was a philosophy of the outsider. Otherwise, philosophy became historical — the great works of philosophical history were written around this time (Johann Eduard Erdmann, Eduard Zeller, Kuno Fischer); or it was restricted to specialist areas (such as aesthetics or psychology) and was given the problems which the other sciences could not solve. Generally speaking, therefore, philosophy became a specialist science.

In idea at least — and in comparison with today — an overall scientific education still maintained a sense of unity amongst the multiplicity of sciences. In truth, however, as specialisation in the sciences increased, so did the problems of their contradictions, and any such unity gradually dissolved amidst a whole number of half-truths and an increasing fragmentation of the world and of knowledge. Scientification of the world did not lead to a synthesis, and this made German society vulnerable to ideologies founded merely on half-truths. It was Nietzsche, the philosopher of the outsider, who would be the first to make the problems and restlessness of the time one of his themes during the 1870s, and who began to question the problems and ideals of the sciences, of 'culture' and the *Bildungsreligion* in the light of the new concept of 'life'.

4. Aesthetic Culture: Music, Art and Literature

In the 19th century, art and aesthetic culture occupied a new central role in bourgeois society; and indeed, art and culture played a very important part in all areas of life at that time. The art world had its own laws, its own importance, and art sought to offer many ways of understanding reality and the mysteries of life. It also sought to establish meanings, and find ways of explaining them, it took part in the recent debate over the individual and the world. Art was central to an understanding of man's spiritual nature at a certain period in history, a mark of his feelings and sensibilities, his mode of expression, and a record of his experiences, a chronicle of how man perceived himself and the world. Art is not just a clue to this history, it is an agent in it.

Art acquired this new function, first of all, because the social class which supported art had changed. This is referred to as the 'embourgeoisement' of aesthetic culture, phenomenon that first occurred in the field of belles-lettres in the 18th century. Art broke away from its connections with the court and the world of estates, and from its close ties to the church, having previously served to enhance prestige and perform liturgical traditions and functions. Art also freed itself from its usage as a decorative and frivolous accessory at courtly and social gatherings, and became accessible to the general bourgeois public. In short, art became a fundamental part of the educated bourgeois world, art for the 'common people', as it were. At the same time, art was no longer merely an incidental entertainment, but acquired a value of its own. With the emergence of new institutions, which had arisen primarily for the bourgeois classes, and new modes of social behaviour, the role of art and cultural life intensified and developed a whole new meaning. Hence, a specific cultural life came into being, alongside the creation of an art, music and literature 'business'.

By taking music as an example first of all, we will consider in more depth how art and culture affected all classes of society. Music had developed from being predominantly a feature of the courts and the church to become an essential part of the bourgeois world. In the first half of the 19th century, music concerts as we know them today became fashionable. Societies and clubs organised concerts; admission was charged and programmes printed. Initially, only amateur musicians took part, and then also professional musicians and orchestras, who at first came from the world of court and opera. Concerts became an institution, not just one-time events or during the theatre holidays; instead performances were held on a regular basis, and a season-ticket arrangement was also introduced. Examples of this were the Leipzig 'Gewandhaus' founded in 1781, the Museum Society in Frankfurt in 1808, the Music Academy in Munich in 1811, the Society of the Friends of Music in Vienna in 1812, the Philharmonic Society in Berlin in 1826 and in Hamburg in 1828, and the Cologne Concert Society in 1827. In the 1840s, public concerts charging admission replaced the private concerts, which had flourished up until then, and professional musicians, who outside the state capitals were often still mediocre, badly paid and poorly prepared — frequently only with one rehearsal — pushed out the amateurs. At the same time, virtuosos were more in demand, and the travelling virtuoso and popular soloists became a new phenomenon of musical life. Paganini, Liszt and the singer Jenny Lind were the first celebrities, along with a good number of actors, to receive general public adulation. Such admiration was a strange combination of passion for music, a craving for sensation, and an effect of the cult of genius, which all served to compensate for a growing spiritual deficiency. The advent of the railways also helped make of such musical events possible. But one should not forget the role played by the promoters and agents of concerts in stirring up public interest in musical events. Music joined forces with private enterprise and became a marketable commodity, a development against which Richard Wagner, for one, campaigned so fiercely.

The second pillar of musical life was opera. Originally an activity confined to court circles for purposes of prestige, opera evolved to become a customary part of bourgeois life. The bourgeois public was no longer confined to the stalls, while the places that really mattered, the theatre boxes, were reserved for nobility and members of court society. Not just in the Paris of Napoleon III, opera became the centre of bourgeois social life up until the time of Richard Wagner; this is evident from the great opera houses of the time. The bourgeoisie now had a say in what the major opera houses put on, and the courtly aristocrats with their preference for Italian opera no longer held sway; historical and bourgeois themes appeared in place of those of the ancient world and mythology, for instance in the 'opera seria' and French grand opera, but even the bourgeoisie demanded tragedies. In addition, romantic and patriotic themes became popular, as in the German opera, which had been gaining in popularity since *The Magic Flute*, *Fidelio* and *Der Freischütz*. In the centres where opera flourished, people took sides, and all issues relating to the opera became news; the cultural battles over music, such as Richard Wagner's opera, which were so typical of the epoch, had their origins here. Germany's federalism and the number of royal seats with a court theatre and/or orchestra allowed opera and concert music to flourish; institutions that had been funded by the princes continued as such, or became public and state-sponsored institutions. The bourgeois cities, i.e. first Hamburg, Frankfurt, Leipzig, then Cologne and Aachen, and later many others, competed with the royal culture, and travelling operatic companies performed at many of the repertoire theatres. In 1850, there were twenty-three court opera houses in Germany and already about a hundred municipal theatres staging operatic productions.

The third major institution of musical life were the laymen's choirs and choral societies; these were particularily characteristic of the 19th century and represented a large spiritual and secular oratorio culture which today has almost been forgotten. A characteristic feature, especially during the Vormärz period, was the regional music festival in which these choirs would be joined by the local orchestra, e.g. the festival of the Lower Rhine region, which was in existence from 1818. In 1832 in Düsseldorf, there were twenty choirs and thirty choral delegations altogether. Both national and traditional, the musical programme of such orchestras was serious and comprehensive, a 'musical Olympia', as they described it. Such choirs survived because of the enthusiasm and endeavours of the laymen themselves. In addition to these concert choirs, male choral societies became a new feature throughout Germany, enjoying a widespread popularity and communal singing, freed from estate-based ties, flourished everywhere, e.g. in the modern bourgeois social organisation of the 'Verein' as choral societies starting from 1809 and then after 1815, and particularly in the 1820s and 1830s. Communal singing was at the same time associated with certain ideas, for instance the idea held by Hans Georg Nägeli, a follower of Pestalozzi, regarding the education of the people, whereby the culture of ordinary folk could be united with 'the rest of higher culture', the patriotism of the Wars of Liberation and the national movement, and the democratic, populist ideas of liberalism. In the medium of this type of singing, people of nearly all classes got together — in the words of one song, 'the petty barriers of the estates fall before the power of song'. Folk music which was both plain and simple, yet also evocative and verging on sentimentality, brought to everyday life a glimmer of a higher, more 'noble world'. Choral societies also spread from the cities to the country, and the regional and national festivals became in turn a part of the popular music culture. At the same time as the songs developed political tendencies, so the people became more politically conscious. The societies were an important part of and also promoted the principles of liberalism and the national movement, and it was for that reason they were at times oppressed, for example under Metternich's regime in Austria before 1848. However, in 1862 in Coburg — already a centre of national associations, the *Turner* and *Schützen* (gymnastic and shooting clubs) — these societies founded the *Deutscher Sängerbund* (German Choral Union), a symbol of the desire for German unity. It was only natural that the workers' movement too should lay claim so early on to this political music culture, and for a considerable length of time this important role of music and song was kept alive in schools as a part of the national popular culture.

Finally, it is imperative to mention private musicianship, which included piano-playing, (solo) singing and domestic chamber music. Music lessons and private performances quickly gained popularity as an integral part of cultural life in the family and as a component of a 'better' education. However, this development certainly had its drawbacks. Musical activities were seen as a symbol of education and status, becoming a convention regardless of a person's talent or inclination, hence the saying 'one learns music, because music is made everywhere' or 'the question was not who was musical, but who wasn't'. The 'young lady' who played the piano or who sang was a product of this vogue, and in its role of flattering social vanities or acting as a marriage bureau, music became contrived and perverted — a fact which E. T. A. Hoffmann had already complained about. A type of music also evolved which was part 'petty bourgeois', part *nouveau-riche* 'salon' music, e.g. opera adaptations, musical medleys, sentimental virtuoso entertainments, against which the conservative critic Riehl set the genuine, serious 'family music', although such distinctions do not really separate the middle-class drawing-room from the bourgeois salon, especially not in Germany. Yet in spite of such occurrences, the immensely serious and active interest of ordinary people in music and the shaping of the social structure through music were of crucial importance. Artistic standards of musical composition and the capabilities of amateurs had not quite parted company at this time. The spread of sheet music, particularly after the invention of the lithograph, including 'four-handed' piano scores of the large orchestral works, oratorios and operas, and an increase in the number of private music teachers were also symptoms of this laymen's culture and its very serious attitude towards art. Music was an essential part of bourgeois life, and it is absurd, as any comparison with England or Italy shows, to trace it back to the 'non-political' or 'introspective' nature of the Germans or the non-existence of a 'society' of the western European type. But certainly the facts that 'feeling' and 'introspection' were the qualities Germans liked to find expressed in music, and that work of Richard Wagner was at the centre of the critical discussions surrounding modern life and modern culture, were brought about by this broad musical culture, and indeed were the very basis that Germany was the leading country of a great history of music in the 19th century from Beethoven up until the time of Brahms and Wagner.

Further examples of 'embourgeoisement' can be found in the fine arts. The monarchy and communities decorated courts, castles and public places with frescoes, in order to bring art to the public eye, both as an education and a self-portrait of the bourgeoisie. Works of art were made accessible to the public, and art museums were founded from the royal art galleries and private art collections. At first museums were open to the general public, and later they became state-sponsored; the Fridericianum in Kassel (already founded in 1779), the Glyptothek in Munich (1816–30), the Grossherzogliches Museum in Darmstadt (1820–34), the Altes Museum in Berlin (1823–30) and the Alte Pinakothek in Munich (1824–36) marked the start of this development in the royal capitals. In general, it was considered that works of art were the property of the nation and that museums served 'the nation's spiritual education'. Especially in the second half of the 19th century, donors, art collectors and patrons established their own museums in the bourgeois cities, e.g. in Hamburg, Cologne, Frankfurt and Hanover, and in many others. In addition to art museums, history museums and museums of the history of civilisation were founded, and later, in accordance with the model of the Victoria and Albert Museum in London, arts and crafts museums, which were frequently established through the initiative of the bourgeoisie and their 'Vereine' (associations). The fame of the Germanisches Nationalmuseum, founded in Nuremberg (1852–53), was widespread; it was a 'national institute' which preserved and increased the knowledge of 'prehistoric times', a testimony to the historic and cultural orientation of the national movement, which seized upon art — and not just painting — as the ultimate expression of the 'nation's spirit'. It was out of a similar, though more particularist, spirit that the Bayerisches Nationalmuseum was founded in Munich in 1855.

Other public art institutes founded alongside the museums were the academies — the state art colleges with teachers were paid by the state. These institutes were not only of importance as educational establishments, but they were also a place where contemporary art was brought to the people through regular art exhibitions, competitions and awards ceremonies. As well as these art institutes, and partly as a contrast to their official, didactic and, at times, ossified nature, a new entity emerged which was characteristic of the century: the free art 'Verein' which was not state-sponsored, e.g. in Karlsruhe founded in 1818, Munich in 1824, Berlin in 1825, Dresden in 1828 and Düsseldorf in 1829. These 'Vereine' wanted to bring together artists and bourgeoisie who were sympathetic towards the arts; they gave artists a new status within society outside the courts and the academies; they organised exhibitions, sales of art and lotteries, and awarded 'yearly donations'; and they increased the circulation of art and contributed to the 'embourgeoisement' of art. Many new and different engraving techniques also made works of art accessible to ordinary people, although the development of the art trade as a marketable commodity was only gradual in Germany, particularly from the 1860s. As in the case of music, art education at home became the norm for the bourgeoisie, and occasionally even a symbol of status. Private art lessons were popular, and it is important not to forget the work of amateur artists who etched and painted in watercolours at a time when photography had not been invented. At the end of this period of time, with the advent of photography and technical reproductions, art was no longer solely a part of bourgeois education, but through imitations as well as kitsch it became a part of the world of the petty bourgeois, the farming communities, and even the respectable working class.

Sculpture also became 'bourgeois', to a small extent privately with plaster and bronze castings and small figurines to be found in all the best bourgeois drawing-rooms, but to a much greater extent in public. New parks and gardens were decorated with fountains and statues, and monuments were erected, especially in town squares (about 800 of them had appeared by 1883). Alongside monarchs and generals stood the giants of the intellectual world, beginning with Luther, Dürer, Schiller, Gutenberg and Mozart and followed by many more, and also the leading figures of the historical world who were deemed worthy of remembrance. The bourgeoisie celebrated themselves in these memorials to middle-class society, and the monarchy competed with them: Ludwig I built the Walhalla and the Münchener Ruhmeshalle, and the statue of 'Bavaria' became a symbol of a new Bavaria, the town of Munich and the *Oktoberfest*, and similar 'allegorical ladies' were erected elsewhere. This memorial 'craze' also spread to the countryside, not everywhere at first, but with several famous examples, i.e. the Walhalla outside of Regensburg, the 'Befreiungshalle' outside of Kelheim and the statue of Arminius in the Teutoburger Wald. In addition, and again a new development, an enormous number of memorials were erected for people killed in the war — in glorification of dying for the fatherland — e.g. the war and peace memorials for the years 1813–15, which ranged from Schinkel's memorial on the Kreuzberg outside of Berlin, down to simple marks of respect in countless villages. As well as the monarchy, the towns, bourgeoisie and *Vereine* offered various kinds of patronage, and occasionally — as in the case of the statue of Arminius — there were public collections of money throughout Germany. The wider popular appeal of such memorials, such symbols was their obvious and quite popular prestige value; they belonged to the tangible world of everyday life and especially to the days of worship. Many of the memorial celebrations (*Denkmalsfeste*), particularly those held in the Vormärz period, were primarily celebrations for the bourgeoisie and common people, and they showed, above and beyond their political influence, how widespread and how popular the response to this kind of aesthetic culture was.

The prestige value of architecture was no longer primarily the coin of the courts, but of public administrations and the bourgeoisie. This development was reflected in the fact that new town halls built after the middle of the century were often larger than practical usage dictated.

Finally, in the field of literature and the literary culture, the boundaries surrounding printed works without aesthetic standards, for instance in the press or commercial literature, become blurred; therefore it is sufficient to mention this area principally in connection with the 'reading revolution'. In this context it is enough to point to the spread of literature, magazines, novels, and especially poetry anthologies, and the increasing number of books being bought by the educated bourgeoisie. Literature played an important role in public as well as in private, in social gatherings and debates. Young boys had their family albums — kept in poetic and bourgeois style — and the young girls their poetry albums, ; the boys dabbled passionately in literary activities, striving to express themselves in 'verse form'; young people enjoying poetry became a characteristic feature of the educated bourgeois world. Of the institutions, the theatre above all should be mentioned here. Alongside court and privately owned theatres, municipal theatres emerged everywhere, often with the support of *Vereine* and various patrons, the first being in Mannheim in 1839, and all municipal theatres were eventually made permanent and subsidised. Gradually and with a few setbacks, a more professional management eventually won out in the court theatres; in addition, it should be noted that they were in general more independent than the municipal theatres, despite their consideration to the courts, as the town theatres were under more pressure to secure revenue and therefore were obliged to pander to the public's whims. Touring actors also played starring roles at the theatres, in the same way as concert and opera virtuosi, generating great enthusiasm; and at about the same time the job function of the director developed into a separate position where he became responsible for the whole conception of a performance, which was a new step in theatre. The theatre became a focal point of bourgeois life (even more so than the opera, which was performed less frequently), not only for its entertainment value, but also because it was a place where the meaning of life was debated and where the tensions of contemporary life as well as 'eternal' human fate were played out. The theatre was regarded as an uplifting place, a place where all human emotions were voiced, both true and false, it was a sort of educational shrine, a place of worship where a young person could go to see a performance of, say, *William Tell* and thus graduate through a kind of initiation rite in bourgeois culture.

The debate regarding music, art and literature continued to grow and spread. In the first half of the century, literature, art and music criticism became an accepted part of public communication in newspapers and periodicals as well as in social gatherings, and hence a part of systematic historical and aesthetic thought. The bourgeois *Vereine* nurtured this culture, even if they did not specialise in any particular area of cultural activity. Art played a significant part both in private and public education: literature above all at the secondary schools, which was reflected in the teacher-training academies and in the reading-books; and music in elementary schools and in state-owned and private conservatories. A state policy for the arts developed — Ludwig I of Bavaria and Friedrich Wilhelm IV of Prussia were particularly characteristic of this tendency — the idea of promoting education to the nation, even down to the lowest classes, through 'beauty', i.e. through art, particularly through museums, monuments and architecture, but also through theatre and music. It was this intention which formed the basis of art sponsorship, first of all from the monarchy and then from state, parliamentary and municipal subsidies, which went a step beyond simple patronage. All the great cultural buildings and the controversy surrounding the 'style' of public buildings — the most visible and common products of the artisitic world — arose from this idea. Art is not merely an accessory, but a vital, formative element, and for that reason, in a constitutional age, a topic in the debate about political ideas.

All in all, life in and around culture became part of the bourgeois existence, and to a certain extent it was taken for granted, it became obligatory, no matter whether one sought to follow the serious life or follow fashion. At the same time, there were groups within the bourgeoisie who were released or excluded from 'real life', i.e. earning money, the economy, career and politics, who played a special role, for example young people and women. There was an ideology with regard to the sexes, for instance, which inferred that 'higher things' were more relevant to women, emphasising their significance to aesthetic culture. Yet this culture extended way beyond the realms of home and the upper strata of bourgeois society. It should be noted, for example, that when Beethoven died in Vienna in 1827 not only were the schools closed, but 20,000–30,000 people followed his coffin. And as, from the 1830s onwards, monuments were erected to commemorate poets, painters, musicians and learned men, and as public celebrations for various centenary anniversaries began to become common, this widespread response was shown again and again, until its culmination in the Schiller celebration of 1859, which was sc popular that it reached all levels of society, and although it was certainly an outlet for liberal and nationalistic tendencies that politics had failed to satisfy, it was nonetheless a festival of national identification on the occasion of the anniversary of a great and popular poet.

So art had an unusually high position in the life of bourgeois households — at least this was the impression they wished to create — and art became an integral part of Sundays and holidays. Consequently, art developed a quasi-religious function; one can speak of the religion of art in this century. From the early Romantic age onwards, art was described as an object of 'devotion' and 'consecration', piety and reverance; and from the age of Wackenroder, concerts were seen as parallel to the church, and immersion in music or painting was regarded as analogous to religious worship. Museums, theatres and concert halls were presented as temples devoted to religious edification, as 'aesthetic churches': that was their claim and their function, to be a visible expression of art's sacredness. This subjective sanctity of art corresponded with the clear understanding that art was a being that transcended this world: art was a piece of transcendence; it became an agent and expression of the infinite and divine, of the absolute, and of the profound nature and secrets of the self and the universe, and art itself was unearthly, divine, ideal, perfect, it represented a higher sphere. In art man was able to perfect himself, in art he found the infinite and gained eternity, and in art, as in philosophy, science and religion — perhaps even more than in these — there is authentic truth. The beautiful was the true, the good, the sacred; in the second third of the century, when people were leaving the church, whether through faint-heartedness or firm resolve, it was expressly art which preserved, for this age, the truth of religion in itself. Art consoled, reconciled, redeemed, and it became a sort of idea of salvation. Finally, the artist too had his role to play; as a messenger and prophet of the divine, mythical and religious qualities were attributed to him, elevating the effect of the cult of genius, which was characteristic of the 19th century, even higher. A typical example of this genre was Beethoven, idolised as Prometheus, a revolutionary, sorcerer, saint and martyr, the prophet of a heroic gospel of sorrow and overcoming.

This, as it were, self-evident 'emphatic' concept of art took various forms, e.g. among atheists, agnostics or Christians, optimists or pessimists, and especially in the differing notions regarding the relationship between art and reality. Beauty could be an end in itself, and art, especially music, its own higher world, in which man lost himself in reverie in order to perceive some sort of perfection. Or art became the art of ideas, elevating and idealising reality and reconciling its contradictions — as, for example, that of naturalness and reflection, or that of the inner world and the alienated 'outer' world; art was a reflection, or utopia, of such reconciliations. Art revealed ideal truth, a true life purpose, however fragmentary and tragic it might be, and however much it might be, as with Schopenhauer, the emptiness of all worldly desires. In an increasingly 'material' world of work and service, economy and technology, money and power, achievement and success, art became a new alternative world, for religion alone no longer had the power to enclose or control or stand up against this 'material' world and to explain life's purpose. Art stood opposed to the world of profit, mediocrity and hypocrisy;

and through buildings and pictures, for example, art became a necessary and vindicating elevation of one's own already quite high demands, even for the modern bourgeois 'economic' citizen, who was orientated toward work, profit and this life on earth. The liberation of the individual, the dissolution of traditional codes of behaviour, the rise of the bourgeois world of work and capital, the weakening of religious ties and the rise of art to become a life-force — all these factors corresponded with each other.

Indeed, it was the great question of the century — whether the truth of art was the ideal, the idea which was the basis of reality and which transfigured reality, or whether art revealed precisely the naked truth of reality — that of the moment, of the individual — opposed to convention and sentiment, to idealisation and stylisation, whether the 'transcendence' of art was perhaps not found above and beyond the world, but rather completely within the world. From the middle of the century, and in contrast to idealised art, there was a growing move towards reality and realism in the communicative and fine arts. At the same time, opinion shifted as to which reality was 'worthy' and 'capable' of art, and certainly at that time art still had in essence to correlate with what was socially acceptable. Increasingly, however, art was turning towards a wider reality, including subjects which at first did not seem 'worthy' of art, i.e. 'coincidental' realities such as poverty, the world of money and work, and the anarchistic tendencies of people as well as society. Admittedly, this immediately created the problem of whether an almost naturalistic realism would not lead to content triumphing over form — which was, after all, what made art in the first place — and thereby destroying art's autonomy and causing the public to ask only rather primitive questions such as: what is it about, what is it representing? Towards the latter part of the century this problem led to the conflict between naturalism and anti-naturalistic 'art for art's sake'.

All forms of the emphatic concept of art shared the idea that art no longer needed to serve a direct purpose, but could be an end in itself. In this sense art was free and autonomous. No external power set its goals or issued instructions concerning it; art could define and fulfil its own standards, follow its own laws, its own essence. Art had no concrete obligations to anyone, only to itself, and at most only to the universal abstract counterpart of such obligations: mankind.

The emphatic concept of art tended towards the exclusion of entertainment, variety and pleasure from art. Art had a right to be esoteric and elitist, contrary to the public's preferences, and it either created or subjugated its public. A basic fact of the 19th century was that, in order to counterbalance the demands of 'high' or 'serious' art with its quasi-religious claim, an individual 'branch' of entertainment, 'light' art and kitsch was seperated out. Of course, there had been earlier examples of light entertainment, but it was only at this time that it flourished in its own right, and going beyond the old simplicity, the achievements of 'high' art were adopted and trivialised and sentimentalised. This expansion of the arts had a basic, close connection with a number of factors: the mass of consumers, technical reproductions, the incipient large 'market' for art, and, among other things, the function of art breaking away from estate-based, traditional norms, art's individualisation and its new multi-faceted nature. In the elitist society of estates, art had come under the controlling influence of artists and those who understood art, but in a 'democratised' and individualistic public and with an increasing number of competing 'producers', a need for light entertainment and triviality could evolve autonomously, and this situation arose when such factors were excluded from 'serious' art. Another factor was that the period no longer had a formative style — not even one that guided the mediocre — and, therefore, no possible adequate pre-ordained ritualistic expression of feeling. Without such fixed forms, this feeling, which increased as life became more individualised and which differentiated further outside of the upper and educated social classes, manifested itself as a need for sentimentality. Characteristic of this was the emergence of 'light' entertaining music and salon music, which were closely related to folk and dance music, yet were more refined, full of effects, more virtuoso, complaisant, imitative and often conventional and insubstantial, importunate, sentimental, wheedling, and squeezing every drop of 'sweet sensuality' from the music. The two successes of 'light entertainment' in the 1850, and 1860s came from this music, the Parisian operetta of the brilliant Offenbach, still in the shadow of the grand opera, and the Vienna waltzes from the king of waltz, Johann Strauss. In literature, 'mere' entertainment and adventure novels were more sharply divided from 'highbrow' narrative works, and in Germany more so than, for example, in England, e.g. Dickens. In painting, the adoption of bourgeois principles led to the spread of kitsch, e.g. decorating a room with one or more pictures, new reproduction techniques, the flourishing of genre painting, and, as in the late Nazarene style, the sentimentalisation of religious painting. Of course, there were wide areas of overlap between 'light' and 'serious' art, and the audiences for both 'sectors' were by no means completely different — a complete separation of ways is always a slow and irregular process. For example, the theatre was still regarded as an educational temple, a discussion forum and a place for entertainment all rolled into one; even when Goethe was a theatre director, only about a tenth of the productions were classical (Shakespeare, Lessing, Schiller and Goethe), and so it remained during this period. The border between serious and entertaining novels remained fluid, as in many serialised novels. In the first half of the 19th century, concert programmes were still varied, there was a sprinkling of opera, virtuoso and salon pieces, the basic principle of 'variety' prevailed, and the order of pieces was in medley format. Very often only a few individual movements of great works were played, or they were split up; for example, in the original performance of Schubert's posthumous Symphony in C major the order of movements was 'lightened up' by the addition of a Donizetti aria, and it was only from the middle of the century that musical scores became quite serious and orientated around complete works.

As art's function and purpose altered, so did the role of the artist. In the old world of estates and court, for instance, musicians or painters had a set function in society; they were skilled craftsmen employed by the church, monarchy or aristocracy, and principally they were assigned tasks and given commissions; they played music or painted for society's benefit within a framework of pre-ordained rules, even if they did overstep those rules. In general, artists grew up in an artisan family, and then moved through no actual 'choice' into an artistic trade, where they received an education of sorts, learning painstakingly and by heart the canonised 'craft' of their art at that time. In the emergent bourgeois society, and according to art's new concepts, the artist was 'emancipated', liberated from a structured society of estates and its ensuing order of rank and position, and he became a free individual, opposed to and isolated from society, which in the 19th century was also true for those individuals who earned their living as 'officials' of art — e.g. as professors and

Kapellmeister — or for the numerous painters who lived from the commissions of their noble rulers. Poets and writers were less and less bound to rank and office, yet it was only in the early part of the 19th century that the 'independent writer' became an ideal, which was also the standard by which writers lived who were in normal, i.e. official 'breadwinning', positions. Artists were now able to 'choose' their profession (for example, one of the first among the great composers was the bookseller's son Robert Schumann), and they no longer learned their skills according to the ways of the old 'trade', but 'studied' at academies and conservatories or by their own methods. They no longer created their art, at any rate not primarily, for commissions or occasions, nor for a specific purpose, and not even to live up to the expectations of the public or, if they had one, of their royal patron. The artist lived in obeisance to an eternal duty, to an ideal, and to art, and he created for the sake of himself and for God, for eternity and the future (at least in the case of composers and painters) and for a distant, abstract concept of mankind. He defined his own laws in his own world, free from all pre-ordained ties to established criteria and symbols. In fact, the artist was accountable only to himself and to his 'art', and it was this singular responsibility to art which was so distinguished the artist, frequently spoken of as a duty to one's own genius.

The artist was no longer a tradesman, nor was he naïve; he became increasingly educated and interested in theoretical reflection. Philosophical and aesthetical reflection and commentary, programmes and pamphlets became important for musicians, painters, architects and poets, although in the case of poets this was not a new development. Schumann, Liszt and Wagner, Caspar David Friedrich, Cornelius, Blechen, Feuerbach and Marées, Schinkel, Hübsch and Semper were all typical of this tendency. Furthermore, from the middle of the century, a kind of literary stylisation of non-literary art evolved, including programmatic music, symphonic poems or historical paintings; thus music and painting required a literary, even scholarly background for their composition as well as in their understanding.

As a result of the new concept of art and the new role of the 'artist', artists emerged as an opposition to the bourgeoisie or 'philistines', as they had been called since the age of Romanticism. The artist, in accordance with his role and function, was a loner, an outsider, opposed to an ignorant, prosaic and narrow-minded society, whose conventions he shunned, and in so suffering, he developed another 'nature' far removed from the 'commonplace', with a feeling for the 'higher life', the divine realm of beauty. The fact of the matter was that since the age of Romanticism the very decision and conscious effort needed to become an artist already created a special position, independent of an artist's achievements and work. The myth of the misunderstood and misrepresented artist/genius was typical of the century, and the sensitive souls of bourgeois society identified with this model in order to distance themselves from a part of society which had become bereft of feeling and understanding. The artist also became a recognised hero of bourgeois life, because he was creative, independent and productive, capable of self-fulfilment and asserting himself above sorrow, disappointment, failure and having to prove his worth, although admittedly, in general, this idea of the artist only existed in the distant, literary representation of the artistic way of life.

Originality became the standard of the artist and of art. The artist's work was an expression of his individuality, of his view of the soul and the world or of the artistic realm, that of his individual creation, and it was viewed objectively, a specific piece of infinity or perfection. The principle of originality in art posed the typically modern problem of tradition and style. In the 18th century, tradition and the period style, at least in the areas of fine arts and music — things were changing already in literature — were marked by a supra-individual, objective guiding force, which carried along even lesser talents, and which, especially in music, provided a lushness and agility. The great and original works of genius were created as a continuation and restructuring of tradition; stepping beyond tradition or breaking slightly with it, but still remaining within it; thus tradition and convention did not present any real problem to the artist. However, this situation changed at the beginning of the 19th century. There was a greater call for individual works to contain profundity, gravity and cohesion, originality and autonomy, and no longer could a great composer write almost fifty or even over a hundred symphonies (as with Mozart or Haydn respectively). There was a heightened demand on the originality of the artist; outside of society and its pre-ordaineds, the artist is left to his own devices to free himself, to emancipate himself from tradition and convention; once the latter were no longer the fundamental basis of art, they became a problem. At the same time, for example, in poetry and painting the stock of shared forms of expression, symbols and mythology, and the set order of representative roles began to break down. This was a consequence of individualisation and rationalisation, of secularisation, and of the 'embourgeoisement' of the world and of art, e.g. Venus was seen as a naked girl, and His Majesty as a man with a crown. In the same way, genre theory, which divided genres up according to — socially adequate — categories of matter and form, also fell apart. Tradition and convention lost their stabilising power; there was no longer an integrated aesthetic canon, and 'taste' was no longer an unified social standard, but had become individualistic and diverse. The artist lost the unproblematic, naïve certainties of the old world, and directly experienced tradition became a burden; its shadows, the Goethes and Beethovens, grew longer, and it was a problem to be an epigone. There was a feeling that art was ageing, and its styles, form and themes seemed used up; under the postulate of originality, if tradition was continued it became trivial.

At the same time, it seemed that art was becoming historical, and the historical awareness already present in education spread to art. Art from the past was fully represented alongside contemporary art, and the present day lost its natural precedence and self-assurance, which had been undisputed up until that time, neither relativised nor tarnished even by the tendency to look back on the norms of the ancient world. The 'classics' appeared in concerts, in the repertoires of music played at home, in the theatre, on bookshelves and in museums, and knowledge of the classic works was as important for the aesthetical education of artists as it was for the public. Research, preservation and the presentation of art from the past became characteristic of the 19th century, as was evident in the professional institutions set up for the conservation of monuments, and the emergence of large publishing houses, confirming the widespread rediscovery of past works and artists. The new performance of Bach's *St Matthew Passion* by Mendelssohn in 1829, and its transference from church to concert hall, is only one classical example. Certainly a lot of areas remained explored, e.g. the baroque, and admittedly artists and anyone appreciative of art still had the option of choice. An obligatory reverence for all things historical regardless of their worth was not yet an established feature, although there were the first indications of antiquarian and museum-like attitudes. However, contemporary art did recede under the long shadows of history and eternity, its self-assurance was relativised, and the critical engagement with tradition was intensified. This created a paradox, for in using originality as a yardstick, this made all originality of the past equal, and to be original in the present day was ever more difficult. There was a series of answers typical of the century to this reformulation of the problem of the relationship of art to its time. For example, art was seen as an opposition, opposed to tradition and convention, to the schools and the academies, and to the court and the public, and, in the name of truth, ideals and inspiration, and was characterised by excitement. Many of the young rebels within art, if they were succesful, eventually became academic popes and tyrants, e.g. Peter Cornelius, Friedrich Overbeck and Julius Schnorr von Carolsfeld. A stronger reaction was that art became *avant-garde*, the champion of modernity, progress; accordingly, there developed a faith in the 'future' of art and the art of the future, a prophylactic against increasing trivialisation, which both Liszt and Wagner expressed with regard to music, and 'youth' became the new watchword. The artist who was ahead of his time, or who had been ahead of his time in the past, was the new legend of the century. A more moderate view was that art was an expression of the present day and wanted to be in accordance with it, but in this situation art always had to be new, and that was then the positive turning-point, that art advanced with progress to become 'better'. The renaissance of historical tendencies was opposed to all these precepts, for it went against its own time and reached back to the past, e.g. in the revival of the Nazarene style, historic architecture and the Palestrina renaissance in church music. Another answer was that classical traditions were adopted, as with Brahms, and then developed further in the style of the present day. Hans von Bülow's well-known characterisation of Brahms's First Symphony as the 'Tenth', after the, as it were, 'absolute' symphonies of Beethoven, gives an idea of the situation.

Closely linked with his relationship to the age was the artist's relationship to the public. His public was no longer simply a given; it could no longer be taken for granted that it consisted of the upper classes of society. The 'serious' artist had an uncomfortable relationship to his public, as his art was somewhat esoteric. He was able to address the people who appreciated art, the initiated, as August von Platen and the poets of 'formalistic art' had done. He could distance himself from his public, as Beethoven did by writing sonatas more difficult than his contemporaries were able to play, which deprived them of their social and entertaining utility. An artist could turn against his public with a gesture of reproach, the feeling of being unrecognised, as was characteristic of Blechen and Feuerbach among the painters, or with the feeling of being independent of the public and applause, as was the case with Hans von Marées. He could first of all educate and 'elevate' his public, creating and winning them over, as Beethoven and Wagner did. Finally, there was the suffering caused by the alienation of the artist from his public, as art became more esoteric, complicated, intellectual, *avant-garde* and pluralistic, and as the shared system of symbols and social values declined. Parallel with this were the attempts to establish a new understanding, whereby man could reach back, for instance to the ancient world, to archetypes, which were simple and recognised, historical, characteristic and national. The concurrent view that art should (re-)create the community was reflected in the fresco paintings of the Nazarenes in public buildings, the stylisation of popular life by Ludwig Richter, and the role of 'folk' songs in music.

Even apart from these efforts, the art of this period was not uninfluenced by the national movement and the new religion of the nation; art became nationalistic, or at least had a nationalistic tone. National themes were popular, for instance from the areas of history and mythology, and national elements and forms, e.g. the folk-songs and other folklore. There was a commonly held idea of the 'national style', which was sometimes thought to be the Gothic style, and national monuments were founded, e.g. the Cologne Cathedral and Wartburg. National memorials were of increasing importance, and art from the past was interpreted as an expression of Germanness and the German soul; and in the debate surrounding the revival of art, the specific Germanness or intention to arouse national feeling through art played an important role. What was 'German' in art was very subjective and very relative; for example, Weber's *Der Freischütz* only became a national opera through the results of critical interpretation (analyses of its treatment of 'the German forest' or of the music). However, art's new connections with nationality were decisive.

In conclusion, the aesthetic and social circumstances of art's existence created a modern pluralism, which was unknown until that time, the juxtaposition of art from the past and present, of divergent art intentions and styles, and the simultaneity of the non-simultaneous. Firstly, this created obvious conflicts and splitting up within the art world, which changed bourgeois society; secondly, it brought about a speeding up of the changes of such intentions and directions; and thirdly, it led to the advance of relativism against the claims of an absolute ideal of art. The diversity and fragmentation of the modern world also developed out of this.

The individual areas of art, to whose history we now turn, are obviously linked throughout by their own autonomous, aesthetic problems, and with artists' individuality, which cannot be understood simply as an 'expression of the time'. For our purpose, we can only concern ourselves with pressing developments which give us stories revealing the history of soul and mind, feeling and imagination, experience of the self and interpretation of the world, of the people of that century.

(a) Music

Music will be discussed first, the favourite art form of the Germans, which brought them renown like nothing else in this period. The music of the 19th century was primarily romantic in the shadow of Beethoven, who was both the last of the Classicists and the father of Romanticism; his image, as interpreted by the Romantics, dominated the century. The music was characterised by the high ideals and high-mannered styles of the most developed forms of instrumental music such as the symphony, the sonata, the quartet and the concerto. In both the explicit and the implicit aesthetics of the 19th century, music was no longer concerned with mere entertainment or emotion — it was an end in itself; it was autonomous; it represented the spirit; it was 'form animated by sound'; it represented the thematic development of musical ideas and motifs, creating a balanced order within the context of works in several movements. It was a world of the spirit and of the absolute, a world which was self-contained and structured, where the listener was called upon to understand and decipher its meaning. Only through listening (silently) to such a world would man be able to arrive at freedom and autonomy; only then would he truly be able to value himself — that was the classical and humanist function of music. At the same time, music represented another world, which — even if it was no longer supposed to be the expression of specific emotional effects — was centred around the emotions and the soul; it was filled with tension and resolution, passion and calm, intensity, pathos, conflict; it was filled with gravity and legerity, sorrow and joy. Music brought about a new, heightened and passionate awareness of life. It excited man and edified him; in this sense, too, it was sublime. The great music of Beethoven embodied both of these worlds for the 19th century: the spirit as resonant form and the soul, emotion, grief and heroic pathos. And it was able to combine both these aspects: to subdue chaos through the use of form and create cosmos. Music for the romantics, especially instrumental music, was the key to the innermost secrets of the world and the universe; it was the key to the beyond, to the infinite and the transcendental.

During the period under review music became more and more romantic. Melody, harmony, rhythm and tone colour became more complex, more differentiated, freer and took on greater importance. For example, the timbre of each instrument and of the orchestra developed an importance and 'magic' of their own. The syntax of music — periods (e.g. four-measure phrases) and dominant-tonic harmony — began to lose its stability. The character and spirit of music began to change. Goethe's 'infinite, explosive and overwhelming yearning and restlessness' would come to dominate — dark and mysterious elements, elements of the extreme, the bisected, the unlimited, the fluid, and the fantastic as opposed to the control, clarity, definition and lucidity of classicism. Lyricism, melody coupled with specific harmony, gained in importance, and music became more contemplative. Mood and contrasts in mood began to dominate. Music became — as the doctrine had it — poetic. This meant that classical form, the practice of developing and contrasting themes and the thematic relationship between the various movements of a work slowly became problematic. In his highly reflective later works, where the heroicism of his earlier works no longer dominated, Beethoven pushed abstraction and lyricism to a new esotericism. He freely experimented with new and different formal solutions, without dissolving form altogether. Thereafter, with the rise of the lyric and idiosyncratic — sometimes with the sense that the classical models were outmoded — there was a relaxation in form. Form became secondary to content, to theme, mood and narrative sequence. Freedom of feeling and imagination shattered the discipline of form, and form became hidden and merely schematic. The classical development of a theme or a motif was often replaced by juxtaposing different sounds and lyrical periods. The lyric piano or character pieces which relativised sonata form — those of Schumann, for example — with their pregnant motifs, their literary and esoteric themes and their lyricism, were typical of the 19th century. The same loosening of form could be found in large instrumental works such as the symphony. Schubert, in his last two great symphonies, was able successfully to combine both tendencies, lyricism and form, in very unconventional ways. Brahms was also able to preserve classical form against the overwhelming flood of subjectivity and even combine the two, while remaining decisively modern in other aspects, such as the use of motifs and a greater harshness in melody and harmony. Liszt, on the other hand, following Berlioz, thought that the possibilities of classical form had been exhausted, and he propagated and developed programme music and the symphonic tone-poem (and thereby introduced a new *Bildungsmusik* based on literary themes). While the minor composers of early romanticism, such as Spohr, Loewe and Lortzing, were able to achieve a certain acceptability with their music of compromise, this possibility disappeared as the problem of form was heightened and became more difficult.

As form was relaxed, so subjectivity took the place of the objectivity of musical logic. Without the unifying element of large-scale form, the musical world became more fragmentary and transitory. Both these aspects corresponded to the changing view of the world in general and the position of the self within that world. And yet with the dissolution and relaxation of form came also the diminution of the reconciliatory elements of tragedy and conflict peculiar to the symphonic form, and which can be seen, for example, in the closing rondo movements of classical symphonies — the unreconciled became more and more pronounced.

With all its subjectivity and lyricism, romantic music became more and more expressive and intense. It appealed less to the power of judgment of the listener as classical music had done, and tended to overpower and overwhelm him, to transport, excite and intoxicate, to exhaust and enrapture him. That the classical symphonies of Haydn lost their power of attraction during the period under review is typical of this tendency. Music became polarised between the intimacy of solo and chamber music, piano music and the *Lied* (that supreme romantic combination of poetry and independent music, whose every detail is worked out and carefully placed within the composition as a whole), and the monumentality of orchestral music, of supreme pathos, the ecstasy of passion and excitement — and often associated with this — of virtuosity and great effect. It was especially in the intimacy but also in the monumental pathos that the basic feeling of melancholy in the 19th century — which has since become an inevitable part of our world — the melancholy of Schubert, the feeling of grief and pain and of unreconciled conflict, can be seen. The radiant, the effervescent, the vigorously or serenely emotional elements in this music often — though by no means always — only seem to have been forced from out of this basic melancholic mood. The contrast between the lyrical intimacy and monumental pathos of the music, between the individual soul and the huge mass of public, remains one of the main sources of its tension. This contrast is typical of the emotional situation of society in general, of the polarity of inwardness and pathos, of isolation and community, of intensification of emotion and ambivalence, spiritual climax and instability, of melancholy and change. And it is astonishing that after 1848 music remained completely unaffected by the *Zeitgeist* of realism; indeed, it took on a compensatory role as a means of expressing and describing the range of emotions in a realistic world.

Alongside the great instrumental music was another distinct and separate type of music — namely opera, which was associated primarily with the name of Rossini and consequently with Italian and French operas. It found popular support in Germany as it did throughout the whole of Europe, and was a complete music culture in itself — laying no claim to the high aesthetic goals of perfected form — in the tradition of the older divertimento. Weber's 'romantic opera' *Der Freischütz* was romantic in its subject-matter as well as its meticulously composed music, highly original in its instrumentation, harmony and rhythm, and, in contrast to the five hundred other penny-dreadful-like romantic operas of the first half of the 19th century, can be considered as serious and great music. Only later, however, would it achieve the status of a 'national' opera.

It was the creator of a new type of opera who would prove to mark a new era in Germany — Richard Wagner, the most successful and controversial musician of his time, who stood at the end of a period which had begun with Beethoven, and who would become the supreme representative of both his art and his age. Only a tiny part of the vast amount of critical reflection on his life and work can be touched upon here.

As a dramatist, Wagner wanted to create a new mythology in the face of the escalating detail, reflection and education of the novelist's art, and of everything intellectual and subjective. For this, he needed music, for only music as the language of emotion could lead the way to the absolute in a godless world. He also wanted to reform opera — musical theatre should be a work of art in an emphatic sense, not merely for entertainment or social prestige, a game, a mere effect (without a cause). By adopting the ambitions of the symphony, it would become the leading musical form; indeed, as a music drama, a *Gesamtkunstwerk*, it would come to embody the metaphysical nature of art. For music drama had a universal significance for Wagner, who was always intensely aware of the relationship between art and society. It represented truth in and for an age, and it represented it musically and dramatically — that is to say, it was not isolated theory, but a living whole. In this way it had a political, social and religious function, as Greek drama had done. It had the ability to transform mankind; it was a temple of consecration, a place for celebration, removed from daily life. It created a community and a common (national) culture in the face of the individualistic dissolution of capitalist bourgeois society. And by transporting both expert and layman with its irresistible force, it created its own public. Its success can in part be explained by this ambitious claim and its unique power to convince people that it applied to them; that they understood it and could live up to it; and that therefore they belonged to the spiritual, social and national elite. But what Wagner in fact achieved was no new nation, but simply a community of his own — how could it have been otherwise?

For his purpose Wagner used Germanic and medieval mythology in a modernised form. He used modern men, in conflict with themselves, self-tormenting — like Wotan — and the mythical dimension served to raise their conflicts, their feelings and their fates to the superhuman, to the point of pathos, monumentality, even ecstasy and to the restless longing and *Liebestod* of *Tristan und Isolde*. The romantic heightening of expression, subjectivity and emotion, the romantic notion of fate, and the desire for an ardent, intense and poetic fulfilment of life culminated in Wagner's work. These myths were fascinated by death and night, by the destruction and end of the world. They placed bourgeois life in tragic darkness and interpreted life and the world, suffering and salvation in a Schopenhauerian light. The combination of intensity of feeling, the prevailing mood of tragedy and a religious view of the world — leaving out the extraneous factors in Wagner's success — must have hit a nerve.

Musically speaking, beginning with *Das Rheingold*, Wagner adopted the thematic language of the symphony and incorporated it into his tissue of leitmotifs. Out of its logic, the form develops by way of a musical prose in which — in the wake of the disintegration of traditional musical syntax of the four-measure phrase — irregular groups of measures are juxtaposed to form the 'endless melody'. He took chromatic differentiation of harmony to its logical consequence in *Tristan*, endowing the music with a nervous sensibility, allowing it to rise to new heights of ecstasy and intoxication — once again, overpowering and sweeping the listener along, violently and bewitchingly — without avoiding, of course, the pitfalls of mere theatricality, hollowness, false pathos and excessive obtrusiveness of the leitmotif, which even the untrained ear could not fail to hear. But all these elements of Wagner's work corresponded to the imaginary worlds of most of his contemporaries. It was precisely in the pompous monumentality and artificial archaicisms, in the intoxication, the transfiguration of eroticism, in the metaphysics of redemptive self-destruction in face of a world consumed by lust for power and wealth, and in his irritating nervousness that Wagner and his work was to prove so modern, like no one else amongst the poets up to this point except perhaps — despite the many differences — Heine.

(b) Architecture

Architecture, as an applied art, is especially closely connected to the political and social history of a country, and even today it continues to fulfil specific tasks which have been set by and for others. More than any other art, architecture is part of reality, not an alternative one. As an art, it should express the desires and needs of a particular age; and yet as part of the everyday environment, it should also shape that age. During the 19th century, where symbols played a far more important role than they do today, architecture — and the public debate that surrounded it — was one of the most important areas of art, and one where aesthetics, social representation and political decision-making were all closely interwoven.

First of all, the different tasks of construction will be considered. In the pre-revolutionary world the central tasks were the construction of church and castle, and, in fact, during the 18th century everything else was secondary and subordinate to the castle — it represented a whole complex of rule and authority, as could be seen in the still 'new' royal seat of Karlsruhe. The strict hierarchical order gradually dissolved, however. As the populations and the towns grew, so more churches and more castles were built. During the latter part of the 18th century, however, and in line with the changing role of the monarchy, these castles became more intimate and more personal, even 'cosier'. They lost their element of power (e.g. Schinkel's Charlottenhof), or they became places for art and education, where the décor or the art collection took on a role of its own. In some cases, in the neo-Gothic castle at Hohenschwangau, for example, they would take on an historicist function.

More interestingly, other buildings became equally or even more important: the autonomous buildings of culture and education, for example — the theatre, the museum and the concert hall. They would portray the new value of art and serve its new purpose — to ennoble mankind. They became the new temples and sanctuaries, magnificent and monumental — such as Schinkel's Altes Museum, Klenze's Glyptothek and Alte Pinakothek and Semper's Galerie in Dresden. The theatre was no longer a place of social division, but something which drew the attention of all to the centre, to the stage (Schinkel's Schauspielhaus in Berlin, for example, or Semper's opera houses in Dresden and Vienna). In addition to this were the buildings of education, the colleges and academies, the schools and the *Gymnasia* — more modest, but still characteristic of these tendencies. Then there were the public buildings — some functional, some for the sake of prestige — the ministries and administrative buildings, the parliaments, the palaces of justice, which all corresponded to the growing importance of the law, justice and the legal process. There were the ubiquitous post offices, the city halls, the buildings of the bourgeois commercial society and the stock exchanges. All these buildings sought to visualise their public prestige. They wanted to be more than merely functional, they wanted to impress. Town halls, for example, were often larger than they needed to be, as we pointed out earlier. When the Ringstrasse (ring road) around Vienna was tackled towards the end of the period under review, eight new buildings appeared which would be used as theatres, museums and academies, along with three educational buildings, one parliament, one city hall, one judicial building, a stock exchange and a church. Finally, there was the peculiar phenomenon of 'political architecture' — such as Schinkel's Neue Wache in Berlin or Gärtner's Siegestor in Munich. And last of all, there were the architectonic national memorials, such as the Walhalla, or the Hall of Liberation, or the Hall of Fame in Munich, with their ideals of visualising something which was absolute and invisible in the form of a quasi-holy place.

These were the tasks of 'monumental' architecture, undertaken mostly by state architects. Living accommodation and urban development lay outside their field. The simpler normal houses were built by master-builders following architectural models, such as those of Schinkel. Urban development and growth eluded architects for the most part, and in some places there were simply no plans at all. The exception to this was Munich, and it would only be in the 1860s with the construction of the ring roads (around Vienna and Cologne, for example) that there was any connection between architecture and urban development.

Construction of roads and industry were similarly not a matter for architects. They were the province of engineers, and for the time being the two fields had little effect on the work of architects. The early factories and industrial buildings made use of already existing forms of architecture, so long as they were suitable, when the capacity of the old rural buildings for machines and the new working processes no longer sufficed. This was the reason for the similarity of many of the first of the early hall buildings to churches (e.g. the Sayn ironworks). Indeed, the technical functionalism of a building was often disguised by historicist and monumental architecture, so that the winding towers in the Ruhr during the 1850s and 1860s (the so-called Malakoff towers), for example, resembled a fortress. Railway stations constituted the other new phenomenon in construction, combining engineer-designed hall buildings (similar to exhibition halls such as the Glaspalast in Munich), with monumental architecture. They were concerned less with function than emphasising prestige and history, thereby serving as the gateway to the city.

Finally, there was one more task for architecture — the public garden or park. During the 18th century, the 'English garden' had triumphantly overcome the strict order of the architecture of authority. It represented the plurality of an artificial, well-planned but nonetheless free nature. It had no centre and seemingly no limits, and it was a place where the individual on a stroll could see things from his own perspective, and where he could pursue his own dreams, feelings and memories, inspired by waterfalls, temples, ruins or memorial stones. In contrast to the formal garden, it was an individual and liberal world. The English garden had a lasting effect on the perception of nature and the visible order. It became a public garden, bourgeois, even if the people who built them were still mainly monarchs and nobles. Since the beginning of the 19th century, the notion of a public park became generally accepted as a place where people could not only relax by walking, but where they could also educate and ennoble themselves through the contemplation and direct experience of an ordered nature. The park was an humane, edifying construction with a 'higher' purpose. The aesthetic idea of the beauty of a garden became deeply embedded in tradition. With the triumph of the English garden, however, the initial quasi-liberal components of such a model gradually lost their significance, and, in a purely aesthetic reversal, the elements of the formal garden once more came to dominate.

The problem of 19th-century architecture became the problem of historicism — styles from the past came to dominate the present and there was a lack of any common style. At the turn of the century, as throughout the whole of Europe since the late 18th century, architecture recalled classical ideals and the style of antiquity, especially of the ancient Greeks. Classicism, the last true architectural style, was represented by the works of Schinkel, Klenze or Weinbrenner even in the fifteen to twenty years after 1815. Simplicity, clarity and austerity, the proportion and logic of contrasting and complementary cubical forms, of the juxtaposition of the horizontal and vertical of the measured, architectonic, plastic connecting links (Schinkel's Schauspielhaus, 1821, or his Altes Museum, 1830, in Berlin), of the architecture of public squares surrounded by blocks of houses (Weinbrenner's Marktplatz in Karlsruhe, 1805-25, Fischer's Karolinenplatz in Munich, 1805–11) — all these characterised the architectural style of the time. It was primarily, of course, a rejection of the baroque and rococo styles of the feudal world, and its sobriety, rationality, moderation reflected the bourgeois character; later the (Doric) republican severity during the 1790s had a revolutionary character; at least it conformed to the bourgeois spirit, even when it was taken over by the new bureaucratic and monarchical styles. For classicism, the architecture of the Greeks was practical, full of character, 'sublime' and perfect in its beauty — a true and lasting ideal. For a different world, however, with different tasks, different technologies, one should not simply build a copy, but a variation, a translation based on a mastery of the Greek forms — as the ancient Greeks themselves would build if they were here today; thus Klenze was able to build a Greek temple for Walhalla with an iron framework for the roof. The invocation of the ancient Greeks in construction was more than just an architectural style, however — it alluded to the humanity of the Greeks, to history as tradition, to ancient truths. The style was full of ethical, cultural and political implications, evocations and associations, and education had been entrusted with the task of realising them. Classicism saw its architecture as a means of participating not only in the aesthetic education of man, but also in his social renewal. It sought continuity and permanence against the crisis of the age, against fracture and discontinuity. It was an architecture of ideas and of education, in which the visible building was able to point to something invisible, something which should command respect and fill the onlooker with a corresponding humanity.

This tension in classicist architecture between historical reference, contemporaneity and a claim to immortality, despite some of the magnificent buildings classicism produced, proved precarious. In view of the 'prosaicism' of the age and the acute awareness of the losses and failures of the revolution, the demand for continuity and the past and thus the significance of the monuments of the past began to grow, especially after 1815. Churches became monuments of history and of art. In a culture which was becoming more and more aware of its history, people were beginning to restore and preserve the various monuments of past ages, such as the Marienburg, the Schöner Brunnen in Nuremberg or the cathedrals in Cologne and

Speyer. Other styles began to appear and gain in aesthetic, moral and ideological importance, styles such as the 'Old German' style, above all the Gothic style, which had proved so popular with the Romantics. The Gothic style came to symbolise romanticism, the eternal, the spiritual; it came to symbolise Christianity and the Middle Ages, as well as the very essence, or 'soul' of the Germans and the bourgeoisie. Architects began to question whether beauty should be restricted to an historical form such as the Greek form, and — in a view that was both historical and anti-historical at the same time — whether style should not be tied to a specific age or a specific place through the changes in materials and technologies of that age, and through considerations of climate and the different problems architecture was faced with. Should each age not have its own non-Greek style? Even in his mature classical period, Schinkel was designing and building buildings in a Gothic style, and in the church at Werder, for example, he drew up plans in both Gothic and Renaissance styles. He even began to consider whether a 'pure' style could not be developed using the masterpieces of every age. Munich classicism adopted many Renaissance elements, as can be seen in Klenze's Alte Pinakothek. Despite the clarity of composition and the powerful structural logic, the Munich classicism was rather eclectic, taking Roman, Renaissance forms (as in Gärtner's Staatsbibliothek) or early Christian and Byzantine forms (as in Gärtner's Ludwigskirche or Church of St Boniface), and even synthesising them. Out of this grew the so-called *Rundbogenstil* or 'round-arch' style of the 1830s and 1840s which would last for many years and can be seen in the Johanneum, Alster-Arkaden and Alte Post in Hamburg, the Trinkhalle in Baden-Baden, and the railway stations in Karlsruhe, Freiburg and Munich. Schinkel's pupils in Berlin would also refer to early Christian and early Renaissance models in their works and attempt to develop them in modern ways.

In 1828, Heinrich Hübsch wrote a pamphlet which would quickly become very famous: *In What Style Shall We Build?* He answered the question by examining the tasks and circumstances of modern architecture in the northern Alps. Style should be 'functional'. It should not be 'educational' with historical associations and references, even though it should be justified historically and fit in with national tradition. The result was the *Rundbogenstil* as it might have been, had it been allowed to develop freely. Even if an architect did not make use of a past style, his style would have to be justified historically, whether as a synthesis or summation of previous developments. When King Maximilian II of Bavaria began his Maximilianstrasse in 1851, there was a competition to foster a new style with an historical basis.

But more symptomatic than the historical foundation of a new style was the question of Hübsch's title. There was no longer simply one style, or simply a conflict between old and new styles. There were numerous styles, and people could choose which one they wanted to build in. It was a totally new situation. There was no longer any overriding obligation to one style in particular. The whole of history was at a person's disposal: the historicisation of even the classical norm led to a relativism and pluralism of the traditional styles. This was primarily a result of the 'architecture of ideas'. If the 'meaning' of a building could not be physically seen, but could be found in the reactions of the onlooker, then the form of the building could become a means of representing various ideas, and could take any form whatever.

Alongside the attempts to create a new, synthetic style were a whole group of different historicist styles. Such styles were connected with the increasing importance of the ideology of their different historical associations. They recalled traditions and ideas which people wanted to follow, and they represented a whole range of different social symbols. There were also newer references, such as those to the Nordic renaissance (first apparent in the reconstruction of the castle in Schwerin in 1844), and these appealed particularly to the new individuality and subjectivity of the modern middle classes. Certain styles were associated with certain types of buildings. On the Vienna Ringstrasse, for example, parliament and stock exchange were Greek, the church Gothic, the town hall renaissance-Gothic, museums and university were High Renaissance, and the theatres in the eclectic style of the Second Empire. Or the clients would decide which style best suited their picture of themselves — the sober severity and aristocratic air of classicism, the respectability and chivalry of Gothic, or the pompous and regal brilliance of the Renaissance. The magnates of Silesia, who had become industrial lords, built their new castles in all three styles during the 1850s. In every programme of construction there were ideational and ideological tendencies — even the new style of the Maximilianstrasse in Munich symbolised something: the constitutional monarchy, the agreement between the king and the people.

It was above all the 'Gothic' style which had very close connections with ideology. Like classicism before it, it laid claim to being the only style — throughout the whole of Europe. For the champions of the neo-Gothic style, the Gothic period was the last period to have a style of its own. Indeed, it was regarded as the most perfect of all architectural styles, and one which, in an age which had lost its style, would be a worthy one to follow — a far more nostalgic and historical view than that of the classicists of 1800. The Gothic style stood for Christianity, for Catholicism and for pre-Reformation Protestantism. Or it stood for freedom in religion, for the middle classes and urban existence, for community, for the greatness, depth and spirituality of the German people, for their national identity, and it was a continual reminder of what was missing in the new age. By building in the Gothic style, people could reawaken and conjure up these old ideals — or so they thought, and different parties and denominations, even the different nations of western and north-western Europe, fought over the interpretation of the style. After building had recommenced on Cologne Cathedral in 1842, there was a boom in the neo-Gothic style. A huge wave of public protest in Hamburg in 1842 overthrew the decision to favour Gottfried Semper in the reconstruction of the Petrikirche and ensured the victory of the neo-Gothic design of the Englishman Gilbert Scott. The movement moved from churches to castles (Hohenschwangau, 1832–37, is an early example), town halls, post offices and town houses. Later on, the neo-Romanesque style experienced a similar revival, although to a much smaller extent as it was restricted to the construction of churches.

Historicist architecture therefore developed along two different lines. On the one hand, it was no longer a matter of simply adopting a past style, but of reconstructing it scientifically by means of art historians and scholarly architects. It was no longer a matter of simply copying details, but of following the fundamental and intellectual principles of a past style, which organised and shaped the different elements into a unified whole. Justifying a design was more than a simple matter of aesthetic truth, it was a matter of historical faithfulness and accuracy. By mid-century, people viewed the world from an historicist point of view. That applied even to antiquity, which further weakened its claim to supra-historical classicality. Churches were cleaned up — everything which had come after the Middle Ages was replaced. But restoration work such as this, the painting of Speyer cathedral in 1852, for example, or the reconstruction of the castle at Lichtenstein in 1841, are typical of the 19th century. Even where the reconstruction of a Gothic building and its 'spirit' was succeessful, the architects were no longer limited by their materials or their technology as their predecessors had been. What they achieved may have been theoretically accurate, but it remained purely abstract — it was simply 'drawing-board' architecture.

On the other hand, however, historicist architecture and its historical references were no longer tied to the laws and aims of the old buildings. Its various forms could be used at will; they became independent, mere decoration, pieces of façade which could added later. They could be seen as quotations or merely a means of creating an historical atmosphere or historical associations, like the Gothic disguises of many factory buildings and of engineering constructions generally, or the growing 'façade culture' of the large residential buildings during and after the 1860s. Sometimes they lost their moral-historical references altogether and became purely decorative. The most important architect of the central years of the 19th century, Gottfried Semper, who himself combined an early functionalism and an historicist monumentalism in his work (for example, the Galerie and the — twice-built — opera house in Dresden, the Technical University in Zurich and a few buildings on the Vienna Ringstrasse), mockingly criticised the eclecticism and arbitrariness of such historicism in 1854: 'The aesthete traverses the world and stuffs his herbarium full of his sketches, then returns home contented, in pleasant anticipation of that fine day when his order for a Walhalla à la Parthenon, a basilica à la Monreale, a boudoir à la Pompeii, a palace à la Pitti, a Byzantine church or even a Turkish bazaar.' 'Our capital cities blossom with the quintessence of every age and every culture' to the extent that we forget which century we are in; styles are 'begged and borrowed', they do not form part of 'our flesh and blood'. In 1847, Hübsch spoke of the 'architectonic carnival'. Historicism had gone wrong — it was a consequence of minute historical thinking. But it was also a result of the democratisation of architecture — of the new multitude of clients whose tastes were no longer bound to a closed and hierarchical society. The variety of architectonic forms, the juxtaposition of styles and the overall lack of style were all a product of the new competitive freedom of the clients and of society. Only now could people see that what was successful was not necessarily good.

Despite the criticisms made at the time and those made today, it is still necessary to understand the impetus of that historicism, in both its purest and eclectic forms. On the one hand, architecture was a testimony to the new-found self-confidence of bourgeois society. Their buildings were there to impress, for they were certain and confident of what they stood for, and the clients at least saw the historical traits as an affirmation of their prestige and their ideas. And on the other hand, architecture was an attempt to safeguard tradition and continuity; it was an attempt to compensate for the loss of stability and tradition brought about by industrialisation. The past was 'quoted' in order to breathe life into everyday life. Historicist buildings created an emotional base for society, and sought to introduce humanity into reality by evoking the past and raising it to an ideal — that had also been the aim of Schinkel, Hübsch and Semper. Behind the masquerade to which architecture was trivialised and behind that ideology that uses history to justify or condemn according to its self-interest, there still remained those two impulses conjuring up old ideals and compensating for loss. Admittedly, both the self-confidence of modern society and the conjuring up of a past humanity remained in a peculiar tension to one another — and it became one of the central problems for the bourgeois world.

(c) Painting

We turn now to painting, concentrating first on the subjects which were considered worthy of depiction. The traditional hierarchical classification and delineation of pictoral genres disintegrated. It was superseded by an art form which was gradually gaining an autonomy free of predetermined tenets. There was a shift in the balance of the genres: 'lower' types such as landscape and genre-painting were 'emancipated' and began to enjoy a greater respect.

Despite the trend towards secularism and the religious function which art in general took over, the classic genre of religious painting continued to play a significant role in this period. Indeed, religious painting was infused with new life in the work of the 'Nazarenes', one of the Romantic schools. Their aim was to overcome the disintegration and alienation of the age by returning to religion (specifically to a Catholicism rich in imagery). They sought to renew society and religion through art, which would itself be renewed in this process. The profoundly pious style of the early Renaissance was appropriated and practised by the collaboration of a community of artists based on the organisational principles of a holy order. Clearly, however much they aimed for a new naïvety, their lofty claims for their art could only result in a laboured and ponderous effect. Moreover, the attempt to resurrect the art of monumental fresco painting stemmed from a new reflexive and sophisticated religiosity, which took as a given the fundamental questioning of faith expressed by the melancholic Romantic consciousness. This type of painting also reveals another trait, which, like reflexivity, was characteristic of the century: the dominance of subjectivity, of emancipated feeling. Neither objective events nor objective forms were paramount in these pictures (leaving aside the work of Peter Cornelius for the moment), but rather subjective experience and the sensibilities of the soul. They portrayed, for example, Jesus' 'mood' and its reflection in his countenance, or the proverbial dread of the shepherds. Parallel to this was the presumption that the viewer could share in the various emotional states represented. Previously, everybody would have been so well acquainted with biblical stories that such subjective portrayals had been superfluous. Thus, a theme would be chosen according to its ability to arouse sympathy and empathy in the observer. Piety, pious feeling, the pious disposition of the believer and edification inherited the pride of place once reserved for religious artifacts and the objective truth of belief. 'I weep, therefore I believe.' With these words, Chateaubriand provided the world with a Romantic justification of religion. It was a sentiment which was also expressed in art, underpinned by the modern liberation of the emotional subject. In the work of the Nazarenes, the significance of bold lines and sketching (as opposed to colour), pointed to an intellectual demand for objectivity. However, this style of drawing failed in its attempt to cancel out excessive emotionalism. Even Friedrich Theodor Vischer had mocked the studied pseudonaïvety of these pictures. According to him, Nazarene Madonnas looked as though they had been brought up in girls' schools, sipping tea and reading Zschokke's fashionable devotional work, *Hours of Devotion*. By the middle of the century, it was quite clear that religious art had become quite cloyingly sentimentalised.

The process of subjectification is evident in a different and less problematic way in the approach to another classic pictoral style: the portrait. The portrait was a significant genre throughout the century, which was mastered time and again. Biedermeier was, in fact, the golden age of bourgeois and intimate portraiture. In the days before photography gave permanence and perpetuity to people and the very moment, the great culture of portraiture conveyed the century's spirit of individualism, self-determination, the liberation of the private sphere and the rise of the bourgeoisie. Family culture, so closely bound to modern individualism, found expression in the characteristic family portraits of Romanticism and Biedermeier. The differences between the portraits of the 19th century and the portraiture of earlier times are, however, even more interesting for the history of art (and human history). That the old world was a culture of status can be seen in its portraiture. The subject of the portrait would stand before the world, his class and his social position signified by an objectively prescribed bearing. His dignity and his inner being would be revealed through a certain ritualised 'roles', poses and expressions, and he would appear as a totality. During the bourgeois epoch, this public code for status disintegrated. This prescription for poses largely disappeared, preserved only for portraits of soldiers, clergymen and, occasionally, intellectuals. As stated above, people now had a 'personal status', they were 'private' and 'natural', individual and driven by internal compulsions. Pose and expression became individual and subjective. By means of this change, a stylisation, indeed a *mise en scène*, painters created a new, individualised representation (for example, Runge's painting of his parents, and Gottlieb Schick's portrait of Mrs Dannecker). The subject's pose might be carefully planned during the sitting, yet no attempt would be made to hide the fact. Alternatively, the pose would seem quite detached from both artist and viewer, subjects being immersed in themselves and their activities (such as Georg Friedrich Kersting's 'Girl Reading' or represented quite informally simply being themselves. Finally, there was the intimate (family) portrait of the Biedermeier style, which was not about status, and was the precursor of the photographic poses of the subsequent decade.

The actual artistry of portraiture — especially in the second third of the century — lay in its emphasis on the psychology of the individual. Artists sought to make the subject recognisable as an individual from the inside out, so to speak, according to his 'inner drives'. Indeed, they sought to enable the viewer to experience them himself, or, in the case of the self-portrait, to turn the moment of confession into a portrayal of feelings not normally put on public display. The nonchalant, chance moment (as in Menzel's portrait of his brother-in-law, for example) and the efforts to capture the essence of the soul were both facets of this new emphasis on the private sphere, yet in stark contrast to this apparent indiscretion, the expression of the true inner self was also concealed and restrained. Tact and discretion became new, individual characteristics, which were no longer a function of status. Finally, the image no longer presented a comprehensive view of the subject, but just one aspect of him. His relationship to the image, and indeed, to the beholder was entirely personal. The boundary between picture and beholder became fluid and at times would disappear altogether. A new balance was struck between photographic realism and the subjective perspective.

To digress for a moment, we might note a similar process of subjectification occuring in one of the few new domains of sculpture: the tombstone, now in all its artistic splendour. If one thinks of Schadow and Rauch, say, the mausoleum of Queen Luise, the tombstone can be seen as no longer a monument to fame or even to death, but a monument to mourning. This corresponded to the new significance bestowed on death, as mentioned above: death as the death of the other. Moreover, this mourning was no longer a subjective mourning that could be objectified through ritualised expression. It was the pain of individual emotion which still found form in great sculpture.

Alongside religion, the second great theme of traditional painting had been mythology. Despite echos in 'official' art (for example, the painting of the interior of the Glyptothek in Munich), mythological themes gradually disappeared during the 'bourgeois epoch'. In their place came 'historical' painting, which, in spite of various precursors, only now became a new and great genre of painting. 'History', said the Hegelian aesthetician Friedrich Theodor Vischer in 1841, 'is where ethical forces announce God's presence,' and is — in place of religious painting — the rightful concern of the modern artist; and the Munich artists remarked: 'We must paint history. History is the religion of our time. Only history is in keeping with our times.' The triumph of historical painting was especially characteristic of the second third of the century — from the revitalisation of monumental fresco painting (thanks to the aristocratic patronage and the Nazarenes), through the decoration of palaces, castles, town halls, courts and stately rooms, to the great canvases from Cornelius, Schnorr von Carolsfeld and Schwind, through Karl Friedrich Lessing and Rethel, Piloty and Kaulbach up to Menzel. This type of painting excited admiration and enthusiasm and dominated aesthetic debate.

Patrons, artists and critics alike acknowledged the eminently public and artistically pedagogical effects of historical painting. Moreover, historical painting was deemed to cultivate and form both a common consciousness and the symbols of that consciousness. The connection between art and society, the (re-)integration of art into a common purpose, appeared here at its most intensive and noteworthy. Naturally, art's recourse to history took place within the framework of the prevailing trend to accentuate history in other contexts, which we described above as historicism. Taking the pictures as a starting-point, two dominant forces and trends demand attention. On the one hand, historical painting responded to a need for continuity which, in a century of revolutionary transformations, was no longer self-evident, a need for reassurance of one's own national, cultural and human origins, a need for identification, and, at the same time, a need for historical legitimisation of personal desires and goals. The themes of national history were central: medieval Germany — above all in the age of empire, chivalry and municipality — and then early Teutonic history and legend ('Barbarossa in the Kyffhäuser' being a typical example of the politico-historical legend). Here, art and nationalism and patriotic enthusiasm, often tinged with liberalism, all merged, but the presentation and celebration of national history did not necessarily always coincide with the political vision of the foundation of a national state (consider, for example, the Bavarian King Ludwig I). There were other political trends aside from nationalism (witness the immediate fame of Karl Friedrich Lessing's painting of Johannes Huss) which inaugurated a new and, as its contemporaries felt, 'modern' phase following the the Nazerenes. This type of painting displayed an explicitly liberal and anti-clerical bias and was intentionally partisan. On the purchase of one of these pictures by the Städel Gallery in Frankfurt, a savage row ensued, during which the old Nazarenes Overbeck and Veit answered in their art the challenge to their belief in Catholicism. Alongside self-confirmation in national terms, there existed, especially in cycles of paintings, the depiction of philosophies of history which had universal human import. When Rethel painted 'Charlemagne Topples the Irminsul' in the Aachen town hall, its situation within a national context showed that it was not only intended as a representation of a heroic saga, but as an expression both of the collision of two epochs and of Charlemagne's 'world-historical mission'. After the turn of the century, Kaulbach painted some rather derivative pictures of decisive world-historical moments with remarkable success, (e.g. 'Battle on the Fields of Catalaun'). These pictures were designed to make visible the spirit of God in history.

In this style of painting, history became a realm of events and figures, wherein greatness could be experienced — fate, conflict, passion, mood, the guilt and innocence of heroes — and where this greatness could be experienced with much pathos and intensity, transcending the sphere of the private and the commonplace, in the knowledge that everything in the painting had once been reality. With the demise of mythology, only history was still capable of forging a supra-individual and coherent world of ideas. History became the great theatre of life, the stage on which fate was played out. Characteristic of this type of painting was a certain tension, the intensification of effect which gave it its sensationalist character. Similarly characteristic was the skilful employment of authentic historical detail. These characteristics ensured the huge popular success of these paintings, from Theodor Hildebrandt's 'Murder of the Children of Edward IV' to Karl von Piloty's 'Seni by Wallenstein's Corpse'.

Both trends presupposed, to varying degrees, a knowledge of history, and to that extent they could be described as *'Bildungskunst'* (educative art). To an extent, they wanted to promote such education, they wanted to teach — history became a *'Bildungserlebnis'* (educative experience). In time, historical painting turned away from the lofty claims which lay behind the original interest in history, and sought merely to satisfy simple curiosity about the past. In these paintings, history was no longer envisaged as it was in historicism generally, as an (educative) model for human situations which basically remained the same. History was no longer painted to suit an objectified canon of fixed emotive gestures and airs. It was rather the particular qualities of the time and situation which were of the essence. The image relied on a new type of relationship between the beholder and the subject-matter of the work of art. The new relationship was predicated on comprehension. Feelings, emotions, moods — in short, the subjective experience of the people portrayed — was frequently, but not always, represented. The beholder was invited to 'enter this world in confidence', sharing the experiences and feelings of the subjects, experiencing his greatness or his degeneracy, looking through the other's eyes. It all came down to the modern preoccupation with empathy. Along with the apotheosis of an intensified and completed historical moment, there was a tense anticipation of the future progress of history. Education and empathy had now become essential features of art.

As might be expected, there existed, from the middle of the century, a realistic counterpart to this whole style of historical painting with its national or broadly political appeal, its interpretation of world history, its staging of fate, its monumentality and its pathos. Adolf Menzel, in presenting the past in terms of milieu, mood and psychology in his 'Friedrich' pictures, was typical of realistic historicism.

Another dominant theme in painting was the 'landscape', a theme which also had relevance outside of art. For seeing and experiencing nature became one of the points of reference and one of the basic forces of individual existence and attitudes to life in the bourgeois epoch, together with work, family, art, science, history, freedom, progress and nation. An aesthetic, sentimental, often almost religiously tinged relationship to nature existed alongside the scientific objectification of nature, its techno-industrial domination and economic exploitation, and with its the growing separation from people in the wake of urbanisation. Art fed on this relationship, expressed it and formed it. The experience of the landscape was mirrored in the art of landscape painting. The origins of this modern relationship to nature went back some way, certainly to a time before the rise of industry and the city. The most important prerequisite could well have been the latent pantheism of the 18th and 19th centuries. God, divinity and transcendence were experienced in nature. Indeed, nature, wherein the self was experienced, was itself divine. Therefore, nature was worthy of worship. In addition, a powerful wave of Rousseauism — in Germany as well, perhaps especially so — amounted to a rejection of conformist, alienating, prismatic civilisation. Nature was to represent purity, virginity and intrinsic prosperity. Alternatively it could represent savagery and the elemental, as it did in the '*Sturm und Drang*' (storm and stress) movement. Nature and soul were aligned, they mirrored each other, in sentimentalism. The elements of the landscape became the bearers of emotion, where nature and soul became one. This individualistic and bourgeois tendency was, by the way, aimed against nobility, hierarchy, class and convention.

In the paintings of the old world — in the landscapes of Claude Lorrain and Poussin, like those of the Dutch masters — nature, with its predominantly idyllic human foreground and unified background, was a totality imbued with law and harmony. It was ideal and symbolic, unrealistic, referring to God and humanity. This totality was present in each and every detail. In the wake of secularisation, with the breaking down of barriers and the discovery of the depths of subjectivity, all this was to change.

At the beginning of our period, landscapes were a feature of both Classicism and Romanticism. The Classical landscape, with its well-defined order, its harsh, almost geological construction and stark contrasts showed the purity, greatness and power of nature. Nature symbolised the laws of the universe, but, at the same time, the antagonistic powers of pathos reflected the way fate and conflict touched the heart. In its greatness and power with respect to man — whose environment it was, after all — nature was a moral force, unleashing in him a consciousness of freedom and sublimity, and a consciousness of an heroic pathos in the face of this force. In other words, nature unleashed a feeling of sublimity (a concept Kant and Schiller were later to develop). Such landscapes were heroic: the landscapes of Joseph Anton Koch in the first decades of the century represent this new concept of nature particularly well.

In contrast to the Classical landscape was its Romantic counterpart, so magnificently and unforgettably imprinted on our memories by the work of Caspar David

Friedrich. No longer were the images determined by lucid construction, brightness and the balancing of oppositions, but by transition and change, darkness and the dominance of a 'tone'. New Romantic themes appeared: twilight, dusk, sunset, moonlight and mist, skies, plains and oceans, mountain peaks and the lifeless paralysis of ice. The landscape was no longer confined, but was limitless. It stretched out into an eternity beyond the image. Man is outside, exposed and always related to this remote distance (and beyond it). Nature was no longer the nature of the creation in which man laboured, nor was it sublime in the Classical sense of human struggle or moral self-assertion. Eternity, loneliness, and transitoriness now provided the fundamental tone (the symbol of ruins, for example); transitoriness was no longer compensated by the certainty of divine redemption, the certainty of eternity. Nature was now seen as transcendental, divine and unfamiliar. Yet humanity was metaphysically connected to nature; it was the site of greatest attraction, of the true, namely 'poetic', experience of self and world. To the infinity of the landscape in which the beholder might lose himself, corresponded the endlessness of human subjectivity; the prevailing mood of the landscape corresponded to that of the soul. Nature mirrored the 'plaintive cries' of an existence unfulfilled in metaphysical terms: forlornness and mourning for the world, pain and melancholy, loneliness, isolation, silence and worship — and longing. These were the fundamental tones of the new experience which individuals had both of themselves and of nature (and inasmuch as Friedrich was so often able to draw the beholder into his pictures, it could be said that he managed to capture this particular experience of nature, too). In short, this type of intense Romantic experience of nature gained a directly religious — revelatory — character; it was the experience of a transcendence which bound individuals in '*schlechthinnige Abhängigkeit*' (absolute dependency) and which at the same time withdrew painfully from them. It was a transcendence which no longer penetrated everyday life — as it had once done so unquestioningly in the old world. It was devotion to and an outlook on the transcendence and grief of world and self in the context of a developing chasm between the real world and this transcendental reference. They were no longer bound by the undisputed exegetic certainty provided by religious tradition.

The landscape painting of the subsequent period picked up on both these extreme possibilities. The classic-heroic landscape was reshaped (in the work of Karl Rottmann, for example) as an architectonic monument to the drama of geological history, indeed — according to the intellectuals of the day at least — it was a monument to human history ('Marathon'). Nature here was immutable; the individual had been exiled from it, but the emotional power of the sublime bound the observer to the observed. Outside his Dresden circle (Dahl and Carus), Friedrich's lofty claims for art were toned down considerably. The widespread sense of a penetrant and luminous infinity, the sense of a fundamental metaphysical emotion declined, although it did not disappear altogether. Nature opened itself up and became more intimate. Objects and motifs became autonomous, multiplied and became more tangible. Moods varied and ranged from pain to sweetness. Immersion in the overpowering forces of nature transformed into a bond with nature, into a 'pleasure' in nature whose 'poetry' stimulated the 'heart'. But the perceptual discoveries of great Romanticism were nevertheless incorporated in this style of painting. Nature was now a completely autonomous entity, no longer bound to work or culture. People (and all human activity) became a mere shell. Landscape became something which existed for its own sake, lacking that all-pervading sense of trans-cendence, and yet it remained interlaced with the romantically informed individual soul. The artistically appreciative town-dweller of the mid-century saw through the eyes of a romanticising landcape painter. Art informed the experience of nature because nature had been set free in aesthetic terms. Of course, in the flood of landscape paintings which followed, the motifs and moods became conventionalised in paintings of 'summer prettiness'.

All of these landscapes were authentic in terms of detail, but they were nevertheless ideal constructions, built upon a thought, an idea, a mood. But Realism was advancing on various fronts — among the early Munich landscape painters, in the work of Waldmüller and Blechen. Importance was attached to the unmistakable scenery of a particular area — Switzerland or Upper Bavaria, for example (as in Dillis, Wagenbauer, Christian Morgenstern and Eduard Schleich). Artists turned their skills to recording the features of mountain ranges, distinctive rock formations, and characteristic flora. Land-scape painting expressed a new consciousness of *Heimat* (homeland) and a love of local scenery. Nature was no longer primarily regarded as the realm in which individual feelings were reflected. Nor was it any longer symbol of the order of things, but was regarded as a purely visual affair. Of greater consequence was the intrinsic value of pain-terliness, of light and colour, and the capturing of the moment. Blechen, the only truly great German painter between Friedrich and Menzel, still took the atmospheric and symbolic character of the landscape as his starting-point. The moment of light and colour was for him the artistic means whereby the symbolic and atmospheric content took shape. For the emergent artistic Realism, everything in nature became worthy of portrayal, on the one hand, and yet the idea of a harmony and a totality of nature was on the wane. Modern transformations of the landscape — the railway, the rolling mill, industrial and urban landscapes, backyard and building site — everything which until then had been considered 'unsightly', was passionately seized upon as worthy of portrayal (the work of Menzel is a case in point). Hence, both the Romantic devotion to the infinite and the emotional subjectification of nature to a poetically tuned and attuned landscape, diminished. The central concern was no longer the coherence of the object world by mood, idea and emotion. Optical impression, optical coherence — line, light and colour — and the 'pure' object began to gain independence. Vision became photographically objective, and it thereby gained a new and unsentimental subjectivity. Aspect, cropping perspective, chance and moment now formed the basis of a new experience of reality.

The displacement of an idealised (and sentimentalised) nature and its corresponding conventions of perception was a gradual process. Even for the most confirmed realists, nature retained an intrinsic and irreplaceable value, even if this was different from the Classical-Romantic tradition. It represented the 'free' in the face of restriction and abnormality (as in the work of Menzel), or the 'true' and 'authentic' (as in Leibl), which the painter serves by painting the strictly visible. Nature could no longer be taken for granted. In particular, there was a focus on the countryside and the village. Both for the painter who had abandoned the town and for the bourgeois who bought his pictures, hoping thereby to be able to follow the artist to these landscapes, albeit only in his imagination, nature was presented unconventionally and, hence, 'truthfully'.

Romanticism and Classicism attempted to defend themselves against the onset of Realism. Feuerbach sought to preserve the connection between mood and landscape in his antiquated-modern figures. Böcklin tried to preserve the ideal atmosphere of landscape and subjective experience within a new mythological motif ('Pan in the Reeds', 1857). The nature depicted here was different to that of earlier art and represented a crucial stage in the history of emotional reactions to nature. These paintings were concerned with neither morality nor the poetic mood of the soul. Nature became elementary, magical and seductive. It conjured up terror and stillness, it was transcendental, yet anti-divine, and as such it was worshipped. This attempt at a new mythology is characteristic of the last third of the century (witness Wagner's compositions), motivated as it was by an overwhelming desire for effect at any price. This new mythology, however, suffered from a somewhat inauthentic and laboured quality.

One last 'classic' theme of the bourgeois epoch, was 'genre' painting — the depiction of customs, everyday social activity and private scenes. Taking up the mantle of the Dutch school, genre painting was consciously middle-class. It was the self-representation of the bourgeois world which desired thereby to determine the deeper meaning of everyday bourgeois life, its actions and emotions. Admittedly, the claims of this genre to be on a par with other supposedly higher genres was restricted on two essential counts. On the one hand, it quite consciously maintained a penchant for entertainment and merriment, anecdotes, sentimentality, busyness, and comedy. But the rigid social roles and rituals of old Dutch peasant life no longer existed, and thus many of the new genre paintings conveyed a sense of arbitrariness and fortuity. Secondly, genre painting tended towards the presentation of idylls, optimistic emotions, and an harmony which smoothed out contradictions. It had an insistent cheerfulness and rendered everything harmless. The parameters of the genre were fluid. If the criterion for inclusion in this genre is subject-matter, many Romantic, Biedermeier and even early Realistic paintings may be counted in its ranks. We will concentrate here on some of the groups within this genre which are especially valuable in charting the history of this particular outlook. Firstly, there were the hugely successful village and peasant paintings (Waldmüller, Peter and Heinrich Hess, Defregger). These pictures did not show peasants at work, but idealised and sentamentalised them as peasants in Sunday (or even salon) finery, hunters and poachers. Traditional costumes and traditional customs were celebrated in these projections of urban bourgeois fantasies and desires. There was a certain kind of idyll that took in both genre and landscape painting, especially in Biedermeier: it depicted nature as a state of contented and harmonious peace. People lived here in harmony and contentment, their naïvety and simplicity contrasting to the ailments of the epoch. God held this harmony together. Ludwig Richter was the master of this idyll: 'the contemplative and the edifying' (*Beschauliches und Erbauliches*). It portrayed the devout in small and familiar circles, bound to their region (*heimatlich*), provincial, rural, *volkstümlich*, at work, at home, on the land. Children, women and the elderly were represented most frequently — the children were naïve and touching, the women domestic. Backgrounds hinted at days gone by, the days of castles, legend and fairy-tales. Industry had not yet reared its ugly head, nor did the crisis of poverty come into the picture. It was a world without conflict. This style was hugely successful, albeit somewhat trivial, because it corresponded as much to a disappearing reality as to the bourgeoisie's nostalgia for an homeland in this uncanny bourgeois epoch. Moritz von Schwind had a poetic vision of nature, filled with figures from legend and folk-tales. The Austrian Waldmüller's vision, meanwhile, was somewhat more realistic. At the end of the 1840s there was a move towards social critiques (the Düsseldorf school is a case in point), but the mainstream trend remained wedded to the conventions of pathos and emotion. Finally, there was a trend towards the humorous, the scurrilous, the eccentric, the ironic and to caricature. It was a trend which sought to balance detachment with harmony, commonplace objects with the subjective perspective of artistic representation, instinctual emotion with reflection. It portrayed philistine narrow-mindedness, but in simultaneously fracturing and reconciling it, it was remarkably successful artistically. One example was Carl Spitzweg's portrayal of provincial eccentrics and the discrepancy between what was claimed to be true and what was true in reality. The more bitter and revealing work of the greatest German humorist, the poet and caricaturist Wilhelm Busch, is another case in point. He exposed the human weaknesses in the 'petty-bourgeois' milieu. His profound pessimism nevertheless did nothing to dent his enormous popularity.

The subject-matter of this type of painting was 'realistic' and less ponderous. It shied away from symbolism, idealism and sophistication. Everyday matters took precedence. In that sense, these paintings were closer to artistic realism and to the precise representation of optical reality which did not ignore minor details. Even the trend towards idyll made use of realistic, or at least more realistic, techniques — the use of light, atmosphere and space (e.g. Waldmüller), although it must be said that on the whole the idealist perspective overshadowed the realistic presentation of reality. The relative ambivalence of this type of painting (as well as the bourgeois understanding of reality which was therein expressed) became evident when its twin transformations in the last third of the century are considered. On the one hand, it culminated in trivial art (even after being accepted by the academies, indeed all the more so) and in kitsch. On the other hand, it culminated in the great paintings of Realism and Impressionism: in Leibl's village pictures and in Liebermann's depiction of rural labour and craftsmen at work.

Having dealt with the various genres and themes which tell us so much about the history of ideas and feelings of the period, it now remains for us to say something about the changes in technique and style. In general, one can identify a move towards realism and reality. The pre-modern unity of rationally recognisable meaning and rationally perceivable appearance was crumbling, initially under the impact of secularisation and then because of the decline of idealistic and romantic metaphysics, a decline in the centrality of idea and thought, the idealising, spiritualising and transfiguring of reality. Art's claims to be something other than an imprint of perceivable reality were no longer accepted. The idea of art as metaphysical reference (consider, for example, the unnatural light of old paintings) or as artistic reference to the invisible was superseded by 'real', factual, visible, unmediated unmediated reality. The autonomy of optical experience and values — light and atmosphere — was of the essence. These were the greatest artistic achievements of the epoch. Painting sought to depict the visible, and nothing but the visible. Truth did not lie behind or above the 'positive' reality, but within it. This represented not only a change in aesthetic terms, but also, in part, a change in the consciousness of and emotional responses to reality in general, which art was obviously well suited to express. At the height of its triumph, however, this turn to an inherent sense of reality fell immediately into a new dilemma. Photography came to dominate the fashion for realism, and painting, could either compete, — hence, Naturalism — or give up ground. Optical impressions and — subjective — modes of perception were the rightful domain of art, and in asserting their independence they swam against the tide of Realism. A new autonomy of art developed, culminating in the anti-Realism of 'l'art pour l'art'. Art drew from reality and yet was able to create a reality that was all its own.

Classicism sought an ideal nature and overlooked all that did not accord with its conception of ideal beauty: bold line and sketching clarity, austerity and harmony were of the utmost importance. Beauty was bound to the idea of the good and the true. For that reason, the human figure remained central. Romanticism, as stated above, was dominated by the unlimited, the transitional, the fluid, symbolically indicative (as in Runge), the uncanny, the subjective and the disquieting. Biedermeier and Vormärz can be characterised as something of a lull: the Nazarene renaissance of religious painting and religious-historical frescoes, the new history painting, with its pathos and public nature, and, despite all its subjectification, with its nevertheless objective containment of the world and the preservation of an atmospheric landscape against unfamiliarity and excessive subjectivity and emotion. Biedermeier resorted to solid forms and to detail (all perceived realistically). It advocated bourgeois cleanliness and brightness, and a return to simplicity in pictures of urban and rural life, cosy interiors and imposing façades. The peculiarly exotic themes of foreign climes, strange wildernesses, the glamour of adventure, desert heat and harems arose in the middle of the century. All this contrasted to the solid, conformist world of work from which artists had broken loose, and so performed a compensatory function for the owners of their paintings.

At the end of our period, the Realists come into their own. Menzel and Leibl, who — along with Friedrich and Runge, and perhaps Blechen too — belong to the few truly great German painters of the 19th century. Genres and their peculiar problematics — nature, history, individual and society — were beginning to break down. Methods of observation and of painting relegated the interest in subject-matter to second place. Reality — visible reality — possessed its own artistic worth independent of stylisation and the ideational schemes of signification, independent too of transfiguration, illusion and sentimentality. 'Reality' was analytical and intolerant of illusions. Not only artistic conventions but ways of seeing themselves were destroyed. Admittedly, ugliness, the unacceptable, could still not be featured naturalistically or at least not emphasised in a provocative way. Part of Menzel and Leibl's greatness consisted in the fact that their realism was wrested from the tension between the new reality of facts and optical impressions, and the spirituality of tradition. It is possible to identify parallels to scientific, 'positivist' conceptions of reality in this new mode of seeing (and painting). Positivism was reflected in the determined, if not fanatical, seriousness of artists' quest for reality, and nothing but reality, although German Realists were not directly concerned with 'positivist' science.

The collapse of a whole world of conventional ideals, feelings, figures and scenarios certainly constituted a revolution in the realm of art, setting free the elements of the visible and the painterly — light, aspect and colour. But considered from a social and political point of view, realistic art was far from revolutionary — though it derived its themes from observing the everyday world, the contemporary situation, because it was there before their eyes, and in that sense it was bourgeois, but it was not a democratic phenonomen, let alone a socialist one. It rejected the intellectualism and partisanship of historical painting and was apolitical, concentrating solely on the visible. The revolution in art had nothing to do with the art of revolution.

The aesthetic appropriation of the world reflected the essence of the century, but in turn moulded it, too. In the process, the new realities of history and nature were involved, as were new trends toward an individualising of the ego and a subjectifying of emotions and ideas. Transcendence and meaning became immanent; suffering in the here and now and its transfiguration unleashed a positive, factual, and visible reality. All came together under the weighty emotiveness of a liberation in search of truth.

(d) Literature

Literature — and by this we mean 'serious' literature and 'belles lettres' — was even more closely in tune with the times than art, though, of course, this took place in a variety of ways. First of all, in the bourgeois epoch, now that religion had lost its monopoly as the forum for debate and discussion about the purpose and meaning of life, the baton was passed to literature. In a time of growing mobility and increasingly diverse notions of life's substance, the voice of tradition was no longer implicitly obeyed, nor did it determine what people did, thought, felt or questioned; nor could philosophy or science take on this mantle, owing to their growing specialisation and complexity; and so literature took on a greater social relevance. Second, literature, especially in so far as it struck a chord with the public, voiced the preoccupations of the age, taking up contemporary themes and experiences, reflecting underlying emotions and contemporary theories about the world and the self. Third, literature distilled the experiences of the age, charted new possibilities, and offered a conflicting account of the age to the familiar one given to us by politics, the economy, society, the church, science and private testimonies about contemporaries. Literature had an outsider's view, it stood at a critical distance to social and individual reality. It was a counter-world, and, as such, the experiences and view of life condensed within it cannot easily be related to contemporary reality. But even as counter-world, literature had a compensatory relation to its time; indeed, literature expressed the hidden history of the contemporary psyche. Finally, whether it swam with the current of the times or ran counter to it, literature exerted a major influence on the experiences, feelings and attitudes of its readers. Primarily a leisure activity, something to occupy Sunday, it therefore primarily affected those freed of the necessity to work (women and young people), it nevertheless had a significant part to play in 'normal' life, at work, in the family and in social life.

The famous north German decade of peace, 1795–1805, which helped to usher in the period we are considering, heralded what was to become the golden age of German culture, which was characterised by the two great (if not always mutually exclusive) literary and aesthetic movements, Classicism and Romanticism, whose impact was felt throughout the rest of the century.

For our purposes, a rough sketch of these characteristics will suffice. According to the tenets of Classicism, (1) All human existence is determined by a number of typically modern antagonisms: self *versus* world, individual *versus* society, ideal *versus* real, mind *versus* nature, fate endured *versus* individual autonomy, self-doubt *versus* self-certainty in emotion and action, specialisation *versus* universality, tradition *versus* modernity, 'being' as opposed to 'having' and 'achieving': Classicism sought to relax these tensions. The essential goal of life, perhaps its only goal, was the cultivation of a rounded personality, consisting in the development of individual potential, talents, and principles — now contradicting, now reconciled to society. With the example of Goethe's *Wilhelm Meister* before them, writers turned to the *Bildungsroman* (a novel concerned with the spiritual and intellectual development of an individual) to exemplify this view.

(2) Reality still pointed to the ideas and ideals of *Humanität* — the ever-present 'firmament of ideas'. One of these ideas was freedom. Freedom as an ideal, even when unrealised, remained a touchstone (as in Schiller's dramas) above tragic guilt and suffering. Or the 'unfathomable' which demanded calm respect — law, ethos and harmony; here too the pantheistic or Kantian reformulations of Christian ethics. In short, this peculiar constellation of secularity, individualism and idealism — this 'faith in the world' — provided certain fixed points in the quest to ascertain the elusive and impalpable meaning of life.

(3) It was through the medium of art that the task of restoring man to his ideal state, despite his doubts and even resistance. Art was the mediator between culture and humanity, hence its unique status. In the last analysis, the classical ideals of life and art were characterised by moderation. All extremes — excess, endlessness, the hereafter, darkness, chaos, unworldly forces, irrationality, the unconscious, uninhibited fantasy, overpowering emotions, destructive tensions and excessive subjectivity — all were tamed and sublimated by Classicism, and a sense of harmony wrested from them. This set Classicism apart from conventional forms of art. '*Humanität*', it was argued, needs clarity and constraints, form and order; it needs 'renunciation', to live in the here and now, and to conform to the ultimate order of things. Art aspired to harmony and ideality, unity and objectivity, typicality and universal validity. Harmony and *Humanität* could best be represented in strict form, in effect as a means of imposing order on disorder, assimilating chaos into the cosmos. In his old age Goethe was the archetypal Classicist; both in his writings and in the way he mastered — and commented on — his own life, he typified Classicism's view of, and mastery of, life; in so doing, he was either revered or vilified. In his late work especially, he dealt with human passions, but extracted from them an ethos of moderation and renunciation, a lofty and formal serenity. He interpreted the world symbolically and created, in the figure of Faust, one of the few epochal myths of modern man.

Once Hölderlin had fallen silent, it was left to Heinrich von Kleist and Jean Paul to bridge the divide between Classicism and Romanticism. To us, Kleist seems remarkably modern, with his crisis of understanding, his confusing dialectic of emotions and his loss of orientation. But his contemporaries and immediate successors deemed him an outsider. The most popular writer of this period was Jean Paul, whose work took from both the Enlightenment and the sentimental, movement, 'speaking' to the reader in a loose and open fashion and striking an happy balance between sympathy and humour.

Romanticism was not just a German phenonemon, but a thoroughly European movement. It charted the powerful revolt of intellectual and spiritual subjectivity against the maxims of rationalism and utilitarianism of the Enlightenment. It challenged the harmony and order of Classicism and undermined the domination of austere reality, conventional morality and mediocrity. Romanticism redrew the boundaries of human reality and, whether we like it or not, has shaped the contours of our subjectivity ever since. The world of the Romantics was irregular and enigmatic, wondrous, magical and chaotic. Darkness and 'night' were all-pervasive. The self was infinite, complex, ambivalent, torn, unfathomable, original in its thought as well as its emotion — more intense than ever before. Man, the Romantics argued, was not first and foremost a rational being, but a creature of emotions, moods and passions. But Romanticism's greatest discovery was that of the unconscious. New priorities emerged. In contrast to Classicism's culture of personality, which emphasised universal human traits, Romanticism emphasised individual characteristics and recognised their inherent value. Subjectivity was radicalised to a position of the utmost importance. Romanticism may be seen as the revolt of the contemplative, sensitive subjectivity against the objectivity, immutability, restriction and finality which had informed not only the ideals of the Enlightenment, but also Classicism. Whereas Classicism sought to harmonise conflicting inner forces, Romanticism went a step further and explored the most intensive, extreme, imbalanced and bizarre possibilities. Subjectivity thus contradicted objective reality. It could not be squared with the normative categories dictated by objective reality.

The sentient self, its expectation and view of the world, was 'poetic'. Emotion and experience coincided in the typical Romantic encounter with nature, love, art, wonder and adventure. Reality, on the other hand, was 'prosaic'. The dissonance between self and world determined experience, interpretation and sentiment, and opposed the Classical idea of equilibrium, the ideal of personal development, the restrictions of conformity and all relative harmony. Individuals inhabited an alien, alienated world, which constricted and diminished them and subordinated them to commonplace and tedious utility. The self was riven by the contradictions inherent in this world. Gone were the days when religion had bridged the gap between self and world. Gone too was the exhortation to dutiful obedience on God's earth, gone the active cultivation of personality and the sense of freedom even in tragic failure. This experience manifested itself as an increasing sense of melancholic mourning for the world and for life. There was a sense of loss of the childlike unity of self and world, of the naïvety of earlier cultural epochs; a sense of a loss too of 'totality', of unified worlds and peoples. The Romantics gave voice to transience, sadness and 'homesickness' (*Heimweh*), to the unrealised and the unrealisable. They longed for that which was lost, and that which has never been found. They yearned for some knowledge of the eternal Other and longed to flee from the present, from the factual and mundane, into a remembered past and a future aspired to, to a place that is home but can never be reached, into fantastic transcendence or a religion which would forever defy definition. All this promoted a rejection of regimentation, middle-class mentality and the humdrum world of work, and opened the gates to the 'poetic' provinces of life.

Art was entrusted with all that is 'poetic' in the world. The 'unhappy' consciousness and its discontent in the face of all that is 'prosaic' in life required the 'divine' realm of art, as it were, as compensation. Art, like the true and proper life, was not bound to morality, probability or reality, but was able to relativise and disempower reality through creative, non-utilitarian play. Employing the great human gifts of dream and fantasy, art countered reality with infinite subtlety and irony, now abandoning, now restoring the self. Art was the highest expression of human freedom and its true totality. It shattered the rigidity of the objective world, the self and all classical forms. Subjective fragments were presented in an attempt to emphasise the unfinished and fragmentary nature of the world. Art challenged any entity which made claims to permanence, transforming the world into an infinite chain of codes and symbols. In short, the Romantics counterposed a world of art (and feeling) to the world of reality. In doing so, they were reaching back to find genuine simplicity and naïvety. They rediscovered the folk poem (*Des Knaben Wunderhorn*, 1806–8), legends and fairy-tales and immersed themselves in the Middle Ages, seeking all that was elemental and archaic, for they saw this as a world of symbolism and poetry, as distinct and self-contained as the alien and distant cultures and literatures they so relished.

At the start of our period, the differences between the early and late schools of Romanticism are, naturally, of importance. The early Romantics (Novalis and the Schlegel brothers) thrived on a combination of *raison* and *sentiment*. Central to their work was intellectual reflection and aesthetic subjectivity, the self-realisation of the ego in opposition to the 'prosaic' world, and the redemption of the world through art. For the generation of 1810, the 'Heidelberg Romantics' (Brentano, Arnim, Görres, Jacob Grimm and, again, Friedrich Schlegel), the perils of an untrammelled subjectivity — in the peaks and troughs of mood, in fantasy and reflection — became clearer. Loss of identity and orientation and the 'gospel' of poeticising the world were no longer so attractive. Subjective liberty and intellectualism gave way to a commitment to tradition, history, supra-individual community, *Volk* and religion. Significant new impulses included the pathos of the elemental and the forces of darkness, the idea of letting oneself be swept along by the currents of the age, and the glorification of the ancestral past.

Much as Goethe's mature work (and especially the posthumous influence and popularity of Schiller) kept the spirit of Classicism alive, the resonance of Romanticism lingered on through the first third of the 19th century in the work of its two greatest exponents. One was E. T. A. Hoffmann, who formulated a surreal and grotesque Romantic counter-world, highlighting the theme of the failure of self-realisation in society. Out of this interest in the darker side of life grew the demonic realism of crime fiction. The other great exponent of Romanticism was Baron Joseph von Eichendorff, who perfected the Romantic nature poetry of longing, bliss and mourning, in images of sylvan solitude, twilight and darkness, in opposition to the regimented world. His Catholic faith shielded his eternal 'homesickness' from the descent into world-weariness.

If one takes the experiences and interpretations of writers from 1815 onwards as a yardstick, the existential problem of modern subjectivity can be seen to have intensified during this period. Classicism's solution had consisted in harmonising self and world, ideal and real, and in individual development through education, a 'faith in the world' which glossed over all contradictions. The function of art in this process had been to achieve a mastery over life and the world. This solution, however, began to break down. The Romantic attempt to create a world of poetry, both alongside the world of prose and in opposition to it — in other words, the Romantic attempt to poeticise life — was similarly unsuccessful and dissatisfying. The equilibrium of the ego and the world became ever more difficult to sustain. Human subjectivity became more complex, more sensitive and fractured; reflection grew more important; emotions were ever more ambivalent and changeable; actions less fluent. The self was more contradictory and incoherent; identity more difficult to sustain, was threatened, insecure. The individual was barely able to come to terms with himself. The objective nature of the world became starker, more impenetrable and darker. The modern world of economics, bureaucracy, the division of labour, collective restraints, anonymity, achievement, competition and mobility was experienced as a colder, more prosaic, more alienating, inhospitable place which could never be home. It was impossible even to conceive of the world as a fitting and coherent place. The world became contradictory and fragmented, its unity and order uncertain. Traditions, which informed attitudes and provided certainties in the conflict between self and world, became questionable and fragile, as did the bonds which tied people to the world. People turned against traditions, but at the same time suffered from their dissolution. Not only did organised religion lose its self-evidence and force, but so did the secular religion of Classicism — the religion of ethos or cosmos, the belief in God, freedom and immortality. The 'firmament of ideas', however it was interpreted, became increasingly unrecognisable and contrived. The sense of mundanity increased, but the ideals of this world — love, work, progress, political, social and human emancipation — became as relativised as were the absolute norms. Individual liberty was called into question now that it was faced with the experience of determination by nature, time, society, chance, and an unfathomable, i.e. no longer divinely ordained, fate. Individuals experienced themselves as isolated when confronted by social processes and the emergent public praxis. First and foremost, they inhabited the private sphere. Public and private were experienced as separate and divided. This was not a consequence of specifically German circumstances, as is often claimed, but rather a structural characteristic of the modern age in which the public sphere became vague, anonymous and prosaic. So the private sphere — fate, life, emotion — became the stuff of poetry. The human soul had apparently been banished from the real world. Genuine feeling floundered. The mediation between inner life and everday praxis at work and in society became more complex. Characteristically for modernity, the meaning of life became problematic, because religion, tradition, and socio-political plans for the future were no longer able to provide answers. Questioning took on a new urgency, and answers were relativised. In short, the dissonance between the sensitive, contemplative self and its desires on the one hand, and social reality, questions of identity and the sense of the self on the other, became a typically modern experience, and found expression through literature. This was a European phenomenon, not limited to a German context. Yet it cannot simply be put down to the evils of capitalism, for its appearance long predates the capitalist system. That this experience became a fundamental problem of literature had to do with the fact that art's place in the world had become problematic: science claimed to comprehend modern social reality; politics, economy and technology claimed to mould it. Confronted with such competing 'claims to truth', art moved to the individual and private realm. But even there, claims to truth and aesthetic demands might diverge. Hence, to some extent, we are able to understand the striking contradiction which existed between the existential experiences voiced in literature and the experiences arising in science, politics and the everyday, which were shaped by a belief in a post-idealist *Humanität*, in progress, nation, constitution, work, and the family — in short, a belief in the gods of the day.

The fundamental modern experience of dissonance between self and world, which was thematised and discussed in literature, determined the predominant moods and mental dispositions expressed in literature: turmoil, restlessness, sensibility, nervousness, melancholy, resignation, rebellion, despair, world-weariness (*Weltschmerz*). Even where fracture, subjectivity, boundlessness and forlornness were harnessed and ordered, and reconciliation and agreement were reached, where reality is taken seriously, where the substantial world is present, where there is an effort to explain the world, where there is utopia or even happiness, where humour characterises the view of life — all this seems to be wrested from an underlying sense of malaise and conflict (in the greatest poetry at least). In Germany especially, literature tended to emphasise inwardness and idealistic inner reality, isolated from the age, society and the public sphere, notwithstanding the difficulty of separating the legitimate presentation and preservation of the private self from society's ideologisation of it.

Yet it would be quite wrong to emphasise the fixation with the 'loss of centre' alone, important though it may be, for alongside this there was often the equally emphatic will to reality, the rejection of the ideal and mere imagination, as well as of the abstract opposition of poetry and prose. The substantiality of both inner and outer worlds was discovered, a broadening and deepening of the experiential world. Moreover, the fragmentation and doubtfulness of meaning was the very foundation for the curiosity and adventurousness of the inner self. It was also the basis for entering new dimensions and realms of subjectivity, human relationships, nature and the social world. Moreover, there frequently arose a desire to inhabit this reality, accepting its law. Reality would be the starting-point in the quest for alternative and more appropriate ways of life.

These were the two general, fundamental problems of the age, which went beyond the specifically aesthetic problems enunciated in literature. There were various attempts at resolution, new perspectives on life and the world, and divers stylistic positions. Thus arose a pluralism of differentiated and yet concurrent philosophical positions and styles. Even so, three major movements stand out: Biedermeier, 'Young Germany' and Realism.

Biedermeier primarily comprised the very formal post-Classical and post-Romantic literature of the restoration period and Vormärz. It cannot be ascribed to the oppositional literature of the 1830s and 1840s. It too stemmed from the conflict described above, namely the agonising separation of self from the world, the painful experience of life and its interpretation. Three contingencies formed this basic situation. Firstly, it was formed in opposition to Classicism's individualism, its secular humanist religion and its aestheticism, wherein art became the central medium for mastering life; the revolt against Goethe — the heathen, the hedonist, the courtier, the aesthete divorced from the people — is a case in point. Biedermeier similarly eschewed Romanticism, with its arbitrariness and intensity of subjectivity, and its fascination with chaos and the void, its unchecked reflection and irony, its rampant imagination, its sentimental excesses and its vision of a world of poetry beyond the prose of reality (work and family) and its elimination of all forms. Finally, Biedermeier incorporated an insight which, though going against the grain of the actual Biedermeier ideal, was quite typical of the age. This was Romantic pain and suffering, which intensified during the Vormärz to *Weltschmerz*, that is, to a metaphysical desperation with the world and 'demonic' inner conflict, to boredom and cynicism, pessimism and nihilism. *Weltschmerz* was not solely the product of the authoritarian German restoration, however. It had been fashionable throughout Europe since Byron's time, but German readers came to know it through the works of Nikolaus Lenau and Christian Grabbe, and to some extent through Heine, but best of all through Georg Büchner.

Weltschmerz was cut free from religion, from mere sentimental causes (like unrequited love) and entered the realms of the inexplicable: pain became shrouded in mystery, no longer neutralised by Christian or idealistic theologising, it was beyond comprehension. Even the Biedermeier revolt against the uncontrolled and immodest subjectivity of *Weltschmerz* was wrested from the very permanence of its threat to life. Karl Immermann, certainly no sufferer from *Weltschmerz*, called his generation, the youth of the Napoleonic era, not only hopeless and powerless 'epigones' but just so many 'Hamlets'. This feeling of insecurity and threat was accompanied by doubts about the validity of such ethical norms as the sense of historical progress. The age was perceived in terms of crisis. One seemed to suffer as much from the losses, threats, destabilisation and excitement of modernity as from the pressures and stagnation of the restoration. Biedermeier's 'answer' to the challenges of this situation, was the quest for composure and calm, peace and simplicity, and for order. All excesses were rejected, as was concentration on self, the emancipation of the ego, and aesthetic hedonism. There was a move against mere 'topicality', against the large-scale, against principles and theories in favour of the small-scale, the modest and the familiar. It was a move towards the tangible and the detailed, to the empiricism of experience and the objectivity of the real and natural world. It built on the Romantics' concern with forces which transcend the individual — *Heimat* (homeland) and family, nation and work. Biedermeier aspired to a moral code, to history and religion, and revered 'being' itself and its (divine) guidance, which ultimately led to a new confidence in the world. It revolted against the 'drives' of the times — politics and society — retreating to the private realm and peace of mind, taming and suppressing the passionate, the elemental and the strange. In short, it withdrew to a culture of inwardness, to a certain passive acceptance of the world. It embraced an ethos of renunciation and relinquishment, tinged with gentle resignation, and yet not without a sense of fulfilment. It seemed to retreat to the idyllic lull of a smaller world (such as Friedrich Hebbel criticised in Adalbert Stifter, the greatest writer of this genre after Eduard Mörike and Annette von Droste-Hülshoff). In fact, Stifter's ideal world, later so maliciously denounced, had been wrung from disastrous reality, chaos and resistance, from the stimulation and emancipation of the time, from subjectivity and negativity. Against this backdrop, Biedermeier tried to regain a beautiful rational, harmonious and moral order, to bring the individual once again under the 'gentle law' of little things and the nature of being. There were various refinements and literary renditions of this basic position: Stifter's epic subjugation; the emphaticturn to Christianity of Droste-Hülshoff and Jeremias Gotthelf; the lyrical appeal to nature and the objective world, whereby the self objectified its own relationship to both (Mörike, Droste-Hülshoff); the widespread exploitation of the themes of history and *Heimat*; the Classical form of Grillparzer; the humour of Raimund or, in a more acerbic form, of Nestroy, who exposed the illusions and delusions of the world. It was perhaps in Austria that Biedermeier enjoyed its greatest triumphs. It grew from a variety of traditions — Catholicism, baroque, theatrical folk customs, from Josephinist bureaucracy, anti-clericalism and the supra-national empire — and from the particularly intense form of Metternichian restoration.

In engaging the times, political and oppositional literature played an important role in the 1830s and 1840s. It challenged Biedermeier literature and the attitudes contained therein, although both shared a common starting-point. First of all, there was a revolution of the literati in the 'Young Germany' movement, led by Karl Gutzkow and Heinrich Laube, who in the 1830s put emancipation on the literary agenda in the form of the *Zeitroman* (timely novel) and the *Tendenzroman* (tendentious novel). They dealt with emancipation — of the here and now, of women and of the 'flesh' — promoting an emancipation from Christianity and morality. Stimulated, intellectual, bohemian, and elitist in their attitudes, puerile and impudent in their religious critique, more provocative than significant as literature, they acquired a reputation for opposing the status quo, largely as a result of having their publications banned by the Deutscher Bund (German League). They were, however, rather ephemeral — certainly not worthy of the claims to posterity which today's progressives try to ascribe to them. Left-wing 'Young Hegelians', such as the young Friedrich Engels, emphatically rejected this 'revolution of the literati'.

Political poetry was of greater importance. While failing to become part of the canon, it was nevertheless very popular and representative of the times. This poetry included the songs of the early 1820s and 1830s about Greece and Poland, which provided an outlet for a suppressed public debate on freedom. It also included the Rhineland songs of 1840 and the great oppositional poetry of the 1840s, such as that by Anastasius Grün, Franz Dingelstedt, Hoffmann von Fallersleben (who lost his office because of it), and above all that by Georg Herwegh and the most powerful poet of them all, Ferdinand Freiligrath, both of whom were forced into exile. The importance of this group for the formation of political parties has already been mentioned.

We turn now to the *Zeitroman*, which undertook a mixture of contemplative observations and politically committed social critiques of the times. Various works illustrate this, from Immermann's *Epigonen* (1825–36), which has more in common with Biedermeier, through Gutzkow's *Ritter vom Geiste* (1850–51) to Friedrich Spielhagen. There was also a lot of 'committed' trivia, as well as the portrayal of a counter-world — free America — in the work of the Austrian writer Karl Postl (writing under the pseudonym of Charles Sealsfield).

Finally, there are the two great writers of the 'opposition', who, like the leading exponents of Biedermeier, imprinted themselves indelibly in the history of the German language, and on feelings, experiences and consciousness. The first was Georg Büchner — romantic, world-weary, disillusioned and disillusioning, despairing of metaphysics and understanding, a materialist-nihilist and a fatalist, a democratic and a social revolutionary, whose language expressed so memorably both the justness and the sheer inescapable tragedy of revolution. The second was Heinrich Heine. A baptised Jew, he suffered from his enforced role as outsider. He was rooted in the Romantic tradition of emotion, pain and song, which accounted for his popularity and resonance. He broke with self-confirming and reflective subjectivity in a rational, sceptical and ironic way. Using the new form of the feuilleton, Heine developed a new style of prose in his travel reports, newspaper articles and critical descriptions of the age. From 1830 onwards, writing mostly form Paris, he fought vehemently against the conditions in Germany — the lack of freedom in the political realm, the inequality of the social order. He crusaded against religion and ascetic morality as a Saint-Simonist and sensualist. He was enraptured by the magic of emancipation and promulgated countless emancipatory causes. But, ever the aesthete, he insisted on the sovereignty of art, in opposition to the zealots of tendentious literature. And, close as he was to accepting the idea of egalitarian revolution, his position on art, and the curious adoption of the religion of his fathers at the end of his life, meant that he remained permanently distanced from communist socialism. Leaving aside his personal opinions, Heine must be regarded as a modern poet, primarily because he put into words the modern experience of uncertainty, fragmentation, the tumultuous mood of the times and its sublation in reflection; he even conveyed the fragmentation of expression.

Even beyond the middle of the century, Romanticism and, to a certain extent, Classicism, persisted as literary genres, alongside Biedermeier and Young Germany. An epigonic tradition and convention of literary expression arose, to which even the more original minds contributed. The tradition could be seen in the themes and requisites, in the emotions and forms, which profoundly affected the readers. This movement was to produce some of the most successful poets of the age. The powerful Romantic works of Ludwig Uhland, for example, were tamed for bourgeois consumption and appeared in the form of folk-songs and ballads, which presented a patriotic and outmoded demo-cratic vision of the German (and, more particularly, Swabian) Middle Ages. These didactic songs came to be a feature of popular songbooks and even schoolbooks. Another popular poet was Friedrich Rückert, a master of both Classical and exotic forms, such as orientalism. Although his poetry was occasionally shocking, there was no subject from which he would shy away. He too found immortality in music, most famously in the compositions of Gustav Mahler. Emanuel Geibel, an eclectic and educated bourgeois, who exuded pathos, virtuosity, and a consciousness of form in his writing, continued the genre beyond 1848. By means of quite average methods, he managed to give 'noble' and sublime expression to quite average sentiments, and to the now prevailing nationalist mood. Notwithstanding variations in quality, all three writers were basically undemanding poets. The fine arts were toned down to suit a domestic, everyday context. They were leisure-time poets who reined in their imaginations and represented a 'higher' sphere with which the reader could identify without having too many demands being made on the average emotional state of mind. They were the heirs to a Classicism which had been placed upon a pedestal and which, in spite of all its rhetoric, could no longer claim to be a binding force and was reduced to an empty gesture. Only August von Platen was more ambitious, attempting to realise esoteric and great artistic claims for a new Classical ethos of art and form, which would drown out melancholic *Weltschmerz* with the pure beauty of unexhausted forms.

It was a similar story for most of the epigonic *Bildungsdramen* (didactic dramas), which for the most part have since been forgotten, which sought to individualise the world spirit (*Weltgeist*) by their portrayal of historical figures. (In the 1850s and 1860s these accounted for approximately three-quarters of all dramatic productions!) The verse epic is another case in point. Not very demanding, these poems were generally idyllic, reconciliatory and mostly dressed in historical and romantic garb. Josef von Scheffel's endearing *Trompeter von Säckingen* is a good example. Eventually it became a bestseller (ten years after it first appeared in 1854, it was in its fourth edition). Finally, there was the work of Paul Heyse, whose epigonic, aesthetic, individualistic, mundane, mortal, and intellectually elitist prose defied bourgeois *tristesse* in its formal perfection and freethinking spirit. He gave new voice to a *joie de vivre*, to self-fulfilment. He defended the right to be passionate, even if it meant flying in the face of conventional mores. His setting was another world, a world of beauty, greatness and freedom. Yet precisely because of its themes of the purification and renunciation of worldly things, his work remained bound up in bourgeois norms and conventions.

We come now to Realism, the important new movement of the 1850s and 1860s. The division in the world, the existential problem of the 19th century, apparently became still more intense. Schopenhauer's pessimistic philosophy matched the prevailing mood: suffering born of the impenetrability and irrationality of the world and self, the disappearance of context, the loss of meaning and purpose, elementary egoism. The freedom of the ego was less tangible now that there were deterministic explanations of the world. The threat to human life posed by modernity, capitalism, alienation, destabilisation, and the paralysis of tradition was enhanced. Contradictions became more intractable. For the major writers at least, religion declined in importance, or lost its relevance altogether. Moreover, the belief not only in a hereafter, in immortality and transcendental reconciliation, but also in an idealist metaphysics, the faith in 'spirit' (*Geist*), also diminished. On the other hand, however, the departure of religion and metaphysics did not lead to nihilism, despite all the doom and gloom. For Feuerbach, the death of God was a positive experience, in that it indicated a return to the here and now, an exclusive affirmation of the moment, of the individual and of the species itself. It represented a move towards a happiness which was realistically attainable, albeit a more modest one. Or to put it less boldly, the prohibition of transcendence, the agnostic dismissal of such questions, the contentment with life, were all in keeping with the loss of transcendence.

A moral and aesthetic resort to Realism grew out of this idea. Once again, it was a movement which was set against Romanticism and world-weariness, but also against Young Germany; it was set against the excesses of subjectivity and know-it-all radical intellectualism, against all that was tendentious, against ideological constructions, against rhetoric, bias, pathos, arbitrariness and all that was crass and sentimental. It challenged the bias in favour of fracture and disharmony and set itself against the merely subjective protest of the ego, against its distortions and exaggerations. But more than this, it was also set against the forced contentment and harmony of Biedermeier, against the retreat to the past, to the leisured 'Sunday' mentality and the order of the private sphere. It rejected an idealised objectivity which was remote from ordinary objectivity. In short, it opposed the estrangement from the times. Instead, Realism embraced the forms and conditions of the real world, a world which could be experienced. It accepted the ego, not in opposition to, but in conjunction with, reality. Thematically, this meant a rejection of the leisured mentality in order to incorporate everyday experience; a rejection of exceptional situations, marginal experiences, outsiders; a move away from the domination of love and friendship, exceptional fate, religious and metaphysical problems, in order to enable an encounter with 'normal' situations, occurrences and figures. It entailed a move away from 'poetically' informed heroes, artists and intellectuals to the common citizen, to people living in the 'prosaic' world. Instead of highlighting historical themes, the old order, *Volk* and *Heimat*, Realism put the emphasis on objective circumstances, and above all modern society, social milieux and the everyday world. Subjectivity became the object of analytical and psychological explanation, in terms of cause and interaction.

Of course, it was not a question of photographic objectivity. The continuing theme was still the bourgeois problem of existence, fulfilment, happiness and individual self-determination in the context of a world which conditions and constricts; in addition, there was the problem of mediation between the predominance of objective necessity and the unrelinquishable claims of individuality. The sentient self, the 'psyche', the 'soul', and indeed the painful failure of self in this world continued to loom large, as did the problem of the enduring and threatening antagonism of inner and outer realities. Confronted with threat and disintegration, the connection between world experience and self-experience was considered, the tension between the isolation of individuals and their habitation in the world. Meaning, which had become problematic, was investigated. At the same time, at least according to contemporary understanding, 'objective' reality was present only in subjective perceptions, moods and perspectives. Aesthetically, the main task for the Realists was to offset an objective reflection of reality and subjective interpretation, according to the laws of probability, for example. They were simultaneously to objectify and subjectify. If the problem of meaning and panoramic objectivity are taken together, it becomes clear that art was designed to represent a meaning that was no longer provided by religion, philosophy and science. Furthermore, art was designed to represent the meaning of the world, and the context of the self therein, in terms of the emotion and the moment. According to the contemporary philosopher Hermann Lotze, art should bring the 'deepest substance of life' to recognition on the basis of the 'sentient soul'. This substance had now, according to the aesthetician Friedrich Theodor Vischer, taken the place of the 'absolute', the psychological and historical experiences of mutable life. In this sense literature had import for more than just reality; it dealt with truth. Such was its 'higher' beauty.

Art thus preserved humanity, ethos, the sparkle of hope and justice, the 'golden glister of reconciliation', as transfigurations of a reality which it both discovered and countered. Thence derived the particularly literary tendency of Realism to blunt and balance out conflicts and breaches, to mellow and 'suppress' them. It aspired to establish an equilibrium, mediating between the unpredictable fortunes of the real and the ideal, and bringing together idea and experience, great and small, thought and action. The two most prevalent stylistic tools of this literary movement were, on the one hand, humour, which united the agonising distance from and the attachment to life, and, on the other, reminiscence, which elegiacally regarded the real conflict from a temporal distance, while nevertheless reconciling it. Of course, meaning broke through only in a vague, fragmented and doubtful way. Only for Schopenhauerian pessimists was absolute truth represented by art alone, in its exposing the apparition of the reality of the will. The peace which art established was on a higher plane than reason ever could be. Realistic art demanded a contemplative reading which incorporated all the tensions and ambivalences between pessimism and the assertion of meaning, between pain and confidence, resignation and security, laughter and tears. For that reason, on the whole, the effect of realistic art was to encourage a reconciliation with life. In the last analysis, Realism was concerned with enduring metaphysical uncertainty, finding one's way in the real world, taking a stand against the loss of meaning with an unpretentious and unambiguously courageous affirmation of life. This was a classic bourgeois 'position' — in a world abandoned by religion where politics, science, work and family were not sufficient to forge and maintain the meaning of life.

The ambivalence of the Realist position towards life and the expectations of art conditioned the variety and differentiation of both literature and ideology. Novels and novellas became the leading genres. The novel dealt with the conflict between the individual and society. Plot and events were subordinated to descriptions of spiritual processes and reactions to the world. 'Private' existence was central to the novel. The novella, dealt less with events, than with a specific issue. Moreover, the novella, in approaching the aesthetic ideal of strict form and objectivity, was one of the classic vehicles of Realism, precisely because the notion of social totality (which the novel originally hoped to encompass) was on the wane. The German novel — and prose writing in general — has been accused of having an absolute lack of social awareness because of this emphasis on the inner world. Certainly, in comparison with the French and English novels of Stendhal, Balzac, Dickens and Thackeray, social criticism and social typology were in no way central to the German novel. The distance between author and protagonist was negligible, the identification between them great. The hero was pivotal, but that can hardly be grounds for reproach. For one thing, the notion of tracing the development, reactions and thoughts of an individual was a legitimate theme for the bourgeois novel. Moreover, the basically coherent bourgeois society, which had been the prerequisite of English and French social novels, was not yet fully developed at this point in German history.

Soll und Haben (Debit and Credit, 1855), Gustav Freytag's investigation of the German people and the bourgeoisie at work, was the most successful novel of the day, publishing 20,000 copies in just a few years; it has been a bourgeois 'classic' ever since — the gift at many a confirmation. It affirmed a faith in the harmony of individual and social development, a faith in progress, in the liberal-nationalist rise of the bourgeoisie and in the ultimate triumph of virtue.

With the exception of the bitter social criticism of his early epic on agricultural working life, *Kein Hüsung* (1858), the work of Fritz Reuter, victim of the political suppression during the Vormärz, was typical of the trend towards the nostalgic, gently humorous, contemplative idyll. Wilhelm Busch, meanwhile, typified the combination of Schopenhauerian pessimism and petty-bourgeois grotesquerie, mellowing it by way of epic verse and everyday idyll.

The two greatest Realist writers in Germany before Theodor Fontane were Theodor Storm and Wilhelm Raabe. Storm expressed in a particularly idiosyncratic way the experiences of nemesis, loss and contradiction, insurmountable transitoriness, and the tragedy of bourgeois existence. He articulated the dilemma of meaning and the problem of grasping an increasingly intangible reality. He depicted transfiguration and appeasement in memories tinged with melancholy which reconcile truth and its loss, and the calm endurance of life. Raabe, meanwhile, presented a humanity threatened both by a world of old-fashioned narrowness and oppression, and by modern-day alienation with its clattering progress, its wealth and power. He proffered a solution: an exodus from present-day reality into a private world of eccentricity. In the face of disillusionment, he illustrated the assertion of the self against society, charting a heroic and resigned retreat into the self and to the world of inner freedom and truth. Yet Raabe still embraced the outside world with fond humour. This peculiar unmodernity — to some extent also a feature of a small-town mentality — determined the greatness and significance of these works and the perspective endorsed therein. It showed very clearly the discrepancy between emotional and social reactions to the rapid onset of modernity in the German world. Gottfried Keller was the third great Realist in the

German language, adding new weight to a positive perspective on life. (Incidentally, he was no less important than the others for readers in Germany, despite his Swiss nationality.) This was naturally of great importance for the literary restoration of an equilibrium of the mood, morale and outlook of educated readers.

In conclusion, the examination of a few contemporary literary themes will furnish us with an authentic sense of the prevailing attitudes and conditions in Germany and the ways in which they changed. One such theme was nature. As part of the heritage of pantheistic nature worship and the fusion of nature and spirit of the sentimental movement, together with Rousseau's critique of civilisation, nature became, for the Romantics, both an expression of and location for sentient subjectivity. Nature was a place of origin, of freedom from civilisation, convention and social pressures; it was a place of individuality and solitude, a place of eternity, transcendence, beauty, harmony and bliss, a place of pain and longing. The variety and intensity of the encounter with nature paralleled the experience of the inner self. Nature, in all its enticing melancholy, became an essential and satisfying reality in which the difficulties of the poetic soul with the prosaic world were subsumed. Long before industry and the city turned nature into a compensatory reality, the relationship to nature took on a religious character and assumed an elevated and ethereal position in the scheme of things.

It was, above all, Brentano and Eichendorff who brought the Romantic experience of nature unforgettably into the German language. They called the tune for subsequent poetic experiences of the natural world, in terms of the perception of nature and the *'et ego'* reaction of the sentient soul; they provided the now conventional repertoire of 'nature perceptions' — forest and brook, springtime, birds, rustling of leaves, floating clouds, moonlit nights, twilight and so on. It was they who shaped literary expectations and actual experience. For literature did not only mirror the bourgeois aesthetic experience of nature, but formed it at the same time. Nature experienced was at once nature expressed and recalled.

During the Biedermeier period, nature gained a firm and unassailable character, which had been comforting in the face of worldly turmoil. The experience of cultivated nature — flowers and gardens, not just uncultivated parks — was characteristic of the non-literary mentality. But something quite different happened as well. In the great lyric poetry of Mörike and Annette von Droste-Hülshoff, and to a certain extent that of Storm, and in the nature prose writings (as in Stifter, for example), new and original experiences of nature found a voice which contrasted with Romanticism's *'et ego'* topos. Nature became more tangible, more detailed and objective, no longer the reflection of a sentimental self. It became wilder, uncannier, less penetrable. For Stifter, it was precisely in this uncanniness and in the descriptions of natural catastrophes which were appearing in literature for the first time that nature became a symbol both of the riddle of existence and fate and of the harnessing of passions. For Droste-Hülshoff, nature became an image, sign and symbol of reality. For Mörike, nature was mute, and the ego left to itself, but his literary form objectified the ego and showed the world in a new light. At the same time, subjective experiences were differentiated. Highly emotional ambivalence and disturbance entered the language, but such self-expression was fractured in the process of reflection or, in Droste-Hülshoff's case, by religion. Strangely enough, it was Droste-Hülshoff and Mörike, reputedly apolitical Biedermeier conservatives, who were the great innovators and creators of a new language and experience of reality.

The second great literary theme which appealed to the bourgeois sensibility was love. Unlike conventional sentimentalism, Romanticism elevated love to a central category. Romantic, fateful and highly individualised love became the key to experiencing the world. It was the vital metaphysical point at which sentient subjectivity, nostalgia for one's homeland (*Heimatsuche*) and eternity coincided. All this determined the literary expression of the bourgeois dream, and the excessive importance attached to it. The failure of love was inevitable, faced with such an overbearing burden, and it became the actual poetic crisis-point of inner existence. Lovesickness and disappointment in the affairs of the heart gained metaphysical weight and became the core of the individual's inner self and his suffering in society.

Biedermeier idealistically appealed to family in order to oppose the Romantic subjectification and intensification of love and lovesickness (and to prevent the release of the daemon Eros which lay behind it). Love in itself was insufficient. Marriage was the true and lasting union between individuals, but it went beyond the relationship of man and woman to embrace family, home and a close continuity between past and present generations. Marriage thus led to a sense of peace in a restless world, to something holy, a veritable 'heaven on earth' — as evidenced in the thoroughly modern writing of Karl Immermann. Here, happy and harmonious human existence was at home, as was the soul. Indeed, the family was regarded idyllically. Mothers were the focal point; grandmothers and fathers handed down experience and wisdom; the children — more so than adolescents — were touching in their mixture of 'purity' and 'mischieviousness' and were the great love of the age. Romantic, ideal and painful love was poles apart from the Biedermeier family, yet they found a synthesis in the average bourgeois imagination.

The containment of eroticism and, indeed, its repression belonged to the Biedermeier treatment of the theme of love — in contrast to its treatment in (at least early) Romanticism. In this sense, Heine was initially an outsider in the literary world, calling for erotic sensuality and sexuality to replace the increasingly 'bland' idealisation of love. The Realists had indeed appropriated the dominant attitudes to love and marriage, but in turning away from the idyllic and the sentimental, and by analysing human relationships in psychological terms, they had not only grasped this thematic realm in a new and more modern way, but had problematised it.

Part of contemporary literature, much as in the fine arts, was a new concern with history, which in turn became a sort of new mythology. Historical motifs had exerted a fascination over writers ever since the international success of Walter Scott, and of Wilhelm Hauff's *Lichtenstein* (1826), through Willibald Alexis's Prussian novels to the professorial novels of the 1860s (Georg Ebers and Felix Dahn). The ballad, the historical drama and, of course, above all, the historical novel were the preferred modes of expression. History became more tangible, no longer the battleground of ideas, but a tapestry of circumstance and fate, which, in part, accounted for its fascination for writers and readers alike. The prevailing notion was that public and private fate were more poetically linked in history than in the prosaic present, and so could be more representatively portrayed there. The world of the past was more complete and vivid than that of the present, but, being rooted in fact and not fiction, it satiated the age's hunger for reality. The emphases of historical novels were, of course, many and varied: the consolidation of a regional or national past; the romantic, imaginary depiction of foreign lands, be they Roman or Egyptian; the realisation of liberty or national unity and glory; critical images to counter present reality; motifs of escape, and hopes for the future, whether progressive or conservative. Citizen and *Volk* crowded in from all sides, perhaps at times appearing archaic and orchestrated, but always playing an active part in history. Underlying all this lay the need for identity, continuity and political legitimation. The recourse to history served to orientate life — that is reflected in this literature, just as much as the literature itself served to consolidate and form it.

Literature also mirrored social changes and political constellations. The world of the court and the nobility, together with the 'free' existence of students and travelling artists, had been the dominant milieux of Romanticism. With Biedermeier, Young Germany and Realism, the literary world became increasingly 'bourgeois'. The educated, bureaucratic and artisanal segments of the provincial bourgeoisie rose to prominence. They were critical of both the nobility and the new industrial bourgeoisie; even Gustav Freytag, who had hoped in *Soll und Haben* to present an examination of the German nation at work around the 1850s, chose as hero an old-style bourgeois merchant rather than a factory-owner or worker. Up until the middle of the century, such a choice would certainly have struck a chord with the reality of the situation in Germany — thereafter, however, it seemed inappropriate in the light of the great social changes which were under way, and certainly it was a less contemporary vision than Balzac's Paris or Dickens's London. Land, village and peasantry had, since the 1830s, played an important role in prose as counter-images to the bourgeois world, as for example in Berthold Auerbach's slightly sentimentalised in accordance with urban prejudices, yet exceedingly popular *Schwarzwälder Dorfgeschichten* (Tales from Black Forest Villages, 1843–54) or in the secure and flourishing counter-world of Immermann's *Oberhof* (1838–39). Village life represented a simpler, more genuine counter-world to urban bourgeois decadence. Here was a *Volk* in the pre-industrial sense, corresponding to the political inclinations of liberals and conservatives alike.

At this point, we should note that the literature of this period, from Biedermeier to Realism, had a strong inclination towards the regional and the 'homeland' nostalgic (*heimatlich*), both in terms of content and theme as in mood and tone. From Mörike and Annette von Droste-Hülshoff, Grillparzer and Stifter to Storm, even the great poets were drawn to and captivated by the landscape of their homeland. The (re-)emergence of serious poetry written in regional dialect, as in Klaus Groth and, above all, in Fritz Reuter, went along the same lines, not to speak of local popular plays in the provenance of Berlin, Vienna or Hesse. Germany still was not organised around the capitals, even in the age of nationalism. It remained a land of regions, of *Heimaten*. And the will to concrete, visible reality and intersubjective alliances instilled this provinciality in literature. The provinces were no intellectual desert even in federalist Germany, and were in no sense negative or worthy of scorn.

A final theme on which to close, a theme typical of the changes in philosophical understanding in drama and in prose: human fate. The Classical conviction was that fate is bound up with the liberty of the individual and the 'firmament of ideas' which exists over us, and that tragedy is a product of the clash of an indefinite desire with a definite reality. This conviction was now relinquished. During the 19th century, writers increasingly felt that fate was inescapable. At the same time, action became more complicated and lost its uniformity of meaning, and the unintentional consequences of action became more important. The identity of the *dramatis personae* headed into the realms of doubt, through the discovery of an 'id' in the 'ego'. Humanity became caught up in dreadful fate and was rendered passive. The logical sequence of actions disintegrated. This was true initially of the great dramas of Grillparzer and Hebbel. It was they who, at that time, preserved the Classical form, the Classical gesture and, to a certain extent, the Classical thematic. Furthermore, they tried to justify the claims of tragedy and myth to challenge the pattern of the times. For Grillparzer, fate and tragedy were determined by the status quo, the general morale and the forces of reality. One major theme addressed not only the destruction of order by a heroic protagonist, but also the destruction of the protagonist by his passion, and then the distrust of the liberated action itself. Even for Grabbe, no matter how large a role was played in his plays by the failure of the 'great' individual before the pettiness of the masses and the times, the protagonist underwent a fundamental transformation — from being the subject of history to becoming its object. For Hebbel, it was existence as will, and not its aim, which signified guilt (thereby implying the existence of guilt in innocence). The very fact of the battle of the sexes, for example, unleashed tragic forces. The laws of the world mercilessly contradicted the individual, his greatness and his essential inadequacy, and these contradictions were absolute. Both these dramatists were before their time in psychologically analysing behaviour and, in Hebbel's case, even intellectualising it. In the process, it became obvious that behaviour is determined. Under these conditions, tragedy lost its — Classical — reconciliatory and comforting character, even where great social orders won through against the self-assertion and rebellion of the individual even to the point of denial and downfall.

Of course, the bourgeois lifestyle became alienated from tragedy. Unlike the tragedies of the inherited Classical canon, bourgeois tragedy seemed remarkably inappropriate to the time. Bourgeois fate found its way into the novel and the novella. Biedermeier, and above all Realism, witnessed the demise of chance and 'daemonic' undoing, which had been so important in Romanticism. Action and fate were greatly differentiated and were largely explained by internal and external necessities and the connections between them. Further explanations were found in psychological development, historical and social positions, by the wealth of circumstance and detail, and sometimes by a sequence of barely perceivable changes. Action virtually became something that happened to the individual. Liberty was limited, but not overwhelmed, by determinate necessity, for the form of the work of art (and the distancing stylistic tools of humour and reminiscence) was supposed to sustain it in the face of all restrictions. Of course, the question of the meaning of an individual life or of worldly happiness in such a view became ever more entangled in the web of historical and social limitations on the one hand and psychological limitations on the other.

5. The Reading Revolution and the Rise of the Press

During the first two-thirds of the century, Germany progressed from an illiterate to a literate nation. If the ratio of non-readers to potential readers is estimated to be 3:1 around 1800, this ratio would be reversed by 1870. This phenomenon can rightly be called the 'reading revolution', the more so when one takes into account the qualitative change from intensive and repetitive consumption of a few books — like the Bible — to the extensive consumption of a wider range of publications. One factor in this process was, of course, an effective literacy programme in the school system. Another and more general impetus came from casting off the old world of tradition, a world in which class and custom, and the living inheritance passed down by word of mouth, determined conduct, and, together with religion, informed the interpretation of life and individual existence. The static world in which old and permanent truths had been central and where communication had been practised on a one-to-one level was abandoned. The new world of the 'estate of the individual', of reflection about social behaviour, of freedom of choice and self-education. This was a world of change and progress in which novelty and the future were more important than the here and now. It was a world which related more closely to abstract, universal communities and criteria: a world in which curiosity had been unleashed. A world, then, of language. In a universe which harboured a growing need for new formulas to understand life and self, new ways to reach out beyond the answers offered by the established church, reading acted as a medium for the problems arising from the need to adapt to an increased social mobility.

Bourgeois enlightenment and the bourgeois culture of feeling stood at the threshold of this new development, which first appeared in the critical discourses, primarily in utilitarian and fictional genres, but also later manifesting itself on occasion in political literature. The epicentre of the reading revolution was located in the largely urban, educated bourgeoisie (and upper classes). The shock-waves reached far and wide. This literature, in contrast to the scholastic and court literature of the old world, was capable of filtering down to more of the population. The numbers of intellectuals and readers in general grew significantly. Not only did they read more, but most importantly, a new way of perceiving and challenging the world permeated through to other groups.

The production of books rose dramatically. Measured by the number of titles, book production trebled between 1821 and 1843 (4,181 in 1805, 4,505 in 1821, 14,059 in 1843). Between 1801 and 1828, it grew by 28%, and between 1828 and 1845 by 153%, i.e. by around 700 new titles a year. Until the end of the 1860s, it fell back to under 10,000 titles in total, but since the number of copies of each individual title rose, book production as a whole expanded. Technical, commercial and publishing innovations revolutionised the book business. The flourishing of encyclopaedias since the 1830s and 1840s was part of this phenomenon. There were 2,000 copies of the first edition of the six-volume *Brockhaus*, for example. The fifth edition of ten volumes, published in 1818–19, comprised 32,000 copies. By 1870, the copy-run was 300,000. There were, of course, other encyclopaedias, such as *Meyer* and *Herder*. In this period, there was a general burgeoning of cheap books in circulation; from the mid-century, it is possible to speak in terms of large publishing firms and mass production. Reading societies, in which the personal study of texts was combined with discussion, encouraged the educated bourgeoisie in its reading of books and periodicals. Some organisations among the upper middle class provided libraries and reading-rooms. Later, up until about 1860, lending libraries became more typical. This, of course, led to an expansion of the reading public which could cut across class boundaries. But it was not to last. Broadsheets, falling book prices, the loss of the lending library's prestige and the expansion of the book trade since the middle of the century all led to domination of private ownership and private consumption of reading matter among the educated classes.

If one looks at the content of this mounting production, one sees an increase in the proportion of belles lettres and light literature (novels and almanacs in particular). The serialisation of novels in newspapers, and even newspapers that only printed novels, appeared around the middle of the century, and later also in journals. There was also an increase in children's books, schoolbooks and 'factual' literature, especially in the fields of economics and technology. The prevailing preoccupation with entertainment popularised trivial literature, such as Gerstäcker and Hackländer's surprisingly good prairie stories and travel novels, which filled a need for entertainment and information, while satisfying curiosity. In the early 19th century, these trends were not yet class-specific. Light fiction, for example, found a response among the thousands of women readers, even among the educated. The lending libraries had a levelling effect, as did the writings of Walter Scott and other bestsellers of the first half of the century. Later, a sharper division began to emerge between readers of both trivial and more demanding literature, *grosso modo*, between the educated and the petty bourgeois.

The 'reading revolution' also gripped the rural population and the urban lower classes. A decisive role in this period was played by (door-to-door) pedlars selling books, especially outside the cities. They traded not only in traditional religious literature in the form of almanacs and improving tracts, but also in inexpensive chapbooks, so-called *Kolportage* (pedlar's) novels, adventure and horror stories, tales of knights in shining armour and, from the middle of the century onwards, penny dreadfuls.

In addition, this period witnessed the peculiarly ambivalent trends of popular enlightenment and education. The authorities and conservative factions grew apprehensive about reading, or at least about 'too much' reading. Fearing that reading might lead to revolution, the demise of tradition and the distortion of reality by illusions or demands, they moved towards forms of direct and indirect censorship. Prohibitive measures alone were not enough. A movement grew up in opposition to 'bad' and 'harmful' influences. It demanded 'decent' and 'good' literature. It was mainly confessional associations which devoted themselves in the 1840s to the spread of popular writing, looking to establish their own particular type of folk literature — like the stories of the Catholic priest Christoph von Schmid. They wanted to counter 'trashy literature' with new almanacs and books of wisdom and guidance which would disseminate knowledge, information and indeed their own brand of 'reason'. This movement encouraged the growth of popular literacy. For all the tenacity of tradition, the upheavals of the time found expression both in *Kolportage* fiction and 'good' oppositional literature. The comparison with foreign climes also affected the rural population and the lower classes. The expansion of newspapers hastened the demise of the traditional mentality by confronting readers with novelty and otherness.

One result of the reading revolution, which manifested itself in the later years of the period under discussion, is the involvement of the masses in the formation of public opinion, thanks to the influence of the press. Germany had become a nation of newspaper-readers. It was, moreover, a self-perpetuating process: the press both represented and shaped public opinion, which had become a powerful force in the 19th century. No longer the community, the workplace or the church, but rather newspapers brought people into daily and continual contact with the universal, with the Hegelian 'world spirit'. People thereby entered into a new relationship to the times and to the daily routine — away from the familiar and the repetitive towards change and dynamism. They adopted a new relationship to modernity, to distant places in Germany and abroad, and to the abstractions and ideas beyond the ideological world. The direct experience of people's immediate vicinity, the public sphere and politics was put on the agenda.

And at the same time, the newspaper — 'my newspaper' — was a token of self-affirmation and a pledge of hope in a world of enormous transformations and political conviction. Such a multiplication of communication, based on technical intensification and economic innovations (the high-speed printing-press and the telegraph, for example), was an essential feature in the cultivation of modern society, which, in its promotion of mobility and integration, was no longer particularised or bound by convention.

The first impetus for information, discussion, reflection, for a public forum, and hence for the press, came from the bourgeois liberal side. Established powers — governments, for example — had no love of the press, still less for a free press. For them, the press was nothing but a disturbing vehicle for criticism, lobbying and revolution, a symptom of the liberal system. But despite the censorship, neither the objective force of the new communication processes nor public opinion could be ignored. The likes of Metternich, arch-conservative enemy of press freedom, and his near-genius journalist colleague, Friedrich Gentz, joined in this new system of communication and traded in the market-place of public opinion, as did the Prussian government and the Catholic church during the 1837–38 conflict, or again the Prussian conservatives with their *Kreuzzeitung* of 1848. Bismarck too, on assuming office, made 'press policy' a fundamental part of his politics with extraordinary mastery.

The history of the press — newspapers, periodicals and political journals — is a history of press freedom and changing newspaper styles. During the Napoleonic era, papers were centred entirely on Paris — take the *Moniteur,* for example — or, in the case of Vienna and Berlin, bound up closely with governmental policies of appeasement. An independent, politically committed press acting as a mediator of opinions was not established until the wars of liberation. The most famous publication was Joseph Görres's national-democratic *Rheinischer Merkur* produced in Koblenz (1814), which even the thoroughly modern Napoleon appraised as a 'great power' in its own right — though it was a paper of just four pages, appearing only every second day! This paper, along with comparable publications, was to be a victim of the restoration after 1815. Censorship and the Karlsbad Decrees, together with the ban on voicing critical opinions, determined the fate of the daily papers. The bane of liberal publishers, these measures moulded the Metternich era. Of course, one must add a caveat here. Censors and censorship vacillated between rigorous and less stringent phases — there were chinks, and there were also differences between the German states. Moreover, there was the possibility of evading the law by turning to ever new forms of publication — like periodicals, for example — or by going into exile or taking up smuggling. The 'police state' was far from foolproof in comparison with 20th-century experience; there was a constant see-sawing of advantage between the press and the censors. The censor sacrificed the opposition to the courts and to society (a sixth of the parliamentary representatives of 1848 had been dealt with in this way), and thereby radicalised a section of the intellectual opposition to extremes. Guaranteed public freedom of expression had been successfully curtailed, but the growth of liberal, nationalist and democratic opposition, encouraged by the press, could not be entirely suppressed. In fact, political parties themselves were first formed as groupings around the various organs of the press.

The daily papers of the restoration period (in a similar way to the court and state journals, which were gazettes enjoying a state monopoly on advertising) and the so-called 'intelligentsia' broadsheets were, in the main, politically neutral. Abstaining from politics, they contained rather colourless reports, initially limited to the local neighbourhood. Only the *Allgemeine Zeitung*, published by the firm of Cotta in Augsburg, had a interregional importance, thanks to its wealth of content, which was presented in a quietly objective style, plotting a course down the middle of the road that was by no means undistinguished. In Austria, while it enjoyed a certain freedom, the paper had to adopt certain stratagems to guard its interests, being, as it was, a tool in Metternich's foreign policy (it had to give up its Paris correspondent, Heine, in 1832, for example). During 1830–31, and again from the end of the 1830s, there was a rising and ever-changing tide of new oppositional publications, most of which were founded by Young Germany and the Young Hegelians, including the *Hallesche Jahrbücher* (1838–43) or the *Rheinische Zeitung* (1842–43), which was financed by members of the Rhineland *haute bourgeoisie* and written by radical intellectuals like Karl Marx. Furthermore, there was also a greater number of periodicals and journals touching on politics.

A part of the radical journalist community was forced into exile; others, for example Johann Georg August Wirth with the *Deutsche Volkshalle* in Constance, and Karl Grün with the *Mannheimer Abendzeitung*, were able to sustain relatively radical publications within Germany. Further titles included the *Mannheimer Journal*, and the *Westphälisches Dampfboot*, which appeared in Minden from 1844 to 1848, and Robert Blum's *Sächsische Vaterlandsblätter* in Leipzig. Equally important, indeed even more influential, was the fact that the larger dailies, like Königsberg's *Hartungsche Zeitung*, Bremen's *Weserzeitung*, Hamburg's *Neue Zeitung* and the *Vossische Zeitung* in Berlin, pursued a decisively liberal course. Circulation of these papers rose sharply during the 1840s — that of the *Vossische Zeitung*, for example, nearly doubled to 20,000 from 1840 to 1847. The *Kölnische Zeitung*, published by Joseph Du Mont, had a circulation of almost 10,000 in 1847. It enjoyed an influence beyond the immediate environs of Cologne owing to its extensive coverage of current affairs and the arts under the direction of Karl-Heinz Brüggemann, a former member of a student fraternity. The year 1847 saw the first interregional party-political paper, Gervinus's liberal-nationalist *Deutsche Zeitung*, printed in Heidelberg. Not surprisingly, it did not survive the revolution. Liberal political periodicals developed in a similar way, such as the *Deutsche Vierteljahresschrift* or Leipzig's *Grenzboten* (1841–42), which was highly influential in the 1850s and 1860s. It was not only the liberal parties which had their journals; conservatives founded the Berlin *Politische Wochenblatt* in 1831, and in 1838 the

Catholics founded the *Historisch-politische Blätter für das katholische Deutschland*. These papers addressed themselves to the politically committed and educated upper middle classes.

The year 1848 was the year of the newspaper; old and new titles thrived. Even in Austria, classic haven of Vormärz censorship, the number of titles rose from 79 to 388! Newspapers became the political forum and were now read even by the masses. Even after 1848, the experience of this process could not easily be swept aside. The state could plague the press, as it did in the 1850s, with securities, licences and fees, and with police and court actions; but it did not reintroduce censorship. Circulation figures and numbers of titles continued to increase, as the changing ratio of papers to population indicates: from 1:25 in 1841 to 1:5.6 in 1865. Fifty-eight weekly papers and thirty-two dailies (six of which had twice-daily editions) were published in Berlin in 1862. The scope of papers grew in line with the quantity. There was increasing differentiation between sections — from economic and feuilleton pages to the serialisation of novels, and, with the discontinuation of the state monopoly, an increasing devotion to advertising. Popular papers were cheaper and more modest than the larger papers, costing three, as opposed to six, thalers a year; but a penny press like the ones in London and Paris did not develop. Most newspapers remained regionalised, although news agencies and correspondents did produce a certain uniformity. The *Kölnische Zeitung*, with its remarkable circulation of 60,000 in 1866, was the foremost liberal-nationalist interregional organ. The leftist liberal, anti-Prussian camp gradually (from 1856-8) came to be served in a similar way by Leopold Sonnemann's *Frankfurter Zeitung*. The majority of papers were bourgeois liberal, and were either moderately or radically progressive. The conservatives too had their journals: in Prussia there was the *Neue Preussische Zeitung* (called the *Kreuzzeitung*, the 'Cross Paper', after its emblem), which was brilliantly edited by Hermann Wagener; political Catholicism had 126 papers at its disposal, with a combined circulation of over 320,000 in 1871. Moreover, with district and small-town newspapers, the press reached into the provinces and the countryside in the 1850s and 1860s. It was the press which gradually integrated the rural population into 'literary' life, the changing society, politics, and into the nation as a whole. Needless to say, these newspapers, with their traditional style and educative standards (as indicated, for example, by their inclusion of extensive parliamentary reports), generally had little success in courting workers and day-labourers — in other words, the lower classes.

Equally important for the development of bourgeois politics and culture was the development of a (necessarily) national press, whose ideas were further disseminated through organised reading circles. Its readership far exceeded that of Romantic and Classical literary magazines and the journals of the Enlightenment period. Political periodicals belonged to this new national press, whose debates assembled and articulated the various positions of the political classes. For the liberals, there were the famous *Preussische Jahrbücher* (1858), along with the above-mentioned *Grenzboten*, now run by Gustav Freytag. Then there were the political and cultural revues — copying the literary pamphlets of the Vormärz period — like *Westermanns Monatshefte* (1856) and *Cottas Morgenblatt für die gebildeten Stände*. Alongside these were the satirical magazines after the English and French pattern, like the *Fliegende Blätter* in Munich (1845) and Berlin's *Kladderadatsch* (1848), whose circulation reached

39,000 in 1861. In addition, there were countless specialist papers for every subject and every profession, a symptom of two of the traits of modern society — diversification and the division of labour.

Finally, there were a number of woodcut-illustrated newspapers and family and entertainment-orientated magazines, of the type founded in Leipzig in 1853 by Ernst Keil. His paper, *Die Gartenlaube*, had a circulation of 160,000 in 1863, 200,000 in 1866, and, after the publication of novels of Eugenie Marlitt, 400,000 by 1875. Its circulation was therefore in the order of two million, and it found a loyal audience among the various *Vereine* (societies): sharpshooters, choruses, gymnasts. There were other family magazines competing with *Die Gartenlaube*, like *Über Land und Meer* or the conservative *Daheim*. These new journals were entertaining, literary and informative about subjects such as nature, foreign lands and history; they were pleasantly informal, but in no way entirely apolitical. But above all, they were liberal, nationalist and integrative, albeit somewhat contrived, idealistic and sentimental. They were a phenomenon of the rising bourgeois and petty-bourgeois mass culture. In their utopias and surrogate worlds, their bourgeois and universal ideals endowed these papers with a relevance extending beyond German borders — more so after 1871 than ever before. It is easy for the modern intellectual to pour scorn on this utopianism, but even today's 'anti-*Gartenlaube*' world of magazines and media is scarcely more down-to-earth.

With the rise of the press, there arose a new social group — journalists — who, in part, melted into the new political class. In the Vormärz, part-time editors began to be outnumbered by full-time ones. The majority continued to have a university education with a doctorate — the newspaper industry at that time demanded a mastery of modern foreign languages. Many also had scholarly or academic ambitions, and just wanted to have had experience of a different profession. They were philosophical and political intellectuals. After the revolution, philologists, those with doctorates and those who had come from other professions declined in number; trained lawyers, economists and people who had started out in newspapers played a larger role. In short, the job was professionalised. The reporter gained column inches alongside the opinion-maker, likewise the local reporter and the news editor alongside the leader-writer. For politically committed and ambitious members of the bureaucratic, academic and free intelligentsia, part-time journalism still played an important role. Journalistic talents provided the basis for the political careers of men of such diverse political persuasions as the conservatives Hermann Wagener and Joseph Edmund Jörg, the liberals Heinrich von Treitschke, Gustav Freytag, Eduard Lasker and Leopold Sonnemann, and the socialist Ferdinand Lassalle.

Journalists liked to identify themselves with the task of the press to articulate 'what's on everybody's mind', 'what everybody agrees on', to function and be recognised as an 'opinion leader' of the people, not simply to relate facts 'slavishly', but to judge, as Görres had said in 1814. Here, party opinion and public opinion in general — what everybody thought and what everybody ought to have thought — were merged unquestioningly into one. This was also typical of the 'philosophical-political' journalists who emerged after 1830. Life, literature and other realms were subordinated to philosophical and political norms. Alongside civil servants and poets, men of the church and universities, journalists appeared as formulators of universalities and champions of change. They constituted an *avant-garde*. The press was an 'organ which allowed the epoch to converse with itself', said the Young German Robert Prutz. Daily journalism, he argued, appealed for a change from the extant 'limited' opinion to 'unlimited' educated opinion and to discussion. There was a widespread conviction, born of liberal argument, that demagogy and untruth would disappear in such discussion, and that the 'truly' universal would come to light. But the journalism of opinions was also the attempt to propagate ideas and to court adherents. In any case, partisanship, judgment and critical reflection were the usual concerns of journalists, rather than the compilation of reports and information. Published opinion was, therefore, only partly identified with public opinion. Certain things, such as rural life or the Catholic community, were almost completely excluded; others, such as the church enlightenment groups of the 1840s, were over-exposed. After 1848, a new realism won out against philosophical doctrine and the dominance of critical reflection; a new value was ascribed to factual accuracy. Only a newspaper which reflected actuality could, so it was thought, convincingly form a realistic political opinion.

The rise of the press and of journalism was accompanied by constant criticism. 'Everywhere there are fools infernal, who, lacking all skills, start a journal' (*Der Narren gibt es überall, wer sonst nichts kann, schreibt ein Journal*), wrote Baron Adolf von Knigge, a typical man of the Enlightenment, as early as 1785. 'Whoever wanted to reap without having sown, became a man of letters,' said Riehl after 1848 in his sociological analysis of the opposition of journalists ('proletarians of intellectual labour') to the state and the existing society. The more robust conservatives complained that a good deal of the press 'finds itself in the hands of the most degenerate subjects who are religiously, morally and economically impoverished and speculate on nothing other than dissolution and overthrow' or are blind to reality and experience (*Historisch-politische Blätter*, 1849). The liberals, on the other hand, believed that dishonest and incapable journalism could not remain popular very long with the public. Lassalle formulated the critique from the left: the journalist, otherwise dishonest, dissipated and incapable of the most elementary craft, working in this capitalist newspaper industry said just what the largest group of consumers wanted to hear, instead of gradually 'raising' the public to loftier ideas. With the rise of the press, the debate about its 'true' function became virulent.

There is one final criticism to mention, which stretched from Goethe through Burckhardt and Kierkegaard to Nietzsche. It was not a criticism of journalists, but of the effect of newspaper reading: a tendency to lose oneself in daily affairs, in the multiplicity of the world, and in mediated experience alone. It was a criticism of newspapers' tendency to construct a prefabricated relationship to the world. Karl Immermann, who was certainly no conservative, said in the 1830s that the reading of journals changed the culture, commanded an essential place in the life of the individual and challenged the importance of the family. It promoted the readers' pretensions that they were informed about everything and understood it all, thereby making superficiality a sign of the times. But this type of media critique did not influence the subsequent course of events.

V

The Revolution of 1848–49

1. The March Revolution

All the tensions and hopes of political and social life of the German people are gathered together in the outbreak and explosion of the great German revolution of 1848–49.

Despite the eschatological fear of revolution that the conservatives harboured, and despite the hunger revolts of 1847, the revolution in Germany came unexpectedly; and indeed, it was not planned by activists or conspirators. The liberals that led the revolution had not wanted it, and it was not inevitable. It had been triggered by the February revolution in Paris. The clash between the forces of movement and of resistance was a European one. The Germans were keeping one eye on Europe and one eye on France, the country that was the model for revolution. The news of the events in Paris — on 24 February Louis Philippe's throne was burnt on the Place de la Bastille — was the spark that struck at the tension in Germany and set in motion the wave of unrest; that, at least, was the trigger. But, of course, revolution was not imported. It was also a German phenomenon that grew out of German crises and problems. The German revolution was part of the wider European revolution, but it had its own specific elements and its own goals.

What happened in March was firstly a chain of revolutions in the individual German states — some in the state capitals and some in the larger provincial centres — accompanied by social unrest, particularly out in the country; in some places the revolutions were simultaneous, while in other areas they were more of a chain reaction. The sequence of events was similar, as were the claims that the many revolutions were directly and indirectly linked, and inasmuch as they brought together ideas of want, sentiment and action they did indeed form one united German revolution, despite the different geographical areas — and this was not all that was different about the individual revolutions — in which their events unfolded.

Typical of the course of events of these revolutions were the events in Baden. On 27 February, influenced by the news from Paris, a large public gathering in Mannheim, at which the liberal Karl Mathy and the radical Friedrich Hecker were still able to appear together, decided to petition the parliamentary chambers. They demanded that the people be armed; in other words, they wanted a militia. The royal army, it was said, should no longer have a monopoly on arms. They also demanded freedom of the press, the end of censorship and freedom of political expression; in short, they were calling for the end of the ban on political parties. They called for courts with juries, which meant the democratisation of judiciary, especially in political cases. They also wanted a national parliament. Demands such as these no longer meant the straight-forward amendment of laws; the people wanted to alter the system and the balance of power, both in Baden and in Germany. The same demands, in similar guise, were taken up throughout the country and have become known as the classic *Märzforderungen* (March Demands). On 1 March a deputation, accompanied by a mass demonstration, went to Karlsruhe. The masses were to constitute the power base of a revolution: they included city-dwellers, apprentices, workers and students, and peasants and country people from the whole state. Some had come to Karlsruhe by train; some were armed; all had been inspired by speeches and the spirit of a joint alliance. Tumultuous, they gathered near the buildings of the parliamentary chambers. The lower chamber took up the March Demands and added to them: the army should swear an oath to the constitution; feudal rights should be abolished; ministers should held accountable. Initially, the grand duke resisted the demands, but he rejected Prussian military aid and gave in. On 9 March, appointing the liberal party leaders, he formed a new government which not only recognised the March Demands but also began to implement them. This was a typical case of the new 'March government'.

It was the same story right across the Third Germany: public meetings led to demonstrations, addresses, petitions, unrest and pressure. None of the governments dared to send in the police or the army. In those places where the governments hesitated or made only partial concessions, a military arsenal or town hall would be stormed, as happened in Munich and Frankfurt. Other demands were added to the classic March Demands, including new elections, the liberalisation of voting rights, revision of the constitution and the liberation of peasants. The monarchs agreed in the end, and they installed new, liberal 'March governments'. Only in Munich did the monarch, Ludwig I, an autocratic ruler unwilling to work with the new liberal powers, abdicate and hand the throne to his son, Maximilian.

The revolution spread through the two great states, grasping even the bastions of the old system, Vienna and Berlin. And it was here, for the time being, that the fate of the German revolution was decided. In Vienna, Metternich had initially believed that it would be possible to block first the French revolution and then the Italian revolution from crossing the borders into Germany. The Viennese knew what this would cost and stormed the banks to redeem their paper money. But Metternich's belief proved to be an illusion as the revolution spilled over into Germany and Hungary. On 7 March, the Viennese liberals, organised into associations, circulated a petition; the students drew up a somewhat stronger version, the 'Aula'. When the moderately oppositional Estates of Lower Austria discussed similar demands on 13 March, there was a mass demonstration in front of the assembly building, which the crowds then stormed. The intervention of the military, which was hesitant, only added to the tension. There was serious unrest in the areas around the city, which led to a sort of 'proletarian' revolution. Pawnshops, tax offices and factories were stormed, and in places shops were looted. The *Bürger* and the militia allied themselves to the revolutionaries. There was a call for the withdrawal of troops and for Metternich's resignation. The *Staatskonferenz* (government) submitted. Military suppression of the uprising was abandoned; the state had no more self-confidence and had almost lost its ability to act. Metternich was dropped, and the state was pleased to have found a sacrifice — it also thought that it would now perhaps be possible to follow a course of conservative reforms and that he would be little more than a nuisance to it. The establishment was crumbling and filled with contradictions from within; and that increased the chances of the revolution. Metternich had not given the fight his all, and, pessimistic about the future, he gave up his struggle as a lost cause and resigned. He fled quietly to England, although he was still one of the most powerful men in the ongoing events. The army was withdrawn, and a citizens' national guard and an Academic Legion were sanctioned. Promises of a constitution, which were initially stalled, were then given, but only after a further siege of the Hofburg; and censorship was lifted. The government was restructured, but, of course, only within the framework of the old bureaucracy of the establishment.

The events of the March weeks gave the Vienna revolution its own character. Firstly, the radical element played a far greater role in the Vienna revolution than elsewhere. The Viennese masses of the emerging working class lent the revolution part of its clout, they represented potential radicalism. And it was only in Vienna that students were particularly affected by the established privileged and caste system, and hence had acted independently and led the way; they had been more radical than the middle classes, and with the founding of the Academic Legion they had temporarily consolidated their influence. That meant that the radicals did not abandon the leadership of the revolution, as had happened elsewhere. For this reason, the dialectics of radicalism and counter-revolution had made a greater impression in Vienna than anywhere else; and this had far-reaching consequences for the whole of the German people. Secondly, the state leadership did indeed make concessions, agreeing to consider the introduction of agri-cultural reform, faced as it was with the threat of an agricultural revolution. But for the time being there was no 'March ministry' that, within the context of the monarchic state, would have been able to implement such a reform. It was precisely for this reason that in Vienna there was no temporary consolidation of the revolution. The revolution was carried on by the Bürgerausschuss (citizens' committee), the Demokratischer Klub (democratic club), the national guard and the Academic Legion, and thus it was that the left held on to its position. When, on 25 April, the government proposed a constitution, similar to that in Belgium, and limited voting rights, there was savage protest. Such things were not a matter for the government, it was said. On 15 May the government had to agree to a national assembly — which would draw up a constitution — and to universal suffrage, and it had to make concessions to the national guard and the Academic Legion. On 17 May, the royal court 'fled' from radical Vienna to Innsbruck, and in so doing gained a little freedom to act. The attempt by the government in Vienna to limit the students' power failed. Instead a security committee, led by the one-time moderately radical student Adolf Fischhof, was set up, which acted rather like a supplementary government. The actual government was democratised. One of the leaders of the citizens' democratic opposition, a certain Alexander Bach, who had been at the barricades, became Minister of Justice.

The empire, however, had not only been shaken by the revolution in Vienna; it had been seriously rocked by the national revolutions in its other territories. The continued existence of this realm was itself now in question. The Italian provinces had risen up and made themselves independent. Piedmont had begun the war, and England and France had encouraged the Italian revolution. Revolutionary Hungary seemed to have removed itself from the realm as a whole. In Prague too there had been a revolution in March. As everywhere else, it had been a liberal constitutional revolution with social elements, but it was also a nationalist Bohemian movement. Demands were made for the right of autonomy and participation for the Estates and the union of the lands of Wenceslaus's crown, which meant the incorporation of Moravia and Silesia. Of course, these two states showed little interest in this plan. At the outset, Germans and Czechs worked together; Prague was still a staunchly German city. But this unity crumbled, and the national difference became an explosive issue. There were claims to power and feelings of threat; should there be equal rights or should the Czechs dominate in an autonomous Bohemia? Social tensions which, in the face of the more bourgeois status of the Germans, took on a nationalistic feeling: these were the matters which had taken centre-stage. The estate-orientated party of the nobility, which was more Bohemian than Czech, joined forces with bourgeois Czech powers. This ran contrary to German–Bohemian interests. What was then decisive was that the Germans wanted to take part in the pan-German reorganisation, whereas the Czechs did not, and they were unable to come to any agreement on this matter. We shall return to this later.

The Austrian government, faced with the revolution and the threat to the existence of the entire state, was in a weak position. For the German people as a whole, this meant that Austria was temporarily a power unable to act; she was also discounted as an opponent of or a partner to a German policy.

Then there was the revolution in Prussia. At the beginning of March, there was agitation and unrest in the Rhineland. A gathering of over 5,000 people in Cologne (3 March), led by the communist doctor Andreas Gottschalk, made more than just the usual demands. In radical spirit, their demands were as follows: legislation and administration by the people and its revolutionary committees; protection of work and a guarantee to meet everyday needs. The army dispersed the demonstration. As a result, there then followed a liberal and also a left-wing liberal petition; the liberal one in particular found an audience in other provinces. But in Prussia attention was focused on Berlin. From 7 March, there had been a whole chain of initially small but then increasingly better attended gatherings of people 'Under the Tents' in the zoo, where addresses calling for the usual demands to be met were given. The unrest grew. Talk was of social revolution, and there was indignation that the army had occupied strategically important positions. On the evening of 13 March, the army and the demonstrators clashed; then barricades were erected and street fighting broke out; and finally there came the first casualties. Civilian deputations demanded the withdrawal of troops. The king, uncertain of what to do and influenced by Metternich's fall, finally decided to agree to the demands. On 18 March, he lifted censorship, summoned the United Diet, and promised a constitution and the reorganisation of the confederation. A large crowd that had gathered outside the palace, originally with the intention of forcing the king to accept the demands, gave him a lively ovation; but the bayonets were cause for some disquiet, and there were some calls for the soldiers to withdraw. Thereupon the troops were ordered to clear the square, a few untargeted shots were fired, and cries of 'Treason' and 'To arms' went up, and the fighting began again. This, of course, was more than an unfortunate coincidence, misunderstanding or panic. In fact, it represented the conflict that was the basis of the Berlin revolution, namely the conflict between civilians and the army. The question of whether the troops would be withdrawn or remain was one that reached to the very heart of the Prussian monarchy; it questioned the king's unchallengeable authority. Calls of 'abolish the army' meant that the king should renounce the military state and become 'civilian'; this revolutionised the basis of the Prussian state.

The whole of Berlin, from house-owners to workers, was in uproar. Hundreds of barricades were erected, and there was bitter street fighting and house-to-house battles. More than 230 people lost their lives. The troops pushed forward, sometimes making use of artillery. But on the night of 19 March, there was a change of mind (*Entschlüsse*). The commander, General von Prittwitz, began to doubt the morale and the capability of troops to keep up the street battles; he decided it would be better to besiege the city from outside. The king, shocked by all that had happened, had a change of heart. Everything, he declared in an appeal 'to my dear people of Berlin', had been a terrible mistake. He withdrew the troops and submitted to the revolution. On 19 March, he honoured the revolution's dead. The militia was provided with arms from the military arsenal and now guarded the palace. Prince Wilhelm, the king's brother, the much-hated champion of the military party, had to leave Berlin and fled to England. The collapse of the old order seemed clear; the people's revolution had defeated the authorities — and this in the strongest military state in Germany. On 21 March, the king, accompanied by princes and ministers and wearing black, red and gold armbands, rode ceremonially through Berlin. No calls of 'Long live the Kaiser of Germany' were allowed, but next to the royal group walked the veterinarian Urban, with his long beard and flowing hair, carrying a painted imperial crown. In a speech, Friedrich Wilhelm declared himself to be in favour of German unity, freedom and a constitution. 'Prussia is from henceforth merged with Germany,' he said. Was this then the new call of Prussia, the new call of the monarchy? In any event, it was an attempt, directly after the defeat, to introduce a policy that represented both a moral conquest and a German policy. The following day the king defined more clearly his promise of a constitution. On 29 March, he appointed a 'March ministry' led by the two *haut bourgeois* Rhineland liberals, Ludolf Camphausen and David Hansemann. This was a curious victory for the new Prussian west over the old Junker east. The ministry was set the task of uniting the kingdom and the civilian movement and of thereby transforming Prussia into a constitutional monarchy and 'civil society'. When, on 25 March, the king called on the officers of the guard in Potsdam to honour fully the spirit of the times (as he put it, 'I have never been freer and safer than under the protection of my people'), there was much grumbling. Ultra-royalists were waiting for the order for a counter-revolution. Bismarck wanted to organise such a revolution in the name of Prince Wilhelm, employing peasant farmers and the army; one of the generals wanted to arrest Bismarck for these plans, on a charge of high treason. But the king did not exploit the army's readiness for counter-revolution. The officers, who were more Prussian and more monarchic than their king, stood about like soaked poodles. It was in this difference of attitude between the king and the army that the revolution's greatest opportunity lay. The king stuck by his political decision; he was, of course, uncertain of the outcome, but in the first instance he supported the idea of a Germany policy and felt that he would then be able to isolate the more radical trends.

So much for the events. Let us now look more closely at the aims and the supporters of this revolution. The March Demands, even in their initial formulation, were only a meagre and not always completely understood — indeed, more of a symbolic — expression of what was moving the people to act. Everyone had a different idea of these demands, felt more strongly about certain hardships and harboured different expectations of the new order. There was, however, a general basic feeling, and it was one of indignation concerning the existing power hierarchy and the state. This was an authoritarian state, a state with a patronising bureaucracy, a state of administrative offices and laborious procedures. It was a state of courts, soldiers, tax-collectors and gendarmes, founded on orders and obedience, on bans and permissions. The state established duties but guaranteed few rights. It was a state that continually checked, rebuked and harassed youth and students, craftsmen, workers and humble people. The state prohibited free speech and threatened those who criticised with censor, trial and deportation. It was a state where taxes were used principally to finance the royal court and the army, matters on which the people had little say. Finally, it was a state of dynastic and, above all, feudal privileges which were oppressive and violated any feeling of justice. Of course, politically and legally the Germans were far better off than in 1789. They were not so oppressed, they were treated less unfairly, and they were not bled so dry. Freedom and security were greater, as was respect of human dignity —there were less beatings, for example. Corruption and wastefulness by the authorities was considerably less. But standards had changed, and self-awareness had grown; such things went against the grain of the old system. There was a seething discontentment that had been building up over a long period of time, and it finally exploded. The feelings of indignation and hatred were greater than any positive aims that existed, but what was certain was that the order of power should become more liberal and move closer to the people. Words like constitution and participation were symbols of a new order. It was for these reasons that the people gathered behind the liberal-democratic demands, originally put forward by the politically-minded bourgeois elite. And lent them their revolutionary weight. This applied equally to states with or without a constitution, because even the former were authoritarian, unpopular and not liberal. The early constitutions did not work like the safety-valve that their creators had envisaged; equally, rejection of a constitution did not work like a dam. Before the revolution this distinction had become immaterial.

Constitution was the cardinal value, then the idea of a nation-state. This is quite astonishing, because the national aim was far less concretely concerned with everyday life; the logic of the connection between freedom and unity was an abstract idea for the man in the street, and it was really only the educated who were concerned with identity. It is, however, a misunderstanding of political thinking to ask only for direct interests and expectations. The national aim had become self-evident for the people of the city. Of course, the nation-state was also a symbol of freedom and of a citizens' state that was opposed to both the evil confederation (Bond) and the familiar authoritarianism. But the nation was also a unique reality, and an end in itself.

It was to these aims that the curious mood of the revolution adhered; they also fill all the reports on the issue. The mood was one of awakening, of 'spring', as was often said; it was a mood of great, if somewhat indeterminate, hopes and expectations; everything would now be renewed and better. There was merrymaking, celebratory processions and banquets, a feeling of unity; everywhere people embraced one another in public; there was a curious compulsion to go out into the streets and to keep moving. There was a desire to be participating in some united action, and since one didn't always know what that would be, it often came in the form of the wish to take up arms, to be a soldier or to join the militia. The expectations of a new era and the readiness to act determined not only the atmosphere, they also determined the character of this revolution.

Let us look further at the social aims and causes of the revolution and at those who supported it. The revolution was accompanied by social movements — indeed, they formed a combined force. The most significant was the peasant unrest during the weeks of March. In Austria, the liberation of the peasant had not yet been carried out. In the regions with *Grundherrschaft*, i.e. in south and central Germany, the *Ablösung* (redemption) of peasants' debts to their former lords had been put off and remained incomplete. This was particularly the case for the regions controlled by the mediatised princes, and it was most notably they who constituted with the help of their public rights a kind of subsidiary sovereignty. At the same time, however, in the constitutional states of the Third Germany, the self-confidence and politicisation of peasants continued to flourish. In March, there was a major peasant revolution in many areas of south-west Germany, the Hessian states, and then in Thuringia and Franconia. The revolution was directed against the aristocratic *Grundherren* and the major mediatised princes — the Hohenlohes, Neippergs, Fürstenbergs and Leiningens, for example; but the revolution was particularly strongly targeted against the state demesne, forestry and tax officials, and against Jewish creditors. The revolution took the form of a civil war and included spontaneous demonstrations and marches outside the palace or the town hall where calls were made for documents to be handed over so that they might be burnt. In Weinsberg, five hundred peasants, intimidating an official who offered them the key to the wine cellar, declared that they 'had not come to eat and drink; all we want is to burn those papers which reduce us to begging, and then we want to go and see the king and tell him of our suffering and poverty'. Events were not always so orderly. There were also cases of looting, destruction, arson and violence, the aim of which was, of course, to force the rapid capitulation of state and feudal violence. In Nassau, many thousands of peasants went to Wiesbaden and demanded the transfer of royal demesnes to state ownership and then that they be divided up. Some came with money-bags and went to the tax-collectors to demand their share. '*Sicherheit-sausschüssee*' (Committees of Public Safety) in the villages dismissed the mayors and wardens. The farmers temporarily stopped paying their taxes and assumed all rights to use of the forest and all hunting rights. Whole villages were then able, often with rusty shot-guns, to set out on great shoots.

This rural revolution was a revolution of the peasants against the lords and the state. The poverty and social conflicts in villages were not significant in this revolution; it was not the farm labourers and the lower peasant classes that were participating in the revolution.

The rural revolution was kept almost entirely within the boundaries of the area defined by the old Germany. In Prussia, the countryside remained calm for the most part; it was only in Silesia that there was any unrest — and this included the small-peasant classes. But Silesia was the province in which peasant liberation was most affected by delays and restrictions. In Austria, the possibility that a rural revolution might take place was sufficiently threatening to force the authorities to introduce agricultural reforms.

The peasant revolution would never have taken place had it not been for the urban revolution which preceded it. It then became an independent social revolution with its own motives and aims and its own dynamism. Politically, however, it was subordinate to the liberal bourgeois revolution. Both the peasants and the urban bourgeoisie wanted the abolition of the old feudal order and freedom of property. Of course, the peasants' vigour was greater and their methods more radical. They wanted their own farmland, but they were not bothered about historical property rights and law and order. In a country with no capital city and where two-thirds of the population were still living in the countryside, violence and the readiness of the peasants to adopt violent means represented a major part of the foundation of the masses and the power of the bourgeois revolution to win through, even though the liberals rejected the violence. The 'March ministers' on the one hand distanced themselves from the tumult and forced abandonment of property — Heinrich von Gagern tore up a declaration to this effect in the Darmstadt chamber — and indeed, they used the military to suppress such ideas. But on the other hand they immediately promised to fulfil the peasants' demands for emancipation and the abolition of privileges for the nobility and began to tackle these issues. The peasants had quickly achieved their aims. And one very important consequence of this was that the peasants then withdrew from the revolution. They could only think in terms of their villages and what they could see with their own eyes; the notions of a nation-state put forward by the inhabitants of the city were of no interest to them; they remained particularist. Once they had what they wanted, it became clear that the liberal and democratic policies and the policies put forward by the city-dwellers were alien to them. In the spring of 1848, the peasants were one of the forces behind the revolution; but then the revolution had to continue without them. It had to consolidate or die.

Even in the urban revolutions, social protest and social revolutionary motives were playing their part. We have already discussed the working classes and the troubles of the poverty crisis of the 1840s; there was still an enormous gulf between the growth of the population and the stagnation in the numbers required in the workforce; factories and factory workers were still at a very early stage in their development. In 1846–47, following a failed harvest, Germany (and Europe) was hit by a serious agricultural and food shortage crisis. Increasing food prices, decreasing purchasing power, a drop in sales and a drop in production in the trades and the growing problem of under-employment were all part of a situation worsened by an industrial and commercial recession. This background of increased poverty was a significant factor in the readiness for and tendency towards revolution. Things had to change, and it seemed that social and political power structures were to blame for the situation; it was generally felt that they had to change. Unrest in the working classes motivated by social conditions was part of the March revolution. A major part of its protest was directed — somewhat outmodedly — against factories and machines; this was particularly the case in Mannheim, Hanau and Mainz, Leipzig, Schmalkalden and other Thuringian towns, as well as in Solingen, Krefeld and other parts of the Rhineland. Machines were destroyed by workers and craftsmen; steamships and railway installations by coachmen and boatmen. The Krefeld silk-weavers, within the framework of a guild, wanted to share out the looms; no one was to have more than four. This was described as small-business privatisation of the means of production. But all these actions were very localised and cannot be seen as a great revolutionary programme against the state or the bourgeois society as a whole; they were actually only offshoots and undercurrents rather than a united social revolution. The textile workers in Saxony, in the Bergisches Land and the majority of those in the Lower Rhine area, for example, made almost no protest.

What is more important in this context is that the workers in large cities such as Cologne, Mannheim and Vienna took part in the revolution. In Berlin, the workers did not initially take part in the gathering in front of the palace, but then students called on the workers of Borsig to join the protests; they asked to be paid their week's wages, and then they came armed with axes to the barricades. From then on, however, no distinction was made between the factory workers and the mass of day-labourers and the poor. Together they represented a reservoir of unrest, quite prepared to overstep the boundaries of police order, to demonstrate and to man the barricades. But the same was also true of the craftsmen living on the edge of the middle class, the proletarian master-craftsman and the restless apprentices who were threatened by both the decline of the crafts and the rise of the factories. They were particularly active and mobile and quick to put forward new ideas of opposition; everywhere they represented a major supporting faction of the revolution. Among the dead of the March battles in Berlin were many joiners, metalworkers and tailors, who in this instance were skilled workers and were on the verge of becoming salaried workers. These lower-middle-class and marginally middle-class masses took part in the bourgeois revolution, they supported it with feeling, force and determination. But social deprivation and unrest in the working classes were not the causes of the revolution.

It is possible to identify other social groups that supported the revolution, such as the intellectuals, journalists, literary figures, booksellers, former theologians and students. They did not make the revolution, but once they were part of it they played a specific role in it, especially in the radical wings. Of the middle classes, it tended to be the younger and less well off who took part in the struggle, rather than the established, property-owning educated members of that class. But the revolution remained a revolution for all the people.

Both the left and the right have tried to explain events differently. In fact, it has been said, the lower classes, the apprentices, the workers, the students and the peasants were all pursuing the revolution for social and not political reasons. Furthermore, it has been said, there were in fact two revolutions: the revolution of the masses, which was based principally on social issues and cleared the way for the revolution of the notables, of the middle classes with property and an education, who then proposed a liberal programme and placed themselves in the top positions in order, it has been claimed, to force the government to adopt their course to respond to the existing revolutionary forces, but also to channel and to stem the revolution, to reinstate the old order and to avert complete social revolution. This, of course, is a mere construction. Clearly, the liberal notables did not want the revolution, but of course at the same time they did want to exploit it and channel it; but there were not two revolutions. The political demands were the main issue from the very outset; the opposition leaders of the Vormärz were the recognised leaders from the start, and they stated what the masses also wanted. Social forces and interests — that is, those of the peasants, craftsmen and workers — were heterogeneous, united only by their political goal. The social motives lent the revolution its dynamism and power and played a major role in its success; they coloured the revolution. It is not easy to separate the political issues from the social issues; this becomes a question of priorities and emphases. The revolution was not, however, primarily one of exploited and oppressed classes; rather the demands rose out of a cross-section of a civilian society calling for a liberal, popular restructuring of state and society. If one uses this basic fact as a starting-point, it is, of course, possible to say that the social impetus for the March revolution veiled a tendency to go beyond the liberal March Demands; it veiled the potential for more radical action. The expectations from the revolution of those who took part in it showed considerable difference of emphasis. The egalitarian demands of the radical democrats and the calls by the socialists for a guarantee of provision of basic human necessities were the basis of the social protests in the city. This became a problem for the further development of the revolution. It was the leaders of the liberal bourgeoisie who were most aware of this problem. Confronted with the French examples and the crisis discussions of the 1840s, they feared that the revolution would become more socially radical. Social revolution was not the main issue of the March revolution, but it was a possibility. This possibility influenced the policy of the 'March ministers' and the liberal centre — in an atmosphere of concern and fear. And this, indeed, was the true significance of the social complex.

In considering the results of the March events, we must bear in mind three points.

(1) It is astonishing how quickly and completely the old powers capitulated. They surrendered having offered very little decisive opposition. The restoration collapsed like a house of cards. The self-confidence and robustness of the old forces were as if crippled by an irresistible earthquake; indeed, the very awareness of their legitimacy melted away. Of course, the revolution stopped short of the thrones, as had been the case with all the first revolutions in Europe; this demonstrated the monarchical sentiment of the majority and the liberal, bourgeois notions of continuity and accord. The monarchy was maintained, therefore, to some extent precisely because it had capitulated so quickly. It was weak, but it had not fundamentally lost its power. The question of where power now lay, and where it was to lie in the future, remained unanswered. None of the monarchs contemplated counter-revolution, but the monarchy remained a potential for counter-revolution. In the meantime, the monarchs were in favour of constitutional compromise to counter a radicalisation of the revolution. Before criticising the revolution for stopping short of ousting the monarchs, one must bear in mind that the French revolution of 1848, while abolishing the monarchy, had resulted in the Caesaristic empire of Napoleon III.

(2) The revolution's victory was in fact a chain of victories in the individual states. The states — the capitals, governments and parliaments — were all small centres of revolution, and everywhere each state had taken its own position on a consolidation of the revolution and a restructuring of a new Germany. In short, the revolution was decentralised — indeed, what else could have been expected from the confederation of states that was Germany? — and this was to become one of its greatest weaknesses.

(3) The result of the March revolution was not the total overthrow of the power structure, monarchy and constitution (where one existed). There was, however, a

fundamental reform and a change of system. It led to the pragmatic self-evident truth that the government appointed by the monarch governed in agreement with the parliament. And the governments energetically took in hand the task of extending political freedom, the right to vote, the rights of the chambers of power, self-administration, and the reform of the judiciary and agricultural reform. The 'March ministers' had not wanted the revolution, and they certainly had no affection for it. But it was only through force that they had been able to come to power, and the revolution alone was the basis of the evolution now sought. These ministers had been created by the revolution, but they no longer wanted to be revolutionaries or to have their legitimacy dependent on the revolution. They wanted to channel the revolution and consolidate it. That was their reality and their ambivalence — and their tragedy. They based their effort on continuity and legality, and not on the revolution, the aim of which was to replace all that had gone before. They wanted to avoid chaos and radicalisation; they wanted both order and reform at the same time; they wanted to ride roughshod over the revolution by continually achieving new goals and thereby being able to shake off their links with it. They wanted the revolution to be over and done with; all that needed to be done was to reap its rewards. The revolution had been victorious, so long live the reforms: that was the liberal strategy. It was also the strategy of accord and compromise, but in view of the weakness of the old forces, it seemed more promising than ever. The strategy of the developing far left — namely the continuation of the revolution in order to secure the ground gained from the old powers — seemed almost life-threatening. The liberals calculated that the arming of the people was sufficient safeguard against any unlikely reaction by the weakened former powers.

2. The Road to the Paulskirche

The revolution revolutionised the German states. But over and above that, its aim was also the creation of a German nation-state and a German parliament. That was — with no model to follow — the parliament of the revolution; it was its creation. There were many differing ideas about how this national assembly and the restructuring of Germany should be reached.

As early as 5 March, fifty-one politicians, primarily from the south-west, were meeting in Heidelberg in order, with the authority of the revolution, to advise on the next steps to be taken. A contrast between the liberals and the democrats was immediately obvious. Friedrich Hecker and Gustav von Struve, the democrats, wanted the formation of a German republic, and this was to mean that the national assembly 'alone' would draw up the constitution and be the highest state institution. Heinrich von Gagern and the liberals wanted a constitutional monarchy, and they wanted to keep open the issue of the competence of the national assembly and the possibility of accord with the governments. The disagreement was left unresolved. The governments were asked to hold elections, and at the same time a new assembly, made up largely from all the current and former 'states' deputies' of parliament, was convened in Frankfurt and given the task of preparing and implementing the elections. It was a revolutionary organ which became known as the *Vorparlament*. Shortly afterwards the existing pan-German 'national' institution, the Bundestag or diet of the German Confederation, which in the meantime had been briefed by the 'March governments', decided to appoint the so-called Committee of Seventeen made up of 'men trusted by the general public', which from the end of March advised on reform of the Confederation. The attempt by a few liberal governments in the south-west and especially the Gagern brothers to use diplomacy to win over the German governments and persuade them to introduce a reform of the Confederation and transfer provisional executive power to Prussia did not succeed, largely because of Bavaria and Prussia. It was an attempt at one stroke and from above to combine the revolutionary movement and the governments quickly into one working whole; indeed it was an attempt to constitutionalise and channel the revolution, based on the *kleindeutsch* solution. But such a move had no future.

Between 31 March and 3 April, the *Vorparlament* met in Frankfurt's Paulskirche. There were 574 members, still for the most part from the south-west, the south and west. Two-thirds of the Prussian representatives came from the Rhineland. There were only two members from Austria. But no one doubted the moral authority of the assembly. Clashes between liberal and democratic ideas became more marked. The liberals wanted a preliminary decision on their constitutional programme — which Gagern defined as 'Liberty, Sovereignty of the People and the Monarchy'. They then wanted to try to implement the programme by agreement with the Bundestag, because, they said, it represented 'the only actual existing authority in Germany'. Struve presented the counter-motion for the radicals. It called for the abolition of the monarchy and the establishment of a republic. In addition, it called for the removal of the standing armies, the tenured civil service and the monasteries; it also proposed protection of work. The *Vorparlament* should become a permanent institution and hand executive power to an implementation committee. This was, of course, the strategy of the continuing revolution; instead of accord with governments and the Bundestag, it proposed the founding of a revolutionary 'convention' which was to retain all power. But then both groups refused to prejudice the national assembly through the unelected *Vorparlament*; the principle of democratic legitimacy prevented such resolute *avant-garde* political strategists from anticipating events in this way. There followed a rapid agreement to hold elections. In addition to the states of the German confederation, Schleswig and East and West Prussia were to vote; the question of Posen was left unresolved. It was decided to use the system of majority vote and equal and universal — though indirect — suffrage; in the minutes, the talk was of suffrage for all 'independents', but the problem remained unresolved and was not discussed further. The renewed proposal put forward by the left that the assembly should declare itself a permanent institution was again rejected by 356 to 142 votes. This was a victory for the liberals. They did not want to push the revolution any further; instead it was their intention to achieve the aims of the revolution through agreement and amalgamation with the existing legal system. Of course, it was intended that the assembly 'alone' should decide on the constitution; that had been one of the demands made by the revolution. But this did not preclude conferring with the governments. The left then issued an ultimatum stating that the Bundestag should dissociate itself from those members who had played a part in the emergency laws. The liberals toned down the ultimatum and turned it into a declaration. This prompted Hecker and forty of his supporters to leave the assembly, but the moderate left led by Robert Blum remained. Hecker had hoped his action would cause the demise of the *Vorparlament* and deprive it of its legitimacy, but this did not happen. As well as the split in the bourgeois movement between the liberals and the democrats, there now developed a split of the left between moderates and extremists. Though Hecker — following the Bundestag's lifting of the emergency laws and the resignation of their 'accomplices' — did return, the extreme left fared badly in the election of a 'Committee of Fifty' — which was supposed to advise the Bundestag and, in event of an 'emergency', reconvene the *Vorparlament*, — and the votes were cast generally between the Gagern and Blum positions.

The *Vorparlament* had not become a revolutionary convention; it sought to implement liberty and unity in conjunction with the now 'liberalised' former powers. This reflected the overriding mood of the March revolution. But it also meant forgoing, at a time when the states were weak, the establishment of a liberal, national restructuring and forcing the governments to commit to it. For the time being, the revolution hung between the national movement on the one hand and the individual state governments on the other. Of course, the policies of the liberals were realistic, and there was a chance that they might be successful. But their failure shows the tragedy of the initial decision.

The two extreme alternatives, between which the majority swayed, failed in the following weeks. A liberal restructuring of the Confederation such as was planned, for example, by the new Bundestag representative from Baden, the famous liberal Karl Theodor Welcker, came to naught. And the draft constitution, which was worked on by the Committee of Seventeen until the end of April, was rejected by the larger states and by the 'parties'. The national assembly was supposed simply to accept the draft and then endorse the appointment of a Kaiser elected by the princes; but this amounted to the revolution and the parliament depriving themselves of power and would have meant a reform of the Confederation and an abandonment of the establishment of a Reich: it was not acceptable. The mistrust of the Confederation remained, even once the liberals had gained power in it. 'Once a Jesuit monastery, always a Jesuit monastery, even if it does have new inhabitants,' Robert Blum stated. In those weeks Germany could not be restructured by the governments.

Hecker and Struve for their part had not accepted their defeat. Their supporters in Baden, even as early as the middle of March, had organised themselves into a radical party and had called for the chambers to be 'purged of all unprincipled and reactionary elements' and for the formation of national associations for 'right-thinking' people, who should also lead public life. This was the Jacobin democracy of the clubs; it was party dictatorship. On 12 April in Constance, Hecker, supported by his extraordinary popularity as a people's hero, proclaimed a provisional government and the fight for the German republic. Accompanied by 6,000 men, he went on to Freiburg and believed he could win over the peasants, the militia and even soldiers; but on 20 April the troops of the Confederation, who in the interim had been mobilised, were victorious and the uprising collapsed. Hecker had to flee into exile and has since become part of the legend of south German democracy: 'If any one should ask you / "Is Hecker still alive?" / Then you just tell him / Hecker is still alive. / He's not hanging from a tree, / He's not hanging from a rope, / He's hanging on to dreams / Of a German Republic.' The attempt to instigate a second revolution had failed. But the gulf between the left and the liberals had grown even wider and was now almost irreparable. In the eyes of the centre ground, this 'putsch' had shown where the continuation of the revolution and the policies of the left would lead. Robert Blum, the spokesman for the moderate left, was in despair. He felt that Hecker and Struve had 'betrayed' the people and had held them back just as they were winning, because their minority radicalism had discredited the democratic legitimacy of the left and thereby its policies; Marx and Engels, who were less fussy about the question of majority, were equally damning of the action, calling it hopeless 'putsch' mania.

In the meantime, the elections to the national assembly went ahead. The framework of voting rights laid down by the *Vorparlament* was satisfactory to the governments. There were, however, a few differences of opinion, particularly with regard to the definition of 'independent'. Prussia excluded from voting only those who were receiving poor relief; Braunschweig, Schleswig–Holstein and the Hessian states followed suit. Saxony also excluded those who received food and accommodation from their employer; in the cases of Austria, Württemberg, Hanover and Baden some servants, some pieceworkers and some craft apprentices were also excluded. Much was made of these exclusions later, but judged by the standards of the era, the restrictions were not immense. In all probability there was hardly anywhere where less than 75% of men were eligible to vote; in some instances the figure was as high as 90%, the average being perhaps 80%. The consequences of voting restrictions were not yet clear to those involved in the elections. The left was not particularly annoyed by the requirement that voters be independent; and, indeed, it was aristocratic and *haut bourgeois Vereinigter Landtag* in Berlin that was most generous with the criteria for suffrage. The electoral process was for the most part indirect (occasionally even public). 'Direct voters' voted for 'delegates', and this favoured the dignitaries: a system which naturally favoured the notables. As far as we are able to assess, voter participation varied widely and ranged from 40 to 75%. In Bohemia, the Czechs did not take part in the vote, because they felt it had nothing to do with them. In 40 of the 68 constituencies (and in Moravia in 5 of the 28), voting did not take place at all.

The elections took place at a time of peculiar transition. Apart from the small collection of 'politicians', there were no established parties; there was only the diffuse middle-class movement, which was a long time consolidating and displayed differences of opinion, and its opponents. Following the March revolution, in no time at all, a political public had grown up — indeed, political life had come into being. There were meetings, demonstrations and marches; there were communications, announcements and discussions, reading-halls, clubs and associations, petitions and addresses, newspapers, pamphlets, brochures and caricatures; all these elements spread like wildfire, and for one year in Germany it created a climate of intense political activity. Meetings and committees were active in selecting candidates and conducting the elections, but the most active were undoubtedly the liberal-democratic associations. At the beginning the associations included virtually the whole spectrum of the bourgeois movement, but then they subdivided themselves into 'constitutionalists' and 'democrats'. But the distinctions between the various parties took a long time to be clearly defined, and there were several cross-overs; and at the time of the elections — mid-April to mid-May — the defining process was by no means over. It was with these conditions as a backdrop, and not only because of the process itself, that the elections were to a large extent a matter of personality. The range of possible candidates was limited; the eminent people of the pre-revolutionary era, the notables and those in the professions, had an advantage, not least because they were well known. In the cities, there were, of course, people who had only stepped into the public arena with the coming of the revolution. And another important factor, even outside the cities, was the place within the constituency from which the candidate actually hailed. In short, candidates were often selected, and indeed elected, simply because they were personalities known to the general public. For those supporters of the revolution in the broad centre, the individual direction of the particular party did not seem as important. For this reason, the members were for the most part free to make up their own minds as to which particular *Fraktion* (parliamentary grouping) they wanted to join, particularly those who represented areas where the election campaign had been an easy ride. Reputation was often more important than political leaning. On occasion, the defeated candidate was elected as a deputy for the winner; and the Prussian voters elected somewhat more left-wing candidates to the Berlin national assembly than they elected for Frankfurt, simply because the candidates were different. Where there were political election campaigns, the issue was predominantly one of contrast between the moderates and the hardliners, the liberals and the democrats. In the Rhineland and Bavaria especially, the influence of the Catholics played its part, exercised through the clergy and the pastoral letters of the bishops, though this was more marked in the direct elections than in the actual voting for members of parliament.

These elections produced the first German parliament, the so-called 'Paulskirche'. It is foolish to expect a parliament to reflect the social structure of the electorate, and then to criticise it when this does not happen. But the social make-up of the 830 members and their deputies is nonetheless interesting. Over 600, that is almost 75%, had a university education; the majority were jurists in the civil service; 124 were from the teaching profession; 184 were from the free professions, and of these, 106 were lawyers; 312 were state or municipal civil servants and judges, and with the teachers and professors, the total number of civil servants came to 436. By contrast, only 60 were from trade and commerce, 4 of those being craftsmen, and only 46 were from agriculture, one of whom was a smallholder farmer. A slightly greater number, 85, i.e. 10%, were from the nobility. In other words, it was in fact a parliament of academics, civil servants and jurists. 'Only' 49 professors were members, but as they play a particularly important role, talk of a parliament of professors is understandable. The result was not one of class voting rights or manipulation; rather it was the traditional social hierarchy that had asserted itself despite, or rather precisely because of, universal suffrage. The Paulskirche was a democratic parliament and at the same time a parliament of notables, but these were not notables noted for the fact that they came from the bourgeoisie; they were noted for the fact that they were educated. It was symbolic that Professor Ernst Moritz Arndt and former *Burschenschaftler* Heinrich von Gagern became the first presidents of the assembly. Even the democrats deviated only slightly from this social character, with fewer representatives of the bourgeois, civil-service establishment. Finally, what is also interesting is a comparison with the national assembly of Prussia, elected on the same day. In the Prussian assembly, there were more representatives of the non-academic middle classes of society. The reason for this is simple: the better-known notables from the Vormärz and revolutionary periods had preferred to go to Frankfurt. For the electorate, it is important to note that political orientation did not simply correspond to social status. The liberals were not simply the bourgeoisie and the notables, and the democrats were not simply the lower classes; there was much overlapping. The social spectrum covered, for example, by the democratic and the liberal associations was in the main the same.

What did the political result look like? There were no ultra-conservative or socialist members in this universal-suffrage and majority-vote parliament. Political Catholicism was not as strongly represented among the members of parliament as it had been in the political public life during 1848 and the Catholic-clerical deputies were dispersed throughout different factions: Radowitz, Döllinger, Ketteler and Buss joined the right, whilst August and Peter Reichensperger and Max von Gagern joined the centre. It was only for issues relating to the relationship between church and state that they formed a separate parliamentary grouping. The political leanings in the parliament subdivided themselves into *Fraktionen*, which then took their names from the inns in which they met. There were the right-wingers, who were called the 'Café Milani' (originally the 'Steinernes Haus'); they were moderate conservatives who stood for the preservation of the existing order and advocated accord with the states' governments, and they believed passionately in federalism and the church. In October they were supported by 40 members of parliament, 23 from Prussia, 7 from Bavaria and 6 from Austria. Then there were the *Fraktionen* of the centre; they wanted to implement unity and liberty against reaction, and order against anarchy. The right centre, the 'Casino', was the constitutional wing of liberalism; they were supporters of pragmatic parliamentarianism to be balanced by the absolute right of veto of the crown; they supported a balance between state and individual. They saw themselves as the true 'realists' where all the other groups were utopian, and they built upon the principle of accord, because they believed that it was only by working with the governments 'of the German states' that it would be possible to achieve unity. In cases of conflict they were therefore prepared to accept restrictions imposed on the demands for liberty; and they were resolute opponents of the democratic, radical and egalitarian tendencies of the left. This was the party of Heinrich von Gagern, the party of the majority of the prominent professors, including Dahlmann, Droysen, Waitz, Duncker, Haym, Welcker, Beseler and so on, and the party of the Rhenish *haute bourgeoisie*. The Casino was the strongest *Fraktion*, with 120 to 130 members including sympathisers, but it accounted for no more than a quarter of the assembly; and yet its influence on decisions taken was strong. Next came the left centre, which met in the Württemberger Hof and was the left wing of liberalism, which gave a stronger emphasis to the sovereignty of the people and parliamentary rights — thereby including the sovereignty of the Paulskirche — and wanted to grant the monarch only a suspensory right of veto; it was the party that valued individual rights above state and tradition and which, as in the issue of voting rights, was orientated towards the early liberal ideal of a broad classless society. Robert von Mohl from Württemberg, Heinrich Simon from Breslau, Karl Biedermann from Leipzig, Gabriel Riesser from Hamburg and Franz Raveaux from Cologne were some of its most outstanding members; at the end of June they were supported by about a hundred members of parliament. In October the group split up into three *Fraktionen* of roughly equal strength. To the right the 'Augsburger Hof' group was formed, and to the left the 'Westendhall' ('the left in top-hat and tails'); combined with the remaining centre ground, they had some 120 members of parliament. And finally there was the left, the Democrats, who stood for a republic, for the sovereignty of the people and for real parliamentary supremacy; they wanted revolutionary restructuring and were against the strategy of accord with individual governments, against historic rights and for a high degree of equality. This group was further subdivided on the one hand into the moderate democrats, the 'Deutscher Hof', Robert Blum's party, who recognised the principle of majority and a society based on lawfulness and were prepared to compromise; at the outset they numbered a hundred members of parliament, although later this number fell to sixty. The other subdivision of this group was the 'Donnersberg', friends of Hecker, who if necessary were prepared to continue the revolution; they were the radicals from Baden, the Palatinate, Hesse and Saxony, and they included 'Young Hegelians' such as Arnold Ruge and, to a certain extent, Julius Fröbel. In total they numbered forty.

The effective role played by these newly formed organisations is quite astonishing. The *Fraktionen* with their programmes, memberships and preliminary discussions, and, of course, the requirement to vote in accordance with the policy of the *Fraktion* (if a matter was declared an issue supported by the party, no member was allowed to vote against it, although he could abstain) gave life to the organised parliament. Despite liberal-revolutionary tendency to interminable discussions, they helped to give the Paulskirche a certain function and use. Of course, one ought not to overstate the significance of the forming of *Fraktionen* and their delimitation. In the beginning, some members of parliament were members of two *Fraktionen*, many changed allegiance, and some — the so-called 'wild ones' — allied themselves to no particular *Fraktion*. The members of parliament felt quite definitely that they had a free mandate, and parliament was like one large fluctuating discussion. On many of the individual issues discussed there were always alternative points of agreement and disagreement that surpassed the boundaries of the *Fraktionen* in parliament. There was also a strong feeling of sharing a common ground; this came both from the experience of the Vormärz and the awareness of a common purpose and a common starting-point. This sentiment certainly stretched from the right centre ground to the moderate democrats. Robert Blum worked resolutely against it, however, using the differences of opinion to create a breach. Blum himself was highly regarded in all camps, as was the Casino man, Heinrich von Gagern, who became a true authority in parliament — even in the eyes of the left, and, of course, of its president.

From the autumn of 1848 the *grossdeutsch/kleindeutsch* question had reshaped and regrouped the *Fraktionen*. This national-political question added another political dividing-line on top of those relating to the constitution: the *kleindeutsch* 'royalists' met in the Weidenbusch inn, while those in favour of the *grossdeutsch* solution, excepting the left, met in the Mainlust.

Even before that happened, one could draw the dividing-lines rather differently. Sometimes the division between the centre left and right was clearer than that between the centre left and the democratic left. The term 'centre' is, of course, relative. If one takes into account the party movements out in the country and then takes ones bearings from the overall make-up of the society, that becomes even clearer. Then there were the liberals, who wanted a state made up of the middle stratum of society, as well as a system of census voting, a monarchy and an accord with the governments; the idea was that the lower strata of society should gradually merge into the state, and in this respect it was a 'class state on credit' (to quote Langewiesche). For this group, the formation of a republic would be social revolution, rule by the mob or the proletariat and its demagogues. Then there were the 'republicans', from the less extreme left. They wanted evolutionary modernisation, social reform and an open society for the citizen into which the sub-bourgeois elements would also be integrated. The 'republic' — which was a synonym for a liberal, socially just, people's polity, even if it took the form of a monarchy — was supposed to ensure the success of the revolution while at the same time bringing it to an end. These, therefore, were the two camps. But life, both in the parliament and in the country in general, has no time for single divisions, either then or now; the centre left was simultaneously centre and (monarchic) republican, and at the same time it was allied to the centre right and the moderate left.

The Paulskirche was then faced with two tasks. It was to found a state and provide a constitution, to establish unity and liberty. Of course, these were linked, but it was nonetheless a twofold task. Given the fast-moving current of German affairs, however, the Paulskirche needed an executive which would be empowered to act during the transition to safeguard the revolution or implement reform while the state and the constitution were coming into existence. This indeed was the programme for the provisional central authority, and, irrespective of all constitutional theory, it made political sense. This, however, raised two important questions. Firstly, what was to be the relationship of the new power and the Paulskirche to the existing powers? Was the Paulskirche a sovereign body and thus permitted to create such an executive, or should it come to some sort of accord with the German governments? This amounted to the question of how the Paulskirche viewed its relationship to the revolution and the question of strategy. The second question asked what sort of executive should be strived for. The decision on the form the executive should take and its relationship to the national assembly had to be a preliminary decision on the constitution of the future state, and that was a matter that was hotly disputed. After his election to the post of president, Gagern said on 19 May that the assembly should create a constitution from the 'sovereignty of the nation' — he did not use the relevant term 'sovereignty of the people' — and that it was part of the assembly's 'calling' to 'obtain the co-operation of the state governments'. This marked out a route between sovereignty and accord. The assembly itself at the same time laid claim to higher sovereignty, thus opposing the competing institutions in Austria and Prussia which were also drawing up constitutions. This, of course, led to renewed conflict. Indeed, the first major parliamentary debate (19 to 25 June) was on the nature and appointment of the central authority. The left called for the setting up of a parliamentary executive committee from its own ranks; the right wanted a (federal) directorate of three, following an accord with the governments. The suggestion to transfer the central power to the Prussian king was met with roars of laughter. It was in this situation that Gagern made his 'bold move'. 'I am going to make a bold move', he said, 'and say to you that the we must create and elect the provisional central power ourselves.' This meant that the new legislative authority was based on democratic, parliamentary sovereignty. But the pinnacle of power was to be a constitutional monarchy. There was to be no republican president and no directorate. Instead there was a single *Reichsverweser* (imperial vicar) who, like a monarch, was not answerable to the parliament; he would appoint a ministry which was answerable to the parliament and which, as long as it retained his trust, was able to govern. This was a *de facto* parliamentary system. Finally, Gagern proposed the

Austrian Archduke Johann as *Reichsverweser*; he was popular, led a non-aristocratic life and had a non-aristocratic marriage; since the Napoleonic era he had been linked to the German movement, and this, it was said, was not because of but in spite of the fact that he was a prince. This idea was approved of even by those in favour of the *grossdeutsch* solution and those in favour of the monarchic, dynastic solution. The objective underlying this suggestion was to bind together revolution and accord with the governments; it represented a quasi- monarchic head of the empire based on parliamentary democracy in which the agreement of the governments — retrospectively, of course — seemed to be assured. It was a policy of agreement using revolutionary means, and it reflected the mood of the majority in the Paulskirche, who in no way felt that they were a convention and revolutionary tribunal. The idea was also a long-term strategy with considerable prospects, inasmuch as — and as long as — one could assume the relative weakness of the monarchy.

The law was passed by 450 to 100 votes, and even one-third of the republican left voted in favour. The archduke was also elected, by 436 to 112 votes, while 52 of the dissenting left actually voted for Gagern. The impression made by the election and the taking up of office was great, and the mood was one of euphoria and enthusiasm. Gagern spoke of the beginning of a completely new era. The governments recognised the election; the Bundestag demonstrated anti-revolutionary legality by transferring its power to the newly elected *Reichsverweser*. On 13 July, the latter named Prince Karl Leiningen, half-brother of Queen Victoria and one of the leading German 'Whigs', as Minister-President. The cabinet was made up predominantly of members from the right, although the centre left was also represented, and the Austrian Anton von Schmerling was the Minister of the Interior and became the strong man of the government.

In forming the central power and the government, the Paulskirche was not limited to its principal task of advising on and deciding upon a constitution. The fact that there was now a government drew the parliament into everyday politics and all the major internal and external problems that that entailed. These issues became as important as discussions on the constitution.

The new central imperial authority was supported by the authority of the Paulskirche and the consensus of the German people, but it had no real power; it had no money and very little credit, no offices, no paper, no secretaries, and not even any subordinate authorities in the country. And, of course, it had no army; only an outright revolutionary government could have tried to create that from such an unpromising situation. It was successful at that time only in Hungary. The new imperial authority had dissolved the Bundestag; even the moderate centre had no more use for it, as we have seen. But in so doing the imperial power had 'unhooked' (in Faber's phrase) itself from the institutional reality of the German people and the individual states. It was dependent on the goodwill of (and the financial contributions made by) the individual states to implement its policies; and this goodwill was now only available on a case-by-case basis, if at all. The revolution threatened to add to its other problems by also running into trouble on the question of federalism and on the issue of the relationship between the central power and individual states. This was clear from the very outset. The new War Minister, Edward von Peucker, a Prussian general no less, was quite prepared to co-operate with the governments, but he first insisted that all troops should 'pay homage to' the *Reichsverweser* and don the colours of the Reich; this was a symbolic act which would have entailed the army, the nucleus of the monarchic and particularist power, being declared part of an army of the Reich. The smaller states accepted the idea, but Prussia, Austria, Bavaria and Hanover rejected it. Even the attempt by those with sympathy for the civil-nationalist right and left to build up an imperial fleet was hardly more successful. And finally there was deep disappointment at the realisation that, with the exception of the United States of America, foreign powers did not recognise the diplomatic status of the central power.

The Paulskirche and its government had created an authority which, based on a broader moral authority, was a factor in the political process of that year, which in turn firmly represented the majority opinion for the outside world through its dealings and declarations. But, for all its great efforts, the government had won only fragments of power. The left had severely criticised and mocked the impotence of the government, its ministers and the parliament. But such impotence was not the fault of the government. It stemmed largely from the moral authority of the Paulskirche and the relative weakness of the old powers.

The second major decision under consideration related to the creation of a constitution. In the early summer, the issue seemed open to debate. The old powers were laid low; Austria seemed to be in a state of dissolution; and the authority of the Paulskirche was great. That could have been the opportunity to realise the pan-German aims of the revolution — in other words, to occupy the position of power, given that a power vacuum existed; indeed, the setting up of the central power was a step in this direction. The time seemed right. In order to exploit it, a constitution had to be drawn up quickly before a counter-revolution or second revolution was allowed to break out and before the opposing views in Paulskirche were allowed to become more marked. But the opportunity was missed.

The Committee of Seventeen appointed by the Bundestag — most strongly influenced by Dahlmann — had worked out a draft constitution. It was, however, rejected; for some it had been too monarchist and for others too unitarian. But above all it gave the national assembly no creative power, and it was unable to give a consensus suggestion as to who should be the *Erbkaiser* (hereditary emperor). The strategic idea of firstly establishing a state and then of safeguarding liberty was also a failure. It was difficult to imagine that there could be a rapid solution. And was not the formation of the central power the necessary step towards power? By 24 May, a thirty-man constitutional committee had been set up, and as it was not yet formed with the input of different *Fraktionen*, the centre right had the majority. The committee decided to begin discussions on *Grundrechte* (fundamental rights). On 3 July, the negotiations had their first plenary session, and it took two readings and until 20 December to finalise them, as the proceedings were constantly interrupted by major debates and everyday politics. It was not until the end of October that debates began on the territorial organisation of the new 'Reich' and its institutions.

The *Grundrechte* then came to the forefront of discussions, and the actual political questions took a back seat. The Paulskirche was thus fighting a battle against time, and many initiatives and possibilities for negotiation were lost. Was this the fault of the theorists and the professors who, in holding great discussions about their views of the world and the problem of freedom of the individual in the state, failed to appreciate the seriousness of the major power issues and allowed unity and freedom to slip away? This indeed has been the criticism levelled ever since by critics from both the left and right. One has to understand the decision to be able to understand the situation. The *Grundrechte* were the palladium of the liberal, popular new order against the feudalism and absolutism of the authoritarian police state, against both of which the revolution had so vehemently fought. The *Grundrechte* were an elementary, emotional and popular reality; they were like the articles of the civilian faith and represented the very meaning of the constitutional state. They were not rhetorical clauses of a programme; they actually changed people's lives and the structure of power. They were a weapon. They were revolutionary, and they were realistic. And moreover, they were also the palladium of national unity; they were to be valid throughout Germany, above any particularist laws; they were to guarantee the liberty of the individual throughout all the German states, and that was the liberating meaning of unity. It was a force against provincial absolutism and particularism. To put this at the top of the agenda, particularly if one takes into account the voters' expectations, was understandable and legitimate. But there were also other motives of a more tactical and perhaps political nature. The *Grundrechte* represented an area of great unity of purpose, an area on which there could be agreement. Some hoped that the more difficult issues would be resolved as time passed. Some who adhered to the *kleindeutsch* 'realist' group felt that the Prussian solution would take time to gain popularity and that in the meantime the other solutions should be worn down. And almost everyone, both left and right, saw the *Grundrechte* as a way of counterbalancing or offsetting social revolution. This much is quite understandable and beyond dispute. But one failing still remains, namely that an hour of strength was allowed to pass without taking advantage of it, and the tough questions relating to what should become of Austria, what to do about a Kaiser, and what should happen with parliament and voting rights were not dealt with that summer; no decision was made. Of course, the question of *Grundrechte* would be merely a paper issue if a German state did not exist. And the longer the major decisions were put off, the more forceful the opposition became, firstly from the particularists and then from the threat of counter-revolution. Of course, it is likely that these major issues could not actually have been settled in the space of that summer, nor would the early resolution of the issues have significantly increased the revolution's chances. This we cannot tell. But there was simply no attempt made to resolve the issues.

3. Extraparliamentary Movements: Denominational and Social Problems

Suddenly Germany had seen the birth of intensive public political life. The abolition of the old authorities released new forces. Everything about German life was now a subject for discussion. This had led to the setting up of a whole array of movements and organisations outside parliament and in parallel with the political parties. These movements and organisations expressed and mobilised the interests, desires and positions of the general public. This added a new dimension to the political process. Elementary-school teachers, grammar-school teachers, professors and university lecturers, students, doctors, large property-owners, skilled manual workers, labourers, free traders, supporters of protective tariffs, Catholics, Protestants — and many more —

came together, formed organisations or movements and wanted to make themselves heard. Virtually all the groups turned to the national assembly to present their petitions and the like. And the national assembly was under constant pressure from such movements and interacted with them. Some had a considerable influence on the course of the revolution.

An important movement was that of the Catholics. A large number of the members elected to the Paulskirche were strong Catholics. In contrast to the anti-revolutionary conservative Catholicism of the 1840s, they supported the constitutional state, but they did not form their own party. As early as the spring a large Catholic group was formed which led to the first Catholic daily newspapers, the *Rheinische Volkshalle* (Cologne) and the *Mainzer Journal*, meetings, congresses, associations, petitions and so on. The most important of these movements were the 'Piusvereine für religiöse Freiheit' (Pious Associations for Religious Freedom), which were first formed in Mainz on 23 March. By October, there were some 400 branches, with approximately 100,000 members, mostly led by priests, and all linked to one another by central associations. In August, they set in motion a large action petitioning for the civil rights and liberties of the church; 1,142 petitions with over 273,000 signatures were presented to the Paulskirche. From 3 to 6 October, they held a general meeting in Mainz, which they called the 'spiritual parliament of the Catholic people'; this was the first German Catholic convention, as it was later to be called. Franz Joseph Buss, who mocked himself as a 'subversive' and people's agitator, was the president. Ignaz von Döllinger spoke on the political demands and Baron Wilhelm Emanuel von Ketterler on the social tasks of Catholicism. Shortly afterwards the first German bishops' conference was held and drew up a church policy programme; a national German church organisation, with a primate and synod, was rejected by Rome and came to nothing. Of course, the national and the liberal-democratic tendencies of the age were also present in these movements. But the central issue was the demand for the liberation of the church from the state and within the state. Many of the ideas were included in the *Grundrechte* drawn up by the Paulskirche. The Catholics won through against attempts by the radicals to break the power of the church by separating it from the state, or to force it out of society and democratise its own internal structure; even the Jesuit ban was defeated. This movement had mobilised and integrated the Catholic masses and had given Catholicism its strong political base. Within the Catholic structure itself, the ultramontane and strongly hierarchical direction, which encouraged isolation from the outside world, grew stronger.

Politically, in the long term, the movement turned against the left. The anti-clericalism and crude atheism which many democrats tried to encourage with unrestrained power of conviction was bound to provoke rejection of this kind. To say that the Catholics had a 'braking effect' is therefore to fudge the issue. What is far more important is that this movement was the expression of a reality which had a power outside parliament, the political parties and politics in general. It demonstrated the interests and opinions of the people; and it was this reality that was barely represented in the parliaments and in what was negotiated by them. The denominational differences of opinion and passions were a reality of prime importance. These had been cleverly brought under control and filtered on a national scale by the Paulskirche; but out in the country they were debated much more vehemently, either in public or behind closed doors. And the Catholic movement accentuated and highlighted these differences. The great national political alternative, the *grossdeutsch* or *kleindeutsch* solution, was very closely linked to the issue of religious orientation, and this had considerable bearing on whether one supported Archduke Johann or the Prussian king, despite the fact that such things were not mentioned in parliament. In private, Buss could say that 'our Slovene hound', the Austrian general, could turn against Berlin. But such things, of course, were not a result of the Catholic movement. But it would be to fail to understand the German revolution at all if one were to ignore the depth of religious differences and the fact that these differences reached far beyond the parliament and the political parties. This remained a critical burden to both a liberal-democratic and to a national solution of the German question.

The religious issues aside, and indeed more significantly, it was social issues that set in motion movements outside the parliamentary political parties. In March, the social motives had been politically re-formed and repackaged. But they continued to have effect; the various social interests were more starkly articulated and emerged more independently with the advent of political grouping. However, as we have already noted, the strongest social movement, namely the peasants, for the most part withdrew from the revolution. This was not the case with skilled workers and labourers however.

On 15 July, a congress of German artisans and tradesmen was held in Frankfurt. The message of the skilled workers was loud and clear: they were against freedom of trade and competition, and against capitalism and industry. The cure was the guild and the protection and intervention of the state; they were expected to guarantee stability against massive change and the threat of downgrading. In fact, they wanted things to return to the way they had been before industrialisation. And the apprentices in the skilled trades, who had to hold a congress separate from the master-craftsmen, were of a similar opinion. The Kassel trade-school teacher Karl Georg Winkelblech, who called himself Marlo, was the great theorist and spokesman of the movement; he propagated the idea of a harmonious, co-operative model of society based on the solidarity of the people. The master-craftsmen were also against the republic and in favour of the monarchy. This meant they were against the egalitarian radical democrats and all property experiments. This was not, however, a turn to the right; rather it was basic liberalism. Of significance was the fact that the craftsmen, like so many, and seeing that the citizens now had a say, wanted a solution to those problems that affected them directly; these were social and economic issues. They had different priorities from the politicians so concerned with ideas of a constitution and a nation-state. And the craftsmen were socially and economically predominantly conservative, something that was generally true of the lower middle classes; and on this point they were at odds with their moderate or democratic political liberalism.

This view did not only arise at this particular congress, it is something we can see from many other statements, particularly on the local and regional level, and from a whole array of petitions. The liberal politicians found themselves faced with an impossible dilemma. The ideal of the harmonious property-owning society gave way in the push to take firm decisions. It was not possible to continue with the policies of the Vormärz which, where economic and social order was at issue, had held back. If discussions on *Grundrechte* and on competition and the freedom of residency were to take place, then some basic decisions had to be made. The liberals at the Paulskirche, who came more from the realms of academia and less from the practical professions, took a majority decision to support competition and industry and thus to accept the consequences of modernity. This decision must have lost them support from some of their citizens, more so than the priority hearing that they were prepared to give to the policies on the constitution and the nation. A similar problem arose on the issue of self-administration. Citizens of the municipalities and liberals were united in their opposition to bureaucracy; but the liberals were opposed to authoritarian bureaucracy, while the citizens of the municipalities opposed modernising bureaucracy. Then the cities — as they always had done in the previous decades — called for restrictions to be imposed on the freedoms of residency, marriage and commerce. But the citizens' party and the parliament of the *allgemeiner Stand* (general estate) could not oblige. They decided in principle, in accordance with the general libertarian principles and ultimately in accordance with progress and growth, in favour of the freedom of residency; and as a result of their introduction of government control of local police, which itself had the last word on commerce and marriage and thus on all things important, all the communities of old Germany were revolutionised. In the Paulskirche the committee on the national economy was more open to these opinions presented, in a vast number of petitions, by the 'grassroots', but the committee usually remained in the minority. None the less, law regulating domiciliary rights and an edict regulating the trades were supposed to control the individual; this was a concession and a consolation for the future as opposed to the rigidity of a principle. But it did not alter the fact that the relationship between the social base and political representation was now one of considerable tension, and indeed it was at this point that the relationship broke down. What else was to be expected from a non-homogeneous society like that in Germany, which was in the midst of social change and a stagnation crisis? This was a serious blow to the German revolution.

In principle, although it was somewhat less harsh, the same thing happened with the differences of opinion relating to free trade and the protective tariff. The 'Allgemeiner Deutscher Verein zum Schutze der vaterländischen Arbeit' (Universal German Association for the Protection of German National Work) arranged more than 3,700 petitions with some 370,000 signatures; the free traders, for their part, were only able to collect 20,000 signatures. Protection of work was supported not only by the industries whose interests were involved, but also by craftsmen, small merchants, peasants and even labourers; and entrepreneurs, in the framework of such a coalition, also supported universal suffrage, or 'ultra-democratic ideas' as their free-trade opponents critically called them. Liberalism and protective tariffs were not, of course, mutually exclusive, but the academics' parliament that was the Paulskirche was against state protectionism, both in terms of a trade policy and a commerce policy, and tended towards free trade.

The third large extraparliamentary group was the German workers' movement, the movement that during the revolution first came on the scene, as it were, in the pan-German context. The workers, as we have already seen, were not yet a united class. In the revolution it was not the farm labourers, railway workers, home-workers or the day-labourers, nor indeed the factory workers, who had led the way; it was in fact skilled workers and craftsmen. Even this group wavered between traditionalism and utopianism, ideas of revolution and ideas of pragmatic conformity, attacks against machinery, enthusiasm for the future, social reform and social revolution. It is possible, in rough terms, to distinguish between three trends.

Firstly, there were the true apprentice craftsmen — they were essentially ambivalent, socially conservative and in favour of security through the state and the guilds, and opposed to economic and social risks; but they were also opposed to restrictions on their liberty imposed by the patriachalism of their masters and the guilds and by the regulations imposed by the state. They wanted the best from the old conservative world and a socialist-like world of 'organisation of work' by state and society; they wanted freedom and security at the same time. By means of a pan-German workers' congress, one part of the apprentices' congress joined the organising workers.

The second group were the social democrats, the social-reforming 'Workers' Brotherhood'. All over Germany, workers' associations had been springing up since March; some were associated with existing organisations, but many were completely new, particularly in Prussia, Saxony, Württemberg, Berlin, Cologne and Frankfurt. What in March had been a peripheral matter was now a major issue, namely solving the social question relating to the 'organisation of work' by state or society. In April, in part as a result of the worsening economic situation, there were a great many strikes over pay in the large cities of north Germany. In the same month, a 'Central Workers' Committee' was formed in Berlin, and many of the other workers' associations became members. Stefan Born, an apprentice printer of Jewish origin, led the committee. At a workers' congress in Berlin at the end of August at which thirty-one associations and three committees were represented, the 'Workers' Brotherhood' was founded as an association of workers' groups. The central committee moved to Leipzig; the majority of the associations became members; in 1849 there were 170 associations with as many as 15,000 members; the first unions that were then beginning to be formed were also close to this group. The programme of this movement was not a well-worked-out theory; rather it was an appeal by all its members for solidarity and brotherhood. Born himself had been squarely influenced by Marx. But for him the central issue of all efforts should be social reform, and this indeed sums up the mood of the organising workers. 'We workers', said Born, 'have now come of age and we must take our cause into our own hands.' He called for a 'legal' and ordered revolution, because, he claimed, the workers were by nature the pillars of peace and order. He attacked the hollow rhetoric of 'raging dreamers', uncontrolled activism, the playing-off of class differences and the radicalisation of the revolution. Reform meant only one thing, namely that the workers had to help themselves. Co-operatives, unions, the establishment of treasuries and education were things that, above all the aspirations, bound the movement to the bourgeois world of values. Reform, on the other hand, meant the implementation of a 'social state' in place of the police state; there should be a fair tax and school system, with welfare and support, recognition of the brotherhood as a legal body. This also had a political dimension, it was 'social democracy', it presupposed equal rights for the worker, and was in favour of a liberal-democratic state and the participation of all citizens in political life. This reflected what the workers wanted. They did not want to wage a historic battle; all they wanted was a little more bread, more justice and more humanity. It was taken for granted that in May 1849 the supporters of 'social democracy' would come down on the side of the bourgeois democrats and defend the achievement of the revolution — i.e. a liberal constitution — against an attack from the counter-revolutionaries. It is true that this movement's emphasis was on reform. But just as the forward-looking vision of a 'fair wage' bore certain social-revolutionary characteristics, so we cannot overlook the fact, especially in the case of the movement's leaders, that social democracy also encompassed a potential for social revolution: the distinction between 'reformism' and revolution was far from clear-cut. In retrospect — over and above the Marxist polarisation of the working class and the bourgeoisie — this movement is of considerable significance. It might perhaps have been able to introduce a different, perhaps more Anglo-Saxon, developmental trend into the German workers' movement.

Finally, there was the social-revolutionary movement, which itself was, of course, part of the emerging workers' movement. This movement included Marx and Engels, the 'Bund der Kommunisten' (League of Communists), with its network of bases and supporters, who were predominantly intellectuals or skilled workers. Marx and Engels, however, were not at first even remotely interested in having their own workers' organisation; even during the revolution they had not been interested in the communist alliance. Marx was not active in any workers' association; he was active only through his newspaper, the *Rheinische Zeitung*, which reappeared in Cologne on 16 June. The strategy of Marx and Engels was to follow completely the course chosen by the radical democrats and to further the revolution, on the terms set out by this group, in support of egalitarian ideas and opposed to all compromises. They wanted to be the most radical faction of the democracy, tending possibly towards infiltrating it and exploiting it — the proletariat as a sort of *avant-garde* — but they rejected the idea of putting forward their own worker demands. This line was also of little interest to the workers themselves; and it was for this reason also that the communists remained on the fringes. When Marx and Engels withdrew, in December, from the alliance with the democrats and began to propagate communist social demands, the effect was very limited.

The liberals saw such movements as a great and acute danger. The freedom to exercise a trade and economic unity had surely been their own policy, which was intended to end pauperism. Protection of work, on the other hand — where the slogan did not simply provoke class fear — would surely lead to a police state and lack of freedom. But there was another more fundamental objection, namely that the outbreak of the social question put in jeopardy the struggle for political freedom and the constitution and weakened the people's unity against reaction. Therefore this problem was to be put off, whenever it could not be denied or dispelled. Even the democrats were of a similar point of view. In fact, they promoted their radical, egalitarian demands and exploited the social poverty to promote agitation not only against the pre-revolutionary establishment, but predominantly against the bourgeois establishment. In one way they were the party of the little people, but they had no solutions for the problem created by industry. They too were in favour of politics taking priority, looking after their political revolution as they were, over the explosive effect of the social question.

A very important factor was the curious notion that the middle classes had of the social movement and the possibilities of a social revolution; indeed, it was a worry, a fear even, of a social coup and the 'red spectre'. The events in Paris, the bloody struggle between the unruly worker masses and the army of the republic, the memory of the Jacobins, the radical rhetoric of the left-wing democrats — far more than the rhetoric of the workers — encouraged this fear. The proletariat and the masses of dependent workers, the middle classes thought, were not following a path of reason; they were blatantly pursuing their own interests, they were capable of being manipulated by demagogues, they had anarchist tendencies, and they wanted to abolish property.

Objectively there was no potential for a social revolution, and as such this fear was exaggerated. But the Jacobin revolution could develop unwittingly out of radical democracy, as it had in 1793; and thus the fear of the middle classes was not unfounded. This point was not without significance for the progress of the revolution.

4. Germany and Europe

The German revolution was also a European and foreign affairs problem. Europe was still the continent of the ideological civil war, and the question still remained as to what extent far opponents and supporters of the revolution would take sides. Europe was a system of states and, it would seem, enjoyed relative stability; there was no question that a new, potentially stronger state in central Europe, in other words a new great power would affect the *raison d'être* of all the other powers; rather the question was whether such a state could even be tolerated, and to what extent the other states were ready and willing to prevent it from being founded. Europe was also a Europe of *Völker* (peoples). Historically, central Europe had been organised on the basis of a dynasty and feudalism. The revolutionary formation of a German nation-state was bound to cause conflicts relating to frontiers and nationality; and these conflicts would be with the old states and with the new peoples, whether they were organised as a state or not.

Let us turn firstly to the major powers. Russia was the most decisive opponent of revolution and remained so; it was the great power behind counter-revolution and supported such moves in Prussia and wherever else it could. On a power-political basis too, Russia opposed the idea of a German nation-state, which would have weakened either Austria or Prussia and which would thus block the Russian dynastic influence in the smaller and medium-size German states and threaten the Russian position in Poland. Even the Prussian king was not allowed to make a pact with the national movement. The threat of Russian intervention hung constantly over the German revolution; everyone knew this and it was no coincidence that politicians ranging from moderate Liberals to the radicals were decidedly anti-Russian. Of course, no one knew at what point and under what overall European circumstances Russia would deem it necessary to invade. In the early summer of 1848, things had not yet come to that.

France, to the disappointment of the left, had not followed a policy of revolutionary solidarity. In the spring, the Prussian Foreign Minister, Count von Arnim, tried to create an alliance with France: the prospects of this included French support of Italy, the restoration of Poland, and the inclusion of Schleswig into the new German state. The new government in Paris rejected the idea, the main reasons for which were a concern about the situation at home and a dislike of war. The French policy was not aggressively opposed to the national German movement, but the idea of a German nation-state, of course, gave France cause for concern; and for this reason France sympathised with Russia, despite their vastly differing ideologies. Of course, in June 1848, France — now clearly opposed to a German nation-state — temporarily withdrew from the circle of active powers; for the Germans, this was a great relief.

In England, opinions differed. The Conservatives saw in a German nation-state — 'that dreamy and dangerous nonsense called German nationality', as Disraeli put it — a threat to European peace. The Queen and the Prince Consort, himself from the House of Coburg, supported and encouraged a moderately liberal (thoroughly anti-radical) and national solution led by Prussia; Karl Leiningen was in close contact, by letter, with the Prince Consort. As the House of Coburg came to be a symbol of liberal princes, it is justifiable to talk of a 'Coburg' policy. Palmerston, a senior minister, for reasons of tariffs and trade policy alone, was sceptical; he was not a supporter of Germany, but nor was he opposed to a liberal, national new order, and because Austria was a European 'necessity' for England in the south-west, he favoured a solution led by Prussia. In the early summer, a Prussian liberal solution might have been able to win English patronage perhaps even over Russian objections. But there was an obstacle to this in the form of the national claim made by the Germans on Schleswig. Both public opinion and the government opposed the nation-state precisely because of this issue; this was the real point of conflict. England, as well as Russia, thus opposed the Frankfurt assembly. The revolution came into direct conflict with Europe. Schleswig–Holstein became the revolution's most essential problem.

It is at this point that we reach the other main issue, namely that of national boundaries. Who should belong to the nation? Should it be all German-speakers and only German-speakers? Or all those peoples who historically were seen as inhabitants of German countries? What should happen to minorities, both Germany's own and foreign minorities? The aim was to found a nation-state. But Germany was not a nation-state; ethnic and historic boundaries do not necessarily coincide, and there were so many wide areas of national intermixing. With the appearance of the German national movement had come the first national political conflicts. These conflicts were a part of the European power situation, and they influenced the latent argument in Germany over who should lead, namely the argument concerning the position of Prussia and, above all, the position of Austria in Germany. It was for this reason that these conflicts had been of the utmost importance to the revolution, and not only for the century of nationalism that was now dawning.

There were three conflicts that were particularly important. Firstly, there was the conflict over Schleswig–Holstein. Here the issue before the revolution, as we have already discussed, was concerned with whether Schleswig should be included into the Danish state (the 'Eider Dane' solution), whether it should maintain its link with Holstein, or whether it should be removed from the Danish state and annexed to 'Germany' — and in the 1840s the issue had become a key question for the Pan-German national movement. When Schleswig was annexed into the Danish state by revolutionary means on 21 March 1848, the Germans proclaimed their opposition to such annexation, saying that it was contrary to the old law; and so they set up a provisional state government. The king-duke was not deposed, but he was relieved of his duties. The revolution had not stopped short of the throne, and even the Lutheran pastors turned against the 'authorities'; the reason for this was that it was a national revolution. The Bundestag also recognised the new government, and Schleswig took part in the elections to the national assembly. At the request of the provisional government, Prussia then moved in and occupied Schleswig. The Confederation accepted this action as lawful. This then led to war with Denmark. It was no longer a war of governments, it had become a war of peoples, and Germans right across the political spectrum supported the cause passionately. At the end of May, the Prussian troops — as a result of English mediation — retreated to southern

Schleswig. In a wild protest the Frankfurt National Assembly declared Schleswig–
Holstein a 'national affair'; Prussia could not be allowed to make decisions alone. In the
meantime, the issue had become a European one. The Tsar — mostly for reasons of
maritime strategic interests — took Denmark's side and threatened Prussia. Thereupon
England — with interests in 'the Bosphorus of the North' — joined the debate.
England wanted a peaceful solution and to hold Russia at bay. The sensible suggestion
to divide Schleswig, made by the English, was unacceptable to the parties in the
conflict, and national sentiment was in any event far too aroused. The Germans were as
unwilling to recognise the national right of the Danes in northern Schleswig to self-
determination and separation as the Danes were to recognise a similar situation for
Germans in southern Schleswig. It was not the principle of nationality that concerned
the two sides here; they were concerned about the principle relating to the country's
history. Under pressure from the two major powers and as a result of the success of the
Danish sea blockade, the Prussians negotiated a ceasefire. This was agreed on 26
August in Malmö. It was very nearly a capitulation: it included the withdrawal of
Prussian troops, the end of the provisional government, the abolition of the measures it
had introduced and the imposition of another government in collaboration with
Copenhagen. This led to fiery protest from the general public and in the Paulskirche; it
was national 'treason' and a violation of 'national honour'. It also had an effect on
Frankfurt's relationship with Prussia; the latter had seriously overstepped the limits of
its authority in its dealings on this matter and had excluded the imperial government.
This was an attack on the Paulskirche and an attack on the revolution. Nevertheless, the
Paulskirche was expected to recognise the ceasefire. This was a serious dilemma. The
balance of power left neither Prussia nor Frankfurt any other choice, and Frankfurt,
without its forces, was dependent on Berlin. For part of the *kleindeutsch* supporters of
the right there was the added consideration that Prussia should not be snubbed; Prussia,
after all, had been assigned a leading role in the solution of the German question. In the
course of such realistic considerations — as well as the strong, indeed immense,
pressure from the English — the imperial government proposed to accept the ceasefire.

Against all national sentiment, the government bowed to the power of the facts; there
was no point in hitting heads against brick walls, and it was not possible to correct the
European power situation merely using moral authority. On the other side of the argument stood national sentiment, national right, the adherence to self-legitimisation and
self-determination. Foreign powers would build on Germany's inner conflict and weakness if Germany did not now act correctly and honourably. 'If the lion ceases to flex its
muscles, people will think it had only borrowed its fur,' declared Robert Blum; better to
be defeated honourably rather than accept this disgrace. It was the left in particular that
talked in such terms. They also harboured a justified concern that submission to Prussia
would weaken both the revolution and Frankfurt. The revolution, even in the moderate
form of the strategy of accord with the state governments, was based on the fact that one
could threaten to continue it at any time. By accepting the ceasefire, this position would
be gambled away. A curious alternative then came to light which even the radical left, in
the figure of Karl Marx, for example, supported. Would it not be possible — as had
happened in France in 1792–93 — to unleash a universal people's war against Denmark,
reactionary Russia and Prussia, with the Prussian people fighting against the Prussian
government? Would it not be possible in this way simultaneously to save and to

radicalise the revolution? But such alternatives seemed to both the right and centre as dangerous as they were unrealistic. Finally, the politics of compromise and adjustment stood opposed to the politics of principle, of all or nothing. This policy had frequently been used rhetorically; but it was only realistic if what was sought was a new revolution and a large war — only then could it be seen as an alternative. But the majority was not in favour of such a result; even the moderate left had not really wanted it. The left was justified in wanting to keep open the revolution, but they could offer no suggestions as to how to solve the crisis. It was not until 5 September that the Paulskirche, with a small majority (238 to 221), including the left and a section of the right led by Dahlmann, decided to reject the ceasefire. The government — in true parliamentary style — resigned. But Dahlmann was unable to form a majority government with an otherwise incoherent coalition that was based only on rejection of the ceasefire. Threatened with the defeat of its foreign policy — and this was eased as a result of a few Danish concessions — a few members from the centre, including some from Schleswig–Holstein, changed their minds; on 16 September, the ceasefire was accepted by 259 to 234. The former government, now led by Anton von Schmerling, was reinstated and had to represent this totally unpopular policy. This was the tragedy of the situation. The National Assembly had 'given in', because it had taken a realistic decision in preference to a demonstration of patriotism; there was far from a majority in favour of a people's war. The liberals accepted the situation and thereby lost considerable influence; the left failed in their attempt to keep open the revolution. And thus it was that the national conflict and interference by the powers on the eastern and western flanks of Europe played a significant part in the demise of the revolution. We shall turn in a moment to the extraordinary effects that these events had on the internal situation in Germany. The Schleswig–Holstein issue, once the ceasefire had come into force, remained temporarily unresolved. But in the non-German countries, despite this submission, unrest was growing about the demands made by this evolving German nation-state.

The second major national political problem was Posen. Here, the March revolution had had Polish nationalist characteristics. A national committee had, to a large extent, won authority. Initially, a mood of supra-national solidarity seemed to dominate. The leaders of the 1846 Polish uprising were granted amnesty immediately and became heroes of the Berlin revolution. The mood was one of enthusiasm, especially of the Germans within Germany (the *Binnendeutschen*), for a free Germany and an independent Poland. The new March government in Berlin promised 'national reorganisation' in Posen to suit the Poles. This also reflected the policies of the new Foreign Minister, Count von Arnim, who placed Prussia at the head of the national movement and wanted to restore the Polish state against the wishes of the Russians. France rejected this policy, and the king turned away from it. On the question of reorganisation, the struggle on nationalities flared up in Posen after a short period of liberal unity. The Germans organised themselves against this; the Polish national movement set up militia groups. The Prussian troops, after a short delay, took action against them. On 9–10 May, they had to capitulate. The government divided Posen and limited the reorganisation to the eastern, Polish sector. In June, the boundary lines were moved once again; more Polish territory was given over to a German Posen. In this province twelve members had been elected to sit in the Frankfurt National Assembly, but they were now only temporarily granted access; the looming conflict was deferred. People wanted to have it both ways:

they wanted a free Poland, which was the classic liberal-democratic conviction, and the inclusion of the Prussian east into the new Germany. The illusion that the Internationale of the national movement, the *Völkerfrühling* (peoples' spring), would prevent conflicts from occurring was very quickly shattered. A choice had to be made between the national interests of the Poles and those of the Germans in the east. All mediation was difficult because the nationalities were dispersed amongst each other.

In a major and very lively debate (24–27 July), the Paulskirche dealt with this issue. One part of the left came out very strongly on the side of Poland and the Poles. In view of the significance of Poland for European liberty, the Germans were obliged, Arnold Ruge said, to strive for the re-creation of a free Poland, using violent means if necessary; a German minority would have to be sacrificed. On the one hand, reference was made to the ethnic principle on which the nation was founded, namely to the self-determination of Poland. On the other hand, there were historic, territorial arguments against the division of Posen, which was, after all, according to Robert Blum, completely Polish. If Posen was to be divided because of the German minority, then in many places non-German nationalities, such as Danes, Trentiners and Czechs, would have to be released from the German union. But the majority was of a different opinion. The East Prussian member of parliament, Wilhelm Jordan, who at that time was still a Democrat, expressed it particularly strongly, 'not despite, but precisely because' he was a Democrat. He was opposed to what he called this 'cosmopolitan idealism', this 'nonsensical sentimentality' of 'Poland mania', and proposed in its place 'healthy people's pride' for the Germans. This was no longer a question of the rights of the Germans living in Posen; what was now at issue was the 'natural historic fact' of German superiority over the Slavs. Poland, it was said, should not and ought not be restored. Others were less harsh. The majority did not think and speak in the aggressively naturalistic way that Jordan did. But they pleaded in favour of German interests and the interests of the German people. With a large majority, 342 to 31 (predominantly from the extreme left), it was decided to incorporate the western part of Posen into Germany and to redraw the dividing-line, though the *Reich* commissioner subsequently altered it once again to the disadvantage of the Poles. There was no more talk of the re-creation of Poland. Even the majority of the moderate left could suggest no solution to the dilemma; they tried to postpone dealing with the problem. Today we know the disastrous route that chauvinism — as Jordan called it — and staunch nationalism took, particularly between Germany and Poland. It cannot, of course, be overlooked that there were real conflicts for which, at that time, there was no solution. The clash between nationalities and nationalisms could not be avoided by what was, after all, a national revolution; the Poles too had claimed dominance over the Germans. The conflict was legitimate, but it was also tragic. And it was, above all, among the Germans in the east that this led to a nationalism based on a sense of being threatened, which then spread to other parts of the nation, and consequently has become one of the great tragedies of our history.

The third major national political issue was Bohemia. Franz Palacky, the recognised leader of the evolving Czech nation, had turned down an invitation from the Committee of Fifty. He replied that there was no place for him or his nation or for an autonomous Bohemia in a German nation-state. Rather, the Austrian empire, he said, was the natural protector of the small nations in this part of Europe, especially against Russia. If, he said, Austria did not already exist, 'in the interest of Europe and of humanity in general it would have to be created, and quickly'. As we have already said, the Czechs did not take part in the elections to the Paulskirche. This was not only a demand for self-determination on the part of the Czechs; it was also a rejection of the claim to self-determination by the Germans — in Bohemia and in Austria — who, it was said, should not be allowed to join the new nation-state; it was a rejection of Austria's claim to lead Germany; and it was a rejection of the claim by the *grossdeutsch* Germans within Germany for the right to belong to Austria. The Pan-Slav Congress held in Prague in early June, at which harsh words were used against the Germans — the Slovak Jan Kollár even claimed that Dresden and Leipzig were pure Slavic cities in which the Germans had simply taken over — debated on a new pro-Slavic reorganisation of Austria outside the German alliance. This considerably increased the national tension towards the Germans, particularly in Bohemia. Even in Bohemia, by early summer at the latest, the nationalities were opposing each other, a point to which we shall return later. The Paulskirche now held fast to Germany's claim on Bohemia, the country of the old Reich, as well as the Confederation. There were neither conditions nor justification for independent national development, a view espoused by Gagern and more or less universally shared. That attitude was very different from that towards the Poles, who had been a symbol of the struggle for freedom for more than fifty years. Behind this idea was the conviction that the Germans — especially in the south-east — were the heroes of liberty and progress and were leading a 'world historic mission' (August Reichensperger) with their superior culture; there was also the idea that the lives and integration of the smaller groups of people could only be ordered if they were part of a large and, of course, German empire. The left largely shared these ideas: even Karl Marx believed that Bohemia was and should be part of the German sphere of culture and power, even if the Czechs would retain their own language for a few decades yet. It was believed that the Czechs had no right to be a nation, because, it was said, they were reactionary. The Paulskirche, with its eye firmly on Bohemia, wanted to solve the problem of national minorities in the nation-state by the implementation of a generous constitution. A liberal inter-pretation of the rights of the minority was to guarantee free national, cultural development; the new empire was also to be a comfortable home for the non-German groups. Those in Frankfurt, partly influenced by German-Bohemian members, were much more confident and content about the Bohemia issue; it was not until the summer that the opposition to all efforts by the resolute Czech nationalism grew stronger.

The Paulskirche wanted two things. It wanted to retain possession of every part of the old Reich and the Confederation, not only if it was now made up of mixed nationals, but even if it was no longer German at all. The application by the Italian members from Trentino to release their country from the Confederation — and thereby to divide the Tyrol — was rejected by a large majority, and even the Democrats pleaded only for an autonomous status; and all the members were in favour of the continued adherence of the duchy of Limburg, which was actually Dutch but belonged to the Confederation, to Germany. The Paulskirche also wanted to incorporate into Germany German and even non-German areas in the north and east which historically had belong to German or German-dominated areas — Schleswig and at least the larger part of Posen. Of course, with the exception of claims by marginal figures, there were no claims made on other

German people — in Alsace and in the Baltic, for example; the extent of the spirit of German nationalism had not yet become quite so broad. The arguments sought to confirm these claims; they were contradictory, sometimes they changed, and they were not logical. The subjective right to decide on national allegiance applied only to the Germans in question. The same was also true of disputes on the ethnic principle; this was, of course, a fundamental issue; in controversial cases, the historical, territorial concept of a nation was preferred — but in the case of Schleswig the argument was different from that used for Posen. In contrast to the later harsher nationalism, preference was given to a liberal, tolerant nationality policy; it was felt that in this way the problem of areas of mixed nationality and national injustices could be overcome. The position of the Germans in these conflicts was, of course, a reflection of common European nationalism and was a part of its destiny; the Danes, Poles and Czechs behaved in precisely the same way. One should avoid apportioning blame. It was the tragedy of the situation.

Part of the problem of Germany and Europe was the result of ideas and dreams of imperial power which lay behind the concept of the German nation-state. Thoughts were of a great, German empire to which the marginal peoples and states of Europe, from Switzerland, the Netherlands and even Scandinavia to the countries in south-east Europe, would link up; it would be a hegemony from the North and Baltic Seas to the Adriatic and Black Seas; it would be a maritime and commercial force. There was an emphatic demand for power — for great power. Dahlmann said in the September crisis that 'the road of power is the only one which will satisfy and fulfil this seething desire for liberty. For it is . . . not only liberty that the Germans want, it is to a large extent power for which they crave.' Of course, the background to this was the Schleswig–Holstein experience, which had shown that freedom could not be protected without power. And on questions of boundary and nationality the security interests of Germany were also of considerable significance, interests that were not illegitimate. But power was also an end in itself. Dahlmann was a moderate, but more expansionist rhetoric also abounded. Everyone was talking about German shame and German honour: 'Germany's freedom and rights over all other considerations' was the motto of the Peoples' Rights (i.e., international policy) Committee. According to the Democrat Karl Vogt, no cannon should be fired anywhere in the world without Germany's involvement. Germany, it was said, would be the most important power in the world once it was united; the Prussian envoy Baron von Bunsen bemoaned the 'nonsensical demands' of the Teutons. One of the favourite references was to the 'strength of the German sword', to which appeal was made, because, it was said, only this strength could ensure peace. There was a general view that the struggle between the Germanic and Slavic peoples in the east and south-east was a 'world historic fact', which did not make the possibilities for coexistence any easier. War remained a strong possibility. The left was enthusiastic about a popular war against what Vogt called 'the barbarism of the east'; reborn peoples called for a 'baptism by fire'; even Ruge, the sole pacifist and supporter of a people's alliance, at first wanted the 'final war' against war, namely the war with Russia. This was all, of course, the talk of a weak and divided nation that felt it needed to catch up and claim some sort of compensation; it was a nation that wanted to win what was normal, namely the power enjoyed by large states.

This nationalism, this unrest over power and ambitions of power, was supported by both the right and the left. In 1848, the left — with the exception of Ruge — was no less nationalistic than the right, with a few exceptions on the Polish issue. The force of the democratic claim and the appeal to the people and their power significantly increased the strength of traditional claims. This was perhaps more noticeable in the case of the left because, unlike most of the centre and the right, it was not damped down by being filtered through considerations of political realism. The rhetoric that fifty years later was right-wing was at this time rather more left-wing. Even nationalism was still basically a phenomenon of the left.

Of course, we should not overestimate this situation, particularly in the light of what was to come. Rhetoric was not the order of the day, and the decisions — with the exception of the serious problem of the national boundaries — were more moderate and more realistic than the wild talk that was sometimes heard. Despite all ambitions, the main aim was and remained the creation of a German nation-state and not the creation of an empire. The decision ultimately taken to create a *kleindeutsch* nation-state shows this clearly. The majority had thereby decisively limited the potential for international conflict. Germany could, after all, be tolerated by the rest of Europe.

5. Between Radicalisation and Counter-revolution

The liberal revolution, the revolution of the middle-class centre, had been victorious, it seemed. It held the power in the individual states, in parliament and in the state governments. With the Paulskirche and the *Zentralgewalt* (central power) it had an institutional centre for the Pan-German revolution. The national state, the liberal constitution and the civil society seemed to be evolving. The liberals' strategy was now one of accord and agreement. Accord with the existing powers, but also with those powers which had renewed themselves, was intended to protect the achievements so far of the revolution and at the same time uphold civil order. Behind this strategy lay the rejection of an abrupt break and the past, and the belief in evolution, continuity, order and legality. Also behind the strategy was the fear of a continuing revolution, of both radical and reactionary masses, of Jacobin-like dictatorship and terror — of a social coup and a new autocracy, as there had been in 1793. This is something for which the liberals have since been severely criticised. One need not share this fear, but it cannot be denied historical legitimacy. It was not based solely on class interests but also on a very realistic insight: the existing powers could still depend on the loyalty of a large proportion of the people, especially those out in the country. Confrontation and the continuation of the revolution would be bound to lead to civil war, and that was not a sensible alternative. So the strategy of accord was based on the expectation that the old powers were forced to submit, for the most part, to the liberal demands, because it would then be possible to work together to create social order opposed to a 'republican' radicalism. It would have to be possible to employ the moral weight of public opinion; it was necessary to be able to appeal to the potential for revolution; they could not be cut off from it completely, but at the same time the aim was to bring it to an end. This was the liberals' dilemma.

The liberals' position was precarious, despite their success. The Reich government had no instruments of power. The governments of the individual states soon found themselves stuck between crown and parliament. The vast number of opposing views weakened the unity of the liberal movement; social conflicts and social disappointment diminished its strength. European feeling, in view of Schleswig–Holstein, turned against the revolution. The location and division of power were unstable. But above all, since the summer of 1848 the position of the liberals and the policies of the centre had been under threat from a double movement: firstly from attempts by the left to continue the revolution and to radicalise it and make it a 'second', true revolution, and secondly from attempts by the vanquished of March to regroup and start a counter-revolution. Both groups pursued their aims on their own initiative, both wanted to remove completely the liberal system, but both were counteracting each other, provoking each other and propagating fear of the other extreme. Both sought to polarise the situation, and the policies of the centre became more difficult.

Of course, the political public and political movements were still predominantly orientated toward the centre. This was true of the majority of the extraparliamentary movements, of which we have already spoken. It was also true of the journalists and the party-orientated political associations. They continued to grow and were now more clearly differentiated: right-of-centre liberal 'constitutionalists', left-of-centre liberals and moderate democrats. But it was the extreme positions that had the greater influence on events.

The conservatives, who still held positions of bureaucratic or military power or were influential at court, once again found their footing and began, firstly in Austria and Prussia, to reconsider plans for a counter-revolution. In Prussia they were especially public. The strongly conservative group led by the Gerlach brothers were already planning a newspaper in April; this then appeared in July with the title *Neue Preussische Zeitung*, and because of its iron cross emblem it became known as the *Kreuzzeitung*. This was the organ of counter-revolutionary conservatism. The Junkers organised the defence of their economic interests and privileges by forming the Verein zum Schutz des Eigentums und zur Föderung des Wohlstandes aller Klassen (Association for the Protection of Property and the Promotion of the Prosperity of All Classes). Initially it had been intended to give it the blatant title of Wahrung der Interessen des Grundbesitzers (Protection of the Interests of Property-Owners); in August they held a general assembly which became known as the Junker parliament. In June the Preussenverein für das konstitutionelle Königtum (Prussian Association for a Constitutional Kingdom) was founded; a whole network of similar associations linked up with this group, bearing names such as Pastoral Association or Fatherland Association, especially in the country, and they all began working on the members of parliament by means of addresses and petitions. Even the church orthodoxy took the side of the counter-revolution. Of course, the army was particularly important. An informal military party was formed which wanted to make the army the instrument of the counter-revolution; it opposed reform generals such as the War Ministers Eduard von Peucker in Frankfurt and Ernst von Pfuel in Berlin. As a result of the developments during the Vormärz, the officer corps for the most part took the side of the counter-revolution and persuaded the non-commissioned officer corps to do the same. The liberals' criticism of the army and the civil aversion to an effective constitution for the armed forces were strong influencing points on the issue. The army claimed that it was defending itself against poor plans that threatened its very existence and its striking power against real threats to peace. Typical of the situation was one of the spokesmen for the 'army party', Lieutenant-Colonel Griesheim, the Director of the General War Department and an eminent authority in the War Ministry, who went out into the streets bearing propagandist pamphlets. The title of his fourth pamphlet, which appeared at the end of November, became a byword and a slogan: *Only Soldiers Can Help against Democrats*.

On the other side of the argument were the radicals. The events from March up to the founding of the Paulskirche had played out for them; the liberals were in power; the April revolution in Baden had failed. But there were still the radical Democrats grouped around the Donnersberg faction in Frankfurt. They wanted a republic, sovereignty of the people, and egalitarian democracy as opposed to rule by bourgeois notables; they wanted to continue the revolution against compromise, accord and mere evolution; they wanted to oust the conservatives altogether and force the liberals onto the sidelines. They were quick to scent the danger of counter-revolution and wanted to defend the revolution precisely by continuing it — this was their brand of realism. They were different from the moderates who supported Robert Blum because of the means that they chose to achieve their goals. They were not only parliamentarians, they were also activists. They criticised the parliament and wanted to mobilise extraparliamentary forces. They called for a second revolution. Arnold Ruge, a member from the Donnersberg group until he resigned from the parliament on 10 November, publicly called for this through his newspaper *Die Reform*. They believed the Paulskirche would collapse, and in this event they wanted to be ready, using propaganda, organisation and action, to create the preconditions for a resolute democracy; this would be a sort of Jacobin temporary dictatorship of the true democrats. This bore traits of totalitarianism, such as had been seen in the position on the church since March. In the old major cities such as Frankfurt, Berlin and Vienna, this political wing, supported by the social protest of the urban underclass, was particularly strong. At Whitsuntide 1848, between 14 and 17 June, 200 Democrats met in Frankfurt for the first Democrats' Congress. Julius Fröbel was the leading figure. A total of 89 associations from 66 cities were represented, and a large number of Donnersberg members attended. It was decided that the organisation of democratic associations should strengthen the 'Democratic Republican Party'; there was also to be a central committee in Berlin. Berlin was seen as the centre of all the developments. It was said that there was 'only one constitution that the German people could sustain, and that was a democratic republic; that would mean a constitution in which all responsibility for the freedom and welfare of the individual would be taken on by everyone'. This went against all liberal beliefs and was almost totalitarian. The communist Gottschalk had proposed this formula to the congress, and it accepted it.

The democratic clubs and associations finally separated from the liberals, consolidated and began to spread into the Rhine province, into Rhenish Hesse, Baden and Württemberg, Saxony and central Germany, and particularly into Silesia (here in the countryside as well). The democrats were now agitated strongly against the liberals, against the decline of the Paulskirche and the other parliaments into endless verbalising, compromises and weakness. In the name of direct and true democracy, of the people's assemblies and the decisions of the associations, they turned against the parliament completely; they wanted an almost imperative mandate and declared that they had no confidence in the present deputies referring to a change in opinion of the electorate. This mood was later summed up in poetic form by Georg Herwegh in the line 'Im Parla-Parla-Parlament, das Reden nimmt kein End' (In parla-parla-parliament, talk is never-ending). This is a curious precursor of a completely different sort of criticism of the parliament that was to come much later. The aim was to put parliament under pressure, to remove its power and to replace it. Its proponents wanted a second revolution. The social protest by the lower classes and the man in the street, strengthened by the recession, fed this agitation.

This development came to a head in September and was caused by the Paulskirche's acceptance in Malmö of the ceasefire. With the abandonment of Schleswig–Holstein and the capitulation of Prussia, which was already seen as a leader of the coming counter-revolution, the Paulskirche's self-imposed limitation on its own power and the crippling of the revolution led to widespread anger. In the Rhineland and central and north Germany there were protest demonstrations as early as the beginning of September. But Frankfurt was the deciding factor. The radicals, who were strong both in the city and its environs, had asked the left to leave the Paulskirche in protest. This meant they were to set themselves up as an opposing parliament. The moderate left rejected this idea. After demonstrations in front of the Paulskirche, a meeting of a thousand people declared that those who had authorised the ceasefire were traitors to the German people and that their mandate was thereby removed. It was then announced that there was to be an armed meeting in the city centre. The government and the Frankfurt senate called on Austrian, Prussian and Hessian troops to protect the Paulskirche. On 18 September the parliament held a heated debate on the situation; demonstrators tried to occupy the building, but they were prevented from doing so by the army. The demonstration led to a riot against 'treason', against the foreign army and against the Prussians. It was not until the evening and after bitter battles that the army was able to bring the uprising under control; there were some eighty dead, with casualties from both sides. Two conservative members, Prince Lichnowsky and General von Auerswald, were murdered by the rioters. The *Reichsverweser* declared a state of emergency. In Cologne and Düsseldorf, where there were demonstrations influenced by Marx and Engels and the young Ferdinand Lassalle, the government also declared an emergency.

The events in Frankfurt had a powerful effect. As the centre saw it, out of rage over the situation in Schleswig–Holstein had risen an attempted revolution of red republicans; from the demonstrations had come violence and terror, anarchy and murder; for them this was not a sad, terrible side-effect of political conflict, it was the authentic manifestation of the second revolution. It was the murder of the two members of parliament that discredited the entire left, although they could not be remotely identified with this outbreak of rage. This increased the fear of renewed revolution and strengthened the resolve to maintain order. On the Rhine, in the Palatinate, in Hesse, in Baden and in central Germany there seemed to be a threat of seething anger and uprising. The radicals' view that it was now only the property-owning and educated middle class that had any power in the parliament led to renewed social protest by the masses. The *Reich* government sent in imperial commissioners and a concentration of troops. In retrospect, the threat of a new revolution seems very remote, but that is generally the case with failed revolutions.

Had the coup in Frankfurt succeeded — and it was possible — it would most probably have resulted in all-out civil war under the banner of national unity and social democracy. Only in Baden did an actual new revolution occur. The wounds of the April uprising had not healed. The Paulskirche had not admitted the great Hecker as a member. The republican emigrants in Switzerland and Alsace were agitating to bring about the overthrow of the Frankfurt parliament, to create a United States of Germany, and they set up an armed military corps. Struve, believing the coup in Frankfurt had been successful, returned from Switzerland and on 21 September in Lörrach declared a German republic. He declared prosperity, education and liberty for everyone — that was the social slogan. Rich merchants and Jews were to finance the revolution by way of special taxes. The Baden Oberland took on this task, but after four days the army in Baden had suppressed the uprising.

The authority of the *Reich* and of Paulskirche had held their own during the crisis. But they had been weakened. The left had attacked the centre, and the centre had reacted against the left. The centre wanted freedom and justice, but it wanted them in safety and order. They wanted to demonstrate their freedom to decide against pressure from the radicals, and they did not want to see their liberal-democratic aims discredited by attacks on order and property. The centre turned against a second, permanent revolution. This deepened the gulf between it and the left. The centre wanted to assert itself, but because it did not have any real power of its own, it had to go along with the state powers; by maintaining law and order, the centre was forced onto the side of the old powers. This was dangerous, because the willingness of the individual states to compromise with the centre receded as a result of this change of stance. Clearly, it was felt, there was no longer any need to be too wary of the centre; and perhaps also in the end it was only soldiers that could help against democrats. This was a stimulus for the counter-revolution; and among the middle-class and peasant majority in the country the emphasis that had been placed on freedom and justice could now be placed on safety and order. Lines of common ground and division were moved. The centre, however, according to the beliefs which had brought them to office, and in the mêlée of the Schleswig–Holstein crisis, had no choice. This was another tragedy of the situation.

Despite their defeat, the Democrats continued to agitate, even more strongly than in the summer, against the counter-revolution that loomed in Berlin and Vienna. On 3 October the Democratic central committee protested against the Paulskirche. It demanded meetings of the electorate, the annulment of the mandate, the recall of the members and new elections; and as there was no likelihood of their demands being met, there was yet another call for a second revolution. When the second Democrats' Congress met in Berlin between 26 and 31 October — 260 associations from 140 cities were now represented — the counter-revolutions in Berlin and Vienna were already well under way. The Paulskirche's mandate was declared expired. But on other issues there was no longer a great deal of unity; they could agree neither on their aims nor on their methods. Disagreements between socialist and non-socialist Democrats split the congress, as did the question of what they could do about the Vienna revolution. The attempt to bring together all the German extreme left-wing members of parliament to form a sort of opposition parliament in Berlin also failed. A concrete alternative to the liberals' strategy was not forthcoming; the extreme left collapsed; despair at the coming counter-revolution was widespread.

In November, it was the moderate left in Frankfurt who once again gave impetus to a powerful reorganisation. The 'Central March Association' sought to bring together the left in parliament and in the countryside to fight for the March achievements and to unite the Democrats to fight against the counter-revolution. By the spring almost 500,000 people had organised themselves into 500 local associations.

There were three interweaving threads of negotiation in the process of counter-revolution and radicalisation: the Pan-German, the Austrian and the Prussian; the centres of the action were Frankfurt, Vienna and Berlin. These all interacted, but it is necessary to understand each of these threads in its own right.

The developments in Austria were of decisive significance for the Pan-German revolution. This was really rather remarkable because in the early summer of 1848 Austria seemed almost paralysed; the liberal and national revolution seemed to usher in the end of the old dynastic, supra-national state. This development had various centres, although it was ultimately centred on Vienna.

Firstly, let us consider Prague. A constitution, autonomy and its own government had been promised, but, of course, in the early summer such things still hung very much in the balance. This was cause for unrest. On the basis of the March achievements, an alliance had been formed between the moderately liberal bourgeois Czech nationalists and the rather more conservative aristocracy, and this alliance then laid claim to the leadership. This naturally provoked the left. After all, there had been a sharpening of the difference of opinion between the Germans and the Czechs. The majority of Germans did not want equality of the languages to be interpreted in such a way that the Sudetenland or Prague universities became bilingual; and the Czechs did not want a two-nation country, but rather a Czech Bohemia with rights for minorities. The most important point was that the Germans, in contrast to the Czechs, wanted to belong to a united Germany and a German-led Austria. They felt threatened by Czech ambitions; they formed their own organisation — indeed, in the German border areas there was a tendency to separate from the Czech provinces. The Pan-Slav Congress in Prague at the beginning of June, which was made up almost exclusively of Austrian Slavs, supported the rejection of the Paulskirche and its Greater Germany (*Grossdeutschland*) and the *grossdeutsch* Austrians (it also rejected the idea of the Hungarian estates assembly for a Greater Hungary). It called for a federal Austria in which it would no longer be the Germans alone who would lead; instead the Slavs would share power with them. The congress was not particularly successful, but it provoked sharp reaction. On 12 June, there was an uprising by the left, the Democrats and students, supported by unemployed cotton workers and the poor; it had no clearly defined programme other than the continuation of the revolution, opposition of the counter-revolution and above all the continued presence of the military. The military commander, Prince Alfred von Windischgrätz, turned down all offers of talks and initially allowed the uprising to go unchecked, presumably quite consciously, in order then to crush it all the more harshly. There were 400 victims of bloody battles before the rebels were forced to surrender on 16 June. Windischgrätz assumed power. There had been Germans and Czechs on both sides, but social-radical excesses against the wealthy German bourgeoisie were seen as anti-German and further increased national tensions. Windischgrätz was not met with rejection, however; on the contrary, the German bourgeosie saw him as their protector against Czech radicalism. And the anti-radical Czech bourgeosie saw his victory as the victory of the black and yellow of Austria over the black, red and gold of the German national democracy, which was so radically rejected; it was also a victory over the black, red and gold of Vienna. The whole thing could not yet be called the first major victory of the counter-revolution, but for the first time the power of the army had not only defeated a radical revolution, it had also stemmed the liberal national revolution. The left in Vienna took it quite rightly as the defeat of the revolution, but they too had nothing in common with the Czech autonomists or the federalists.

The second scene of the revolution was Italy. The Italians could not agree among themselves, and the French had not intervened to protect the revolution. The old institutions of the imperial state were successful in strengthening the army in Italy; Croatian and Magyar leaders hoped that they would gain national political advantages by supporting the Emperor militarily in Italy. On 25 July, the Austrian multi-national army, under the leadership of the eighty-two-year-old Radetzky, defeated the Piedmontese at Custozza; Johann Strauss's Radetzky March has since immortalised him. Radetzky rode victorious into Milan and forced a ceasefire in Piedmont. Only a French invasion could have prevented the Austrians from securing its position and would thereby have exacerbated the dissolution of Austria. But General Cavaignac's republican 'dictatorship' could not afford such a policy, as it had hardly recovered from its suppression of the workers' revolt in June. This victory in Italy returned the self-confidence to the empire and the powers supporting it; but public opinion in Austria and in the rest of Germany greeted this victory as a national victory. Despite ongoing commitments in Italy, the empire had won a new military strength. The victory became the basis of the assault on Hungary, and part of this process was first to suppress the revolution in Vienna; and this was the beginning of the victory of the counter-revolution in Germany. In the summer the belief had been widely held that Austria would not only be paralysed, but that it would be dissolved. Anton von Schmerling in Frankfurt, a committed Austrian and an intelligent man, was expecting the cession of Lombardy and Galicia and a three-way division of the core area of the country into Bohemia, Hungary and German Austria, each to be governed by an archduke; this would have eased the German problem. The victory in Italy altered the outlook not only of observers, but also of the state itself.

The question of Hungary's fate remained unresolved. The Emperor and the Viennese government, in essence, had no say over the matter. As a result of the revolution, the country had its own parliamentary government and was autonomous. Things seemed to be heading towards independence from the united state: a personal union perhaps or a complete break-away; this would mean confrontation. In the early summer, both the court and the government were manoeuvring, especially since it was hoped that Hungarian troops could be employed against Italy. But following the victory in Italy, Vienna demonstrated more resolute opposition to Hungarian separation. In addition, a new conflict arose; it was an opposition of nationalities, namely that of the countries subject to Hungarian rule against Magyar nationalism. The Hungarians, like almost all the national movements at that time, stood firmly by their historical claims; though they made up only a very slim majority of the population, they wanted to be the ruling nation. They did not want autonomous areas on their soil. Everyone was to speak Magyar — this was, of course, a symbol of such a policy. This was a move against Vienna. And the Magyars felt that they were quite within their rights; they saw themselves as forerunners of freedom and progress, and other nationalities were to be admitted into politics only with the agreement of the Magyars. In short, the other nationalities were expected to adapt. But these nationalities — the Croatians, the Serbs, and above all the Rumanians, all of whom had until then remained outside political life — then rose up against this idea. The rejection by the Hungarians of the united nation and the rejection by the nationalities of Magyar nationalism were not compatible; this was the primary factor central European balance of power. Count Jellacic, put forward by a self-formed Croatian national committee in Agram, was declared the Ban (state governor) of Croatia by the Emperor. After much to-ing and fro-ing, the Emperor revoked his recognition of complete independence for Hungary at the end of August, and on 12 September Jellacic, at the head of an army, rode over the demarcation lines which until then had been respected. This meant war. It was a war of the national minorities against the Magyar majority; it was a war of what remained of the united nation against a rebellious Hungary; it was an internal Hungarian and an all-Austrian civil war.

The loyalties, alliances and oppositions all intersected in this situation in the most remarkable way. The supporters of a united Austria, regardless of whether they were Germans or Slavs, counter-revolutionaries, moderately liberals, centrists or Slavic autonomists, rose up against Magyar Hungary. The left was pro-Hungary. It believed in the internationality of the nationalists; but apart from German, Polish and Italian nationalism, it recognised only Magyar nationalism, and not that of the Slavs. This was a case of an ideological dividing-line between progress and reaction. But it was not clear whether progress was on the side of the Hungarian petty nobility or that of the emerging Slavic ruling classes. As usual, the national conflict plunged the opponents of the absolutist status quo into a dilemma and transgressed the usual lines of conflict. This caused a crisis for the revolution in Austria. Before we go into this in any more detail, however, we must first turn to the events in Vienna.

The revolution in Vienna was decidedly liberal-democratic, and it was national and German in its outlook. Since April, the black, red and gold flag, the symbol of the student 'Academic Legion', had dominated public life. The fact that there was no 'March government' and that the constitution promises came only hesitatingly, as well as the fact that the capital — with its students, intellectuals and foreigners, its workers, poor people and strongly politicised and economically threatened petty bourgeoisie — had become a bastion of radicalism, prevented the liberal consolidation of the revolution. The 'second Viennese revolution' on 15 May, led by the Academic Legion, the workers' associations and the national guard, had forced an unconditional promise of a national assembly and a constitution from the government; but at the same time it had resulted in the royal court fleeing to Innsbruck. The attempts by the government to stabilise the situation in Vienna failed; the power of the democratic organisations and their revolutionary Committees of Safety under Adolf Fischhof, who was no ultra-radical, was too great. There remained, therefore, two power centres side by side, even when the government, under pressure from the left, was reformed at the beginning of July, and when, in addition to two other new ministers, the Democrat Alexander Bach was appointed Minister of Justice.

Vienna, of course, was in a situation of latent opposition to the provinces. The peasants and citizens of the smaller towns were out-and-out opponents of the old system, and they were especially anti-feudal, but they were not radical. And, in part, the often talented intellectual spokesmen of radicalism had discredited themselves in the eyes of the Catholic people by their anti-clericalism, their German Catholicism and their ideas of independence from Rome. The peasants lost all interest in the revolution once agrarian issues had been settled. The provinces were not republican — indeed, they were moderately monarchist — and since the summer there had been a growing feeling of rejection of radical red Vienna.

In the summer, throughout the whole empire with the exception of Hungary and northern Italy, an imperial diet (the Reichstag) was elected under the electoral law of the Paulskirche. On 22 July, it met in Vienna. Of the 383 members — and this was the first reality, the national reality — 160 were German, 190 were Slavs, and 39 were Italian, Rumanian and so on. By social status some 94 were peasants, 74 were civil servants, 70 were doctors and advocates, 24 were priests, and 42 were from the nobility. Aside from the usual academic element, it was striking that agriculture was so strongly represented. Some of the peasants even turned up in their country dress. Politically the situation was unusual, because national and constitutional orientation overlapped. Only the Germans formed a conservative and liberal centre and a democratic left, made up of 80 members. On the whole, this parliament too was a parliament of the centre ground. The dealings were difficult, if only because German was not understood by all those present. The first act of this assembly, at the request of the young Silesian member Hans Kudlich, was the emancipation of the peasants and the abolition of compulsory labour and feudal encumbrances. Despite the wishes of the left, peasants were required to pay compensation, but the amount was only small and taken over partly by the state. This then was the end of the feudal system. Many of the peasants then left the Reichstag. The government then gave the Emperor's resolution force of law; this was intended to guarantee the crown's right of involvement, but such issues remained unresolved. On the whole, the Reichstag did not become a centre of action, nor was it a major centre of power. It discussed the constitution. An attempt in September by the left to declare the Reichstag permanent, by making it a convention and giving it executive power, was rejected by the centre and the right. Revolution and counter-revolution in October then forced it even further onto the periphery.

In the summer, the Emperor and the court finally returned to Vienna. But the unrest continued. The potential for social unrest among workers, day-labourers and the smaller craftsmen had considerably increased; the revolution had led to a decline in sales, unemployment and increased prices; public relief works, which employed some 50,000 people, further fuelled the tensions. There was also the social unrest of the radical democrats, concern about the slowness of the Reichstag, and a feared reaction by the army; the Jacobin radicals tended to perceive, and pursue, enemies of the people at every turn. There was still much disagreement, subjects for conflict were still rife, and the situation was confused. In August, there were serious clashes over pay for the workers engaged in emergency relief operations; eighteen people were killed and 300 injured. As a result, the government was able to move workers engaged in emergency relief operations; away from the city, it was also able to bring the national guard under its control and to abolish the Committee of Safety. But again in the middle of September, as a result of demands made by small craftsmen and the unemployed, there were serious clashes. The situation had become polarised. On one side there was the radicalism of the republicans, who based their ideas on social protest and presented themselves as a people's front wanting to continue the revolution and act with resolution against all counter-revolutionary moves; and despite several cracks, this group managed to hold together. On the other side there were the moderates; in March they had been revolutionaries, but now they were horrified by radicalism; in a Thermidor-like mood they had become more conservative and more monarchist; they were supporters of order. Because the radicals now monopolised the black, red and gold flag of German unity, some of them became more Austrian, under the black and yellow colours; Franz Grillparzer was an example of this. In two days a monarchist constitutional association gained 6,000 members. Tendencies towards the right of this kind only served to intensify the left's radicalism. At the end of September, the radical associations formed a central committee.

The Germans left outside Austria accurately sensed that what was happening in Vienna would be decisive for Germany and Europe and therefore attempted to exert influence there. At the end of the summer, Friedrich Hecker, Johannes Ronge, Julius Fröbel and Karl Marx were in Vienna. Their political awareness was such that they were able to assess the practicalities of the balance of power. Unlike Frankfurt, Vienna was the place of real decisions. 'If the democratic alliance of the United States of Central Europe is not founded in Vienna, then the Russian borders and despotism will soon be knocking at the city's gates,' said Fröbel. Later Blum's comment that 'it is in Vienna that Germany's fate will be decided' also summed up the mood of that late summer.

The spark that ignited the great conflict was the Hungarian question. In mid-September Jellacic moved against Hungary. A Hungarian delegation that was supposed to request the intervention of the Reichstag was not even heard; the pro-Hungarian left was in the minority. Provoked by the murder of its commissioner in Hungary, the government nominated Jellacic as the Emperor's representative; after a few military setbacks, it ordered the deployment of German troops as well against Hungary. On 6 October, one group of troops — from Vienna, naturally — staged a mutiny: German and Hungarian freedom were one and the same thing. This led to general insurrection in Vienna; the War Minister, Count Theodor Baillet de Latour, was lynched and hung from a street lamp. There were violent battles which overran and split even organisations of the left. All attempts to negotiate failed; the Reichstag ordered the government troops to clear the arsenals; the royal court and the majority of ministers fled; many members left the Reichstag; the city was taken over by the rebels. The Democratic associations and their central committee, students' and workers' committees and a new militia wearing red cockades ruled the streets. A new Committee of Safety and the city council assumed power. They appointed a 'supreme commander', Wenzel Messenhauser, a lieutenant and a writer, who was more a man of letters than a dictator. Even on the day before his execution he was negotiating with the Burgtheater on a performance of a social drama. It was the Polish general Joseph Bem who became the real military leader; he was an adventurous character of the Napoleonic era. On 17 October, Blum and Fröbel, members of the parliament, and two others from Frankfurt arrived; they were given honorary membership of the Academic Legion and girded with swords. Another 200 men would have to become 'Latourists', Blum said with great emotion, before freedom could be saved.

This Viennese revolution had many different aims. It changed from being national to international, and from being liberal to radical. Only in this way could the revolution still be saved; this was the rational heart of the matter. And behind this was the emphatic belief in a permanent revolution that would abolish everything relating to the order of the state and society and even to the church, and would ultimately lead to a social revolution. It was now a minority that ruled, but with its rational argument that the revolution must be defended, it still had some supporters from the centre. The revolution was also a last attempt to revolutionise the entire state, with the capital as a starting-point. But they were unable to win the support of the country people. The peasants could not be talked into joining a militia, least of all by Vienna. And the majority of the petty bourgeoisie tended to be more intimidated and passive. The German left, of course, backed the Viennese revolution with body and soul. 'If we could still kneel, we would kneel down, and if we could still pray, we would pray for Vienna,' said Ferdinand Freiligrath. But in reality they could do nothing; and any hope of Hungarian help melted away.

This 'red revolution' was the long-awaited signal for the counter-revolution led by Windischgrätz. He amalgamated his troops with Jellacic's Croatians, and in hard-fought battles at the end of October, in which more than 2,000 men were killed, Vienna was taken. The reaction of the Viennese was curious and characteristic. The deployment of the counter-revolution was greeted enthusiastically with cheers, probably for opportunistic reasons and for fear of being killed, but there was also a feeling of relief. The city council, which had recently referred to Windischgrätz as the new Brutus crushing the law of the people and of nature under his feet, now grovelled to him, thanking him for saving the city and restoring order and true freedom and for showing such mercy. Windischgrätz got rid of the 'Rotzbubenwirtschaft' ('snotty-nosed brat-ocracy'). The President of the French Republic, Louis Cavaignac, congratulated him on his 'great favour for Germany and Austria, which was also a decided service to France and the rest of Europe'. The punishments then imposed were not as harsh as one might have expected. Twenty-five men were executed, including Robert Blum, and the Paulskirche understood this as it was intended, namely as a provocative attack against the immunity of members of parliament and against the Paulskirche itself; in short, it meant that Austria was now turning against the common German and liberal principle. All in the Paulskirche were incensed and in a mood of protest, and Robert Blum became a martyr of the liberal-democratic revolution. The sending of two commissions from the Reich's government to Vienna was now rejected by Austria as interference, and the commissions were sent back to Frankfurt; seemingly the Paulskirche was now powerless.

Why was the counter-revolution victorious in Vienna of all places, and in Austria? For half a year it had seemed that Vienna was the weakest member of all the states that had seen revolution. All the world was astonished that this broken giant of an imperial state had been able to reassert itself so forcefully. Was it the 'reactionary' Slavs, under the command of Windischgrätz and Jellacic, or the peasants and the medium and petty bourgeosie, who had deserted the Viennese revolution and turned to the camp of the reactionaries? Such ideas are too simplistic. But the question is extremely important — indeed, it is the key question of this period — because the victory of the counter-revolution in Austria formed the basis for its victory in Germany. In Vienna, Germany's fate was determined. And it is for this reason that questions about the causes are so pressing. Firstly, the counter-revolution was victorious because the dynastic, military state and its institutions had more power and reserves than the victory of the liberal movement in Vienna or Prague and the resolutions of the victorious associations and committees had suggested. Conservative loyalty came from non-political masses of soldiers, and here the system of command and obedience was clearly still functioning. The monarchist temperament, especially, coupled with the tradition of the institution, particularly in the army, and the allegiance to authority and tradition, constituted a reality which, when it came to conflict, was reactivated. The same also applied for the state tradition of the unity of the countries within the whole empire, which the majority of the new, liberal government figures, except those in Hungary, now entered. The 'state' had more support than the old or new incumbents of the senior offices. The state was more than pure power, more than a house of cards; it had legitimacy, and that was able to mobilise loyalty.

Of course, the counter-revolution was also victorious because the revolution had splintered. The radicalism of the capital meant that it had cut itself off from the provinces and, most importantly, from the rural masses. The revolution in Vienna, even if it was a step taken in desperation, was doomed to failure; by October, it was no longer possible to try to bring about change in Austria by working from Vienna. The radical tendency of the Viennese revolution, which had persisted throughout the summer, had made it impossible to consolidate and form a liberal government; although it is unlikely that even such a government would have been able to consolidate the revolution. Of course, this radical tendency had forced the centre, and perhaps even the masses of the Viennese petty bourgeoisie, further towards the right; it had increased people's fear of anarchy, of people on barricades and of Jacobins, and created concern about order. But this was not what determined the situation that then developed; Vienna was not taken from within, but rather by an exterior force. It was taken because the army was still intact, because the provinces did not rebel, and because conflict between nationalities weakened the revolution, thereby enabling the former powers to bring themselves to the helm. The precarious split in the bourgeois movement into the radicalism of the left and the wariness of the centre, which in Vienna was a situation that became increasingly acute, had facilitated the victory of the counter-revolution, but it was not its real cause. Even if the radicalism had been more unified and stronger — for example, in the form of alliance of the bourgeoisie and the workers — it would not have won the battle; it would not have had a chance. And even if things in Vienna had remained more moderate and there had not been the wildness of the second revolution, the counter-revolution would have won through, as it did in Italy and in Prague. The October revolution, the most decisive second revolution that took place in Germany, had only succeeded in assuring the early and complete victory of the counter-revolution. In other words, because the second revolution attempted to meet the challenge of the Hungarian separation and the Magyar suppression of nationalities, the old state slipped into an emergency situation — unlike anywhere else in Germany — and it was precisely this that mobilised the forces that it still had at its disposal.

The determining factors — and indeed, this is the whole basis of this discussion — were the national conflicts and the fact that there was a double revolution: that the political (and social) conflicts were eclipsed and overlapped by the national conflicts. As we saw earlier, the national demands brought into question both the united state and the unity of the historic countries, and they were at odds with the liberal programme — which included, for example, a parliament for the entire country — and with the sovereignty of the people, if such sovereignty actually belonged with the individual states. The revolution in Austria in reality represented the revolutions of the nations, because each of them asked the question of how the united state would be structured, what form it would take, although they did this in a variety of ways, as they did not form a unity. It was for this reason too that they crippled each other. The question about the united state was especially complicated within the context of German history because the issue always revolved around what position the Germans would play in the Reich that was to be created. The struggle for closer unity of the Reich was at the same time a struggle by the Germans to take up the leadership and for them to impose themselves as the key national group within the state; the struggle of the nationalities for more autonomy was also a struggle against the Germans assuming this leadership; in the Hungarian part of the empire the same was true of the resistance to the Magyars. This also characterised the political desire of the Germans. They wanted at the same time to belong to both Austria and Germany. Nearly all were convinced of the legitimacy and the merit of preserving the united state, and they wanted to retain their leading role, at least in the non-Hungarian sector. The latter aim too seemed to be something that was not only self-evident but also legitimate, because, spread throughout all the areas, they represented the progressive bourgeois nation. But in the people's revolution this position had been placed in danger, and the Germans began to adopt a seige mentality. Their position in Austria was closely related to their position in a united Germany; by belonging to Germany they should secure their leadership of Austria. On this point, however, as we discussed in the case of the Bohemians, they were at odds with the growing nationalism of the Slavic peoples. In other words, the German, the Magyar and the Slavic — first the Czech and then the Croatian — revolution had opposing national aims which can be summarised as follows: a German-led and united state; the separation of a Magyar Greater Hungary; the preservation of a united state, which would be independent of Germany, with autonomy for the Slavic peoples and their participation in the running of the country. It was also these opposing ideas that caused the failure of both a liberal, federal, united reorganisation of the state and its division into the several main entities. It was principally the Slavic peoples who had to oppose the German and Magyar national revolution, because they had a very pressing interest in the preservation of the old state; however, they did not want this state to be governed by Germans or Magyars. Their nationalism was as legitimate as that of all the other groups, and the accusation by Marx and Engels that it was reactionary is unjustified. But the national conflicts and the Slavic interests especially resulted in the former imperial state being re-legitimised and indeed revitalised. It had to strengthen those forces which were rooted in the traditions and necessity of the united state. As the national conflicts seemed impossible to resolve, the united state seemed something like a parallelogram of the powers; that was the unifying factor for the interests that supported it. Of course, as the national conflicts continued unresolved, so the position of the Slavic peoples against the Magyars and the Germans not only strengthened the former united state, but also *de facto* the counter-revolution. It was the national conflicts that had made the counter-revolution victory possible. And at that time these national conflicts were unavoidable. This was the true tragedy of this revolution.

The victory over the Viennese revolution almost meant victory over radicalism. Windischgrätz, who was at once Vienna's Cavaignac and an imperial officer, a man of order and a man of traditional legitimacy, proceeded legally and moderately, against his usual tendencies. For a time, the victory could be seen as a sensible solution, a victory of order, security and freedom over anarchy and terror. But in reality, it was the centre that had now been decidedly weakened. The centre had not simply turned into a supporter of reaction; it had thrown itself at the feet of military despotism, preferring the terror from above to the terror from below. And the events had not compromised the legitimacy of the centre and its programme for a constitutional solution for the reconciliation of freedom and order, because the centre, as we have already noted, did not submit out of cowardice or fear of the masses — quite simply it was worn down by the national conflicts. The centre was still intact, but its position, of course, had been permanently weakened; its power had stemmed from having the option of recalling the revolution, if its achievements appeared to be threatened. It had been completely consumed by radicalism and national conflict. The old authorities now had the power; and as they now propagated the alternatives of anarchy or authoritarian order, so they further weakened the position of the centre.

It was not, of course, the counter-revolution's military man Windischgrätz who formed the new government; this was carried out instead by his brother-in-law, Prince Felix von Schwarzenberg. He was a great politician, resolute and full of purpose, and had a sense of power and a readiness to take risks. He was not a man of tradition or of the status quo, and he saw that feudalism was out of date and that the monarchy was breaking up. He did not value very highly the political capabilities of his own class, and he realised that the social and political groupings were now different. His response was revolution from above; he followed a policy of conservative modernisation. He appointed the most significant bourgeois politicians of the previous government to his cabinet, including Alexander Bach, who had begun as a Democrat and a man of the barricades, and Baron von Bruck, the son of a Rhineland petty bourgeois who, having remained in Trieste, had become a major ship-owner. On 2 December, the Emperor, incapable of governing, was persuaded to abdicate and his eighteen-year-old nephew, Franz Joseph, was named his successor, by the grace of God and not on the basis of a constitution, a symbol of the renewed ability to take action. For the time being, the government continued to give the impression that, in conjunction with the Reichstag, its intention was to implement the transition to a constitutional state. In view of the open German question, the position of the Paulskirche, public opinion and Prussian competition, as well as with an eye towards Hungary, this seemed a clever move; it was most certainly a tactically move, although perhaps Schwarzenberg really did intend to keep that option open. The Reichstag continued to meet in Kremsier and brought the discussions on the constitution to an end. It was a decidedly liberal constitution, and it represented a clear attempt to accommodate federalism of the historic countries, the demands of the nations and the interests of the empire. Within the different states, regional districts enjoying considerable autonomy were to be set up for the different nationalities; in the central institutions the Germans, partly because of the number of German states and partly because they were the minority that was present in every part of the empire, were to have occupied a strong position. When it came to the oath, however, the authoritarian monarchy did not want to accept a constitution that had been drawn up by parliament. This would have reversed the new balance of power. Before the constitution was adopted, the government responded with a *coup d'état*. On 4 March, the Reichstag was quietly dissolved, whereafter a constitution was imposed; it was utterly more monarchist than that proposed by the Reichstag and somewhat more centralist, but it too contained a universal system of self-administration. But this was clearly not the point. Firstly, what was politically critical was the fact that the constitution decreed Austria's indivisibility. This presupposed the solution of the Hungarian question and was a demonstration against any *grossdeutsch* division of Austria. The fact that this constitution did have some liberal content was a weapon in the battle against the Paulskirche and Prussia, and in the national struggle in Austria. The constitution was a façade which hid the intention to restore absolutism. Its institutions and the necessary elections were never implemented. What ruled was a state of emergency, and in reality the liberal, conservative solution merged with reaction.

Austria had re-emerged as a German and European major power. This had important consequences for the development of the German revolution and the German question. Schwarzenberg's policy reflected the Austrian *raison d'état*. Austria was to be preserved as an empire and, of course, as a great power. It was to maintain the leadership in northern Italy, in the south-east and in Germany; Austria was determined not to be forced out of Germany. In the situation as it was, this was no longer the old balanced policy; it was a new imperial power policy, and Schwarzenberg, with his enthusiasm, was the man to lead it.

Of course, in the first instance Austria remained committed in Italy and Hungary. The suppression of the Italian provinces — which led to a new war with Piedmont — dragged on into late spring (battle of Novara). Then the subjugation of Hungary failed in the winter of 1848–49. In the spring, Hungary declared itself completely independent. Austria, utterly displeased at the prospect, requested the assistance of the Tsar; and, for reasons of ideology and power politics, the Tsar was more than willing to oblige. By August, Hungary had been conquered. Thus it was the Russian army that crushed the Hungarian revolution. Hungary could not expect assistance from any quarter, and the revolution was over. England and France were entirely in favour of a strong Austria, as a bulwark against Russia, and they had no sympathy for the radicalism of the Hungarian revolution's leader, Lájos Kossuth. One may well ask if Austria could not have been victorious without assistance from Russia. It is likely that it would have been, but it would have taken considerably longer and would have kept Austria away from the issue of the German state. Russia therefore had become Austria's saviour and a bastion of the counter-revolution. Thus Austria had in fact only regained its position as a major power by borrowing power from another state, and for the time being it remained more allied to Russia than ever. The Austrians' criminal court in Hungary, condemning a hundred people to death and hundreds more to prison, later turned public opinion in western Europe against what it called 'brutal' Austria. The consequences for Germany and the foreign policy of this Russian-Austrian joint action were serious. The gratitude that Russia expected from Austria was not in the long term compatible with the Austrian *raison d'état*; we shall return later to this point.

Let us turn finally to the developments in Prussia. The character of the Berlin National Assembly was less learned and academic than that of Frankfurt. Its members were made up of more peasants and more craftsmen (46 of each from a total of 402 members), commerce was more strongly represented, and there were more middle-ranking civil servants (34) and fewer professors. But here too it was judges, communal civil servants, teachers and clergymen who played the more important role. Politically speaking, here too the majority was constitutional, but the centre was further to the left. The parliament was less moderate, more decisive, but less pragmatic and, in part, more doctrinaire. The centre left was strong and emphatically anti-feudal; the left, moderate and radical, with more than 120 members, was the strongest *Fraktion*, and it formed itself around the uncrowned king of the parliament, the jurist Benedikt Franz Waldeck. This somewhat greater orientation to the left also stemmed from the fact that the circumstances this body found itself in appeared more straightforward. Its goal was to renew the state and not to found a new one; it was possible to pursue the goal of liberty without having to bear in mind the question of unity, which lessened the tendency towards compromises. Connected with this was something more, however; the parliament, including the left, had developed a curious parliamentarian, Prussian particularism. It felt duty bound to the sovereignty of the Prussian people, and there was no question that the decisions made in the Paulskirche should be accepted uncon-ditionally in Prussia. This revealed one of the major latent tensions of the revolution.

The fate of the revolution in Prussia was decided on the one hand by discussions between the crown, government and parliament, and on the other hand by the extra-parliamentary movements and actions. These two threads interacted with one another. The king made the assumption that the National Assembly had been appointed to agree on a constitution, and for this reason he had set in motion a Second United Diet; this was the monarch's proviso against the constitutional sovereignty of the people. The left made reference to this sovereignty based on the revolution, while the centre tried to build revolution and legality, sovereignty and accord into both the assembly's strategy and its understanding of its own purpose. This is where the latent conflict between the crown and parliament lay. Berlin was also experiencing problems typical of a major city and a capital city; these were strong radical democratic movements and tensions between the employed or unemployed dependent workers and the middle class, represented here by the militia which, because everyone armed himself, excluded these strata of society. When, at the beginning of June, Prince Wilhelm, the grand champion of the military monarchy, returned to Prussia and even presented himself as a member of parliament, and after a narrow majority in the National Assembly had blocked a request by the left for 'recognition of the revolution', the radicals were able to see the looming threat of counter-revolution. On 14 June, the military arsenal was stormed. Because the militia surrendered, military units moved to break up this revolt of which even the parliamentary left had disapproved; the workers were disarmed. The National Assembly, despite all this, did not want 'armed protection'; it was this issue that caused the collapse of the Camphausen ministry, which was then replaced by the moderate-liberal but generally more decisive Auerswald ministry. Despite this, the king was also thinking of recalling the army. The Gerlach brothers began talking about the possibility of dissolving parliament and initiating the counter-revolution. But this for the moment was little more than pie in the sky.

The assembly's constitution committee had prepared a draft by 26 July — which was fast compared with Frankfurt — the so-called Waldeck Charter. This proposed a strong parliamentary system; the king would have only a suspensive veto; the first chamber was to be a communal parliament; feudal rights were to be abolished without compensation; the state army and a militia-like people's army were to be strengthened, and they would become more independent and more distant from the command of the king. This was decidedly liberal, although not in fact radical. The conservatives, however, saw an opportunity to agitate against such 'republican' plans.

It was, however, the question of the place of the military that sharpened the conflict. Until that time, the National Assembly had put off rendering the army constitutional; in May, in Posen, the king had shielded his command against the War Minister responsible in parliament. An incident in Schweidnitz on 31 July then triggered the crisis. The military acted against civilians who were demonstrating in favour of the civilian militia. Fourteen citizens were shot. On 9 August, the National Assembly requested the War Minister to require the officer corps to uphold the law of the constitution and ensure that it was enforced; anyone who did not accept this was to leave the army. The king and his followers rejected this as an intrusion on the rights of the executive, as a restriction on individuals' views and as an attack on the last bastion of royal power. The government rejected the resolution because it saw it as impossible to implement and wanted itself to decide how to implement loyalty to the constitution. The great majority remained firm on the resolution; on 8 September the government resigned. One may ask whether the parliament had pushed through a declaration of views and thereby took on board the fall of a liberal government. The majority saw this course of action as the only way to fend off the counter-revolution and to forestall a second revolution. It was to this extent a considered strategy. In any event, this then finally set the counter-revolution in motion. On 11 September, the king set out a battle plan. This included the adjournment of the assembly and the imposition of a constitution. He appointed General Wrangel as commander-in-chief 'in the [Brandenburg] marches'. But things were once again adjourned, and the revolution's potential still seemed strong. The king appointed a cabinet of civil servants with a reform-minded general, Ernst von Pfuel, at its head. Pfuel, a man of courage, issued the controversial 'Anti-Reactionary Decree', albeit in a somewhat milder form, which was the greatest concession that even a man of such talent for negotiation could extract from the king. But this policy of equilibrium did not succeed. The National Assembly, in its discussions on the constitution, had sharpened its parliamentary, democratic character, even with regard to the army. The assembly no longer sought compromise and equilibrium; now it wanted decisively to push through its goals and claims, even at the risk of causing conflict. In so doing it had, of course, seriously overestimated its freedom to act. The rights of the police and the judiciary were to be further limited, the death penalty was to be abolished, as were feudal hunting rights, without compensation. They also included some symbolic gestures, such as the abolition of the nobility, decorations and titles and the king's formulation 'by the Grace of God'. This led to an outpouring of violent emotions: the king may well have to forgo certain competencies, but surely not his divine right to the throne. It was against such deprivation of power of the king and government, the army and the nobility, and against the overthrow of all of Prussia's traditional foundations, that the king and his followers now put up a resistance; they could not stand idly back and allow this to happen. The king reverted to a firm anti-constitutional stance. The conservatives and high officer corps drew him back onto their ground (and thereby secured their positions). Even the civilian-minded king did not want to subject the army to a constitution. Questions on the military and the constitution came together. The army began preparing the counter-revolution and the king dismissed his civilian ministers.

This was the main thread of the conflict. It was made worse and eclipsed by the beginnings of a second revolution in Berlin, which in addition brought to the fore the tension between the bourgeois centre and the radical left. A law passed by the National Assembly on 13 October legitimised the militia as the only armed force of the people. This was aimed against the informal units set up by the radicals, and against 'street democracy' (Valentin). It triggered further insurrections, and even the militia itself was very nearly destroyed. In addition, since 16 October there had been considerable unrest among workers. Canal workers destroyed a steam-pump installation, and others protested about sackings. This ended in bloody barricade battles; the militia won, but even at the burial of the eleven dead there were more demonstrations by the radicals against the moderates. The National Assembly rejected a request from Waldeck for the government to intervene in the Vienna revolution by 229 votes to 113. Democrats in the capital saw this as treason, and there were more demonstrations, with torches and groups shouting in unison; they now also shouted against the parliamentary left. The Democrats' Congress at the end of October increased the unrest. On 31 October, the militia was supposed to protect the National Assembly. On 28 October, Pfuel, who had been been minister on call from the beginning, and had tried to achieve compromise, resigned. On 1 November, the king appointed the Graf von Brandenburg as Prime Minister and Otto von Manteuffel as Minister of the Interior. The demands from the National Assembly not to make these appointments and to introduce a 'constitutional' government were rejected by the king. 'The tragedy of the kings is that they do not want to listen to the truth,' was Johann Jacoby's response to the king's rejection. An attempt by the Paulskirche, and more particularly by Gagern, who did not want to endanger the connection between the *kleindeutsch* liberals and the Prussian king, was also unsuccessful. The new ministry was the ministry for counter-revolution. On 5 November, the National Assembly, using the excuse that it had to be protected from the pressure from the streets, was adjourned and moved to Brandenburg. The assembly opposed this and continued to convene, but it no longer had any power. The militia, however, refused to abolish the assembly, but neither did it protect it, and no people's resistance came to its assistance. Wrangel and his troops marched into Berlin, a state of siege was declared, the militia was abolished, and the National Assembly was dispersed. Nevertheless, 227 members met on 15 November in an inn and declared that the ministry was not authorised to raise taxes. This led to a call for the non-payment of taxes which was taken on by the democratic organisations in the provinces. But this move too backfired, because it was precisely those people who were eligible to pay taxes who were more in favour of calm and order. There were only isolated cases of unrest and or of mutiny in the mobilised *Landwehr*. The *coup d'état* had won the day without leading to civil war, without the spilling of blood, and without a shot being fired. But it was not only the left that had been conquered; so too had the liberal centre and the March revolution.

The rump assembly that met on 27 November remained unable to pass any resolutions. On 5 December, it was dissolved. The king imposed his own constitution. Although it had been the army that had led the counter-revolution, the event had not ended in a military dictatorship; this was also due to the fact that there had been no resistance and no civil war. The king, who wanted to arrest the party leaders and reinstate a united estate-based *Landtag*, distanced himself from such ideas. The ultra-conservatives, opponents of every type of constitution, were as unable to impose themselves as the moderates, who for their part were recommending a conservatively revised compromise. The political realists had the say. The imposed constitution was for the most part the Waldeck Charter. The second chamber was even permitted to maintain universal suffrage, while the first chamber was, of course, intended as a chamber for the major taxpayers and property-owners. The ministry even forced the king to promise to make the army swear allegiance to the constitution. This was extremely hard for the officers to swallow, and some grumbled that the army would not step in a second time to save the state. In cases of conflict, of course, the government had effective subordinate legislation and the right to emergency decrees; this made the government more independent. Furthermore, the imposed constitution aimed to revise the constitution, and this was to be the first task of the chambers. The meaning behind this policy was threefold. The first aim was to win time. Secondly, it was thought that, even if Frankfurt were to intervene, only by transferring to a constitutional system could the crisis be brought under control. Finally, the intention was to hold all the trump cards for the implementation of a German policy, and even Brandenburg was very open-minded about the idea of a Prussian-German empire, but this would require a constitution. Public opinion seemed for the most part to be in favour of this idea. The Liberal opponents of the *coup d'état* and of the imposed constitution reacted positively in part, the hidden conditions remained undetected, and many saw only victory over radicalism and were unaware of the fact that the Liberals were just as much the vanquished. Those in favour of the *kleindeutsch* solution found themselves in an impossible dilemma and, when their mediation failed, wanted to continue to wager on Prussia. Of course, in the winter of 1848–49 Prussia's ability to act was still limited because the king and the government were still of different opinions with regard to the German question, and thereby cancelled each other out.

In Prussia, unlike Vienna, the existence of the state, separation and anarchy and the polarisation of extremes had not been the issues; what had been at the heart of the events in Prussia was the classic question of the right of power between the crown and parliament. Had Prussia had a constitutional history, the shifting of responsibilities and power in favour of the parliament would have been more feasible. But this was not the case. And for this reason the policies of the National Assembly set in action the counter-forces and what until then had been the basis of the state, namely the army. The king had not been as thoroughly defeated as the assembly thought. But the Liberals' policy of negotiation was not a real alternative; this had been demonstrated by the conflicts on the issue of the army. A parliament that did not want to give itself up and deprive itself of all power was bound in the long run to come into conflict with the crown and the old powers, even if it had spoken less provocatively and made less inflammatory decisions.

The counter-revolution could not rely solely on a conservative camarilla, an army of noble officers and the highly disciplined non-commissioned officers and soldiers. The Tsar also played a role in the events, encouraging the king to pursue a counter-revolution; indeed, the Tsar's army was the emergency reserve of this policy. An influencing factor was also the victory of the counter-revolution in Vienna. The Prussian king would probably have acted in the same way, even if the events in Vienna had been different; but the events in Vienna had altered the situation in Berlin in the counter-revolution's favour. The internal situation in Prussia itself must also be borne in mind. The conservative elements, especially in the country, in a certain way had gained more strength. Prussian associations and military agitation had had an effect. The petty bourgeoisie and the middle-stratum bourgeoisie were experiencing what we might call the Thermidor spirit; they were people who took the radicalism, social protest and the red revolution more seriously than they actually were, and who, concerned that the red in the black, red and gold flag might become more dominant, reverted to the black and white of the Prussian flag. It was in any event a fact that in Berlin there were no longer any revolutionary masses rising up to show solidarity with the revolution, and the will to resist was now less than the mobilisation force of the events in March. This was not only out of fear or opportunism; it was also a result of disappointment as well as of Democratic agitation. It would be wrong to say that this is what caused or made possible the counter-revolution. But it did make its path easier.

6. The Imperial Constitution and the Empire

Let us now return to the Paulskirche. As we have already seen, it had not been possible to set up a constitution quickly, and the members had begun with the basic rights. It was not until 20 December, after two readings, that these were adopted. The plenum had not turned its attention to political questions, to the issue of Austria belonging to the Reich, and to the decision on the head of the Reich, until the end of October, and the discussions on these issues then went on until March 1849. By comparison with the summer, the political scene had changed fundamentally. Prussia and Austria were in the throes of counter-revolution. The Paulskirche had lost its authority and its freedom to make a sovereign decision on the constitution and then be able to implement it. The discussions in parliament that winter were continuously entangled with the changing political situation and the division of power, and also with the continued attempts by the states' governments to influence the resolution of the issues concerning the constitution. These discussions and the results were of great significance to the character of the revolution, to its aims and its problems, and to its progress and conclusion.

As we have already noted, the members dealt firstly with the basic rights. These were intended to create and guarantee a civil society and a state governed by the rule of law. They would also provide individual rights of freedom and property, equality before the law, the end of the feudal system and the police state, political freedom, and the right to a public trial. There were, however, no social rights, as the constitution did not set out to provide welfare reforms. In the eyes of the liberals, this would have impaired freedom. Overall, it was the moderate views that were adopted. Historic rights and traditions had, where possible, been protected against the rationalism of natural law. Of course, as we have already seen, in the major points of dispute relating to the economic and social order and the freedom of trade, and the right of residency, for example, the fundamental decision was in favour of the new, liberal order, although the actual implementation was postponed. The constitutional jurists won through against the 'economists'. On the issue of schools and the church, a compromise was reached. The radicals with their anti-clerical ideas — including the decrease of the church's power and an insistence that its structure be made more democratic — were unable to defeat the common sense of the majority and their shying away from religious conflict. Even one of their favourite ideas, namely that the Jesuits should be banned, did not succeed in the end. The church was free to govern its own affairs and — thanks to the Catholics — was subject only to the universal laws, i.e. there would be no special laws to govern the church. The opportunity for civil marriage was opened up, and responsibility for education in schools was taken on by the state. These were all liberal stances. But on the other hand, the church retained responsibility for the centralised religious education. It was now possible to found private schools, which in effect were religious schools. Most importantly, issues relating to (elementary) schools were to be dealt with by the community, which was closer to the church and the parents than the far-off and bureaucratic state. In short, this seemed to be a tolerable compromise to one of the most divisive of the fundamental issues of German life.

The Germany that the Paulskirche wanted to create was to be a federal state. For this reason it was, above all else, a *Reich* (empire), and, of course, the almost sacred memories of an historic-minded nation were encapsulated in this term. The word *Bund* (confederation) had been used in a reactionary way. There were a few — left-wing — unitarians, but the majority wanted a federation, and they all took their model from the United States, though that model was interpreted variously. The left would have preferred a federation of republics, preferably organised as new imperial districts without reference to the historical states. This, of course, was not very realistic. If one wanted to retain the monarchy — even a constitutional one — the monarchs would have be taken on board; Germany could not create new monarchies, so the federation would have to take as its starting-point the existing individual states. Germany's federal plurality was a fact that reached far beyond the dynasties. Even the parliaments of 1848, for all their efforts to create a unified state, had strongly represented the interests of their own individual state, the result being something like a parliamentary particularism. The problem of how to deal with the imbalance of the German states, some being too large and others too small for a federal state, was fully appreciated, but no one could suggest a solution. Mediatisation of the small states was considered, but the idea was then dropped. The federalisation of Prussia into its provinces, and even the abandonment of a Pan-Prussian parliament, were among the ideas about how Prussia's size should be dealt with; but they remained no more than ideas. The aim was to create a federal state, but it was to be a unitary federal state — which meant that while the individual states could remain, the maximum amount of responsibility should lie with the central government and not *vice versa*. There were to be two chambers: a democratic and unitary *Volkshaus* (people's house) and a *Staatenhaus* (states' house). The one-chamber system preferred by the left was rejected. The *Staatenhaus* was to have the same degree of competence with regard to the passing of laws as the *Volkshaus*; thus a strong left majority had been voted down. There was not, however, to be a special organ of the government, in the form of a *Reichsrat* (imperial council), as had been wanted by a strong right minority. The *Staatenhaus* was to be made up half of deputies from the state governments and half of representatives of the people.

The new Germany, of course, was to be a constitutional state, with a head of state, a government and a parliament. The question remained of how power and competence was to be divided between these organs; and, as had already been the case in the Vormärz period, there were many different opinions on this matter. Firstly, the role of the parliament was discussed. The great majority, without explicitly professing the principle, were in favour of a parliamentary system of government. The government should only be able to act with agreement from the majority of the people's representatives. There followed much muddled discussion, and quite understandably so, about the relationship between the Reich's government and the Paulskirche parliament. The fact that the government was to appoint the head of state, however, remained for the most part undisputed. Of course, behind the scenes there were other varying and opposing ideas. The left wanted a strong parliament and strong controlling rights over the government, but it was for the most part thinking more of a rather old-fashioned dualist system. The fact that someone who had fought for liberty had now become a 'man of government', as it was called, was more often regretted than welcomed. The left saw the parliament's relationship to the government rather like that of the Congress to the President of the United States. The right, by contrast, was most concerned about the prospect of 'parliamentary absolutism', which they accused the left of seeking and about the fact that an excess of controls could hinder the state's ability to act and govern. The right too wanted a strong parliament, but they also wanted a strong government and a strong head of state. The head of state, they said, should be able to dissolve parliament and have powers to act, especially on issues of foreign and military policy. Alongside the theories on the constitution, the national political aspect also played an important role in this argument: it was said that a strong executive was needed to act as an integrating element in the face of particularist forces and in the domain of foreign policy. The left sensed in this idea a threat to freedom and democracy. As far as they were concerned, the Reich parliament itself constituted a sufficient integrating force. But these issues were not discussed to their conclusions. The major issues became the question of whether the head of state should have an absolute or a suspensive right of veto over the parliament. Dahlmann spoke with great passion in favour of the absolute veto, calling it 'right of the saving act', although he did not want thereby to touch on the parliamentary way of governing. He may also have been bearing in mind the realistic consideration that the constitution should be such that it would be accepted by the Prussian king. The clear majority, however, in part because tactical points of view of the *grossdeutsch/kleindeutsch* factions did not yet play a role, rejected the absolute veto and voted instead for the suspensive veto. It seemed that only in this way could a parliamentary method of government be really guaranteed. This regulation, it should be noted, also limited the parliament's power to a degree, particularly when one considers that the head of state was also given the right to dissolve the parliament, in other words, the right to appeal directly to the people. Where there was conflict, it would be possible to delay a decision for two to three years.

Another central issue for the coming constitution was the question of voting rights. Even before the revolution this had been a major point of dissent between the parties. The right-of-centre liberals, who had the majority on the committee for the constitution, wanted to secure overwhelming influence for the middle strata of society, at least for the foreseeable future, because, they claimed, they represented 'the main emphasis of the state'. Freedom of the individual for them seemed to be linked to natural social inequalities, and they believed it was only in this way that they could prevent despotism of the masses. Therefore they felt that participation in the political process should be linked to education and knowledge, and those who were without property should not have command over property. Universal suffrage, it was said, would encourage the demagogy of the radicals and social revolution, as well as conservative or authoritarian reaction. It would, according to Georg Waitz, first produce 'the most radical and then the most servile members of parliament'. The liberals had to forgo the indirect voting system that they favoured, but voting should be exercised publicly, not secretly, and employees, apprentice craftsmen, factory workers, day-labourers and servants should, be excluded. Thus it was that, following the events of those months, they retreated to the voting rights that had preceded the Paulskirche; according to a contemporary estimate, half of the electorate in Prussia that had voted for the Paulskirche would have lost their right to vote under such a system. This, of course, was pure class interest. The liberal argument, however, that to give voting rights to the politically immature masses would threaten freedom, was not without foundation. In France it led to the dictatorship of Napoleon III. And no matter how crucial the basic democratic right may be to us, it is fair to ask whether Germany, in 1848, was ready for it. When universal suffrage was finally introduced in 1867–71, which was still very early in comparison with other European nations, its effect was to work against the liberals and against the building of the constitutional state into a democracy. The programme of the liberal right, however, was not able to win majority support. Only the left was in favour of the universal, equal, direct and secret right to vote, but many sought to compromise. The debate was then overtaken by events. As the taking of the decision was placed on the agenda in February 1849, the respective supporters of the *grossdeutsch* and *kleindeutsch* solutions were competing for the votes of the left. The draft put forward by the liberal-right Casino party was rejected by 422 votes to 21, and on 2 March the majority accepted the universal, equal, direct and secret right to vote; its *grossdeutsch* opponents voted partly for tactical reasons in favour of the law, in order to make it impossible for the Prussian king to take the crown; others voted in the expectation that the law would later be revised.

Finally, there was the question of the head of state and the form the state should take. The left was basically republican, anti-monarchist, although outright hatred of the princes — reflected in the saying 'Only when the last prince is hanged by the guts of the last priest . . . !' — was evident only on the extreme margins of the group. Even the majority of the left could see that the monarchy could not be removed from individual states, at least not yet. What they sought above all was a republican head of state for the Reich, and it did not seem to matter that he might be a prince-president. With the exception of the south-west, one can reasonably assume, the masses were for the most part still very much in favour of the monarchy. 'Republic', as we have already seen, was a not a term of constitutional law; it meant a liberal constitution, a civil kingdom, 'monarchy by the grace of the people', a 'monarchic republic'; it also meant little or no taxation and more equality. But a republic as a form of state was not in the offing. Federalists still imagined that there might be a tripartite directorate, but this too had little prospect of becoming reality. Thus the discussions continued to focus on a monarchy — indeed, to be more precise, on a *Kaisertum*, an empire. This was not due to any ideas of imperial romanticism or medieval nostalgia, but rather because a Kaiser could be superior to all the kings the empire already had. It could be a *Wahlkaisertum* (electoral empire), an idea preferred by the centre left; or it could alternate between Prussia and Austria, or it could be hereditary, with the first Kaiser being elected by the parliament, this being the national democratic side of the monarchy; and this evolved into the idea of an *Erbkaisertum* (hereditary empire). But Austro-Prussian dualism divided the supporters of the monarchy. The question of the head of state was no longer a question of theories on the constitution, but rather it depended on the solution of the German question.

The fact that there were two competing great powers in Germany, and that one of these included other countries beyond the boundaries of the German Confederation and of the German nation, was decisive, politically, for the constitution and the revolution as a whole. The question then became critical when it was asked how Austria could be part of the German empire. In spite of its geographically marginal position, and in spite of Metternich, Austria was self-evidently part of Germany; of this there was no doubt. The first reply to the question was therefore the *grossdeutsch* one. Austria and its German and Bohemian territories should belong to the empire, but it should belong only with those territories; and they, together with the other foreign parts of the *Kaiserstaat* as it had existed until that time, should only be bound by personal union. The connection of German Austria to the new Reich amounted to the division of the whole of the old Austrian empire and the surrendering of its national unity. This was the plan proposed by the constitution committee. On 27 October the plenum passed the proposal with a large majority. There were only 90 votes against, which, apart from conservative Catholics and a few *kleindeutsch* liberals, included 41 from Austria (the black-and-yellows, one might say). The majority of the Austrians, 74, voted for the *grossdeutsch* solution. Even those who supported Prussian leadership of the new Reich voted, for the most part, in favour. When this solution had been drawn up, the general opinion was that Austria, as a united state, would collapse, and then the question of German and Bohemian provinces belonging to a new Reich would no longer present a problem. Many members also understood this decision to be a 'request to Austria' to say its piece and make some suggestions. The alternative envisaged was the *kleindeutsch* solution, which would have meant excluding Austria from what would then have become a Prussian-led Germany and a confederate link of such a Germany with a united Austria. Here we see what Heinrich von Gagern referred to as the 'narrower' or 'wider' federation. The proposed *grossdeutsch* solution was bound, in the long term, to lead to the division of the Austrian states. A personal union would not be able to stop this from happening. A state, and a major power at that, could not remain a state and a major power if one half of it was part of another major power. Indeed, without the German centre that was Vienna, the other component territories would probably have severed their mutual links and the Habsburg empire would have crumbled into small, unconnected states. Had this been the case, Germany's leadership in south-east Europe would not have been sustainable. In taking *grossdeutsch* unity for granted, the special position of a supra-national major power had not been fully appreciated. This was also true of the majority of Austria's Germans, as we have already seen. They were ambivalent and wanted opposing things at the same time. On the one hand they wanted unity with Germany, but they did not actually want to join together, because they did not want to be separated from the whole of the Austrian state, unless the latter was to collapse by itself. It was a long time before the dilemma of reality and the possible solutions became clearer.

In the meantime, however, the counter-revolution had been victorious in Austria. Felix von Schwarzenberg's answer to the question posed by the Paulskirche constitution came on 27 November in the form of his Kremsier programme. Austria, it stated, had to remain a unified single state. This was effectively a rejection of the *grossdeutsch* solution, the solution that would have divided Austria. Austria, as Schwarzenberg declared at the end of December, also stuck firmly by its claim to participate in the constitution as a 'German federal power'. He thus also decisively rejected the idea of linking Austria with the rest of Germany only in the form of a 'wider', extended federation. In March, this issue was made clear by the Austrian *coup d'état*. The imposed constitution fixed in law the national unity of the German and non-German areas of the monarchy. Furthermore, in a note dated 9 March, Schwarzenberg requested that the whole of Austria be allowed to join the new Germany. This therefore was the third alternative: the Greater Austrian solution, and the idea of a Reich of 70 million people. This Reich was to be organised as a confederation of states and, given the array of nationalities, there was no other option; there was to be a directorate and no real parliament. There was to be only a *Staatenhaus* made up of delegates from the individual state parliaments, in which the Austrians, in line with the population ratio of 38 to 32 million, would have had the majority. And this parliament was to convene only once every three years. This plan did indeed link up with certain of the Paulskirche's imperial, central European ideas about the German hegemony in the south-east; it could not, however, be adopted. The national democratic revolution wanted the unity of German people in a nation-state; but did not want to take in millions of non-Germans. It did not want a confederation of states, it wanted a federal state. It did not want Austria's hegemony, the foreign policy interests of which were quite different; it wanted sovereignty for the German people. The revolution wanted a democratic, parliamentary state.

Of course, in the winter of 1848–49, these last consequences were not yet foreseeable to the members of parliament. Once, however, the first rejection of the *grossdeutsch* solution by Austria came, in November, the *kleindeutsch* alternative took on particular significance. It was, even though some of the supporters of the *kleindeutsch* solution had foreseen it, simply the escape route, the only remaining option. The supporters of the *grossdeutsch* solution, however, still hoped that a compromise could be reached and that a final concession would be made by the Austrian government. In view of the situation, the parties on the right and in the centre split up and regrouped. New alliances and new majorities were formed. Anton von Schmerling, still Prime Minister, became the leader of the *grossdeutsch* coalition which met in the Pariser Hof; Gagern became the leader of the supporters of the *kleindeutsch* solution who met in the Weidenbusch. On 15 December, Schmerling resigned from his position as Prime Minister and Gagern became his successor. In a complicated parliamentary, diplomatic game, both sought the support of Austria and Prussia and both tried to obtain a decision from the Paulskirche, which was still a factor in the power structure. But neither group had a majority. This was clearly demonstrated when, between 19 and 23 January, the parliament's discussions on the question of the head of state for the Reich were unsuccessful. Both groups were reliant on the left to make up a majority. This was a completely new situation.

The supporters of the *grossdeutsch* solution were made up of different groups with varying motives. On the one hand, there were the true *grossdeutsch* supporters, who favoured the solution out of emotion and will, such as the Austrians, who did not want to be thrown out of Germany or, put more harshly, feared that Gagern's policy would hand over millions of Germans to what Moritz Hartmann called the 'whip of the Slavs'; then there were all those who felt that, as Schmerling put it, Germany had a 'divine right' to Austria's German territories; and then there were the conservatives, who were in favour of Austria's historic sense of belonging to Germany and of the principle of compromise, and who also saw Austria as a force of counter-revolution outside parliament. Then, on the other hand, there were those who favoured the *grossdeutsch* solution out of less direct motives: these included the federalist supporters of the tripartite directorate, particularists, south and west Germany's Catholics and the greater majority of democrats and republicans. They were first and foremost anti-Prussian; they did not want a Prussian leadership and did not want to be left alone with Prussia in the new Reich. But, of course, this *grossdeutsch* sentiment, in concrete terms, could only indicate what was not wanted. They did not have a political solution as an alternative to the Austrian policy or even the Greater Austrian alternative. The Reaction in Vienna made the situation more difficult. Franz Joseph was not a suitable candidate as 'Kaiser of the Germans'. And the *grossdeutsch* left wanted a nation-state — not the monarchic, federal empire of the *grossdeutsch* right; the left wanted in essence the dissolution of Austria.

On the other side were the supporters of the *kleindeutsch* solution. For Germans living in the main German territory, Austria was relatively foreign and far away. Prussia was near. The picture that these Germans had of Prussia was ambivalent, just as Prussia itself was ambivalent. Prussia was in no way seen as a stronghold of aggressive power politics, and the left especially felt some affection for Frederick the Great. The conservative, old-style Prussians were opponents of power politics. The problem lay elsewhere. Prussia was one of the bastions of reaction as well as being a military state. But it was also the heir of the Reform Era, the state of reason, as Hegel and a large part of Europe had seen it. Another positive point was that Prussia, unlike Austria, was a German state. The supporters of the *kleindeutsch* solution, predominantly liberals, believed that Prussia could not remain reactionary for ever; it was only reactionary, they said, out of 'caprice' (Max Duncker), and not due to its real *raison d'état*. It was, of course, the state of liberal bureaucracy, of the west German bourgeoisie, of the Zollverein and of *Wissenschaft*. It was also the state of Protestantism, a fact that marked out a strong emotional dividing-line, and a fact that in the eyes of the liberals meant it was the foundation of freedom and intellect. The spokesmen for the *kleindeutsch* group were neither Prussians nor 'old Prussians', they were north, west and south-west Germans like Dahlmann and Hansemann, Gagern or Pfizer. The *kleindeutsch* supporters were by no means advocates of Greater Prussia; they were attracted by Prussia, or saw Prussia as the only real power capable of participating in and taking in hand national union. But they wanted Prussia 'to merge into Germany' — indeed, they calculated that this is what would happen were the Hohenzollern king to be made head of state. The unfinished nature of the German great power made it easier for her to become a true German great power. People spoke of making Prussia a state within the Reich, or of dividing her into provinces. Theodor Reh, a member of parliament, went as far as to say that he was in favour of a hereditary empire, because otherwise Prussia's suicide would not be possible. But neither was it a bugbear if Prussia did not immediately become part of Germany, but instead became powerful. This too it was believed, would destroy that specific, out-and-out exclusively Prussian nature which was so disliked. That, at least, was what people hoped. But much of this was illusory. People had misjudged the strength of both the old and the new parliamentary Prussia. But it was also no utopia, as people have been inclined to think since 1871. The picture of the Reich that the *kleindeutsch* supporters of 1848 had was not one of a great military power stamped with the identity of Greater Prussia.

In January and February there seemed to be a coalition looming on the constitution questions between the supporters of the *grossdeutsch* solution and the left, which blocked the *kleindeutsch* solution. But Austria's request, following the coup in March, to enter the new Reich as a unitary state split the coalition. Schmerling distanced himself from Schwarzenberg. Welcker, the *grossdeutsch* liberal, defected to the *kleindeutsch* supporters, because Austria, he said, was making the federal state, the parliament and the liberal constitution impossible. The *kleindeutsch* supporters won some backing from the left. In the end, they had, of course, to make major political concessions relating to the constitution. Fifteen members from the left were persuaded to support the idea of an hereditary empire, after 114 members from the centre agreed to drop their challenge, in the second reading, to the suspensive veto and universal suffrage. Eighty-six also promised not to take part in any later attempt to revise the constitution. This was the 'pact' between Heinrich Simon and Gagern. The force of the *grossdeutsch/kleindeutsch* decision had bridged the gap between the centre and the left. The Casino party were realists; unity and the fact that at least something should be brought into existence were more important than the disliked democratic concessions. The constitution was accepted; the hereditary empire was also accepted by a slim majority of 267 to 263, and even four Austrians voted in favour. On the following day, 28 March, Friedrich Wilhelm IV of Prussia was elected by 290 votes, with 248 abstentions, as Emperor (Kaiser) of the German people. Many had acted on the idea that they would have 'ardently desired the contrary, but that it was better to have a small Germany than to have no Germany at all'. The victory won by the supporters of the *kleindeutsch* solution was a result of this very sentiment.

The Paulskirche therefore had completed a constitution. It had taken on this area of authority 'alone'. Thus the constitution was not 'negotiated'. But after the first reading in January, Gagern had turned to the government and asked for its position on a second reading. Both the unitary and the democratic traits aroused feelings of concern in the government. Austria, Bavaria, Württemberg, Hanover and Saxony were more or less decisive in their rejection of the draft proposal. The great majority of the other states, most notably Prussia, agreed with it in principle, although they all wanted to add their own minor alterations. Prussia's stance was important with regard to the election of the Kaiser. Of course, with the conclusion of the constitution the leeway for further negotiations was considerably reduced.

The Paulskirche had also come out in favour of the hereditary empire and had voted for a Kaiser. The Kaiser of the German people, voted by parliament, was symbolic of this revolution. It was a monarchy that was no longer based on legitimacy and the grace of God, but instead was founded democratically on elections. But it was also a monarchy that had escaped the principle of democratic change; indeed, it was hereditary, and its incumbent, departing from the democratic principles of power, was 'not responsible' in the constitutional sense. This was the curious expression of the liberals' policy of mediation and compromise, and it was intended to bind together freedom and order, democracy, the will of the people and authority. It had also given the monarchy an opportunity to modernise itself and to renew its legitimacy.

The election of the Prussian king, given the actual situation in Germany, was not absurd. After Austria had withdrawn, there was simply no one else for the job. The question had been there to be dealt with since the beginning of the revolution. The *kleindeutsch* liberals had courted Friedrich Wilhelm; the Coburg princes had suggested to him that he head this movement because, they said, the new Reich would be better governed with an imperial parliament and a royal house than with a democratic, Prussian *Landtag*. The king had until then wavered; by imposing a constitution he had completely kept open the constitutional route to a Prussian policy for Germany. Now, in the spring of 1849, many influences were being brought to bear on him. The ultra-conservatives saw revolution, usurpation and the demise of Prussia in the constitution and empire. Both chambers declared that they would accept. What was more important was that a part of the establishment, the majority of the ministers, officers, the heir to the throne, national conservatives and supporters of the Greater Prussia notion declared that they too would accept, of course with a few provisos, including the agreement of the princes, the absolute right of veto and a different suffrage. It was thought that the National Assembly would agree to these conditions in order to save unity and the constitution. This is precisely what the left had feared, and the right had taken it into account. But the king rejected it. He was imbued with the legitimacy of the Habsburg empire in Germany, and he was particularly imbued with the position being granted by the grace of God, and this was incompatible with this parliamentary crown of 'dirt and clay' and with 'the dog-collar with which people want to chain me to the 1848 revolution'. And even though he did not actually say so, he did not want to relinquish the military monarchy and the royal command over the army. We cannot know if a different decision — that is, the acceptance of the constitution under certain conditions — could have worked. It was likely that the left would have resisted, that Russia and Austria too would have shown resistance, and indeed that it might have led to war. Prussia's power options were severely restricted. But this was not to be tested by history. Furthermore, the king had not rejected the constitution for rational, political reasons. He quite simply did not want to link himself with the now tamed liberal revolution.

7. The End

Following the rejection of the imperial crown by Friedrich Wilhelm IV, the policy of the new majority in the Paulskirche, which was the policy of the *kleindeutsch*, liberal hereditary empire, had failed. The fruits of the stalled revolution, constitution and unity, slipped away. The end of the revolution is quickly told. After the initially verbal and somewhat hedged rejection by the king at the beginning of April, Gagern and his supporters still hoped that mediation would be possible: that agreement by the other princes and a revision of the constitution would change the king's mind. This did not happen, however. Neither Friedrich Wilhelm IV nor the Paulskirche could be talked into accepting this idea. The National Assembly had implemented the constitution on 28 March; at the final count, twenty-nine states had recognised it, although of course the major powers, namely Austria, Prussia, Bavaria, Hanover and Saxony, had not. The Paulskirche did not want to revise the constitution. It wanted simply to declare the constitution valid, as it made clear in its call on 4 May to the governments, parliaments, communities and 'all the German people'. The majority that had existed until then, however — indeed, the parliament itself — collapsed. Gagern, who wanted to support a legal battle for the Reich's constitution, thereby lost the confidence of the *Reichsverweser*, and on 10 May, he resigned. A new left majority backed the ongoing campaign for the Reich's constitution, but the *Reichsverweser* joined forces with a new conservative ministry and opposed the campaign. On 14 May, Prussia declared the mandates of its members of parliament to be dissolved. Saxony and Hanover followed suit. The Austrians, for the most part, had already abandoned the parliament some time before; many members, especially from the right centre, now also left. The parliament became a rump parliament with a left majority. On 30 May, it moved to Stuttgart, but on 18 June the liberal government in Württemberg closed the meeting hall and used military force to disperse the last few remaining members. But by then these events had become insignificant. The Paulskirche was steamrollered by a new wave of counter-revolution and the last attempt at an armed revolution. In Prussia, on 26 April, the lower chamber, which had accepted the imperial constitution, was dissolved and Prussia was then placed under emergency laws and a state of siege. This was a new, counter-revolutionary *coup d'état*. The German left, both inside and outside the parliament, now made the implementation of the Reich's constitution their mission. This may seem paradoxical, because it was precisely the left that had been opposed to the constitution and because the supporters of the constitution were opposed to the left; but in a deeper sense it was, of course, legitimate because the constitution had, after all, been the achievement of the revolution, and it was at least a certain measure of freedom and unity that could be asserted in the face of reaction. The defence of the liberal and national revolution was now taken on by the left. All the energy of the second revolution and the social revolution too was poured into this struggle. It was predominantly the Zentralmärzverein (Central March Association) and its member organisations which had been organising this 'campaign for the constitution of the Reich' since April, firstly by way of demonstrations and addresses — in Württemberg, for example, on 25 April the reluctant king had had to recognise the constitution — but as the prospects of war worsened, so the dividing-line between demonstrations, resistance and active struggle became more blurred. This was the May revolution, a tragically sad and ineffective story of failure.

In Prussia too there was insurrection and even mutiny in the ranks of some of the conscripted Landwehr, particularly in the west. It was in the west that the radical, democratic and communist intellectuals, such as Gottfried Kinkel, Friedrich Engels and Fritz Anneke, and the workers and day-labourers played a very significant role. But the Bürgerwehr was able, for the most part, to suppress them. It was only in Iserlohn that a rebellion was crushed by the regular army; the more than one hundred people who were killed were the first victims. The actual bourgeoisie was not ready for armed rebellion, much less for another social revolution. Engels too was ushered out of Elberfeld by the supporters of the constitution campaign.

The actual centres of this revolution were Saxony, the Palatinate and Baden. In Saxony, there was a rebellion against the counter-revolutionary course followed by the government. A provisional government was even formed, though it effectively remained within the confines of Dresden. Workers, craftsmen and intellectuals, including Richard Wagner and Gottfried Semper, Mikhail Bakunin and Stefan Born, the workers' leader, belonged to this provisional government. The middle classes remained on the whole outside these events. After harsh street battles, Prussian troops crushed the insurrection. In the Palatinate, a provisional state defence committee announced it would defend the constitution of the Reich with the declaration, 'With the government having turned to rebellion, it is the free citizens of the Palatinate who must now execute the law.' They managed for the most part to take control of the state; even soldiers defected to the rebels. On 17 May, a provisional government was proclaimed. This revolt instantly became a cause taken up by the radical left in Germany and indeed in central Europe. Radical irregular volunteers and refugees arrived from everywhere, including Austria and Poland. At the beginning of June, Prussian troops were able to crush the revolution in just a few days. One of the reasons why this was possible was because hardly any of the rural population took part in the battles. All the revolutionaries now poured from Saxony, the Palatinate, the Rhine province and from exile, into Baden. Even though the government in Baden had recognised the Reich constitution, in May the new revolution was now developing here as well, out of the agitation by the 'people's associations' along the lines of the old Struve–Hecker radicalism, and out of mutinies by the troops; a provisional government, led by Lorenz Brentano, a lawyer from Mannheim, then assumed power. But this revolution too was ultimately crushed by Prussian troops, though it took many weeks, until 23 July, to do so. Calm was reinstated by courts martial and executions, high treason trials and prison sentences. Every tenth prisoner in the fortress at Rastatt was shot. Although there was also a revolutionary terror with many 'wild loudmouths', this counter-terror was to be ingrained in the minds and hearts of the people of Baden; it triggered immense bitterness and seemingly for a very long time prevented the people from experiencing any feelings of inner peace, something reflected in the lines of a Baden song: 'Sleep, my child, sleep quietly, the Prussian is outside, we must all be still, just like your father beneath his stone.' Emigration, the political and social motives for which, of course, we cannot distinguish, began once again in earnest.

The revolution was defeated once and for all; it was over.

8. The Failed Revolution

Why the German revolution failed is a question that puzzled both the participants and their contemporaries as well as succeeding generations of historians. And because this failure was one of the most important episodes, though not the most important, in the destiny of democracy for us, and because it still fills us with mourning for a lost opportunity, it is indeed a question that, over and above all the learned efforts and the desire for intellectual insight, still touches the perception we have of ourselves.

Historic failure nearly always prompts questions about the responsibility or share of blame borne by those who were involved in the failure. Did they fail, and in what way? Or who, of those involved, really failed? Why did those involved not seize the opportunities they were given? Would things not have been different if only this or that person had acted differently? And even though we know we cannot write a history based on 'if onlys', such questions still serve as a goad. The answer to such examinations of the consciences of those who led the revolutionary action is, then, firstly from an objective point of view, that it was the split in the bourgeois movement into, on the one hand, liberal constitutionalists and, on the other hand, radical democrats, which led or considerably contributed to their failure. This had a sustained weakening effect on the revolution in comparison with the old powers. And if one thinks back to the causes of the split and to the various and indeed opposing aims and even to the strategies of the centre and the left during the revolution, then one easily begins to apportion blame. Was it the radicals' radicalism, and perhaps their utopian illusionism, which thwarted the revolution's possible opportunities (one thinks of Robert Blum's anger over Hecker and the Baden revolution, something we have already discussed)? Or was it the wariness and the authoritarian, conservative traditionalism of the liberals, their class-based fear of democracy, of social change and of the 'red revolution' which led them to fight against the left, to co-operate with the old powers and to become resigned to the situation? By doing this, did they give away the opportunity for victory, enable the old powers to recover and thereby facilitate a successful counter-revolution? In short, did the liberals abandon the revolution too early, if indeed they did not actually abandon it from the very outset, and did they in fact 'betray' the revolution? Or did they get too entangled with theory — this is another, older accusation — and, without an awareness of power or reality, allow the hour for action to pass them by? Today, the accusation against the liberals, the centre, the bourgeoisie — even if it rejects the betrayal theory — is common currency. For this reason, we must address it. The liberals were liberals, they were from the centre ground; they were not the left, nor did they want to be. Their goals and their strategies were different from those of the left. They pursued a policy of the centre, which of course opposed that of the left, but it also opposed the old powers, the status quo and the counter-revolution. They were not resolute revolutionaries; they were revolutionaries against their will. They stopped short of the throne. They wanted to end the revolution and transfer to a system of legality. Permanent revolution as a basis for their legitimacy and their power was an abomination to them. Nevertheless, they were standing on the foundation of the revolution, more so than they were at times prepared to admit. The things they wanted, namely the new constitution, a new society and the new state, represented a real revolutionising of the existing system. And if they wanted to safeguard or realise the achievements of the March revolution and its Pan-

German aims along the road to reform, or to achieve freedom and unity on the road to establishing order; then the revolution was indeed the basis of accelerated evolution. The liberals wanted to build dams against chaos and they wanted to limit the revolution precisely because they wanted to implement those goals that they shared with the revolution. One cannot expect liberals or middle-class notables, lawyers from a society of civil people or property-owners to defend the social and egalitarian, democratic norms of our society in the 20th century. And indeed, it was their right to hold fast to and represent their ideas of a liberal, democratic constitutional state and of a civil society against the 'republican' — in the broad sense — concept. One might well say the liberals' fear about social revolution was exaggerated, in view of the social division of power in Germany, but it was not unfounded in so far as the Jacobin, radical, democratic wing, which was activist and concentrated in certain regions and major cities, was a real power. The chance of a second revolution was quite real, and it was not possible to tell what the result of such a revolution would have been. The French example of 1792–93 was not simply conjured up, and the displays of street democracy must have increased their fears. The liberal objective and the double-front stance was a reflection firstly of the central element of the liberal strategy, namely accord. But this was in fact a double strategy, because revolutionary elements were also contained in the policy of accord. In many ways this was a policy of small steps, and also of compromise, and an abandonment of the continuation of the revolution, but without excluding the potential for revolution. The solution to the question of the power within the Reich is typical of this stance. It was a gentle and gradual but still decisive process, and not a sharp and abrupt one, that was pursued. As long as the monarchs were weak and the revolution was controlled by the liberals, of course this strategy remained a sensible possibility. From September, however, this became doubtful, but the difficulties with the *grossdeutsch-kleindeutsch* question still lent the strategy its clout. In short, the policy and strategy of the liberals were thoroughly comprehensible and legitimate. The liberals also did not move towards the right; they stood by their centre policies. What did move, of course, was the political spectrum, which gave their policies a different complexion.

If the liberals can claim legitimacy for themselves, then so too can the left, and, of course, the 'republican', parliamentary left as well. Their goals went far beyond those of the centre, and their strategy was quite different; it was less concerned with accord and more with the masses and revolutionary legitimacy; it was more led by its worry about the counter-revolution than by the extreme-left radicalisation of the revolution, which it believed it would be able to bring under control by the adoption of a sort of all-embracing strategy — namely by the rejection of a putsch-based policy.

Of course, it would be possible to discuss *ad infinitum* the various objectives and strategies in respect of one's own political stance and standards; it is certainly not possible to come to any sort of scientific decision about the situation. We can, however, ask about the reality content of both concepts and about their chances of success. Clearly, the liberals had the majority behind them, and in a movement which made reference to people and democracy, that is not simply a question of *Realpolitik*, but also of revolutionary legitimacy. It was this that had to be upheld against the self-imposed claims of an *avant-garde* minority. The voters and the people did not followed the line taken by Hecker and his noisy successors. This was something that Robert Blum and the moderate Democrats were well aware of, but they too did not represent the majority. If one believes the success of a revolution claims a higher legitimacy than that of the majority — which is then usually discredited with the epithet 'ostensible' majority — there remains the question of how legitimate each respective strategy was. The centre claimed precisely this realism for its policy; it was far more aware than the left of the weakness of the revolutionary forces, and this lent their behaviour something of a Hamlet character. They lacked any sort of revolutionary self-assurance beyond mere realism. This realistic assessment clearly became part of their weakness. But was the assessment not correct? The masses, despite all the 'republican' stirrings, were still orientated towards the monarchy and individual states; they did not want 'yet more' revolution. A counter-revolutionary mobilisation of the masses against a republican revolution was a direct possibility. Such a revolution would therefore inevitably have led to civil war, the outcome of which was more than uncertain; indeed, it might even provoke Russian intervention, which could and most probably would mean the end of all freedom. This is the often overlooked realism of the strategy of accord (and some of its defenders were far from docile when it came to contemplating the possible use of revolutionary means). In short, in addition to the politically based and the class-determined arguments for the strategy of the centre stood these politically realistic arguments. And the core of the *kleindeutsch* supporters, who had a sense of the power relationship of states, however they may have been constituted, was also convinced for reasons of *Realpolitik* that the revolution could only be successful with Prussia's support, and therefore that it was necessary to work for accord. The chances of a republican policy — even if one ignores the Jacobin second revolution, the consequences of which were always incalculable — therefore seemed remote. Confrontation and perseverance for the full sovereignty of the people and the revolution were unlikely to succeed with the bourgeois and peasant majority and the governments in the individual states, which had since become liberal. Nor were the lower strata prepared to be mobilised fully for the cause. This brings us closer still to the question of the possible alternatives; not those that we may dream up for ourselves, but rather those that were existing in the situation as it was. There were two, what we might call right-liberal alternatives. The first alternative was a far-reaching reform of the Confederation, *de facto* without the participation of the National Assembly, as had been suggested by the Committee of Seventeen. This perhaps would have led to rapid consolidation. But this was totally incompatible with the claim of the revolution, with the idea of a new Reich. Even those ostensibly timid liberals, who favoured accord rejected the idea. Then there was the 'Coburg solution'. If in the spring Friedrich Wilhelm IV had really found and implemented a policy of accord with German liberalism, this may have led to something. But he did not do so. It is also likely that this solution was at that time still too much to ask of the liberals, and the clarification of the *grossdeutsch/kleindeutsch* issue was not so advanced that it would have been accepted by a working majority. When considering the alternatives put forward by the left, one must realise that the left was not a single unit and it did not have a single united strategic programme. The only truly realistic alternative proposed by the radical left was in fact to fight a great European war against Russia. This would have been a real opportunity, though of course with enormous risks, and some people were thinking in terms of a policy of catastrophe; they wanted to risk the Flood, because they believed that they themselves would come after it. The two other alternatives are less clear. One was to place the political questions relating to the constitution ahead of the debate on basic rights, which would perhaps have meant that the Paulskirche could have won its race against time — we have already discussed why things happened as they did with regard to this issue. This refers to the enormous internal difficulties of the revolution, to which we shall turn in a moment. It is likely that a different sequence of events would also have run aground on the *grossdeutsch/kleindeutsch* problem. But this is pure speculation. The other alternative was a possible centre–left alliance from Gagern to Blum, in other words excluding the extreme left. This could have happened. This would have made for a harder-line approach in Frankfurt policy. The Paulskirche would have taken on a certain air of the revolutionary tribunal. There were objections to this. The link between the moderate and the extreme left led the centre right to reject such an alliance, and even prevented the moderate left from entering into it. On concrete issues their views were very much opposed. This possibility was hardly even tested. Whether or not it would have been successful, however — by making earlier decisions by consensus while the states were still weak, for example — is unclear, and I believe it to be unlikely. The Paulskirche could not be turned into a revolutionary tribunal. Had it been, then it would probably have failed completely much earlier in a mishmash of lack of response, civil war and counter-revolution.

The strongest argument against the liberals is, of course, the fact that they failed. The policy of accord proved to be no more successful than the policy of confrontation put forward by the radical forces. Of course, the liberals overestimated their chances with accord, legality and reform and, of course — this must now be said, after so much defence of the liberal stance — their policy against the left, which was provoked by the left, had been used against all intention to strengthen and rejuvenate the old powers, the powers of order and the military; and it lent support to the Thermidor feeling, evolving at that time among the petty bourgeois, against too much revolution. The centre did not fall into the arms of reaction. But its conflict with the left benefitted reaction. But the policy of accord, however much it may have reflected the mood of the majority, lessened and disrupted the liberals' contact with the masses, and it took from them a large part of its popular basis (although the radicals were not able to win this liberal loss over to their side). The National Assembly lost a major part of the support it had from the masses without winning the support of the individual governments. Both liberals and Radicals alike wanted to save the revolution. Because this conflict, which was provoked more by the left than the centre but was pursued by both sides, could not be avoided, we may justifiably describe it as tragic.

Of course, the points we have noted above are points over which we could argue for a very long time; it would be possible to have sympathy for the 'republicans' and offer better odds for the realisation of their ideas, or out of a sense of morality to accuse the realists of wanting simply to accommodate, without looking at the opportunities open to them. But what is now more important in our considerations is the fact that the revolution did not fail because of a rift between the left and the centre. The rift did, of course, assist the counter-revolution, and the polarisation did weaken the revolution, which was threatened by time running out; but the rift was not the main cause of its failure. Even a united movement in the form of a revolutionary 'people's front policy' would not have had a better chance of success — except perhaps by means of the great

European war. In other words, neither a more moderate nor a more decisive occurrence of an all-out revolution would have been any more successful. Certainly, there was both too much and too little revolution: too little to drive out the old powers once and for all — although the majority of citizens did not want this and it was unlikely to succeed; and too much because the radical democrats destroyed the united front and thereby effectively forced the centre to the right and discredited the revolution. And initially there was really a question of whether the weakened monarchies were still a partner, and then whether moderation had not actually destroyed the credit of the moderates. But this did not affect the outcome. The rift, as the drawing up of the constitution shows, was not so deep that it could not be bridged and joint action be taken. But this did not alter the final result, and even earlier understanding would have made very little difference. It is for this reason that the apportioning of blame between republicans and liberals is basically irrelevant. Their conflict was legitimate, unavoidable and tragic. It is unlikely that the revolution would have had a definite and long-term chance had the conflict not existed.

The failure of a political action, and hence of a revolution, is not necessarily the fault of those who failed nor of their — avoidable — mistakes, nor of their unavoidable fundamental philosophies. The vanquished are not always to blame for their defeat. The actual cause of the failure was the fact that the resistance was too diverse and too great, as were the problems to be solved. It was the fact that there were too many and too great a variety of confusingly interconnected problems that needed to be solved all at once. The revolution ran up against the resistance of the old powers; this much is clear. But these powers were stronger than it had first appeared. A monarchic sense and a sense of legality were still widespread among the people. The military still functioned and did not, or at least very rarely, defect to the revolution. The constitutional, political unity of the revolution was made more difficult and weakened by the internal tensions among the German people. Similar effects were also created by the social tensions; by the peasants' withdrawal from the revolution; by the increasing distance between the politicians, the central elites, for whom the constitutional questions were the central issues, and the social and local interests of the people outside; by the discrepancy between liberal constitutional policy and liberal social policy; by the distance of the Paulskirche from elementary needs; by the conflicts over economic and social interests outside of the political community. In short, the liberal civil society, which was only just coming into being, was under threat from the particularism of German society, which itself was still so utterly heterogeneous. The social problems of the early industrial era were also occurring at the same time as the implementation of civil society and the civil constitutional state. And the social tensions and conflicts that had been so useful to the revolution's cause were then all negated by the agricultural reforms and the healthy economic situation of 1848–49. In addition there was also the strong undercurrent of politico-religious tensions between the faiths and between the clerical and the anti-clerical. This placed a burden on the upswing of freedom as it was to be realised in concrete terms.

As with freedom, unity too had its major problems. It clashed with the European powers and the new nationalism of the peoples — the borders, minorities, the position of a new great power — and Schleswig–Holstein, for example, became an major factor in the history of the failure of the revolution. Indeed, it had to become so, because the German national democracy was as unable as the Danes to give up its claims, just as the major powers were unable to give up their interest in maintaining a balance of power. And the demand for unity thrust against the old and the new federalism and particularism of the German political world; it was the conflict between individual state and evolving united state. It also hit against the problem of German dualism. There could not be national unity without Austria or without Prussia; but as long as these two existed as states, the problem of leadership remained. There was also the problem of how to reconcile the German nation-state and the claim of the nation to include the Germans in Austria with the existence of this supra-national state. This was the double problem. Put a different way, the national revolution of the Germans clashed with the particularist states, with the European powers, the neighbouring revolutionary nations, and with supra-national Austria.

German unity, German borders, German freedom and a bit of social justice already made four problems, all of which needed to be dealt with and which older (and in this respect happier) nations had been able to attempt to solve one after the other. But this was no coincidence: without national unity, or a civil society, there could be no civil rule. Freedom and unity were indivisible.

It was the large number of problems and their insolubility that led to the failure of the revolution. The wish had been to found a state and to set up a constitution, both at the same time; and all this in a situation of serious social tension. In France too, where the problems were more straightforward, and in Italy the revolution had failed. These facts must be considered in any judgment of the German revolution. If one wants to evaluate the individual causes of the failure of the revolution in Germany, then in my opinion one would have to conclude that among the most important factors were the *grossdeutsch/ kleindeutsch* problem and the problem of Austria's states based on nationality and the resulting national conflicts. It was these that in the summer had made a rapid decision impossible, and made the first major victory of the counter-revolution possible in Austria; from autumn onwards they had so disturbed the unity of the revolution that joint action was no longer possible; this in turn then directed the decision towards Prussia. It is was these factors that placed the revolution in a race against time, a race the revolution could not win. This view may seem old-fashioned, but this specifically German predetermined moulding of the national question was the deciding point.

The outcome of the revolution was not only its failure. The revolution had created a national public, over and above all the elites, and a national democratic nation. The revolution had brought to an end the era of Metternich and the era of restoration, and had abolished the major elements of feudal society. Despite the failure, the age then became more civilian. And indeed, Prussia's transition to a constitutional state fits into this context. The rise of the Bürger was not blocked for ever, it had simply been curbed, and ten years later it began again. After the revolution, nothing was as it had been before. The crisis between the state and society, however, remained unresolved. And this was a burden to German history.

9. Epilogue: Germany as a Union of the States?

The failed revolution ended with a curious epilogue, arising from the fact that the question of how Germany was now to be organised still remained an open question even for the victors. Prussia attempted to solve the issue on a *kleindeutsch*, national conservative basis. The king and the government had not intended their refusal to the Paulskirche to be the renunciation of an active German policy. National conservative ideas linked up, much to the annoyance of the 'old Prussian' ultras, with the romantic tendencies of the king. He wanted in an agreement with the governments to have a *kleindeutsch* federal state under Prussian leadership, and an agreed constitution with a royal veto and limited voting rights, and an extended alliance with Austria. The chances of success of such a plan, which would have revolutionised German and European relations, seemed to be reasonable. The medium-sized states were dependent on Prussian troops; Austria still had ties in Hungary and Italy. But the king and his advisers did not pursue this policy with concentrated resolve or true will for power. They did not want radically to shut out Austria. Their policy remained hesitant and yielding, and they allowed the favourable hour, if it really had come, to pass them by.

Then at the end of May, Prussia, Saxony and Hanover formed an alliance to realise these ideas. This soon became known as the Erfurt Union. The majority of German states joined the Union. But Bavaria refused. In the interest of its own *raison d'état*, it did not want to shut out Austria, nor did it want Prussian leadership. The Bavarian minister, Baron Ludwig von der Pfordten, warned against the dismantling of Europe into nation-states and against the centralised power state, which was revolution by the back door. Württemberg also came out of the Union. The Union thus lost considerable appeal. At the beginning of 1850, Saxony and Hanover, which had linked their approval of the Union to all states, except Austria, joining, left just as the Reichstag elections for the Union were called. They formed an alliance with Austria, now fully active again, the aim of which was to include all of Austria in a new order for central Europe. This represented a rejection of the idea of a nation-state. What was now wanted was a new Confederation with a directorate, a customs union and even some kind of 'parliament', which was to be an organ that would be voted in by the parliaments of the individual states and, it was thought, would convene once every three years. Despite its absurdity, Schwarzenberg said, this would enable the Austrians to join this new alliance and run with the pack, up to a certain point.

Nevertheless, Prussia pursued its utopian plans. In January 1850, the union states elected a parliament, using a system of three-class voting rights, which was then to draw up a constitution: this was the Erfurt parliament. The left had rejected these plans and boycotted the election. The supporters of the hereditary Kaiser, predominantly from the right although some were from the left centre, held discussions at the end of June in Gotha, which is why they then became known as the 'Gothaer'. They gave their consent, partly out of conviction and partly for tactical reasons. They stated that the 'goal' that was to be achieved with the Reich constitution was far more important than the 'form' it took; an attempt had to made, they continued, to create unity, even at the cost of the Paulskirche constitution. On 20 March, this parliament convened. Eduard Simson, the spokesman for the Paulskirche delegation which had offered Friedrich Wilhelm the throne, was president, and Bismarck was one of his clerks. There were only two parties namely the Conservatives and the Liberal Gothaers; they had the majority. The Paulskirche constitution was used as a starting-point, and after only five weeks of debate a new constitution had been drawn up. It was a conservative version of the Reich's constitution. The majority wanted to achieve something and therefore gave in to the

wishes of the governments. Of course, the Conservatives were still opponents of this constitution, and the majority of the governments were far from being in complete
agreement with it. But of decisive importance was Austria's stance. By the late summer
of 1849, Austria had consolidated with the help of Russia, which was actually the great
power of the counter-revolution. Austria then laid claim, more decisively than it had
done for a long time, to being the German and central European great power.
Schwarzenberg was playing realistic power politics, without emotion and without regard
to ideology; he was decisive and resolute. He did not shy away from power conflict,
which Austria's German stance threatened, or from conflict with Prussia; he was not
interested in agreement, because he wanted victory. He wanted to eliminate the Union
and to force Austria's entry into the new organisation of Germany, the so-called 'seventy
million empire'. He wanted Austria to retain the hegemony, or as much of it as possible;
and now his chances of success seemed ripe. As the threat of revolution was now over, it
was now possible to take up the concerns of the kingdoms about the loss of sovereignty
from which they would be unavoidably threatened were a Confederation led by Prussia
to be established. A suggested compromise, which involved the abolition of the Union
and agreeing to the 'seventy million empire' in return for giving Prussia a limited special
position, was rejected by Prussia. The signs were that a conflict was looming.

Thus part of Austria's strategy was the continuity of the German Confederation. In
May 1850, Austria organised a congress to commemorate its restoration, and on 2
September it set up a rump Bundestag. Prussia and the Union boycotted the congress
and disputed the legality of the rump body. Thus in the late summer of 1850, two blocs
stood opposing each other in Germany.

The situation focused on two problems, which in essence were legacies of the
revolution. The first was that in August in Schleswig–Holstein the war, which in April
1849 had still been open war, had once again reached a ceasefire. Under pressure from
the powers, including Russia, and fearing the Tsar would otherwise completely take
Austria's side, Prussia had agreed on 2 July 1850 to a peace formula and given up the
dukedoms. It was once again recognised that Holstein belonged to the German
Confederation. In the so-called London Protocol, the major powers had guaranteed both
this ruling and the integrity of the whole Danish state. But as a revolutionary
governorship was asserting itself in Holstein, Denmark asked the Confederation to
intervene. Austria used this as a pretext for pushing the Confederation forward. The
rump Bundestag prepared to intervene in the area, but Prussia resisted such measures.
The second problem was that the government of the Electorate of Hesse, formally a state
of the Union, also was calling for intervention by the Confederation. This government,
which acted against the constitution of the state in using emergency regulations, tax
increases and other counter-revolutionary practices, saw that it would be faced with
massive resistance from the *Landtag*, the civil servants, the courts and even from the
officers who had sworn allegiance to the constitution, this being the so-called *Renitenz*
(literally, 'obstinacy'); this had to be broken. The Austrian group, including Austrian and
Bavarian troops, was quite prepared to intervene. This threatened not only the Union, it
also threatened the civilian and military routes connecting Prussia to the west, and at the
same time created a direct route via Hanover all the way to Holstein. Prussia opposed
this, although in so doing it was supporting opposition to a reigning monarch. Both sides
mobilised. It seemed that the issue could now only be settled by war.

The conflict became an issue of European politics. Prussia had no allies abroad. The Tsar had taken on the role of mediator and exercised pressure on Prussia, because he was decidedly opposed to the policy of the Union. As Prussia was about to give way to Austria, the latter decided to march into the Electorate of Hesse on 1 November in order to intensify the crisis and thereby obtain a clear decision against Prussia. After much to-ing and fro-ing in the corridors of power in Prussia, the king gave way; pressure exerted by the Tsar, the king's aversion to the Union parliament, and his fear of a radical break with Austria and the kingdoms had clearly influenced his decision. Joseph von Radowitz, the force behind the policies of the Union, had to go. But the threat of war remained because Austria now gave Prussia an ultimatum to clear out of the Electorate of Hesse. Prussia responded by ordering a general mobilisation, but then she submitted. In the Treaty of Olmütz of 29 November, Prussia gave up the Union policy and its resistance to intervention in Hesse and Holstein; it also had to demobilise. Austria had won the day without having to pay any direct price. For this reason, contemporaries and their liberal descendants spoke of 'capitulation', Prussia's 'humiliation' and of the 'shame' of Olmütz. It was a defeat. However, the Confederation was to be restored only after new and free negotiations, and Austria's federal policy was thus not attested. More significantly, Schwarzenberg was not yet able to implement the entry of the whole of Austria into a German union and thereby assure Austria's hegemony. This too was postponed, which, in end result, meant that it had been blocked. Thus, to some extent, there was some compensation for Prussia's renunciation of the Union, despite its defeat. Peace had been ensured, and the attempt at a national revolution from above had failed; the question of national unity had been removed temporarily from the agenda, and dualism had been consolidated anew, as had the supremacy of the Russian Tsar.

The speech made by Bismarck, as a member of parliament, in defence of this treaty is now famous. He defended the courage and the morality of the diplomatic retreat, and he then turned to a counter-attack. A war for the Union or for the Electorate of Hesse would have been absurd, he claimed. 'It is easy', he continued, 'to blow the war trumpet using the breath of popular support, and then to sit back and warm yourself by the fire, or to make thunderous speeches.' He added that Prussia was to be mediatised in the Union by the smaller states, and it would have to remain allied to the German power, which was now Austria. This was a masterly performance of tactical rhetoric in the best traditions of the conservatives. Of course, the speech demonstrated the conservative rejection of the Union. But of more significance were the new ideas which until then had lain on the margins of conservatism. He declared his support for state egotism and for policies that were inspired solely by self-interest. This, Bismarck said, was the only sound basis for a great state. This was a comment directed against the left: it represented the *raison d'être* of the state against the *raison d'être* of the party. But the rejection, in this way, of a policy of ideology could also turn against the conservatives. This was to be a crucial point for the decade that was to follow.

VI

Between Reaction and Liberalism: Bismarck and the Problem of German Unity, 1849–66

1. Reaction in Germany, 1849–59

The policies of the German governments in the 1850s were policies of reaction. There was an attempt to re-establish firmly the conservative, bureaucratic state of authority and order, and to protect against all forms of liberalism and all those tendencies that had governed the revolution. But this was more than a mere return to the times as they had been before the revolution. In the first place, this would have been impossible, because those who took part and those who were affected by it were post-revolutionary people. For this reason, the means that the governments used to achieve this aim were different. They were more modern and at times were themselves revolutionary. And it was not possible to reverse all the results of the revolution — indeed, there was no desire to do so. The Reaction paradoxically, was more modern than the restoration after 1815.

The Reaction ran different courses in the individual states. It was also, however, a unity; and in concrete terms it was the German Confederation that the united reactionary approach was attempting to implement. The constitutions of the individual states were to be organised on a strongly statist and conservative basis, and any of their liberal or democratic elements were to be curtailed vigorously. The individual states were ordered to revise the changes that had taken place during the years of the revolution to fit in with the 'principle of the monarchy'; this was to cover such things as the budget rights, the army's oath of allegiance to the constitution, the democratic voting processes and the extended freedom of the press. A committee of the Confederation, the 'Reaction Committee', was to monitor this process. The Confederation used admonishments, rebukes, directives and even commissioners — in Bremen and Frankfurt, for example — to ensure that this revision process was carried out. In 1854, it passed a press and associations laws along these lines, for the entire

Confederation. Of course, it was even more eager to compel the governments to, as Bismarck put it, 'carry out the break with the revolution themselves and seriously to compromise themselves with respect to the revolution'; they should not be able to unload the enmity of public opinion onto the Confederation or the governing powers.

The majority of the individual states reversed the 1848 alterations to the constitution, partly through coup-like measures, the dissolution of chambers, alterations to the voting laws and the imposition of decrees, and partly with the assistance of governmental chambers and enormous influence exerted at elections. Indeed, this is what happened in Saxony, Hanover and the two Mecklenburgs, in Thuringia, Nassau and Hesse–Darmstadt; it also happened in the model reactionary state, namely the Electorate of Hesse, where an imposed constitution dated back beyond that of 1831. And it was also in the Electorate of Hesse, that the state of war continued until 1854. The events in Württemberg were similar, though here, in 1850, the government put forward a draft constitution containing liberal concessions; it was not until the chamber rejected it that the government reverted to the constitution of 1819 and, after a coup and new elections, moved over to reaction. By contrast, the monarchy in Baden, adopting a policy of pacification, renounced constitutional amendments. The liberal civil servants retained their posts, and as there was no actual conservative programme, the government's path did not extend beyond immobility and a few mild restrictions. In Bavaria, Minister von der Pfordten, until 1852, continued to follow a policy of conservative liberal reform and had nothing to do with reaction, partly out of a sense of particularist independence, and partly because the government did not want to shut out the thoroughly moderate liberal and conservative opposition in the *Landtag* using imposed measures or other strategies of conflict. In 1852, with the appointment of two Conservatives to the posts of Minister of the Interior and Minister for Culture, here too the government's course became more reactionary, with pronounced clericalist and police-state overtones, and there was now continuous conflict between the government and the chamber which repeated abrogation and prorogation could only hide with great effort. In all states, authority over legislation and administration was increased, giving the police, the government and the bureaucratic administration more power. The rationale of 'public safety' was used not only against insurrection but also most vigorously against the freedom of assembly, the freedom of association and the freedom of the press. The civil service was purged of all radical elements, and discipline was sharpened. Schools, especially the *Volksschulen* (elementary schools), which were seen as hotbeds and the origins of revolution, were particularly severely controlled, especially where the training of teachers was concerned; the schools were to revert to a basis of simplicity, obedience and religion. Socialists and democrats who had not emigrated along with many others in 1849 were monitored and pursued by the police; people's and workers' associations were suppressed; and the left in general was intimidated so that they repeatedly boycotted the elections. The political climate surrounding the administration, the courts and the police, was one of pressure and conformity.

Of course, the majority of the German states continued to be constitutional states — although their constitutions had, needless to say, been revised — and they retained their constitutional institutions and procedural rules. This is one of the most significant reasons why the era of reaction came to an end after ten years. More importantly, the social achievement of the revolution, namely the liberation of the peasants, was not revoked. From Hanover to Austria, there was no return to the old system of manorial privileges. Even in Prussia, where there was a certain restoration of the rights of the nobility, patrimonial jurisdiction remained abolished. It was similar with the formal equalisation of commoner and nobleman. Reaction was well aware, even where it lacked insight into the necessary modernisation, that the state needed a solid social foundation. It was also for this reason that its proponents sought to damp the unrest among craftsmen by imposing a temporary limitation on the freedom to practise a trade; similar attempts were also made to satisfy even the workers with rudimentary worker-protection measures. And once again some of the states outside Prussia gave in to demands from the community to impose limits on the freedom of settlement and the freedom of marriage. Self-administration also remained in place; only in Austria was its introduction blocked; in other places self-administration was restricted by state supervision and increased power given to the community executive over the city representatives; in places the voting rights became more plutocratic, but self-administration remained an institution from which, at a later stage, a new political life was able to develop.

As well as trying to increase its authority and social basis, the Reaction also tried to strengthen its foundation of political ideas. The connection with the church, and, where necessary, with the conservative, counter-revolutionary powers within the church, assisted this foundation. Life was to become more religious. The state avoided conflict with the Catholic church or tried to resolve any such conflicts, by renouncing the old state-church rights, through concordats; this is, in fact, what happened in Württemberg, Hesse–Darmstadt and in Baden. In Baden, as we have seen, it was only after wild conflict between the Archbishop of Freiburg and the government, a conflict that involved excommunication and imprisonment, that such agreement could be reached. It was in Austria that this tendency was strongest. Here the state gave up the Josephist church rights and the church became free to deal with its own affairs; in matters that involved both church and state, it was primarily the church that had the final say. For the most part, the state handed responsibility for the schools, especially the *Volksschulen* (elementary schools), to the church, extending to the supervision and control of books and control over removing teachers. Catholic couples were subject to the Catholic marriage laws. The state undertook to implement religious measures against recalcitrant clergymen and even to prevent the spread of books banned by the church. Professors were not to teach anything that was incompatible with religious teachings (and this was also the case in Baden). In practice, things were, in general, not quite so rigid, but these standards were an attack on everything that at the time was considered as being liberal. It was precisely as a result of the policy of concordats that the unity of the conservatives broke down. The emotional surge against these concordats brought back support, firstly in Baden and Württemberg, for liberalism and forced the governments to the change of course known as the 'New Era'. In the strongly Protestant states of Prussia and Hesse–Kassel, there were similar alliances between the governments and the high-church Protestant orthodoxy; and there was also similar uproar, if not quite as loud, from the liberals.

One thing must be stressed. It was precisely the reaction in the small and medium-sized states, over and above that of the three large states of southern Germany, that the opposition liberals found particularly intolerable. In view of the bureaucratic, 'particularist' rule of Minister Dalwigk in Hesse–Darmstadt and his alliance with Bishop Ketteler of Mainz, the leader of the opposition there made the following statement in 1859: 'We would rather have the harshest Prussian military rule than this small-state misery.' This was not untypical, and it explains why the majority of the new Prussians welcomed the annexation of 1864–66 — in spite of Bismarck's policy of conflict.

Of particular importance to the course of German history were conditions in the major states. Austria in the 1850s was the classic state without a constitution. At the end of the revolution, this was not yet a certainty. In March 1849, with the dissolution of the Reichstag, a constitution had been imposed, and although it was not immediately implemented because of the tensions of the situation, the constitutional and liberal ministers like Bruck, Schmerling, Krauss and Bach, just like Stadion, the actual author of the constitution itself, tried to base their policies on it. Schmerling began with a reform of the judiciary; the promised self-administration was prepared. There were also conservative motives for such solutions inasmuch as the constitution could help integration and could assist in finding a solution to the potentiality crippling financial problems of the state. But the Emperor, supported by the former ministers from the Metternich era, Kübeck and the senior military circles, favoured the opposite approach. In August 1851, 'ministerial liability' was expressly lifted, and with it the collegiate form of government. At the same time, the ministers were demoted, as it were. The liberal ministers, with the exception of Bach, resigned. On 31 December 1851, after Olmütz, and after the coup of Napoleon III, the constitution was revoked with the so-called 'New Year's Eve Patent', and monarchic absolutism was reinstated. Following Schwarzenberg's sudden death in 1852, the Emperor became the true autocrat. Of particular importance to him was the role played by the military cabinet, led by Count von Grünne. This system became known as 'neo-absolutism'.

The system was anti-liberal, as everywhere else, and it was a police and military system. A central gendarmerie, made up of elite units from the military, guarded over the country, and the military even had judicial powers. It was called the 'Bach system' after the Interior Minister and former Democrat Alexander Bach. The state of siege remained in Vienna and Prague until September 1853, and in other revolutionary zones it remained until May 1854. The system was bureaucratic. The liberal reforms of the judiciary, self-administration, the press and the associations were revoked, and even the division between judiciary and administration was, in part, reversed. But administration was modernised and rationalised, as was, at least, the indirect taxation system. The civil service, now better paid, was more effective, and it was loyal. The system was centralised, and the responsibilities of the historic states were moved up and down, partly by a reorganisation of the states. The power and control exerted by the central power in Vienna were significantly increased. Hungary's special position was not continued, but neither did its neighbouring states/provinces win any special position. This was a system based on a statist counter-revolution, not a feudal one.

The system did not merely modernise the state apparatus; its aim, unlike that of the Vormärz period, was to modernise society. The emancipation of the peasants was implemented under the conditions of 1848, which had been extremely favourable to the peasants. This was one of the great achievements of the era. The nobility's requests were rejected. The minister for education, Count von Thun, who was actually a

Bohemian federalist, brought highly successful and far-reaching modernisation to the school and university system, which in places lagged far behind the other German states. The legal system, principally by way of liberating property-ownership, was also reformed. The government, demonstrating what was also a Bonapartist trait, attempted to satisfy bourgeois society by pursuing an active and dynamic economic policy under the leadership of Minister von Bruck. This involved the extension of the infrastructure, especially the railways, the abolition of internal duty levies, standardisation within the economic zone, the support of industry, the founding of joint-stock companies and banks, less protectionism in foreign trade, and more liberal commercial regulations. This led to the evolution of an economic upper class, for the most part German, that was linked totally to this system, even though the question of protectionism placed part of industry and the economy in opposition to the government.

The last aim of this rigid policy of neo-absolutism, pursued with such energy, was to make Austria a major power, in other words the acquisition or implementation of the hegemonic claim — in Germany, Italy and in the south-east. Here domestic and foreign policy were inextricably intertwined.

The system was based primarily on the support of the army and the civil service; then on the support derived from satisfying economic interests; finally it depended on the alliance with the Catholic church. This last strategy was intended to help against liberalism and nationalism and against the attempts by the individual states to gain autonomy. The 1855 concordat made Catholicism the *de facto* state religion. Outside Hungary, there was no noteworthy resistance to this. The general upturn in the economy was damping discontent and social protest. The middle class reached the obvious conclusion about its experience of radicalisation and the defeat of the revolution; the effectiveness of the system and the police seems to further consolidate this view. After one decade, however, the system failed and the cracks were very clear. One factor was that the liberal, constitutional tendencies of the middle class could not be neutralised indefinitely. It was precisely the concordat policy that mobilised the German-Austrian middle class, which was Catholic but of the Josephist philosophy and liberal, against the system. Even in Catholic Austria a definite atmosphere of *Kulturkampf* evolved. It was on this that German-Austrian liberalism lived. It also had a nationalist side, with an eye to the German Question. The concordat, it was feared, would shut out Austria from Germany and further reduce pro-Austrian sympathies.

A second factor was that the bureaucratic centralism was geared up for national unity with all of Austria, and as such it was an opponent of national and federal tendencies. But the reality of the states and nations and the growing nationalism were stronger than the fiction of the supra-national state. In the non-German states, the church together with the nobility spoke up for state and national interests. Hungary could not be satisfied, and its neighbouring (states/provinces) Croatia and the Serbian provinces, which in 1848 had placed their hopes on Vienna, were deeply disappointed. There was also the fact that the centralised state employed Germans and used the German language. German was the language of administration; only the German text of laws and orders was accepted as authentic; every civil servant, every judge and every officer had to be able to speak German. In higher education, in the Czech secondary schools or at the University of Cracow for example, German took on a much stronger role. Of course, the aim of this policy was a supra-national state and a united nation-state, but the leadership also included outspoken slavophiles, such as Minister von Thun. But the leadership worked in favour of the Germans and of groups who were both able and willing to adapt, particularly certain Czech groups. In short, centralism was implemented, against the nation's desire for autonomy, by Germans and with Germans. This turned the nationalistic sentiments even more decisively against the system, and intensified the Germans' national conflict with the people of the German Reich for a long time to come. Because it was the Germans who were the imposers of this centralism, opposition to, and indeed hate of them, grew.

Finally, and indeed what was the most directly important factor, was that the system failed because of a lack of finance. The debts incurred during the Metternich era, the costs of the military operations during the revolution and immediately following it, the state's share of the compensation for large-scale landowners and the expansion of bureaucracy and public works had all added up. New taxes and other levying methods, which expanded to include Hungary, did indeed significantly increase the state's income; economy measures limited expenditure; and the economic climate of the 1850s did benefit the state; but the deficit did not decrease. It was not possible to modernise the state and society that quickly. Hungary's administration remained ineffective, even from a taxation point of view. The need for finance was met by loans and ultimately by the sale of the state railway; the conditions of such deals became more and more unfavourable. It was barely possible, however, to modernise the army. Each mobilisation during the Crimean War, for example, brought the state to the brink of financial collapse. The major power policy was being pursued without a financial basis. The system was living beyond its means. An economic crisis, such as that in 1857, struck right through to the state finances. The Jewish banks, on which the lending system was based, became increasingly reserved — which was also, in part, a consequence of the concordat policy of discrimination. By 1859, money could be obtained only through forced loans at an interest rate of 5% and a rate of issue of 70%. The Italian war of 1859 led inevitably to a crisis for the system; things could not go on in this way.

Finally, let us turn to the other German major power, namely Prussia. In December 1848, the counter-revolutionary government, not only for tactical reasons, had imposed a constitution, of course on condition that, in conjunction with the chambers, it would be considerably revised. When, in 1849, the second chamber, which tended to be politically more moderate, accepted the Reich constitution, the king dissolved it. A state of siege was declared and, with the help of an emergency order, on 30 May the three-class voting system was imposed. This was yet another coup. The three-class voting system was universal, but it did not provide equal voting rights. The system was supposed to represent the whole of society and reflect the unequal interests therein. This was not old-fashioned conservatism, because the voters were not categorised by estate but rather by the bourgeois principle of ability to pay taxes. But the system was less modern than the census voting system because it created a new, non-civil privilege order. Most importantly, it was a public, open system. Putting to one side the moral idea that an opinion should be expressed openly, this was intended to guarantee that 'natural authority', and more particularly state and government influence would be exerted on the voters. As with every voting system, this one had a varied effect in various historical situations. In the 1860s, it was the basis of liberal opposition to

Bismarck, and he was one of its harshest opponents. In 1849, it reflected a compromise right-of-centre liberals and conservatives. This was the voting system used. Of the electorate, 4.7% belonged to the first class and therefore fielded one-third of the electors; 12.6% belonged to the second class, and 82.7% to the third. The poll was still relatively high (35.4% in the first class, 44.7% in the second, and 28.6% in the third, giving an average of 31.9%). In 1852, the poll dropped to only 21.6%. The appeal by the left to boycott the election was effective only against the delegates fielded by the third class. The centre, also horrified by the May revolution, voted; the majority of liberals had now moved further towards the right. The newly elected chambers recognised the voting rights decrees.

It was therefore with these chambers, up until February 1850, that the crown negotiated a revised version of the constitution. The rights of the crown were now strengthened: veto, emergency decrees and state of emergency. The military was not included in the constitution, and they would not have to swear allegiance to it. The special relationship between the monarch and the army remained. The commando authority was extended to all military and personal political acts; it was no longer a matter for the War Minister, who was responsible to parliament, but rather for the royal military cabinet, which was responsible only to the king. The military was a decisive agent in the declaration and enforcement of the state of emergency. The government, particularly where the budget was concerned, became more independent of the parliament. The king, albeit reluctantly, finally took the oath to uphold this constitution, and thereby abandoned the hope for another direct coup. Another revision of the constitution in 1854 included the reorganisation of the first chamber, a long and hard-fought issue. Initially it was a body of property owners based on a high census, but then it became a nobility body, a *Herrenhaus* (house of peers). The king actually wanted a house for the higher nobility and persons appointed by him, from which he expected a strengthening of his position. The Junker nobility, however, wanted its own chamber and for the most part pushed this idea forward. The king finally guaranteed privileges for the smaller rural nobility, which in turn supported his power. The relationship between the king and the Junkers, which was not necessarily of an enduring nature, had thereby been newly secured. The *Herrenhaus* remained part of Prussian reality until 1918. The majority of its members were hereditary or lifelong members of the nobility and included predominantly the introduced representatives of the 'old and established landowners', a group from which all bourgeois lords of the manor were excluded. There were also a few urban, church and university representatives. The king had the right to create peers; in other words, he could appoint new hereditary members. On the whole, however, the upper chamber was a representation of the interests of the Junkers. It could take part in the legislation process, and it had a *de facto* right of veto against both the government and the people's chamber. This flew in the face of all ideas of a constitutional state and a state under the rule of law.

Let us try to characterise this Prussian system as a whole. On the one hand, the monarchy was once again in control of the state power. The king controlled executive power, the authority of the military, foreign policy and the state of emergency. He summoned the chambers and influenced, in one way or another, their make-up. The king was in charge of all actions taken. He was the actual force of initiative behind his government, and he was the centre of politics. The military and bureaucracy were the pillars supporting this rule. The state remained a state of the king, of the civil service and of the military. Furthermore, the political privileges of the nobility, namely its power to participate in political decisions, was maintained and newly consolidated by means of the *Herrenhaus*. On the other hand, Prussia was now a constitutional state and a state under the rule of law; it was no longer an absolutist state. There were now guaranteed basic rights and the separation of powers; there was a people's representation — and despite the class voting system, this was not a representation of estates or interest groups, because it represented the whole; these representations were able to participate in the legislative process and in the drawing up of the budget, and they had a right of veto. The ministers did not have parliamentary responsibility, although they were legally and politically liable. And in the long term it was for this reason that the independence of the government from the parliament was not absolute, as it may seem on paper. The old powers were once again in control of the state, but things were no longer as they had been before the revolution. There was now a constitution, and the crown had had to compromise with the civil constitutional movement. The revisions made between 1850 and 1854 and governmental practice rendered this constitutionalism conservative; it was weakened and brought to the brink of being sham constitutionalism. The emphasis of the politics lay with the crown and the government, and the conservatives were able to build a new, more modern, but constitutional power position. The constitution survived these pressures, however, and thus there remained the possibility for a realisation or renewal more faithful to the original meaning of the constitution and a different distribution of power.

The practical consequences of the constitution were reactionary. It was principally with the help of enormous influence applied during the elections that the government guaranteed the governmental make-up they wanted for the second chamber (in 1855, for example, there were 205 pro-government members and 147 others; made up of 181 conservatives, 51 Catholics, 48 right-of-centre liberals and 72 other members). A large number of them were civil servants. These were the so-called *Landratskammern* (Chambers dominated by the *Landräte*). With this group in power, a conservative legislative process was possible. This seemed to make a total revision of the constitution or even a coup superfluous. Sometimes the chamber appeared to be a subordinate authority. The conservative arrangement with the constitutional state seemed to function in a conservative fashion.

Reaction in Prussia otherwise operated much as it did elsewhere. A police system appeared, of which the Berlin police chief Carl von Hinckeldey became the notorious symbol. There were trials against communists and democrats — Waldeck, of course, was acquitted by the courts. A surveillance system was introduced using informers and agents, and grotesquely exceeding its powers, it spared neither the Gerlachs, nor the heir to the throne, nor the king himself. The press was controlled by censorship, a system of licences (*Konzessionszwang*) and taxation on the one hand and by a new press policy on the other. The civil service was subjected to increased controls: the disciplinary system was strengthened as was the execution thereof. Liberal-conservative *Regierungapraesidenten* and *Landräte* were relieved of their duties; and now even judges were replaced. The government no longer demanded mere neutrality; it demanded support and positive commitment to its course of action. Careers depended on having the right party 'attitude' and acting in the right way. The *Conduitenlisten* recorded everything that was of importance. The term 'political civil servants' — including the *Landräte* and state prosecutors — was clearly defined: unlike other civil servants, they could be 'pensioned off', i.e. removed from office; they were bound very closely to the ministry's course of action. This, particularly by way of hiring and promotion, reshaped the civil servants in the administration into a more conservative mould, especially younger ones and those in the country. The actual ministerial civil servants, those serving on councils and judges were subjected somewhat less to the pressure applied from above. The judicial monitoring of administrative documents was further restricted. The state lawyers' monopoly on prosecutions — which was a liberal achievement — was strictly governed by ministerial instructions; political and press offences, wherever possible, were deprived of a trial by jury. Urban self-administration was more closely supervised, and in the Rhine Province urban and rural government were completely separated. The policy for schools, especially *Volksschulen*, was corrected along conservative lines. All these measures were intended to tighten up the state apparatus and to control, discipline and depoliticise society. There was also a sort of 'compensation policy' in operation, the aim of which was to reconcile the different classes with the state's new course. The conclusion of the peasants' liberation, now to include the smaller peasants, was pushed through with the aid of annuity offices. The craftsmen too were to be better 'protected' by an amendment to the law governing the trades. The new factory inspectors, introduced in 1853 against resistance from the liberal manufacturers, were supposed to stress the restrictions on child and youth labour and fight dangers to health and safety. When the Berlin police chief Hinckeldey was buried in 1856, ten thousand people attended because this man of reaction, on such issues as, for example, fire protection and sanitation measures, had been the defender of the poor. The position of the capitalist bourgeoisie was further improved by the freer regulations on the establishment of joint-stock companies, by the state bank policy and finally by the liberalisation of the mining law. Of course, it was the nobility, more than anyone else, who were the beneficiaries of this political realism. However, the pre-1848 conditions were not re-established, although with the return of the nobility's manorial policing rights and the appointment of village mayors, Junker domination out in the country in the east was once again consolidated, and temporarily at least exemption from taxation remained in place. Of course, the bureaucratic and military state of Prussia was a constitutional state and a state governed by the rule of law, but it was also a Junker state. The strength of the feudal elements made the problem of the constitution particularly explosive.

Also of great importance, finally, was that the reaction in Prussia was even less unified than it was elsewhere. On the one side was the trend towards a bureaucratic, authoritarian statism with certain Bonapartist elements (i.e. a tendency to seek the consent of the masses). This was the line of the Minister-President, Otto von Manteuffel. The state was supposed to be based on the army and the civil service, and not on the nobility and the estates. They wanted to make a decisive break away from the revolution. It was for this reason that the constitution had to be revised and reinterpreted. But the intention was also to abide by the constitution. It was to be possible to incorporate society into the bureaucratic state using the constitution and also to block the political parties. In opposition to this bureaucratic reaction stood — if one ignores the neo-absolutist tendencies towards a government without any parliament — feudal reaction, which was more doctrinaire and decisive; these were the ultra-conservatives. They opposed absolutism and favoured chambers constitutied according to corporate principles and a state constructed on federalism; they favoured a coup and a complete revision of the constitution; they were also in favour of the restoration of manorial rights. They saw Manteuffel as their greatest enemy, and they had considerable influence over the king. The latter, of course, felt bound by his oath to the constitution, but he encouraged his heir not to take a similar oath. Finally, in 1851, on the occasion of the planned restoration of the corporate provincial estates (*Provinzialstände* and *Kreistage*), a conservative-liberal group of diplomats and state employees was formed under the leadership of Moritz August von Bethmann-Hollweg; it was called the *Wochenblattpartei* after their newspaper. They opposed any break with or undermining of the constitution; they stood up against the reintroduction of feudalism and against romantic notions of Christian estates; at the same time they also opposed the Treaty of Olmütz and all of Prussia's policies to renounce involvement in the German Question. Of course, this was largely a case of officers without soldiers, but under the electoral system as it stood, soldiers, to continue the metaphor, were of little significance; this party's weight stemmed from the fact that it seemed to be close to the king.

The revision of the constitution was in part a victory for the bureaucratic statists. The defeated were the ultra-conservatives and the liberals. Under these conditions, however, the Prussian leadership was hardly a united one. There was much to-ing and fro-ing to win the ear of the king and influence his decisions. Basically it was the double alternative of a 'right ministry' under Gerlach and a 'left' ministry under Bethmann-Hollweg that kept Manteuffel at the helm of the regime. The tensions, however, demonstrated the cracks among the reactionaries, and these were soon to become more visible.

2. German Policy in the 1850s

Reaction was not a return to the conditions of 1848. In view of the German question, this would hardly have been possible. After 1850, however, the Confederation and the Bundestag were restored, though there was no return to the informal co-operation, such as had existed under Metternich, between the two leading powers of Austria and Prussia. The revolution had led to the rebirth of dualism. The rivalry between the two powers that for some time had lain dormant now reared its head once again. The confrontation on the question of the Union may well have passed, but Olmütz, as had been demonstrated, was only a ceasefire. Even their joint interest in reaction was no longer strong enough to neutralise the competing claims of power.

The new Austria — i.e. with Schwarzenberg's demand to join, together with all the provinces, the German alliance and follow the idea of the 'seventy-million empire'— set a completely new tone. Bismarck, who at the time was the Prussian envoy to the Confederation, saw that the Austrian policy was a result of internal difficulties. He felt that the centralisation of the Reich, because it must in fact be a Germanisation, would make a 'revival' of its relationship to Germany necessary, but this would have to be under its hegemony. But, he also felt, Prussia could not tolerate such a situation, because it would mean Prussia losing much of its power and sovereignty. On the other hand, Prussia with its Zollverein and plans for a Union had in fact proposed, at least as a political possibility, an anti-Austrian, *kleindeutsch*, Prussian hegemony. Whatever the Prussian policy may have been in concrete terms, this was one of the persistent options of a Prussian Germany policy. Every realist had to reckon with this option. A new king or a liberal government would only have made it more likely. Austria was still in danger of being forced out of Germany. Avoiding this had to be the defensive aim of Austrian policy; it was the counterpoint to the offensive achievement of a true hegemony.

At Olmütz the question of a new reform of the German Confederation was relegated to a separate conference which met in Dresden from December 1850 to May 1851. Austria's 'seventy-million empire' project failed. And Prussia's attempt to establish at least a north German regional union and to create a sort of duumvirate within the Confederation was also unsuccessful. As a result, Prussia moved towards support for the status quo, at least in order to prevent an Austrian hegemony. The Confederation and its diet, the Bundestag, were restored in the old form.

The scene for the German policy of both the major powers was the German Confederation. Austria wanted to use the Confederation, if hegemony could not be achieved, as a way of keeping Prussia in second place. Austria tried to extend its responsibility for the order of business to become a sort of 'presidial power'; she also tried to make the Confederation more capable of acting and to widen its competencies and to overcome the paralysing principle of unanimity. Austria further attempted to use the fear of Prussia harboured by the medium-sized states, which in 1849–50 had again increased, to its advantage. A return to an accord with Prussia was not completely excluded, but it was less likely. Prussia had little interest in an active policy within the Confederation. Prussia wanted to be placed on a par with Austria, as this would secure Prussia's position as a European power and was further the nucleus of its *raison d'état*. For this reason, Prussia was opposed to setting a federation in motion, opposed to greater authority for the presidial power, opposed to the strengthening of the majority principle and against more competencies being allocated to the Confederation. Such things could have driven Prussia out of the Confederation. Therefore Prussia insisted on unanimity on crucial issues; in other words, it wanted a right of veto. It also insisted on full sovereignty for the other states, and to this end it was able to mobilise the support of the medium-sized states. Over and above this, the unity of reaction was no longer of any help. Austria, for example, wanted to extend the jurisdiction of the Confederation and the federal executive by introducing a federal press law, which would also be used against all published attacks on Austria and against the Confederation in the Prussian press. Prussia allied itself with Bavaria and prevented the Austrian plan; without strong centralisation the law remained more or less ineffective. And there were many more such instances of this sort.

Bismarck was the man for struggle. As the defender of Olmütz, as a member of the conservative party appointed as envoy to the Bundestag, he quickly developed into the champion of Prussia's interests, as he saw them. He gradually relativised the fundamental conservative policy which held that there should be solidarity where political ideas were concerned. The interests of his own state were now the priority. If, in his Olmütz speech, he had played 'state interests' off against party interests — which at that time was left — then this stance was now turned against the conservative 'party interests'. Ultimately there were even thoughts of using 'revolutionary' powers, as was done in the France of Napoleon III, and revolutionary means to impose Prussia's own goals. At a very early stage he saw the relationship between Austria and Prussia in terms of an essential conflict. Austria, he said, had to continue to strive for hegemony in Germany. 'But', he continued, 'we stand in its way, however much we may drive ourselves to the wall; a German Prussia of seventeen million people will always be too great a throng to grant Austria the leeway for which it is striving. Germany is the sole parade ground for our policy, but it is Germany that Austria thinks it needs. There is no room for both of us, and so in the long term we would not be able to tolerate each other. Each one of us is sucking the life blood from the other, so one of us has to give way.' This was a realistic analysis, but it was a polarisation of the situation. The *raison d'être* of power was the final reality of the policy, and this *raison d'être* of power was, as shown by Bismarck's use of the term 'parade ground', not only defensive but also offensive and expansionist.

Of course, there were other ideas for Prussian policy. The ultra-conservatives assumed that there would be an alliance with Austria, as demonstrated by Gerlach in his slogan 'Preussen und Österreich Hand in Hand, Deutschland sonst ausser Rand und Band' (Prussia and Austria hand in hand, otherwise Germany will be out of control); they took it for granted that there would a new Holy Alliance, an alliance of the three black eagles. For them power struggle was not the highest reality. Their consciousness of Prussian power was more restrained than Bismarck's. But the idea that Prussia's power should fall below that of Austria was something that they too did not wish to see. The solidarity of political ideas was not strong enough to quiet the dualism. Even the old triadic policy was revived with the idea of increasing the weight of the medium-sized states and bringing it to bear more resolutely in the tensions of the major powers, thereby to strengthen the Confederation so that it guaranteed its own existence and kept the major powers in check. But this was as unsuccessful as it had been on the previous occasion.

In practice and over the long term, the politics of the confederation stagnated during the 1850s. Bismarck pursued his line of opposition to Austria using very brusque methods. He not only blocked every change for which Austria strove, he also intensified every little conflict until it became a fundamental one. The latent antagonism became more apparent and permanent.

Alongside the Confederation, the Zollverein was the other no less important level of the German policy, and no matter how strong the connection between politics and economics, the political and economic institutions at that time remained separate. Schwarzenberg's Greater Austria policy was accompanied by a political trade and tariffs offensive, introduced by the eminent Trade Minister, Baron Karl von Bruck. This idea was one of a central European customs union. Austria in its entirety was to enter an Pan-German customs alliance. This economic amalgamation was, for Bruck — as in reverse it had previously been for the Prussian minister Friedrich von Motz — a path to political unity under Austrian leadership. Austria wanted to underpin its claim to political supremacy in economic terms as well as political. According to these plans, Prussia would have been incorporated, economically as well, in an Austrian-led central

Europe. The moves and countermoves on the policy of union were accompanied for this reason by offences relating to the politics of tariffs; and after Olmütz the time to implement the Austrian plans seemed almost perfect. The idea of a central European economic zone — with all the great perspectives that resulted from it — was also attractive economically and met with much support; indeed, especially since Bruck was prepared to open up the Austrian market by toning down his country's protectionist actions. In concrete terms, the question was in fact one of Austria joining the Zollverein. This was also politically tempting, particularly for the medium-sized states which, in spite of all the material advantages, still feared Prussia's superior strength in the Zollverein. It was predominantly Bavaria and Saxony who propagated the idea of tariff accord with Austria; and by suggesting the possibility of not renewing the customs treaties in 1853, they seemed to have a means of persuasion at their disposal. But Prussia put up a fight against Austria's entry; Prussia did not want to be deprived of the customs union that it led; and it did not want an economic Olmütz. It thwarted the plans of the pro-Austrian group by negotiating, at first somewhat hesitantly, and then by setting up a customs treaty (and then the so-called tax union) with Hanover. In so doing it had guaranteed a sustainable, north German customs zone and the linking together of its western and eastern provinces; and it now had the German north and east coasts, which were also important for the south, under its *de facto* control. As before, the considerable financial advantages had overcome the reserve in Hanover with respect to the Prussians. When the pro-Austrians threatened to quash this treaty, Prussia, of its own accord, announced in November 1851 that it would cancel the Zollverein contract of association effective in 1854; it was prepared to reach a new agreement only if Hanover was to be included. The other medium-sized states continued to try to force through Austria's entry and threatened to form a new Zollverein excluding Prussia. This attempt failed, partly because Austria's claims to take the lead and the triadic policy followed by the medium-sized states were incompatible, but principally because Austria had too little to offer economically and the Zollverein states were more clearly orientated around the Prussian economic zone. The government of Saxony, for example, in view of its industry, was not in a position to enter a customs war with Prussia. At the end of 1852, Austria revised its policy of confrontation on the customs issue and aimed for a balance. In February 1853, it signed a twelve-year trade agreement with Prussia; the issue of customs unification was not supposed to be discussed again until 1860. Thereupon, the Zollverein was renewed. This was in fact only a ceasefire, but on the whole it was a Prussian success. The weight of the Zollverein and the economic might of Prussia had won through against the combination of Austria and the medium-sized states. Of course, as had happened even after 1834, the recognition of Prussia's economic hegemony had no direct repercussions on the political situation. Economic dependency on Prussia tended rather to have the effect that the medium-sized states turned to depend on Austria politically. Economic and political fronts were not identical. Economic and political developments, on the other hand, were closely intertwined, although they did not necessarily run in parallel.

3. Germany in Europe:
from the Crimean War to the Italian War

In spite of the tensions between Prussia and Austria, the 1850s in Germany began as a time of calm. The elements of movement which also affected German issues were in fact the major European crises, namely the Crimean War and the Italian War. Many people at the time, both the vanquished of 1848 and Bismarck too, after the experiences of the revolution years, were convinced that the internal and the German political conditions could only be blown open from outside as a result of the effects of foreign crises. They hoped that this would happen.

After the revolution, irritation caused by popular and national movements during the two years of revolution seemed temporarily to have been overcome, as far as European diplomacy was concerned. European diplomacy had once again become a matter for the governing establishment. In eastern and continental Europe, Russia had become both the champion of monarchic, conservative order and the supreme power. At Olmütz, Prussia had had to submit to Russian pressure. Austria and Prussia seemed to be dependent on Russia. Russia had long since been at odds in terms of political ideas and political realism with England and with England's close ally, France; in general terms, it seemed that the eastern powers stood against the western powers. But at that time there were no points of conflict.

The situation changed when Louis Napoleon, by way of a coup at the end of 1852, made himself Emperor of France. It was he who for the next two decades was to become the element of unrest in Europe. He, as heir of the revolution and as a Caesar, who was more dependent on popular legitimacy than others, attempted to revolutionise what still remained of the 1815 order of Europe; this he did by presenting himself as the champion of the modern principle of nationality. In doing so, however, he was trying to strengthen France's importance, and indeed to establish as a sort of quasi-hegemony. This was bound to upset the balance of power in Europe and thereby irritate England, however much England supported the national and liberal forces in Europe as well as the smaller nations and states. It was also bound to provoke above all the conservative and multi-national powers of the east. Napoleon wanted to destroy the Holy Alliance and free Poland, and most of all he wanted to unite Italy. This threatened Austria's position.

The beginnings of the Italian crisis were at first overshadowed by a new crisis in the East, of the kind that had accompanied political events in Europe since the times of Napoleon I. The main point at issue was the continued existence, the restraint or the partition of the Ottoman Empire; the issue focused on the question of whether the straits should be dominated by Russia or remain neutral. This was a problem of world importance, because for Russia it was a question of securing the politically strategic Black Sea, and, from a trade point of view, it would also secure the export of grain; at the same time, the issue was crucial to the question of hegemony. At stake for England was the sea route to India, the freedom of the Mediterranean and the maintenance of the balance of power in Europe. Both world powers feared that the other would win more power, and they tried to prevent this. It was more the fear and the situations that developed rather than the resolute will of the powers involved that ultimately led to war. The Tsar wanted to increase his influence and used, to this end, his position as the protector of Orthodox Christianity in the Ottoman Empire. The Sultan, supported by

England, resisted the Russian demands. The result was war. In July 1853, Russia marched into the Danube principalities, later to become Rumania, and annihilated the Turkish fleet. In response England, France — and Piedmont — entered the war, sent a fleet to the Black Sea and finally landed on the Crimean peninsula, the name of which was to be given to the war. The war had become an international war. It was a curious war, a cabinet war, an old-fashioned war with limited objectives and fought with limited means; it was not a war of ideological fronts, but rather a war of foreign interests. Parliamentary England and caesaristic France joined forces to protect despotic Turkey.

This war forced the German powers to question their own position. The western powers were eager for them to take part in the war, in part in order to elicit a true theatre of war; by contrast, Russia, no less fervently, sought allies or positive declarations of neutrality. It was primarily Austria, because of its geographical position, that was faced with the greatest challenge to its power. Austria was closely allied to Russia, but if it was Russia's aim to free the Balkans and to revolutionise the national situation, this represented a threat to Austria's claim to hegemony in the south-east, the freedom of the Danube — so important from an economic point of view — and Austria's very existence as a multi-national (and anti-nationalistic) empire. In Vienna three trends tried to influence the decision: the first was pro-Russian, ultra-conservative and anti-revolutionary, and it wanted to solve the Balkan problem by a division of influence; the second favoured a neutral stance, which proposed active negotiation to secure Austrian hegemony in the south-east; the third was pro-west and wanted to form an alliance with the west to break Russia's supremacy, to safeguard Austria's position in the Balkans, and to bring under control France's pressure on Italy. This last trend, under the leadership of the Foreign Minister, Count Buol, was the one selected for the time being. In the summer of 1854, Austria — still in the alliance with Prussia — presented Russia with an ultimatum; thereupon Russia moved out of the Danube principalities; Austrian and Turkish troops then retreated. Then, in conjunction with the western powers, Austria formulated sharper and more offensive war objectives and demanded peace negotiations and, *de facto*, a Russian retreat. When Russia refused, Austria mobilised and using her troop concentrations encircled strong Russian forces. Austria was trying, by half-alliances of this type with the west and without having to enter the war itself, to force Russia to submit and to bring the west round to offering acceptable conditions. In December 1854, Austria finally had to come down on the side of the west; it signed a treaty of alliance with the western powers and promised to join in the war if Russia did not accede. The solidarity of the monarchs had finally collapsed. A group of Austrian politicians were seized by visions of a great war and the transition from the protection of the status quo to hegemonic expansionism. Buol hoped that he could force Prussia to side with the Russians and then, with the help of the French, defeat Prussia. 'We shall take Silesia, Saxony will be restored, and France can have the Rhineland; what do we care if they are German or French.' Such were Buol's dreams. People everywhere were now expecting a great war which, were Austria to participate, would make it the biggest ever. But in March 1855 the anti-war party won through in Vienna. Austria's alliance with the west proved to be an illusion; Austria proved to be no more decisively pro-French than it had been pro-Russian. The west had proclaimed an additional war objective, namely the neutralisation of the Black Sea. This was no more an adequate reason for continuing the war than the status of the straits — and the peace negotiations now dealt only with this issue. The armies, with good reason, were opposed to a war that was likely to make Austria the target of a Russian attack — indeed, that would entangle Austria in a fight for its very existence. Equally, the financial situation was against the war. There were good reasons for not entering the war. But, despite the course of events up to this point, the result was: Austria shied away, temporarily at least, from war. This prevented a limited war becoming a universal war, in other words, a 'world war'. But this action did not improve Austria's situation.

Even in Prussia, which was less directly affected, there were opposing tendencies. The ultra-conservative principle politicians favoured co-operation with Russia to a greater or lesser degree. The Minister-President Manteuffel, and others supported strict neutrality. The '*Orient*', they said, was of no significance to Prussia. Neither Russia's defeat nor its victory was in Prussia's interest; a balance of power alone would favour its interests. There, they said, Prussia had to try to play the role of the honourable middleman. Finally, the *Wochenblattpartei* and the heir to the throne stated that it was not principles but self interest that had to be pursued; Prussia should opt for the west in order to be able to pursue the Union policy again with its backing. Basically these opposing views within the establishment paralysed Prussian policy. Then the diplomats from the *Wochenblattpartei* took the initiative. The Prussian diplomat, Count von Pourtalès, negotiated along these lines in London in December 1853. The intention was to keep a free hand to be able to force Austria out of the German Confederation. For this reason, it was seen as desirable, of course with certain provisos with regard to French troops marching through the country, to enter an alliance with the west. England rejected the idea. It neither wanted nor was it able to sacrifice Austria, which was more important for the war. But the pro-west Prussian politicians did not give up; in the spring of 1854, they tried once again to ally themselves to the west, to obtain pro-west neutrality status, or even to enter the war, because they believed that in this way they would be able to reintroduce the Union policy without even a formal agreement. Baron von Bunsen, the envoy to London, wanted war against Russia in order that Europe might be restructured. In war they saw an end to Russia's supremacy and confinement to its 'natural' borders, the restoration of Poland, the expansion of Austria and Prussia, and a free hand for Prussia's German policy; it was thus on this basis that he negotiated. The problem with this policy was that the potential opponent, namely Austria, was also drawing closer to the west and it was not immediately clear how Prussia would have been able to cut it off in this way. This attempt, however, ended in April and May 1854 with the fall of the *Wochenblattpartei*. Eduard von Bonin, the War Minister, and Bunsen were sacked. The ultra-conservatives won back their influence over the king. His tendency towards solidarity of political ideas and towards neutrality won the upper hand. Of course, Prussia was itself on the verge of a crisis. Friedrich, a future heir to the throne, protested at the sacking of the pro-western War Minister Bonin. Thereupon he was suspended as an officer and sent on leave. His English wife had already sought asylum in England. But taking a pro-western stance was no longer an option. When the western powers and Austria tried to commit Prussia at least to agree to a declaration supporting Turkey's integrity, Prussia refused, not because it opposed such a motion, but because it did not want to be part of a display of anti-Russianism.

The to-ing and fro-ing of the Austrian and the Prussian policies on this European question always seem to lead back to the German question; it was either a question of imposing offensive objectives or of blocking opposing objectives. In the spring of 1854, Austria was successful in committing Prussia and then the Confederation to a protection and truce alliance along a common line, namely on Austria's peace demands and retreat from the Danube principalities. Prussia even agreed to provide military support were a conflict to arise. Prussia was clinging, out of fear of isolation, 'to Austria's coat-tails', Bismarck said. Of course, a decisive difference of view remained. Austria tried to suck Prussia and the other states of the Confederation into its intervention policy, while these states had aimed for permanent neutrality and wanted to hamper Austria in its endeavours in this direction. This led, in December 1854, to a crisis. Austria, unlike Prussia, had now entered an alliance with the west. The war was offensive, its aim being to force Russia to retreat. Austria, referring to the protection alliance of April 1854, requested the mobilisation of the Confederation with Austria assuming the supreme command. Austria wanted the backing of the Confederation, because it could only continue its active policy in the south-east if Prussia at least neutralised the Confederation, or rather made the Confederation a partner in the western alliance. For this reason, Austria wanted to draw the Confederation out of its neutral position and into the war to which it so greatly aspired. As Bismarck saw it, Austria was trying to 'Germanise' the crisis in order then to be able to stand up in the name of central Europe and 'let Prussian thalers and German bayonets rattle behind its sick state' and defend the Turks on the Vistula; but, he continued, this was all to serve Austria's own interests. Buol believed that despite Prussia's obstruction the whole of Germany would 'rise up as one, should ever the day come when an Austrian village was occupied by a foe'. But, in a situation such as this, he was wrong. The medium-sized states viewed the Austrian policy as warmongering; they saw in it a coalition with anti-German France and ultimately the break-up of the Confederation. They felt they had been left in the lurch. Bismarck, whose diplomatic talents knew no bounds, was successful in persuading the medium-sized states to oppose the Austrian advance. The Austrian idea and the call to the duty of the alliance were rejected. A more formal willingness to go to war was declared, not however against Russia, but to maintain the Confederation's neutrality. Austria seemed to have been ostracised from the Confederation. Bismarck had used the situation in Europe to secure Prussia's position against Austria in the Confederation for the first time since Olmütz, and it represented a major success. Of course, this was in the interest of Prussia's power and competition status. But behind it all — and this is what Bismarck took into account — was a very real fact, namely that Austria was a European major power with significant extra-German interests and Germany was being forced to become involved in these interests that were foreign to it. It also showed, according to Bismarck, that Prussia on the other hand was an almost pure German power whose European interests and security requirements were for the most part identical to those of the rest of Germany. But without Prussia, the Third Germany would not have been able to resist Austria's insistence; to this extent it seemed that the German states, in matters of European politics, were reliant on Prussia.

In March 1856 — by this stage Russia, albeit incompletely, was beaten — the war leaders met in Paris and agreed to a peace. It was no longer Austria, which had disappointed both sides, that was the mediator, and it most certainly was not Prussia, whose policies were considered to be weak; instead it was France and Napoleon III. The Danube principalities, under European guarantee, became partly independent, the maritime straits and the Black Sea were declared neutral, and Turkey remained independent.

Russia had been checked and its Balkan ambitions postponed; the alliance of the conservative eastern powers had collapsed. This weakening of Russia had given the rest of Europe a new-found freedom of movement. It had made it possible firstly for France and later for Prussia–Germany to become the leading power on the continent. In addition, however, Russia was no longer a status quo power. Like France and Prussia, it became revisionist in matters of foreign policy. From a world political point of view, England had been victorious, but in Europe it was France, from a diplomatic point of view, that was the true winner. France, freed from the pressure of the eastern powers, had won considerable clout. Napoleon seemed to be the arbitrator of Europe. While the Anglo-Russian differences, the differences between the 'whale' and the 'bear', remained the constant factor of world politics, a rapprochement between France and Russia seemed to be in the offing. The interests of the powers had won through against the solidarity of political ideas. The European order of 1815 had lost its near-sacrosanct status. This was an important precondition that over the next one and a half decades allowed the setting up of a new order in central Europe and in Italy. The situation of the German powers had also changed. Austria had lost the support of Russia, on which in the final analysis its German and European power positioned had been based; indeed, Russia was now an ardent enemy of Austria and had received an emotional reproach for 'ingratitude' from Russia — this went beyond rationality, because the Balkan difficulties were by no means dominant and the unity on the Poland question was a fact. But Austria had not won any partners in the west either and now seemed isolated. The possibility of giving up northern Italy and acquiring Rumania, in other words of orientating itself completely towards the southeast, was rejected by Austria. Prussia on the other hand was almost completely excluded at the peace conference as a neutral 'great' power and now only appeared to be in a weak position. Disinterested in the east as it was, Prussia had won back a freer hand. Despite all the fluctuations in the situation, Prussia had maintained good relations with Russia without having alienated the west to any great degree. For Russia, Prussia replaced Austria as the second conservative major power. The political structure drawn up at Olmütz was no more. The pressure exerted by the west on the rest of Europe was no longer concentrated on nearby Schleswig–Holstein; it now turned to the distant Danube principalities. This all represented international relief. And at last Prussia had been successful in the German Confederation.

Immediately after the signing of peace, however, the medium-sized states moved closer to Austria; they found Bismarck's obstructionist policy offensive. But it was widely felt that the Confederation could no longer function in terms of foreign policy, and that it was thus in a crisis. The reform of the Confederation was then placed on the agenda, and the experience with Austria's European interests again aroused calls for a specifically German foreign policy. The experiences of Germans in the Crimean War had altered the options of any German policy in the long term.

The Crimean War had started to prise open the German situation. The Italian war of 1859 continued this even more forcibly. This was now no longer a cabinet war, it was a national war with thoroughly revolutionary traits. The Italian unity movement had its champions in the kingdom of Piedmont and Sardinia, especially among the members of Count Cavour's government. The formation of an Italian nation-state meant the destruction of the Austrian position in northern Italy. This was not a question of diplomatic negotiations and compromises; it was a conflict of vital significance. Of course, Piedmont and the Italian national movement on their own were too weak to force Austria out. The issue became critical because Napoleon wanted Italy to be united. He made this possible internationally and militarily. He transferred from the status quo alliance with England to a revisionist, indeed revolutionary foreign policy. As we have already seen, he wanted to use the national question to change the order that had existed in Europe until then to France's advantage. He was thinking of an Italian confederation under the indirect protection of France, because he believed that he could keep the national movement under control. He wanted Nice and Savoy from Piedmont as territorial compensation; behind this was the idea of 'natural borders'. By way of weakening of Austria, he wanted to increase considerably France's clout against Germany and any solution of the German question. Napoleon's Italian policy and his — to express it in a word — Rhine policy were closely linked.

On the other side of the argument, Austria's status as a European great power had been based, since 1815, partly on its position in Italy; indeed, the division of Italy was a considerable part of Austria's existence as a supra-national state. As such, the Italian question was not a marginal question; it was a question central to the position of Austria in Europe and thus also to the balance of power in Europe.

In 1858, France and Piedmont formed an alliance. This was the preparation for the offensive, indeed for the attack. Russia, not exactly a friend of the nationalist policy, had nothing against a weakening of Austria in Italy and promised to remain neutral. England, for reasons of balance that tended to be more pro-Austrian, remained passive. Cavour's masterly diplomacy succeeded in provoking Austria into war and making Austria the aggressor, and this was of great significance to Prussia's stance and to that of the German Confederation. After an ultimatum issued because of armament in Piedmont, Austrian troops began the war on 29 April 1859. In the battles with the French–Piedmontese armies in May and June, the Austrians were defeated on 4 June near Magenta, on 24 June near Solferino, and they lost Lombardy. This was no longer a case of bad luck at war, it was also the fault of the system. Financial misery and the protection of the nobility who filled the higher and highest command positions had seriously weakened the fighting force and the army. But the war was by no means decided by these battles.

The rest of Germany was, of course, embroiled in this conflict from the beginning. War and theatres of war were near to them. The very heart of a German power, albeit one outside Germany, was under threat. If Austria were defeated it would be bound to have some effect on Germany. If France ruled over the plains of the Po and European balance moved in France's favour, then the danger on the Rhine would, by necessity, almost double. The Italian war raised the question of German security. Was it not vital, as Friedrich Engels said, to protect the Rhine at the River Po? This was more than a question of *raison d'état* that the governments had to weigh up; it was a question about the nation itself. The Austrians were brothers, and the Rhine was a sensitive and symbolic life-line for the German people. Security policies and national passions melted into one. Unlike during the Crimean War, it was now difficult to remain netural.

It was equally self-evident however that the question of what stance Germany should take with regard to the Italian war was linked to the conflict between Prussia and Austria. Every decision was tainted by this conflict, and each decision was bound to have an enormous impact on internal German balance. Austria at the very beginning of the crisis had asked for guarantees from and the help of the Confederation in its Italian provinces, because even though these provinces did not lie on federal territory, losing them would represent a danger to the Confederation. Prussia opposed Austria's requests. Prussia threatened that to be outvoted on this issue would mean a break up of the Confederation, and if this were to happen, Prussia would leave the Confederation. In April, Prussia forced the Confederation to maintain its neutral stance, and in May it prevented even defensive mobilisation. The Prussian policy, which as always was the result of varying tendencies, did not want to come down automatically and unconditionally on Austria's side and thus in opposition to France and Russia. But Prussia also did not want to become a tool of French policy working against Austria. The desire was to protect German security interests along the Rhine and in Italy. The consequence of this dual consideration was qualified support for Austria with appropriate service to be rendered in return. Prussia wanted to set a 'price' for its support of Austria. Prussia wanted equality in the Bundestag, supreme command of the Rhine, and political and military primacy in north Germany. In June, such calculations even extended as far as armed mediation whereby Prussia, with its army intact and after a mutual weakening of France and Austria, would be able to dictate the peace in Italy and be seen as the saviour of Germany and the Austrian position in Italy; thereby Prussia would reassert its claim to leadership. It was also for this reason that there was much hesitation about making any commitment to Austria. Austria, however, believed that Prussia would be as unable as the Third Germany to refuse to commit the help of the Confederation. What was a duty and a right, it was said, would be forced upon Prussia by self interest and public opinion. For this reason, Austria did not want to make any real concessions.

In June and July, the Prussian calculations seemed nonetheless to be coming true. The mobilisation began, and Prussia had a prospect of obtaining the supreme command it sought. Of course, there was still some dissent on the condition of whether Prussia should act in the name of the Confederation or as a free, European major power. Before the matter could be resolved, however, on 11 July a preliminary peace was drawn up in Villafranca between France and Austria. Austria thereby handed Lombardy — but not Venetia — to Napoleon, who in turn handed it back to Piedmont. Thus Napoleon avoided fighting the battle to the bitter end. It was wariness of England and Russia and a long war, concern about Prussia's diplomatic or military intervention, fear of the Italian national movement becoming independent in central and lower Italy, and political consideration of the ultramontane element in France, who must have feared for the existence of the Pope and the church state, that together determined Napoleon's action. Austria, in spite of — and indeed in the face of — the offer of Prussian assistance, decided to surrender. Of course, the financial misery in Austria at the time was also an influencing factor. The main reason, however, was that Austria's renunciation of Lombardy, which, it believed, represented a masssive loss to its position in Germany and put an end to her claims of hegemony, but which also spoilt Prussia's opportunity for triumph. Austria had accepted a heavy defeated in Italy, but it had also prevented a Prussian victory. Prussia's plans had failed precisely because Austria had accepted defeat.

This back and forth on major political decisions was accompanied by intense discussions within the political establishment and among the general public. Even during the Crimean War the question of the foreign policy option, particularly in Prussia, had become a subject of passionate public debate, over and above all institutional responsibility and authoritarian monopoly over foreign policy. This then intensified considerably during the Italian crisis. Social forces brought their opinion, with considerable vehemence, to the attention of the whole country, and thereby also claimed the right to participate in any decision-making processes. Foreign policy became an internal policy issue. The result was that suddenly all the questions relating to the nation and the constitution were on the agenda; every issue was now set in motion. And is so often the case with crucial political issues, the fronts quickly ran straight across the paths of the existing parties.

Three camps can be identified. Firstly, there were the resolute anti-Austrians. This group argued that Prussia should exploit the situation and force Austria out of Germany. Bismarck, who was somewhat neutralised diplomatically by his being in Petersburg, said that Prussia should not become 'intoxicated' with an Austrian imitation of '1813' and pull someone else's chestnuts from the fire. Prussia should, he continued, solve the German question under protection from Russia and France, annex south Germany, where 'on the following day everyone will give us their enthusiastic support', particularly if the king were to 'rebaptise' the Prussian Reich the German Reich. Bismarck was at that time still just an isolated figure, but his conservative-liberal opponents from the *Wochenblattpartei* were thinking along similar lines to his with regard to this issue, as indeed were the *kleindeutsch* liberals such as Constantin Rössler and radical democrats like Ludwig Bamberger and Arnold Ruge. It was the socialist Ferdinand Lassalle who expressed the idea most harshly: 'If Napoleon revises the map of Europe in the south based on the principle of nationality, that's fine; we shall do the same in the north. If he frees Italy, we shall take Schleswig–Holstein.' France and Germany ought, he continued, as civilised people to move against Austria, which had to be 'ripped to pieces and crushed' — these were radical-national but at the same time *grossdeutsch* notions. He continued that, in the spirit of Frederick the Great, Prussia must unite Germany. But such voices were in the minority.

The second group, comprising a large majority, supported Austria. This support was further backed by a great national mood of opposition to French hegemony and France's hegemonic tendencies. This, temporarily at least, bridged the gap between the supporters of the *grossdeutsch* and *kleindeutsch* solutions. They were united in their support for the Austrians, their brothers. This mood found expression in old and new Rhineland songs such as 'Oh Deutschland hoch in Ehren', as had happened in 1840. The ultra-conservatives such as Gerlach and Stahl were also part of this majority. So too was the national conservative Moltke, the chief of staff, who thought that together with Austria a preventative national war against France, under Prussian leadership, was necessary; of course, the main intention was to secure Prussia's leadership position. The Catholics, of course, also belonged to this majority, but so too did liberals such as Heinrich von Gagern, the *kleindeutsch* supporter of 1848, and *grossdeutsch* democrats like Julius Fröbel, but also emphatically Prussian democrats like Benedikt Waldeck. Finally, socialists such as Marx and Engels believed that Napoleon was the representative of the counter-revolution, that his destruction was in the interest of the working class, and that at the same time it would also be a blow to Russia; they also believed that the German western boundary had to be protected by an alliance with Austria.

Finally, there was a third and much smaller group. These were the *kleindeutsch* advocates of *Realpolitik* who, like the Prussian government, propagated the repulsion of French hegemony, assistance to Austria, but concessions to Prussia. David Hansemann and Max Duncker belonged to this group, for example, as did the non-Prussians Gustav Rümelin, Rudolf von Bennigsen and Hermann Baumgarten. More pointedly, Johann Gustav Droysen said that Austria should remain engaged in Italy because only then could a solution to the German question be found. Even more pointedly, Heinrich von Treitschke stated that Prussia should help Austria in this war precisely in order to inflict on her this 'delicate blow'.

In this debate there was also a curious ambivalence demonstrated by the liberal national movement towards the Italian national movement. The Italian national movement, with its civil, state-orientated, political realist character under the leadership of Cavour, was a model for the German national movement, and therefore there was a great deal of sympathy with it. But national self-interest was stronger than feelings of sympathy and solidarity. Italy's struggle for unity and independence seemed to threaten even Germany, and it also served Napoleon's egotistical, hegemonic interests, or at least it was exploited by him. Therefore, Germany's own self-interest had to take priority.

The outcome of the war was seen by most as disappointing. For the majority of the *grossdeutsch* supporters, and of course for Austria, Prussia had been disloyal, indeed even a traitor to Germany. It was said that it had put too high a 'selling price' on what was only, after all, support for Austria in line with its duty; and if Prussia's claim to hegemony was recognised, it was said that Prussia had not been prepared to take a risk. But similar reproaches were also made against Austria. It was said that it had surrendered to Napoleon too quickly so as not to be saved by Prussia. The most cutting criticism came from the radicals who said that Austria was an anachronism with its anti-national aristocracy and its pact with the ultramontane Catholics. In concrete terms this distrust and dissatisfaction with both Prussia and Austria was a call for a Confederation reform that served neither Austrian nor Prussian power interests, but instead served German security interests. Frequently at the root of this idea was a longing for a great and strong man — the image of Cavour was even more at work here than that of Napoleon — who would solve the national question; or even a Caesar who, following the path to power, would cut Germany's Gordian knot.

4. The New Era

The reaction proper came to an end after almost a decade, at the end of the 1850s. Once again, the liberal and nationalist movements were increasing in strength; compromises seemed to be developing between them and the governments, an evolutionary development in the questions of the constitution and the national state. This period is often not taken seriously enough; it is overshadowed by the alternatives of 1848 and the later foundation, by imposition from above, of the Reich. It was, however, an alternative in itself, and the possibilities and turning-points of German history are particularly clear here. This period is called the 'New Era', after the name which has become customary in Prussia for this change of monarch and government.

In October 1858, Crown Prince Wilhelm took on the regency of Prussia, in the place of Friedrich Wilhelm IV, who suffered from mental illness. Once again, many hopes were pinned on this event, some justified, others groundless. The successor to the throne was harder and more sober than his brother, with a greater sense of duty and reason. He was definitely more of a Prussian, but was more interested in power than ideology. He was an opponent of Olmütz, who was close to the Prussian–German ambitions of the *Wochenblattpartei*; the reason for his giving hope to the *kleindeutsch* nationalists. But he, the grapeshot prince of 1848, was a soldier through and through, a man of the Prussian military state, and it was this which eventually led to the great conflict. In the early period of his regency, however, it was his opposition to the arch-conservatives and the reaction which was the main trend. In contradiction of the last will and testament of Friedrich Wilhelm IV, he took the oath on the constitution on taking over the regency. As the constitution existed, he argued, it ought to be upheld, and not falsified by forced interpretations. A conservative-liberal cabinet, whose principal members were Prince Hohenzollern, the 1848 traditional liberal minister Rudolf von Auerswald, and above all the leader of the *Wochenblattpartei*, Bethmann-Hollweg, formed the government, with the arch-conservatives and the bureaucratic-absolutionist reactionaries in opposition. This was English-style politics, as favoured by the Coburgs, the wife of the Prince Regent, Augusta, and her relatives and advisers, and the liberal Prussian aristocracy: a balance between the elite classes, an expansion of the traditional ruling class, and the integration of at least part of the bourgeoisie, in order to strengthen the authority of the state and preserve it from the shocks of a (social) revolution. An alliance with the liberals and the introduction of reforms — this was the way to retain the monarchic and aristocratic nature of the existing order. This was a sensible programme with a good chance of succeeding, and it was widely accepted. The English example made this system attractive to the monarchy and the aristocracy, to the educated and the monied members of the bourgeoisie alike. It was a realistic option. The range of people who were in favour of this method was indeed a wide one, including determined reformers, those for whom only the ultras were too extreme, those who considered the older generation too old-fashioned, and those who purely for reasons of tactical compromise wished to reconcile the educated and monied sections of the bourgeoisie to the existing social and political order.

As always, the Prince Regent developed the programme of this New Era in a speech. The government must satisfy the justified needs and demands of the time with a 'careful and improving hand'; Prussia must be at the forefront of the intelligentsia through its system of schools and universities; religion must not become the cloak of politics (this remark was aimed at the hyper-orthodoxy movement and was particularly welcomed by the liberals); Prussia must conduct an independent foreign policy. But he then went on to say: 'In Germany, Prussia must make moral conquests by means of wise legislation at home, by the elevation of moral elements and the use of unifying elements, such as the customs and excise organisation. . . . The world must know that Prussia is prepared to defend the cause of justice everywhere.' This seemed to be a clear rejection of the reactionary course, which had cost Prussia so much credibility in Germany. The Prince Regent, it seemed, had finally adopted the liberal views of Prussia's historical role in Germany. Other points mentioned by Wilhelm in this speech concerned a healthy, strong, conservative basis for government, the need to improve and modernise the army, and a rejection of the liberal notion that the government should always be striving to develop new ideas — this was not perceived so clearly. Nevertheless, it remained a conservative-liberal and moderate nationalist programme. Even Bismarck advised the Prince Regent to allow the press and parliament more freedom and to encourage the uniform co-operation of all the institutions and resources of the nation, in keeping with the requirements of the time. He also believed that some kind of reconciliation with the liberals was an important part of the great hegemonical politics of Prussia.

The government took a number of steps to defuse the atmosphere of conflict. There was a government reshuffle — Bismarck, for example, was banished to Petersburg; the camarilla was stripped of its authority. The next elections to the lower chamber were no longer 'controlled' by the state, with the result that the number of conservatives was reduced from 224 to 16. As the democrats were still boycotting the elections, the cautious 'old liberals', who were certainly open to negotiations, won the majority of seats. In the long-running conflict in the Bundestag concerning the constitution in the Electorate of Hesse — the regime in the Electorate of Hesse was the most provocative of the German reactionary establishments — Prussia demanded, with public opinion now behind it, the reinstatement of the 1831 constitution, which it finally got, by working together with other governments of the New Era and exerting hefty pressure, including threats of war, at the end of 1862, now against a completely different political background at home. But the planned decisive reforms did not come about — at least not yet. In 1860, a whole series of draft reforms failed, e.g. concerning municipal and district authorities and marriage law, largely because of rejection in the upper chamber. The abrogation of the landed gentry's exemption from land tax was pushed through by nominating a batch of new peers, but that was about all. The freedom of movement for such policies became ever more restricted. The golden rule of politics in the New Era was not to challenge the existing powers; 'Don't push too hard' was the motto — to avoid driving the king into the conservative camp. The old liberals were hoping that time was on their side; but in the emergence of the conflict over the army, the military and the military cabinet around the king began to play a more important role. A law concerning ministerial responsibilities, which was of particular importance to the Liberals, was not passed because the military cabinet and the new War Minister, Roon, persuaded the king to withdraw the draft. It now became clear that the purely coincidental and personal fact of the king being a man from the first decades of the century meant that the change of monarch in Prussia had not been a change of generation, and this limited the reform programme decisively.

A new political era was also beginning in other countries. In Austria, as we shall be discussing shortly, neo-absolutism ended after the Italian defeat. In Bavaria, where, as we have already seen, the reaction was not as sharp as elsewhere, there was a serious conflict between the chamber and the government after the election of a liberal majority in 1859. The chief minister von der Pfordten had to choose between a *coup d'état*, dissolution of the chamber, and the imposition from above of new electoral laws or resignation. The king decided, not without considering the New Era in Prussia, in favour of a peaceful solution — 'I want to be at peace with my people' — and von der Pfordten resigned. This was the beginning of a phase of moderate liberal bureaucratic governments, which co-operated with the Liberal majority in the *Landtag*. In Baden, the grand duke used the resistance of the Liberal majority in the chamber to the concordat to effect a change of government; the Liberal party leader, August Lamey, became Interior Minister; the Liberals became the governing party, although there was no direct changeover to a parliamentary system. Conciliation and reform: that was the order of the day. This also coincided with the German policies of Baden and of the adviser to the grand duke, Baron Franz von Roggenbach; a liberal-nationalist, federal-*kleindeutsch* unification was the goal; it was to be achieved by means of negotiations by the governments and the pressure of public opinion. The participation of the bourgeois movement and the parliaments in the development of political objectives in the individual states was a prerequisite for this. Baden was supposed to be an example of the ability of such liberal policies to work; at the same time, these domestic policies were meant to guarantee Baden the necessary freedom of action regarding foreign policy. There was, it is true, no change of government in Württemberg, but the reaction did stop; the government adopted a kind of middle-of-the-road style; and in Saxony, in Hanover, in both states of Hesse, the conservative regime continued, but the general style was now much more moderate. Everywhere liberalism was making huge gains; the 'old left' entered the political arena once again, to become part of the one great liberal movement. 'Progress' and its party, the Progressive Party (*Fortschrittspartei*), which sprang up in many countries after 1861, was marching forward.

One may well wonder how such a change can occur in a whole series of important states, why the apparently unwavering reaction should come to an end after just ten years. Changes of monarch, sometimes also changes of generation, obviously played a certain role; there also arose a liberal-conservative group among the monarchs, as represented most obviously by Friedrich von Baden and Ernst von Coburg. In the establishment of the reaction, as we have already seen, the cracks became more apparent; in Prussia, there was tension between the arch-conservatives and the *Wochenblattpartei*; in Austria and the states of southern Germany, there was an ongoing conflict between the state and the Catholic church, which no concordat was able to resolve permanently; it was as a result of this rupture that liberalism regained ground and freedom. It was, of course, over foreign policy, especially after the Italian War, and the German Question that the unity of the reaction was finally broken and there was a drive for new policies. The competition between the old powers depended on the power of the modern principle of a public sphere, and even a conservative government, if it wished to achieve anything in the German Question, could not do so without winning the support of the public and of the power bases within society. In Austria, it was the catastrophic economic and financial condition of the state — which was hardly able to continue to fulfil its claim to be a great political power — which forced the government to attempt to negotiate with the powers within society. Indirectly, of course, this is a universal law; without a basis of consensus, without 'peace with the people', even a conservative system cannot hold on to power indefinitely, let alone develop itself. In that much (though, indeed, only in that much), the developments within society caught up with the politics of the states and the old powers. Liberalism, which survived the years of reaction with the impulse of the reforms, was now slowly gaining power again through new reforms and the Liberal-Conservatives.

The reactionary laws were relaxed. The old intended liberal reforms in the areas of justice, self-government, laws regarding the press and clubs and organisations, and new liberal reforms concerning schools, business and the economy — in short, civil freedom and civil equality and a liberal market economy — were introduced and encouraged. Freedom of choice of residence and settlement was finally established, as a result of a healthy economy, over the old restrictiveness of the traditional communities. All this applied especially to Bavaria and Baden.

The case of Baden is particularly interesting, because the Liberals were the governing party. Here the latent *Kulturkampf* came to the surface; measures against the religious control of schools, conceived by Interior Minister Lamey as, among other things, a tactical means of keeping the Liberals together, provoked resistance from the church. Furthermore, the liberal economic and trade laws were met with protest from protectionist and traditionalist groups, especially in the rural areas and small towns. The result was the formation of an anti-liberal, Catholic opposition, which, on a national scale, could also mobilise the support of the strong, nationalist, anti-Prussian sentiments. Also, the politics of dignitaries, which liberalism in effect was, naturally provoked populist-democratic opposition. The Baden experiment, which was supposed to lead, slowly and quietly, to an altered constitution, did not succeed. Stated candidly, liberalism proved itself to be not yet capable of government. In the face of the extraordinary challenges of these years, it was not capable of unified action. During the conflicts regarding the church and the *Kulturkampf* there developed a division of the movement into a more decisive radical wing and a moderate wing, and this difference also played a role in other areas. In 1865, the radical wing became an independent organisation. At the same time, and this is even more important, the national division between the pro-Prussian and anti-Prussian liberals became deeper. In 1865, Roggenbach, the representative of the Liberal government's *kleindeutsch* national policy, had to resign as Foreign Minister; he no longer had an adequate political base. The policies of the Liberal government were alienating many supporters of the Liberal party (and any other polices would have done the same). This was not due to normal wear and tear, but to the inhomogeneity of German society, which caught up with the liberals in the religious, social, economic and national political conflicts. The party base and unity were not stable enough to support the co-operation between the government and the party. It would hardly have been different anywhere in southern Germany. From 1864 onwards, in particular under the weight of the German Question, the democrats were once again separating from the liberals everywhere, and everywhere the liberals were struggling with the dilemma of the Prussian and anti-Prussian options. In Baden, the experiment of liberalism as a governing party ended in 1866 with the return of a constitutional government which presided over the parties and forced the parliament into a secondary role. This episode did not show that the liberal hopes of a transition to a liberal and parliamentary type of governmental system were unrealisable — six years was not long enough for that — but it did reveal the difficulties involved on account of the conflicts and tensions within German society, particularly in connection with the question of nationhood. But if in Prussia, for example, the conservative-liberal Crown Prince Friedrich had succeeded to the throne on the abdication of King Wilhelm (which was most certainly considered as a possible course of action), then German domestic politics might well have followed the 'English way'.

The rather different special case of Austria was, of course, also very important, even for the development of Germany as a whole. Here the Italian defeat led to the collapse of neo-absolutism. This system had isolated Austria internationally; it had made a German policy for the Confederation — in competition with Prussia, which was, after all, a state with a constitution — more difficult, and it had completely destroyed the financial basis of the state, or was at least unable to restore its inner strength. Austria needed a constitution in order to give the state a stronger economic and social base and be able to conduct a German policy, and it needed a reconciliation with the national monarchical powers, in particular with Hungary. These were conflicting objectives, and this was part of the dilemma of Austrian constitutional policy, and the reason for the constitution being developed as a series of experiments. First of all, in October 1860, the Kaiser tried a type of conservative federalism, primarily with an eye toward Hungary; the states were to be restored as autonomous entities; there was to be a federal council (*Reichsrat*) for advising on laws and authorising taxes, which would comprise, as well as the appointed members, representatives of the *Landtage*, who were recruited from the aristocracy and the upper class. This programme met with more or less general resistance. For the Slavic representatives and the Hungarians, it was not federalistic enough, and the Hungarians wanted an agreement and not an imposed solution. To the Germans, on the other hand, and in particular to the liberals, it was not organised on a sufficiently 'one-state' basis; only in a more heavily centralised Reich could a real constitution exist; and they found it too conservative: Austria would be run by the aristocracy and the clergy, and the taxpayer would have no say in budgetary affairs. The fear of the Germans, for example in Bohemia, of being at the mercy of other nationalists naturally influenced their attitude.

In the face of this resistance and the hopelessness of an appeasement policy concerning Hungary, the other alternative was selected — a more strongly constitutional and more strongly centralised solution with the German liberals. The man from the Paulskirche, Anton von Schmerling, became the leading minister. The February patent of 1861 turned the Reichsrat into a national parliament with full legislative rights, consisting of an upper house and a lower house; the members of the latter were elected from the *Landtage*. The states had their *Landtage*, and in the composition of these the urban bourgeoisie would now be favoured alongside the landed classes; compared to the rural districts it was hugely over-represented, in Bohemia, for instance, by a ratio of 4.5:1. In the smaller Reichsrat, which was responsible for the non-Hungarian parts of the Reich (this became a new expression in the political vocabulary), the bourgeoisie had 65 seats to the 59 of the landed classes. Owing to the social and economic structure of society, this system *de facto* favoured the Germans. The German liberals were in no way German irredentists; they in particular did not want to represent any one group, but society as a whole, they believed in a one-state system; but objectively this was in their national interest. The one-state solution and the leading role of the Germans necessarily went hand in hand.

These constitutional-liberal policies had a domestic Austrian purpose, but were also part of the German policies of Austria. They were designed to establish Austria's legitimacy and appeal with the German Confederation, the small and medium-sized states and German public opinion in the struggle against Prussian ambitions. The fact that between 1862 and 1865, while Prussia was in the midst of the constitutional conflict and under the reactionary Bismarck regime, Schmerling was leading the government in Austria with a liberal constitution, obviously had a great effect on the development of the German Question. The Austrian constitutional policies were closely connected to the Austrian policies of federal reforms. Many politicians in the medium-sized states in the non-Austrian and particularly the Catholic parts of Germany, supporters of the *grossdeutsch* solution, convinced of the indefeasible, natural and necessary affiliation of Austria to Germany and with anti-Prussian attitudes, were very influential in the ministries and higher levels of administration, as well as in government propaganda; such views were held by people like, for example, Ludwig von Biegeleben. But a view towards Germany was not enough to consolidate the constitution.

This constitution also was met with resistance, which was, in the end, the cause of its failure. The Hungarians boycotted the new system; the Slavs — especially the Czechs and Poles — the aristocracy and the clergy, and to a certain extent the German Alpine states as well, were all in favour of a more federal and conservative system. In the smaller Reichsrat, the German 'left', i.e. the liberals, with 118 seats, although divided among themselves, were in the majority; the Ruthenes, Italians and Rumanians usually supported them, mainly for reasons of nationality politics; the actual opposition was 70 strong. In 1863, the Poles and the Czechs withdrew in protest from the parliament. The relationship between the government and the majority remained tense. The government had, it is true, revised its particularly offensive church policies in 1861 with the introduction of a Protestant patent, but it remained dependent on the concordat and the Kaiser and had to employ careful tactics. The usual liberal reforms were only introduced very slowly. The tragic result of the policies of the reactionary period was rather peculiar: an anti-clerical stance was adopted by the *Catholic* liberals as almost their main objective. There were reasons for this, connected with the German Question: to eliminate the liberal proscription of Austria in the rest of Germany on account of the concordat. The Austrian Germans won support for their anti-clerical policies in the 1860s from the increasingly powerful German-Jewish bourgeoisie; but in the long term this anti-church stance did not favour the development of the constitution. More so than elsewhere in Germany, it alienated the liberal bourgeois and educated sections of society from the peasant and petty-bourgeois masses. But this was not the reason for the experiment failing. More decisive was the inability of the Schmerling system to bring the Hungarian problem closer to a solution. Neither the exertion of pressure, nor patient waiting, nor the attempt to negotiate with the neighbouring Hungarian countries bore any results, and the passive resistance of the Hungarians continued to exacerbate the financial misery. The Kaiser reverted to his federal stance on account of the possibility of a war over Germany and Italy and of negotiations with Hungary and a Magyar–Croatian settlement. On 26 June 1865, Schmerling resigned and in July was replaced by the conservative-clerical Count Belcredi; the February constitution and the Reichsrat were suspended; the Hungarian *Landtag* was convened, and a conciliatory speech from the throne signalled the start of negotiations with the Hungarians. After the collapse of neo-absolutism, the centralised constitutional-liberal system also failed, mainly owing to Hungarian opposition, but also to that of the other non-German nations and conservative-clerical elements. Because Austria was a great power and wanted to conduct great-power politics, and because it was under the acute pressure of financial misery, it was impossible simply to play a waiting game, let alone get to grips with a fundamental reorganisation of the whole question of states and nationalities; there had to be negotiations with Hungary, with the old Greater Hungary, now of the Magyars. When Austria left Germany in 1866, such a step had finally become unavoidable.

The difficulties which the supra-national 'Kaiser's state' had with the liberalism of the New Era were not the same as those experienced by the other German states. But this is premature. First, we must again deal with the context of the Pan-German policies.

5. The German Question, 1859–63

At the end of the 1850s, the German Question once again became the major topic of discussion for the Germans, the governments and the public. The Italian War had raised anew and urgently the problem of German security. In the matter of providing assistance from the Confederation, Prussia had renewed its claims in a decisive manner; Austria had clearly decided to give priority to its German policies in the Villafranca Agreement; the dualism was intensified. The dawning of the New Era and the new European and Pan-German constellations meant that, for the remaining governments also, the former priority of domestic politics, the reaction, was being pushed into the background; it was now the German Question that was right at the top of the agenda. This change meant that public opinion became more important and gained new influence, and the question of nationhood was most definitely the central theme with the general public. As now nobody could pin their hopes on a national revolution or, indeed, a violent, warlike solution, the German Question became one of the reform of the German Confederation. This dominated the politics of the subsequent years, apparently on its own at first, until the German Question then became inseparably linked to the question of European power politics.

The German policies of these years were a confusion of plans, actions and counter-actions, irritations and fluctuations; the men of that time explored and portrayed it with great passion, both *kleindeutsch* and *grossdeutsch*. To the post-war generations, this topic is not so important; the vital questions nowadays are those of constitution and rule, of the relationship between the citizenry and the monarchical, feudal and military authoritarian state; in other words, the question of freedom has become the central theme, the question of social and economic conditions and conflicts. However, these plans for the Confederation remain for the present generation, and for any history of the Germans, of epochal importance. Basically, we are concerned with the question of the alternatives to the unification policies of Bismarck: to the Little German, Great Prussian, violent foundation of the Reich as an authoritarian state, to the resultant inner structure of this Reich and the accommodation of the liberals, to the formation of a powerful national-imperial state, which did not contain the explosive power of German nationalism in Europe, but rather mobilised it; to the separation of Austria and to the first modern division of the German nation. Of course, the German policies cannot be separated from the party movements and the domestic policies of the individual states; they interacted intensely with the Prussian conflict, and in the same way were naturally coupled with the Zollverein policies. A chronological account would make these interconnections clear. But we have no time for that here. In order to make things more transparent, we want to separate the various developments and problems, and extract from the complexities of Confederation policies only the typical possible solutions, which presented themselves one after the other, and the moments of great decision.

Going on the assumption that all those involved were agreed on the necessity of a federal reform, we shall look firstly at the Prussian idea for federal reforms. This idea aimed at a dualistic hegemony within the Confederation, equal rights, an alternating presidency and prior negotiations between the hegemonical powers, reform of the war constitution in order to bring about a better solution of the German security problem, and finally, either as an addition or an alternative, the claim to independent hegemony in the north, i.e. a division of influence along the line of the River Main, whereby Prussia demanded a free hand in Schleswig–Holstein and the Electorate of Hesse. This solution had clear priority in Prussian politics before Bismarck; the other alternative, the smashing or paralysing of the Confederation, was only a temporary, emergency solution. There were two possible ways of getting Austria to accept this reform: not only confrontation and the exertion of pressure, but also co-operation. For example, in the face of the rather opaque plans of Napoleon III, the Prussians for a time preferred an understanding with Austria, and Bismarck had included this aspect in his calculations. Of course, considering the difficult position of Austria internationally, Prussia definitely had something to offer, e.g. the guarantee of the remaining Italian position of Austria in Venetia; to that extent, a co-operation and division of influence was not without its attractions for Austria as well. However, Austria did not want to give up its leading role in Germany, nor have it reduced in any way; it wanted to block Prussia's efforts at change as far as possible, and to accomplish this it wanted, if necessary, to strengthen the Confederation. It is true, though, that Austrian politics also fluctuated between the alternatives of an anti-Prussian confrontational style and dualistic co-operation; a permanent decision was never arrived at. Initially there seemed to be a Prussian–Austrian rapprochement beginning in the autumn of 1859; in July 1860 Prussia was willing to guarantee Austria's position, including in Italy, and Austria gave priority to the federal alliance with Prussia. By the spring of 1861, however, these arrangements had been reduced to nothing. In the end, Austria drew back from a policy of division of influence; one reason for this was that it would then have to reckon with ever-increasing Prussian claims — an argument which cannot be rejected out of hand.

Opposition to both the Prussian and the Austrian ideas came from the 'triadic' ideas of the medium-sized states, who had been holding their own conferences in Würzburg since 1859. They were just as horrified by ideas of a Prussian–Austrian duumvirate as they were by the hegemonic ambitions of Prussia and the possible exclusion of Austria. They wanted a federal reform, which would guarantee their existence and at the same time strengthen the authority of the Confederation. In 1859 they called for a standardisation of the legal system by the Confederation and the involvement of delegates from the *Landtage* in the running thereof. Then, in 1861,

Count von Beust, the Prime Minister of Saxony, demanded a more powerful executive, in fact a triumvirate, and an increase in the authority of the Confederation and the formation of a federal assembly consisting of delegates from the *Landtage*. This was the concession of the politicians of the medium-sized states to the nationalist movement, although in fact this assembly of delegates was remodelled into a particularist-federal institution. But this triad suffered from the same old problems: Bavaria wanted a special role, and time and again the unity of this group was revealed to be very fragile on the important questions.

After the Prussian–Austrian attempts at agreement failed in the summer of 1861, Austria once again drew closer to the medium-sized states. A different development was the new increase in popularity of *kleindeutsch*, liberal-nationalist unification plans, with Baron Franz von Roggenbach, the minister from Baden, as their main champion. In July 1861, he addressed the King of Prussia: Germany must be fundamentally reformed, with a parliament and a constitution. Such a reformation would, however, only be possible without Austria; Austria should be given a military guarantee as 'compensation' and allied to a narrower Germany. These were basically the policies of that wing of the German nationalist movement which in 1859 had constituted itself as the Deutscher Nationalverein (German National Society), in order to campaign publicly for such goals. Bismarck had also been airing his opinions during these months: Prussia should lodge an official complaint with the federal authorities against the policies of the Confederation, against the particularism of the princes and the failure in the real issues of German security; furthermore, it should initiate negotiations with the individual governments regarding a reformation of the Confederation; it should make plans for the establishment of a parliament, as this would be a necessary organ of integration against the divergent, dynastical and particularist politics of the time; and the parliament and the governments of the Confederation would mutually limit and balance each other's powers. This was a different tone of voice, more Machiavellian, borne of *raison d'état*, security considerations and Prussian hegemonical ambition. The motives and aims were different to those of the nationalist movement. But Bismarck recognised this movement and public opinion as a power with which one could, or indeed must, ally oneself in order to achieve one's own goals; there were signs of an unusual alliance developing in the long term. The Prussian Foreign Minister Bernstorff, was also, in December 1861, thinking in terms of a Prussian-led *kleindeutsch* union, albeit without a parliament. Initially, however, Prussia chose not to pursue such policies seriously.

It was exactly in opposition to such plans that Austria and the medium-sized states came closer together. They once again took up the idea of an assembly of parliamentary delegates, who were to debate a code of civil laws and a standardisation of the legal system; this would have been a substitute parliament which could not have inflicted any real harm on the individual states. At the end of 1862, they attempted to outvote Prussia in the Confederation; Prussia threatened to leave the Confederation. Bismarck, by now Prime Minister, even threatened war if Austria did not recognise the parity in the Confederation and Prussian hegemony in the north; Austria would have to choose between Prussia and the medium-sized states — a threat which, in view of the European situation, was not very realistic. In December 1862, he offered, instead of permanent confrontation, a policy of power-sharing and co-operation, if Austria was prepared to pay the price demanded. This would have been a policy of conservative, counter-revolutionary solidarity, and Bismarck certainly made use of this ideological concept in argument, because the confrontational politics of Prussia, paradoxically enough, were aimed at a national policy along the lines of that favoured by the liberals, or even together with them. But Austria did not further pursue such surprising and grand perspectives. Nevertheless, faced with the alternative of Prussia leaving the Confederation, the motion to outvote it was defeated. Prussia then prepared a counter-attack. Under the leadership of the 'minister of conflict' Bismarck, who had shortly before said how the great questions of the time would be decided by iron and blood, it now spoke out in favour of a parliament, elected directly and in proportion to the size of the population. This was directed against the supra-national Austria, which could not allow such a parliament. Initially this suggestion brought only mockery and scorn upon Prussia, but the national parliament was a revolutionary weapon, even in the hands of the Prussian government; it was a grand prospect for the future.

Then, however, in 1863, Austria once again took the initiative. This was the time of the *grossdeutsch* liberals in Vienna: they wanted to embark upon a massive programme of genuine reform and thereby solve the German Question in such a way, naturally, that would allow Austria's political existence to remain intact and its leading role to be guaranteed. The basics of the Austrian plan were presented in July 1863. The Confederation was to remain federal, but the 'federal state' elements were to be strengthened alongside those of the 'federation of states', in particular with regard to the competences and power of the federal executive. The organs of state would be a directorate consisting of five or six members, an assembly of princes and a federal parliament, to be elected from the state parliaments and with limited rights. This was a grand plan to reorganise Germany and central Europe, compromising between particularist sovereignty and common interests, supra-national central European ideals and that of the nation-state, and between the governments and the civil-populist movement, albeit without a parliament. There was mention of a temporary solution, if necessary, without Prussia; a sort of reversed Little Germany. The Austrian Emperor sent out invitations to a conference of princes in Frankfurt in August 1863, where this plan was to be debated, without the arrangement of prior ministers' conferences, which the Prussian king had immediately demanded. The way in which Bismarck went to great lengths to prevent the Prussian king from attending this 'birthday party of princes in white', and succeeded, is now famous. As far as Prussia was concerned, the plan was aimed purely at strengthening the Confederation in Austria's favour; Prussia would be reduced to the role of one of five members of a directorate. This, however, was probably a negotiable point. But Bismarck did not want that either. In the end, his realistic power-political views prevailed over all the king's dynastical solidarity and loyalty to tradition. Wilhelm turned the invitation down, with the strange argument that the king can only act in consultation with his ministers. The 'king of conflict' was now, apparently, advocating the constitutional and originally liberal theory of a constitution. Had the king gone to Frankfurt, then Bismarck would have resigned. The king would not have been able to resist the *grossdeutsch* reform plans entirely, and German history would have turned in a very different direction.

In Frankfurt the majority of the medium-sized states, except Baden, accepted a federalistically even more moderated version of the Austrian project. Prussia was absolutely opposed to the idea, and demanded a right of veto for the major powers and parity in leadership, and it wanted a real parliament. This was in tune with public opinion, as expressed by a conference of delegates in Frankfurt and the German National Society: a reform of the Confederation without a genuine parliament would not be acceptable for the liberal-national movement. Of course, when Bismarck, of all people, called for a parliament it was for tactical reasons, the aim being to counteract Austria's plans while at the same time pacifying domestic opposition in Prussia. But, as we have already mentioned, there was also a long-term aspect. Bismarck was rallying the nation against the princes, he also considered that the German Question could only be solved with a parliament. In that much he was in agreement with the basic demand of the liberals. This was a completely new situation, which could revolutionise the battle-lines which had previously been drawn up. It was no coincidence, but rather an objective identity of interests, when the nationalist movement was closer to Prussia than the reform plans of the Greater Germans and the medium-sized states. In the end, these reforms were not aimed at creating a nation-state — they were too particularist and too Greater Austrian for that, and without a real parliament they were also not democratic. It is easy to regret the failure of these Greater German federalist plans, considering the fate of German and central European nationalism. They were unable to deliver the nationalistic, democratic unity which the liberal-nationalist movement wanted. They were only an alternative if one was prepared to forgo the nation-state or, historically speaking, regard the nation-state as a form of political existence which could be bypassed.

Naturally, for the liberal-nationalists the identity of interests with Prussia had been disturbed by Bismarck, and even his nationalist-parliamentarian demagogy could not change that. But Prussia would not always be identified with Bismarck, and it was believed that Prussian *raison d'état* would eventually lead Prussia to move with the prevailing trends of the times and that, in the end, unity would bring about an advancement of freedom.

The reform failed owing to the determined resistance of Prussia. The original Austrian idea of a special federation (*Sonderbund*) failed, as did any idea of a tougher stance against Prussia, on account of the reservations of the medium-sized states. They were not brave enough to act without, or worse still against, Prussia, and they also feared that a special federation would eventually lead to an Austrian hegemony. Thus these efforts were to no avail. Austria, for the time being, did not further pursue its plans. The Schleswig–Holstein crisis of 1863–64 gave rise, once again, to a co-operation between Austria and Prussia. The matters of Confederation reform and the German Question were shelved for a while.

German policies and the reform of the Confederation were matters concerning not only the governments but, as we have already said, public opinion and the great political movements as well. Furthermore, they were not merely an accompaniment to the comings and goings of governments, but influenced such manoeuvres considerably, even though the laws concerning inter-state and federal activity was quite definitely a matter for the governments. Here, as well, the nationalist commitment of the forces within society came to the forefront with the end of the reaction in 1859. It was in this year that the German National Society was founded, in the shadow of the Italian War — which had posed anew the problem of German security and unity — along the lines of the Italian Società Nazionale of 1856. Liberals and moderate Democrats from various German states came together to form this organisation: Rudolf von Bennigsen, a Liberal delegate from Hanover, Hans Viktor von Unruh, president of the Prussian National Assembly of 1848, Hermann Schulze-Delitzsch, founder of the co-operative associations and politically a Democrat — these were the principal leaders. Fedor Streit, a Democrat, became general secretary, and the headquarters of the organisation were in Coburg. The programme of the organisation followed on from the Reich Constitution of 1849: a German nation-state with a central government, a powerful national parliament and universal suffrage — liberal-federalistic and *kleindeutsch* under Prussian leadership; even the more moderate ideas of the 'Gotha' Union politicians of 1849–50 reappeared here. People were seeking an 'Italian solution', because one of the things they had learned from the failed revolution of 1848 was that union in central Europe could not be achieved directly by the people, but rather by means of a co-operation between a large popular movement and one or more of the leading states. The society was designed to be an organ of agitation and propaganda, which would, by means of publicity and rallies, influence public opinion in favour of freedom and unity and against particularism and foreign threats — such as Napoleon's speeches about natural boundaries.

The society received a great deal of support and built up a cross-frontier membership in all the German states — which in itself was a revolutionary feature — of 25,000; the Confederation could no longer suppress such a movement in the face of opposition from the constitutional governments and the mood of the New Era. The society did, however, remain one of dignitaries; the fact that the membership fee was an annual one made sure of that. This was completely in tune with the liberal style of politics; even the Democrat members of the main committees, who tended to rely more on the support of the masses, could not change that. Even so, this society was a large, spontaneous and popular movement; the nationalist motive brought 'Old Liberals' and 'Old Democrats' together and helped to establish peace between these two parties. The society very much brought public opinion back into the discussion of the German Question and in favour of the *kleindeutsch* solution. It is true that the organisation was a pressure group and not a political party; it did not have to make political decisions or carry through political actions. It did not need to resolve differences within its own ranks, but could cope with these by means of verbal compromises, tactics and careful manoeuvring. The *kleindeutsch*, pro-Prussian aims were never completely publicised. The genuine *kleindeutsch* supporters believed that, in the face of the brutal Prussian–Austrian dualism, a decision would have to be made one way or the other, and this decision would have to be for Prussia; this was because Prussia was the only power capable of uniting Germany, and because the Prussian ambition and spirit of self-preservation would objectively lead to a German national policy. The differences between Greater Prussian power politics and the policies of national unification, which were always being highlighted by the anti-Prussians, were of little importance to them; they believed that it would be the very unification of Germany which would bring about a liberalisation in Prussia. But the existence of a great deal of anti-Prussian feeling, the persistence of an emotionally based sympathy for *grossdeutsch* ideals, and a reluctance to talk in the hard terms of power politics about sharply contrasting attitudes and opinions or, put another way, because nobody wanted to be held responsible for the division of Germany — all these factors explain why the society was so very cautious in its tactics. This, however, did not spare it from the dilemma of nationalist politics. When Prussia, since the autumn of 1862 under Bismarck, embarked upon the policies of confrontation and reaction, of iron and blood, the society started its downward slide: Prussia lost prestige in liberal Germany; no liberal (before 1864 at least) could imagine agreeing on any kind of nationalist policy with such a Prussian regime; Prussia seemed to be failing once and for all in its German mission. The question of nationhood seemed to be blocked — neither Austria nor the medium-sized states nor a democratic revolution were able to offer an acceptable or realisable alternative. The only hope was that there would be a change of government in Prussia. The situation began to change, very slowly, after 1864.

In opposition to the Lesser Germans, just as in 1848 but now with renewed strength, were the Greater Germans. It is important to understand the force of this fundamental difference of view: in this decade it was the nationalist-political split which ran deeper than all the other party political contrasts, which made people overcome old differences and form new alliances, which caused the battle-lines to be redrawn. In October 1862, in connection with the federal reform plans of an ever more liberal Austria, the Deutscher Reformverein (German Reform Society) was set up in opposition to the German National Society. The objectives of this organisation were to mobilise popular opposition to the *kleindeutsch* monarchical programme. Alongside the universalistic and particularistic opponents of the nation-state, the Catholic anti-Prussians and Greater Germans, there were also liberals and democrats, and not just from Austria: the old politicians of the Paulskirche, the constitutional-liberal and originally *kleindeutsch* Heinrich von Gagern, the left-wing liberal Moritz Mohl and the 1848 radical Julius Fröbel. This society had a wide membership base, particularly in Bavaria and Württemberg, in Hesse and Hanover. Of course, this peculiar alliance of conservatives, clericals and democrats could not really survive in the long term. The programme of reforms to turn the Confederation into more of a federation of states — the directorial executive and the indirectly elected, almost powerless parliament — could only cover up the differences between the supporters of the status quo and the liberal-democratic proponents of *grossdeutsch* unity and power; it could not resolve them. The aim of the reforms, to renew the 1815 foundation of the Confederation with more unity and more freedom and to unite Prussia and Austria — the dream of the *grossdeutsch* patriots — could not be achieved; after all, this did not conform to the crisis of the Confederation, it did not correspond to the crisis of the times. In the end, agreement could only be reached on the negatives. The estrangement between the Austrian 'Kaiser's state' and the democratic-parliamentary nationalist ideal turned out to be irrescindable, and in 1866 it was even more marked than that between Prussian military monarchy and nationalist democracy. When the reform policies of Austria and those of the medium-sized states failed after 1863, the German Reform Society also lost respect and influence. The dilemma clearly appeared to be that a nationalist solution was not possible with Austria, while a liberal solution was not possible with Prussia.

The *kleindeutsch* and *grossdeutsch* arguments over federal policies were accompanied by the great propaganda and academic arguments of both schools of thought. In no way was the open or latent pro-Prussian liberalism the prevailing force. Both the *kleindeutsch* historians, for example, and the *grossdeutsch* federalist historians played an important role: Johann Friedrich Böhmer of Frankfurt, Onno

Klopp of Hanover, Constantin Frantz and the Bavarian Edmund Jörg, editor of the *Historisch-Politische*. They all employed historical arguments in the struggle against the 'Prussianisation' of Germany. In 1860, Klopp described Friedrich II as the 'vitiator' of German history, warned of Prussia's expansionism and oppressive military system, and later of the *kleindeutsch* 'architects' of history. The argument in Innsbruck between Heinrich von Sybel and Julius Ficker about the German 'Kaiser politics' of the Middle Ages is now famous: Sybel's criticism of the universalistic and Italy-orientated policies of the Kaisers and their disintegrating effects on the organisation of the Reich, a criticism which is gauged on the norms of the nation-state, and Ficker's riposte, an historical explanation of the Kaiser system, based on its own presuppositions and not ours. In academic terms, Ficker was right, but even he used this to defend and legitimise his own political, i.e. *grossdeutsch* universalistic, views. This is only one example of many which show how political conflicts can be argued out in the form of an historical debate and how the *kleindeutsch/grossdeutsch* conflict determined the battle-lines both in the world of *Realpolitik* and political ideology.

At least as important as the arguments about reform and hegemony in the German Confederation was the conflict concerning economic union and hegemony, the fight over the Zollverein. The question of Austria joining the Zollverein was postponed in 1853; negotiations were rescheduled for 1860. Prussia had been able to fend off this assault on its dominant position in finance and trading. But the question was now up for discussion. It was a great political question, but it was also a question of economic interests. Prussia, economically strong and relatively advanced, saw its interests best served in a system of free trade; it was not only the bureaucracy, businessmen and academic intelligentia who supported this position, but also the majority of producers, the large-scale landowners in the north-east who produced and exported corn, and most parts of industry, despite resistance in the iron and textile sectors. By contrast, Austria had for decades been practising very protectionist policies; the Austrian economy, which was only in the initial stages of industrialisation, was dependent on the continuation of these protectionist customs regulations. The worldwide recession of 1857 had reinforced both these tendencies. Furthermore, Austria was not particularly attractive as a market; it was in an advanced state of financial ruin; the war of 1859 had more or less led to a collapse.

However, Austria stuck firmly to its economic policies and power-political plans. In 1859, Bruck once again undertook an intensive attempt to get Austria into the Zollverein; this was in the interests of Austria, but also held out the possibility of a great central and south-eastern European economic bloc. Naturally, a Zollverein which included Austria would have been more protectionist than suitable for Prussian trade and industry, but Bruck was quite prepared to lower customs tariffs for Austria — although this did provoke determined resistance from the Austrian textile and mining industries. Initially, however, it was all a question of power politics. The states of southern Germany supported, just as they did at the beginning of the 1850s, Austria's efforts to join for federal-political reasons; Prussia opposed them. In 1860, it even refused to carry out the agreed negotiations on the grounds that a positive result was not to be expected. At the same time, Prussia started negotiating a trade agreement with France. This was a prudent move from the point of view of trade, as France had just completed a trade agreement with England (the Cobden Treaty) which marked the final transition of the world economy to the free-trade phase; the Zollverein could not remain unaffected by that. But the exchange of trade with France was not of primarily important economically — at least as important for both Paris and Berlin were the power-political motives. Prussia kept the momentum of these negotiations going in order to pre-empt Austria's counteractions, and especially in order to seal Austria's exclusion from the Zollverein once and for all; Austria, it was realised, would never be able to accept the free inflow of French goods as well, and furthermore Austria would lose, on account of the 'most favoured status' clause, all the benefits it had under the trade agreement it completed with the Zollverein in 1853. Apparently Prussia wanted, as the military hegemony was not realisable, to guarantee and reinforce its economic hegemony in Germany. In a great counter-offensive, Austria mobilised almost the entire Third Germany against this blackmail by Prussia, apparently with success. But in spite of this pressure, Prussia and France completed the treaty in 1862 — a kind of trade-policy Villafranca for Austria.

But the final, decisive battle was now about to begin. Austria categorically demanded to be admitted to the Zollverein in 1865, and therefore that the agreement with the French be rescinded. At first, Prussia seemed to be isolated. Württemberg, Bavaria, Hesse–Darmstadt and Nassau were all staunch allies of Austria, mainly for federal-political reasons; they rejected the ratification of the French treaty and declared that they would only renew the Zollverein in 1865 if Austria were allowed to join. Otherwise they planned either a special union with Austria or a triadic solution. Public opinion and the interested parties, now concerning themselves with the economic aspects, participated in the decision-making process on a hitherto unknown scale; they attempted to influence the governments concerned. The *kleindeutsch* liberals, the German National Society and the Kongress Deutscher Volkswirte (Congress of German Economists), primarily a north German free-trade lobby, all decided in favour of Prussia; the Deutscher Handelstag (German Association of Trade and Commerce), in which Austria was also represented, narrowly decided in October 1862 in Munich by 102 votes to 93 in favour of the Prussian solution. Many of the pressure groups and representatives of interested parties in the medium-sized states were opposed to the French contract and in favour of Austria's admission to the Zollverein. The majority of Austrian industry, on the other hand, was opposed to Austria joining the Zollverein, as this would have meant that Austria would have had to relinquish its protectionist policies. Such a step would, *de facto*, have considerably hindered Austrian industrialisation, if not thrown it backwards; the political energy of the government was continually being weakened by this opposition. Regardless of all these shifts and stratagems, Prussia ratified the French agreement on 2 August 1862 and made the planned renewal of the Zollverein in 1865 dependent upon everybody accepting this treaty. Prussia put everybody under pressure by threatening to disband the Zollverein, and Bismarck now quite intentionally set out to mobilise the 'material interests' of the German people for Prussia and the Zollverein and against Austria. In the end, Prussia won. Not even Austria was able to promote the triadic solution favoured by Bavaria. The overriding economic considerations meant that the medium-sized states had to ally themselves with Prussia, and the pro-Austrian protectionist minority, including, for example, the industry of Württemberg or the textile industry of southern Germany as a whole, could not change this. Austria's attempt, for instance, to win the support of Saxony for a disbandment of the Zollverein failed; the anti-Prussian minister Beust explained in unequivocal terms that an industrial state such as Saxony was unfortunately not able to dispense with the advantages of free trade with France and the links with Prussia. The economic fact that Prussia was in control of about nine-tenths of the mining and metal industries, two-thirds of heavy industry and almost one-half of the textile industry now came to bear. During 1863–64, on account of the common policy with Prussia in the Schleswig–Holstein question, Austria was no longer able to sustain the confrontation. In the end, there was not even a compromise in the form of a conservative solidarity between the great powers. A customs union was definitely out of the question; indeed, the Prussian Trade Minister considered — in disagreement with Bismarck — that even a trade agreement with Austria would be economically and politically damaging and superfluous. The life-and-death struggle over trade policies ended in victory for Prussia. Austria's offensive failed in the face of the counter-offensive from Prussia. The trade agreement which Austria did in the end complete with Prussia and the Zollverein in 1865 sealed it.

This was a preliminary round in the resolution of the German Question. German unity was not based on iron and blood alone, but in at least equal measure, to use a famous quote from Keynes, on iron and coal. It is true that this decision was not final; the medium-sized states continued to believe that they could be economic allies of Prussia and federal-political allies of Austria. We know from the development of the EEC that there is no automatic concurrence between economic union and political union. If, for instance, the question of German unity had not become acute until after 1873, then the conflict of interests would have been accompanied, within the framework of the Zollverein by the new confrontation between the protectionists and the free traders; the customs-political interests would have been less clear. Despite the economic decisions that had now been made, the power struggle, which was to be decisive in the final event, had merely been postponed.

6. Politics and Society: Changes in the Parties

Counter-revolution and reaction were, for a while, able to govern, supported by the army, the police, and the once again disciplined state machinery, regardless of the political movements and forces within society; to discipline, suppress and ignore the opposition. But they could not do so permanently. This was not a totalitarian age. It was not possible to govern against the people, to levy taxes, to expect loyalty and motivation. The peculiarly peaceful and bloodless end of the reaction and the transition into the New Era are clear evidence of that. But all the politicians of the reaction knew that the shock of defeat would not immobilise the activist party for ever, and neither would the fear of a radical, red revolution. The more clever ones also realised that they would have to base their politics on forces within society. After all, politics was dependent on the condition of, and especially the changing political currents within, society.

Let us remember: the 1850s and 1860s were a time of great surges forward in industry and the economy, the time of the breakthrough of the Industrial Revolution and, despite setbacks and crises, a time of accelerated growth and a booming economy. This had considerable effects on all sectors of the economy and all social levels and for society in general. The pauperism crisis was cushioned, the scissor-effect of an expanding population and stagnant labour market was stopped, and although the situation of the working classes did not markedly improve until the 1860s, it had certainly stabilised since the crisis of the 1840s. The danger of a social revolution was diminishing. The situation of the peasants, including the small peasants, was improving. Even the crisis in the handicraft trades was bottoming out, and the new co-operatives provided a means of modernising the handicraft trades and helping them to come to terms at least somewhat with the modern market economy. For the bourgeoisie, the middle classes, the dynamic development of the economy became increasingly important; they were able to improve their station in life by means of employment and investment opportunities, the boom in building and railways etc., the spread of share ownership, and speculation. Incomes and prospective living standards grew; the middle classes became wealthier. Altogether the world became more modern, urban, industrial, commercial, rational, mobile and dynamic, and less traditional. Class differences became more apparent. The entrepreneurs, the economic bourgeosie, arose from the traditional middle classes; a proportion of the smaller artisans became members of the working classes, which were formed by the amalgamation of these craftsmen and the old rural and urban lower classes. The non-bourgeois power of the big landowners, the social basis of conservatism, was further established and reinforced; the economic successes resulting from the modernisation of agriculture proved to be of particular benefit to the Junker class and thereby lent a new, material basis of support to their claims to authority, even in the modern world. Furthermore, the middle bourgeosie, not only became wealthier, they also underwent social changes; they became more differentiated as far as situation and employment, income, interests and values were concerned. Seen through the eyes of history it was, in fact, a fast and very concentrated social modernisation.

However, we must not overlook the strengths and remnants of traditions which quietly survived these upheavals. Germany was still a country of rural areas and small towns; industry still did not play a dominant role by any standards, and mentalities were naturally much slower to change than were economic relations. Both industrialists and craftsmen still felt that they belonged to the bourgeoisie, the middle classes. Of course, more than a century later it has become much more obvious, but the writers were already beginning to observe it in those days: this modern world had become less safe, more uncanny; there was a price to be paid for modernity, and there would be crises of modernisation, especially where modern social and economic situations were coexisting with traditional mentalities and institutions. This was the case in the Germany of concentrated modernisation; it became, after the crisis of the 1870s and until 1933, a major problem of the political culture. But the effects of this were cushioned during the two decades we are concerned with here; these were principally times of growth: because there were no crises, resistance to modernisation decreased while confidence therein increased.

Naturally, the bourgeoisie and the modern economic forces became stronger; they gained influence in comparison with the old, aristocratic, military and bureaucratic power elites, despite the advances made by agriculture and the landed classes. Because the bourgeoisie became the leading group, or at least one of the leading groups, in the modern economy, tension grew between the new social power structure and what was, in effect, the old, pre-industrial, pre-bourgeois system of rule. But this was not a clear and simple confrontation between opposites, and the tension was not revolutionary; it was cushioned by the growing, if unevenly distributed, prosperity. Furthermore, it was weakened by the differentiations among the non-aristocratic classes, the non-identity of members of the bourgeoisie and peasantry, and the blatant contrasts between the bourgeoisie and the workers. The peasants and workers were social forces outside the polarisation of the world of commoners and the world of the aristocracy. In short, the balance of power within society was unstable and ambivalent.

This meant that, as far as questions of the distribution of power were concerned, decisions were made by means of political processes. But these decisions had a new character; they were now more closely related to the relationships of social forces. The character of politics was altered; in particular, the liberal concept of politics became more difficult. Where the conflicts of interest become sharper and perhaps reach a crisis point, the idea that a consensus can be arrived at by means of discussion and compromise, or that a majority decision can be made, becomes less convincing; the 'common good' would seem to lie outside the sum of liberal individual and group interests; the old state, the new nation, the socialist people would perhaps be better suited to solving the problems of the time. In any event, the simple comparisons of movement and inertia, monarchy and democracy were no longer sufficient. In Germany, as in France, the problem of new forms of politics became obvious: Caesarist–Bonapartist, plebescitary, nationalistic, socialistic. The basic left–right scheme of things remained, but now it was a very chequered version. The questions of how to solve the social problem, how to solve the national problem, and how to resolve the conflict between the modern civil society and the church, challenged the classic battle-line formations — neither the ideal of the proscription of power nor that of the maintenance of stability and traditional structures was sufficient. The age-old question of means and ends was also a topical subject. If politics was a struggle between classes, where the aim was to mobilise the forces within society in favour of one's own interests and against one's political opponents, i.e. if politics was a fight about class, could not conservative ends also be achieved by revolutionary means, and revolutionary ends by conservative means? In the face of such questions, the previous contrasts and styles of the political parties became outdated; new liaisons and new versions came into existence, in particular a new liberalism and — with Bismarck — a new conservatism.

Along with the sociological and political changes came also great changes in the psychological climate, in the general view of life and the world. We discussed this earlier in connection with religion, science and the arts: the end of idealistic philosophy, the dominance of the empirical sciences, the natural sciences and the historical sciences, and the gradual separation from their romantic-idealistic origins; the insistence on the principles of experience, fact, experiment, i.e. positivism; the decline of organised religion, at least in leading and educated Protestant circles, the advance of agnosticism and occasionally of vulgar materialism, and of the substitute religions, of belief in the family, work, art, the nation, the society of the future; the turn to 'reality', i.e. to realism in the arts; belief in progress and a feeling of alienation; a split in the view of the meaning of life — on the one hand, an optimistic belief in development, which should not be judged on its platitudes and trivialities, but on the seriousness of the scientific, technical and economic mastery of the world, and on the other hand, pessimism, sorrow and a loss of meaning, for which the popularity of Schopenhauer and the redemptive music of Richard Wagner became so important. One cannot simply put these trends and factors in the interpretation of life itself on a parallel with the social and economic developments of the time. They are *sui generis*. For political orientation they became as important as the material displacements.

(a) The Liberals

It was the great political movements, the parties, which tried to shape the politics and society of the times. The centre of the political stage in Germany during these decades was occupied by the Liberals.

The Liberals were the defeated party of 1848–49; they had to come to terms with this. People have often spoken of the retreat of the liberal bourgeoisie into private life and a loss of interest in politics, of withdrawal into introspection or a diversion of attention to economic activities, a passion for earning money. This, however, is inaccurate, even fundamentally untrue, and is merely the result of the moralising of literary critics. Naturally there was a wave of disappointment, resignation and frustration, particularly among the average citizens (Wilhelm Raabe's novels bear reliable witness to this fact), and certainly there was a forced exclusion from the political arena. But when the reaction came to an end in 1859, all the Liberals, who had supposedly given up politics altogether, were once again on the scene, and a whole new generation was there with them; the emerging economic bourgeoisie supported liberalism. The story of a retreat is merely a legend.

The Liberals of the 1850s were coming to terms with their defeat and pondering on the reasons for it. The power of the opposition and the size and variety of the problems concerned were part of this; the debate still continues about whether it was the hesitation of the Liberals or the vehemence of the radicals which forfeited what could have been achieved, and what role social problems had played. At the same time, people tend to think much more in political terms and put a political meaning on what were primarily social tensions. In any event, the defeat is regarded as a temporary one; it was the loss of a battle, not of the entire war.

Some liberals persisted in the old ideas — the dualism of parliament and government, the ideal of a moderate constitutionalism and the politics of consensus or, in weaker terms, the left-wing liberal-democratic idea of the people's state and the alliance between the bourgeoisie and the masses; this was their way of trying to come to terms with the experience of revolution and defeat. Of course, there were still idealists and doctrinaires who wanted to preserve the ideals and not dilute them with compromises, who had an unshakable belief that right was right and that it would eventually triumph over unpleasant reality.

More interesting, and in the long term more important, are those who, in the self-critical analysis of their own failure, underwent a reorientation. This was a change in favour of realism, a move to 'Realpolitik'. In a famous essay in 1853, *Principles of Realpolitik as Applied to the Current Political Situation in Germany*, the journalist Ludwig von Rochau was the first to explain the new position, and the catchword of the following decades — *Realpolitik* — was thereby firmly established in the political vocabulary. The opposition of the Vormärz and the liberalism of the Paulskirche were unworldly, idealistic and utopian — concerned only with theories, doctrines and arguments of principle and justice; without a sufficient awareness of what was possible, of what could be done, they allowed the hour of decisive action to pass them by. In politics, it is reality alone that counts; it is not ideas, but only forces that can unite Germany. Politics is not concerned with norms — so the polemical version went — but with experience, and the world of political experience is based upon power, the 'natural law' of power. This is Machiavellian realism — especially when, alongside power, success is identified as the goal and yardstick of politics. This may sometimes seem cynical, the reality of power against norms, and naturally we do not want to have moral norms pushed completely to one side. But we also know that politics with a moral base, e.g. the claim on the zones of eastern Germany, can become unreal, that responsible politics has to make allowances for reality. A nostalgia for the upright politics of feeling, ideals and norms alone destroys all real politics.

We should not overburden the angry confrontation between *Realpolitik* and the politics of feeling in 1853. The objective was not to abandon one's own beliefs and simply adapt to the prevailing circumstances for the purpose of gaining power. The aim was to reorganise one's own goals with regard to the long-term prospects and to develop a corresponding strategy for altering reality. The liberals had to come to power, but first they had to become capable of governing. In order to do this, they had to understand what is meant by the 'forces' which supposedly are the only factors which count in politics. These include not only the ruling political powers, but also — and this is the bridge between ideas and reality — public opinion, generally held convictions; it is here that ideas and justice become tangible political power. A further factor is the major social class, as it is this class which will eventually also become the dominant political group. This was, of course, in the middle of the nineteenth century, the bourgeoisie. The expectations and goals of this class of society derive their force not because they are based on some abstract truth, but because they are based on its own social and economic interests. This is where liberalism derived its power to change prevailing circumstances; this is why it had time and the trend of history on its side. But it had to adjust to this, its real self-interest basis. If liberalism is not based on theory and principle alone, then it must, more decidedly than ever, recognise that it is a movement of the bourgeoisie, a middle-class party, even though it will never relinquish its claim on being based on a classless principle.

In all this realism one cannot fail to see a peculiar optimism, which recognises one's own ideas within reality and sees them making advances. This is the realistic-empirical reforming of the old idealism. It is this which sustains the difficult distinction between realistic politics and purely opportunistic adaptation.

This change of attitude in favour of reality and pragmatism, and against the abstract 'what should be', pure ideals and what is 'right', was in tune with the general trend of thought at the time; it involved the rejection of ideal constructions, a building of rules and norms, and of deductive inferences. There are many such moves towards reality and *Realpolitik* within political liberalism. Rudolf Haym, for example, a moderate constitutionalist, in a very influential book, *Hegel and His Times* (1857), made this change in a completely different, i.e. a philosophical, manner: he relativised Hegel by describing him as a philosopher of the Prussian restoration, and deliberately and decisively separated politics and political objectives from the functions of abstract and speculative reasoning and from the pre-historic theory of natural laws, basing it instead on experience and history.

This change in favour of 'realism' also entails a new and now even more intensive orientation on that science of experience, history; the connecting link of idealist tradition. The 'fantastic idealism' of philosophy is replaced by the 'real idealism' of history — this is the way in which Max Duncker, the historian and liberal politician, described the process. History becomes, for a time, the leading science for the legitimisation of objectives or circumstances; it delivers arguments; it is referred to in political debate; people expect history to provide a solution. It destroys the normative reasoning of explanation and the idealism of philosophy, but it firmly anchors once again the norms and goals in the historical trends and conditions. The part of German history we are concerned with here, that of the 1850s and 1860s, turned against Ranke's 'objectivity' and against the idea that the context of history is unrecognisably conveyed to us only in God, and it turned against a straightforward positivism of historical facts (or laws). It was 'engaged' history, and intentionally so. It was concerned with norms and values, and, more precisely, with the liberal and nationalistic objectives. These were based on the course of history, its telos; because history is the progressive march to freedom, the progressive march to nationhood. In concrete terms, this means that history is against reaction; it is on the side of liberalism. The rise of the bourgeoisie and the development of a nation-state were inexorable; the state had to be liberal and nationalistic, in order to meet the historical requirements of the times. Only in this way does it gain élan and force, only in this way could it function properly. Once again, this is the peculiar optimism of history: power shall go to the bourgeois forces. This engaged history is not solely, but is certainly mainly, *kleindeutsch*. But all liberals were now using history to justify and support their programmes. That was part of the new realism. This was by no means a surrender of liberal ideas; rather it was, in the final analysis, aimed not at confrontation with the prevailing relations, but instead at reforming them, at a gradual and continual alteration; liberal historicism is — in contrast to socialist historicism — not revolutionary, but reformist.

Another part of the change to realistic liberalism — and this is much more modern and lies outside the idealism and traditions of the Vormärz — was the attention to the area of economics. Economic interests, economic growth, and economic crises became basic socio-political factors and were recognised as such. Economic policy became a central part of politics as a whole. Economic interests within the — liberal — parties formed their own pressure groups and influential wings; but all politicians, everybody who was interested in politics, everyone who took part in public debates, now realised the importance of economic matters. This was a completely different situation than in the Vormärz.

Reality: experience, facts, power; public opinion and classes of society as political forces; the dynamic rise of the bourgeoisie and its productivity; history, economics — these are the new points of orientation of the new, changing liberalism. The justifications were altered. What this meant in terms of concrete political goals and strategy, we shall discuss shortly. The following point must be made clear first of all. Of course, liberalism still included a very wide range of political positions; there had been wings and groups since the 1840s. The reasoning and justifications were also not uniform. There were still the old positions of constitutionalism and dualism and the varying attitudes on the importance of the state and the individual, institutional limitations of power and people's rights, and it was by no means only the chief actors of the Vormärz or the revolution who thought in these terms, but also new liberals, younger people. There were various links between the old-fashioned idealism and the new realism. From the basis of the new realism, it was possible to draw left-wing or right-wing conclusions, to set various priorities, and to engage more decidedly in either co-operation with the existing powers or in confrontation. More important now, though, was the exact opposite situation. The liberalism of 1860 was, for all its diversity, a unified force, a great political movement; the divisions of the Vormärz and revolutionary periods pale into insignificance against this new unity. Even the Democrats, who in the 1850s — in so far as they had not been forced to emigrate — were resentfully withdrawing from political life and boycotting elections, were now, since their re-entry into politics during the time of the New Era, allying themselves with the Liberals, albeit with the exception of a handful of radical loners. The common goals and common opponents became more important; what was now significant was the bourgeois, liberal-democratic and nationalist movement, the legacies of 1848 and, first and foremost, the renewed activist party.

With the end of the reaction and the beginning of the New Era this liberalism returned from its withdrawn position, from its semi-silence almost, and quite suddenly re-entered public life. It also proved itself to be the leading force in bourgeois society; its branching into the various sections of this society became more concentrated and intense, and this was the basis of its popularity.

One could say, with the historian H. Seier, that liberalism had taken possession of the rostrums and in part also of the pulpits, the arts and the offices. Liberalism dominated in municipal government and the chambers of commerce, in the universities and the secondary schools, in learned organisations and other academically biased clubs and associations; it was dominant in the newly founded national institutions of the educated and business-orientated bourgeoisie, at the Deutscher Handelstag the convention of municipal authorities, the jurists' convention (and, of course, the older learned associations). Furthermore, where necessary, the liberals founded their own organisations, for example the Kongress deutscher Volkswirte towards the end of the 1850s, which became the most important lobby for free trade and Manchester Liberalism, or the Protestant Association of 1863, which was the voice of the liberal and nationalist anti-orthodox clerical Protestantism. The liberals determined the great popular organisations, which now began to engage in political activity: the choral societies, the gymnasts and the marksmen, who formed national organisations at the beginning of the 1860s and celebrated their great national festivals. Coburg, on account of its liberal administration and association procedures, became a centre of the new, Pan-German, liberal organisations. The Vormärz tradition of commemorative festivals and monuments was revived, and it accompanied the liberal movement. The Schiller festivals of 1859, which were dedicated to the popular libertarian, nationalistic, bourgeois poet and moralist — as opposed to the aristocratic and non-nationalist Goethe! — had an effect on a much wider section of society than just the educated classes, extending, for example, among artisans and craftsmen as well; this was symbolic of the new feeling of awakening. New monuments to Schiller, Stein and Jahn were planned, and old, shelved plans were revived, e.g. the Hermann monument in the Teutoburg Forest or the monument to the Liberation of 1813, which the representatives of the German towns — dissatisfied with the princely, federalistic monument of Ludwig I in the Hall of Liberation in Kelheim — recalled with passion in Leipzig in 1863, fifty years after the event. It was almost a foregone conclusion that science and literature, students and all young people were liberals. In addition to this, at last, came the spreading of publicity and propaganda on a local, regional and national basis. The majority of newspapers and journalists became more and more vociferously liberal. Magazines played a particularly important role in the communication and exchange of information among liberals themselves: these ranged from the academic basis of publications such as the *Historische Zeitschrift* (1859), which was inspired by the *kleindeutsch* liberal Heinrich von Sybel, through the elite publication of moderate, constitutional liberalism, the *Preussische Jahrbücher* (1858), which was run by Rudolf Haym and later Heinrich von Treitschke, the older *Grenzboten*, which Gustav Freytag made into one of the great liberal magazines, to the family and household publications, from *Westermanns Monatshefte* to *Die Gartenlaube*. This fundamental wave of bourgeois-liberal attitudes and intentions was registered and articulated by such institutions, organisations and publications, and it was in this way that it was caused to spread out even further.

This great liberal movement came to a head politically in two new organisations. One was the German National Society, which we discussed in the foregoing section of this book. The other new formation was the German Progressive Party. This party first came into being in Prussia during the constitutional conflict, when determined liberals organised themselves as the 'Executive of the National Organisation', as the party of progress. We shall discuss this in more detail a little later on. In almost all parts of the medium-sized states, an equivalent 'party' was formed in 1861–62. These parties, which regarded themselves as one party, had, in contrast to the old liberalism, a concrete programme, better adapted to suit the needs of the times, and clearer lines of demarcation. The old character of a movement was concentrated into a party, although the natural tensions and directional differences were covered up, rather than settled, by generalised principles and liberal rhetoric. This party then began, in contrast to previous practice, to form links, although loose ones at first, between the factions in parliament and like-minded people around the country.

In all places where there were now free elections, and not government-manipulated ones, the Liberals won a majority: 1858 in Prussia — 55% old liberals; 1861 — 40% old liberals and liberal centrists and 29.5% progressives; 1862 — 32% left centrists and 38% progressives; 1865 — 30% and 40% respectively. In Baden 48 of the 63 delegates in 1861 were united liberals; they also had a majority in the Hesse states and in Württemberg.

In sociological terms, liberalism did not limit itself to the educated and wealthy bourgeoisie, but gained access to a relatively wide spectrum of bourgeois groups through the popular associations of chorists, gymnasts and marksmen — it is estimated there were 60,000 chorists and 170,000 gymnasts — and through the more popular magazines and newspapers. But as a party, the Liberals remained an organisation of dignitaries. The style of their politics was that of a political elite, and their decision-making process was no different. This corresponded to the inclinations of this elite group, and corresponded also to the real socio-political situation in Germany. The position of the Liberals regarding the people and the masses was ambivalent; they needed the support of the voters and wanted to represent them, but they did not want a general mobilisation of the masses. They did not want to appeal to elementary emotions and interests; in that respect they believed in ideas and an 'intellectual' programme content, in educating and enlightening the voters. They were not sure whether they could depend on the masses, whether the enlightened people, the representation of which was the primary legitimisation of Liberal claims to power, were identical with the real masses. When, after 1863, the Democrats tried to mobilise the masses, the Liberals again saw in this the methods of the Jacobin revolution. The Liberals certainly wanted to be a party with a wide base of popular support, and they wanted more public participation in affairs of the state and other public matters — but all this had naturally to come about in a well-ordered, controlled manner, led by the educated dignitaries. Intensive contact with the voters and a correspondingly extensive party organisation were not matters for the Liberal dignitaries; this was not their political style. While it is true that the left-wingers were more optimistic, believing that they had the people in the palm of their hand and that they could therefore give way to popular currents of feeling without any fear, the right-wingers were more sceptical. But this was not a decisive split. In fact, the fears and intentions of the Liberals were not as important as their critics, democratic and anti-elitist through and through, claim a hundred years later. The dignitaries' style of politics was conducive to the social situation of the times. There was no politicisation of the masses in Germany at this time; it was decades before this happened, despite social democracy and the centrists. There was much apolitical apathy; politics was still a matter for the ruling classes. A look at the electoral turnout figures for Prussia (Table 36) does, in fact, show an increase in all three classes with the dawning of the New Era and conflict; but in the third class, i.e. the class of the masses, the turnout remains low and only ever reaches about one-third of those eligible to vote.

Table 36: Electoral turnout in Prussia (%)

	Class I	Class II	Class III	Total
1855	39.6	27.2	12.7	16.1
1858	50.2	37.1	18.5	22.6
1861	55.8	42.4	23.0	27.2
1862	61.0	48.0	30.5	34.3
1863	57.0	44.0	27.3	30.9
1866	60.4	47.5	27.6	31.5

Even the conflict, then, did not lead to a mobilisation of the masses; and in the third class the Liberal votes came mainly from the urban and not the rural areas. Of course, the systems of indirect election and public voting safeguarded the political leadership of the bourgeois dignitaries. But on the whole, this corresponded to the situation of the people.

There is an important conclusion to be drawn from these reflections: the Liberals represented the people in as far as they were politically active, enfranchised and actually voting under the prevailing electoral system. They had no mandate over the 'masses'. Liberalism was — although this was only partially apparent — discovering the limits of its popularity: a proportion of the peasants, a large section of the lower classes and the majority of the Catholic sections of the population all lay outside these limits. These factors, then, determined Liberal strategy; the possibility of an extraparliamentary offensive was not available.

One last point on the social character of the Liberal Party: this party of dignitaries continued to come, surprisingly enough, from the educated bourgeoisie. The wealthy and business-orientated bourgeoisie, the new middle classes, were mainly Liberal and voted Liberal, but left the leading role in politics in the main to members of the academic professions. Most of the delegates in the Prussian *Landtag* were still civil servants (50% in 1862) and jurists, who were joined by some members of the independent academic professions.

When talking about the concrete aims of the Liberals during these decades, it must first of all be emphasised that these were the old and classical liberal objectives: a national constitutional state and a civil society. This remained so, this was the continuity which linked them with the traditions of the Vormärz. But the accents and prospects had changed.

Of course, the aim of the Liberals was a liberal state, a state with a constitution without ifs and buts, a state in which the citizens finally get their rightful and major say in the political decision-making process. They were not concerned with a different state, a new constitution or, indeed, democracy. Neither were they concerned (in contrast to the situation in the Vormärz) so much, or finally, with a strengthening of parliament in the dualistic opposition to the government. They were now concerned with the liberalisation of the governmental system, and with the transition to liberal governments, even if this did not necessarily mean government by the Liberal Party. They wanted to transform the existing monarchical state into a civil one, tie the crown to a relative consensus with the parliamentary majority, and break the power of the aristocracy, particularly the 'Junkers', and the military; and they wanted finally to end absolutism and aristocratic rule. One could also say that the English example was now the one to be followed, the French one having been exhausted and devalued by revolution and Caesarism.

There was a stronger sense of the meaning of the state; the tendencies of the right-wing liberals of the Vormärz now became more general. Naturally, they were still concerned with the legal definition and limitation of the power of the state over individuals and their private associations and organisations of self-administration, but the early liberal dichotomy of the individual *versus* the state, the people's parliament *versus* the totalitarian government, freedom *versus* authority, had definitely become less important. The state is not a necessary evil and not a simple means of furthering individual interests, it is also an end in itself. Its function in the international organisation of power, in the control of social processes, in the organisation of education is more than a simple safeguarding of rights; all this means that the state also has its own rights over individuals. Indeed, the state is the agent and guarantor of freedom; this old reformist euphoria retained its effect, or regained it. Even determined left-wing liberals, such as the Prussian Karl Twesten, were now pleading, in contrast to the Vormärz period, for the necessity of a strong state and a strong executive. But they drew liberal conclusions from all this: under the prevailing conditions, the power of the state can only be strengthened by increased participation; what the state needs is a liberal constitution — this would not limit its power, but reinforce it. Others, such as Treitschke, had quite early on assigned the state a superior position with respect to the socio-economic interests of society; this, in turn, meant a strong government. Behind this theory was the doubt as to whether parliament, as a place where opposing interests were balanced or a majority interest was formed, was the only appropriate institution in the face of the conflicts of interest in a class-divided society. With the conservative liberals, the fear of an abuse of freedom, of revolution and anarchy also led to the advocacy of a strong state capable of maintaining order. But, once again in contrast to the Vormärz period, the fear of revolution during these decades of upswing was not widely held or significant.

The old debate on suffrage remained unsettled. The left-wingers, such as Hermann Schulze-Delitzsch, were in favour of universal suffrage; the voters, so went the optimistic theory, would surely vote for wealth and education. Even the Vormärz liberal Karl Theodor Welcker now thought along these lines, although as a safeguard he wanted the minimum voting age to be raised to about thirty or thirty-two years. The right-wingers were concerned by doubts about obtaining a majority and an aversion to plebescites and too much democracy; the plebescite Caesarism of Napoleon and also the mass movements of the Catholics reinforced fears of the 'reactionary' effects of universal suffrage. But the right-wing liberals were under pressure from all those who, for whatever reasons, were in favour of universal suffrage.

The post-revolutionary liberals were also nationalists, and nationalism was still opposed to the ruling elite and the prevailing conditions, i.e. it was left-wing and revolutionary. In the great dilemma between unity and freedom, which had emerged in 1848–50, the emphasis probably shifted slightly in favour of unity. Unity was regarded as a prerequisite to freedom, because freedom could not exist without national security and could not surmount the privations and problems of life in the small, individual states without a great national apparatus and public life, great tasks and responsibilities. Furthermore, unity would, according to the commonly held belief, on account of its reducing Prussia's military burden, give freedom more room for manoeuvre within a military state. On the other hand, liberalisation was a prerequisite for national unification by one of the two great German powers; only a more liberal Prussia, for instance, could make moral conquests. Therefore, freedom was also a prerequisite for unity. The principal fact remained that unity and freedom were closely linked with each other, were two sides of the same coin. Even those who were aware of the chronological priority of unification did not want to postpone freedom *ad calendas Graecas*. For a long time, no liberal could contemplate a national policy in the hands of a Prussia under the leadership of Bismarck; when Bismarck spoke in such terms, it was considered merely as the demagogy of a reactionary. It was not until after Schleswig–Holstein crisis in 1864 that the situation began to change, albeit slowly; it now seemed possible, to a number of Prussian liberals at first, to put foreign policy above, or better still before, domestic policy, in order to achieve freedom through unity. Now the dilemma between unity and freedom became acute and precarious. We have already spoken about the *grossdeutsch/kleindeutsch* dilemma, in which the liberal-nationalist movement unavoidably remained caught up. The nationalist-political split could not be isolated, for instance, in the opposition of the German National Society and German Reform Society; it involved the entire Liberal Party in Germany and was a major factor in its fundamental problems and its breakup. We shall discuss this a little later on.

A central element of post-revolutionary liberalism was the strained relationship with the Catholic church, a tendency to engage in a *Kukturkampf*. The ultramontane reforming of Catholicism increased the tension on both sides. The liberals, who regarded themselves as the leading power of the age, did not merely remain defensive, but quite deliberately adopted an offensive stance; their anti-clericalism, which was also supported by some sections of the Catholic population, easily developed into an anti-Catholicism. The liberal-Protestant interpretation of history — of the Germans and of freedom — and the *kleindeutsch* recourse to the Reformation and the Protestant 'principle' only served to compound the antagonism. Sometimes it seemed, for instance in Austria, that the struggle against the church was the main content of liberal politics. In the 1860s, of course, apart from in Austria and Baden and perhaps Bavaria, this subject was in general not such a dominant theme; the sharp and exclusive demarcation between liberals and Catholics even in day-to-day life was not yet a normal circumstance. But this emotional theme was on the political agenda. On one occasion, the liberals joined forces with the state in the struggle against Catholicism. The state was involved in a fight over 'infringements' of the church, and the liberals allied themselves with the state, or rather attempted to mobilise the state in the first place. Certainly the liberals believed that when they called on the state to act against the church in matters such as schooling, it would be a liberal state that did so. But *de facto* they could not (or did not want to) wait for such a liberal state to come about, and so, wherever possible, they allied themselves with the existing state; in the long-term fight for freedom this was more than problematical. It is, of course, a known fact that the anti-clericalism of this century, even in democratic states such as the French Third Republic, became militant and unscrupulously forced through its own version of freedom administered by the state against the Catholic concept of freedom. But in Germany anti-Catholicism became a basis for negotiation and communication with the bureaucratic, authoritarian state.

Finally, questions concerning the economic and social order, as we have already seen, became a central part of liberal politics in the wake of extensive industrialisation. Against the backcloth of economic upswing and the surmounting of the pauperism crisis, those liberal economic policies which advocated the principles of the free market and competition — freedom of movement, freedom of occupation and, above all, free trade — were generally accepted. The apostles of free trade and Manchester Liberalism at the head of the Kongress deutscher Volkswirte, such as John Prince-Smith, were not, it is true, representative of the entire liberal establishment — they were too missionary, sometimes too doctrinaire, in their belief in economic freedom as a creative force for all other freedoms; they attached too much importance to the dominance of economic policy for that. But almost all liberals were convinced that a free market economy was the best guarantor of stability and growth and the best way of solving the problems of the economy and society and reinforcing liberalism as a way of life and a political force. These political objectives initially strengthened liberalism. The programme was attractive, and the socio-economic conflicts between the upper and lower middle classes, between modern and traditional forces, which had done much to damage liberalism in 1848, had now, in the wake of the economic upswing, been defused for the moment or even overcome. The new economic forces were vehemently opposing all vestiges of state tutelage, obsession with rules and regulations, and high-handed bureaucracy, and were demanding real powers of co-determination for parliament. Of course, the more the state itself adopted the principles of liberal economic policy, the fewer specifically economic reasons and motives there would be for demanding a liberalisation of the system as a whole. This meant that a strategy of co-operation, rather than one of confrontation, would seem to have been the most advisable. Only a minority of liberals were in favour of concentrating on the material foundations of progress. The majority advocated the inclusion of economic interests in the overall liberal system, and for many the tradition of morality (which was independent of markets) played an important role. Gneist, Treitschke or Bluntschli — whose *Deutsches Staatswörterbuch* (Dictionary of the German State), published in eleven volumes between 1857 and 1870, in many ways replaced the old 'Rotteck' *Staatslexikon* — also advocated action by the state, declaring that the state must control the liberated interests of individuals and groups, not least on account of the social consequences of a free market society. On the whole, we can speak here of a kind of bilateral approach: the liberation of economic interests and the market on the one hand, and the priority of 'spiritual (*geistig*) values and the inclusion of the economy in the state system on the other. This argument was never really balanced in this way; these were really the ideological and rhetorical reservations of the educated classes — the establishment of the free market was of primary importance where the current problems of the time were concerned.

We shall deal with the attitude of the liberals to the workers and the social question later on. In general, the liberals still wanted a bourgeois, middle-class society. Of course, they realised now, more so than in the Vormärz, that different classes of society existed, and naturally they also wanted to win the support of, and represent, various groups and interests etc., and certainly they wanted to be regarded as a class themselves. But the liberal and constitutional objectives were supposed to bridge all the gaps between the various middle-class groups; the liberals regarded themselves as a united non-aristocratic society — and this included the peasants. This unity was much more important than many of the differences. This is why the demarcation was so important, particularly that excluding the upper classes, the aristocracy. The opposition of the bourgeoisie to the aristocracy — in so far as the aristocrats had not adopted bourgeois norms and standards — was still elementary and powerful. This extended from parliament to the *Gartenlaube* magazine, daily social life, and the clubs and associations. It also applied to the emerging bourgeoisie, despite a certain tendency to adapt or achieve a balance, as we have observed earlier. In Prussia especially, this opposition to the Junkers, the spirit and rule of the Junkers, was the basis of the political power struggle; Bismarck's provocative style served to polarise the political world in a social way and engender even more solidarity among the liberals. There was also a demarcation against the lower classes. The liberal claim to power was the claim of an advancing, enlightened social class, and it is certainly fair to say that liberal politics were also bourgeois class politics; but — and this was the important factor now — the majority of liberals still believed that bourgeois ideals could be applied to society in general; that the bourgeoisie were the *allgemeiner Stand* (general estate). Members of the other classes would in the long term be given, as a result of liberal policies and the economic developments, the chance to rise to an equal status and participate in political life; this was, at any rate, the ideal.

The liberals wanted power; they wanted to govern. We want now to discuss the strategy they employed to achieve this goal. The change to *Realpolitik*, as became quite clear with August von Rochau, was a move away from the revolution, that mishmash of utopia and anarchy. The revolution, it was proved in 1848–49, had not been a realistic, calculated event, even if this or that aspect could have turned out quite differently: 'A people which gets richer by the day does not make a revolution.' This confirmed the old liberal antipathy. Right-wing liberalism drew from this the conclusion that a stronger emphasis on co-operation would be the correct strategy. Politics — according to Rudolf Haym — needs power; the liberals, who were not yet in possession of power, had to win power; in order to do this they had to co-operate with the existing powers, make compromises, slowly penetrate the opponent from inside, as it were, and draw him towards their own position, to become able to govern in alliance with the old powers and then win power for themselves — because, after all — and this was the reason for such optimism — in the long term the old powers would need the new ones. The politics of the old liberals and the New Era consisted, then, of negotiations, compromises, concessions: reformism as a strategy. Naturally, the liberals were able to carry out this strategy in a much less uncertain, a much more determined manner. But they always had to remember that the essential strategy was to remain within the existing system, for the eventual purpose of altering it in such a way that it would, in the end, be a completely different system. They did not want to engage in 'all or nothing' policies, but in a piece-by-piece reform of small and large steps; they wanted to be not an opposition of principle, but a parliamentary one. This was, in all German parliaments, the difference between the situation of 1840 and that of 1860. This was a sensible, realistic, non-illusionary strategy with definite chances of success; one only had to look at the example of England.

The left-wing trend — even on the basis of the new realism — was confrontation, determined pressure and conflict both in parliament and in public. The liberals believed that they would win this defensive or offensive conflict in the end. No government, no state, could govern against public opinion, against the educated and wealthy bourgeoisie and against the people, which it was supposed to represent, on a long-term basis; the trends of the times would prove to be stronger in the end; the state would only be able to retain power and maintain domestic order with a civil society and a liberal constitution and government. As we have already seen, the liberals were not — on account of their experiences in the revolution, the social problems, their reservations about democracy and the masses, their class position and elitist style — inclined to foster closer connections with the masses or to mobilise them or adopt a radically democratic stance. Only Georg Gottfried Gervinus, who was more of a right-wing liberal in the Vormärz period, made a determined change to a democratic line during the 1850s. Even left-wing liberals who thought on more egalitarian lines and favoured more contact with the masses, such as the founder of the co-operatives, Schulze-Delitzsch, did not, when it came to a conflict, subscribe to a radically democratic strategy. This was, of course, in accordance with reality: the people and the masses could not easily be mobilised further and also were not unreserved supporters of the liberals. Their strategy in the event of conflict, therefore, was based largely on hope.

Liberalism in Germany was, surprisingly enough, from the dawning of the New Era to the climax of the Prussian constitutional conflict, i.e. between 1859 and 1864, a unified force. There were various wings and directions: in Prussia, for instance, the old liberals of Baron Georg von Vincke's faction, always ready to negotiate, and then the determined men of the Progressive Party, and in between them a faction of 'left centrists', who, however, tended to align themselves with the Progressives on the major issues; and there were also various factions and groupings within the Progressive Party itself, in Prussia as in other German states, consisting mainly of moderates and radicals, constitutionalists and democrats, all of whom had varying views on the principal subjects — constitution, the economy and society, the church, nationalist policies, and so on. From this it can be seen that, especially with regard to Germany as a whole, German society was still very much particularised and not very homogeneous. There was still no civil political nation, no common political culture upon which liberalism could base itself. The political and social experiences and objectives in the individual states, in the regions, in the various sections and classes of society were different, and these divergences could not easily be joined together and integrated. This heterogeneity was damaging to German liberalism. The existence of various wings was only natural and need not have destroyed the unity in any way. But the heterogeneity did make unity more difficult and did, without a doubt, impair the appeal of liberalism beyond the one-third of voters who were politically active. It is precisely for this reason that it is surprising how the common liberal and nationalist goals engendered a great feeling of unity.

It was the national political differences which split the liberal movement again in the middle of the 1860s, and revived the socio-political divergences and the old division between Liberals and Democrats. Outside Prussia, *grossdeutsch* and *kleindeutsch* trends within the liberal movement were blocking progress on decisions and actions and in some places, such as Baden, virtually paralysing the movement. In other places, particularly in connection with the Schleswig–Holstein crisis of 1864, the Democrats split from the Liberals. Württemberg is a classic example. Here the *grossdeutsch*, anti-Prussian tendency united with the egalitarian-popular one, an anti-Manchester economic policy, a disapproval of a moderate strategy, and support for an alliance with the workers. Similar situations arose elsewhere, especially in the Rhine–Main region and in Saxony. The root cause of all this — despite the many differences over constitutional and social policies — was anti-Prussianism. Unity was maintained in those states where the movement was under great pressure — in Prussia under Bismarck's government, in Baden and Bavaria in the face of the conservative and Catholic, and sometimes particularistic, opposition.

The Democrats wanted a great Pan-German democrat people's party, based on popularity with the masses, to mobilise the masses, the marksmen, gymnasts and the workers. For example, their idea of defensive gymnastics was aimed at the formation of a national, revolutionary people's militia; this was a particularly topical theme during the Schleswig–Holstein crisis of 1863–64, when Schleswig–Holstein associations were springing up all over the place. These associations regarded themselves as being nationalistic and revolutionary and wanted, more or less as in 1848, a republic, even if this did have to be some type of monarchical republic. The large majority of them were bluntly anti-Prussian. But this party and this strategy remained a dream. Outside Württemberg, Saxony and Frankfurt, the party hardly rose above a sect-like status; its potential supporters were unable to agree on a programme or a common stance in either the national or the social issues. It was not able to present a realistic alternative in the areas of freedom and unity.

But even without this separation, the liberals would have split over nationalist policies. They could not simply cover up the national political alternatives with wishful thinking for ever. They had to ally themselves with either the Prussian or the anti-Prussian conservatives in order to be able to continue in active politics. Otherwise, they would have to postpone their politics until some uncertain day of hope and great changes, or wait for a new Caesar. When Bismarck recognisably embarked upon his nationalist foreign policy in 1864, the hitherto evaded question concerning the priority of freedom or unity became acute; this was bound to split the liberals, and even the *kleindeutsch* advocates, once again.

The liberals were the leading political force of the middle classes, of the politically articulate sections of society. But they were hardly the majority of the people, and the existence of non-liberal masses considerably limited their capacity to act in situations of conflict. The liberal movement contained all the inhomogeneous elements of German society; this meant that its unity was always rather precarious. But it was the national political double dilemma, the *grossdeutsch/kleindeutsch* polarisation and the question of the priority of unity or freedom, which impaired liberalism's unity and its capacity to act as a leading political force in the middle of the 1860s. It is, of course, also a fact that it was Bismarck, the exception to the norm, who finally determined what shape German politics would take, forced the liberals into a reactive position and eventually split them. How things would have turned out without Bismarck — what would have happened, for instance, if Wilhelm I had really abdicated in favour of his son Friedrich in 1862 — we do not know. The liberals would undoubtedly have got nearer to achieving their goal of becoming the governing party; maybe they would have had a greater degree of influence on the eventual national solution. But, in the confusion of the German Question and in the face of the national revolution which Bismarck set in motion, it is difficult to see a clear liberal alternative.

(b) Conservatives and Catholics

There is much less to be said about the principal opponents of the liberals: there were fewer new developments and occurrences, and the changes the liberals went through were incomparably more important for the development of German history than those of the conservative and Catholic parties, particularly as the power of conservatism lay with the governments, and that of Catholicism with the church.

The conservatives tended, as a party, to remain unchanged. They fought against the revolution and against the liberals — the extreme arch-conservatives went as far as to consider a *coup d'état* and a revision of the constitution, or even a reversion to an estate-based system, all organised along the lines of their old doctrines and theories; the bureaucratic-statist conservatives, more realistically, were thinking along the lines of neo-absolutism or the reactionary limitation of the constitutional concessions and the manipulation of the parliamentary elections. Eventually the conservatives, particularly in Prussia after 1848, adjusted to the facts of a constitutional system with certain decision-making powers for parliament; the political philosophy of Friedrich Stahl undoubtedly gave both foundation and justification to this change. The constitutional system could certainly be of advantage to the conservatives, because it bound — by means of the upper chamber, in a much stronger manner than previously — the crown to the origins and interests of the old elites, especially the aristocracy, and it fortified — again by means of the upper chamber, the franchise system and constitutional guarantees — the influence and role of the conservatives. Appreciation of these facts resulted in a parliamentary conservatism which used the new system to consolidate its own influence and tried to prevent any expansion of citizens' or parliamentary rights against the crown or the aristocracy. But, because the position of the conservatives did not depend on elections, and certainly not on free elections, popular support was not so important; authority and conviction are what counted. Marginal developments included modern versions of reformist conservatism such as that of the *Wochenblattpartei* ('Weekly Journal Party').

The cleverer and more modern theoreticians and publicists among the conservatives recognised the connection between any form of modern politics and displacements in the relations of social forces and any attempt to found a new, more modern style of conservative politics, e.g. Wilhelm Heinrich Riehl or, even before 1848, Lorenz Stein with his idea of a social kingdom, or the editor of the *Kreuzzeitung*, Hermann Wagener, who later became one of the inspirators of Bismarck's social policies. After all, there were enough strong social groups who were more or less orientated towards conservatism, opponents of the urban, commercial, industrial, academic bourgeoisie, opponents of modernisation and the market economy. The conservatives had merely to mobilise the traditional interests and powers, the old estates, the peasants and the craftsmen, and, of course, orthodox Christian traditionalism, which was so threatened by liberalism, and its wide following among the people. The conservatives, according to these modernists, could not rely on monarchy and the state machinery, on the patriarchal authority of the aristocracy and the church alone, even though the German world was not yet a world of the masses and mass politics. When the New Era and the many liberal organisations came into their prime, the clever Hermann Wagener founded the Prussian people's clubs (*Volksvereine*) in order to win popular support for the conservatives, especially in the towns. This was, however, rather an anticipation of future developments; in the authoritarian world of the normal conservatives these events did not play a decisive role. More important were the conflicts about the reaction and the constitution, liberalisation of the government and the power of the crown, particularist states and German politics. As we have already seen, one of the more pragmatic aspects of the conservative politics of the governments of the reaction was the 'Bonapartist' concept of a policy of economic pacification: an attempt to carry through successfully the emancipation of the peasantry, and to quell the agitation of the craftsmen by means of a limitation or delay in the free choice of occupation, the inception of workers' protection and other social policies, and also an attempt to compromise with the capitalistic bourgeoisie by stimulating the economy and reducing bureaucracy. This was naturally in the general interests of the state, but it also had a purpose as far as domestic policy was concerned: to reduce, or even divert, the pressure of social forces on the ruling authorities. A healthy or, better still, growing economy could, in the long term, benefit the conservative system. But this was, as we have already seen, more an exercise in pragmatic statesmanship than a new conservative recipe.

Alongside the reformist conservatives of the *Wochenblattpartei* and their idea of the reconciliation of the elites, and alongside the social conservatives with their very realistic social analyses — but in a much stronger and, in the long term, more effective way — it was Bismarck who decidedly modernised the ageing style of conservatism, even against the will of the conservatives themselves. In all areas of politics, he turned away from the old politics of ideas, even those of his conservative friends. He relied on realism and self-interest, and did this often with a marked anti-idealistic cynicism. He recognised and accepted the modern conditions of politics, the necessity for a consensus based on plebescite, the people or parliament, the irreversibility of democratic mobilisation and liberal-civil modernisation, and, of course, as we shall discuss later on, the unavoidable reality of the nationalist movement and the question of nationhood. He did not reject and therefore negate the modern movements in politics and society on grounds of political ideology; instead he accepted them as reality. Then he tried to use them in his own plans; to include them in his own, conservative brand of politics, to found a powerful state and a strong government, and to fence liberalism in, but to do all this in partial alliance with these modern forces and, without reservations, to make use of some very unconservative and modern means in order to achieve these ends. This revolutionised conservatism. From the 1850s onwards, Bismarck, particularly in confrontation with the Gerlach brothers, carried out a gradual move away from the old conservative theories; 'Bonapartism' was the charge made by his original supporters, the designation for this rejection of outdated policies. It was the chess-player logic of the realist power-politician, his lack of prejudice against actual and modern forces, against the irresistible currents of the times, and finally the priority he gave to the Prussian reasoning of power over metapolitical conservative principles, which turned Bismarck from a conservative party politician to a man on the sidelines of his party and then between the fronts. In the long term, after 1866, this in turn resulted in the reform of conservatism.

We turn now to the Catholics. Political Catholicism was, even after the revolution, still a mighty latent force, opposed to old or new bureaucratic statism, to modernity and anti-clerical and mostly Protestant liberalism. How, and if, Catholicism organised itself as a party varied and depended on the prevailing situation. In the 1850s, it was regarded as a matter for the church, the clergy and the bishops to formulate and represent the interests of Catholicism. Politics was excluded from the flourishing Catholic associations; these clubs wanted to remain non-political, purely religious organisations. Furthermore, the co-operativeness of most governments during the period of reaction meant that a special Catholic party would have been superfluous; in Baden, the church fought its wild confrontation with the state at the beginning of the 1850s without popular support, without a party.

In Prussia, even the reaction had not completely settled the differences between the Protestant-conservative state and Catholicism. In the Prussian parliament a Catholic faction was formed in 1852, led by August Reichensperger, initially in order to defend the rights of the church and Catholics. This faction, which was dominated by dignataries from the Rhineland, supported constitutionalism and the rights and freedoms embodied in the constitution, and opposed the reaction of both the Junkers and the bureaucrats. In 1853, six conservative aristocrats who did not share this position were forced to leave the group. This is the legacy of constitutionally liberal Catholicism. Of course, this group was otherwise opposed to the liberals; it was more inclined to moderation and mediation. It did not take the side of the liberals in the constitutional conflict, and this weakened its position considerably; it did not yet represent the majority of Catholic voters. In 1866, the survival of this 'party' was uncertain.

As we have already seen, political Catholicism supported, in the main, the *grossdeutsch* side in the great national political conflict; in 1863, for instance, it supported the German Reform Society against the German National Society. In Bavaria, Hesse–Darmstadt and Nassau there was an amalgamation of Catholic, particularist (in Bavaria this is called 'patriotic'), *grossdeutsch*/anti-Prussian and conservative tendencies. In Baden, where there was no great Catholic establishment, this amalgamation resulted, in the middle of the 1860s, in a populist-Catholic movement, a kind of people's party. The *kulturkampf* promoted by the clergy and the bureaucrats, usually the liberals, had finally made its impact felt on the masses: the opposition of so many groups of the 'old' society to the liberal economic legislation and the emotional anti-Prussianism came together here. The situation of the 'clerical' people's party in opposition to the liberal and, in the main, *kleindeutsch* bourgeois party had an enormous effect in the special circumstances of 1870–71. In Württemberg there were different developments: here the *grossdeutsch*-Catholic element remained allied to political democracy, i.e. the people's party, and there was no segregation. The situation in Austria was different again. Here the combination of reaction and the politics of the concordat had unleashed a tidal wave of Catholic and anti-clerical liberalism in the urban bourgeoisie — something unheard of anywhere else in Germany. It is a part of the almost forgotten fate of German Catholicism and its political tendencies that this liberal Austrian element died out in 1866.

(c) The workers' movement and workers' parties

The fate of liberalism during these decades was of tremendous consequence for the fate of the Germans, and it influenced German history for half a century. But a development that in the 1860s was still modest, namely the formation of first one, and then a second, workers' party, was also a matter of great consequence for the period that followed, and is therefore especially interesting. Of course, it is true that in the wake of industrialisation workers' parties were formed in all European societies; in that much German history is nothing extraordinary. But in Germany this happened much earlier than anywhere else. This fact had an influence on both the workers' movement and on German history as a whole. An explanation is necessary.

Let us remember what we have already observed about the developments in society. The working class, the proletariat, dominated by factory workers, only arose very slowly from the masses of manual workers, from rural and urban poverty, from day-labourers, home-workers, apprentices and junior craftsmen. More important than the differences were the common elements of these people's fate and circumstances: unpropertied and reliant on selling their labour and on wages; the fundamental insecurity and lack of social rights, the result of the severing of old ties under the principle of abstract contractual freedom; the persistent and extreme inequality of opportunity, which the modern economic society was to countercheck by means of efficiency and competition; the social and political exclusion from civil society. Slowly, a group or class consciousness developed. One cannot, of course, project the later circumstances and the theories of the proletariat back to the situation of the 1850s and 1860s. At this time, factory work, or even large-scale enterprise as a whole, were not a dominant feature; owing, in particular, to a high degree of mobility, there was as yet no inherited 'workers' lot'; the qualifications, working practices, norms and expectations of the craftsman's lifestyle still played an important role. The beginnings of the workers' movement were shaped by apprentices, small-scale masters and skilled specialists trained in the craft tradition, not by unskilled or semi-skilled factory workers or day-labourers. But the experiences of the new socio-economic system were becoming more intensive, and people were increasingly trying to interpret and understand the new situation.

The beginnings of the workers' movement, both in the Vormärz and during the revolution, were remembered individually and collectively by those involved. But the reaction had suppressed not only the democratic organisations but also the workers' associations, the League of Communists and the Workers' Solidarity Clubs. Furthermore, the strict application of the laws governing associations made it very difficult to form other apparently less 'dangerous' organisations. Even so, there were remains of the old movement both underground and in exile; and assistance and support funds, which were used in local and isolated strikes during the 1850s, were built up and not challenged by the governments.

The New Era saw the revival of workers' associations, which came into existence and spread quickly; in the early 1860s, there were at least 225 of them. These groups, together with the workers' education societies and bourgeois foundations for workers or with workers in them, were part of the liberal-democratic movement and formed the basis of the common opposition to the authoritarian feudal system. It was, in the main, craftsmen and skilled workers who were active in such organisations. Workers in the large and medium-sized factories, the core of the working classes, were much less interested in the formation of these associations.

The next question which we must ask ourselves is: What was the liberal concept of a policy concerning the workers? In general, the liberals believed that the emancipation and free development of society would naturally lead to economic growth, progress and, finally, harmony. They believed in the self-healing properties of society; the social problems were regarded as transitionary symptoms and teething troubles, and not the necessary result of the development of capitalism or even the conflicts between the classes. These views were evidence of a peculiarly trivial optimism. During these times people still believed in the ideal of a society of common citizens which had not yet disintegrated into various antagonistic classes. There was still that old-fashioned trust in individual ability, hard work, thrift and talent, still the belief in the self-improvement of the individual — and reality certainly was not yet contradicting these ideals. The liberals did not believe in the power of collective groups, and they did not believe in an objective and permanent conflict of interests or class between the bourgeoisie and the working classes; they did not believe that the confrontation between these two classes over political or social power was, or would later be, an important theme. As far as the workers were concerned, this meant two things. Firstly, it meant a free market economy. Freedom of movement, freedom of occupation and free trade would not only be in the interests of the bourgeosie, but also in the interests of the workers; it was the system of craftsmens' guilds and the proliferation of state regulations which hindered the free utilisation of labour. This liberal insistence on these rights and freedoms was certainly popular with the workers, who were used to being harassed and checked up on by the guilds, the local authorities and the police. They believed that the state should at long last allow the self-organisation of the labour market. Secondly, when the bourgeoisie was fighting for freedom and unity, constitution and the national state, it was fighting in the interests of everyone, in particular the workers. In the conflict of the age, the important thing was the unity of the one great progressive movement. Every splinter group formation, or special workers' organisation, was in effect a division, and a corresponding weakening, of the movement. This, as Schulze-Delitzsch had continually been stressing since 1862, was the lesson to be learned from the defeat of the revolution in 1848. The workers were a part of the nationalist-liberal movement and nothing more; their economic and political interests were those of progress, identical with those of the bourgeoisie.

It was, then, within this framework of general identity of interests that a policy programme for workers was evolved. This programme was characterised by the central elements of co-operatives, education and self-help. Hermann Schulze-Delitzsch, the propagandist and organiser of the liberal middle-class system of co-operatives, was the recognised champion of a liberal workers' policy in the late 1850s and the 1860s. Co-operatives were supposed to solve not only the problems of the craftsmen and small merchants, but also those of the workers on the basis of the existing structure of society. Co-operatives were supposed to 'democratise' capital, to give the workers a share in capital; this was the idea of the harmonistic social programme. According to Schulze-Delitzsch, the consumer co-operatives were the most important from the workers' point of view, as they represented an approach to deproletarianisation. Next came the production co-operatives, which were designed to turn workers into self-employed small entrepreneurs, to counter the influence of the monopolistic entrepreneurs, and consequently bring about a long-term increase in wage levels. In the event, these ideas did not prevail; the co-operatives became primarily banking co-operatives for the lower middle class, providing finance and capital for their businesses. Consumer co-operatives and production associations were on the decline even under Schulze-Delitzsch, and this trend became even more pronounced in the practice of the new co-operatives. But these developments did not affect the programme or its attractiveness in any way at this stage. Co-operative and association — these were the magic words of the time: they stood for individual self-help and therefore the will to achieve, for responsibility and self-respect, the middle-class thrift ethic, and finally for the solidarity which seemed to be missing in the market economy and consumer society; this satisfied a deep emotional requirement and filled the people with a supersensible pathos of expectation. Even Lassalle, despite all his wild attacks on Schulze-Delitzsch and his petty-capitalist co-operatives, used the production association as a central part of his programme. In terms of social history, the association idea represented the transitional phase of the worker from craftsman to wage-worker; it was in many ways an ideal from the world of craftsmen. When large factories and paid labour spread further and became typical, and the idea of individual advancement lost some of its attractiveness, the production association idea also became less interesting.

The co-operative idea was effective also because all practical suggestions concerning social reform for both the bourgeoisie and the workers could be linked to it. The risks of the lifestyle and working conditions of the proletariat were more of a threat to the livelihood of the workers than the low level of the wages. Help and support funds were started to counteract this; these were financially managed in a variety of ways, but were always based on the co-operative idea. Various other components of the liberal-bourgeois social reforms, e.g. those propagated by the Central Association for the Welfare of the Working Classes, such as company pension funds, industrial tribunals organised on the basis of parity, and other bodies which were designed to replace simple discipline by co-operation, were all based on the idea of solidary self-organisation and member participation.

The liberal co-operatives were not designed as a model for trade unions, that is, they not intended to be strike organisations. In this respect, the liberals were ambivalent. In accordance with their Manchester view of political economy, they were convinced that strikes were useless. If the economic prerequisites for a wage rise existed, then wages would rise without a strike; if these prerequisites were not fulfilled, then even a strike would not bring about a rise in wages. Strikes could only worsen the situation of the workers as well as the companies involved. But it was the libertarian aspect that influenced the majority of theoreticians and parliamentarians to come out in favour of the principle of freedom to organise; the state should not get involved in the nature of employment contracts through bans and prohibitions. When, however, the question of freedom to organise became acute, the liberals found themselves under pressure from Bismarck, who planned to use the freedom-to-organise principle as a weapon against the entrepreneurial bourgeoisie.

The other magic word of liberal worker politics was *Bildung* (education) — meaning useful, practical, occupation-related knowledge and qualifications, a basis for individual vocational advancement. It also meant, from a humanistic point of view, general education, knowledge of heaven and earth, of nature and history, economics and society; it meant rhetorical technique and civilised customs and behaviour; it was the basis of successful co-operative activity and proper participation in politics; it was liberation from the constraints of ignorance and prejudice, the passport to civil society, the beginnings of integration and belonging, of full acceptance of the working classes. Education, for the liberals, was also, of course, an understanding of the basic harmony between capital and labour, and of the wrongness of socialist/communist demagogy. Behind all this was the liberal belief that education itself was the key to the solution of human problems, both of an individual and community nature; science, enlightenment, rationality. The liberals wanted to impart all this to the workers, too. Of course, there were differing views among liberals. The liberals themselves regarded the shortcomings in education primarily as the cause of the problems and the dissatisfaction; they emphasised the integrational function of education. The democrats preferred to stress the critical function of knowledge with regard to the traditional powers, particularly the church; knowledge was ammunition and power, and its purpose was to give the workers an equal place and rights of participation in the democratic people's movement. Seen objectively, this educational activity was the assimilation of bourgeois knowledge, but it was more than that; it was the practising of reflective thought, the basis of self-awareness. This educational motivation and activity later led to the leaders of the workers' parties adopting the not uncomplicated theories of socialism. The workers' educational associations, which were founded to integrate the working classes, were also catalysts for the formation of an independent, political workers' movement.

The liberal passion for learning was keenly adopted by the upper working classes. In particular, the craftsmen took on the educational norms of the bourgeoisie with enthusiasm; this was part of their new horizon of expectations. This was indelibly imprinted into the consciousness of the rising proletarian movement as heirs to the bourgeoisie.

The liberal concept as a whole was aimed at the industrious worker who wanted to become middle class, and these were indeed the people it reached. It was suited to those who still worked as craftsmen and lived in a world shaped by the working conditions and expectations of craftsmen. It was the qualified craftsmen and better-paid workers who were active in these associations. To that extent, the movement was originally the result of a transitionary situation.

The liberals, then, wanted to integrate the workers by means of self-help, co-operatives, education and various reforms. But there was a fundamental ambivalence in all this. On the one hand, they wanted to integrate the workers into the one, great, bourgeois freedom and unity movement, to use them when exerting pressure on the governments. On the other hand, they were afraid of the possibility that the workers would in some way become independent and radical. This fear manifested itself in two different ways. All the workers' education associations were presided over by the bourgeoisie, and they were founded as an integral part of bourgeois politics. Some liberals wanted a paternalistic relationship with the workers, so to speak, seeing them, at that time, as unquestioning followers of the bourgeois movement; they wanted to lead, to create politics for the workers, but to exclude the workers themselves from politics. This was the style of dignitaries. The German National Society, for instance, had an annual membership fee, thereby effectively preventing workers from joining. In 1862, this organisation rejected a call from some 'left-wing' politicians to alter both the amount and the annual collection of the membership fee, so that workers would more easily be able to join. Evidently the bourgeoisie did not want the middle-class character of either the membership or the leadership of the organisation to be altered in any way. The rather badly chosen words of Schulze-Delitzsch, when he spoke of the workers as the born 'honourable members' of the organisation, made this point absolutely clear. Even he believed that the workers would only be able to grow into a role of active participation in democratic processes at a later date and over a long period of time, by virtue of having attained a position of 'comfortable', accumulated affluence. As we have already seen, a large proportion of liberals had strong reservations about universal suffrage, not only because of their own class interests but also on account of a justified fear of a reactionary mobilisation of the masses. The other faction, the democrats, already regarded the workers as a part of the great people's movement and considered that they already had the right of self-articulation; they wanted equal rights for the workers, both in society and in politics. Put another way, the men of the Progressive Party saw their relationship with the workers as a kind of teacher–pupil relationship; they differed in their views of the rights of the pupils to speak out. The liberals were afraid of the possibility of the formation of a left-wing splinter group, and wanted to keep the workers, as well as every other people's or mass movement, out of politics, neutralised or at least canalised; the democrats wanted to mobilise the workers as part of their planned mass movement. But they also wanted to integrate the workers into the common people's movement, and to prevent the formation of any separate workers' organisation, because it would have damaged the common political goal.

There were divisions — and not only towards the liberal paternalists and opponents of universal suffrage, which was an essential issue for the workers. All the policies, both liberal and democratic, relating to the workers were harmonistic and played down the conflict of interest between workers and employers, and all liberal concepts overlooked one of the decisive components in the workers' lot: the level of wages. Everyone wanted to shape the workers in their own image and paid scant respect to what the workers themselves wanted to be, and everyone, as far as possible, ignored and excluded the latent political tensions.

However, the workers' movement, which was revived towards the end of the reaction, was initially a part of the great bourgeois liberation movement. The conflict between capital and labour did not yet dominate everything. Primarily the workers felt, like the socially committed intellectuals, that they were a part of the German unity movement; the social-democratic element was closely related to the nationalist-democratic element. The workers were regarded, like the chorists and gymnasts, many of whom were also workers, as 'pillars of the emerging German nation'. The workers, according to the pointed remark later made by August Bebel, had seen their ideal in the realisation of German unity; socialism and communism were nonsense in their eyes. National unity seemed to be an essential prerequisite to a solution of the social problem, or, expressed in stronger terms, the national-democratic revolution was a prerequisite for the social revolution. A united and free Germany and the abolition of the system of class rule were just as closely related in the eyes of Bebel and Wilhelm Liebknecht as they were for Lassalle. The 'sacred right' to nationhood and to membership of the nation was expressed as a self-evident truth at all workers' meetings; and in 1863–64, of course, solidarity with their brothers in Schleswig–Holstein was also included in these declarations. The tone was the same as that of the German National Society. The leaders of the workers' movement were also convinced that national unity had at least a chronological priority over social emancipation; some even believed that unity would lead to freedom. Furthermore, this goal of a democratic nation-state was not, as Marx believed, merely a functional step in the development of history, but it was an end in itself, and one dear to the heart at that. This is why the conflict between *kleindeutsch* and *grossdeutsch* orientation was such an important aspect of the early history of the workers' movement. But there were completely different reasons for the first splitting away of a socialist party from the liberal-democratic movement as a whole.

This is where Lassalle came onto the scene. In 1862, the German National Society sent a workers' delegation to the world exhibition in London. This visit, incidentally, turned out to be only a moderate success. A question in the public report of this delegation led to concrete plans being made in various places for the formation of a general German workers' congress. A mass meeting of workers in Berlin (2 November 1862), by no means anti-liberal at that time, decided upon Leipzig as the location of the congress, following the example of the Workers' Brotherhood of 1848. Another meeting then elected a committee in Leipzig to take over the leadership of the congress movement. This committee quite clearly distanced itself from the principles of liberal policies regarding the workers; it demanded the right of independent political activity for the working classes, i.e. the wage-workers. The liberals were not exactly enthusiastic about these ambitions; they feared the loss of a section of their mass support and consequently began, under the leadership of Schulze-Delitzsch, a massive, modern, well-organised campaign of propaganda and mass meetings and mobilised the workers' education associations against the congress in Leipzig. In this situation of tensions and divisions, the Leipzig committee — almost by coincidence, some members of the committee had read the 'Workers' Programme' and were impressed by it — turned to the writer Ferdinand Lassalle and asked him to articulate the situation of conflict which the congress found itself getting into with the liberals, and particularly with their pope, Schulze-Delitzsch. Lassalle responded to this request with a new programme, contained in the 'Open Reply' of 1 March 1863. This gave a completely new direction to the developments which now unfolded.

Ferdinand Lassalle, of Jewish descent, had become renowned as a writer on philosophical, legal and political matters. He was also a well-known radical and nationalist democratic revolutionary and socialist; in 1848–49, he had worked in the same area as Karl Marx in the Rhineland. His themes were the state, nationhood, democracy and the social question. Lassalle had failed with his conception of radical-democratic politics; according to his analysis, the nationalist-revolutionary and democratic impetus, even of the new Progressive Party, was broken; the party was not prepared, for example, to take the radical step of a parliamentary strike, and also did not seem willing to risk a revolution. Therefore, a revolutionary democrat would have to turn against the cowardly 'bourgeois liberalism' and its politics of compromise. This is why Lassalle now advocated the formation of a workers' party. He did not begin with social demands, but with the democratic one, which was looking for an advocate. Lassalle now brought a new idea and a new strategy to the more radical groups of workers. The central matter for him was the question of universal suffrage. This, he argued, was the original, primary democratic right, and must therefore come first; the solution of the social problem depended on this. The reality of capitalism is shaped by the 'iron law of wages', which keeps the workers on the breadline, perpetuates the process of impoverishment and firmly establishes the principle of exploitation. All talk of harmony or balance between capital and labour is hopeless twaddle and illusion. This system must be broken by the formation of production associations by the workers themselves; this was the link with the idea of co-operatives. But such associations would have to be financed by the state from tax revenues; only then could they survive and be effective. Therefore, the state must become a democratic one, because only a democratic state can also be a socially just one; and universal suffrage is a prerequisite for this. These were demands for revolutionary reforms. State loans and associations were only a means of eventually turning the state itself into an association of the working classes. Lassalle's democracy of universal suffrage and production associations did not correspond with the general idea of a parliamentary democracy — even though his followers understood his demands for universal suffrage to mean just that; his democracy was basically one of conventions and public assemblies, a plebescitary dictatorship.

In this very short description of Lassalle's programme the following three points need to be stated. (1) In contrast to Marx, Lassalle was a voluntarist. His primary belief, despite his Hegelist roots, was not in an automatic evolution of society towards the end of world history, but in the conscious and deliberate self-determination of the working classes. (2) Lassalle believed in the state; he did not advocate allowing the state simply to wither away, and he caricaturised with biting sarcasm the liberal concept of the 'night watchman state'. He considered the state to be an absolutely essential feature of political life; it completed the development of people — towards freedom. Lassalle was an opponent of liberal individualism; freedom, he believed, is not based on the rights of the individual, freedom is solidarity, and it is therefore the workers who will have the real power in democracy, because they have no individual or special interests but devote themselves entirely to the 'species'. This is where the tendency towards totalitarianism originates: if the state is democracy, then it has rights and power; hence the sympathy for authoritarian systems based on an autocratic plebescitary principle, whether in the state or in the party — one's own party. In the final analysis, the state is the true instrument of socialism. The state about which Lassalle is talking, the one which will bring about a redistribution of wealth, is not the existing one, but the state of the future, i.e. democracy. But he was already addressing his demands for social reform to the existing state; for it was not the socialist state of the future, but the actual present-day state which could, unless it was a bourgeois state, adopt policies which would lead to a socialist democracy. He therefore included the existing state in his strategy. These were the roots of his negotiations with Bismarck, and also the basis for the later social-democratic tendency towards reformism. (3) The democratic-socialist ideas are linked with the idea of nationhood. Lassalle was a staunch nationalist-democrat, and it was precisely this which motivated him to join forces with the workers' movement. Democracy and nationhood are related in that together they constitute self-determination both internally and externally; therein lies their unity. Both freedom and nationhood are valid aims: the national question is the means of achieving democracy; it was this which shaped the movement's tactics. Finally, the victory of the working classes is a precondition of national existence, of a unified and liberated people's state.

Within the socialist movement, Lassalle's new concepts amounted to a clear break with Marx and Marxism as such. This was to have far-reaching consequences for the later, second workers' party, which competed with Lassalle's party, and therefore also for German social democracy.

As far as the actual situation in 1863 was concerned, it was other matters which played a decisive role. Lassalle saw the question of the workers no longer as one of education, and also not primarily as a socio-economic question, but as a political one. Even the fashionable idea of workers' associations was given a very political emphasis by Lassalle. He maintained that the working class must separate itself from the bourgeoisie and the Progressive Party, because these groups, despite the constitutional conflict, were only representing their own class interests and a system of class suffrage. In contrast to this, the workers must organise themselves as a party, achieve the establishment of universal suffrage and reform the state. Lassalle went even further than those workers who were beginning to distance themselves from liberalism: he rejected any form of alliance with the liberals. They were the arch-enemy. This was the new aspect of the situation of 1863. Lassalle's appearance on the scene exploded the unity of the workers' and liberal-democratic movements, destroyed even the possibility of an alliance, and led to the independent formation of a social-democratic political party.

The Leipzig committee adopted Lassalle's programme on 17 March. On 23 May 1863 the General German Workers' Association (Allgemeiner Deutscher Arbeiterverein, the ADAV) was founded in Leipzig; eleven cities were represented at the inaugural meeting. This was a centrally organised agitational movement, primarily standing for universal suffrage; in addition, it was an association of political action during election campaigns, but which also remained active even when there were no elections being fought, just like a modern political party. In some ways, the fact that there was now an organised party of the working classes was more important than all the ideology; this was the really new and astounding feature. Lassalle was the first president of the party, and he was an enthusiastic and inspiring speaker, their charismatic and dictatorial leader.

Lassalle broke into the existing 'elementary' workers' movement and its liberal style with his idea; he confronted it with his new concept; he rejected it, or overpowered it. Thus was the new party formed, and the wild conflict and competitive struggle between liberal and Lassallean organisations became, after 1862, the major phenomenon in the political history of the working classes. The workers themselves were split — Lassalle or Schulze-Delitzsch — this is how the struggle was personalised and, with the formula state assistance *versus* self-help, trivialised. After all, Lassalle's criticism of Schulze-Delitzsch was not a general rejection of self-help, but a different political interpretation of it. But the confrontation had to have symbolic labels, and the ones chosen really fired the emotions and feelings of those involved.

The ADAV developed into a party of political faith, a party with which one could identify, which gave meaning and had an effect on life as a whole. Hamburg provides a particularly good example of how an agitational organisation can very quickly become the central feature of the life even of an entire family. This was certainly also a result of the charismatic personality of Lassalle. Particularly after his death in 1864 in a duel, there developed a distinct personality cult around Lassalle, which certainly outdid the liberal Schulze-Delitzsch cult. The religious structure of this anti-clerical, secular cult movement soon became clear — poems, songs, festivals, symbolic words and symbolic acts were all part of the life of this workers' movement. Even so, there were still only 3,000 members on Lassalle's death in 1864, and in 1865 the party almost disintegrated as a result of sect-like conflicts over the legacy of Lassalle and the dictatorial party leadership. It was not until 1866, when Johann Baptist von Schweitzer took over the leadership, that a certain consolidation was brought about.

It was not known, at that time, whether the split between the working classes and the liberal bourgeoisie was final. Lassalle and his new movement had the initial effect of consolidating the liberal-social workers' movement. In the spring of 1863, the liberals embarked upon a massive campaign against Lassalle; Schulze-Delitzsch was making speeches and giving lectures everywhere; his *Workers' Catechism* became one of the most popular and widely read books of the time. The campaign was fairly successful. Lassalle's ideas were, after all, eccentric and must have met with the instant disapproval of many workers. The criticism of education, the co-operatives and self-help affected the highest values of the organised workers, their hopes and the basis of their self-respect; it was incomprehensible, even defamatory. With his reforming of the workers' organisations into agitational associations, or pressure groups, for universal suffrage, Lassalle seemed to have completely ignored the subculture of these organisations, which was so dear to their members. The suggestion that the workers had until then not had the right to speak out, and that they should now, with the help of Lassalle, acquire that right, was an insult to their pride. Furthermore, the call for state assistance, even from the existing state, and the break with the Progressive Party or rather the attack upon it, seemed to be reactionary to them. The liberal reproach, that Lassalle was driving the workers into the arms of the reaction, was an effective weapon; seen objectively, it was the decline of the liberals, intentional or not, which would really have strengthened the reaction. In any event, it was initially the liberal workers' movement which was strengthened by the Lassalle agitation.

It is true that it also resulted in a certain radicalisation of the workers' associations; they began to advocate a more decisive style of politics from the liberals, the German National Society and the Progressive Party. They also wanted, in contrast to the ADAV, a federal unification. Under the aegis of the Frankfurt Democrat Leopold Sonnemann, the Congress of German Workers' Associations united the liberal educational associations in June 1863. This move was aimed against the creation of a high-profile independent workers' movement or even a special workers' party; it was intended to keep the workers within the liberal-democratic movement. But the workers did want a little more independence. They wanted to place more emphasis on specific workers' problems — the problem of industrial unrest could not be excluded forever — and they wanted to be a type of co-ordinated left wing of liberalism.

The competition between the liberals and the democrats for the newly organised workers, and the conflict between the two new groups were the main features of the development of working-class politics after 1862–63.

The highly important question of which workers became liberal and which became socialist cannot be conclusively answered. While the liberal labour politicians found in the majority of organised workers' associations, the new party relied more on public meetings at which non-members and other workers, not just craftsmen, were able to speak out. Even so, the craftsmen were initially in the majority in both groups. Lassalle's followers had their initial successes in the more rural, smaller industrial areas, where there were no liberal organisations or workers' associations and also no powerful local authorities. It was not until later that they made gradual advances in the industrial cities in the west, such as Duisburg, Solingen, Wuppertal, and then Düsseldorf and the industrial area of Bradenburg. They were successful in those areas where both conservative laws on the trade and relative political freedom had combined to make the workers anti-capitalistic and radically democratic in their views, such as in Hamburg or Frankfurt; where, as in the western provinces of Prussia or in Leipzig, the confrontation between the workers and the liberal local authorities or the state bureaucracy was particularly marked; where, as in the impoverished weaving areas of Saxony, in their general misery people saw a fundamental change as their only chance; where, such as in the Rhine provinces, socialist-communist traditions and members of the League of Communists played an important role. They had little success in areas where the liberals were well organised and had plenty of support, such as Berlin, or in areas where there were strong liberal-democratic traditions, such as Württemberg, where the strong agricultural base of the workers probably also played a role; in fact anywhere, such as in the south, where the class barriers were less prominent and there was a strong tradition of anti-Prussianism. As can be seen, there was some overlapping of motivations, and all statements such as these have exceptions: in Saxony, for instance, both factions were strong despite the democratic traditions. Such anomalies increased with time, particularly after 1866 when the pro-Prussian/anti-Prussian dividing-line became an important factor.

For both groups, and for the course of their conflict, the national-political problem was of considerable importance. Both wings of the workers' movement were part of the nationalist movement, were national-democratic. Lassalle was in this respect decidedly anti-Austrian and therefore pro-Prussian. In his opinion, Austria would have to be destroyed; only the German-Austrians should be allowed to belong to the German democratic nation-state. The party also adopted this view, which meant, in the concrete situation, that it was *kleindeutsch*. The opposition to 'bourgeois liberalism' kept the opposition to the Prussian state in check. In 1866, the vast majority of the ADAV were on the side of Prussia; national unity was a goal in itself — they supported the strategy of 'Through Unity to Freedom'. In 1867, in a second ballot in the Elberfeld constituency, the party even instructed its members not to vote for the Liberals, but for Bismarck. This was, of course, a tactical move and one affected by domestic politics: Bismarck had established universal suffrage and held out the prospect of the right to organise — but it was also characteristic of the national-political consensus. Of course, it was because the party was in agreement with the 1866 solution that it was now making a central issue of the demands of the workers and the call to make the nation-state a democratic people's state.

In the movement conducted by the liberal-democratic associations, however, the traditions of the 1848 democracy persisted. They also considered that the national question and democracy, by which they meant social democracy, were identical. But they gave priority to opposing the enemies of German unity and freedom, rather than opposing the liberals. In this movement, as time went on, a strong anti-Prussian feeling and *grossdeutsch*, democratic orientation developed, particularly outside Berlin and Old Prussia. 'With Prussia against Germany, with Germany against Prussia' is how the 1848 democrat Wilhelm Liebknecht described the situation of 1866; the result of a Prussian victory would be the surrender of the German border regions, the violent division of Germany and its conversion to a barracks. Where this was the prevalent attitude, particularly in Saxony and in the south, the workers' associations movement was a part of the *grossdeutsch*, democratic, anti-Prussian peoples' party; and when the followers of Lassalle joined forces with Bismarck in 1867, the Saxon workers' association members, despite doubts, allied themselves to the conservative Saxon particularists. This anti-Prussian tendency had made the majority of the liberal workers politically more radical. This, in turn, had two consequences. The opposition of the workers to the state became a more concrete opposition to the Prussian state, Bismarck's state, the arising German nation-state — not because it was a nation-state, but because it was *kleindeutsch*, Prussian, militaristic and undemocratic. This had a long-term and profound effect on the emotional attitude of the workers' movement. The *grossdeutsch*, democratic trend also had a formative and long-lasting effect on certain elements of the liberal tradition, counteracting the influence of Lassalle, within the rising workers' movement, as manifest, for example, in its determined anti-despotism. In the short term, the anti-Prussian national-political tendency of the workers' associations, particularly in competition with the Lassalle movement, cemented and even prolonged (in 1866) the incorporation thereof in the democratic, people's party wing of the bourgeois movement.

The question of nationhood, then, was of considerable importance to both movements. But they answered the question in opposing ways, and in a double sense: pro-Prussian with a split from the liberals, *grossdeutsch* in alliance with the democrats.

The national question and the question of alliance or independence were inseparably connected in those times.

In this connection, we must now discuss the end of the promising prospects of a liberal workers' movement, brought about by the founding of the Social Democratic Workers' Party by Bebel and Liebknecht in 1868–69. The workers' associations became more radical, in terms of both social and general politics; the separation of the Democrats from the Liberals led to the majority of the workers' associations moving to the Democratic camp. But the tendency of the associations to keep social and political issues apart from one another could not be sustained. The bourgeois politicians rejected 'socialism'; the workers were not prepared to abandon it. Of course, being German as they all were, they wanted a clarification of principle, and they were not prepared to leave anything undecided. In addition, they had the competition from the Lassallean movement to cope with: as a pure workers' party, they were always accusing the associations of being appendages of the bourgeoisie, thereby forcing them to distinguish themselves. Once again, the national question was of decisive importance. Hopes for a civil constitution were fading; the Prussian solution seemed a more probable outcome. The defeat of the Progressive Party, the weaknesses of bourgeois, *grossdeutsch* radicalism after 1866 led the workers affiliated with it to found their own organisation. To that extent, the foundation of a second workers' party was the result of the polarisation in the national question, a result of the national-political decision of 1866. But there were also other causes that led to its foundation, such as the competition from the Lassallean movement, and the fact that important groups in the ADAV had formed splinter organisations. When the liberal-democratic workers' associations formed their own party, they adopted a Marxist version of socialism and decided in favour of the internationalism of his International Workers' Association. They adopted, in a break with their own previous practice, a much more radical theory; this was also a result of tactics and the prevailing situation, a response to the competitive pressure from the Lassallean movement, the influence of converts, and the necessity to emphasise their class point of view in contrast to that of their erstwhile allies, the democrats. Furthermore, the declaration in favour of internationalism was in no way meant to be understood as a desertion from the nationalist movement. But this decision did have an extraordinary, formative effect on future developments.

In the midst of the competitive struggle between the workers' organisations, there began a new, independent development: the rise of the trade unions. In the middle of the 1860s, particularly in 1865, there were more union-organised and successful strikes than ever before. The first Pan-German trade unions were being formed at this time: book printers, cigar-makers, tailors. In the discussion about the free choice of occupation, the question of the right to organise once again became a topical theme. The Lassallean movement rejected these first socially reformative initiatives of the trade unions on the grounds that they were senseless; the liberals adopted them with definite reservations. When, however, they became successful, they were, from 1866 onwards, also sponsored by the competing political organisations and parties. This is how they developed, and it was particularly interesting in the liberal camp. The liberals, who wanted to prevent a desertion by the workers, had to tolerate a greater representation of workers' interests, a more decisive emphasis on social matters; and the liberal workers' movement became more active in social politics through the trade union organisation. In the long term, this was bound to result in a conflict with the employers, thereby jeopardising the political links. This also applied, for example in Prussia, to the workers who had nothing to do with the *grossdeutsch*, populist party concepts.

To sum up: the workers' movement in Germany, earlier than elsewhere, separated itself from the bourgeois movement and formed its own political parties. The liberal workers' movement, which at first seemed to have a great future, was threatened by the foundation of Lassalle's movement in 1863; it reached the limits of its potential after 1866. An explanation is needed for the early, even premature formation of the political workers' movement in Germany. The social conflict between the workers and the bourgeoisie resulted because it was so closely linked to the political conflicts over freedom and unity, because the democratic and nationalist goals had not been achieved, and because the struggle over this had brought a different polarisation to the situation. Certainly the appearance of Lassalle affected the situation: this one man set the direction for everybody — even his competitors; without him, everything would have turned out differently. But there were also structural conditions. The skilled workers of the 1860s wanted to be integrated into the bourgeois state — indeed, one reason why they formed their own independent movement was that the state was not bourgeois enough. This is why Lassalle caused such a sensation; he had a programme for achieving the democratic and then the social goals in an individual, radical manner. The second workers' party was also founded because both the workers and the people's movement were so far removed from anything like equal rights status; that was why they liberated themselves from the bourgeois bureaucracy, and that was why Marx was so popular with them. But it was then the national-political conflict — between the *kleindeutsch* and *grossdeutsch* solutions and the relationship between freedom and unity — which further shaped events. Lassalle's party could well have disintegrated, but the decision of 1866 and the failure of national democracy made the foundation of a second party in 1869, in competition with the Lassalle movement, unavoidable, and hence also the separation of the 'socialist' and the liberal-bourgeois democratic movements.

Certainly there were also other reasons. One of these would have been the lack of any kind of early socialist/anarchist tradition, such as existed in France. Another would have been the fact that the workers, at least the Protestant ones, had left the church in much greater numbers than, for example, in England, that they were less integrated culturally or religiously and also more crudely rationalistic in their outlook and therefore more receptive to socialist ideas. Furthermore, because of the political system and later industrialisation, there was no established trade union movement, which could, even by means of strikes etc., have kept the workers' movement within the framework of the liberal system for a long while, as happened in England. But the political constellation in Germany was what directly affected events.

The peculiar tension of this founding decade — between reformism and revolution, coping with the present and believing in the future, trust in the state and fundamental opposition, nationalism and internationalism — remained the legacy of the German workers' movement and continued to keep it, too, in a state of tension. But it was the premature formations and foundings which in the long term isolated the workers' movement both in bourgeois society and in the national state and also led to a weakening of liberal-democratic potential in Germany. Here, too, the national question led to a tragic dilemma in German history.

7. The Constitutional Conflict in Prussia and Bismarck's Minister-Presidency

In Prussia, the tame beginnings of the New Era did not lead to a gradual and moderate liberalisation, but instead to the great conflict over the army and the constitution. Between the revolution and the foundation of the Reich this was one of the monumental events of domestic German history. It was here that the future course of Prussian and German history was reset. The conservative nature of the state was reaffirmed. This had decisive consequences for the German Reich of 1871 and for its history to 1918 and beyond. Therefore, we shall discuss this conflict in great detail.

As soon as he took over the regency in 1858, the Prince Regent Wilhelm announced a reform of the army. It was a matter which had been on the agenda for some time, and there were three reasons for this. The main reason was that, in the face of the prevailing defence and security problems, full use was not being made of the military potential of that great German and European power — Prussia. The strength of the army had remained constant for nearly half a century and had thus not reflected the increase in the size of the population. Whereas in 1820 Prussia had 40,000 fewer soldiers than France, the difference had now risen to 200,000, and similar discrepancies had arisen elsewhere. Austria's army was much larger than that of Prussia, and Russia could count about one million men in the ranks of its armed forces. The army was the guarantor of Prussian and German security, and it was the basis of an active and, should the occasion arise, expansionist Prussian foreign and power politics. A reform of the army was definitely called for after the two great European wars of the 1850s, and also to bring it into line with the other great European armies; its modernisation was most certainly due; it was not just a whim of the Prince Regent. There was also the problem of conscriptional equity. The number of conscripts had not been increased in line with the size of the population since 1814, during which time the population had risen from 11 million to 18 million. Since the 1840s, the length of service had, in many cases, been practically reduced to two years, and, furthermore, two-thirds of those eligible for conscription were excused; less than one-third had to actually serve in the army. Those who did serve then belonged to the Reserve of the *Linie* (Line), i.e. the regular army) for a further two years and thereafter were members of the *Landwehr* (national guard, the militia), 1st Reserve (i.e. the field army) — for a further seven years. These people were then also called up on mobilisations, such as during the Crimean and Italian Wars. This was obviously a very unfair system with inequalities between the generations but also within age groups. There was also the problem of the military quality of the *Landwehr*: its officers were poorly qualified, some of them were old, some had only served for one year as regulars, and their organisational incorporation into the regular army had not been satisfactorily resolved. There was, basically, no disagreement on these matters. There was, in any event, a debate on the tightening up of the whole organisation of the regular and reserve armies.

As can be seen, a reform was definitely necessary. Of course, the unmilitary Friedrich Wilhelm IV had not further committed himself to this. In that much, it was rather a historical coincidence that the new Prince Regent was so close to the military, and therefore gave the matter a very high priority and lent momentum and shape to the reform. Great political motives were now added to the objective reasons for the reform. First, came the old disapproval of the *Landwehr* on the part of the military men. They considered the *Landwehr* to be not only relatively useless militarily, but also a 'false institution politically'. It was a civilian and therefore necessarily an unmilitary organisation; the *Landwehr* man was quite simply not a soldier; he was concerned with his work and his home, not his country's flag. Discipline, that essential prerequisite of fighting ability, was underemphasised, and the appeal to a sense of patriotism and morality did therefore not have the desired effect. Furthermore, effective leadership in military fighting could not be expected from lawyers and businessmen, but only from trained career officers. Some even alleged that the *Landwehr* was politically unreliable, the potential troops of the revolution; a number of counter-revolutionary military men pointed to the very small number of mutinies in the *Landwehr* in 1848–49 — ignoring the fact that the vast majority of the *Landwehr* had remained loyal and had not become a revolutionary civil guard. General von Roon, who formulated all these arguments more clearly than most and certainly had political acumen, put this more pointedly: in this age of universal suffrage the basic principle that the army did not hold debates was under threat in a fundamentally civilian organisation such as the *Landwehr*; the government was becoming too dependent as a result of the discussion about the reliability of the *Landwehr* and consequently was losing the necessary freedom of decision and room to manoeuvre. In short, the civilian and politicised *Landwehr* should not be improved, but should — by means of reform, discipline, new leadership, de-civilianisation and de-politicisation — be stripped of its uniqueness.

Wilhelm's own convictions were running along similar lines, namely that a three-year period of service was absolutely necessary for the army. The soldier must be completely removed from civilian life, must become a soldier with body and soul, must make discipline, blind obedience and the military spirit an integral part of his personality; only then could the monarch rely on the army in every situation — including the fight against revolution. Counter-revolutionary spirit and military professionalism combined in the mind of the king to produce the *idée fixe*, which was by no means shared with all the experts, that only a three-year period of service could turn a person into a soldier; anything else was merely putting a civilian into a military uniform.

Behind both points of view was basically the pre-revolutionary idea of a professional army. Even an army sustained by universal conscription should be run and in the spirit of a professional army. The army should not be a civilian organisation; it should be completely separate from society and its organisational structure and political constitution. This basic idea reflected the views of the military as they had developed in Prussia since the reform and during the revolution. The army was distanced from, if not opposed to, the civilian world. The corps of officers was still overwhelmingly aristocratic — there were 750 aristocratic officers in the infantry and cavalry, compared with 91 from non-aristocratic society, and only in the pioneers and artillery was the relationship 50:107. Officers were a caste unto themselves. These tendencies had been reinforced by the military cadet schools and the priority of military training over general civilian education. During forty-five years of peace, the corps of officers had become very insular and inward-looking, filled with the spirit of the counter-revolution: they regarded the army as the protector and saviour of the monarchy, law and order; and often this was more important to them than their national defence role. Even after the defeat of the revolution they still felt threatened, regarded themselves as the Praetorian Guard of the monarchy, swimming against the current of the times, against the throng of the revolutionary masses. This did not mean that the majority of officers were arch-conservatives, like the camarilla, or that they were planning a coup; but they did want to be a counterweight to the civilian, parliamentary, popular forces. The army remained, even in the process of transfer to a constitutional state, outside the constitution. It was, and intended to remain, the army of the king. The army was based on strict discipline and absolute loyalty to the 'war master', outside of all politics and deliberations as to whether something was just, good, constitutional or not. This was its preconstitutional basis, and it included the power of command of the 'war master'. It is true that Wilhelm had accepted the constitution, and nobody could alter that. All the important military matters were his concern alone, and he made the decisions in consultation with his war cabinet; the authority of the 'responsible' war minister was almost a separate matter and in any event carried less weight than the royal power of command.

All in all, the reform of 1813–14 seemed to have petered out; the army was, and intended to remain, a state within a state. The conscripted army was supposed to take on the spirit of a professional, king's army. In this respect, the army was meant to become the 'nation's tutor'; the army was not supposed to adopt civilian norms and standards; on the contrary, it should neutralise and repel them. Where the military men were not only thinking in defensive terms, but also offensively, they wanted more or less to reverse the idea of the old reform; they wanted to discipline and militarise the nation, without the civilianisation of the army, and to turn the peoples' army of the (rural) masses into a king's army. In fact, the army should have remained unpolitical, as indeed it wanted to, but in its opposition to civil society it stood firmly in the counter-revolutionary camp.

These attitudes of the military were bound to impede the planned reform; indeed, they were the potential cause of conflict. This was because, in spite of its special status, the army was, in a constitutional state, dependent on parliament for its budget, dependent on the approval of the bourgeois civilian delegates, even on popularity with the voters. This was a new situation.

The first War Minister of the New Era, Eduard von Bonin, had intended to conduct the reform in co-operation with parliament; he wanted to preserve the *Landwehr*, because its dissolution would have impaired the people's trust in the army, and he wanted to strengthen the position of the constitutional war minister in relation to the war cabinet. In this he was defeated by the Prince Regent, who had already taken it as fact that the chamber of delegates would oppose the necessary reforms. In December 1859, he appointed General von Roon as War Minister. Roon worked out a concept for reform: the annual number of new recruits was to be increased from 40,000 to 63,000, which would effectively increase the strength of the army from 150,000 to 220,000 men. This would entail a reorganisation of the cadre units and an increase in the number of officer and NCO posts. The period of active service should once again be set at three years. There should also be a reorganisation of the *Landwehr* and the reserves. Instead of just two recruitment classes added to the reserves, there would in future be five, i.e. three recruitment classes would be taken away from the *Landwehr* 1st Reserve; the remaining four recruitment classes of the *Landwehr* would be allocated to the 2nd Reserve, which would only be used for home and rear duties. The *Landwehr* officers would gradually be replaced by reserve and professional officers selected by the officers of the line (*Linie*).

That an existential conflict would arise from this reform could not be anticipated at this stage, despite the attitudes of the military that we have described. In terms of numbers, Roon's planned reform was a limited one; even the estimated cost of 9½ million thalers per annum was not exorbitant. The reaction of the liberals was by no means fundamentally negative. They were in favour of a strengthening of the army, because the army was not only the instrument of Prussian/German security, but also that of any German policy of Prussia. They accepted the scale of the planned reinforcements and were prepared to approve the necessary additional expenditure. Of course, the liberals had different ideas concerning the status of the army within the constitution, and they wanted a more strongly non-aristocratic army. The increase in cadres for officers, NCOs and long-serving soldiers, and especially certain other features which favoured the guards and cavalry regiments, engendered suspicion among the civilian population; there was anger over the privileges of the officer caste and of the preference given to the aristocracy and a suspicion that the landed gentry and reactionary officers wanted to build up a 'party army' — not just in opposition to the revolution, which the liberals also did not want, but also against the country, against the liberal and civil society. There was a liberal myth which held that only the *Landwehr* could be a genuine people's army and a safeguard for freedom. During the climax of the conflict in 1862–63, the more radical liberals once again strongly emphasised these military-democratic arguments: the 'people in arms' was not the active army led by a caste of warriors, but the *Landwehr*; the *Landwehr* had never been, and never would be, the troops of the revolution, but, and this is where the liberal argument turned the tables, it would be an effective force against any coup. But trends and opinions such as these were not decisive at this stage. The old liberals of the New Era were prepared to negotiate with 'their' government. They did not overestimate the political importance of the *Landwehr*, and they did accept the military criticism of its shortcomings; in short, a compromise could have been reached on the reorganisation of the *Landwehr* and the reserves. The real bone of contention was the length of service. The shortening thereof would have been a 'normal' compensation for the increase in the financial burden of the army, and as such would have had the desired effect on the electorate. Furthermore, this was where the limit was set on the effective building up of a professional army for the king, on the militarisation of society; the liberals did not want to reverse the process of integration of the army into society. In fact, the liberals really did want civilians in uniform; they did not want the existing balance of power between the army and society to be completely altered. This is why they opposed the superfluous burden of a three-year period of service. This was the defensive position adopted by the liberals; and as far as the political motives behind this reform of the army were concerned, they were undoubtedly right. As the arch-conservative Gerlach remarked in 1859, if the liberals had just accepted the reform as it was, they would effectively have had no real power.

One could ask whether it would not have been better for the liberals to yield in some way in order to preserve their influence. Even a three-year period of service would not be incompatible with a constitutional system; this was later practised for a long time by the French Republic. But such a calculation would have been illusionary. The liberals had no prospect of winning power and influence by giving way in the military debate. There was a symbolic limit beyond which they could not go. Without relinquishing their own right to exist, they could not dispense with the parliamentary right of co-determination, or the integration of the army into the constitutional state and civil society.

Initially, then, no agreement could be reached on the matter of the reorganisation. The liberals, still prepared to negotiate and compromise, approved the required additional expenditure for the government in May 1860 in a so-called 'provisional arrangement'. They set their hopes on a compromise at a later date and hoped that they would be able to establish the two-year period of service in the end, and subscribed to the peculiar illusion — encouraged, naturally, by the government — that a provisional reform could, if necessary, be reversed at a later date. In 1861, the liberals, still hesitant and undecided, once again approved a similar 'provisional arrangement'.

After the first failure of the reorganisation laws, the conflict worsened; the military party around the Prince Regent embarked upon a new offensive. They now wanted to abolish, as far as military matters were concerned, the parliamentary right of co-determination. The so-called 'power of command' was substantially extended. According to the new strategy, the king alone could now decide on matters of troop strength and the organisation of the army, the *Landwehr* and the *Linie*, the number of regiments and the number of officers, conscription and strength of presence, and even the period of service, or at least the relevant procedures and arrangements, and he could do so without consulting parliament. This new law, according to Roon, was merely a modification of the existing military service act of 1814. This had the effect of increasing the importance of the army debate, and more precisely the pragmatic questions concerning the *Landwehr* and the period of service, to the level of a fundamental conflict between the monarchy and the 'revolution'. An army of the king or an army of parliament? — this was, in reality, the question. The anti-constitutional tendency of the reform was intensified to become an existential fight for power: against parliament and for monarchical absolutism, at least in military matters. Edwin von Manteuffel, head of the war cabinet, and other arch-conservatives were all for abolishing the constitution and bringing about a real, and if necessary bloody, counter-revolution. But they all wanted to force back that little bit of parliamentary co-determination. The army should not be based on the law, but on the decisions of the king. This, however, meant a review of the constitution, and not only defending or stabilising the authority of the crown, but extending and increasing it at the expense of parliament. Behind this was the 'either/or' thinking of the extreme right-wingers. The modest claim of parliament to co-determination in legislation and a little 'civilianisation' of the army was blown up by the conservatives to be a parliamentary claim on the command of the army as a whole. These were, of course, remotely possible consequences, and this was in the background of the conflict. Initially, however, in the face of obvious compromises regarding the *Landwehr* or period of service, such matters were not on the table. In short, it was an offensive by the military party with an aim towards polarisation and confrontation. They wanted to subjugate parliament and, in the concrete situation, topple the liberal-conservative government of the Prince Regent; in practical terms, they wanted to use the prejudice of the king in the matter of the period of service — which was by no means shared by everyone — to bring about a change of course. In these circles, the revolution seemed less frightful than the existing state of affairs: out of the 'mudbath of a new revolution' Prussia could rise anew with increased strength, whereas it would, in the 'sewer of doctrinal liberalism', irretrievably rot away, as Roon said. 'If Prussia goes red, the crown will roll in the mud' — that was the attitude to these harmless attempts at a moderately liberal course. However, it was not only a question of the crown, but also one of the position of the military itself. The military wanted the right to decide on the correct politics and the preservation of the existing balance of power, even against the civil government. They put the Prince Regent under pressure — for example, in their speeches about the discontentment within the army — and attempted to bring him back onto their own ground, so that he would break with the government of the New Era.

The government attempted, in accordance with the new theory, to negotiate on the subject of the new power of command: Roon reorganised the army, installed the new units, and even put them on public show. He used the willingness of the opposition to compromise and made a definite military arrangement out of the provisional financial one.

From the beginning of 1861 to September 1862, the conflict worsened and came to a dramatic head. In February 1861, a left-wing splinter group, called 'Jung-Litthauen' (Young Lithuania) because of its East Prussian base, split away from the old liberals. From this group, the German Progressive Party, which we have already discussed, was founded on 6 June 1861. This was the first German party which was based on a programme; it was the 'executive of the German National Society in Prussia', and it united decided liberals and old 1848 democrats. Its leadership included Leopold von Hoverbeck and Max von Forckenbeck, Rudolf Virchow and Theodor Mommsen, Hermann Schulze-Delitzsch and Benedikt Waldeck, Johann Jacoby and Wilhelm Löwe-Calbe. This was more than a party of opposition to the conservative course, and in that respect it was new. From the disappointment over the standstill of the reform policy and the stagnation of German politics there now arose the call for a liberal development of the constitution, a reform of the *Herrenhaus* (the upper chamber of parliament), ministerial responsibility and, lastly, a liberal government. In the December 1861 elections, the Conservatives shrivelled to a mere 14 seats; the Progressive Party walked straight in with 109 delegates; in between the two were 54 members of the Catholic faction, which was rather conservative where the constitution was concerned, 91 old liberals and about 50 members of a (liberal) left-of-centre party. In military party circles, there was a mood of civil war; secret operational orders were issued; Manteuffel was seeking a coup and military dictatorship. Of course, nothing came of this; the king wanted to freeze the constitution to suit his own interests as far as military matters were concerned, but not otherwise interfere with it; and the liberals did not want a revolution: they believed in the superiority of law and order, and in the strategy of a legal, parliamentary opposition.

But the opposition now entered into the conflict and mounted a counter-attack. They no longer wanted a provisional arrangement, but instead demanded a detailed analysis of the hitherto very generally defined military budget (31 million thalers 'for provisions, clothing and weaponry'), not least in order to prevent the covering up of the military reorganisation. In other words, they were demanding an extension of parliamentary rights over the budget. In fact, then, the conservative attack on the guaranteed rights of parliament led to these rights being defended by reinforcing and extending them. The king then dissolved the lower chamber on 11 March and replaced the government of the New Era with a conservative one on 14 March. But the subsequent elections did not herald any considerable changes. There were now 133 supporters of the Progressive Party and, after the disintegration of the old liberals, 96 left liberals. Of the 352 parliamentary delegates, 285 were liberal. Once again, a compromise seemed possible. One of the great liberal leaders, Karl Twesten, who had called Manteuffel 'an unholy man in an unholy hour', was challenged by Manteuffel to a duel, in which he was injured; it belonged to the style of the times that he could not turn down a challenge of this nature. Twesten, together with Heinrich von Sybel and Friedrich von Stavenhagen, then held out the prospect of giving their approval if the government would agree to the two-year period of service. The government seemed willing to accept this, demanding in return an increase in the number of long-serving soldiers to the equivalent of one-third of the army and the permanent fixing of military strengths and finances, i.e. a partial reduction of the influence of parliament. Parliament, however, did not have to decide on this matter, because the idea was rejected by the king. As far as he was concerned, the question of a three-year period of service and parliamentary participation in the organisation of the army had become a matter of the highest principle, and he stuck to his position with unusual obstinacy. To yield in this matter, he believed, would have meant a handing over to parliament of the power of command, the army and the state; this was tantamount to a 'mummification' of the monarchy, cold revolution and monarchy by the grace of the people.

Now that the conflict had been so thoroughly brought to a head by the conservatives, the reverse was true. A victory for the crown would have meant a shift in the existing compromise over the constitution in favour of the rule of the king. The crown had made the structure of the state and the balance of power the actual theme of the confrontation; cold revolution or cold state coup. Naturally, before the conflict the military had been excluded from the constitution and stood in opposition to civil society — that was nothing new; but in the new confrontation any decision in favour of this state of affairs would have meant a shift of power to the military and the king. It was not the liberals who wanted to use the question of military reform and the military budget to extend the authority of parliament or, indeed, to 'parliamentarianise' the government; they were very definitely on the defensive in the beginning. But the natural wish to persist in the conflict which had, effectively, forced upon them, and to assert their position, now led to an ambition to further develop the constitution as related to the military question and more; the self-assertion of parliament was an objective victory in itself, and had to shift the balance of power in favour of all concrete liberal objectives over and above a mere maintaining of the status quo. The existing situation could not be held in a state of conflict; it had to be altered in favour of one or other of the parties.

The conflict over the army became a conflict over the budget and thus turned into a real constitutional conflict. The majority of parliamentary delegates had decided to reject the military budget and thus the entire budget as well. This was the basis of their power and they wanted to use it. The liberals were acting on the assumption that the government would not be able to govern without a budget. They would probably have to call fresh elections, and if they could not obtain a majority, they would have to resign; the king would then have to appoint a government which would be able to govern in consultation and agreement with parliament. This was, it is true, an exceptional method of solving an otherwise insoluble conflict, but it would lead to an alteration in the system of government; a moderate parliamentary style of governing. Of course, the king and the conservatives saw things completely differently: the king could and must continue to govern even if parliament did not approve the budget; the constitution did not stipulate what was to be done in the event of such a conflict between the crown and parliament — it had a 'gap' in this respect (this was the so-called *Lückentheorie* (theory of the gap) with which Bismarck then argued). In this situation, it was claimed, the king, and only the king, as the giver of the constitution, had the right to make a final decision. The ultra-conservatives, of course, regardless of all these arguments, wanted to use the situation to eliminate parliament, or at least decidedly weaken it. In September 1862, when the attempted compromise in the matter of the period of service had failed owing to the obstinacy of the king, the crisis came to a head. The rejection of the budget was due to occur very shortly. The government considered another set of fresh elections to be pointless; but they did not want to govern, at least not all of them, without a budget, as this would have been in contravention of the constitution. The king felt let down by his ministers. He did not want to give in; he would rather have abdicated than that. He drew up a statement of abdication and summoned his son, the Crown Prince Friedrich, for consultations. Friedrich argued resolutely against the abdication. At the same time, Bismarck, who was now an envoy in Paris, came to Berlin. He had long felt that he would be a suitable candidate for a ministry; the crisis was his hour, and Roon gave him a further signal with the now famous telegram: 'Periculum in mora, dépêchez-vous.' After a long consultation between the king and Bismarck in Babelsberg, Bismarck was appointed Minister-President on 22 September. The abdication was no longer valid; a fighting cabinet was formed.

This was a decisive event which would have far-reaching consequences for the future. It is certainly worth pondering on the fact that the conflict had reached the point where the only alternatives available were Bismarck or the abdication of the king, and abdication was a very real possibility. Of course, there was no threat of revolution in Prussia; all the shouting of the ultra-conservatives was not to be taken seriously. The military and monarchical structure of Prussia was not about to collapse. What was being debated was merely a little less power of command for the military and a reduction in its special status, along with a little more responsibility for the ministers and greater influence for parliament, a gradual integration of the old and new elites, and the continuation of the New Era and its conservative-liberal English–Coburg course. These were definite possibilities in Prussia at that time, despite all the restrictions of the prevailing political structures. Even the Crown Prince, later Kaiser Friedrich, was in favour of these changes. For sound personal and political reasons, he was not impatient to become king; nobody at that time could have foreseen that his succession to the throne would not take place until more than a quarter of a century later. But the time for embarking upon a different course had passed. Despite all belief in structural restrictions, it must be emphasised that at that time both Prussian and German history could have taken a different turn, and that it was left to one solitary man, namely Bismarck, to save and retain the position of the monarchy. The individual attitudes of an old king, obstinately clinging on to the traditional military-monarchical system, a more liberal Crown Prince who was, however, loyal to his family, and the 'strong man', Bismarck, were responsible for the historic choice between the two options open to Prussia at that time. This is why it was individual qualities which were so important then. Despite all recognition for the outstanding greatness and achievements of Bismarck, for German liberalism and a liberal penetration of the German style of life, this was a tragic decision.

We have already come across Bismarck a few times since the 1848 revolution and his speech in defence of the Olmütz agreement. It would not be inappropriate at this juncture to relate the exciting and fascinating biography of Bismarck up until those days. Bismarck was born in 1815 into an old Junker family from the Mark Brandenburg. His mother was dominant and little loved, herself coming from a family of bourgeois civil servants. After a wild youth as a student and trainee civil servant, he left the service of the state, full of a thirst for independence and an anti-bureaucratic attitude. After a deep religious crisis he abandoned sceptical deism and, in connection with his engagement to Johanna von Puttkamer and his association with the pietistical Pomeranian aristocracy, returned to the Christian Lutheran faith. Completely dissatisfied with the existence of a 'mere' landowner and full of ambition and a thirst for action, he entered politics, something which had now become possible outside of a career as a civil servant or diplomat in the parliaments. Initially in the United *Landtag* and then during the revolution he began his political career as a party man, an arch-conservative Junker royalist and counter-revolutionary who immediately attracted attention with his almost genial as well as original and provocative oratorical style. After the revolution, with the support of the arch-conservative leaders, he went into the diplomatic service, first as an envoy to the Bundestag in Frankfurt and then, during the New Era, in Petersburg and lastly in Paris. He was full of initiative and ideas, sharp but difficult; he was passionate and unreserved, egocentric and self-confident, yet deep down he felt threatened; only his wife and his religion were able to contain this feeling. For him, politics was first and foremost a fight; but he was pervaded by a profound Christian sense of realism, critical of all illusions and sceptical with regard to the possibilities of the individual, always aware of the limits of his own actions within the context of the great way of the world. Bismarck's ambition, in the years before 1862, was to become a minister, if not Minister-President; he wanted to win power and leadership, to 'call the tune', to put his political ideas into practice; his personal ambition and passion for the subject were closely connected.

During his years in Frankfurt, he departed from the ideology of his arch-conservative friends, and effectively from his own party base; he became, if one were to exaggerate the situation somewhat, a man between the fronts, certainly still a conservative, but one of a new and modern kind hitherto unknown in Germany. Bismarck developed his own version of *Realpolitik*: critical (and sometimes cynical) with regard to ideals, theories, doctrines and principles and the obstinacy often associated with them. Politics was a matter of interests, not ideas; politics was concerned with states, their realities, their interests, their power motives, and that meant, for the individual politician, one's own state, i.e. Prussia and Prussian power interests. A Prussian foreign policy which subjugated itself to principles motivated by domestic politics — legitimacy, counter-revolution, international solidarity among conservatives — would paralyse itself and therefore be a bad foreign policy. It would not serve the interests of self-assertion and the assertion of power, nor would it serve the interests of the potential advancement and extension of power. As far as Bismarck was concerned, these two were inseparably linked to one another. Politics was also Machiavellism and a chess game, and this was in contradiction to the precedence of the politics of ideology and the position of fronts in the great struggle of peoples throughout Europe. States were more real than parties. For Bismarck, the interests of Prussia — of monarchical and conservative Prussia, naturally — became the central theme, albeit only as a shift of accent initially; this then shaped the style and the vehemence of politics and led to the formation of new alliances and enemies.

His politics in Frankfurt were, therefore, not just a repulsion of Austrian advances, but a clear, blunt and permanent counter-offensive. With an unusually impartial sense of perception, and the sobriety of an international statesman, then, he took note of the new forces and movements of the age and considered, unabashedly and without ideological inhibitions, how he could include them in his political calculations. This applied to the France of Bonaparte and to so-called Bonapartism, it applied to the nationalist movement, from which he was far removed, it applied to social interests and forces — the Junkers, the bourgeoisie, the lower classes. It applied also to revolutionary forces, means and methods, to unconventional alliances — to the mobilisation of nationalist and bourgeois interests against Austria, to the interests of the lower classes against liberalism, and it applied internationally to the diversified interests of the European powers — England's interest in the balance of power, the hegemonical interests of France, for instance — in the service of one's own political objectives. Bismarck was a Prussian through and through; Prussian power, self-assertion, expansion and consolidation — that was the core of his politics. His objective was to carry out those policies in these revolutionary times, in the face of the risks of revolution and using revolutionary means. Bismarck was also a passionate and dedicated international statesman; Prussia's assertion of power in Europe was, in his opinion, only possible through a hegemonical Prussian solution to the German Question, against Austria, but at the same time with the semi-agreement, or at least tolerance, of the rest of Europe; this was because, for Bismarck, the German Question was a question of the European power-political constellation. In fact, he basically believed that the existence of the Germans in Europe could only be guaranteed and safeguarded under a new and unified federation under Prussian leadership — that was not nationalism, that was his international realism. A lot has been said about the relationship between foreign policy and domestic policy; his contemporaries regarded Bismarck as advocating the 'primacy' of foreign policy; nowadays a lot of people tend to regard him as advocating the primacy of domestic policy. Both these views are one-sided. Bismarck knew, of course, that foreign policy was subject to the conditions of domestic policy and could fulfil domestic political functions, and he consciously included this fact in his calculations: his nationalist foreign policy, e.g. his alliance with the nationalist movement or, even more simply, his striving for successes in foreign policy, had a disburdening effect on domestic politics. But this foreign policy also had, and sometimes in a much greater way, its own aims, purposes and laws. Put another way, Bismarck was certainly a symbol of Old Prussianism; that was part of his original political nature. He wanted to retain the Prussian state of royalty and order, and the power of the military and the aristocracy. This coloured his hegemonical politics. But this was what mattered, and not primarily the conservation of an existing order. It was this, and not any particularly cunning move to preserve conservative power, which separated him from his comrades of his class and way of thinking, thereby enabling him to ally himself with the nationalist movement and sometimes with the liberal movement.

Bismarck was — and this has to be said in a description as brief as this — much more difficult, complex and contradictory than the old clichés reveal: the man of blood and iron, the power-politician, the hero of German unity, the Iron Chancellor, the Junker genius, the great diplomat, the politician of responsibility; more difficult even than the various modern versions such as the cleverest and most modern representative of his class or the 'white revolutionary' — accurate as these are in many respects. Bismarck was one of the very few great and meaningful people in 19th-century German history, a political genius, full of contradiction and tension, someone who could not be described in terms of a simple formula. To understand him means to relate his story in an understandable way.

Bismarck had repeatedly been considered as a ministerial candidate even before 1862. His talent and energy, his perception and courage, in short his stature, could not be missed. But on the other hand, there was a certain mistrust, a suspicion that he was a man of unscrupulous power politics, unpredictable and unruly, with a tendency to embark upon adventures and escapades in both domestic and foreign policy, an ambitious and unprincipled careerist, always ready to turn everything upside down, to govern by the bayonet and then suddenly make a pact with the liberals. This led many people to have, and keep, reservations about him; these included both the old and the new king, the majority of the government establishment and the ideological wing of the *Kreuzzeitung* party; and Queen Augusta, especially, was and remained an influential opponent of his candidacy. But, in September 1862, the political crisis had become so intense that the king simply ignored both his own reservations — he had expressed them to the Crown Prince just three days before — and those of the people around him. This was because Bismarck was the only candidate who was willing and seemed able to carry out the king's policies, i.e. to establish the military reforms in every detail and to govern against parliament and without a budget. Bismarck was the last and only card the king had against the alternative of abdication. Bismarck had convinced the king in an unusual way. He presented himself as a 'vassal of the Electorate of Brandenburg' at the unconditional service of his *Lehnsherr* (feudal lord); he wanted to strengthen unreservedly the power of the monarchy and oppose the threat of parliamentary rule. It was for this reason that he came to power. He did not want to be a 'constitutional minister': he was going to govern on behalf of the king, even when he acted against the king's advice; in that much there was no longer any further need for a government programme. This was, then, an old-fashioned, royalist-absolutist tie to the king. But this also meant that he did not have to tie himself to any particular programme. This was the basis of his power for the future, because Bismarck neither wanted to be the man of Roon and the military party, nor did he want to engage in a foreign policy which was conceived in the court of the king. He wanted, within the framework of a strict loyalty to the monarchy, to determine the course of politics himself. He came to power in a crisis, and, by unreservedly making himself available to the king, created a position of power for himself which really could only be shattered by another great crisis.

In 1862, Bismarck wanted to become minister and Minister-President, not because he wanted to lead the conflict, or realise the 'period of dictatorship', but because for him, the uncanny outsider of the establishment, in between the various fronts and various camps, the chance to get to the centre of power, to 'call the tune', lay in the milieu of conflict and crisis. Nor was it because he wanted to fight liberalism, but rather because he wanted to make Prussian politics, and to do it in the form of hegemonical policies. But in concrete terms, the struggle with liberalism was the most immediate matter of importance, and the new minister threw himself into this challenge with passion. He began, this was in a way coincidental as far as his motives were concerned, as an energetic defender of the Prussian military monarchy. This had the effect of establishing an initial and basic profile which later continued to shape Bismarck's image and style and which never completely disappeared. Bismarck was much more than a 'minister of conflict', both before and after 1862; but the fact that he had started as such was always a basic factor in his style of politics. Bismarck had not created the conflict, and also had not wanted it in the form it eventually took, but the fact that he took hold of it with all his energy was everything but coincidental. This was in accordance with that part of his being which we shall call 'Old Prussianism' and which, however well he transformed it into modern forms, was part of the fundamental basis of his political being. This was the monarchical/landed aristocracy/military 'complex', the lack of ability to relate to the urban bourgeois, liberal, parliamentary world. As much as he, in his modernity, recognised the latter world, attempted to use it or formed alliances or compromises with it, his deepest identity lay in Old Prussianism. This is why it was through Bismarck, the moderniser of quite unmodern origins, that this 'Old Prussianism' has grown so markedly and decisively into modern German history.

Bismarck began by attempting a compromise. He offered the old liberals and the left liberals three ministerial posts; in the matter of the army, however, he could only hold out the hope that he would, in time, be able to persuade the king to accept a two-year period of service, which he himself favoured. This solution would have led to a new link between the government and parliament, and we cannot deny that the idea had some historical chance of developing along the lines of the English system. But it is understandable that, in the situation of conflict, the liberals did not want to be drawn into any deals of this nature; they would have been in danger of becoming officers without soldiers, prisoners of Bismarck. Parliament rejected the military budget. On 30 September 1862, Bismarck announced in committee that he would, if necessary, govern without a budget, and he added: 'The great questions of the time will not be decided by speeches and majority decisions' — that had been the mistake of 1848 — 'but by iron and blood.' This remark provoked a colossal reaction and is to this day a central feature of the image we have of Bismarck. Had not this man, who during the following eight years started, provoked or at least happily accepted three wars, revealed himself with this remark to be an unscrupulous politician of force and violence right at the very beginning? Bismarck was not naturally a worshipper of iron and blood and power; he was definitely aware of the limitations of power and the necessity for peace. What Bismarck meant was, at the time, quite simply true: that the existential questions of politics and the state were a matter of power and military force; that German unity could only be further advanced by means of Prussian military power; and that there were conflicts which could not be avoided. It was not his intention to provoke or offend anybody with this remark; he was trying to appeal to the parliamentary delegates, to win their support. The liberals were by no means opponents of iron and blood. The myth of 1813, which still played such an important role in the military debate, was their myth; they also still considered war and armies to be a completely legitimate means of conducting politics. But it now depended upon who made such statements, in what situation, and with what overtones. In this remark the opposition heard the voice of a gambler, who for domestic political reasons was looking for foreign political adventures and successes. This minister was, according to Gall, a 'security risk'. 'When I hear this shallow Junker Bismarck talking of iron and blood, with which he wants to subjugate Germany, it seems to me that its nastiness is only exceeded by its absurdity' — this was the opinion of Heinrich von Treitschke, who later became an admirer of Bismarck and a propagator of an almost naturalistic power politics. Certainly, the almost brutal frankness with which Bismarck spoke of realities, in contrast to the usual civil, pacifying and moralising style of rhetoric, was unusual, rash and shocking. It was perfectly acceptable to think in such terms, but one was not supposed to speak in this manner. Despite all this, however, we must not completely discount the 'iron and blood' reputation. By speaking in this way, Bismarck was putting the reasoning of power and real interests on an equal footing with norms and laws, or possibly even above them. While this may, in certain situations, have been suited to the tragic seriousness of reality, one could not lightly, even as a liberal realist, go against the conscious mood of the times, which was a striving for justice and peace in the world, at least as an ideal.

The government carried on without a budget. The liberals protested. The government declared that resolutions of parliament were invalid. The delegates declared the actions of the government to be in violation of the constitution. The government regarded any giving of ground to be a surrender of the royal prerogative and power of command. The liberals saw the actions of the government as a manifestation of naked, absolutist force and the abolition of justice and the state under rule of law — as an insidious coup. By means of continual and deliberate provocations of both parliament and the public, Bismarck intentionally made the conflict more intense and emotional. The government, particularly on the initiative of Bismarck (the other ministers were less important or even independent figures), resorted to ever sterner suppressive measures against the opposition and individual members thereof. Civil servants were placed under surveillance, harassed, reprimanded, pursued in the courts, threatened with loss of career, financial status and even respectability as citizens. The judiciary was to be brought into line with the goverment's course at last, by means of postings and the ruthless use of public prosecutors. The mass of suppressive measures, their ostentatious arbitrariness and the deliberate personalisation of the political struggle by Bismarck gave rise to a deep and long-lasting feeling of bitterness among the educated bourgeoisie, which, within the left wing of the liberal movement, continued for decades after the foundation of the Reich. A press directive of 1 June 1863 used every conceivable form of ban and censorship to strangle the free press; it was, according to Treitschke, 'an attack on the holiest element of our national character' — even the Crown Prince publicly protested it. Because parliament, naturally, refused to give its consent to these measures in accordance with the constitution, they had to be withdrawn. The *Landtag*, in which the government and the Liberal majority were constantly clashing, was suspended in 1863 and later dissolved. The subsequent elections were a triumphant success for the Liberals, despite massive pressure from the government; they won over two-thirds of the seats, and the Progressive Party alone had 141. The conflict now became a war of position. Parliament was able to hinder the government even in important matters, for instance in rejection of a loan for the government's Schleswig–Holstein policies. Bismarck tried to wear down both parliament and the opposition by simply governing with the apparatus of state, delaying many matters, and not summoning the *Landtag* for long periods of time. But the conflict continued. On 9 May 1866, just before the war, the government once again dissolved the *Landtag*.

Certainly, in the first instance, the government had the longer arm. They were in charge, they were in possession of the instruments of state power. But whether they would always have the upper hand was highly questionable. Any failure of foreign policy would have severely damaged them, if not finished them off. They had to find a way out of the conflict sooner or later, on account of their German policies if nothing else. On a long-term basis, foreign and military policy was linked to financial and fiscal policy, and this could hardly be carried out against parliament and the civil society. What were the possibilities of ending the conflict? The chances of a compromise were small. In May 1863 the opposition would certainly have accepted a limitation of budgetary rights (*de facto* a fixed military budget) if the crown had accepted a two-year period of service and a formal law concerning the organisation of the army. But the conflict had now run too deep; the king resisted anything that even resembled an extension of parliamentary power. The left wing of the Progressive Party considered that negotiations would only be possible after the dissolution of Bismarck's government of conflict. After the attempts at reaching a compromise failed, this view was also adopted by the vast majority of the liberals.

In their resistance to the government's military and budget policies, and, indeed, its violation of the constitution, the liberals remained completely within the bounds of the law. They did not boycott parliamentary sittings; they did not refuse to give their consent to other laws and agreements, e.g. in the areas of the economy or customs and excise. They did not attempt to mobilise the masses; they were not working towards revolution. This was in accordance with their dislike of revolution and the special position of liberalism, which we discussed earlier. The liberals were not simply the 'people' — electoral turnout in the third class was not high. Their basis within society, then, was a narrow one. A revolution would have been hopeless; neither the peasants nor the workers and the poor would have supported it, and the bourgeoisie itself was not revolutionary by nature. This was also partly because the opposition was of more or less the same opinion as the government in economic and customs matters. It must be made clear that there was no 'material' question with which to mobilise the masses against the government. In England, for example, the movement for the liberalisation of the political system in the 1830s and 1840s had, with the agitation against the corn laws, a tangible, material cause which even captured the imagination of the workers' movement and the Chartists. This, however, was missing in Germany: the big grain producers, the majority of the industrial and commercial bourgeoisie, the consumer masses, the government and the administration were all in favour of free trade. Indeed, the policies of the government concerning the economy and the Zollverein had effectively undermined the opposition of conflict: the substantial successes of the government on the basis of a wide consensus had to result in the loosening of the oppositional bloc. Furthermore, with the economy in generally good shape in this period of economic upswing, which had tamed various forms of social protest, the conflict between parliament and the government, between the civil society and the state was effectively isolated and localised, thereby limiting the oppositional possibilities of liberalism. Sociologically, the conflict was a fight between the bourgeoisie and the Junkers — the latter of whom were accustomed to describe themselves in the *Herrenhaus* as the pillars of the militaristic monarchy — which is exactly how people saw it. But the bourgeoisie was, in society as a whole, not as strong as it sometimes may have appeared. This also shaped the cautious strategy of the opposition. Basically, the liberals wanted to persuade the crown to terminate its old alliance with the Junkers and enter into an alliance with themselves. This also meant that they were obliged to stay strictly within the law and to refrain from using any methods of total obstruction or confrontation. But, even though they did not have the 'masses' at their disposal, they did represent the upwardly mobile section of society, the bourgeoisie, and this was the basis of their self-confidence and their claim to power. They believed, as they always had done, in *Recht* (law, justice), which would always work in the end; the crown and the state could not — on a long-term basis — persist in opposition to the strongest forces in the economy and society. It was said that Prussia would ruin itself with its anti-liberal and anti-nationalist policies, that it was digging its own grave. These ideas were not so very wrong; they were basically shared by no less a person than Bismarck himself. In any event, the goal of the liberals remained, contrary to what the counter-revolutionaries thought, fairly limited; they were not demanding a full parliamentarian-ism of the state, but rather a parliamentary constitutionalism in the style of the New Era and the Coburg/early Victorian ideals, like the model system which was being tried out in Baden. Admittedly, as far as the conservatives were concerned, even that was a decisive shift of political and constitutional power; seen objectively, and in the long term, of course, they were not wrong in this view.

On the other side there was Bismarck. It would be wrong to see him only through the eyes of the liberals, as a 'minister of conflict'. Admittedly, he carried out this conflict in his hard and tough manner, but this is because he wanted to put an end to it. He wanted to reassert the power of the Prussian crown and the specifically Prussian character of the strong state, but he had certainly realised that this would only be possible in co-operation with a part of the opposition, i.e. their participation would be necessary; this was not an end in itself for him, but merely a means to an end, and it would in any event considerably alter the political situation. Furthermore, he had also realised, gradually, that his policies for Germany were only workable in co-operation with the liberal-nationalist forces in society. In this respect, he believed that the only programme which was suited to the times and which had good future chances was the liberal one. Because this was the case, Bismarck, as the historian Gall accurately pointed out, simply took the liberals' programme from them; in opposing the Austrian reform plans of 1863, he was supporting the aims of the Progressive Party, i.e. the confirmed domestic opposition. This in itself was paradoxical. This is where the close interconnections between domestic and foreign policy took effect right down to the smallest detail.

As we have already said, Bismarck did not conduct his policies for Germany in order to get out of the domestic political blockade, which in the long term would become an unbearable stalemate for the crown as well, and to conclusively win it for the crown. But he certainly intended to alter the domestic political situation, to break down the solid fronts, by means of national politics and foreign-policy successes. This was certainly a calculated and desired effect of such policies. Bismarck believed that after he had taken office he would soon be able to win the nationalist (and moderate) liberals over to his way of thinking. He made them various offers of co-operation, some hidden, some open, ranging from foreign policy to areas of domestic policy outside the military question. In these endeavours he failed, particularly in 1863 and again in 1865. In this situation of failure, Bismarck felt he was pushed into a corner and consequently reacted to the liberals in an especially fierce and aggressive manner; the intensification of the conflict was the result of disappointment and dashed hopes. But there was more. Bismarck rejected the plans of Manteuffel and his associates for a *coup d'état* whose objectives were counter-revolutionary and aimed at a fundamental revision of the constitution; he considered that the idea of a quasi-absolutist subjugation or taming of the opposition was without a future. But in opposing such an ultra-conservative option and its propagators around the king, he had to hold his position and weaken the suspicion that he was seeking to negotiate and compromise with the liberals or even follow their line on nationalist policies, and he could only do this by presenting himself as an unswerving supporter of the crown and tough opponent of the liberal opposition. This also explains in part his verbal and administrative toughness against the liberals; it was designed to outmanoeuvre the supporters of the *coup d'état* idea. In 1864, after the victory over Denmark, he was able to fend off these attempts, but in 1865 the military did succeed in getting the king, and not just the liberals, to reject Bismarck's planned attempts at compromise.

In this connection, it must be mentioned that Bismarck had also been considering a coup of his own, although it was admittedly one of a very different nature. In May 1863, and again in June 1864, he planned the introduction of universal suffrage. It was in this context that Bismarck conducted his astounding talks with Ferdinand Lassalle. The conservative and the socialist had their opposition to the bourgeoisie and liberalism in common; furthermore, they both had state-socialist tendencies. Bismarck, conservative revolutionary that he was, certainly considered the use of such revolutionary means as universal, democratic suffrage. This may well have led to a Bonapartist style of politics, a plebescitary despotism. No 'normal' conservative had dared to think in such terms until then. But nothing came of these plans at that time. Lassalle was not a power, and in any case it was questionable whether such a solution would have had any prospects of success in the monarchistic Prussia of those times. But such ideas were definitely effective as a potential threat to the liberals. Even Bismarck's national-political call for a Pan-German parliament based on universal suffrage was not so much an offer of alliance with the nationalist-democratic movement as an attempt both to entice and to threaten the bourgeois liberal-nationalist movement into a political alliance. First of all, then, Bismarck's strategy of conflict was aimed at breaking the stalemate by means of a nationalist policy and a successful foreign policy. He was not able to win support for this from the old arch-conservatives or the supporters of a coup, but he did manage to get the statist military men, such as Roon, and the king on his side. In the same way that a failure of foreign policy would probably have made Bismarck's position untenable, a success in this area would have to improve his standing.

This now became the liberals' problem. After all, the Liberal Party was also the German nationalist party. If freedom and unity were inseparably linked with one another, then any progress made towards unity would, by necessity, also influence the policies concerning freedom. The liberals would probably have been prepared to give way more easily at the beginning of the conflict if there had been a strong and effective German policy in Prussia, and if they could have been reasonably certain that the reorganised army would be used in the execution of such a policy. But as the conflict became more and more intense this possibility temporarily faded away. This was due to the fact that the nationalist policies of the *kleindeutsch* Prussian liberals were based on the concept of Prussian moral conquests, the moral authority of the Prussian constitution and the expectation of at least the style of politics of the New Era. But Bismarck's politics of conflict destroyed not only the liberal hopes but also the nationalist ones; it was for this reason that the liberal-nationalists were so deeply bitter. The nationalist programme of the liberals was anti-particularistic, anti-feudal, constitutional; Prussia was not living up to its 'calling', it was apparently withdrawing as a champion of the national solution.

However, this situation, as well as the perception thereof, changed in 1864 when Bismarck, in solving the Schleswig–Holstein question, recognisably adopted a nationalist policy and was successful with it. It was shown that nationalist policy was also possible outside the scope of liberalism. Now there were the beginnings of a separation between unity and freedom. Some of the liberal-nationalist Progressive Party politicians had become uncertain since the Schleswig–Holstein crisis. They advocated the Prussian annexation of the duchies; Treitschke, for instance, propagated this. The military state on the border would become, just like in Italy, 'the core and starting-point of a modern state structure', i.e. of the nation-state. This was altogether a new situation: the dilemma between freedom and unity had opened up, and some pleaded for the priority of unity, but now without the 'moral' conquest. Theodor Mommsen, a confirmed liberal, said in 1865 that the present alternatives were: domination by the — unloved — great German state of Prussia, or the fall of the nation. This was not capitulation or defection in the face of successful policies. It was not as simple as that. The Prussian liberals saw, as we have already indicated, a fundamental, if admittedly dialectical link between unity and freedom, which, particularly in conflict, was topical. They believed that the inherited structure of the Prussian military state could only be relaxed and liberalised if Prussia were freed from the over-proportional military burdens with which it was encumbered in the defence of Germany as a whole, i.e. if it became part of a German nation-state. German unity was, therefore, one way, the sure way, of making Prussia more civilian and its constitution more liberated. This was definitely a valid line of thought, and it led one faction of liberals to accept compromises in the face of decisive and successful unification policies, or in any event motivated them to accept such compromises in the face of the blocking of liberal and nationalist hopes and the emerging tragic dilemma between unity and freedom. This tendency started rather feebly in 1864 and had still by no means penetrated the movement on the outbreak of war in 1866. But it was a tendency which went in the direction of an alleviation of the conflict and was also a concession to Bismarck's strategy. It led to an intensification of his efforts to gain the support of the nationalist movement.

8. The Decision concerning Germany: German and European Politics, 1863–66

Since the Crimean and Italian Wars the European scene had been determined by the policies of Napoleon III. He wanted to revise the existing power structure in Europe, in particular with the assistance of the nationalist movements; this was supposed to increase the importance and prestige of France and also bring him — as in Nice and Savoy — some territorial compensations. Naturally, because any shift of power in Germany, and particularly the formation of a great new German power, would not go unobserved by the great neighbouring power, France, there were also objective reasons why the German Question played a central role in his turbulent politics; any solution to this question, any alteration in relations between the German powers, would first have to come up against Napoleon. This is why the German powers had, since 1859, been competing for Napoleon's goodwill. Admittedly, Napoleon's politics, which were aimed at revision, the acquisition of power and hegemony, and which caused so much disquiet and, indeed, seemed to be posing a threat to the English glacis, Belgium and the Rhine, were mistrusted in Europe and particularly in England ('a nation so warlike as the French' remarked Foreign Secretary Russell). Napoleon's politics were indeed regarded as the threat to the balance of power in Europe. Russia was still involved in an informal half-alliance with France, but was becoming more suspicious.

Among the German powers, it was particularly Prussia which benefited from this European situation. Austria remained isolated from both Russia and France and its junior partner, Italy. Prussia, on the other hand, was on good terms with France, despite Napoleon's worries, which had led to the Villafranca peace agreement, because the latent opposition to Austria was a strong basis of mutual interest. Furthermore, Prussia benefited from the increasing English and Russian mistrust of Napoleon. It is true that neither England nor Russia had supported any expansive national policy of Prussia's, and, additionally, the constitutional conflict completely ruled out any closer links between Prussia and England; but Prussia could hope for a certain amount of goodwill and neutrality from the flanking powers; the Olmütz situation, where Prussia had both England and Russia opposing it, was over, because it was now no longer Prussia but Napoleon who was threatening the balance of power. Admittedly, as long as the Franco-Russian half-alliance continued to exist, Prussia would have no freedom to reshape Germany. This is why its balance-of-power policy, to achieve parity with Austria against a guarantee of its European position, was also a result of the European situation.

This constellation was altered in 1863 when the Poles staged a revolt against the Russians. This development led to a European crisis. The revolt did have some chance of success, in so far as it was about a relative degree of autonomy, particularly as there was a liberal tendency of appeasement in Petersburg. Moreover, Napoleon was, for many reasons — including domestic political ones — on the side of Poland, although in consideration of Russia he did avoid any appearance of an intervention. But in Petersburg, the pro-Polish and pro-French tendencies were connected. Bismarck used this Polish crisis in an exceedingly clever way; by nature not a nationalist, for purely power-political reasons he turned on the Poles, who were striving for independence, and their friends and allies with maximum toughness and a good measure of Junker brutality. Prussia was also affected by this revolt: directly, because it could well have spread into Prussia's eastern provinces; and indirectly, because an independent Poland would have presented a danger to the Prussian state. This was the long shadow of division; an independent Poland, according to Bismarck, would be 'a French encampment on the Vistula River'. Prussia mobilised its troops, and Bismarck came to an agreement with Russia, the so-called Alvensleben Convention, which concerned mutual and cross-border assistance in the pursuit of the rebels. Admittedly, that was not the real purpose of this act. It was in fact a pro-Russian and anti-liberal move, which was primarily intended to thwart the Franco-Russian rapprochement and to outmanoeuvre the pro-French and pro-Polish elements of appeasement around Foreign Minister Gorchakov in Petersburg, which at the same time would lead to Russia being discredited in western Europe. The rest of Europe now considered this to be an 'intervention', and Napoleon placed himself at the head of a protest movement, supported by western European public opinion, against this 'breach of neutrality', and attempted to intensify this protest to the level of a diplomatic offensive and, indeed, massive pressure, not against Russia but against Prussia. He approached Austria. The Empress Eugénie held out the prospect, to an Austrian diplomat, of a grand revision of the map of Europe: Venetia to Italy, Silesia to Austria, the left bank of the Rhine to France, a new Poland, the expansion of Prussia to the north — certainly an adventurous plan, but one taken seriously by all those involved. England, however, was opposed to an isolation of Prussia; it was more interested in disturbing the alliance between Russia and France. In the face of this diplomatic pressure, Bismarck dispensed with the execution of the Alvensleben Convention; this was in any case no longer necessary, as it had served its purpose. In this respect, Napoleon's protest had the wind taken out of its sails. He could no longer avoid a clear pro-Polish, anti-Russian stance.

The result of all these manoeuvres was that Napoleon suffered a defeat. He had had to turn against his potential partners, Prussia and Russia; the dissent with England was intensified. In Russia, not least because the revolt continued and because western support for it had provoked deeply emotional counter-reactions, the result was that the hard and old-fashioned non-Pan-Slavic view prevailed, and this meant an anti-French, pro-Prussian stance. The Franco-Russian alliance was as good as finished, and with it the potential pressure on two fronts against Prussia, for twenty-seven years in any event. Prussia had more international political power; it guaranteed Poland for Russia, and it guaranteed Belgium for England. Both England and Russia had further distanced themselves from Napoleon; he lost his role as arbiter in Europe. England began to favour the idea of a power-political consolidation in Germany. Russia — still an enemy of Austria — extended its benevolent neutrality towards Prussia to include a Prussian solution of the German Question. Prussia's room for manoeuvre had increased: it was now the potential partner of both the flanking powers and their anti-Napoleonic policies of containment. Admittedly, Prussia's other potential partner, Napoleon, its ally in the national revision of central Europe against Austria, had now been seriously alienated; in terms of the situation in 1863, the success of Bismarck's policies was not as great as it may seem from the standpoint of 1866 or 1871.

Public opinion in Prussia and Germany, although not in favour of 'releasing' the Prussian Poles, but certainly anti-Russian, was in stark opposition to Bismarck's policies; in the people's eyes he had made himself an unscrupulous accomplice of Tsarist despotism and as such had blood on his hands, or had certainly done nothing other than engage in the politics of adventurism and brinkmanship.

Immediately after the events in Poland there occurred the next big European and German crisis. The thorny problem of Schleswig–Holstein was once again on the agenda. In 1852, as we have already seen, the question was resolved internationally by means of the so-called London Protocols: the Danish state was to remain fully intact; in all parts of the country, including Holstein and Schleswig, the succession of the female line was to apply; the candidate from the male line, the Duke of Augustenburg, relinquished his claims; but at the same time the special position not only of Holstein, but also of Schleswig, was guaranteed. But such international agreements as these could neutralise neither Danish nor German nationalism. The Eider Danes were working towards the gradual assimilation of Schleswig into the kingdom of Denmark and its separation from Holstein; in 1863, this was decreed by a 'patent' in March and the new state constitution in November, and the new king, Christian IX, the so-called Protocol Prince, confirmed this brand-new constitution immediately after his accession to the throne in November. This was a violation of European agreements.

The German nationalist movement protested wildly at this turn of events. Did they not now have a free hand in dealing with the matter, particularly as other accepted norms of international law had been ignored, e.g. the acceptance of the king by the Holstein estates? They demanded the separation of the duchies from Denmark. The son of the Duke of Augustenburg, the one who had relinquished his claims, now raised claims of inheritance in his own name, and, as he was considered to be both German and liberal, became the candidate of the liberal-nationalist movement, despite the old-fashioned, dynastic, legitimistic nature of his claims. The Liberals now became the 'Augustenburg' party; they proclaimed and supported his rights with passion and enthusiasm. Here was a chance, at last, to advance the cause of nationalism. A massive campaign of agitation was started, mass meetings were held everywhere, Schleswig–Holstein societies were founded. For the first time since 1849, there was once again a great mass movement of the people; all the pent-up political will and zest for action went into this movement. *Grossdeutsch* and *kleindeutsch* advocates, the National Society and the Reform Society, Liberals and Democrats, everyone was agreed; this was a matter of nationhood, and a matter of law and justice as well. A conference of almost 500 German delegates in Frankfurt at the end of 1863 demanded the separation of the duchies from Denmark under the Duke of Augustenburg. The medium-sized states were also making the same demands; their nationalist policies went this far, at least; and a new medium-sized state in the north could only strengthen the German Confederation and their own position between the great powers.

In contrast, the Prussian government adopted a completely different position. It came out in support of the London Protocols and the recognition of Christian IX, i.e. it placed itself firmly on the basis of the legality of European agreements and international law. It demanded only that the new Danish king adhere to the agreements entered into in 1852. There were several motives for doing this. Bismarck was convinced that any realistic politics in this matter had to be based on European agreements, by which all the powers were bound; anything else would have been nationalist illusion and would certainly have provoked the intervention of both Russia and England, as in 1848–49. He also saw the danger of a Paris–Petersburg axis, particularly as the Tsar had favoured a third candidate for the throne, the Grand Duke of Oldenburg, to whom he was related, and that fit in with the nationalist politics of the medium-sized states. Furthermore, and particularly in the long term, Prussia had no interest in the formation of a new medium-sized state on its northern border. If there were to be any changes, the only development which would have been in the interests of Prussia would be an annexation of the duchies. Basically, Bismarck thought a military solution to be the only possibility. Great changes would also bring internal alterations. But internationally he could not leave the European camp, and internally he could not leave the conservative one; hence this policy of apparently strict compliance with international law. This policy of Bismarck's made him, in the eyes of the public, the traitor of the nationalist cause, or even the violator of federal law. But he did succeed in getting Austria onto his side, despite the fact that he had so recently dealt that country a severe blow by his rejection of the Conference of German Princes. Austria did have its reasons. As a European power whose existence and structure was based upon European agreements, it had, in the event of a conflict, to adhere to those international laws and agreements. There was also the question of whether a nationalist and liberal candidate such as the Duke of Augustenburg was in its interests. Furthermore, there was the factor that the Austrian Foreign Minister, Count von Rechberg, after the failure of his German policies, was now in favour of co-operation and negotiations with Prussia, in contrast to the *grossdeutsch* liberals, who supported Augustenburg. Also, because Austria, as long as it wanted to conduct German policies, could not stand back from the Schleswig–Holstein question, it joined the side of Prussia in this matter. Even so, with this move Austria let itself in for a Prussian policy without making any concrete agreements regarding the Schleswig–Holstein question or even detecting Prussia's real intentions; and it was a policy which had nothing to do with its own interests and, indeed, in some respects ran counter to them and, furthermore, was bound to alienate Austria's real allies in the Confederation, namely the medium-sized states. It was a masterpiece of Bismarck's diplomacy, to entice and lock Austria into his own politics in such a way.

The next development was a confrontation in the Confederation. The medium-sized states wanted nothing to do with the London Protocols and the legal validity of the succession to the Danish throne; instead they wanted to deal with the illegal rule of Christian IX in Holstein by means of 'federal intervention' or 'occupation', which basically meant war, whereas the great powers 'merely' advocated an 'execution' against the legal king and duke, because he refused to withdraw the illegal constitution. This was the legal culmination of very different political conceptions. Prussia and Austria threatened to dissolve the Confederation and forced their policies and legal views through with a majority of just one vote and in the face of fierce resistance from the medium-sized states. Holstein was occupied by federal troops. On 1 February, Austria and Prussia began the 'surety occupation' of Schleswig, and in March they moved into Jutland as well, and all the while the argument in the Confederation concerning the basis and aim of the war continued. Bismarck and Roon, who wanted a prestige success, ordered the now famous storming of the Düppel entrenchments on 8 April 1864, in the face of opposition from local commanders.

The European powers, meanwhile, had not been inactive. Of course, they were not so greatly interested in the Eider Danes, but much more so, geographically speaking, in the Sound, the Vistula and the Rhine, in the power structures in Europe. Russia wanted to prevent the revisionist, Napoleon, from opening the 'Pandora's box', initiating the national revolutionising of Europe, intervening in the north or allying himself with Bismarck; and it also wanted, for reasons of conservative solidarity and worries about liberal German policies, to prevent Bismarck from suffering a defeat and hence a fall from power. In England, there were two different attitudes. The Prime Minister, Palmerston, was pro-Danish and wanted to contain Prussia, but without help from Napoleon as this would give the latter advantages on the Rhine. Other sections of the English government establishment, and also the queen, were opposed to any inter-vention at all. Basically, though, the two flanking powers were in favour of maintaining the status quo; Napoleon, however, wanted to use the situation to bring about changes. At a conference in London, delegates had been debating a diplomatic solution to the crisis since 25 April. This conference, however, was not successful. Denmark, blindly trusting in some kind of pro-Danish intervention, flatly and stubbornly refused to accept any form of compromise, even a division. The threatened English intervention did not come about; there was no support for it in Europe. The only military potential that counted was France's, and England did not want use this at the price Napoleon had to demand; he could not fight an anti-nationalist war for the London Protocols, but only a European war, which meant in Italy and on the Rhine as well. Furthermore, it was the peace faction which won the day in England, supported by public opinion which, particularly because of the adherence to agreements of the German powers, had not been provoked to bellicosity. Palmerston was defeated by the queen. The main danger to the balance of power lay not with Prussia and on the Sound, but with Russia and France; that is why England was able to give way. Russia did not insist on maintenance of the status quo, because the concern about Napoleon and his containment, and the desire to keep Bismarck and Prussia on its side, were stronger; and Bismarck certainly used the chance of negotiating with Napoleon as a means of exerting pressure. In the end, France was able to win neither the unconditional support of the flanking powers nor compensation for its defence of the right to national self-determination. The London Protocols had become defunct. At the end of June, the war was continued without even one of the great powers protesting; the end result was a victory for the German powers. In the peace agreement (1 August–30 October), Denmark surrendered Schleswig–Holstein to Austria and Prussia, and they took it on as a condominium.

It had been a peculiar war. It would be oversimplification to describe it from the standpoint of 1866 and 1870 as a war of annexation or hegemonical interests. The antagonisms had existed for a long time, and the crisis and the ensuing war were a direct result of Danish politics. Admittedly, Bismarck gladly accepted both the crisis and the war, subsequently steering further developments himself and in a direction which was conducive to his own interests. The war was an old-fashioned cabinet and coalition war. It was not, initially, a national war; it was conducted in opposition to the popular movement. Bismarck had not nationalised it; on the contrary, he had internationalised it. But it was precisely because of this that he had managed to prevent any international involvement and had, in the end, made it an issue of German national interests and achieved one of the great national political goals of 1848. Because he had adhered firmly to the European agreements of 1852 — which were in opposition to the goals of the nationalist movement — Bismarck had been able to win the support of Austria and prevent, or at any rate destroy, a pro-Danish front of the great powers, such as had existed in 1848–49. In the face of national protest and opposition from the medium-sized states and the Augustenburg claimant, he had achieved this national success in his own way.

The European consequences were no less important than the national German ones. Russia had remained neutral and had not, this time, allied itself with France; it had remained neutral — perhaps benevolently so — with regard to Prussia and its possible German policies. But the position of England was the really new feature. For one thing, England's continental policies were now primarily determined by the opposition to Napoleon, his hegemonical tendencies and his restlessness. This had the effect of lightening the burden on Germany — both Prussia and Austria. But more than this, the political mood in England had changed. There was still, it is true, a strong dislike of the anti-liberal Prussian regime, but the politics of halves and wholes, of attempted and completed interventions, the politics of Palmerston, had been discredited. England now adopted a neutral stance with regard to the continent; it turned its back on the continent. It was now concentrating on its own problems and those of its empire. England was now no longer a potential opponent of a Prussian national German policy. This situation had not existed in central Europe for 300 years: that one could count on the neutrality of the two strongest European flanking powers in German matters. In terms of international politics, that is the reason why Prussia and Austria had to contend only with Napoleon in 1866; why it was Napoleon alone, once again, who had to play the role of arbiter.

Public opinion in Germany reacted to the result of the war with ambivalence. On the one hand, people disapproved of the 'false' character of the war, which had been dictated by Prussia and Austria, and were opposed to the violation of the right to self-determination of the people of Schleswig–Holstein, who wanted to be ruled by their own Augustenburg. On the other hand, they could not deny that the war had resulted in a national success. Some of the Prussian liberals, from both wings of the movement, from Waldeck and Mommsen to Droysen, Treitschke and Sybel, from the *Grenzboten* to the *Preussische Jahrbücher*, altered their position and became supporters of the Prussian annexation, considering it to be a suitable means of solving the German Question as a whole. The attitude to Bismarck's policies began to change; right in the middle of the domestic political confrontation there appeared to be the possibility of a national political consensus.

The conflict over the 'spoils' of 1864, i.e. the condominium, then, as is well known, led to the war of 1866, to the questions of German dualism and German nationhood being settled by means of military force, to Austria being excluded from Germany, and to the Prussian foundation of the Reich. But this was not an intended or necessary development. It was also not the only or even the obvious direction of Bismarck's politics. These were not aimed at a *kleindeutsch* foundation of the Reich. Apart from simple tactical manoeuvring and thought-games, there were other alternatives and options; there was the possibility of a dualistic settlement on the basis of a division of spheres of influence.

Let us first look at the interests and initial positions of the two powers. Prussia wanted to annex the duchies. Or, if — out of respect for the wishes of Austria, the medium-sized states, and public opinion — it had to accept the Duke of Augustenburg, then the new medium-sized state should at least be militarily and economically incorporated into Prussia. It was with this in mind that Bismarck conducted negotiations with Augustenburg in the summer of 1864 and again in February 1865. This was all a step in the direction of north German hegemony for Prussia. Additionally, Bismarck wanted to use the Schleswig–Holstein question as a lever in the furtherance of his German policies. Of course, this was Prussian power politics, aimed at increasing power and the expansion of Prussia. But there were various aspects to this policy, regarding both its means and its ends. There was the tendency to expel Austria from Germany, and there was the possibility of reaching a settlement. There was the possibility of diplomatic solutions (and victories), and there was the *ultima ratio* of war. Bismarck was more than a clever diplomat; he was — if we can use the well-worn word just once — a demonic power-politician, he was a 'tiger', and one cannot, as Heinrich von Sybel's official history of the foundation of the Reich was criticised for doing, restyle him as a 'domestic cat'. In the final analysis, he did want Prussian hegemony in Germany, and a European position of power for Prussia — if necessary, at the expense of Austria. But he was also a realist and a politician with a sense of the finite. Whatever his ambitions and aims may have been, his politics were always related to actual situations and real possibilities; he may well have tried to shape situations, but he never believed (or presumed) that he alone could decide upon future developments or plan them in advance.

As early as the summer of 1864, Bismarck held discussions with the Austrian Foreign Minister, Rechberg, on the possibility of an extensive negotiated settlement. In a joint war against France, Austria was to recapture Lombardy, and Schleswig–Holstein was, once and for all, to become Prussian; in other words, there would be a Prussian expansion in the north and an Austrian expansion in Italy. The position of Austria in Italy was connected to its position in Germany. This was a peculiar, old-fashioned and pre-national power-political calculation, but during these times the idea of great territorial revisions was always coming up. Bismarck did not push this plan with all his energy; it was for him more of a tactic, playing with a policy of conservative solidarity. Behind this tactic was the possibility of a Prussian guarantee of Austria's European position, on a *quid pro quo* basis. Of course, whether Bismarck really believed that this policy — against France and against the most powerful tendency of the time — had any real chance of success is a matter open to doubt. In any event, he experimented with it. Admittedly, at the time these plans were rejected by the monarchs. Franz Joseph did not want an Italian compensation, and an insecure one at that, but a German one, and Wilhelm was still very reluctant about an annexation of Schleswig–Holstein; he wanted some level of Prussian hegemony in the Confederation. At any rate, there definitely seemed to be possibilities for a compromise and a division of influence.

In 1864, Austria had got into an almost absurd situation. It was allied to Prussia but was combating its annexation tendencies, and it had alienated its natural allies in the Confederation, namely the medium-sized states. Schleswig–Holstein was also strategically an untenable and remote position. As a great power, it had little room for manoeuvre in the game of European power politics. An alliance with France could only have been achieved by surrendering Venetia; Austria was not yet prepared to do this. An understanding with Russia was impossible on account of the tangible competition over Rumania, not to mention the other, more wide-reaching antagonisms. A compromise with Prussia would only have been possible with a surrender of both the position in the north and a portion of German hegemony. This may have improved security in Europe, but in the final analysis, and in the long term, Austria was not prepared to do this (at least not yet). Because it stubbornly clung to its position on all fronts, it was unable to win any allies. Where Prussia was concerned, it was uncertain. Austria had co-operated with Prussia in connection with the Schleswig–Holstein crisis, and this policy was not entirely without success. Rechberg had tried to continue with this policy after the victory; in view of Austria's precarious financial and security position, it had its advantages; the alliance with the medium-sized states had become very fragile, the Schleswig–Holstein movement was too liberal, and the Tsar was still threatening with the Oldenburg candidacy. Apart from the attractions of a realistic settlement, Rechberg also had some sympathy for traditional conservative solidarity. But in the summer of 1864, as we have already said, this did not produce any tangible results. When Rechberg did not succeed in obtaining Prussia's agreement for Austrian membership of the Zollverein, it seemed that the policy of co-operation had failed on account of the resolute obstinacy of Prussia, which was defending its position of power with all available means. Rechberg was forced to resign. He, in any event, was no longer the right man for achieving a settlement. After much hesitation and repeated changes of course, Austria finally adopted a policy of confrontation. From this Bismarck drew the conclusion that the policy of settlement had failed; that the politics of conservative solidarity in the German Question were not compatible with Prussian interests. On another occasion this pointed him in the direction of the liberal-nationalist movement, but that depended on the situation.

Austria then returned to the candidacy of Augustenburg. But it rejected the Prussian version of a satellite state. 'He would rather be a potato farmer than regent of this state,' remarked Biegeleben, the leading official of the Austrian diplomatic service. The crisis came to a head in the early part of the summer of 1865. As an occupational power, Austria supported the vociferous pro-Augustenburg movement, which also had the administrative state government on its side. The medium-sized states were also pushing for the Augustenburg solution in the Confederation. The great powers were arguing over the various aspects of the formation of an assembly of estates. On 29 May a Prussian royal council decided that a full annexation should now be attempted, even at the risk of a war. This was the final departure from the (traditional) conservative idea of dual sovereignty. But Bismarck decided against waging a war at that juncture. He too found the condominium on his own doorstep unbearable. He by no means excluded war as a means of achieving his political ends, and he did everything to make the international, national and domestic political climate favourable for a war; but he also did not discard the possibility of achieving his goals by the exertion of pressure, without war. The situation was not favourable for a war, at least not yet, particularly if such a war was to help overcome the internal Prussian deadlock, to reverse the domestic antagonisms, as Bismarck wished. The European situation was, it is true, not entirely unfavourable, but France had not yet been neutralised and that was an essential prerequisite if one wanted to risk an open conflict. German public opinion could not yet be mobilised for a policy of conflict; the nationalist movement was pro-Augustenburg; the annexation advocated by Bismarck was regarded as a particularistic Prussian policy. As long as a peaceful settlement still seemed possible and there was no compulsive reason for going to war, this war would not have the backing of the country. But without the basis of popular support, Bismarck considered that a policy of annexation and of war would not be possible, would have no hope of succeeding. Finally, Bismarck wanted to defeat the ultra-conservative pro-coup faction at home and eliminate the chief of the war cabinet, Manteuffel, before tackling the Schleswig–Holstein problem again; in August 1865, Manteuffel was appointed military governor in Schleswig and so removed from the centre of power. It was these considerations that determined Bismarck's politics in 1865.

Threats of war and ultimatums then once again led to a settlement between Austria and Prussia, the Gastein Convention of 14 August 1865. The administration of the duchies was provisionally divided: in Schleswig Prussian, in Holstein Austrian with special rights for Prussia. That was, first of all, a success for Bismarck. He had, it is true, originally wanted to share the sovereignty, but later found the new solution perfectly acceptable: it left the future open and concealed new issues of conflict. He had once again persuaded Austria to co-operate and to hold on to the untenable positions in the north. The reasons why Austria went along with this policy of appeasement were, for one, the looming threat of bankruptcy, which would have made a mobilisation of the army a highly dangerous venture. The other reason was a general change of tack in Vienna: the constitutional and national political course of Schmerling, which was liberal, *grossdeutsch* and anti-Prussian, had been abandoned. The new Minister-President, Belcredi, even sought an understanding with Hungary; in terms of German politics, the alternative to appeasement seemed to him and his followers to be too risky; they were afraid that supporting Augustenburg would strengthen liberalism too much in Germany, and, what was more dangerous, in Prussia. But the Prussian–Austrian understanding turned out to be only an interlude. Bismarck would have been prepared to enter into a lasting settlement only if all the important concessions had come from Austria, i.e. if Austria had surrendered Holstein and agreed to the division in terms of German politics. In the event, however, Gastein was merely a temporary settlement.

Public opinion and the medium-sized states protested almost unanimously — because Prussia had long since been written off in this matter — against Austria: it had left Augustenburg out in the cold and had, furthermore, completely ignored the emotional matter of the unity of the duchies — '*up ewig ungedeelt*' (never to be divided). But by the beginning of 1866, it was already becoming clear that the new agreement was untenable. For Prussia, it had only been a step towards annexation; for Austria, it was an extreme concession. It was in fact the pro-Augustenburg movement which split the powers again. Austria favoured this movement in Holstein; Prussia protested and laid claim to rights of objection. Bismarck used all these antagonisms to raise the temperature of the conflict. Prussia considered that Austria had violated the terms of the agreement. The crisis was approaching a state of war. On 28 February 1866, a Prussian royal council decided that the 'unavoidable war' for Prussia's position in Germany, at least in the north, should not be directly entered into, but should certainly be prepared for internationally by means of negotiations with Napoleon and Italy. One week before this, the Austrian council of ministers had decided not to evade the war. Prussia, therefore, was determined, if necessary, to fight for a strengthening of its position of power, and Austria was equally determined to defend its position by force, even at the risk of another war in Italy.

Prussia's desire for war was quite clear. It arose, initially, from *raison d'état*, from Prussia's power-political interests. But war and the will to war could not be separated from the German questions and the national interests of the Germans. Bismarck believed that in these times a war could not be started arbitrarily and without the support of public opinion; it could only be successfully fought if a national goal was at stake. Therefore, it was necessary to identify the Prussian interests and national requirements which were at stake. This, however, was not just a pretext; it was more than just tactics and propaganda, more than a retrospective legitimisation of a desire for war by skilfully manipulating the arguments of the times, more than just a skilful appeal to the alliance with the modern forces of public opinion and popular movements. Of course, it was all this as well, and it is indicative of the greatness of the conservative Bismarck, whose background was, in fact, the tradition of cabinet politics, that he clearly recognised this modern style of politics and adjusted himself to it. As far as Bismarck was concerned, Prussian interests were paramount; he was a man of the state and of the states. But he was convinced that Prussian interests and the interests of German security were identical. If Prussia became the leading power in Germany, then that would be in the German interest. For Bismarck, the war was a Prussian one and a national one at the same time: that was an integrating element of his politics. In this regard, the Prussian liberals held more or less the same convictions.

The conclusions which Bismarck drew from these considerations were admittedly revolutionary. He aimed at an alliance with the nationalist movement. He wanted an 'alliance with the people' in order to take away Austria's hegemonical position and to explode completely the way in which Germany was organised. The means with which this was to be done was federal reform. On 9 April 1866 Bismarck lodged the application for a reform of the Confederation: the federal assembly should become a parliament, the composition of which should be decided by means of universal and equal suffrage in direct elections. A directly-elected parliament would mean, however, as we have often seen, the exclusion of Austria. This was a despotic method, the mobilisation of the nationalist movement, revolution from above. With this manoeuvre, Bismarck wanted to overwhelm Austria; he wanted to make the European powers frightened of intervening, and he wanted to establish the leadership of Prussia. As Bismarck himself later remarked, in a situation of extreme emergency, it is sometimes necessary to use revolutionary methods, he 'threw into the pan' what was 'at the time the strongest of freedom's arts', i.e. universal suffrage, in order to frighten the European powers out of the temptation of 'sticking their fingers into our national pie'. But there were also national and domestic reasons for this tactic, namely to put both the medium-sized states and the liberals, neither of whom were wild about universal suffrage, under pressure. But in the prevailing situation, it was precisely this part of Bismarck's plan that had no success. At that time, public opinion gave no credit to the man of conflict and the violater of Schleswig–Holstein. Not only *grossdeutsch* advocates, North German particularists and clerics, but also supporters of Augustenburg and *kleindeutsch* liberals in south Germany saw in Bismarck's suggestion merely a cunning trick, with which he sought to get applause and praise for his own selfish motives. The medium-sized states, whose support Bismarck had been hoping to win, rejected the suggestion. A parliament which would have squeezed Austria out was not a matter for discussion as far as they were concerned; consequently, they once again moved closer to Austria. Last-ditch efforts, particularly on the part of Bavaria, to reach some sort of negotiated settlement along the lines of a triadic agreement, failed.

The possible war, which apparently the German powers were conditionally determined to fight, had, as well as this national German dimension, also an international European one; it was most definitely a matter of the international power-political constellation. Prussia made international preparations for the war. On 8 April, it entered into an offensive alliance with the kingdom of Italy, valid for a period of three months. In the pact, Italy undertook to enter into a war with Austria; Prussia was in a position to start this war. That was, so to speak, in international terms the alliance with the nationalist revolution, because Italy wanted to complete the foundation of the Italian nation-state; it wanted, at last, to take Venetia from Austria. But it was the great powers who were of decisive importance as far as the international situation was concerned. We may recall: England and Russia were relatively uninvolved as far as the German Question was concerned, both being occupied with matters either outside Europe or at home, and they both saw Napoleon as the potential source of danger, and not the German powers; Russia was in fact rather pro-Prussian, and England was certainly not anti-Prussian. Admittedly, even Prussia could never be absolutely certain of Russia's behaviour; even in Bismarck's calculations there was always a residue of risk.

In contrast to the Olmütz situation of 1849–50, Austria had, since the Crimean War, lost the support of Russia. Even if an understanding with Russia had been possible, it was not an option for Austria: it would at this juncture have produced very negative results for Austria, as well as the hostility of France and Italy, Prussia and Rumania, and that of public opinion in Germany.

Everything now depended on France, on Napoleon. He could either remain neutral or intervene; he could strengthen one or other of the sides in such a way that it would win — either with or without a war. In any event, he wanted to use the German conflict to advance his position of power and supremacy on the continent. The position of France in Europe was the big question at stake; the German Question was only an initiator and aspect of this matter. Both the German powers tried to win assurances from Napoleon. Napoleon, however, did not have a free hand in questions of foreign policy. As a son of the revolution, a plebescitary despot, he had to rely, more than others, on popularity and international successes, and this meant, above all else, that he had to satisfy the growing and peevish nationalism of the French. Personally he was pursuing two main objectives. He wanted, at long last, to finalise the unification of Italy by integrating Venetia; that was, subjectively speaking, the strongest motive; he wanted to achieve that before he died. He also wanted, in the event of a shift in the balance of power in Germany, 'compensations'. His ultimate goal was not, as people in Germany subsequently believed for three generations, a border on the Rhine. But as he himself once said to the Prussian ambassador, 'all the eyes of France are fixed upon the Rhine', and he therefore had to take account of French nationalism; thus he always kept this Rhine objective alive. If it could not be the Rhine, for instance a Rhineland buffer state under French protection, then other compensations would certainly be acceptable, e.g. border alterations in the Palatinate or along the Saar. Furthermore, the formation of a German nation-state, a new European great power, could not be in the interests of even one single French politician. In the prevailing situation, Napoleon did not want an understanding between Prussia and Austria; that would have left Venetia under Austrian rule and completely excluded France from the reorganisation of central Europe. In a rather obscure series of diplomatic moves, he tried to play the two countries off against one another, allow them both to hope for French assistance and obtain promises of compensation from them both.

Bismarck did not need an alliance with France, but he did need France's neutrality. Initially it seemed that he was successful in making sure that France would remain neutral, as this was conducive also to French power-political interests. He wanted, if at all possible, not to have to pay a price for this neutrality, but he also, without committing himself, aroused Napoleon's hopes of a compensation, possibly Luxemburg. Indeed, it was Napoleon who persuaded Italy to accept the Prussian offer of an alliance; he therefore seemed to be virtually committed against Austria, and the level of his potential threat to Prussia was reduced. The prospect that, under French patronage, Schleswig–Holstein would fall to Prussia and Venetia would become Italian seemed to guarantee some sort of French supremacy. Admittedly, Napoleon did not allow himself to be drawn into any formal agreements, but retained his freedom of room to manoeuvre, and this was the uncertainty which Prussia always had to take account of. Certainly the Austrian option was tempting for France. The Prussian–Italian alliance would also endanger French hegemony. But the primary consideration was that French public opinion and many of Napoleon's advisers believed the Rhine to be more important than Italy or the principle of nationality, and for this reason Austria was the better ally, because it was the most suitable partner for great exchange deals concerning Venetia, Silesia and the Rhine. In May, Austria attempted to reach a definitive understanding with France. Austria was prepared to surrender Venetia if Italy would guarantee neutrality. But Italy refused — despite French attempts at mediation. It wanted more than just a diplomatic victory; it demanded, in the interests of national-democratic legitimisation, a plebescite — which Austria had no choice but to reject. Napoleon suggested the formation of an international congress for the settlement and arrangement of 'compensations', something which Bismarck could hardly refuse, even though a congress of this nature would have thwarted all his calculated plans and real hopes for Prussia. But the other powers reacted very reservedly to this suggestion, and Austria, with Italy in mind, rejected it outright. This meant that war was now even more likely. Then, at the last minute, just as war was about to break out, France and Austria entered into a secret agreement on 12 June. In this agreement, Austria undertook to surrender Venetia, even in the event of a victory; France promised to remain neutral and also to persuade Italy to do the same; Austria and the medium-sized states were to expand within Germany, but not to the level of full hegemony; a Rhine state within the Confederation was considered a possibility. Austria believed that it had a good chance of victory. Napoleon, like all the others, was preparing for a long war in which he believed he would play a decisive role because everyone else was dependent on him.

That was the international situation in the early summer of 1866. Bismarck, in consideration of this, played the card of nationalist revolution. He issued a threat to Russian and French diplomats that he would instigate a revolutionary, national war if France intervened; and he meant it.

The negotiations of the German powers were not a matter of the German policies of Prussia and the 'un-German' policies of Austria, as the *kleindeutsch* nationalist movement later believed. Both states were propagating their own power-political interests and, within that framework, their ideas as far as German policies were concerned. But Austrian *raison d'état* was more old-fashioned, and thus Austria still found it easier to think in terms of dividing and sharing out countries and regions, whereas the Prussians were able to be modern and objective and were therefore more able to think in terms of the tendencies of national self-determination.

Prussian politics in the crisis were superior to those of Austria; Prussia was determined, took initiatives and made exact calculations, whereas Austrian politics sometimes had an air of helplessness about them. But that was not only due to the politicians, it was also a result of the situation. Prussia was quite definitely at an advantage because, among other things, it was on the attack. Austria was, as the Tsar revealingly remarked at the beginning of 1866, 'resigned to war'. As early as 21 April, it had mobilised its border troops in the face of the Italian military preparations. It was unable to effect a standstill agreement. Furthermore, Austria needed six to eight weeks to be ready for war. Prussia, on the other hand, needed only three weeks.

There was one final, private mediation attempt by a Saxon-Prussian aristocrat, Anton von der Gablenz, which entailed a division of German hegemony along the line of the River Main. Bismarck initially seized upon the idea and toyed with it for a while, although possibly only to help the king overcome his last scruples about the war. In any event, it was now the turn of the Austrian Kaiser to reject the proposal; distrust of Bismarck had become overwhelming, and the proposal did not even include a guarantee regarding Venetia. But Bismarck was quite happy about this failure. On 1 June 1866, Austria brought the Schleswig–Holstein question before the Bundestag and at the same time called up the assemblies of the estates in Holstein, its 'zone of occupation'. This was a decisive step in the direction of war. Prussia protested and invaded Holstein on 9 June. With this move, Prussia had taken the law into its own hands and had violated the federal agreement. On 10 June, Prussia presented its detailed plan for a reform of the Confederation, one excluding Austria. This was, of course, nothing more than a demonstration, a demonstration of the national and constitutionally legitimised objective of war. On 11 June, Austria applied for a mobilisation of the non-Prussian federal army, on account of the Prussian military action; this application was granted on 14 June. Bavaria, Württemberg, the Hesse states, Saxony, Hanover and a number of smaller states voted for Austria; the majority of the small states in northern and central Germany voted against it; Baden abstained. Prussia declared the Confederation to be dissolved, and issued an ultimatum to Saxony, Hanover and the Electorate of Hesse, all of whom rejected it. On 15 June, Prussia invaded these states. On 16 June, the Bundestag including Baden, voted in favour of the dissolution of the Confederation. It seemed that the opposing interests could now only be settled by force. The cold war had now finally become a hot war.

Public opinion had naturally been taking an intense interest in these developments. The war which was looming was an unpopular one. Everywhere there were demonstrations and proclamations against the 'war of brothers'; even the Prussians were not enthusiastic about it. The conservatives of the *Kreuzzeitung* newspaper saw the interests of Prussia and Austria as being on an equal basis; even if we win, Gerlach told Bismarck, we are threatened with 'severe ruin'. The liberals wanted either unification without a war, or, if there had to be a war, then certainly they did not want this one, the war of a Prussia which since 1848 had so rudely disappointed all liberal hopes, the war of the hated government of conflict, the war of Bismarck, who was only conducting it in his own interests and as a means of escaping from the conflict. In short, even those who in the cause of the national constitutional state would not shy away from war, could not identify, or even associate, themselves with the reactionary Prussia. Bismarck's nationalist-democratic rallying-cry could not work, not any more, not after the years of conflict. The liberals in the medium-sized states were helpless; any victory in this war would be a defeat from their point of view. In Bavaria, in Württemberg and in Saxony, people were afraid of Prussian hegemony, afraid of the French, whom they considered to be using Bismarck for their own ends, and afraid of a division along the River Main. Admittedly, Lassalle's workers' organisation supported Bismarck's war because Bismarck was in favour of universal suffrage, and they trusted the nationalist revolutionary dynamism. On 16 June, workers demonstrated for the flag of Bismarck and Garibaldi, and Bismarck released the president of the organisation, Johann von Schweitzer, from prison; his newspaper, the *Sozialdemokrat*, was granted a loan.

What sort of a war was this? Certainly it was not, as Moltke said, 'defence against a threat to one's own existence'. It was not born of the 'tempest' of the people, but was a war which had been 'recognised as necessary by the cabinet and intentionally and deliberately planned over a long period of time, not for the purpose of winning land or other material values, but for an ideal'; such was Moltke's description of Prussian hegemony. First and foremost, then, it was a war of the cabinet, of the state, a hegemonical war. Prussia had wanted this war, Bismarck had instigated it; out of an elementary interest of state and power, Prussia had placed itself in opposition to Austria and finally also against the Confederation. As a 'halved and divided' great power Prussia had to push for change; it was the only way in which it could permanently consolidate its existence. The dividing-line between self-assertion and power expansion was necessarily a moving one. The clarity with which Prussian politics then aimed for power expansion was admittedly the work of Bismarck. It may not have begun that way, but, in the end, this had to lead to war. It was the only way in which Prussia's hegemonical policies could be realised, because Austria was not prepared to tolerate any devaluation of its leading position — not least because it believed that a surrender of its position and claims in Germany would automatically lead to a surrender of its position as a great power — that it would, in fact, be the beginning of the end.

Prussia's will to power and Austria's will to assert itself, then, clashed with one another; the tensions of German dualism finally led to this war. It did not have to be so. Austria was now merely resigned to war; Prussia was the driving, dynamic, initiating power, determined to go to war. But, historically speaking, this war was not an improbable event or a freak occurrence; it was not the result of deliberate or reckless politics. War was still regarded by the politically active, indeed, by all contemporaries, as a completely legitimate means of achieving vital, or even not so vital, political objectives; the Crimean War and the Italian War were two very different examples of this. The human race had not yet become morally preoccupied with the problem of war guilt. The hundred-year-old Prussian–Austrian dualism was a power-political phenomenon in which a military solution was never outside the realms of possibility as far as any of the participants were concerned. In that respect, the war was an existential clash between two opposing political claims to power, each with its own legitimisation, which in the final analysis proved to be irreconcilable with one another. Even Austria was not acting purely in self-defence. The question of whether the war could be described as 'just' was unanswerable. That was the tragic aspect of this war, despite the clear division of offensive and defensive tendencies in 1866. This aspect went beyond both Bismarck and the politicians in Vienna. But this war of cabinet and hegemony was still a national war, or, as the people and the nation had distanced themselves from one another, at least a war of unification. There was a revolutionary right of the German nation to a nation-state, a right to revolutionise the Confederation, because reform of the Confederation had proved to be impossible. This right could only be realised by excluding Austria, whose existence made the formation of a nation-state impossible, and this therefore clashed with Austria's equally legitimate right to belong to Germany, and the right of the Germans to live together with Austria in a political union. This was the tragedy of the clashing of two legitimate but opposing rights. But the right to nationalist revolution remained a right. In making itself the promoter of this right, Prussia assured itself of the national legitimisation of its destruction of the Confederation and of its war.

The chances of the warring parties were by no means clear in the eyes of the contemporary observers. Prussia was much weaker in terms of population size, its territory was divided by hostile states, its army unused to war. Austria, admittedly, had to fight a war on two fronts, in Italy and in Germany, and in Germany it had to fight a war in coalition with the uncoordinated armies of the medium-sized states, and it was also less advanced than Prussia in some respects. But people were expecting a long war, some even expected a new Seven Years' War, and they were expecting other European powers to intervene. Prussia's position was by no means regarded as favourable. The stock exchange in Berlin was speculating on an Austrian victory, despite the fact that the minister of conflict, Bismarck, had secured funds for financing the war from his banker, Gerson Bleichröder. In short, and this is something that was forgotten very quickly after the victory, Bismarck had taken a big risk.

Among the political strategies which Bismarck adopted for this expectedly long war was one which is especially worthy of our attention. This was the plan to mobilise the nationalist revolution of the peoples against the Habsburg state. The authorities in Berlin were incredibly well informed: they had contacts with revolutionaries and émigrés, and they had agents. All this was intensified in 1866, and the revolution and the 'diversion' were prepared, particularly with the Hungarians and the southern Slavs. Hungarian and Italian legions were stationed in Silesia, later also with prisoners of war; Garibaldi was supposed to move into Dalmatia and then Hungary, and this was then supposed to instigate the kingdom of Italy to move on Vienna; similar preparations were made from Belgrade and Bucharest. In a proclamation to the Czechs, which was worded in co-operation with an anarchistic-socialist refugee, they were promised a national position similar to that of the Hungarians; in the event that the Tsar did not hold his peace, they even hoped for a Polish uprising.

Certainly Bismarck did not want to destroy the Habsburg Empire; these manoeuvres were threats which were designed to force Austria into making concessions. But Bismarck also considered the extreme case of an existential conflict to be a possibility and made appropriate preparations. In a fight of life and death, so he said, he would have to take any allies he could find. The conservative monarchist Bismarck, the Prussian, the politician who had so distanced himself from nationalism, allied himself in this situation with all the forces of nationalist-democratic revolution. That was his *Realpolitik*.

Contrary to expectation, the war was only a short one. After Prussia had very quickly (by 29 June) defeated the armies of Hanover and the Electorate of Hesse, which had stood between its western and eastern halves, the decisive victory over the Austrians came a mere three weeks after the beginning of the war, at the battle of Königgrätz (known to English-speaking historians as Sadowa). The strategic concept of the Prussian chief-of-staff, Moltke, which was not accepted without a struggle, was that three armies would march separately to Bohemia and not unite until they reached the battlefield; 'march apart, fight together', that was the recipe for success. The Prussian armies managed to outmanoeuvre the strategic advantage of the Austrians, the inner line, and the immobility and mistakes of the Austrians enabled the Prussians to take the best tactical starting positions even before the battle. It is true that the battle did not end in the surrounding and annihilation of the Austrian army; most of the Austrian troops managed to escape. But the victory for Prussia was categorical and sufficient. Prussia, even though it was on the attack, lost only 9,000 men, while Austria lost 25,000. The Austrian victories in the Italian land battle (Custozza, 24 June) and sea battle (Lissa, 20 July) were of no comparable consequence, and even the later Prussian victories over the armies of the southern German states, particularly in Bavaria, were of relatively minor significance.

If we try to discover the reasons for this quick and surprising victory, we could say that it was the victory of the modern army of a modern state over the old-fashioned army of an old-fashioned state. The organisation of the Austrian army was outdated; it still did not have divisions; the command structure was clumsy; the role of the senior planning staff was unclear; the leadership was inflexible. The decades of financial shortages in the Reich showed their effect; the periods of service had often been unrealistic and consequently the standard of training had suffered; effectiveness was reduced. Where leadership was concerned, dynastic and feudal aspects played a greater role than expertise and performance. An archduke, Albrecht, was given supreme command in Italy because a victory was more likely there and the Austrians did not want to make him suffer a defeat at the hands of the Prussians; Count Ludwig von Benedek, whose only experience was in Italy, was given, against his will, supreme command in Bohemia. The structure of the state affected decisions such as these, and this aspect was at least as important as the individual fact that anyone would have had a hard time against a military genius such as Moltke. At long last, the basic structural weakness of the German Confederation worked to Austria's disadvantage; even in war, the medium-sized states remained particularistic; the Bavarians did not come to Bohemia; there was no overall concept; the problems of a coalition war remained unsolved.

On the other side was the modernity of Prussia, and this amounted to more than just the absence of the Austrian shortcomings. The Prussian army was well organised and well trained; the initiative of the junior commanders, the functional co-operation and the clear channels of command complemented each other; the senior commanders had also received excellent tactical training; the planning authority of the general staff had been more or less established, although even in Prussia this was in the face of resistance from the old soldiers and the court; the chief of staff was actually in charge in the field. Moltke was a military genius, but he was also the product of a specific type of Prussianism: schooled on Clausewitz, he based his work on a thoroughly realistic, rational and unemotional analysis of war; far removed from all feelings of prestige, he was guided by a clear objective, which was to destroy the enemy forces by surrounding them; his campaign was based on rational and thorough planning. That was the basis of his strategic successes, the likes of which had not been seen since the first Napoleon, and it was the basis for a war being won in one great battle. The Prussians were better equipped; between 1849 and 1866 the entire army had been given the needle-gun, which could be used in the lying position and deliver seven shots in one minute (the previous rifles could only manage two), although it did have a shorter range and a number of other defects. The Prussians were much more mobile, primarily because they used their extensive railway network for military purposes, a very modern scheme. Since the 1840s, Moltke had been using the strategic possibilities of the railways in all his plans and manoeuvres. This had revolutionised all the previous concepts of forces, distances and times. In 1866, all six Prussian railway lines were available for a mobilisation; the Austrians had just one, and even that was not used effectively. Moltke had already sent his army to Bohemia before the Austrians were able even to concentrate their forces. There was a similar story where the use of the telegraph was concerned; Moltke conducted the war from Berlin right up until immediately before the battle by using the telegraph.

The victory of Königgrätz made an enormous impression in Europe. 'Casca il mondo,' was the comment of the Pope. All the expectations had been overturned. In particular, Napoleon's calculation that he would end up being the arbiter in a long war had totally failed to materialise. But the continued progress of the war became an international problem for precisely this reason. Austria looked to Napoleon as a mediator, initially in Italy; Napoleon then led the negotiations, which began on 5 July. Admittedly, a ceasefire was not agreed. Austria was involved in negotiations, but had to be prepared for a Prussian invasion of Vienna. A possible French intervention was a threat to the victors, Prussia and Italy, and Napoleon certainly used this threat as a means of exerting pressure. Seen objectively, however, the danger of an intervention was not so great. The French army was poorly equipped; Napoleon was gravely ill, and he feared that the Germans, under Prussian leadership, would embark upon a nationalist revolutionary offensive against France. He also saw the difficulties involved in leading France, the representative of the nationalist principle in Europe, into an alliance with the supra-national and anti-nationalist Austria. Even so, the situation was an open one. Napoleon's Foreign Minister, Edouard Drouyn de l'Huys, was moving towards an alliance with Austria. The feeling which was expressed by Louis Adolphe Thiers on the founding of the North German Confederation was a widely held one: France had not suffered such a defeat for 400 years. Bismarck realised, immediately after Königgrätz, that peace could only be achieved internationally if Prussia spared Austria; it would have to go for a negotiated peace rather than a victorious peace. On 14 July, Prussia and

France reached a peace agreement. This included the union of Venetia with Italy, the dissolution of the German Confederation and the exclusion of Austria from Germany, although Austria's existence and constitution as a state was otherwise to be guaranteed; recognition of a Prussian-led North German Confederation; the annexation of Schleswig–Holstein by Prussia, with the reservation of a vote in the northern part of Schleswig concerning the question of nationality; undeclared further annexations in northern Germany, i.e. Hanover, the Electorate of Hesse, Nassau; and finally the right of the independent states of southern Germany to form their own internationally independent southern confederation. This was a three-way division of Germany and the limitation of Prussia along the line of the River Main. This was the price which Bismarck had to pay for Napoleon not intervening and also for accepting the Prussian annexations in northern Germany. Admittedly, Bismarck had his own reasons for stopping at the River Main; the consolidation of the new Prussian North Germany would have been much more difficult with the anti-Prussian southern states. But that was not the main reason. There were limits to what could be achieved in the face of the other powers in Europe. From Napoleon's standpoint, the conditions of this agreement were moderate ones, which did not contravene his role as a pioneer of a Europe of nations and possibly even guaranteed France some influence over the independent southern zone — and perhaps indeed even win some kind of gratitude on the part of the Italian and German nationalist movements. He had finally refused any kind of commitment for Austria, after intensive negotiations on the subject in Paris between 4 July and 10 July. An acceptance may have better served French power-political interests, but not the legitimisation principle of Napoleonic rule. In that much, Napoleon's decision did have its inner logic.

On the basis of this understanding, Bismarck quickly brought the peace negotiations with Austria to an end. Austria was, in defeat, ready to accept these conditions of peace. Now that France had come to an understanding with Prussia, Austria had no other choice. Even so, there arose a very characteristic difficulty. The Prussian king, still thinking in his old-fashioned way, wanted the defeated foe to be 'punished' by means of a surrender of territory by either Austria or its main ally in northern Germany, Saxony. On the other hand, it went against the dynastic nature of the king to simply dethrone fellow monarchs, such as those of Hanover, the Electorate of Hesse and Nassau, and annex their countries, as Bismarck wanted to do. Bismarck finally got his way after many heated arguments, in which he was supported by the Crown Prince, and which he classically and dramatically described in his memoirs. He followed the cool calculation of *raison d'état* contrary to all traditional ideas that a surrender of territory had to be the end result of a war. Politics should not have the 'objective of a Nemesis'; on the contrary, it must orientate itself towards that 'which is necessary for the Prussian state'. He regarded the existence of 'amputated' parts of states within the new North German Confederation as much more dangerous than full annexation, which he also favoured on account of his Prussian sense of power; in the case of Saxony, there was also the additional factor that both France and Austria had insisted that it remain intact. Certainly he was opposed to any 'amputation' of Austria; in his calculating manner, he was thinking of the long-term prospects for peace and future developments. Austria was a great European power and should remain so, and Prussia had to keep its options for a future alliance with this power open; Bismarck did not want to provoke a prolonged enmity or retaliatory policies. This peace, then, revealed a typical 'double face' of Bismarck's politics. In a completely unconventional manner, he spared the southern states and Austria, because these were the allies of the future. Also completely unconventional was the radical destruction of the northern states by annexation, a Napoleonic total revision of the map in contradiction to all legal standards and historical rights. This, once again, was a rejection of conservative principles. Here was a national revolution, comparable with the elimination of the Italian dynasties in the wake of the unification of Italy, annexations based on a Greater Prussian *raison d'état*, but also legitimised by the national desire for unification — it was both Prussian and nationalistic at the same time. Thus arose a new Prussia. On 26 July, on the basis of the Franco-Prussian agreements, the preliminary peace of Nikolsburg was formalised. This forced Italy, as well, to be satisfied with Venetia and to relinquish its demands in Trient and South Tyrol.

Admittedly, this preliminary peace did not solve the international crisis once and for all. Napoleon did not initially discuss the question of compensations and did not react to the allusions of the Prussian envoy. But then the nationalistic, compensationalist politicians in Paris began to exert more influence. On 16 July, Benedetti, the French envoy in Berlin, spoke of revisions to the borders of the Saar and the Palatinate (the borders determined in 1814) and of the annexation of Luxemburg. Bismarck reacted in a dilatory manner. On 5 August, the talk was of the Bavarian Palatinate and the left bank of the Rhine in Hesse; it is clear that even in France the traditions of gaining territory were still strong. This was categorically rejected by Bismarck; not one German village could or would be surrendered — and this was something which everybody, from King Wilhelm to the anti-Prussian radical democrat Wilhelm Liebknecht, agreed upon. As far as Bismarck was concerned, this would have been the end of any Prussian nationalist policy and a severe diplomatic defeat; he once again threatened a nationalist revolutionary war on the basis of the 1849 Constitution of the Reich, and a revolutionising of the Habsburg Empire. Of course, he was assuming that Napoleon would relent, and this is indeed what happened on 12 August when he was informed that it had all been a misunderstanding, and that the chauvinistic Foreign Minister had now been sacked. In subsequent negotiations, there was still talk of French compensations in Belgium and Luxemburg, but Bismarck did not commit himself. France offered Prussia an alliance in return for Prussian support, but such an alliance would have been of no value to Prussia now that the war was over — indeed, because it would have provoked Russia and England, it would even have been damaging. Furthermore, the demand which Bismarck could have made, namely the annexation of the southern German states, was not something which France could have guaranteed, and was also, in consideration of the German and European situation, not feasible. France was no longer the spokesman of (western) Europe, as it had been at the end of the Crimean War and during the Italian War; it had been isolated by England. This reduced Napoleon's room for manoeuvre and increased Bismarck's.

Once again it must be said, in consideration of the long tradition of anti-French nationalism in Germany, that it was completely normal for France to have to react to any shifts in the balance of power in central Europe. It must also be remembered that compensations were not as disreputable in those times as they may now seem in our democratic age. But naturally one can no more deny the very aggressive and peevish nationalism of the French than that of the Germans.

Napoleon believed that he could live with the new, enlarged Prussia; indeed, the national reorganisation was a contributing factor of order and the balance of power; he believed that only the nation-states would be able to maintain Europe's position between the giants of the future, i.e. Russia and the United States. It was for this reason that he did not regard the result of the war as a defeat; he wanted to appear as the protector of the new order, and Bismarck had done everything to keep his relationship with Napoleon open and positive. It was a different matter with the radical nationalists. They, like Thiers, considered the result of the war to be a catastrophe. The need for security and a sense of power played an equally important role here as the peculiar need for prestige and a collective feeling of glory. This is how that odd sentiment, characterised by the call 'Revenge for Sadowa' came into being. French policy concerning Germany developed between these two positions over the next five years.

Finally, Russia also tried to intervene in the new order in Europe. Russia attempted, in an anti-revolutionary and dynastic manner, to prevent the fall of entire dynasties. The Tsar announced his disappointment over the nationalist revolutionary war policies of his Prussian allies and the 'democratic' character of the new Confederation; the Prime Minister, Gorchakov, was, despite all the allegiances between Russia and Prussia, pro-French and tended to side more with Austria in this matter. Russia tried to secure a position in south Germany for Austria. To counter the mediation monopoly of Napoleon, Russia suggested a congress of the powers. This would have posed a threat to the entire consolidated solution and Bismarck's policies. England rejected this suggestion, and so did Bismarck; again he threatened to instigate a nationalist revolution in the south-east and east, but he also held out the carrot of support for the Russian demands of a revision of the neutralisation of the Black Sea, and he promised to protect those German dynasties that were related to the Tsar's family. Russia dropped the plan. In the face of the passivity of England and the ambivalence of France, it was too weak to prevent the overthrow of the old system. Furthermore, the new Prussian order in central Europe, even though it was nationalist and revolutionary, was still more acceptable than a Napoleonic system, which would have been anti-Polish and, in fact, essentially conservative.

In the end, England had managed to adhere to its new policy of non-intervention. Despite some antipathy towards Prussia, the interests of England were, in fact, well served by a consolidation of Germany in relation to the continental flanking powers. If the dualism did not last, the Prussian leadership was more stable than the Austrian. The balance of power was not yet being threatened by Prussia or by Germany, but by Napoleonic France, the troublemaker of the decade, and, in the longer term, by a once again powerful Russia.

In short, the European powers in the end accepted — had to accept — the new order of German affairs without any intervention.

In accordance with the preliminary peace agreement, the formal peace treaty was completed on 23 August in Prague. This treaty, in accordance with the wishes of France, internationally guaranteed the independence of the southern states. But the idea of a separate southern confederation, as favoured by both Austria and Napoleon, was now no longer pressing. Baden and Württemberg were opposed to the Bavarian ambitions of supremacy (the old dilemma of triadic politics); in fact, Baden was opposed to any isolation from the north. Bismarck could have no interest in such a Confederation. He had used the French wish for compensations to form secret defensive and offensive alliances with the south German states at the peace negotiations; these were to consist of a mutual guarantee of territorial and political integrity and the placement of all troops under the supreme command of the Prussian king in a defensive emergency. This was directed not against a revisionist Austria but against an interventionalist France.

9. Consequences

The primary consequence of the events of 1866 was the defeat of Austria. It had tried to simultaneously uphold its position as ruler in northern Italy, as a keeper of the peace in the Danube region, and as a leading power in Germany; this proved to be too much for it. It no longer had any sufficient cover in Europe, and it was in a state of continual existential crisis domestically — constitutionally, financially and with respect to the nationalities. Even though the contemporaries had not foreseen Austria's defeat, in retrospect the reasons were only too clear.

Austria had to leave Germany. Once and for all, the idea of a 'Reich' in the sense of universalistic rule, the inheritance of the Roman Empire, as had been represented by the Habsburg Empire, was buried, and neither Bismarck nor any nationalist liberal wanted to revive such a Reich. Also buried was the German Confederation of 1815. This confederation had, as a result of its structure as a federation of states and the fact of German dualism, proved itself to be incapable of developing further, of solving the problems of the time, or of satisfying the demands of society for security, constitutional order, economic and legal union. Hardly anybody longed for a revival of this confederation.

Austria pulled out of Germany, the German Austrians left the national union of the Germans. It was the end of an era which had lasted nearly a thousand years. It was the first modern division of the nation. Yet it was at the same time, rather paradoxically, the establishment of a German nation — by means of the rejection of the supra-national Austria and the concept of letting Germany exist as merely a part of a supra-national state in central Europe. The core of the tragedy of German history is that the Germans could only constitute a political nation by means of division. These developments caused sadness, bitterness and disappointment both at the time and later, and the feeling of sadness — unrelated to any revisionism — concerning this tragic course of German history can still affect one today. After 1871, this wound of division apparently healed quite quickly in non-Austrian Germany; in Austria, it seemed, this process took longer; but then the wound was opened again during the national conflicts. Then, after 1918, it once again became the trauma of the national existence of all Germans and had an infinite effect on our shared history. The Austrian German Adolf Hitler was a belated consequence of that division of 1866, which through him, more than half a century later, cast its unholy shadow on the history of the Germans, the Europeans, and the human race. Such a great historical development, such a tragic turn of events, cannot be that easily forgotten.

Division of the nation, the exclusion of Austria — there is also in this a charge against Bismarck, against Prussia, against the *kleindeutsch* advocates, because there can be no doubt that this development was the result of a Prussian war. But one must consider what the alternatives would have been had Austria won, or the status quo continued. This was, basically, a *grossdeutsch*, central European federal system, as the federalist publicist Constantin Frantz propagated at the time and continued to do so well into the 1870s in his grumbling and critical way. In the wake of the criticism since 1945 of the national political wrong direction of the Germans, this possibility has once again been presented as the better alternative. But a system like this did not hold out much promise of stability or integrational effectiveness. Without a strong leadership and without a genuine parliament, it would hardly have been able to solve the internal conflicts or even relatively satisfy the demands of society. Just like the Austria-Hungary of 1867, it would have been pulled down into the quagmire of nationality conflicts. The century was a century of nations, it ran counter to supra-national formations; the dissolution of Austria-Hungary into 'successor states' was no coincidence. Furthermore, it is uncertain whether Europe would have accepted even a loose amalgamation of the central European powers, entailing the merging of two great powers into one. In short, these considerations are all arguments against the long-term stability of a federal universalistic solution. The Germans, like the Italians and then all the nations of the east and south-east, felt the need to catch up in terms of having a nation-state. It is the stuff of post-nationalist dreams to believe that the national democratic will of the Germans could have been pacified and satisfied by a federal central Europe. An order of nation-states could only be surmounted after that order had existed and been consolidated. Even if, and particularly when, one is not minded to laud the victory in battle and the established facts, one must realise that the *kleindeutsch* solution had the logic of historical probability on its side. This was totally obvious to one opponent of both Bismarck and Prussia, who had a keen sense of world history, namely Karl Marx. But the historical logic of this solution does not mitigate the tragedy of it.

The division of the German nation had quite considerable and direct consequences for both Austria and the Germans in Austria. The events of 1866 were also unfortunate for Austria's internal structure and its ability to exist. It is true that the 'monarchy' continued to exist for more than fifty years — and this is a fact, despite all the nostalgic misinformation to the contrary. But the problems of the monarchy became even more insurmountable after the exclusion from Germany. A centralistic and German-led reorganisation of the Reich was now no longer a possibility. A federal solution which included the Slavic peoples, a tripartite solution, also did not come about; instead, a German–Magyar dualism prevailed. The defeat of Königgrätz did not for one minute endanger the cohesion of the Kaiser's state; even the Hungarians did not use it to split off. The state did have that much stability. The settlement with Hungary in 1867 was the result of the defeat of 1866; from the Austrian Kaiser's Reich arose the double monarchy. After the defeat, the Kaiser dropped the luckless federalist Slavophile minister Count Richard von Belcredi; in his place came the active, energetic minister Count Friedrich von Beust, previously of Saxony. Beust was hoping to be able to continue the struggle for German hegemony as a matter of priority. In order to do this, he needed not only the Hungarians but also the German liberals in Austria, because it was through them that he wanted to uphold the connection with the German medium-sized states. But because of this he too was in favour of a dualistic settlement and opposed to a pro-Slavic federation.

The reorganised state was based on the two strongest nationality groups, the Germans and the Magyars. Vienna largely conceded to the demands of the Magyars for autonomy; they remained in the Reich, but they became a separate people of the Reich. It was the Magyars, in particular, who wanted to exclude any federation which would have given the Slavs equal status or rights of co-determination, not only in the Hungarian sphere of influence, but also in the non-Hungarian half, in 'Cislithania', because this would also have undermined Magyar dominance in the Hungarian half of the Reich. The leading Magyar politician of the settlement, Count Gyula Andrássy, wanted a link between Hungary and Austria, a German-led Austria, for this very reason, since it would serve to secure the leadership of the Magyars over the Slavs in Hungary. In short, the dualism was based on the dominance of the Magyars and the Germans, and the effective exclusion of the Slavs from any position of power on either side. 'We Hungarians shall deal with our Slavs, and you Germans can deal with yours,' Andrássy is reported to have said. This is why there was an undeclared alliance between the Hungarian nationalist liberals and the Germans, especially the Germans in Bohemia, who feared the predominance of the Czechs. The Magyars, then, arranged the settlement in such a way that the non-federation of the Cislithania was a prerequisite, thus effectively blocking all other solutions in the long term.

Austria, and the Germans in Austria, had since 1866–67 been living under a double burden which they had to carry for over fifty years. One of these was dualism. In place of the Austro-Prussian dualism was now the internal Austro-Hungarian version; it was this which now dominated political and economic life. It did not function particularly well and was, in fact, a permanent problem which hobbled along from one provisional solution to the next and was never conclusively solved, and as a result it severely hampered the efforts of this state to carry out political action and reform, affecting even its ability to exist. The second burden was the fact that a federal solution regarding the coexistence of the Slavs and the Germans in their own, i.e. the Cislithanian half of the Reich never came about. Here the Germans were not in the same dominant position as the Magyars were in their half of the Reich. One possibility which was mentioned from time to time, namely for Poland to provide relief for Austria in this respect, thereby securing the Germans a majority over the Czechs and the Southern Slavs, was never put into practice. Cislithania remained an old-fashioned conglomerate of different states, artificial and with little cohesion or national appeal, which became so important during this age of nations. The special status of the states remained intact, and the government in Vienna, which was organised predominantly along the lines of a unified state, was still dependent on the Slavs. The Germans were admittedly the people of the Reich, but they were also one nationality among many, and they felt this more and more; they felt that their status was threatened — as indeed it sometimes was — and they reacted aggressively, as anyone would have done. This double status between people of the Reich and nationality and the resulting ambivalence intensified the nationality problem in the Austrian half of the Reich as well, thereby making it more or less insurmountable. Without 1866 things may have developed in a different way. But the fact that a federalistic multinational solution of the Austrian Reich problem did not come about after 1866 would seem to demonstrate the scant chances of success which a general federalisation of central Europe and a federal universalistic solution of the German Question would have had at that time.

The events of 1866 had made a *grossdeutsch* solution of the German Question impossible, had excluded Austria from Germany, and had divided the nation. Admittedly, the result was not just a bipartite division of Germany and the German nation, but a tripartite one, because even non-Austrian Germany was divided into northern and southern regions. Bismarck had achieved the first objective of Prussian power politics, namely Prussian hegemony in the North. He had also managed to get the great powers to accept this, either actively or passively. In addition, Prussia had consolidated its newly-won position by means of the (ruthless) annexation of Schleswig–Holstein, Hanover, the Electorate of Hesse, Nassau and the free city of Frankfurt. It was the end of North German federalism. There were few reservations or protests about the annexations, despite the existence of a Guelfic opposition in Hanover and a democratic free-city one in Frankfurt. Prussia now possessed a single, unified territory for the first time in its history. It now was in a position of absolute dominance in the North, despite the preservation of Saxony. This Northern region was now organised along the lines of Bismarck's earlier suggestions for federal reform, i.e. as a North German Confederation, a centralistic, federalistic and constitutional state. For the time being, the Prussian new order in Germany stopped at the River Main. This was the result of the European and German power-political constellations. But there were other, internal reasons for stopping at the River Main: according to Bismarck, the new North German order had to be 'given a limit which would ensure a stable amalgamation'; and the Catholic South German 'element' would not, 'for a long time yet willingly allow itself to be governed' by Prussia.

Germany, therefore, was divided into three. Prussia had overshot its original objective of hegemony in the North by the exclusion of Austria from Germany. But the future of the relationship between the Prussian-led North and the South was left open. A unification, an 'annexation' of the South, remained an objective of both Prussian and national politics, but a Prussian attack on the South was shelved, at least for the time being; the European power-political constellation had prevented such a move.

Certainly, the theme of a unification of the North and the South was on the agenda; it was a possibility, and there were strong tendencies in this direction. The defensive and offensive alliances, for instance, were 'eternally valid', i.e. could not be terminated. It is true that they were formally only defensive alliances, but in those days, the differences between a defensive war and, for example, a preventative war, were a lot less clear than they later became; in the long term, these alliances were also designed to bring about a military unification and adaptation. This meant that, in effect, the line of the River Main had now been crossed not only in terms of the customs organisation, but in terms of military organisation as well, thus linking the South to the North. This was not just a result of Prussian power-politics, but of the legitimate security interests of the South. Bismarck continued to aim for unification in his subsequent German policies; for him, the line of the River Main was not a 'wall', but a 'gate'. However, things were not as they may seem to have been from the standpoint of 1871, i.e. that the division along the River Main was only a delaying factor and that developments over the next five years ran directly towards the foundation of the Reich. There was quite extraordinary resistance and hindrances. The particularistic powers and the anti-Prussian tendencies were strong. 'Pay your taxes, serve in the army and keep your mouth shut': as far as the Württemberg democrats or the Bavarian patriots, for example, were concerned, this was the essence of the Prussian state and of a Prussian-led Germany. Neither the military alliances nor the Zollverein proved to be a satisfactory vehicle for speeding up the process of reform. The chances of an annexation of the South did not immediately improve after 1866 — on the contrary, they declined. There were many, and conflicting, ideas as to how to overcome these hindrances. The supporters of unification were thinking long-term, and of a peaceful growing together, and so was Bismarck; it was also clear to him how much every move forward depended on concrete situations and economic circumstances. The alternative of settling for what had already been achieved, at least temporarily, was certainly a real one. After all, the European situation now also seemed to preclude any great movement or alteration in circumstances. Both France and Russia had, until 1866, only been expecting an alteration in the distribution of power in Germany, and were counting on Prussia in this respect. Now the prospect of German unity had really become topical for them. France had to resist this prospect, both in terms of its security interests and its peevish nationalism, and because Napoleon was dependent on successes. Napoleon now embarked upon a policy of containment regarding Prussia, and attempted, together with Austria, to out-manoeuvre Prussia in the South. This could have led, once again, to a war, and Bismarck had certainly included the possibility of a war in his calculations, but, in contrast to the period before 1866, he did not now consider that a war was almost inevitable.

Admittedly, in 1866 Bismarck and Prussia had allied themselves more than ever before with the nationalist movement, and had counted on the nationalist revolutionising of the European system of states. The cabinet war of 1866 became, in the end, a national war, and this had consequences. Bismarck was no longer able to turn away from the German Question; he had become, as A.J.P. Taylor put it, a prisoner of his own political success. That was the dynamic element of the future. The line of the River Main could hardly be a permanent border, even though the foundation of a *kleindeutsch* nation-state was in no way a certainty, either in terms of German politics or power politics. Prussia was a conservative power, but it was also a modern power, with all the resources which a modern power could create or mobilise. This is why it was stronger than the traditional powers, the German Confederation and the Habsburg Empire. This is why it was able to ignore the rift between conservative and liberal forces and ally itself with the other modern power of the times, the nationalist movement.

Finally, war and victory changed the internal situation, particularly in Prussia, and altered the German political party structure. The government's German policies were in most respects those policies which the liberals had been demanding since 1848. This fact could certainly have been the basis of a new consensus between the government and the opposition. Public opinion changed, thus revealing how insecure the electoral base of the liberals was. In the elections on 3 July, the day of Königgrätz, the number of conservative mandates rose from 35 to 136; the liberals, who had wanted to reject the war expenditure programme, shrank from 247 to 148 mandates. After the victory, Bismarck introduced an 'indemnity' bill. He was trying to obtain the retrospective mandate of parliament for the expenditure of the government, which had been incurred without any normal budget, thereby implicitly recognising the budgetary rights of parliament, without relinquishing the theory of the gap, and simultaneously legalising the controversial reform of the army and the decisive matter of the monarchical power of command. Whether the acceptance of this bill had the effect of exonerating the government for its actions during the period of conflict, in the form of a retrospective 'absolution' and approval, remained an open question, as both possible answers could be considered to be correct. In the face of much resistance from both the left and right, parliament adopted this bill. With this bill, Bismarck had decided against the idea of using the victory to carry out a coup, against resistance in the government establishment, against the old-Prussian reaction, and against a reversal of the constitution. He had also decided against the temptation of a Bonapartist solution, and against a directly despotic regime, such as some liberals had feared he would adopt. Furthermore, he had decided against continuing the confrontation until the liberals capitulated. He did not over-exploit his victory; he did not use his foreign political success to further his domestic political ends. The belief of the liberal opposition, that his foreign policies were merely an instrument of his domestic policies, was not confirmed. Indeed, he separated himself from the ideologies and front formations in which he had previously been involved. He decided, after talks with the non-Prussian leaders of the German National Society, Rudolf von Bennigsen and Johannes von Miquel, and with leaders of the Prussian Progressive Party, such as Karl Twesten and Hans Viktor von Unruh, in favour of this form of understanding with the liberals. The conflict could not go on for ever. His alliance with the nationalist movement had to have an effect on the domestic situation. Only in this way could he make any further progress with his national policies. Certainly, the government was now in a position of strength. But Bismarck did not want to demonstrate a parliamentary victory, but to arrive at an amicable peace agreement by means of formulated compromises. The question of power remained in the balance.

People often see only the defeat of parliament in this ending of the conflict, interpreting it as the final fortification of the authoritarian state and the military monarchy — although, admittedly, on the other hand conservatives criticised Bismarck's acceptance of the basic principle of the parliamentary system. In truth, the indemnity was primarily a compromise. One could argue that, in the long term, the arch-conservative idea of a coup would not have been a tenable solution, and that therefore Bismarck's compromise did not really amount to any giving of ground. But a continuation of the conflict or a despotic solution was not so unrealistic. One could argue that, in the original central issues of the conflict, the crown had its way. The army was neither civilianised nor integrated into the constitutional state; on the contrary, its special position in the state and in society was established and confirmed. More paradoxically, it was the victories of the non-civilianised army that closed the rift between it and society; the army no longer had to be civilianised in order to be accepted by society, because this was achieved by the military successes. The military state, with its power structure, its monarchical power of command and feudal elements, had asserted itself, and the liberals had to approve retrospectively the financial cost of this military system. That, certainly, was a defeat of the liberal bourgeoisie. This was the result of the unique coincidence of three factors: the power structure in Prussia; the personal relationship between this king Wilhelm and this leading minister Bismarck; and finally and decisively, the extraordinary foreign-policy and military victory of a state governed in this way. Once again, it was a defeat of the parliamentarian tendencies — a success for the crown and the government that was fighting off these tendencies; the unstable balance of power shifted to their advantage.

But that is only half the truth. It was not a case of the subjugation of the citizens, but more one of an alliance between the crown and the citizenry, admittedly not under the conditions of the New Era — far from it — but an alliance all the same. The government avoided making the final decision, on the 'clarification' of the issue of power. There was no capitulation. Thus the way to a more parliamentary system was left open. The whole matter had been delayed and postponed, and the liberals were left with the idea of furthering their own objectives either with Bismarck or after Bismarck, this exceptional man, the man one had to put up with. Whether this end to the conflict meant that a final decision had been made on this system, or whether the system was capable of being developed and reformed, was the question which had been left open. That is why this particular ending to the conflict was primarily a compromise.

This solution was also conducive to the other great constitutional new order, the constitution of the North German Confederation. This constitution, largely determined by Bismarck, was also a ceasefire and a compromise. It was a balance of federalist and parliamentarian principles. Certainly, this constitution limited, or even blocked, the power of parliament by means of a federal congress and the position of the government, but it also created and consolidated a dynamic parliament on the basis of universal suffrage. It guaranteed a non-parliamentary system of rule for a time, but it also installed a dualistic system of balanced power, which offered many possibilities for development, particularly for the parliament. But these are matters for another age, more recent than the one we are dealing with here.

There is one last point which has to be discussed: the alterations in the party-political structure in Germany in the wake of the Prussian victory of 1866. Firstly, the majority of conservatives distanced themselves from Bismarck. They disapproved of his pacts with the nationalist movement and, worse, his adoption of a nationalist revolutionary course, they were opposed to his Caesarist-Bonapartist tendencies, his policy of reconciliation and allegiance with the liberals, and his method of accepting a nationalist revolution as a means of avoiding a democratic one. Ernst Ludwig von Gerlach expressed, in exaggerated form, all the principles and emotions of an old conservative; he opposed the anti-Austrian tearing apart of Germany, the illegal destruction of the Confederation, and the godless annexations ('crown robbery and nationality swindle'). Bismarck was the revolutionary; whether he was a 'white' revolutionary or any other colour did not matter. The mainstream conservatives were less principled and also Greater Prussian in outlook, but they were basically opposed to the indemnity, even if they did reluctantly vote for it, and they were opposed to the Caesarist tendencies and to too much nationalism; they were Prussian-particularist. They did not want any compromises with the liberals, which would have robbed them of their newly-won victory, and they were opposed to a policy of embrace and conciliation; they did not want to be the unconditional supporters of Bismarck. This man was too modern and too alien for them; he had fallen from favour and was no longer one of them. They went into opposition. The Conservative Party split into an oppositional wing, the specifically Prussian Old Conservatives, and a completely pro-governmental wing, which was also willing to make concessions to the liberals, calling themselves the 'Free

Conservatives', the party of 'Bismarck *sans phrase*'. The conservatives in the annexed countries, particularly the 'Guelfs' in Hanover, and those in the other countries of North and South Germany were in any case in opposition to Bismarck.

The Catholics, who were in an apocalyptic mood over the defeat of 1866, remained, in their majority, anti-Prussian and opposed to anti-clerical liberalism, and this was compounded when the right wing of liberalism and Bismarck moved towards one another. But they did accept the realities of the times — the North German Confederation and the exclusion of Austria from Germany. In the South, though, particularly in Baden and Bavaria, they formed the core of the anti-Prussian and anti-liberal political parties.

The most important development was the new orientation in the liberal camp. In the Prussian *Landtag*, one-half of the delegates of the Progressive Party and two-thirds of the left centrists changed their stance from one of confrontation to co-operation with Bismarck. They voted in favour of the indemnity law. They accepted Bismarck's astonishing offer of peace and a compromise after, as Twesten said, history had given an indemnity in favour of his ministry itself. Even the determined fighters of the Progressive Party, such as Twesten and Forckenbeck, Unruh and Lasker, were thinking along these lines. They no longer wanted to be in a position of unconditional and fruitless opposition, but at last wanted to achieve something positive. They wanted to conduct national politics with Bismarck, and they wanted, now, to achieve those liberal objectives which could be achieved in co-operation with the government, particularly with regard to the internal development of the new Confederation. The liberals in the annexed areas and in the other North German federal states also followed this new course. From this, there arose a new faction of liberalism and then a new party, the National Liberal Party. This was one of the great turning-points in German party-political history, the history of democracy in Germany. A famous essay by Hermann Baumgarten, *German Liberalism — A Self-Critical Analysis*, which appeared towards the end of 1866, became characteristic of this turning-point. According to this work, it was not liberalism but Prussia, the monarchical and military state, which proved to be the pioneer of national unity, and this was a result of its realistic politics. But this state could not easily be turned into a parliamentary state. The strategy of the liberals, to achieve unity through freedom, had failed. But the root of the German problem, and also the weakness of liberalism, was German particularism. That is why German unity was an absolute prerequisite for German freedom and, particularly with regard to the prevailing circumstances of the time, had to have priority. The other core element of the *Realpolitik*, then, was this: one cannot conduct politics on the basis of normative ideas. In concrete terms, this meant that the liberals could no longer remain in opposition and without any real influence, holding on to their dreams in the face of a very different reality; instead, they now wanted to have a real say in the development of policies, and so gradually become what they were not yet: capable of governing, and therefore a real power. Finally, the third element of the *Realpolitik* of those decades was the absolute necessity for a powerful state with a strong leadership; the liberals had to learn this, even if they did find it difficult. Alongside this, there was also a peculiarly defeatist ideological view of the situation, which held that the bourgeoisie had failed, that it was not yet a political class, and that it would, for a long time, have to join forces with the old powers and the leadership of the old political class, namely the aristocracy.

Was that the 'Fall' of liberalism or its capitulation? Was it an opportunistic accommodation to success, an option for power and against principle, for unity but against freedom? Was it the reconciliation with the authoritarian state, which gambled away the future of liberalism and led to its eventual decline, and also set the scene for a unique path for German political history outside of the development of western democracy? It is these and similar critical questions and reproaches which have been voiced, particularly since Hitler and the fall of the German Reich.

The people who make these criticisms are always keen to point out the economic and social interests which would have driven the liberal bourgeoisie to ally themselves with the old establishment and protractedly domesticated their will for freedom: the economic interest in unity and economic success, the fear of a social revolution and democracy; or they attribute these tendencies, more exactly, to the upper and middle bourgeois forces, who, they claim, had separated themselves from the liberal 'petty bourgeoisie', who were still in opposition. They are right in so far as, on a long-term basis, with increasing prosperity and increasingly intense class struggles, the bourgeoisie became more conservative. But that was a perspective of later decades. These interests did not play a significant role in the nationalist liberal decision of 1866. They were not, at that time, clearly defined; people were not primarily concerned with the danger of a social revolution; after all, universal suffrage had been an important aspect of the compromise. It was not just those who had always been right-wing liberals who adapted to the new political direction, although the vast majority of them did, but even decided left-wingers, even old radicals of the revolutionary period, such as Kinkel or Ruge, also, in this situation, supported Bismarck's policies. The decision was definitely a political one, although economic growth and a consensus concerning customs policy were certainly aspects that would have been taken into consideration. The dilemma of unity and freedom, which the liberals had wanted to avoid for decades, had now become acute. In this situation, the nationalist liberals now decided that unity would have priority. They did not make the nation absolute, but they did — in contrast, initially, to both the political right and the political left — accept or even welcome the exclusion of the Austrian Germans. But they did want the nation-state. This national programme, the will for unity, it must be said again, was a manifestation of the bourgeois will for self-improvement and freedom, in opposition to any kind of reaction, as the gymnasts wrote in 1872 on their monument to Jahn. The nationalist slogan in 1866 was still very much anti-feudal and progressive. The unity of the nation was still the embodiment of the general political and liberal progress. We have already discussed the belief that the expansion of the Prussian power base to that of a nation-state would be a step towards its liberalisation, because it would lead to a reduction of its over-proportional military burden, which was having such an effect on its internal politics. The old Baumgarten argument basically continued by saying that the supersession of the old elites would be possible in a new nation-state, whereas it was not possible in the old particularist ones. Unity was a road to freedom, and people were optimistically believing in the inevitability of progress. This is why they were prepared to accept, from a strategic point of view, the concept of 'postponement': immediate unity on the basis of an understanding with the Prussian state and the 'exception', Bismarck; freedom would then come in the medium and long term, and what had been postponed could be achieved at a later date.

In other words, the liberals had in no way surrendered their objectives. They had, for the time being, surrendered their claim to leadership — liberalism as the governing party. They were ready to compromise with the existing order, and they were prepared to accept a limited realisation of their objectives for the time being, but they did want an expansion of the constitutional state and the continued development of civil society, within the pre-liberal and pre-civil system, but in such a way that they could win significant influence. They wanted to get further in the realisation of their objectives by means of co-operation and sharing power, further, at any rate, than pure opposition and confrontation had brought them. This was not crude opportunism, but simply realism, arising from the knowledge that the threat of a revolution was, in the face of Bismarck's successes and a people who were getting richer by the day, not available to them. This change in liberal policy was not only, as some have claimed, a result of the development of moderate liberalism since the 1840s, but was rather a factually legitimised and reasonable decision in the new situation of 1866.

One had to consider what the alternatives were. These were an ultra-conservative coup or a despotic dictatorship by Bismarck; his game with universal suffrage certainly had a potential anti-liberal striking ability once the mood of the people had changed, and this was something which no liberal could possibly want. That the victor, Bismarck, made such an astounding peace offer, aiming not at subjugation, but rather at an understanding, was, after all, evidence of the real power of liberalism; to reject this offer of co-operation and co-determination would hardly have been justifiable. The other alternative would have been to remain stubbornly in opposition; and this is what the opponents of the compromise did, for this was the policy of the last remnants of the Progressive Party, which did not want to surrender or postpone its demands for freedom or its unconditional ideals for the mess of pottage of national unity or the Bismarck-dominated liberal-conservative compromises. This policy had, certainly in retrospect, its own legitimisation. But, the National Liberals argued, that was merely an acceptance of the existing situation, despite all the verbal radicalism; it was merely the surrender of an opportunity to co-determine policy, a moral protest against Bismarck's politics of force; it was a display of purely theoretical politics which would not take on any responsibility with all its incumbent burdens and ambivalences. For the old Progressive Party could not and would not bring about a revolution, and it also had no prospects of ever obtaining a majority, which is normally the strategic goal of any opposition. In the eyes of the National Liberals, this was not a policy worth pursuing. The compromise was conducive to the situation, the balance of forces and the liberals' own prospects, without them having to surrender their objectives in the long term. The nation-state and the constitutional state would come from the same roots. The compromise could be developed.

Admittedly, it must be said that the compromise also harboured great dangers; the long-term developments could have turned out to be completely different from what the liberals were hoping; their peculiar brand of optimism could have turned out to be misguided. The argument of the opponents of the compromise, namely Waldeck, Schulze-Delitzsch and Jacoby, who constituted the core of what remained of the Progressive Party, was also a viable one. It would be the high point of Bismarck's Machiavellianism to corrupt his opponents by allowing them to share in his own success; this would be bound to de-naturalise liberalism. The compromise favoured, and made possible, a shift of accent in the liberal system of values: from freedom and justice to unity, order and power. The realism was able to become a purpose in itself, the sheer belief in success and power; the compromise was ideologised far beyond its meaning as a realistic political strategy — as an ideal solution, a fulfilment of German history and its special destiny. The temporary toleration of the authoritarian state was able to become a justification of the same. The attitude that a victory for Prussia was also a victory for the Protestant bourgeois principle of freedom was one component of such ideology. The intended 'relief of burden' for Prussia in fact ended in a militarisation of the entire nation. The new Reich, instead of bringing about a replacement of the elites, actually seemed to strengthen the old elites. The postponement of basic liberal demands in fact led to them eventually being surrendered altogether. In short, the compromise did not have to develop in a liberal direction. The fact that the liberal hopes and expectations were not, or at least were only very partially, fulfilled in the long term makes our judgment on the decisions of 1866 that much more difficult. The new politics opened up possibilities for the National Liberals, and they attempted, for more than a decade, to make use of these possibilities in the furtherance of their liberal objectives. In retrospect, one can say that they overestimated the opportunities and underestimated the dangers. But those who fail are not always at fault. In 1866 their assessment was not unrealistic. Their failure was their tragedy.

Contemporaries, both of the left and the right, regarded the events of 1866 as a revolution, a German revolution and a revolution from above: Bismarck's revolution. Bismarck revolutionised the political order of Germany and central Europe. He ended two centuries-old facts of German history: the inclusion of the Austrians and the particularistic organisation of Germany. He significantly altered the power structure on the European continent, although admittedly not decisively until 1871, and this was a revolutionising of the international situation in itself. Certainly, these events were the end of a long development, but they were still astoundingly new. At the same time — and this is what is really meant when people talk about a revolution — the internal order and the prevailing political norms were fundamentally altered and reformed. Bismarck achieved self-assertion and the expansion of Prussian power within the trends of the times. He placed himself at the head of a great popular movement which had nothing to do with the world from which he originated. He firmly based the current balance of forces within the society in the institutions of the Prussian and North German new order. This was intended to strengthen the state and the government, to secure and maintain power. Bismarck allied himself with the nationalist movement. This was, as we have already said, more than just tactics, especially in 1866. It was an alliance with the power of the time, without which nothing was possible any longer. Nationhood was the dominating principle of the age. By making this realisation the maxim of his politics, he initiated the great reformation of German nationalism. Nationalism changed from being an oppositional ideology to being an integrational ideology. The principle of nationhood was the basic factor integrating civil society, whose heterogeneity we have so frequently referred to, and combined it with the state, which had started out on the road to becoming a nation-state. That, as well, was a revolutionary change.

We have reached the end of this history. Like the beginning, the end is also characterised by a revolution from above. This revolution, once again, but this time in a different way, put an end to the federalistic, universalistic, *grossdeutsch* tradition of the old Reich, German dualism and the German Confederation. It also ended the existence of old Prussia. The year 1866 was an epoch in the history of the Germans. The ending was also a new beginning, both influencing the other. That is history. It was the end of a centuries-old history, and the beginning of the German nation-state, which itself ended only eight decades later. This need not have been the case. The new foundation was neither built on sand nor against the tide of history. The fact that it came to such a sudden end does not diminish its legitimacy in the slightest. Admittedly, the new foundation stood in the shadow of the failed revolution of 1848; it was Bismarck's foundation and, in spite of the alliance, not that of the liberals. Therein lay its crisis potential, its contradictions and its dangers; these were not mistakes or faults, but a result of the tragic development of German history. No history is without tragedy, and this is particularly true of German history. There were many possible developments, some of them quite different from those which actually came to pass. The future was burdened and overshadowed, and it was, as always, fated. But it was open.

Epilogue

On concluding this book, which has been a part of my life for many years now, I not only feel relief, but also a profound sense of gratitude. What we are and what we do are not things that come from within. We stand in the continuity and community of the historians, our predecessors, our teachers, our colleagues, our students, who have prepared and taught us, who motivate and provoke, criticise and revise, particularly with regard to those aspects which lie outside the scope of the direct material and problems of a book like this. That is why my friends and my academic adversaries have a large share in this book, greater than they realise. We live in academic institutions in which, more than previously, we suffer and from which we have to wrestle time for writing books, but which do enable us to carry out our work in the first place. We live in a society and in a state which are free and at peace, which support and tolerate us; that is our good fortune and is something which cannot be taken for granted, and this fills us with gratitude. We live from a past and a life story to which many people have contributed many things which, in turn, have made us the individuals we are; we live in circumstances which keep us healthy and sane, and have friendships which enrich us. Over and above all the pain of history and the world, we have the happiness of history understood, and beyond all doubt the satisfaction of having completed something and of being able to leave it behind us. Indeed, we live in the hope, albeit challenged, that the world, our world, which bears the fruits of our labour, shall continue. We also live from the hope that there is, beyond our subjective analysis, something objective: the truth, which we can approach and which can relieve us from our subjectivity. For all this I am grateful.

As well as thanking my colleagues and assistants, who have made a lot of things easier for me, there are two particular expressions of gratitude I would like to make. I thank the Institute for Advanced Study in Princeton, in which I began this book in 1978, an academic heaven indeed, in which I certainly felt at home, liberated and assisted; without the Institute — and without Felix Gilbert and John Elliot, Albert Hirschman and Harry Woolf and many others — I would not have attained the mental peace or been able to engage in the thought-games which a book like this requires. I would also like to thank my wife and our children, who have had to go without many things and who not only did this without grumbling, but also provided relief, support and happiness and, indeed, continue to do so. It is due to them, more than anything, that I was able to complete this book.

Easter 1983   Thomas Nipperdey

Index

Aachen, 473

Abel, Karl von, 311, 371

Abitur, 49, 179, 402, 405–7, 409, 422

Ablosung, 34, 125, 126, 134, 135, 145, 146, 148, 309, 533
  amounts, 147
  Hanover, 325
  Saxony, 325
  United Diet, 352–3

Ablosungsbanken, 146

Ablosungsbauern, 138, 139

absolutism, 63, 64, 66, 77, 258, 312, 338, 446, 574
  Austria, 65, 298
  conservative opposition to, 277–8
  enlightened, 55–6
  neo-absolutism, 602–4, 608, 622, 625, 626
  Prussia, 606

Ackerburger, 93

ADAV, 661–5

Addresses to the German Nation (Fichte), 248

Adel, 295

Adelsbauern, 61

administration. *see also* constitutional policies
  Austria, 65
  decentralisation, 288
  reform, 240, 282–3
  reforms, Confederation of the Rhine, 56–8
  reforms sought, 240, 282–3, 286–8
  southern Germany, 303–12

agnosticism, 397

agricultural associations, 129

agriculture, 116, 125–54, 339
  animal husbandry, 134
  Austria, 65, 66, 299
  combinations banned, 216
  crops, 131–4
  developments in, 125–37
  employment in, 169–70, 174, 191, 205
  income levels, 135
  land prices, 125–6, 129
  land reform, 137–42, 146–9
  market-oriented, 135–7
  reform, 28–36, 54, 61, 64, 157, 193
  statistics, 130–34
  status of labourers, 142–4

Ahrens, Heinrich, 341

Aix-la-Chapelle, 95, 166, 168, 215, 321, 331
  Congress of, 246

Albert, Prince Consort, 554

Albrecht, archduke, 699

Albrecht, Professor, 332–3

alcohol consumption, 107

Alexander I, Tsar of Russia, 10, 67, 69–70, 74
  Austro-Hungarian war, 574–5
  and constitutions, 237, 243
  and *Deutscher Bund*, 79
  foreign policy, 320
  Holy Alliance, 82–3
  and Napoleon, 5–6, 15, 72

Alexander II, Tsar of Russia, 351, 352, 555, 579, 696, 687, 698, 703
  Crimean War, 612–16
  opposes union policy, 597, 598

Alexis, Willibald, 517

All-German Song Festival, 1845, 274

Allgemeine Deutsche Burschenschaft, 245
Allgemeine Deutsche Frauenverein, 106
Allgemeine Zeitung, 300, 440
Allgemeines Burgerliches Gesetzbuch, 65
Allgemeines Landrecht, 21, 30, 32, 283, 296
Alpine regions, 94, 149, 162, 167, 410
Alsace, 74, 82, 265, 327–8, 362, 559
Alsace-Lorraine, 85
Alte Pinakothek, Munich, 475, 488, 491
Altenstein, Karl Friedrich Freiherr von
        Stein zum, 40, 294, 402, 423
Altenteil, 129
Altes Museum, Berlin, 475, 488
Altona, 96
Alvensleben Convention, 685
Amalie Sieveking poorhouses, 377
Andrassy, Count Gyula, 706
Andrian-Werburg, Viktor Freiherr von, 301
Anhalt, 166, 312, 317, 318
Anneke, Fritz, 589
Ansbach, 4, 75, 238
Anschluss, 15
anthropology, 393
anti-clericalism, 252, 338, 548–9, 626, 647, 654
antisemitism, 217–23
Antwerp, 166
Apprentices' Societies, 339
architecture, 113, 115, 476, 484
        development of, 488–94
        Gothic style, 491–2
        historicism of, 490–94
        'Maximilian style', 117
        restoration, 268
*Archive for Pathological Anatomy,
        Physiology and Clinical Medicine*, 434
Archive for Physiological Medicine, 434
Aretin, Johann Christoph von, 16, 315
aristocracy, 2, 181, 281, 301, 304, 312–13,
        407, 421–2. *see also* Junkers;
        mediatisation
        and associations, 234
        Austria, 66, 298–9
        benefits of *Ablosung*, 147
        in civil service, 285–6
        and constitutions, 238
        in *Deutscher Bund*, 78
        edict opposed, 308–9
        effects of reforms, 224–5
        as entrepreneurs, 178
        estates broken up, 125–6
        and industrialisation, 156
        land reform, 29, 137–42
        liberalism, 342
        and middle classes, 230–31
        public administration, 288
        and reforms, 25, 33–4, 39, 54, 145–6, 240
        restoration, Prussia, 294–5
        role of, 148
        strata within, 142, 225–7
        taxation, 37, 60
        in universities, 421–2
Arminius, 268, 476
army, 8, 39, 68, 316
        aristocracy in, 139, 148, 294
        Austria, 66, 289–90, 667
        auxiliary corps, 15–16
        budget opposed, 308–9
        cadet schools, 39, 224, 407
        citizenship rights, 27
        Confederation of the Rhine, 57
        German Confederation, 315
        Jewish inclusion, 218
        Linie, 41, 42, 242, 289, 667–71
        military service, 152, 398, 405, 415, 422
        nationalism in, 18
        officer corps, 38–9
        and Paulskirche, 545–6
        Prussia, 37–42, 667–74, 699–700
        punishments, 38
        riot control, 293
        role of state, 281
        social status, 227–8
        and state power, 288–90
        troop levies, 17
Arndt, Ernst Moritz, 29, 67, 244, 247, 248,
        350, 387, 541
        nationalism, 18, 42, 68–9, 72, 76, 81–2,
        266
Arnim, Achim von, 18, 507, 553, 556
Arnoldi, Bishop of Trier, 364
Arnoldi, Ernst Wilhelm, 168
Arnsberg, 92
Arnstein, Fanny, 222
art, 475, 477, 480. *see also* culture
        emphatic concept of, 479–80
        and nationalism, 267, 484
        public art, 475–6
        role of artist, 480–83
*Articles on the History of the Church in
        19th-Century Germany*, 370

artisans' associations, 347–8
Aschaffenburg, 75
Aspern, battle of, 12
Assembly of Notables, Prussia, 52–3
Association Catholicism, 365
Association for the Protection of Property
    and the Promotion of the Prosperity
    of All Classes, 561
Association of German Engineers, 160
Association of Iron and Steel Trades, 182
Association of Writers' and Artists'
    Concordia, 302
associations, 188, 353. *see also* choral
    societies
  artisans, 347–8
  Catholic, 365
  cultural, 234–5
  democratic, 562–3
  development of, 233–6
  liberal, 343, 648
  people's clubs, 652
  repressed, 600
  scientific, 436–7
  student. *see* student associations
Aston, Luise, 106
Athanasius (Gorres), 338, 371
Auerbach, Berthold, 221, 518
Auerspberg, Anton Alexander, Count von, 302
Auerstadt, battle of, 5
Auerswald, Rudolf von, 342, 563, 575
Augsburg, 161, 163–4, 166, 168, 206, 300, 427
  newspaper, 523
Augusta, queen of Prussia, 621, 677
Augustenburg, Herzog Christian von, 273,
    686, 690, 691–2
Austerlitz, battle of, 3, 4, 14
Austria, 2, 6, 11, 83, 90, 147, 165, 166, 169,
    297, 353, 355, 457, 502, 685
  administration, 288, 296–303, 312
  agriculture, 131–2
  aristocracy, 225, 226
  army, 289–90, 667
  Beidermeier, 510
  and Bismarck, 676, 681–2
  Bohemia question, 557–8
  Carlsbad Decrees, 248
  Catholicism in, 366, 654
  censorship, 523
  choral societies, 474
  church and state, 369, 372, 623, 624

civil service, 285–6
Congress of Vienna, 73–5
constitutions, 237–8, 573–4, 623, 625–7
counter-revolution, 566–71, 579, 584,
    585
Crimean War, 612–16
currency, 175
customs policy, 317, 319–20
and *Deutscher Bund*, 78–80
education, 401, 410, 413
foreign policy, 320, 322, 323, 603–4, 684,
    685, 686
and French-Russian war, 68–71
and German Confederation, 82, 314–16
and German unification, 596–8
and Germany, 64–7, 271, 583–7, 627–36
Great Reforms, 64–7
and Hungary, 574–5, 625–7
industry, 158, 162, 172, 173, 177, 179,
    187, 188
Italian War, 612, 616–20
Jews in, 218, 219, 221
July Revolution, 331
land reform, 145, 146
liberalism, 262
May revolution, 589
and Napoleon, 16
Napoleonic war, 12–14
nationalism in, 269
New Era, 622
newspapers, 524
and Paulskirche, 542, 544, 546, 547, 588
population, 85, 87, 93
Reaction, 601, 602–4
revolution, 1848, 530, 533, 534, 553, 554,
    595
rivalry with Prussia, 608–11
and Russia, 15
Schleswig-Holstein question
  consequences of war, 704–15
  Danish war, 687–8, 690–93
  peace negotiations, 700–704
  Prussian negotiations, 692–8
social policy, 216
Third Coalition, 2–3
unification with Germany, 387
universities, 417, 421, 423
Vorparlament elections, 540
workers' movement, 216, 664
and *Zollverein*, 634–6

Austria and its Future (Andrian-Werburg), 301
Austrian Alpine Club, 119
Austrian Architectural and Engineering Association, 160
Austrian Credit Institution for Trade and Commerce, 176
autonomy, 250–51

Baader, Franz von, 212, 213, 214, 278, 339, 361
Baare, Louis, 178
Bach, Alexander, 529, 568, 573, 602–3
Bach, Johann Sebastian, 482
Bacon, 438
Baden, 149, 164, 166, 203, 214, 248, 328, 333, 343
    administration, 56, 287, 288
    aristocracy, 60
    army, 289
    Austro-Prussian war, 696
    and Bavaria, 239, 704
    church and state, 371, 373, 382, 385, 647, 654
    constitution, 238, 254, 305, 306–7, 308–10
    customs policy, 317, 318
    education, 413, 415
    expansion, 2, 3, 55
    and German Question, 629, 630
    industry, 107, 159, 173, 188
    Jews in, 219
    liberalism, 326, 643, 650
    May revolution, 589
    New Era, 623, 624–5
    patriotism, 304
    population, 87
    radicalism, 345, 346, 543, 562, 563–4
    Reaction, 600, 601
    reform, 58, 63, 146, 327
    revolution, 1848, 527–8, 562, 590
    social policy, 91, 124, 216
    ultramontanism, 366
    university, 423, 424
    Vorparlament, 539, 540
    workers' movement, 216
Baden, Friedrich von, 623
Baden, grand duke of, 254
Baden-Baden, 119, 238, 491
Baedeker guides, 119

Baer, Karl Ernst von, 432
Baillet de Latour, Count Theodor, 569
Bakunin, Mikhail, 589
Balkans, 6, 14
Balzac, Honore de, 515, 518
Bamberg, 238
Bamberger, Ludwig, 619
banking, 129–30, 145, 175–6, 214, 299, 604, 607
    and industrialisation, 167–8
Barm, 215
Barmen, 95
Basel, 166
Bassermann, Friedrich Daniel, 343
Battle of the Nations, Leipzig, 71
Bauer, Bruno, 344, 392
Bauern, 295
Bauernschutz, 29, 30, 31, 34, 35
Baumgarten, Hermann, 620, 711, 712
Baur, Ferdinand Christian, 380
Bautzen, 70
Bavaria, 92, 146, 226, 328, 500, 597, 634, 704
    administration, 56, 57, 288, 299
    agricultural associations, 129
    architecture, 491
    army, 289
    Austro-Prussian war, 696, 697
    birth rate, 91
    Catholicism, 361, 364, 366, 654
    church and state, 368–9, 371–2, 384, 385, 387, 647
    church reform, 59
    civil service, 283, 285
    and Confederation of Rhine, 8
    constitution, 62, 238, 239, 248, 310–11, 586
    customs policy, 316, 317, 318, 611
    'despotism of the peasants', 148
    and *Deutscher Bund*, 78–9
    disease, 121
    economy, 184
    education, 401, 410, 413, 415
    expansion, 2, 3, 55, 75
    and German Confederation, 314, 315
    German Reform Society, 633
    industry, 159, 163
    Jews in, 219
    land reform, 145
    liberalism, 326
    medicine, 122

mortality rates, 90
nationalism in, 17, 19, 268, 304
New Era, 622–3
parliament, 305, 306, 307, 308
and Paulskirche, 542, 546
pietism, 376
and Prussia, 609, 708
Reaction, 600
reform, 58, 63
revolution, 1848, 528
sculpture, 476
secularisation, 59–60
social policy, 61, 124, 216, 224
Treaty of Ried, 71–2
Tyrol revolt, 13
unemployment, 193
university, 361, 417
Vorparlament, 538, 541
and *Zollverein*, 635
Bayerisches Nationalmuseum, Munich, 475
Bayer's factories, 173
Bayreuth, 75, 124, 238, 396
Beamtenrecht, 332
Beamtenschaft, 262
Beamtenstaat, 296, 304
Beamtentum, 241
Bebel, August, 659, 665
Becker, Nikolaus, 273
Beckerath, Hermann von, 178, 261, 342
Beethoven, Ludwig van, 268, 300, 474,
477–8, 483, 487
Romanticism of, 484–5
begging, 108
Behorden, 56, 57
Bekker, August Immanuel, 450
Belcredi, Count Richard von, 626, 692, 705
Belgium, 82, 272, 331, 339, 529, 684, 685, 702
founded, 322
industry, 163, 174
July revolution, 323–4
Marx and Engels in, 348
Belgrade, 698
Bem, Joseph, 569–70
Benedek, Count Ludwig von, 699
Benedetti, Vincent, 702
Bennigsen, Rudolf von, 227, 385, 620, 632,
709
Benzenberg, Johann, 241
Berchtesgaden, 13, 163
Berechtigungswesen, 405–6

Berg, 8, 57, 61, 63, 69, 72
Bergau, 157
Bergisches Land, 156, 376, 382, 535
Berlin, 16, 18, 96, 105, 120, 125, 165, 166,
176, 384, 466, 476, 518, 561, 698, 702
architecture, 488, 489, 490, 491
civic improvements, 114–15, 117, 118, 124
counter-revolution, 564
culture, 472, 475
disease, 121
education, 406, 410, 411, 419, 427
female emancipation, 106
home ownership, 112
housing, 113–14
industry, 159, 160, 164, 170, 184
Jews in, 220, 221, 222
July revolution, 331
medicine, 122, 123, 433
newspapers, 522, 523, 524
and Paulskirche, 549
pietism, 376
population, 94, 95
'potato revolution', 194
poverty, 183
radicalism, 350, 562
revolution, 1848, 386, 528, 530–31, 535
unemployment, 193
university, 45, 50–51, 417, 418–19, 423,
424
Vorparlament elections, 541
workers' movement, 551, 659, 663
Berlin National Assembly, 575–8
Berlin Political Weekly, 279, 334, 338
Berlin Trading Company, 176
Berlioz, Hector, 485
Bernadotte, Marshal Jean Baptiste Jules, 15,
72
Bernstorff, Christian Gunther, Count, 316,
629
Berthold, Arnold Adolf, 432
Beseler, Georg, 273, 343, 453, 542
Bethel, 377
Bethmann-Hollweg, Moritz August von,
376, 386, 608, 621
Beuggen, 377
Beust, Count Friedrich von, 629, 637, 705–6
Beuth, Peter Christian, 159, 160, 427
Beuthen, 220
Beyme, Karl Friedrich, 24, 243
Biedermann, Karl, 271, 386, 425, 542

Biedermeier movement, 104, 113, 188, 249, 301, 355, 495, 501, 503, 512, 513
  development of, 509–10
  literature, 517, 518, 519
  nature in, 516
Bielefeld, 172
Bildung, 360–61, 374
Bildungsdramen, 512
Bildungskunst, 497
Bildungsmusik, 485
Bildungsreligion, 389, 390, 398, 471
Bildungsroman, 505
Birkenfeld, 75
birth rates, 90–92, 98
Bismarck, Otto von, 142, 279, 336, 376, 381, 404, 459, 602, 612, 626, 657
  career of, 675–8
  censorship, 522
  conservatism of, 638, 646, 653
  constitutional policy, 679–84
  Crimean War, 614
  Erfurt parliament, 596, 598
  and German Question, 628–36
  and German unification, 599–715
  and Italian War, 619
  and Lassalle, 661
  and liberalism, 622, 648, 651
  Minister-President, 674, 678
  nationalism, 683–4
  opposition to Austria, 608–11
  Polish crisis, 685–6
  Reaction, 600
  revolution, 1848, 531
  Schleswig-Holstein question, 686–90
    Austrian policy, 690–93
    peace negotiations, 700–704
    war, 686–90
  universal suffrage, 257, 605, 682–3
  and workers' movement, 216, 664
Blechen, Karl, 481, 483, 500, 503
Bleichroder, Gerson, 698
Blucher, 5, 72, 82
Blum, Robert, 345, 364, 543, 555, 557, 562, 593
  executed, 570
  newspaper, 523
  revolution, 1848, 590, 591–2
  Vorparlament, 539, 540
Bluntschli, Johann Kaspar, 385, 648
Bocklin, Arnold, 501

Bodelschwingh, Friedrich von, 377
Boeckh, Philipp August, 450, 462
Bohemia, 11, 85, 147, 297, 540, 572, 603, 625
  Austro-Prussian war, 699, 700, 706
  and counter-revolution, 565–6
  education, 410
  and German empire, 583
  industry, 161, 173, 178
  Jews in, 221
  Landtag, 302–3
  population, 87, 89
  question of, 557–8
  revolution, 1848, 530
Bohemian National Museum, 303
Bohmer, Johann Friedrich, 457, 633–4
Bolyai, Janos, 436
Bolzano, Bernhard, 300, 436
Bonald, Louis de, 275
Bonald, Louis Gabriel Ambroise, Vicomte de, 275
Bonaparte, Jerome, 8
Boniface, 268
Boniface Society, 365
Bonin, Eduard von, 614, 669
Bonn, 123, 124, 128, 247, 346, 363, 365, 431
  university, 370, 417
Bopp, Franz, 451
Borbeck foundry, 172
Borne, Ludwig, 109, 330, 331, 391
Borromeo Society, 365
Borsig, August, 160, 164, 173, 178, 427, 535
Bourbons, 82
bourgeoisie. *see* middle class
Boyen, Hermann von, 16, 38, 39, 41, 242–3, 289, 350, 400
Brahms, Johannes, 474, 483, 485
Brandenburg, 30, 34, 136, 352, 410, 577, 578, 663
Brauer, Nikolaus, 63
Braunschweig, 540
Breisgau, 238
Bremen, 6, 105, 167, 192, 523
  customs policy, 318
  Reaction, 599
Bremerhaven, 117, 168
Brentano, Clemens, 18, 358, 507, 516
Brentano, Lorenz, 589
Breslau, 95, 117, 220, 346, 363, 364, 542
  university, 417
Breslau, Bishop of, 370

breweries, 147
Brockhaus, 163
Brockhaus encyclopaedia, 520
Bruck, Karl von, 573, 602, 603, 610, 634
Bruggemann, Karl-Heinz, 327–8, 523
Brummel, Beau, 118
Brunn, 166
Brunswick, 8, 12, 318, 324, 427
Brunswick, Duke of, 13
Bucharest, 698
Bucher, Lothar, 286
Buchner, Georg, 149, 329–30, 391, 396, 509, 511
Buchner, Ludwig, 396
Bulow, Hans von, 483
Bund, 580
Bundesgebiet, 169
Bundesstaat, 314
Bundestag, 80, 238, 309, 324, 538, 622
    attack on, 329
    Bismarck at, 675, 676
    censorship by, 247, 331, 352
    constitution reinstated, 622
    customs policy, 316–17
    'purging' of, 315
    restored, 608
    Schleswig-Holstein question, 554, 696
    transfers power, 545
    and *Vorparlament*, 539
Bundesversammlung, 80
Bunsen, Karl Josias Freiherr von, 559, 614
Bunsen, Robert, 434
Buol-Schauenstein, Count Karl von, 613, 615
Burckhardt, Jacob, 459, 526
bureaucracy. *see* civil service
Burger, 183, 190, 262
Burger, Johann, 128
Burgerausschuss, 529
Burgerliches Gesetzbuch, 453
Burke, Edmund, 17, 22, 275, 276, 444
Burschenschaften, 19, 76, 218, 234, 238, 388, 420–21
    antisemitism, 244
    and constitutional debate, 243–9
    July Revolution, 329
    nationalism, 267
    opposition, 326–30
    radical wing, 245–6
Busch, Wilhelm, 103, 396, 502, 515

Buss, Franz Joseph, 214, 339, 542, 549
Byron, George Noel Gordon, Lord, 509

Calvinism, 382, 384–5
Campe, Joachim Heinrich, 102
Camphausen, Ludolf, 165, 166, 179, 261, 342, 345, 575
canals, 158, 164–5
Canning, George, 321
Cantor, Moritz, 436
capitalism, 53, 155, 211
Carinthia, 69
Carl Johan, Crown Prince (later King) of Sweden. *see* Bernadotte, Marshal
Carlsbad, 119
Carlsbad Decrees, 118, 242, 247, 248, 249, 294, 300, 314, 423
carnivals, 119
Carus, Carl Gustav, 123, 431, 499
Cassel, 130
Castlereagh, Robert, Viscount, 72, 74, 82, 320
Catholic societies, 337
Catholicism, 55, 151, 239, 646, 711. *see also* churches; ultramontanism
    and administration, 286–7
    anti-Catholic historicism, 458–9
    anti-clericalism, 626
    Bavaria, 311
    church-state conflict, 623, 624
    conservative, 154
    cults, 363–4
    development of, 359–73
    entrepreneurs, 179
    'German Catholics', 364
    government opposition, 307
    grossdeutsch support, 585
    independence movements, 290, 325
    and Italian War, 619
    and liberalism, 252, 338–9, 647
    and nationalism, 245
    and natural sciences, 439
    newspapers, 524
    political parties, 334, 337–40, 353, 651, 653–4
    and Reaction, 601, 603
    and regionalism, 290
    relationship with state, 367–73
    religious practices, 363–4
    role of *Volk*, 364–5
    and Romanticism, 358, 365, 431

Catholicism (cont.)
   and secularisation, 58–9
   and social class, 231
   social policy, 213, 214
   Syllabus of Errors, 365–6
   theological development, 360–62
   university appointments, 424
   Vorparlament elections, 541, 542
Cavaignac, Louis Eugene, 566, 570
Cavendish, Henry, 429
Cavour, Camillo Benso di, 617, 620
Celle, 127
censorship, 17, 247–8, 248, 249, 308, 309,
   353, 528
   Austria, 300, 301
   Bavaria, 310–11
   campaign against, 326–9
   incomplete, 334
   intensified, 328–9
   literature, 521
   and nationalism, 303
   newspapers, 522–3
   Prussia, 294–5, 310–11, 606
   Vormarz, 350
Central Association for the Welfare of the
   Working Classes, 657
Central March Association, 565, 588
Central Workers' Committee, Berlin, 551
chamber of commerce, 160–61
charitable work, 377
charivari, 99
Charlemagne, 16
Charlottenburg, 96
Chateaubriand, Francois Rene, Vicomte de,
   275, 494
chemical industry, 173, 179
Chemnitz, 95, 108, 164
children, 107
   charitable care, 377
   child labour, 108, 213, 215, 216, 293,
     409, 607
   in family, 100, 103–4, 110
   mortality, 98, 108
Chladni, Ernst Florens Friedrich, 429
Chopin, Frederic, 300
choral festivals, 343
choral societies, 234, 473–4
Christian IX, king of Denmark, 686, 687
Christian Westphalian Farmer's Association,
   129

Christmas, 100
Chur, Prince-Bishop of, 13
Church Congress, 388
churches, 2
   attendance, 366
   in Austria, 65
   Confederation of the Rhine, 58–60
   and education, 50, 51, 400, 410–11, 413
   spiritualisation, 60
   and the state, 296, 332, 335–6, 367–73,
     383–4, 623, 624
Cislithania, 706
cities, 93–6, 98–9, 108, 120, 230. *see also*
   towns
   administrative reform, 26–7
   Austria, 299
   civic improvements, 114–16
   duties of councils, 124–5
   education in, 410, 411–12
   Free Cities, 312
   housing, 112, 113–14
   and industrialisation, 206
   Jews in, 220–21
   planning, 116
   poverty in, 183
   public buildings, 115–16
citizenship, definition of, 27
Civil Code, 453
civil liberties, 19–20, 22, 217–19
civil service, 18, 57, 305
   aristocracy in, 139, 148
   Austria, 298–9
   bureaucracy, 286–7, 354–5
   conditions for entry, 283, 405–6
   Confederation of the Rhine, 57
   and education, 49–50, 400–401, 404, 405
   and Great Reforms, 46, 48
   Hanover, 332–3
   and industrialisation, 159
   in *Landtage*, 307, 308, 310
   and liberalism, 262, 645
   numbers of, 286
   Prussia, 52, 241, 291–3, 295, 296, 606–7
   and reform, 20, 23, 30, 146, 413
   role and status of, 227–8, 282–6
   role of universities, 419–20
   salaries, 284
class structure, 213
   rural, 139–42
   villages, 149–50

class tax, 37
classical studies, 399, 403, 408
Classicism, 44, 357, 360, 397, 440, 443, 524
    in architecture, 490
    and de-Christianisation, 390–91
    development of, 504–9
    in literature, 508, 512, 518–19
    in music, 484
    in painting, 498–501, 503
    and philology, 449–51
Claudius, Matthias, 357
Clausewitz, Carl von, 16, 38, 700
Clausius, Rudolf, 435
clergy, social status of, 228
Clett, 164
clocks, 199
Cloppenburg, 122
clothing, 118, 153
    fashion, 118
clubs, 119, 234
co-operatives, 35, 186, 214, 336–7, 462, 551,
    649, 656–7
coal mining
    investment in, 169
    production, 170, 172
Cobden Treaty, 634
Coblenz, 17, 361, 522
Coburg, 328, 474, 632
Coburg, Ernst von, 623
Coburg, House of, 554, 587, 621
Code Napoleon, 57, 61, 245
coffee-houses, 120
College of Land Economy, 129
Collegium Germanicum, Rome, 363
Colmar, Joseph Ludwig, Bishop of Mainz, 362
Cologne, 95, 117, 165, 166, 168, 179, 363, 542
    architecture, 489
    'Cologne Incident', 337–8, 370–71
    culture, 473, 475
    'factory children', 409
    Jews in, 220
    medicine, 122
    revolution, 1848, 530, 535
    socialism, 350
    unemployment, 193
    workers' associations, 551
Cologne Cathedral, 350–51, 371, 484, 490,
    492
    Festival, 1842, 268
Cologne Concert Society, 472

Cologne Mining Company, 176
Committee for the Preservation of the
    Czech Language and Literature, 303
Committee of Fifty, 539, 557
Committee of Seventeen, 538, 539, 546, 592
Committees of Public Safety, 533, 567, 569
commonage, 143, 149, 192
communications, 153, 158, 167, 176, 326
communism, 190, 348–50, 412, 552, 659, 663
    and Lassalle programme, 660–61
Communist Manifesto, 348, 349
Comte, August, 438, 440, 462
concordat, 372
Condillac, Etienne Bonnot de, 438
Condition of the English Working Classes
    (Engels), 211, 348
condominium, 691
Conduitenlisten, 607
Confederate Assembly, 238
Confederation of the Rhine, 3–4, 6–11, 12,
    14, 56, 66, 70, 76, 77, 238
    administration, 8–9, 288
    and aristocracy, 224
    church and state, 368
    constituent parts, 7–8
    and *Deutscher Bund*, 79
    differences between states, 62–4
    and French-Russian war, 69–70
    Great Reforms, 19, 22, 54–64
        administration, 56–8
        constitutional reform, 61–2
        secularisation, 58–60
        social reforms, 61–2
    Jews in, 217
    and Napoleon, 16–17
    nationalism in, 19
    Treaty of Ried, 71–2
Conference of German Princes, 687
Congress of Churches, Wittenberg, 386
Congress of German Economists, 635
Congress of German Natural Scientists and
    Doctors, 436–7
Congress of German Workers' Associations,
    663
Congress of Vienna, 73–5, 77, 81–2, 145,
    218, 243, 319, 368
    and aristocracy, 224
    and constitutions, 237
    customs policy, 316
    German Confederation, 313

Congress of Vienna (cont.)
  international treaties, 82–3
conscription, 215, 289
  Austria, 66, 289–90
  Confederation of the Rhine, 57
  France, 38
  Prussia, 40–41, 288
Conservateur, Le, 275
conservatism, 250, 334, 638
  and administration, 286–7
  and Austro-Prussian war, 697, 708, 710–11
  Catholic, 340
  church and state, 383–4
  development of, 274–80, 341–3
  and education, 412–15
  and education reform, 399–400
  ideas behind, 275–6
  in New Era, 651–4
  newspapers, 523–4
  in parliaments, 307–12
  political parties, 335–7
  and Prussian military reform, 672–5
  Reaction, Prussia, 606–7
  reactionary movement, 332–3
  rejection of states' union, 597, 598
  and revolution, 1848, 561–2
  social policy, 216
  and universities, 418–19, 423–4
Constance, 368
constitutions, 23, 28, 336
  Austria, 66, 625–7
  Confederation of the Rhine, 61–2
  conservative support, 651–2
  constitutional movements, 324–6
  effect of, 304–5
  Electorate of Hesse, 622
  Germany, 77–8
  history of, 237–50
  imperial constitution, 579–87
  and integration, 304
  and liberalism, 254–60
  and nationalism, 270
  Prussia, 51–4, 293, 295–6
  Prussian, 351–3
  reasons for adoption, 238–9
  Reichstag, 573–4
  revolution, 1848, 532
  role of monarch, 258–9, 281
  seen as inadequate, 327–8, 330, 343–4,
      353–4

separation of powers, 255–6
  southern Germany, 304–6
construction industry, 173, 207
consumption tax, 37
Continental Blockade, 6–7, 8, 11, 15, 17,
      125, 157–8
Continental System, 7, 8
Convention of Reichenbach, 71
Convention of Tauroggen, 67
Cornelius, Peter, 481, 483, 494, 496
corporatism, 341
Correspondence between Two Germans
      (Pfizer), 270–71
Cortes, Donoso, 276
Cotta, 164
Cotta, firm of, 523
Cotta, Johann Friedrich, 163
cottage industry, 149, 156, 171, 173, 199
  decline, 185
  and factories, 205
  and poverty, 193–4
  'truck system', 209
*Cottas Morgenblatt fur die gebildeten
      Stande*, 524
Council for a Future Age, 439
Council of Heads of Districts, 78
Council of State, 24
Counter-Reformation, 362, 365
counter-revolution
  Austria, 566–71
  pan-German, 565–6
Courts of Honour, 39
Cousin, Victor, 409
Cracow, 302, 323
crafts sector, 156, 182–91, 339, 354, 415,
      607
  and factories, 203, 205, 206
  incomes within, 186–7
  and industrialisation, 190
  middle class, 637
  and socialism, 347
  trade freedom, 187–90
  wages, 195–7
craftsmen
  and industrialisation, 179
credit co-operatives, 186
credit institutions, 129–30
Credit Mobilier, 176
Creuzer, Friedrich, 426, 450
crime, 193

Crimean War, 612–16, 618, 619, 667, 697–8,
  702
Croatia, 13, 566, 567, 570, 572, 603, 626
culture, 233, 425, 472–519
  Austria, 300–301
  influence of, 478–9
  middle class, 181
  and nationalism, 267–8, 274
  spread of, 477–8
currency, 66, 175
customs and excise, 37, 57, 152, 153, 158,
  175, 316, 324. *see also* Zollverein
Czechs, 297, 302–3, 530, 626, 698, 706

Daheim, 525
Dahl, Johann Christian Clausen, 499
Dahlmann, Friedrich Christoph, 300, 355,
  453, 456–7, 542, 585
  constitutionalism, 256, 261, 313, 332–3
  draft constitution, 546
  imperial constitution, 581
  nationalism, 556, 559
  view of state, 341–2
Dahn, Felix, 517
daily life, 111–25
Dalberg, Karl Theodor Freiherr von, 2, 3, 8,
  16, 217
Dalmatia, 3
Danube river, 3, 164
Danube Steamship Company, 165
Danzig, 5, 117, 124
Darmstadt, 128, 324, 427, 475, 534
Darmstadt Bank for Trade and Industry, 176
Darwin, Charles, 380, 396–7, 436
David, J. Ben, 437–8
Davidis, Henriette, 121
de Wette, Martin Leberecht, 246–7, 248
death, attitudes to, 101–2
death penalty, 101, 570, 576
debts, national, 55
Decree of Genuflection, 371
Defregger, Franz, 501
democratic clubs, 529, 562–3
Democrats, 251, 334, 345–6
  failure of revolution, 591–2
  and liberalism, 624–5, 642, 643, 649–51
  and nationalism, 632
  and revolution, 1848, 562–5
  Schleswig-Holstein question, 632
  and working class, 658–9

Democrats' Congress, 1848, 562, 564, 577
d'Enghien, Duc, 2, 17
Denmark, 6, 75, 320, 353, 559
  and Bismarck, 682
  Schleswig-Holstein question, 273–4,
    312–13, 320, 554–6, 595–8
  Schleswig-Holstein war, 686–8
department stores, 186
Deputation of the Imperial Diet, 2
Deputationen, 50
d'Ester, Dr, 350
Deutsch-franzosische Jahrbucher, 344
Deutsche Bundesakte, 80
Deutsche Ideologie, Die (Marx and Engels),
  348
Deutsche Jahrbucher, 344
Deutsche Tribune, 327
Deutsche Vierteljahresschrift, 523
Deutsche Volkshalle, 523
Deutsche Zeitung, 343
Deutscher Bund. see German Confederation
Deutscher Handelstag, 161
Deutscher Zollverein. see Zollverein
Deutsches Staatsworterbuch, 648
Deutsches Volkstum, 266
Dickens, Charles, 480, 515, 518
Diesterweg, Adolf, 351, 412, 413, 425
Dietel, Dr, 433–4
Dieterici, Wilhelm, 92, 192
Diez, Friedrich, 451
Dillis, Georg von, 500
Dinnendahl, Franz, 178
diplomatic corps, 148
Direktionsprinzip, 175, 204
Discount Society, 176
disease, 88, 90, 121–2, 124, 194
  cholera, 121, 124
  typhus, 121, 124, 194
  VD, 121–2
Disraeli, Benjamin, Lord Beaconsfield, 553
district assemblies, 140
divorce, 106, 111
Doblhoff, Anton Freiherr von, 301
Dohm, Christian Wilhelm, 217
Dollinger, Ignaz von, 362, 365, 366, 542, 548
Dombaufest, Cologne, 350–51
Donizetti, Gaetano, 480
Dornberg, Wilhelm Freiherr von, 13
Dorner, Isaak August, 379, 386
Dortmund, 95, 166, 172, 182

Douglas, John, 158
Dresden, 71, 95, 164, 166, 220, 427, 558, 609
  architecture, 488, 493
  art, 475, 499
  May revolution, 589
Droste-Hulshoff, Annette Freiin von, 510,
  516, 518
Droste zu Vischering, Clemens August von,
  Archbishop of Cologne, 269, 291,
  337–8, 370–71
Drouyn de l'Huys, Edouard, 700
Droysen, Johann Gustav, 273, 343, 456,
  458–9, 542, 620
Du Bois-Reymond, Emil, 432, 440
dualism, 260–61, 271, 314, 355, 689
  Austro-Prussian war, 706
  consolidated, 598
  and failure of revolution, 595
  German Question, 627–36
  parliamentarian, 305, 307–12
  rebirth after Reaction, 608
  roots of war, 698
  theory of, 258
duelling, 224, 420, 673
Duisburg, 95, 163, 663
Duisburg-Ruhrort, 165
Dulon, Rudolf, 386
Duncker, Max, 542, 585, 620, 641
Duren, 162
Durer, Albrecht, 268, 476
Durlach, 238
Dussel valley, 377
Dusseldorf, 17, 95, 181, 663
  culture, 473, 475, 502

Eberfeld, 95
Eberfeld System, 215
Ebers, Georg, 517
Echtermeyer, Ernst Theodor, 344
economic policy, 304, 316
  agriculture, 125–7
  Austria, 66, 299, 604
  conservative, 652
  cycles of recession, 177
  and German Question, 634–6
  GNP, 174
  and industrialisation, 157–8
  and liberalism, 260–61, 647–8
  and nationalism, 271
  and pauperism, 194–5

prosperity, 636–7
Prussia, 11
  reforms, 23, 29, 36–7
  and social changes, 228–9
economics, 22, 460–65
education, 57, 152, 179, 198, 213, 377, 473,
  642, 647. *see also* schools
  aristocratic privilege, 224
  Austria, 65, 603
  and civil service, 286
  compulsory, 299, 409–10
  control of, 300, 625
  and counter-revolution, 580
  development of, 398–428
  and family, 100
  gender differences, 102, 104
  Great Reforms, 42–51
  individualisation, 233
  and industrialisation, 108, 159–60
  Jews in, 221
  and nationalism, 269
  philosophy of, 42–7
  and Reaction, 600, 607
  reform, 22, 293
  and religion, 367, 372
  role of state, 281
  and social mobility, 228–9
  and ultramontanism, 365
  women as teachers, 106
  and working class, 657–8, 663
egalitarianism, 47, 260–61, 342
Egells, Franz Anton, 159, 160, 178
Egerstorff, Georg, 164
Egypt, 323
Eichendorff, Joseph Freiherr von, 68, 507,
  516
Eichhorn, Albrecht Friedrich, 317, 351, 413
Eichstatt, 363
Eifel, 162
Eigenkatner, 142–3, 144
Einjahrige, 179, 228, 405, 415, 422
Elbe river, 30, 165, 317
Elberfeld, 166, 589
Elbing, 164
Eldena, 128
elections, 27, 62, 305, 643
  suffrage debate, 27, 256–7, 582, 646, 658
  three-class voting system, 604–5
  universal suffrage, 664, 668, 682–3, 697
  Vorparlament, 540–41

emigration, 92–3, 97, 144, 149, 192, 331, 382, 589
  of Jews, 221
Empfindsamkeit, 360
Ems, 119
Engels, Friedrich, 154, 211, 331, 376, 392, 441, 511, 552
  and Hecker, 540
  and Italian War, 617, 620
  May revolution, 589
  radical demonstrations, 563
  social theory of, 348–9
engineering, 163, 164, 167, 173, 427–8, 489
  entrepreneurs, 178
  investment in, 169
England, 15, 16, 120, 159–60, 163, 189, 207, 270, 355, 394, 489, 676
  after 1814, 83
  agriculture, 29, 35, 127, 135, 136, 137
  aristocracy, 225
  and Austria, 12
  Cobden Treaty, 634
  Congress of Vienna, 73–5
  conservatism, 276
  Crimean War, 612–16
  culture, 100, 110, 118, 474, 480, 515
  economic embargo, 6–7
  economy, 316, 465
  education, 410
  foreign policy, 320–23, 554–5, 612, 688, 694, 702
  and German Confederation, 81–2
  and Germany, 16, 125, 158, 168
  home ownership, 112
  industrialisation, 156, 161–2, 163, 208
  liberalism, 252, 260, 261
  Marx and Engels in, 348
  Metternich in, 529
  and Napoleon III, 684–5
  Napoleonic wars, 2–3, 4–5, 6, 11, 70–73
  parliamentarianism, 256, 310, 342
  religion, 398
  and revolution, 1848, 530, 553–4
  science, 437–8, 460
  social policy, 201, 211, 346, 680–81
  universities, 416
  workers' movement, 665
Enlightenment, 21, 22, 42–3, 44, 46–7, 59, 124, 127, 217, 338, 368, 469, 524, 526
  and conservatism, 274–5

  and education, 49, 413
  and family, 102, 110–11
  and historicism, 443–5, 450, 454–6
  influence of, 63–4, 232, 250
  and law, 452
  and liberalism, 261
  and literature, 505–6
  and religion, 356–7, 360–61, 364, 374–5, 380, 382, 389, 395
  and socialism, 346
  views of children, 91–2
entrepreneurs, 163, 178–82, 202, 261–2
Eos, 278, 361
Erdmann, Johann Eduard, 471
Erfurt, 10, 90
Erfurt Union, 595–8
Erlangen, 376, 387, 419
Ernst August, king of Hanover, 325, 332–3
Eschweiler, 162
Essen, 95, 163, 172
Esslingen, 114, 164, 211
estates, system of, 26–7, 32–4, 223–4
Europe
  and German politics, 684–704
  Germany in, 319–23
European Community, 319, 636
Evangelische Kirchenzeitung, 280, 376
everyday life, 111–25
Ewald, Heinrich, 332–3
Extraordinarius, 418
Eylau, battle of, 5

factories, 115, 198–9, 203, 212
  child labour, 108, 215, 409
  hours of work, 209
  inspectorate, 216
  organisation of, 200–201
  patriarchalism, 201–3
  pay scales, 203–4, 206–8
  piecework, 201, 207
  time management, 198–200
  workforce, 191–216
  working conditions, 200, 206–10, 607
Falke, Johannes, 377
family, 97–111, 397. *see also* everyday life
  and business, 181
  causes for emergence of, 110–11
  children in, 103–4
  gender roles, 99–100, 102–3
  growing individualisation, 232–4

family (cont.)
  and industrialisation, 210
  lower class, 106–9
  nuclear family, 100–101
  privacy of, 98–9, 100, 104–5, 112–13
  relationships within, 151–2
  and sexuality, 109–10
  and social class, 151
Faraday, Michael, 429, 431
fatherland associations, 331, 561
Fechner, Gustav Theodor, 440
Federal Act, 238
federalism, 77, 249, 292, 327–8, 343,
    580–81, 583–4, 625
  German Confederation reforms, 693–4
  and nation-state, 271–2
  and Paulskirche, 545–6
  Prussia, 628–9
Ferdinand I, emperor of Austria, 77, 298,
    566–7, 573
  Napoleonic wars, 70
fertilisers, 128, 132
festivals, 100, 119, 129, 274, 343, 353
Feuchtersleben, Ernst Freiherr von, 123
feudalism, 19, 20, 34, 135, 153, 156, 260,
    341, 655
  agrarian, 28–9, 31
  Austria, 299
  and the church, 60
  compensation for property, 32–4
  and conservatism, 279
  defeudalisation, 146, 152
  privileges abolished, 141
  Prussia, 21, 353
  reform of, 241, 312
  remnants of, 63, 193, 325, 354, 410
  social order, 27
Feuerbach, Anselm, 61
Feuerbach, Ludwig, 344, 392, 394–7, 470,
    471, 481, 483, 501, 513
Fichte, Johann Gottlieb, 18, 22, 44, 45, 248,
    377, 466, 467
  nationalism, 265–6
Ficker, Julius, 459
Fidericianum, Kassel, 475
financial institutions, 175–6
Finckenstein, Friedrich Ludwig Karl Graf
    Fincke von, 53
Finland, 6, 12, 83
fire safety, 116–17

Fischer, Kuno, 471, 490
Fischhof, Adolf, 529, 567
Fliedner, Theodor, 377
Fliegende Blatter, 223, 524
Flottwell, Edward von, 272
Flurbereinigung, 35
Flurzwang, 28, 29, 35
folk culture, 153, 274, 462, 507, 521
  music, 474, 480, 483, 512
Follen, Karl, 97, 245–6, 267, 358, 388
Fontane, Theodor, 142, 515
food, 119–21, 144
  famine, 120–21, 126, 131, 171, 193, 354
  proportion of income on, 209
  riots, 194
  rising prices, 195
Forckenbeck, Max von, 672
Forster, Therese, 336
Fraktionen, 542–3, 562
France, 13, 83, 100, 118, 120, 121, 124, 187,
    259, 267, 270, 486, 515, 555, 638, 676
  army, 38, 667, 671
  banking, 176
  chambers of commerce, 160–61
  Charte 1814, 237
  Cobden Treaty, 634–5
  confederate model, 22
  and Confederation of Rhine, 8–9
  Congress of Vienna, 72–4
  conservatism, 276
  and counter-revolution, 570
  Crimean War, 613–16
  economy, 7, 316
  education, 409, 410, 426
  family in, 110
  female emancipation, 106
  foreign policy, 14, 320–21, 323, 353
  and Germany, 2, 4, 16–19, 63, 81–2, 708
  in Germany, 290, 299, 326
  'Great Empire', 3–4
  industrialisation, 157, 158, 161, 174
  influence of, 63, 64, 146, 341
  Italian War, 617–20
  July Revolution, 322, 323
  liberalism, 252, 261
  Louis Napoleon coup, 612
  nationalism, 263
  postitivism, 441
  Protestantism in, 381
  and Prussia, 4–5, 11

reform model, 23
religion, 154, 398, 647
revolution, 1848, 528, 530, 595
Rhine crisis, 272–3
and Russia, 612
Schleswig-Holstein question, 688,
    690–91, 692, 694–5, 700–704
science, 437–8, 460
separation of powers, 256
social policy, 211, 346
socialism, 349, 465, 665
universal suffrage, 582
universities, 416
war with Russia, 15, 62–73
Franck, J.P., 124
Franco-Prussian war, 62–73
Franconia, 58, 149, 328, 533
Frankfurt, 6–7, 57, 63, 117, 168, 192, 309,
    327, 330, 336, 561, 566, 633, 663,
    675–6, 686
    Austro-Prussian war, 707
    conference of princes, 1863, 630–31
    culture, 472, 473, 475, 497
    customs policy, 318
    Democrats, 650–51
    free city, 75
    grand duchy, 8
    Jews in, 219, 220
    Paulskirche riots, 563–4
    radicalism, 565
    Reaction, 599
    storming of the guards, 329
    Vorparlament elections, 541, 542
    workers' movement, 549, 551
Frankfurt National Assembly, 14, 190, 219,
    221, 386, 396, 424, 458, 554, 575, 625,
    633, 639–40
    aims of, 544–7
    and aristocracy, 226
    Blum executed, 570
    Bohemia Question, 557–8
    Catholics in, 340, 548–9
    collapses, 588
    and counter-revolution, 565–71, 574,
    577, 578
    coup attempted, 563–4
    Democrats in, 562
    elections, 540–41
    established, 540–47
    failure of revolution, 592–3

Fraktionen, 119, 190, 542–4
Gottingen Seven, 333
    imperial constitution, 579–87
    Posen question, 556–7
    and radicals, 562–4
    Schleswig-Holstein question, 554–6
Frankfurt/Oder university, 417
Frankfurter Zeitung, 524
Frantz, Constantin, 634, 705
Franz I, emperor of Austria, 12, 297, 298
    renounces empire, 2, 4
Franz Joseph, emperor of Austria, 60, 118,
    573, 602, 630, 690
    Austro-Prussian war, 705–6
    and mediatised aristocracy, 238
    reform, 625, 626
fraternities, 99
Fraunhofer, Joseph, 163, 429
Frederick the Great, 21, 279, 585
free trade, 550, 647–8. *see also* Zollverein
Freemasonry, 234
Freiburg, 7, 261, 373, 426, 491, 539
    diocese, 368
    Mining Academy, 426, 429
    university, 305, 309, 339
Freie Stadte, 312
Freiheit zum Staat, 22
Freikorps, 68
Freiligrath, Ferdinand, 334, 345, 570
French Revolution, 1, 14, 17, 18, 30, 38, 55,
    387, 444, 470
    and conservatism, 274, 275–6
    influence of, 19–20, 251
    Jewish emancipation, 217
    and nationalism, 264–5
    Reign of Terror, 246
    and religion, 357
    and socialism, 346
Frey, Johann Gottfried, 26, 27
Freytag, Gustav, 223, 398, 459, 515, 518
    newspaper, 524, 525, 643
Friedland, battle of, 5, 14
Friedrich, Caspar David, 481, 498–9, 500, 503
Friedrich, crown prince of Prussia, 625, 634,
    651, 674–5, 677
Friedrich, king of Wurttemberg, 63, 315
Friedrich Wilhelm Foundry, Mulheim, 162
Friedrich Wilhelm III, king of Prussia, 50,
    68, 167, 240, 242–3, 292–3
    army reforms, 38–40

Friedrich Wilhelm IV, king of Prussia, 141,
    224, 243, 254, 281, 336, 358, 376, 549,
    592
Friedrich Wilhelm IV (cont.)
    army reform, 668, 673–4, 675
    arts policy, 477
    and Bismarck, 677–8
    church and state, 371, 382–3, 386
    conservatism, 279, 424
    and counter-revolution, 577–9
    and education, 402
    elected kaiser, 586–8
    Erfurt Union, 596–8
    general synod, 384
    and Herwegh, 345
    illness, 621
    nationalism, 268, 272
    reign of, 350–51
    revolution, 1848, 530–32
    Schleswig-Holstein crisis, 597–8
Friends of Light, 384, 386
Fries, Jakob, 218, 244, 245, 248
Friesen, Friedrich, 18, 244
Frisia, East, 75
Frobel, Julius, 103, 344, 345, 543, 562, 620
    counter-revolution, 569–70
    German Reform Society, 633
Fuggers, 168
Fulda, 368
furniture, 113, 114
Fursorgepflicht, 30, 32
Furstenberg family, 147, 533
Furth, 166, 220

Gagern, Friedrich von, 271
Gagern, Heinrich von, 63, 227, 328, 334,
    342, 343, 534, 537, 538, 542, 558, 593
    German Reform Society, 633
    and Italian War, 619
    kleindeutsch solution, 583–6
    and Paulskirche, 541, 543, 544–5
    resigns, 588
Gagern, Max von, 538
Galerie, Dresden, 488
Galicia, 302, 323, 566
Gall, Franz Joseph, 260, 429, 431, 679, 681
Gallitzin, Princess, 360
Galvani, Luigi, 430
Gans, Eduard, 212, 454
Garde de Corps, 240
gardens, public, 489–90

Garibaldi, Giuseppe, 697, 698
Gartenlaube, Die, 122, 181, 223, 230, 525,
    643, 648
Gartner, Friedrich von, 489, 491
gas industry, 164
gas lighting, 114
Gastein Convention, 692–3
Gaus and Weber, 167
Gauss, Carl Friedrich, 429, 436
Geestemunde, 168
Geibel, Emanuel, 512
Geissel, 371
Geist, 374
Geisteswissenschaften, 441, 442, 449
Gendarmerie-Edikt, 25, 141
General Commissions, 34, 139
General German Trade Law Handbook, 175
General German Workers' Association
    (ADAV), 661–5
Gentz, Friedrich, 12, 17, 18, 238, 248, 280, 522
Gerlach, Ernst Ludwig von, 276, 279, 351,
    376, 606, 608, 610, 619, 653, 670, 697
Gerlach, Leopold von, 279, 351, 376, 606, 653
German Association for Liberation, Inner
    Renewal and the Ultimate Unification
    of the German People, 18–19
German Association for Trade and
    Commerce, 316, 635
German Bank, 178
German Catholic Conference, 1865, 365–6
German Choral Union, 474
German Confederation, 83, 218, 247–8, 308,
    313, 336, 511, 583, 708, 715
    army, 289
    and Austria, 303, 626, 690, 691
    Austro-Prussian war, 699, 701, 704
    Bismarck's reforms, 693–4
    censorship, 309
    church and state, 368
    constitutions, 237–8
    customs policy, 316
    decline of, 353
    decrees, 1832, 310
    established, 78–82, 313–16
    and extra-parliamentary opposition, 328–9
    foreign policy, 320, 322, 612–20
    and Hanover *coup d'etat*, 333
    Jews in, 221
    July Revolution, 326–30
    as model, 343
    nationalism in, 268, 270–72

policy in 1850s, 608–11
political parties in, 333–50
population, 85–7, 93
Reaction, 599–608
reform of, 592, 627–36
repression, 355
restoration, 249–50
revolution, 1848, 538
Schleswig-Holstein question, 597–8, 696,
   697–8
union of states, 596–8
and *Vorparlament*, 539
war with Denmark, 686–7
German Congress of Trade and Industry, 182
German empire, 77
   kleindeutsch solution, 583–6
   unification, 599–715
German Federation
   sexuality, 109
German League, 511
German National Society, 629, 631–3, 635,
   643, 646, 654, 658–9, 709
   and ADAV, 663
German People's Association, Paris, 331
German Protestant Society, 385
German Protestantism (Hundeshagen), 386
German Question, 623–4, 626–36, 651, 691
   and Bismarck, 676, 708
   and European politics, 684–704
   and Schleswig-Holstein, 689, 694
German Reform Society, 633, 646, 654
German societies, 244
German studies, 451
German triad, 315
German Women's Society, 106
Germania, 326
Germanisation, 350
Germanisches Nationalmuseum,
   Nuremberg, 475
Germanistik, 453
Germanists, 274, 343, 425
Germany, 1–2, 165
   agriculture, 126–7, 130–34, 144–6
   aristocracy, 226
   army, 228
   centralisation, 76–81
   constitutions, 237, 238–9, 242
   and counter-revolution, 568–73
   craft risings, 190
   crafts sector, 187

currency, 175
and Europe, 319–23
in French Empire, 6–11
Great Reforms, 19–67
and Hungary, 572–3
imperial constitution, 579–87
industrialisation, 172, 173, 209
Jews in, 217, 219
liberalism, 154, 252–4
nationalism, 263–74
police state, 249–50
public opinion and Napoleon, 16–19
Reaction, 599–608
rural life, 152
social mobility, 230
territorial reorganisation, 1814, 73–6
trade, 125
war with Napoleon, 67–73
Germany and the Revolution (Gorres), 242
Germany in its Period of Deep Humiliation, 13
Gerstacker, Friedrich, 521
Gervinus, Georg Gottfried, 332–3, 343, 364,
   523, 649
Gesenius, Wilhelm, 374
Gesindeordnung, 33, 150, 216
Gesinderecht, 454
Gesindezwangsdienst, 29–30
Gewerbefreiheit, 187
Gewerbeinstitut, 160, 427
Gierke, Otto von, 453, 462
Giessen, 245, 330, 363, 434
   university, 418, 419
glee-clubs, 274
Glyptothek, Munich, 475, 488, 496
Gneisenau, August Graf Neidhardt von, 5, 10,
   13, 15, 16, 23, 38–40, 72, 76, 82, 248
Gneist, Rudolf von, 462, 648
Goethe, Johann Wolfgang von, 4, 379, 429,
   444, 526, 642
   admirer of Napoleon, 16, 265
   Classicism, 440, 505, 507
   influence of, 390, 485
   monuments, 268
   and religion, 357, 360–61
   sexuality, 109
   and theatre, 480
'Good Comrade' (Uhland), 13
Gorchakov, Alexander, 685, 703
Gorres, Joseph, 18, 76, 77, 246, 252, 348,
   358, 361, 507, 525

Gorres, Joseph (cont.)
  Athanasius, 371
  church and state, 338
  conservatism, 278
  constitutional petition, 241–2
  on German Confederation, 81, 82
  nationalism, 17, 18, 265
  newspapers, 72, 79, 522
Gossen, Hermann Heinrich, 460
Gotha company, 168
Gothaer, 596, 632
Gotthelf, Jeremias, 510
Gottingen, 43, 123, 128, 187, 325, 429, 450
  university, 332–3, 350, 419
Gottingen Seven, 252, 269, 332–3, 350, 418,
  424
Gottschalk, Andreas, 350, 530, 562
Grabbe, Christian, 509, 519
Grassmann, Hermann, 436
Great Exhibition, London 1851, 132, 162
Great Reforms, 19–67
  Austria, 64–7
  Confederation of the Rhine, 19, 22, 54–64
  Prussia, 21–54
  resistance to, 40
Greece, 44–6, 263, 272, 274
  independence struggle, 319, 321–2
Greifswald, 128
Grenzboten, 523, 524, 643, 689
Griesheim, Lt-Colonel, 562
Grillparzer, Franz, 300, 372, 510, 518, 519,
  569
Grimm, Jacob, 18, 332–3, 507
Grimm, Jakob, 450
Grimm, Wilhelm, 18, 332–3, 450
Grolman, Karl von, 38
Gross-Hoffinger, Anton, 302
gross national product, 174
grossdeutsch solution, 387, 459, 565, 581,
  626
  Catholic support, 654
  effects of Austro-Prussian war, 705, 707
  end of, 715
  and failure of revolution, 591, 593, 595
  and Italian War, 619–20
  liberals split, 650–51
  and Paulskirche, 547, 549
  rejected, 583–6
  and Schleswig-Holstein question, 686, 694
  and workers' movement, 659, 664–6

Grossgorschen, 70
Grossherzogliches Museum, Darmstadt,
  475
Groth, Klaus, 518
Grun, Anastasius, 302
Grun, Karl, 348, 523
Grundentlastung, 146, 149, 304, 308, 354
Grunderzeit, 113
Grundherren, 28
Grundherrschaft, 34, 61, 146, 533
Grundrechte, 546–7, 548, 549
Grundsteuer, 37, 142
Gruner, Justus, 16, 67, 76, 81–2
Grunne, Count von, 602
guilds, 43, 98, 156, 211, 288
  factory demarcations, 203
  numbers in, 183–4
  reforms, 304
  and social class, 231–2
  and trade freedom, 187–90
Gunther, Anton, 360
Gustav Adolf Society, 377, 381, 388
Gute Stube, 113
Gutenberg, 268, 476
Gutsbezirke, 25
Gutsherren, 28, 32
Gutzkow, Karl, 330, 391, 511
Gymnasia, 45, 48–9, 269, 399, 422, 428
gymnastic associations, 19, 244, 248, 274
gymnastics, 123
gymnastics clubs, 76

Habilitation, 418
Habsburg Empire, 77, 93, 272, 303, 321,
  587, 698–9, 702, 708
Habsburg lands, 3
Hacklander, Friedrich Wilhelm, 521
Haeckel, Ernst, 397, 436
Hahnemann, Samuel, 123, 431
Halle, 50, 374, 419
Halle Almanacs, 334
Haller, Karl Ludwig von, 245, 278–9
Hallesche Jahrbucher, 344, 523
Hallgarten, 343
Hamann, 357
Hambach festival, 269, 270, 310, 326–7, 329,
  332, 351, 391
Hamburg, 6, 95, 96, 105, 115, 168, 192, 542,
  663
  architecture, 491, 492

culture, 472, 473, 475
  Jews in, 219
  newspapers, 523
  prostitution, 122
  reconstruction, 117
  unemployment, 193
  water system, 124
Hanau, 324, 534
Haniel, 163, 178
Hanover, 4, 38, 75, 91, 145, 146, 166, 188,
    324, 427, 632, 634
  administration, 288
  aristocracy, 225, 312
  Austro-Prussian war, 696, 699, 701–2, 707
  church and state, 385
  constitution, 325, 586
  coup d'etat, 269
  culture, 475
  customs policy, 318, 611
  and *Deutscher Bund*, 78–9
  education, 413, 427
  English rule, 71, 74
  Erfurt Union, 596–7
  and France, 2, 8, 82
  Guelfs, 711
  industry, 95, 164, 168
  Jews in, 219, 220
  land reforms, 147
  New Era, 623
  and Paulskirche, 546, 588
  population, 96
  Reaction, 600
  reactionary movement, 332–3
  Vorparlament elections, 540
  workers' organisations, 216
Hanseatic towns, 71, 75
Hansemann, David, 178, 180, 215, 261–2,
    342, 353, 530, 585, 620
HAPAG, 168
Harburg, 96
Hardenberg, Carl August Freiherr von, 5,
    11, 15, 52–4, 74, 78, 109, 293
  child labour, 215
  Congress of Vienna, 81–2
  and constitution, 241–3
  Jewish rights, 218
  and Metternich, 246
  nationalism, 18
  and power of aristocracy, 141
  reforms, 23–5, 33–4, 35, 36–7

Riga Memorandum, 20
  and student associations, 248
Harkort, Friedrich, 163, 165, 214, 262, 412
Harless, Adolf, 386, 387
Hartmann, Eduard von, 164, 396
Hartungsche Zeitung, 523
Hassenpflug, Ludwig, 332
Hauff, Wilhelm, 517
Hausmannskost, 121
Hausser, Ludwig, 343, 385
Havlicek, Karel, 303
Haydn, Franz Joseph, 482, 486
Haym, Rudolf, 542, 640, 643, 649
health care, 117, 121–5, 150
  health and safety legislation, 216
  regulations, 116–17
  sickness benefit, 202
Hebbel, Freidrich, 510, 519
Hebel, Johann Peter, 375
Hecker, Friedrich, 343, 345
Hegel, Georg Wilhelm Friedrich, 16, 212, 291,
    296, 419, 455. *see also* Young Hegelians
  admirer of Napoleon, 265
  on agriculture, 127
  and art history, 460
  and historicism, 361, 380, 448–9, 456, 457
  influence of, 465–71
  and jurisprudence, 453
  natural philosophy, 430
  and Prussia, 291, 350, 585
  and religion, 360, 377, 385
  social theories, 111, 461–2, 465
  taught in universities, 423, 424
Hegelianism, 294, 522, 660
Hegewisch, 244
Heidelberg, 19, 57, 75, 166, 247, 327, 361,
    433, 452
  'Heidelberg Romantics', 507
  liberalism, 343
  rationalism, 374–5
  university, 417, 419, 427
Heilige Family, Die (Marx and Engels), 348
Heine, Heinrich, 193, 221, 222, 358, 488
  admirer of Napoleon, 17
  conservatism, 276
  de-Christianisation, 391
  influence of, 330–31, 348, 511–12
  Paris correspondent, 523
  revolution, 1848, 386
  Weltschmertz, 509

Heinroth, Johann Christian August, 431
Heligoland, 6
Hellenism, 44–6, 47, 263, 404, 450, 490
Helmholtz, Hermann, 432, 433, 434–5
Hengstenberg, Ernst Wilhelm, 280, 376
Henle, Jacob, 432
Henning, 131, 147
Henschel, Carl, 164, 178
Heppenheim, 343
Herbart, Johann Friedrich, 415
Herder, 520
Herder, Johann Gottfried, 444, 445, 451
Hermann, Friedrich Benedict Wilhelm von,
    460
hermeneutics, 450
Hermes, Georg, 360, 370
Herrenhaus, 224, 605, 606, 672
Herrmann, Gottfried, 450
Hertz, Henriette, 222
Herwegh, Georg, 334, 345, 563
Hess, Moses, 348, 350
Hess, Peter and Heinrich, 501
Hesse, 148, 327, 518, 533, 543
    Austro-Prussian war, 696, 702
    banking, 176
    church and state, 382
    education, 413
    German Reform Society, 633
    radicalism, 153, 563
    regionalism, 290
    revolutionary movement, 329–30
    Vorparlament elections, 540
Hesse, Elector of, 312, 313
Hesse, Electorate of, 145, 149, 313, 332, 628
    absolutism, 312
    administration, 288
    Austro-Prussian war, 696, 699, 701–2, 707
    church and state, 385
    customs policy, 317, 318
    Jews in, 219
    Reaction, 600
    revolutionary movement, 328
    Schleswig-Holstein question, 597–8
    uprising, 324–5
Hesse, Grand Duchy of, 149
Hesse, Rhenish, 303–4, 562
    regionalism, 303–4
Hesse-Darmstadt, 2, 3, 75, 92, 238, 239
    Catholic politics, 654
    customs policy, 317, 318

Reaction, 600, 601, 602
    and Zollverein, 635
Hesse-Kassel, 8, 12, 13, 601
Hessischer Landbote, 330, 391
Heyne, Christian Gottlob, 450
Heyse, Paul, 398, 512–13
Hildebrand, Bruno, 213, 461
Hildebrandt, Theodor, 497
Hinckeldey, Carl von, 606, 607
Hirscher, Johann Baptist, 361–2, 363
Historical and Political Journal, 334, 457
Historical and Political Magazine, 334
historicism, 254, 341, 457, 647
    in architecture, 490–94
    in art, 482–3, 496–8
    cultural history, 459
    development of, 441–71
    and economics, 461
    in literature, 517–18
    political aims, 457–8, 641
    roots of, 442–6
*Historisch-Politische Blatter fur das
    katholische Deutschland*, 338, 524
Historische-Politische, 634
Historische Zeitschrift, 459, 643
History of Bohemia (Palacky), 303
Hitler, Adolf, 142, 217, 262, 704, 712
Hobbes, Thomas, 275
Hobrecht, James, 118
Hoechst factory, 173
Hoesch foundry, 162, 178
Hofer, Andreas, 13
Hoffmann, Doctor (*Struwwelpeter*), 103
Hoffmann, E.T.A., 474, 507
Hoffmann League, 244
Hoffmann (statistician), 92
Hoffmann von Fallersleben, August
    Heinrich, 273, 345, 351
Hofmann, 387
Hofmann, August Wilhelm von, 430, 434
Hofschlachterei, 130
Hohenheim, 128
Hohenlohe family, 147
Hohenlohe-Ohringen family, 148
Hohenschwangau, 488, 492
Hohenzollern, Prince, 621
Holderlin, 505
Holland, 6, 7
Holstein, 96, 125, 312–13, 454. *see also*
    Schleswig-Holstein

Holy Alliance, 82–3, 323, 612
Holy Roman Empire, 3–4
Homburg, 119
homeopathy, 123, 431
Horder foundry, 172
hospitals, 123–4
housing, 111–14, 174, 202, 210
Huber, Ernst Rudolf, 327, 333
Huber, Victor Aime, 214, 336–7, 389
Hubsch, Heinrich, 481, 491, 493
Hufeland, Doctor, 123
Hugo, Gustav, 452
humanism, 263–4, 389–98, 401, 402–3, 404, 441
    and technical education, 426, 428
Humanitat, 44, 47, 505, 508
humanities, 460
    evolution of, 441–71
    historical, 449–52
Humboldt, Alexander von, 418, 429–30
Humboldt, Wilhelm von, 44–51, 57, 78, 102, 109, 423, 438, 440
    constitutional struggle, 242–3
    historicism, 445
    Jewish rights, 218
    linguistics, 451
    and Metternich, 246
    nationalism, 266, 267
Hundeshagen, Karl Bernhard, 386
Hungary, 66, 297, 302
    and Austria, 596, 625–7
    Austro-Prussian war, 698, 705–6
    and counter-revolution, 566–8, 570, 571–3
    Reaction, 602, 603, 604
    and Schleswig-Holstein question, 692
    war with Austria, 574–5
Hungerpastor, 223
Hunsruck, 75, 162
hunting rights, 141, 146
hygiene, 112, 117, 124
hypnosis, 123

Ibell, Karl von, 236, 246
idealism, 44, 390, 395
    and historicism, 447, 448–9
    philosophy of, 466–71
Idstein, 128
Ihering, Rudolf von, 454
illegitimacy, 91–2, 108–9, 110, 151, 152
Illenau, 124

illiteracy, 409–10
Illyria, 71
Immermann, Karl, 510, 511, 517, 518, 526
immigration, 183
impeachment, 308, 310
Imperial Knights, 3, 23, 29, 60
income tax, 37, 52
individualisation, 232–4, 341–2
industrialisation, 95, 107, 131, 135, 144, 149, 155–82, 160, 271, 293, 339, 636–7. *see also* factories; labour movement
    class division, 654–5
    and education, 415
    effects of, 174–8
    employer-labour relations, 201–3
    financing of, 148, 167–9
    ideas of time, 198–9
    and liberalism, 261
    motivation to work, 199–200
    numbers employed, 164, 169–70
    opposition to, 190, 534–5, 549
    and pauperism, 192–8
    preconditions for, 156–8
    role of entrepreneurs, 178–82
    share of economy, 171–4
    southern Germany, 304
    wages, 203–4
infallibility, 363, 366
inflation, 66–7
Ingolstadt, 417
inheritance, 151, 152
Inner Mission, 213, 377, 388–9
Innsbruck, 459, 529, 634
Innviertel, the, 13
insanity, 124
Institute for the Study of Austrian History, 457
Instleute, 143
insurance, 136, 168, 213
integration, 238, 240–41, 292, 296, 312
Ireland, 303, 339
Iron Cross, 68
iron industry, 162, 167, 169, 171, 172, 178, 205
Isar river, 164
Istria, 3, 13
Italian War, 612, 623, 627, 630, 667, 697–8, 702
Italy, 172, 321, 474, 553, 604, 626, 683, 685
    and Austria, 70, 73, 83, 596, 612–13, 628, 690, 693

Italy (cont.)
  Austro-Prussian war, 694, 695, 698, 699,
    701
  counter-revolution, 566, 568, 571
  and German Confederation, 558
  July Revolution, 322, 323–4
  music, 486
  and Napoleon, 2, 3, 6, 7
  revolution, 1848, 528, 530, 595
  Societa Nazionale, 632
  unification of, 82, 302, 617–18, 620, 702
  war with Austria, 616–20
Itzstein, Johann Adam von, 309, 343

Jacobi, Carl Gustav, 418
Jacobinism, 265, 338
  Democrats, 562, 568
  fear of, 552–3, 560, 571, 643, 658
Jacobins, 242, 251, 357, 361
Jacoby, Johann, 346, 351–2, 577, 672, 713
Jahn, Friedrich Ludwig, 18, 19, 76, 118, 244,
    245, 247, 266, 350
  monument, 642
Jarcke, Karl Ernst, 338
Jeggle, Dr, 150
Jellacic, Joseph Graf, 567, 569, 570
Jena, 19, 128, 245, 397, 466
  university, 245
Jena, battle of, 5, 14
Jesuits, 251, 363, 364, 366, 369, 372, 580
  ban lifted, 548
  expelled from Freiburg, 373
Jew Laws, 1847, 219
Jews, 53, 179, 564
  assimilation, 221–3
  banking, 167–8, 299, 604
  citizenship rights, 27
  embourgeoisement, 220–21
  in Prussia, 348
  reform movement, 222–3
  and students' associations, 244
  treatment of, 153, 217–23
  university appointments, 424
Johann, Archduke of Austria, 14, 66
joint stock companies, 168–9, 175, 176, 179,
    182, 293, 607
Jordan, Sylvester, 324, 332
Jorg, Joseph Edmund, 525, 634
Joseph II, 65, 297
Josephinism, 364, 366, 369, 372, 601, 603

Joule, 434
Journal of Rational Medicine, 434
journalists, 525–6, 561, 643
judiciary, 57, 576, 606
  aristocracy in, 285
  liberalism, 645
  reforms, 25, 26
  and the state, 294
July Revolution, 145, 310, 322
  associations, 331
  effects of, 323–33
  extra-parliamentary opposition, 326–30
  literature, 330–31
Jung-Stilling, Dr, 123, 357
Junkers, 25, 29, 35, 139–40, 141, 142, 280, 295
  Catholic opposition to, 654
  compensation for, 33–4
  counter-revolution, 561–2
  and education reform, 400
  High Conservatism, 335–6
  and liberalism, 645, 648, 681
  and Reaction, 605–8
  and reform, 32, 52–3, 144, 241, 312
  revolution, 1848, 531
  status of, 226
jurisprudence, 451–4

Kaiserswerth, 124, 377
Kalisch, Proclamation of, 69
Kant, Immanuel, 28, 29, 360, 374, 377, 389,
    440, 498, 505
  historicism, 445, 456
  idealism, 21–2, 44, 55, 498
  influence of, 250–51, 253, 465–7, 469
  and jurisprudence, 454
  liberalism, 269
  and natural law, 451
  on science, 395
Karl, Archduke of Austria, 12, 66, 82
Karl, Duke of Brunswick, 324
Karl of Mecklenburg, Duke, 240
Karlmarsch, Karl, 427
Karlsruhe, 164, 427, 435, 475
  architecture, 488, 490, 491
Kassel, 8, 13, 164, 324, 427, 475, 549
Katholik, Der, 362, 365
Kaulbach, Friedrich, 496, 497
Kehr, E., 68
Keil, Ernst, 525
Kein Husung (Reuter), 144

Kekule, August, 434
Kelheim, 476, 643
Kelheimer Hall of Liberation, 268
Keller, Gottfried, 398, 515–16
Kerner, Justinus, 123, 430
Kersting, Georg Friedrich, 495
Kessler, 164
Ketteler, Wilhelm Emanuel Freiherr von, 214, 339, 548, 602
Kieler Blatter, 313
Kierkegaard, Soren, 526
Kiltgang, 99
kindergartens, 103
Kinkel, Gottfried, 346
Kirchhoff, Gustav Robert, 434, 435
Kissingen, 119
Kladderadatsch, 524–5
kleindeutsch solution, 75, 271, 300, 301, 387, 538, 555, 624, 683, 690
    accepted, 583–6
    anti-Catholicism, 367
    anti-imperial, 560
    and counter-revolution, 577, 578
    effects of Austro-Prussian war, 705, 707, 708
    Erfurt Union, 596–7
    and failure of revolution, 591–3, 595
    German Question, 627–36
    and historicism, 458–9, 641
    and imperial constitution, 581
    and Italian War, 619–20
    liberals split, 650–51
    and Paulskirche, 547, 549
    and Schleswig-Holstein question, 686, 690, 694, 696
    support for, 623
    and workers' movement, 659, 664–6
Kleist, Heinrich von, 12, 18, 266, 505
Kleist-Retzow family, 376
Klenze, Leo von, 488, 490, 491
Kleve, 4
Klopp, Onno, 633–4
Kneipp, Sebastian, 123
Knies, Karl, 461
Knigge, Baron Adolf von, 526
knights, 32, 33, 140
Koch, Joseph Anton, 498
Koch, Robert, 434
Kocka, Dr, 180
Kolberg, 5

Kollar, Jan, 558
Kolnische Zeitung, 523, 524
Kolowrat, Franz Anton Graf von, 298
Kolping, Adolf, 339
Kolping Brotherhood, 365
Kolportage novels, 521
Kongress deutscher Volkswirte, 642, 647
Konig, Friedrich, 163–4, 178
Koniggratz, battle of, 415, 699–700, 705, 708
Konigsberg, 18, 22, 27, 29, 52, 95, 128, 129, 346, 419, 523
Konzessionswang, 606
Koppe, Johann Gottlieb, 128
Korner, Theodor, 68
Kossuth, Lajos, 574
Kotzebue, August von, 109, 238, 245, 246
Kraus, Christian Jacob, 22, 29, 164
Krauss, Philipp von, 602
'Krautjunkers', 142
Krefeld, 95, 190, 534–5
Kreis, 25, 28, 33, 35, 52, 56, 78, 140
    and aristocracy, 224, 225
    constitutions, 296
Kreisdirektoren, 56
Kreisoberen, 78
Kreisordnung, 54, 141
Kreistage, 141, 285, 294
Kremsier programme, 584
Kreuzzeitung, 522, 524, 561, 652, 677, 697
Kries
    reform, 241
Kronig, Karl, 435
Krumper system, 40
Krupp, Alfred, 159, 162, 178, 180, 181
Krupp factory, 120, 202, 204, 205
Kubeck, Baron von, 299, 602
Kuhn, Thomas S., 431
Kulturkampf, 366, 367, 371–3, 414, 426, 603–4, 625, 647, 654
Kulturnation, 265, 267–8
Kunth, Christian, 159
Kutusow, General, 69

labour force, 31, 32–3
    crafts sector, 183–6
    effects of industrialisation, 169–70, 198–201
    minimum working age, 215–16
    mobility, 210–11
    proportion of factory workers, 204–6

labour force (cont.)
   social policy for, 211–16
   wages, 195, 196–7
   welfare of, 202–3
   working conditions, 171, 206–10
labour laws, 293
labour movement. *see* workers' movement
Lachmann, Karl, 450, 451
Lagarde, Paul de, 398
Lagrange, Joseph Louis, 429
Laibach, 321
Lamennais, Abbe, 338
land. *see* agriculture
land tax, 57
Landau, 82
Landrate, 141, 241, 285, 287, 293, 294
Landratskammern, 606
Landschaften, 32, 130
Landshut, 19, 57, 360, 417
Landsmannschaften, 244
Landstandische Verfassungen, 313
Landsturm, 41
Landtage, 53, 182, 214, 224, 292, 294, 412
   Austria, 625
   autonomy reduced, 328–9
   Bismarck suspends, 680
   Catholics in, 337, 339
   and constitutions, 324–5
   Hungary, 626
   Jewish exclusion, 218, 219
   July Revolutions, 324–6
   liberalism in, 261, 262
   nationalism in, 274
   role of, 295–6, 306–7, 352, 628–9
Landwehr, 12, 40–42, 66, 68, 228, 289
   army reforms, 667–71
   mutiny, 589
   position of, 242–3
Landwirtschaftlicher Verein, 129
Langen, Johann Jacob, 179
Langewiesche, 544
language, 263, 265
   use of French, 9
Lanz, Heinrich, 132
Laplace, Pierre Simon, Marquis de, 429
Lasker, Eduard, 525
Lassalle, Ferdinand, 222, 525, 526, 563, 619,
   656
   and Bismarck, 682, 697
   programme of, 659–66

Lassbauern, 137
Laube, Heinrich, 330, 511
Lauenburg, 75
Lavater, Johann Kasper, 357
Lavoisier, Antoine Laurent, 429
League of Blacks, 245–6
League of Communists, 348, 552, 655, 663
League of Outlaws, 331, 347
League of the Just, 331, 347, 348
League of Virtue, 18, 382
Legal and Political Readers' Association, 302
legal system, 175, 204
   Bavaria, 57
   equality, 255
   and historicism, 451–4
   and liberalism, 257–8, 259
   Prussian code, 240–41
   worker protection, 216
Leibig's Meat Extract, 120
Leibl, Wilhelm, 500, 502
Leiningen, Prince Karl, 342, 545, 554
Leipzig, 115, 120, 123, 166, 542, 558, 643,
   663
   congress, 1862, 659–60
   culture, 472, 473
   newspapers, 344, 523, 525
   revolution, 1848, 534
   trading centre, 6, 7, 95
   Workers' Brotherhood, 551
Leipzig, battle of, 244–5, 388
leisure occupations, 119
Lenau, Nikolaus, 509
Leo, Heinrich, 248, 457
Leopold, Grand Duke, 309, 310
Lerchenfeld, Maximilian von, 314
Lessing, Karl Friedrich, 43, 217, 496, 497
Levin, Rahel, 222
Leyer und Schwerdt (Korner), 68
Liberal Party, Baden, 624–5
liberalism, 154, 251–3, 277, 332–3, 334, 474,
   648
   and administration, 287
   aristocratic support, 227
   and associations, 234–5
   attitude to army, 290
   Austria, 301, 372, 626–7
   and Austro-Prussian war, 697, 708,
      710–11
   and Bismarck, 678–84
   and Catholicism, 338–9, 340, 647

changes after 1848, 639–51
church and state, 371
in civil service, 282, 284–5
conflicts within, 261–2, 650–51
and Democrats, 624–5
development of, 250–62
and economy, 260–61, 647–8
and education, 404
egalitarianism, 260–61
extra-parliamentary opposition, 326–30
'German triad', 315
and historicism, 458–9
and imperial constitution, 581–2
and Jews, 222
and July Revolution, 323–6
and jurisprudence, 454
and Lassalle programme, 659–66
and nationalism, 269–70, 297, 632, 646
New Era, 601, 621–4
newspapers, 523–4
and North German Confederation,
    711–14
opposed to revolution, 251–2, 355, 643,
    658
in parliaments, 307–12
political parties, 334–5
popular movement, 341–3
and Protestantism, 377–81
Prussia, 294–5, 670–74
and Reaction, 600–602
revolution, 1848, 536–7, 560–61, 590–94
role of constitution, 254–60
role of monarch, 258–9
Schleswig-Holstein question, 686
social policy, 214, 216
and socialism, 552–3
and universities, 424–5
and *Vorparlament*, 538–9
and working class, 643–5, 655–9
liberation of peasants. *see* peasants
libraries, 521
Lichnowsky, Prince, 563
Lichtenberg, 328
Lichtenstein, 493
Lichtfreunde, 345
Lieber, Franz, 97
Liebermann, Leopold, 362
Liebermann, Max, 502
Liebig, Justus von, 128, 408, 418, 419, 432,
    434, 440

Liebknecht, Wilhelm, 659, 664, 665, 702
Liebl, Wilhelm, 503
Lieder eines Lebendigen (Herwegh), 345
Life of Jesus, The (Strauss), 380, 391
Limburg, 322, 368, 558
Lind, Jenny, 472
Lindau, 3
Lindenau, Bernhard von, 325
linguistics, 451
Lippe, 75, 164, 237
Lissa, battle of, 699
List, Friedrich, 97, 146, 149, 159, 212, 260,
    271, 460
   on bureaucracy, 286
   customs campaign, 316
   in parliament, 308
   and railways, 165
Lister, Joseph, 433
Liszt, Franz, 472, 481, 483, 485
literacy
   reading revolution, 520–21
Literarisches Comptoir, 345
literature, 312, 353, 476, 480, 521
   book-burning, 245
   de-Christianisation, 398
   development of, 504–19
   and nationalism, 267
   oppositional, 510–12
   radicalism in, 330–31
   Realism, 514–16
Lobachevski, N.I., 436
local government, 117, 124–5, 140, 287–8.
    see also self-administration
   Prussia, 291–3
Loening, Karl, 246
Loewe, Carl, 485–6
Lohe, Wilhelm, 377
Lombardy, 165, 566, 617, 690
London, 168, 347, 524
Lornssen, Uwe Jens, 273
Lorrach, 564
Lorrain, Claude, 498
Lorraine, 82
Lortzing, Albert, 485–6
Lotze, Hermann, 440, 514
Louis Napoleon. *see* Napoleon III
Louis Philippe, emperor of France, 527
Louise, queen of Prussia, 11
Lowe-Calbe, Wilhelm, 672
Lower Austrian Trade Association, 302

Lubeck, 5, 6, 274, 343
Luchentheorie, 674
Luden, Dr, 244
Ludwig, Karl, 432
Ludwig I, king of Bavaria, 19, 239, 268, 281,
    361, 476, 497, 528, 643
  arts policy, 477
  and electors, 62
  and parliament, 310–11
Ludwigshafen, 165
Ludwigskanal, 164
Luther, Martin, 99, 335, 361, 377, 476
  and modernism, 376, 379
  and nationalism, 267, 268
  scholarship, 253
Lutheranism, 325, 335, 374, 382, 384–5,
    386, 387, 416, 554
Lutzow Rifles, 68
Lutzow Volunteer Corps, 244
Luxemburg, 75, 272, 322, 695, 702

Mack, Karl Freiherr von, 3
Maffei, Joseph Anton, 164
magazines, 525
Magdeburg, 95
Magenta, battle of, 617
Magyars, 297, 302, 566–7, 571–3, 626–7
  Austro-Prussian war, 705–6
Mahler, Gustav, 512
Main river, 164, 628, 696, 697, 701, 707–8
Mainz, 75, 165, 220, 247, 368
  Catholic convention, 548
  ultramontanism, 362–3
Mainz commission of inquiry, 315
Mainzer Journal, 548
Maistre, Joseph, Count von, 275
Malakoff towers, 489
Mallinckrodt, Arnold, 241
Malmo, 555
malnutrition, 120–21
Malthusianism, 90, 91
Mangoldt, Hans von, 460
Mannesmann, Reinhard, 178
Mannheim, 75, 95, 165, 166, 220, 476, 589
  industry, 173
  revolution, 1848, 527–8, 534, 535
Mannheim, Karl, 280
Mannheim-Friedrichsfeld, 166
Mannheimer Abendzeitung, 523
Mannheimer Journal, 523

Mansfeld, 157
Manteuffel, Edwin von, 671, 672, 673, 683
Manteuffel, Otto von, 577, 607–8, 614
Marburg, 330, 363
Marees, Hans von, 481, 483
Marienburg, the, 490
Marlitt, Eugenie, 223, 525
marriage, 36, 87, 90–2, 98, 108, 111, 134, 151
  dowries, 104, 129
  laws, 144, 224, 304
  mixed, 337, 367, 369–70
  restrictions, 205–6
  romantic love, 99, 101, 109
  and social class, 106–7
Marschall von Bieberstein, Karl Wilhelm
    Freiherr, 63
Marwitz, Friedrich August von der, 32, 53,
    278
Marx, Karl, 110, 154, 186, 392, 397, 551,
    620, 659, 705
  on Bohemia, 558
  and counter-revolution, 569
  criticism of religion, 393–4
  economic theories, 460, 462–5
  and Hecker, 540
  and Lassalle programme, 660–61
  newspapers, 182, 344, 345, 523, 552
  radical demonstrations, 563
  and Schleswig-Holstein question, 555
  social theory of, 136, 348–9, 470, 471
  and workers' movement, 665, 666
Marxism, 441, 462–5
Marz government, 176
masturbation, 110
materialism, 396–7
maternity care, 123
mathematics, 436
Mathy, Karl, 343
Maximilian II, king of Bavaria, 491, 528
Mayer, Robert, 434–5
Mazzini, Giuseppe, 331
Mecklenburg, 29, 62–3, 85, 144, 312, 385
  administration, 288
  education, 410, 413
  Jews in, 219
  population, 93
  Reaction, 600
media. *see* newspapers
  free press, 247
  technical journals, 160

mediatisation, 60–61, 75, 77, 80, 145, 304
edict opposed, 309
effects of, 224–5
and parliament, 305
Prussia, 295
medicine, 122–3, 428–41
romantic medicine, 430–31
Meersburg, 360
Mehemet Ali, 323
memorials, 476, 484, 489, 496
Mendel, Gregor, 429
Mendeleev, Dmitri, 434
Mendelssohn, Felix, 482
mental illness, 124, 431
Menzel, Adolf, 495, 496, 498, 500, 503
Menzel, Wolfgang, 109
Mesmer, Franz Anton, 430
Mesmerism, 123
Metternich, Clemens Lothar Graf, 14, 17,
        79–80, 82, 109, 277, 309, 423, 583,
        602, 604, 608
    administration, 297
    and associations, 245–7, 474
    and bankers, 168
    church and state, 369
    conservatism, 275, 277, 354
    and constitutions, 237–8, 239, 243
    and emperor, 351, 352
    foreign policy, 321–3
    and German Confederation, 313, 314–15
    Hanover *coup d'etat*, 333
    Holy Alliance, 83
    influence of, 298
    and Jewish rights, 218
    and July Revolution, 328–9
    and nationalism, 82
    opposition to, 353
    press control, 522, 523
    on Prussia, 291
    and reform, 300–301, 302
    and revolution, 1848, 528–9, 530
    and Russia, 15
    war with Napoleon, 12, 69–73
    on Zollverein, 319
Mevissen, Gustav, 176, 179, 180, 261, 342,
        345, 412
Meyer, 520
Meyer, Lothar, 434
middle class, 29, 36, 62, 354, 355, 397
    art and culture, 474, 475–8, 518

Austria, 300–301
    and Bismarck, 678–84
    Catholicism in, 366
    and constitutions, 238, 241–2
    education of, 404
    fear of revolution, 552–3
    and liberalism, 252, 260, 342–3, 643–5,
        648–9
    New Era, 621
    society, 636–8
    in universities, 421–2, 426
    and working class, 655–9
migration, 31, 144, 205–6, 210
    banned, 29–30
militia, 228, 242–3, 289, 528, 575, 577
Minden, 92, 166, 523
mining, 156, 157, 159, 172, 203, 204, 607
    coal-mining, 162–3, 167
    employer-labour relations, 201
    industrialisation, 162–3
    laws, 216
    social welfare, 216
    wages, 207–8
Miquel, Johannes von, 709
missionary societies, 377
missions, 372
Mittermaier, Karl, 343
modernisation. *see* Great Reforms
Moers, 413
Moglin, 127, 128
Mohl, Moritz, 633
Mohl, Robert von, 213, 259, 260, 462
Mohler, Johann Adam, 361
Moleschott, Jakob, 396
Moltke, Helmuth Graf von, 398, 619, 697,
        699–700
Mommsen, Theodor, 459, 672, 683, 689
monarchy
    Austria, 298
    divine right of kings, 576
    effect of constitutions on, 304–5
    in imperial constitution, 582–3
    Prussia, 292–3
    role of, 24, 64, 280–81
monasteries, 59, 356, 364, 372
Monchen-Gladbach, 161
Montecuccoli, Albert, Count, 301
Montez, Lola, 311, 372
Montgelas, Maximilian Graf von, 58, 61, 63,
        117, 239, 368–9

744   *Index*

monuments, 268, 274, 353, 476, 478, 489,
    496, 642–3
Moravia, 85, 161, 530, 540
Morgenstern, Christian, 500
Morike, Eduard, 510, 516, 518
mortality rates, 87, 89–90, 121–2, 150
Moser, Justus, 29, 275, 444
Motz, Friedrich von, 317, 610
Mount Isel, battle of, 13
Mozart, Wolfgang Amadeus, 268, 476,
    482
Mulheim, 162
Muller, Adam, 12, 18, 127, 213, 278, 339,
    358, 462
Muller, Johannes von, 16, 418, 419, 432
Mulvany, William T., 158, 178
Mundt, Theodor, 330
Munich, 58, 95, 117, 124, 128, 166, 278,
    326, 365, 431
    administration, 288
    architecture, 488, 489, 490, 491, 492
    Catholic politics, 338
    culture, 163, 472, 475, 476, 496, 500
    education, 427
    'Hall of Fame', 304
    hospitals, 123, 124
    industry, 164
    Jews in, 220
    newspapers, 524
    Oktoberfest, 129
    revolution, 1848, 528
    Romanticism, 361
    ultramontanism, 363
    university, 417, 419
Municipal Ordinance, 1808, 26, 28
Munster, 92, 360
Munster, Count, 325
Murat, Joachim, 8
Murhard, Friedrich, 315
Museum Society, Frankfurt, 472
museums, 475, 488
music, 472–4, 480, 481
    debate, 477
    development of, 484–8
    and nationalism, 268
Music Academy, Munich, 472
musical associations, 234
Nachmarz, 223, 231
Nageli, Hans Goerg, 473
Naples, 168

Napoleon I, emperor of France, 14, 64,
    79–80, 145, 146, 238, 270, 357, 700.
    see also Confederation of the Rhine
    banking, 168
    battle of Waterloo, 81
    despotism of, 9–11, 13, 62
    and German public opinion, 16–19
    and German reform, 1–6
    and industrialisation, 157
    influence of, 55
    nationalism, 265
    Prussian army restrictions, 40
    road development, 165
    social reforms, 61
    topographic survey, 163
    war with Russia, 15, 62–73
Napoleon III, emperor of France, 118, 257,
    473, 582, 602, 610, 612, 616, 628, 632,
    646
    and German Question, 684–9
    Italian War, 618, 619, 620
    Schleswig-Holstein question, 688, 694–5,
        700–704
Napoleonic Wars, 70–73
Nassau, 2, 63, 75, 92, 128, 146, 236, 246, 326
    Austro-Prussian war, 701, 707
    Carlsbad Decrees, 248
    Catholic politics, 654
    church and state, 382
    constitution, 238
    crafts sector, 187–8
    customs policy, 318
    education, 410
    medicine, 122
    Reaction, 600
    revolution, 1848, 533
    and Zollverein, 635
national guard, 529
National Liberal Party, 227, 711, 713, 714
National Representative Assembly, Prussia,
    52–3
nationalism, 68–9, 250, 265, 267–8, 271–2
    attitudes to Napoleon, 16–19
    Austria, 12–13, 14, 297
    and Bismarck, 676–7, 683–4, 709, 714
    and Catholicism, 339–40
    and conservatism, 279, 336
    cultural, 265, 473–4, 484, 496–7
    development of, 262–74, 302–3
    and education, 402, 404

and failure of revolution, 594–5
and foreign policy, 271
German, 81–2, 244
and German Confederation, 315
and German Question, 630–33
Hungary, 566–7
and liberalism, 269–70, 297, 632, 646
'national uprising', 267
New Era, 621–2
obstacles to, 268–9
in Paulskirche, 558–60
Posen question, 557
problem of nationalities, 297, 302–3
and Protestantism, 387–8
and Reaction, 603–4
and reforms, 22
and religion, 339–40, 357–8
and Romanticism, 448
Schleswig-Holstein question, 273–4, 686–9
Slavs, 572–3
spread of, 353–4
Nationalverein, 227, 424
natural law, 341
natural sciences, 428–41
Nazarenes, 483, 494–5, 497, 503
Neander, August, 376
Nebenius, Karl Friedrich, 159, 304, 310
Neipperg family, 533
Nelson, Horatio, 3
neo-humanism, 44–5, 401, 402–3, 404, 406,
    408, 419, 426, 443
    and jurisprudence, 451
Nestroy, Johann, 300, 510
Netherlands, the, 2, 3, 73, 75, 82, 320, 322,
    559
Nettelbeck, Joachim, 5
Neue Zeitung, 523
Neuenahr, 119
Neuendettelsau, 377
Neumann, Salomon, 125
Neustadt, 327
New Era, 142, 620–27, 632, 636, 649, 681, 710
    Democrats, 642
    liberalism, 219, 424, 601, 644
    Prussia, 667, 670, 672, 673, 674
    religion, 385, 387
New Year's Eve Patent, 602
newspapers, 152, 160, 521–6, 643
    Catholic, 548
    censorship, 522–3, 606

counter-revolution, 561
    free press, 247
Nice, 684
Nicholas I, Tsar of Russia, 321
Nicolovius, Georg, 48, 376
Niebuhr, Barthold Georg, 40, 81–2, 268,
    454–5
Niethammer, Friedrich Immanuel, 401
Nietzsche, Karl Immanuel, 379, 395, 397,
    404, 425, 471
Nikolsburg, peace of, 702–4
nobility. *see* aristocracy; Junkers
North German Bund, 122
North German Confederation, 219, 700,
    701–2, 707, 710
    liberalism in, 711–14
North-German Lloyd, 168
Novalis, 390, 507
Nuremberg, 95, 164, 165–6, 427, 475, 490
nursing, 109–10, 124
nutrition, 120–21

October Edict, 1807, 31–4
October revolution, 571–2
Oder river, 10, 11, 165
Oerstedt, 431
Oettingen-Wallerstein, Prince, 227, 311
Oettingen-Wallerstein family, 147
Offenbach, Jacques, 480
Offenburg, 346
Ohm, Georg Simon, 429
Oken, Lorenz, 244, 248, 418–19, 430, 436
Old Germans, 245–6
Old Hegelians, 470
Old Lutherans, 97
Oldenburg, 15, 75, 318
Oldenburg, grand duke of, 687
Olmutz, Treaty of, 598, 602, 608–12, 615,
    621, 675, 684, 694
opera, 268, 473, 480, 484, 486–8
Oppenheim, Salomon, 168
Order of St Vincent de Paul, 124
orthodoxy, 374
Osnabruck, 325
Otto-Peters, Louise, 106
Overbeck, Franz, 358, 398
Overbeck, Friedrich, 483, 497

Paganini, Niccolo, 472
Pagerie, Bavaria, 224

painting, 494–504
 historical, 496–8
 landscape, 498–501
 portraiture, 495–6
Palacky, Franz, 303
Palatinate, the, 149, 153, 154, 179, 187, 239, 247, 695
 Austro-Prussian war, 702
 under Bavaria, 75
 church and state, 382
 constitution, 238
 under France, 9
 July Revolution, 326–7
 May revolution, 589
 radicalism, 543, 563
 reform, 56
 regionalism, 290, 303–4
Palestrina, Giovanni, 483
Palm, bookseller, 13
Palmerston, Lord, 554, 688
pantheism, 389
papacy, power of, 359–60, 362–3
papalism, 359
Paris, 168, 522, 524, 675
 exiles in, 330, 331, 344
 revolution, 1848, 527–8
Paris, Peace of, 73
Paris, Second Peace of, 82
Paris, Treaty of, 10
parishes, reform of, 241
parks, 489–90
parliamentarianism, 306–12, 340
parliaments, 140, 305–12, 326–30, 528. *see also* constitutions
 liberal views of, 256–60
particularism, 239, 252, 269, 270, 274
Pascal, Blaise, 362
Pasteur, Louis, 433
pastoral associations, 561
patriarchalism, 99–100, 102–3, 107, 111
patriotism, 12–13, 14, 18, 68–9, 76, 265, 304. *see also* nationalism
 societies, 473–4
Paul, Jean, 246, 505
Paulskirche, 14, 190. *see also* Frankfurt National Assembly
Paulus, Heinrich, 374
pauperism, 192–8, 208, 211, 230, 231, 260, 271, 304, 354. *see also* poverty
 Jewish, 220
 and social policy, 211–16

peasants, 142–4, 143, 218
 land reform, 137–42
 liberation of, 26, 28–36, 61, 260
  Austria, 65, 66
  Germany, 144–6
  and industrialisation, 157
  poverty factor, 150–51
  Prussia, 241, 293, 294
  southern Germany, 304
 uprisings, 30, 139
People's Rights Committee, 559
Pertz, Georg Heinrich, 457
Pestalozzi, Johann Heinrich, 22, 44, 45, 49, 65, 360, 377, 415, 473
Pettenkofer, Max von, 124, 433
Peucker, Eduard von, 545–6, 561
Pfizer, Paul, 256, 270–71, 310, 585
Pfordten, Baron Ludwig von der, 596, 600, 623
Pforzheim, 193
Pfuel, Ernst von, 561, 576, 577
pharmacies, 122, 124
Philharmonic Society, Berlin, 472
philology, 49, 404–5, 449–51
philosophy, 419–20, 638
 and Catholicism, 360–61
 and de-Christianisation, 395–6
 development of, 465–71
 and education reform, 42–7
 and liberal Protestantism, 377–8
 natural philosophy, 430–32
 and reforms, 21–2
 and science, 440
 in universities, 50–51
photography, 502–3
phrenology, 431
Piedmont, 566, 574, 613
 Italian War, 617–20
pietism, 374, 375–6
pilgrimages, 337, 364
Piloty, Karl von, 496, 497
Pious Associations for Religious Freedom, 365, 548
Pius IX, Pope (1846–78), 700
Platen, August von, 483, 512
poaching, 149
Poensgen, Carl, 178
poets, 481, 488, 512–13, 525
 political, 345
Poland, 13, 14, 15, 67, 71, 626, 698
 and Cislithania, 706
 constitution, 237

and Germany, 81, 319
July revolution, 323–4
May revolution, 589
nationalism, 272, 274, 302, 339, 559, 560
Polish in Germany, 239, 241, 272, 274,
        326, 331, 350
reforms, 141
and revolution, 1848, 553
and Russia, 6, 68, 70, 74, 83, 616, 684–5
uprisings, 5, 322, 684–5
police, 9–10, 141, 249, 291
Austria, 300, 301
reforms, 26, 35
secret police, 247
political parties, 353
changes in, 637–67
formation and restructuring of, 333–50
liberalism, 639–51
political societies, 236
politics, 153–4, 182, 190–91
aristocracy in, 148
and social movements, 636–67
Politische Wochenblatt, 523
polytechnics, 415, 427
Pomerania, 34, 35, 128, 131, 136, 352, 675
agriculture, 136
illiteracy, 410
pietism, 376
Swedish, 75, 239
Western, 187, 266
poorhouses, 377
Pope. *see* papacy; Pius IX
Poppelsdorf, 128
population, 134, 667
average age, 93
density, 85, 88
details of, 85–97
growth of, 126–7, 143–4, 149, 192, 354
internal migration, 93–6
Portugal, 6, 70, 321
Posen, 35, 74, 141, 187, 331, 350, 538, 576
administration, 285, 287
constitutional struggle, 239, 241
education, 409, 410
Jews in, 218–19, 220, 221
nationalism in, 272
regionalism, 290
and revolution, 1848, 556–7, 559
Posen, Archbishop of, 370
Positivism, 503

postal service, 119
Postl, Karl, 511
potato blight, 126, 131
Potsdam, 115, 166, 530
Poussin, Nicolas, 498
poverty, 191–3
crafts sector, 183, 189
and industrialisation, 175
poverty factor, 150–51
rural areas, 149
Prabenden, 32
Prague, 95, 303, 427, 530, 558, 571, 703
counter-revolution, 565–6
Jews in, 219, 221
Reaction, 602
Prato, Katharina von, 121
press. *see also* censorship; newspapers
Press- und Vaterlandsverein, 326–7
Pressburg, peace of, 3
Preussische Jahrbucher, 524, 643, 689
Preussische Seehandlung, 159
Priessnitz, Vinzenz, 123
Priestley, Joseph, 429
Prince-Smith, John, 647
printing, 163–4, 207
Prittwitz, General von, 531
Privatdozenten, 418, 422, 424
Pro-Gymnasium, 406
professions, 228, 234
Progressive Party, 623, 643, 650, 658, 680,
        709, 711, 713
aims of, 672
and Bismarck, 682, 683
and Lassalle programme, 660, 661–3
and workers' movement, 665
property rights, 92, 151–2, 255
Proskau, 128
prostitution, 110, 122, 193
protectionism, 299, 304, 550, 610–11, 634–6.
        see also Zollverein
Protestant Association, 642
Protestant Society, 387
Protestantism, 179, 191, 338, 377, 439. *see*
        also churches
anti-Catholicism, 381
church and state, 369, 371–2, 381–7
development of, 373–89
'German Catholics', 364
and historicism, 458–9
and industrialisation, 156

Protestantism (cont.)
　influence of, 151, 381
　internal organisation, 382–5
　and liberalism, 154
　mixed marriages, 369–70
　and nationalism, 245, 267–8, 339–40,
　　357–8, 387–8
　'positive' religion, 375–6
　and regionalism, 290
　social policy, 192, 213, 388–9
　social status of clergy, 228
Proudhon, Pierre-Joseph, 349
Provincial Assembly, East Prussia, 67
Provinzialstanden, 241, 242, 294, 295
Prussia, 2, 3, 62, 67, 83, 89, 90, 121, 150,
　　168, 260, 292, 328
　administration, 52, 283, 285, 286, 291–6,
　　312
　agriculture, 125–6, 129, 131, 136,
　　137–42
　aristocracy, 224–5, 226
　army, 14, 228, 288–9, 388
　and Austria, 12–13, 608–11, 626
　Carlsbad Decrees, 248
　Catholicism in, 337, 338
　church and state, 369, 370–71, 372, 373,
　　382, 383–4, 385, 653
　cities, 94
　Congress of Vienna, 73–5
　conservatism, 280, 335–6, 651–3
　constitution, 237, 239–43, 295–6, 351–3,
　　372, 384, 667–84
　counter-revolution, 561–2, 575–9
　crafts sector, 187, 189
　Crimean War, 612–16
　customs policy, 316–19
　defeudalisation, 147
　and *Deutscher Bund*, 78–80
　economy, 175, 184, 304
　education, 401–16
　Erfurt Union, 596–7
　and European politics, 684–704
　family in, 111
　foreign policy, 320, 676–7
　Franco-Prussian war, 1806, 4–5
　and German Confederation, 81–2,
　　314–16
　and German empire, 584–7
　and German nationalism, 271, 272
　and German Question, 627–36

Great Reforms, 21–54, 55–6, 63–4
　agrarian constitution, 28–36
　army, 37–42
　compensation for, 32–4
　constitutional policies, 51–4
　economic policy, 36–7
　education, 42–51
　government and administration, 23–8
　influences and aims, 21–3
industrialisation, 108, 157, 159, 161, 170,
　　172, 173, 182, 209
Jews in, 217–19, 221
July Revolution, 329, 331–2
and liberalism, 154, 262, 643
May rebellion, 588–9
medicine, 122, 123
mining, 163, 204
and Napoleon, 10–11
nationalism, 18–19, 268
New Era, 620–27
and Paulskirche, 542, 544, 546, 559
philosophy, 466, 470
pietism, 376
population, 85, 87, 91–2, 93, 134
and Posen, 556–7
poverty, 192
press control, 522
Protestant reform, 385–6
radicalism, 344, 345
Reaction, 601, 604–8
regionalism, 290
restoration in, 293–5
revolution, 1848, 530–32, 533–4, 592, 595
and Russia, 15–16, 68–9
Schleswig-Holstein question
　Austrian negotiations with, 692–8
　Bismarck's policy, 686–90
　consequences of war, 704–15
　peace negotiations, 700–704
social mobility, 230
social policy, 215
socialism, 348
split reinforced, 75
student associations, 247
taxation, 159
transport, 164, 166
and unification, 459
universities, 420, 423, 424, 425
and Vormarz, 350–55
Vorparlament, 538, 540, 541

war with Denmark, 554–5
workers' movement, 551, 663–6
Prussian Association for a Constitutional
    Kingdom, 561
Prussian Auxiliary Corps, 67
Prussian Bank, 175
Prussian Congress of Trade and Industry, 182
Prussian National Assembly, 1848, 541–2, 632
Prussian Police Laws, 245
Prussian Rhine Steamship Company, 165
Prussian Shares Law, 175
Prutz, Robert, 526
publishing, 163, 345–6
Puchta, Georg Friedrich, 454
Purkinje, Johannes Evangelista, 418
Puttkamer, Johanna von, 675
Puttkamer family, 376

Quadruple Alliance, 82

Raabe, Wilhelm, 223, 396, 515, 639
Radetzky, Joseph Graf von, 566
radicalism, 249–50, 341, 344–6, 355
    development of, 343–6
Radowitz, Joseph von, 269, 336, 351, 598
Raiffeisen, Friedrich Wilhelm, 130
railways, 115, 116, 119, 135, 136, 153, 158,
    193, 205, 700
    boom, 163, 164
    bureaucracy, 180
    construction, 144
    development of, 165–7
    effect of, 304
    expansion of, 173–4
    ownership of, 166
    Prussia, 352–3
    social clauses, 293
    station architecture, 489, 491
Raimund, Ferdinand, 300, 510
Ranke, Leopold von, 334, 455–6, 457, 458,
    459
Rask, Rasmus Kristian, 451
Rass, Bishop of Strasbourg, 362
Rasselstein-Neuwied, 162
Ratingen, 157
rationalism, 294, 339, 374–5
Rau, Karl Friedrich, 460
Rauch, Christian Daniel, 11, 496
Raumer, Friedrich von, 457
Raveaux, Franz, 542

Reaction, 599–608
    Austria, 602–4
    Austrian-Prussian rivalry, 608–11
    foreign policy, 612–20
    Prussia, 604–8
reading societies, 520–21
Realgymnasium, 408, 409, 422, 427, 428
Realism
    development of, 513–16
    in literature, 509, 517, 518, 519
    in painting, 500–504
Realpolitik, 77, 620
    of Bismarck, 675–6, 699
    liberal change to, 639–44, 649
    North German Confederation, 711
Realteilung, 148–9
Realteilungsgebiete, 85, 98, 134, 192
Realteilungslander, 92
Rechberg, Johann Bernhard Graf von, 667,
    690, 691
Rechtfertigungslehre, 379
Recke, Elias von der, 377
'Red Book', 370
Redemptorists, 364
Redtenbacher, Ferdinand, 427, 435
Reform, Die, 562
Reform Era, 223
Reformation, 338, 376, 381, 388, 459, 466
Reformed Church, 384–5
reforms, 240. *see also* Great Reforms
    end of, 237–50
    and German Confederation, 313
    Prussia, 240
    and universities, 423–4
Reformverein, 424
Regensburg, 476
Regenwalde, 128
Regierungsbezirke, 25, 56, 240
regionalism, 76–7, 274, 290, 292, 295, 303–4
Regulation Edict, 1811, 33
Regulierungsbauern, 138, 139
Reh, Theodor, 586
Reich Concordat, 2
Reichenbach, Georg von, 163
Reichenhall, 163
Reichensperger, August, 339, 542, 558, 654
Reichensperger, Peter, 339, 542
Reichsrate, 307, 625
Reichsstande, 243, 352
Reichstag, 52

Reitzenstein, Sigismund Freiherr von, 58, 63

religion, 55, 91–2, 179, 181, 230, 264
  anti-clericalism, 154
  and art, 472, 478, 494–5, 497
  and associations, 234
  Austria, 301
  de-Christianisation, 375, 389–98
  decline in, 638
  and emigration, 97
  and family, 106, 110
  and nationalism, 267–8
  return to, 356–9
  and rural life, 151
  and science, 439–40
  and social class, 232
  and social policy, 213–15
  state and, 367–73
  and workers' movement, 665
Religion of the Old Testament (Vatke), 380
religious orders, 124, 372, 416
Renan, Ernest, 264–5
repeal movement, 303
republicanism, 562, 563–4, 582–3, 591, 593
restoration, 290–91, 312–13, 358
  Austria, 298–9
  German Confederation, 315–16
  Prussia, 293–5
Rethel, Alfred, 496, 497
Reuleaux, Franz, 427
Reussia, 312
Reuter, Fritz, 144, 312, 329, 515, 518
Reventlow, Fritz, 313
revolution, 1846, 302
revolution, 1848, 146, 153, 190, 527–98. *see also* Reaction
  aims and participants of, 532–6
  and Catholicism, 372
  counter-revolution, 560–79
  development of nation-state, 537–47
  emperor elected, 586–7
  end of, 588–9
  European reactions to, 553–60
  extraparliamentary movements, 547–53
  imperial constitution, 579–87
  March revolution, 527–37
  May revolution, 588–9
  and Protestantism, 384–5, 386–7
  radical reaction to, 562–5
  reasons for failure, 590–95

reforms, 139, 141
  results of, 536–7
  union of states, 595–8
Rheinische Volkshalle, 548
Rheinische Zeitung, 182, 334, 345, 348, 523, 552
Rheinischer Merkur, 72, 81, 522
Rheydt, 161
Rhine
  Upper, 3, 166
Rhine river, 22, 164, 617
Rhineland, 9, 22, 35, 119, 145, 148, 149, 167, 181, 182, 187, 295, 327, 685
  administration, 72, 285, 286, 287, 288
  attitudes to France, 17
  church and state, 369, 382
  constitutional struggle, 239, 241–2
  craft risings, 190
  crisis, 272–3
  culture, 473
  disputed territory, 239
  entrepreneurs, 260
  French control, 1, 7, 9–10
  French threat, 351
  importance to France, 694–5
  industrialisation, 157, 158, 162, 163
  Landtage, 296
  liberalism, 261–2, 339, 342
  life expectancy, 89
  population, 85, 91
  to Prussia, 74–5
  Prussian legal code, 240–41
  radicalism, 562, 563
  Reaction, 607
  reforms, 63, 224
  regionalism, 290
  revolution, 1848, 530, 534
  Rhenish model, 141
  secularisation, 59–60
  separation of estates, 294
  social policy, 215
  unemployment, 193
  university, 417
  Vorparlament, 538, 541
  workers' movement, 663
Ricardo, David, 460, 464
Richter, Ludwig, 104, 483, 501
Ried, Treaty of, 71–2
Riehl, Wilhelm Heinrich, 288, 474, 526, 652
  humanism, 404

on peasants, 152, 154, 459
social theories, 103, 108, 214, 414, 462
Riemann, Bernhard, 245, 436
Riesser, Gabriel, 221, 542
Riga Memorandum, 20
Ringseis, Johann Nepomuk, 361, 418, 431
risings, 141, 146, 190, 193–4
Ritter, Carl, 460
Ritter, Johann Wilhelm, 140, 429
rivers
    control of, 153
    transport, 158, 164–5
roads, 136, 153, 158, 193, 205, 489
    construction, 117
    development of, 117, 165
    maintenance, 116–17
Robespierre, Maximilian, 246
robot, 145–6
Rochau, August von, 649
Rochau, Ludwig von, 639
Rochling, Karl, 178
Rodbertus, Carl von, 460–61
Rodenberg, Julius, 221
Roggenbach, Franz von, 623, 629
Rokitansky, Karl, 433
Romanticism, 102, 123, 254, 481, 524
    and Catholicism, 360–61, 365
    and conservatism, 32
    and de-Christianisation, 390–91
    development of, 505–9
    and historicism, 445, 447–8, 450, 451,
        456, 458
    and jurisprudence, 452
    in literature, 512, 517, 519
    in music, 484–6
    and nationalism, 264, 265, 267, 270
    in painting, 494–5, 498–501, 503
    romantic love, 99, 101, 109
romanticism
    and religion, 357–8
Ronge, Johannes, 364, 569
Roon, Albrecht Graf von, 668–72, 674, 678,
    683, 688
Roscher, Wilhelm, 461
Rossini, Gioacchino, 486
Rossler, Constantin, 619
Rothe, Richard, 379
Rother, Christian von, 159
Rothschild, House of, 168, 176, 220, 299
Rotteck, Karl von, 270, 305, 309, 328, 341
    dualist, 259, 261

on family, 111
historicism, 456
on role of army, 290
Staatslexikon, 261, 334
Rottenburg, 368
Rotterdam, 165
Rottmann, Karl, 499
Rousseau, Jean Jacques, 29, 103, 123, 443,
    446, 467, 498, 516
Ruckert, Friedrich, 68, 267, 512
Rudhart, Ignaz von, 310
Ruge, Arnold, 344, 543, 557, 559, 562, 619,
    712
Rugen, 18, 75
Ruhr, 113, 164, 173, 174, 205, 211, 489
    entrepreneurs, 179
    foundries, 162
    industrialisation, 158
    joint stock companies, 176
    mining, 163, 172
Ruhrgebiet, 172
Ruhs, Professor, 218
Rumania, 321, 567, 568, 613, 616, 626, 691,
    694
Rumelin, Gustav, 620
Rundbogenstil, 491
Runge, Philipp Otto, 495, 503
rural areas, 125–54, 354
    class structure, 149–50
    contrast with urban, 230
    housing, 113
    influences on, 152–3
    politics in, 153–4
    poverty, 144, 149, 150–51
Russell, Lord John, 684
Russia, 4, 6, 12, 14, 34, 83, 559, 592–3, 675
    army of, 667
    and Austria, 13, 691
    Austro-Hungarian war, 574–5
    Austro-Prussian war, 694, 696, 702
    balance of power, 703
    and Bohemia, 557–8
    Congress of Vienna, 74–5
    Crimean War, 612–16
    foreign policy, 320–23
    and Germany, 2, 81, 587, 708
    and Napoleon, 10
    opposes union policy, 597, 598
    Polish revolt, 684–5
    and Prussia, 5
    and revolution, 1848, 553, 554

Russia (cont.)
  Schleswig-Holstein question, 687–8
  war with France, 15, 67–73
Ruthenia, 302, 626

Saar, 159, 175, 695, 702
Saarbrucken, 82
Sachsische Vaterlandsblatter, 523
Sadowa, battle of, 699
Sailer, Johann Michael, 360–61
Salzburg, 13, 75, 85
Samwer, Karl, 273
Sand, George, 106
Sand, Karl Ludwig, 246–7, 267, 358
Savigny, Friedrich Karl von, 452–3
savings banks, 168
Saxe-Weimar, 237, 238, 248
Saxony, 5, 30, 35, 62–3, 70, 72, 95, 183, 317,
    586, 613, 629
  administration, 287, 288
  agriculture, 128, 136, 145
  Austro-Prussian war, 696, 697, 701–2, 707
  church and state, 385
  constitutional movement, 239, 325
  crisis, 79
  customs policy, 318, 611
  education, 409, 410, 415
  Erfurt Union, 596–7
  industry, 7, 107, 161, 167, 170, 184, 187,
    209
  Jews in, 219
  Landtage, 296
  May revolution, 589
  New Era, 623
  and Paulskirche, 588
  population, 85, 87, 90
  and Prussia, 74
  radicalism, 345, 543, 650–51
  Reaction, 600
  and reform, 312–13
  revolution, 1848, 535
  social policy, 216
  Vorparlament elections, 540
  workers' movement, 216, 551, 663, 664
  and Zollverein, 635–6
Sayn iron-works, 489
Scandinavia, 154, 559
Schaaffhausen, Abraham, 168
Schaaffhausen Banking Society, 176
Schadow, Johann Gottfried, 496

Schaezler, Johann Lorenz, 168
Schapper, Karl, 347
Scharnhorst, Gerhard, 5, 10, 12, 18, 38, 39
Scharnweber, Christian Friedrich, 33
Schauspielhaus, Berlin, 488
Scheffel, Josef von, 512
Schelling, Friedrich Wilhelm, 351, 424, 430,
    466
Schenckendorf, Max von, 68
Schenk, Edward von, 310–11
Scherr, Johannes, 459
Schichau, Ferdinand, 164
Schick, Gottlieb, 495
Schill, Major, 5, 13
Schiller, Friedrich, 188, 252, 357, 498, 505,
    507
  celebration, 1859, 478
  censored, 300
  Classicism, 44
  culture and religion, 389–90
  festivals, 642
  idealism, 102, 109
  monuments, 268, 476, 642
Schinkel, Karl Friedrich, 476, 481, 488, 489,
    490, 493
  Gothic style, 491
Schlayer, Johannes von, 311
Schlegel, Friedrich, 12, 18, 278, 358, 361,
    507
Schleich, Eduard, 500
Schleiden, Matthias Jacob, 432
Schleiermacher, Friedrich Daniel, 48, 244,
    247, 248, 266, 357, 450
  liberalism, 375, 377–9, 382, 383, 385
  nationalism, 387
Schleswig, 313, 320, 538, 559
Schleswig-Holstein, 87, 144–5, 273–4,
    553–6, 559, 563, 616, 619, 636
  Austro-Prussian peace, 700–704
  Austro-Prussian war, 704–15
  and Bismarck, 680, 683, 686–9
  condominium, 689–90
  crises, 564, 630, 646, 650
  and failure of revolution, 595–6
  Gastein Convention, 692
  and Prussia, 597–8, 628
  revolution, 1848, 386, 388, 561
  Vorparlament elections, 540
  workers' movement, 659
Schlosser, Friedrich Christoph, 456

Schmalz, Theodor, 245
Schmerling, Anton von, 545, 556, 584–6,
    625, 626, 692
    counter-revolution, 566
    liberalism, 301, 342
    reforms, 602
Schmid, Christoph von, 521
Schnaase, Karl, 460
Schnorr Carolsfeld, Julius von, 483, 496
Scholler, Robert, 178
Schon, Theodor von, 28, 30, 32, 286, 292, 351
Schonbrunn, Peace of, 13–14, 66
Schoneberg, 96
Schonlein, Johann Lukas, 418, 431, 433
Schonleutner, Max, 128
schools, 48, 116, 400, 406, 407, 408, 411,
    414, 415, 428, 441. *see also Gymnasia*;
        Volksschulen
    architecture, 488
    fees, 405
    middle schools, 399, 407–8, 409, 415
    number of, 48–9
    secondary schools, 401–9, 415
    Sunday schools, 415
    Tochterschulen, 416
Schopenhauer, Arthur, 395–6, 471, 478,
    513, 514, 515, 638–9
Schorlemer-Alst, Baron von, 129
Schreber, Dr, 123
Schubert, Franz, 301, 480, 485, 486
Schubert, Gotthilf Heinrich von, 431
Schuchard, Johannes, 215
Schuckmann, Friedrich, 423
Schuler, Friedrich, 326
Schulze, Johannes, 403, 408
Schulze, Max, 432
Schulze-Delitzsch, Hermann, 186, 214, 632,
    646, 649, 656, 658, 672, 713
    workers' movement, 659–60, 662
Schumann, Robert, 124, 481, 485
Schurz, Karl, 97
Schuselka, Franz, 302, 303
Schutzverwandten, 27
Schwann, Theodor, 432
Schwartzkopff, Louis, 164
Schwarzenberg, Felix von, 573, 574, 584,
    586, 596–8, 602, 608
Schweidnitz, 576
Schweitzer, Johann Baptist von, 662, 697
Schwerin, 144, 492

Schwerz, Johann Nepomuk, 128
Schwind, Moritz von, 496, 501–2
science, 422, 423, 424
    development of, 419, 428–41, 638
    and education, 43–4, 47–8
    and industrialisation, 159
    journals, 436–7
    and medicine, 123
    natural sciences, 435–6
    physics, 434–5
Scott, Gilbert, 492
Scott, Walter, 517, 521
sculpture, 476
Sealsfield, Charles (Karl Postl), 511
seamen's guilds, 165
Secret Society of Young Europe, 331
secularisation, 58–60, 232, 356
Sedlnitzky, Josef, 300
Seier, H., 642
self-administration, 26–7, 35, 287, 288, 309
    Prussia, 607
    and Reaction, 601
self-government
    liberal reforms, 259–60
Semmelweiss, Ignaz, 433
Semper, Gottfried, 117, 481, 488, 492, 493, 589
separatism, 268–9
Serbs, 567, 603
serfdom, 61, 65
servants, 104–5, 112, 150
Servants' Ordinance, 216
sewerage systems, 117, 118
sexuality, 109–10
shipping
    modernisation, 168
shops, 116
Siebenpfeiffer, Philipp, 326, 327, 329
Siegburg, 124
Siemens, Georg von, 159, 178, 180
Siemens factory, 202
Silesia, 15, 33, 70, 97, 142, 364, 530, 568,
    613, 685, 695, 698
    agriculture, 125, 128
    architecture, 492
    aristocracy, 226
    church and state, 382
    communications, 176
    formation, 292
    industry, 148, 157, 158, 167, 178, 179,
        193–4, 350

Silesia (cont.)
Jews in, 221
poverty, 144
radicalism, 562
revolution, 1848, 533–4
Upper, 85, 87, 175, 178, 179, 194, 221
uprisings, 30, 139, 350
Simon, Heinrich, 346, 542, 586
Simson, Eduard, 596
Sisters of Mercy, 124
Six Articles, 1832, 328–9, 332
Sixty Articles, 1834, 329
Skoda, Joseph, 433
slander, 39
slaughterhouses, 124
Slavs, 302–3, 567, 568, 570, 585, 603–4, 626
Austro-Prussian war, 698, 705–6
Congress, 1848, 565
nationalism, 772–3
Smith, Adam, 22, 29, 127, 180, 318, 460
smuggling, 6–7
social class, 92, 198
bourgeois society, 223–36
in civil service, 285–6
and education reform, 46–7
family types, 98–109
and industrialisation, 176, 178, 191–216
and liberalism, 262
and revolution, 1848, 533–6
role of universities, 421–3
social mobility, 228–9
Social Democratic Workers' Party, 665
Social Democrats, 110, 381
social policy, 17, 304
of conservatives, 336–7
development of, 211–16
health care, 124–5
paternalism, 180
Paulskirche, 549–53
and Protestantism, 388–9
Prussia, 293
reforms, 23, 27, 52, 61
role of state, 215–16, 281–2
unrest, 354
social sciences, 460–65
socialism, 250, 331, 334, 346–50, 665
and atheism, 393–4
Christian socialism, 388–9
and Jews, 222
Lassalle programme, 659–66
and revolution, 1848, 535–6

Socialism and Communism (Hess and
Grun), 348
societies. *see* associations
Societies of St Vincent, 365
Society for Morality and Science, 18
Society for Old German History, 457
Society for the Advancement of
Employment for the Female Sex, 106
Society for the Promotion of Diligence,
214–15
Society for the Welfare of the Working
Classes, 215
Society of the Friends of Music, 472
Solferino, battle of, 617
Solingen, 190, 193, 663
Soll und Haben, 223
Sonderbund, 631
Sonnemann, Leopold, 524, 525, 663
South America, 321
south Germany, 4, 292. *see also*
Confederation of the Rhine
administration, 285, 303–12
church and state, 623
July Revolution, 326
and Prussia, 701, 707–8
and Zollverein, 634
Sozialdemokrat, 697
Spain, 6, 9, 10, 12, 70, 321
Spandau, 96
spas, 119, 123
Spessart, 149
Speyer, 490, 493
Spielhagen, Friedrich, 511
spiritualism, 430–31
Spitzweg, Carl, 502
Spohr, Ludwig, 485–6
Spranger, 414
Staastand, 284
Staatenhaus, 580–81
Staatslexikon (Rotteck and Welcker), 261,
334, 648
Staatsnation, 268, 269–70
Staatsrat, 24, 238, 240, 292–3
Staatsvolk, 264
Stadion, Count Philip, 12, 66, 82, 602
Stadteordnungen, 217
Stadter, 295
Stahl, Friedrich Julius, 248, 335–6, 351, 386,
424, 619, 651
Christian state, 387

state
    role of, 37, 47–8, 152–3, 215–16, 277–9,
      341–2, 354–5
State Council, Austria, 298
statism, 51–2, 53, 64, 65, 77, 268
Stavenhagen, Friedrich von, 673
steamships, 165
steel industry, 156, 162, 167, 169, 172
Steffen, 430
Steffens, Heinrich, 244, 267
Stein, Heinrich Friedrich Carl, Baron vom,
      9, 17, 77, 240, 248, 279, 283, 457
    administration, 72, 140, 286, 287
    administrative reforms, 53
    banished, 10–11
    on Christianity, 382
    class struggle, 213
    and constitution, 241
    and *Deutscher Bund*, 78, 79
    dismissal, 5, 16
    on feudalism, 29
    and German Confederation, 80
    nationalism, 18, 19, 69, 266
    October Edict, 30–34
    on political education, 22
    on political parties, 334
    Provincial Assembly, 67
    and reforms, 23–4, 26–7, 34, 35, 38, 48,
      51, 52
Stein, Lorenz von, 124, 211, 462, 652
Stendhal, 515
Stettin, 166
Stiehl, Ferdinand, 414
Stifter, Adalbert, 301, 510, 516, 518
Stinnes, Matthias, 163, 178
stock exchanges, 116
Storm, Theodor, 398, 515, 516, 518
Straits Convention, 323
Strauss, David Friedrich, 344, 380, 391, 397,
      398, 471
Strauss, Johann, 480, 566
street lighting, 114, 116–17
Strelitz, 144
Stroussberg, 180
Struve, Gustav von, 343, 345, 539–40, 564,
      589
Struwwelpeter, Der, 103, 112
student associations, 19, 76, 234, 264,
      420–21
    anti-semitism, 218

    and constitutions, 243
    investigation commission, 248–9
    radicalisation, 238
student fraternities, 358, 418, 420–21, 423
Stumm, 162, 178, 180
Stunden der Andracht (Zschokke), 375
Sturm und Drang, 389, 498
Stuttgart, 95, 128, 427, 588
Stuve, Johann, 145, 325
subjectivism, 246
Sudetenland, 94, 366, 410
Suvern, Johann Wilhelm, 48, 49, 399–400
Swabia, 3
Sweden, 6, 15, 70, 72
Swiss Federal Polytechnical College, 427
Switzerland, 3, 69, 73, 260, 331, 500, 516, 559
    civil war, 355
    emigres in, 345, 459, 564
    independence struggle, 319
    peasant revolt, 154
    socialism, 347
    Third Coalition, 2
Sybel, Heinrich von, 459, 634, 643, 673, 689,
      690
Sylt, 273
Symbolik (Mohler), 361

Tagewerk, 198
taxation, 8, 17, 27, 52, 54, 57, 60, 66, 124,
      156, 238, 308, 398
    civil service, 227
    'class taxation', 140
    exemptions, 146
    increases, 148
    and industrialisation, 159
    and land valuation, 129
    property tax, 142
    Prussia, 292
    reform, 33, 35, 36–7
    role of state, 281
    Saxony, 325
    withheld as protest, 69
Taylor, A.J.P., 708
teachers, 49, 106
    pay, 412
    role of, 413–15
    secondary schools, 404–5
    training of, 411, 412, 413, 416
    university staff, 418–19, 422, 423–5
Volksschule, 411

teaching associations, 414
technical education, 415, 426–8
technical journals, 160
telegraph, 167, 173, 700
Teplitz, 247
Teplitz, Treaty of, 71
Teutoburger Wald, 476
textile industry, 7, 156, 157, 158, 161–2, 163,
        167, 200, 206
    Austria, 177
    investment in, 169
    Jews in, 221
    mechanisation, 172–3, 183, 185
    wages, 207
    worker uprisings, 193–4
Thackeray, W.M., 515
Thadden family, 376
Thaer, Albert, 127, 130
Tharandt, 128
theatre, 300, 476–7, 480, 488, 512
Theologische Quartalsschrift, 361
theology, 49, 50, 360–62
    development of, 374–81
    historical-critical theology, 379–80
    mediatory theology, 379
    'positive' theology, 386
Thibaut, Anton, 452
Thiers, Louis Adolphe, 323, 700, 703
Thiersch, Friedrich, 401
Third Coalition, 2–3
Third Germany, 7, 315, 360
Tholuck, Friedrich, 376
Thomas, Edward, 158
Thorn, 74
Three Emperors, Battle of the, 3
Thun, Leo Graf von, 417, 602
Thunen, Johann Heinrich von, 127–8, 460
Thuringia, 75, 149, 153, 216, 317, 318, 533, 600
Thurn und Taxis family, 147
Thyssen, August, 181
Tilsit, peace of, 5, 10, 12
time, idea of, 198–9
tobacco, 121
Tocqueville, Alexis de, 342
totalitarianism, 265, 562
towns, 37, 144, 153
    conscription, 41–2, 66
    poverty in, 192–3
trade, 17, 120, 125, 261, 603, 634–5
    Austria, 299
    Continental Blockade, 6–7, 11

expansion, 174
free trade, 36, 260, 550, 647–8
free trade agreements, 175
growing influence of, 177
modernisation, 168
pre-industrial, 156, 158
protectionism, 177, 190
trade associations, 234
trade councils, 216
trade unions, 213, 214, 657, 665–6
Trades Edict, 1810, 36
Trafalgar, battle of, 3
transport, 95, 115, 136, 158, 162, 174
    revolution in, 164–5
travel, 119
treasury, role of, 145
Treaty of Submission, 52
Treitschke, Heinrich von, 317, 324, 343,
        525, 620
    and Bismarck, 679, 680
    on king's policy, 351
    newspapers, 643
    role of state, 645–6, 648
    Schleswig-Holstein question, 683, 689
Treves, 348
    Holy Coat of, 337
Trier, 364
Trieste, 85, 166, 573
Troppau, 321
tuberculosis, 122, 123
Tubingen, 316, 361
Tulla, 427
Tulla (planning official), 164
Turgenev, Ivan, 396
Turkey, 5, 15, 321, 322, 323
    Crimean War, 612–16
Tuvora, Joseph, 302
Twesten, Karl, 645, 673, 709, 711
Tyrol, 3, 69, 75, 85, 301
    revolt, 13, 14

Uber Land und Meer, 525
Uberweiblichkeit, 103
Uhland, Ludwig, 13, 512
Ulm, battle of, 3
ultramontanism, 301, 337, 360, 362–73, 548
    church and state, 369–73
    development of, 362–3
    religious practices, 363–4
    resistance to, 366–7
unemployment, 192–3, 354

United Diet, 166, 352–3
United States of America, 123, 137, 160,
    166, 342, 433, 546
    California gold rush, 175
    emigration to, 97, 221, 382
    federal model, 580, 581
    separation of powers, 256, 258
    social mobility, 228
Universal German Association for the
    Protection of German National Work,
    550
universalism, 268
universities, 43, 50, 253, 286, 329, 345,
    419–21, 421, 466. *see also* student
    associations
    censorship of, 294
    development of, 416–26
    nationalism in, 269
    and politics, 424–6
    rationalism, 374–5
    reform of, 43, 49–51, 57
    revolution, 1848, 528–9
    and social class, 226, 407, 421–3
    and state, 423–4
urban areas. *see* cities; towns
urbanisation, 93–6, 108
    eating habits, 120
    and family, 98–9
    home ownership, 112
    and industrialisation, 206
Urwahler, 305
usury, 130
Utzschneider, Joseph, 163

vaccination, 121
vagrancy, 108
Valhalla Enterprise, 268
Vaterlandsverein, 326
Vatican Council, 1870, 363
Vatke, Wilhelm, 380
Vegesack, 167
Veit, Philipp, 497
Venetia, 628, 685, 691, 694–5, 701
Venice, 3
Verein. see associations
Verein zur Berforderung der Arbeitsamkeit,
    214–15
*Verein zur Forderung der Erwerbstatigkeit
    des weiblichen Geschlechts*, 106
Vereinigte Provinzialstande, 166

Verona, 321
Vicari, Hermann von, Archbishop of
    Freiburg, 373
Victoria, Queen, 545, 554, 688
Vienna, 12, 69, 105, 115, 161, 165, 166, 300,
    303, 433, 518, 613, 630, 692, 698, 700
    architecture, 488, 489, 492, 493
    aristocracy in, 226
    banking, 168
    coffee-houses, 120
    constitutions, 248
    counter-revolution, 564, 566–71, 577, 585
    education, 427
    housing, 113
    Jews in, 220, 221, 222
    liberalism, 630
    and Magyars, 706
    medicine, 123, 429, 433
    music, 472, 477–8, 480
    nationalism, 18
    newspapers, 522
    population, 85, 95
    radicalism, 562
    Reaction, 602
    reform movement, 302
    revolution, 1848, 528–9, 535
    Ringstrasse, 117
    Romanticism, 361
    water system, 117, 124
Vienna Final Act, 314
*Vier Fragen, beantwortet von einem
    Ostpreussen* (Jacoby), 352
Villach, 13
Villafranca Agreement, 618, 627, 684
Vilmar, August, 384
Vincke, Baron Georg von, 40, 342, 650
Vincke, Ludwig von, 292
Virchow, Rudolf, 432, 433, 434, 672
    exiled, 419, 424
    on public health, 122, 124, 194
    on science and church, 395, 439–40
Vischer, Friedrich Theodor, 494, 496, 514
Vistula river, 10
Vogt, Karl, 315, 396, 559
Vogt, Niklas, 16
Volksammer, 256
Volksgeist, 447, 452, 453
Volksschulen, 45, 49, 58, 407, 427
    control of, 601, 607
    development of, 409–16

Volksschulen (cont.)
   and politics, 412–15
   pupil numbers, 411–12
   Reaction, 600
Volskunde, 462
Volta river, 429
voluntary collectives, 233–6
Vorarlberg, 3, 85
Vormarz, 142, 190, 226, 243, 255, 309, 476,
      602, 642
   administration, 284–5
   agriculture, 129, 143
   art, 503
   censorship, 524
   church and state, 384
   conservatism, 645–6
   counter-revolution, 561
   culture, 473, 509, 515
   defeudalisation, 145–6
   education, 408, 411, 412, 414, 418–19,
      421, 424
   family under, 105, 106, 181
   historicism in, 456–7
   history of, 350–55
   Jews under, 222, 223
   liberalism, 222, 270, 332, 460, 543,
      639–40, 649
   nationalism, 268
   poets, 17
   politics, 182
   population, 94
   poverty, 149, 211
   religion, 181, 386
   revolution, 1848, 535–6
   social policy, 214
   social status, 228, 231
   taxation, 148
   Vorparlament elections, 542
   workers' movement, 655
Vorparlament, 538–40, 542
Vorschussvereine, 186
Voss, Johann Heinrich, 312
Vossische Zeitung, 523
voting rights, 27, 256–7

Wacht am Rhein, 273
Wagenbauer, Max Joseph, 500
Wagener, Hermann, 213, 214, 216, 336, 652
   newspapers, 524, 525
wages, 150

Wagner, Richard, 222, 396, 397, 473, 474,
      481, 483, 486–8, 501, 589, 639
Wagram, battle of, 12, 14
Wahlkaisertum, 583
Waitz, Georg, 343, 457, 542, 582
Waldau, 128
Waldeck, Benedikt Franz, 75, 575, 576, 577,
      578, 620
Waldmuller, 500, 501, 502
Wallonia, 328
Wangenheim, Karl von, 315, 316–17
War Ministry, Prussia, 39–40
Wars of Liberation, 387, 452, 473
Warsaw, 5
Wartburg, 244–5, 267, 484
   festival, 358, 388
Waterloo, battle of, 81
Weber, Wilhelm, 268, 332–3, 435, 484, 486
Weende, 128
Wegscheider, Julius, 374
Weiderecht, 35
Weidig, Friedrich Ludwig, 330, 391
Weihenstephan, 128
Weimar, 246, 377
Weimar, Grand Duke of, 245
Weimar, Karl August von, 76
Weinbrenner, Friedrich, 427, 490
Weitling, Wilhelm, 347, 349
Welcker, Friedrich Gottlieb, 247, 450
Welcker, Karl Theodor, 244, 247, 250, 261,
      271–2, 334, 539, 542, 586, 646
Welcker, K.T., 309
welfare institutions, 226
welfare state, 454
Weltgeist, 16
Weltprinzip, 445
Weltschmerz, 391, 395, 509–10
Wenceslaus, king of Bohemia, 530
Wendel, Francois de, 178
Werder, 491
Werner, Zacharias, 358
Werner Siemens, 167
Weser river, 87, 165
Wesermunde, 168
Weserzeitung, 523
Wessenberg, Heinrich Ignaz von, 360, 368
Westbote, 327
Westermanns Monatshefte, 524, 643
Westphalia, 5, 8, 9, 35, 55, 57, 63, 69, 72,
      89–90, 145, 187, 295

administration, 287
agriculture, 129, 136
church and state, 369
constitution, 62, 239, 241
education, 410
liberalism, 262
reform, 292
regionalism, 290
Westphalisches Dampfboot, 523
Wichern, Johann Hinrich, 213, 214, 377, 388
Wieland, Christoph Martin, 109
Wienbarg, Ludolf, 330
Wiesbaden, 119, 533
Wilhelm I, king of Prussia, 39, 118, 531,
     575, 625, 651, 701
  army reform, 667–74
  Austro-Prussian war, 702
  and Bismarck, 709
  regent, 621
Wilhelm II, king of Prussia, 701
Wilhelmshaven, 168
Wilkelblech, Karl Georg (Marlo), 549
Winckelmann, Johann Joachim, 43, 443
Windischmann, Karl, 431
Winter, Ludwig, 309, 310
Wirth, Johann Georg August, 270, 326–7,
     329, 523
Wissenschaft, 45, 48, 333, 417, 585
  and historicism, 445, 447
  and universities, 420–21, 425, 439
Wissenschaft des Judentums, 222
Wittenberg, 386
Wittgenstein, Wilhelm Ludwig Georg, 240
Wochenblattpartei, 608, 614, 619, 621, 623,
     652
Wocher und wohin? (Schon), 351
Wohler, Friedrich, 427, 434
Wolf, Friedrich August, 44, 450
women
  education of, 415–16
  emancipation of, 105–6, 330
  employment of, 107–8, 203, 205, 206
  role of, 99–100, 102–3, 377, 477
  and sexuality, 109–10
woodlands, 135, 143, 147, 149
worker protection, 293
workers' associations, 210, 234–5, 655
Workers' Brotherhood, 551, 659
workers' combinations, 211, 216
workers' movement, 211, 212, 394, 441

and Austro-Prussian war, 697
  Lassalle programme, 659–65
  and Paulskirche, 550–52
  and politics, 654–67
  and socialism, 346–50
Workers' Solidarity Clubs, 655
working class, 211, 354
  alienation, 195, 198
  industrialisation, 191–216
  and liberalism, 643–5, 648–9
  'proletariat', 212
  revolution, 1848, 534–5
  strata within, 231
Wrangel, General, 576, 577
Wrede, General, 239
Wunsiedel, 246
Wuppertal, 156, 376, 663
Wurttemberg, 58, 59, 72, 75, 82, 134, 149,
     226, 271, 311, 316, 542, 704
  Ablosung, 147
  administration, 56, 288
  agriculture, 149
  Austro-Prussian war, 697
  church and state, 371, 373, 381, 654
  civil service, 283, 286
  and Confederation of Rhine, 8
  constitution, 237, 238, 239, 248
  customs policy, 318
  defeudalisation, 146
  and *Deutscher Bund*, 78–9
  disease, 121
  education, 401, 415
  emigration, 97
  Erfurt Union, 596
  expansion, 2, 3, 55
  and German Confederation, 315
  German Reform Society, 633
  and imperial constitution, 586
  Jews in, 219
  liberalism, 650
  nationalism, 304
  New Era, 623
  parliament, 305–6, 308, 310
  and Paulskirche, 588
  population, 87, 91
  and Prussia, 708
  radicalism, 562
  Reaction, 600, 601
  reforms, 63
  taxation, 60

Wurttemberg (cont.)
  university, 421
  Vorparlament elections, 540
  workers' movement, 216, 551, 663
  and Zollverein, 635
Wurzburg, 8, 57, 75, 163, 238, 433, 628
  university, 417, 418–19
Wuste-Giesdorf, 159

Yorck, General, 18, 39, 67, 91
Young Germany, 106, 330–31, 391, 509,
    510–12, 513, 518
  newspapers, 523, 526
Young Hegelians, 344, 348, 391–2, 424, 470,
    511, 543
  newspapers, 523
Young Lithuania, 672

Zachariae, Heinrich, 259
Zeller, Christian Heinrich, 377
Zeller, Eduard, 471
Zentner, Georg Friedrich, 63, 239
Zeuner, Gustav, 427
Ziller Valley Protestants, 301, 369
Zollverein, 165, 175, 177, 324
  establishment of, 158, 293, 316–19, 351
  German Question, 634–6
  industry, 161, 164, 172, 182
  as model, 343
  number of workers, 169
  in 1850s, 609, 610–11
Zschokke, Heinrich, 375, 494
Zurich, 419, 427, 433, 493
Zwanziger, 193